THE HOLOCAUST CHRONICLE

Publications International, Ltd.

Front cover: This young girl was discovered by British troops in the typhus ward of the Bergen-Belsen, Germany, concentration camp in April 1945. She was one of approximately 60,000 inmates found alive at the camp. Of that number, at least 10,000 were so ravaged by disease and the effects of overwork that they died after their liberation. The girl's name, background, and ultimate fate are unknown.

Louis Weber, CEO
Publications International, Ltd.
7373 North Cicero Avenue
Lincolnwood, Illinois 60712

Manufactured in China

8 7 6 5 4 3 2 1

ISBN: 0-7853-2963-3

Library of Congress Card Number: 99-067861

A Message from the Publisher

A booklet published in Jerusalem in 1940 by the United Aid Committee for the Jews in Poland termed the extermination of Europe's Jews *sho'ah,* a Hebrew word for mass slaughter. In the 1950s the word "Holocaust" came into common usage to describe the catastrophe that befell Jews during the war years.

The Holocaust Chronicle is a remembrance designed to be held in one's hands. It is a portable archive that demands to be looked at and read. Although its weight and heft cannot capture the immensity of its subject, the volume's size does suggest that this is a topic that must be openly confronted.

The book is a not-for-profit enterprise made available to the widest possible audience via a low price that will allow widespread distribution to schools, universities, synagogues, public libraries, churches, and retail outlets. Its goal is the truth, scrupulously researched and vividly expressed in words and pictures.

Equally notable is the book's companion project, a detailed, cross-referenced *Holocaust Chronicle* Web site that will include the book's complete text and a revolving selection of images. Because Holocaust-related developments cross news wires daily, the Web site will be updated continually.

Black-and-white photographs and mottled motion picture footage may lead young people to conclude that the Holocaust happened so long ago as to be unknowable, even irrelevant. Some older people may have convinced themselves that the past is past, and that the Holocaust is a dead issue. But in the great continuum of history, the horror took place only yesterday. Thousands of Holocaust survivors still live, and those who were the youngest and most helpless are not elderly but merely middle-aged.

We owe it not merely to the Holocaust victims to remember what happened, but to all people now living, and to all those yet to be born, to remember, and to ponder. Only in our remembrance and open discussion is there a chance, a hope, that another Holocaust will never happen.

Louis Weber

3

Publisher
Louis Weber

Editor-in-Chief
David J. Hogan

Editor
David Aretha

Art Director
Patrick Murray

Vice President, Acquisitions
Jeff Mintz

Acquisitions Editors
Kelli Christiansen
Roger Marsh
Anton Pav
Patty Wetli

Production Director
Steven Grundt

Production Editors
Jennifer Geraci
Margaret McConnell

Electronic Publishing Specialist
Kym Condon

Manager, Visual Resources
Larry Glickman

Visual Resource Specialists
Elizabeth Haydon
Harry Kapsalis
Kelly Swett

Assistant to the Publisher
Renee G. Haring

Editorial Assistants
Molly Dynan
Kathline Jones
Catherine Ploetz
Rachel Winstead

Cover Design
Linda LaCroix

Vice President, Publishing Operations
Mona Syring

Publications Manager
Kristine Z. Hnat

Director, Pre-Press
David Darian

Pre-Press Coordinator
Laura C. Schmidt

Imaging Specialists
Keith Browne
Paul Fromberg
Bill Hutchinson
Kurt Suesse

Director of Manufacturing
James R. Zimmermann

Director of Purchasing
Rocky Wu

Manufacturing Manager
Kent Keutzer

Vice President, Strategic Technologies
Rich Franco

Director of Database Development
Pat Hagle

Web Site Development
Thomas Anastasi Carr
Jeff Krakow

Adviser to the Publisher
Bonnie Weber

Legal Adviser
Michael R. Shelist

Public Relations Adviser
Nancy Kahan

Contributing Writers
Marilyn J. Harran, Ph.D.
Dieter Kuntz, Ph.D.
Russel Lemmons, Ph.D.
Robert A. Michael, Ph.D.
Keith Pickus, Ph.D.
John K. Roth, Ph.D.

Consultant
Abraham J. Edelheit, Ph.D.

Contributing Consultants
Marilyn J. Harran, Ph.D.
Robert A. Michael, Ph.D.
Alexander Rossino, Ph.D.
John K. Roth, Ph.D.

Appendices
Eric Epstein
Philip Rosen, Ph.D.

Fact Checkers
Robert Brown
Julie Courtwright
Wendy Henry
Ann Mann Millin
Jennifer Rosenberg
Alexander Rossino, Ph.D.

Photo Researchers
Rose Lerer Cohen
Oliver Gottfried
Marla Seidell

Map Illustrators
Susan and Mark Carlson

Indexer
Rita Tatum

Contributing Authors and Consultants

Marilyn Harran, Ph.D., is professor of religion and history at Chapman University (CA). She has taught courses on "Germany and the Holocaust: From Anti-Semitism to Final Solution" and "Topics in the Holocaust: Perpetrators, Victims, and Bystanders." She also assisted Thomas Blatt in preparing his publication *Sobibor: The Forgotten Revolt*. She has served on the Orange County Advisory Board on Pluralism and Diversity of the National Conference of Christians and Jews. She is a member of the Leo Baeck Institute.

Dieter Kuntz, Ph.D., has taught at the University of Kansas, and was a visiting assistant professor of history at the University of Iowa, where he taught modern German history. Courses taught include "Hitler and Nazi Germany," "Inside Hitler's Germany," and "Germany Since 1914: Weimar, Hitler, and After." He is coauthor and editor of *Inside Hitler's Germany: A Documentary History of Life in the Third Reich*. As a guest speaker, he has lectured on "The Rise of the Nazis." He also has prepared materials for the television video course "Never Again: Understanding the Holocaust," which was sponsored by the American Institute of Jewish Studies.

Russel Lemmons, Ph.D., is associate professor of history at Jacksonville State University (AL), where he served as a member of the Holocaust Commemoration Committee. He has developed and taught courses such as "Rise and Fall of Hitler" and "History of the Holocaust." He is the author of *Goebbels and "Der Angriff,"* and contributed to *Representations of Jews Through the Ages*. He has presented papers on "Confronting Holocaust Denial" and "Nazi Propaganda and the Proletariat."

Robert Ashley Michael, Ph.D., is professor of European history at the University of Massachusetts, Dartmouth, where he has taught the Holocaust for 21 years. He has published extensively on the Holocaust and the history of antisemitism, including the books *The Holocaust: A Chronology and Documentary*, *The Radicals and Nazi Germany*, and *Fatal Vision*. His articles often appear in publications such as *Holocaust and Genocide Studies*, *Martyrdom and Resistance* and *Menorah Review*, where he served as contributing editor. He is coeditor of the scholarly Internet interest groups H-ANTISEMITISM, H-W-CIV (History of Western Civilization), and formerly of H-HOLOCAUST. In addition to his contributions as a writer on this project, he also served as map and timeline consultant.

Keith Pickus, Ph.D., is assistant professor in modern European and German history at Wichita State University. Courses taught include "Hitler's Third Reich," "The Holocaust," "The Jewish Experience in Christian Europe," and "Antisemitism and Nationalism in Modern Europe." He is the author of the forthcoming book *Constructing Modern Identities: Jewish University Students in Germany, 1815–1914*, and has published numerous journal articles including "Tapestries of German Jewish Identity" and "German Jewish Identity in the Kaiserreich." He has lectured publicly on "Making Meaning of the Holocaust." He is a member of the Association of Jewish Studies and the Leo Baeck Institute.

John K. Roth, Ph.D., is the Russell K. Pitzer Professor of Philosophy at Claremont McKenna College (CA). He has served as Visiting Professor of Holocaust Studies at the University of Haifa, Israel, and received a grant from the National Endowment for the Humanities to develop the course "Perspectives on the 20th Century: The Holocaust." He has published hundreds of articles and reviews and is the author, coauthor, or editor of more than 25 books, including *A Consuming Fire: Encounters with Elie Wiesel and the Holocaust, Approaches to Auschwitz: The Holocaust and Its Legacy* (with Richard L. Rubenstein), and *Different Voices: Women and the Holocaust* (edited with Carol Rittner). He presently serves on the selection committee for the Elie Wiesel Prize in Ethics and on the editorial board of *Holocaust and Genocide Studies,* and has served on the United States Holocaust Memorial Council. In addition to his contributions as a writer, he also served as sidebar consultant on this project.

Consultant

Abraham Edelheit, Ph.D., is a researcher on the President's Commission on Holocaust Assets in the United States and an adjunct professor of history at Kingsborough Community College of City University of New York (CUNY). He serves as Jewish history editor for *Jewish Book World,* published by the Jewish Book Council, and has worked as a researcher/writer for the United States Holocaust Memorial Museum. His numerous publications include the three-volume *Bibliography on Holocaust Literature* and books such as *History of the Holocaust: A Handbook and Dictionary, A World in Turmoil: An Integrated Chronology of the Holocaust and World War II,* and *The Yishuv in the Shadow of the Holocaust: Zionist Politics and Rescue Aliya, 1933–1939.* His latest book is, *History of Zionism: A Handbook and Dictionary.* He served as editor on and contributed articles to the *Encyclopedia of the Holocaust* and also contributed articles to the *Students Encyclopedia of the Holocaust.*

ACKNOWLEDGMENTS

Thanks are expressed to the following people for special assistance, materials, and/or information:

Michael Berenbaum
Jack Berger
Dodge Color, Inc.
Phil Drell
William Elperin—President, The "1939" Club
Genya Markon—United States Holocaust Memorial Museum
Valerie Ben Or—Yad Vashem Photo Archives
Frau Berit Pistora—*Bundesarchiv*
Zippi Rosenne—Beth Hatefutsoth Photo Archives
David Shore
Herman Spertus—Spertus Institute of Jewish Studies
Howard Sulkin—President, Spertus Institute of Jewish Studies
Leslie Swift, former director, United States Holocaust Memorial Museum Photo Archives
Ed Vebell

Special thanks are extended to the employees of Publications International, Ltd., who helped make this not-for-profit book possible: David H. Achord, Amy Adair, Jack Alexander, Michael Allen, Debra Almgren-Horwitz, Charles Aluyi, Mike Anderson, Wes Antczak, Sara Armstrong, Kristin Ashley, Sherise Marie Ayuso, Patrick Bachler, John Baker, Lucy Banak, Diane Baskette, Lori S. Baxter, Richard N. Beals, Becky Bell, David Bellm, Amy Berman, Susan Bezanes, Brett Bickler, John Biel, Mark Bilek, Kevin Biron-Bomis, Heather Blaha, Ana Boyer, Earl Brosnahan, Tom Broughton, Sharon Broutzas, David Brown, Lisa Brutto, Zachary B. Burkons, Juliane Bylica, Donald Callender, Brent Cardillo, Charlotte Caron, William Carp, Bruce Carroll, Jeffrey Casemier, Larry T. Castleman, Ginger Cervantez-Sanchez, Christine K. Cesal, Ike Chavez, Cynthia Ann Childers, Cynthia Colby, Marissa Conner, Frank Cordaro, Richard Cotta, Bob Coutteau, Jeffrey Coyle, Michael D. Cross, Kim Curran, Jane Curtain, Jacqueline Lisa Curtis, David M. Darakjian, Robert L. Davis, Jr., Kimberly M. Desmedt, Paula DeSmet, Onelia DiBartolomeo, Lynn Dolan, Elenelia Dorado, Kris Dresen, Jamie Elder, Charlene Epple, Vanessa Ettkin, Susan Barbee Ewald, Fiona Fargo, Kerry Finnamore, Jennifer Firlotte, Roland Flessner, Ronald B. Flickinger, Michael Franck, Martha Frey, Janet Fuglsang, Ronald Gad, John Gale, Anna Galkowska, Eliana Gallego, Susan Garard, Theresa Gavin, Maria Georgouses, Ed Geraghty, Charles Giametta, Jennifer Goldstein, Daniel Gordon, Lori Grabarek, Mike Graf, Jeffrey D. Gray, Rebecca Grazulis, Julie Greene, Jonathan P. Gross, Nicole Guagliardo, Amy Gundersen, Matthew Hampton, John Hansen, Jeff Hapner, Rhoda Hapner, Jim Harbison, Robin Harris, Sara D. Hauber, Brigette Heath, Christopher Hellman, Ila Henderson, Daniel C. Henrick, Laura Henry, Michelle Hickok, Linda Hillesland, Cherylette Hilton, Janice Himmel, Elizabeth C. Howell, Sarah Huegen, Don Hutson, Valerie Iglar-Mobley, Josh Iskra, Donald P. Jacobs, Andrea Jacobson, William Jahnke, Kat Johnson, Stephen Johnson, Valerie Kim Johnston, Ann Kahlenberg, Paul Kelly, Heather Kennedy, Kerri Kennedy, Jeanne Kim, Deena Kindahl, Jim King, John A. King, Mary Kolleth, Terese Kolodziej, Jerry Kurtzweil, Mary L. Laffey, Katherine Lane, Lois R. Levin, Joanne Lewis, Bryan Libbin, Phyllis Licata, Timothy Light, Elizabeth Mackey, Laura Madalinski, Amy Madden, Richard Maddrell, Connie Malone, Marvella Marion-Bowen, Curtis Marolt, Steven Martin, Astrid Master, Jay McHugh, Shawn McNichols, Naida Meyers, Martin Michalek, Lisa Mierzwa, Tabatha Miller, Anna Misfeldt, Scott Mitchell, Shirley Mong, Rose Montegna, Adam Cain Morgan, Liz Mork, Fred Moss, Michael Murphy, Jacqueline Najera, John Neiman, Francine Neuman, Henry Ng, Denise Noncek, Kevin Oatess, Anne O'Connor, Ginny O'Donnell, Leslie Okamura, Jill Oldham, Ann-Marie Olson, Margie Omotosho, Elizabeth Panzer, Nes Pastrana, Frank E. Peiler, Alice Pekarek, Debbie Pekarek, Deborah Pinkston, Stephen Polanek, Susan Polsky, Chris Poole, Robert Ralph, Barbara Rasbid, Beth Reichert, Michelle Rhodes, Dana Richter, Carolyn Riehl, Barbara Rittenhouse, Colleen Rohan, Linda Roth, Janet Rowe, Natalya Ryabova, Karim Sabur, Lori Saleh, Lynette Santiago, Mark Schindler, Gizel Schwartz, Jackie Schwarz, Christopher Sciabica, Anne-Michele Selover, James Senhauser, Nahrin Shamoon, Donald Shea, Stuart Shea, Kurt Sholly, Ruth Siegel, Charles K. Simpson, Randy Skach, James Slate, Charlotte Anne Smith, Darcy Smith, Jeanne Smith, Doug Sohn, Joanna Spathis, Dave Stahl, J. Robert Stanik, Jenny Stein, Tracy Stetson, Jack Stewart, Susan St. Onge, Lynne Suesse, Gail Swanson, John Tasigeorgos, Ann Taylor, Shirley Taylor, Brett Thornsberry, Jordan Trais, James Travnicek, Roberto Trento, Judy Tribbey, Deborah Upton, Georgia Vasilopoulos, Rey Verceles, Diwata Virtusio, Eran Wade, Arthur Walker, Lynn Wallschlaeger, Jeanne Wang, Charles W. Watkins, Jeremy Weber, Vida Wei, Marilyn Weiner, Patricia Weiss, Thomas Werner, Randy Whitlock, Graham Wiemer, Robert B. Williams, Jr., Renee Witherwax, Ronald A. Witt, Sara Wolfsmith, Michael J. Woodard, Kelly Wright, Jerry Yamamoto, Leah Yarrow, Steve Yonkelowitz, Max Yu, Kathy Yurkovich, Brooke S. Zimmerman, David Zino, Deena Zymm

Contents

Foreword

WHEN I first began to teach the Holocaust more than a quarter of a century ago, students often inquired about its relevance. What does the Holocaust have to do with our world? The Holocaust was regarded as a scar from the past. Other issues were far more central. Much has happened in that quarter century. Perhaps too much.

Sadly, students today do not have to ask whether what they are studying is relevant. The images of Bosnia, Rwanda, and Kosovo are embedded in their consciousness, more deeply engraved in their being than images of Cambodia or Biafra two decades ago. We live in a world of CNN, where events from remote parts of the world are integrated into our daily viewing. Students and their parents have heard such words as ethnic cleansing and genocide and have seen the pictures of corpses, villages bereft of their populations, refugees in flight. They have seen films such as *Schindler's List,* and perhaps they have even visited one of the Holocaust museums—the United States Holocaust Memorial Museum in Washington, D.C., or another Holocaust museum in many major cities in the United States, Canada, Europe, and Israel. They are interested and they want to know more.

The role of the survivors also has changed over these many years. Once they were silent, willing to speak but unable to find those who would listen. In the first years after World War II, they were politely but ever firmly told that "the past is past." In Israel the future beckoned, the free future of an independent Jewish state. Exile was exile, bitter and tragic, but now they were home. In the United States, new refugees were told that everyone came to the new world with a story from the old world, but America is future-oriented—not really interested in the past.

I know because I first encountered the Holocaust in silence, in the unspoken; I saw teachers with fists but no fingers, teachers with tattooed numbers on their arms. In later years, as I started my teaching career, survivors were afraid of burdening their children, so they guarded their words. Only hints of what happened emerged. But by now they have written their memoirs and told their stories. The recording of video testimonies that was begun in 1978 at New Haven, Connecticut, in a project later named the Fortunoff Video Archives for Holocaust Testimonies has been a model for other projects in other cities. And since 1994, more than 50,000 testimonies of Holocaust survivors, liberators, rescuers, and eyewitnesses have been taken in 32 languages in 57 countries by the Survivors of the Shoah Visual History Foundation in Los Angeles. So the documentation from the survivors is ample, and survivors have come to be regarded as witnesses and teachers, speaking to this generation and beyond. They have spoken, and their words are a cry against indifference, a plea for tolerance and pluralism, for human values and human dignity.

It is now our turn to listen.

As we enter the new millennium, the Holocaust has taken its place as a defining moment of 20th century humanity, the moment we learned something about what we are as individuals, about human capacity for good and evil. But we have learned more than about ourselves as individuals. We have learned about the power of states and institutions to shape the world and to accomplish so much, even the annihilation of a people. As we make the transition to the 21st century, one has an uneasy feeling that there is a struggle between tribalism and globalism.

There is a paradox in the study of the Holocaust: The more distant we are from the Event, the more interest seems to grow. Why study the Holocaust? The answers are complex, but the underlying reason is simple.

Because it happened.

Much is known about the Holocaust. The killers left meticulous records of actions, of plans, of orders. They documented the crime. Indeed, they were proud of it.

Photos were taken, even films. You will see many of those records in this book.

Still, there is much that is unknown or in dispute. Some people have portrayed the Holocaust as an aberration, a world apart from the ordinary world in which we dwell. Yet more frightening to me, the Holocaust is not an aberration, but an expression in the extreme of what is common to the mainstream of our civilization.

Because it happened, we must understand the evil—systematic evil, state-sponsored evil, industrialized killing, mass murders—that was the essence of the Holocaust. We must understand its emblematic invention, the death camp, as well as the people who staffed such camps. Their assignment: mass murder. Some were sadists and criminals—people unlike us—but many more were ordinary men and women trying to do their best, to fulfill their obligations. Some were professionals, even doctors, who used the skills they had learned to become more efficient killers. Some were enthusiastic, others more reluctant; all became party to mass murder.

We must understand the circumstances of the victims, who had to make choiceless choices between the impossible and the horrific, and who faced conditions of such utter powerlessness that they could do so little to determine their fate. And we must understand the indifference of neutrality. In the struggle between powerless victims and an overwhelmingly powerful killing machine, neutrality is anything but neutral. Indifference is a death sentence.

We can learn so much about evil while studying the Holocaust that it leaves us numb, that despair overtakes us, that we sense our own helplessness. Indeed, the Holocaust was an atrocity, senseless and anguishing. But there were a few—a precious few men, women, and even children—who opened their homes and their hearts and provided a haven for the victims, a place to sleep, a crust of bread, a kind word, a hiding place. What makes such goodness possible? Why were some people immune to the infection of evil? These are the people whose deeds we may wish to emulate, who can serve as models for how we want to behave and what we want to become.

The Holocaust began slowly. Age-old prejudice led to discrimination, discrimination to persecution, persecution to incarceration, incarceration to annihilation. And mass murder, which culminated with the killing of six million Jews, did not begin with the Jews nor did it encompass only the Jews. The violations of one group's rights are seldom contained only to that group.

The study of the Holocaust is not an easy undertaking, emotionally or intellectually. What you have before you is a tool, a chronicle that takes you year by year, month by month, through the events of the Holocaust. You will see the images of the Holocaust, meet the people who perpetrated the killing and the processes by which they worked. No significant issue is avoided. Your guides are not only writers who know their subjects, but teachers who know what to offer those who yearn to learn.

The book is large because the Event is large. A word of advice: Don't let the book's size overwhelm you; instead, let it empower you to learn at your pace. You will have to confront death in this book, yet the study of these deaths is in the service of life. To study this evil is to strengthen decency and goodness.

The Holocaust shatters faith—faith in God, secular faith in human decency, and faith in meaningful progress. Although the Holocaust provides few answers and raises many questions, the questions invite moral struggle against that evil.

The call from the victims—from the world of the dead—was to remember. Today we hear from those who were there and those who were not the urgency of memory, its agony and anguish, the presence of meaning and meaning's absence. To live in our age, one must face that absence as well as that presence.

Rabbi Nachman, a great Hasidic master of paradox, once said that nothing is as whole as a heart that has been broken and mended.

The Holocaust shatters. Our task is to mend.

Michael Berenbaum
Autumn 1999

Michael Berenbaum, Ph.D., was Project Director for the creation of the United States Holocaust Memorial Museum, and the first director of the United States Holocaust Research Institute. In addition, he was President and CEO of the Survivors of the Shoah Visual History Foundation. Dr. Berenbaum is the author and editor of 14 books, among them The World Must Know, After Tragedy and Triumph, *and* Witness to the Holocaust. *For almost two decades he was the Hymen Goldman Professor of Theology at Georgetown University, and currently is an Adjunct Professor of Theology at the University of Judaism.*

A Letter from Herman Spertus

I believe in people.

Of all the virtues we bestow upon ourselves and others, one of the greatest is education. The educated person has learned to be empathetic to the origins, needs, and feelings of others. Education fosters tolerance and the capacity for love—the love for one's family, and for the greater human family that includes us all.

I have lived in every year of this century. I have been a son, an immigrant, a husband, a businessman, a community leader, a father. Over many years I have turned much of my energy to the preservation of Jewish memory and the heritage that has shaped me. The Holocaust is an unavoidable part of that memory and heritage.

The unreasoning hatred that was at the core of the Nazi persecution and the murder of Jews and others cannot be eliminated altogether, but it can be tempered and diminished. It must be discouraged from gaining a toehold in the minds of the world's young people.

The Holocaust is a blow that affects Jews and Judaism—indeed, all people and all faiths—deeply, perhaps beyond reckoning. It demonstrates with fearsome clarity that democracy cannot thrive in an atmosphere of callous indifference. The Holocaust was deliberate and carefully conceived. It was carried out because too many people *allowed* it to be carried out. When each of the Holocaust's 11 million people perished, including six million Jewish victims, humankind was diminished and the flame of Judaism flickered. But that flame was not extinguished. It burns today and will continue to burn as long as we remember that the past informs our present, and provides priceless guideposts for our future.

When we study history, we pause to reflect upon moments in the unending continuity of life and experience. To be sure, study of the Holocaust does not make the event comprehensible. Study does not neatly tidy up the Holocaust or transform it into something that can be looked at dispassionately. Rather, proper Holocaust study stirs the blood and fills us with indignation. It awakens our better instincts, and teaches us to recognize and avoid the moral and intellectual failings that encouraged that enormous and sorrowful crime.

And so by learning and teaching, we aspire not just to knowledge but to compassion and understanding. We make ourselves *whole*.

Herman Spertus
Autumn 1999

The institution that bears the Spertus name, Spertus Institute of Jewish Studies, was founded in 1924 as the Chicago College of Jewish Studies. In 1971, the name of the institution was changed in honor of a major gift provided by Herman and his brother Maurice. Herman has served as a Life Trustee and active leader since that time.

Introduction

IT exists alone in history.

It is the Holocaust, the systematic, state-organized persecution and murder of six million Jews—as well as other targeted groups—by Nazi Germany and its collaborators. With poison gas, bullets, the noose, clubs, fists, starvation, and overwork, the perpetrators slaughtered two-thirds of Europe's Jews and one-third of the world's Jewish population. In addition, Nazi Germany's genocidal policies annihilated millions of other defenseless people, including Sinti and Roma (Gypsies), Polish citizens, Soviet prisoners of war, homosexuals, the handicapped, Freemasons, Jehovah's Witnesses, and other political and religious dissidents.

The Holocaust was the most profound expression of the anti-semitism that had flourished in Germany and other European nations for many centuries. By 1918, when the victorious Allies held Germany responsible for World War I, the German nation found itself staggered with forced reparations payments scheduled to be made from 1919 to 1988. Throughout the 1920s, the new, shakily democratic Weimar German government struggled with mass unemployment, grotesque inflation that made currency worthless, terrible national debt, and political strife and street fighting.

Adolf Hitler took control of the insignificant National Socialist People's Party in 1921, and subsequently agitated loudly throughout Germany. By 1933, he had manipulated the democratic process so skillfully that he was named chancellor. A year later, Hitler assumed absolute, dictatorial control of the German government.

German citizens had responded positively to Hitler's promises of full employment, a rebirth of German pride, the supposed superiority of the Nordic "race," and his outspoken hatred of Jews, on whom he blamed all of society's ills.

Germany's thorough persecution of its Jewish citizens began almost immediately after Hitler assumed national office in 1933, and steadily escalated. State-sanctioned boycotts of Jewish businesses; gross vandalism of synagogues; vile, antisemitic propaganda; the pushing of Jews from the mainstream of German life—these insults and others were turned by the Nazis against the nation's Jewish population.

Germany touched off World War II on September 1, 1939. Persecution of Jews expanded and intensified rapidly as the Nazi military machine swept across Europe. In the Berlin suburb of Wannsee on January 20, 1942, Reinhard Heydrich, Adolf Eichmann, and 13 other Nazi leaders attended an 87-minute conference to discuss the elimination of Europe's Jews. The genocidal plan that was agreed upon was euphemistically dubbed the "Final Solution."

The groundwork for genocide had been laid well before Wannsee. Beginning in the fall of 1939, the Nazis and their collaborators organized a complex and far-reaching machinery of death throughout conquered Europe. The system encompassed walled-in Jewish ghettos, rail transport of deportees, and concentration and slave-labor camps. It later grew to include horrific extermination camps built in conquered Poland. So the system was put in place, and a vast Nazi bureaucracy proceeded to torment and destroy millions of innocent human beings.

The Holocaust Chronicle—a not-for-profit book written and fact-checked by respected scholars—recounts the complex story of the most terrible crime of the 20th century. So complex is the subject, in fact, that no single volume could hope to cover it all. With this in mind, *The Holocaust Chronicle* has been designed as a richly illustrated survey that will introduce students and lay readers to the basic facts of the Holocaust, and help guide them to an increased understanding of the event.

The scale of the story is so vast that a temptation to view it as an abstraction is understandable. The sum of Jewish victims, six million, invites a certain numbness of response. The mind wants to shut down, turn itself off. The figure, finally, cannot be comprehended. And then you realize that millions of *individuals* were killed. One death at a time—an end to mortal existence for a person like you. Someone with past happiness and dreams, someone who loved and was loved by others. All of that, gone at the instant of death, destroyed in the name of "racial purity."

To express this reality in a comprehensible way has been one goal of this book. Above all else, the Holocaust is a human story. There is nothing abstract about the victims or about the perpetrators. The Holocaust was conceived by men; was carried out by men and women; and was the destroyer of men, women, and children. This is an obvious insight that can be overlooked in the striving for proper scholarship. Hard facts and figures can overwhelm the flesh-and-blood truth of the Holocaust.

The human factor must remain at the forefront. The work toward this goal is particularly evident in the book's 80,000-word timeline of Holocaust-related events covering some 3000 years of history. The timeline is unprecedented in its scope and thoroughness and yet is, admittedly, not complete. No Holocaust timeline or book could hope to be. Of the numberless events that occurred during the Holocaust, most were never recorded. Many facts of the Holocaust died with the victims. Still, much information about events large and isolated *has* been preserved, not least by the

Nazis themselves, who were dedicated photographers and record keepers.

As you peruse the timeline, and as you look at the book's photographs and read the captions and sidebars, keep in mind that not every piece of information is of equal weight, at least not in the historical sense. But history is not momentous events only but an accumulation of "small" ones that loomed large to the people involved. In order to impart to the reader a feeling for those "small" stories of the Holocaust, *The Holocaust Chronicle* relates the fates and exploits not merely of people whose names you will find in encyclopedias and in standard works on the Holocaust, but of hundreds of heretofore anonymous people who played roles: as resisters and partisans, as victims, as planners and bureaucrats, as Nazi collaborators, as witnesses, as killers. Taken as a single piece, the book invites the reader to trace the ebb and flow of Holocaust-related events without losing sight of those six million people mentioned earlier.

The Holocaust happened more than a half-century ago. Why study it today? Although it is a very specific, clearly defined historical event, the human and political motivations that helped to create it—fear, envy, sadism, hatred, ignorance, territorialism—are ever-present. Even as the 21st century begins, genocidal "ethnic cleansing" and other state-sanctioned crimes against humanity take place across the globe. And antisemitism, maddeningly, remains a powerful force. To study the Holocaust, then, is to begin to understand not just that event, but the still-potent forces that motivated it.

Holocaust studies are marked by academic controversy. The subject brings with it numerous tricky historical and philosophical issues. Did the Holocaust evolve over time during the war years, or was it planned from the beginnings of the Third Reich? Was it hatched earlier still, in the mind of the ragtag, young Adolf Hitler? Did Hitler the *Führer* know every detail of the Holocaust? Why did the Allies never bomb Auschwitz? Is it possible to retain a faith in God after surviving the Holocaust? These are difficult questions that are debated somewhere every day. The book notes these issues and others of equal difficulty and controversy, but does not attempt to provide irrefutable answers. To do that was never the book's mandate. It is sufficient, we believe, for these and other thorny issues to be noted; readers who independently pursue answers to such questions will have put *The Holocaust Chronicle* to good use.

Holocaust historians have part of the answer to the question "why?" but not the whole answer. "How?" may be somewhat less difficult to deal with, but even here things are far from clear. In a 1954 essay called *"Der Führer,"* writer Herbert Luethy warned that Adolf Hitler, the evil engine of the Holocaust, must not be regarded as an unstoppable force of nature, an elemental being who is both nonhuman and more than human. Hitler was not "natural" or "elemental," Luethy wrote, but rather a small man of few real convictions, who "fell upon Europe not out of the steppes [like Attila] but from the Viennese gutter." Göring, Hess, Himmler, and the rest of Hitler's inner circle were small men as well. Gray and rumpled in the dock during the war-crimes trials at Nuremberg in 1945–46, they were described by historian Irving Kristol as "petty and colorless and superficial . . . without dignity, fanaticism, obsessive hate, or the stature that large-scale wickedness often bestows. In comparison with John Dillinger, Hermann Göring looked like an indignant pickpocket."

Hitler himself was of this ilk. Cold of heart and incapable of partaking in the normal joys experienced by other people, Hitler viewed human life as a blunt and never-ending struggle for power, territory, and racial dominance. To him, people were animals and little more, and it was the responsibility of the "Aryan race" to subjugate—indeed, to destroy—the menace Hitler saw embodied in Jews and other so-called *Untermenschen*—subhumans. That he did not hesitate to sacrifice the lives of millions of Germans who had become his enthusiastic supporters proves the monomaniacal emptiness of his struggle. The people of his adopted Germany meant nothing to Hitler except as the means to a philosophically hazy end. What, then, was there to deter him from the wholesale murder of millions of Jews and others?

No document with Hitler's signature —no "smoking gun"—has yet been discovered that directly links him to the Holocaust. However, there is little doubt that just as the Holocaust would not have been possible without the long and demeaning European tradition of antisemitism, so too would the Final Solution have been unlikely without Hitler and National Socialism. Hitler fancied himself an infallible

puppet master, and for a while it appeared as though he was. His resolute rebuilding of Germany's military and his illusive reinvigoration of German self-esteem convinced him of the rightness of his cause. So too did his brazenly unblinking expansionism of 1938, his world-shaking paper alliance with the Soviet Union in 1939 and his almost gleeful plunge into war late that summer, and the astonishing victories that followed for the next two years.

And even later, when Hitler paced and mumbled in his bunker below the streets of Berlin as the Third Reich literally crumbled around him, he did not give up his hatred of the Jews. The enormous crime he had inspired affected him only insofar as it would remain unfinished. In his final political testament, dictated just hours before his suicide, Hitler exhorted the Aryan race to carry on the fight against the Jews. The monstrousness of the man's mind, and the minds of those who carried out his will, is exceeded only by the monstrousness of the crime.

For all of this terrible travail, Judaism was not destroyed. Jews persevered, gathered themselves, and fought for and won a homeland. Today, Judaism thrives, but the price that must be paid is a constant vigilance. The fervor and excellence of the Israeli armed forces are well known, as is the nation's policy of meeting aggression with unblinking force. For a nation that was born from the ashes of the Holocaust, to do otherwise is an impossibility.

Although Hitler and his sycophants failed, that is cold comfort in light of the millions who were hounded and murdered. It is for

those millions that *The Holocaust Chronicle* endeavors to speak.

Finally, a few words about this book's use of the word "antisemitism," rather than the commonly seen "anti-Semitism." The latter iteration dates from the 1870s, when a German journalist named Wilhelm Marr coined it based on a wholly erroneous racial belief of long standing. According to this belief, Jews are a *race,* distinct from other races and distinguished by undesirable, genetically inherited qualities unique to Jews.

Marr exploited the term "Semite" to set Jews apart from non-Jews, and to reinforce the race-based perception of Judaism. In its original meaning, however, "Semite" encompassed Arab peoples as well as Jews, and yet "anti-Semitism" connotes hatred of Jews only, not of Arabs. Marr helped to encourage anti-Jewish minds to indulge in this too-convenient, wholly prejudicial distinction.

Jews do not comprise a race. Rather, they are united by faith, history, tradition, and other cultural qualities. They share no distinguishing genetic feature, no biological marker that identifies them as Jewish. Because Judaism is a religion, one does not have to be "born into" the faith in order to be Jewish. Many Jews are converts from other religions.

Continued use of the term "anti-Semitism" inadvertently perpetuates its unfounded racial connotation. The alternate "antisemitism" retains the sound of Marr's term—that is, its prejudicial meaning is quickly comprehensible—while implicitly denying the erroneous reasoning indulged in by Marr and others like him.

PROLOGUE

NIGHT, Elie Wiesel's famous Holocaust memoir, tells what happened to him in Auschwitz, the Nazi concentration, forced-labor, and extermination camp in Poland that he entered as a teenager in May 1944. The narrative concludes in April 1945 as Wiesel looked into a mirror. Seeing oneself in a mirror is a small thing, but the boy had not done so since he and his family were deported from Sighet, their hometown in Hungary, more than a year before. What Wiesel saw, moreover, was not ordinary at all. "From the depths of the mirror," he wrote, "a corpse gazed back at me."

Even though he was officially "liberated" from Auschwitz, Wiesel could never be free from the catastrophe that had befallen him and his people. He and the other survivors had witnessed so much senseless violence and useless dying in "the kingdom of night" that their living would ever more include the death-with-life that he must have recognized when he set himself and gazed into the mirror. "The look in his eyes, as they stared into mine, has never left me," he wrote.

From time to time, Elie Wiesel has returned to Auschwitz. He has done so first and foremost as a witness for the dead and the living. But he has also returned because his accomplishments as a distinguished author, influential humanitarian, and Nobel Peace Prize

> **"The beginning, the end: all the world's roads, all the outcries of mankind, lead to this accursed place. Here is the kingdom of night, where God's face is hidden and a flaming sky becomes a graveyard for a vanished people."**
>
> —*Elie Wiesel, "Pilgrimage to the Kingdom of Night"*

recipient in 1986 have given him leadership responsibilities for preserving memory of the Holocaust, including accurate conservation of its most important sites. In the summer of 1979, he led a delegation to visit significant places in the Holocaust's history. Auschwitz-Birkenau was among them. The main killing center in the large Auschwitz system of camps, Birkenau was the place where more than one million Jews were gassed.

The visitors accompanying Wiesel were from the President's Commission on the Holocaust. It had been charged by Jimmy Carter, the American president at the time, to recommend an appropriate Holocaust memorial for the United States. That initiative resulted in the opening of the United States Holocaust Memorial Museum in Washington, D.C., in 1993. During the Auschwitz stop on his 1979 journey, Wiesel read "Listen to the Wind," a poem he had written. The poem urged people to listen—to listen to the wind, stones, and sky—in a place that Wiesel aptly called "the grave of man's heart." Later in 1979, reflecting on his "Pilgrimage to the Kingdom of Night," as his November 4 article in *The New York Times* called it, Wiesel referred to Auschwitz-Birkenau as "the beginning, the end: all the world's roads, all the outcries of mankind, lead to this accursed place."

As Wiesel stood with other survivors at Auschwitz-Birkenau in 1979, "at the place where we had

Many medieval European monarchs expelled Jews or condemned them to death. Philip V of France orders this Jewish woman to burn at the stake.

lost our families," he reports that "there were no words.... There was nothing to say." But then, Wiesel recalls, out of memory in the Auschwitz wind, ancient words could be heard, words that also go back to the beginning: "*Shma Israel.* 'Hear, O Israel, God is our God, God is one.'...*Ani maamin.* 'I believe with all my heart in the coming of the Messiah....'" Centuries and even millennia old, those words from the Jewish tradition hearken back not only to the origins of the Jewish people but also to the beginning of time and creation themselves. Heard from Auschwitz, those words ask: How did it happen that Birkenau scarred the earth and left humankind to cope with the Holocaust's enduring anguish? Why did that ending result from the beginning?

Long after the last page of this book has been turned, those questions will remain. How could they not, for no event challenges human understanding more than the Holocaust. To grasp how and why it happened, detailed analysis of the years 1933 to 1946—the focal point of *The Holocaust Chronicle*—is essential. However, just as it is incomplete to say that the Holocaust ended in 1946, it is also insufficient to say that the

Why Antisemitism?

In 1879 and 1880, Heinrich von Treitschke, an influential German nationalist historian, published a series of articles that drew attention to a fateful phrase: *"Die Juden sind unser Unglück"* ("The Jews are our misfortune"). Eventually, that slogan would be written on banners at Nazi Party rallies. Just before Treitschke's essay appeared, another German writer, anti-Jewish journalist Wilhelm Marr, coined the term *antisemitism*. But what that term denotes—discrimination and hatred against Jews—is arguably the world's longest hatred.

In the year 70 C.E., the Romans under Titus starved and/or slaughtered at least 600,000 Jews at Jerusalem. Early-day Christian theologians said the Jews brought the massacre upon themselves because they had rejected Jesus as their Messiah. Violence subsequently raged against Jews for centuries. Jews were expelled from England in 1290, from France in 1306, and from Spain in 1492.

As religious toleration and civil rights developed in 18th- and 19th-century Europe, Jews became almost equal citizens under the law. Those liberal trends, however, did not eliminate hate for Jews. In the late 1800s, for instance, anti-Jewish pogroms broke out in Russia and Poland, killing thousands.

Over the centuries antisemitism has taken different but related forms: religious, political, economic, social, and racial. Jews have been discriminated against, hated, and killed because prejudiced non-Jews believed Jews belonged to the wrong religion, lacked citizenship qualifications, practiced business improperly, behaved inappropriately, or possessed inferior racial characteristics. These forms of antisemitism, especially the racial one, all played key parts in the Holocaust. Without antisemitism, the Holocaust could not have happened.

Religious faith and a keen grasp of the world before the Holocaust have helped to sustain author and Holocaust survivor Elie Wiesel.

● **c. 1500 BCE:** Based on biblical chronology, Hebrews move to Egypt.

● **c. 1250 BCE:** The Hebrew Moses receives the Ten Commandments, which is crucial to the Hebrew religion's evolution into monotheism.

● **c. 1000 BCE:** Kings Saul, David, and Solomon reign. Jerusalem becomes the capital of the Israelite Kingdom. The great Solomon's Temple is constructed in Jerusalem.

● **c. 700 BCE:** Assyrians deport ten of the 12 Jewish tribes—the Ten Lost Tribes.

● **c. 600 BCE:** Babylonians conquer Jerusalem and destroy the Temple. They exile many Jews to Babylon. This diaspora is called the Babylonian Exile.

● **c. 500 BCE:** The notion of a Messiah, a political/military-religious/moral leader, develops. • The Persians conquer the Babylonians and permit the return of the exiled Jews and reconsecration of the Temple.

Auschwitz survivors reenter the camp in April 1965, 20 years after its liberation by the Russians.

Holocaust's beginning was in 1933.

The Holocaust's impact lives on. In that way the past is present. When the Holocaust is concerned, moreover, the presence of the past stretches awareness back and forth. Efforts to understand the Holocaust take one back in time to the origins of the Jewish people and the modern German state. It leads to a consideration of anti-Jewish discrimination that was rooted in Christianity as well as in racial stereotypes that preceded the existence of National Socialism.

As the 21st century unfolds, the Holocaust recedes farther into the past. As something that happened in an earlier century, it may appear to be increasingly distant from us. Nothing, however, could be further from the truth. The genocide happened; it casts shadows upon the earth. The genocide makes no darkness unthinkable, no destruction unimaginable, no devastation impossible. Post-Holocaust ethnic cleansing in Kosovo and genocides in Bosnia and Rwanda testify to that. Only if the Holocaust's warning is heeded and not forgotten can the cry "never again!" keep from being mocked by a resounding "again and again!" The warning can be best heeded by starting at the beginning. We start by paying attention to broken eyeglasses that belonged to a German journalist named Fritz Gerlich.

Fritz Gerlich's Spectacles

Born in 1883, Dr. Fritz Gerlich grew up in Munich. There he studied university science and history, writing a dissertation on a medieval Germanic emperor to obtain his doctorate. Hampered by the poor eyes that led to his wearing the steel-rimmed spectacles for which he became well known, Gerlich was unable to serve in the German Army during World War I. Instead he worked in the national archives while becoming increasingly attracted to political journalism.

Staunchly defending German nationalism in the aftermath of his country's defeat in 1918, Gerlich soon became editor-in-chief of the *Münchener Neueste Nachrichten,* one of the city's most conservative newspapers. By the early 1920s, Gerlich was a significant figure in Germany's postwar nationalist movement. In the spring of 1923, he received a visit from a controversial man, six years his junior, who was the leader of the right-wing National Socialist German Workers' Party. That man was Adolf Hitler.

Hitler's 1923 visit to Gerlich took place in troubled times. Sad-

Although a political rightist, Munich newspaper editor Fritz Gerlich abhorred Hitler. His opinion was unwavering throughout Hitler's rise to power, and ultimately cost Gerlich his life.

• **c. 4th–2nd centuries BCE:** Greeks attempt to destroy Judaism and impose Hellenistic culture and religion on the Jews. The Jews fight back. (Jews still celebrate these events in their holiday Chanukah.)

• **c. 3rd century BCE:** The Pentateuch (first five books of the Jewish Scriptures) are translated into Greek. This version becomes known as the Septuagint.

• **140 BCE:** Judea and Rome are allies.

• **63 BCE:** Pompey, one of the three rulers of Rome, conquers Palestine.

• **c. 4 BCE–30 C.E.:** This is the approximate lifetime of Jesus of Nazareth.

Pontius Pilate, the Roman governor of Judea, orders the execution of Jesus, who has been opposed by some Jewish leaders. A complication is that at this time many Jews belong to distinctly different sects of Judaism: The Sadducees are an aristocratic, priestly group who collaborate with the Roman authorities to maintain the status quo; the Pharisees are devoted

dled with the huge debt incurred in financing World War I and the misery of soaring inflation, the Weimar Republic (as the parliamentary government of Germany was called from 1919 to 1933) was stressed and strained. To glimpse what was to happen between Gerlich and Hitler, it is important to note in more detail a few of the reasons for Germany's distress at that time.

Germany's defeat in World War I was officially sealed on Armistice Day, November 11, 1918. Seven months later, on June 28, 1919, the Versailles Treaty, which established the peace terms, was signed in Paris. The treaty pronounced Germany guilty for starting the war and required the Germans to pay for all the damages the Allies had suffered. A reparations commission would determine the amount. The terms of an agree-

In sharp contrast to the mechanized Nazi *Blitzkrieg* into France 17 years later, French soldiers occupied the Ruhr by bicycle in 1923.

ment subsequently reached in London in May 1921 put Germany's war reparations bill at 132 billion gold marks (about $31 billion at the prevailing exchange rate). The debt was to be paid at six percent interest over 37 years. The annual payments would amount to two billion gold marks plus 26 percent of German exports. Estimated to be about seven percent of Germany's national income, the annual payments were judged by British economist John Maynard Keynes to be three times what the country could afford. The financial burden created deep resentment that Hitler and his Nazi Party would exploit to the fullest.

From the beginning, Germany had difficulty meeting the reparations schedule. Already at the end of 1921, for example, the

government declared that it could not make the payments due in January and February 1922. Several times Germany asked for a moratorium, but France, in particular, saw payment defaults as an opportunity to weaken Germany further by reoccupying the Rhine-Ruhr area, a region of industrial and strategic importance for Germany's postwar recovery. On January 11, 1923, using a shortfall in German wood and coal deliveries as his pretext, French Premier Raymond Poincaré sent troops into that part of Germany to oversee French interests.

Unable to offer military resistance to the French occupation, which was augmented by Belgian forces, the Germans responded with passive resistance. When 130,000 German laborers refused to work, the region's productivity declined by half. The French met

Upon their return home from the Great War, German soldiers found that their prospects were limited. Many of them wound up on welfare lines.

to the traditions of the Mosaic laws and seek religious purity among God's chosen people; the Essenes withdraw from society into quasi-monastic conclaves; the Zealots agitate for political freedom for Judea from Roman rule; and the Jewish Christians believe Jesus is the promised Messiah.

● 1st century C.E.: About five million Jews live outside Palestine, 80 percent of them within the Roman Empire.

● 70: Following a Jewish revolt, General Titus and his Roman army surround Jerusalem, entrapping the city's population. Jews who try to escape are killed. The rest are held

under siege for several months before being attacked by the army. Between starvation and slaughter, at least 600,000 Jews die. The Romans destroy the Second Temple. Many early-day Christian theologians will say that the Jews brought the destruction upon themselves because they had rejected Jesus as their Messiah.

this resistance with arrests, imprisonments, evictions, and even executions. By the summer of 1923, the woes of the slumping German economy had grown worse and the French occupation force in the Rhine-Ruhr area had risen to 100,000 men, a number equivalent to the size permitted for the entire German Army by the Versailles Treaty. These outcomes added insult to German injury, especially for those who erroneously believed, as Hitler did, that Germany's defeat and especially the Versailles Treaty had been the result of a *Dolchstoss* ("stab in the back") inflicted from within Germany by Jewish traitors and their left-wing collaborators.

In 1923 Germany experienced one of the most desperate inflationary spirals any industrialized nation has known. The country's wartime financing had depended less on increased taxation and much more on loans and bonds, which then were repaid by the government's already inflationary policy of increasing the money in circulation at the time. As quickly as the paper money was printed, its value depreciated.

Unfortunately, the problems plaguing Germany's economy went well beyond both the debts that had accumulated during wartime and the reparations demands that

The Versailles Treaty

The signing of the Versailles Peace Treaty in June 1919 marked the formal conclusion of the war between Germany and the former Entente powers. Written entirely by the victors, the treaty was universally loathed by Germans.

The treaty required Germany to relinquish the territories of Alsace, Lorraine, Poznan, West Prussia, and Upper Silesia as well as its prized colonial possessions in Africa. In addition, Germany lost control of its coal mines in the Saarland. The military provisions of the treaty removed German troops from the Rhineland, dismantled Germany's navy, and limited its army to 100,000 men. Exorbitant reparations, 132 billion gold marks (about $31 billion), were also exacted.

The most devastating feature of the treaty was the infamous "war-guilt clause." Article #231 stipulated that Germany must accept complete and total responsibility for the war, a demand that humiliated even moderate Germans who recognized Germany's obligations to make restitution.

Saddled with the burden of defeat and the humiliation of the Versailles Treaty, Germany's postwar government, the Weimar Republic, was accused by its critics of having stabbed Germany in the back. A call to overturn the treaty was the most salient feature of the Nazis' political platform before their ascension to power in 1933.

were another immense price for defeat. The war had harmed Germany's industrial capacity. Its stock of raw materials and goods had been severely depleted. Then there were the high costs of converting the economy from wartime to peacetime operation, a difficulty compounded by Germany's high unemployment. That problem, in

This poster of a bawling baby reflects German anger that those born after the war would spend their entire lives paying reparations.

• **313: Roman Emperor Constantine issues a decree that grants tolerance for all religions, including Christianity.**

• **4th century: Jews are discriminated against by the Christianized Roman Empire.**

• **4th–6th centuries: Several Church councils and dozens of Roman laws** attack Judaism and Jews, forbidding, for example, marriage between Christians and Jews. • **Christians begin to attack Jews as "Christ killers" in league with the devil.**

• **c. 500–1000: During the early Middle Ages, European Jews, generally working as merchants, suffer scattered persecution.**

• **1096–1099: The first Christian Crusaders massacre Jews in Europe and capture Jerusalem.**

• **11th–13th centuries: Many Christian Crusades include massacres of Jews. Thousands are slaughtered, and synagogues and homes are plundered.**

Economic Calamity

In Germany in 1923, a typical workingman carted his weekly salary home in a wheelbarrow. Housewives used the nearly worthless government currency to light household fires. An armload of banknotes might buy a loaf of bread. These absurdities were some of the more visible results of the economic inflation that wiped out people's savings and crippled Germany's Weimar government during the interwar years before Hitler.

From its inception in 1919, the democratic Weimar Republic faced serious economic problems, foremost among them staggering reparations payments demanded by the victorious Entente powers after the Great War of 1914–1918, and set forth in the Treaty of Versailles. Because German financial manipulators became fabulously wealthy by taking advantage of middle-class misfortune, those who had been ruined became receptive to right-wing political extremists who blamed the nation's ills on the Weimar government and, frequently, on Jews.

Although inflation came to a halt in 1924, the German recovery was fragile. The New York stock-market crash of October 1929 set off an international economic crisis that devastated Germany. Business failures and unemployment reached unprecedented levels. Argument in the *Reichstag* led to virtual paralysis of Germany's political decision-making process.

Throughout these years Adolf Hitler campaigned tirelessly, vowing to repudiate Versailles and restore Germany's pride and prosperity. A desperate electorate responded. In the 1930 elections, the NSDAP scored a dramatic political breakthrough, winning 18.3 percent of the vote and increasing its *Reichstag* representation from 12 delegates to 107—the second largest in parliament.

Nazi rhetoric encouraged the middle class to remember the awful inflation of 1923, and to resent the indignities of the Versailles Treaty. Nazis blamed Ger-

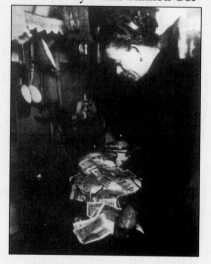

many's calamitous situation on "November criminals" (a reference to Social Democrats deemed responsible for Germany's prostrate position in 1919), on Marxists, on economic profiteers, and on the Jews, who supposedly were behind it all.

The shouting matches in parliament found increasingly more violent expression on Germany's streets, where pitched battles were fought by competing political armies. Youthful Nazi thugs relished clashes with Social Democrats and other political opponents. The summer of 1932 was particularly bloody, as Nazi Storm Troopers made good on their promises to "break skulls" and "smash up the goddamned Jewish republic." In June in the state of Prussia alone, nearly 500 skirmishes left more than 80 people dead.

As the Depression deepened, vigorous Nazi propaganda efforts paid even more dramatic dividends. The July 1932 elections gave the Nazis a stunning 37 percent of the vote. Now, with 230 *Reichstag* members, they became Germany's largest political party. Emboldened by this ballot-box success and apparent public approval of his grandiose economic plans, Hitler intensified his demand to be named chancellor.

● **11th–15th centuries:** Medieval Jews experience a significant deterioration of their status in Europe. Jews are viewed as the devil's agents; Europe's greatest sinners; rapacious usurers; malicious murderers of Christian children (ritual-murder defamation); drinkers of Christian blood (blood libel); conspirators who seek to destroy Christianity (poisoners of wells); and continued enemies of Jesus Christ (desecrators of the Host). These frequent defamations against Jews are not born out by the facts. Nevertheless, whole Jewish communities are slaughtered as a result of the animosity behind these charges.

● **1171:** In the town of Blois, southwest of Paris, Jews are falsely accused of committing ritual murder (killing of a Christian child) and blood libel (using the blood of the child in Jewish religious ritual). The adult Jews of the city are arrested and most are executed after refusing to convert. Thirty-one or 32 of the Jews are killed. The Jewish children are forcibly baptized.

This 1924 election poster urged Germans to vote for the German Nationalist People's Party (DNVP) and against the traitorous Democrats and Socialists.

turn, was made no easier by the fact that in 1920 Germany still maintained 660,000 soldiers. To meet the provisions of the Versailles Treaty, 560,000 had to be demobilized and then, somehow, absorbed into the German labor force. That goal could scarcely be accomplished in an economy whose inflationary instability was rapidly destroying confidence in the government.

In the early 1920s, one dollar was worth 100 marks. In January 1923 the mark fell to 18,000 per dollar. Hyperinflation had replaced inflation. Later in the year, the exchange rate soared to 4.2 billion marks to the dollar. Before the spiral could be brought under control at the end of 1923, the hyperinflation had ruined millions of ordinary Germans who depended on wages, fixed incomes, or savings that had been carefully accumulated during better times. At the inflation's peak, a liter of milk or a loaf of bread could cost billions of marks. Prices changed not only daily but *during* the day as well. Currency held in the morning was worthless by nightfall.

Hyperinflation benefited some financial manipulators who obtained huge bank loans, used them to buy businesses or property, and then were able to repay their loans with devalued currency. Most Germans, however, found themselves in dire economic straits, for it was not unusual for them to receive word from their banks indicating that their deposits no longer had any value.

An early mecca for Germany's postwar nationalist movements, the region of Bavaria—and in particular Munich, its chief city—not only was affected by economic instability in 1923 but was also a place where plans to restore order by revolutionary means were under way. It is likely that such plans led to Hitler's meeting with the bespectacled Fritz Gerlich. Gerlich was no Nazi, but the two men shared interests, and they might have become allies. As it turned out, the opposite happened. Gerlich became one of Germany's most persistent and adamant opponents of Hitler and the Nazis. The origin of his loathing for Hitler is less than crystal clear, but it probably stemmed from assurances that Hitler gave Gerlich in the spring and then broke in the autumn of 1923.

As Ron Rosenbaum documents the story in his 1998 book, *Explaining Hitler,* Gerlich backed the political aspirations of Gustav von Kahr, the right-wing nationalist governor of Bavaria. Hitler may have promised Gerlich that he, too, would support Kahr and not resort to illegal methods to advance the Nazi agenda. Subsequently, Gerlich witnessed the Munich Beer Hall *Putsch* on November 8–9, 1923, in which Hitler rashly attempted a takeover

As inflation rose, the Weimar government printed even more money. A ten-billion mark note, like the one pictured here, could buy practically nothing at the end of 1923.

● **1215: The Church's Fourth Lateran Council decrees that Jews be differentiated from others by their type of clothing to avoid intercourse between Jews and Christians. Jews are sometimes required to wear a badge; sometimes a pointed hat. • The Papacy sometimes protects Jews but makes it clear to one and all that the Jews are stateless beings who depend** on the kindness of the Church for their very existence within Christendom.

● **1290: Jews are expelled from England. Hostility toward Jews will persist in the British Isles for the next 350 years, despite the absence of Jews until the mid–17th century.**

● **1306: Philip IV orders all Jews expelled from France, with their property to be sold at public auction. Some 125,000 Jews are forced to leave.**

● **Early 14th century: Gypsies establish themselves in Southeastern Europe.**

of the Bavarian state. The coup began on the evening of November 8, when Hitler and other Nazi Party leaders interrupted a patriotic meeting in Munich's *Bürgerbräukeller*, where Kahr was the featured speaker. With Nazi Storm Troopers surrounding the building, Hitler put Kahr under arrest and extorted his support at gunpoint.

Once Kahr was free of intimidation, he renounced his coerced support. He also directed Bavarian police forces to be ready by midday on November 9. That afternoon Hitler and other Nazi leaders—including General Erich Ludendorff, a German war hero, and Hermann Göring, an ace fighter pilot who would become a

Gustav von Kahr, the nationalistic state commissioner of Bavaria, squelched Hitler's grab for power in Munich in 1923.

key figure in the Third Reich— advanced toward the *Odeonplatz* in Munich's center with some 2000 of their followers. Blocking the Nazis' path, the state police opened fire. Sixteen Nazis and four members of the police were killed. Hitler and Göring were injured. The coup failed, but far from forgetting it, the Nazis made this early revolutionary upsurge a key part of their party's identity. The fallen Nazis became martyrs. Those who survived became specially honored heroes among the *Alte Kämpfer* (old fighters), the Nazis who belonged to the Party before Hitler's rise to governmental power on January 30, 1933.

Meanwhile, Hitler was arrested two days after the

Frustrated by long-term unemployment, German workers rioted in Berlin in October 1923. Police quelled the riot and marched the demonstrators to prison.

failed coup. He stood trial for treason three months later. The court, however, was not overly concerned about Hitler's attempt to overthrow the government. Sentenced to five years in Landsberg Prison, Hitler was released after nine months, in December 1924. He had put his comfortable prison term to good use by starting to write one of the 20th century's most influential books, *Mein Kampf (My Struggle)*, which was published in 1925. By 1933 *Mein Kampf* had sold more than one million copies. The 500th printing took place in 1939, and by 1945 sales had reached ten million copies. The royalties made Hitler a wealthy man.

By 1933 Fritz Gerlich was a marked man as far as Hitler and the Nazis were concerned. For a decade, he had neither forgotten nor forgiven Hitler's broken promises. Gerlich never lost the conviction that had been driven home to him in 1923: namely, that deception, treachery, and ruthless violence were at the heart of Hitler's character. Gerlich determined that he would use his expertise and influence as a journalist to do his best to expose Hitler in any way he could.

Gerlich was not the only German journalist who opposed Hitler and the Nazi Party during

---

• **1348–1349: As the Black Death (bubonic plague) sweeps across Europe, killing indiscriminately, Jews are cast as scapegoats by people desperate to find an explanation for the terrible scourge. In Frankfurt and Worms, Germany, and at many other sites, Jews are murdered and their communities destroyed.**

• **15th century: Gypsies establish themselves in Western Europe.**

• **1490: The Spanish Inquisition charges both Jews and *conversos* (converted Jews) of plotting against Christians. Each group is accused of desecrating the Host. Between 1480 and 1520, perhaps 2000 to 4000 Marranos (converted Jews) are**

condemned to death as heretics or crypto-Jews.

• **1492: Jews are expelled from Spain.**

• **1516: The closed Jewish Quarter in Venice, Italy, is dubbed the *Geto Nuovo* (New Foundry). "Geto" will later become the basis for the word "ghetto."**

the 1920s and early 1930s. Even before Gerlich used his pen against Hitler, a group of now largely (but undeservedly) forgotten editors and reporters at the *Munich Post*—Martin Gruber, Erhard Auer, Edmund Goldschagg, and Julius Zerfass among them—used a savvy combination of investigative and tabloid styles to expose the Nazis as scandal-ridden, blackmailing, murderous thugs who would stop at nothing to put their racist, antisemitic politics into practice. Arguably the first public voices raised against Hitler, their opposition was from the political left more than from Gerlich's conservative perspective, but their themes and his had much in common.

For 12 years, up to and even including Hitler's early days as Germany's chancellor in the winter of 1933, the *Munich Post* battled Hitler and the National Socialists in print. Regarding Hitler as a political criminal and the Nazis as a reckless gang, the newspaper portrayed Hitler as controlling every move the Nazis made. The Nazis, the *Post*'s journalists typically underscored, were the "Hitler Party." Its cartoons lampooned Hitler; its stories aimed to topple him. The paper exposed murderous blackmail-driven purges within the Nazi

Party, and denounced Hitler's lie that a Socialist "stab in the back" had brought about Germany's World War I defeat. *Post* reporters implicated Hitler criminally in the mysterious death of his half-niece, Geli Raubal, and they insinuated that Hitler's antisemitism was unsuccessfully cov-

These are the most important defendants at the trial following the Beer Hall *Putsch*. Hitler is fourth from the right.

The Beer Hall Putsch

In November 1923 Adolf Hitler and Nazi Party followers attempted to overthrow the Bavarian government in what has come to be known as the Beer Hall *Putsch*.

Backed by armed members of the SA, Hitler stormed an official rally held in one of Munich, Germany's ubiquitous beer cellars on the evening of November 8. With a melodramatic proclamation that the national revolution had begun, Hitler and his followers took over the meeting and discussed strategy to gain popular support for their uprising. The next day, a mass Nazi demonstration in the center of Munich turned into a fiasco. Confronted by police barricades and following a brief gun battle in which 16 Nazis and four policemen were killed, Hitler and his followers fled for their lives.

The treason trial against Hitler and his underlings received national attention in Germany and resulted in a propaganda victory for the upstart politician. Accepting full responsibility for his actions, Hitler claimed that the real criminals were the signatories of the Versailles Peace Treaty and supporters of the Weimar Republic.

Right-wing judges sympathetic to Hitler's political vision sentenced Hitler to five years in prison, of which he served nine months. While in jail, Hitler dictated (to Rudolf Hess) his political manifesto, *Mein Kampf* (*My Struggle*).

● 1516–1918: Palestine is under control of the Ottoman Empire; *See* October 1918.

● 1542: Martin Luther, father of Protestant Christianity, publishes the pamphlet *On the Jews and Their Lies*.

● 1648–1649: The Cossack-led pogroms of Bogdan Chmielnicki

erupt in Poland and Russia. Charges of ritual murder and Host profanation lead to the destruction of about 300 Jewish communities and the murder of about 100,000 Jews.

● 1780s: Prussian chemists formulate "Prussian blue," a toxic compound that will be refined some 155 years later and called Zyklon B, used by the

Germans to gas Jewish death-camp inmates.

● September 27, 1791: France grants citizenship to Jews who swear an oath of loyalty to the nation.

● 1796: The Netherlands grants citizenship to Jews.

Fascism

Fascism was founded about 1920 in Italy by Benito Mussolini *(pictured, left)*. Fascist governments eventually came to power in Germany, Romania, Slovakia, and Croatia. Virtually every European country spawned its own Fascist organization.

Although lacking a common political manifesto, Fascist movements shared a number of similar features. Fascism, in its many varieties, stressed movement and action, and typically had a large following among the youth. Fascist governments were antidemocratic and anti-Marxist. Some but not all Fascist movements incorporated antisemitism into their political platform. Without exception, Fascist movements were closely identified with their leaders. No Fascist regime survived the death of its founder.

Mussolini's *Fasci di Combattimento* (Band of Combat) came to power in 1922. A show of force by the Italian "Black Shirts" on October 27, 1922, resulted in Mussolini's appointment as Italy's prime minister. Although Mussolini acquired power legally, months of terrorist disruption and intimidation strengthened his position. As prime minister, Mussolini cautiously consolidated his power before imposing a dictatorship. By the end of 1926, Italy had been transformed into a single-party dictatorial state.

A dramatically rendered illustration from this Hitler biography glorifies a Nazi Storm Trooper. The implication is clear: A movement worth fighting for is one worth dying for.

ering the likelihood that he was himself at least partly Jewish. In "The Jews in the Third Reich," a forecast published on December 9, 1931, more than two years before Hitler took power, the *Post* reported that it knew of a secret Nazi plan to deprive Jews of civil rights, confiscate their property, and achieve "the Final Solution of the Jewish Question"

by removing them from German society through slave labor.

In Nazi circles, the *Munich Post* became known as the "Poison Kitchen." Prior to the Nazi takeover in 1933, "the Hitler Party" tried to silence the *Post* with libel suits and death threats against its staff. Nevertheless, the newspaper's anti-Nazi resistance continued. Well into February 1933, the *Post* continued to publish reports about political murders carried out by the Nazis. Among its final anti-Hitler accounts was a three-part series that valiantly tried to counter what the *Post* had long regarded as Hitler's most destructive characteristic: his willful falsification of history. The *Post* foresaw Hitler's aims as disastrous for Germany and the world. Its views, however, did not prevail. Before the 1932–33 winter had ended, the *Post's* anti-Hitler reporting was smashed, its courageous journalists imprisoned or killed.

While the *Munich Post* attacked Hitler from the left, Fritz Gerlich and some of his journalistic colleagues became the most vociferous anti-Hitler critics among German conservatives. Moving on from his position with the *Münchener Neueste Nachrichten*, Gerlich led his own anti-Hitler newspaper, *Der Gerade Weg (The Right Way*

---

or *The Straight Path*) by the mid–1920s. One of the peaks of Gerlich's mounting hatred of Hitler was *Der Gerade Weg*'s sensational attack against him on July 17, 1932. Gerlich's paper featured a racially provocative photo composite image that aimed to assassinate Hitler's character. It suggested that Hitler had married a black woman. Headlining this "wedding" picture were provocative words that asked: "Does Hitler Have Mongolian Blood?"

At the heart and soul of Hitler's political creed stood the ideal of racial purity. Above all else, German or so-called Aryan blood

Erhard Auer was one of many *Munich Post* journalists who worked to expose the lies behind Hitler's supposed patriotism.

must be kept vital and strong. Taking this ideology to be the fraud it was, Gerlich went for the jugular by spreading the impression that Hitler, the champion of "pure blood," was not only a lying hypocrite but an aspiring German leader whose character and political ambitions were rotten to the core.

No one went further than Gerlich to state publicly what others may have suspected: namely, that Hitler's appearance was scarcely like the Nordic ideal about which he could wax so eloquent. In the article that Gerlich wrote to accompany the photo montage and its scathing headline, he brilliantly used satire to argue, in particular, that Hitler's nose could not stand the scrutiny of the "racial science" that Nazism advocated. Putting Hitler's nose on trial, Gerlich's article concluded that Hitler miserably failed his own racial test. Gerlich's attack on Hitler's

physiognomy, moreover, went more than skin deep. Persistently using the Nazis' own imagery against Hitler, Gerlich contended ironically that there could be nothing truly German about Hitler because "blood," according to Nazi ideology, was a matter of spirit as well as the key element in physical life. In Gerlich's view, Hitler's theories and political practices—despotic and corrupt at once—were profoundly at odds with the highest Germanic ideals.

Hitler was not pleased. Soon after Gerlich's article appeared, Nazis attacked the journalist's apartment building. Undaunted, Gerlich used the next week's issue of *Der Gerade Weg* to press the issue further. On July 24, 1932, he made clear that his lampoon had in no way been an endorsement of the Nazi racism he found so abhorrent. His point had not been to put Hitler on the low end of a racial hierarchy. To the contrary,

Although it eased some Versailles Treaty demands, the Young Plan required Germany to pay reparations until the 1980s. It met with fierce opposition from the German right, including the NSDAP.

not be seated as a member of Parliament because he will not swear the oath of office, which affirms Christianity as the true faith.

● 1851: Norway allows Jews to enter the country.

● 1860s: Europe sees its first stirrings of Zionism, as a nationalistic Jewish

movement to establish a Jewish homeland in the location that will become Israel.

● 1864: A satire by Maurice Joly called the *"Dialogue aux Enfers entre Montesquieu et Machiavel"* ("Dialogue in Hell Between Montesquieu and Machiavelli") attacking Napoleon III is published in Belgium.

It becomes the basis for the antisemitic *Protocols of the Elders of Zion*.

● 1865: The Ku Klux Klan is founded in the United States. It is anti-black and antisemitic.

● 1867: Hungary grants citizenship to Jews. • German journalist Wilhelm Marr publishes a popular book, *The*

The Depression hit Germany hard, forcing proud parents to send their children to soup kitchens operated by the Salvation Army.

he stated, all people are essentially equal because their souls are "bestowed on them by God." Furthermore, invoking religious tradition, Gerlich insisted that no man or woman could be racially inferior because "we are all descendants of one father and one mother, children of Adam and Eve."

Gerlich wanted his fellow Germans to understand that Hitler's way was neither the right way nor the German way. As 1932 wore on, Gerlich and the other anti-Hitler journalists had some reason to hope. Although the Nazis had achieved their high-water mark in freely contested national elections by winning 37.3 percent of the popular vote (230 seats in the *Reichstag*) on July 31, 1932, their popularity declined during

the next elections. On November 6, 1932, they received 33.1 percent of the popular vote and their *Reichstag* seats declined to 196. But overall the political tide was running with Hitler more than against him, and the anti-Hitler journalists could not stem it.

Still, Fritz Gerlich did not give up. On March 9, 1933, more than five weeks after Hitler took power, Gerlich prepared to publish yet another anti-Hitler attack in *Der Gerade Weg*. Perhaps he wanted to make new charges about Hitler's role in the untimely death of Geli Raubal. Perhaps he intended to arouse suspicion that the Nazis themselves—not Communists, as

Hitler addresses the NSDAP leaders' meeting in Munich in August 1928. He argued that the Nazis' poor showing in the May elections necessitated radical changes in strategy.

the Nazis claimed—had torched the *Reichstag* building on February 27, an action that Hitler used to convince the German president, Paul von Hindenburg, to issue the "Presidential Decree for the Protection of People and State." Its emergency measures, which remained in place throughout the Nazi period, suspended freedom of speech, press, and assembly; eliminated freedom from invasion of privacy; and abolished freedom from house search without warrant. These measures also made distribution of politically unacceptable material a treasonous crime punishable by death.

Apparently a last-ditch effort to derail Hitler, the contents of Gerlich's March 9 report remain unknown because on that day, as journalist Ron Rosenbaum aptly summarizes the situation, "Storm Troopers burst into Gerlich's newspaper office, ripped his last story from the presses, beat him senseless, and dragged him off to Dachau." Gerlich was imprisoned in the German concentration camp for more than a year. Then, his wife got the message that the Nazis had killed the journalist who had seen through them all. The notice contained no words,

---

Victory of Judaism over Germanism. **He coins the word "antisemitism" so that** *Judenhass,* **or Jew-hatred, can be discussed in polite society.**

● **1868: Benjamin Disraeli becomes prime minister of Great Britain—and the first prime minister of Jewish descent in Europe.**

● **1869: Italy grants emancipation to Jews.**

● **1870: Sweden grants citizenship to Jews.**

● **1870–1871: German states are unified under autocratic and militaristic Prussia. The king of Prussia becomes German Kaiser (emperor). Prussia's**

capital city, Berlin, becomes Germany's capital.

● **1871: Great Britain grants full emancipation to Jews.**

● **January 12, 1871: A new German constitution gives German Jews full legal equality for the first time since the region's first Jewish settlement,**

just his steel-rimmed, blood-spattered spectacles.

Adolf Hitler's Vision

Adolf Hitler wore no signature spectacles, but his racist, antisemitic vision meant that the pair Sophie Gerlich received in the early summer of 1934 were by no means the only ones that belonged to Nazi victims. When the Soviet Army liberated Auschwitz-Birkenau 11 years later, they found huge amounts of loot, which had been taken from the Jews who were murdered there. The loot included not only millions of pieces of clothing and tons of human hair but also mounds of eyeglasses. None of those spectacles or any others that could have been prescribed would have corrected Hitler's vision, however. His outlook—distorting and defacing human life nearly beyond recognition—won a following strong enough to govern Nazi Germany and to dominate most of Europe from 1933 to 1945. *Mein Kampf* contains the core of Hitler's vision. But as we shall see, it raises questions that go farther back than the 1920s or the turn-of-the-century world into which Hitler was born in Braunau, Austria, on April 20, 1889.

Disagreements persist about the precise origins of Hitler's antisemitism. No reputable scholar would deny, however, that Hitler was incorrigibly antisemitic well before he met Fritz Gerlich in Munich during the spring of 1923. Nor would any serious interpreter repudiate the view that Hitler's antisemitism was unwavering. His hatred for Jews was so unrelenting that the political testament he signed on April 29, 1945—one day prior to his suicide and less than ten days before the Third Reich surrendered—ended by ordering "the government and the people to uphold the race laws to the limit and to resist mercilessly the poisoner of all nations, international Jewry."

Hitler's own account of the beginnings of his antisemitism is sometimes at variance with sources that locate them prior to his first visit to Vienna in May 1906. Nevertheless, Hitler's emphasis on the formative quality of his experiences in that city, before he moved to Munich in 1913 at the age of 24, reveals that he found the imperial capital of Austria-Hungary to be very differ-

---

The Young Hitler

Adolf Hitler *(center)* grew up in an authoritarian household. His father, an Austrian customs official, was quick-tempered and overly strict, and Adolf drew much closer to his overindulgent mother. It was from his father that Hitler acquired many of his personality traits.

Hitler was born on April 20, 1889, in Braunau am Inn, an Austrian town on the German border. Little Adolf was spoiled by his mother, but did not have a happy childhood. He and his father quarreled frequently, and the boy was moody and discontent. A lazy and disinterested student, he dropped out of school at the age of 16 to pursue his dream of becoming a painter.

Crushed and bitterly disappointed when he failed the entrance examination to the Vienna Academy of Art in 1907, Hitler spent the next five years enduring a miserable existence in Vienna. Living in men's hostels, unshaven, and shabbily dressed, he barely eked out a living by hawking his sketches at local cafes and taverns. This period in Vienna was, he remembered, "the hardest, but also the most thorough, school of my life." There, his ideological foundations became established.

---

which dates to Roman times. This "equality" does little to stem German antisemitism.

● **1874:** After a long process, Jews in Switzerland receive full rights of citizenship under the new constitution.

● **1878:** The antisemitic German Christian Social Party is founded by Adolf Stoecker, a court chaplain. The party demands that Jews convert to Christianity.

● **1880:** Petitions signed by 250,000 Germans demand that the government ban Jews from German schools and universities—and from holding public office.

● **1880s:** Anti-Jewish pogroms break out across Russia.

● **1881:** Eugen Karl Dühring publishes an antisemitic book in Germany, *Die Judenfrage als Rassen-, Sitten-, und Kulturfrage* (*The Jewish Question as a Racial, Moral, and Cultural Problem*).

Richard Wagner

Born in 1813, Richard Wagner was a leading proponent of *völkisch* nationalism, the movement that defined Germany in highly xenophobic and exclusive terms. Wagner's operas, especially *Der Ring des Nibelungen* (*The Ring of the Nibelung*), attempted to recapture Germany's grandeur and mystical past.

Wagner was also notorious for his political and racial antisemitism. His essay *"Das Judenthum in der Musik"* ("Jewry in Music") claimed that Germans were "instinctively repelled" by Jews. According to Wagner, Jews had a destructive effect on German culture. Their financial power enabled them to dictate public opinion.

Wagner's racial antisemitism attracted a large following among Germany's educated elite. Although the composer sank into insanity before his death at 70 in 1883, his political essays and music were greatly admired by Adolf Hitler. Wagner's works were performed at many Nazi festivals.

ent from provincial Linz, his hometown, where he first heard the music of the antisemitic composer Richard Wagner, who long exerted strong influence upon him. Vienna alienated, captivated, and educated Hitler all at once, and in decisive ways that he could not have anticipated.

Hitler's artistic ambitions—his traditionalist style of painting featured landscapes and buildings—led him to seek admission to Vienna's Academy of Art. After clearing the preliminary hurdles, he took the crucial drawing examination on October 1 and 2, 1907. The faculty evaluating this examination—none of them were Jewish—admitted 28 of the 113 candidates. How different the 20th century might have been if Hitler had been among those accepted, but he was not. Although rejected from the academy, Hitler remained in Vienna, where he supplemented family funds that were available to him by occasionally selling his pictures to art dealers, most of them Jewish.

Protestant minister and noted antisemite Adolf Stoecker was appointed court chaplain for Kaiser Wilhelm I. In this position he influenced the Kaiser and his ministers against Germany's Jews.

While living in Vienna, Hitler became acquainted with Viennese versions of the racism and antisemitism that some European politicians frequently used to blame the Jews for any and every difficulty that non-Jews encountered. One who did so was Dr. Karl Lueger, who served as mayor of Vienna from 1897 to 1910. Lueger was a popular mayor. He worked hard to revitalize his native city, whose population of two million in

As this color sketch attests, Hitler had artistic ambitions. Rejected twice by Vienna's Academy of Art, he turned his frustrated energies toward reactionary, antisemitic politics.

● **1881–1884:** Violently anti-Jewish pogroms sweep Poland, the Ukraine, and Russia; *See* 1903–1906.

● **1881–1903:** Waves of immigration of European Jews to Palestine and the United States occur.

● **1883:** Sir Francis Galton coins the term "eugenics" to encompass the

notion of positive modification of natural selection through selective breeding of human beings; *See* 1910.

● **April 20, 1889:** Adolf Hitler is born in Braunau am Inn, Austria.

● **1894:** In France, Army Captain Alfred Dreyfus, a Jew, is falsely accused and convicted of treason, set-

ting off a wave of French antisemitism, bordering on the hysterical. Dreyfus will spend nearly five years on Devil's Island before being freed and ultimately exonerated. ● In France, the antisemitic Edouard-Adolphe Drumont and *La Croix*, the newspaper of the Assumptionist Order of the Roman Catholic Church, lead the attack on the Jews. ● In Germany,

1908 made it the sixth largest in the world. One of Lueger's political slogans was that "Greater Vienna must not turn into Greater Jerusalem." He was a mesmerizing speaker who rarely missed an opportunity to use antisemitism for his political advantage.

Jews had lived in Vienna since the middle of the 12th century. In 1623, however, the inner city became off-limits to them. Ghettoized for a time, they were completely expelled from Vienna in 1670 by Emperor Leopold I, who subsequently invited them back when economic interests led him to do so. Though they were more or less oppressed for centuries, the prospects for the Viennese Jews improved in 1867 when emancipating changes in the Austro-Hungarian law—the changes were late-arriving in comparison with most European states—gave them full civil rights. These freedoms meant that Jews could own property in Vienna, enter government service, and enjoy greater access to universities—freedoms that brought the city a wave of Jewish immigration. In 1860, for example, Vienna's Jewish population numbered 6200. By 1910 that number had grown to 175,300 (8.7 percent of Vienna's total population).

Educational opportunities were especially attractive to Vienna's growing Jewish population. By the turn of the century, nearly one-third of Viennese university students were Jews. In 1913 the percentages of Jews studying medicine and law were 40 and 25, respectively. In business, too, and in the artistic fields, Jews had also achieved considerable success. Far from being celebrated throughout Vienna, however, the gains made by Jews—especially when those gains created unwanted competition—produced resentment among non-Jews who felt that they were being hurt by Jewish success. Vienna's antisemitic currents, moreover, had been intensifying not only in reaction to Jewish success stories but also from fear that impoverished Jews from Eastern Europe and Russia, fleeing for their lives from pogroms directed against them, would flood Vienna with an even more alien Jewish presence, which was embodied in the traditional dress that characterized those predominantly Orthodox Jews.

By the time Hitler took up residence in Vienna in 1907, antisemitism ran high. Much of it was based on a two-part principle: (1) all Jews, no matter their differ-

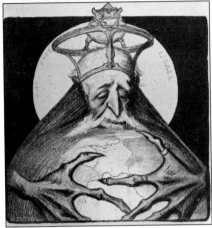

Top: These Jews, awaiting customers on Berlin's *Grenadierstrasse,* struggled to make a living on the black market during the lean interwar years. *Bottom:* Antisemites fixated on Europe's Jewish Rothschild family, decrying them as political and financial manipulators.

ences, were essentially—ethnically or even racially—the same; (2) all Jews were different, dangerously so, from Vienna's non-Jewish population, no matter how much or how little they seemed to be part of it. Newspapers and political

---

Social Darwinist Alfred Ploetz describes selective breeding of human beings as "racial hygiene."

● **1896: Anti-Jewish violence accompanying the Dreyfus Affair inspires eyewitness reporter and Hungarian Zionist Theodor Herzl to publish *Der Judenstaat (The Jewish State),* a work that promotes Zionism; *See* 1897.**

● **1897: The World Zionist Organization (WZO) is created at Basel, Switzerland. Zionist leader Theodor Herzl, who has covered antisemitic violence as a journalist, calls for a Jewish state. ● Antisemitic politician Dr. Karl Lueger is elected mayor of Vienna, running on the electoral ticket of the antisemitic Christian Social Party.**

● **1899: *Die Grundlagen des 19. Jahrhunderts (Foundations of the Nineteenth Century),* an antisemitic book by Houston Stewart Chamberlain, is published in Germany. It holds that human history is a battle between Jews and Aryans. ● *Action Française* (French Action), an antisemitic group, is founded in France.**

"One does not have dealings with pests and parasites; one does not rear and cherish them; one destroys them as speedily and thoroughly as possible."

—Paul Anton de Lagarde, 19th-century German political theorist, nationalist, and antisemite, on Jews; 1881

German soldiers, once part of a massive wartime army, found solidarity during the interwar years within the ranks of a nationalist veterans organization called *Stahlhelm* (Steel Helmet).

tracts were full of antisemitic commentary. Local politics was charged with antisemitic rhetoric. Antisemitism, in short, filled the Viennese air that Hitler breathed.

Still, it remains a question whether Vienna's antisemitism simply became Hitler's during the period from 1907 to 1913. Documented antisemitic remarks from the young Hitler are hard to find. Viennese eyewitnesses reported that Hitler got along well with Jews at the time. The picture that emerges in *Mein Kampf*, however, suggests something else. There, Hitler highlights what he describes as a converting experience. "The visual instruction of the Vienna streets," wrote Hitler, "performed invaluable services." According to Hitler, he initially "wandered blindly" through the city, but as time passed he saw the city's people "with open eyes." In particular, he emphasized seeing "an apparition in a black caftan and black hair locks. Is this a Jew? was my first thought . . . but the

longer I stared at this foreign face, scrutinizing feature for feature, the more my first question assumed a new form: Is this a German?" In *Mein Kampf*, Hitler went on to say that this decisive encounter convinced him that the Viennese Jews were not Germans of a particular religious persuasion but "a people in themselves."

Mein Kampf says that Hitler's antisemitic vision became focused in Vienna, but that account was written more than a decade later, and much had happened during those intervening years. Of crucial importance was Hitler's experience in World War I. In 1913 Hitler avoided serving in the Austrian military by leaving Vienna. He lived in Munich for a time and then returned to Austria, where he was found physically unfit for military service. Nevertheless, when World War I began in August 1914, Hitler was elated, and he volunteered enthusiastically for the German Army. He spent the next four years on the

Western Front, serving in France and Belgium as a dispatch runner, an often-dangerous duty that entailed carrying orders—on foot or by bicycle—from regimental commanders to leaders at the front. Hitler received a promotion to corporal on November 3, 1914, but rose no higher for reasons that remain unclear. Some accounts indicate that he refused to be considered for promotion; others suggest that his superiors found his leadership potential wanting.

Nevertheless, Hitler, who was wounded in October 1916, served with distinction. His military decorations included the Iron Cross First Class, a special achievement for a corporal, which he received on August 4, 1918, thanks to his

---

• **1899–1902: The term "concentration camp" is coined by the British during the Boer War to denote holding areas for potentially threatening Afrikaners (descendents of Dutch who immigrated to South Africa in the mid-1800s).**

• **1903: The party platform of the nationalistic and aggressively anti-**semitic *Narodowa Demokracja* **(National Democratic Party) is established in Poland. It encourages anti-Jewish pogroms and forced immigration.**

• **1903–1906: A second wave of violently antisemitic pogroms sweeps Poland and the Ukraine;** *See* **1881–1884; 1919–1921.**

• **1905: A revised version of the apocryphal *Protocols of the Elders of Zion* is published in Russia.** • **In Germany, the International Society for Racial Hygiene is founded to advance theories of Social Darwinism and selective breeding of human beings.**

• **1907: Adolf Hitler is rejected for study at the Vienna Academy of Art.**

Influences on Hitler

The foundations of Hitler's worldview took shape during the six poverty-stricken years he spent in the Austrian capital of Vienna, from 1907 to 1913. His attitudes developed from the frustrations he experienced there, and were based on the interrelated concepts of social Darwinism, antisocialism, and antisemitism.

Reduced to living among Vienna's dregs of society and robbed of his self-esteem, the young Hitler deeply resented being denied access to the splendor and gaiety of the city. There, in what he termed a world of "repugnant filth," he saw himself engaged in a struggle for survival, in which only the fittest, most brutal, stood a chance. Applying this lesson to his Machiavellian perception of life, he declared in *Mein Kampf* that "he who wants to live should fight, and he who does not want to battle in this world of eternal struggle does not deserve to be alive."

Hitler contemptuously perceived working-class ideologies to be intrinsically weak doctrines that "reject the aristocratic principle of nature, and replace the eternal privilege of power and strength by the mass of numbers." This, he was sure, would result in the "collapse of human civilization." It was no mere coincidence, he reasoned, that Jews were behind these "doctrines of destruction."

Hitler's nationalist and antisemitic ideology began to crystallize as a result of his exposure to an abundance of poisonous literature. Antisemitism became the driving force in his life.

Among his favorite reading was the gutter journal *Ostara*, edited by Lanz von Liebenfels, an eccentric ex-monk. This crackpot racial theorist imagined blue-eyed, blond Aryans waging a monumental struggle against the "race defilement" danger posed by what he termed "monkey people."

Hitler acquired his first political education by studying the propaganda techniques and demagoguery of Dr. Karl Lueger *(pictured)*, the antisemitic mayor of Vienna. Lueger was a skillful manipulator of mass audiences who pushed for the removal of Jews from influential positions. From Adolf Stoecker, the leading German antisemite of the late 19th century, Hitler borrowed the notion that Jews who controlled corporations and banks were the inevitable cause of the economic misfortunes of small-business owners.

Hitler also studied the *völkisch* (racist-nationalist) extremist philosophy of politician Georg von Schönerer, who demanded that all culturally German lands within the Hapsburg Empire be incorporated into the Reich. Perhaps the most influential writers shaping Hitler's formulation of race theory were philosopher Eugen Dühring and journalist Wilhelm Marr. Basing their shrill message on pseudoscientific arguments, they expounded a biologically based antisemitism. Warning that the German race was in grave danger, they urged the adoption of special laws against Jews, and—hauntingly—called for their deportation.

● **October 23, 1907:** A Berlin libel case, *Moltke v. Harden*, leads to the exposure of considerable homosexuality and sodomy in the German military and the Kaiser's inner circle. The case will later help to justify Nazi abuse of homosexuals.

● **1907–1941:** Approximately 38,000 mentally disabled men and women are sterilized in American mental institutions.

● **1910:** British Home Secretary Winston Churchill, inspired by eugenics theories of Sir Francis Galton, urges that some 100,000 "degenerate British citizens" be sterilized or interned in labor camps.

● **1911–1913:** In Russia, Menahem Mendel Beilis, a Jew, is put on trial for the ritual murder of a Christian boy. After two years followed by a "show trial," Beilis is acquitted.

● **1913–1915:** The Leo Frank Affair occurs in Atlanta, Georgia. Frank, a northern Jew, is falsely accused of murdering a 13-year-old Christian

nomination by a Jewish officer named Hugo Guttman. By that time, huge German losses—about 800,000 men had fallen in the previous four months—made the German leadership recognize that the war was lost. In October 1918, shortly before the war ended, a mustard-gas attack temporarily blinded Hitler. By the time he recovered in the Pasewalk military hospital, Germany had surrendered. Along with many other Germans,

Hitler was stunned by the news of defeat.

Up to the end, the German leadership did little to prepare people for war's outcome, which proved to be disastrous. More than 13 million men, almost 20 percent of the German population, had served in the Army. About two million were killed, another five million wounded. Contrary to Hitler's oft-repeated claim, no "stab in the back" had defeated

Germany. Rather, superior Allied resources and German exhaustion eventually brought this devastating war to an end. From March to July 1918, 750,000 German soldiers were wounded and about 1.75 million more were incapacitated during one of the world's most severe influenza epidemics. Nevertheless, the Hitler who had gone off to war elated became the revengefully determined Hitler of *Mein Kampf*, where he recalled his bitterness about the outcome of World War I during his Pasewalk convalescence from gas-attack blindness: "And so it had all been in vain. . . . The more I tried to achieve clarity on the monstrous event in this hour, the more the shame of indignation and disgrace burned in my brow. What was all the pain in my eyes compared to this misery?"

While World War I and its immediate aftermath gave Hitler's antisemitism its distinctively virulent form, what he had heard, seen, and observed in Vienna proved to be a formative influence nonetheless. For as Hitler sought an explanation for Germany's defeat, Europe saw an outbreak of Socialist- and Communist-inspired revolutions. This, plus the sanctions of the Versailles Treaty and the antisemitism he had encountered in Vienna, struck

Alfred Rosenberg

Alfred Rosenberg, self-styled National Socialist "philosopher," joined the Nazi Party in 1919 and became editor of the Party newspaper, *Völkischer Beobachter*, four years later. He is most widely remembered for his book, *The Myth of the Twentieth Century* (1930), which made him the chief ideologue of the National Socialist movement.

Rosenberg's book was among the most widely circulated of the Nazi years, with more than one million copies in print by 1942. Permeated with hatred for the Jews, it promoted "purity of blood" for the German people "under the sign of the swastika." Rosenberg characterized all of history as a conflict between the forces of light (the Nordic or Aryan peoples) and the powers of darkness (the Jews). The Jews were the most virulent enemy of German culture and racial purity, and their influence, according to Rosenberg, had to be eradicated.

From July 1941 Rosenberg had, as minister of Occupied Eastern Territories, the opportunity to put his ideas into practice. In spite of his apparent influence, the Nazi leadership widely despised him as a crackpot, and his underlings regularly circumvented his authority. This caused him to quit in disgust in October 1944. After the war, Rosenberg was arrested and tried at Nuremberg. Convicted of crimes against humanity, he was hanged on October 16, 1946.

girl. Amid an intensely antisemitic environment, which makes a fair trial impossible, Frank is convicted. Even though the governor commutes his death sentence, a mob breaks into prison and lynches Frank.

● **1914: The first American-Jewish movie with an all-Jewish cast, *A Passover Miracle*, is released.**

● **1914–1918: The First World War devastates Europe.**

● **1915: The Jewish Anti-Defamation League (ADL) is created in the wake of the Leo Frank Affair.**

● **1917: The Russian Revolution develops.**

● **April 6, 1917: The United States declares war on Germany.**

● **November 2, 1917: The Balfour Declaration is published. This letter, from British Foreign Secretary Lord Arthur Balfour to British-Jewish leader Lord Rothschild, promises qualified British support for the establishment of a Jewish homeland**

This letterhead of the antisemitic Thule Society states: "Remember, you are a German! Keep your blood pure!"

Hitler profoundly, with renewed clarity: The Jews, he believed, *were* to blame. Writing in retrospect about his immediate postwar experience, Hitler put the point this way: "There is no making pacts with Jews; there can only be the hard: either-or. I, for my part, decided to go into politics."

By the time Hitler wrote those words in 1924, he had been in politics for a relatively short time, but during those postwar years he took steps that proved to be especially important. First, discharged from the Pasewalk hospital but not yet demobilized from the Army, he traveled through a crisis-ridden Germany—250,000 Germans starved to death in 1918—and arrived in Munich. That city was a center of violent postwar unrest that produced, among other things, a short-lived, left-wing political takeover, which was crushed on May 1, 1919. To

accomplish that task, regular army formations had to be augmented by so-called *Freikorps* (Free Corps) units. These right-wing paramilitary groups consisted largely of World War I veterans who blamed Germany's defeat on the Jews and the Social Democrats, the largest—and considerably Jewish—political party in the Weimar Republic, which had been proclaimed on November 9, 1918. Although still in the regular Army, Hitler played no major part in suppressing this revolutionary attempt, but his awareness that it included Jewish leadership reinforced his linking of antisemitism with anticommunism.

More decisive in Hitler's political development was the fact that in May 1919 he got a position in the Army's information department, whose Munich unit was under the command of Captain Karl Mayr. Mayr's tasks included inculcating German troops with the proper nationalist and anticommunist attitudes. Hitler was one of the men he selected for training as an instructor in this project. Soon given the opportunity to lecture German troops, Hitler found his element: He proved to be a brilliant and persuasive speaker. Significantly, Hitler's talks to German soldiers in the spring and summer of 1919 were

the first occasions in which Hitler spoke publicly against the Jews.

Apparently regarding Hitler as something of an expert on Jewish issues, Mayr told Hitler to answer a letter, dated September 4, 1919, that had been sent by a man named Adolf Gemlich, who had participated in one of the troop instruction courses. Gemlich wanted clarification about the "Jewish question." The reply that Hitler sent to Gemlich, dated September 16, 1919, was his first explicit writing about the Jews. Hitler told Gemlich that "Jewry is unqualifiedly a racial association and not a religious association. . . . Its influence will bring about the racial tuberculosis of the people." He then drew an important dis-

To attract new members from the ranks of Nationalists and Socialists, the German Workers' Party changed its name to the National Socialist Workers' Party at a meeting in Munich on February 24, 1920.

---

in Palestine. The declaration contradicts the earlier McMahon-Faisal agreement, which promised the same territory to Arabs.

● **1918: The antisemitic group** *Schutz und Trutz Bund* **is established in Germany.** ● *Sin Against the Blood*, **an antisemitic novel by Artur Dinter, is published.** ● **The** *Thule-Gesellschaft*

(Thule Society), **a radical right-wing group in Munich, Germany, is established. The group uses the swastika as a symbol of German nationalism.**

● **July 16–17, 1918: Russian Czar Nicholas II and his family are executed by Bolsheviks following a long period of captivity.**

● **1918–1920: The Russian civil war, pitting Bolsheviks against anti-Bolsheviks, is won by the Bolsheviks.** ● **About 100,000 Jews are murdered in western Ukraine.**

● **October 1918: Britain and Turkey agree to an armistice, taking Turkey out of the world war. Palestine falls under British control, freeing it from**

The Rise of the Nazi Party

Employed in the Political Department of the District Army Command in Munich, a 30-year-old veteran of World War I was instructed to reply to Adolf Gemlich, a soldier who had wondered why Germany had lost the war. The reply, dated September 16, 1919, blamed Jews for Germany's defeat. It was written and signed by Adolf Hitler.

In this letter, his first explicitly anti-Jewish writing, Hitler drew a pair of crucial distinctions. He emphasized, first, that Jewish identity should be defined not by religion but by race. Second, Hitler separated *emotional* and *rational* antisemitism. Emotional antisemitism, he claimed, periodically erupts in violence, but it lacks the systematic qualities necessary to achieve anti-

semitism's "final objective," which ought to be "the removal of the Jews altogether."

On September 12, 1919, Hitler attended his first meeting of the German Workers' Party (DAP), a small, right-wing political group. Four days later, Hitler not only dispatched his message to Gemlich but also joined the DAP as the seventh member of its executive committee. By 1920 the German Workers' Party had become the National Socialist German Workers' Party (NSDAP). Now led by Hitler, who had quickly assumed dictatorial control, its members were known as Nazis (a contraction of National Socialists).

The Nazis' unsuccessful attempt to take over the German government in November 1923—known as the Munich (Beer Hall)

Putsch—led to a prison sentence for Hitler in 1924. While in prison at Landsberg, Hitler wrote *Mein Kampf* (*My Struggle*), whose two volumes were published in 1925 and 1926. By 1945, this book had sold more than six million copies.

Inflaming racist antisemitism, *Mein Kampf* asserted that some races create civilization and others corrupt it. These races struggle for survival of the fittest. According to Hitler, the best and most desirable race was the Nordic-Aryan-German "master race." Jews were the worst enemy of all. Wherever he saw a threat to the "master" race's survival, Hitler found the Jews. The German people, he proclaimed, must eliminate this Jewish menace. Under his leadership, *Mein Kampf* affirmed, the Nazis would do so.

Benefiting from Hitler's power as a spellbinding speaker, the Nazis gained in popularity as Hitler promised a better life for the German people and renewed glory for Germany. According to Nazi ideology, that way of life would be based on nationalism that emphasized antisemitism and German racial "purity," ferocious anticommunism, a single-party dictatorship and a state-controlled economy, and, eventually, expansion of German territory. Although still a minority in 1932, the Nazis were the largest political party in Germany. Soon they gained control. Calling their state the Third Reich, Adolf Hitler and his Nazi followers ruled Germany from 1933 to 1945.

Turkish rule for the first time since 1516.

• October 4, 1918: An exhausted Germany asks the Allies for terms of an armistice.

• November 1918: Germany's Kaiser Wilhelm abdicates.

• November 11, 1918: An armistice signed between Germany and the Allies ends the First World War, but not the root troubles that plague Europe.

• December 25, 1918: The nationalistic, antisemitic *Stahlhelm* (Steel Helmet) is established by war veterans in Germany.

• 1918–1933: Antisemitic policies of the Polish government prompt 60,000 Polish Jews to immigrate to Germany.

• 1919: Germany adopts a democratic constitution. • The nation also passes laws restricting Gypsy movement, camping, and settlement.
• German nationalist Albert Leo is executed by the French after defying

Storm Troopers, responsible for fomenting riots and disrupting political meetings, stand at attention before Nazi banners that proclaim, "Germany awake."

tinction. "Antisemitism on purely emotional grounds," said Hitler, "will find its ultimate expression in the form of pogroms. Rational antisemitism, however, must lead to a systematic legal opposition and elimination of the special privileges which Jews hold.... Its final objective must unswervingly be the removal (*Entfernung*) of the Jews altogether. Only a government of national vitality is capable of doing both, and never a government of national impotence." Whether this statement meant that already in 1919 Hitler intended to exterminate the Jews is far from clear. But other parts of this early and carefully focused statement remained constant throughout his political life, notably antisemitism defined racially, and Hitler's call for a unified and systematic national policy to combat Jewish power.

On September 12, 1919, Mayr sent Hitler to the *Sterneckerbräu*, a Munich beer hall, to obtain intelligence about a group whose name led the Army to think—mistakenly—that it belonged to the political left. In fact, the ideology of the *Deutsche Arbeiterpartei* (DAP; German Workers' Party) was just the opposite.

Established in January 1919, this little-known party's leaders included Anton Drexler, a Munich railroad worker, who envisioned a *völkisch* German state resting on broad middle-class interests and purged of Jews and foreigners. At first, Hitler found the September 12 meeting boring and was about to leave, but when the discussion turned to the possibility of Bavarian separatism, Hitler intervened in strong disagreement. Impressed by Hitler's vigorous rebuttal, Drexler gave Hitler a copy of *My Political Awakening*, the DAP leader's political credo, and invited Hitler to return if he wanted to join. A few days later, before Hitler had decided what to do, he received a postcard. It said that he had been accepted as a party member and urged him to attend a DAP leadership meeting for further discussion. Hitler went to this meeting—it was held in another

Munich beer hall, the dimly lit *Altes Rosenbad*—where his sympathy for the DAP's views and his sense of personal opportunity impressed him. The exact date remains unclear, but one day during the second half of September 1919, Hitler joined the German Workers' Party as member No. 555 (the DAP's numbering began at 501 to magnify its size). He also became the seventh member of its executive committee.

Hitler's political energy, canny use of advertising and propaganda

Young supporters of the Nazi Party parade through the streets of Munich during the first annual Party Day rally. The NSDAP did not create a formal youth organization until 1926.

techniques, and speech-making ability gradually lifted the DAP from oblivion. On February 24, 1920, nearly 2000 people, including several hundred Socialist opponents, came to the party's first mass meeting, which was held in the *Festsaal* (banquet hall) of

French authority in the Ruhr. In later years, the Nazis will elevate Leo to martyr status. • *Action Nationale*, an antisemitic and Fascist group, is founded in Belgium by Pierre Nothomb. • The Treaty of St. Germain guarantees minority rights to Austrian Jews. • The German translation of *Protocols of the Elders of Zion*, the alleged minutes of a

secret meeting of conspiratorial Elders of Zion, is published.

• **January 5, 1919:** The German Workers' Party (DAP) is founded in Munich.

• **Mid-September, 1919:** Adolf Hitler joins the German Workers' Party.

• **Late 1919:** Hitler meets Dietrich Eckart, a Munich playwright and the publisher of *Auf gut deutsch* (*In Plain German*), a rabidly antisemitic, anti-Marxist weekly.

• **1919–1921:** A third wave of violently antisemitic pogroms sweeps Poland and the Ukraine. Overall, more than 60,000 Jews are killed, and several

Munich's *Hofbräuhaus*. When it was Hitler's turn to speak, he harangued the audience, amplifying party platform themes that he and Drexler had set down a few days earlier. Among the platform's standard right-wing articles—for example, pan-German nationalism and denunciation of the Versailles Treaty—there were also proposals to revoke the citizenship rights of Jews, to exclude them from the civil service, and to deport Jews who had come to Germany after World War I began. None of these proposals particularly distinguished the DAP from other right-wing German parties, but Hitler and his fiery rhetoric did.

By early March 1920, the DAP had a new name. Henceforth, it would be known as the *National-sozialistische Deutsche Arbeiterpartei* (NSDAP; National Socialist German Workers' Party). Its members became known as Nazis, which is a contraction of National Socialists. A month later Hitler left the Army to devote himself full-time to the political future of the renamed party. Hitler's speeches—typically they were delivered from rough notes and lasted two hours—drew crowds that often numbered in the thousands. He rapidly became virtually synonymous with the NSDAP. At a party congress on July 29, 1921,

Hitler obtained dictatorial leadership of the NSDAP, which he was then able to control as he wished. His plans included the aim of making the Nazis the champions not of special social classes or interest groups but of the German people as a whole—a goal that, of course, found no room within it for Jews or other "non-Germans."

By the following summer, the NSDAP had 6000 members. It also had a paramilitary organization known as the *Sturmabteilung* (SA; Storm Troopers). Organized by Hermann Göring, the ace flyer from World War I, and under the command of former Army captain Ernst Röhm, the SA drew its membership mainly from the *Freikorps* and other Germans who distrusted the Weimar Republic's

Hitler got almost everything he asked for while confined in Landsberg Prison. He had a suite of rooms and could even receive visitors.

democratic orientation. The SA's taste for street fighting and intimidation not only kept hecklers at bay but also gave the NSDAP an image of strength and loyalty that Hitler prized.

Hitler argued in *Mein Kampf* that nature's basic law is one of eternal struggle in which conflict is the means to greatness. In addition, Hitler claimed that there are two other natural laws that are vitally important: the laws of heredity and self-preservation. Nature, contended Hitler, balks at the mixing of species in reproduction. It also preserves the strongest while eliminating the weakest. Human life is not exempt from nature's ruthless, unrelenting process, which always favors the strongest. The crucial difference, however, is that human beings can know—they must know—that their individual and social existence unfolds in an arena of unending mortal struggle. The strong, therefore, will not flinch from embracing a principle that was self-evident to Hitler: namely, that national survival may well depend on aggression and violence. Crucial in these considerations, Hitler urged, is the additional fact that a people's survival and movement toward excellence depends on geography. Sufficient land (*Lebensraum*) is essential for a vital people and for

---

times that number are injured and wounded.

● **1919–1923: Romania grants citizenship to Jews.**

● **1920: The League of Nations** (which the United States has declined to join) holds its first meeting, at Geneva, Switzerland. • A Jewish

underground militia, *Hagana* (Defense), is founded in Palestine.

● **February 24, 1920: The first mass meeting of the National Socialist Party (NSDAP) takes place at Munich's *Hofbräuhaus*. Despite disruptions by adversaries, Adolf Hitler establishes the party program.**

● **April 1, 1920: Adolf Hitler is honorably discharged from the German Army.**

● **1921: The Allied Reparations Committee assesses German liability for World War I at 132 billion gold marks (about $31 billion);** *See* January 1923.
• The NSDAP, also known as the Nazi Party, establishes the *Sturmabteilung*

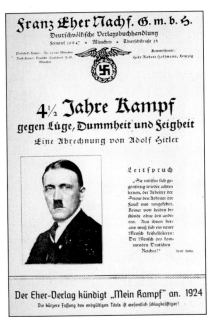

This advertisement was issued in 1924 to announce the publication of Hitler's "autobiography," *Mein Kampf*, under the title *4½ Years of Struggle Against Lies, Idiocy, and Cowardice*.

the purity of its way of life. To achieve greatness and the space it requires, brutal means may be necessary. A people's spirit is tested as it is required to apply maximum force in subduing its enemies.

As Hitler drew selectively on Social Darwinism and racial theory that could be traced back to the 19th century, the links between these dimensions of his worldview and his racist antisemitism were not difficult to recognize. In fact, these components were interfused because Hitler thought that

nature and history are of one piece. Not only are there different human races, which should be kept apart as much as different species are naturally separated, but also some human races are culture-creating and others are culture-destroying. These enemies, he believed, are locked in a struggle for survival of the fittest. According to Hitler, at the top of the culture-creating races is the Nordic-Aryan-Germanic "master race," which deserves to dominate "inferior" races. In Hitler's view, however, the racially superior German people were especially threatened by racial "pollution." Thus, Poles, Russians, Ukrainians, and other Slavic peoples, as well as "defective" and "asocial" Germans (for example, the mentally and physically disabled, homosexuals, and habitual criminals), would become Hitler's targets. The Jews, the racial enemy that Hitler regarded as the most unrelenting of all, headed this target list.

By 1924, according to *Mein Kampf*, wherever Hitler saw a threat to the racial and national survival he treasured, wherever he sensed an obstacle to the geographical expansion he craved, he ultimately found the Jews. According to Hitler, Jews plundered, subverted, and infected the very people who deserved to dominate

The Swastika

Today people in Western cultures associate the swastika with Nazi Germany. Actually, the symbol dates to ancient times, and it is still widely used in Eastern cultures.

The word derives from the Sanskrit *svastika*, which means "conducive to well-being." The symbol appeared in art from the Byzantine era (5th and 6th centuries) as well as from Indian tribes in North, South, and Central America, including the Navajos. Today in India, it is an auspicious symbol of the Hindus and Buddhists.

In 1910 German nationalist Guido von List suggested the swastika (*Hakenkreuz* in German) as a universal symbol for antisemitic organizations. The Nazi Party adopted it as their emblem in 1920. In 1935 the black swastika on a white circle against a red field became the national flag of Germany. Today, it is illegal to display the symbol in that country.

(SA; Storm Troopers; Brown Shirts). • The *Times* of London pronounces the *Protocols of the Elders of Zion* a forgery. • *Völkischer Beobachter* (People's Observer), the official National Socialist newspaper, begins publication.

• **March 21, 1921:** Anti-Jewish riots break out in Jerusalem.

• **July 29, 1921:** Adolf Hitler becomes the Nazi Party's first chairman with dictatorial powers.

• **1922:** *Jungsturm Adolf Hitler* (Adolf Hitler Boys Storm Troop) is established; *See* 1926. • *Stosstrupp Adolf Hitler* (Shock Troop Adolf Hitler) is established as Hitler's personal bodyguard contingent. This is the nucleus

for what will become the *Schutzstaffel* (SS). • Benito Mussolini establishes a Fascist government in Italy. • Antisemitic professor and social anthropologist Hans F. K. Günther publishes a racist book, *Race Lore of the German Volk*.

• **June 24, 1922:** Walther Rathenau, Jewish foreign minister of Germany,

the world. Following Hitler's lead, Nazi propaganda depicted the Jews in at least three major ways at once: as international anti-German conspirators, criminals, and life-threatening pestilence. The German people had to beat back the challenge of these "culture destroyers" once and for all. Under his leadership, Hitler believed, the Nazis would do so by making good their promise of a better life for the German people. As Nazi ideology developed, it understood that way of life to be based on ultranationalism that emphasized German racial "purity" and antisemitism. It also needed a single-party dictatorship and a state-controlled economy, plus ferocious anticommunism and, eventually, aggressive imperi-

Such works as this, a weekly 1932 installment of Fritz Reuter's antisemitic novel *The Russian Jew,* were quite popular with right-wing fanatics.

alist expansion of German territory through war.

Although no one—not even Hitler himself—could know in 1924 the catastrophe that such thinking would create, Hitler's influence and the visibility of the Nazi Party had grown significantly from the most improbable origins. The Nazis were on Germany's political map.

Without the Nazis, the Holocaust was unlikely. Without Hitler, neither Nazi domination nor the Holocaust were probable. Without antisemitism, however, Nazism, Hitler's dictatorship, and the Holocaust were plainly impossible. Antisemitism was constitutive of them all.

But now issues arise that reach further into the past than Hitler's efforts in Munich during the 1920s, or his experiences in World War I, or his formative years in Vienna. Neither Hitler nor any of his contemporaries were the first to practice what has sometimes been called "the longest hatred." Hitler was born into a world, and specifically into a European environment, in which antisemitism was already present. Not even his racial version of it was novel, although his antisemitic vision definitely produced something completely new: a call for the physical destruction of human beings.

This Polish broadside makes the outrageous, but then popular, claim that "Jews are lice; they cause typhus."

Tracing the beginning of the history that moves back from Elie Wiesel's Auschwitz to Fritz Gerlich's spectacles and Hitler's vision requires asking: How did antisemitism arise? What have been the key moments and features in its development? What made it a cause that, if not sufficient to produce the Holocaust, was certainly necessary for that disaster to take place? One approach to that story can start by stepping into the shadow world of pseudoscience and racism.

The Justification for Hatred

Uses of the terms *antisemite* and *antisemitism* have become so common that one might suppose them to be of ancient origin. In

---

is assassinated by members of Organisation Consul, a clandestine, right-wing political organization led by Captain Hermann Ehrhardt.

● **July 24, 1922:** The League of Nations grants Great Britain a mandate for Palestine, guaranteeing Jewish immigration.

● **1922–1933:** Two hundred Jewish graves at Nuremberg, Germany, are desecrated.

● **1923:** Rampant inflation throughout Germany makes the nation's currency worthless. • The first issue of the pro-Nazi, antisemitic newspaper *Der Stürmer* (*The Attacker*) is published in Nuremberg, Germany. Its

slogan is *"Die Juden sind unser Unglück"* ("The Jews are our misfortune"), a phrase picked up from Heinrich von Treitschke. • Noted Fascist and antisemite Arthur Moeller van den Bruck publishes *Das Dritte Reich* (*The Third Reich*), a book that will become a major influence on Hitler. • Jewish homes in Berlin are burned.

fact, a German journalist named Wilhelm Marr is credited with inventing and popularizing them in the late 1870s. Marr's often-reprinted political tract, "The Victory of Judaism over Germandom," warned that "the Jewish spirit and Jewish consciousness have overpowered the world." He called for resistance against "this foreign power" before it was too late. Marr thought that before long "there will be absolutely no public office, even the highest one, which the Jews will not have usurped." For Marr, it was a badge of honor to be called an antisemite.

Marr and others employed the word *antisemitism* in the largely secular anti-Jewish political campaigns that became widespread in Europe around the turn of the century. The word derived from an 18th-century analysis of languages that differentiated between those with so-called "Aryan" roots and those with so-called "Semitic" ones. This distinction led, in turn, to the assumption—a false one—that there were corresponding racial groups. Within this framework, Jews became "Semites," and that designation paved the way for Marr's new vocabulary. He could have used the conventional German term *Judenhass* to refer to his hatred of Jews, but that way of

speaking carried religious connotations that Marr wanted to de-emphasize in favor of racial ones. Apparently more "scientific," Marr's *Antisemitismus* caught on. Eventually, it became a way of speaking about all the forms of hostility toward Jews throughout history.

Over the centuries, antisemitism has taken on different but related forms: religious, political, economic, social, and racial. Jews have been discriminated against, hated, and killed because prejudiced non-Jews believed they belonged to the wrong religion, lacked citizenship qualifications, practiced business improperly, behaved inappropriately, or possessed inferior racial characteris-

This poster from Poland seeks to link Jews with communism and big capital. The caption reads: "Plutocracy or bolshevism—both are invented by Jews."

Wilhelm Marr

Known as the father of modern antisemitism, Wilhelm Marr led the fight to overturn Jewish emancipation in Germany.

Born in 1819, Marr entered politics as a democratic revolutionary who favored the emancipation of all oppressed groups, including Jews. However, when he became embittered about the failure of the 1848–49 German Revolution to democratize Germany, and about his own rapidly declining political fortunes, he turned his venom against the Jews. His essay *"Der Sieg des Judenthums über das Germanenthum von nicht confessionellen Standpunkt"* ("The Victory of Judaism over Germandom: From a Non-Denominational Point of View") reached its 12th edition in 1879.

Marr's conception of antisemitism focused on the supposed racial, as opposed to religious, characteristics of the Jews. His organization, the League of Antisemites, introduced the word "antisemite" into the political lexicon and established the first popular political movement based entirely on anti-Jewish beliefs.

● **January 1923: France and Belgium occupy the Ruhr after an economically broken Germany is unable to meet the annual installment of its war-reparations payments designed to pay off Germany's $31 billion war debt. Many Germans, especially veterans of the Great War, are deeply angered by this humiliation.**

● **March 1923: The *Schutzstaffel* (SS; Protection Squad) is established. It is initially a bodyguard for Hitler but will later become an elite armed guard of the Third Reich. This Nazi terrorist organization, completely loyal to Hitler and headed by Heinrich Himmler, will be made responsible for carrying out the "Final Solution of the Jewish problem."**

● **November 1923: The German mark trades four billion to one U.S. dollar. Weimar inflation is halted by the introduction of a new hard currency based on land values.**

● **November 8–11, 1923: Hitler's so-called "Beer Hall *Putsch*" takeover attempt at Munich fails, temporarily rattling the National Socialist Party**

tics. These forms of antisemitism, but especially the racial one, all played key parts in the Holocaust.

Importantly, Hitler and his followers were not antisemites primarily because they were racists. The relation worked more the other way around: Hitler and his followers were racists because they were antisemites looking for an anti-Jewish stigma deeper than

any religious, economic, or political prejudice alone could provide. For if Jews were found wanting religiously, it was possible for them to convert. If their business practices or political views were somehow inappropriate, changed behavior could, in principle, correct their shortcomings. But antisemites in the line that ran from Marr to Hitler believed that Jews

were a menace no matter what they did. As Marr put the point, "the Jews are the 'best citizens' of this modern, Christian state," but they were that way, he added, because it was "in perfect harmony with their interests" to be so. Undoubtedly, Marr believed—and Hitler agreed even more so—that the interests of Jews were irreconcilably at odds with Germany's.

For antisemites of Marr's stripe, converted Jews were still untrustworthy Jews. Jewish behavior might change in any number of ways, but the "logic" of racist antisemitism did not consider such changes as reasons to give up antisemitism. To the contrary, this antisemitism interpreted Jewish assimilation as infiltration, Jewish conformity as duplicity, and Jewish integration into non-Jewish society as proof of Jewish cunning that intended world domination. On the other hand, if Jews insisted on retaining their distinctively Jewish ways, that insistence provided evidence of another kind to show that Jews were an alien people. Added to earlier forms of antisemitism, racial theory "explained" why the Jews, no matter what appearances might suggest to the contrary, were a threat that Germans could not afford to tolerate.

Jews, of course, are not a race, because any person, irrespective

Christian Antisemitism

Nazi antisemitic propaganda drew inspiration from a 2000-year, anti-Jewish tradition that had been cultivated by Christian churches. The stereotyped and wholly false image of Jews as the "killers of Christ" persisted through the centuries. Desecration of the crucifix *(pictured)* has been another common theme.

At times, Jews were humiliated, expelled from countries, and even massacred. Forbidden from marrying Christians, Jews were

 forced to wear identifying clothing, restricted to certain occupations, and often segregated in certain sections of towns. Failure during the medieval period to convert Jews to Christianity resulted in greater fear, suspicion, and hatred. Caricatures depicted Jews in satanic imagery. Even more harmful was "blood libel," charging Jews with ritual murders of Christian children. The myth circulated even into the 20th century that Jews used the blood of Christian virgins in baking *matzo* for Passover.

Sixteenth-century Protestant reformer Martin Luther was a virulent antisemite in his later years. Angered by the Jews' refusal to convert, he unleashed the scathing tract *On the Jews and Their Lies*, depicting them as Christ killers and criminals bent on ruling the world. Luther advocated burning synagogues, schools, and homes, and driving Jews "like mad dogs out of the land." The Nazis prominently displayed this treatise at Party rallies.

and leading to Hitler's arrest in Bavaria, Germany, on the 11th. Hitler will serve only nine months and receive several privileges from the judiciary.

• 1924: The United States Congress passes the Immigration Restriction Act, which effectively bans immigration to the U.S. from Asia and Eastern

Europe. This and other American anti-immigrant activity is noted by Germany.

• May 4, 1924: The Nazis win 6.6 percent of the vote in the *Reichstag* (Parliament) election.

• July 1924: While in prison, Hitler begins work on a book, *Mein Kampf*

(*My Struggle*). His loyal secretary, Rudolf Hess, transcribes Hitler's ramblings; *See* July 18, 1925.

• 1925: The *Tannenbergbund* is founded in Germany by General Erich Ludendorff and his wife, Mathilde Ludendorff. The *Bund* attacks Jews, Communists, Catholics, and Freemasons. • *Jeunesse*

Left: Jesus, a Jew, taught and lived by the tenets of Judaism. He was killed by Romans who feared his unique leadership. *Middle:* Rome brutally put down Jewish rebellion in 70 C.E., destroying Jerusalem and the sacred Second Temple. *Right:* A converted Christian, Emperor Constantine ended persecution of Christians and granted the religion official recognition. He imposed a series of edicts oppressive to Jews.

of "blood" or any other biological feature, can become a Jew by conversion. Nevertheless, the belief that Jews are a race caught on. Such thinking had immense implications and vast consequences. If Jewishness was a racial matter, then it could be argued that Jewish identity was determined by heredity, Jewish character by biological inheritance. According to this racist outlook, Jews could do nothing to change their identity and character. It made no difference whether they converted to Christianity or displayed patriotic love for their country. According to the beliefs of racist antisemites, a Jew was a Jew no matter what, and Jews were a menace to the "superior" non-Jewish societies in which they lived. Racial anti-

semitism meant that the very existence of Jewish life had become a problem that required a solution.

Once linked, antisemitism and racism energized each other. But racial antisemitism could never have arisen had it not been for the nonracial forms of antisemitism that were at its roots. Although Jewish identity is ordinarily passed from parent to child, anyone, in principle, can be Jewish. Therefore, Nazi ideology to the contrary notwithstanding, racial characteristics cannot define Jews in any "essential" way. Jews have to be identified in other ways before it is possible to impute racial identity to them. Thus, behavior—what Jews do or do not do—becomes critical in defining identity prior to the imputation of racial differ-

ences. Behavior, however, is also problematic in establishing distinctively Jewish identity—at least that is true if one focuses only on the work that Jews do, the professions they practice, the economic plans or political persuasions they possess. For in and of themselves, those roles can usually be filled by all kinds of people. There is, however, at least one distinguishing and far-ranging behavioral difference.

Not all Jews are religious. Nevertheless, religion is at the core of differences that originally set Jews apart. Religion involves more than particular beliefs. It lives in specific practices, too. Jews not only worshiped one God exclusively, but they also observed a special Sabbath and distinctive holidays, such as Passover. They practiced circumcision, adhered to special dietary restrictions, and regarded Jerusalem as the Holy City. Informed by Judaism, their singular religion, Jews were unique. In addition, religious particularity is crucial when it comes to understanding the anti-Jewish feelings that have long been embedded in Christianity. Absent Christian hostility toward Jews, it would be extremely difficult, if not impossible, to explain why Jews were so consistently targets for discrimination and persecution in Western

---

Nationale, a youth-group offshoot of the antisemitic, Fascist *Action Nationale,* is founded in Belgium.
• In the United States, Rev. Gerald B. Winrod founds Defenders of the Christian Faith, an antisemitic group that attacks "Jewish bolshevism." Winrod is dubbed "the American Streicher."

● **February 27, 1925: A large rally in Munich, Germany, relaunches the Nazi Party. Four thousand people attend.**

● **March 24, 1925: Publication of the pro-Nazi, antisemitic newspaper *Der Stürmer* resumes after being banned by the Weimar government in November 1923.**

● **April 26, 1925: Paul von Hindenburg is elected president of Germany.**

● **June 1925: The Geneva Conventions Protocol prohibits wartime use of asphyxiating, poisonous, and other gases, as well as bacteriological warfare.**

civilization and why, specifically, they were eventually set up for the kill in Hitler's Germany.

Well before the Nazi Party struggled its way into existence in the aftermath of World War I, antisemitism was so entrenched in some Christian-dominated cultures that, with few exceptions, Jews could not be fully included within Western civilization's fundamentally Christian-defined boundaries of moral obligation. Christianity's anti-Jewish ways were not sufficient to cause the Holocaust, but it's doubtful the Holocaust would have happened if it weren't for the long history of Christianity's negative views about the Jews. To clarify these points, it is important to ask about the origins of the Jewish people.

Descending from people who were enslaved in ancient Egypt—

In this German woodcut from 1493, Jews are burned alive after having been forced into a pit. The horned hats worn by some of the Jews are symbolic of a presumed shameful stigma borne by all Jews.

sometimes called Hebrews—Jews traditionally trace their origins to the biblical figures named Abraham and Sarah, who lived in Mesopotamia about 4000 years ago. Judaism is rooted in the formative experience of a miraculous exodus from Egyptian slavery and in what that tradition takes to be God's ancient revelation to Moses at Mount Sinai more than 3000 years ago. The Ten Commandments, only one of the many civilizing contributions that Jews have given to Western culture, come from those early times. They are part of the Torah, the teachings found in the first five books of Jewish Scripture. The Ten Commandments make clear that the God who bestowed them is an exclusive God: "You shall have no other gods before me" (Exodus 20:3). The biblical narratives assert that God and Israelites, as the ancient Hebrews came to be identified, were linked by a covenant that included ritual laws and ethical rules. As a result, the life of this people became distinctive and different from other groups around them.

After the revelation at Sinai, 12 Israelite tribes occupied the Mediterranean coastal land of Canaan,

In the First Crusade, Christians attempted to regain the Holy Land from the Muslims. The Crusade generated massive violence against European Jews, who were characterized as "Christ killers."

which they believed God had promised them. In time they established a nation, with David as their king. Its capital was Jerusalem. Unable to sustain the unity and autonomy it enjoyed from about 1000 to 922 BCE, the kingdom was split by internal divisions and then besieged and occupied by a variety of conquerors: the Assyrians, Babylonians, Persians, Greeks, and eventually the Romans.

In the year 70 C.E., the Romans ruthlessly put down a sustained Jewish rebellion. The Romans' massive reprisals included the destruction of the city of Jerusalem and its Temple, the most sacred Jewish site. Most of the surviving Jews were forcibly dispersed from their traditional homeland to various parts of the Roman Empire. As a result, exiled Jews have lived in European lands—from Portugal and Spain to Poland and Russia, from Greece and Italy to Great Britain, France, and Germany—for more than 2000 years.

In all of these places, Jews found ways to flourish and enhance the vitality of the regions they inhabited. But the Jews, always a minority people in these circumstances, lacked the power to control their own destinies. In particular, set apart from the Christian majority by their Jewish traditions, Jews in the European diaspora (scattering) often became the targets of suspicion, prejudice, hatred, and violence that the majority Christian population directed against them.

Why that hostility existed can be understood further by noting that Christianity grew historically out of Jewish monotheism (worship of a single God) and the traditions of Judaism as they existed nearly 2000 years ago. Although Jesus of Nazareth came to be understood as the founding leader of Christianity, he did not intend to start a new religion. Jesus was a practicing Jew, and he died as one.

The World That Was Lost

Approximately nine million Jews lived in the many European countries that Nazi Germany would occupy during World War II. All of them were eventually targeted for death—not for anything they had done, but simply because they were Jewish.

In 1933 German Jews numbered about a half-million, less than one percent of Germany's population. Like the Jews in other Western European nations, German Jews often adopted the culture, but not the religion, of their non-Jewish neighbors. Thousands of Jews had served in the German Army during World War I. Many were decorated for bravery. From 1905 to 1933, Jews won 11 of the 37 Nobel Prizes awarded to Germans.

The largest Jewish population was in Eastern Europe (*pictured*), where many lived in predominantly Jewish towns called *shtetls*. These Jews were less assimilated than those in Western Europe. Yiddish—a mixture of German, Hebrew, and Slavic languages—was usually spoken, and Orthodox religious observance was the norm.

In many places, Jews had their own schools, libraries, banks, athletic and cultural organizations, and a variety of political groups. In spite of antisemitism, European Jews maintained their traditions, sustained a vital cultural and religious life, and contributed impressively to Western civilization wherever they lived.

His original followers were practicing Jews as well. In agreement with Jewish traditions, Jesus' teachings emphasized love of one's neighbor, the need for repentance, and liberation for the oppressed. Although he rejected violence, Jesus suffered a violent death when Pontius Pilate, the cruel Roman governor of Palestine, took Jesus' execution as the most expedient way to stop the politi-

Martin Luther, founder of Protestantism in the 16th century, advocated "abandonment" of Jews who refused to convert.

Jewish rioting that is organized by Romanian students. • Seventy-seven percent of university students in Prussia—feeling threatened by Jewish intellectual and commercial accomplishments—demand an "Aryan paragraph" that will exclude Jews from organizations, federations, parties, and eventually all public life.

● **March 10, 1927:** Germany's Weimar government lifts its speaking ban on Hitler.

● **May 2, 1927:** The U.S. Supreme Court rules in *Buck v. Bell* that compulsory sterilization is constitutional.

● **July 4, 1927:** Joseph Goebbels publishes the first issue of the antisemitic *Der Angriff* (*The Attack*). It is founded to rally Nazi Party members during the nearly two-year ban on the Party in Berlin.

● **1928:** The Kaiser Wilhelm Institute for Anthropology, Human Genetics, and Eugenics is established in Germany.

The Protocols of the Elders of Zion

In the late 1800s, European antisemites depicted the Jew as an alien and corrupting element within society. They published inflammatory literature that reviled Jews, depicting them as plotting to undermine Western Christian civilization in order to take over the world.

By the turn of the century, antisemites firmly believed that Jews were collectively scheming to achieve world domination. One of the most influential writings fueling this belief was a widely read publication entitled *The Protocols of the Elders of Zion*. This document was, however, actually a carefully crafted forgery fabricated by the secret police of czarist Russia to justify that government's persecution of Jews. *The Protocols* offered "proof" of a widespread international Jewish conspiracy. It featured a fictional account of minutes of an alleged secret meeting of subversive Zionist leaders in Basel, Switzerland, in 1897. It even outlined technical plans for a Jewish world state.

Exiles from Bolshevist Russia brought copies of *The Protocols* with them. Alfred Rosenberg, a Nazi Party ideologue, published his own "edited" version in 1923. Adolf Hitler, like many other avowed antisemites, was utterly convinced that the *Protocols*—and the Jewish conspiracy—were real.

cal upheaval that Jesus and his followers might cause.

Roman, not Jewish, power put Jesus to death by crucifixion. Jesus' death left his followers dismayed and scattered. Indeed, Jesus probably would have been little more than a footnote in history if his Jewish disciples had not come to believe and convince others that Jesus had been resurrected from death, that he was the Mes-

siah promised in Jewish tradition, and that he was the Son of God.

Most Jews, however, believed neither that Jesus had been resurrected nor that he was the promised Messiah, let alone the Son of God. Nevertheless, with Paul, a converted Jew, leading the way, the early Christians began to experience greater success in sharing their faith with the gentiles (non-Jews) of the Mediter-

ranean world. By the time the Romans destroyed Jerusalem in the year 70 C.E., what had started as a small, struggling sect within Judaism was on its way to becoming the Christian religion that would gain cultural dominance in Western civilization.

The divorce between Christianity and Judaism was not a happy one. Jews came to be depicted as "Christ killers"—in part because it was Judas, a Jew, who betrayed Christ—and demonized as the devil's agents. According to this sort of Christian view, the Jews were guilty of *deicide*, the most heinous of crimes because it was nothing less than the murder of the unique incarnation of God. Over the centuries, such perspectives developed into a full-fledged Christian "teaching of contempt" against Jews and Judaism. From Augustine in the 5th century to Martin Luther in the 16th century, some of the most eloquent and persuasive Christian theologians taught that the Jews were rebels against God. They preached that Jewish misfortune was God's judgment against them for rejecting Jesus. It was no coincidence that acts of violence against Jews often occurred in the spring, the season of Easter and Passover.

In European Christendom, the Jew was the "other," the "outsider."

• **May 20, 1928:** The Nazis win 2.6 percent of the vote and 12 seats in the *Reichstag* election.

• **September 22, 1928:** An antisemitic "blood libel" in Messina, New York, inspires violence against Jews.

• **1929:** The eugenics-preoccupied National Socialist German Physicians'

League is founded in Germany.
• Alfred Rosenberg founds the antisemitic, anti-Bolshevist *Kampfbund für Deutsche Kultur* (Combat League for German Culture), which is dedicated to the eradication of *entartete Kunst* (degenerate art). • An Arab mob attacks Jews in Jerusalem; 70 are killed on August 24. The violence spreads to other parts of the country.

• **The first talkie film produced in Yiddish,** an American feature called *Style and Class*, is released.

• **1929–1939:** Another wave of *aliya* (immigration) of Jews to Palestine occurs.

• **January 20, 1929:** Hitler appoints Heinrich Himmler *Reichsführer-SS.*

Theodor Herzl, a Hungarian journalist and father of the Zionist movement, urged European Jews to immigrate to Palestine in the face of increasing anti-semitism.

Thus, contacts between Jews and Christians were carefully regulated. Intermarriage was prohibited. Jews were excluded from the army, most administrative posts, and the legal profession. They were barred from owning land. Commerce remained open, however, and many Jews earned their livings in such fields. For example, since the early Church did not permit usury by Christians (lending money at interest), Jews came to fill the vital but unpopular role of moneylenders for the Christian majority.

Jewish circumstances took a major turn for the worse in 1096 when crusading Christian fervor to recapture holy places from Islamic forces took its toll on Jews as well. Massacres followed as Christians used early forms of "ethnic cleansing" to "purify" their European territory. Following on the heels of those bloodbaths, Jews were obliged by the Lateran Council of 1215 to wear specially marked clothing. Different styles developed, but in France the insignia was a yellow patch, the precursor of the yellow star later decreed by the Nazis. Ghettos were established, and in the popular imagination Jews became increasingly identified with Satan. Falsely, the "blood libel" held that Jews murdered Christian children for religious purposes. Jews were held responsible for the plagues and famines that ravaged Europe in the 14th and 15th centuries. Violence exacted payment in blood for these "crimes." Outright expulsion occurred as well—from England in 1290, from France beginning in 1306, and from Spain in 1492.

Five centuries later Christian teaching about Jews has changed significantly. With relatively few exceptions, Christians have repudiated the "teaching of contempt," and they have revised their understanding of Jews and Judaism in positive ways. The price for those changes, however, has been immense. The Nazis and their collaborators used religious history, and specifically Christian teachings about Jews, to obtain precedents for many of the measures that they exacted against the Jews.

Christianity alone would not have been sufficient to cause the Holocaust. The reason is that validation of the Christian faith's claim to exclusive truth required that Jews continue to exist—as potential converts to Christianity or as living reminders of God's judgment. Nonetheless, typical Christian attitudes about Jews—which included a desire for Jews to simply disappear through conversion—were a necessary condition for the Holocaust. Without the anti-Jewish feeling that Christianity sustained for centuries, it is barely conceivable that the European Jews would have been eventually targeted for annihilation.

By the late 18th century, secular ideas about human equality, religious toleration, and basic civil rights were becoming more widespread in Western civilization. One

In the wake of the Dreyfus Affair at the close of the 19th century, French antisemitism rose to the boiling point. Anti-Jewish riots were commonplace.

• **August 3–4, 1929: The Nazi Party Day rally at Nuremberg, Germany, draws well over 100,000 people.**

• **1930: Hjalmar Schacht, financier and president of the *Reichsbank*, begins a long-lasting financial relationship with the National Socialists, providing them with considerable funding. • In Yugoslavia, Croatian** nationalists establish *Ustasa* (Insurgent), an organization that will murder 500,000 Serbs and 20,000 Gypsies during World War II.**

• **September 2, 1930: Hitler becomes supreme leader of the SA (Storm Troopers). He will encourage and utilize their thuggery.**

• **September 14, 1930: The National Socialist Party wins 18 percent (6.4 million) of votes cast in the *Reichstag* election, jumping from 12 seats to 107 and becoming the second largest political party in Germany.**

• **November 1930: In Denmark, Frits Clausen establishes a collaborationist organization, *Danmarks National-***

result was Jewish emancipation. In many European countries—England, France, and Prussia, for example—economic and social restrictions were removed, Jews received civil rights, and they became almost equal citizens under the law. Yet by no means did antisemitic feelings and beliefs yield completely to these liberal trends that were part of the European Enlightenment. In France, for example, even Count Stanislas de Clermont-Tonnerre, a strong advocate for Jewish civil rights, contended in December 1789 that "the Jews should be denied everything as a nation, but granted everything as individuals," which meant that, unless Jews assimilated to the point of giving up their distinctiveness and separateness, they would still be suspect.

By the mid-19th century, the popular appeal of theories about

A Russian-Jewish soldier returns home on leave only to find his family massacred during the 1906 pogroms against the Jews incited by the czarist government.

racial differences among people was growing in Western society. These views stressed that some racial groups—white Europeans, for example—were "superior" to others who were less "civilized" or "weaker." In the hands of antisemitic thinkers such as Wilhelm Marr, racial theories legitimized the claim that Jews are a race that is both threatening and inferior.

Meanwhile, in imperial Russia during the late 1800s, the governments organized or at least did not prevent large-scale violence against Jewish communities. These attacks became known as "pogroms." The brutality of the pogroms forced Jews to flee these areas, which was an outcome both welcomed and intended by the perpetrators. In the late 1890s, antisemitism also raged in France during the "Dreyfus Affair." A Jewish captain in the French Army, Alfred Dreyfus had been falsely accused and convicted of spying for Germany. Covering the Dreyfus case for the Viennese newspaper *Neue Freie Presse,* a Jewish journalist named Theodor Herzl heard Parisian mobs shouting, "Death to the Jews." Reversing his earlier view that emancipation and assimilation could provide a viable

future for Jews in Europe, Herzl became convinced that Jews must have a state of their own, a decision that led to his becoming a founder of modern political Zionism.

At about the same time, an antisemitic forgery, the *Protocols of the Elders of Zion,* began its notorious circulation. Originating in Russian circles, this fabricated document "revealed" a Jewish conspiracy to take over the world. Few writings have done more to fuel antisemitic fires. Especially between the two worlds wars, this antisemitic publication was translated into many languages and distributed worldwide. Much to Hitler's delight, American industrialist Henry Ford gave the *Protocols* extensive positive publicity in the 1920s. For Hitler, whose antisemitic logic led him to think that forgery claims were "proof" that the *Protocols* were true, this "document" became, as scholar Norman Cohn has called it, a "warrant for genocide."

Hitler's Rise to Power

In its varied and interconnected forms, antisemitism was widespread in Europe—and in the United States as well—as 20th-century developments led to World War I and the subsequent emergence of Adolf Hitler's Nazi

Socialistiske Arbejder Parti (Danish National Socialist Workers Party).

● **1931: Joseph Goebbels orders that Party members address Hitler as "Führer" (Leader). ● The *Rasse-und Siedlungshauptamt* (RuSHA; Race and Resettlement Main Office) is established by SS chief Heinrich Himmler and Richard Walther Darré.**

● **July 13, 1931: Germany's *Danat-bank* collapses, leading to closure of all German banks until August 5.**

● **September 12, 1931: On the eve of the Jewish New Year, Nazis attack Jews on the *Kurfürstendamm* in Berlin as they return home from synagogue.**

● **October 11, 1931: German industrialist Alfred Hugenberg forms the Harzburg Front, an alliance between the NSDAP, the German National People's Party, Steel Helmet, the All German Association, and the so-called Fatherland associations.**

● **October 30, 1931: Baldur von Schirach assumes leadership of *Hitler***

Party. Germany was by no means the only place where antisemitism was entrenched, but the rising Nazi Party kept sounding its antisemitic drumbeat. It resonated with many Germans, who agreed with Heinrich von Treitschke. In 1879 and 1880, Treitschke, an influential, nationalistic historian, had published a series of articles that drew attention to a fateful phrase: *"Die Juden sind unser Unglück"* ("The Jews are our misfortune"). Before long, that slogan would be festooned at Nazi Party rallies.

Measured by 1925 census figures, it would have seemed unlikely that Jews were Germany's misfortune. They numbered 564,379, or only 0.9 percent of the total population. Two-thirds of the German Jews, however, were concentrated in six large cities; Berlin's Jewish population was 180,000 at the time. Such urbanization encouraged a vibrant cultural and religious life but also made the German Jews visible, despite their largely middle-class and frequently assimilated status.

At the time of the unsuccessful Nazi coup in November 1923, the NSDAP had about 55,000 members. Briefly banned from German politics, the Party fell into disarray. Vowing to pursue parliamentary means to power, Hitler relaunched

Urging voters to break the shackles of the Treaty of Versailles, this poster trumpeted, "End it now! Elect Hitler."

it in February 1925. Membership had fallen to 27,000, but by 1926 the decline had been reversed, and 108,000 Germans belonged

Nazi Party Structure

The Nazi Party functioned on three levels, all theoretically based on the *Führerprinzip* (leadership principle) that defined organizational structure. The system emphasized discipline and a chain of command culminating in the charismatic position of the *Führer*. It also, however, fostered fierce competition, internal feuds, jurisdictional overlap, and incompetency that resulted in much inefficiency.

The Nazi Party's highest level was its leadership cadre. Adolf

Hitler sat atop this hierarchical pyramid, dictating to the levels below. Immediately subordinate to Hitler were the heads of the Party Chancellery and Treasury. Next in importance were the *Reichsleiter*, in charge of departments such as propaganda and foreign policy. Below them were the heads of the Party's territorial administrative machinery. Germany was divided into *Gaue* (regions) administered by *Gauleiter* (regional Party leaders) responsible only to Hitler. Each *Gau* was subdivided into

smaller districts, then towns, neighborhoods, and finally blocks. The block warden, or *Blockleiter*, was the lowest official above the ordinary member, or *Parteigenosse*.

The Party's second level consisted of the paramilitary and auxiliary division hierarchies, including the Hitler Youth, SA, SS, and NS Women's Organization. The third tier included the affiliated associations representing professional groups, such as the German Labor Front and the NS Teachers' League.

Jugend (Hitler Youth). Young and outwardly personable, he will mold the organization into an inescapable part of German life.

● **December 14, 1931: In Holland, a collaborationist political organization, *Nationaal Socialistische Beweging* (National Socialist Movement), is established.**

● **1932: The Nazis establish the Faith Movement of German Christians, which is intended to encourage fierce German nationalism and to undercut the authority of the German Protestant Church with exhortations to antisemitism, anti-Catholicism, and anti-Marxism. ● In Holland, a collaborationist combat arm, *Weer Afdeeling* (Storm Troops), is established. ●** *I Saw*

Hitler!, an anti-Nazi book by American journalist Dorothy Thompson, is published; *See* 1934.

● **January 26, 1932: Hitler charms German industrialists in a speech at Düsseldorf Industry Club.**

● **February 25, 1932: The Austrian Hitler is granted German citizenship.**

to the NSDAP. Those gains, however, did not translate immediately into ballot-box success. After the 1923 hyperinflation, the German economy stabilized considerably. The Nazis did not achieve major political gains until the world was plunged into the severe depression whose origins included the American stock-market crash in October 1929. Unemployment's misery scourged Germany.

During the winter of 1929–30, more than three million Germans (14 percent of the population) were jobless. By the autumn of 1932, five million were out of work, a figure that climbed to six million by January 1933. Unfortunately, the Weimar Republic's economic woes—industrial production fell 42 percent from 1929 to 1932—benefited the Nazis. Party membership doubled from 1928 to 1930. In September 1930 the Nazis won their first major breakthrough in Germany's national elections—nearly 6.4 million votes and 107 seats in the *Reichstag,* which made their delegation's size second only to the Social Democratic Party.

The Nazi Party had more than 1.4 million members by the end of 1932. The reasons why Germans joined the Party or voted for Hitler were diverse. Party members and the Nazi electorate came from varied socioeconomic classes. Nazism attracted them because it took a strong stand against communism, or because other parties did not back their economic and political interests as the Nazis promised to do. Antisemitism played a part, too, although not the most decisive one. Hitler sensed when and how to stress "the Jewish

"By warding off the Jews, I am fighting for the Lord's work."

—Adolf Hitler

Hitler literally demonstrated his slogan "The *Führer* over Germany" as the first candidate to use an airplane during the 1932 presidential-election campaign.

question" and when and how to downplay it.

Although Hitler had led the Nazi Party for more than ten years, he did not become a German citizen until mid-February 1932. At the time, the Nazis needed to field a candidate against the Weimar Republic's aging incumbent president, Field Marshal Paul von Hindenburg. Hitler, the only Nazi with a chance to win, had to be naturalized before he was eligible to run. In a Germany wracked by economic depression and increasing political chaos, Hitler campaigned "for freedom and bread," hoping that idealistic young people and a beleaguered lower middle class would bring him victory. Hindenburg, perceived by moderate Germans as the last bulwark between communism or Nazism, defeated Hitler by more than seven million votes. The splintering of the electorate, however, forced a runoff, since Hindenburg had not received a majority. The field marshal won the second contest, but not before Hitler had narrowed the margin by nearly 1.2 million votes.

Hindenburg's victory brought Germany neither peace nor unity. The Weimar Republic's parliamentary system had been especially shaky since September 1930,

---

● **March 13, 1932: Hitler receives 11.3 million votes in the German presidential election.**

● **April 10, 1932: In a run-off election for president of Germany, incumbent Paul von Hindenburg defeats Hitler.**

● **May 30, 1932: German Chancellor Heinrich Brüning resigns.**

● **June 1, 1932: Franz von Papen is appointed chancellor of Germany.**

● **June 14, 1932: The German government lifts its ban on Nazi Storm Troopers.**

● **June 30, 1932: A pro-Nazi American organization, Friends of the New Germany, is founded. The name will**

later be changed to *Amerika-Deutscher Volksbund* (German-American Bund).

● **July 31, 1932: In elections for the *Reichstag,* the National Socialists receive 37.3 percent (13,750,000) of the total votes cast. The number of seats held by National Socialists increases to 230 (of 608).**

Showing a German impaled on the Nazi crown of a monocled monarchist, this poster from the Social Democratic Party cautioned voters to reject reactionary parties.

when it became clear that no government could rule Germany without Nazi support. On July 31, 1932, elections for the *Reichstag* brought the Nazis nearly 14 million votes (37 percent of the total and 230 *Reichstag* seats), a total higher than the combined results of the Nazis' two closest rivals, the Communists and the Social Democrats. Braced by this showing, Hitler was determined to be chancellor, the prime minister of the German government. Political opponents still had sufficient strength to frustrate Hitler's ambition, and the tide turned against him—momentarily.

Hitler's subsequent refusal to join any coalition government

forced new elections, which were held on November 6, 1932, at a time when the worst of the economic crisis was starting to subside. The election results were far from those that the Nazis desired; the NSDAP received two million votes fewer than it polled in July. Although the Nazis remained the largest party in the *Reichstag*, they had lost 34 seats. Their momentum seemed to be stalling. Although Hitler was stunned and discouraged at the end of 1932, his fortunes soon improved dramatically.

Faced by the prospect that no sustainable government would emerge after the November election, Hindenburg used his constitutional authority on January 30, 1933, reluctantly appointing Hitler, a man he despised, chancellor of Germany.

Hitler had not seized power. In fact, the power he wanted had nearly eluded him. Instead, it was handed to him by those who thought he could be controlled. Hindenburg's decision was taken to prevent an overthrow of the existing order, but unintentional though the outcome was, his appointment put Hitler's vision in control. That result led to Fritz Gerlich's bloody spectacles. It also plunged Germany into the unprecedented evil of the Holocaust.

On February 1, 1933, Adolf Hitler spoke to the German people on the radio for the first time as chancellor. He ended by appealing to the Almighty to bless his government's work. On that day, Elie Wiesel was not yet five years old. Forty-six years later, Wiesel would write about Auschwitz-Birkenau: "The beginning, the end: all the world's roads, all the outcries of mankind, lead to this accursed place. Here is the kingdom of night, where God's face is hidden and a flaming sky becomes a graveyard for a vanished people."

Darkness was poised to fall across Europe.

The "Hitler cult" embraced by many Germans was expressed, in part, by postcards such as this. The stylized rays of the sun suggest that Hitler heralds the dawn of a new, greater Germany.

• **August 13, 1932: German President Paul von Hindenburg offers the vice-chancellorship to Hitler, who refuses.**

• **October 1932: The Nazis, now in power in the region encompassing Dessau, evict the Bauhaus design school from the city, signaling the Party's abhorrence for forward-thinking art and aesthetics.**

• **October 17, 1932: The Paul Reveres, an anti-Communist and antisemitic organization, is founded in the United States and chaired by Colonel Edwin M. Handley.**

• **November 6, 1932: In elections for the *Reichstag*, the last free elections before Hitler's ascension to power, votes attracted by National Socialist**

candidates fall to 33.1 percent. The number of seats held by National Socialists dips from 230 to 196.

• **December 3, 1932: General Kurt von Schleicher, a political conservative who will prove no match for Hitler, is appointed chancellor of Germany.**

1933

DURING the night of May 10, 1933—100 days after Adolf Hitler legally became chancellor of Germany—more than 20,000 books burned in the *Opernplatz* (Opera House Square) opposite the Humboldt University in Berlin. This event was not an isolated incident during that night. In some 30 German university towns, brown-shirted Nazi students along with many of their professors purged "un-German" writings from libraries and shops and set them ablaze. Enthusiastic crowds witnessed the destruction, which was launched with torchlight parades and accented by speeches that proclaimed the death of "Jewish intellectualism" and the purification of German culture. Thus, writings by such Jewish intellectuals as Albert Einstein and Sigmund Freud fueled the huge bonfires. Also engulfed in flames was the work of Heinrich Heine, a German poet of Jewish origin.

A century earlier Heine had stated, "Where books are burned, in the end people will be burned." Heine could scarcely have imagined how true his statement would become, specifically for the European Jews who found themselves under Nazi domination during the Third Reich. German Jews were harassed, beaten, arrested and imprisoned. Their businesses were boycotted, and Jewish lives were proscribed by a long list of new anti-Jewish laws.

Though antisemitism in Germany had simmered for centuries, it had reached a boiling point by 1933. The reasons were largely economical. In the early '30s Germany was suffering the effects of a severe worldwide economic depression. It put millions out of work, increased social unrest, and undermined confidence in the post-World War I German government, which was known as the Weimar Republic. These discouraging conditions were made even worse by the bitterness many Germans felt over Germany's defeat in World War I. They wanted decisive leadership and national rebirth, yet political instability left both of those aims in doubt.

Although the National Socialists (Nazis) could never win an absolute majority in any freely contested national election, by 1932 they were the largest political party in Germany. Fearing continued chaos and unable to see a better solution, Germany President Paul von Hindenburg, age 85, reluctantly made a fateful decision on January 29. He used his constitutional authority to appoint Hitler as the head of a coalition government.

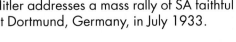

Hitler addresses a mass rally of SA faithful at Dortmund, Germany, in July 1933.

1933

Hitler took the chancellor's oath on January 30, and that night Nazis celebrated the victory with spirited torchlight parades in Berlin.

Hindenburg and his conservative advisers hoped Hitler could restore social order and yet be controlled. The plan backfired disastrously. Six months after Hitler's appointment, democracy was dead in Germany. Hitler's decrees had the force of law, civil rights had disappeared, and the Nazis were the only legal political party.

As the terror tactics of the Nazi state became ever more obvious, thousands of the Third Reich's suspected political opponents were sent to concentration camps, such as the one established at Dachau, Germany, on

March 20. In 1933 50 concentration camps were opened in various parts of Germany. By July more than 25,000 Socialists, Communists, and Jews had been sent to concentration camps or to prison.

Jews were especially hard hit by the Nazi takeover, for Hitler and his followers had long been convinced that Jews posed the most deadly threat to German life. According to the Nazi worldview, Jewish "blood" was indelibly different and inferior to that of the German "master race." Although the Jewish population of Germany—it numbered about 565,000—was less than one percent of the nation's total when Hitler became chancellor, Nazi ideology required the elimination of Jews from German life. Soon after taking power, Hitler began to implement the racial antisemitism that stood at the center of his party's policy.

During the first two months of Nazi rule, anti-Jewish violence mostly hit individuals. Those circumstances changed irrevocably on April 1, when the Nazis took their first nationwide, planned action specifically against German Jewry as a whole. It was a boycott of Jewish businesses. All across the country, Nazi Storm Troopers and SS men posted signs that advised "Don't Buy from Jews" and "The Jews Are Our Misfortune." They smeared the word *Jude* (Jew) and painted the six-pointed Star of David in yellow and black across thousands of doors and windows. They stood menacingly in front of the homes of Jewish lawyers and doctors as well as at the entrances of Jewish-owned businesses. Germans were "encouraged" not to enter, while Jews were arrested, beaten, harassed, and humiliated.

Top: German students eagerly participate in the public torching of "un-German" books. *Bottom:* The Nazis opened 50 concentration camps in 1933, including this one at Dachau, Germany.

The boycott was not a complete success. It caused too much economic and emotional turmoil within Germany and provoked negative international reactions as well. Nevertheless, the boycott marked the beginning of an unrelenting nationwide campaign against all of Germany's Jews.

If the 1933 German economy was too fragile to withstand a boycott's disruptions, other measures could be taken to deprive and isolate the nation's Jews. Within a week of the boycott, the Nazis enacted the first of hundreds of national laws that would define, segregate, and impoverish the Third Reich's Jews from 1933 through 1939. The first instance of this "paper violence" was the April 7 Law for the Restoration of the Professional Civil Service. Affecting more than two million state and municipal workers, it was intended to ensure that government employees would be firmly controlled by and loyal to the Nazi regime. Paragraph 3, which came to be known as the "Aryan paragraph," targeted Jews by requiring that "civil servants of non-Aryan descent must retire." On April 11 a supplement to this law clarified that any person who had a Jewish parent or grandparent was "non-Aryan," a definition that would later be refined.

Increasingly, the Nazis used law to separate Jews from German society, but such measures could not be effective unless Jews were "defined." The discriminatory and definitional measures enacted in early April became the foundation for many other "legal" persecutions that followed.

In the early months of the Nazi regime, anti-Jewish laws were enacted on an almost daily basis. Though out of practical necessity the laws were not always thoroughly enforced, in one way after another Jewish life—religious, educational, and cultural as well as professional—was increasingly restricted. On April 21, for example, Jewish ritual preparation of meat was outlawed. A few days later, the April 25 Law Against the Overcrowding of German Schools introduced a quota system to restrict the number of "non-Aryan" students in German schools and universities. Its implementation meant that new Jewish students in any German school or university would be limited to 1.5 percent of the total of new applicants. Overall, the number of Jewish students could not be more than five percent.

Additional laws implemented that April barred Jewish physicians from clinics and hospitals that were funded under the national health insurance system. Pharmacy licenses were no longer available to Jews, and Jewish lawyers found severe restrictions on their practices, too. The month ended with the banishment of Jews from German sports organizations.

Meanwhile, millions of non-Jewish Germans felt the effects of the anti-Jewish legislation, for it became essential for them to prove their "Aryan" ancestry. The task of certifying people's Aryan indentities soon fell on priests and pastors, clerks, and archivists. The process led to an expanding network of investigations and bureaucratic offices that became one of the hallmarks of Nazi Germany's racial state.

The assault begins: Storm Troopers urge Germans to boycott Jewish-owned shops.

Germany's Jews did their best to cope with the mounting decrees that were segregating them, robbing them of liberty, and depriving them of their livelihoods. About 37,000 German Jews emigrated from Germany in 1933, including writers such as Walter Benjamin and Hannah Arendt. However, the costs of flight were high, both financially and psychologically. Thus, most of the German Jews remained in the country that they regarded as home. They hoped that the storm of discrimination would pass, and they rallied their communal solidarity until such time as it did.

Far from passing, the storm was gathering a ferocity that no one could foresee in detail. Still, as the weeks and months accumulated, it became clearer that Nazi law was excluding Jews from every aspect of German life. Within Germany and throughout the world, it was no secret that Hitler's regime had started a systematic process of persecution that was intended, at the very least, to segregate the German Jews. Although exceptions could be found, inside and outside of Germany relatively few voices were raised in protest as 1933 drew to a close.

Newly appointed Chancellor Adolf Hitler shakes hands with German President Paul von Hindenburg on January 30, 1933. Fourteen years after he entered the political arena in the chaotic aftermath of World War I—and only seven years after serving a prison sentence for treason—Hitler legally assumed Germany's top elected position. Once in office, Hitler took decisive action against his primary political foes, the Communists and Socialists. By July all political parties besides the NSDAP were outlawed.

In 1932 Kurt von Schleicher was appointed German chancellor by President Paul von Hindenburg as a last-ditch effort to prevent Hitler from obtaining the post. A veteran of the German Army and an official of the Weimar Republic, Schleicher proved incapable of establishing a coalition government. He was dismissed by Hindenburg on January 28, 1933, paving the way for Hitler to become chancellor January 30.

Hitler's cabinet in 1933. To the right of Hitler are Vice Chancellor Franz von Papen, Minister of the Interior Wilhelm Frick, and Foreign Minister Konstantin Baron von Neurath. With only two fellow Nazis in the cabinet—Frick and minister without portfolio Hermann Göring *(bottom row, second from left)*—Hitler was dependent upon the support of right-wing nationalists Alfred Hugenberg and Fran Seldte *(first and third from left in middle row)*.

1933

• 1933: Arrests for German citizens for sedition are up sharply from 1932.
• Concentration camps are established this year in Oranienburg, Esterwegen, Sachsenburg, and Dachau.
• Jewish Social Democratic politician Ernst Heilmann is arrested. • An antisemitic, anti-Communist organization, *Gesamtverband deutscher anti-kommunistischer Vereinigungen*

(General Association of German Anti-Communist Societies), is founded .
• The antisemitic *Glaubensbewegung deutscher Christen* (Movement of German Christian Believers) becomes the semiofficial religious organization of Germany. • The *Volksempfänger* (People's Radio Receiver) debuts in Germany; *See* August 5, 1938.

The Nazi faithful enthusiastically salute their leader as Hitler looks out from the second-story window of his new office in Berlin. This scene creates the impression of unflagging loyalty to the new chancellor. The Nazis effectively choreographed Hitler's every appearance to highlight his power and give the impression of mass support. The Nazi swastika, the *Sieg Heil* salute, and the ever-present stone-faced SA and SS troops reinforced the image of an omnipotent Nazi state.

What Is the Holocaust?

The Holocaust was the systematic, state-organized persecution and murder of at least six million Jews—as well as other targeted groups—by Nazi Germany and its collaborators. They slaughtered two-thirds of Europe's Jews and one-third of the world's Jewish population. In addition, Nazi Germany's genocidal policies destroyed millions of other defenseless people, including Roma and Sinti (Gypsies), Polish citizens, Soviet prisoners of war, homosexuals, the handicapped, Jehovah's Witnesses, and other political and religious dissidents within Germany itself.

At least four terms name this immense tragedy, which continues to raise questions concerning why and how it happened. Masters of euphemistic language, the Nazis spoke of *die Endlösung*, the "Final Solution" of their so-called "Jewish question." In the early 1940s Eastern European Jews turned to Jewish scripture and used the Yiddish word *churb'n*, which means "destruction," or the Hebrew term *sho'ah*, which means "catastrophe," to name the disaster confronting their people.

Sho'ah is widely used in Israel, and the official remembrance day for the Holocaust is called *Yom ha-Sho'ah*. However, "Holocaust," a term that began to achieve prominence in the 1950s, remains the most common term in the English-speaking world. It derives from the Septuagint, an ancient Greek translation of the Hebrew Bible, which employs *holokaustos* for the Hebrew *olah*. Those biblical words refer to a completely consumed burnt offering. While the destruction perpetrated by Nazi Germany must be named lest it be forgotten, the problematic religious connotations surrounding the term "Holocaust" suggest that no name can do it justice.

• *Schlageter*, a pro-Nazi play by Hanns Johst, premieres. It is a tribute to Nazi "martyr" Albert Leo Schlageter, who was executed by the French in 1923 after defying French authority in the Ruhr. • German-Jewish physicist Albert Einstein criticizes the new Nazi regime: "I shall live in a land where political freedom, tolerance, and equality of all citizens reign." Einstein subsequently takes his genius to the United States. • The Silver Shirts, a Nazi-like political group, is founded in America. • The first issue of the antisemitic *National Worker* is published in London by Colonel Graham Seton-Hutchinson. • An antisemitic feature film entitled *Pettersson and Bendel* is produced in Sweden.

• January 1933: A pastoral letter of Austrian Bishop Gfollner of Linz states that it is the duty of all Catholics to adopt a "moral form of antisemitism."

• January 4, 1933: Hitler and former Prime Minister Franz von Papen meet secretly to discuss Hitler's future in the German government.

Roll call at Oranienburg, Germany, the concentration camp built on the Havel River. Like other camps within Germany before the war, Oranienburg was not as harsh a camp as those that would open during the war. In addition to the standard fatigue duty and drill, prisoners were allowed occasional recreational opportunities. Nevertheless, the regimentation of daily routines and the ever-present armed guards reminded prisoners of their status.

Three young Polish Jews—Szaja Dershowitz, Meyer Fliegelman, and David Saleschutz—pose aboard the *San Marco* en route from Trieste, Italy, to Palestine. Increased antisemitism at home coupled with Zionist activism spurred individuals to forsake their troubled native land for promises of a new and better life in the Jewish homeland. While more than 40,000 Polish Jews journeyed to Palestine before 1933, most refugees went to the United States and the urban centers of Western and Central Europe.

A German Jew is forced to carry a sign that says he had "ravaged a Christian girl." The public humiliation of Jews was the Nazis' first step to systematically removing them from German society. SA members also cut the beards off Jewish men and forced wealthy Jewish women to scrub the streets with their undergarments.

Joseph Goebbels founded *Der Angriff (The Attack)* in Berlin in 1926. An official organ of the Nazi Party, the paper cynically incited violence against German Jews. This January 23, 1933, headline states, "The day has come: Berlin belongs to us!"—an exultant reference to Hitler's imminent ascension to real power in the German government.

1933

● **January 28, 1933:** German Chancellor Kurt von Schleicher resigns.

● **January 30, 1933:** German President Paul von Hindenburg appoints Hitler chancellor of Germany; Franz von Papen is named vice-chancellor. The Nazis refer to this as *Machtergreifung* ("Seizure of power").

● **February 2, 1933:** Political demonstrations are banned within Germany.

● **February 12, 1933:** "Bloody Sunday" riots in Berlin lead to the death of one Communist and injuries to hundreds of other citizens, including Jews.

As the *Reichstag* went up in flames on February 27, 1933, the Nazis prepared to move against their primary political opponent, the Communist Party of Germany. Blaming the fire on a Dutch Communist, the Nazis suspended civil liberties on February 28. Thousands of Communists were arrested and hastily sent to the recently opened concentration camps at Dachau, Germany, and other locations.

The Fire

On the night of February 27, 1933, the *Reichstag* building in Berlin was set on fire. German police arrested a Dutch Communist, Marinus van der Lubbe, whom they discovered at the scene. Hitler interpreted this clear case of arson as the first step of a Communist revolution, and he pushed for the arrest of several German Communist leaders as well as representatives of Communist International.

Van der Lubbe, however, was the only one of the accused convicted. Even at the time, many observers believed that the Nazis set the fire themselves, using it as a pretext to crack down on their political enemies. Scholars remain divided on the issue. Some argue that van der Lubbe started the fire and that Hitler was the beneficiary of a remarkable stroke of good luck.

Members of the German Communist Party (KPD) were arrested and closely guarded following the burning of the *Reichstag* building in February 1933. Hermann Göring's boast that "whoever raises a hand against us shall lose his head" led to mass arrests and many executions. Not only were political opponents taken into custody, but members of the Nazi Party suspected of being disloyal were also rounded up. Estimates vary greatly regarding the number of summary executions carried out by Nazi Storm Troopers, but thousands of "enemies" disappeared after the imposition of martial law in March.

● **February 19 and 26, 1933:** Father Charles Coughlin, a Jew-hating priest—Canadian but working in the Detroit, Michigan, diocese—sermonizes on the radio that "Shylocks" (Jews) are causing the Depression. He receives 80,000 letters of support a week, about 70 percent from Protestants. His editorials often parallel those of the Nazi press. He is friendly with several U.S. senators and representatives.

● **February 20, 1933:** Hitler wins over a group of leading German industrialists at a meeting designed for that purpose.

● **February 27, 1933:** The German *Reichstag* building is set ablaze. The Nazis are quick to blame the fire on Communists.

● **February 28, 1933:** A presidential decree gives Chancellor Hitler emergency powers. All 100 Communist Party members of the *Reichstag* are arrested. One Berlin man is given 50 lashes for being a Communist and 50 more for being a Jew.

Who Is a Jew?

As early as 1919, Adolf Hitler defined Jews as "a racial and not a religious group." His judgment was wrong and deadly.

Not all Jews practice Judaism, but any person can become Jewish through religious conversion. Traditionally, anyone whose mother is Jewish has been identified as Jewish, but that condition is not necessary for Jewish identity, either. Presently, many Jews are citizens of the modern state of Israel, but a majority of the world's Jews do not fit that description. Who is a Jew? It's a complex question.

Jews trace their origins to the biblical patriarch Abraham, who lived almost 4000 years ago. Judaism, a distinctively monotheistic religion, is rooted in the exodus of the ancient Hebrew people from Egyptian slavery and in experiences they shared under Moses' leadership at Mount Sinai. The early Jews' ritual laws and ethical rules distinguished them from other groups.

Eventually occupying the Mediterranean coastal land of Canaan, the Jews established the kingdom of Israel. Unable to sustain the unity and autonomy it enjoyed from about 1000 to 922 B.C.E., the kingdom was split by internal divisions, besieged, and occupied by a variety of conquerors. In 70 C.E., the Romans ruthlessly put down a sustained Jewish rebellion. Most of the surviving Jews were dispersed to various parts of the Roman Empire. Exiled Jews have lived in European lands for more than 2000 years.

Whether their outlooks are secular or religious, their homes in Israel, Europe, the United States, or anywhere else in the world, Jews are not a race but a people unified by memory and history, culture, tradition, and religious observances that are widely, if not identically, shared.

Established in March 1933, Esterwegen in Germany was a "protective custody" camp. Like other concentration camps, Esterwegen housed Communists, high officials of the Weimar Republic, Jews, and common criminals. The SS guards often brutalized Jews and prominent inmates, and summary executions were not uncommon. When the camp was dissolved in September 1936, its inmates were transferred to a camp at Sachsenhausen, Germany.

While the Nazis unleashed a terror campaign against political opponents at home, it was business as usual on the diplomatic front. Here Hjalmar Schacht, president of the German *Reichsbank,* shakes hands with U.S. President Franklin Delano Roosevelt *(right)* at an economic conference in Washington, D.C. Roosevelt was inaugurated as U.S. president on March 4, 1933, and would remain his country's leader for nearly the duration of the Holocaust.

1933

● **March 4, 1933:** United States President Franklin Delano Roosevelt makes his inaugural address. He will remain as president throughout the Holocaust.

● **March 5, 1933:** The Nazis win 288 of 647 seats in the *Reichstag* election.
● Individual German states are stripped of power.

● **March 9–10, 1933:** A wave of riots begins against German Jews by the SA, so-called Storm Troopers of the Nazi Party, and *Stahlhelm,* a nationalist organization comprised of World War I veterans.

● **March 19, 1933:** The Jewish War Veterans of America announces it will boycott German goods and services.

A Berlin police officer *(left)* and a member of the SA patrol the streets after the burning of the *Reichstag* building. Granted police authority by Hitler's government, members of the SA and SS used their powers to suppress political opponents. The government approved of the intimidation tactics of Nazi shock troops, who effectively hounded Communists and Socialists—as well as Jews—into submission.

With the full powers of government at their disposal following passage of the Enabling Act, the SA unleashed a terror campaign against opponents of the Nazi regime. Unauthorized beatings and periods of police detention were common occurrences. The brown-shirted Storm Troopers were feared throughout Germany, and the Nazi swastika became a symbol of the repressive, omnipotent state.

Police struggle to hold back enthusiastic crowds waiting to greet the chancellor and president at the opening of the *Reichstag* in Potsdam on March 21, 1933. Marching together into the Garrison Church, the young chancellor, Adolf Hitler, and the aged president, Field Marshal Paul von Hindenburg, symbolized the joining of Germany's glorious past with its vibrant future.

• **March 21, 1933:** Special Nazi courts are set up to deal with political dissidents. • **This is the Day of Potsdam—the first opening of a Nazi-controlled *Reichstag*.**

• **March 22, 1933:** The first concentration camp, Dachau, is established in south Germany. By 1945 the Nazis will build more than 1000 camps.

• **March 23, 1933:** *Ermächtigungsgesetz* (Enabling Act), passed by the *Reichstag*, gives Hitler's government dictatorial powers. Hitler promises that Germany's artistic growth will be fueled by "blood and race."

• **March 27, 1933:** A gigantic anti-Nazi protest rally, organized by the American Jewish Congress, is held in

New York City. 55,000 people attend and threaten to boycott German goods if the Germans carry out their planned permanent boycott of Jewish-owned stores and businesses.

• **April 1, 1933:** The German government institutes the first official boycott of Jewish lawyers, doctors, and merchants. Due to international out-

Dachau

The Dachau camp, near Munich, Germany, was the first official concentration camp established by the Nazi Party. Staffed initially by local SA and SS men, Dachau was the scene of excessively cruel punishments.

Reorganized and brought under SS control in early 1934, Dachau became the model for the more orderly, horrifyingly efficient concentration camp system. Heinrich Himmler's appointee, Theodor Eicke, reorganized the camp's administration and refined procedures guiding the brutalization of inmates. He demanded utmost discipline and instilled fanatical hatred of prisoners, whom he regarded as subhuman enemies of the state. The most severe and most psychologically devastating punishments were reserved for Jewish inmates. Among Eicke's favorite punishments were long periods of solitary confinement with only bread and water; lashings; and the tying of prisoners to stakes.

The camp was also the scene of hundreds of illegal and inhumane medical experiments. Prisoners were subjected to diseases. Others were immersed in cold water for long periods to test the effect on the human body. The camp still stands today as a grim memorial.

Hitler's personal magnetism and charismatic speaking abilities were key to the Nazi Party's political fortunes. A tireless campaigner and self-proclaimed man of the people, Hitler was relentless on the stump. He is pictured here speaking to loyal followers in the basement canteen of the Munich Brown House. Membership in the Nazi paramilitary organization offered a surrogate family structure. Food, clothing, shelter, and camaraderie were tremendous attractions for many wayward and alienated young men.

National Socialist youth offer the *Sieg Heil* salute while viewing a parade in Berlin. No child was considered too young to identify with the Party, and great effort was put forth to recruit. Clubs and activities geared for the young attracted thousands of German children into the Nazi fold. The leadership of the Nazi Party recognized that children were central to their plans for a thousand-year Reich.

1933

rage and the apathy of many non-Jewish Germans, Hitler orders the boycott limited to a single day.

• April 4, 1933: A front-page article in the German-Jewish newspaper *Jüdische Rundschau* exhorts Jews to wear the identifying Yellow Star with the headline, *Tragt ihn mit Stolz, den Gelben Fleck!* (Wear it with Pride, the Yellow Badge!). • A series of articles by German Jew Robert Weltsch follows the theme, "Say 'yes' to our Jewishness."

• April 7, 1933: Hitler approves decrees banning Jews and other non-Aryans from the practice of law and from jobs in the civil service (Law for the Restoration of the Professional

A gathering is held in London's Hyde Park to protest the Nazi treatment of German Jews. Free to express their opposition, thousands of Londoners listened to the speaker detail the campaign against German Jewry. And yet for all this, the British government seemed willfully oblivious to the German terror tactics.

Rabbi M. Z. Margolies addresses the crowd at New York's Madison Square Garden on March 27, 1933. An estimated 55,000 people joined the demonstration to protest the Nazi treatment of German Jews. Speeches by leading rabbinical authorities, politicians, and celebrities had little impact on the Nazi regime. While Jewish religious leaders called for a day of fasting and prayer to publicize the plight of German Jews, the effort was impotent in the face of the Nazi assault.

Thousands of American Communists take to the streets in New York City on March 25, 1933, to protest the actions of the German government. Carrying banners that professed solidarity with their political brethren and the Jews of Germany, this crowd made its way through the streets of lower Manhattan to the nearby German consulate.

Civil Service). Jewish government workers in Germany are ordered to retire.

• April 11, 1933: The German government begins employment and economic sanctions against Jews that are widely perceived as being racially based. The Lutheran Church opposes the sanctions.

• April 14, 1933: The *Nationalpolitische Erziehungsanstalten* (National Political Educational Institutes) are established as training schools for Nazi Party cadets.

• April 25, 1933: The Law for Preventing Overcrowding in German Schools and Schools of Higher Education takes effect; the law restricts

enrollment of Jews. Similar extralegal discrimination against Jews already exists in the United States.

• April 26, 1933: Hermann Göring establishes the Gestapo (*Geheime Staatspolizei*; Secret State Police).
• Hitler meets with Bishop Wilhelm Berning of Osnabrück and Monsignor Steinmann, prelates representing the

Ludwig Müller

Calling themselves the "Storm Troopers of Jesus Christ," and believing Hitler was an instrument of God, a group of Nazi Protestant theologians spearheaded a drive in 1933 to align the Protestant churches of Germany with pagan Nordic ritual and the goals of the Nazis. Their goal, one Reich church under cen-

tralized leadership, produced the coerced election of Ludwig Müller, Hitler's advisor on church matters, to the new post of Reich bishop of the Protestant Church.

Müller was an antisemitic nationalist, a military chaplain who believed racial "mongrelization was immoral and should be prohibited by law." Protestant pastors opposed to Müller's "positive Christianity" created a rival organization, the Confessing Church. Müller persecuted dissenting pastors, having many of them arrested. The resulting public furor, however, forced Hitler to tone down his assault on the Confessing Church.

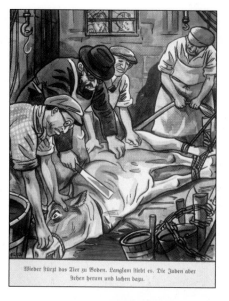

Wieder stürzt das Tier zu Boden. Langsam stirbt es. Die Juden aber stehen herum und lachen dazu.

Jewish ritual slaughter was a frequent target of Nazi propaganda. Seen as barbaric and demonstrative of Jewish cruelty, ritual slaughter was prohibited by the German government in April 1933. This page from the antisemitic children's book *Der Giftpilz* (*The Poisonous Mushroom*) contained the following text: "Again the animal falls to the ground. It is slowly dying. The Jews, however, are standing around and laughing about it." The message to impressionable German youth was clear: Jews took pleasure in and were entertained by killing innocent animals.

Nazi Storm Troopers prepare to launch the boycott against Jewish-owned stores and professional establishments in Berlin in April 1933. Party members stationed themselves in the doorways of Jewish businesses, discouraging patrons from entering. The move to divide German society into gentile and Jewish sectors was a major initiative of the Nazi regime.

1933

Roman Catholic Church in Germany. Hitler claims that he is only doing to the Jews what the Catholic Church has already done to them for 1600 years. He reminds the prelates that the Church has regarded the Jews as dangerous and pushed them into ghettos. Hitler suggests that his anti-Jewish actions are "doing Christianity a great service." Bishop Berning and Monsignor Steinmann later describe the talks as "cordial and to the point."

• April 27, 1933: The German government prohibits the practice of ritual Jewish slaughter of animals for meat.

• May 6, 1933: The Institute of Sexual Studies in Berlin is destroyed by pro-

"I am a Jew but I have no complaints about the Nazis."

—Sandwich board forced on an elderly Jewish man who had been stripped of his shoes and pants; Frankfurt, Germany, 1933

The arrest of Jewish merchants was a familiar scene in Germany during Nazi boycott against the Jews. Observant Jews clothed in traditional garb were frequent targets of persecution and harassment. Although only a small minority of the German-Jewish community was Orthodox, the Nazis commonly displayed them as both quintessentially Jewish and "un-German."

Three young women read a sign warning German citizens against Jewish propaganda. While signs like this were common throughout Germany, the initial boycott against Jewish-owned businesses instituted in April was short-lived due to lack of support, the need to shore up the German economy, and the Nazis' fear of an international outcry. The use of bilingual placards was limited to international cities, such as Berlin, Munich, and other major shopping areas.

Jewish lawyers wait in front of the Lawyers' Chamber building in Berlin to apply for admission. Following passage of legislation in April, the number of Jewish lawyers admitted at the Berlin courts was sharply reduced. For more than 50 years, German antisemites had campaigned to limit Jewish influence in society by restricting the numbers of Jewish lawyers, judges, and teachers.

Nazi students, likely because of its academic interest in homosexuality.

• **May 10, 1933:** Books deemed of "un-German spirit," most of them Jewish, are burned on Unter den Linden, opposite the University of Berlin, and throughout Germany. More than 20,000 volumes are destroyed, including works by John

Dos Passos, Thomas Mann, Karl Marx, Ernest Hemingway, Upton Sinclair, Émile Zola, H. G. Wells, André Gide, Sigmund Freud, Maxim Gorky, Helen Keller, Friedrich Forster, Marcel Proust, Jack London, and Erich Maria Remarque.

• **May 17, 1933:** The Bernheim Petition, named for imprisoned Silesian

Jew Franz Bernheim, is presented to the League of Nations to protest Germany's anti-Jewish legislation. • In Norway, Vidkun Quisling establishes the Norwegian Fascist Party as well as the *Hirdmen* (King's Men), a collaborationist organization that's modeled on the Nazi *Sturmabteilung* (SA).

The closing of German gay bars spurred the creation of this collage, *Der Notschrei* (*The Scream for Help*). The pictures offer a poignant but ultimately futile plea for help. The Nazi attacks on homosexuality, particularly after the murder of Ernst Röhm and the crushing of the SA in 1934, were rooted in their campaigns against all forms of "degeneracy." Hitler feared that homosexuals in positions of leadership undermined his government's ability to rule effectively.

The *Führer* digs the ceremonial first shovelful of dirt to inaugurate the building of the *Autobahn.* Hitler's participation in this and other groundbreaking ceremonies created the impression of a government addressing the financial woes of Germany's legions of unemployed. Instituted in the summer of 1933, the Nazi economic program known as the Reinhardt Plan allocated an enormous amount of money for public works projects. Directed by Fritz Todt, the *Autobahn* program was highly visible and popular, bringing jobs for construction workers and engineers while simultaneously stimulating the automobile industry. The *Autobahn* would also be helpful during the war, providing quick transport for troops and materiel.

Gatherings of Nazi Storm Troopers, such as this one in Dortmund, Germany, were common in the early years of Nazi rule. Arranged to accentuate Hitler's popularity, public rallies replete with swastika banners and paramilitary organizations (outfitted in starched uniforms and polished boots) appealed to the militaristic values deeply embedded within German society. Positioned as the antithesis to the weak and disgraced Weimar Republic, the Nazis effectively presented themselves as the legitimate heirs to the mythical Teutonic knights and the legendary Prussian military machine.

1933

• **June 1, 1933:** Germany introduces the Law for Reduction of Unemployment, which provides for marriage loans and other incentives to genetically "fit" Germans.

• **June 16, 1933:** Unknown assailants murder Chaim Arlosoroff, a Labor Zionist leader.

• **June 26, 1933:** The *Akademie für Deutsches Recht* (Academy for German Law) is founded to rewrite the entire body of German law to NSDAP specifications.

• **June 27, 1933:** At a rally in London, speakers protest antisemitism in Nazi Germany.

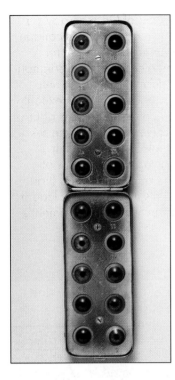

Classifying humans according to their physical features was central to Nazi plans for the racial reordering of Europe. This metal case with 20 glass balls of different eye colors was used to identify and designate one's racial group according to the pseudoscience of the Nazis. Although first-hand observations often contradicted the theoretical basis of race-based science, many German doctors and scientists enthusiastically pursued the research agenda set by the regime.

A pedestrian eyes the National Socialist paraphernalia on display at a Nazi headquarters in Yorkville, Pennsylvania. Biographies of Hitler, the party newspaper (*Völkischer Beobachter*), and other items could be purchased by individuals who either supported or were curious about the Nazi movement. Hitler's government was seen by many native Germans living in the U.S. as a needed corrective to the ineffective governmental regimes of the earlier Weimar Republic.

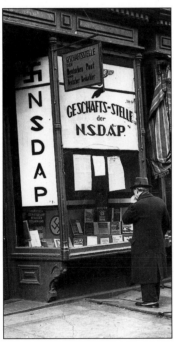

Aryanization

Arisierung, or "Aryanization," was a vital part of the Nazi Party's plan to reduce Jewish influence in Germany. This scheme, which began almost immediately after Hitler came to power, consisted of two components: cultural and economic Aryanization.

The cultural portion began in 1933, with the government's efforts to drive Jews out of the Reich's cultural life. Jewish intellectuals, actors, journalists, and musicians lost their posts in important cultural institutions, and Jewish enrollment in universities was severely restricted.

From the outset of the Third Reich, many Jews found it prudent to sell their property at a loss and flee the country. In 1938, however, the Aryanization of Jewish property began in earnest. On April 26 Hermann Göring promulgated the "Order Requiring the Declaration of Jewish Property," which obligated all German Jews to declare the value of their economic holdings both at home and abroad. Increased pressure forced Jews to sell their businesses at 30 to 60 percent of their value.

The effects of Aryanization were devastating to Germany's Jewish population, severely undermining the economic well-being of the Jewish community. This was, of course, the Nazis' main goal in carrying out this practice.

• **June 28, 1933:** In a speech to German newspaper publishers, Hitler describes the government's new journalistic regulations.

• **July 1, 1933:** The German government states that "Reich Chancellor Hitler still belongs to the Catholic Church and has no intention of leaving it."

• **July 14, 1933:** The Nazi Party is made Germany's only legal political party; political opposition is punishable by law. The Law Regarding Revocation of Naturalization and the Annulment of German Citizenship strips German citizenship from Eastern European Jews living in Germany. Also, Germany enacts the Law for the Prevention of Offspring with

Hereditary Diseases, which provides for sterilization of "unfit" parents and potential parents, as well as "euthanasia" of the "defective" and of "useless eaters." The government terms these people *lebensunwertes Leben* ("life unworthy of life"). The law is endorsed by the American Eugenics Society.

The Haavara Agreement

In 1933 the German government signed a pact, called the *Haavara* (Transfer) agreement, with the Zionists. German law, formulated under the Weimar Republic, severely restricted the amount of property Jews could take with them if they emigrated to Palestine. Under the terms of the *Haavara* agreement, the assets of Jews leaving Germany for Palestine would be placed in special accounts, portions of which would be transferred (in the form of German goods) to Palestinian banks.

The pact not only encouraged Jewish emigration—a positive development from the point of view of the Nazis—by allowing refugees to take a portion of their assets with them, but it also assured that those German Jews who arrived in Palestine would not be penniless. That was an extremely important consideration for the British, who held the mandate on the region. Under the terms of the agreement, about 40,000 Jews escaped the Holocaust by emigrating to Palestine.

Students and Nazi Storm Troopers carry reams of blacklisted materials to a bonfire on Berlin's *Opernplatz*. The nazification of public schools and universities proceeded at a breakneck pace during the first year of Hitler's rule. Teachers and professors who opposed the Nazis' intellectual agenda were dismissed, and curricular materials that reinforced the racial ideology of Nazism were implemented throughout the country. Because Germany's youth were instrumental in Hitler's plans to dominate the world, their education and upbringing greatly concerned the Nazi authorities.

On May 10, 1933, organized book burnings occured throughout Germany. Libraries, public buildings, private offices, and homes were searched for offensive materials. The campaign to homogenize German cultural and intellectual life undermined the principles on which democratic societies are based. Nazi terror and public apathy led to the disintegration of the freedoms and institutions central to Western democratic traditions.

1933

• July 20, 1933: The Vatican signs a concordat with Germany. Pope Pius XI considers the treaty as protecting Catholic rights in Germany. However, by this action the Vatican helps legitimize the Third Reich in the eyes of the German Catholic hierarchy and laymen as well as of the international community. As a result, the concordat helps pave the way for the Nazi totalitarianization of German society and later German attacks on the European state system.

• July 31, 1933: Approximately 30,000 people are by now interned in Nazi concentration camps.

• August 20, 1933: The American Jewish Congress announces its mem-

The transport of these arrested leaders of the Socialist Party through the streets of Karlsruhe, Germany, was choreographed to feed the Nazi propaganda machine. Guarded by SA and SS personnel, the "criminals" were jeered by hostile crowds along the entire route to the prison at Kislau, Germany. Photographs of the staged event were later used as part of a postcard series glorifying the elimination of the subversive elements within German society. According to Nazi lore, the Socialists shouldered responsibility for the failures of the despised Weimar Republic.

JEWISH POPULATIONS IN EUROPE'S NATIONS, 1933

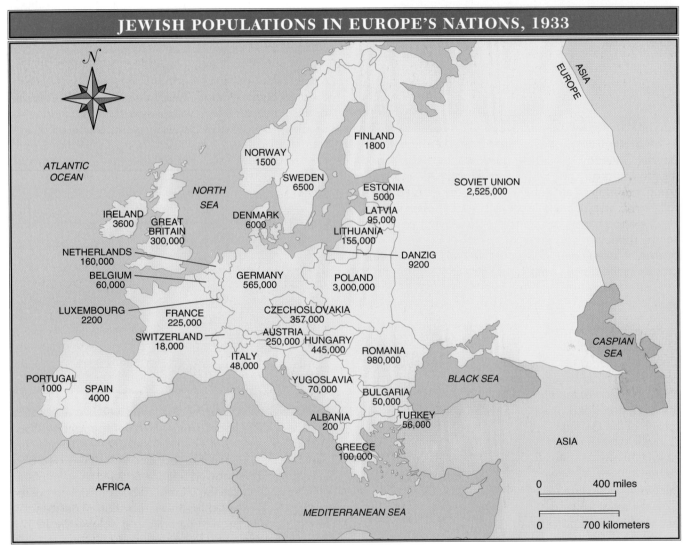

bers will boycott German goods and services.

• **August 25, 1933:** The *Haavara* (Transfer) agreement between the German Ministry of the Economy and the Zionist Organization facilitates a large-scale emigration of Jews from Germany to Palestine.

• **September 1933:** Heinrich Himmler is appointed overseer of all police units in the Reich, except Prussia.
• The *Reichsvertretung der deutschen Juden*, the central representative body of German Jews emphasizing education, is established; it is led by Otto Hirsch and Rabbi Leo Baeck. It is the only organization officially allowed to represent German Jews.

• **September 22, 1933:** The Reich Chamber of Culture is established.
• German Jews are banned from the fields of journalism, art, literature, music, broadcasting, and theater.

• **September 29, 1933:** Hitler approves the decree forbidding German Jews from the occupation of farming.

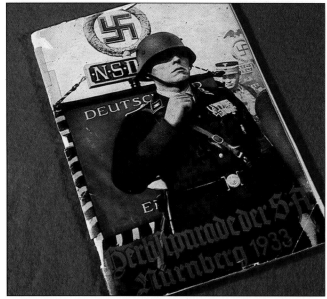

The sensationalized portrayal of the mentally ill reinforced Nazi ideology regarding the worthiness of life. Pictured here as "idiots," mental patients were hidden and isolated, as if they were members of another species. Their days in Germany were numbered.

SA Storm Trooper, symbolizing a proud and purposeful Germany, graces the cover of the program for the *Herbstparade der SA* (Autumn Parade of the Storm Troopers). At the September 1933 Nuremberg Party rally, the SA celebrated the Party's rise to power with Hitler's appointment as chancellor earlier that year. In songs, speeches, and processions, solemn remembrance of fallen comrades was joined with joyous celebration at the dawn of the Third Reich.

Pope Pius XI, leader of the Roman Catholic Church, signed a Concordat with Hitler in July 1933 that guaranteed the legal status and protection of the German Catholic Church and its organizations. In spite of the agreement, however, the Nazis imprisoned Catholic religious leaders and harassed parochial schools.

"Life without hope" is how Nazi propaganda artists portrayed patients in Germany's mental institutions. The mentally ill, the handicapped, and those convicted of sex crimes were labeled inferior and were systematically removed from the German *Volk*. Legislation passed in July 1933 allowed for the sterilization of persons suffering from "incurable" hereditary problems. By 1937 200,000 people had been sterilized.

1933

- **October 4, 1933:** The Editor Law calls for racially pure journalism and forces the dismissal across Germany of Jewish reporters and publishing executives. A codicil strips newspaper editors of power over content.

- **October 21, 1933:** Germany withdraws from the League of Nations.

- **October 27, 1933:** Arabs riot in Palestine to protest immigration of Jews.

- **November 1933:** The *Deutsche Christen* organization stages a rally in Berlin to honor "Christ the Hero."
- The first issue of editor A. Ristow's antisemitic *Blick in die Zeit* (*A Look at the Times*) is published in Germany.

While the government program against German Jews continued unabated inside Germany, the Council of the American Jewish Congress and the Jewish Labor Committee urged their members to boycott German goods and services. The organizations' relatively small memberships, combined with the devastating effects of the Depression, undermined their campaigns. Outside of direct government intervention by the former allies of World War I, little could be done to stop the Nazi juggernaut.

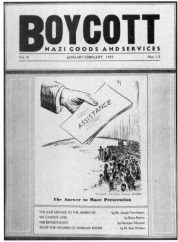

Ernst Röhm (left), Heinrich Himmler (center), and other Nazi officials arrive at Berlin's Grunewald Stadium for a Party rally. As leader of the Storm Troopers (SA), Röhm commanded a paramilitary force of more than 400,000 men that was charged with eliminating the regime's political opponents. The SA's brutal tactics helped consolidate Hitler's power and made Röhm the second most powerful man in Germany.

The Nazi faithful march in formation at the first Reich Party Day ceremony in Nuremberg, Germany. Battalions of SS soldiers carry eagle standards and flags that proclaim, "Germany Awake." The festivities offered visual evidence of Nazi power.

Stephen S. Wise

Rabbi Stephen S. Wise was president of the American Jewish Congress and the World Jewish Congress. Determined to help ease the plight of Germany's Jews, both through the boycott of German goods in the U.S. and an increase in emigration from the Third Reich to Palestine, Wise placed a great deal of hope in U.S. President Franklin Roosevelt. Sadly, Wise's pleas were largely ignored.

Wise and other Jewish leaders in America learned about the slaughter of Jews as early as 1942, but their efforts to do something to help Hitler's victims fell on deaf ears. In the end, Wise and the organizations he ran were unable to save many Jews because there was so little interest in their efforts among non-Jews. In a terrible abrogation of responsibility, the international community abandoned Europe's Jews to their fate at the hands of the Nazis.

• **November 12, 1933:** Nazi candidates win 93 percent of the vote in the *Reichstag* election. However, only the Nazi Party was permitted to nominate candidates.

• **November 24, 1933:** The German Law Against Dangerous and Habitual Criminals allows for compulsory castration of "hereditary" criminals.

• **November 27, 1933:** *Kraft durch Freude* (KdF; Strength through Joy) is established to tie leisure activities of the German *Volk* (people) to the aims of the Nazi Party.

• **December 1, 1933:** A legal decree issued by Hitler declares Germany and the Nazi Party one.

• **Late 1933:** The German News Bureau (DNB) is established to feed propagandistic "news" to Germany's newspapers. • Hermann Göring orders closure of all SA "wild camps" (locally mandated concentration camps).

• **1933–39:** More than 1400 anti-Jewish laws are passed in Germany.

1934

THOUSANDS of Nazi supporters flocked to Nuremberg in September 1934 for the city's annual weeklong celebration of Nazi solidarity. Among the sights and sounds of various parades and rallies: enormous Nazi banners that reached halfway to the heavens, 130 searchlights that beamed 25,000 feet into the night sky, and a gathering of tens of thousands of brown-shirted Storm Troopers. Bands blared "The Badenweiler March," while delirious Nazi supporters waved swastika flags and punctuated the air with cries of "Heil Hitler!" An impassioned Adolf Hitler spoke of the Party's solidarity and strength, proclaiming, "There will be no other revolution in Germany for the next 1000 years!" Filmmaker Leni Riefenstahl captured the pageantry and drama of the Nuremberg rally, creating a propaganda documentary that would be entitled *Triumph of the Will.*

Nuremberg had hosted Nazi rallies annually since 1927, but never before had spirits been so high. Just weeks earlier, Hitler had been elected *Führer* of the German state in a landslide vote. It was the ultimate political victory for Hitler—a true "triumph of the will." Yet, ironically, that triumph did not come easily.

During the first two years of Nazi rule, Hitler had to deal not only with the formidable tasks of *Gleichschaltung*—a term referring to a streamlined process to put all aspects of German life under Nazi control—but also with troublesome factions inside the Nazi Party itself. The Nazi Party's populist wing and especially the Storm Troopers (*Sturmabteilung,* or SA) thought that the Nazi revolution was incomplete and resented that it progressed so slowly. These radical Nazis believed that big business, the traditional German bureaucracy, the military, and especially Jewish life had been left too much intact.

The SA posed a particularly difficult problem for Hitler. Led by Ernst Röhm, one of Hitler's close friends from the Nazi Party's earliest days, the SA originated in the summer of 1921. With membership drawn from disgruntled World War I veterans, it became the Nazi Party's private army. At the time of Hitler's appointment as chancellor in 1933, there were more than a half-million SA men. By early 1934 that number had soared to about 4.5 million, which made the SA a force much larger than Germany's post-World War I army. Though Röhm and the SA felt they were securing Nazi Germany's interests, Hitler and many other Party leaders—to say nothing

A proud *Führer* reviews parading Storm Troopers at the Nuremberg Party rally.

1934

of the allies Hitler needed from German industry and the military—saw Röhm and the SA as threats to stability, particularly because it was Röhm's ambition to make the SA the true army of the Third Reich.

In the spring and early summer of 1934, another complication arose. President Paul von Hindenburg, who had been giving his reluctant blessing to most Nazi initiatives, was now in failing health. Hitler had to protect his flanks. If Röhm's SA was not checked, the organization could be put to use by Röhm as the linchpin of a revolution at odds with Hitler's. However, if Röhm's leadership of the SA could be neutralized, Hitler reasoned, Germany's military establishment would endorse *Der Führer* as Hindenburg's successor.

Under growing Nazi oppression, the Hugo Brill family celebrates the Passover seder.

Thus came to pass the notorious Night of the Long Knives, a bloodbath ordered by Hitler that ensued on June 30 and July 1. The exact number of people who were killed during this purge remains uncertain. Although some tallies put the number in the hundreds or even the thousands, probably fewer than 100 people were killed. Among them, however, were not only Röhm and other senior SA men but also conservatives who were perceived as threats to Hitler, men who might try to depose him and restore monarchy in Germany.

A key figure in the Röhm purge was Heinrich Himmler, who headed the black-shirted SS (*Schutzstaffel*, or Protection Squad). Initially formed in the summer of 1925 as Hitler's personal guard unit, the SS was originally part of the SA. When Himmler took command in January 1929, the SS consisted of a few hundred men. By the spring of 1934, it had already become everything that the SA was not—a disciplined, armed elite of more than 50,000 men who were intensely loyal to Hitler. At this time, Himmler's influence expanded further as he gained increasing control of Nazi Germany's political police, whose main branches included the SD (*Sicherheitsdienst*, or Security Service) and the Gestapo (*Geheime Staatspolizei*, or Secret State Police).

Once his rival, Röhm, was out of the way, Himmler reaped the benefits. For its part in the purge, his SS got independence from the SA, a move that enhanced Himmler's authority. Meanwhile, Himmler bestowed some rewards of his own. On July 4, for example, he appointed Theodor Eicke, commandant of the Dachau concentration camp, as inspector of concentration camps. Eicke, who had followed Himmler's execution order by personally murdering Röhm, instituted in other camps the systematically brutal methods of control and punishment that had characterized his administration at Dachau. With the help of Eicke and other SS subordinates, Himmler soon controlled a vast state security empire. In this capacity, Himmler would later use his SS and police power to become a key architect of the destruction of the European Jews.

While Himmler expanded his power, Hitler still had to shore up his political authority. The Röhm purge had removed threats to that authority, but it left Hitler with the need to explain what had happened and why. Hitler's strategy was to argue that Röhm and his closest SA associates were guilty of treasonous activity and sexual deviance—Röhm was a homosexual—and to portray himself as a protector whose intervention had saved good German lives.

Speaking to the *Reichstag* on July 13, Hitler took responsibility for the purge, referring to himself as the "highest judge of the German people," and affirmed that "in the state there is only one bearer of arms, and that is the Army; there is only one bearer of the political will, and that is the National Socialist Party." The Army leadership's satisfaction in hearing that proclamation was matched by the *Reichstag*'s applause as it passed a law legitimating the purge as "emergency defense measures of the state."

Hitler's good fortune continued. He received a congratulatory telegram from President Hindenburg, who wrote that Hitler had "nipped treason in the bud" and "saved the nation from serious danger." But an even bigger reward was his on the morning of August 2 when President Hindenburg died. With the plan already arranged, a government announcement was made within an hour of Hindenburg's death: The offices of president and chancellor were to be merged. Hitler would be Nazi Party chief, head of state, and supreme commander of the armed forces as well.

Adolf Hitler salutes a monument to fallen Nazi comrades at the Nuremberg Party rally.

Hitler was now the nation's ultimate authority. Signaling that fact on the same day, German soldiers took a personal oath of loyalty to Hitler: "I swear before God this sacred oath: I will render unconditional obedience to Adolf Hitler, the *Führer* of the German nation and people, supreme commander of the Armed Forces, and will be ready as a brave soldier to risk my life at any time for this oath."

Less than three weeks later, the German people were given an opportunity to ratify Hitler's new position and title: *Führer* and Reich chancellor. The turnout for this plebiscite was more than 90 percent of the 45.5 million people who could vote. Thirty-eight million Germans—about 90 percent of the votes cast—said "yes." Not every German agreed, however. More than four million voted "no," and about 870,000 voting papers were defaced.

Hitler could go to the 1934 Nazi Party rally at Nuremberg a much more confident man than he was when the year began. As Hitler's confidence was bolstered and as Himmler's authority increased, the vise on Germany's Jews was tightening even if the year's major events in Germany had not been focused primarily on them. By no means, however, had the Jews been forgotten while Hitler and his loyal followers consolidated and expanded their power. "Paper violence" against Jews had continued.

One important measure, enacted on March 23, was the Law Regarding Expulsion from the Reich, which would pave the way for East European Jews to be expelled from the Reich. Other decrees were aimed particularly at removing Jews from German educational institutions and professions. In early February, for instance, "non-Aryan" medical students had been prohibited from taking state medical examinations. In early May tuition exemptions were discontinued for Jewish university students.

The year 1934 was a triumph of the will for Hitler and his followers. For the European Jews, that triumph would prove to be a catastrophe.

Hitler loyalist Theodor Eicke (*pictured*) murdered SA leader Ernst Röhm during the Night of the Long Knives.

The SD (*Sicherheitsdienst;* Security Service) was the intelligence arm of the SS. Led by Reinhard Heydrich, it ruthlessly sought out the enemies of National Socialism. Increasingly focusing upon eliminating Jews from German society, the SD drew Adolf Eichmann *(pictured)* to its ranks soon after its founding in March 1934. Eichmann had joined the SS in 1932, serving as a corporal at Dachau and attracting the attention of Heydrich and his superior, Heinrich Himmler. The SD offered Eichmann new opportunities to rise in rank and become a "specialist" in Jewish affairs, leading him to play a key role in implementing the "Final Solution."

Her face brimming with youthful joy and optimism, 19-year-old Gerda D. was hospitalized in the psychiatric emergency ward of a hospital in Berlin. Although the diagnosis of Gerda as schizophrenic was uncertain, she was released only after being sterilized under the Law for the Prevention of Progeny with Hereditary Diseases. Passed the previous year, this vicious measure was one of a series of actions against those deemed a threat to Germany's racial purity and health.

After immigrating from Frankfurt, Germany, with her family in 1934, Anne Frank *(right)* plays outside her Amsterdam home with her friend, Sanne. In response to open anti-semitism and increasing Nazi attacks, about 50,000 Jews had left their German homeland to seek safer havens by the end of 1934.

1934

● 1934: "Twenty-Five Points of the German Religion" are issued in Germany by Professor Ernst Bergmann. It holds that Christ was not a Jew but a Nordic warrior put to death by Jews, and whose death spared the world from Jewish domination; Adolf Hitler is the new messiah sent to Earth to save the world from Jews. ● Heinrich Himmler is given responsibility for police in Prussia, making him the chief of police forces throughout the Reich. ● The *Institut für Erbbiologie und Rassenforschung* (Institute of Hereditary Biology and Race Research) is founded at the University of Frankfort am Main by Dr. Otmar Freiherr von Verschuer to study racial and hereditary issues.

In 1928 the Nazis publicly made known their opposition to the repeal of Paragraph 175, which stipulated imprisonment for same-gender sexual activity. Once Hitler became chancellor, the government moved quickly against gays, forbidding the mention of homosexuality in magazines and closing gay bars. The Eldorado, a popular gay gathering spot in Berlin, was closed in early March 1934. Accusations of homosexuality resulted in imprisonment in concentration camps, where gays were particularly abused.

Der Giftpilz (The Poisonous Mushroom) was one of the many antisemitic books written for German children. Highlighting the medieval theme of Jews as Christ-killers, it urges children: "When you see a cross, then think of the horrible murder by the Jews on Golgatha."

Sinti and Roma

Ever since their arrival in Central Europe in the 1400s, the Gypsies had been social outcasts. In the 1930s, when Heinrich Himmler vowed to rid Germany of "asocials," Gypsies were among the targeted groups.

Consisting of different "tribes" or "nations," these ethnic minorities were called "Gypsies" because they were thought to have Egyptian origins. The Sinti and Roma tribes were the most common in Germany and Austria, respectively. Labeled by the Nazis as racial "inferiors," Sinti and Roma were regarded as so "unfit" that Himmler's circular of December 8, 1938, "Combating the Gypsy Nuisance," recommended "the final solution of the Gypsy question."

Throughout Nazi-occupied Europe, tens of thousands of Gypsies were hunted down and shot or deported and killed in camps. At least 23,000 Roma and Sinti were sent to Auschwitz-Birkenau. During one night alone—August 2–3, 1944—2897 men, women, and children were gassed there during the liquidation of the "Gypsy family camp." The Nazis and their collaborators killed between 20 and 50 percent—220,000 to 500,000—of the Sinti and Roma, who call this genocide the *Porrajmos*, or "great devouring," of their people.

• Dorothy Thompson, an anti-Nazi American journalist whose 1932 book *I Saw Hitler* is critical of the *Führer*, is expelled from Germany. • Restoration work begins at *Wewelsburg*, a 17th-century cliff-top fortress in Westphalia, Germany. When complete, the castle will be used by Heinrich Himmler and the *Schutzstaffel* (SS) as a mystical fortress, complete with a

12,000-volume Aryan library and a center for racial research. • In the United States, the American Christian Defenders (the World Alliance Against Jewish Aggressiveness) is founded by antisemitic propagandist Eugene N. Sanctuary.

• Early 1934: Hitler Youth members are turned loose throughout Ger-

many to intimidate members of Catholic youth groups.

• January 1, 1934: The Nazis remove Jewish holidays from the official German calendar. • German laws allowing sterilization of the "unfit," which were passed in July 1933, are promulgated. Hitler orders the German government to undertake a building

This poster reflects the antisemitism of the Polish organization *Obóz Narodowo-Radykalny* (National Radical Camp). It asserts that Jews are "the whip [oppressors] of all mankind." Founded in April 1934, the National Radical Camp was banned by Polish leader Józef Pilsudski three months later.

Renowned for her inventive artistry as a filmmaker, Leni Riefenstahl converses with Nazi cameramen at a rally. In her film *Triumph des Willens (Triumph of the Will)*, a record of the 1934 Nuremberg Party rally, Riefenstahl portrayed Nazism with powerful images and hypnotic grandeur.

Their handshake symbolizing the transfer of power, Hermann Göring *(right)* confirms Heinrich Himmler as director of the Gestapo, the Secret State Police, in April 1934. When he assumed broader powers as head of all German police in 1936, Himmler in turn passed the torch to Reinhard Heydrich. Begun in Prussia during the Weimar Republic, the Gestapo was intended to protect the security of the state. Under the Nazis, it became a tool of terror, often placing people in "protective custody" before sending them to concentration camps.

1934

program that will produce 4000 aircraft by October 1935.

• January 24, 1934: A Lutheran minister opposed to the Reich Church is beaten by Nazi thugs.

• January 26, 1934: Germany and Poland sign a ten-year nonaggression pact.

• January 30, 1934: Hitler publicly insists that Germany will not be deterred from its program of rearmament.

• February 1934: Germany native Anneliese Frank joins other family members in Amsterdam. Anne is three years old.

At an April rally in Rome, a unit of the Italian Black Shirts proclaims its loyalty to Benito Mussolini. Standing at attention with their spades emblazoned with the words *Il Duce* (the Leader), these militant Fascists prepare to modernize the country and ready it for war by reclaiming more land for agriculture. Originally a separate militia, the Black Shirts were later incorporated into the Italian Army.

Adolf Hitler and Julius Streicher stroll together outside a German factory in Nuremberg, Germany. As editor and later publisher of the newspaper *Der Stürmer (The Attacker)*, Streicher fed the Nazi propaganda machine with his virulent attacks on Jews. At its height, the newspaper reached about 600,000 readers. Streicher played upon people's fears by reviving the medieval accusation that Jews murder Christian children and use their blood in perverted religious rituals.

For liberty and truth we fight With words and deeds and song

Promoting unity and understanding between the two countries, the organization Friends of the New Germany largely drew Americans of German heritage to its ranks. Known also as the German-American Bund, the organization encouraged American support for Nazi Germany. On May 17, 1934, the Bund attracted 50,000 to a rally at New York City's Madison Square Garden.

• **February 17, 1934:** Great Britain, France, and Italy warn that Austria's independence must be maintained.

• **April 1934:** Germany establishes the *Volksgericht* (People's Court) to deal with enemies of the state; there is no trial by jury and no right of appeal.

• **April 7, 1934:** Several thousand Americans attend a pro-Nazi rally in Queens, New York.

• **April 14, 1934:** An antisemitic organization in Poland, *Obóz Narodowo-Radykalny* (National Radical Camp), is established; *See* July 10, 1934.

• **May 1, 1934:** Julius Streicher's Nazi periodical, *Der Stürmer*—one of Germany's most popular periodicals and a favorite of Hitler—reminds its readers that during the Middle Ages, the Jews were accused of committing ritual murder of Christian children and of using their blood for religious ritual purposes. • The *Rassenpolitisches Amt der NSDAP* (Racial Policy Office

---

The SA

The Nazi Party owed much of its early success to its brown-shirted army of violent thugs, the SA. The *Sturmabteilung* (Storm Troopers), or SA for short, was created to maintain order at meetings and protect Party speakers. In time it became much more than that.

After the refounding of the Party in 1925, the SA developed into a powerful propaganda tool. Vowing to "win the streets" for the Party, SA men sold newspapers, distributed leaflets, posted placards, and marched at mass rallies. The SA also took delight in provoking violent confrontations with political opponents. Most SA men were street toughs who relied on fists, knives, clubs, and guns during brawls.

Numbering almost four million men by June 1934, the SA's strength ironically became troublesome for Hitler. Its continued radicalism, talk of a "second revolution," and scheme to become the new "people's army" clashed with Hitler's plans. During the night of June 30, 1934 , Hitler unleashed an assassination campaign against the SA's top leadership. Among the most prominent victims slaughtered was SA chief Ernst Röhm. With the purge of the SA, its rival organization—the SS—rapidly rose in power in the Nazi state.

Among the most outspoken American critics of the Third Reich's persecution of Germany's Jews was newspaper columnist Dorothy Thompson. A journalist in Germany during the early days of the Hitler regime, she reported on the antisemitic atrocities of the new government. When news of the Holocaust reached the United States in December 1942, Thompson was one of the few Americans to call for concerted action to stop the genocide. Her pleas fell on deaf ears.

Reichstag members enthusiastically salute Hitler after his address justifying the death of several dozen Nazis in the Night of the Long Knives on June 30,1934. The Blood Purge eradicated the leadership of the Brown Shirts (SA), the quasimilitary organization led by Ernst Röhm, along with scores of other potential enemies.

1934

of the National Socialist German Workers Party) is established by Hitler's friend and secretary, Rudolph Hess.

• **May 2, 1934:** Congressman Louis T. McFadden delivers an antisemitic speech on the floor of the United States House of Representatives.

• **May 17, 1934:** At New York's Madison Square Garden, thousands attend a pro-Nazi rally sponsored by the German-American Bund.

• **June 9, 1934:** The SD (*Sicherheitsdienst;* Security Service), an intelligence service of the SS, is now designated the sole intelligence service for the SS and Nazi Party. • The Soviet

Among the earliest of Hitler's supporters, Ernst Röhm proved a threat to Hitler's goal of seizing power through political means. Röhm joined the 1923 Munich Beer Hall *Putsch,* but he left Germany in disappointment two years later. Success in the 1930 elections led Hitler to send for Röhm and appoint him SA chief of staff. Röhm proved a formidable leader, transforming the Storm Troopers into a vicious force, controlling the streets by terror. The Nazis' political victories made Röhm expendable. His vision of a soldier's state uniting the Army with the SA alarmed military leaders, who pressured Hitler to eliminate him.

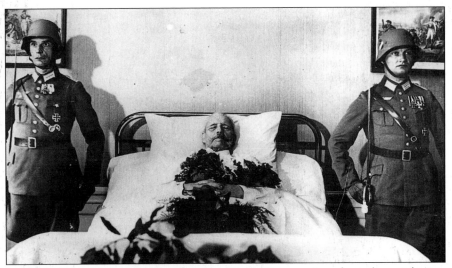

Flanked by Army officers, Paul von Hindenburg, twice elected president of the Weimar Republic, lies in state in his simple room at Neudeck, East Prussia. With the death of the 87-year-old president on August 2, Hitler moved immediately to claim absolute power as *Führer.* Senile and under the sway of advisors, the field marshal and hero of the Battle of Tannenberg had proven no match for his ambitious chancellor.

Placing one hand upon the Nazi flag and raising the other in obedience, these German soldiers swear their allegiance to the *Führer.* With President Paul von Hindenburg's death, Hitler consolidated power by joining the offices of chancellor and president. He solidified his position by requiring that all soldiers swear a personal oath of loyalty to him as *Führer.*

Union, Poland, and Romania pledge to respect their common borders.

• **June 14–15, 1934:** In Venice, Hitler and Italy's dictator, Benito Mussolini, meet to discuss the fate of Austria.

• **June 30, 1934:** Hundreds of actual and presumed opponents of the Hitler regime, including many high-ranking officers of the Nazi Storm Troopers (SA), are rounded up and executed in what will come to be called the "Night of the Long Knives." Victims include Ernst Röhm, chief of the SA, and Gregor Strasser, former Reich organization leader of the Nazi Party. • Nazi persecution of homosexuals begins in earnest.

• **July 4, 1934:** An Inspectorate of Concentration Camps is established, headed by Theodor Eicke.

• **July 10, 1934:** The Polish anti-semitic organization *Obóz Narodowo-Radykalny* is banned by Polish leader Marshal Józef Piłsudski, three months after its formation.

Within weeks of President Paul von Hindenburg's death, Hitler sought a public mandate for his policies. This poster announces a plebiscite for August 19. With an "X" in the box marked *Ja* (Yes) and the bold banner proclaiming "the entire people answer this question with a unanimous yes" running underneath, opposition to the Nazis was strongly discouraged. As it turned out, nearly 90 percent of German citizens voted yes to the mandate.

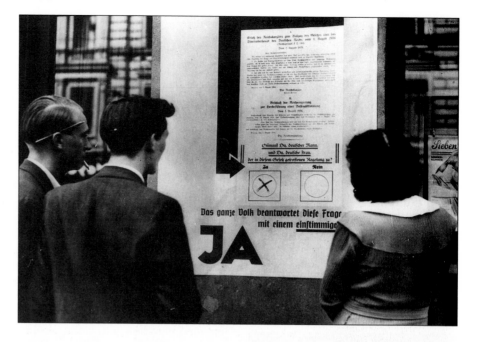

With Hitler looming god-like behind him, a blond-haired German youth gazes into the future on the cover of this Hitler Youth publication. The title reads *Youth Serves the Führer*. The Hitler Youth was aggressively loyal to the *Führer* and militaristic in spirit. In early 1934 the group was used to intimidate Catholic youth groups.

A festive group of schoolgirls, led by their teachers, offers the Nazi salute at a rally in Coburg, Germany. German girls joined the Nazi youth organization *Jungmädelbund* (League of Young Girls) at the age of ten. At 15 they were promoted into the *Bund Deutscher Mädel* (League of German Girls). From childhood, girls were taught to prepare for motherhood and conform to the motto of the BDM: "Be faithful, be pure, be German!"

1934

• **July 25, 1934:** Chancellor Engelbert Dollfuss is killed when the Nazis unsuccessfully try to seize power in Austria.

• **August 2, 1934:** German President Paul von Hindenburg dies; Hitler declares himself *Führer* of the German state and commander-in-chief of Germany's Armed Forces. Members

of the Armed Forces must take a personal oath of allegiance to Hitler.

• **August 5, 1934:** One hundred Jews are killed in an antisemitic pogrom at Constantine, Algeria.

• **August 19, 1934:** In a plebiscite on Hitler's expanded powers, 89.9 percent of voters approve. Although an

The *Führer* offers a paternal embrace to a circle of Bavarian children. Nazi propaganda pictured Hitler as both a strong leader and a gentle and protective guide. The Nazi caption to this photo read: "One always sees the *Führer* surrounded by children in pictures."

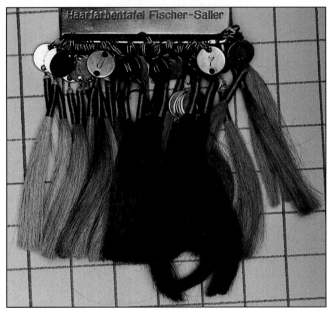

Nazi scientists developed this kit, which contained 29 samples of human hair. The samples were used by geneticists, anthropologists, and doctors to determine ancestry. Hair color also became a means to prove the supposed superiority of Aryans and the inferiority of Jews, Gypsies, and those of "mixed breeds."

The SS

For Heinrich Himmler, leader of the SS, the extermination of the Jews was a "moral right," an "historical task," and "a page of glory in German history."

The SS became the chief instrument of Nazi terror, as well as the carrier of its racial ideals. Officially known as the *Schutzstaffel* (Protection Squad), the organization came into being in 1925, as Adolf Hitler's personal bodyguard. Once Hitler appointed Himmler to head the SS, in 1929, it rose beyond its bodyguard role and developed into a Party police.

Subordinate to the much larger SA until the so-called "Blood Purge" in 1934, the black-shirted SS expanded dramatically from a few hundred Germans in 1929 to almost a quarter-million by the beginning of the war ten years later. Controlling all police forces, the SS pursued domestic enemies of the Nazi Party and assumed responsibility for the "Final Solution." Membership

was selective and based on racial criteria. Aryan racial purity was demanded even of prospective SS brides.

Himmler developed his forces into an elite brotherhood, complete with cult-like rituals and Teutonic symbols of a sacred order. Dabbling in an obscure occultism, he believed himself to be the reincarnation of a medieval German king who had conquered eastern territories.

---

overwhelmingly Christian nation, most Germans will generally support Hitler's actions until near the end of the war.

● September 1934: In Denmark, a collaborationist SS organization, *National Socialistike Ungdom* (National Socialist Youth), is established.

● September 4–10, 1934: A massive Nazi Party Congress is staged at Nuremberg.

● September 24, 1934: The Nazis establish *Verfügungstruppen* (Militarized Standby Troops) as part of the SS. In wartime, the *Verfügungstruppen* will serve as conventional troops under the *Wehrmacht*.

● September 27, 1934: Hoping to deter Hitler's expansionist goals, Great Britain, France, and Italy declare support for the independence of Austria.

● October 1, 1934: Hitler secretly orders a quick buildup of the German Army and Navy, and the creation of an air force.

1935

AFTER the Nazis took power in 1933, Germany's loosely affiliated Jewish communities established a new national organization. It was called the *Reichsvertretung der Deutschen Juden* (Reich Representation of German Jews). Led by Rabbi Leo Baeck and Otto Hirsch, the *Reichsvertretung* faced a thicket of problems: Jewish educational needs, vocational training, welfare, emigration assistance, and much more. Still, Baeck, Hirsch, and others worked gallantly to help their people. They even remained hopeful for a truce with the Nazi Party—a hope that, in retrospect, was sadly naive.

In 1935 government authorities required the *Reichsvertretung* to change its name to *Reichsvertretung der Juden in Deutschland* (National Representation of Jews in Germany), a nuance that exemplified the Nazi intention to cut off the Jews' German identity. Nevertheless, the *Reichsvertretung*—like most individual Jews in Germany—did not fully perceive the Nazis' uncompromisingly anti-Jewish position. Jews just could not believe that the persecution would escalate.

On September 24, 1935, the *Reichsvertretung* published an article in the newspaper *Jüdische Rundschau* (*Jewish Review*). Written for Jews and Germans alike, it spoke about the ways in which "a tolerable relationship" could be established "between the German and the Jewish people." The *Reichsvertretung*, the commentary continued, was "willing to contribute to this end with all of its powers."

This newspaper article was the *Reichsvertretung*'s response to a speech by Hitler at the 1935 Nazi Party rally at Nuremberg on September 15. Hitler defended the German rearmament that had begun in the spring. He denounced Communists, then attacked Jews. Hitler contended that a threatening Jewish problem required the government "to bring about, by means of a singular momentous measure, a framework within which the German people would be in a position to establish tolerable relations with the Jewish people." If Jewish agitation continued despite the government's action, Hitler warned, "a new evaluation of the situation would have to take place."

Although the words "establish tolerable relations" may have sparked some hope for Jews, Hitler had no diplomatic intentions. In fact, his "framework" consisted of three vice-tightening laws, which the *Reichstag* would soon enact unanimously.

The Nazis posted a clear warning: "Jews not wanted in Behringersdorf (Germany)."

1935

The first of the "Nuremberg Laws," as the decrees came to be known, was the Reich Flag Law. It established red, black, and white as the official colors of the Nazi state and determined that the nation's flag would be the swastika flag. If that law did not target Jews directly, the other two did so with a vengeance. The Reich Citizenship Law and the Law for the Protection of German Blood and Honor, both carrying Hitler's signature, became centerpieces of Nazi Germany's anti-Jewish legislation.

The Citizenship Law drew a fundamental distinction between "citizens" and "subjects." It restricted citizenship to those who were of "German or related blood." Only citizens, the law stipulated, could enjoy "full political rights in accordance with the law." Furthermore, citizenship was "acquired through the granting of a Reich Citizenship Certificate."

Although the word "Jews" appeared nowhere in its text, this law was clearly targeted against them. Henceforth, Jews would only be subjects in Nazi Germany. Stripped of citizenship, deprived of civil rights, they would live as foreigners—if at all—in their German homeland.

The Law for the Protection of German Blood and Honor contained several numbered paragraphs. Four of them especially showed how sharp the previous distinction between citizen and subject was meant to be, for this law used the word "Jew" explicitly. The preamble to the law's detail expressed that "the purity of German blood" was essential for the ongoing existence of the German people. As the key paragraphs of the law went on to make clear, that purity depended on control of the polluting racial threat claimed by the government.

Paragraph 1 immediately prohibited marriage between Jews and persons of "German or related blood." Violations of this provision were punishable by a prison term. Paragraph 2 made extramarital sexual relations between Jews and Germans illegal.

To discourage the skirting of Paragraph 2, a third provision made it unlawful for Jews to "employ in their households female subjects of German or kindred blood who are under 45 years old." To defy this provision was to risk a year in prison, a fine, or both. The same penalty awaited those who disobeyed Paragraph 4, which established a link to the Reich Flag Law by forbidding Jews to fly the Reich flag and to display the Reich colors. The Law for the Protection of German Blood and Honor took effect the day after it was enacted at Nuremberg, except for the provisions in Paragraph 3, which were delayed until January 1, 1936.

The Nuremberg Laws did not completely doom Jewish life in Germany. The Reich Citizenship Law still allowed Jews to be subjects of the German state, and a subject was defined as "a person who enjoys the protection of the German Reich and who in consequence has specific obligations toward it." That possibility influenced the *Reichsvertretung*'s hope that "a tolerable relationship" might exist between "the German and the Jewish people."

What the Nazis considered tolerable, however, was scarcely the same as what the *Reichsvertretung* had in mind, for the Nuremberg Laws were race laws. They found Jewish "blood" to be inferior and dangerous. Jews could never be Germans. To the contrary, Jews were threats to German purity;

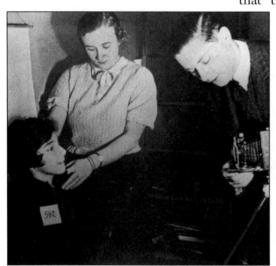

"Scientists" measure a Jewish girl's "racial characteristics."

their very presence on German soil undermined the nation's health and vitality. At the very least, they needed to be segregated, isolated, and ever more removed from the mainstream of German society.

The three laws proclaimed at Nuremberg on September 15, 1935, advanced those policies. Yet Hitler had correctly called them a "framework." By themselves they remained inadequate to reach the goals they were intended to achieve. Some of their paragraphs, for example, used the word "Jew" but did not define it. Who, then, counted as a Jew? Establishing that definition was no trivial matter for Germans and Jews alike, because these laws, which aimed to bring about a thorough racial separation, could not be systematically implemented unless one knew to whom they applied.

Back in April 1933, a vague formula had defined a "non-Aryan" as any person who had a Jewish parent or grandparent. Later, a draft of the Reich Citizenship Law contained the provision that the law applied "only to full-blooded Jews," but that phrase was absent from the text read to the *Reichstag* on September 15, 1935. A sensitive problem in a society where there had been considerable intermarriage, the crucial questions persisted: Who was affected by these laws? How should "Jew" be defined? After lengthy debate within the Nazi leadership, the First Implementation Order to the Reich Citizenship Law decided the issue on November 14.

This order restated that no Jew could be a citizen of the Reich, decreed that Jews had no right to vote on political issues, specified that Jews could not hold public office, and required the retirement of Jewish civil servants. Then its decisive fifth paragraph defined the word "Jew" in a way that distinguished between full Jews and part-Jews. A person was fully Jewish if he or she had at least three Jewish grandparents. If a person had two Jewish grandparents but did not practice Judaism or have a Jewish spouse, then he or she was a part-Jew—specifically a *Mischlinge* (crossbreed).

The *Mischlinge* category was eventually refined to distinguish between *Mischlinge* of the first or second degree, the latter classification referring to persons who had only a single Jewish grandparent and who did practice Judaism or have a Jewish spouse. From the Nazi perspective, it was much worse to be a full Jew than, say, a *Mischlinge* of the second degree.

Detailed though it was, however, this racial classification rested on a paradoxical foundation. Nazi science could not identify a specifically Jewish blood type because no such thing exists. The identity of Jewish grandparents was not determined by "blood" but by membership in the Jewish religious community instead.

For the Nazis, logical consistency was less important than the fact that the Nuremberg Laws, now buttressed by the November definitions, had established race as the fundamental legal principle in German life. The definitions themselves were important steps in the process that destroyed Jewish life. They were used to identify who the targets for persecution—and eventually death—would be. The *Reichsvertretung*'s hopes notwithstanding, the actions taken at Nuremberg in September 1935 meant that there could be no "tolerable relationship" between "the German and the Jewish people" as long as Nazi rule prevailed.

Otto Hirsch, chairman of the National Representation of Jews in Germany.

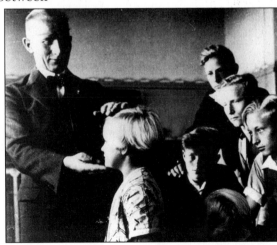

An Aryan child is singled out by a teacher for having especially desirable physical characteristics.

The Netherlands, long recognized as one of Europe's most tolerant countries, admitted about 34,000 refugee Jews from Germany. Of these, about 15,000 became permanent residents of the country, only to be captured by the Germans after the 1940 invasion. This 1935 photograph shows the mayor of the Dutch city of Naarden, Boddons Hosang, holding a refugee Jewish girl.

The year 1935 witnessed a series of violent pogroms in Poland, a country long notorious for its vicious antisemitism, deeply rooted in Polish Catholicism. In response, many Jews fled the country. This greeting card celebrating the Jewish New Year portrays some of the thousands of Polish Jews who emigrated to Israel in spite of severe restrictions imposed by the British, who held the mandate on Palestine.

Sir Oswald Mosley (center) was leader of the British Union of Fascists during the years 1930 to 1940. Fascism's appeal in Britain lay not only in its invocation of traditional English antisemitism, but also in Hitler's apparent success in dealing with the Great Depression. The British Union of Fascists experienced significant appeal, with one source claiming 50,000 members and another source 100,000.

1935

• 1935: The *Reichswehr* (Reich military; the German force whose size was severely proscribed by the Treaty of Versailles) is renamed the *Wehrmacht* (Armed Forces) in brazen acknowledgment of Adolf Hitler's military expansion and defiance of the treaty. • Hitler mandates the creation of the state-controlled Union of Protestant Churches. • German film-maker Leni Riefenstahl's *Triumph of the Will*, an epic documentary film of the 1934 Nazi Party Congress at Nuremberg and a deification of Hitler, is released. • The *Sturmabteilung* (SA) is incorporated into the *Schutzstaffel* (SS).

• The first issue of the antisemitic *Deutsche Wochenschau für Politik,*

The Gestapo headquarters looms ominously on Prinz Albrechtstrasse in Berlin. A benign residence was transformed into a place of terror and torture after it was occupied by the notorious Gestapo. Germany's secret police used all methods available to wring information out of people. Individuals unfortunate enough to be introduced to the building's torture chambers and dungeons emerged battered and psychologically broken.

The Nazis went to great lengths to justify their "scientific" racism. This is a chart from *Genetics and Racial Science: A Photographic Portrayal,* one of their numerous textbooks on the subject. The photographs are designed to show that the European racial type is aesthetically superior to the Australian, Negro, and Mongoloid races.

Pro-Nazi Groups in U.S.

The German-American Bund was the most consequential pro-Nazi political movement to emerge in the prewar United States. Under the leadership of its *"Führer,"* a notorious antisemite named Fritz Kuhn, the Bund at its height claimed about 15,000 members in addition to 8000 Storm Troopers.

A 1939 rally in New York City's Madison Square Garden attracted an audience of 20,000. In spite of efforts to portray themselves as patriotic Americans, even going so far as to combine images of George Washington and the swastika in their propaganda, Bundists were overwhelmingly German immigrants whose thoughts were with Nazi Germany. Membership was concentrated in large cities, and the party never had much grassroots support. Never a serious threat to the American government, the Bund's fortunes experienced a downturn in 1939, when Kuhn was sent to prison for embezzling funds.

Another avowedly antisemitic political movement to emerge

between the wars was William Dudley Pelley's Silver Shirts. Pelley claimed that a "near-death experience" influenced his spiritualist antisemitism. Like the Bund, the Silver Shirts could never claim an extensive membership; they had only about 15,000 members, mostly middle-class, by 1934. The movement's strength dwindled to only 5000 four years later.

Wirtschaft, Kultur und Technik (German Weekly for Politics, Economy, Culture and Technology) is published in Germany. • The first issue of the pseudoscientific, antisemitic *Zeitschrift für Rassenkunde (Journal for Racial Science)* is published. • The American Jewish Congress joins with the Jewish Labor Committee to form the Joint Boycott Council, aimed at

German purveyors of goods and services. • The Nazi government forces the closure of Masonic lodges across Germany. • Anti-Jewish riots occur across Romania. • Poland adopts a new constitution that abolishes parliamentary democracy.

• America's pro-Nazi Silver Shirts political group merges with the Chris-

tian Party. • In Britain, the first issue of Sir Oswald Mosley's *Fascist Quarterly* is published. • The German government permits the publication of Martin Luther's *On the Jews and Their Lies,* in which Luther advocates a program to arrest Jews, expropriate them, force them into the kind of labor the government determines, and, finally, to exile or murder them.

On March 16, 1935, the *Führer's* cabinet met and decided to announce publicly that Germany was reintroducing military conscription. Although this policy violated the Treaty of Versailles, the French and British governments did nothing in response, choosing to believe Hitler's assertion that the policy was a purely defensive measure. The resulting rejuvenation of the German Army was important to the future of Nazi Germany's expansionist policies.

Germany lost the Saar region as a result of the First World War. On January 13, 1935, the people of the Saar voted overwhelmingly in favor of a return to Germany. The result of the plebiscite was an important propaganda victory for Hitler, who could claim to have the support of the vast majority of the German people. This photograph shows a demonstration in Trier following the annexation of the territory. The banner reads, "The Saar is ours."

As part of their effort to prepare Germany for war, the Nazis made a concerted effort to promote paramilitary organizations, such as the Hitler Youth. In 1939 participation in this organization became mandatory, and its membership rose to 8.9 million. The Hitler Youth helped the Nazis to indoctrinate German boys with racist ideology as well as give them rudimentary military training.

1935

• **January 13, 1935:** A plebiscite conducted under the auspices of the League of Nations brings the Saar region into Greater Germany.

• **March 1, 1935:** Germany retakes the Saarland; *See* April 1, 1935.

• **March 16, 1935:** Germany initiates conscription, in defiance of the Versailles Treaty. France, England, and the United States do not do anything to reverse the Reich's decision.

• **April 1, 1935:** Anti-Jewish legislation in the Saar region is passed.

• **April 30, 1935:** Jews may no longer display the German flag.

"When Jewish blood spurts from the knife, things go twice as well."

—SA celebratory chant; Berlin, 1935

In 1935 Hessy Levinson Taft, then six months old, appeared on the cover of the Nazi family magazine *Sun in the House.* Hessy was presented as the archetype of Aryan babyhood. Ironically, the baby wasn't Aryan at all. In fact, her parents were Latvian Jews. When confronted by Hessy's frightened mother, the photographer admitted that he had submitted the photograph to a beauty contest for Aryan babies, hoping to mock Nazi racial theory. He succeeded beyond his wildest dreams.

It was important to Nazi officials that those who cared for German children were themselves of Aryan ancestry. This student nurse, or "little blonde sister," was painstakingly screened before being permitted to look after these infants. The Nazi flag, and banner with SS runes, bring a spooky irony to this otherwise idyllic scene.

Racist ideology became part of the curriculum in German schools. Students, like these girls in a home economics class at the Luise-Otto-Peters School in Berlin, regularly made posters incorporating racist themes. The text reads: "Your first duty is: To take care of your race, to ensure that the race remains healthy, and to protect the race from foreign influences."

• **May 12, 1935: Polish dictator Jozef Pilsudski dies.** From here on Jews will experience more antisemitism in Poland. The government and most Polish political parties will call for discrimination, economic boycott, expulsion, and physical violence against Jews. The Polish Catholic Church, most priests, the Catholic press, and schools will sanction dis-crimination and/or violence against the Jews.

• **May 14, 1935:** A court in Bern, Switzerland, pronounces the German edition of the *Protocols of the Elders of Zion* a forgery.

• **May 31, 1935:** Jews are banned from the German Armed Forces.

• **June 9, 1935:** Anti-Jewish riots occur in Grodno, Poland.

• **June 18, 1935:** The Anglo-German Naval Agreement permits the expansion of the German Navy.

• **June 26, 1935:** The Law for the Prevention of Offspring with Hereditary Diseases (*see* July 14, 1933) is

Among the most infamous cases prosecuted under the Nuremberg Laws was that against Albert Hirschland, a Jewish school principal in Magdeburg, Germany, accused of having illicit sex with "hundreds of non-Jewish students." Among the German newspapers to cover Hirschland's trial was Julius Streicher's notorious antisemitic rag *Der Stürmer.* The headline reads: "Albert Hirschland: The Race Defiler from Magdeburg." The accused was convicted on the trumped-up charges and sentenced to life in prison.

Wilhelm Stuckart *(pictured)* helped Wilhelm Frick draft the infamous Nuremberg Laws of 1935. A Nazi Party member since 1922, Stuckart became a Party judge in 1930. He rose through the ranks quickly, holding a variety of law-oriented bureaucratic Party posts throughout the 1930s and early '40s. Stuckart joined the SS in 1936; six years later he was a participant at the Wannsee Conference, at which the "Final Solution" was planned. Lack of evidence caused him to be sentenced to only four years' imprisonment following his arrest by the Allies in 1945. Stuckart was killed in an auto accident in 1953.

Opposition to the Nazi regime was vigorously attacked. In the city of Stuttgart, Germany, the *Sturmabteilung* (SA) launched a move against Jews and Catholics who had dared to challenge the government. Members of the SA paraded through the streets on a truck bedecked with a picture of Nazi enemies. The inscription reads: "We don't tolerate any sabotage to the *Führer's* constructive work."

1935

amended to provide for compulsory abortion of "unfit" fetuses up to six months in utero.

● **July 1, 1935:** The antisemitic *Ahnenerbe Forschungs- und Lehrgemeinschaft* (Society for Research into the Teaching of Ancestral Heritage) is founded to study the racial history of the German people.

● **August 25, 1935:** Pastor Martin Niemöller, the leading Protestant anti-Nazi, sermonizes that Jewish history is "dark and sinister" and that the Jewish people are forever "under a curse" because they not only "brought the Christ of God to the cross" but they also bear the responsibility for the "blood of all the righteous men who were ever murdered."

Wilhelm Frick began his career on Munich's police force, a job he lost because of his support for Hitler's failed coup in November 1923. In 1924 he was elected to the *Reichstag*, becoming leader of the Nazi delegation in 1928. As Thuringia's minister of the interior (1930–1931), he nazified the state's police force, which became notorious for its brutal antisemitism. Frick coauthored the infamous Nuremberg Laws (1935) and, as Germany's minister of the interior, oversaw their enforcement. His political career had, however, reached its zenith, and he played only a small role in the final years of the Third Reich.

"Original Sin"

In 1924 Adolf Hitler warned that "blood desecration" (*Blutschande*) and "defilement of the race" (*Rassenschande*) were the "original sin." His book *Mein Kampf* condemns the deleterious effects of "racial cross-breeding." The laws of nature, Hitler said, dictated that "every animal mates only with a member of the same species.... The titmouse seeks the titmouse, the wolf the she-wolf, etc."

Since the bedrock of Hitler's race theory was his belief in the biological superiority of the Aryan race, he vowed to end what  he believed to be the harmful contamination of Aryan blood and maintain its purity. For Hitler, the worst violation of blood occurred in the mating between Jews and Aryans. The 1935 "Law for the Protection of German Blood" made sexual intercourse between Aryan and non-Aryan a crime. By 1945 race defilement was punishable by execution.

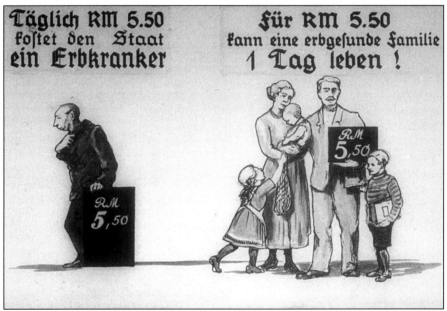

This illustration from a filmstrip produced by the Reich Propaganda Office demonstrates that for the 5.50 *Reichsmarks* it costs to feed, house, and clothe one disabled person for a single day, an entire healthy German family could survive. Propaganda such as this helped prepare the German people for the murder of those deemed genetically inferior.

• **September 15, 1935:** The first Nuremberg Laws are passed, including the Reich Citizenship Law and the Law for Protection of German Blood and Honor. The Jews are returned to the legal position they had occupied in Germany before their emancipation in the 19th century. Jews can no longer exist as German citizens or marry non-Jews.

• **Another new Nuremberg Law, the Reich Flag Law,** defines the official flag of Germany: a black swastika in a white circle on a red field. • The 1935 National Socialist Party rally marks the first display of the product of Germany's illegal rearmament.

• **October 18, 1935:** The German government introduces the antisemitic

Law for the Protection of the Hereditary Health of the German People.

• **November 1, 1935:** An addition to the Reich Citizenship Law disqualifies Jews from German citizenship.

• **November 14, 1935:** The National Law of Citizenship is instituted throughout Germany, establishing

Defining "Race"

Nazi efforts to safeguard the "purity of blood" by codifying racial distinctions affected Jewish life in Germany at every turn. This was acutely illustrated by the case of a Jewish doctor sent to a concentration camp after giving a life-saving transfusion of his own blood to a non-Jew.

The precise terminology of the Nuremberg Laws defined "degrees of Jewishness" based on one's number of Jewish grandparents. Distinctions between "full Jew" and "half-breed Jews" (*Mischlinge*) became critical, designating not only legal status but also determining Jewish economic survival—and ultimately life or death. Panicked Germans besieged Church registries to secure documentation of their non-Jewish heritage.

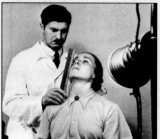

Intensified Nazi propaganda about the evils of race defilement thoroughly poisoned relations between Aryans and Jews. Aryan veterinarians even refused to treat the pets of their Jewish owners. Jews became social pariahs, as Germans avoided all contacts that could be construed as traitorous association with the enemies of Aryan blood. Jews were wantonly accused of sexual relations with Aryan women, and even simple casual public encounters with Aryans were risky.

German children, too, became caught up in the newly defined racial distinctions. Indoctrinated and desensitized by Nazi rhetoric, Aryan children were quick to brutalize their Jewish counterparts.

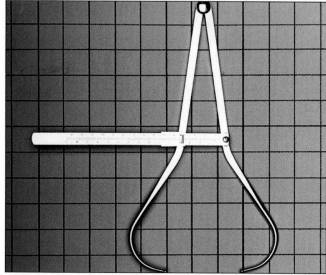

Nazi racial experts used instruments such as this caliper to determine racial background "scientifically." Physicians used this device to measure body parts. The Nazis believed that such measurements indicated who was of superior racial stock (in their minds, Aryans) and who came from an inferior strain (Jews, Gypsies, and Africans).

Another law promulgated in Nuremberg in September 1935 was the Reich Flag Law, which made it illegal for Jews to fly the Nazi flag, the official banner of Germany. The swastika had long been a symbol of racist political movements in Germany. The photograph shows German women sewing Nazi flags in Berlin.

1935

for the first time official definitions of "Jew" (anyone who has two Jewish grandparents and is a member of the Jewish religious community, and anyone with three or more Jewish grandparents) and *"Mischlinge"* (mixed race; that is, part Jew). Anywhere from 250,000 to 500,000 German citizens fall into the *Mischlinge* category. Marriages between Jews and second-generation *Mischlinge* are prohibited.

● November 15, 1935: The German Churches begin to collaborate with the Nazis by supplying records to the government indicating who is a Christian and who is not; that is, who is a Jew.

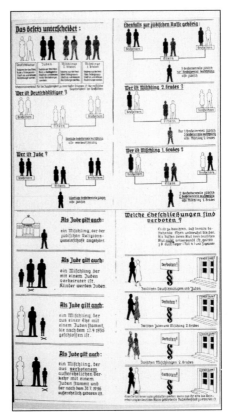

International reaction to the Nuremberg Laws was generally negative. Here, Baltimore, Maryland's *The Sun* attacks the laws as an unprovoked assault upon the rights of Germany's Jewish population. Nevertheless, few Americans were willing to go beyond *pro forma* protests.

The Nuremberg Laws forbade marriages between Aryans and Jews. But the question remained: Who was a Jew? This chart, produced by the German government, explains which unions were forbidden. These included marriages between those of "German blood" and full or "half Jews," as well as those between Jews and people of one-quarter Jewish heritage. Further, the state prohibited marriages between "quarter Jews" and any other marriages that might somehow "pollute" the German blood of one of the partners. Moreover, those Aryans who had married half or quarter Jews before 1935 were encouraged to seek divorce.

A Christmas greeting from Hitler to Heinrich Himmler. Eventually, the Nazis officially replaced the word "Christmas" with "Yuletide," lest anyone's birth be celebrated more fervently than Hitler's.

• **December 1935:** SS chief Heinrich Himmler orders the Race and Settlement Central Office (RuSHA) to establish the *Lebensborn* (Fountain of Life) network of maternity homes. The purpose of the homes is "to accommodate and look after racially and genetically valuable expectant mothers."

• **December 31, 1935:** The last Jews remaining in Germany's civil service are dismissed by the government.

• **1935–1938:** Poland models its policy regarding Jews on that of Nazi Germany. Jews are attacked throughout Poland. Tens of thousands of Polish Jews emigrate to Holland, France, Belgium, and Palestine. Anti-Jewish riots erupt in Polish universities, where Jewish students are restricted to special seats. • University quotas for Jews also exist at this time in United States universities. American discrimination restricts the Jewish presence in education, jobs, and housing just as it keeps Eastern European Jews out of the United States.

1936

ADOLF Hitler was quite the host at the 1936 Summer Olympics in Berlin. His people were gracious and hospitable, their parties festive and extravagant. And his Opening Ceremonies were the grandest ever held, climaxed by the release of 20,000 birds that soared to the sky wearing colored ribbons. Many foreign guests left the Games impressed and bedazzled. Hence, the manipulative Hitler had achieved his goal for the Olympics: to give the illusion that the Nazis weren't as villainous as they were often portrayed abroad.

The International Olympic Committee had awarded the 1936 Games to Germany back in 1932, a year before Hitler came to power. Berlin was to be the venue for the summer competition, while the Winter Olympics would be held in Garmisch-Partenkirchen in Bavaria. At the time of the IOC's announcement, no one knew (at least for sure) that *Nazi* Germany would host those Games. Indeed, the Olympics' internationalist ideal—uniting the world's people through a festival of sport—seemed so much at odds with the Nazis' racist and antisemitic nationalism that the very idea of a Nazi Olympiad seemed wildly contradictory.

The IOC subsequently considered moving the '36 Games to another venue, but the savvy Hitler made just enough concessions to keep the events in Germany. He knew that the upcoming Olympics would be a public relations boon for the Third Reich. As it would turn out, the success of the '36 Olympics would also help seal the fate of millions of European Jews.

Publicly, the Nazis downplayed their feelings of antisemitism throughout the Olympics, even though German Jews, including Jewish athletes, had been severely discriminated against. Jews were banned from sports clubs and athletic facilities where they had been members. Separate and inferior facilities were all that remained for Jewish athletes in Germany.

During the training period prior to the 1936 Summer Olympics, Gretl Bergmann, a world-class high jumper (and a Jew), matched the German women's record—five feet, three inches. On June 13 she received a letter from the German Olympic Committee. Criticizing her recent high-jumping performances for being too erratic, it informed her that she had not been chosen to be a member of her country's Olympic track and field team.

By the summer of 1936, German Jews had lost their citizenship rights. Their businesses had been boycotted, their professional lives restricted.

The Summer Olympic Games in Berlin begin with the traditional torch lighting.

97

1936

They were excluded from public facilities and prohibited from marrying non-Jews. Meanwhile, as the Nazis expanded their anti-Jewish policies, they also understood that German physical fitness and athletic prowess could build nationalism, foster racial purity, and spur military preparedness. Consequently, Jewish opportunity for places on the 1936 Olympic team was all but eliminated. Those positions had to be saved for those who could bring the most honor to the German people and the Nazi state.

Bowing ever so slightly to pressure, Reich officials placated the IOC by allowing one Jewish athlete to compete for Germany in the 1936 Summer Games: Helene Mayer. Mayer had competed for Germany in two previous Olympiads, and she announced she would be pleased to return to her homeland from California to do so again. Mayer was half Jewish, a *Mischlinge*. She was also tall and blonde, nearly fitting the prototypical Aryan image. As Mayer received the Olympic silver medal in the women's foil competition, film coverage from that day shows her giving the stiff-armed Nazi salute. Brief and ambivalent though it seems to have been, her salute signaled that perhaps Hitler's Germany wasn't such a bad place.

Earlier, on March 7, 1936, Hitler had made a speech to the *Reichstag*. As he announced the restoration of German sovereignty over the Rhineland, German military forces reentered that territory, which had been demilitarized after World War I. Although that action clearly violated the Versailles Treaty, and was condemned by the League of Nations, Hitler's decision was not revoked and German troops were not withdrawn. Nevertheless, as the Olympic appearance of Helene Mayer suggests, Hitler and his followers were shrewd about advancing their national interests without straining international opinion too much.

Before the Games began, movements in several countries, including the United States and the Soviet Union, urged a boycott of Olympic competition in Germany. Not wanting to risk that outcome, the Nazi regime made concessions to improve its image. Some of those concessions involved taking down the vicious anti-Jewish signs that proliferated along German highways, at the boundaries of towns and cities, and on many streets and stores. "Jews are not wanted in this place," some of them asserted. "The Jew is our misfortune," others proclaimed.

The Winter Games began at Garmisch-Partenkirchen on February 6. By the time Hitler officially opened the Games, the antisemitic signs in the immediate area were dismantled. They remained, however, along the highways that led to the competition site. Count Henri Baillet-Latour, the Belgian president of the IOC, saw these antisemitic displays as he traveled to the opening of the Winter Games. He immediately demanded to see Hitler and told him that such practices were unacceptable. Hitler argued that Olympic protocol could not override concerns of paramount importance within Germany, but when Baillet-Latour threatened cancellation of the 1936 Olympics, Hitler ordered the road signs removed.

Such concessions were matters of expediency. They represented no change of heart or policy regarding the "Jewish question" in Nazi Germany. On June 17, for instance, Hitler issued a decree that made Heinrich Himmler chief of all German police forces. Combining that power with the author-

German-Jewish high jumper Gretl Bergmann was later removed from the team.

ity he already enjoyed as the leader of the SS, Himmler expanded the vast terror apparatus that was now under his control. As preparations for the Summer Olympics continued, Nazi Germany was becoming an ever-more centralized police state.

Appearing to be clean, hospitable, and prosperous, Berlin greeted the opening of the Summer Games on August 1. Antisemitic signs and publications were not in view. The German press was instructed to report "non-Aryan" victories without racial commentary. Forty-nine countries sent teams to the Nazi Olympics, which concluded on August 16. They included the United States, where the boycott effort, which tried to deny Nazi Germany the legitimacy that the Olympics conferred, narrowly failed.

Hitler presided over the opening in Berlin's immense Olympic stadium. The ceremony culminated in a newly created "torch run," which brought fire from the site of the ancient Greek Olympic Games to Berlin. Leni Riefenstahl and her film crews were there to capture the pageantry and athletic competition. Her film, *Olympia*, would win first prize at the 1938 Venice film festival.

Some of *Olympia*'s best footage focused on an African-American athlete named Jesse Owens. Owens had experienced racism in the United States, but at the 1936 Olympics his four gold-medal performances were hailed by critics of the Nazi regime, who argued that Owens's victories refuted Hitler's claim of white superiority.

Embarrassing though Owens's victories were for the Nazis, Hitler and his followers were more than satisfied by their Olympic success. The German team won more medals than any other. Hitler played well the parts of world statesman and beloved national leader. German hospitality persuaded most foreign visitors that the Third Reich's intentions were as peaceful as its economic revival was efficient, its goals as benign as its culture was healthy and vigorous.

At least ten Jewish athletes won medals at the 1936 Olympics, among them Samuel Balter, who played on the American basketball team. For her part, Gretl Bergmann emigrated to the United States, continued her championship career in track and field, and kept her vow never to return to Germany. Other Jewish athletes were not so fortunate. Their fate indicates that the deception created by the Nazi Olympics was colossal and deadly.

Nazi power took the life of Victor Perez, a French Jew who was the world's flyweight boxing champion in the early 1930s. He was murdered at Auschwitz. Lilli Henoch, a world record holder in the shot put and discus, was deported from Germany in 1942. She was murdered and buried in a mass grave near Riga, Latvia. Attila Petschauer, a Hungarian fencer who won a silver medal at the 1928 Olympics, froze to death in a Nazi labor camp in 1943. A German Jew named Alfred Flatow, winner of three gold medals and one silver in gymnastics during the 1896 Games in Athens, died in the Theresienstadt (Czechoslovakia) camp/ghetto in 1942.

Top: Adolf Hitler makes his way to the opening ceremonies of the 11th Olympiad. *Bottom:* African-American Jesse Owens embarrassed Hitler by winning four gold medals.

Germany's relaxing of anti-Jewish pressure ended soon after the 1936 Games. By the year's end, the antisemitic campaign to drive Jews out of Germany was again in full force.

David Frankfurter *(foreground),* a Jewish student in Switzerland, was sentenced to 18 years in prison for his role in the murder of Nazi Party Foreign Section official Wilhelm Gustloff. In addition to his prison sentence, Frankfurter was deprived of his civil rights and expelled from Switzerland, but not before he paid court costs and restitution.

The title of this children's book is *Trau keinem Fuchs auf gruener Heid und Keinem Jud bei Seinem Eid (You Can't Trust a Fox in a Heath and a Jew on His Oath).* The book disseminated antisemitic propaganda to Germany's unsuspecting youth. This illustration leaves nothing to the imagination.

August Cardinal Hlond, the head of the Polish Catholic Church, called for discrimination against Polish Jews unless they converted to Catholicism. Thought to be less antisemitic than many Polish clergymen, Hlond's pastoral letter blasting the Jews for their "harmful morality" revealed the growing influence of Nazi ideology in Poland. Church-sanctioned anti-Jewish policy undermined the tenuous position of Polish Jewry and exacerbated tensions between Jews and Gentiles.

1936

• 1936: A leading Jewish-German jurist, Gerhard Leibholz, is stripped of his position at the University of Göttingen. • The first *Lebensborn* home for expectant Aryan mothers opens near Munich. • The *Institut der NSDAP zum Studium der Judenfrage* (Institute of the NSDAP to Study the Jewish Question) is founded by Joseph Goebbels. • The first issue of *Forschungen zur Judenfrage (Research into the Jewish Question),* a magazine devoted to the quasi-scholarly exposition of Nazi racial ideology, is published.

• The Nazis establish public television viewing rooms for the dissemination of government propaganda. • Romania's Iron Guard explodes a bomb in a

Judges and clerks of the National Socialist regime conclude an evening's celebration with the singing of *"Deutschland Über Alles"* as well as the Horst Wessel song. The vast majority of German jurists quickly accommodated themselves to the dictates of Nazism. The legal system was entirely subverted, as legislation predicated on race replaced the fundamental structures of civil society. Emphasis on the national community resonated throughout the Nazi law code. Individuals who were defined as outsiders, such as Jews and Gypsies, lost all access to legal recourse.

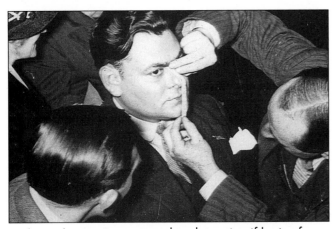

A man's nose is measured to determine if he is of Jewish ancestry. The Nazis utilized a wide range of tactics and implements to determine the ancestry of potential victims. Race-based "science" was nothing new, however. It had been developed by scholars and medical professionals in the 19th century.

The SD

Crucial to the Nazi apparatus of terror was the work of the regime's highly efficient surveillance system. The Nazi Security Service (*Sicherheitsdienst*, or SD) maintained a network of thousands of informers and confidence men that pried into the private lives of all Germans. During the war, the SD expanded its role to encompass all of Occupied Europe. And after eliminating the regime's "domestic enemies," the SD began its assault on "racial enemies."

Founded by Heinrich Himmler (*pictured, left*) in 1931 as a special section of the SS, the SD ferreted out disloyalty and treachery within the Nazi Party and guarded against infiltration by spies. After the seizure of power, the SD played a crucial role in monitoring the moods and attitudes of the German public.

Chief of the SD was Reinhard Heydrich (*pictured, right*), a tall, blue-eyed "blond beast" who embodied Himmler's Aryan ideal, and who became the Nazis' master spy. Heydrich recruited intelligent, young university graduates for the SD, using their skills to perfect his surveillance network. Their more murderous assignments during the war included the "Night and Fog" decrees, whereby victims vanished without a trace. As members of the *Einsatzgruppen* killing squads, they liquidated partisans and Jews in Occupied Eastern Europe.

Jewish theater in Timisoara, Romania, killing two Jews. • The America-based German-American Bund funnels currency to the Reich.

• Following the same anti-Jewish path as German Lutherans during the Nazi regime, America's foremost Protestant journal, *Christian Century*, argues that America is a Christian nation with a Christian culture and has to remain that way. Christians are indifferent to Jewish suffering because the Jews deserve God's punishment due to their denial of Jesus. Judaism is a racial, religious, and nationalist prototype of Nazism. These attitudes are reflected in much of the American Protestant press during the Holocaust.

• February 4, 1936: David Frankfurter, a Jewish student in Switzerland, assassinates Wilhelm Gustloff, the head of the NSDAP in Switzerland.

• February 29, 1936: August Cardinal Hlond, the head of the Polish Catholic Church, considered less antisemitic than many Polish clergy and a

The Hitler Youth

Adolf Hitler preached in *Mein Kampf* that the education and training of each young German "must be so ordered as to give him the conviction that he is absolutely superior to others." The Nazis energetically recruited the younger generation of Germans, who were both impressionable and enthusiastic.

The *Hitlerjugend* (HJ; Hitler Youth) was established in 1926, and by 1934, under the leadership of Baldur von Schirach, it reached a membership of 3.5 million. By 1939 membership in the Hitler Youth—and its companion organization, the *Bund Deutscher Mädel* (BDM; League of German Girls)—became compulsory, and its numbers rose to almost nine million Germans between the ages of 10 and 18. Youths were attracted to the camaraderie, the semimilitary hiking and camping, and the HJ sports competitions.

Some young Germans resisted assimilation. Working-class youths formed anti-Nazi gangs, called the "Edelweiss Pirates." They hiked and camped, too, but they often attacked Hitler Youth patrols. Others, from upper-middle-class backgrounds, such as the so-called "Swing Youth," engaged in counterculture activities, such as dancing to American jazz, which was considered "Negro music" by the regime.

Baldur von Schirach rose to prominence as the leader of the Hitler Youth. His organizational skills and fanatic devotion to the *Führer* propelled him into Hitler's inner circle. Schirach became Reich Youth Leader in 1928, National Youth Leader in 1931, and Youth Leader of the German Reich in 1933. He led the Hitler Youth, the National Socialists Schoolboys League, the League of German Girls, and the *Jungvolk* until he was dismissed in 1940.

German troops march through a Spanish city in support of Francisco Franco's military campaigns against Republican forces. German involvement in the Spanish Civil War served as a training ground for Hitler's troops and a test arena for new military equipment and tactics. The *Luftwaffe,* the new German air force, experimented with terror bombing of civilian populations.

1936

careful follower of Vatican policy, issues a pastoral letter advocating discrimination against Polish Jews "so long as they remain Jews." He writes that Polish Catholics "ought to fence themselves off against the Jews' harmful moral influence of Jewry" and "ought to separate themselves from its anti-Christian culture." He states that Polish Catholics "ought to boy-cott the Jewish press" and other "demoralizing Jewish publications," although "Catholics should not assault Jews."

• March 1936: Anti-Jewish pogroms occur in Poland. Polish Cardinal Hlond speaks out against Jewish "usury, fraud, and white slavery."

"The Devil is the father of the Jew.
When God created the world,
He invented the races:
The Indians, the Negroes, the Chinese,
And also the wicked creature called the Jew."

—*Verse in a German children's book; 1936*

A German girl pins a native flower on a trooper. The remilitarization of the Rhineland was a public relations bonanza for the Nazi regime. Local inhabitants—few of whom were Nazi Party members—applauded their "liberation," while the myth of Hitler's invincibility received additional reinforcement.

German troops cross the Rhine River on March 7, 1936, en route to reoccupying the Rhineland. The demilitarization of this border region had been mandated by the Versailles Treaty and was integral to the post-World War I security system designed to prevent future German incursions into France. Although the move was publicly deplored by Western diplomats, nothing was done to prevent it. The remilitarization of the Rhineland enhanced Hitler's stature within Germany and demonstrated the defensive nature of French military strategy.

Carl von Ossietzky, a leading German pacifist and editor of the left-wing political weekly *Die Weltbuehne* (*The World Stage*), stands before an SS guard at the Esterwegen, Germany, concentration camp. Arrested after the *Reichstag* fire in 1933 and sentenced to a labor camp, Ossietzky contracted tuberculosis while in Esterwegen. When his disease grew worse, he was transferred to a Berlin hospital in May 1936; he died there two years later. Ossietzky became an international cause célèbre when the Nazi regime refused to let him accept the 1935 Nobel Peace Prize.

• **March 3, 1936:** Henceforth, Jewish doctors are denied the right to practice medicine at German government hospitals.

• **March 7, 1936:** In defiance of the Versailles Treaty and other international agreements, German troops occupy the Rhineland. Although publicly denouncing Hitler's action,

France, Great Britain, and the United States accept it—another important step in appeasing Hitler and in encouraging him to make further demands in Europe.

• **March 9, 1936:** Jews are killed and injured during an antisemitic pogrom at Przytyk, Poland.

• **March 17, 1936:** A mass demonstration of Polish Jews, left-wingers, and liberals protests antisemitism in Poland.

• **March 29, 1936:** SS guard formations are renamed SS-*Totenkopfverbände* (SS-Death's Head Units). They provide guards for concentration camps. • A *Reichstag* "election" is

A formal meeting of the Berlin Jewish community is held at the *Prinzregentenstrasse* synagogue on May 4, 1936, to protest the recent onset of Arab terrorism in Palestine. In spite of their own tenuous legal and economic situation, German Jews remained attuned to events in the Middle East. As governmental efforts to encourage emigration intensified, the Jews of Germany remained painfully aware of the need to keep Palestine and other possible points of destination open to them. Arab-Jewish violence brought pressure on the British government to curtail Jewish immigration into Palestine.

Riots in the Arab city of Jaffa, Palestine, including this melee in June 1936, inaugurated a period of intense social conflict between Arabs and Jews. Caught between the World Zionist Organization's demand for increased Jewish immigration to Palestine and Arab hostility to it, British authorities came under fire from both sides. The Arab-Jewish conflict lasted for three years and resulted in the virtual prohibition of Jewish immigration into the region.

Jewish-owned businesses and homes are set ablaze during an anti-Jewish riot in Mińsk Mazowiecki, Poland, in June 1936. A sharp increase in antisemitic activity punctuated Polish-Jewish life in 1936. Pogroms, rallies, and an antisemitic legislative agenda exacerbated Polish-Jewish relations. Increased German economic and military strength convinced many Poles that the time had come to settle their differences with their troublesome Jewish minority. Jews comprised about ten percent of Poland's population.

1936

held. Hitler's policies are approved by 98 percent of the voters.

• April 1936: French conservatives condemn French Socialist leader Léon Blum because of his Jewish ancestry and his strongly anti-Nazi orientation. A popular slogan at the time condemns the future French premier: "Better Hitler than Blum."

• April 15, 1936: Two Jews are murdered during an Arab general strike in Palestine in protest against Jewish immigration.

• April 19, 1936: Arabs kill nine Jews in Jaffa, Palestine.

• April 21, 1936: Arabs in the Palestine cities of Tel Aviv and Jaffa riot

In 1936 Heinrich Himmler was appointed head of Germany's police forces, a position that allowed him the tools necessary to carry out his race-based agenda. It also simultaneously placed fellow Nazi Hermann Göring in a subordinate position. Himmler was amassing tremendous powers. He was the lord of the Nazi concentration camp system and would become the second most powerful man in Germany during World War II.

A group of Jewish girls in Berlin participates in a vocational training course in anticipation of emigrating. By 1936 German Jews were deprived of an economic livelihood and encouraged to leave Germany. Though never official Nazi policy, the increased social isolation of Jews in the Reich, along with intensive economic discrimination, made it painfully clear that hopes for the future had to be realized in other countries.

Creating a Police State

The Nazis realized that control of the police was vital to the regime's maintenance of power. By fusing the SS with all police forces in Germany, Heinrich Himmler was able to construct a police state based on coercion and terror.

Responsible only to the *Führer*, Himmler circumvented legal systems and state bureaucracies. The Nazi police apparatus was free to define "legality," and was unhindered by moral constraints.

Already chief of the SS, Himmler launched his quest for police power in 1933, becoming police president of Munich and then commander of the Bavarian political police. The following year he was appointed chief of political police in all German states, and also gained control of the Prussian Gestapo. Formally named chief of all German police in 1936, he restructured it into two main departments: Order Police, including municipal police and rural constabularies; and Security Police, comprising the Gestapo and the Criminal Police. Later, the Security Police and SD were amalgamated, thereby consolidating an astonishing amount of power.

The Central Office for Reich Security, created in 1939, included numerous subdivisions of "preventive surveillance." As a result, a vast and diverse array of individuals and groups were under constant watch. Targets included Jews, Marxists, churches, and homosexuals, among others.

---

to protest Jewish immigration to Palestine.

● **June 17, 1936: Heinrich Himmler is appointed the chief of German police.**

● **June 19, 1936: German heavyweight boxer Max Schmeling, a former world champion, defeats promising African-** American heavyweight Joe Louis. Hitler turns the fight into a propaganda victory for Aryan superiority; *See* June 22, 1938.

● **June 26, 1936: Reinhard Heydrich is appointed by Heinrich Himmler to head the SD (Security Service branch of the SS).**

● **June 30, 1936: Polish Jews strike to protest antisemitism.**

● **July 3, 1936: German Jew Stefan Lux kills himself in the assembly room of the League of Nations in Geneva, Switzerland. The suicide is in protest of Germany's persecution of Jews.**

German heavyweight boxer Max Schmeling took on the up-and-coming Joe Louis at New York's Yankee Stadium on June 19, 1936. (Scheduled for the 18th, the match was delayed one day because of rain.) Billed in Germany as a fight between the Aryan "master race" and an inferior African, Schmeling's victory provided ripe fodder for the Nazi propaganda machine. Two years later, when Louis knocked out Schmeling in the first round of their rematch, the Nazi press quietly downplayed the event.

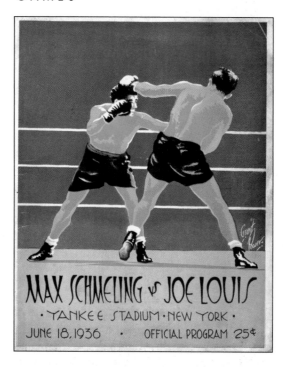

MAX SCHMELING vs JOE LOUIS
• YANKEE STADIUM • NEW YORK •
JUNE 18, 1936 • OFFICIAL PROGRAM 25¢

Reinhard Heydrich's "prototypical Nordic" features and cunning administrative talents made him the Nazis' favorite advertisement for the "master race." As Himmler's right-hand man, Heydrich in 1936 became chief of the Berlin Gestapo and head of the *Sicherheitsdienst* (SD), the security apparatus for the entire German Reich. Heydrich was instrumental in building the SS terror system and designing the "Final Solution" to the "Jewish question."

Father Charles E. Coughlin was the founder of the Union for Social Justice, an isolationist, antisemitic organization that he promoted on his national radio program. Here he addresses an audience in Cleveland, Ohio, on July 17, 1936. Heating up an already sweltering auditorium, Coughlin attacks President Franklin Roosevelt's social agenda and its Jewish supporters.

1936

● July 17, 1936: The Spanish Civil War begins.

● August 1936: Poland's Ministry of Commerce orders all small businesses to display the owners' names as the names appear on the birth certificates. The directive is intended to expose Jewish-owned businesses.

● August 1–16, 1936: The Summer Olympic Games are held in Berlin, allowing the world its first (stage-managed) look at the Third Reich. The Germans disguise any outward signs of antisemitism. Avery Brundage, head of the United States National Olympic Committee, successfully fights against an American boycott of the Berlin Olympics, insist-

Signs bearing the words "Jews are unwanted here" humiliated Jewish people throughout Nazi Germany. Parks, stores, restaurants, and other locations were declared off-limits. In an effort to whitewash their treatment of Jews before the international audience at Berlin for the 1936 Olympics, the Nazis systematically removed the signs before the start of the Games. The signs were reinstalled after the Games were over.

A Nazi propaganda filmstrip showing different racial types portrays the Jew as a racial "bastard." According to Nazi race ideology, Jews were the antithesis of Germans and the scourge of the earth. The constant barrage of antisemitic depictions of Jews effectively dehumanized them.

Sachsenhausen

The Sachsenhausen concentration camp was established in Oranienburg, a town about 15 miles northeast of Berlin, in September 1936. Among the first of the major concentration camps built to house the Third Reich's thousands of political prisoners, it was conveniently located close to the German capital.

While Sachsenhausen remained primarily a camp for political opponents of the regime, Jews began to arrive there in significant numbers in 1938. From 1942, most of the Jews who entered the camp stayed only temporarily, eventually being sent eastward to the death camps in Poland.

Many of those who remained in the camp were victims of the cruel medical experiments carried on there. Among these was research into the causes, effects, and cures for jaundice. The subjects of these experiments were eventually killed (sometimes in the camp's small gas chamber), autopsied, and cremated in the camp's ovens.

In total, about 100,000 people died in Sachsenhausen during the years of the camp's operation (1936 to 1945), making it one of the most lethal of the concentration camps located on German soil.

ing that the Olympic boycott lobby is led by Jewish "special interests." Once in Germany, Brundage is entertained by top Nazi official Hermann Göring.

● September 7, 1936: A 25-percent tax is imposed on all Jewish assets in Germany.

● September 23, 1936: A concentration camp opens at Sachsenhausen, Germany.

● October 1, 1936: Criminal-court judges in Berlin swear a mandatory oath of allegiance to Hitler.

● October 25, 1936: Hitler and Italian dictator Benito Mussolini sign a

treaty forming the Berlin-Rome Axis in preparation for war.

● November 18, 1936: Germany's volunteer Condor Legion leaves for combat in Spain, on the side of Francisco Franco's Fascists.

● November 25, 1936: Germany and Japan sign the Anti-Comintern Pact in

This German, antisemitic cartoon is entitled "The Progress of 'Modern Art'—Dance with a Prostitute." Pictured is a Jewish "degenerate" artist whose palette bears the words *Schulchan Aruch* (a medieval compendium of Jewish law). Also pictured are a Jewish journalist and a filmmaker, symbolizing the alleged Jewish control of the media. The wealthy, well-fed Jewish man in the foreground parties with a prostitute while dancing on the cross. Other details suggest capitalism (the woman's top hat), Freemasonry (the symbol on the dancer's cummerbund), and African-American jazz (the saxophone).

The right-wing, anti-Jewish weekly Polish publication *Samoobrona Naradu* (*National Self-Defense*) lobbied extensively to remove all Jews from Poland. Urging its countrymen to pay heed to their Jewish "problem," the paper led the campaign to "clear Poland of its Jews." This edition carried the following text: "POLAND FOR THE POLES! A feeling of national pride, solidarity, and unity must be aroused. Each of you must lend support to the Polish worker, shopkeeper, et al. JOBS AND BREAD IN POLAND FOR THE POLES!" The cartoon at the top of the announcement portrays a Pole carting Jews off to Palestine.

Persecution of Homosexuals

Homosexuals were prime targets of persecution by the Nazis, who considered them defilers of German blood. Declaring homosexuality a crime of degeneracy contrary to "wholesome popular sentiment," the regime moved to eradicate it.

From 1933 to 1944, the Nazis convicted and sent to concentration camps tens of thousands of men on charges of homosexuality. There they were humiliated, tortured, subjected to medical experimentation, and killed. An estimated 5000 to 15,000 homosexuals perished behind barbed-wire fences during the Holocaust.

The campaign against homosexuals was especially fierce from 1936 to 1939. In order to identify homosexuals, the Gestapo compiled lists of known individuals, encouraged all citizens to report deviant behavior, pressured victims to denounce others, tracked down names in address books, raided gay bars and clubs, and confiscated subscription lists of gay magazines.

Thrown into concentration camps for "rehabilitation," homosexuals were forced to wear identifying triangular patches of pink cloth. There they were subjected to degradation and sadistic beatings by guards. Many were castrated or became human guinea pigs for hormone experiments conducted by SS doctors. Political enemies of the regime, such as Catholic priests, were also conveniently eliminated through charges of homosexuality.

1936

order to block Soviet activities abroad.

• November 27, 1936: Nazi Minister of Propaganda Joseph Goebbels declares that film criticism is henceforth banned, freeing the Nazi-controlled German film industry to pursue its own agenda, which includes blatantly antisemitic films. • During the same period in the United States, Hollywood is self-censored in that it fears dealing with Jewish issues because of the high level of antisemitism existing at the time in the United States.

• November 29, 1936: Germany's Minister of Agriculture, Walther Darré, declares that democracy

German Chancellor Adolf Hitler and Italy's Benito Mussolini stroll together during Hitler's official visit to Italy in 1934. The spring rendezvous in Venice between the leaders of Europe's two most powerful Fascist regimes laid the groundwork for a formal military alliance in October 1936. While the two countries shared common concerns, they had a different understanding of racial issues. Before becoming formally aligned with Germany, Mussolini's Fascist Italy did not enact antisemitic legislation. The "Jewish question" was not a burning issue for Italians.

The back page of the September 1936 issue of *Jüdische Auswanderung (Jewish Emigration)* included an advertisement for the Atlantic Express travel agency. The monthly publication was put out by the *Hilfsverein der Juden in Deutschland*, the assistance organization for German Jewry, to provide information about emigration and resettlement. From 1933 through 1938, thousands of Jews sought to flee the increasing persecution of the Nazis.

Two SS guards and their highly trained German shepherds patrol the snow-laden perimeter of the concentration camp at Sachsenhausen, Germany. Electrified fences, specially trained police dogs, and armed guards made escape nearly impossible. Attempts to break out of the camp were further discouraged by the fact that if one was caught, execution was certain.

and liberalism were invented by the Jews.

• December 27, 1936: Great Britain and France agree on a non-intervention appeasement policy in regard to the Spanish Civil War.

• 1936–39: The Spanish Civil War rages on for three years, during which Hitler sends German forces to fight for General Francisco Franco's Nationalists against the Republicans. The Germans use this opportunity to test both weapons and tactics. Even more help is provided by Italian dictator Benito Mussolini, who sends tens of thousands of Italian troops to fight the forces remaining loyal to Spain's leftist, democratic, and legally elected government. • The antisemitic "colonels' clique" in Poland, *Obóz Zjednoczenia Narodowego* (Camp of National Unity), becomes active. It is headed by Pulkownik Adam Koc and controlled by Polish President Ignacy Moscicki and Minister of Defense Marzalek Edward Rydz-Smigly.

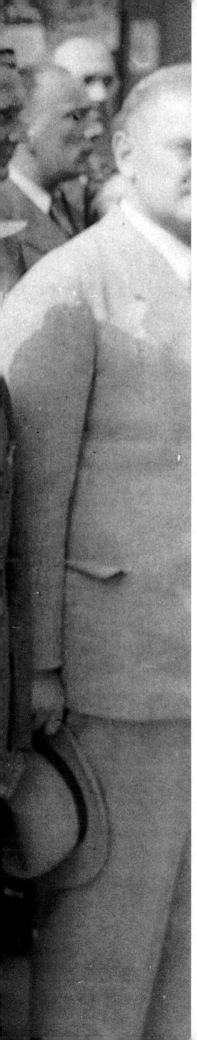

1937

ON January 1, 1937, a 25-year-old German doctor began his research assistantship at the University of Frankfurt's prestigious Institute of Hereditary Biology and Racial Hygiene. Soon he joined the Nazi Party and the SS. Six years later, on May 30, 1943, his career in the service of Nazi Germany's "racial purity" would reach its climax by taking him to Auschwitz and placing him at the center of the "Final Solution." Specifically, during his 20 months at Auschwitz, this Nazi doctor would conduct notorious medical experiments and preside at "selections" that would determine who would be gassed. His name was Josef Mengele.

Mengele identified himself as a Catholic. It is worth noting, therefore, that as Mengele began his research at the University of Frankfurt, Achille Ratti, 79—who had earned a triple doctorate in philosophy, theology, and law—was working in Rome. Ratti would die before World War II began, but in the relative quiet before that genocidal storm, he faced important decisions about his relationship to Nazi Germany. Ratti was better known as Pope Pius XI, leader of the Roman Catholic Church.

Pius XI and Josef Mengele never met. Nevertheless, the Pontiff knew about Mengele's Nazi masters and their devotion to "racial hygiene." From the beginning of Adolf Hitler's power, Pius XI had recognized two other realities as well. First, he understood that Nazism jeopardized the Catholic Church's authority. Second, he knew that Germany's Jews were besieged with difficulties. Pius XI's feelings about those matters coincided with the description that Winston Churchill offered on April 14, 1937: "We seem to be moving," Churchill said, "toward some hideous catastrophe."

Hitler realized that official Vatican recognition of his authority could be politically valuable at home and abroad. He sensed correctly that the Papacy would consider it wise to safeguard the status of the Roman Catholic Church in Germany. In the spring of 1933 Nazi inquiries were favorably received by the Vatican's secretary of state, Eugenio Cardinal Pacelli, a former papal diplomat to Berlin. During an elaborate ceremony on July 20, 1933, a concordat between the Holy See and the German Reich was officially signed and sealed by Vice Chancellor Franz von Papen and Cardinal Pacelli. It affirmed legal status and protection for the Catholic Church and its organizations in Germany if—but only if—they were dedicated to purely religious activities.

A clergyman is among the prisoners in the Buchenwald concentration camp.

1937

The concordat gave no comfort to Germany's Jews, for the treaty conferred important international legitimacy on the Third Reich. Indeed, Hitler regarded the concordat as a useful tool to be wielded in the Reich's battle against the Jews. Meanwhile, the Nazis' anti-Catholic pressure did not relent, and by 1937 a mounting list of arrested nuns and priests, closed convents and monasteries, and harassed parochial schools led Pope Pius XI to write *"Mit brennender Sorge"* ("With Burning Concern"). Issued on March 14, this encyclical protested the Catholic Church's difficulties in Germany, accused the Nazi government of violating its word, and warned against the deification of race, nation, and state. Smuggled into Germany, printed secretly, and distributed to the clergy, it was read from Catholic pulpits throughout the Reich on March 21, Palm Sunday.

"Mit brennender Sorge" spoke of "God-given rights" and invoked a "human nature" that went beyond national boundaries. It even stated that rejection of the Old Testament, which some leaders—religious as well as secular—advocated in Nazi Germany, was blasphemous. Yet, failing to mention the racist Nuremberg Laws that had stripped civil rights from Germany's Jews in 1935, it offered no condemnation of the persecution of German Jews. Instead of protesting antisemitism, in fact, *"Mit brennender Sorge"* referred to the Chosen people as those who were "constantly straying" from God and who had crucified Christ.

Pius XI's pronouncements sent mixed signals about the "Jewish question," but he became an increasingly strong critic of the Nazi state. In June 1938 he summoned Father John LaFarge, an American Jesuit priest, to confer with him. Impressed by LaFarge's antiracist work in the United States, Pius XI went outside the usual Vatican personnel and assigned LaFarge to draft *"Humani Generis Unitas"* ("The Unity of Humankind"), an encyclical that would denounce racism and the persecution of Jews by advocates of racial purity. As the fate of German and Austrian Jews worsened under the Nazi grip, LaFarge and a few trusted colleagues worked in Paris, writing and revising a text that grew to almost 100 pages.

A heart attack took the life of Pius XI during the night of February 9, 1939. LaFarge's draft of *"Humani Generis Unitas"* was reportedly on the Pope's desk at that time. Delayed for several months by the Vatican's bureaucracy, it had reached the Pope too late to be of consequence. Cardinal Pacelli, who feared Communists more than Nazis, succeeded to the papacy on March 3, taking the name Pius XII. His leadership record during the Holocaust years would be problematic at best. Six months later World War II began. *"Humani Generis Unitas"* was shelved in Church archives. Nothing much was heard of it until long after the Holocaust took place.

Had the encyclical appeared in the 1930s, it alone would not have been sufficient to prevent the Final Solution. One reason is that even as LaFarge's text attacked racism and racially motivated persecution of Jews, it by no means freed itself entirely from traditional anti-Jewish teachings that had been part of Christian tradition for centuries. Nevertheless, the disappearance of *"Humani Generis Unitas"* stands out as a significant example of lost opportunities that might have helped Jews by bringing international pressure to bear on the Nazi state.

Pope Pius XI's encyclical "With Burning Concern" protested Nazi attacks on the Church.

In 1937 some alternative actions were tried. On March 15 an anti-Nazi protest rally, sponsored by the American Jewish Congress (AJC) and the Jewish Labor Committee, took place in New York's Madison Square Garden. Inside Germany, David Glick, an American lawyer who had connections with the American Jewish Joint Distribution Committee, successfully negotiated the release and emigration of 120 of the 300 Jews who were then prisoners in the Dachau concentration camp. In late December 1937 the official leadership of German Jewry publicly urged its people to carry on with resoluteness and self-confidence.

Noble though they were, such efforts were not strong enough to check the power they faced. They lacked support from a larger collective will—inside Germany and internationally as well—that would have been necessary to check the persecution of Jews, which had already begun to spread beyond Germany's borders. For example, 350 attacks on Jews were recorded in Poland during August alone. Earlier in the year, on June 11, 1937, one of the few remaining legal protections given to German Jews was further stripped away when Jews were prohibited from giving testimony in German courts. Five months later the German Interior Ministry required Jews to carry special identity cards for travel inside the country.

The Nazis also stepped up arrests to enforce the laws forbidding sexual relations between Germans and Jews. Those arrests often resulted in concentration camp sentences. That summer the Nazi camp system expanded, most significantly with the opening of Buchenwald, which became operational on July 16.

Top: Policemen march for the *Führer* at the annual Nuremberg Party rally. *Bottom:* Graffiti on a Frankfurt, Germany, window suggests that Jews should move to Palestine.

Three days later a Nazi exhibition of "degenerate art" opened in Munich. Ordered by Hitler himself, this exhibition denigrated innovative art, including many works by Jewish artists. The Nazis eventually destroyed some of this art, but much of it was auctioned off for foreign currency that the Third Reich needed to advance its ambitions. A few months later, on November 8, Munich witnessed the opening of another destructive exhibition, The Eternal Jew, an antisemitic art and poster show sponsored by the Nazis.

Nazi ambitions in 1937 included solidified relationships with Italy, which opened the way for German annexation of Austria the following year. Germany cultivated an alliance with imperial Japan and continued the rapid growth of its own military forces, which would be needed for the even larger territorial expansion to which Hitler's talk increasingly referred. Nazi ambition also embraced young Dr. Mengele's research. All too soon, it would take him from the Institute of Hereditary Biology and Racial Hygiene to the racially inspired experiments and "selections" that would destroy millions of Jews and other defenseless people who were branded less than fully human. In the twilight world of Auschwitz, there would be little concern for the "God-given rights" cherished by Pope Pius XI.

If 1937 was one of the Holocaust's quieter years, it was certainly ominous enough. The storm's full force was not far off. No papal encyclical, protest rally, or emigration project would be enough to keep it at bay. Churchill was right. The "hideous catastrophe" that he anticipated in 1937 was fast approaching.

The Jewish War Veterans called for a boycott of German-made goods in response to Nazi persecution of Jews. The boycott proved ineffective, and in fact had an adverse effect: It supplied the Nazis with an excuse for oppressing Jews even more severely. No amount of economic pressure would stop the process by which Germany's Jews were driven out of German public life.

During the years 1933 to 1938, the German government made a concerted effort to force Jews out of public institutions. By 1937, for example, more than 60 percent of Jewish children had been driven out of German schools. In response, Jewish associations established their own schools with activities paralleling those of the "Aryan" majority. Pictured is a certificate awarded to Trude Kirchhausen for winning the long jump in her school's sports festival.

These young German women are pictured in a nurse training camp. Camp life allowed the regime to mold the bodies and minds of Germany's young people. Healthy bodies were important not only for the defense of the Fatherland, but also for the propagation of the Aryan "race." The creation of sound minds meant creating the proper respect for National Socialist ideals, especially the notion of racial purity.

1937

• 1937: At the Nationalist Socialist Party rally at Nuremberg, Adolf Hitler announces the Third Reich will last a thousand years. • *Adolf Hitler Schulen* (AHS; Adolf Hitler Schools) are established to educate and train future Nazi leaders. • The Baum Group, a Jewish resistance organization, is established in Berlin by Herbert and Marianne Baum. • The

Central Conference of American Rabbis officially abrogates the Pittsburgh Platform of 1885, which declared that Jews should no longer look forward to a return to Israel. This new policy actively encourages Jews to support the establishment of a Jewish homeland. • *Stronnictwo Pracy* (Labor Front), a right-wing labor and antisemitic party, is established in Poland.

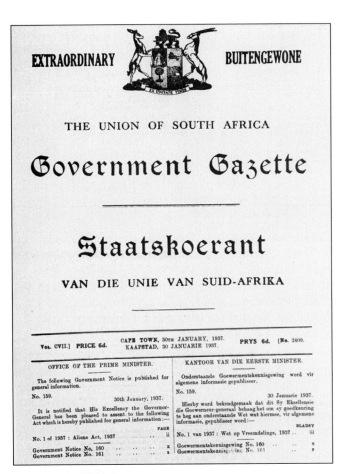

Germany's persecuted Jewish minority had few places to go. Legislation such as South Africa's Aliens Act *(pictured)* severely restricted the number of Jews that country would accept. The unwillingness of other nations to accept Germany's Jews fueled the Third Reich's antisemitic propaganda and led Hitler to question the sincerity of international protest against his anti-Jewish policies.

Lebensraum

Adolf Hitler's ideology made war with the Soviet Union inevitable. Early in his political career, he announced National Socialism's "mission" to "secure for the German people the land and soil to which they are entitled on this earth." Numerous references in his book *Mein Kampf* point to the "necessity" for German territorial expansion—for *Lebensraum* (Living space) for the German people. Hitler was convinced that more land was needed as a "source of a people's food," and that Germany had to become a great military and political power if it were to win and safeguard this territory.

This was not a new idea. German expansionists had coined the *Lebensraum* slogan before World War I, justifying their colonial empire and European annexation plans. Hitler also was influenced by the teachings of Karl Haushofer, a professor at the University of Munich, whose geopolitical theory centered on "space as a factor of power."

Hitler believed Germany's required living space could be taken from Eastern Europe and Russia. He not only considered Slavic people inferior, but he felt the Soviet Union was ripe for conquest because of the weakness of its "Jewish Bolshevik" leadership. On November 5, 1937, Hitler outlined his expansionist plans in a secret conference with his top military staff.

Herbert Baum led a clandestine Jewish Communist cell in Germany from 1936 until his death in '43. In 1937 he and his wife, Marianne, established a Jewish resistance organization called the Baum Group. The group met weekly in the young couple's Berlin home to discuss politics and plot strategy. Members also informed and educated Jews about important matters.

• In Hungary, Ferenc Szálasi establishes the *Nyilaskeresztes Part-Hungarista Mozgalom* (Arrow Cross Movement), dedicated to antisemitism. • Britain proposes an Arab and a Jewish state separated by a mandated area incorporating Jerusalem and Nazareth; Arabs demand a single state with minority rights for Jews. • SS functionary Adolf Eichmann,

posing as a journalist, visits Palestine to investigate the feasibility of mass deportations of German Jews to that area. • The first issue of *Die Judenfrage* (*The Jewish Question*), edited by Georg Haller, is published in Germany. • Poland investigates the possibility of deporting resident Jews to Madagascar.

• January 1, 1937: The *Volksdeutsche Mittelstelle* (VOMI; Ethnic German Assistance Office) is founded to act as an intermediary between Berlin and ethnic Germans (from nations other than Germany) who are to be resettled in Eastern Europe.

• March 1937: Jewish film star Paul Muni receives an Academy Award for

Buchenwald

In the summer of 1937, the Buchenwald concentration camp opened in the hilly woods just outside Weimar, a German city famous for its cultural heritage. The camp soon became a torture center.

Ilse Koch, the wife of camp commander Karl Koch, developed a morbid taste for tattooed skin stripped from the corpses of inmates. Another camp commander habitually unleashed vicious dogs against Gypsy prisoners who refused to undergo sterilization. The victims were torn to pieces. Homosexual prisoners underwent pseudoscientific experiments, in which they were injected with typhus bacillus. Tens of thousands perished at Buchenwald between 1937 and 1945—victims of disease from overcrowding and poor sanitation, hard labor, torture, medical experiments, and gassings.

The camp initially housed political prisoners, but was enlarged in 1938 to take in large numbers of Jews. In the wake of *Kristallnacht*, more than 10,000 Jews filled the barracks. During the war years, inmates were exploited as slave labor for the armament industry. By 1945 the evacuation of camps in Eastern Europe brought a tremendous influx of inmates into Buchenwald; at war's end in April 1945, more than 47,000 were imprisoned there.

The Buchenwald concentration camp was among the most infamous in Germany. Here, as elsewhere, the Third Reich's officials kept extensive records on each prisoner, and each prisoner had to go through registration *(pictured)*. Most of the Jews sent to Buchenwald were soon shipped out to other camps.

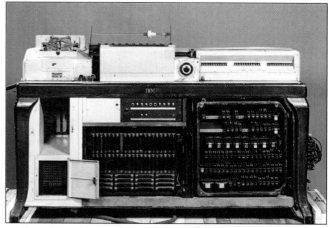

Devices such as this Dehomag D11 tabulating machine permitted the SS to keep track of the huge numbers of prisoners held in concentration camps. Manufactured by the German Hollerith Machine Company, a subsidiary of IBM, this data processing apparatus was state of the art in the 1930s.

1937

playing the title role in *The Life of Emile Zola*. Although the film deals with French antisemitism, the dialogue never mentions the word "Jew."

• **March 14, 1937:** Pope Pius XI issues an encyclical, *"Mit brennender Sorge"* ("With Burning Concern"), repudiating Nazi racism and totalitarianism. Pius XI respectfully chastises the Nazis for violating their concordat with the Church by attempting to control Catholic education. The wording of the encyclical implies that Pius is seeking a rapprochement with the Third Reich. The Pope does not denounce widespread German-Christian antisemitism. Indeed, Pius reminds his readers of the Jews' crime of deicide.

"Today almost six million Jews are doomed to be pent up in places where they are not wanted, and for whom the world is divided into places where they cannot live, and places into which they cannot enter."

—Chaim Weizmann, president of the World Zionist Organization; 1937

Prisoners called Ilse Koch, wife of concentration camp commander Karl Otto Koch, the "Bitch of Buchenwald." Notorious for her corruption and cruelty to the prisoners, as well as her promiscuity with the camp's guards, she also possessed a collection of tattooed human skin. Arrested in 1943 for her unscrupulous financial practices, she spent the last two years of the war in a Weimar, Germany, prison. After the war, she received four years' imprisonment for war crimes, later extended to a life sentence by the German government. Eventually going insane, she committed suicide in Aichach Prison in 1967.

"Kneeling Woman," a sculpture done in artificial stone by Wilhelm Lembruck, was one of the many art pieces labeled as degenerate by the Nazis and displayed in an exhibition called *Entartete Kunst* (Degenerate Art). The exhibit opened in Munich on July 19, 1937. It contained more than 650 important paintings, sculptures, and books that up until a few weeks before the exhibit had all been in one of Germany's 32 public galleries. The works were assembled to clarify the type of art that was unacceptable to the Reich and, thus, "un-German."

Nuremberg became the center of the Nazi universe for one week each September. The populace decked out the entire city for the benefit of the *Führer* and other Party officials. Parades, designed to exhibit the solidarity of the German people, were a vital component of the festivities. Here, spectators cheer SA men marching through the medieval part of the city.

● **March 15, 1937: An anti-Nazi rally attracts large crowds in New York City. Mayor Fiorello La Guardia, whose mother was Jewish, condemns Nazism.**

● **Spring 1937: Without justification, Jewish merchants in Germany lose their businesses.**

● **April 24, 1937: Pastor Martin Niemöller, one of the foremost leaders of the German opposition forces to Hitler, preaches that it is unfortunate that God permitted Jesus to be born a Jew; *See* July 1, 1937.**

● **May 28, 1937: Neville Chamberlain becomes prime minister of Great Britain.**

● **July 1937: The *Entartete Kunst* (Degenerate Art) exhibition of "unacceptable" artwork by Jews and others opens in Munich. A concurrent event of "approved" art held nearby attracts far fewer people than the *Entartete Kunst* exhibit.**

● **July 1, 1937: Pastor Martin Niemöller's antisemitism does not pre-**

The Zeppelin field in Nuremberg became the center of the annual Nazi Party rally. Hitler and other leaders of the Third Reich gathered there before a mass audience designed to show the popularity of the regime. The impressive light dome, designed by architect Albert Speer, added an awe-inspiring spectacle to the assembly. One hundred and thirty searchlights illuminated the night sky to a height of 25,000 feet.

National Socialists objected to any secret society, especially the Masons. The Nazis viewed such groups, which could not be controlled by the state, as tools of the imagined international Jewish conspiracy. This fanciful reproduction of a Masonic altar was constructed for The Eternal Jew exhibition that opened in Munich on November 8, 1937.

On November 5, 1937, at the Hossbach Conference, Hitler informed the German High Command of his plans to dominate Europe. Named after Colonel Friedrich Hossbach, who took minutes, the conference marked the first time that Hitler openly shared his views on the racial reordering of Europe. To Hitler's left is Propaganda Minister Joseph Goebbels. To Hitler's right is Dr. Karl Brandt, his personal physician.

1937

vent the Nazis from arresting him because of his opposition to Hitler.

• July 15, 1937: A concentration camp is established at Buchenwald, Germany.

• July 27, 1937: A ritual-murder trial of five Jews opens in Bamberg, Germany.

• August 1937: Jews are accused of sacrilege at Humméné, Czechoslovakia. • 350 incidents of physical assaults against Jews are recorded this month in Poland.

• September 6–13, 1937: 600,000 German troops parade before Hitler at Nuremberg.

This portion of The Eternal Jew exhibition held in Munich shows representations of stereotypical "Jewish" facial features. The Jew was characterized by a large hooked nose, enormous lips, and sloping forehead. Such characterizations had been part and parcel of European antisemitism since the Middle Ages, but Nazi Germany gave them the veneer of scientific respectability.

Martin Niemöller

When the Nazis took power, Martin Niemöller was minister of St. Anne's Lutheran Church in Berlin Dahlem. Like many Christian leaders, he initially welcomed Hitler's rise to power as the opening stage of a national revival. Niemöller was especially sympathetic to the Nazis' anti-Communism, but he soon concluded that Hitler's regime was also anti-Christian.

In 1934 Niemöller founded the Pastors' Emergency League, which became the foundation of the Confessing Church. The church sought to counter the increasing influence of the openly antisemitic and pro-Nazi "Positive German Christians." In May 1934 Niemöller was among the Confessing leaders who drew up the "Barmen Declaration," which reaffirmed the Jewish roots of Christianity and the validity of the Hebrew Bible.

In 1937 Niemöller was arrested and sentenced to seven months in prison and a 2000-*Reichsmark* fine. Under Hitler's orders, he was rearrested shortly after his release and spent the next eight years in several concentration camps, including Sachsenhausen and Dachau. He lived until 1984.

The Eternal Jew, a degenerate-art exhibition in Munich, opened on November 8, 1937. The largest prewar antisemitic exhibit produced by the Nazis, it depicted Jews as vile, subhuman creatures. The exhibit featured photographs pointing out the typically "Jewish" features of political figures, such as Leon Trotsky, and entertainers, including Charlie Chaplin. The display placed heavy emphasis upon supposed efforts of the Jews to bolshevize Germany.

● **September 7, 1937:** Hitler declares the Treaty of Versailles invalid and ended.

● **October 12, 1937:** The SS assumes control of Grafeneck, a crippled-children's institution in Württemberg, Germany, and begins the facility's transformation into a "euthanasia" center.

● **November 5, 1937:** Hitler chairs a secret conference in which he informs the High Command and others of his racial, geopolitical, and military plans to dominate Europe. The conference is recorded by Colonel Friedrich Hossbach and called after him.

● **November 8, 1937:** The German Museum in Munich mounts the *Der*

Ewige Jude (The Eternal Jew) exhibition. It links Jews with bolshevism.

● **November 25, 1937:** Germany signs a military agreement with Japan.

● **1937–1939:** Synthetic fat derived from coal is tested on inmates at the Sachsenhausen, Germany, concentration camp.

1938

IN 1930 Sigmund Freud published an important book entitled *Civilization and Its Discontents.* The famous Jewish psychoanalyst stated that civilization had developed so that human beings "would have no difficulty in exterminating one another to the last man." Freud hoped that awareness of this fact might check humanity's death-dealing inclinations.

The book sold well. When his publisher brought out a second edition in 1931, Freud added a final sentence. "Who can foresee," he wondered, "with what success and with what result, how the great struggle between life and death will play out?" Freud raised that question shortly after the Nazi Party's influence surged in Germany's 1930 elections.

By the end of the 1930s, Freud's worries about "civilization and its discontents" were more specific than they had been when the book first appeared. On March 12, 1938, for example, Freud, 82, was still living in Vienna, the city that had long been his home, when German troops crossed the Austrian border. By the next day the *Anschluss,* as the annexation of Austria became known, had made that country a part of the Third Reich. Hundreds of thousands of enthusiastic Viennese greeted Hitler's triumphal arrival. "As *Führer* and chancellor of the German nation and Reich," Hitler proclaimed from the balcony of the *Hofburg* on March 15, "I now report to history that my homeland has joined the German Reich."

Caught in life-and-death struggles with Nazism, Austria's 190,000 Jews would find themselves targeted by a campaign of persecution, expropriation, and forced emigration that moved more rapidly and thoroughly than anything the German Jews had as yet experienced. On June 4 Freud left Vienna, but only after the Gestapo had twice searched his apartment, interrogated his daughter Anna, seized family property, and extracted an emigration tax. In addition, Freud was required to sign a Nazi document to testify that he had not been mistreated. Getting away with risky sarcasm, he added: "I can most highly recommend the Gestapo to everyone."

Freud died in London on September 23, 1939. Meanwhile, the *Anschluss* posed a crucial problem for Nazi Germany, for it gave the Third Reich a Jewish population larger than the total number of Jews who had managed to leave Germany in the previous five years. National Socialist strategies had aimed at making life so uncomfortable for German Jews that they would emigrate, but these tactics had not been very successful. The dimensions

Jewish merchants sweep up following *Kristallnacht,*
the "Night of Broken Glass."

121

1938

of the "Jewish problem" created by the Anschluss called for more effective measures. Austria became the place to test them. One of those put in charge was a young, recently promoted *Untersturmführer* (second lieutenant). This rising expert on Jewish affairs was Adolf Eichmann.

During the spring of 1938, Eichmann started an assembly-line process of forced emigration for the Austrian Jews. Intimidated by a severe reign of terror, these Jews were eager to leave. Recalling Eichmann's system, a Jewish leader named Franz Mayer described emigration as follows: "You put in a Jew at one end, with property, a shop, a bank account, and legal rights. He passed through the building and came out at the other end without property, without privileges, without rights, with nothing except a passport and order to leave the country within a fortnight; otherwise, he would find himself inside a concentration camp." In six months Eichmann expelled nearly 45,000 Jews from Austria. By May 1939 some 100,000 Jews—more than 50 percent of Austria's Jewish population—had left.

The *Anschluss* and Eichmann's program of forced emigration in Austria escalated an international refugee problem. U.S. President Franklin D. Roosevelt called for an international conference to address the issue. From

Pro-Nazi propaganda on the streets of Vienna urged citizen support of the *Anschluss*.

July 6 to 15, 1938, the delegates of 32 nations and the representatives of 39 private relief agencies (21 of them Jewish) met at the French resort of Evian-les-Bains on Lake Geneva, near the Swiss border. Nazi Germany did not attend but permitted representation from the German and Austrian Jewish communities. Although the delegates expressed sympathy for the Jewish refugees, they also made excuses: The doors of their countries could not be opened.

The most important result of the Evian Conference was that it undermined the illusion that forced emigration could really solve the Nazis' "Jewish problem." Later in the year, German Foreign Minister Joachim von Ribbentrop would succinctly sum up the situation for Hitler by recalling a conversation with Georges Bonnet, Ribbentrop's French counterpart. Bonnet had insisted that France did not want to receive any more Jews from Germany, and in fact wanted to ship 10,000 Jews elsewhere. Ribbentrop told Hitler that he had replied to Bonnet "that we all wanted to get rid of our Jews but that the difficulties lay in the fact that no country wished to receive them."

Poland was one of the countries that fitted Ribbentrop's description. On March 31, 1938, just a few weeks after the *Anschluss*, the Polish Parliament passed legislation that made it possible to revoke citizenship for Poles who lived abroad. Both before and after that date, the Polish government took related steps, all of them aimed at preventing the return of thousands of Polish Jews who lived in Germany. Many of those Jews would lose their Polish citizenship on November 1, 1938. In late October the Nazis made a preemptive decision and tried to deport the Polish Jews to Poland. The Polish authorities refused them entry.

The family of Herschel Grynszpan, 17, was among the Polish Jews who ended up in a Polish concentration camp near the border town of Zbaszyń. Living in Paris at the time, Herschel did not know in detail what was happening to his family, but word received from his sister Berta indicated that the Grynszpans had been forced to leave their home in Hannover, Germany. In reprisal, Grynszpan went to the German Embassy in Paris on November 7 and shot a diplomat named Ernst vom Rath, who would die two days later.

News of the shooting led some local Nazi leaders to instigate violence and rioting in parts of Germany during the evening of November 8. The following evening, after Rath's death, Propaganda Minister Joseph Goebbels gave the signal, sanctioned by Hitler himself, for a nationwide pogrom against the Reich's Jews to avenge Rath's murder. Evidence that these November pogroms, which came to be known collectively as *Kristallnacht* (Crystal Night, or Night of Broken Glass), were anything but spontaneous is illustrated by the telegram that Gestapo chief Heinrich Müller sent to all police units at 11:55 on the evening of November 9: "In shortest order," Müller instructed, "actions against Jews and especially their synagogues will take place in all Germany. These are not to be interfered with. . . ."

Evian Conference attendees failed miserably in their attempts to find refuge for Europe's Jews.

The "actions" were devastating. Throughout the Reich, Jewish synagogues, cemeteries, hospitals, schools, businesses, and homes were looted, wrecked, and often set aflame. Scores of Jews were killed; thousands more were arrested and marched off to concentration camps. The Jews' German neighbors inflicted much of this damage, while police not only followed Müller's orders not to interfere but went on to arrest many of those who had been victimized. Meanwhile, fire brigades followed their orders, too: Let torched synagogues burn, but protect Aryan property nearby.

Kristallnacht ended the illusion that anything resembling normal Jewish life was still possible in the Third Reich. Its violence also smashed some Nazi illusions, for the shattered glass that littered the streets symbolized the high cost that the November pogroms had exacted for Germany. Property valuable to the Reich had been wantonly destroyed. Despite their antisemitism, many Germans also found the violence abhorrent.

On November 12 *Reichsmarschall* Hermann Göring, who controlled the Reich's economic planning, convened an important meeting to deal with *Kristallnacht*'s consequences. Göring opened the meeting by announcing that it would be of "a decisive nature," for he had received "a letter written on the *Führer*'s orders . . . requesting that the Jewish question be now, once and for all, coordinated and solved one way or the other." At the time, Göring remained convinced that the solution was "mainly an economic one." His stated goal was "the elimination of the Jew from the German economy."

Herschel Grynszpan *(pictured)* assassinated Ernst vom Rath, igniting the pogroms of November 9–10.

The policies that emerged from Göring's meeting on November 12 were not yet overtly genocidal, but those brainstorming talks led to harsh segregation measures and lethal economic restrictions that soon barred Jews from theaters, denied them admission to German parks and schools, and made it increasingly difficult for Jews to earn a living in the Third Reich. It was increasingly hopeless to think that Nazi Germany's anti-Jewish policies would relent. The end of that illusion was at hand.

Göring aptly concluded his November meeting—and summed up the year 1938 as well—when he said, "I would not like to be a Jew in Germany."

Teaching Antisemitism

According to children's textbooks in Nazi Germany, Adolf Hitler had been a great Nordic warrior. Jews couldn't be trusted. And non-Nordic people were something less than human.

The nazification of the German school system began soon after Hitler's seizure of power. Schools were centralized and purged of Jewish teachers, while indoctrination courses retrained the rest. Reshaped school curricula underscored race theory, discouraged analytical thinking, and overemphasized physical training.

Textbooks and children's literature reflected this nazification of academic subjects. War stories replaced fairy tales. Nordic legends and  sagas of heroic personalities became reading staples. A typical kindergarten primer depicted a caricature of a "dishonest Jew" on its cover; inside, it would feature pictures of soldiers. Elementary readers fictionalized the *Führer's* childhood.

More ominous was the introduction of pseudoscientific racial biology. Hermann Gauch's textbook on race taught that humankind could be divided into Nordic people and non-Nordic people—or, as he called the latter, subhumans. In classrooms, students measured each other's skulls and classified their racial types. Teachers singled out Jewish children to demonstrate and test racial hypotheses. Though they were already limited to 1.5 percent of the student body, a 1938 law banned Jewish pupils altogether from German public schools.

With the Star of David at its center, this official *Jüdische Winterhilfe* (Jewish Winter Aid) symbol urges Jews to remember the needy during the cold winter months. As the Nazis pressured Jews to leave Germany, even those Jews in cosmopolitan Berlin experienced growing isolation and need. Berlin Jews established a model for welfare services, running everything from soup kitchens to orphanages.

General Werner von Blomberg *(left)* resigned when his wife was exposed as a registered prostitute. Because Hitler did not wish to deal with Blomberg's logical successor, the independent General Werner von Fritsch, Heinrich Himmler and Hermann Göring produced fake police reports suggesting that Fritsch had homosexual inclinations. These scandals allowed Hitler to name himself supreme commander of the *Wehrmacht*, and to create a new High Command structure that he controlled completely.

1938

• 1938: Of Germany's 500,000 Jews in 1933, about 200,000 emigrate by the end of 1938. • The first issue of *Jüdisches Nachrichtenblatt* (*Jewish Newsletter*), a Nazi-controlled publication, keeps German citizens abreast of Nazi regulations regarding Jews. • Ludwig Schemann, a leading German advocate of racism, dies. • In Romania, a Fascist and antisemitic government, established in December 1937 and headed by Octavian Goga, falls early in 1938. • Right-wing Catholic priest Jozef Tiso becomes prime minister of Slovakia and establishes ties to Nazi Germany.

• Adolf Hitler tells Minister of Justice Hans Frank that he has come to fulfill the curse imposed by the Jews them-

The *Führer* inspects the Sachsenhausen concentration camp, located near Berlin. Built in 1936, Sachsenhausen followed Dachau as one of the first camps built to imprison political enemies of the Nazis. After *Kristallnacht,* about 1800 Jews were arrested and sent there, of whom some 450 never left. Forced to run a gauntlet of vicious beatings, many died from their injuries while others were executed.

GERMANY'S MAJOR CONCENTRATION CAMPS, 1933–1939

In the 1930s the Nazi camps housed mostly political opponents. In the wake of *Kristallnacht,* however, thousands of Jews were incarcerated.

Henry Ford, industrialist and owner of the Ford Motor Company, was also an outspoken antisemite. In 1920 his newspaper, *The Dearborn Independent,* published an edition of the faked *The Protocols of the Elders of Zion,* fueling American fears of a Jewish conspiracy. Hitler reprinted Ford's edition of *The Protocols* in German and awarded him the medal of the Grand Cross of the German Eagle. When war in Europe began, Ford blamed the "Jew bankers" for causing it.

selves in the New Testament: "His [Jesus's] blood be upon us and upon our children." Hitler, born and raised as a Roman Catholic, observes that had Martin Luther, the founder of Protestantism, been fully aware of the Jewish threat, he would not have criticized Catholicism; instead, he would have put all of his energy into attacking the Jews.

• January 1938: The concentration camp at Dachau, Germany, is enlarged. • In Holland, a collaborationist organization, *National-Socialistische Vrouwen Organisatie* (National Socialist Women's Organization), is established. • The Swedish government institutes strict immigration standards.

• January 21, 1938: The Romanian government strips Romanian Jews of their citizenship.

• February 1938: Hitler appoints Joachim von Ribbentrop foreign minister.

• February 4, 1938: Hitler names himself supreme commander of the

Viennese children salute Hitler and his entourage during his first official visit to Vienna after the *Anschluss*, the forced union with Germany. Displaying a banner that reads, "We sing for Adolf Hitler," the young Austrians enthusiastically welcome their new leader. Although Austrian Chancellor Kurt von Schuschnigg attempted to resist German encroachment, intense pressure by the Nazis forced him from office.

An SS officer guards the entrance to the offices of the Jewish community center of Vienna during the raids of March 18. Following the *Anschluss*, the entire corpus of antisemitic legislation that had developed during the preceding five years in Germany was enacted overnight in Austria. Austria's nearly 200,000 Jews were deprived of citizenship, while Jewish organizations and congregations lost their government funding.

The union of Austria with Germany unleashed a torrent of antisemitism. Not only were Austrian Jews systematically deprived of their citizenship, but they were publicly humiliated as well. Here, Austrian Nazis and local residents look on as Jews are forced to get on their knees and scrub pro-Schuschnigg slogans off the pavement (Kurt von Schuschnigg was the recently ousted chancellor of Austria). A favorite sport of the Austrian Nazis was to force wealthy Jewish women to scrub the sidewalks with their lingerie.

1938

Wehrmacht. Hitler's Cabinet meets for the final time. • Austrian Nazis prepare to take over every Jewish business in the nation.

• March 1938: The Polish government threatens to revoke the citizenship of Polish Jews who are living in Germany.

• March 12, 1938: The German Army enters Vienna, Austria. Austria is annexed (the *Anschluss*) by Germany and is immediately subject to all anti-semitic laws in effect in Germany. Jewish organizations and congregations are subsequently forbidden.

• March 28, 1938: Jewish community organizations in Germany lose their

Immediately after the *Anschluss* in March 1938, the Nazis moved to seize control of the Jewish community in Vienna. Standing outside the Ministry of the Interior on March 18, Adolf Eichmann *(left background, facing camera)* and the SS prepare for a raid on Jewish offices. Eichmann and his men intimidated community leaders and established a climate of fear to spur emigration. German antisemitic laws were now applied to Austria, and Jewish organizations and congregations were abolished.

Enthusiastic participants in a wheelbarrow race, these members of the Hitler Youth demonstrate the pro-Nazi sentiment of many Austrians after the *Anschluss*. While these young people were frolicking, others were finding the parks of Vienna far less hospitable. On April 23 numerous Jews were rounded up on the Sabbath and forced to eat grass at the Prater, Vienna's famous amusement park. Some suffered heart attacks and a few died from the ordeal.

Fate of Austria's Jews

When the Germans annexed Austria on March 12, 1938, its 190,000 Jews came under the control of the Nazis. Attacks upon these unfortunate Jews began almost immediately, and the isolation and persecution of Jews, which happened over five years in Germany, took place in just a few months in Austria.

Jews were assaulted by Nazis on the street, and became subject to the infamous Nuremberg Laws. The Nazis also subjected Jews to numerous forms of humiliation. Jews had to run in circles until they collapsed, while some men had their beards publicly shaved. Many elderly Jews died as the result of heart attacks caused by their torment, and hundreds of others committed suicide rather than be subjected to Nazi oppression.

Germany's Aryanization of Jewish property also extended to the newly annexed region. Over the first few months after the *Anschluss*, for example, 78 of Vienna's 86 Jewish-owned banks fell into Aryan hands. By the end of the year, about two-thirds of the city's Jewish-owned apartments had been Aryanized.

The Nazis established concentration camps in Austria, among them the infamous Mauthausen, to confine their Jewish victims. Most of Austria's Jews died during the seven years of Nazi rule.

---

official status; they are no longer recognized by the government.

• April 5, 1938: Anti-Jewish riots spread across Poland.

• April 15, 1938: Jews are killed and injured during an antisemitic pogrom at Dabrowa Tarnowska, Poland.

• April 21, 1938: Germany issues a decree that effectively eliminates Jews from the nation's economy and provides for the seizure of Jewish assets.

• April 23, 1938: Jews in Vienna, Austria, are rounded up on the Sabbath by Nazis and forced to eat grass at the Prater, a local amusement park. Many

of the victimized Jews suffer heart attacks and a few die.

• April 26, 1938: The German government demands that all Jews register with the authorities all real estate and other assets exceeding 5000 marks. This is the first step toward expropriation of Jewish property; that is, Aryanization, a process whereby

The *Führer* meets in the *Reich-chancellory* with pro-Nazi Slovakian Premier Jozef Tiso. Following the Munich agreement and the occupation of the Sudetenland, the Nazis continued to extend their grasp over Slovakia. In Tiso, a Catholic priest and Slovak nationalist, the Nazis found a willing partner. While Slovakia retained some political autonomy, Germany set the racial policies. In 1942 an unknown number of Gypsies and perhaps 70,000 Jews were sent to death camps. Tiso fled to Austria in 1945, where he was captured by the American Army. Extradited to Czechoslovakia, he was tried and executed for war crimes.

Warsaw, Poland, police intervene to quell an antisemitic riot. While some Jews huddle next to buildings to escape harm, others have already fallen under the force of fists and bats. After Marshal Jósef Pilsudski's death in 1935, the new Polish government used antisemitism as a tool to rally the nation and to win German goodwill. While the government did not advocate violence, right-wing parties such as the *Endecja* did, and during April 1938 anti-Jewish riots swept across Poland.

Well dressed and appearing optimistic, the Simon family from Hamburg, Germany, arrives in New York before continuing its journey to San Francisco, California. While some Americans made Jewish emigres feel welcome, others, such as broadcaster Father Charles Coughlin, were openly hostile. In late 1938 supporters of Coughlin took to the streets of New York proclaiming, "Send Jews back where they came from in leaky boats."

1938

the Reich government seizes Jewish property and auctions it off to gentiles.

• April 29, 1938: Jews are killed and injured during an antisemitic pogrom at Vilna, Poland.

• May 1938: Following the *Anschluss*, Austrians force Jewish men and women to scrub the streets with small brushes and with the women's fur coats.

• May 3, 1938: A concentration camp is established at Flossenbürg, Germany.

• May 4, 1938: Carl von Ossietzky, an anti-Nazi German journalist and win-

Prospective buyers view confiscated property of German Jews before it appears on the auction block. Early in 1938 Hermann Göring, the plenipotentiary for the Four-Year Plan, initiated plans for systematically expropriating Jewish wealth. Jews were required to submit a comprehensive list of their domestic and foreign property; the property then was seized.

Prisoners of the Flossenbürg concentration camp in Germany endure hard labor while working in this stone quarry. Opened in May 1938 near the Bavarian town of the same name, the Flossenbürg camp was relatively small. Approximately 65,000 inmates were incarcerated before it was liberated on April 23, 1945, by U.S. troops. About 14,000 prisoners were reported to have died or were executed during the last 14 months of the war. Among the fatalities was German Pastor Dietrich Bonhoeffer.

Adolf Eichmann

As the "Jewish specialist" of the SS, Adolf Eichmann zealously and efficiently organized the arrests and transportation of millions of Jews to death and concentration camps. Convinced of the importance and "necessity" of his task, he asserted that he performed his job "with all the fanaticism that an old Nazi would expect of himself." He found his work "fascinating" and admitted that doing it well gave him "uncommon joy."

Eichmann joined the SS in 1932, and in 1934 he took a position in Reinhard Heydrich's Security Service (SD). Within the SD's Jewish Department, he became the leading expert on Jewish affairs. Disguised as a journalist, he traveled to Palestine in 1937 to study the possibility of deporting Jews to that region, but he concluded that the creation of a Jewish state "should be impeded." After the annexation of Austria in March 1938, he headed the Office of Jewish Emigration, acquiring expertise in "forced emigration" techniques: systematic physical violence, blackmail, and concentration-camp threats.

At the 1942 Wannsee Conference, Eichmann received the task of implementing the "Final Solution." With utmost bureaucratic efficiency, he organized the technical aspects of the extermination policy—from roundups and train convoys to devising gassing procedures and setting death quotas in extermination camps.

---

ner of the 1935 Nobel Peace Prize, dies at age 50 after five years' captivity in concentration camps.

● **May 28, 1938:** Jewish businesses in Frankfurt, Germany, are boycotted.

● **May 29, 1938:** Hungary restricts the proportion of Jews holding jobs in commerce, industry, the liberal pro-

fessions, and the Hungarian government to 20 percent.

● **May 31, 1938:** German legislation outlaws "decadent art."

● **June 9, 1938:** The main synagogue at Munich is burned to the ground by Nazis.

● **June 14, 1938:** All Jewish businesses that have not already been registered and marked must now comply with the Reich requirement.

● **June 15, 1938:** Throughout Germany, any Jew "previously convicted" of a crime (even a traffic offense) is arrested.

While Jews were prohibited from working as journalists for "German" newspapers during the Nazi years, a number of Jewish periodicals were allowed until 1938. Although closely scrutinized by censors, the papers provided an opportunity for Jews to protest their increasingly perilous existence. Jewish journalists challenged the racial basis of Nazi citizenship and the ill treatment of Jews at the hands of their Nazi oppressors. After 1938 the only journal published for Jews was the *Jüdisches Nachrichtenblatt*.

The *Liberation* was the newspaper of the Silver Shirts, an antisemitic organization in the United States that patterned itself after the Nazi Party. This headline insinuates that Jews were ringleaders in an international drug trade, and it questions whether Americans should be duped into going to war to save such criminals.

Like Hitler, Italian dictator Benito Mussolini appealed to the young for support. Here, a large crowd salutes *Il Duce* at this Fascist youth gathering in Rome in June 1938. Mussolini's early victories, including securing much-needed Ethiopian oil, helped his popularity and spurred his desire to gain more territory. To solidify his standing with Hitler and to win approval for his expansionist plans, Mussolini enacted antisemitic legislation in 1938, a move few Italians supported.

1938

• **June 22, 1938:** German heavyweight boxer Max Schmeling, a symbol of "Aryan supremacy," is knocked out in the first round by world champion Joe Louis. Schmeling had defeated Louis in 1936.

• **June 25, 1938:** German-Jewish doctors are allowed to treat only Jewish patients.

• **July 6–14, 1938:** An international conference at Evian-les-Bains, France, is called by United States President Franklin Roosevelt to deal with the Jewish refugee problem. Roosevelt's aims, some say, are to deflect American Jewish appeals to help the German Jews. Aside from Costa Rica and the Dominican Republic, which want enormous

Promoting the caricature of the Jew as puppet master, this cartoon from a Budapest, Hungary, antisemitic publication played on people's fears and animosities. The rich Jew is pictured as manipulating all society. Under racist Prime Minister Gyula Gömbös, who controlled the government from 1932 to 1939, Hungary pursued a policy of economic and political cooperation with Germany. In May 1938 Hungary, following the German example, enacted a law restricting Jewish participation in the country's economic life.

With increasing persecution, many Jews sought refuge in Palestine. However, the British were fearful of alienating their Arab allies and hence resisted opening up Palestine as a Jewish homeland. An expanding Jewish population angered Arabs, who were also spurred to action by Nazi propaganda. Beginning in 1936, there were sustained attacks on Jewish communities. In an effort both to protect and to control the Jewish population, the British required travel permits. Here, Jews of Haifa are pictured waiting for their permits, without which they could not legally leave the city.

A wary Warsaw Jew peers from his doorway toward his son, who signals that members of the antisemitic *Endecja* (National Democrats) movement are approaching. Fiercely nationalist and with a mono-ethnic vision of Poland, *Endecja* was hostile to minorities, and especially to Jews, who they saw as an obstacle to their goals.

sums of money to allow a small number of Jews to immigrate, the 32 nations attending the conference decide that they will not permit large numbers of Jews to enter their countries.

• July 1938: Under a proposal called the Sosua Project, the Dominican Republic offers to accept 100,000 European Jewish refugees, to be settled in an area near Santo Domingo, in return for payment of millions of dollars from the American Jewish Joint Distribution Committee (JDC). (Under the plan, only about 500 Jews will be admitted to the Dominican Republic before the country halts immigration in 1940.)

• July 14, 1938: Recognizing the intent of the Evian Conference nations in regard to the Jews, a Nazi newspaper headlines: "JEWS FOR SALE AT A BARGAIN PRICE—WHO WANTS THEM? NO ONE."

• July 23, 1938: Jews in Germany are ordered to apply for identity cards to be shown to police on demand.

The Evian Conference

To Jews, the anticipated Evian Conference seemed like a godsend. The international conference, called by United States President Franklin D. Roosevelt, was intended to offer refuge to the hundreds of thousands of Jews in Nazi-controlled Germany and Austria. Instead, in a horrible twist of irony, the conference sealed their doom.

From July 6–15, 1938, delegates of 32 nations and representatives of 39 private relief agencies (21 of them Jewish) met at the luxurious Hotel Royal in the French resort of  Evian-les-Bains on Lake Geneva, near the Swiss border. Prior to the conference, President Roosevelt had made it clear that "no country would be expected to receive a greater number of emigrants than is permitted by its existing legislation." Taking advantage of Roosevelt's qualification, the national delegates, one after another, expressed sympathy for the Jewish refugees but also made excuses to say why their countries' doors could not be opened.

The Evian Conference offered no help to Jewish refugees. Moreover, by legitimating the Nazi claim that "nobody wants them," it became a critical turning point in Nazi-Jewish relations. The conference showed that forced emigration, which had been the centerpiece of Nazi Germany's anti-Jewish policy, was unworkable. Another solution for the Reich's "Jewish problem" would have to be found.

German-Jewish refugee nurses hold five babies at a hospital in Sosua, Dominican Republic. The refugee settlement in Sosua was established after the president of the Dominican Republic offered his country as a haven for Jews persecuted by the Nazi regime. The Dominican government agreed to accept up to 100,000 European Jewish refugees in exchange for a million-dollar payment by the American Jewish Joint Distribution Committee (JDC). Fewer than 500 European Jews made their way to Sosua before the Dominican government halted the immigration project.

Myron C. Taylor of the United States delivers a speech at the Evian Conference, which was called to find homes for the tens of thousands of Jewish refugees. Taylor stated that "the time has come when governments … must act and act promptly." Unfortunately, American isolationism and antisemitism did nothing to spur U.S. politicians to take meaningful action.

1938

• July 25, 1938: Germany cancels the licenses of Jewish doctors. • American radio broadcaster Father Charles Coughlin calls for the establishment of an American Christian Front to combat Communists and Jews. The Christian Front, which will come to fruition, will consist of mostly working-class Irish and German Americans. The organization will adhere to the beliefs that America is a Christian nation and that Catholics should march along with Protestants in a united Christian Front against the Jews.

• July 30, 1938: Henry Ford, an American industrialist and a leading antisemite, accepts the Third Reich's medal of the Grand Cross of the Ger-

Female workers remove the name from a Jewish-owned store located in Hof, Germany. The Aryanization of Jewish property was in full swing by summer. Businesses owned by Jews were systematically seized, and large corporations and branch businesses that were backed by Jewish capital were also targeted. While the "voluntary" transfer of Jewish business to non-Jews continued at a moderate pace, a July 6 decree called for the termination of all Jewish business by the end of the year.

The identification cards of Betty and Nathan Dreifuss issued in 1938 are stamped with the letter "J" for *Jude* (Jew). A decree passed on July 23 required all Jews to apply for identification cards and carry them at all times. A law issued the following month declared that all male Jews must assume the name of Israel and all female Jews the name of Sara. Not only did these laws further alienate Jews from German civil society, but they also placed the Jews under the complete control of the police.

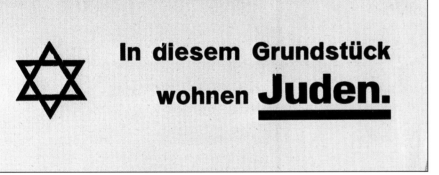

In diesem Grundstück wohnen **Juden.**

At every turn, the Nazis sought to humiliate and ostracize Jews. This sign with a prominent Star of David informs all who pass by that Jews reside in the building. Faced with this warning and fearing guilt by association, many Germans turned away from their Jewish neighbors, friends, and colleagues.

man Eagle. A year later, at the outset of World War II, Ford will claim that "the Jew bankers" are responsible for the war.

● **August 1938:** The *Reichszentralstelle für Jüdische Auswanderung* (Reich Central Bureau for Jewish Emigration) is established in Vienna, Austria, to facilitate Jewish emigra-

tion from the Reich; *See* July 26, 1939.

● **August 5, 1938:** Nazi Minister of Propaganda Joseph Goebbels introduces a new radio for the German people, the German Mini-Receiver also known as the *Goebbels Schnauze* (Goebbels's Snout).

● **August 8, 1938:** The first Austrian concentration camp is established at Mauthausen.

● **August 10, 1938:** The Great Synagogue in Nuremberg, Germany, is destroyed.

● **August 17, 1938:** Male and female Jews in Germany must assume the

Driven Across Borders

During the 1930s it was still possible for Germany's Jews to emigrate. Yet sadly, there were few places to go. Most countries were unwilling to admit Jews, fearing they would become social and economic burdens.

By 1938 the number of Jews seeking refuge abroad increased tremendously. The *Anschluss*, Germany's annexation of Austria, was accompanied by the humiliation, torture, arrests, and expropriation of Austrian Jews. Thousands attempted to flee for the borders of Czechoslovakia, Hungary, Poland, and Switzerland, filling trains and congesting roads with cars and taxis.

The *Anschluss* also marked the beginning of the Nazi policy of expulsion by force. Some Jews were beaten, stripped of their belongings, put onto dilapidated boats, and pushed down the Danube River frontier. In October 1938, 17,000 Polish-born Jews living in Germany were rounded up, loaded aboard sealed railroad cars, and illegally driven across the Polish border by SS guards. Finding shelter in a small frontier village, thousands crowded into pigsties, stables, and warehouses. Although the Poles initially attempted to force them back, most of the refugees were reluctantly admitted.

Kristallnacht ignited further panicked emigration to Palestine, Britain, the Americas, and war-torn Shanghai, China. Some hastily fled eastward via the Soviet Trans-Siberian Railroad. Others frantically accepted passage aboard rickety, unseaworthy ships.

Growing persecution fueled the conviction among some German Jews that their future lay in a Jewish homeland. Others remained rooted in Germany but sought to further Jewish cultural renewal and to strengthen solidarity among Jews. Theologian, scholar, and community leader Martin Buber launched an ambitious program of education to offset Jewish expulsion from German schools and universities. Here he addresses the Berlin Jewish community during "Palestine Week." An ardent Zionist, Buber emigrated to Palestine in 1938.

This poster proclaims that America "challenges anti-semitism and race hatred." However, many—perhaps most—Americans were not willing to help Europe's Jews. A 1939 Gallup poll reported that the majority of Americans opposed increasing immigration quotas for Jewish refugees.

1938

names Israel and Sarah, respectively, by January 1, 1939.

• August 18, 1938: Romanian Orthodox Church Patriarch Miron Cristea calls upon the nation "to fight the Jewish parasites." • The Swiss government denies entry to Jews. However, Paul Grüninger, local police commandant of St. Gall on the Austrian frontier, disobeys his superiors and allows 3600 Jews to pass the border from August through December 1938.

• August 26, 1938: In Vienna, the Central Office for Jewish Emigration (*Zentralstelle für Jüdische Auswanderung*) is set up under Adolf Eichmann.

Desecrated and partially destroyed, this Torah scroll was once the treasured possession of a Jewish family in Pultusk, Poland. The Pole who offered it for sale after the war claimed that it had been used as the backdrop for executions of Jews in a courtyard in Pultusk. Jews Jerome Lipowicz and Abraham Zielinski purchased the scroll and eventually brought it to the United States. Now in five fragments, it is a stark reminder of the sacrilege inflicted upon the Jewish religious community.

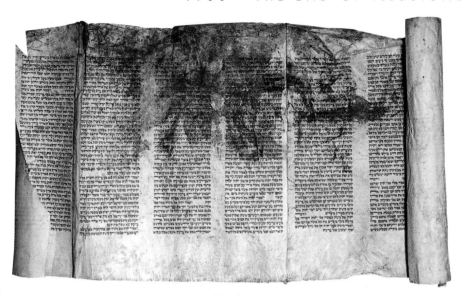

Jews refused to abandon the things that made life tolerable. One of those things was orchestral music, which was administered by the *Kulturbund Deutscher Juden* (Cultural Society of German Jews). The organization had been formed early in 1933 to provide Jews with access to theater, music, sports, and other activities. It existed under increasingly strong Nazi disapproval until 1941, when it was dissolved.

The Nazis viewed Freemasons and Jews as comprising a vast international conspiracy whose aim was to rule the world. Freemasons came under attack as soon as Hitler gained power, and lodges soon closed. In an effort to ridicule Masonic beliefs, the Nazis took over a lodge in Erlangen, Germany, and turned it into a museum *(pictured)*, replete with demonstrations of rituals and initiation rites.

• **September 1938: A concentration camp is established at Neuengamme, Germany.** • **The Berlin** *Putsch*, with the aim of overthrowing Hitler and tossing him into an insane asylum, is planned by generals and influential civilians, but it never comes off because of poor organization and wavering leadership.

• **September 6, 1938: Pope Pius XII informally tells Belgian pilgrims that antisemitism is a movement in which Christians should not involve themselves.** However, Pius says, each Christian has the right "to defend himself, to take means to protect himself against all that threatens his legitimate interest."

• **September 15, 1938: British Prime Minister Neville Chamberlain meets with Hitler at Berchtesgaden, Germany, to discuss the Sudeten crisis.** Hitler has demanded that the Sudetenland, which was part of Austria up through the end of World War I, be ceded by Czechoslovakia to Germany.

An SS officer intently observes the forced-labor operations at the Neuengamme concentration camp in Germany. As was the case with many camps, the first prisoners were responsible for constructing the facilities. The site at Neuengamme was selected because of the abandoned brick factory that was part of the complex. The SS wanted to reactivate the factory and use the bricks to supply the public structures being planned for Hamburg.

German Chancellor Adolf Hitler greets British Prime Minister Neville Chamberlain upon his arrival at Berchtesgaden, Germany, for the Munich Conference. The meeting was called to discuss Hitler's demand that Czechoslovakia hand over the Sudetenland territories of Bohemia and Moravia, two regions that were largely inhabited by ethnic Germans. During the meetings, Hitler promised that the Sudetenland would be his last territorial demand in Europe.

Upon his return to London following the Munich Conference, Neville Chamberlain declared that he had secured "peace in our time." Chamberlain began his speech by saying that he had just concluded a series of meetings with the "honorable" Mr. Hitler. Describing the talks as forthright and earnest, Chamberlain downplayed the fact that Britain had agreed to the territorial dismantling of the independent democratic state of Czechoslovakia.

1938

● **September 22–23, 1938: Neville Chamberlain again meets with Hitler, this time in Godesberg, Germany.**

● **September 26, 1938: Hitler promises that the Sudetenland will be his last territorial demand in Europe.**

● **September 27, 1938: Jews are barred from practicing law in Germany.**

● **September 29–30, 1938: The Munich Conference is attended by French Premier Edouard Daladier, British Prime Minister Neville Chamberlain, Italian dictator Benito Mussolini, and Hitler. Climaxing the**

The cover page of this German passport, issued to Karoline Ruelf, is stamped with the letter "J" for *Jude* (Jew). Heinrich Rothmund of the Swiss federal police instigated the recall of all Jewish passports. Swiss officials were worried that German Jews would attempt to pose as Christians and smuggle themselves into Switzerland. The large, red "J" on their passports was an attempt to curtail the movement of German Jews and reassure the Swiss government.

Mauthausen

The Mauthausen concentration camp near Linz, Austria, specialized in working prisoners to death in its rock quarry. Of the 200,000 men, women, and children who passed through its gates, about 120,000 perished from neglect, overwork, and sadistic torture—the highest percentage of all camps within the Reich.

The camp was designed according to the "Dachau model" and followed the established method of mistreating prisoners. But in addition to murder through starvation and beatings, Mauthausen also featured a unique brand of torture. It was devised by camp commander Franz "Babyface" Ziereis. Prisoners were forced to run up 186 steps from the camp's granite quarry, carrying stones weighing over 100 pounds. If dropped, they crushed the feet of those behind. Every Jew who dropped his load was beaten mercilessly, and the stones were again lifted to his shoulders. In despair, many committed suicide by leaping into the quarry from the cliff above. Some were thrown over the edge by guards, who referred to their victims as "parachute troops."

Prisoners were also murdered by being forced to run into electrified fences, through shootings in the back of the neck, and with chemical injections directly into the heart.

Allies' appeasement policy, France and Great Britain permit Germany to illegally annex the Sudetenland of Czechoslovakia. Most of Europe breathes a sigh of relief because war is averted. Daladier, observing the huge crowds awaiting him at the Orly airport near Paris, fears that they will tear him apart for betraying France's Czech ally. After he lands, he is relieved when his people throw roses at him.

• The Czech representatives to the conference, who had been forced to wait helplessly in the corridor outside the conference hall, break down into sobs after hearing the news of the Allied concessions to Germany. Also at the conference, Chamberlain signs a Friendship Treaty with Germany without informing his French ally. Arriving home, he triumphantly holds this scrap of paper up to the crowd that surrounds his airplane and promises "peace in our time."

● October 1938: The Polish government revokes passports of all Jews who have lived outside of Poland for

The Madagascar Plan

In 1938 the Nazis explored the idea of shipping Germany's Jews to Madagascar, an island off the eastern coast of Africa. The plan was never implemented since Britain controlled the seas, but Hitler toyed with the idea for years. He reasoned that "the Jews must be sent to Africa, where climatic conditions have a debilitating effect on the human organism and lower its resistance."

The scheme to ship Jews to this French colonial possession in the Indian Ocean was first dreamed up by German antisemite Paul de Lagarde in the 19th century. The plan reemerged in the 1920s within antisemitic circles in Poland. In 1937 the Polish government negotiated the possibility with France.

The Nazi plan proposed exiling four million Jews to Madagascar. French inhabitants of the island would leave, isolating the Jews from contact with white Europeans. German naval bases would be located on the island. The remainder of the land would be a Jewish reservation, with its own mayors and postal service, but with a Nazi police governor responsible to Heinrich Himmler. Envisioned in this role was Philip Bouhler, head of the Nazis' "euthanasia" program.

Graffiti written above the window of this Jewish-owned clothing store in Vienna conveys the antisemitic spirit of the times. The Star of David and the word *Jud* (Jew) are accompanied by a gallows and the sardonic announcement that the proprietors are vacationing in Dachau.

Hitler's tour of the Czech lands took him to the resort town of Karlsbad. Known for its fine waters and spas, Karlsbad was often host to Europe's royalty. Upon arriving in the famed town of the western Czech lands, Hitler was received by a military honor guard, replete with an armored division of the *Wehrmacht*. The Czech people quickly learned of the military pageantry favored by their new rulers.

1938

more than five years, rendering them stateless. • *Civiltà Cattolica*, the foremost Jesuit journal, which is published in Rome and controlled by the Vatican, calls Judaism sinister and accuses Jews of trying to control the world through money and secularism. The journal says that the devil is the Jews' master; Judaism is evil and "a standing menace to the world."

• October 1–10, 1938: The German *Wehrmacht* occupies the Czech Sudetenland.

• October 5, 1938: Following a request by Heinrich Rothmund, head of the Swiss federal police, the German government recalls all Jewish passports and marks them with a large, colored "J." This is to prevent

Three women greet Hitler with the Nazi salute during the German chancellor's tour of the newly acquired Sudetenland. The range of emotions portrayed in this photo is telling. While the woman on the far left is clearly enthusiastic and the one in the middle somewhat reserved and respectful, the woman on the right weeps openly as she salutes. Her tears suggest that she may have harbored deep-seated reservations about the incorporation of her homeland into Hitler's ever-expanding Third Reich.

Hitler accepts bouquets of flowers from children of the Sudetenland. Accompanied by Heinrich Himmler and other top officials, Hitler's staged tour through the Czech lands was choreographed to perfection. Cheering crowds, grateful schoolchildren, and members of the Austrian Nazi Party met him at every stop. The incorporation of the Sudetenland into the greater German Reich was a tremendous propaganda victory for Hitler. Since entering politics in 1919, Hitler had argued passionately for the creation of a German nation to house all ethnic Germans.

The incorporation of the Sudetenland into the German Reich included thousands of nonethnic Germans along with the German-speaking majority. After the signing of the Munich Treaty, approximately 200,000 people were expelled or fled from their homes. In this photo, armed Nazi soldiers supervise the expulsion of Czech citizens from Falknov and Ohri.

German Jews from passing as Christians and smuggling themselves into Switzerland.

• **October 8, 1938:** The Slovak Peoples' Party establishes *Hlinkova Garda* (Hlinka Guard), an antisemitic militia that will collaborate with the Germans.

• **October 28, 1938:** Germany expels Jews with Polish citizenship to the Polish border. Poles refuse to admit them; Germans refuse to allow them back into Germany. Seventeen thousand are stranded in the frontier town of Zbaszyń, Poland.

• **November 1938:** Father Bernhard Lichtenberg, a Roman Catholic priest in Berlin, condemns the German assault on Jews. One of the few German Catholics to denounce the immoral behavior of the government, Father Lichtenberg sermonizes: "Outside the synagogue is burning, and that also is a house of God."

• **November 2, 1938:** Sections of Slovakia as well as the Transcar-

Members of the newly formed Hlinka Guard of Slovakia march in formation. The incorporation of the Sudetenland into Germany propelled the Hlinka People's Party, a right-wing nationalist group, into action. Hoping to create an independent Slovakian state, Hlinka leaders quickly aligned themselves with the Nazis. The nearly 90,000 Jews of Slovakia braced themselves for troubled times.

"They shouted to us, 'Run! Run!' I myself received a blow and I fell in the ditch. My son helped me and he said, 'Run, run, Dad—otherwise you'll die!'"

—German Jew Zindel Grynszpan, on the forced march of 17,000 German Jews toward the Polish border

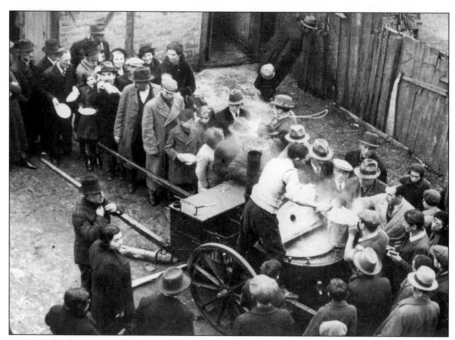

Jewish deportees line up for soup at a mobile cooking facility in the Zbaszyń, Poland, refugee camp. Nearly 6000 Jews arrived in Zbaszyń during the first two days of the expulsion. Initially, the refugees were provided with warm water and food by local residents, but since the crisis lasted several months, the Joint Distribution Committee sponsored an organized relief effort. After high-level governmental talks, Polish and German officials finally agreed to allow Jewish deportees back into Poland after they had returned to Germany to liquidate their assets.

1938

pathian Ukraine are annexed by Hungary.

• November 7, 1938: A distraught young Jew named Herschel Grynszpan, whose family has just been deported to Zbaszyń, enters the German Embassy in Paris and mortally wounds Third Secretary of Legation Ernst vom Rath. The Nazis will exploit this event by instigating a long-planned terror campaign against all Jews in Germany and Austria.

• November 9, 1938: Hitler authorizes Hermann Göring to deal with all Jewish political issues.

• November 9–10, 1938: *Kristallnacht* (Night of Broken Glass) occurs across

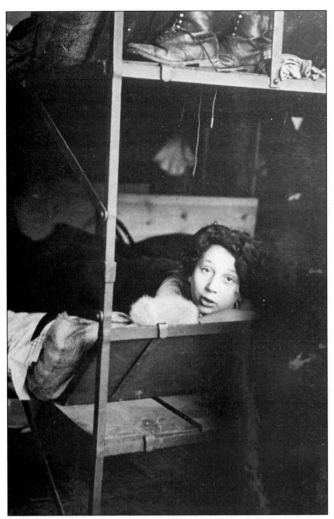

Nettie Stub Katz peers out from her wooden bunk at the Zbaszyń, Poland, refugee camp near the German border. About 17,000 Polish Jews were stranded in the frontier town of Zbaszyń after the Nazis expelled Jews of Polish nationality from Germany and the Poles refused to admit them back into their country. Katz spent almost a year in the camp before obtaining an entrance visa to Sweden, where she survived the war.

Neuengamme

In December 1938 the SS bought a closed-down brick factory at Neuengamme, a town near Hamburg, Germany, on the marshy bank of the Elbe River. Inmate labor from the nearby Sachsenhausen concentration camp was brought in to renovate the factory. Within two years, the SS converted the site into a concentration camp that provided cheap labor for the armaments industry.

More than 100,000 prisoners were sent to Neuengamme and satellite camps, including 14,000 women and hundreds of children. The camp imprisoned Poles, Russian POWs, and others of diverse nationalities. Most Jews were shipped to Auschwitz. Exhausted, underfed inmates slaved at back-breaking work. They cut, loaded, and transported wet, heavy clay from the morass surrounding the camp. They dug mud from a nearby canal. They lifted hot, glowing bricks without protective equipment.

Skilled inmates manufactured pistol and grenade parts, or repaired U-boat engines. Women made gas masks and concrete products. Production quotas were extremely high, penalties severe. Failure meant death. Saboteurs were hanged. Overwork, disease, and medical "experiments" caused more than half of Neuengamme's inmates to perish.

Germany and Austria. Ninety-one Jews are killed; others are beaten. Thirty thousand male Jews are sent to concentration camps, though most will be released in a few weeks. 267 synagogues are desecrated and destroyed (almost all of the synagogues of Germany and Austria). SS Security Service chief Reinhard Heydrich instructs security agencies to burn the synagogues unless German lives or property are endangered. Jewish businesses are looted and destroyed.

• Hitler mentions to Hermann Göring that he would like to see all German Jews forcibly resettled on the island of Madagascar. Opportunistically chosen by the Nazi leadership, the date of the pogrom is of great symbolic importance. It coincides with two important national holidays, the Nazi Blood Witness Day of November 9 and Martin Luther's birthday of November 10. Blood Witness Day commemorates the Nazi "martyrs" who died for their cause. Martin Luther advocated the destruction of Jewish homes and synagogues as well

In celebration of Propaganda Minister Joseph Goebbels's birthday, 500 new radios were distributed to needy countrymen in Berlin. Both Hitler and Goebbels recognized that radio was an effective way to get their message to the German masses. Once the Nazis were in power, Goebbels's news broadcasts became the sole responsibility of the Propaganda Ministry, and Hitler delivered numerous radio speeches every year. The Nazi regime encouraged radio listening at every opportunity. Radios were set up in factories, restaurants, and offices. By 1939 70 percent of German households owned radios, the highest ownership rate in the world.

Ernst vom Rath (pictured), a German diplomat serving in Paris, was shot by a Polish Jew named Herschel Grynszpan. Grynszpan shot Rath thinking that he was the German ambassador. In reality, Rath was a legation secretary in the German Embassy. The shooting and eventual death of Rath served as a pretext for the Nazis to initiate a pogrom against the Jews.

Herschel Grynszpan is taken from police headquarters in Paris after being interrogated about the shooting of Ernst vom Rath. Grynszpan spent two years languishing in French jails before the Vichy regime turned him over to the Germans. The time and place of Grynszpan's death have never been determined.

1938

as the impoverishment, forced labor, exile, and death of Jews.

• November 10, 1938: 100,000 people in Nuremberg, Germany, attend a rally celebrating *Kristallnacht.*

• November 11, 1938: Jews are killed and injured during an antisemitic pogrom at Bratislava, Slovakia.

• November 12, 1938: Hermann Göring leads a discussion of German officials that results in a one-billion-mark ($400-million) fine against the German-Jewish community to pay for *Kristallnacht.* Göring calls this extortion an "expiation payment." Seizing the money German insurance companies were paying the Jews for their damages, the Nazis require

The interior of the Eberswalde synagogue located in a Berlin suburb stands in ruins following the "Night of Broken Glass." In destroying Jewish places of worship, the Nazis unleashed their hatred with bitter violence. Not only were synagogues set on fire, but sacred religious objects were plundered, Jewish holy books were desecrated, and German Jews were attacked and occasionally murdered.

Curious women shoppers gather outside this ladies' apparel shop to survey the damage of *Kristallnacht*. The store next door, presumably owned by "Aryans," remains untouched, its display cases fully stocked and its windows intact. While many Germans were privately appalled at the violence unleashed that night, few publicly spoke out against what had occurred.

Local residents in the German-annexed Sudetenland town of Opava watch the synagogue go up in flames. Of the more than 200 synagogues destroyed during the orgy of violence unleashed during *Kristallnacht,* many were located in Austria and the Sudetenland. As the Nazis' empire expanded, their virulent antisemitism was disseminated throughout the realm.

the Jews to pay for the repair of their own properties damaged in *Kristallnacht.*

• The Nazis decide on a decree to remove all Jews from the German economy, society, and culture. Reinhard Heydrich suggests that every Jew be forced to wear a badge. Nazi Minister of Propaganda Joseph

Goebbels suggests that Jews be kept from using public parks. Hermann Göring mentions that Hitler told him on the phone on November 9 that if war breaks out, Germany "will first of all make sure of settling accounts with the Jews. [Hitler] is going to ask the other nations: 'Why do you keep talking about the Jews? Take them!'" In the Nazi Party's principal newspaper,

Goebbels writes: "We want only one thing, that the world loves the Jews enough to rid us of them all."

• Speaking at a meeting with the South African minister of economics and defense, Hitler remarks that Europe's Jews will be killed in the event of war.

Kristallnacht

On November 9, 1938, Adolf Hitler attended a dinner in Munich to honor Nazi Party heroes. During the course of the evening, he received word of the death of Ernst vom Rath, a German diplomat in Paris. Upon receiving the news, Hitler spoke intensely with his propaganda minister, Joseph Goebbels, and then left without giving his customary speech.

Goebbels took the floor. After announcing Rath's death, he referred to the anti-Jewish violence in Germany earlier that week. According to Goebbels, Hitler did not wish for such demonstrations to be "prepared or organized" by the Nazi Party. However, Goebbels added, Hitler did say that if those actions "erupted spontaneously, they were not to be hampered."

This encrypted signal was the product of Rath's murder. A Jewish teenager named Herschel Grynszpan provided the excuse for the Third Reich's worst prewar pogroms, which left the German streets littered with shattered glass from Jewish synagogues and store windows. These pogroms came to be known as *Kristallnacht*—"Crystal Night" or "Night of Broken Glass."

On November 7, 1938, Grynszpan, 17, was eking out his existence in Paris. At that time, his family was among some 17,000 Polish Jews—many of them, like the Grynszpans, longtime residents of Germany—whom the Nazi government had deported to Polish territory in late October. When the Polish state refused them entry, most of these hapless Jews ended up in a miserable Polish refugee camp near the border town of Zbaszyń.

Grynszpan correctly inferred that his family was in serious

trouble. "We don't have a cent," his sister Berta wrote in a letter to him. Her brother did not have much more, but he had enough money to buy a pistol. Next he went to the German Embassy, asked to see an official, and then shot and fatally wounded Ernst vom Rath.

As Rath lay dying, Nazi plans were laid to give free rein to the "spontaneous" eruption of "popular anger" that news of the shooting had provoked. Within 48 hours of Rath's death, hundreds of Jewish synagogues were torched—while fire brigades idly stood by. More than 7000 Jewish businesses were looted without intervention by the police. Jewish cemeteries were desecrated. Some 91 Jews were killed, and 30,000 Jewish men were placed under arrest and sent to the newly enlarged concentration camps at Dachau, Buchenwald, and Sachsenhausen.

Jews were blamed for the pogrom and had to pay for the damages as well. A fine of one billion *Reichsmarks*—equal to some 400 million U.S. dollars at 1938 rates—was imposed on the Jewish community. *Kristallnacht* showed that no Jew could ever expect to live a normal life within the Nazi dictatorship.

1938

• **November 15, 1938:** All Jewish students are expelled from German schools. From now on, they may only attend Jewish schools. • In the wake of the bloody pogroms of *Kristallnacht*, United States President Franklin Roosevelt withdraws his ambassador from Germany; *See* January 22, 1944.

• **November 18, 1938:** Hitler recalls Hans Heinrich Dieckhoff, German ambassador to the United States, after President Franklin Roosevelt recalled the U.S. ambassador to Germany. • The American Virgin Islands Assembly offers the islands as a haven for Jewish refugees. The American government does not explore this possibility.

In an act of vile desecration during *Kristallnacht,* the members of the Baden-Baden Jewish community were compelled to listen to a reading of Hitler's *Mein Kampf* from the pulpit. Hours before the synagogue was torched, 60 Jewish men were paraded through the streets by members of the SS. Once they reached the synagogue, they were forced to listen to Dr. Flehinger, a fellow Jew and *Gymnasium* (high school) teacher, read selections of *Mein Kampf.* Afterwards, the Jews had to rehearse the song about Horst Wessel (a Nazi martyr) until they could recite it perfectly. The public humiliation of the Jews accompanied the violence of *Kristallnacht.*

Thousands of newly arrived prisoners stand at attention in their civilian clothes during a roll call at the Buchenwald concentration camp. These prisoners were among the more than 30,000 Jews arrested during the *Kristallnacht* pogrom. With their heads shaved, these German Jews were introduced to the terror system of the Nazi concentration camps. More than 1000 Jews arrested at this time died while incarcerated. The rest were released after the Nazis extracted written promises that they would leave Germany as soon as they could liquidate their holdings.

● **November 20, 1938: Using Nazi documents, American radio commentator Father Charles Coughlin contends that Jews are responsible for Russian communism and for Germany's problems. All of Coughlin's radio programs are approved by his archdiocese as not contradicting Catholic faith or morals. Some Catholics protest Coughlin's broad-** casts, including Chicago's Cardinal George Mundelein, but most of the American Church is silent.

● **November 21, 1938: The British House of Commons objects to German persecution of minorities.**

● **November 24, 1938: British Conservative Party leader Winston** Churchill decides that Palestine cannot be considered a primary refuge for Jews.

● **December 1938:** *Reichsbank* president Hjalmar Schacht travels to London to propose to George Rublee, of the Intergovernmental Committee for Political Refugees, an extortionate scheme: German Jews could emigrate

Four days after *Kristallnacht, The Philadelphia Inquirer* reported that Germany's Jews had to pay a one-billion *Reichsmark* fine for the violence and damage they had suffered. Sympathy for the Jewish plight in the U.S. press and among the public ran high, leading President Franklin Roosevelt to recall the American ambassador, Hugh Wilson, to Washington. No other official action was taken.

Americans reacted with widespread outrage at the events of *Kristallnacht*. Some took to the streets to demonstrate their opposition to Nazi policies. In this New York City demonstration, participants called for an end to "Hitler's bloody pogroms." President Franklin Roosevelt proclaimed his disbelief that such actions could occur "in a 20th-century civilization." Nevertheless, relatively few Americans advocated changing immigration quotas to allow more Jews a safe haven.

Formerly owned by Jews, this Frankfurt, Germany, rubber-ware store was turned over to "Aryan" proprietors Stamm and Bassermann. Aryanization of Jewish businesses began in 1933, as Jews were excluded from the nation's economic life. It accelerated after *Kristallnacht* with Hermann Göring's Decree Excluding Jews from German Economic Life. Stores, factories, and banks—often Jewish concerns for generations—were now forcibly Aryanized.

1938

if they put up cash assets that would be transferred to the Reich upon emigration. This Schacht-Rublee plan will be abandoned in January 1939, when Schacht will be dismissed by Hitler after Schacht objects to the high cost of Germany's rearmament.

• The British Cabinet allows 10,000 unaccompanied Jewish children into Britain in an action called the *Kindertransport*. (Britain, however, refuses to allow 21,000 more Jewish children into Palestine.) The rescued children come from Germany, Austria, and Czechoslovakia with the help of British, Jewish, and Quaker welfare organizations. Because of the Holocaust, most of the children will never see their parents again, and many of

As Hitler's leading economics advisor in the early days of the Third Reich, Hjalmar Schacht played a major role in lifting the nation from the Depression and furthering rearmament. In December 1938 Schacht proposed that German Jews could emigrate if they offered cash assets that would be transferred to the Reich at their departure. Schacht resigned from his post as plenipotentiary for the war economy in 1937. Two years later he was dismissed as head of the *Reichsbank*. Implicated in the 1944 plot against Hitler, Schacht was confined to a concentration camp. He was tried at Nuremberg in 1946 and acquitted of all charges.

Arriving in Harwich, England, Helga Kreiner, a member of the first *Kindertransport* (children's transport) from Germany, clutches her doll while waiting to be taken to her new home. In response to burgeoning violence against Jews, some 10,000 refugee children from Central Europe were permitted entrance into England from December 1938 to September 1939. Some lived in foster homes or hostels; others were housed on training farms run by the Youth Aliya organization in Britain. The vast majority would never see their parents again.

Clutching an American flag, three-year-old Trudel Levy holds the hand of 74-year-old Mrs. Emilia Herz as the pair descends the gangplank in New York. Sailing aboard the *SS President Roosevelt,* these refugees arrived on the last day of a year of hatred and open violence toward Jews in Germany. Many America-bound refugees, unable to speak English and feeling adrift in a foreign land, sought support from each other and established a strong community in Washington Heights, in upper Manhattan in New York.

the Jewish children will be converted to Christianity.

• **December 3, 1938:** The German government decrees that all Jewish industries, shops, and businesses must be forcibly "Aryanized."

• **December 6, 1938:** Germany and France sign a nonaggression pact.

• **December 18, 1938:** Thousands of Father Charles Coughlin's followers take to the streets of New York City, chanting, "Send Jews back where they came from in leaky boats!" and "Wait until Hitler comes over here!" Many Christian policemen are sympathetic to the Coughlinites. The protests will last until April 1939. They are opposed by other Catholic

organizations and by leftists and liberals.

• **December 24, 1938:** Several members of the American Catholic hierarchy and leading Protestants sign a Christmas resolution expressing "horror and shame" in response to the *Kristallnacht* pogrom.

1939

ON September 21, 1939, Reinhard Heydrich, head of Nazi Germany's Security Police, dispatched a secret message. It went to the chiefs of special task forces (*Einsatzgruppen*), whose responsibilities covered Polish territory controlled by Nazi Germany after its successful invasion of Poland on September 1. The subject of the message was the "Jewish Question in Occupied Territory," and Heydrich wrote about the final and intermediate goals.

Heydrich did not define the *Endziel* (final goal), but his memo was clear about many of the intermediate stages. Jews should be concentrated; that is, moved from the countryside and villages into large cities, where railroad transportation was readily available. Certain parts of Occupied Poland would become *Judenrein* (cleansed of Jews) to facilitate the resettlement of ethnic Germans. Jewish councils (*Judenräte*) were to be appointed and held responsible for carrying out "the exact and prompt implementation of directives."

Heydrich also ordered his *Einsatzgruppen* chiefs to give him updates on the number and location of Polish Jews as well as their property. These orders contained an ambitious demographic plan. Specifically, it was an order to start the ghettoization of Polish Jewry, a deadly decision that would eventually doom millions of Jewish children, women, and men. Under the cover of conventional war, a different war—one against all of Europe's Jews—was beginning.

Eight months earlier, on January 30, 1939, Hitler spoke to the *Reichstag* about the future of Europe, and the fate of European Jewry in particular. The evening's two-and-a-half-hour speech included his by then familiar anti-Jewish tirades, but on this occasion Hitler's menacing forecasts were more ominous than usual. "If international Jewish financiers inside and outside Europe again succeed in plunging the nations into a world war," Hitler insisted, "the result will not be the bolshevization of the earth and with it the victory of Jewry, but the annihilation of the Jewish race in Europe."

Hitler did not detail what he had in mind. Forced emigration or large-scale Jewish resettlement were the anti-Jewish objectives most in play at the time. But Hitler also had plans to annex Czech territory, and he may have intended to keep international interference at bay by signaling that the Reich's Jews would be held hostage. Be that as it may, few listeners took Hitler's murderous threats literally. Nevertheless, as the search continued for "solu-

A young boy ponders his fate while sitting among
the ruins of his Warsaw, Poland, home.

149

1939

tions" to Nazi Germany's "Jewish question," Hitler's speech advanced the idea of annihilation, which would eventually become the Reich's policy.

Hitler's threats about annihilating European Jewry were not especially credible in early 1939 because a comparatively small number of Europe's Jews—fewer than 400,000—were directly under Nazi domination as 1939 began. With time's passage, however, those numbers soared. As they did, Hitler's *Reichstag* threats, though still far from being implemented, became more plausible. Steps in that direction took place on March 15, when Czechoslovakia disappeared from the map of Europe.

Already in the autumn of 1938, Nazi Germany had annexed parts of Czechoslovakia known as the Sudetenland. Six months later Hitler engineered Slovakian secession from Czechoslovakia and the establishment of a Nazi puppet government in the new state of Slovakia. Then, on March 15, he sent the German Army into the Czech provinces of Bohemia and Moravia, declaring them a protectorate whose ethnic German inhabitants would become Reich citizens. Two days later British Prime Minister Neville Chamberlain publicly proclaimed that his government would resist any further German aggression. Unfortunately, that vow came too late for the 118,000 Jews of Bohemia and Moravia, who were now subject to German control. Another 90,000 Jews lived in the highly antisemitic puppet state of Slovakia.

A Jew in Poland is publicly humiliated by the forcible trimming of his beard, a symbol of his faith.

Trying to flee the enlarging Nazi web, Jews found restrictions and obstacles increasingly in their way as 1939 unfolded. On May 17, for example, the British government issued a document known as the White Paper. It restricted Jewish immigration to Palestine, which a League of Nations mandate had placed under British rule following the First World War.

Other doors remained closed to Jewish refugees. On February 9, 1939, Senator Robert Wagner of New York and Representative Edith Rogers of Massachusetts introduced legislation in the United States Congress. The Wagner-Rogers Child Refugee Bill would grant entry to 10,000 refugee children under the age of 14 in each of two years, 1939 and 1940. These girls and boys would be beyond the number of immigrants allowed under the German quota. However, the often-amended bill became bogged down in committee. Lacking support from President Franklin D. Roosevelt as well, the Wagner-Rogers Bill was put aside early that summer.

Earlier that spring, having played his winning Czechoslovakian card, Hitler turned his attention toward Poland. Undeterred by Britain's promise to defend Polish borders, which was affirmed on March 31, Hitler issued important orders on April 11: The *Wehrmacht* should prepare "Operation White," the code name for Nazi Germany's forthcoming attack on Poland.

Before that attack could be launched, the Germans needed to check potential opposition from the Soviet Union. When Hitler opened negotiations with Joseph Stalin, he found the Soviet dictator receptive. On August 23 the foreign ministers of Nazi Germany and the USSR—Joachim von Ribbentrop and Viacheslav Molotov, respectively—signed the German-Soviet Non-Aggression Pact. Beyond guaranteeing that the two countries would not attack one another, this treaty contained a secret provision: It stipulated the spheres of influence that would belong to each side in case of war. Specifically, Poland would be partitioned.

Without fear of Soviet intervention, Nazi Germany invaded Poland on September 1. Two days later Britain and France responded to the plight of their Polish ally by declaring war on Germany. Before September ended, however, German forces had crushed Polish resistance.

Like Czechoslovakia, Poland disappeared from the map of Europe. Soviet forces occupied eastern Poland on September 17. In October the Germans annexed Poland's western and northern districts to the Reich. Much of the country's central heartland—it included the cities of Lublin, Kraków, and the Polish capital Warsaw—became a German colony known as the *Generalgouvernement*.

In the autumn of 1939, Poland's total population numbered about 33 million. Ten percent—3.3 million—were Jews. Nazi Germany's *Blitzkrieg* military tactics and the partition of Poland brought two million Jews under German domination. For the Third Reich, this "Jewish problem" was one of unprecedented proportions. In some ways, however, the "Jewish problem" was more manageable in Poland than it had been in Germany, Austria, or the Protectorate of Bohemia and Moravia. According to Nazi racial ideology, Poles were much inferior to Germans. Eastern European Jewry—Polish Jews among them—ranked even lower. As part of what the Nazis called "subhumanity," Polish Jews should have no reason to expect even the modicum of respect that German Jews had received.

Still, the sheer number of Polish Jews—Warsaw alone was home to almost 400,000—created difficulties that the Germans had not faced before. What should be done with the Polish Jews? Acknowledging that "it is obvious that the tasks ahead cannot be laid down from here in full detail," Reinhard Heydrich's September 21 dispatch from Berlin was intended nonetheless to be an important part of the answer to that question.

While plans to ghettoize Polish Jewry were under way, other parts of the

Top: Reinhard Heydrich called for the establishment of Jewish ghettos in German-occupied Poland. *Bottom:* Lublin was one of the ghettos created shortly after the German invasion of Poland.

answer to the "Jewish question" were beginning to emerge, however dimly at the time, through Hitler's authorization of a so-called "euthanasia" program. The program targeted Germans who were physically or mentally disabled. During the winter of 1939–40, these "useless eaters" were being put to death at institutions in Germany and Austria that were equipped with gas chambers. Later, officials who worked for the euthanasia program would take their skills to such Nazi killing centers as Belzec, Sobibór, and Treblinka. There, Jews would be gassed by the tens of thousands.

After the Nazi seizure of power, Julius Streicher's pornographic, antisemitic rag, *Der Stürmer,* became one of the most widely read newspapers in Germany. Established in Nuremberg in the 1920s, the paper had a national distribution by 1939. This photograph shows a young man gazing at a poster taped to the daily's Danzig office. The poster reads, "The Jews are our misfortune," a widely held sentiment embodying the Nazi position on the "Jewish question."

This photo montage, "The Scourge of God," by an unknown artist or artists, shows the Nazis' view of Poland's Jews at the time of the invasion. The image, used as evidence at the postwar Nuremberg Trials, appeared in the antisemitic hate sheet *Der Stürmer.*

JEWS!   JEWS!
Jews Everywhere!

The Roosevelt Administration is Loaded with Jews

12 Million White American Workers Jobless

OVER ¼ MILLION EUROPEAN JEWS ARE NOW COMING TO UNITED STATES TO THROW WHITE AMERICAN WORKERS OUT OF JOBS

Benjamin Franklin Said:
"Jews are a menace to this country if permitted entrance And Should Be Excluded."

Samuel Roth Said:
"We Jews are a people of vultures, living on the labor of the rest of the world."

The Jewish Talmud Says:
"Jews are human beings, Gentiles are not human beings, but beasts." (Baba Mezia, 114, 6.)

Samuel Roth Says:
"WE JEWS, who come to the Nations PRETENDING to escape PERSECUTION, are really the MOST DEADLY PERSECUTORS OF MEN."

Communism is Jewish

OUT WITH JEWS!!
LET WHITE PEOPLE RUN THIS COUNTRY AS THEY DID BEFORE THE JEWISH INVASION

Wake up!   Wake up!   Wake up!   Wake up!
Get in touch with your nearest Anti-Communist Organization

Antisemitism was, of course, not confined to Europe. This antisemitic flier, printed in the United States in 1939, links Judaism and communism, just as German anti-Jewish propaganda did. Like so much anti-immigrant propaganda of the 1930s, the flier blames the Jews for the severe unemployment brought on by the Great Depression. Such appeals, based upon the economic concerns of a mass audience, were among the most effective utilized by antisemitic groups.

1939

• **1939: Approximately 78,000 Jews leave Germany. Jewish valuables throughout Germany are confiscated.** • **Hermann Esser's antisemitic book, *The Jewish World Plague,* is published in Germany.** • **SS chief Heinrich Himmler is appointed Reich commissioner for strengthening German nationhood. Eager to increase the growing Aryan birth rate, Himmler orders his SS men** to impregnate their wives and to act as "conception assistants" to childless women over the age of 29. • **The first issue of *Die Aktion: Kampfblatt für das neue Europa (The Action: Newspaper for Fighting for the New Europe),* an antisemitic propaganda periodical distributed outside of Germany, is published.**

This poster links antisemitism with the strong anti-immigrant sentiments that characterized American politics during the 1930s. According to the poster, Judaism equals communism, which should have no place in the United States. Note the Jewish features, complete with the stereotypical elongated nose, on the Statue of Liberty.

WAKE UP AMERICANS!
DO YOU WANT THIS?

COMMUNISM IS JEWISH

Clean up America! Break the Red Plague!
BOYCOTT the JEW!

The Nazi leadership proclaimed a woman's battlefield to be the home, producing children for the Fatherland. Beginning in May 1939, prolific mothers were celebrated at ceremonies with the awarding of the Honor Cross of the German Mother. Recipients were granted special privileges and saluted by the Hitler Youth. The award had three classes: bronze for women who bore five children; silver for those with seven; and gold for those who truly excelled, producing nine or more children.

Heinrich Himmler

Heinrich Himmler has been called the "architect of genocide." He was the leader of the SS, head of the German police and *Waffen-SS*, and minister of the interior. In Nazi Germany, only Adolf Hitler held more power than Himmler.

Himmler was born into a middle-class Catholic family in Munich in 1900. He studied agriculture and economics but was most intrigued with Nazi politics. He joined the fledgling SS in 1925 and became its leader four years later.

Once the Nazis took power in 1933, Himmler gained control of the police in both Munich and Bavaria. He opened the Dachau concentration camp in March of that year. By the summer of 1936, he controlled the political and criminal police throughout the Third Reich. Himmler gained a reputation as a ruthless perfectionist skilled at organizing terror tactics.

Ruling the concentration and death camps, Himmler directly controlled the Holocaust's process of destruction. In a speech to his SS leaders on October 4, 1943, he called the extermination of Jews "a page of glory in our history," and praised the "decent fellows" who were carrying it out.

Himmler's end was as inglorious as his Nazi career had been indecent. Captured by British troops while wearing a clumsy disguise, he evaded trial when he killed himself by swallowing poison on May 23, 1945.

• An antisemitic film comedy, *Robert und Bertram*, is produced in Germany. • In the United States, the House Un-American Activities Committee (HUAC) investigates the pro-Nazi German-American Bund. • An Elmo Roper poll claims that 53 percent of Americans feel Jews are "different" and require "social and economic restrictions." • A Gallup poll reports that 83 percent of Americans oppose the admission of a larger number of Jewish refugees. • Based on instructions coming from the State Department, a United States consular official in Stuttgart, Germany, tells Ernest Michel, a German Jew who has an American sponsor, that all U.S. immigration quotas are filled and that he should reapply for admission to the United States in three years. Ironically, 1939 was the *only* year in which U.S. quotas were filled.

• January 1939: "Illegal immigration" begins from Germany to Palestine. 27,000 Jews will illegally immigrate by the end of 1940. • *Reichsbank* President Hjalmar Schacht informs Adolf Hitler that Germany's economy is on the verge of a disastrous inflation.

Adolf Hitler celebrates the sixth anniversary of his appointment as German chancellor with a major foreign policy address. Standing in front of the newly reconstituted German *Reichstag,* Hitler threatens to exterminate the Jews of Europe if war breaks out between Germany and the Western Allies. Seen as sensationalist propaganda at the time, the threat to destroy European Jewry assumed prophetic proportions in the aftermath of the Holocaust.

"Today I will once more be a prophet! If the international Jewish financiers inside and outside Europe should again succeed in plunging the nations into a world war, the result will not be the bolshevization of the earth and thus the victory of Jewry, but the annihilation of the Jewish race throughout Europe."

—*Adolf Hitler, addressing the Reichstag;*
January 30, 1939

In February 1939 leaders of the Jewish Agency for Palestine met with Arab leaders at the St. James Palace Conference to discuss the future of Palestine. The London meetings were called by the British government to ease the escalating tensions between Arabs and Jews living under the British Mandate. When the conference participants failed to reach an agreement, the British issued the MacDonald White Paper, which severely curtailed Jewish immigration to Palestine and limited Jewish land purchases.

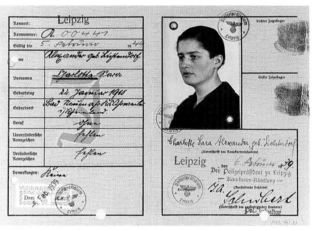

In order for the Nazis to carry out their antisemitic policies, they had to know who was a Jew. One way of determining a person's "racial" background was through the use of identity cards, which all Jews were required to carry. The large "J" on the left identified the bearer as a Jew. After August 17, 1938, all Jewish women had to adopt the middle name "Sara" and Jewish men "Israel."

1939

• **January 1, 1939: As decreed on August 17, 1938, Jewish men in Germany must adopt the middle name of "Israel"; Jewish women must take the middle name "Sara." • Jews are eliminated from the German economy; their capital is seized, though some Jews continue to work under Germans. • At the Buchenwald, Germany, concentration camp, Deputy Commandant Arthur** Rödl orders several thousand inmates to assemble for inspection shortly before midnight. He selects five men and has them whipped to the melody played by the inmate orchestra. The whipping continues all night.

• **January 5, 1939: Germany declares Karaite Jews exempt from enforcement of the Nuremberg Laws.**

As part of a propaganda effort to ready Germany's civilian populace for war, ration cards were issued in 1939. This card, issued to 26-year-old Brunhilde Brandt in Berlin, stipulated the number of products that she could purchase, from milk to potatoes to sugar. Ration cards brought home the need for sacrifice on the home front, as well as on the battle front.

German passports issued to Jews became invalid after October 5, 1938, unless stamped with a "J" indicating the Jewish origin of the bearer. This passport, granted to Lore Oppenheimer of Hildesheim in 1939, allowed Oppenheimer to emigrate to the United States via the United Kingdom. Note that the middle name is given as "Sara" in accordance with German law.

A department of the SS, the *Rasse- und Siedlungshauptamt* (RuSHA; Main Office for Race and Resettlement) was originally charged with maintaining the racial purity of the SS. Following German expansion to the East, it orchestrated "Germanization" of the newly conquered areas and monitored the welfare of the settlers. Ethnic Germans were transplanted to areas designated for settlement by the SS. Here, a female representative of the Nazi Party and an official of RuSHA explain the new measures to several ethnic German (*Volksdeutsch*) women in German-occupied Poland.

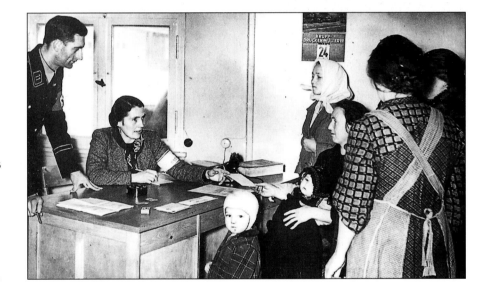

• **January 24, 1939:** Nazi *Generalfeldmarschall* Hermann Göring orders Reinhard Heydrich to establish a Jewish Emigration Office. Heydrich appoints Gestapo chief Heinrich Müller to head it.

• **January 30, 1939:** On the sixth anniversary of his appointment as chancellor, Hitler threatens in the *Reichstag* that if war breaks out, the result will be the extermination of Europe's Jews. Ridiculing the Western Allies' lack of humanitarian action in regard to the Jews, he notes that "it is a shameful spectacle to see how the whole democratic world is oozing sympathy for the poor, tormented Jewish people, but remains hard-hearted and obdurate when it comes to helping them."

• **February 3, 1939:** A bomb destroys a Budapest, Hungary, synagogue, killing one worshipper.

• **February 7–20, 1939:** The St. James Palace Conference is held in London to find a peaceful solution to the political stalemate in Palestine. Jewish delegates withdraw when Arab delegates refuse to meet with their Jewish coun-

The Occupation of Prague

When German troops marched into Prague, Czechoslovakia, on March 15, 1939, Hitler declared that history would remember him as the greatest German of all time. To Prague, certainly, he was the most destructive of interlopers.

By seizing the Czech provinces of Bohemia and Moravia, Hitler delivered 120,000 Jews into the hands of the SS. Half of Prague's roughly 50,000 Jews were refugees from Germany. Forced to flee again, many sought refuge in Poland and Hungary. Thousands appealed in vain for asylum in Western Europe. Within a half-year, more than 30,000 Jews were forced to emigrate.

Of the 90,000 who remained, only 10,000 would survive Nazi rule.

Nazi ordinances stripped Czech Jews of their livelihoods. Laws excluded them from professions, shut down businesses, froze bank accounts, and allowed for confiscation of property. SS terror campaigns featured staged anti-Jewish riots, antisemitic exhibitions, and systematic beatings of Jewish children in city parks. Strict curfews with heavy fines prompted special "hunts" for violators.

The Gestapo's mass expulsion policy demanded the emigration of 70,000 Jews within one year. Rounded up from the provinces and herded into Prague, a quota of 200 had to leave daily—and pay a "flight tax." With no place to go, many were loaded onto trains, transported to unknown destinations, or dumped at borders.

A poster advertising a "Pro-American Rally" sponsored by the German-American Bund was distributed throughout New York City. With the event scheduled to be held in Madison Square Garden, organizers hoped to attract thousands of sympathizers. Most of the 20,000 people who attended the event were members of Father Charles Coughlin's right-wing Christian Front.

A crowd of sullen-faced Czechs looks on as German motorized divisions enter Prague on March 15, 1939. The occupation of the remaining independent Czech lands openly violated the accords reached at the Munich Conference six months earlier. At those meetings, Hitler had assured the naive prime minister of Britain, Neville Chamberlain, that he had no desire for further territorial expansion. The fact that no nation took forcible action against his moves in Czechoslovakia greatly emboldened Hitler.

1939

terparts—and when British delegates support the Arab position.

• February 9, 1939: Anti-Jewish legislation is passed in Italy.

• February 10, 1939: Pope Pius XI dies. His unpublished encyclical on racism and antisemitism does not go beyond the Vatican's traditional policy concerning Jews. This policy is based on the doctrine of St. Augustine that the Jews are Cains who must not be killed but who must wander in suffering for all eternity, until they see the light and choose conversion to Roman Catholicism.

• February 20, 1939. The German-American Bund stages a rally in New

Among the groups persecuted on racial grounds in the Third Reich were the Sinti and Roma, or Gypsies. The Nazis considered the "criminal" lifestyle of the Gypsies to be genetically determined, like that, they felt, of the Jews. On September 21, 1939, Nazi authorities decided to deport Germany's Gypsies to Poland, where they were interned in special camps. Above is the title page of an article entitled, "Vagabonds: New Ways of Combating the Gypsies."

George Rublee, a confidant of U.S. President Franklin Roosevelt, led the Intergovernmental Committee on Political Refugees, a panel created by the British and American governments in 1938. They hoped that Rublee could negotiate with the German government to gain more favorable economic conditions for German refugees. Rublee, for example, wanted the German government to permit emigrants to take more of their property with them. His efforts ultimately failed, and he quit his post. This photograph shows Rublee as he arrived in the U.S. on the *Queen Mary* on February 23, 1939, shortly after his resignation.

Signifying ferocity and fearlessness, the gruesome skull and crossbones insignia was initially worn by men of the *Totenkopfverbände* (Death's Head Units). Wearing black uniforms and chosen for their toughness and discipline, these men comprised a special branch of the SS with responsibility for guarding the concentration camps. With the onset of war in 1939, these units became the core of the *Waffen-SS*.

York City. About 20,000 enthusiasts attend; they come mostly from Father Charles Coughlin's Christian Front.

• February 21, 1939: German Jews are required to surrender all gold and silver to government authorities.

• February–June 1939: New York Democratic Senator Robert F. Wagner, a German American, and Massachusetts Democratic Representative Edith Nourse Rogers jointly propose the Wagner-Rogers Bill to permit 20,000 German children (specifically, Jewish children) into the United States over a two-year period. The bill is tagged with so many amendments that, after hearings, it never leaves the the House or Senate. The bill does receive considerable support from the press and certain churches, and many individuals and organizations testify for or against the bill. But the antisemitism rife in the American public and Congress—and the lack of support from President Franklin Roosevelt—sink the bill. The Wagner-Rogers Bill's foremost opponent, Senator Robert Reynolds of North Carolina, has a secret relation-

German inhabitants of Memel salute a German armored column as it enters the city in late March 1939. A part of East Prussia since the 16th century, Memel and its environs were removed from Germany in 1919 and annexed by Lithuania in 1923. After assuming power in 1933, Hitler agitated for Memel's return to Germany. Before sending troops into Memel, the Nazi Party gradually seized control of local politics by supporting the efforts of Dr. Ernst Neumann.

Jeering members of the SA and SS laugh at this Jewish family from Memel as it flees the Nazi invaders. Most of the city's Lithuanian and Jewish population had left before the German takeover. The uncertainty and fear on the faces of these people illustrate the plight of those unfortunate enough to confront the Nazi juggernaut.

A crowd of 10,000 men, women, and children gathers at Columbus Circle in New York City to listen to speakers condemn the recent German takeover of Czechoslovakia. Many of the crowd were dressed in native Czech costumes and had participated in a "Stop Hitler Parade" held earlier in the day. Nazi activity in Europe polarized Americans of European descent. While those of Jewish, Czech, and Polish heritage campaigned against Hitler, many within the German-American communities supported the Nazi government before the outbreak of war in September 1939.

1939

ship with German-American Nazi agent August Gausebeck. Gausebeck's partner is Walter Schellenberg, the coordinator of Gestapo activities in the United States.

• Asked for her opinion on the bill, Mrs. James Houghteling, wife of the commissioner of immigration, whispers that the only problem with the Wagner-

Rogers bill is "that 20,000 ugly [Jewish] children would all too soon grow up into 20,000 ugly adults." Mrs. Houghteling is Laura Delano Houghteling, President Roosevelt's cousin. • As a result of Roosevelt's administration's policies, the United States offers refuge to fewer Jewish children—about 1000 from 1934 to 1945—than Belgium, France, Britain, Holland, or Sweden.

In March 1939 the British government attempted to expel ten Jewish refugees from Czechoslovakia because their passports were not in order. In response to threats that they would leap from an airplane flight scheduled to land in Warsaw, Poland, the pilot refused to take off. The following day, all ten were forced aboard a ship leaving for the Continent.

Fearing a possible German invasion, Polish cavalry train with lances that would be used to "joust" with tanks. While such tactics evidenced a great deal of bravery on the part of Polish soldiers, they were, of course, useless in the face of the Germans' modern machinery.

Hermann Göring

Hermann Göring, No. 2 in the Nazi Party, seemed the most accessible of all Nazi leaders. He was not a committed antisemite, and he claimed that he joined the Party as a "revolutionary—not because of any ideological nonsense."

A jovial, ebullient extrovert, able to laugh heartily at jokes about his rotund appearance, Göring seemed more human than Hitler or Joseph Goebbels. However, his jolly outward demeanor masked his inhumane traits. He was highly intelligent yet could be as brutal as any of his fellows, lacking conscience and moral compunctions when it came to treatment of prisoners at concentration camps. He thought himself a "Renaissance man," but vanity and greed proved him a Nazi sybarite, as he reveled in power and shamelessly acquired wealth.

An accomplished fighter pilot in World War I, Göring joined the Party in 1922 and rose rapidly in its cadre. He was elected to Parliament in 1928 and received a ministerial post in 1933. In 1934 he was appointed commander of the Air Force, and in 1936 he headed the Four-Year Plan that readied Germany's economy for war.

Failing to prevent Allied bombing of German cities, Göring fell into disfavor and retreated into drug use. After being sentenced to death at the Nuremberg Trials, he committed suicide by swallowing cyanide.

● **March 2, 1939:** Eugenio Cardinal Pacelli is elected as Pope Pius XII.

● **March 11, 1939:** Hungary enacts a law permitting the establishment of the Hungarian Labor Service System (*Munkaszolgálat*). Under the law, Jews of military age will be employed in construction, mining, and fortification work for the military.

● **March 15, 1939:** Nazi troops enter Czechoslovakia and occupy Prague. No nation takes forcible action against the move. Of roughly 50,000 Jews in the city, only 19,000 will escape from Europe. Tens of thousands of Jews are trapped when Nazi troops enter the Czech provinces of Bohemia and Moravia. Slovakia becomes a German satellite.

● **March 20, 1939:** About 5000 paintings, drawings, and sculptures deemed "degenerate" by the Nazis are burned on an enormous pyre in Berlin.

● **March 21, 1939:** Nazi troops enter Memel, Lithuania, forcing Jews there to flee. ● The French government passes legislation outlawing incitement to race hatred; *See* August 27, 1940.

Franklin Delano Roosevelt, president of the United States from 1933 to 1945, was acutely aware of the growing crisis in Europe. Confronted on one side by American Jews who wanted to throw open the doors of the United States to Jewish refugees, and on the other side by antisemitic and xenophobic groups that desired to keep out unwanted foreigners, Roosevelt attempted to remain above the fray. Ever the astute politician, Roosevelt welcomed lobbyists from both sides into the Oval Office, listened intently to their appeals, and perpetuated the status quo. Faced with an array of domestic problems, the crisis in Europe did not yet command his complete attention.

Female inmates at the Ravensbrück concentration camp in Germany are initiated into the Nazi terror system. The women's camp at Ravensbrück, 50 miles north of Berlin, officially opened on May 15, 1939. Like their male counterparts, female prisoners built the facilities that housed them and were required to work without regard to the weather. The spring rains of northern Germany made excavating activities extremely laborious.

Members of the Jewish community in Palestine took to the streets to protest a British decision to restrict Jewish immigration into Palestine. The MacDonald White Paper of May 17, 1939, limited Jewish immigration to 10,000 people a year for a period of five years. British government policy kept the actual numbers of Jewish immigrants far below the quotas set for Palestine.

1939

● **March 25, 1939:** As 500,000 people watch, 20,000 protestors march in a "Stop Hitler" parade held in New York City.

● **March 31, 1939:** British Prime Minister Neville Chamberlain announces that the U.K. and France will guarantee Poland's sovereignty.

● **April 1, 1939:** The Spanish Civil War ends, with Francisco Franco's Fascists the victors.

● **April 3, 1939:** The German government issues a secret directive for the seizure of Danzig, Poland, a "free city" that will figure in German preparation for a larger war.

HAMBURG-AMERIKA LINIE
(Compañía Hamburguesa Americana)

No. 2067

Touristenklasse
Clase Turista
Tourist Class

Motorschiff / St. Louis
motonave
motor vessel

am / 13. Mai 1939
à salir
sailing

von / Hamburg
de
from

nach / Havana
à
to

Name des Reisenden:
nombre del pasajero:
passenger's name:

The Hamburg-America Line issued this ticket to Moritz Schoenberg on the *St. Louis* for passage from Hamburg, Germany, to Havana, Cuba. Note that the fare was RM 508.75, a princely sum.

The St. Louis

The tragic story of the journey of the German ocean liner *St. Louis* epitomized the desperate and futile struggle of Jews trying to escape Germany.

On May 15, 1939, the Nazis allowed more than 900 Jews on the liner, which set sail for Cuba. Hopeful passengers carried what they

believed were valid permits guaranteeing them temporary stay until visas and permanent refuge in the United States could be secured. Shockingly, on arrival at Havana, Cuba, only 29 were allowed to disembark. The rest were refused entry under revised Cuban immigration restrictions. When the ship was ordered to leave the harbor, several passengers attempted suicide. Cuban police boats shadowed the *St. Louis* in case passengers tried to jump ship.

For three days the liner cruised slowly off the U.S. coast, waiting in vain for America to accept its human cargo. In mid-June, after 35 days of aimless sailing, the *St. Louis* was forced to return to Europe, where the governments of England, France, Holland, and Belgium finally agreed to divide the passengers between them. The world's press followed the ship's sad journey, even recording it on newsreels.

Renate and Innes Spanier, twin girls on board the ill-fated refugee ship *St. Louis,* look from a porthole while waiting to set sail for Cuba. When the *St. Louis* was denied entrance to both Cuba and the United States and forced to return to Europe, the Spanier family was granted asylum in Holland. During the war they were deported to Westerbork, Holland, where their father served as the head physician. After their liberation, the family emigrated to the United States.

● **April 4, 1939:** The *Institut zur Erforschung des jüdischen Einflusses auf das deutsche kirchliche Leben* (Institute for the Study of Jewish Influence on German Church Life) is founded.

● **April 7, 1939:** Great Britain institutes conscription. ● Italian forces occupy Albania.

● **April 10, 1939:** Voters in Greater Germany approve the *Anschluss–* Germany's annexation of Austria in 1938.

● **April 15, 1939:** United States President Franklin Roosevelt asks Hitler to respect the independence of European nations; *See* April 28, 1939.

● **April 18, 1939:** Anti-Jewish legislation in Slovakia defines Jews by religion.

● **April 20, 1939:** The *Wirtschafts- und Verwaltungshauptamt* (WVHA; Economy and Administration Main Office) is upgraded. It is concerned with SS economic matters, particularly at concentration camps.

Julius Streicher

Next to Hitler, Julius Streicher was arguably the Nazi Party's most outspoken and most virulent antisemite. He was surly and utterly crude. His fondness for beating political prisoners with a riding whip was exceeded only by his shameless eagerness to amass personal wealth from confiscated Jewish property.

A decorated veteran of World War I, Streicher blamed Jews for the loss of the war and for Germany's misfortune. In 1919 he became leader of an antisemitic political party in Bavaria, and two years later joined the Nazi Party, bringing his own supporters with him. By 1923 he had established his own journal, the notorious *Der Stürmer (The Stormer)*.

The illustrated weekly consisted of lurid, coarsely written stories of Jewish ritual murder and rape of Christian girls. Displayed in public places and widely read, *Der Stürmer's* vulgar pornographic cartoons graphically depicted stereotyped images of Jews. Bold headlines warned of Jewish plots against Aryans and urged boycotts of Jewish businesses. During World War II his paper supported Nazi extermination policies.

Streicher rose within the ranks of the Party to become *Gauleiter* of Franconia. However, corruption, sexual depravity, and conflict with other high Party officials ultimately led to his dismissal from Party posts. He was hanged for crimes against humanity in 1946.

Not everyone was unsympathetic to the plight of Europe's Jews. Among those who favored helping them was American comic film actor Joe E. Brown. He's pictured here testifying before the House Immigration Committee in support of a bill that would admit 20,000 German refugee children to the United States. Brown did his part by adopting two German-Jewish boys.

A group of German-Jewish refugee children enjoys a game of leapfrog at a suburban estate outside of Philadelphia, Pennsylvania. Approximately 50 children received free ocean passage and were housed at this estate until foster homes were found. Securing entry into the United States required a combination of money, connections, and luck. Without all three, European Jews were prevented from entering the United States, in spite of the fact that the immigration quotas remained unfilled.

1939

• **April 28, 1939:** Hitler offers a mocking response to United States President Franklin Roosevelt's April 15 request to respect the independence of European nations.

• **April 30, 1939:** Tenancy protection for Jews in Germany is revoked. This will pave the way for their relocation to "communal Jewish houses."

• **May 1939:** In Hungary, discriminatory laws are passed against Jews engaged in law and medicine. Jewish participation in the economy is restricted to six percent.

• **May 3, 1939:** Hoping to establish rapprochement with Nazi Germany, Soviet leader Joseph Stalin replaces his Jewish commissar for foreign affairs, Mak-

French Premier Edouard Daladier *(left)* and British Minister of War Leslie Hore-Belisha stand shoulder to shoulder during a military parade marking the 150th anniversary of Bastille Day on July 14, 1939. The staged demonstration celebrated the military might of the "United Front" and included British planes, sailors, and marines. A few days prior to the parade, 100 British bombing planes flew from England far over French territory and back in a formidable display of potential power.

The headline of this June 1939 edition of Julius Streicher's *Der Stürmer* reads, "Search for Jewish Legacy: Jews and the German Waltz King Johann Strauss/The Intrigues of the Jewess Menszner-Strauss/A Lamentable Talmudism." It was typical of the Nazis to blame perceived faults in German cultural figures upon those figures' Jewish wives. The cartoon shows the "Jewish Devil-Snake" assaulting an Aryan maiden. The Talmud is in the background. Many National Socialist publications regularly depicted Jewish religious texts as founts of evil, eternally dangerous to the German people. Typical of *Der Stürmer*, this front-page graphic skates close to pornography. The paper's unashamed emphasis on titillation—typically via the cartoons of "Fips," a pseudonym for artist Philip Rupprecht—attracted more than its share of undiscriminating readers. The weekly paper's paid circulation was by this time about 500,000.

Czech and German Jews arrive in Rhodes on a refugee ship en route to Palestine. Following the *Kristallnacht* pogroms, the pace of Jewish emigration from the greater German Reich intensified in spite of the limited space aboard ships, the rarity of visa entries, and the difficulty of obtaining the necessary travel documents. Between November 1938 and September 1939, approximately 150,000 Jews fled Germany.

sim Litvinov, with the less British-oriented Viacheslav Molotov.

• May 15, 1939: A women's concentration camp opens at Ravensbrück, 50 miles north of Berlin. • The German refugee ship *St. Louis* leaves Hamburg. Most of the thousand or so passengers are Jewish escapees from Nazi Germany. They have landing passes for Cuba as well as quota numbers that could allow them entry into the United States three years hence; *See* June 1939.

• May 17, 1939: The British government issues a White Paper (commonly called the MacDonald White Paper) that limits Jewish immigration to 10,000 a year for five years. The White Paper allows 75,000 Jewish immigrants (up to 10,000 per year, plus an additional 25,000 if certain conditions are met) to enter Palestine. The White Paper also restricts Jewish land purchases in Palestine. British government policy will succeed in keeping the actual numbers of Jewish immigrants far below the quotas for settlement in England and Palestine.

Among the activities sponsored by the Jewish Cultural League were productions of operas composed by Jews. This photograph shows children engaged in promoting the League during the intermission of a performance of the operetta *Gräfin Mariza* in Berlin in July 1939. The League's leadership believed that getting children involved was vital to maintaining the existence of German-Jewish culture.

Jewish children wave goodbye as they depart from the Zbaszyń, Poland, refugee camp set up in October 1938. As part of the *Kindertransport* program that brought Jewish children to Britain, the youths pictured here could look forward to a secure future. Most of the 10,000 Jews interned in Zbaszyń, however, were not so fortunate. An agreement between Poland and Germany brought most of the Jews back to Poland.

The Executive Committee of the *Jüdische Kulturbund* (Jewish Cultural League) meets in July 1939. Among those present were the director, Fritz Wisten *(extreme left)*, conductor Rudolf Schwarz *(third from right)*, and Werner Levie, a former journalist for the Ullstein papers *(far right)*. In 1937 1425 artists were members of the league, which played an important role in the preservation of German-Jewish culture until the following year, when increased persecution caused the league's influence to wane.

1939

• **May 22, 1939:** Germany signs a "Pact of Steel" with Italy. • Ernst Toller, a German-Jewish playwright in exile in New York City, commits suicide.

• **June 1939:** The German refugee ship *St. Louis* reaches Cuba. But after extortionate demands for money are made by the Cuban government, the *St. Louis* departs Cuba and sails along the east coast of the United States. President Roosevelt orders the Coast Guard to prevent any of the passengers from landing in the U.S., even should they jump ship; *See* June 17, 1939.

• **June 2, 1939:** The Boston, Massachusetts, newspaper of the Christian Science Church attacks Jewish refugees as causing their own troubles, a posi-

Smoke billows from the ship *Rim* off the island of Rhodes, while local residents look on from the shore. The boat was carrying 600 illegal Romanian immigrants bound for Palestine when it ran aground and burned. Although the British government had effectively closed Palestine to legal migration, thousands of European Jews attempted to escape the Nazi onslaught by entering Palestine illegally.

Left: Jewish refugees from the ship SS *Patria* make their way to shore in lifeboats after sailing from Europe to Tel Aviv. British restrictions placed on Jewish immigration compelled these Jewish refugees to enter Palestine illegally. *Above:* After a deliberate landing of the boat on a sand bank off the coast of Tel Aviv, the 850 European Jewish immigrants on board the *Patria* were arrested by British officials and interned in a detention center near Haifa.

tion taken by many important Protestant journals of the time.

• June 17, 1939: After being denied access to Cuba and the United States, the German refugee ship *St. Louis* docks in Antwerp, Belgium. Belgium offers to take 214 passengers, the Netherlands 181, Britain 287, and France 224. Ultimately, the Nazis will

murder most of the passengers except for those accepted by Great Britain.

• July 30, 1939: Reacting to German anti-Jewish policies and reflecting the attitude of many other officials in Great Britain and Western Europe, British Prime Minister Neville Chamberlain writes: "No doubt Jews aren't a lovable people; I don't care about them myself.

But that is not sufficient to explain the pogrom."

• August 2, 1939: Concerned that the Germans could be the first to develop an atomic bomb, expatriate German physicist Albert Einstein writes to President Franklin Roosevelt about developing an American bomb.

Joachim von Ribbentrop

The Non-Aggression Pact between Germany and the Soviet Union, signed on August 23, 1939, postponed the inevitable military clash of the two powers, and set the stage for the German invasion of Poland. The Ribbentrop-Molotov Pact, as the agreement also was called, contained a secret protocol that divided Poland between the two larger nations. Seen here, from right, are Russian Foreign Minister Viacheslav Molotov, Russian dictator Joseph Stalin, and German Foreign Minister Joachim von Ribbentrop.

Ecstatic with the foreign policy triumphs of 1938–39, Hitler hailed his foreign minister, Joachim von Ribbentrop, as "a second Bismarck" and a "genius." Most others saw Ribbentrop as an arrogant, incompetent upstart (nicknamed "von Ribbensnob") and a fawning flatterer of the *Führer.*

Joseph Goebbels, the Reich press chief, described Ribbentrop as "witless and undiplomatic, touchy and subservient." Goebbels contemptuously remarked that Ribbentrop had  "bought his name, married his money, and swindled his way into office."

Ribbentrop's marriage into a wealthy champagne-producing family, his foreign business contacts, and his command of languages made him appear to Hitler as a man of the world. Although Ribbentrop was a latecomer to the Party, Hitler nonetheless rapidly promoted him within the foreign office. In 1935, as ambassador-at-large, Ribbentrop negotiated the Anglo-German Naval Agreement.

Ribbentrop became ambassador to Britain in 1936 and the Reich's foreign minister in 1938. He convinced Hitler that Britain was weak and unwilling to oppose aggressive German policies. In negotiating the 1939 nonaggression pact with the Soviet Union, Ribbentrop paved the way for the conquest of Nazi *Lebensraum.*

The unscrupulous diplomat was found guilty of war crimes in 1946. Showing no remorse, he was the first Nazi defendant hanged at Nuremberg.

Hitler addresses the *Reichstag* on September 1, 1939. Germany's war with Poland—and his biggest-yet grab for "living space"—had begun. Hostilities were initiated following a foolish masquerade in which German soldiers dressed in Polish Army uniforms attacked a radio station in the German border town of Gleiwitz.

1939

- **August 17, 1939:** The Reich Ministry of the Interior publishes a listing of allowable first names Jewish parents may give their new babies.

- **August 19, 1939:** The Romanian-Jewish refugee ship *Rim*, bound for Palestine, runs aground and burns at Rhodes, Italy.

- **August 22, 1939:** Hitler's speech to generals urges the liquidation of Poles in the forthcoming war in order to gain *Lebensraum* ("Living space") for Germans.

- **August 23, 1939:** The German-Soviet Non-Aggression Pact (Ribbentrop-Molotov Pact) is signed in Moscow, freeing Hitler for the moment from the

A German military train bound for Poland at the outbreak of the war bears an inscription that reads, "We are traveling to Poland to thrash the Jews." With 3.3 million Jews residing in Poland, Nazi plans for the racial reordering of Europe were put to their first major test. Rapid military victories were followed by massive relocations of Polish gentiles and Jews. Jews were concentrated in urban centers and placed under the authority of the SS. The process of ghettoization was an important step in the future destruction of Polish Jewry.

Orthodox Jews in Poland were pressed into service once the war with Germany began. Unlike in Western and Central Europe, where most Jews were highly acculturated and difficult to distinguish from their fellow countrymen, many Jews of Eastern Europe were readily identifiable by virtue of their traditional garb and use of Yiddish, the vernacular language of East European Jewry. The two bearded men in the foreground wear clothing typical of Poland's Orthodox Jews.

German troops and Polish civilians stand on the outskirts of Warsaw as smoke rises from the burning city. The German ground invasion of Poland on September 1, 1939, was accompanied by an extensive aerial campaign that decimated Warsaw and other Polish cities. Although the Poles fought valiantly against the invading Germans, the Polish Army was no match for Hitler's finely tuned military machine. The Nazis threw 1.5 million men against a Polish Army that was outnumbered three to one and unprepared to defend against the lightning-fast pincers movements that were executed by Nazi armor and ground forces.

worry of an Eastern Front war. The pact contains a secret protocol on the disposition of Poland, which will be divided between the two larger nations.

● August 25, 1939: The Anglo-Polish Alliance is signed, by which Great Britain will assist Poland should Poland become the victim of aggression.

● August 27, 1939: The German economy shifts to a wartime footing. The Nazi government issues restrictive *Lebensmittelkarten* (ration cards) to Gypsies and resident aliens within the borders of the Reich. Ration cards for Jews restrict the holders to a starvation diet of 200 to 300 calories per day.

● August 30, 1939: Because of a protracted shooting schedule in New York, popular Polish-Jewish film stars Leon Liebgold and Lili Liliana miss their ship back to Poland two days before the Nazi invasion of their homeland. The couple remains in New York.

● August 31, 1939: Sixty German-Jewish children are shepherded by

"If we lose the war, then Heaven have mercy on us!"

—*Hermann Göring, September 1939*

Before the Nazi invasion, Warsaw, Poland, was one of Eastern Europe's centers of Jewish culture, with a vibrant population of well over 350,000 Jews. This is a photograph taken in the city's Jewish Quarter. Polish Jews had heard about Nazi atrocities against their German co-religionists and were justifiably concerned about the future.

The invading German Army passes through a burning city in Poland. The overwhelmingly superior firepower of the Germans crushed cities and towns alike. The wood-framed houses common in Poland went up in flames like matchboxes. While the German military machine relied on its air force and tank divisions to annihilate the enemy, many Poles utilized horse-drawn wagons to escape the advancing armies. Speed was critical, however, and whole Polish divisions that attempted to pull back were surrounded and wiped out. By September 3, just two days after the *Wehrmacht* crossed the Polish border, Poland's air force had ceased to exist.

Hitler authorized the "euthanasia" program known as Operation T-4 with this letter signed in October 1939, but backdated to September 1. *Reichsleiter* Philip Bouhler and Dr. Karl Brandt administered the program, in which doctors identified individuals as incurable and, after superficially examining them, put them to death. Operation T-4, which went into effect immediately, exemplified the radicalization of Nazi racial policies: Those deemed unworthy of life were systematically destroyed.

1939

train and boat through Holland to safety in the British port city of Harwich.

• **September 1939:** Nazis intern tens of thousands of Spanish Republicans in France before sending them to slave labor at stone quarries at Mauthausen, Austria. • Leading Jewish-German jurist Gerhard Leibholz, stripped of his

position at the University of Göttingen in 1936, escapes to Switzerland with his wife and two daughters.

• **September 1, 1939:** German forces overrun western Poland, instigating World War II. Three thousand Jewish civilians die in the bombing of Warsaw. German troops enter Danzig, trapping more than 5000 Jews. Throughout Ger-

"Euthanasia" and Operation T-4

In October 1939 Adolf Hitler wrote the following memo: "Reich Leader [Philip] Bouhler and Dr. med. [Karl] Brandt are charged with the responsibility of enlarging the authority of certain physicians, designated by name, so that patients who, on the basis of human judgment, are considered incurable, can be granted a mercy death after a discerning diagnosis."

Those words authorized a systematic Nazi program to eliminate *lebensunwertes Leben* ("life unworthy of life"). These "worthless" people included mentally and physically disabled Germans and Austrians, children and adults, who were regarded as a blight on the Third Reich's "racial integrity" and as an unacceptable economic burden for the state. Although Hitler signed the authorization for this so-called "euthanasia" program in October 1939, the document was backdated to September 1—the day World War II began—to create the impression that the "mercy killings" were a wartime necessity.

The euthanasia campaign, called Operation T-4, was code-named after the address of the confiscated Jewish villa at *Tiergartenstrasse* 4, which was the address of the program's central

administrative offices. Hitler chose Bouhler, the head of his private Chancellery, and Dr. Brandt, one of his doctors, to oversee T-4. However, responsibility for its day-to-day implementation fell to Viktor Brack and his deputy, Werner Blanken-

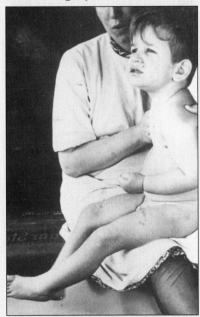

berg. Statistics show that under the leadership of these men, 70,000 to 80,000 people—including 4000 to 5000 Jews—became victims of the euthanasia killings.

The Nazis tried to conceal what was happening, but when public protests exploded—many of them from Germany's Catholic and Lutheran leaders—

Hitler officially halted Operation T-4 on August 24, 1941. Nevertheless, the killing continued in greater secrecy until the spring of 1945. From 1939 through 1945, Operation T-4 and other euthanasia actions murdered between 200,000 and 250,000 disabled people.

Medical personnel selected who would die based on data gathered from hospitals, nursing homes, and other public health facilities. The patients selected to die were transported to one of six euthanasia centers in Germany and Austria: Hartheim, Sonnenstein, Grafeneck, Bernburg, Hadamar, or Brandenburg. The doctors, nurses, and other specialists who worked at these centers employed different methods of murder. Starvation and lethal injection were used at first, but eventually the method of choice was gassing with carbon monoxide in chambers disguised as tiled showers. After gold teeth were harvested, the corpses were burned in crematoria.

Operation T-4 anticipated the Holocaust. The euthanasia program's ideology of racial purity, methods of destruction, and administrative personnel would play key roles in the "Final Solution."

many and Austria, Jews may not be outside after 8:00 P.M. in the winter and 9:00 P.M. in the summer.

• **September 1–October 25, 1939:** Operation Tannenberg, carried out by SS *Einsatzgruppen* (mobile kill squads), leads to the murders of Polish Jews and Catholic intellectuals and to the burnings of synagogues in Poland.

• **September 2, 1939:** In Stutthof, Poland, a subcamp is established for "civilian prisoners of war." • As 1400 Jews escaping from Poland, Romania, Bulgaria, and Czechoslovakia land on a Tel Aviv, Palestine, beach, British soldiers shoot and kill two refugees.

• **September 3, 1939:** Great Britain and France declare war on Germany. The

British government cancels all visas previously granted to "enemy nationals"; one effect is that German Jews can no longer immigrate to safety in England. • At a meeting of the Jewish Agency Executive, an organization informally recognized as the ad hoc Jewish government of Palestine, David Ben-Gurion vows that Jews will fight Hitler. A total of a million and a half

Young Jewish men volunteer for service in the British Armed Forces at a recruitment office in Tel Aviv, Palestine. The poster in the background reads, "Your place is here, enlist!" With the outbreak of war in Europe, David Ben-Gurion of the Jewish Agency Executive encouraged Jews to join the struggle against Hitler. About 26,000 Palestinian Jews as well as 90,000 from the British Commonwealth fought in the British Army.

This photograph, which would eventually become an antisemitic postcard, pictures Jews from the Polish town of Biatek, which the Germans destroyed during their invasion. A German caption accompanying the picture reads: "The Jews are the first to return to the completely destroyed town of Biatek, where they descend like vultures upon the empty shops." The Nazis had very little sympathy for their victims, whom they demonized even as they ruthlessly persecuted them. Hitler ordered that all Poles be evicted from their homeland or killed in order to create *Lebensraum*—"Living space"—for arriving Germans.

A group of Poles from the town of Czestochowa awaits execution at the hands of the Nazi *Einsatzgruppen*, special SS murder squads charged with capturing and eliminating enemies of the German Reich. In Poland the executions were limited largely, but not exclusively, to gentiles. The primary victims were political opponents of Nazism—individuals who were seen as threats to German hegemony.

1939

Jews will fight in the armed forces of nations opposing Germany: 555,000 Jewish servicemen and women in the American Armed Forces; 500,000 for the Soviet Union; 116,000 for Great Britain (26,000 from Palestine and 90,000 from the British Commonwealth); and 243,000 Jews for other European nations.

• September 6, 1939: German forces occupy Kraków, Poland.

• September 8, 1939: German forces occupy Lódź, Radom, and Tarnów, Poland.

• September 14, 1939: German forces occupy Przemyśl, Poland.

Two Polish Jews are forced to dig their own graves. This was a common practice throughout the Holocaust. Not only did this reduce the work of the Nazi murderers, but it also had the effect of further denigrating the victims as they went to their deaths. The dehumanization of the victims made it easier for the Germans to carry out their grisly tasks.

The Jews of the *Generalgouvernement* had to make way for German resettlement in the region. For this reason, increasing numbers of Jews were deported to urban ghettos. This photograph shows a German policeman posting a notice stating that this house has been requisitioned for a German family who will eventually settle in the region. The Jews received no compensation for the property seized from them. This widespread practice contributed dramatically to overcrowding in the ghettos.

Jehovah's Witnesses

From 1933 to 1945, the Nazis imprisoned 10,000 Jehovah's Witnesses, executing more than 200 for refusing military service. As many as 5000 died in concentration camps. Despite persecution, Witnesses clung fervently to their religious beliefs, which did not allow the bearing of arms, and steadfastly refused to swear allegiance to the Nazi state.

Even before the Nazis came to power, SA thugs routinely disrupted Witness Bible-study sessions, beating up participants. After 1933 the regime launched a vigorous attack, banning the organization. The Gestapo compiled membership lists, and raids confiscated illegal literature, such as *The Watchtower*. To defy the ban meant arrest, imprisonment, and loss of jobs and social welfare benefits. Children were shunned, ridiculed, and expelled from school for refusing to give the *Sieg Heil* salute.

In 1935 the Nazis sent 400 Witnesses to the Sachsenhausen concentration camp in Germany for rejecting the newly enacted military draft. By 1939 camps held approximately 6000 Witnesses. After 1939 the Nazis deported Witnesses from occupied countries to camps as well. Marked with purple triangular patches, Jehovah's Witnesses continued to proselytize in camps, despite threat of execution, hard labor, brutal torture, and savage beatings with steel whips. Few accepted the Nazi offer of freedom in return for signing a declaration renouncing their beliefs.

• September 17, 1939: Eastern Poland is invaded by the Soviet Union.

• September 20, 1939: All radios owned by Jews in Greater Germany are confiscated.

• September 21, 1939: SS Security Service chief Reinhard Heydrich orders chiefs of *Einsatzgruppen* to establish, in cooperation with German civil and military authorities, Jewish ghettos in German-occupied Poland. He decrees that all Jewish communities in Poland and Greater Germany with populations under 500 are to be dissolved, so that deportations of Jews to urban ghettos and concentration camps can be accelerated. Further, Heydrich orders the establishment of ghetto *Judenräte* (Jewish councils). The main goals of the ghettoization process are to isolate Jews, force them to manufacture items for Germany, and provide easy Nazi access for murder and deportation.

• September 22, 1939: The *Reichssicherheitshauptamt* (RSHA; State Security Main Office) is founded.

Jewish Responses

Of the half-million Jews living in Germany when Hitler came to power, most critically underestimated the danger confronting them. Considering themselves loyal members of the German community, they hoped to persevere and ride out the Nazi storm. Most awakened only slowly to the full extent of the terror. By then it was too late.

A large number of Jews fled in panic during 1933, but mass emigration was unrealistic. Jewish community leaders advised that the best response was to rally together and organize for mutual aid. Local and national Jewish community groups called on the Jewish public to contribute funds for those who had lost livelihoods and homes. Monetary aid and soup kitchens for the poor provided immediate help. Employment agencies, as well as technical and agricultural retraining programs, focused on long-range economic support.

Social and cultural needs sparked a revival of Jewish traditions that boosted morale. The Jewish Cultural Association sponsored work for Jewish actors and musicians. Sports competitions and newly created Jewish schools tried to provide stability and normalcy for young people, while adult-education classes, lectures, and increased synagogue attendance fostered an awareness of religious heritage and shared experience. In effect, persecuted German Jews created a parallel society—separate and, of course, unequal.

This response was based on a not-unreasonable Jewish assumption that, although the Nazis had declared themselves enemies of the Jews, surely they would allow Jews to exist in segregated communities. Deportation and mass murder were considered by hopeful Jews as impossibilities.

After the German invasion, the Polish corridor, including the disputed city of Danzig (today called Gdansk), returned to Germany. Hitler utilized the disagreement over the region to increase pressure on Poland in the months preceding the attack. This photograph shows Germans in Danzig saluting the removal of the Polish eagle from one of the city's buildings.

The radio was the most important method of communication in Nazi Germany. Because authorities wished to cut off the Jewish population from the outside world, Jews had to surrender their radios to local authorities or face severe punishment.

1939

• September 23, 1939: On this Jewish Day of Atonement, Jews across Poland are publicly humiliated by SS troops: forced labor, coerced shavings of beards, destruction of property, beatings, and forced dancing. At Piotrków, Poland, Jews are compelled to relieve themselves in the local synagogue school, then use prayer shawls and holy books to clean up the mess.

• September 24, 1939: Jewish prisoners of war kept at Zyardow Stadium in Poland for ten days without food are forced to clean latrines with their bare hands.

• September 27, 1939: Warsaw, Poland, falls to German troops. • Berlin issues a command to establish Jewish ghettos in Poland. • Inmates at the Dachau,

Among the thousands of Eastern European synagogues destroyed by the German invaders was this one in Inowroclaw, Poland. The demolition of synagogues was part of Nazi Germany's efforts to eradicate Jewish culture in the lands they conquered. Often, before they destroyed Jewish religious centers, the Germans would desecrate the sacred objects held there, such as Torah scrolls.

Jews from Tluste, a small village located in the Ukraine, are forced to remove their clothing before being killed. Expected to relocate Jews from the Polish countryside to urban centers, the *Einsatzgruppen* faced a formidable task. They often decided to kill the Jews right on the spot rather than transport them hundreds of miles to the nearest ghetto. After eradicating Polish Jewry from the countryside, the *Einsatzgruppen* completed their missions by burning Jewish houses and places of worship.

One of the favorite forms of "entertainment" for the German invaders of Poland was to shear the beards of Orthodox Jews. This photograph shows SS troops from the *Leibstandarte* (bodyguard regiment) "Adolf Hitler" forcibly shaving an Orthodox Jew in Lublin, Poland. Not only was this humiliating for the victim, but it also violated the religious scruples of many Eastern European Jews.

Germany, concentration camp are moved to a camp at Mauthausen, Austria, so that Dachau can be used as a training camp for the *Waffen-SS*; *See* February 19, 1940.

• **September 28, 1939:** Poland surrenders, and the country is partitioned between Germany and the Soviet Union. • The SS selects the start of the weeklong Jewish festival of Sukkot to forcibly deport more than 8000 Jews from Pultusk, Poland.

• **September–December 1939:** German administrative divisions of Eastern Europe are established. They are Greater Danzig (northern Poland), West Prussia (northern Europe on the Baltic), Greater East Prussia (northern Europe on the Baltic), and the Warthegau (western Poland). Jews are forcibly expelled from these areas.

• **October 1939:** In Vienna, Austria, *Übersiedlungsaktion* (Resettlement action) is instituted against able-bodied Jewish men. These Jews are deported to Poland for forced labor. • Nazis begin the internment of Polish "men-

Hans Frank

Vanquished Poland became the testing ground for the "Final Solution." There, the Nazis practiced and perfected their extermination methods under Hans Frank, governor-general of Occupied Poland.

Frank, the former Nazi minister of justice, proclaimed Poland a colony and its people the "slaves of the German Reich." He in turn annihilated the Polish aristocracy, military and political leaders, priests, and intelligentsia. He robbed art treasures, exploited material resources, and forced tens of thousands into slave labor. As people suffered, Frank  lived ostentatiously in the royal palace in Kraków.

However, Frank's power steadily eroded in jurisdictional disputes with the SS. Frustrated by the dumping of Jews into his territory, he lamented the difficulty of "shooting or poisoning three and a half million Jews," but pledged to "take measures" which would "lead, somehow, to their annihilation." Six million perished during the Nazi seizure and occupation of Poland; more than half were Jews. In 1946 Frank was executed as a war criminal.

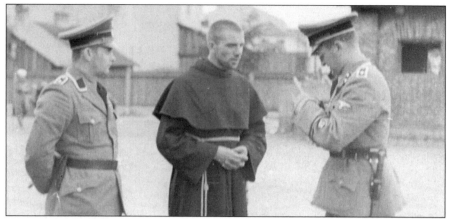

A Polish cleric is detained for questioning by members of the German Security Service (SD). These security forces were commanded by Reinhard Heydrich, the right-hand man of Heinrich Himmler. The SD was a crucial instrument of the German occupational forces, and was especially active in the campaigns against the Jews. Once the German military had defeated the enemy, members of the SD and other branches of the German SS went into action. Members of the SD tended to be fanatically in tune with the ideals of National Socialism.

Inmates at the Stutthof concentration camp in Danzig, Poland, line up for food. Designed to house "civilian prisoners of war," the Stutthof camp was populated by Jews and other opponents of the Nazi regime. As the German military campaigns moved eastward and more concentration camps were built, the Nazis employed the methods that they had perfected in Germany during the preceding six years. Prisoners were collected, shipped to selected sites, and forced to build the camps' infrastructures.

1939

tal defectives" in the Polish village of Piasnica. • Hitler orders that selected physicians be authorized to administer "mercy deaths"—euthanasia—to incurably ill or undesirable German citizens. No legal justification for the killings is necessary.

• October 1, 1939: The Polish government-in-exile is formed in France.

When hostilities escalate, the government will move to London.

• October 4, 1939: A triumphant Hitler tours Warsaw, Poland.

• October 6, 1939: In an address to the *Reichstag*, Hitler offers peace to England and France, but only if Germany's former colonies are returned, Germany

Inhabitants of Warsaw, Poland, sort through the ruins of their city. The combined air and artillery assaults were devastating. Although Hitler declared that Germany did not wage war on innocent civilians, nothing could have been further from the truth. About 50,000 Polish civilians were killed or wounded during the German offensive, and 25 percent of Warsaw's buildings were destroyed.

German infantry troops parade through the streets of Warsaw to celebrate the Nazi victory over Poland. Four short but murderous weeks after Germany invaded Poland, Warsaw fell. Poland was conquered, and the lives of its 3.3 million Jewish inhabitants were imperiled. Hitler took great pleasure in viewing these choreographed victory celebrations, which were utilized by the Nazi propaganda machine to drive home the message of Aryan superiority.

Hitler salutes the passing columns of troops in Warsaw to celebrate the crushing of Poland. After defeating Poland on the battlefield, German troops occupied the western portions of the country. Nazi swastikas were prominently displayed, while German soldiers and members of the Gestapo and SS were deployed throughout the region. The Nazi presence was inescapable.

is allowed to join world trade, and Britain and France allow Germany to solve the "Jewish problem."

• **October 8, 1939:** The restriction of Jews to Nazi-enforced ghettos begins at Piotrków Trybunalski, Poland.

• **October 10, 1939:** The Germans create a *Generalgouvernement* in Poland.

It is an administrative area not incorporated into Greater Germany. The Germans will locate their death camps in the *Generalgouvernement*.

• **October 12, 1939:** The Nazi deportation of Jews from Austria and Moravia to Poland begins. • Hans Frank is appointed governor-general of Occupied Poland.

• **Mid-October 1939:** The SS begins mass killings of "mental defectives" in a forest outside Piasnica, Poland, near Danzig.

• **October 16, 1939:** Kraków, one of the most important Jewish communities since the 1300s, is designated the capital of the *Generalgouvernement*.

Jewish women in Gostynin, Poland, draw water from a well in the town square. Reinhard Heydrich's executive order of September 21 called for the establishment of Jewish ghettos in German-occupied Poland. The dissolution of Jewish communities in Poland and Greater Germany with populations under 500 facilitated the relocation of Jews to urban ghettos. Jews throughout Poland were also required to wear a Star of David emblem. This outward identification mark enhanced the distinction between gentile and Jewish Poles, and furthered the isolation of Jews.

A Jewish woman in Plonsk, Poland, pleads her case with an SS man. The massive relocation of Polish Jews from the countryside to urban centers ruthlessly uprooted people from their homes and communities. With little time to plan and no allowance made for people to bring the majority of their belongings, Jews were thrust into overcrowded and chaotic ghettos. Efforts to dissuade the Nazis were in vain. Once orders were issued and the concentration of Jews into ghettos had begun, virtually nothing could postpone the process.

An SS officer searches a Jew on Grzybowska Street in Warsaw, Poland, as part of a raid for weapons in a Jewish neighborhood. The raid was staged to "prove" that Jews were hiding weapons to use against the German Army. Once ensconced in Poland, the Nazi propaganda machine worked overtime to reinforce anti-Jewish prejudices already present in Polish society.

1939

● **October 17, 1939:** Hitler lectures General Wilhelm Keitel and other top *Wehrmacht* generals on the need for "Jews, Poles, and similar trash" to be cleared from old and new territories of the Reich.

● **October 19, 1939:** A Jewish ghetto at Lublin, Poland, is established.

● **October 24, 1939:** Jews in Wloclawek, Poland, are required to wear a yellow cloth triangle identifying them as Jews; *See* November 23, 1939.

● **October 26, 1939:** The Labor Department of the *Generalgouvernement* of Occupied Poland issues the *Arbeitspflicht* (Work obligation) decree, which makes slave labor mandatory for all

An elderly Jew, wearing what was probably a homemade Yellow Star, engages in forced labor. The Nazis enjoyed making Jews, whom they considered "work shy," engage in heavy labor. Jewish workers toiled under horrific conditions, working at extremely arduous tasks but receiving starvation rations. Thousands of Polish Jews, especially the sick and elderly, died as a result of this abuse.

Partisans proved a thorn in the side of the Germans throughout the course of the war. This Polish-Jewish woman, Bayla Gelblung, appears before a Nazi military court in October 1939. A sharpshooter, she stands accused of firing on German soldiers. Notice her military uniform; civilians accused of sniping were summarily executed.

The Yellow Star

With the crushing defeat of Poland, the Nazis launched the policy of publicly identifying Jews. As a means of identification and humiliation, Jews would be forced to wear the Star of David. Noncompliance was punishable by death.

All Polish Jews over the age of ten were forced "to wear on the right sleeve of their inner and outer garments a white band at least four inches wide, with the Star of David on it." This stigmatizing label became a standard feature of Nazi policy throughout Occupied Europe. The Nazis cynically called the star *Pour le Sémite* (for the Semite), a pun on the German military decoration for valor, *Pour le Mérite* (for the Merit).

Branding Jews with the Star of David turned the symbol of Judaism into a badge of deep humiliation—and a form of torture. To merely go into the street meant being immediately recognized, monitored, shunned, abused, and ultimately marked for death. Jewish children, especially, were easy targets of verbal and physical attacks.

The placement, design, and colors of the badges varied. Initially, most were yellow triangle-shaped patches, some sewn onto lapels. German Jews wore a yellow star inscribed with the word *Jude* in black letters. In Dachau, two overlapping triangular patches formed a yellow star. Armbands in the Warsaw Ghetto featured a blue star. The badges of Greek Jews contained identity numbers. Russian Jews wore yellow badges on the left side of the chest and on the back.

Polish men and women over the age of 14 and under age 60.

● **October 26, 1939–early February 1940:** In a plan devised by Adolf Eichmann, the Nazis deport and "resettle" some 78,000 Jews to a "reservation" located in the Lublin-Nisko region of southeast Poland. The project is temporarily suspended when rolling rail stock is needed for German military campaigns against the Low Countries.

● **October 30, 1939:** SS chief Heinrich Himmler designates the next three months as the period during which all Jews must be cleared from the rural areas of western Poland. Hundreds of communities will be affected, and thousands of Jews will be expelled with nothing but what they can carry with them. ● The British government publishes a report critical of the Nazis' treatment of concentration-camp prisoners.

● **November 1939:** Various German generals plot a *Putsch* designed to overthrow Hitler at Zossen, Germany, but it is never carried out. ● Hans Frank,

Youth Aliya

Thousands of Jews survived the war thanks to Youth Aliya. The goal of this German-Jewish organization was to save lives by helping young Jews, many orphaned, to emigrate from Germany to Palestine to be educated and absorbed into the *kibbutzim* (cooperative farming communities). The movement helped rescue German Jews from the Nazis, mobilized Jews living in the West, and served Jews residing in Palestine.

Ultimately led by American Zionist Henrietta Szold and others, Youth Aliya helped 5000 Jews escape from Germany, operating legally during the 1930s because Nazi government policy called for forced emigration of Jews. After the outbreak of war, more than 3000  European Jewish children were saved. Another 15,000 were brought to Palestine between the end of the war and the establishment of the State of Israel in 1948.

The organization's daring goals contrasted sharply with its conservative structure. Throughout the 1930s it required Jewish children to be physically and psychologically healthy, and they could not be from single-parent families. Once the war began, the goal was to save lives, and the requirements became more flexible. The *kibbutzim* became the hosts for approximately 85 percent of the Aliya youths. After the war Youth Aliya members aided several thousand young Jews in displaced-persons camps and helped even more to immigrate to Palestine.

Hitler was by now the master of European politics. In 1939, with his invasion of Poland, he began his quest for "living space" for the German people, a crusade that would culminate in his June 1941 invasion of the Soviet Union. Hitler realized that, in order to achieve his ambitious goals, which encompassed nothing less than Aryan domination of Europe from the Atlantic to the Urals, he would have to fight a series of wars. The invasion of Poland was just the first step of this bloody enterprise.

German and Soviet officers meet in Brest-Litovsk, Poland, to discuss the partitioning of that country. Once defeated, Poland was partitioned according to the secret protocols of the Nazi-Soviet Non-Aggression Pact. The western portions of Poland were immediately subjected to Nazi rule, and plans for the racial reordering of this territory were implemented. Polish Jews and gentiles were relocated so that ethnic Germans could populate the western regions of Poland. The quest for *Lebensraum* (Living space) was a driving force of the Nazi military campaigns.

1939

governor-general of Occupied Poland, sets up the first "self-governing" Jewish council (*Judenrat*) within Jewish ghettos. The council leaders must obey the demands of the Nazis.

• November 7, 1939: The Nazis begin mass deportations of Jews from western Poland.

• November 8, 1939: Hitler is nearly killed by an assassin's bomb planted at Bürgerbraukeller, Munich, Germany.

• November 11, 1939: Six hundred Jews are murdered by German troops at Ostrow Mazowiecki, Poland. • Two Jews are among six men and three boys taken from Zielonka, Poland, to be shot in nearby woods.

General Franz Halder *(left)*, chief of the German General Staff, discusses military matters with the commander-in-chief of the Army, General Walther von Brauchitsch. Brauchitsch commanded the troops that successfully invaded Poland in the summer of 1939. This, coupled with his leadership of the May 1940 attack on France, led to his promotion to field marshal. Under Brauchitsch, the German Army committed numerous crimes against the Polish people, especially the Jews.

In 1940 the Nazis forced the Jews to construct the Warsaw Ghetto, the largest in Europe, themselves. Before they could begin construction of the wall that would seal off the ghetto, Warsaw's Jews had to clean up the rubble left after the German destruction of the city. Forcing Jews to participate actively in their own persecution—in this case through aiding in the building of the ghetto—was cruelly pragmatic, as the slave labor kept construction costs to a minimum.

The Nazis deported thousands of Czech Jews to ghettos in Poland. Among them were these two men and a small boy from Prague, who loaded their possessions on a cart to take them to Poland. Germany's occupation of the Czech Sudetenland in 1938—a move agreed to by Great Britain, France, and Italy—had put large numbers of Jews under Nazi control.

• **November 12, 1939: SS Security Service chief Reinhard Heydrich orders that all Jews be removed from the newly formed Warthegau province (formerly western Poland) of Greater Germany. The order is made so that the region can be prepared for resettlement by ethnic Germans. • The Nazis begin the deportation of Jews from Lódź to other parts of Poland.**

• **November 13, 1939: SS troops in Poland arrest and execute 53 Jewish men who happen to reside at the same address as a Jewish man who has shot and killed a Polish policeman.**

• **November 15, 1939: The antisemitic *Fideikommissariat* (Estate commission) is established to "Aryanize" Jewish-owned businesses in Occupied Poland.**

• **November 15–17, 1939: Nazis destroy all of the synagogues in Lódź, Poland.**

• **November 18, 1939: Hans Frank, the governor-general of Occupied Poland, reiterates Reinhard Heydrich's order of September 21 regarding the establishment of *Judenräte* in Jewish ghettos.**

Piotr Sosnowski, a deacon from Byslaw, Poland, was executed in what is thought to be the Tuchola Forest. On October 27, 1939, a group of Polish prisoners was transported to an execution spot two kilometers outside of town. When the trucks reached the forest, the prisoners were ordered to empty their pockets and dig a large grave. After the grave was completed, Deacon Sosnowski gave the men absolution before the commanding SS officer, Colonel Wilhelm Theodor Richardt, ordered his men to shoot the Poles as reprisal for the burning of two barns owned by ethnic Germans. Altogether, 45 Poles, including Sosnowski, were killed.

Poles in Grudziadz construct bridges for the Reich Labor Service. Nazi Germany made extensive use of slave labor throughout the conquered territories in Eastern Europe. Almost invariably, Jews were given the most strenuous jobs and the smallest rations. Hence, the number of deaths among Jewish workers was always higher than for non-Jews.

The newly formed *Judenrat* (Jewish council) of Warsaw, Poland, receives its instructions from SD officials. The Jewish councils, comprised of community leaders, were charged with carrying out the orders issued by the Nazis. They were responsible for supplying the Nazis with laborers, allocating housing assignments, collecting taxes, and, eventually, filling deportation quotas. *Judenrat* leaders were in a catch-22: Failure to comply with their orders meant death at the hands of the Nazis, while compliance facilitated efforts to eradicate the Jews.

Nazi Propaganda Minister Joseph Goebbels *(center)* visited Warsaw, Poland, in November 1939. Nazi bigwigs enjoyed their trips to the conquered territories. Goebbels's host was the infamous chief of the *Generalgouvernement*, Hans Frank, a notorious antisemite who wanted all of the *Generalgouvernement*'s Jews deported. When this proved impractical, he became a staunch supporter of murdering Polish Jews in order to make room for Aryan settlers.

1939

- **November 23, 1939: Polish Jews are ordered to wear white armbands with a blue Star of David whenever appearing in public.**

- **November 29, 1939: SS chief Heinrich Himmler orders the death penalty for German Jews who refuse to report for deportation.**

- **November–December 1939: General Johannes Blaskowitz, the commander-in-chief of Greater Germany's Eastern sector, complains to the German High Command that the activities of *Einsatzgruppen* (killing squads) are excessively brutal and a threat to army discipline. His complaints are noted but are largely ignored; *Einsatzgruppen* activities continue as before.**

Senior SS officers meet at Gestapo headquarters in Munich in November 1939. Pictured from left to right are Gestapo chief Heinrich Müller; Franz Josef Huber, leader of the Gestapo in Vienna; SS Chief Heinrich Himmler; Reinhard Heydrich, head of the Security Service (SD); and Arthur Nebe, chief of Kripo (criminal police). They may have discussed the role of the German police forces in the newly acquired Polish territories.

Edouard Daladier, premier of France, inspects the Maginot Line in November 1939. The Maginot Line, which consisted of a series of fortresses built along the Franco-German border designed to halt a cross-Rhine invasion, was the centerpiece of French defense plans. In the end, the fortress complex could not stop the German invasion in the spring of 1940. The Germans simply went around it, invading France through Belgium.

Ghettoization

"What has today brought us?" wrote Chaim Kaplan, a Jew, on November 5, 1939. "A ghetto in Jewish Warsaw!"

First used in Venice, Italy, in 1516, the word "ghetto" originally referred to a city area occupied only by Jews who had segregated there. The Germans made that concept much more deadly. The ghettos they established soon after their 1939 invasion of Poland initially were

intended to be transitional concentration areas to hold Jews, all of whom were to be excluded from Aryan resettlement of desirable, formerly Jewish areas. Later, the only possible Jewish "escape" from the ghettos was via deportation to extermination/slave-labor camps built by the Nazis in Poland.

The Nazis established their first ghetto on October 8, 1939. It stood at Piotrków Trybunalski in the Lódź district of Occupied Poland. A year later Kaplan was among about 500,000 Jews in Warsaw, Poland, who struggled to survive in constantly deteriorating ghetto conditions. Afflicted by hunger, squalor, overcrowding, sickness, and despair, the Warsaw Ghetto and others like it—in cities such as Lódź and Lublin (Poland), Lvov and Minsk (Soviet Union), Kovno and Vilna (Lithuania), and Riga (Latvia)—became places of immense suffering and death.

During 1942 and 1943, the Nazis "liquidated" the ghettos by deporting and murdering their inhabitants. Kaplan was gassed at the Treblinka, Poland, extermination camp.

• November 30, 1939–March 13, 1940: The USSR invades Finland and carries out the Winter War.

• December 1939: German Field Marshal Johannes Blaskowitz, commander-in-chief of the German Army Group East, reports that many Jewish children in transport trains are arriving at their destinations frozen to death. • The Lipowa camp at Lipowa Street in Lublin, Poland, is established. It is initially an assembly point for Polish-Jewish POWs, and it will later be a Jewish work camp. • Lódź (Poland) Ghetto administrator Friedrich Übelhör notes that ghettoization of Jews is only temporary. The final goal is to clean Jews out of Lódź, to "utterly destroy this bubonic plague."

• December 1, 1939: 1350 Jews are murdered by German troops at Chelm, Poland.

• December 1–9, 1939: The forced march of 1800 Jewish men from Chelm and Hrubieszow, Poland, to the Soviet border results in the deaths of all but 200.

Nazi policies in the ghettos made it extremely difficult for Jews to support themselves. This Jewish woman is selling hair pins and ribbons on a Lublin, Poland, street. Through such techniques, some Jews managed to eke out a living in the ghettos. But increasingly severe German regulations made it ever more difficult for ghettoized Jews to survive, and they died of disease and starvation by the tens of thousands.

Jewish children were a particular affront to the Nazis. They were, after all, the future of the Jewish "race." Further, Jewish children were especially "useless" because few of them could work. Hence, they were usually among the first victims of Nazi pogroms. This photo from the Lublin (Poland) Ghetto records a group of Jewish children and their overseer. Note the untrusting eyes of the two children in the foreground.

MAJOR GHETTOS IN OCCUPIED POLAND, 1939–1941

The Nazis established the first Jewish ghetto in Piotrków in October 1939. Warsaw, the largest ghetto with 360,000 Jews initially, was sealed a year later.

1939

• December 5–6, 1939: German authorities seize Jewish property in Poland. Items that are appropriated include businesses, homes, furniture and other household goods, currency and bank accounts, art, jewelry, and other valuables. Now economically helpless, the Jews have virtually nothing with which to sustain themselves.

• December 6, 1939: As an example of its policy of blocking all Jewish escape routes in Central Europe, the British Foreign Office warns Bulgaria that if it ships its Jews to Palestine, the British will "expect the Bulgarian government to take the immigrants back."

• December 8, 1939: Six Jews and 25 non-Jewish Poles, accused of commit-

This photograph shows the last Jew executed outside the city of Ostrow Mazowiecka, Poland. On November 11, 1939, the local population accused the Jews of having set fire to part of the city earlier in the month. In retaliation German police executed (depending upon the account) between 162 and 500 Jews. Polish gentiles often aided the Germans in carrying out anti-Jewish policies. Gentile collaboration was not unexpected, as Poland—like other European nations—had a long history of antisemitism. Anti-Jewish feelings needed only a particular combination of circumstances to erupt into violence and murder.

Before the November 11 executions outside Ostrow Mazowiecka, the men of the East Prussian Police unit dug a series of pits outside the city. On orders from *SS-Obergruppenführer* Friedrich Krüger, the policemen carried out the killings themselves. Witnesses later reported that the perpetrators were troubled by the order but, in the end, were not deterred. The "action" at Ostrow Mazowiecka was among the earliest systematic murders of Polish Jews.

The Nazis needed to be able to identify Polish Jews quickly, and armbands with the Star of David served this purpose effectively. The penalty for failure to wear the proper armband was summary execution. This photograph shows a Jewish boy selling armbands in the Warsaw Ghetto. Once again, Jews were forced to participate in their own persecution. It was a devilish sort of psychological warfare. In time, this bizarre state of affairs assumed an inescapable reality, and the normal world from which Poland's Jews had been wrenched seemed irretrievably lost.

---

ting acts of sabotage, are shot in Occupied Warsaw.

• December 12, 1939: In eastern areas of Greater Germany, two years of forced labor is made compulsory for all Jewish males aged 14 to 60. • Jews are expelled from Kalisz in the Warthegau region of Poland; many flee to Warsaw.

• December 16, 1939: Jewish girls in Lódź, Poland, who have been impressed for forced labor, are forced to clean a latrine with their blouses. When the job is complete, the German overseers wrap the filthy blouses around the girls' faces.

• December 27, 1939: 106 non-Jewish Poles are murdered at Wawer, Poland.

• December 30, 1939: The riverboat *Uranus* reaches the Iron Gates gorge in Romania, on the Yugoslavian border, with 1210 fugitive Jews from Vienna, Austria, and Prague, Czechoslovakia. The boat's journey is halted after Great Britain, holder of the Mandate on Palestine, protests to the Yugoslavian government; *See* October 1941.

1940

IN German-occupied Poland, Mordechai Chaim Rumkowski, a man in his 60s who had organized and directed a well-known orphanage, became the Nazi-appointed leader of his fellow Jews in Lódź, a major Polish city in territory that the Germans had annexed to the Third Reich. The Germans called the city Litzmannstadt. On April 5, 1940, Rumkowski sent to the German authorities one of the frequent petitions that would characterize his doomed efforts to preserve Jewish life in the Lódź Ghetto. Rumkowski emphasized that the ghetto contained thousands of skilled workers. "I could organize matters," he wrote, "so that these people work for the authorities."

Jews of Lódź, Rumkowski believed, could find salvation through work that made them useful, if not essential, to the Germans. Jews in many ghettos held this belief. For some Jews it bought time, although the terms were set by the Germans, not the Jews. "Salvation through work" did not last for long, however, because the perverse "logic" of Nazi Germany's antisemitic racism contradicted that hope. That logic meant that racial threats to German purity and power could not be tolerated and must be removed.

On April 30 Rumkowski got a reply to his April 5 memorandum. Far from responding to his suggestions, it contained a series of orders. These orders gave Rumkowski nearly dictatorial authority in the ghetto, although he had to exercise them as instructed and required. First and foremost, Rumkowski was told that "all residents of the ghetto are forbidden to leave the ghetto, as of April 30, 1940." He would be accountable for "the strict enforcement of this prohibition" and also for the ghetto's "orderly economic life."

In spite of the latter order's virtual impossibility, Rumkowski took it as his mandate and organized the ghetto's labor force. Nevertheless, the fate of most of the 164,000 Lódź Jews was sealed when the ghetto—its area was only 1.54 square miles—was enclosed by barbed wire. That action indicated that the Lódź Jews, valuable though their work might be for a time, were fundamentally unwanted creatures whose place in the Nazi racial hierarchy made them unfit to live where German interests prevailed. As it continued to unfold, that logic would spell mass murder for European Jewry.

A few days before the sealing of the Lódź Ghetto, another decision revealed the logic of Nazi racism even more decisively. On April 27 Heinrich Himmler, head of the SS, decided that a concentration camp should be established on the site of former Polish military barracks near the town

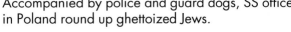

Accompanied by police and guard dogs, SS officers
in Poland round up ghettoized Jews.

1940

of Oświecim. Like Lódź, Oświecim stood in territory that the Germans annexed. They called the town Auschwitz. On April 29 Concentration Camps Inspector Richard Glücks appointed SS Captain Rudolf Höss to be the commandant there. Soon, work began to make the camp operational. The workers included 300 Jews conscripted from Oświecim.

The camp's original mission was to be a regional prison for Poles who opposed German rule. That purpose made Auschwitz a deadly place for tens of thousands of non-Jewish Poles who were killed by slave labor, disease, and execution. In the months and years ahead, Auschwitz would expand into a network of labor and killing installations that would destroy more than a million people. Ninety percent were Jews. They came not only from Poland but from every part of Nazi-controlled Europe. Eventually, Auschwitz revealed the logic of Nazi racism to such an extent that Auschwitz became nearly synonymous with the Holocaust itself.

Nazi racism emphasized German superiority as much as it stressed the inferiority of Poles and Jews. Especially in the spring of 1940, the German spirit of superiority ran high. Having spent several months consolidating their gains in Occupied Poland, German military forces launched a series of quick and successful strikes in Western Europe. Following the invasions of Denmark and Norway on April 9, the *Wehrmacht* attacked France, Belgium, Luxembourg, and the Netherlands on May 10. Only the massive sea evacuation of some 338,000 British, French, and Belgian armed forces from Dunkerque, France, at the end of the month prevented the Germans from decisively destroying the main military forces that opposed them in Western Europe.

On June 5 the Germans launched their final assault against France. Paris fell on June 14. Two days later Marshal Philippe Pétain, the aging French hero of World War I, took over as head of the French government. He quickly asked for an armistice, which was signed on June 22.

The armistice resulted in a two-zone division of the country. The Nazis occupied the northern two-thirds of the country, including Paris. Southern France, with governmental headquarters at the resort town of Vichy, remained unoccupied until early 1942. Under these arrangements, the Germans allowed a collaborationist French government, led by Pétain and then by Pierre Laval, to remain in place in exchange for its cooperation, which included financial exploitation that benefited Germany, labor brigades sent to work in German industry, and punitive measures against Jews.

The total Jewish population of the Western European countries conquered by the Germans in the spring of 1940 was considerably smaller than Poland's alone, but the numbers still were large. In a matter of weeks, more than a half-million Jews in Western Europe, including thousands who had fled from prewar Germany and Central Europe, found themselves under the domination of Nazi Germany and its collaborators. Eventually, these innocents would be rounded up and deported to the East. Many transports sent Jews from France, the Netherlands, Norway, and other Western European states to their deaths at Auschwitz.

The concentration camp at Auschwitz deceived inmates with the words "Work Will Set You Free."

For Europe's Jews, the spring of 1940 went from bad to worse as it continued to reveal Nazi antisemitism and racism in ways that were both known and unknown to them. On May 25, for example, Himmler handed Adolf Hitler a secret memorandum that contained Himmler's recommendations regarding "the treatment of the peoples of alien races in the East." It called for "the racial sifting" of millions of people, an action that would reconfigure the demography as well as the geography of Eastern Europe.

In those areas, the Germans might find some people who would be racially valuable and capable of assimilation. The larger goal, however, would be to turn the so-called inferior populations into "laborers without leaders." They would perform "special tasks," the "heavy work" required for the "everlasting cultural tasks" of the German people. As distinct ethnic groups, these populations should be split up and dissolved into "innumerable small fragments and particles." Himmler envisioned minimal schooling for this non-German population in the East: "simple arithmetic—up to five hundred at the most; writing one's name; the doctrine that it is a divine law to obey the Germans and to be honest, industrious, and good. I don't think that reading is necessary."

Two other features of Himmler's memorandum to Hitler on May 25 are especially noteworthy. Without elaboration, Himmler referred to the possibility that Jewish ways would be "completely extinguished" in the East through "a large emigration of all Jews to Africa or some other colony." In addition, when speaking about racially acceptable children who should be separated from their parents for purposes of assimilation, Himmler stated that "cruel and tragic" though these steps might be in individual cases, they were still the "mildest and best . . . if, out of inner conviction, one rejects as un-German and impossible the Bolshevist method of physical extermination of a people." In Nazi Germany, such inner conviction did not run deep. When Himmler's "large emigration of all Jews" proved impossible, Nazi ideology implied that physical extermination of the Jews was neither impossible nor "un-German."

On May 28 Himmler prepared a summary of Hitler's reactions to the proposal about "alien races in the East." Himmler noted that Hitler had read "the six pages and considered them very good and correct." According to Himmler, Hitler directed that Himmler's report should be handled with "utmost secrecy,"

Top: The conqueror of France poses in triumph with Albert Speer *(left)* in Paris. *Above:* Brick and stone walls seal off the Warsaw Ghetto from the world.

but he also authorized that key Nazi leaders in the East should be informed that "the *Führer* acknowledged and sanctioned this report as a directive." Himmler, who did more than any other Nazi to implement the deadly logic of racism, had obtained one of the authorizations that would help him launch the "Final Solution" when its time came.

That time had not yet come in the spring of 1940, but it drew closer by the end of the year. On December 18 Hitler secretly ordered preparation for Operation Barbarossa, the code name for Nazi Germany's invasion of the Soviet Union. With that 1941 invasion, the mass murder of Jews in Eastern Europe would begin in earnest.

Forced to build their own prison, striped-suited laborers lay the foundation and construct the walls of Auschwitz. Located near the Polish town of Oświecim, the swampy site had housed an army barracks during World War I. At Heinrich Himmler's order, *SS-Hauptsturmführer* Rudolf Höss inspected the area in April 1940 and proclaimed it ideal for incarcerating the rapidly growing number of prisoners, mostly Poles.

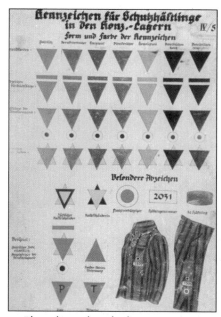

The headquarters of the Nazis' "euthanasia program" was located in this benign building at *Tiergartenstrasse* 4 in Berlin. The T-4 division was created on Hitler's orders and headed by Philip Bouhler and Viktor Brack. The organization was responsible for administering "mercy" killings to the mentally and physically handicapped. Planning began in the spring of 1939, and the first murders occurred in October. Eventually, 70,000 people were murdered under the auspices of the T-4 program.

This chart details the prisoner markings used in German concentration camps. Badges identify the following categories of prisoners: political, professional criminal, emigrant, Jehovah's Witness, homosexual, German shy of work, and others. The hierarchical ordering of prisoners sentenced to concentration camps created a Byzantine world of power relations.

1940

• 1940: Six "euthanasia" centers are set up in Germany to murder Jews, the mentally ill, the elderly, the physically ill, and the handicapped. • Estonia is annexed by the Soviet Union. • Jewish Social Democratic politician Ernst Heilmann dies at the Buchenwald, Germany, concentration camp. • President Franklin Roosevelt puts the question of Jewish immigration into the United States into the antisemitic hands of Assistant Secretary of State Breckinridge Long and associates in the State Department. A political ally of the president, Long opposes "excessive humanitarianism" in regards to the Jews. Tainted by a general xenophobia and a predilection for Mussolini and Italian fascism (Long was ambassador to Italy), Long seems particularly distressed at

In the Palmiry Woods, about 17 miles outside of Warsaw, the Germans shot approximately 2000 Poles during the first four years of the war. This photograph, taken in 1940, shows several blindfolded Polish women standing before a mass grave, awaiting their executions.

Relieved and joyful smiles light up faces in this group of Jewish refugees, who were among the fortunate few allowed entry into Canada, a country hostile to Jewish immigration. While farmers were welcomed, those of most other occupations were not. Scholars and teachers, no matter how esteemed in their homeland, found Canada's universities unwilling to offer them posts.

Sempo Sugihara

Sempo Sugihara, the Japanese consul in Kovno, Lithuania, was one of the true heroes of the Holocaust. He rescued several thousand Jews left stranded in Lithuania after they had fled Nazi-occupied Poland.

A plan devised by Zionist leaders called for the refugees to ostensibly seek asylum in Curacao, a Dutch island in the Caribbean, although there was never any intent to go there. The proposed travel route wound through the Soviet Union and Japan, necessitating transit visas. Soviet approval depended on first acquiring Japan's permission. The Japanese rejected the request. However, seeing throngs of frantic Jews cling-

ing to the iron fences of Japan's consulate, begging for visas, roused compassion in Sugihara. Defying his government, he granted visas to as many applicants as possible—at least 3500.

Ordered out of Kovno, Sugihara continued to sign papers, even as his train pulled away from the station. The refugees journeyed through Russia via the Trans-Siberian Railway to Vladivostok, and from there by boat to Japan, then China. Many eventually reached Israel or the United States.

When the Germans captured Kovno in 1941, they slaughtered thousands of Jews who had not gotten out. As for Sugihara, the Japanese government cited him for insubordination and stripped him of his post.

the prospect of more Jews entering the United States.

• Leslie Hore-Belisha, Great Britain's secretary of state for war, and a Jew, resigns, largely because of the anti-Jewish feelings among members of the British government. Foreign Secretary Lord Halifax and Under-Secretary of the Foreign Office Alexander Cadogan

note that Hore-Belisha's Jewishness rendered him unsuitable as minister of information, stating, "Jew control of our propaganda would be [a] major disaster."

• January 2, 1940: The *Generalgouvernement* in Poland decrees that Jews may not post obituaries.

• January 6, 1940: Shivering Jews in Warsaw, Poland, are forced to burn Jewish books for fuel.

• January 12, 1940: The Gestapo and SS men shoot and kill 300 inmates of a Polish insane asylum at Hordyszcze.

• January 14–16, 1940: The forced march of 880 Polish prisoners of war—

Lódź Ghetto

In September 1939 the Germans annexed the Polish city of Lódź and gave it a new name: Litzmannstadt. They burned down its synagogues and herded its 170,000 Jews into the most neglected, poverty-ridden slum section of town. The ghetto was originally established as a transitional measure, as the Nazis vowed to "cleanse" the city of Jews and "burn out this pestilent abscess." However, the ghetto was maintained for four years.

Wooden fences and barbed wire permanently sealed the Lódź Ghetto in the spring of 1940. Inside, the mostly wooden, overcrowded houses had no toilets, no running water, no sewage. The use of electricity was forbidden at night. Minimal food allocations created chronic starvation. Rats infested  refuse dumps. Dysentery, tuberculosis, and typhus epidemics raged periodically. Heart disease, brought on by constant tension and hardship, claimed even more lives. Some Jews chose suicide by "going to the wire"; guards shot anyone approaching the fence.

The head of the ghetto's Jewish Council, Mordechai Chaim Rumkowski, hoped to keep Jews alive by turning Lódź into a giant slave-labor workshop for the Germans. Nonetheless, liquidation measures began in 1942, when 55,000 Lódź Jews were sent to the gas vans of Chelmno, Poland. By May 1944 only 77,000 remained alive. As the Soviet Army approached, the Nazis consigned the Jews who remained to the ovens of Auschwitz.

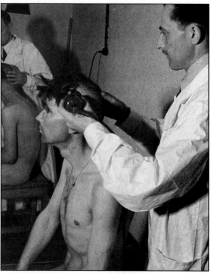

Jewish prisoners of war, newly arrived in Poland's Kraków Ghetto, have their heads shaved, purportedly to prevent typhus. Nowhere was the hypocrisy of the Nazis more apparent than in their management of the ghettos. While they chastised Jews for being unclean and mandated superficial actions to prevent the outbreak and spread of contagious diseases, the grossly overcrowded conditions of the ghettos and complete lack of adequate sanitary facilities virtually assured diseases in epidemic proportions. Disease was a leading cause of death in the ghettos.

This belt buckle is dominated by the Nazi eagle perched on the swastika. The slogan reads, "God is with us."

1940

all Jews—results in the shooting deaths of more than 600.

• **January 18–25, 1940:** 255 Polish Jews arrested at random in Warsaw are taken to the Palmiry Forest outside the city and shot.

• **January 30, 1940:** The British Embassy in Bucharest pressures the Romanian government to prevent its ships from carrying Jewish refugees.

• **February 7, 1940:** Jews in Warsaw, Poland, are prohibited from visiting the city's public libraries.

• **February 8, 1940:** A Jewish ghetto is established at Lódź, Poland.

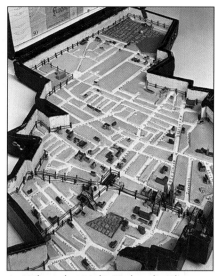

In the midst of increasingly difficult ghetto conditions, Lódź Jews sought to maintain the rhythm of normal life. Here, women are pictured baking matzo in a ghetto factory, in preparation for Passover in 1940. Synagogues throughout the city had been destroyed the previous year, but religious life flourished in the ghetto, with families gathering in homes to observe the holy days.

When the Lódź (Poland) Ghetto was liquidated in August 1944, this intricate model was hidden in the basement of a building. It survived the war and was later returned to its builder, Leon Jacobson, who had survived both the ghetto and Auschwitz. The model, constructed from scrap wood, shows the complexities of the ghetto, with its houses, factories, bridges, ruins of synagogues, and cemeteries. In all, the ghetto comprised a bit more than 1.5 square miles. Of that area, less than one square mile had been developed with buildings suitable for habitation. Some 170,000 Lódź Jews were forced into the ghetto, which was served by only two major avenues, and by wooden pedestrian bridges that were constructed over those streets. The official seals and the examples of ghetto currency *(upper left)* testify to the organization of the ghetto, which was overseen by Jewish Council leader Chaim Rumkowski.

Appointed leader, or Eldest of Jews, of the Lódź Ghetto in 1939, Mordechai Chaim Rumkowski pursued the controversial strategy of "quiet and labor" to further the ghetto's survival. This German and Yiddish sign states his motto, "Our only path [to survival] is [through] work." Rumkowski transformed the ghetto into a bustling manufacturing center, producing mainly textiles. Mocked as "King Chaim" by Jews, Rumkowski ruled as a dictator, forcefully quelling all opposition. Nevertheless, his ghetto strategy fell victim to Hitler's goal of exterminating all Jews.

● **February 12–13, 1940:** The initial deportations of Jews from Germany, mainly from Pomerania, begins.

● **February 18, 1940:** Two Jewish teenage girls are abducted in Warsaw, Poland, and raped in a Jewish cemetery by two German noncommissioned officers.

● **February 19, 1940:** The use of the Dachau, Germany, concentration camp as a training facility for the *Waffen-SS* concludes. Prisoners transferred to the Mauthausen, Austria, camp in September 1939 are returned, and Dachau reverts to its original use as a concentration camp; *See* September 27, 1939.

● **February 21, 1940:** Nazis in Warsaw, Poland, throw a Jewish woman from a moving streetcar.

● **March 12, 1940:** All 160 Jews from the Baltic port of Schneidemühl, Poland, are transported to Lublin, Poland, in sealed freight cars, then are forced to march to small villages 20 kilometers away.

Myron C. Taylor, President Franklin D. Roosevelt's personal envoy to Pope Pius XII, meets with the Pontiff on March 15, 1940. Pope Pius is shown reading Roosevelt's message that was delivered by Mr. Taylor. The purpose of the letter, and the meeting between Taylor and the Pope, was an attempt to bring about peace in Europe. The two men conversed privately for 40 minutes.

Mir Yeshiva students gather on a street corner in the Hongkew district of Shanghai, China. Rescued by the Japanese consul, Sempo Sugihara, some 2000 Jews escaped Kovno, Lithuania, before the German invasion. With transit visas in hand, they made the arduous trip across Siberia to safety in Shanghai, joining a Jewish community that before 1939 had numbered about 5000, mostly from Russia.

Following the surrender of Denmark in April 1940, life remained much the same for most Danish citizens. A stately symbol of national pride, King Christian X continued to take his daily ride through the streets of Copenhagen. Unlike other countries the Nazis occupied, Denmark was not placed under German administration. Fearing a public uproar, the Nazis also refrained until 1943 from implementing decrees against the country's approximately 7700 Jews.

1940

• **Spring 1940:** The first deportations of German Gypsies begin, from western and northwestern Germany.

• **March 22, 1940:** German Field Marshal Hermann Göring halts deportations of Jews to Lublin, Poland, after complaints from Hans Frank, governor-general of Occupied Poland, about "dumping" them.

• **April 1940:** Germany invades Denmark and Norway. The Danes and Norwegians attempt to prevent the Nazis from harming Jews; *See* October 1940.
• The *Institut für deutsche Ostarbeit* (Institute for German Work in the East) is founded to study Polish Jewry.

• **April 1, 1940:** Shanghai, China, accepts thousands of Jewish refugees.

The Nazis adapted buses for use in their "euthanasia" program, the goal of which was to exterminate the physically and mentally unfit. The buses were rigged to pump carbon monoxide from the engines into the passenger compartments, where the victims suffocated. The gassing of the victims provided the perpetrators with a distance from their crimes that other methods lacked. The euthanasia program served as a model for the death camps of Eastern Europe, to which many of the program's personnel were transferred. Protests from the Roman Catholic Church temporarily halted the murder of the handicapped.

Philip Bouhler, chief of Hitler's Chancellery, headed the so-called "euthanasia" program. Soon after the invasion of Poland began, Hitler authorized Bouhler and Dr. Karl Brandt to administer the program. Bouhler, in turn, appointed Viktor Brack to create an organization that would be responsible for administering "mercy" killings to the mentally and physically disabled. This administrative unit became known as T-4.

Rudolf Höss

In May 1940 Rudolf Höss became commandant of the Auschwitz, Poland, concentration camp. During three years there, as Auschwitz was "upgraded" to extermination-camp status, he directed the murders of more than a million people, and was responsible for the deaths of an additional half-million through starvation and disease.

Höss performed his duties so efficiently, his superiors commended him as a "true pioneer in his field." Yet, he insisted he "never personally hated the Jews." He attempted to rationalize his monstrous crimes on grounds that Jews were "enemies of the German people," and claimed his sense of duty compelled him to unquestioningly carry out Hitler's orders.

His devout Catholic parents hoped their son would become a priest. Instead, he enlisted in the Army during World War I, then joined a right-wing paramilitary organization. An accomplice in a 1923 political assassination, he served five years in prison. Höss joined the SS in 1934. He was praised for his work at the Dachau and Sachsenhausen concentration camps, and was subsequently given charge of Auschwitz.

Höss helped perfect the mass-execution process, devising more efficient gassing techniques. He didn't like the long hours, however, and lamented that he couldn't play more often with his children. Arrested in 1946, Höss was tried and executed at Auschwitz in April 1947.

• April 8–11, 1940: Soviet troops massacre 26,000 Polish officers in Katyn Forest near Smolensk, Russia. Many Jews are among the victims.

• April 22, 1940: SS official Odilo Globocnik announces a plan to increase the use of Jewish forced labor and to establish separate work camps for Jewish men and women.

• April 23, 1940: Captive Jews at Stutthof, Poland, are forced to leap into open latrines; many are drowned or beaten to death.

• April 27, 1940: British Foreign Office official H. F. Downie argues that the Jews are "enemies just as the Germans are, but in a more insidious way," and that "our two sets of enemies [Nazis and Jews] are linked together by secret and evil bonds."

• April 30, 1940: The Jewish ghetto in Lódź, Poland, is sealed off from the rest of the city.

• May 1940: Polish and Baltic-area Jews begin to escape to Jerusalem and across the Soviet Union to Japan, the

Aristides de Sousa Mendes

The efforts of Portuguese diplomat Aristides de Sousa Mendes *(pictured, top right)* helped 10,000 refugee Jews flee Nazi-occupied France. In his position as Portuguese consul, stationed in Bordeaux, France, Mendes signed transit visas for thousands of Jews hoping to escape through Portuguese ports.

In May 1940 Mendes defied his government's instructions to curtail the flood of refugees requesting entry into Portugal via Spain. Despite specific orders to issue no visas to Jews, Mendes, a devout Catholic, asserted

that he could not "allow these people to die." Acting on humanitarian principle, he worked day and night signing documents for the unending throng of refugees crowding the offices of the consulate. When supplies of official stationery ran out, he used odd scraps of paper. Even when recalled by his government, Mendes personally escorted a small band of refugees across the Spanish border. Supplying them with makeshift, handwritten visas, he instructed them to walk behind his car through a little-used checkpoint where the guard was unable to notify his superiors.

For his disobedience, the Portuguese government dismissed Mendes from the Ministry of Foreign Affairs and stripped him of all pension benefits. The head of a family of 13 children sank into deep poverty. Forgotten and heartbroken, Mendes died in 1954.

Jews of the Kraków (Poland) Ghetto load coal onto a horse-drawn sled. In the background is a 14th-century synagogue, a structure that attests to the long-standing Jewish presence in the city. On the eve of World War II, 60,000 Jews lived in Kraków, approximately 25 percent of the city's total population. The terror campaigns of December 1940 destroyed Kraków's synagogues and killed many Jews.

German forces swept into the Netherlands in May 1940, quickly capturing its capital, The Hague, and its principal port of Rotterdam, which is pictured. In preparation for the assault, the *Luftwaffe* engaged in massive bombing on May 14, with no concern for civilian casualties. As a result, much of the city was left in ruins. Many Dutch fled the devastation, including a large percentage of Rotterdam's Jewish population.

1940

Dutch East Indies, Australia, Canada, and the United States. In all, only a few thousand Jews from the region manage to escape. • Rudolf Höss, adjutant at the Sachsenhausen, Germany, concentration camp, is ordered to turn the former Polish army barracks at Auschwitz, Poland, into an extermination camp.

• May 10, 1940: German forces invade Holland, Belgium, Luxembourg, and France. • Winston Churchill succeeds Neville Chamberlain as British prime minister. • Poet and essayist T. S. Eliot writes that the Jews are the modern world's foremost "Forces of Evil." He claims that they have "made the modern world vile."

No longer fearing Nazi oppression or deportation to a concentration camp, the Rosenblums, arms linked, smile at their photographer. Refugees from Germany, their search for a safe haven led them around the world to the Hellensville Farm near Auckland, New Zealand. Because they were farmers, the Rosenblums likely were welcomed immigrants.

Under a sign identifying the city limits of Jerusalem, two fortunate refugee couples bask in their new-found freedom to stroll and sit where they choose. While large numbers of Jews from Poland and the Baltic areas sought sanctuary throughout the world, few succeeded in their quest. The British White Paper of 1939 severely restricted the number of Jews allowed to enter Palestine.

Pro-Nazi Dutch parade through the streets of Amsterdam during the occupation of the Netherlands by the Nazis. While some participated in the *Nationaal Socialistische Beweging* (National Socialist Movement), the Dutch equivalent of the Nazi Party, others actively resisted or passively subverted the German occupation. Initially, the Nazis promulgated no decrees against the country's Jews. The situation changed at the end of September 1940, when Jewish publications were banned and civil servants were required to attest to their Aryan status.

• May 15, 1940: Thousands of refugee Jews from Germany, Austria, and Czechoslovakia are trapped behind German lines as Nazi forces push through Holland. The Dutch Army surrenders.

• May 16, 1940: The Nazis launch the Extraordinary Pacification Operation plan to eliminate Polish intellectuals.

• May 19, 1940: Arthur Seyss-Inquart is appointed Reich commissioner for the Netherlands.

• May 20, 1940: A concentration camp begins functioning at Auschwitz in Poland. Because most of Europe's Jews live in Poland and Eastern Europe, the six concentration camps called death camps will be established there:

Auschwitz-Birkenau, Chelmno, Belzec, Treblinka, Sobibór, and Majdanek.

• May 23, 1940: Frustrated by "illegal" immigration into Palestine, British High Commissioner for Palestine Sir Harold MacMichael insists that Hungary accept the return of two Jews who had left Hungary and settled in Palestine in 1934 on tourist visas. The Hun-

Gypsy families from western and northwestern Germany gather at an assembly point in Hohenasperg to await deportation to the *General-gouvernement* in Poland. Like Jews, Gypsies were seen as a threat to the purity of "Aryan" blood, and therefore were targeted for extermination. Beginning as early as 1936, Gypsies living in Germany had been sent to the Dachau, Germany, concentration camp as "asocials." Some 5000 Gypsies were eventually sent to the Lódź (Poland) Ghetto and were among the first selected to die by gassing in the Chelmno, Poland, death camp.

Cots surround the bima of the synagogue at 27 Nalewki Street in Warsaw, Poland. Overcrowding, hunger, and disease dominated Jewish life as the Germans moved some 90,000 Jews from other areas of Poland into Warsaw. These conditions worsened in October with the formation of the ghetto. Some 30 percent of the population lived in less than 2.5 percent of the city.

A young Jewish father stares bleakly into an uncertain future while holding his child in his arms. Child rearing in the ghettos of Poland subjected parents to an endless array of anxieties and cruel choices. Children were the first to be deported and often were the targets of sadistic soldiers. Parents were deprived of adequate food, clothing, and the freedom needed to nurture young human beings, and thus were incapable of protecting their children from tragic and unfortunate existences. The memories of suffering and abandoned children plagued all those who experienced life in the Polish ghettos.

1940

garian government replies that there are an "excessive" number of Jews in their country and the government's aim is "that as many as possible should be encouraged to emigrate."

• **May 27, 1940:** One hundred British prisoners of war are murdered by German troops at Le Paradis, France.

• **May 28, 1940:** Belgium surrenders to Germany.

• **May–December 1940:** Thousands of Polish Jews are sent eastward as forced laborers to construct fortifications along the new Soviet frontier.

• **May 1940–March 1941:** 40,000 Jews are deported from Kraków, Poland.

Celebrating their victory in France, German troops march down the Champs-Élysées through the *Arc de Triomphe*. The armistice signed in June divided France into two areas. One part was occupied by the Germans and placed under military control, while the other was indirectly controlled by the Germans through the government of Marshal Pétain. The latter was headquartered in Vichy in the south of France. Half of the roughly 350,000 Jews in France lived in Paris and were immediately threatened by the Nazis' occupation. The Vichy government, too, moved to segregate Jews from French society, promulgating the *Statut des Juifs* (Jewish Law), which conformed to the German Nuremberg Laws.

General Wilhelm Keitel presents terms of surrender to French leaders on June 21, 1940. Hitler demanded that the meeting be held in the historic Armistice railcar, where Germany's surrender after WWI took place. Seated from left to right, starting with Joachim von Ribbentrop's back, are Hermann Göring, Hitler, Field Marshal Walter von Brautisch *(facing camera)*, and Rudolf Hess *(also facing camera)*. On the right are French generals Jean-Marie-Joseph Bergeret *(nearest camera)* and Charles Léon Clément Huntziger.

Paris Occupation

As German troops marched into Paris on June 14, 1940, millions of Parisians fled southward. Loudspeaker trucks warned that aggression and sabotage were punishable by death, while propaganda broadcasts told Parisians that the Germans meant them no harm. However, for many of the 100,000-plus Parisian Jews, the Nazi occupation meant persecution and deportation to death camps.

A census located all Jews in the city. A card index listed each Jew's address, occupation, and nationality. French identity cards were confiscated. Yellow Star armbands were ordered and nighttime curfews imposed.

Assisted by Paris police, the SS conducted periodic roundups of Jews. Those found were sent to the Drancy, France, transit camp for deportation. A mammoth hunt in 1942 collected 13,000 Jews,

including 4000 children—many of whom had been separated from their parents. After being penned up in a sports stadium for one week, the crying children were then crammed into cattle cars and delivered to Auschwitz.

• **June 4, 1940:** The concentration camp at Neuengamme, Germany, is upgraded to primary-camp status. • French and British troops are evacuated from Dunkerque, France.

• **June 10, 1940:** Italy announces that it has entered the war, as a junior ally to Germany.

• **June 14, 1940:** The first inmates, including teachers, priests, and other non-Jewish Poles, arrive at the Auschwitz death camp. • Paris falls to the Germans. Noted novelist and German-Jewish refugee Ernst Weiss commits suicide in the city.

• **June 16, 1940:** France presses for an armistice with Germany.

• **June 21, 1940:** American radio correspondent William L. Shirer broadcasts details of France's capitulation to Germany.

• **June 22, 1940:** France surrenders and signs an armistice with Germany.

• **June 26, 1940:** United States Assistant Secretary of State Breckinridge Long

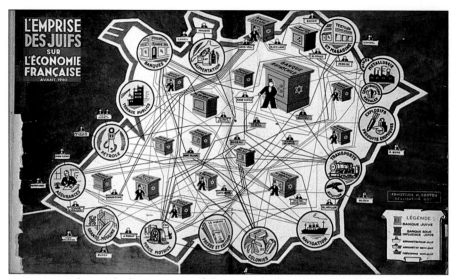

The British White Paper of May 1939 severely limited Jewish immigration to Palestine. Yet many Arab leaders denounced it, demanding that Palestine become an exclusively Arab state immediately. Under the claim, then, to "safeguard the civil and religious rights of all the inhabitants of Palestine irrespective of race and religion," the White Paper satisfied neither Jews nor Arabs. Earlier British attempts to cooperate with the *Hagana*—the Jewish underground army—to put an end to violence, and to deal with Arab leaders via diplomacy, were clumsy and ineffectual. Because Britain finally made it clear that its empire was more important than a Jewish homeland, Jewish agitation for a national state naturally increased. Not surprisingly, antisemitism in Palestine and elsewhere in the Arab world was virulent and widespread. This pro-Nazi Arabic poster reads, "Long Live Hitler."

Supposed Jewish domination of the French economy is graphically depicted in this antisemitic, illustrated map. Following the defeat of France and the establishment of the Vichy regime, antisemitism reemerged as a potent social force. Anti-Jewish legislation was reinforced by popular depictions of traditional negative Jewish stereotypes. Presumed Jewish domination of French capital was particularly resonant given the public's familiarity with the Rothschilds and other Jewish banking families.

A page from an issue of the film magazine *Illustrierter Film-Kurier* depicts a scene from Fritz Hippler's pseudo-documentary *Der Ewige Jude* (*The Eternal Jew*). Films were a particularly important weapon within the Nazi propaganda arsenal. Propaganda Minister Joseph Goebbels recognized their ability to manipulate the masses, especially in the German-occupied countries of Europe. However, the crude and lifeless portrayal of Jewish lust for money in *Der Ewige Jude,* and the film's overt antisemitic messages, resulted in limited appeal for broad audiences.

1940

determines to obstruct the granting of visas to Jews seeking entry into the United States. He seeks indefinitely to "delay and effectively stop" such immigration by ordering American consuls "to put every obstacle in the way [to] postpone and postpone and postpone the granting of visas." His goal will be realized over the next four years.

• July 1940: The America First Committee is formed. It is the most significant American isolationist group, and it is also infiltrated by Nazis, who are working to prevent American intervention in Europe. Several prominent Americans speak in support of the committee. Many in Congress attack the Jews of Hollywood as attempting to involve America in opposition to Hitler.

Inmates of the Sachsenhausen concentration camp in Germany read the inscription posted on their barracks: "There is one way to liberty: Its milestones are obedience, diligence, honesty, order, cleanliness, sense of sacrifice, moderation, truth and love for your Fatherland." While sayings such as this provided good propaganda for Germans outside of the concentration camps, they mocked the realities of camp life. Following incarceration, one's liberty and freedom were brutally taken and seldom returned unconditionally.

Inmates from the Buchenwald concentration camp in Germany construct a gallows while supervised by officers of the SS. Public executions were part of the terror system employed within the concentration camps. Prisoners who violated the Byzantine rules of order were physically punished and often hanged. Survivor testimonies are replete with tales of having witnessed many public hangings.

MAJOR CONCENTRATION CAMPS IN GREATER GERMANY, 1939–1945

Though most of their major concentration camps were in Greater Germany, the Nazis built their death camps in Occupied Poland, "hidden" from the German populace.

• **Bloody anti-Jewish riots erupt in cities throughout Romania.** • **In a letter to German Interior Minister Wilhelm Frick, Bishop Theophil Wurm, head of the provincial Lutheran Church at Württemberg, Germany, objects to "euthanasia" killings at the nearby Grafaneck crippled-children's institution;** See September 5, 1940. • **In Holland, a collaborationist propaganda** group, *Nederlandse Unie* (Netherlands Union), is established.

• **July 1, 1940: A Jewish ghetto is established at Bedzin, Poland.**

• **July 10, 1940: The Battle of Britain begins when the German *Luftwaffe* (Air Force) attacks British targets.**

• **August 1940: The United States Congress passes a law to allow thousands of British children into the U.S. beyond the immigration quotas. The law is widely supported by American public opinion. Exploiting a loophole in America's immigration law never used for Jewish refugee children, President Franklin Roosevelt calls these British children "visitors"; that is, immigrants**

Rescue in France

Although official policy of the United States government during 1940–41 closed gates to Jewish immigration, a handful of private, volunteer-staffed organizations launched rescue operations from America. The New York-based Emergency Rescue Committee (ERC) aided 2000 Jewish refugees—Spanish, German, and Czechoslovakian—who were stranded in France. ERC provided refugees with food, clothing, lodging, and medical care, and attempted to expedite their flight from France.

The valiant efforts of Varian Fry *(pictured)*, ERC's representative in Marseilles, France, made it possible for about 1000 Jews to escape. Among them were many of Europe's leading cultural figures, including artist

Marc Chagall and writers Heinrich Mann and Walter Mehring. For one year, beginning in August 1940, Fry directed the covert escapes of hundreds of refugees. Frustrated by emigration restrictions, Fry set up clandestine operations complete with encrypted codes of communication and secret escape routes. He even established contacts with the underworld to obtain forged papers and boat passages. In one instance, more than 100 refugees—disguised as farm laborers—were smuggled across the French-Spanish border along unpatrolled paths.

Sometimes, though, plans went awry, and French authorities apprehended ships and interned their passengers. Fry was himself expelled in August 1941.

None of the Dunski family pictured here survived the Holocaust. The oldest of four children, Zvi (seated by his mother, Fajga) was active in *Ha-Shomer ha-Tsa'ir*, a Zionist youth organization. He and his friends resisted the Nazis, publishing an underground newspaper and printing leaflets urging Jews of Sosnowiec, Poland, to flee deportation. Arrested by the Jewish police, Zvi was sent to the Gestapo prison in Katowice, Poland, where he was murdered. His mother and sister Sala *(standing right)* were sent to Auschwitz, where they perished, as did Genia *(standing left)*. Only one child, Frania, imprisoned in various labor camps, survived the war.

Ion Antonescu, ruler of Romania from 1940 to '44, smiles warmly as he greets members of the Romanian High Command. After having obtained power with the support of the Iron Guard, Antonescu ordered the expulsion of Jews from villages and towns to urban centers. He also confiscated and nationalized Jewish property. Tried as a war criminal, Antonescu was executed on June 1, 1946.

1940

planning some day to return to Great Britain. Congress amends the Neutrality Act to allow American ships to evacuate these children. • 400 Jews sick with bleeding diarrhea at the Józefów, Poland, labor camp are executed.

• **August 9, 1940:** Hitler orders *Aufbau Ost*, the buildup of military communications and transport in Poland, pre-

paratory to a German invasion of the Soviet Union; *See* June 22, 1941.

• **August 10, 1940:** Romania passes antisemitic legislation.

• **August 15, 1940:** Adolf Eichmann proposes turning the island of Madagascar into a huge Jewish ghetto, where Jews will die out.

Belgian Nazis post a sign that reads "V—sign of German victory." The antisemitic sign on the truck, with its caricature of a bloodthirsty Jew, reads: "The Jewish conspiracy against Europe. Join the Flemish volunteer regiment in the struggle against bolshevism." Established in September 1940, the *Algemeene Schutscharen Vlaanderen* (Flemish General SS) was the first of the Belgian collaborationist units. It was later joined by the *Légion Wallonie* (Wallonian Legion), which earned a reputation even within the SS for its fanaticism.

"**I could not eliminate all lice and Jews in only one year. But in the course of time, and if you will help me, this end will be attained.**"

—*Hans Frank, governor-general of Occupied Poland, addressing his staff*

Hans Frank *(left)* was the head of the *Generalgouvernement*. This region in Poland became a "dumping ground" for Jews, and Frank was intimately involved in the atrocities carried out under his jurisdiction. Under Frank's orders, the Poles were ruthlessly exploited, public treasures were seized, and thousands of innocents were executed. During 1940 the ghettoization of the Jews proceeded at a rapid pace.

A German racial hygienist and a police officer interview an elderly Gypsy woman. With the advent of modern industrial society, the Gypsies' nomadic lifestyle was out of step with the times. Throughout the early 20th century, government authorities attempted to coerce the 28,000 German Gypsies into establishing permanent residences and occupations. Once in power, the Nazis intensified this pressure. The Nuremberg Laws of 1935 were applied to the Gypsies, and thousands of the people were eventually placed in concentration camps. Together with Jews, Gypsies were relocated to the *Generalgouvernement* in Poland.

• **August 25, 1940: The first British air raid is launched against Berlin.**

• **August 26, 1940: German-Jewish philosopher Walter Benjamin commits suicide in Spain, after local authorities threaten to return him to Germany.**

• **August 27, 1940: France's collaborationist government, headed by Marshal** Philippe Pétain, invalidates the March 21, 1939, French decree prohibiting incitement to race hatred.

• **September 1940: Polish underground officer Witold Pilecki penetrates the main camp at Auschwitz with the intention of organizing secret resistance groups inside the camp. • The National Legionary government of dictator Ion** Antonescu assumes power in Romania. • In Belgium, a collaborationist military unit, *Algemeene Schutscharen Vlaanderen* (Flemish General SS), is established.

• **September 1, 1940: Soviet authorities order Japanese Consul Sempo Sugihara to leave Kovno, Lithuania, where he has issued 3500 exit visas to Jews.**

This wedding photograph of Hala Buchwajc and Motek Lichtensztajin, taken in the Bedzin Ghetto, belies the harsh reality of life for Polish Jews. Married in 1940, the newlyweds were separated when they arrived at Auschwitz. After they were transferred to different camps, the young couple lost track of each other and feared the worst. Miraculously, however, Hala and Motek were reunited in 1946 when the two met by chance on the streets of London.

The execution of Jud Süss (actor Ferdinand Marian) provides the climax of the antisemitic feature film *Jud Süss*. Directed by Veit Harlan and released in September 1940, the film was deemed by the Nazis as especially "worthwhile" for young people. Aggressively promoted by Propaganda Minister Joseph Goebbels and backed by a budget of two million *Reichsmarks*, the film portrayed the scandalous financial tricks of Joseph Süss Oppenheimer, the advisor to Duke Karl Alexander of Württemberg, Germany, in the early 1700s. The film's explicit antisemitic message, coupled with powerful performances, had an inflammatory impact on audiences. Attacks against Jews were common after showings of the film.

Two young children of the Bedzin (Poland) Ghetto peacefully bide their time. Occupied by the Germans on September 4, 1939, Bedzin had 27,000 Jewish inhabitants, approximately 45 percent of the town's entire population. Confiscation of Jewish property, forced labor, deprivation, and, ultimately, deportation to Auschwitz were slated for the Jews of Bedzin. After the first wave of deportations to Auschwitz, a Resistance movement attempted to make contact with the Polish underground. The ghetto was liquidated by the Nazis in August 1943.

1940

• **September 5, 1940:** German occupation authorities in Luxembourg introduce Nuremberg Laws. All Jewish businesses are seized and handed to "Aryans." • Bishop Theophil Wurm, head of the provincial Lutheran Church at Württemberg, Germany, sends a second letter to German Interior Minister Wilhelm Frick expressing his objections to "euthanasia" killings.

• **September 7, 1940:** The Germans' "blitz" bombing of Great Britain begins.

• **September 11, 1940:** The Jewish refugee ship *Quanza* stops to refuel at Norfolk, Virginia, after having been denied entry to the United States at New York and to Mexico at Vera Cruz. One passenger, a German Jew, is

Jewish refugees aboard the Portuguese steamer *Quanza* were denied entry to the United States at New York and to Mexico at Vera Cruz. The frantic and futile search for safe havens compelled one passenger, a German Jew, to dive overboard during a refueling stop at Norfolk, Virginia. His escape plans were foiled by an American Army guard who returned him to the ship.

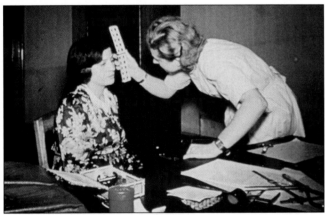

German hygienist Sophie Erhardt checks the eye color of a Gypsy woman during a racial examination. Nazi race science classified humans according to the color of one's eyes and skin, and by body measurements. The Gypsies, who originated in India and traveled to southeastern and east-central Europe through Iran, were readily identifiable by their dark skin and eye color. The Nazis viewed the Gypsies as a threat to "pure" Nordic society and subjected them to relocation and extermination policies.

Jews in North Africa

Vichy's anti-Jewish policies influenced the lives of 300,000 Jews in French colonial North Africa. European immigrants there harbored strong antisemitic sentiments, and the fanatically racist Algerian nationalist movement vigorously terrorized Jews.

The mayor of Algiers, Max Régis, who was also president of the Anti-Jewish League, vowed early in his career to "water Algeria's liberty tree with Jewish blood." Algerian officials stripped Jews of French citizenship, ordered Yellow Star armbands, and applied quotas to education—even primary schools.

In Morocco, where Jewish subjects were granted equal rights, Vichy's "Jewish Statute" was not officially in effect. Still, the French colonial administration vigorously imposed anti-Jewish laws, purging the civil service and barring Jewish children from public swimming pools and scouting organizations. In Tunisia, Jews' independent status ended with the application of the "Statute." Jews lost jobs, and quotas restricted education. Libya's Jews suffered harassment by Italian colonial officials who marked pass-

ports, seized property, limited cultural opportunities, and interned Jews in labor camps, where many died.

No roundups of North African Jews occurred, but over 13,000 foreign Jews deported from Vichy were interned in the desert, where they constituted slave-labor battalions for the Trans-Saharan Railway project. Many died in these remote and desolate camps.

---

returned to the ship by U.S. Army guards after leaping overboard near the shore of Hampton Roads, Virginia.
• In Holland, a collaborationist military unit, *Nederlandsche SS* (Dutch SS), is established.

• **September 15, 1940:** Germany's *Luftwaffe* suffers major losses over London, at last giving Britain's Royal Air Force

(RAF) the upper hand in the Battle of Britain.

• **September 23, 1940:** SS chief Heinrich Himmler authorizes a special SS *Reichsbank* account to hold gold (including gold extracted from teeth), silver, jewelry, and foreign currency stolen from interned Jews. The account is held by the fictitious "Max Heiliger."

• **September 24, 1940:** Director Veit Harlan's antisemitic film *Jud Süss* premieres in Berlin.

• **September 27, 1940:** Japan signs a treaty with Germany and Italy, thus forming the Berlin-Rome-Tokyo Axis. Slovakia, Romania, and Hungary will soon join.

Vichy and the Jews

From 1940 to 1944, all of France was occupied by the Nazis except for the southern third. However, that southern zone, known as Vichy, was ruled by an equally antisemitic government, led by Marshal Philippe Pétain.

The Vichy regime enacted discriminatory and humiliating policies against Jews, which culminated in arrests, internments, and deportations to Nazi death camps. Few victims survived. One-third of the 84,000 Jews deported

from France came from this unoccupied zone. Vichy passed the "Jewish Statute," which racially defined "Jewishness" and barred Jews from positions of authority. A census located Jews and listed their addresses, jobs, and wealth. *Juif* (Jew) stamps marked ration cards and identity papers. Yellow posters identified Jewish businesses, while "Aryanization" robbed them of their property.

Non-French Jews fared worse. Roundups of "undesirable refugees" netted 30,000 Jews. Thrown into special camps, 3000 people died because of deplorable conditions. At Gurs, in the Pyrénées Mountains, 1167 died of starvation, dysentery, and typhoid. At Rivesaltes, where children were imprisoned separate from their mothers, mortality rates were equally high. Horrible sanitary conditions; lack of food, water, and adequate shelter from the cold; and sadistic harassment by guards were standard features of Vichy's concentration camps. In time, deportation to the East emptied the camps.

On October 3, 1940, the Vichy government of France passed the first *Statut des Juifs* (Jewish Statute). The law was modeled on the German Nuremberg Laws. Jews living in Vichy France were required to have their identification cards stamped with the word *Juif* (Jew). Moreover, they were not permitted to change residences, and they had to inform the police about any changes in marital status. The laws effectively enabled the regime to keep tabs on the Jews.

A Jewish refugee and his young daughter stand in Lisbon, Portugal, by the Greek ship *Nea Hellas*. Scheduled to depart for the United States in October 1940, the voyage was canceled after the Italian invasion of Greece. Some 12,000 refugees were stranded in Lisbon, a major gateway for those holding immigration visas.

1940

• **October 1940: 6500 Jews are deported from Germany's Palatinate, Baden, and Saar regions to internment camps at the foot of the French Pyrénées.** • **Jews are forced to pay for and build a wall around the Warsaw (Poland) Ghetto.** • **Reich theoretician Alfred Rosenberg writes an article, "Jews to Madagascar," which suggests mass deportation of Jews to the island** off the African coast. • **German authorities forbid Norwegian Jews to teach and participate in other professions.**

• **October 1, 1940: Young Jewish men return from the Belzec, Poland, camp to Szczebrzeszyn, Poland, after a ransom of 20,000 zlotys is paid to Nazi captors.**

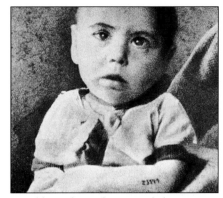

Although mothers tried desperately to hide and protect their children, few as young as this child, tattooed with the number 23141, survived Auschwitz. In the concentration camps, work provided the only hope of survival, a possibility foreclosed to the very young and the elderly. As Auschwitz moved into its final, extermination-camp phase, some children, especially twins, escaped the gas chambers upon arrival only to be subjected to cruel medical experiments.

Accompanied by German Foreign Minister Joachim von Ribbentrop *(near left)* and Army Chief of Staff General Wilhelm Keitel *(far left)*, Soviet Foreign Commissar Viacheslav Molotov reviews German troops during a visit to Berlin in November 1940. Ribbentrop and Molotov were the architects of the Soviet-German Non-Aggression Pact, which secretly divided Poland between the two countries and formed the basis of their peaceful coexistence. Still in effect in 1940, the pact delayed an eventual military confrontation between the Soviet Union and Nazi Germany, two ideological enemies.

Residents of the Warsaw Ghetto cut up dead horses for meat. This was a violation of Kosher laws, but some Jews felt compelled to abandon these rules under the extraordinary conditions imposed on them by life in the ghetto. Many Jews survived only because of their willingness to eat non-Kosher food.

● **October 3, 1940: Vichy (Occupied) France passes antisemitic legislation.** Vichy's anti-Jewish laws, the first *Statut des Juifs*, are modeled on the German Nuremberg Laws, and, like them, are widely accepted. Passed in anticipation of Nazi pressure, the laws' primary aims are to force Jews out of public service, teaching, financial occupations, public relations, and the media.

● **October 4, 1940:** German law gives Vichy France the power to imprison Jews even inside the Unoccupied Zone.

● **October 12, 1940:** On this Jewish Day of Atonement, German loudspeakers in Warsaw, Poland, announce that all Jews in the city must move to the Jewish ghetto by the end of the month.

● **October 14, 1940:** The Nazis move non-Jews out of a designated section of Warsaw, Poland, and import Jews to replace them.

● **October 20, 1940:** More than 7000 Jews from the Saar region of Germany are interned at the camp at Gurs, France.

WARSAW GHETTO

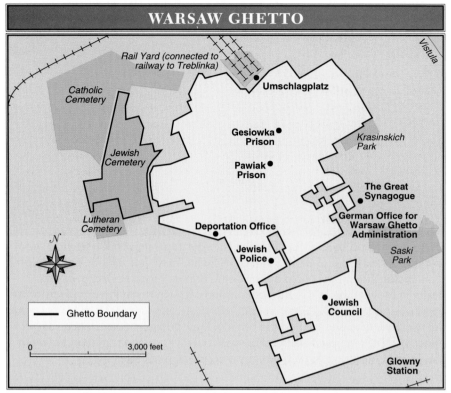

Rail Yard (connected to railway to Treblinka)

Vistula

Catholic Cemetery

Umschlagplatz

Gesiowka Prison

Krasinskich Park

Jewish Cemetery

Pawiak Prison

The Great Synagogue

German Office for Warsaw Ghetto Administration

Lutheran Cemetery

Deportation Office

Jewish Police

Saski Park

Jewish Council

— Ghetto Boundary

0   3,000 feet

Glowny Station

Warsaw's half-million Jews feared the *Umschlagplatz,* an assembly point for deportation.

A group of hungry Jewish children passes the time of day in a crowded room in the Warsaw Ghetto. Children were particularly vulnerable to the harsh treatment of the Nazis. Without proper food, shelter, and clothing, childhood mortality rates were very high. In addition, with schools closed, extracurricular activities nonexistent, and traditional family structures shattered, children of the ghettos were deprived of education and their innocence.

A German soldier checks the papers of a Jewish woman as she enters the Warsaw (Poland) Ghetto. The walls of the ghetto were sealed on November 16, 1940, and from that time until the final liquidation, traffic to and from the ghetto was tightly regulated. At first the ghetto had 22 gates and openings in the wall. By April 1941 only 13 of them remained, all of which were guarded by a cadre of police forces: German, Polish, and Jewish. No one dared to walk through the gates without the proper papers.

1940

• **October 22, 1940:** Jewish business owners in the Netherlands must register their businesses with the occupying Nazis.

• **October 25, 1940:** A German directive issued from Kraków, Poland, prohibits issuance of exit visas to Polish Jews.

• **October 28, 1940:** Italy invades Greece. More than 12,000 Greek Jews help to halt the Italian offensive. • German occupiers in Belgium pass antisemitic legislation.

• **November 11, 1940:** Fifty-five non-Jewish Polish intellectuals are murdered at Dachau, Germany. • German authorities in Poland officially declare

Warsaw Ghetto

The Warsaw Ghetto was the largest of the ghettos organized by the Nazis in Poland. A tiny section of the city, an area of 3.5 square miles, imprisoned a half-million Jews. The ghetto covered merely two percent of the city's area but contained 30 percent of its population.

Unimaginable overcrowding intensified the suffering. Ten percent died from starvation and epidemics during the first year of the ghetto's existence. With the fall of Poland, the Nazis subjected the Jews of Warsaw to a series of repressive measures, including identifying armbands, property confiscations, and forced-labor requisitions.

The Nazis created the ghetto by concentrating Warsaw's Jews in the northern part of the city, the most heavily Jewish-populated district. The announced purpose was to isolate the Jews in order to keep them from spreading typhus. In fact, ghettoization actually spread the disease.

In October 1940 the Nazi governor of Warsaw ordered the remaining 160,000 Jews of the city transferred to the ghetto. An endless stream of bewildered people moved slowly through jammed streets, pushing carts and wheelbarrows and carrying small bundles in a desperate search for shelter. Some found a tiny space in overcrowded rooms. Others took refuge in courtyards, under stairways, or in cellars of bombed-out houses. Each building housed an average of 400 people; rooms held an average of six to seven people.

The barbed wire and wooden fences hastily put up by the Germans gave way to an 11-foot-high brick wall topped with broken glass. It completely enclosed the area and covered 11 miles. About 20 gates allowed limited access to the outside world. These were heavily guarded and locked at night. In November 1940 the gates were permanently sealed, permitting no contact with the outside.

No longer allowed to leave the ghetto even to work, the Jews somehow had to find sub-

sistence. Workers jostled for the few available jobs. Those without work sold jewels and clothing for food. The Nazis provided only minimal food supplies, rationing them in exchange for the output of forced-labor battalions and the products produced by ghetto craftsmen. Daily food allocations, distributed through the *Judenrat*, equaled roughly 200 calories per person. The Nazis permitted no fresh fruits, vegetables, meat, fish, or milk inside the ghetto. Even safe drinking water was scarce. Dozens of soup kitchens helped the neediest. Many subsisted on boiled potato skins and water.

Beggars with skeletal bodies roamed the streets. During the winter, when sewage pipes froze, human excrement was dumped into streets. Without food, heat, or medical supplies, dozens of ghetto residents died daily. Old people and children, too weak to move, simply laid down in the streets and died. Corpses were covered beneath newspaper. Orphaned, naked toddlers sat amidst refuse in gutters, wailing pitifully. All told, about 500,000 residents of Warsaw lost their lives during the Nazi occupation.

---

the existence of the Warsaw (Poland) Ghetto.

• **November 15–16, 1940:** The Nazis seal off the Warsaw (Poland) Ghetto from the rest of the city.

• **November 17, 1940:** In Berlin, Lieutenant Colonel Kazys Skirpa, former Lithuanian ambassador to Germany, establishes the *Lietuviu Aktyvistu Frontas* (Lithuanian Activist Front), a collaborationist Fascist organization dedicated to nationalism and antisemitism.

• **November 19, 1940:** A Christian Pole in Warsaw is killed by Germans after tossing a bundle of bread over the wall into the Jewish ghetto.

• **November 25, 1940:** The ship *Patria*, carrying 2000 Jewish immigrants, is accidentally sunk by the radical Jewish group *Hagana*. About 250 Jews on board are killed.

• **November 26, 1940:** British Secretary of State for the Colonies Lord Lloyd calls those who are working to save Jewish lives by illegally transporting

Antisemitism in Bulgaria

Prior to World War II, Bulgaria's 48,000 Jews were fully integrated into the economic and political life of the country. But that all changed in 1940, when a pro-German government took office. Soon, Bulgarian policy led to the persecution of the country's Jewish population.

The "Law for the Protection of the Nation," passed by Bulgaria's Parliament in 1940, sought to "protect" the nation from Jews, who were now declared state enemies. The law established a definition of a Jew: one who had at least one Jewish parent. Jews could not own farmland or work in the civil service, in banking institutions, or as bookkeepers or clerks.

Legislation forced Jews to register and to use Jewish first names, and prohibited the use of Bulgarian surnames ending in -ov, -ev, or -ich. It barred Jews from military service, and made service in labor squads mandatory. Curfews were imposed, radios and phones were removed from Jewish homes and businesses, and the Star of David had to be worn.

The refugee ship *Patria* sinks off the coast of Haifa, Palestine, in November 1940. With more that 2000 Jews on board, the ship was accidentally sunk by the *Hagana,* the fledgling Jewish army in Palestine. About 250 Jews died in the incident.

Smoke rises from the "euthanasia" center in Hadamar, Germany. Opened in December 1940, the installation at Hadamar became the sixth and final killing center involved in the euthanasia program. New patients were processed on the first floor of the killing facility. The gas chamber and crematorium were located in the basement. The gas chamber was disguised as a shower, and the crematorium consisted of two ovens attached to a single chimney. Although local residents were prohibited entry and kept at bay by stern warning signs, the chimney's smoke and smell could not be suppressed.

1940

them to Palestine "foul people who had to be stamped out."

● November 28, 1940: Director Fritz Hippler's pseudo-documentary, antisemitic film *Der Ewige Jude* (*The Eternal Jew*) premieres in Berlin.

● December 1940: The Vatican condemns Nazi "mercy killings" of "unfit Aryans" as "contrary to both natural and divine law." ● Inside the Warsaw (Poland) Ghetto, Polish-Jewish historian Emanuel Ringelblum begins work on a secret diary of ghetto life. ● In Holland, a collaborationist propaganda group, *Verbond van Nederlandse Journalisten* (Union of Dutch Journalists), is established.

"[Warsaw Ghetto] separation prevented the Jews from coming into contact with non-Jews and left them in a state of isolation, insulation, and choking congestion."

—*Warsaw Ghetto survivor Israel Gutman*

Among the most active Resistance groups in the Warsaw Ghetto was *Ha-Shomer ha-Tsa'ir*, a Zionist-Socialist movement that saw National Socialism as a natural outgrowth of capitalism. Firm believers in "self-help"—that is, Jews looking after Jews—*Ha-Shomer ha-Tsa'ir* had its own soup kitchen located in its secret headquarters at 23 Nalewki Street. Pictured here are the founders of the organization. From left to right: Oskar Handler, Zivia Lubetkin, Yudke Helman, and Yitzhak Zuckerman.

All public facilities in Warsaw, Poland, and other cities with a Jewish ghetto, were strictly segregated. The streetcar above is labeled "Only for Jews." Non-Jews were forbidden to travel in streetcars bearing this distinction, and Jews could use only such cars. Jews careless enough to ride on the non-Jewish cars were executed. The Germans hoped that, by segregating the Polish population, non-Jews would not learn about the living conditions in the ghetto. Even the dead were segregated, as the Jewish "corpse wagon" *(left)* demonstrates.

• **December 5, 1940: British government official Sir John Schuckburgh writes that "the Jews have no sense of humor and no sense of proportion."**

• **December 9, 1940: A German soldier leaps from a car in the Warsaw (Poland) Ghetto and strikes a Jewish boy in the head with an iron bar, killing him.**

• **December 12, 1940: The *Salvador*, a ship that set out from Varna, Bulgaria, a month ago, sinks in the Sea of Marmora; 200 Jewish refugees, including 70 children, drown. T. M. Snow, head of the British Foreign Office's Refugee Section, notes that "there could have been no more opportune disaster from the point of view of stopping this [Jewish refugee] traffic [to Palestine]."**

• **December 17, 1940: Drunk SS guards at the Sachsenhausen, Germany, labor camp awaken Jews during a frigid night and order them to roll in the snow.**

• **Late 1940–early 1941: The Jewish ghetto at Piotrków, Poland, is struck by an epidemic of typhus.**

1941

O N January 30, 1941, the eighth anniversary of his taking power in Germany, Adolf Hitler addressed the *Reichstag:* "I do not wish to forget," said Hitler, "the hint, that I already gave in the German *Reichstag* . . . namely that if the rest of the world should be thrust into a war by Jewry, then all Jewry will have played out its role in Europe! . . . The coming years and months will prove that here, too, my prediction was correct."

By the end of 1940, the number of Jews killed by Nazi Germany approached 100,000. But in 1941 the death toll grew astronomically, as mass murder of Jews became German state policy. How that decisive turn took place, and the relation it bore to Hitler's forecast on January 30, is not exactly clear. What is certain is that in 1941 about one million Jews lost their lives.

A report about a significant part of those losses went to the Berlin office of Reinhard Heydrich, chief of the Security Police and Security Service, on October 2. Designated as "Operational Situation Report USSR No. 101," it briefly summed up the work of *Einsatzgruppe* C at Babi Yar, a ravine-filled area located in northwestern Kiev, the Ukraine's capital city. The report stated: "*Sonderkommando* 4a in collaboration with *Einsatzgruppe* HG and two *Kommandos* of Police Regiment South executed 33,771 Jews in Kiev on September 29 and 30, 1941."

From a bureaucratic perspective, this report required no elaboration. In 1959, however, a German eyewitness, Fritz Höfer, who had been a truck driver in *Sonderkommando* 4a, had more to say. Höfer detailed how the Germans, aided and abetted by their Ukrainian collaborators, rounded up the Jews and forced them to strip, leave their valuables behind, and enter "a ravine that was about 150 meters long, 30 meters wide, and a good 15 meters deep." He said that "no distinction was made between men, women, and children." Once in the ravine, the Jews were "made to lie down on top of Jews who had already been shot. This all happened very quickly. The corpses were literally in layers. A police marksman came along and shot each Jew in the neck with a submachine gun at the spot where he was lying." Until it was too late, said Höfer, the Jews approached Babi Yar "still under the impression that they were being resettled."

In the autumn of 1941, the massacre at Babi Yar was not unusual. It materialized from a planned destruction process that went into effect with the

Minsk partisans Volodya Sherbateyvich *(left)* and Masha Bruskina are hanged, October 26, 1941.

1941

Wehrmacht's (German Army's) invasion of Soviet territory on June 22. As the Germans advanced eastward, army units were accompanied by *Einsatzgruppen,* special squads whose mission was to round up Bolshevik political leaders and intelligentsia, many of whom the Nazis took to be Jews since Nazi ideology saw communism as dominated by Jewish influences.

Following procedures similar to those at Babi Yar, the shooting massacres expanded during the summer. Within a few weeks these mobile killing units devastated hundreds of Jewish communities, slaughtering more Jews than the Nazis had murdered in the previous eight years. About 1.3 million Jews (about a quarter of all the Jews who died in the Holocaust) were killed, one by one, by the 3000 men in the four *Einsatzgruppen,* their support troops, local police, and collaborators—all with the assistance of the *Wehrmacht.* Most of the 1.3 million murders occurred in 1941.

Four members of *Einsatzgruppe* A execute three Jewish men in Kovno, Lithuania.

Although the organization of the *Einsatzgruppen* had been planned in advance of the Nazi invasion of the USSR, the date when a decision was made to kill all of Europe's Jews has not been—and perhaps never will be—precisely determined. No direct written order of that kind from Hitler, for example, has yet been discovered. On July 31, Hermann Göring, the second man in the Third Reich, authorized Reinhard Heydrich to prepare the "Final Solution of the Jewish question," but Göring's authorization did not detail exactly what was to be done, or how.

Heydrich's mandate was to determine how to solve the Nazis' "Jewish problem" once and for all. According to Holocaust scholar Raul Hilberg, what Heydrich obtained was "an authorization to invent." As decisions were taken and events unfolded, invention was called for again and again. Every agency involved would face unprecedented problems because nothing like the "Final Solution" that eventually took place— the mass murder on such a large scale of an entire people, not for anything they had done but simply because of their "race"—had ever been attempted before in human history.

Hilberg sums up the situation succinctly: "Not just how to kill the Jews, but what to do with their property thereafter. And not only that, but how to deal with the problem of not letting the world know what had happened. All this multitude of problems was new." Nazi leaders such as Heydrich; his superior, Heinrich Himmler; subordinates such as Adolf Eichmann; and an immense bureaucracy attempted to solve such problems.

The policy to eliminate Europe's Jews, which was too important to be implemented without Hitler's initiative, probably went into effect during the summer of 1941, after the *Einsatzgruppen* killings had begun in June. Further signs soon appeared to indicate that Hitler had expressed his decision to destroy European Jewry completely. By late autumn, for example, construction of stationary gas chambers was under way at the Belzec and Auschwitz concentration camps in Poland. Even earlier, in September, experiments at Auschwitz showed that a pesticide called Zyklon B could be used to kill human beings in gas chambers. And on December 8, the day after the Japanese bombing of Pearl Harbor brought the United States fully into World War II, the first large-scale gassing of Jews took place: 700 Jews from villages near the killing center at Chelmno, Poland, were executed by carbon monoxide gas in trucks specifically designed for that purpose.

Mass murder by shooting still decimated Jewish communities. However, in the latter months of 1941 it became clear to the Germans that mass murder by shooting was overly stressful on the killers and too inefficient to meet the goals of the "Final Solution." The major change in Nazi Germany's anti-Jewish policy entailed that Jews would increasingly be deported and destroyed at major death camps in Poland.

Employing euphemisms about "resettlement," the Germans tried to disguise their murderous intentions. Abba Kovner, a young, Jewish Resistance leader, was not deceived. When the Nazi slaughter of Lithuanian Jews convinced him that armed resistance against the Germans was imperative, he dedicated himself to organizing Jewish fighters.

At a clandestine meeting held in Vilna, Lithuania, on the night of December 31, 1941, Kovner crafted a manifesto, which was shared more widely with Jewish Resistance members the next day. "Hitler plans to destroy all of the Jews of Europe," the Proclamation of the Vilna Ghetto Resistance Organization stated on January 1, 1942, "and the Jews of Lithuania have been chosen as the first in line." Its exhortation continued: "We will not be led like sheep to the slaughter! True, we are weak and defenseless, but the only reply to the murderer is revolt! Brothers! Better to fall as free fighters than to live by the mercy of the murderers. Arise! Arise with your last breath!"

Based on his early and correct judgment about German intentions to destroy European Jewry completely, Kovner's public call for resistance was the first of its kind. In late 1941 European Jews severely lacked the resources and support needed for effective uprisings. Nevertheless, as the Final Solution's mass murder continued, armed Jewish men, women, and youths found ways to resist the Nazis in ghettos, in partisan units, in underground groups across the European continent, and even in the concentration and extermination camps.

What stands out is not the false stereotype that there was scant armed resistance among the European Jews, but rather that so much of this resistance did take place when Jewish resources were terribly limited. After the

Above: This mobile killing van gassed Jews who were being deported to the crematoria at Chelmno, Poland. *Below:* Billowing smoke testifies to the fierce fighting between German troops, shown driving into the Ukraine, and Soviet defenders. Using flamethrowers and grenades, the Germans destroyed everything in their path.

Holocaust, the examples of Jewish resistance carried out in spite of hopeless odds and almost certain death bear profound symbolic meaning for all people—Jews and non-Jews alike—who understand the human quest for freedom.

Metropolitan Cyril of Plovdiv, Bulgaria, a member of the supreme body of the Orthodox church, protested his country's antisemitic legislation. He was joined by other clerics and a wide range of professionals and politicians in his campaign against the proposed legislation. In spite of the widespread opposition to the racial laws, the Bulgarian government placed its relationship with Germany above all other concerns and implemented the legislation on January 21, 1941.

Dimo Kazassov of Bulgaria delivers a speech in protest of the Jewish laws enacted in 1940. The Law for the Defense of the Nation deprived Bulgarian Jews of their civil rights. Kazassov's written protest to the prime minister was rejected. Kazassov continued his efforts on behalf of Bulgarian Jewry, and he played a key role in preventing their deportation later in the war.

An honorary SS general, Erich Koch was the most important Nazi official in East Prussia, and was *Reichskommissar* for the Ukraine. A German leader in the genocide of Slavic peoples, he was also responsible for murdering hundreds of thousands of Poles and Ukrainians. Koch said, "We are a master race, which must remember that the lowliest German worker is racially and biologically a thousand times more valuable than the population here [the Ukraine]." Koch escaped arrest immediately after the war but was captured by the British in 1949. Finally tried in 1958 and sentenced to death the following year, his sentence was commuted to life in prison. He died in a Polish prison in 1986.

1941

● **1941:** Maximilian Kolbe, a Roman Catholic priest interned at the Auschwitz, Poland, death camp and who volunteered to take the place of a condemned non-Jewish inmate, dies of a phenol injection. ● The first issue of *Sztandar Wolnosci* (*Banner of Freedom*), a Polish-language publication of the Jewish Resistance in Vilna, Lithuania, is published. ● In Holland,

a collaborationist auxiliary police force, *Landwacht* (Home Guard), is established.

● **January 1941:** Denied fuel, Jews in the Warsaw Ghetto are freezing to death.

● **January 9, 1941:** Adolf Hitler officially abandons *Seelöwe* (Sea Lion),

Jewish corpses fill the yard of the morgue in Bucharest, Romania, following an orgy of violence carried out by the Romanian Iron Guard. The three-day killing spree claimed the lives of more than a hundred Jews and left thousands beaten and terrified. Not content to take only the lives of their victims, the murderers also stole their clothing.

Bread and soup were the staples of the starvation diet of prisoners in the concentration camps. Jewish prisoners were allowed only a few hundred calories per day. The restricted number of calories made the Jewish prisoners much more likely to be worked to death or to succumb to typhus and typhoid.

Nazi Euphemisms

Nazi euphemisms played an important role in the dehumanizing process of the Holocaust. From the beginning Hitler spoke of the need to "purify" and "cleanse," to rid the Reich of the Jewish "vermin," and to "decontaminate" or "disinfect" the Reich of the Jewish "bacillus."

Ultimately, the "Jewish problem" was solved through the "Final Solution" (*Endlösung*), a euphemism for extermination. Terms such as "euthanasia" and "mercy death" cloaked the murders of the handicapped (who were designated "unworthy of life"), which were committed for racial reasons—not to ease suffering. "Special treatment" (*Sonderbehandlung*) in euthanasia installations meant killing by gas.

Euphemisms were used in the death camps and in reference to the massacres conducted by *Einsatzkommandos*. Instead of "kill" or "murder," terms such as "special action," "evacuation," and "resettlement" obscured the real intent. "Protective custody" (*Schutzhaft*) of opponents did not mean protection from danger but rather unlimited incarceration without trial. "Jewish residence district" (*Jüdischer Wohnbezirk*) was substituted for "ghetto." The "East" and "Jewish settlement region" (*Jüdisches Siedlungsgebiet*) became collective euphemisms for the killing centers of Poland, with the death camps referred to only as "labor," "preferential," or "POW" camps.

Cruel deception and irony also marked the infamous camp-entrance signs: "Work Will Set You Free" (*Arbeit Macht Frei*). Within the camps, the gas chambers and crematoria received the harmless-sounding names "bath houses" (*Badeanstalten*) and "special installations" (*Spezialeinrichtungen*). Seldom has language been so cynically misused.

---

the German plan for an invasion of England. • Nazi police break into a house in the Warsaw Ghetto, force the women inside to undress, and prod their breasts and genitals with pistols.

• January 10, 1941: Dutch Jews register with German authorities.

• January 21–24, 1941: In Romania, Iron Guard Legionnaires launch a *coup d'état*, during which anti-Jewish violence boils over. Thousands of Jews are beaten and over 120 killed.

• January 22, 1941: The Law for the Defense of the Nation is imposed by Bulgaria, forcing Jews to give up public posts and forcing Jewish doctors, lawyers, and other professionals to forfeit their jobs. Also, a selective tax is imposed on Bulgaria's Jewish shops and homes.

• January 29, 1941: In the Lódź (Poland) Ghetto, Bluma Lichtensztajn leaps to her death from a fourth-floor window. Prize-winning Lódź painter Maurycy Trebacz dies of starvation.

The Holocaust in Romania

Romania was among the most antisemitic countries of prewar Europe. Once war began, the continuing persecution of Romania's Jews culminated in mass murder. Romanian troops rivaled Nazi *Einsatzgruppen* in the brutal killing of Jews, annihilating half of Romania's prewar Jewish population of 760,000.

During the 1930s, economic depression fueled Romanian propaganda that depicted Jews as parasites. Stringent laws stripped Jews of civil rights. In January 1941 Iron Guard Legionnaires stormed the Jewish section of Bucharest, where they burned shops, homes, and synagogues. Thousands of Jews were beaten and tortured. Some Jews were herded into a slaughterhouse and literally butchered

according to Jews' own ritual practices of animal slaughter. The bodies were hung on meat hooks and displayed with "Kosher meat" labels.

The German invasion of the Soviet Union sparked further pogroms. In the recaptured Romanian provinces of Bukovina and Bessarabia, Jews bore the brunt of the killing frenzy. Over 250,000 perished there through mass shootings, through drowning in the Dniester River, or from starvation and disease within ghettos and slave-labor camps. During the siege of Odessa, Romanian dictator Ion Antonescu ordered the execution of more than 35,000 of the city's Jews. *Einsatz* squads even complained of the Romanian soldiers' "undisciplined killing zeal," particularly their disregard for the disposal of corpses.

Residents of the Lódź (Poland) Ghetto stare at a Jewish policeman—seemingly with contempt. The Jewish councils established their own police forces to patrol the ghettos and maintain order. These policemen had to cooperate with the Nazis, but in return they received increased rations and special privileges—for themselves and their families. These advantages often meant the difference between life and death.

A cartoon from the *North-China Daily News* portrays the plight of Jewish refugees. With emigration to Palestine greatly limited by the British and entrance into North America slowed to a trickle, European Jews scattered around the globe. Thousands of Jews made their way to Shanghai, where the Chinese government created a benevolent ghetto for the recent arrivals from Europe.

1941

- **January 30, 1941:** On his eighth anniversary as chancellor, Hitler repeats his threat to destroy all of the Jews of Europe.

- **January 31, 1941:** 3000 Jewish deportees, mostly from the Polish town of Pruszków, arrive at the Warsaw Ghetto.

- **Early 1941:** The population of the Warsaw Ghetto swells to 400,000. Jewish residents are limited to 183 calories a day (Germans are allowed 2310 a day; foreigners 1790; Poles 934).

- **January–March 1941:** 70,000 displaced Polish Jews are forced into the Warsaw Ghetto.

The famed American pilot Charles A. Lindbergh *(left)* testifies before the Senate Foreign Relations Committee. Enamored with Adolf Hitler and the Nazi movement, Lindbergh opposed the Lend-Lease Bill, which would have extended military aid to Great Britain. In a speech in Iowa in September 1941, Lindbergh said Anglophiles and Jews were trying to pressure the U.S. into war. Before Pearl Harbor was bombed, the antiwar movement in the United States had many supporters.

The sign reads: "Plague Area: Only Through Passage Is Allowed." This sign at the entrance to the Warsaw Ghetto kept curious onlookers from getting a close look at the horrible conditions within the ghetto. While Polish gentiles living in Warsaw were aware that Jews were confined to an area smaller than two square miles, the Nazis went to great lengths to hide the reality of life behind the walls.

Three Dutch Jews, arrested for the murder of a Dutch Nazi named Koot, are forced to pose with their weapons in front of an Amsterdam police station on February 11, 1941. After the Germans occupied the Netherlands in May 1940, the Resistance movement to which these Jews belonged waged a valiant but ultimately unsuccessful campaign against the Nazi oppressors.

Nazi sympathizers in Oslo, Norway, stand beneath a banner that reads, "With Quisling for Norway." As leader of the homegrown collaborationist movement, Vidkun Quisling worked closely with the Nazis following the defeat of Norway in the spring of 1940. In a radio broadcast in April, he announced that he was the prime minister of the new government, though the Nazis soon removed him from that post.

Ernst Cahn, a German-Jewish refugee, was part-owner of the Koco ice cream parlors in Amsterdam. Cahn and his partner, another Jewish émigré from Germany, were well liked by both Jews and gentiles of Amsterdam. After the Germans occupied the city, several customers purchased weapons for the owners and installed a 20-inch ammonia flask to the parlor wall to ward off unwanted visitors. When a German police patrol was sprayed with ammonia, a riot ensued. The event became known as the "Koco Affair."

The "Koco Affair" in Amsterdam instigated the Nazis' first roundup of Dutch Jews. German troops entered the Jonas Daniel Meyer Square in the Jewish Quarter of Amsterdam on February 22, 1941. They arrested and physically abused approximately 400 Jews, most of whom were then deported to the Buchenwald concentration camp. Ernst Cahn was shot by a firing squad on March 3 after refusing to name the individuals who had installed the ammonia canister in his shop.

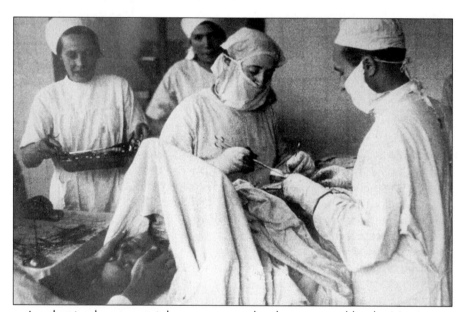

In what is almost certainly a propaganda photo created by the Nazi overseers of the Lódź Ghetto, Jewish surgeons and nurses operate on a patient. The actual state of ghetto health care was considerably more primitive.

1941

• **January–August 1941:** About 13,000 Jews in the Warsaw Ghetto, and 5000 Jews in the Lódź (Poland) Ghetto, die of starvation.

• **February 1941:** Poles caught selling food to Jews in the Warsaw Ghetto are automatically sentenced to three years of hard labor. The daily bread ration for Jews in the Warsaw Ghetto is reduced to three ounces a day.

• Jews deported to slave-labor camps along the Bug River are put to work draining marshes and building fortifications along the Soviet frontier.

• **February 1, 1941:** In France, Marcel Déat establishes a collaborationist Fascist party, *Rassemblement National Populaire* (National People's Rally).

These two German propaganda photographs portray "happy" Jews in the Warsaw Ghetto—celebrating at a cocktail club and performing a play. The Germans created such scenes to persuade Jews that they could expect good treatment as long as they cooperated with the Reich government and went willingly to the ghettos. Once collected into ghettos, the Jews were even more at the "harsh mercy" of the German murderers and their local collaborators.

Martin Bormann

As the *Führer*'s trusted private secretary, Martin Bormann had unmatched direct access to Hitler. This made him one of the most powerful and feared figures in the Third Reich.

Bormann gradually wormed his way into the Nazi elite. In 1941 Hitler appointed him to direct the newly created Party Chancellery. In this post he wielded enormous power, screening all communications and contacts with the *Führer*. Working anonymously behind the scenes, the short, stocky Bormann, dubbed the "Brown Eminence" in Nazi Party circles, manipulated the vague boundaries of his authority. A virtual "secret ruler" of Germany, he strengthened the policy-making role of the Party, launched vicious attacks on Christianity, and issued hundreds of memorandums dealing with Jews and Slavs. "The

Slavs are to work for us," he proclaimed. "In so far as we do not need them, they may die."

Bormann stayed with Hitler to the end, and was apparently killed in May 1945 while trying to escape from Berlin.

• **February 6, 1941:** German General Erwin Rommel is named to command the *Afrika Korps* in North Africa.

• **February 15, 1941:** Germans begin deportations of 1000 Viennese Jewish men per week to a ghetto at Kielce, Poland, as well as a camp at Lublin, Poland.

• **February 19, 1941:** German police who enter an Amsterdam, Holland, ice cream parlor are sprayed with ammonia by a protective device installed by the German-Jewish owners; *See February 22–23, 1941.*

• **February 22–23, 1941:** SS troops raid the Jewish Quarter in Amsterdam, Holland, in reprisal for the ammonia incident of February 19. About 400 Jews are arrested, beaten, and deported to the concentration camp at Buchenwald, Germany, where some are tortured to death. Some will be transferred to the concentration camp at Mauthausen, Austria, where most will be tortured and subsequently executed in the camp's stone quarry; *See March 3, 1941.*

Reinhard Heydrich

On July 31, 1941, Hermann Göring empowered SS Major General Reinhard Heydrich, chief of the Reich Main Security Office (RSHA), to prepare "a total solution of the Jewish question in the German sphere of influence in Europe." This document did not specify what the "solution" would be, but it commissioned Heydrich to handle "the Jewish question" in ways that went beyond "emigration and evacuation." Seizing his opportunity, Heydrich helped orchestrate the murders of millions of Jews.

Joining the Nazi Party and the SS in 1931, Heydrich caught the attention of SS leader Heinrich Himmler, rose rapidly through the ranks, and was appointed head of RSHA in

1939. Working closely with Himmler, he ordered the ghettoization of Polish Jews, organized mass deportations, and directed *Einsatzgruppen* activities in Eastern Europe. On January 20, 1942, Heydrich convened the Wannsee Conference. At this meeting he led top Nazi officials in coordinating plans for the "Final Solution," which had already begun in the latter half of 1941.

Ambushed by Czech Resistance fighters near Prague, Heydrich died on June 4, 1942. The Germans took revenge by razing the Czech village of Lidice and killing all of its male inhabitants.

Many citizens of France felt that Marshal Philippe Pétain had betrayed his people when he became the leader of Vichy, the new puppet government that collaborated with the Nazis. This poster reflects Pétain's desperate pleas to win the support of his people. It states: "People of France, you have not been sold out, betrayed, or abandoned. Have confidence in me!"

Throughout 1941 the Nazis moved thousands of Jews into the Warsaw Ghetto, which would become Europe's largest. Jews from the surrounding towns and countryside were forcibly moved into Warsaw in order to concentrate the "threat" they represented. As a result, Warsaw's Jewish population, which stood at around 340,000 for the entire city at the start of the war, spiraled to 445,000, all within the confines of the ghetto, by March 1941.

1941

• **February 25, 1941:** Tens of thousands of Dutch citizens participate in a general strike in order to protest the deportation of Jews from their country—the only such strike in Europe in reaction to the first deportation of Jews.

• **March 1941:** Hitler's war plans lead him to instruct his generals to conduct an "unmerciful" and "unrelenting" war against the Soviet Union.

• In Frankfurt, Germany, a pseudo-scholarly conference discusses the "problem" of European Jewry.

• Adolf Eichmann, head of the Gestapo section for Jewish affairs, lays plans to restrict Jewish emigration from Europe.

Pictured is the entrance to the offices of the Warsaw Ghetto's Jewish Council. The armband worn by the well-dressed woman indicates that she was employed by the Council, as were the policemen stationed at the entrance. Among ghettoized Jews, the affluent and those of higher "rank" often had better living conditions.

When the order to establish a sealed ghetto in Kraków was implemented, Jews were forcibly conscripted to build the wall. At first Jews were simply pulled off the streets and told to work. Later, however, the Jewish Council worked closely with the Nazi authorities to coordinate the labor pool. Work quotas were established, and the Jewish Council was responsible for delivering the required number of laborers.

Heinrich Himmler and Auschwitz commandant Rudolf Höss share a moment of satisfaction as they ponder the camp's future. During his March 1 inspection, Himmler ordered Höss to expand the facility, including building a new camp called Birkenau for 100,000 prisoners of war. In addition, 10,000 prisoners were to construct an I.G. Farben factory for the production of synthetic rubber. Höss reported that Himmler planned to transform Auschwitz into "one immense prison-cum-munitions center."

- **March 1, 1941:** After failing to maintain its neutrality, Bulgaria joins Germany as an ally. • Heinrich Himmler, leader of the SS, begins plans for the expansion of the Auschwitz complex.

- **March 2, 1941:** German troops enter Bulgaria.

- **March 3, 1941:** A Jewish ghetto at Kraków, Poland, is established.
- Ernst Cahn, co-owner of an Amsterdam ice cream parlor in which German troops were sprayed with ammonia on February 19, is executed by a German firing squad.

- **March 7, 1941:** Thousands of Jews in the Upper Silesia region of Poland

are rounded up and put to work in German mines, metallurgy factories, and textile plants. Jews living in many areas of Germany are put to work in similarly compulsory labor.

- **March 12, 1941:** Thirteen-year-old Wolf Finkelstein is shot through the heart and lungs by a German sentry in the Lódź (Poland) Ghetto.

The main gate to the Kraków Ghetto is adorned with the Star of David and a Hebrew inscription. A center of Jewish learning since early modern times, Kraków provided a hospitable environment for Polish Jews until it was occupied by the Germans in September 1939. About 60,000 Jews came under Nazi authority.

A Jewish couple moves a basket of their belongings into the Kraków Ghetto. On March 3, 1941, the district governor of Kraków, Otto Wachter, decreed that an official ghetto was to be established in the southern portion of the city. On March 20 the ghetto was sealed off behind a wall and barbed-wire fence, and thousands of Jews from neighboring communities were packed into an unimaginably small area. Four to five people were crammed into each room, creating a situation where privacy was nonexistent and sanitary conditions were appalling.

A German policeman checks the identification papers of Jews in the Kraków Ghetto. Jews were required to carry their official papers at all times. Being caught without them resulted in arrest and possible deportation to a concentration camp. When roundups and deportations began in 1942, there was a frenzied rush to establish oneself as an "essential worker."

1941

• **March 13, 1941: A Belgian collaborationist organization,** *Amis du Grand Reich Allemand* **(Friends of the Greater German Reich), is founded.**

• **March 20, 1941: At Baumann and Berson Children's Hospital in the Warsaw Ghetto, nurse D. Wagman writes that she is helpless to prevent death.**

• **Spring 1941: A ghetto is established at Kielce, Poland. German overseers of the ghetto rename some of the streets. New names are Zion Street, Palestine Street, Jerusalem Street, Moses Street, Non-Kosher Street, and Grynszpan Street;** *See* **November 7, 1938.** • **German troops execute 250 members of a Jewish youth group in Subotica, Yugoslavia, who have been**

STADT KRAKAU

Kennkarte Nr. 01664
Karta rozpoznawcza Nr

für den Juden–die Jüdin (dla żyda–żydówki)

Familienname: *Rosenzweig*
nazwisko:

Bei Ehefrauen Geburtsname: *Wiener*
przy mężatkach nazwisko panieńskie:

Vorname: *Cyrla*
imię:

Rosenzweig Cyrla
Eigenhändige Unterschrift (podpis własnoręczny):
Besondere Kennzeichen (Znaki szczególne):

Die Kennkarte ist nur gültig, wenn sie die zeitlich richtigen Gültigkeitsbestätigungen auf Seite 4, bzw. 6 enthält.

Karta rozpoznawcza jest tylko wówczas ważna, jeżeli czasowo obowiązujące potwierdzenia ważności na str. 4 wzgl. 6 zawiera.

This was the official identification card, issued by the Kraków district of the *Generalgouvernement,* of Cyrla Rosenzweig. She survived the war as one of the famous "Schindler Jews." Oskar Schindler saved over 1000 Jews from the death camps by employing them in his munitions factory and using his influence to stave off efforts to deport them.

Jews of the Lublin (Poland) Ghetto wait their turn to draw water from a well. The winter months exacted a heavy toll on the malnourished and diseased Jewish population. The arrival of summer in 1941 was accompanied by a typhus epidemic. Efforts to control the disease were hampered by the overcrowded conditions, widespread starvation, and the absolute lack of medical supplies.

The Commissar Order

In Adolf Hitler's view, the invasion of the Soviet Union was not merely a military operation. It held the key to *Lebensraum* (Living space)—and provided an opportunity to destroy the evils of communism. Hitler regarded the Soviet offensive, therefore, as an epic "battle between two opposing ideologies."

In a forceful speech to his top generals in March 1941, Hitler outlined his plan for the conduct of the campaign. Aiming for the complete eradication of communism, he exhorted his generals *not* to treat the Russian Army according to the rules of civilized warfare. He especially targeted the "Bolshevik commissars" and Communist intelligentsia.

The so-called "Commissar Order" (issued in June in a secret directive to the German Army) established the rules for the treatment of political commissars attached to Red Army units. Reasoning that political commissars constituted a "danger to security, embodied the spirit of resistance," and had "originated barbaric, Asiatic fighting methods," the directive ordered that they be summarily executed upon capture.

carrying out acts of sabotage. • Hungarian troops and German civilians randomly murder 250 Jews and 250 Serbs in Novi Sad, Yugoslavia. • Two Jewish brothers in Zagreb, Yugoslavia, operate a secret Resistance radio. • Many Yugoslavian Jews join anti-Nazi partisans led by Josip Broz (Tito).

● **March 22, 1941:** Vichy France leader Marshal Philippe Pétain authorizes the construction of a Trans-Sahara railway, with labor to be performed by internees composed of Jews, Czechs, Poles, and Spanish Republican soldiers.

● **March 25, 1941:** Yugoslavia joins the Axis countries.

● **March 26, 1941:** The German High Army Command gives approval to RSHA and Reinhard Heydrich on the tasks of the *Einsatzgruppen* in the Soviet Union.

● **March 29, 1941:** In France, the antisemitic *Commissariat Général aux Questions Juives* (General Commission on Jewish Affairs) is established.

German General Erwin Rommel was named to command the *Afrika Korps* in North Africa. His role was to help the Italians defeat the British, which he did brilliantly beginning in 1941. The offensive he undertook at the end of March led him 12 days later to the Egyptian border. Germany suddenly threatened British control not only of the Suez but of the entire eastern Mediterranean. In the fall of 1942, however, Rommel was plagued by lack of supplies and was defeated by the British at El Alamein. Hitler ordered him back to Europe, where he was put in charge of German forces defending against a cross-Channel Allied invasion. Discovered to have connections to the July 1944 conspirators against Hitler, Rommel was blackmailed into suicide.

The German occupation of Yugoslavia in April 1941 enabled the leader of the Croatian Fascist *Ustasa* movement, Ante Pavelić, to proclaim an independent Croatian state. Pavelić collaborated closely with the Nazis and, shortly after assuming power, implemented anti-Jewish legislation that was modeled on the Nuremberg Laws.

Greek civilians are lined up by German paratroopers in preparation for their executions. The occupation of Greece in late April 1941 was swift and brutal. Perceived opponents were ruthlessly eliminated, and the civilian population was divided into three zones of occupation: Italian, German, and Bulgarian.

1941

- **Late March 1941: A Jewish ghetto at Lublin, Poland, is established.**

- **April 1941: A men's annex is established at the Ravensbrück, Germany, concentration camp.** • Yugoslavian collaborationists led by Vladko Macek establish *Hrvatska Zastita* (Croat Militia), a paramilitary force. • Seven Warsaw Jews smuggle themselves into Bratislava, Slovakia, and from there to safety in Palestine. • **The first Croatian concentration camp begins operation, at Danica. Four more Croat camps are opened, at Loborgrad, Jadovno, Gradiska, and Djakovo.** • A pro-Axis officer clique seizes power in Iraq, and prepares airfields for German use.

In 1941, a year before deportations from the Warsaw Ghetto reached their height, ghetto leaders made brave attempts to retain a certain sense of normalcy, and to provide for the physical and emotional needs of the ghetto's children. The care center seen here, and others like it, were vital because they provided children with food and the perception of safe havens. Care centers were possible because a Nazi ban on public and private "gatherings" was rescinded early in 1941. Elementary-school instruction also was allowed. The "normalcy" was illusory, however, and conditions faced by Warsaw's children would shortly be insufferable.

Viktor Brack, a former chauffer to Heinrich Himmler, raised funds for medical experiments during the Holocaust. A colonel in the SS, Brack was Hitler's special advisor on the T-4 "euthanasia" program. So immersed was he in the program that he personally met and interviewed each physician who ultimately participated. Brack also was one of those who decided to use poison gas as the preferred extermination method.

Hitler's ambition and megalomania were boundless. This decorative desktop globe, removed from the *Führerbunker* by Soviet troops in 1945, carries a pair of unnerving German-language inscriptions. Atop the Soviet Union are the words "I am coming." The inscription over North America reads, "I will be there soon."

Professor Julius Hallervorden, a pathologist at the Kaiser-Wilhelm Institute, was one of the many German physicians who willingly participated in the "euthanasia" program to eliminate the mentally ill and physically disabled from German society. Many doctors later collaborated in horrendous medical experiments and in choosing which concentration-camp prisoners were temporarily to live and which immediately to die. German physicians joined the Nazi Party at a higher proportional rate than any other profession in Germany.

From the start of the war, Hungarian Prime Minister Count Pál Teleki wished to expand his nation's territorial holdings while remaining free of philosophical and physical domination by Germany. In the summer of 1940, Teleki acceded to the wishes of many Hungarians when he accepted from Germany the largely Romanian region of Transylvania, home to a substantial Hungarian minority. The price to be paid was closer ties to Berlin and increased antisemitic agitation from Hungarian rightists. On April 2, 1941, the mortified Teleki took his life four days before Germany's invasion of Yugoslavia—a nation with which Hungary had signed a pact of friendship. Teleki's funeral, seen here, closed the book on the prime minister's naive ambition.

> **Alle Juden haben sich am 19 April d. J. um 8 Uhr morgens bei der Städtischen Schutzpolizei (im Feuerwehr-komando am Taš-Majdan) zu melden.**
>
> Juden die dieser Meldepflicht nicht nachkommen, werden erschossen.
>
> Belgrad 16-IV 1941
> Der Chef der Einsatzgruppe der Sicherheitspolizei und des S. D.
>
> **Сви Јевреји морају да се пријаве 19 априла т. г. у 8 час. у јутро градској полицији (у згради Пожарне команде на Ташмајдану).**
>
> **Јевреји који се не одазову овом позиву биће стрељани.**
>
> Београд, 16-IV-1941 год.
> Шеф групе полиције безбедности и С. Д.

This official directive appeared in Belgrade, Yugoslavia. It reads as follows: "All Jews must register with the city police on April 19 by 8:00 A.M. Jews who fail to comply with this mandatory registration will be shot." Posted in both German and Serbo-Croatian, the message clearly communicated the Nazis' serious intent.

The German invasion of Yugoslavia in April 1941 was disastrous for the 80,000 Jewish inhabitants. While the Yugoslav government had enacted anti-Jewish legislation before the war, the campaign intensified after the occupation. The Nazis registered all Jews, restricted their movement, and utilized most Jewish men for forced labor. These men were forced to clean the streets.

1941

- **April 1, 1941: Rashid Ali al-Gaylani establishes a pro-Nazi government in Iraq.**

- **April 2, 1941: Hungarian Premier Count Pál Telecki commits suicide rather than collaborate with Germany.**

- **April 6, 1941: German forces invade Greece and Yugoslavia, setting** off war in the Balkans. Jews in both countries are soon driven from their homes.

- **April 7, 1941: Two separate ghettos are established in Radom, Poland. At Kielce, Poland, 16,000 local Jews and about a thousand Jewish deportees from Vienna are herded into a ghetto area.**

MAJOR DEPORTATIONS OF JEWS TO WARSAW GHETTO, 1941–1942

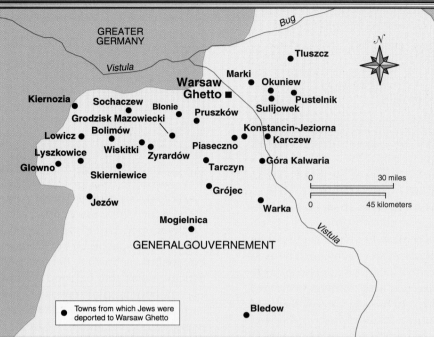

The Nazis deported thousands of Jews from neighboring towns to the Warsaw Ghetto in 1941 and '42, swelling the population to over 400,000. Conditions in the ghetto were so abysmal that 43,000 people died there in 1941.

The German occupation of Radom in 1939 subjected the Jewish populace to severe persecutions. Located in central Poland about 62 miles south of Warsaw, the Radom Ghetto was officially established in March 1941. By April 7 the entire Jewish population was sequestered in two separate ghettos: a large enclosure in the center of the city and a smaller one located in a nearby suburb. The Jews in this photo were held prisoner inside a Radom synagogue.

Many Jews of Radom, Poland, were forced to move into the "little ghetto" located in nearby Glinice. Like many Polish Jews, they had to relocate quickly. They gathered their belongings, loaded them onto carts, and dragged them to their new "home." While the Germans were equipped with the most modern equipment available, many Polish Jews relied on ancient technology to meet the needs of daily life.

• **April 9, 1941: A Jewish ghetto is established at Czestochowa, Poland.**
• **A proclamation of Croatian independence is issued from Zagreb, Yugoslavia. Jews are beaten and murdered, and the process of interning Jews in concentration camps will soon begin.**

• **April 12–13, 1941: German troops enter Belgrade, Yugoslavia; a Jewish** tailor who spits on the arriving troops is shot dead. Jewish shops and homes in Belgrade are ransacked by both German soldiers and resident Germans.

• **April 14, 1941: Hungarian troops occupy portions of northern Yugoslavia. About 500 Jews and Serbs are shot. • Germany and Italy recognize** the independence of the Fascist Croatian state.

• **April 16, 1941: German troops and local Muslims loot and destroy the main synagogue in Sarajevo, Yugoslavia. • Aron Beckermann becomes the first Jew to be shot by the Germans for resistance in France.**

Iraq and the Holocaust

In the late 1920s 120,000 Jews lived in Iraq, including 90,000 in Baghdad alone. Jews coexisted peacefully with their fellow countrymen until 1932, when the British Mandate in Iraq came to an end.

Iraq suffered political instability for the next decade. Nationalism was on the rise, as was a hatred for foreigners and minorities. Fritz Grobba, the German minister to Baghdad, infiltrated the city with antisemitic propaganda. Discriminatory laws against Jews began in 1934, and assaults and pogroms occurred two years later.

A pro-Nazi government led by Rashid Ali al-Gaylani rose to power on April 1, 1941, and sporadic assaults on Jews followed. The new government fell weeks later, with British troops occupying Baghdad on May 30. On June 1, however, furious Iraqi soldiers instigated a city-wide riot against Jews. All told, 179 people were killed and more than 2000 were injured. A new government restored order, but tensions among Muslims and Iraqi Jews (many of whom chose to emigrate to Shanghai, China) continued in Iraq for years.

A Belgian firefighter surveys the wreckage in the wake of the "Antwerp pogrom" of April 1941. Given the go-ahead by the German occupation authorities, Belgian anti-semites looted and pillaged the Jewish neighborhood of Antwerp. Their orgy of violence destroyed two synagogues and the home of Rabbi Marcus Rottenberg, and shattered the lives of many Belgian Jews.

Sitting in this Venetian gondola are Italian government officials Luca Pietromarchi *(front left)* and Raffaele Casertano *(rear left)*. An unidentified Croatian *Ustasa* official sits on the right. The Croats and Italians were participating in the festivities surrounding Croatia's signing of the German-Italian-Japanese Tripartite Pact. The Croatian Ustasa regime under Ante Pavelić killed Jews, Serbs, and Gypsies. Hundreds of thousands were killed, including 80 percent of Croatia's Jews. Ironically, it was the Italian Army that helped save thousands of Croatian Jews.

1941

● **April 17, 1941:** In Warsaw, a Jewish policeman named Ginsberg is bayoneted and shot by German soldiers after asking a soldier to return a sack of potatoes taken from a Jewish woman.

● **April 18, 1941:** Yugoslavia capitulates to the Germans.

● **April 21, 1941:** A mentally ill Jewish woman in the Łódź (Poland) Ghetto complies when a German sentry orders her to dance. Satisfied, the sentry shoots her in the head.

● **April 24, 1941:** One hundred Jews are seized in the Warsaw Ghetto to dig canals and drain swamps in Poland's Kampinos Forest.

Although Hungary never was enthusiastic about its alliance with Nazi Germany, its association did bring it significant new territory and the (temporary) comfort that Hungary would not suffer a German invasion. German-Hungarian links became stronger in the spring of 1941 following Soviet bombing attacks on Hungarian targets. All of this, plus agitation from the Arrow Cross Party and other Hungarian Fascist groups, drove the nation toward closer ties with Germany and into increasing belligerence. The Budapest boys seen here are members of the *Levente*, a paramilitary organization that was mandatory for Hungarian youth.

This photo of a raid on the Jewish ghetto in Warsaw was found on the body of a German soldier killed on the Russian front. During such raids, Jews were lined up in the streets and forced to stand with their hands above their heads for hours. There is no telling why a soldier would carry such a souvenir.

This forged identity card was carried by a man who acted under the pseudonym of Marc Sylvain Camus. In truth, the man was a French Resistance operator. In 1940 a group of Jewish Communists formed a Resistance organization called *Solidarité*, which later became the *Union des Juifs Pour la Résistance et l'Entr'aide* (Union of Jews for Resistance and Mutual Aid). By war's end, the UJRE had saved 900 children from death.

• **April 27, 1941:** Germany completes its conquest of Greece.

• **April 30, 1941:** Racial legislation enacted at Zagreb, Croatia, by the pro-German government removes Jews from public office. • Croat law holds that people with just one Jewish parent are protected from deportation.

• **May 1941:** Thousands of Jews who had fought in the French Foreign Legion against Germany in 1940 are deported to slave-labor camps in the Sahara to build railroads. • 120 Jews are slain in the streets during antisemitic violence in Bucharest, Romania. • Jewish cemeteries, synagogues, and businesses in Zagreb, Yugoslavia, are destroyed. • The *Norges SS* (Norwe-gian SS) is established, with membership taken from Norway's collaborationist *Hirdmen*; *See* May 17, 1933.

• **May 1, 1941:** A concentration camp is established at Natzweiler, Alsace, Germany. • Gross-Rosen, formerly a satellite camp of Sachsenhausen, Germany, becomes an independent camp.

Gross-Rosen

Originally a satellite camp of Sachsenhausen (Germany), Gross-Rosen became an independent concentration camp in 1941 and remained operational until February 1945. The camp was located near granite quarries in Lower Silesia, and inmates performed backbreaking work in the SS-owned quarry. Sick

and emaciated prisoners were sent to the killing centers that were parts of the Nazi "euthanasia" program. Of the 125,000 prisoners who passed through the camp, 40,000 lost their lives.

Jews made up the largest proportion of victims. Many nationalities were represented, and the camp housed women as well as men. As the numbers of prisoners grew, the SS created numerous forced-labor subcamps. There, Jews slaved in mines, steel mills, and armament factories of German industrial giant Krupp—or in I.G. Farben chemical plants set up to produce poison gas. Some toiled on the construction of Hitler's underground headquarters. The hard labor involved in digging subterranean passages, combined with inadequate hygiene, led to exceptionally high mortality rates.

Many women worked in textile factories or in the aircraft industry. Others, assigned to excavate antitank ditches, suffered terribly. One young woman recalled having to dig in freezing weather while standing in deep snow. Many were barefoot because they had not been given shoes, causing feet and legs to freeze. If they attempted to wrap themselves with blankets, they were whipped by the guards.

The main gate at the Gross-Rosen concentration camp in Germany coldly greeted the camp's new inhabitants. Gross-Rosen, which had been a satellite camp of Sachsenhausen, became an independent camp on May 1, 1941. The living and working conditions at the camp, which was near a granite quarry, were particularly brutal. Inmates performed hard labor in the quarry, building the camp's facilities. Jewish prisoners were completely isolated from one another. Each Jewish prisoner was restricted to his own block and denied medical attention.

In May 1941 the German occupation authority in France deported thousands of Jewish men from Paris to a prison camp at Pithiviers. The wretched conditions at the camp strained the relief efforts of French organizations and compelled many Jewish women to protest the arrests of their husbands and sons. Remarkably, their demonstrations outside the gates of the camp earned them the right to visit their menfolk.

1941

● **May 10, 1941:** Deputy *Führer* Rudolf Hess makes an unauthorized solo flight from Augsburg, Germany, to Scotland, where he intends to meet with British Prime Minister Winston Churchill and negotiate an end to the Anglo-German war. He is captured and imprisoned; *See* November 18, 1945.

● **May 11, 1941:** Jewish children in the Warsaw Ghetto are observed tickling a corpse as they play.

● **May 14, 1941:** About 4000 Jews are deported from Paris, most to a camp at Pithiviers, France.

● **May 15, 1941:** Polish Jews who have traveled by sealed train from the

REDARSTVENO RAVNATELJSTVO U ZAGREBU

OGLAS

Određujem, da se u roku od 8 dana imadu preseliti u druge dijelove grada Zagreba svi SRBI i ŽIDOVI, koji stanuju na sjevernoj strani Maksimirske ceste, Vlaške ulice, Jelačićevog trga, ftice do mitnice, kao i iz onih dijelova grada, koji se nalaze sjeverno od označenog cestovnog poteza.

Oni, koji se ne pokore ovoj odredbi, biti će po isteku gore označenog roka PRISILNO EVAKUIRANI na vlastiti trošak i KAŽNJENI po postojećim ZAKONSKIM PROPISIMA.

Marijan Nikšić v r

An order issued by the Croatian government in May 1941 required all Jews and Serbs to vacate specific areas of Zagreb. The Croatian nationalist *Ustasa* movement immediately began to persecute its arch-rivals, the Serbs. Thousands were killed and many more were deported to Serbia. The fate of Croatian Jewry was inextricably intertwined with that of the Serbs. Jews and Serbs who failed to comply with the order were forcibly removed from their homes and severely punished.

Prisoners at Plaszów, Poland, carry loaves of bread to feed workers at the Madritch factory, where German Army combat uniforms were manufactured. Plaszów was first a labor camp policed by Ukrainian guards, but in 1944 it became a concentration camp controlled by the SS.

Marshal Tito *(right)*, a.k.a. Josip Broz, talks with members of Yugoslavian Resistance. Unifying all of Yugoslavia's ethnic and religious groups, Tito commanded perhaps 300,000 partisan fighters who kept 20 German divisions busy in Yugoslavia. More than 2000 Jews fought directly for Tito, who ordered his forces to assist escaping Jews.

Biala Podlaska Jewish POW camp to Konskowola are murdered after the train's Nazi overseers discover that four of the POWs have escaped.

• **May 20, 1941:** Jews in France are prohibited from wholesale and retail trade, nor can they own banks, hotels, or restaurants. • **The Central Office of Emigration in Berlin notifies all**

German consulates that Hermann Göring has banned emigration of Jews from France and all other occupied territories. The directive quotes Göring's mention of the "doubtless imminent final solution," the first official Nazi reference to a scheme for mass extermination of all Jews in Europe.

• **May 21, 1941:** A collaborationist group, *Nederlandse Arbeids Dienst* (Dutch Labor Service), is established in Holland.

• **May 22, 1941:** Jews in Croatia are forced to wear yellow badges.

• **June 1941:** The Bialystok region of Poland is annexed to Greater Ger-

A Jewish prisoner in the Jasenovac, Croatia, concentration camp removes his ring before his execution. In October 1941 the *Ustasa* began to systematically transfer Croatian Jews to Jasenovac. By year's end about two-thirds of Croatian Jewry was incarcerated in the camp, most of whom were later killed by the *Ustasa*. In all, about 600,000 people lost their lives at Jasenovac. These included Jews, Gypsies, Serbs, and political prisoners.

Jews in the Lódź (Poland) Ghetto are restrained behind a barbed-wire and wooden fence separating the ghetto from the rest of the city. A German soldier took this photograph, which, along with others, was found after the war in his abandoned apartment.

Adolf Hitler greets Ante Pavelić, the leader of the collaborationist Croatian state, upon his arrival at the Berghof, Hitler's estate in Berchtesgaden, Germany, for a state visit. The June meeting at the scenic command post in the Bavarian Alps signaled Hitler's pleasure with Pavelić's actions in Croatia. Official visits to the Berghof were an important instrument of Nazi foreign policy.

1941

many. • SS Reich Security Service chief Reinhard Heydrich and *Wehrmacht* Quartermaster General Eduard Wagner meet to determine how the SS and the Army will carry out their respective tasks in the Soviet Union without hindering each other.

• June 6, 1941: The Commissar Order, issued by the German Army, states that all Soviet officials are to be liquidated.

• June 17, 1941: Reinhard Heydrich briefs *Einsatzgruppen* commanders on the implementation of the "Final Solution." • French priests in the Lyon diocese publicly protest the Vichy government's anti-Jewish policies.

Eugen Fischer was the first director of the Kaiser Wilhelm Institute for the study of anthropology, human genetics, and eugenics. Fischer, who specialized in the study of twins, is shown examining pictures of "racial types." Dr. Josef Mengele supplied the institute with blood and skeletons of concentration-camp inmates.

The Iasi Pogrom

In the highly charged atmosphere accompanying Germany's war against Russia, Romanians accused their country's Jews of espionage. Rumors that Jews from the city of Iasi had signaled Soviet aircraft ignited a horrifically violent pogrom on June 27, 1941.

Romanian soldiers, police, and local citizens rampaged through the streets of Iasi, murdering thousands of Jews in their homes and arresting more than 5000. Forcing their victims to march through the streets under a barrage of heavy blows, the police brutally shot those who stumbled. At the railway station, the Jews were robbed of all possessions and herded into waiting cattle cars for deportation to camps.

Over 100 people crowded each padlocked car, which without food, water, or ventilation became an inferno in the summer heat. Reduced to drinking urine, more than 2500 died of thirst, starvation, and suffocation aboard two trains that for eight days crept slowly southward. The Iasi pogrom claimed at least 4000 lives.

This French poster suggests that American Jews are behind Franklin Roosevelt's decision to land U.S. Armed Forces in French North Africa to fight the Germans. The poster states: "Who is stealing our North Africa? Roosevelt. Who urges him on? The Jew." It shows Fiorello La Guardia, the strongly anti-Nazi mayor of New York City, whispering in the President's ear and encompassed by a Jewish star. La Guardia, a dedicated reformer who did *pro bono* legal work for immigrants before World War I, was the son of an Italian father and Jewish mother.

By the spring of 1941, conditions inside Poland's Warsaw Ghetto were hellish. Food was scarce, clothing consisted mainly of old rags, and medical supplies were virtually nonexistent. Under those circumstances, the children of the ghetto suffered horribly. Dressed in rags and bandages, they wandered aimlessly through the streets. Others, orphaned and alone, sought refuge in sleep when their strength escaped them. Heartbroken and shattered parents witnessed the rapid deterioration of their beloved children. Mortality rates for the young skyrocketed during the winter of 1941.

1941

• **June 18, 1941:** Germany and Turkey sign a friendship treaty.

• **Summer 1941:** In Belorussia, a guerrilla collaborationist organization, *Belaruskaya Narodnaya Partizanka* (Belorussian National Guerrillas), is established. • In Denmark, a collaborationist SS organization, *Freikorps Danmark* (Danish

Free Corps), is established. • In Latvia, Viktor Arajs establishes the *Perkonkrusts* (Thunder Cross), a collaborationist paramilitary unit. • Heinrich Himmler, head of the SS, tells Rudolf Höss, the commandant of Auschwitz, that Hitler has ordered that the "Jewish question" be solved once and for all and that the SS is to implement that order. Auschwitz is

"M'hot zei in drerd di rotzchim." ("We shall yet live to see these murderers in their graves.")

—*Popular Jewish aphorism heard in ghettos*

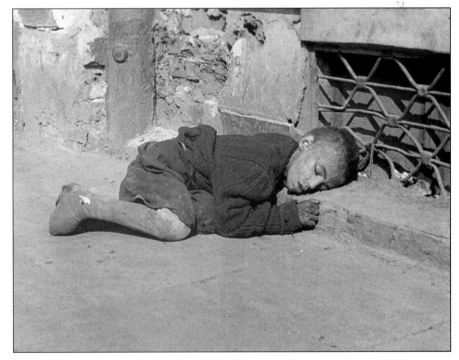

the death camp that is to carry out the greater part of the Jewish extermination. Mass gassings, not shootings, are determined to be the most effective means to exterminate the large numbers of Jews.

• **June 22, 1941: Operation Barbarossa begins, as a massive German force invades the Soviet Union, immersing** Germany in a two-front war and breaking the German-Soviet Non-Aggression Pact of 1939. • Special mobile killing squads—*Einsatzgruppen*—each assigned to a particular area of the Occupied Soviet Union, begin killing Jews on the spot wherever they are found, and often with the help of local antisemites recruited to help. • In the Soviet village of Vir- balis, *Einsatzgruppen* machine-gun all adult Jews and cover the corpses with lime. Local children are seized by the ankles, and their heads are smashed against walls and roads. Many of these children are buried alive.

• **June 24, 1941: The *Wehrmacht* occupies Kovno, Lithuania, where 10,000 Jews will be killed by late July.**

Einsatzgruppen

On December 1, 1941, in Kovno, Lithuania, SS Colonel Karl Jäger completed a report stamped *Geheime Reichssache!* (Secret Reich Business!). A German businessman who had become a member of the SS in 1932, Jäger filed his report as the commander of *Einsatzkommando* 3JC (EK 3), a unit of *Einsatzgruppe* A (EG-A). Jäger's report stated: "Today I can confirm that our objective, to solve the Jewish problem for Lithuania, has been achieved by EK 3. In Lithuania there are no more Jews, apart from Jewish workers and their families."

Jäger claimed that *Einsatzkommando* 3JC accounted for the deaths of more than 130,000 Jewish men, women, and children. Prior to the arrival of EK 3JC in Lithuania on July 2, 1941, he estimated, another 4000 Jews had been "liquidated by pogroms and executions," bringing the Jäger report's total of Jewish dead to 137,346.

Far from being isolated episodes, Jäger's report and the mass murder it tallied were parts of the systematic destruction policy that Nazi Germany implemented when its military forces invaded Soviet territory on June 22, 1941. Prior to the invasion, Hitler resolved that the campaign would destroy both communism and Soviet Jewish life, for part of his antisemitism emphasized that communism was a Jewish invention. *Einsatzgruppen*—special mobile killing squads composed of SS, SD, and other police and security personnel—were ordered to execute Communist leaders and, specifically, "Jews in the party and state apparatus." Nazi interpretation placed virtually all of the Soviet Union's Jews in that category. Thus, with key logistical support from the German Army and enthusiastic help from antisemitic collaborators, the *Einsatzgruppen* specialized in the mass murder of Jews.

About 1.3 million Jews (nearly a quarter of all the Jews who died during the Holocaust) were killed, one by one, by the 3000 men who were organized into the four *Einsatzgruppen* that headed east in the summer of 1941. Deadly contributors to what became known as the "Final Solution," these mobile killing units rounded up Jews and brought them to secluded killing areas. The victims were forced to give up their valuables and take off their clothing. They were then murdered by single or massed shots at the edges of ravines or mass graves that the victims were often forced to dig themselves.

Like Colonel Karl Jäger, most of the *Einsatzgruppen* officers were professional men. They included lawyers, a physician, and even a clergyman. Postwar trials brought some of them to justice. Arrested in April 1959, Jäger said of himself that "I was always a person with a heightened sense of duty." That sense of duty made him and his *Einsatzgruppen* colleagues efficient killers. While in custody, Jäger hanged himself on June 22, 1959.

1941

● June 25, 1941: When 47-year-old Dr. Benjamin From, a Jewish surgeon, refuses to break off an operation on a Christian woman at Lutsk, Ukraine, Germans drag him from the hospital to his home, where he and his family are murdered.

● June 26, 1941: Hundreds of Jews from Kovno, Lithuania, are executed at the fortified Ninth Fort on the city's outskirts.

● June 27, 1941: The second Nazi occupation of Bialystok, Poland, occurs. Hundreds of Jews are burned alive in a local synagogue by a German motorized unit. ● German troops gathered in a synagogue courtyard in Niéswiez, Poland, beat and shoot

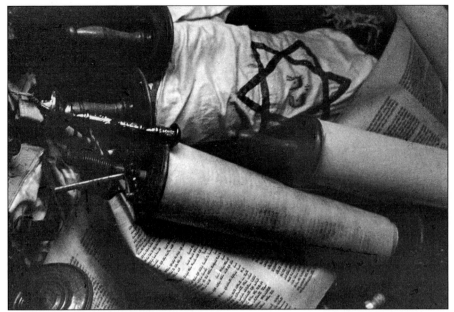

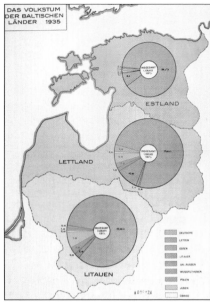

Torah scrolls desecrated by the Nazis were strewn about a synagogue in Kovno, Lithuania. Violence perpetrated against the Jews was typically accompanied by the destruction of Jewish religious articles and places of worship. The clear and intimate connection between the Jewish people and the Torah made the holy book an irresistible target for Nazi vandals.

A chart prepared by Dr. Franz Walter Stahlecker, the first commander of *Einsatzgruppe* A, details the ethnic composition of the Baltic countries (Estonia, Latvia, Lithuania) in preparation for the upcoming invasion of the Soviet Union. The *Einsatzgruppen* singled out Jews and political commissars for extermination. Charts such as this were instrumental in determining the scope of the *Einsatzgruppen*'s operations and the needed manpower.

Heinrich Himmler is greeted by Chaim Rumkowski, the head of Łódź Ghetto's Jewish Council, during an official visit on June 5, 1941. After arriving in a chauffeur-driven Mercedes with a personalized license plate reading "SS-1," Himmler made Rumkowski wait for hours before meeting to discuss the ghetto's work assignment.

In Breslau, Germany, Heinrich Himmler presents new citizens of the Reich with naturalization papers. This Bukovinian and his wife were repatriated from Romania to Germany. Following the 1939 Non-Aggression Pact with Hitler, Joseph Stalin moved his troops into northern Bukovina, annexing it in June 1940. Angered by Stalin's expansion into an area that had once been part of the Hapsburg Empire, Hitler regained the territory a year later, following his attack on the Soviet Union.

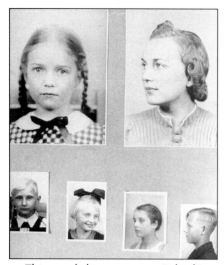

This card demonstrates "ideal" Aryan children from among the *Volksdeutsche,* or ethnic Germans not living within Germany. *Volksdeutsche* were typically gladdened by their incorporation into the Reich; for many, it was a sort of repatriation. For the most part, ethnic Germans collaborated with the Nazis; about 300,000 joined the *Waffen-SS.*

Polish women from Warsaw are led by German security forces into the Palmiry Forest, where they will be executed. While the Jews remained the primary target of the Nazi terror campaigns, individuals suspected of plotting against the occupying German forces faced violent retribution. The Nazis brooked no opposition, and no one was spared from their plans to dominate the continent. Innocent men, women, and children of all backgrounds were killed by the Nazis as they spread their reign of destruction throughout Europe.

An unidentified major general in the German Army and his subordinate officers look over orders for the coming offensive against the Soviet Union. Planning for the attack, code-named "Barbarossa," began in July 1940, 11 months before the invasion took place. The nonaggression treaty with the Soviet Union signed in August 1939 was only a temporary expedient for Hitler.

1941

exhausted Russian POWs. • Romanian Iron Guard Legionnaires, encouraged by the antisemitic policies of dictator Ion Antonescu, undertake to exterminate Jews in Iasi. Thousands are killed. • Jews of Falesti, Romania, are set out on a forced march eastward. • Hungary enters the war, joining the Axis powers.

• June 28–29, 1941: In the German-occupied town of Kovno, Lithuania, Lithuanian police and released convicts use iron bars to beat hundreds of Jews to death in the city's streets. Thousands more Jews are murdered at Kovno, Lithuania, and another 5000 are killed at Brest-Litovsk, Belorussia.

On June 22, 1941, German troops invaded the Soviet Union. Operation Barbarossa was, in the words of historian Alan Clark, "the greatest and longest land battle which mankind has ever fought." Millions of German troops stormed into Soviet territory. The campaigns in the East marked a fundamental shift in operational policy. The war against the Soviet Union was a war of annihilation, as Hitler planned to totally destroy the Bolshevik power. He used the war to unleash the murderous *Einsatzgruppen.* By the end of the year, more than 750,000 Jews would be killed by the *Einsatzgruppen* and their accomplices.

General Alfred Jodl, chief of *Wehrmacht* operations, discusses strategy with Hitler. As Hitler's primary military adviser and close confidant, Jodl knew by mid-1940 of the *Führer*'s plans to invade the Soviet Union. The campaign against the Soviet Union was a logical result of Hitler's worldview. To defeat the enemy in the East would eliminate the Bolshevik foe and provide Germany with the *Lebensraum* (Living space) necessary to feed and house an expanding German nation.

Alfred Rosenberg, *Reichskommissar* for the Occupied Eastern Territories, receives a gift of bread and flowers from a Ukrainian couple who welcomed the Nazi leader on behalf of the Ukrainian people. Joseph Stalin's Communist regime had ruthlessly suppressed all nationalist movements, and many Ukrainians viewed the invading Germans as liberators. The warm reception by the Ukrainians and other nationalist communities of Eastern Europe enabled the Nazis to implement their plans for genocide without fear of local opposition.

• **June 29–July 1941: Romanian soldiers and police in Iasi murder at least 260 Jews in their homes. More than 4000 are marched through the streets and beaten, robbed of their currency and jewelry, and sealed inside railcars and sent south. Fewer than half survive the eight-day journey.**

• **June 30, 1941: Ninety Jews are murdered at Dobromil, Ukraine.**
• **German troops enter Lvov, Ukraine, and beat hundreds of Jews to death after running them ragged at gunpoint.** • **Three hundred young Jews are deported from Amsterdam, Holland, to stone quarries at the Mauthausen, Austria, concentration camp. All will eventually perish.**

• **Late June 1941: American radio commentator Father Charles Coughlin celebrates Hitler's invasion of Russia as "the first strike in the holy war on communism" and attacks "the British-Jewish-Roosevelt war on Germany and Italy."**

• **June–July 1941: More than 62,000 Jews are murdered in western Russia.**

A group of *Waffen-SS* soldiers breaks out champagne to celebrate a recent victory over the Red Army. The early weeks of Operation Barbarossa were marked by rapid and decisive German victories. The German military machine met little resistance as it advanced into Soviet territory.

Three Russian women return to their native Smolensk, one of the many cities destroyed by the rampaging German armies. For centuries, Smolensk had been the object of a bitter struggle involving Russia, Poland, and Lithuania, but never before had the city been ravaged like this.

German troops are greeted as liberators by the residents of Lithuania. The Lithuanians had fought a valiant but ultimately unsuccessful war against the Soviet Union in 1939. Since its defeat, Lithuania chafed under the control of the Communist state. In June 1940, Moscow sent an ultimatum to Lithuania, demanding the resignation of the government. Lithuania complied, but was occupied by the Red Army anyway. When the German armies advanced into their country during the opening campaigns of Operation Barbarossa, the local inhabitants warmly welcomed the Germans.

1941

• **June–November 1941:** Fourteen thousand Bosnian Jews are deported to regional camps.

• **July 1941:** British codebreakers monitoring radio traffic coming from German troops in the Soviet Union become aware of Nazi massacres of Soviet Jews. • Two thousand members of Minsk, Belorussia's intelligentsia are executed by German troops in a nearby forest. • More than 2500 Jews are slaughtered at Zhitomir, Ukraine. • During an *Einsatzkommando Aktion* (murder operation) at Mielnica, Ukraine, a Jew named Abraham Weintraub hurls himself on a German officer and shatters the officer's teeth. Weintraub is immediately shot.

Jews of Kovno, Lithuania, move into the ghetto that was established on the third day of the German campaign against the Soviet Union. The rapidly issued orders to relocate created havoc among the Jews of Kovno. The man in this photo is pulling a disassembled wardrobe that he hoped to set up in his new residence. The limited space in the ghetto houses, however, would compel him and other ghetto inhabitants to hang their clothes from nails.

Pictured is a compilation of German regulations for the Kovno (Lithuania) Ghetto. The cover of this volume is adorned with the statue of justice holding a scale. The Hebrew title expresses the sardonic Jewish reaction to life under the Nazis: "These are the laws—German style."

Elchanan Elkes

Elchanan Elkes, head of Kovno (Lithuania) Ghetto's Jewish Council, was unlike other ghetto council heads. A Lithuanian physician, Elkes was not a dictatorial leader, but rather an exemplary figure of high moral standards who served his community with integrity and selfless dedication.

Elkes left the day-to-day running of ghetto affairs to his deputy. His main function was to intercede with German authorities, who respected him. He worked tirelessly to persuade them to soften harsh decrees. Elkes created work for ghetto residents, and encouraged underground activity that helped many escape to nearby forests.

During the ghetto's final days, Elkes desperately tried to convince the SS to spare the surviving Jews, warning them of accountability for their crimes. Unable to halt the murder of the ghetto's population, Elkes wrote: "My soul is scorched. I am naked and empty." Elkes was deported to the Landsberg concentration camp, where he died in 1944.

• In the Bialystok region of Poland, Nazis murder 300 members of the Jewish intelligentsia. • German killing squads begin to murder Jews remaining in Kishinev, Romania.
• The Hungarian government undertakes a mass roundup of almost 18,000 Jewish refugees for deportation to Kamenets-Podolski, Ukraine.
• Twenty-two-year-old Jew Haya

Dzienciolski finds a pistol, leaves Novogrudok, Ukraine, and helps to organize a group of young partisans in nearby forests.

• July 1, 1941: One hundred Jews are murdered at Lyakhovichi, Belorussia.
• Hundreds of Jews are killed at Plunge, Lithuania.

• July 1–3, 1941: After Germans and Ukrainians spread a rumor that Jews had contributed to the execution of Ukrainian political prisoners, rioting erupts in Lvov, Ukraine. Hundreds of Jews are exterminated by the *Nachtigall* battalion, a Ukrainian militia directed by the Gestapo. • In the Ukrainian town of Koritz, Nazi troops murder Jews and prepare three bur-

Chava and Jadzia Liwer received a gift of life on June 24, 1941: a Polish passport issued in Tokyo, Japan. The certificate was obtained by Abram Liwer, husband of Chava and father of Jadzia. The Liwer family had fled their native Bedzin, Poland, on August 20, 1939, and resettled in Lvov, Ukraine. When Chava and Jadiza were deported to Siberia, Abram Liwer fled to Vilna and then later to Kovno, Lithuania. In Kovno he obtained the passport for his wife and daughter and a visa for himself. The family was reunited in Tokyo on April 1, 1941.

Jews of Bialystok, Poland, participate in forced labor. When the Nazis occupied the city on June 27, 1941, they quickly rounded up Jews for labor brigades, acts of public humiliation, and deadly, sadistic games. German soldiers herded hundreds of Jews into a local synagogue, locked and barred the doors, and set the building on fire. Everyone inside was burned alive.

Of physicians among the Yugoslavian partisans, the vast majority were Jewish. Dr. Rosa Papo, a Yugoslavian Jewish partisan, served as the first woman general in the Yugoslavian Army.

1941

ial pits, one each for men, women, and children. For sport, a man's corpse is propped atop one of the pits, in which some Jews have been buried alive.

• **July 1–August 31, 1941:** Members of the *Einsatzgruppen*, the *Wehrmacht*, and *Esalon Special*, a Romanian unit, kill more than 150,000 Jews in Bessarabia, a region of eastern Romania.

• **July 2, 1941:** Eight hundred Jews are killed at Novo Selista, Ukraine, and hundreds more perish at Kamenka and Stryj, Ukraine. • A German cavalry unit on patrol in Lubieszow, Volhynia, Ukraine, murders Jewish resisters.

The portraits of Fascist leaders Benito Mussolini, Adolf Hitler, Corneliu Codreanu, and Romanian dictator Ion Antonescu adorn the facade of Carroll University in Bucharest, Romania. The portraits were raised during a pro-Antonescu rally held on June 27, 1941. The rally coincided with the extermination of the Jews of Iasi, Romania, carried out by Antonescu's Iron Guard Legionnaires, German soldiers, and Iasi police and residents. The reason for the atrocity was a groundless charge that the Jews had signaled Russian aircraft that bombed the city.

A pile of corpses dumped from an Iasi death train in Romania is evidence of the Iron Cross's murderous campaigns against the Jews. From June 29 through July 7, 260 Jews were murdered in their homes and thousands of others were beaten and robbed as they were marched through Iasi's streets. The pogrom ended when 2500 Jews were sealed inside railcars and sent south. Deprived of food and water, fewer than half of the Jews survived the eight-day journey.

The surviving prisoners of the Iasi death train plunge into the mud near the train tracks. Deprived of food, water, sanitary facilities, and fresh air, the occupants were allowed to disembark for a few minutes when the train stopped. Burning and dehydrated, they immediately sought refuge in the cool mud before returning to the torture chamber of sealed railcars.

The Fate of Lvov

At the beginning of the war, the Jews of Lvov numbered 110,000—the third largest Jewish community in Poland. A flood of refugees brought an additional 100,000. The SS and their Ukrainian helpers murdered all but a few thousand.

The killing began in June 1941. Encouraged by *Einsatzgruppe* C, Ukrainian nationalists unleashed hellish pogroms that over the next two months claimed 6000 Jewish lives. That fall the Nazis forced Jews to move into a section of the city that was sealed with barbed wire. While moving into this ghetto, 5000 elderly and disabled people were murdered; the women were bludgeoned, the men lined against a wall and shot.

In 1941 the SS set up a camp and forced Lvov's Jews to perform slave labor. Sadistic camp commanders used Jews for target practice, aiming at noses or fingers. The injured were finished off with a shot. Those judged unfit for work were marched to a sandy area away from camp, where they were murdered. As many as 200,000 were executed in this "Valley of Death." Tens of thousands were shipped to the Belzec, Poland, death camp.

While liquidating the Lvov Ghetto in 1943, SS members hunted down and killed every Jew they could find. Some fled to nearby forests. A handful survived by hiding in sewers.

Jewish victims of the advancing *Einsatzgruppen* mounted steadily as the invading German Army moved into the Soviet Union. Ordered to kill Jews and political commissars, the notorious *Einsatzgruppen* operated with deadly efficiency. Following on the heels of the rampaging German Army, they quickly rounded up the Jews and systematically executed them. The killing techniques of the early campaigns required the members of the *Einsatzgruppen* and their accomplices to directly confront their victims. Typically, the Jews were killed with a single shot to the base of the skull.

The Jews of Lvov, Ukraine, experienced a wave of violence just days after the Nazis invaded the Soviet Union. From June 30 to July 3, 1941, *Einsatzgruppe* C as well as Ukrainians rampaged through the city, murdering 4000 Jews. Two thousand more died during vicious pogroms in late July.

1941

• July 3, 1941: One hundred Jews are murdered at Bialystok, Poland. • In the Ukraine, 3500 Jews are killed at Zloczow and hundreds die at Drohobycz. • Fifty Jews in Novogroduk, Belorussia, who volunteer for a German-organized Jewish council, "disappear." Another 50, selected at random, are shot in the town square to the accompaniment of music played by a German band. • Soviet leader Joseph Stalin orders the establishment of partisan units to harass German troops in occupied Soviet territory.

• July 4, 1941: Two thousand Jews from Lutsk, Ukraine, are transported to the Lubard Fortress and killed. • Fifty-four Jews are killed at Vilna,

These Belgian Walloon Volunteers for the Struggle Against Bolshevism take an oath to the *Führer* and commander-in-chief, Adolf Hitler. Nazi anti-Marxism was one of its most attractive features in the eyes of many Europeans, and Hitler and his henchmen used it to recruit volunteer soldiers from all of the occupied countries.

Soldiers with a *Wehrmacht* propaganda unit film the anti-Jewish riot that began with the German occupation of Lvov on June 30, 1941. The Nazis incited the Ukrainians to seek revenge against the Jews. They then filmed the murderous four-day rampage to demonstrate how much even their own Ukrainian countrymen hated the Jews. Some 4000 died in the pogrom.

Mass killings of Jews followed quickly in the wake of Germany's invasion of the Soviet Union. Ethnic Germans and many Ukrainians welcomed the invaders with open arms, seeing the Nazis as liberators from the hated Russians. On July 4–11, 1941, 5000 Jews were murdered at Ternopol by Germans and Ukrainians. The Jews were forced to dig their own graves as a prelude to their deaths.

Lithuania. • Germans order Lithuanian militiamen to murder 416 Jewish men and 47 Jewish women at the Seventh Fort.

• July 4–11, 1941: Five thousand Jews are killed in Ternopol, Ukraine.

• July 5, 1941: Ninety-three Jews are shot at Vilna, Lithuania, by an *Einsatzkommando* unit. • Jews in Lvov, Ukraine, are murdered in the streets by antisemitic locals.

• July 6, 1941: In the Ukraine, 3000 Jews are murdered at Chernovtsy; 600 are killed at Skalat. • Jews in Lvov, Ukraine, are ordered to wear the Yellow Star identifying them as Jews. • Two thousand Jews are mur-

dered at the Seventh Fort by Lithuanian militiamen.

• July 7, 1941: Two thousand Jews are murdered at Khotin, Ukraine. • In France, a collaborationist military force, *Légion des Volontaires Français* (French Volunteer Legion), is established. • Thirty-two Jews are killed in Mariampole, Lithuania.

Joseph Stalin's son, Yakov Djugashvili, became a captive of the Germans a month after the *Wehrmacht* invaded the Soviet Union. Stalin's relationship with his elder son had always been cold, and the dictator was unmoved by subsequent German offers to exchange Yakov for Hitler's nephew, Leo Raubal, or for Field Marshal Friedrich von Paulus. Blood ties aside, Stalin was no longer disposed to make deals with Germany. Yakov remained in captivity and died in a German prison camp in 1943—a suicide or, some believe, the victim of British POWs. The SS uniform he wears here was probably a malicious German slap at Stalin.

A column of Jews is herded by Lithuanian auxiliary police into a narrow circular passage. They are en route to their execution at an unfinished construction site in Ponary near Vilna. Auxiliary brigades comprised a critical source of manpower for the Nazis as they unleashed their genocidal fury. Lithuanians, Ukrainians, Latvians, Estonians, and a host of other East Europeans willingly participated in the murder of millions of Jews.

Leaders of the Jewish community from Balti, Romania, await their execution at the hands of the German conquerors. Standing from left to right are Summer Zitterman, Iosif Broitman, Bernard Walter, Sacha Diagot, Aizic Schächtman, Schmerl Schoihat, Burach Blank, Suchar Roitman, Simon Grünberg, Cripps, Leibia Galavata, and Iankel Tenenboim.

1941

• July 8, 1941: Jews in the Baltic states are forced to wear a distinguishing Jewish badge. Within months the Germans and local antisemites will murder most of the Baltic countries' Jewish population of one-quarter million. • Hundreds of Jews are killed at Noua Sulita, Romania. • Executions of Jews begin at Ponary, Lithuania.

• July 10, 1941: All 1600 Jews in the Lithuanian village of Jedwabne are marched to the central market, tortured by SS troopers, then incinerated in a barn.

• July 12, 1941: Great Britain and the Soviet Union sign a military treaty to work together for Hitler's defeat.

A Russian prisoner of war in Berdichev, Ukraine, eats from a can. Many Soviet POWs, however, were not so fortunate. The Nazis were ill-prepared to handle the millions of prisoners they captured, and they were not willing to allocate the necessary resources to provide for them. Many thousands of Russian POWs were forced to do without food and shelter. Russian prisoners were also the first victims to be gassed with Zyklon B at the Auschwitz death facility.

Following the rapid German advance into the Soviet Union and the capture of thousands of Soviet soldiers, SS chief Heinrich Himmler visited this POW camp in Minsk, Belorussia. Himmler stares at a young and already emaciated Soviet prisoner. Millions of Soviet POWs were targeted for destruction by Nazi policies of neglect, abuse, malnutrition, and murder. The *Wehrmacht*, as well as Himmler's SS, were deeply implicated in this brutal behavior.

Jacob Gens

Jacob Gens, leader of Vilna (Lithuania) Ghetto's Jewish Council, ruled his community with almost dictatorial power. Derisively called "King Jacob the First," Gens decided who would live and who would die.

Convinced he could save Jews by demonstrating their value to the German economy, he selected those capable of "productive" labor and surrendered to the Nazis those who were "unproductive." During the 1941 *Einsatzgruppen* roundups, Gens personally  inspected each Jew's work permit. Those too old, too weak, and too ill to work, or not in possession of the prized "yellow card" were delivered by Gens to the SS, who executed them.

When reproached by Jewish religious leaders for his tactics, Gens defended his philosophy: "When they ask me for a thousand Jews, I hand them over. With the thousand, I save ten thousand." The Gestapo shot Gens in 1943, just days before liquidating the ghetto.

• **July 17, 1941:** Twelve hundred Jews are murdered at Slonim, Belorussia. • Alfred Rosenberg is appointed Reich minister for the Occupied Eastern Territories to administer lands seized from the Soviet Union.

• **July 17–31, 1941:** Thousands of Jews are murdered at Kishinev, Romania.

• **July 20, 1941:** A Jewish ghetto at Minsk, Belorussia, is established.

• **July 21, 1941:** Forty-five Jews in Minsk, Belorussia, are forced to dig pits, then are roped together and tossed into the pits. • Belorussians are ordered to bury Jews alive. When they refuse, Jewish and non-Jewish Belorussians alike are murdered by *Einsatzkommandos.* • A concentration camp opens at Majdanek, Poland.

• **July 22, 1941:** France's Vichy government begins expropriation of Jewish businesses.

• **July 24, 1941:** A ghetto is established in Kishinev, Ukraine.

Maximilian Kolbe

Father Maximilian Kolbe, a Polish-Catholic priest and an inmate at the Auschwitz, Poland, concentration camp, sacrificed his life by volunteering to take the place of a fellow prisoner condemned to death. The Nazis agreed to the switch and brutally murdered the priest.

Incarcerated for disseminating his religious and social views, Kolbe continued to practice his faith at Auschwitz. In July 1941, when a prisoner from his block escaped from the camp, the SS ordered the execution of ten inmates as retribution. One of the selected victims, Francis Gajowniczek, pleaded for his life, sobbing over his wife and children. The priest stepped from the numbed, terrified ranks and offered himself, saying he had no family.

Locked naked in a dark, foul-smelling, underground cell, without food or water, he clung to life for two weeks. Impatient, the SS gave him a lethal injection of carbolic acid. In 1982 the Catholic Church canonized Kolbe as a saint.

Members of the Latvian SS practice their marksmanship in preparation for future assignments. The German occupation of Latvia in July 1941 not only filled the jails with political prisoners but also produced some 80,000 men for this SS legion. These troops were used in the campaign against the Soviet Union, and they actively participated in the killing of Jews and Communists. The most lethal Latvian killing unit, the Arajs Commando, killed some 30,000 Latvian Jews.

Hungarian Jews take a moment to rest and eat while en route to their final destination in the Ukraine. Laden with their belongings, this group was one of the many that was expelled from their homes by the Hungarian government. The deportation operations of July relocated almost 18,000 Jews to Kamenets-Podolski, Ukraine.

1941

• July 25, 1941: In five separate incidents, Jews in Belgrade, Yugoslavia, throw gasoline bombs at Nazi cars.

• July 25–26, 1941: About 3800 Jews are killed in a pogrom at Kovno, Lithuania.

• July 25–27, 1941: Local Ukrainians at Lvov seize thousands of Jewish men and women and beat to death at least 2000. The killings are retribution for the 1926 murder of a Ukrainian antisemitic leader, Simon Petliura, by Shalom Schwarzbard, a Jew.

• July 27, 1941: Germans take 1200 Jews from Belgrade, Yugoslavia, to a camp at Tasmajdan, where every tenth captive is shot. • In Holland, a

"I herewith instruct you to make all necessary preparations as regards organizational, financial, and military matters with a total solution of the Jewish question within the area of German influence in Europe."

—*Hermann Göring, in a memo to Reinhard Heydrich; July 31, 1941*

Three Jewish men are hanged in Ternopol, Ukraine, in 1941. They were killed either for having disobeyed German orders or in retribution for any offense someone in the Ternopol Jewish community committed. Placards were often hung around the necks of the executed, to intimidate the living and provide a neat rationale for the executions. Bodies of the murdered might be left hanging for days, until the Nazis felt that the local citizenry had had time to absorb the "example."

Many Ukrainians welcomed the Germans when they took Ternopol in July 1941. What followed was a massacre of 5000 Jews, many of them burnt to death in their synagogues by Germans and Ukrainian nationalists. A few months later the Germans created the Ternopol Ghetto, consisting of more than 12,000 Jews. Only a few hundred Jews survived to liberation by the Soviet Army in 1944.

Dozens of German soldiers observe Jews murdered as a result of the Ternopol, Ukraine, massacres in July 1941. Several of the German soldiers cover their noses with handkerchiefs because of the odor of the decaying corpses. German military commanders exploited local antisemitism wherever their troops went, egging on hateful locals and encouraging German soldiers to participate in the violence. The Ternopol pogrom began on July 4, just two days after German troops took the city.

MAJOR CONCENTRATION CAMPS IN EASTERN EUROPE, 1941–1943

About a third of the population of Minsk, Belorussia, was Jewish by the time the Germans arrived in June 1941. The city's Jews were confined to a ghetto beginning in July, and executions and deportations took place with metronomic regularity. In this photo, Adolf Wedekind, a member of a German police regiment, poses in front of a Nazi display replete with a portrait of Hitler. Wedekind's regiment was involved in the executions of Soviet partisans in the areas surrounding Minsk. As the German Army extended its hold over Europe, the question of manpower became critical. Police regiments like Wedekind's were instrumental in carrying out the racial reordering of Eastern Europe.

Germany occupied Serbia in 1941, interned most of its 16,000 Jews, and shot or gassed most of them. The pro-Nazi *Ustasa* government in Croatia interned about 30,000 Jews, most in the Jasenovac camp, where 20,000 Jews perished.

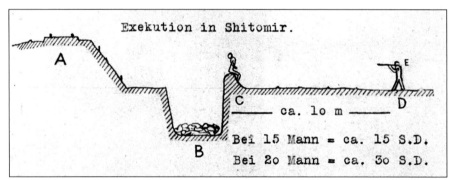

A diagram drawn by an unidentified German soldier describes details of an *Aktion* at Zhitomir in the Ukraine, during which about 500 Jews were shot. As illustrated, Jews were forced to dig a ditch and then kneel at the edge. Each would be shot in the back of the head and then fall into the ditch.

1941

collaborationist military force with ties to the SS, *Freiwillingen Legion Niederlander* (Dutch Volunteer Legion), is established. • The clothing of Jews murdered in Ponas, Ukraine, is sold by the Ukrainian and Nazi killers.

• July 28, 1941: Local police and militiamen, acting with the acquiescence

of SS troops at the prison at Drogobych, Ukraine, use guns, clubs, and fists to slaughter hundreds of Jews. The streets are choked with badly injured fleeing Jews and mangled corpses.

• July 29, 1941: German occupation troops in and around Belgrade, Yugoslavia, execute 122 Communists and

These young women were members of a small but important Resistance movement that existed within the occupied territories of the Soviet Union. Comprised of Soviet Army officers and political commissars whose units had disbanded—as well as Jews who had escaped the marauding *Einsatzgruppen*—partisan groups worked tirelessly to harass the German Army. Most Resistance groups operated in the forests and other remote areas of the Soviet Union.

Partisans with the 26th Division from Baku, Russia, prepare to execute two captured German policemen. After Germany invaded the Soviet Union, Joseph Stalin established partisan units to harass the German Army that remained in Soviet territory. The partisans were not kind to prisoners of war, and summary executions—like the one in this photo—were not uncommon.

The Riga Massacres

In the first six months of their occupation of Latvia, the Germans and their local collaborators annihilated 90 percent of the country's 95,000 Jews. Of the 40,000 Jews living in Riga when the Germans invaded in July 1941, only 4800 were still alive by year's end.

During the first days of the occupation, Latvian "civilian" nationalists initiated savage attacks on Riga's Jews, arresting, beating, torturing, and raping Jews while burning synagogues with people inside. Thousands more were driven toward beaches or nearby woods and shot to death. The Germans then forced the remaining 32,000 into an overcrowded, dilapidated ghetto. In November they sorted "productive" workers from the rest, setting up two separate ghettos. Throwing all available German and Latvian manpower into the "action," the SS transported over 27,000 "unproductive" Jews in modern, blue buses to the Rumbula Forest, where they shot them.

Having wiped out the entire population of the larger ghetto, the Germans brought in 16,000 Jews from the Reich, most of whom they also killed. By late 1943 almost all Latvian Jews had either perished in further SS "actions," been murdered in gas vans, or been worked to death in Latvia's infamous Salaspils camp.

Jews for resistance. • Forty mental patients from Lódź, Poland, are taken from a hospital and executed in a nearby forest.

• July 31, 1941: Hermann Göring instructs SS Reich Security Service chief Reinhard Heydrich by letter to evacuate and eliminate all European Jews presently in German-held territory. The letter mentions a "complete solution" to European Jewry.

• Late July 1941: Germans establish a Jewish ghetto at Dvinsk, Latvia.

• July–August 1941: Tens of thousands of Jews are murdered throughout the western Soviet Union, Lithuania, Romania, and Latvia. The killers are German *Einsatzgruppen*, Romanian troops and militia, Ukrainian peasants, and Lithuanian civilians.

• August 1941: Following the German slaughter of Jews at Cesis, Latvia, German troops and security police celebrate with a *Totenmahl* ("death banquet"). • In Belgium, a

Vilna Ghetto

Known as the "Jerusalem of Lithuania," Vilna was a regional center of Jewish culture. Prior to German occupation, Jews numbered 60,000, over one-fourth of the city's population.

In the summer of 1941, however, *Einsatzkommandos* and Lithuanian collaborators rousted Vilna Jews from their homes and marched them toward the prison yard. Held outdoors for several days, men and women

were separated, put on board trucks, and told they would work. Instead the Jews were dumped in the hilly Ponary Forest. Divided into small groups, they were led to an execution site. "Suddenly the truth hit us, like an electric shock," remembered a survivor. Women with "piteous pleas" kissed the boots of their executioners, futilely offering rings and watches. Up to 20,000 were slaughtered.

In September the Germans set up two ghettos for the remaining Jews. Ghetto No. 1 housed workers, while the smaller No. 2 imprisoned the "unproductive." In October the Nazis exterminated all 11,000 inmates of Ghetto No 2; in November, thousands more from Ghetto No. 1 were killed. By December 40,000 were dead. The 20,000 still alive became a workforce for the Germans until the ghetto was liquidated in 1943. Those fit for work went to labor camps; those "unfit" were banished to extermination camps. Only 2000 to 3000 survived.

The most important Resistance group in Occupied France was the FFI (Free French Insurgency), whose troops are pictured. Commanded by General Charles de Gaulle, the Free French opposed recognition of the Vichy regime, a puppet government established by the Nazis. The FFI coordinated much of the resistance activity within Occupied France and established an army that would participate in the approaching reconquest of Europe.

A Latvian civilian is executed by a member of the notorious *Einsatzgruppen*. This sort of execution—absurdly time-consuming as well as barbarous—was never abandoned by the efficiency-minded Nazis.

1941

collaborationist military organization, *Legion Wallonie* (Wallonian Legion), is established. • German troops in Slobodka, Ukraine, fill the local synagogue with dead cats and force Jews to tear up the Torah scrolls and scatter the pieces atop the dead animals. The Nazi troops then set fire to the building.

• Father Bernhard Lichtenberg, dean of St. Hedwig's Cathedral in Berlin, denounces the so-called euthanasia program. In late October he declares that he wants to share the Jews' fate of deportation to the East so that he can continue to pray for them there. He is subsequently denounced to the Gestapo and arrested.

Many Jews who had escaped the ghettos and camps volunteered to fight Nazis and Fascists. Some 5000 joined the Polish Second Corps, formed in Russia in 1941, while about 30,000 others enlisted in the British Army. Both groups later saw combat in Italy. Here, Arab and Jewish recruits, composing the Auxiliary Military Pioneer Corps of the British Army, march side by side during a training exercise in Palestine.

Julius Lippert, here pictured riding the horse Friedericus, was among the Nazi elite. Extremely well-educated, this longtime acquaintance of Propaganda Minister Joseph Goebbels was also a virulent antisemite. He became mayor of Berlin after Hitler's seizure of power, and was largely responsible for the vicious persecution experienced by Jews of the capital city during the first years of the Third Reich. Lippert also instilled his malignant hatred of Jews into his young son, who became famous for his harassment of his Jewish classmates.

A child of an SS officer is christened in an elaborate and occult-like ceremony. The infant is draped on a wool shawl decorated with a swastika and SS runes, and is placed before an altar covered with the Nazi flag. Each child was given a silver beaker, a silver spoon, and a blue, silk shawl. For every fourth child born to an SS family, the mothers were presented with a silver candlestick engraved with the message, "You are a link in the clan's chain."

• United States Senator Gerald Nye denounces the "Yiddish controllers" of American theater and movies. U.S. Senator Burton Wheeler attacks Jews in the movie business as "Hollywood Hitlers." U.S. Senator Champ Clark sponsors an investigation into Hollywood's "unpatriotic" Jewish filmmakers. (Unpatriotic because their films advocate involvement in the European war.) Other congressmen express antisemitism. Many Americans agree with these sentiments. Many Americans also believe that should the United States go to war, it must be against the Soviet Union, not against Germany. • Hundreds of Jews die during death marches from Bessarukiato, Bessarabia, to the Dniester River.

• August 1, 1941: A Jewish ghetto at Bialystok, Poland, is established. • More than 1000 Jews are killed by an *Einsatzkommando* at Kishinev, Romania. • Shmuel Verble, chairman of the Jewish Council in the Ukrainian village of Kamien Koszyrski, volunteers for death after discovering an execution list with the names of 80 ghetto residents.

Hitler and the Final Solution

Prior to Adolf Eichmann's 1961 Jerusalem trial, Captain Avner Less, an Israeli policeman, spent hundreds of hours interrogating the SS lieutenant-colonel, who would eventually be found guilty and executed for his crimes against the Jewish people. On one occasion, Less questioned Eichmann about "written orders" concerning the "Final Solution," the mass murder of European Jewry. "I never saw a written order," Eichmann claimed. "All I know is that [Reinhard] Heydrich said to me, 'The *Führer* has ordered the physical extermination of the Jews.'"

Recalling events that had taken place 20 years earlier, Eichmann was unsure about the exact date he had heard those words. He thought it might have been two or three months after Germany invaded the Soviet Union in June 1941. His recollection was firmer, however, about the chain of command. Heydrich, said Eichmann, must have gotten his instructions from Heinrich Himmler, who "must have had express orders from Hitler. If he hadn't had orders from Hitler, he'd have been out on his ear before he knew what had hit him."

Coming from an SS officer who played such crucial parts in implementing the Final Solution, Eichmann's testimony—hearsay though it was on these points—is instructive because it involves issues that still puzzle Holocaust scholars. Although Hitler's unrelenting hatred of Jews and his recurring rhetoric about "the destruction of the Jewish race" are thoroughly documented, orders about the Final Solution

written and signed by Hitler have never been found. In fact, such a document may not have existed, for Hitler relied on oral communication to give his subordinates broad authorizations to implement his wishes.

Understanding what Hitler wanted involved interpretation of his tone of voice as well as his choice of words. Citing an affidavit by Albert Speer, the Reich minister for armaments and war production from 1942 to 1945, historian Raul Hilberg puts the point as follows: "When he [Hitler] spoke 'coldly' and in a 'low voice' about 'horrifying' decisions 'also at the dinner table,' then his audience knew that he was 'serious.'" Expert at interpreting Hitler, SS leaders such as Himmler and Heydrich took full advantage of their mandates to solve the "Jewish question" once and for all.

There is little reason to doubt Eichmann's judgment that the Nazi annihilation of European Jewry depended on Hitler's orders. As Hilberg says, "Hitler was the supreme architect of the Jewish catastrophe." The Final Solution was simply too important and vast to be implemented without his initiative. Precisely when Hitler expressed his decision, however, remains less certain. He probably gave his orders some time in the summer of 1941, after the invasion of the Soviet Union and the *Einsatzgruppen* killings that had begun in June. By the autumn of that year, plans for massive Jewish deportations and death camps in Poland were under way.

1941

• August 2, 1941: Four thousand Jews are killed by about 80 drunken Germans at Ponary, Lithuania. • An American Jewish woman is among the approximately 200 Jews killed at Kovno, Lithuania.

• August 3, 1941: Twelve hundred Jews are arrested by the local *Einsatzgruppen* at Chernovtsy, Romania; 682 are executed by German and Romanian police. • Fifteen hundred Jews are murdered at Mitau, Latvia. • Several hundred Jewish professionals are shot at Stanisławów, Ukraine.

• August 5–8, 1941: Eleven thousand Jews are murdered in the Polish city of Pinsk.

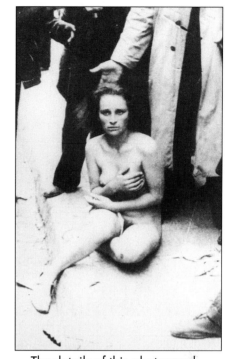

About 110,000 Jews lived in Lvov, Ukraine, before the war. Occupied by the Germans in June 1941, Lvov became the site of brutal Ukrainian pogroms against Jews from July 25 to 27, 1941. They were called the Petliura Days because they commemorated the death of Ukrainian Premier Simon Petliura, who orchestrated pogroms against Jews in 1919. Two thousand Jews were killed in the July 1941 pogroms.

The details of this photograph, which was probably snapped in Lvov, Ukraine, are in doubt. Some sources claim the woman is a captured British agent. Others insist she is a Jew who fell into the hands of antisemitic Ukrainians. Whatever the story behind this disturbing image, there is little doubt that the woman has been stripped and humiliated, probably as a prelude to her execution. The Nazis and their most eager collaborators seemed to take particular relish in this most base sort of domination, degrading Jewish and other women in order to demoralize, as well as for sheer "sport."

These two images portray Jews of Lvov, Ukraine, in July 1941. In the photo above, Jews have been rounded up to be murdered. The image on the right shows a truck carrying the bodies of the executed Jews en route to burial. Most likely, the men accompanying the corpses later buried them. If they were Jews, they were probably shot at the end of their burial detail.

A female inhabitant of the Warsaw Ghetto wears an armband that indicates her status as an employee of the ghetto administration. The task of administering the day-to-day operations within the ghettos of Eastern Europe was delegated to the Jews. In addition to the administrative machinery known as the Jewish councils, there were also Jewish police and a range of administrators. Although many of these people were reviled by fellow Jews for assisting the Nazi conquerors, they typically received preferential treatment. Among the perks were increased food rations, better housing assignments, and access to newer clothing.

Aided by antisemitic Lithuanian partisans, the SS's mobile killing squads organized *Aktionen* (actions) against the Jews. In Kovno, Jews were taken to various forts on the outskirts of town built during Czarist rule. From there they were organized into groups of 500, marched to huge pits a few miles away, and executed. Within the first months of German occupation, nearly 40,000 of Kovno's Jews were murdered.

In August 1941 at Kamenets-Podolski in the Ukraine, members of *Einsatzkommandos* and local Ukrainian nationalists murdered about 25,000 Jews in huge open pits. Victims included 5000 local Jews as well as nearly 20,000 Jews who had been deported from Hungary.

1941

• **August 6, 1941:** In Belgium, a collaborationist military unit, *Legion Vlaandern* (Flanders Legion), is established.

• **August 8–9, 1941:** Thousands of Jews from Dvinsk, Latvia, are transported to the Pogulanka Forest and murdered.

• **August 14, 1941:** All residents of the Jewish community of Lesko, Poland, are transported to Zaslaw, Poland, and executed.

• **August 15, 1941:** Heinrich Lohse, Reich commissioner for Eastern Territories of the Ostland (Eastern Europe) region, decrees that Jews must wear two yellow badges, one on

An identification card issued to Sam Schrijver, a Jew, on August 29, 1941, in Amsterdam. After the Germans occupied Holland, Schrijver was actively involved in the Dutch underground, for whom he fashioned false identification cards and smuggled ration coupons. Arrested in 1943, Schrijver endured numerous beatings and lengthy periods of incarceration. He escaped from Westerbork a few days before the camp was liberated.

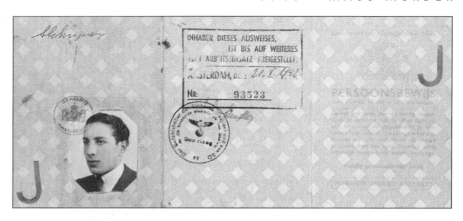

Following their invasion of Yugoslavia, the Germans divided the country into several regions. They placed Serbia and Banat under their direct control and initiated actions against the Jewish population. In this photo, Jews from Zrenjanin in the Banat region prepare for deportation to the Tasmajdan concentration camp, near Belgrade, Yugoslavia. There they would be executed. In August of 1942, German leaders could proudly proclaim the area *Judenrein* (cleansed of Jews).

Life in the ghettos in 1941 remained a torment for the residents, whom the Germans regularly mistreated. Here, a German soldier dangles a Jewish woman in the Vilna (Lithuania) Ghetto by her hair. Germans were taught not to think of the Jews as human, which made it easier for them to liquidate the ghettos once the death camps were established.

the chest and one on the back; that Jews cannot own automobiles or radios; and that their presence in public places will be severely proscribed. • A Jewish ghetto is established at Riga, Latvia. • At the Kovno, Lithuania, suburb of Viliampole, the last of Kovno's 26,000 surviving Jews arrive. Each is allotted three square feet of living space.

• **August 19, 1941:** *Einsatzkommando* 8 as well as local collaborators in Mogilev, Belorussia, kill more than 3000 Jews.

• **August 20–21, 1941:** About 4300 Jews are sent from Paris to Drancy, a transit camp in France. These are the first of 70,000 Jews who will be deported to Drancy and then to

extermination camps, primarily Auschwitz-Birkenau.

• **August 21, 1941:** A concentration camp begins operations at Jasenovac, Croatia.

• **August 24, 1941:** British Prime Minister Winston Churchill broadcasts to the British public that "scores

A German Army patrol searches "suspicious" civilians in Barano-vichi, Belorussia. The faces of the German officer and his men reveal that they are enjoying exercising their power of life and death over civilians. At first, orders emanating from Berlin required German Armed Forces to execute Communists, partisans, and Jews. Unlike these other categories of people to be killed, Jews were on the death list not because of anything they did, but simply because they were born Jews.

Joining his colleagues Burton Wheeler and Champ Clark in condemning Jewish influence in Hollywood, Senator Gerald Nye of North Dakota zeroed in on the "Yiddish controllers" of American theater and movies. Nye was adamant that the United States should stay out of the war and not allow the Jews to drag America into the conflict. Hollywood films, he believed, were swaying American public opinion to the interventionist point of view.

MAJOR EINSATZGRUPPEN MASSACRES OF JEWS, 1941–1942

The Nazi *Einsatzgruppen* followed the German Army into Soviet territory beginning in June 1941. Before the year was out, the *Einsatzgruppen* had shot hundreds of thousands of Jews.

1941

of thousands" of executions of civilians are being perpetrated by German troops in the Soviet Union. In order not to reveal that British Intelligence has cracked the German radio code, Churchill makes no specific mention of the plight of Jews in the Soviet Union or elsewhere in Occupied Europe. • Eighty-six-year-old Dr. Jacob Wigodsky, longtime leader of the Jews of Vilna, Lithuania, is arrested and imprisoned. He will be executed a week later at Ponary, Lithuania.

• **August 25, 1941: German military and civilian authorities meet at Vinnitsa, Ukraine, to discuss the fate of about 20,000 Hungarian Jews impressed into forced labor and**

Estonian police march Jewish men to internment or, more probably, to their deaths. Because of the high rate of antisemitism in the Baltic countries (Lithuania, Latvia, Estonia), the Germans could find large numbers of native people willing to assist with the extermination of the Jews. Most of the Estonian Jews (5000 as of 1933) escaped into the Soviet Union because Estonia was the last Baltic country to be conquered by Germany.

Cloth circles with "J" for Jew at the center identify these women walking on a Lithuanian street. This symbol marked Jews for vilification and abuse as they struggled to buy the basics of life for their families. Life soon took a more ominous turn as *Einsatzkommando* forces (mobile killing units) began to exterminate Lithuania's Jews. Nearly 180,000 of Lithuania's 220,000 Jews were killed by the end of 1941.

British Code Breakers

Despite Nazi attempts to keep secret the *Einsatzgruppen* extermination of Jews, news of mass murders did filter back into Germany and Allied countries. Reports of the unimaginable Nazi atrocities were met with disbelief and skepticism, and were assumed to pertain to military actions involving Russian defense forces.

The British government had detailed knowledge of the killings. On August 24, 1941, Prime Minister Winston Churchill, in a radio address, made public the scope of *Einsatzgruppen* activities in Eastern Europe. He disclosed that "whole districts" were being exterminated, and that "scores of thousands of executions in cold blood" were being perpetrated by "German police-troops upon the Russian patriots who defend their native soil."

Churchill didn't mention that Jews were being exterminated. He could not reveal this since it would have warned the Germans that British intelligence forces had cracked their secret radio codes.

---

interned at Kamenets-Podolski, Ukraine. Lt. General Friedrich Jeckeln announces that all 20,000 will be liquidated by September 1; *See* August 27–29, 1941. • Fifteen hundred Jews are murdered at Tykocin, Poland. • In Yugoslavia, 8000 Jewish residents of Belgrade are transported to Topovske Supe, where they are murdered.

• August 27–29, 1941: Nearly 25,000 Hungarian-Jewish forced laborers are shot to death in bomb craters near Kamenets-Podolski, Ukraine.

• August 28, 1941: A Jewish butcher, one of 2000 Jews forced into a ditch at Kédainiai, Lithuania, resists by inflicting a fatal bite upon the throat of one of the *Einsatzkommando* sol-

diers. The butcher and the other Jews are immediately shot. • Thousands of Jews are murdered at Czyzewo-Szlachecki, Poland. • At Kedainiai, Lithuania, the entire Jewish population is murdered.

• August 31, 1941: More than 3600 Jewish men, women, and children are taken from Vilna, Lithuania, to

Killing Accomplices

During their tireless campaign to annihilate Europe's Jews, the Nazis found thousands of willing accomplices among the populations of Eastern and Western Europe.

Indigenous police forces in France and the Netherlands took part in roundups. Hungarian troops and Fascist extremists joined the hunt and helped slaughter thousands. Slovakia's Hlinka Guard, modeled on Nazi Storm Troopers, attacked Jews while local police organized deportations. The *Ustasa*—a Croatian nationalist, separatist, terrorist organization—tortured and barbarously murdered Jews with axes and hammers. In Romania and the Crimea, the bloodthirsty enthusiasm of volunteer ethnic Germans and Romanian army units who engaged in mass shootings shocked even the SS.

When the mobile killing squads of the *Einsatzgruppen* swept into the Soviet Union, their comparatively thin ranks were augmented by auxiliary troops of native Estonians, Latvians, Lithuanians, and Ukrainians. The *Omakaitse*, Estonian police collaborators, rounded up the Jews of Tallinn and helped the Nazis shoot hundreds. *Selbstschutz*, Latvian police, assisted in the killing of thousands in Riga. Lithuanian police seized and executed Jews, while Lithuanian nationalists killed thousands in pogroms. The particularly brutal *Hilfspolizei* (Ukrainian Auxiliary Police) hunted down Jews escaping from ghettos and killed thousands. Without the work of these sympathizers, the Nazi campaign of genocide would have been noticeably less effective.

Following their occupation of Latvia, Germans and Latvian Fascists moved quickly against the nation's Jews. In Riga, synagogues were destroyed and Jews were beaten, raped, and shot. First marginalized within Latvian society, Jews were then excluded from it in August when they were ordered into the Riga Ghetto. Here, Jewish men and women are forced to perform the most menial and backbreaking labor: clearing the rubble from a street near a Catholic church.

Rallying the German nation to war against the Soviet Union, Minister of Propaganda Joseph Goebbels could reach most of the populace through his radio broadcasts by the end of 1941. War on two fronts did not deter Goebbels from pressing for the removal of Jews from German society. The first deportation of Jews from Berlin occurred in October.

1941

nearby Ponary, where they are shot as retribution for the partisan ambush of a German patrol.

• **September 1941:** The Germans open an exposition in Paris called "The Jew and France." Visitors see sculptures and paintings of hideous mythical Jews, Jews allegedly cursed to wander the world forever because of their supposed attack on Jesus Christ, and Jews allegedly out to control the world. Other exhibits portray the Jew as a repulsive monster destroying France. In the first few days, more than 100,000 Parisians visit the exhibit. • Romanians and Germans force nearly 150,000 Jews into death marches to internment camps in Bessarabia, Ukraine. Many

Bishop Clemens August Graf von Galen supported Nazi nationalism early on. Later, he attempted to stop the "euthanasia" program, denouncing it publicly in 1941. Although he did not participate in the July 1944 assassination attempt on Hitler's life, the Nazis linked Galen to it, and he was consequently imprisoned in the Sachsenhausen, Germany, concentration camp. Pope Pius XII made Galen a Roman Catholic cardinal on Christmas Day, 1945.

French Jews faced increasing restrictions during 1941, including arrest and search by police, as this episode from Paris illustrates. Foreign Jews in France encountered even harsher measures, including detainment and deportation. Beginning in August of that year, foreign Jews were sent to the Drancy transit camp, from which they were sent to labor and concentration camps.

Under the watchful eye of French police, a Jewish man complies with the government order forbidding Jews to own radios. Such measures, enacted throughout 1941, were designed to oppress and isolate Jews as a prelude to their arrests and deportations. Meanwhile, the Vichy government pursued a policy of Aryanization involving the seizure of Jewish property and businesses.

die of beatings, random shootings, fatigue, hunger, thirst, exposure, and disease.

• A nine-block section of Auschwitz is turned into a camp for Soviet POWs.
• Chemists and mechanics at the RSHA (Reich Security Main Office) Criminal Technical Institute develop an execution van with engine exhaust directed to the sealed rear-cargo area.

• September 1, 1941: Jews in Slovakia, Bohemia, and Moravia are ordered to wear Yellow Stars, effective September 19, and to suspend all business activity. • Ukrainian nationalist Ulas Samchuk, editor of the newspaper *Volhyn*, writes that Jews and Poles "must disappear completely from our cities." • Because of Christian-German protests, Hitler suspends the "euthanasia" program. The program will continue unofficially, however.

• September 3, 1941: Six hundred Soviet prisoners of war and 300 Jews are "euthanized" at Auschwitz. • Six

Otto Ohlendorf

From June 1941 to June 1942, Otto Ohlendorf commanded *Einsatzgruppe* D. This extermination squad operated in the Crimea-Caucasus region, where Ohlendorf ordered the slaughter of 90,000 people.

Justifying his actions at his trial in 1947, he asserted his utter conviction in the "military necessity" of the killings. "Jews," he argued, "posed a continuous danger for German occupation troops and might someday  attack Germany." As for murdering children, he reasoned they "were people who would grow up and, being the children of parents who had been killed, would constitute a danger no smaller than that of the parents."

To ease the "immense psychological burden" of personal responsibility, he ordered his executioners to shoot simultaneously at victims. During the trial, women sent flowers to the cell of the handsome defendant, who was sentenced to hang for his crimes.

To counteract the Serbian Resistance movement, the Germans promulgated a harsh retaliatory policy: 100 Serbs would be killed for every German casualty. Many Serbian Jews joined the Resistance, and Jews became special targets of German reprisals. Here, a German soldier orders a group of Jewish and Serbian men into columns to be marched to their deaths.

Under the control of *Einsatzgruppe* B of the SS, these dejected Jewish men in Mogilev, Belorussia, march to forced labor or death. The large size of the Star of David on their clothing suggests that this photograph may have been intended as part of a propaganda film, designed to fuel hatred of the Jew as a subhuman threat to society. Oversized stars, signs hung around necks, degrading labor—all of these were filmed and photographed to transform human beings into the sorts of Jewish caricatures favored by Nazi cartoonists and illustrators.

1941

Jews who refuse to serve on the Jewish Council at Dubossary, Ukraine, are publicly hanged. Later, 600 elderly Jews are driven into Dubossary's eight synagogues and burned alive when the synagogues are set ablaze.

• September 4, 1941: Jewish Resistance members based in Dubossary, Ukraine, and led by Yakov Guzanyatskii assassinate a German commander named Kraft. Another group blows up a large store of German arms.

• September 6, 1941: The Germans establish a "working ghetto" at Vilna, Lithuania.

As part of their campaign to build support for antisemitic measures, the Nazis opened an exposition in Paris entitled *Le Juif et la France* (The Jew and France). Exhibits appealed to French patriotism by portraying the Jew as the enemy, a monster intent on destroying France. In its first days *Le Juif et la France* drew 100,000 Parisians.

A group of young children gaze out at the photographer just prior to their execution by an *Einsatzkommando*. An estimated one million Jewish children died in the Holocaust, most of them in the gas chambers of the death camps. As the Germans swept into Soviet territory, they sometimes turned the task of killing Jewish children over to their Ukrainian allies.

• **September 7, 1941:** British Foreign Secretary Anthony Eden notes that "if we must have preferences, let me murmur in your ear that I prefer Arabs to Jews."

• **September 12, 1941:** German General Wilhelm Keitel exhorts his commanders in the East to be "ruthless" in their treatment of Jews. • 3434

Jews are taken from Vilna, Lithuania, to nearby Ponary and executed.

• **September 13, 1941:** Suspicious that the Allies may be decoding its radio messages, Berlin orders German commanders in the Soviet Union to send future reports of Nazi executions of Jews and other Soviet civilians by courier instead of radio.

• **Eleven members of the Jewish Council of Piotrkow, Poland,** who had cooperated with the city's Jewish underground, are executed following two months of Gestapo torture.

• **Charles and Anne Lindbergh,** members of the America First Committee, attend a rally in Des Moines, Iowa, at which Lindbergh blames the Jews for

Dean of faculty at Berlin University, Dr. Franz Six was an SS general commanding a unit of *Einsatzgruppe* B and responsible for murdering more than 50,000 Jews. He was sentenced to only 20 years in prison and served but four because John McCloy, American high commissioner of Germany, chose to use him in the U.S. counterintelligence service. He later testified on behalf of Adolf Eichmann at Eichmann's trial in Jerusalem.

German soldiers confront a Jewish woman in a Bessarabian transit camp. Many Jews were killed as a result of Romanian leader Ion Antonescu's decree *Curatirea Terenului* (Cleansing of the Ground). Those who survived were relegated to primitive camps with grass huts, like the one pictured here, or to crowded ghettos.

The German conquest of Yugoslavia unleashed new brutality against the country's Jews. With foot raised to deliver yet another blow, a soldier of the German mountain troops kicks a man to death during the campaign to rid the Macva region of all Jews.

1941

"agitating for war... for reasons that are not American.... Their greatest danger to this country lies in their large ownership and influence in our motion pictures, our press, our radio, and our government."

• September 15, 1941: Eighteen thousand Jews are murdered at Berdichev, Ukraine.

• September 16, 1941: All 24,000 Jews of Uman, Ukraine, are assembled at the town's airport and murdered by German troops.

• September 17–18, 1941: A general deportation of German Jews begins.

• September 19, 1941: Germans capture Kiev, Ukraine. • Thousands of

Distraught and terrified, these Jewish women struggle to recover from a severe beating at the hands of Romanians and/or Germans. This violence was the first in a wave of persecution unleashed against the Jews of Bessarabia, Romania. It was followed by deportation and death marches to camps in Transnistria, Romania. Many did not survive the cruel journey, falling victim to shootings, hunger, and thirst. Thousands perished by drowning in the Dniester River.

MAJOR ROMANIAN MASSACRES OF JEWS, 1941–1942

More than 270,000 Romanian Jews were murdered during the Holocaust. Most were massacred in 1941 by Nazi *Einsatzgruppen* and the equally bloodthirsty Romanian troops. Most were shot; others died through drownings, beatings, or other forms of torture. On June 25, 1941, about 15,000 Jews were murdered in Iasi.

September signaled a wave of persecution against Jews in Bessarabia. For two months beginning in September, Romanians and Germans deported some 120,000 Bessarabian Jews from their homes to camps in Transnistria, Romania. Any who fell behind were shot. Those who survived the march told of mothers who could barely stand, carrying their children's corpses until they could receive a proper burial.

A photo of Pola Lenczner appears on a Rosh Hashanah greeting card. The Hebrew inscription over Pola's face translates to "Have a Happy New Year." The German inscription below reads, "Heartfelt New Year's Wishes." Pola was later murdered by the Germans.

Karl Jäger was an important Nazi functionary and SS colonel who took command of *Einsatzkommando* 3 of *Einsatzgruppe* A *and* of security police for Lithuania. He ordered the murder of thousands of Lithuanian Jews by having them shot in pits. Jäger eluded police for many years after the war, but was arrested in 1959. He escaped hanging by committing suicide.

German police and possibly members of an *Einsatzkommando* murder Jews who stand helpless in a trench. Because of the sandy soil, this image may be of an *Aktion* carried out by *Einsatzgruppe* A along the coast of the Baltic Sea in Lithuania, Latvia, or Estonia. Although many German soldiers claimed after the war that they had no choice but to shoot when ordered to do so, the fact is that incidents of punishment of men who refused to participate in execution murders were rare. Men who perpetrated such atrocities did so because they wanted to.

1941

Jews are murdered at Zhitomir, Ukraine. • As per the Nazi decree of September 1, 1941, the Jews of Slovakia, Bohemia, and Moravia are required to wear identifying Yellow Stars.

• September 20, 1941: Several thousand Jews, mostly women and children from Kovno, Lithuania, are

executed at the local synagogue after being held there for three days. • Policemen in Kiev, Ukraine, adopt armbands identifying the wearer as a member of the Nazi-sponsored Organization of Ukrainian Nationalists.

• September 22, 1941: All Jews of Litin, Ukraine, are murdered. • SS-trained Ukrainian militiamen mas-

From an illegal radio that's hidden in a large book, a member of the Dutch Resistance listens probably to a BBC broadcast. Such broadcasts not only maintained the spirits of those in the occupied countries but also provided coded instructions for underground actions against the Germans. Many individual Dutch were sympathetic to, and risked their lives to help hide, Jews from the Germans. However, the Dutch government and police generally cooperated with the German occupation forces in rounding up Jews to be transported to their deaths in Poland.

Slaughter at Ejszyszki

During the autumn of 1941, advancing *Einsatzkommando* units systematically annihilated Jewish communities in villages and small towns in the Baltic states. On September 22, the beginning of the Jewish New Year, the squads swept into the Lithuanian town of Ejszyszki, ready to murder each of the 4000 Jews who lived there.

Some 500 Ejszyszki Jews fled into the countryside, only to be captured by the Germans and their Lithuanian police helpers. Those unable to escape were locked inside three buildings, without food or water. The next day and night, still denied food and water, the Jews were made to stand in the cattle market. Finally, at daybreak of September 25, the healthiest men were taken away. Those remaining were told to not be afraid, that the men were working and preparing a ghetto for the community. But there was no ghetto, only burial pits where the Jews were taken in groups of 250 and shot. A survivor recalled hearing the Lithuanian executioners celebrate with boisterous singing and drinking.

About 300 Lithuanians voluntarily participated in the killing "actions" undertaken by *Einsatzgruppe* A in the Baltic region, which annihilated about 90 percent of the Jewish population. Only 30 Jews from Ejszyszki survived the war.

As the Germans conquered Eastern Europe, they encouraged ethnic Germans (*Volksdeutsche*) to join Nazi organizations. Many of these ethnic Germans participated in the crimes committed by the Nazi regime. In this photograph, uniformed *Volksdeutsche* pose with a group of Serbs and Jews they have executed in Petrovgrad, Yugoslavia, on September 17, 1941.

sacre 28,000 Jews at Vinnitsa, Ukraine. • Nearly 500 Jews escape from Ejszyszki, Lithuania, after being alerted to an impending Nazi sweep; *See* September 23, 1941.

• September 23, 1941: Gassing tests are conducted at Auschwitz. • 3500 Jews unable to escape from Ejszyszki, Lithuania, are locked in a synagogue and then moved to a cattle market, where they are denied food and water; *See* September 27, 1941.

• September 24–28, 1941: Soviet troops in Kiev, Ukraine, booby-trap two hotels, the post office, a radio station, and other major buildings, which are exploded via wireless radio after German troops have settled in. About 1000 Germans are killed. The Germans immediately plot a reprisal; *See* September 29–30, 1941.

• September 26, 1941: Jews of Swieciany, Lithuania, are massacred in the nearby Polygon Woods. Several hundred young Jewish men manage to escape.

The *Einsatzgruppen* were especially active in the Ukraine. Here, soldiers of the *Waffen-SS* and the Reich Labor Service observe the execution of a Ukrainian Jew by a comrade from *Einsatzgruppe* D. In September 1941 the Nazis murdered 28,000 Jews outside of the Ukrainian town of Vinnitsa, burying them in mass graves.

Two Polish Jews doing forced labor pose with their German bosses and tormentors. The pained expressions on the faces of the two Jewish men stand in stark contrast to the smiles of the German overseers. The sight of two well-dressed Jewish men shoveling coal and sweeping the streets apparently brought joy to the faces of these Nazis.

Beginning in September 1941, German Jews had to wear the Star of David on their clothes. The star, which made their "racial" background readily identifiable, contained the word *Jude*. This Jewish couple was photographed on the streets of Berlin. With the stars, they had lost any hope of escaping torment at the hands of Nazis they encountered. The stars also made it easier for the Germans to identify Jews for deportation to the East, which was tantamount to a death sentence.

1941

● **September 27, 1941:** More than 3200 Jews of Ejszyszki, Lithuania, are executed at pits on the outskirts of the city.

● **September 27–28, 1941:** Jews at Kiev, Ukraine, are ordered to assemble for "resettlement"; *See* September 29–30, 1941.

● **September 29–30, 1941:** As a reprisal for the September 24 booby-trap deaths of German troops at the hands of Soviet soldiers in Kiev, Ukraine, 33,771 Jews are shot to death in a ravine at Babi Yar, Ukraine. The massacre is masterminded by *Sonderkommando* 4a commander Paul Blobel.

The Wehrmacht's War of Annihilation

When Hitler launched his campaign in the East, the German *Wehrmacht* (Armed Forces) became direct, active partners in his racial war of annihilation. It engaged not only in military operations but also in ideologically motivated actions.

Military guidelines and pronouncements by high-ranking officers mirrored Hitler's conviction that the campaign against the Soviet Union was no ordinary war. Attempting to justify the planned total eradication of "Jewish Bolshevism" in the quest for *Lebensraum* (Living space), field officers—including Field Marshal Walther von Brauchitsch *(pictured)*—stressed the necessity of brutal measures. Consequently, the ensuing campaign of devastation trampled on the traditional international rules of war. Captured Red Army soldiers were not seen as "comrades in arms" but as "useless mouths to feed" who could be ruthlessly liquidated.

It is estimated that between two and three million Soviet prisoners of war perished at the hands of the German military. Most were allowed to starve to death. Others died of exposure after having their warm clothing confiscated, or from exhaustion or epidemics. Others, if they could not keep up, were shot during long marches to prison camps. Survivors suffered horribly as slave laborers and subjects of medical experiments.

The Army turned over to *Einsatzkommandos* for immediate execution more than 500,000 "politically undesirable prisoners of war." Selected were Communist functionaries, members of the intelligentsia, and all Jews. *Wehrmacht* units also assisted the *Einsatzgruppen* by physically securing areas surrounding mass shootings. They sometimes participated in "combing" operations to ferret out and "cleanse" captured Soviet territory of Jews.

Frustrated by partisan guerrilla activity, the *Wehrmacht*'s reprisal policy featured public hangings and executions of large numbers of defenseless civilians. Jews became easy targets because of their identification as purported supporters of Bolshevism. Troops shot those "walking about" during curfew, burned down entire villages suspected of harboring partisans, drove off livestock, destroyed food reserves, and sometimes forced the rounded-up Jews to clear minefields with rakes.

An *Einsatzgruppe* A report credited the *Wehrmacht* with shooting 19,000 partisans and "criminals," identified as "mostly Jews," by the end of 1941.

The *Wehrmacht* even took part in ghetto liquidations, usually under the guise of "anti-partisan" campaigns. In the fall of 1941, the Army helped murder an additional 20,000 Jews in eight such "actions" in the Belorussian region alone. In Latvia, firing squads that murdered captive Jews included *Wehrmacht* personnel. Anti-partisan reprisal massacres of civilians (again, mainly Jews) and cooperative undertakings between army units, *Einsatzgruppen*, and police also occurred in the Balkans, and typified the *Wehrmacht*'s complicity in the Holocaust.

• September–October 1941: SS murders of Soviet Jews escalate as German troops push east toward Moscow. 48,000 are killed at Odessa, Ukraine, and at Kiev, Ukraine. • More than 20,000 Jews are executed in the former eastern provinces of Poland.

• October 1941: The German government prohibits further Jewish emigration from Germany • At the Auschwitz camp, SS officer Arthur Johann Breitwieser takes note when a comrade is rendered unconscious after accidental exposure to a disinfectant called Zyklon B. A gaseous variant of the compound will eventually be used to kill millions of Jews.
• *Einsatzgruppen* members gather Jews of the Baltic port of Libau and machine-gun them at the local naval base.

• Germans drown 30 Jewish children in clay pits near Okopowa Street in the Warsaw Ghetto. • At the Buchenwald, Germany, concentration camp, Dr. Fritz Mennecke condemns 1200 Jewish prisoners to death by "euthanasia."

Massacre at Babi Yar

Days after the German Army captured Kiev, Ukraine, the bloodiest shooting massacre of the Holocaust took place on the outskirts of that city. Over the course of two days in September 1941, *Einsatzgruppen* and Security Police commandos slaughtered more than 33,000 of Kiev's Jews at a ravine called Babi Yar.

When a series of explosions and fires in Kiev killed many German soldiers and destroyed army headquarters, Jews were blamed. In retaliation, German authorities posted a sign announcing a supposed "resettlement" of the city's Jews. Under threat of death, more than 30,000 were marched to the Jewish cemetery. From there they were marched in small groups to Babi Yar.

Stripped of all clothing, the trembling Jews were led into the ravine. Ordered to lie down, each was shot in the back of the head. The massacre continued uninterruptedly. New victims were forced to lie on those already dead. Corpses stacked up in layers. A survivor recalled being miraculously untouched by the bullets but, clutching her son to her naked body, fell under "a heap of warm, bloody bodies. The bodies of old men rested on the bodies of children, who lay on the bodies of their dead mothers." Commander Paul Blobel later attempted to obliterate all traces of the massacre.

Among the most infamous mass executions perpetrated by the Germans during the war was that at Babi Yar, a ravine near Kiev, Ukraine. On September 29 and 30, 1941, the Germans, with the aid of Ukrainian collaborators, rounded up and executed 33,771 Jews at Babi Yar. This massacre was one of many carried out by German *Einsatzkommandos* and police regiments following the invasion of the Soviet Union.

Paul Blobel was commander of *Sonderkommando* 4a of *Einsatzgruppe* C, which carried out numerous atrocities in the Ukraine during the summer and fall of 1941, among them the Babi Yar massacre. He also headed another enormous massacre at Kharkov, Ukraine, in late December 1941. More than 21,600 Jews were slaughtered.

1941

- **Early October 1941:** Seventy children in the Warsaw Ghetto are found frozen to death outside destroyed houses following the season's first snowfall.

- **October 1–December 22, 1941:** 33,500 Jews are killed in Vilna, Lithuania.

- **October 2, 1941:** On this Jewish Day of Atonement, Jews are taken from the ghetto at Podborodz, Ukraine, and killed. • A Nazi raid on the Jewish ghetto at Vilna, Lithuania, leaves 3000 dead at nearby Ponary. One victim, Serna Morgenstern, is shot in the back by an SS officer after he complimented her beauty and told her she was free to go.

The 33,771 victims of the Babi Yar massacre included Jews of all ages and from all walks of life. The perpetrators showed no mercy for the elderly, women, or even children. Among those murdered were Klara Halef-Miropolsky and her husband, Joseph *(above)*. Their daughter, Mania Halef, here shown in a 1936 photograph *(far left)*, was only seven years old when shot at Babi Yar. The Nazis believed it especially important to murder children, who represented, in their minds, the future of the Jewish "race." Rakhil Mikhailovna Boorakovskaya *(above)* was among the thousands of women killed in the massacre.

● **October 4, 1941:** Fifteen hundred Jews from Kovno, Lithuania, are transported to the Ninth Fort and murdered. In Kovno proper, Nazis lock the Jewish hospital and set it ablaze, incinerating all inside.

● **October 6–7, 1941:** The majority of Jews in Dvinsk, Latvia, are murdered.

● **October 8, 1941:** The Vitebsk (Belorussia) Ghetto is liquidated; more than 16,000 Jews are killed.

● **October 9, 1941:** Hans Frank, governor-general of Occupied Poland, tells ministers of the German *Generalgouvernement* that Jews "must be done away with one way or another."

● **October 10, 1941:** Field Marshal Walter von Reichenau, commander of the German Sixth Army, issues a directive emphasizing the need for harsh treatment of "Jewish subhumanity." ● Thousands of Slovak Jews are sent to labor camps at Sered, Vyhne, and Nováky. ● Slovak, Bohemian, and Moravian Jews are forced from their homes and into ghettos.

Winter comes early to the Ukraine, so in October of 1941 this little Jewish girl at Lubny already is bundled against the cold. More than chill air threatens her, however, for she is part of a group awaiting execution at the hands of a Nazi kill squad, probably *Sonderkommando 4a*, which was active in the Lubny, Ukraine, region in the latter half of October. An official genocide update, euphemistically titled "Operational Situational Report USSR No. 132," describes October *Sonderkommando* activities in the area, and the liquidation of 1363 Ukrainian Jews, Communists, and partisans.

Christian Wirth was a central figure in the Nazi extermination programs. Wirth joined the NSDAP in 1931 and worked for the Stuttgart division of the Gestapo (the Secret Police). As a member of the T-4 euthanasia program, Wirth experimented with gassing those classified as unfit for human life. He organized the first euthanasia installations outside of Germany and supervised the killing installations at the Chelmno, Belzec, Sobibór, and Treblinka death camps. He was assassinated by Yugoslav partisans in 1944.

German soldiers struggle to free their vehicle from the mud during the German attack on the Soviet Union in 1941. Despite the early successes of Operation Barbarossa, the Germans were unprepared for the rigors of the Russian climate. They would be defeated in Russia as much by the weather as by the Soviet Armed Forces.

1941

• **October 11, 1941:** A Jewish ghetto at Chernovtsy, Romania, is established. • Thousands of Jews are murdered at Edineti, Romania.

• **October 12, 1941:** Following the extermination by Gestapo agents and Ukrainian militia of 10,000 to 12,000 Jews at burial pits outside of Stanislawów, Ukraine, German perpetrators throw a "Bloody Sunday" victory celebration. • At Sabac, Yugoslavia, hundreds of Gypsies are murdered. • Three thousand Jews are killed at Sheparovtse, Ukraine.

• **October 13, 1941:** Fifteen thousand Jews are murdered at Dnepropetrovsk, Ukraine.

Wilhelm Kube was a Nazi official who was appointed *Generalkommissar* of Belorussia in 1941. One of the earliest members of the Nazi Party, Kube was a Nazi deputy in the Weimar Republic's *Reichstag* before Hitler's ascension to power in 1933. A political figure to the end, Kube opposed SS deportations and mass murder because he didn't want more Jews brought into his area. He was assassinated by a Russian partisan disguised as a housemaid in September 1943.

These Jews, confined to a German work camp in Occupied Russia, chisel the mortar off the bricks of destroyed buildings. As the Germans made their way through the Soviet Union, they wrought such havoc that many structures had to be rebuilt from scratch, often making use of the materials left in the *Wehrmacht*'s wake.

Kovno Ghetto

Of the 30,000 Jews who made up the original population of the Kovno (Lithuania) Ghetto, more than 90 percent did not survive to liberation.

During the first six weeks of the German occupation in 1941, Lithuanian extremists arrested thousands of Jews, imprisoning them in several old forts that ringed the city. Almost 4000 Jews perished. Many women were raped, then shot. The dead were thrown into pits.

Systematic *Einsatzgruppen* murders began once ghetto gates closed in August. In September some 1600 men, women, and children were shot. On October 4 about 1800 were murdered, including 180 children and infant patients who were burned alive when the Germans set fire to the ghetto hospital. The "Great Action" of October 28 separated Kovno Jews "fit" to work from those "unfit." About 9200 were sent "to the right," to be killed. The remaining 17,000 toiled as slave laborers.

In late 1943 the Nazis began to liquidate the ghetto, deporting many to concentration camps. In March 1944 the SS dragged all children under the age of 12 from homes and hiding paces. This so-called "Children's Action" claimed 1300 lives. A mother's diary recorded the horror of watching her child "tossed like a puppy into the truck...."

• **October 14, 1941:** German Jews are deported to the Lódź (Poland) Ghetto.

• **October 15, 1941:** German authorities in Poland decree that any Jew found outside a designated ghetto will be shot. Further, any non-Jewish Pole who aids a Jew will be executed.

• **October 16, 1941:** German and Romanian forces occupy Odessa, Ukraine. • Three days after the German murder of 15,000 Jewish residents of Dnepropetrtovsk, Ukraine, an additional 5000 Jews are executed in the town. • The first SS deportation train of Western Jews travels to ghettos at Lódź, Lublin, and Warsaw, Poland.

• **October 16–November 4, 1941:** Twenty trains carrying nearly 20,000 Jews travel from Germany, Luxembourg, Czechoslovakia, and Austria to the Lódź (Poland) Ghetto.

• **October 18–20, 1941:** Mass executions of Soviet Jews in Borisov, Belorussia, 50 miles east of Minsk, Belorussia, are carried out by an *Ein-*

"The Jewish women, when they arrived in the first months of pregnancy, were subjected to abortions. When their pregnancy was near the end, after confinement, the babies were drowned in a bucket of water."

—*Marie Vaillant-Couturier, a former French Resistance member, testifying before the Nuremberg Tribunal about Auschwitz; 1946*

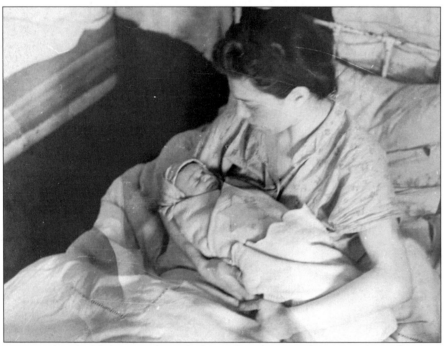

A mother holds her newborn baby in the Kovno (Lithuania) Ghetto hospital. A Jewish star is sewn onto the child's blanket, marking the baby for probable death just minutes after he or she was born. Of the 30,000 original residents of the Kovno Ghetto, which was established in the summer of 1941, less than ten percent survived.

Father Bernhard Lichtenberg was a German Catholic priest and activist based in Berlin at St. Hedwig's Cathedral. He protested to the Nazi regime about the state-sanctioned "euthanasia" program, and exhorted his congregation to denounce the government's deportations of Jews to the East. Lichtenberg was arrested in 1941. When his apartment was searched, notes were found for an undelivered sermon in which he would have told his congregants that the Nazi government's claim that Jews wanted to destroy the German nation and its people was a lie. He was sentenced to prison for a term of two years. He was released in 1943 at age 68. Lichtenberg subsequently was arrested by the Gestapo and sent to be interned at the Dachau concentration camp. Ill from age and his earlier imprisonment, Father Lichtenberg died en route to the camp.

1941

satzkommando following a night of celebration by German troops.

● October 19, 1941: Soviet authorities declare a state of siege in Moscow.

● October 21, 1941: Residents of the Jewish community at Koidanov, Belorussia, are murdered.

● October 21–23, 1941: Thousands of Jews are murdered at Kraljevo, Yugoslavia.

● October 22–23, 1941: Sixty-six German enlisted men and officers, and 17 Romanian officers, are killed when the Romanian headquarters in Odessa, Ukraine, explodes. Three hours later, Jews and Communists are

MAJOR DEPORTATIONS OF JEWS TO LÓDŹ GHETTO, 1941–1943

DENMARK

REICHSKOMMISSARIAT OSTLAND

Hamburg

NETHERLANDS

Berlin

Warta

Vistula

Wloclawek

Vistula

GREATER GERMANY

Warta

Duesseldorf

Cologne

Frankfurt

Oder

Prague

BOHEMIA & MORAVIA

GREATER GERMANY

Kozminek

Kalisz

Warta

Lódź Ghetto

Brzeziny

Pabianice

Lask

Zelow

Vienna

SLOVAKIA

Praszka

Pajeczno

GENERAL-GOUVERNEMENT

SWITZERLAND

■ Cities and towns from which Jews were deported to Lódź Ghetto

0   150 miles

0   250 kilometers

ITALY

HUNGARY

CROATIA

ROMANIA

The Germans established the Lódź (Poland) Ghetto in early 1940, entrapping 150,000 Jews. In 1941 and '42, nearly 40,000 more Jews were deported to Lódź from Berlin, Vienna, Prague, and other areas.

Arthur Nebe

From June to November 1941, Arthur Nebe commanded *Einsatzgruppe* B, operating around Minsk, Belorussia, and along the Moscow front. In those five months, Nebe's unit executed over 45,000 Jews.

After completing his assignment in Russia, Nebe returned to his duties as head of the Criminal Police. During Heinrich Himmler's visit to Minsk, Nebe staged the shoot-  ing execution of 100 people for the *Reichsführer*'s viewing. Himmler, sickened at the sight, became particularly distressed over two women not killed outright. He then instructed Nebe to find more "humane" methods of killing. When given the task of ending the suffering of insane-asylum inmates, Nebe used dynamite on the mentally ill.

Involved in the plot against Hitler, Nebe was himself apparently executed in 1945. He may have survived, however, as witnesses reported seeing him in Italy in 1956 and Ireland in 1960.

Joseph Goebbels speaks at the opening ceremonies of 1941's German Book Week, held in Weimar in October. German books had, by this time, been thoroughly "Aryanized," and works written by Jewish authors had been banned. The goal of publishing, like every other area of German cultural life, was to instill a virulent antisemitism in the German people, and books increasingly became another medium for Nazi propaganda.

hanged in the central square. The next day, 5000 Jews and other civilians are seized and shot.

• October 23, 1941: Thousands of Jews are murdered at Kragujevac, Yugoslavia.

• October 23–25, 1941: At Odessa, Ukraine, thousands of Jews are killed.

• October 24–25, 1941: Sixteen thousand Odessa, Ukraine, Jews are force-marched out of the city toward Dalnik, where they are bound together in groups of 40 to 50 and shot, at first in the open and later through holes drilled in the walls of warehouses. Three of these structures are set ablaze and a fourth is exploded by artillery fire.

• October 25, 1941: Jews at Tatarsk in Soviet Russia revolt against murderous peasants and SS kill squads. The rebellion is put down by regular German Army units, artillery, and air power. All Jews in Tatarsk are murdered. • SS officer Viktor Brack, a member of Hitler's Chancellery, concocts a poison-gas program with which to address the "Jewish ques-

Already massively overcrowded and short on food, the Lódź (Poland) Ghetto became the destination for trainloads of Jews deported from Germany, Austria, and Bohemia beginning in autumn 1941. To accommodate the influx, the Nazis required Chaim Rumkowski, the head of the ghetto administration, to select 20,000 residents for deportation. By late January 1942 Rumkowski had negotiated the number down to 10,000 deemed "asocial"; that is, not contributing to the ghetto's industries.

Nazi authorities often forced the Jews to police themselves, especially in the ghettos. This photograph shows a Jewish policeman at the entrance to the ghetto in Stanislawów, Ukraine. The sign, in German, reads, "Entrance to the Jewish Quarter is Forbidden." The Nazis hoped to completely cut off the ghettos from the outside world. No one was to know what went on there.

The victims of Nazi massacres were almost always buried in mass graves, such as this one in Yugoslavia containing the bodies of Jews and Gypsies murdered by the 750th Infantry Regiment in October 1941. As part of an effort to conceal their horrific crimes, the Nazis would later dig up many of these mass graves so that the bodies could be burned. This is yet another example of atrocity compounded by stupidity. To unearth mass graves was a monumental undertaking, as the Nazis had been *filling* them across Europe for months. Many graves remained untouched until discovered by Allied troops, and even when remains had been exhumed by Germans, considerable physical evidence remained at overburdened ovens and ineffectual outdoor pyres.

1941

tion." Brack's notion is supported by Alfred Wetzel, of the Ministry for the Occupied Eastern Territories, and by SS functionary Adolf Eichmann.

• **October 26, 1941:** Pigeon-keepers at Kiev, Ukraine, are executed on the assumption that the birds could be used to carry messages. • Germans inform Jews of Kalisz, Poland, that

elderly Jews in convalescent homes are to be moved to another home the next day; *See October 27, 1941.*

• **October 27, 1941:** A black van that stops at the Jewish old people's home in Kalisz, Poland, is loaded with elderly and driven off. The van is specially outfitted to route carbon monoxide into the cargo area; *See*

Romania was among Germany's Eastern European allies. On October 16, 1941, the city of Odessa, Ukraine, was overrun by the German and Romanian armies and occupied by the Romanians. Although Jews had been a presence in Romania since the second century, the way for them had been thorny. Romanian governments of the early 20th century prevented Jews from assimilating, and anti-Jewish violence was not uncommon. By 1941 Romania, like other collaborationist states, practiced the same occupation policies as the Germans. This photograph shows Jews waiting to register with the new authorities in the Romanian-controlled city.

Two civilian bureaucrats, Wilhelm Frick *(left)* and Hans Globke *(right)* join their military colleagues in a parade. Frick played a vital role in the Nazi Party's rise to power, first as minister of the interior in Thuringia and later as Reich minister of the interior. Although he never joined the Party, Globke served as the ministry's director of the citizenship department, and was a legal advisor to Frick. In that role, Globke participated in formulating the commentary on the Reich Citizenship Law, differentiating between Jew and German and depriving Jews of their basic rights.

During a roundup of Jews in Poland, a German soldier checks a boy to see if he is a Jew by examining his genitals for circumcision. Despite German claims that Jews displayed obvious racial features that distinguished them from Aryans, sometimes even "experts" with calipers to measure skull dimensions were unable to discover who was a Jew and who was Aryan. Checking males for circumcision was a less scientific but more pragmatic method.

Lebensborn

Nazi racial policy in the conquered Eastern Territories centered on the extermination of undesirables. Yet, Heinrich Himmler, the erstwhile selective breeder of chickens, initiated a further goal: the identification and preservation of "racially valuable" Aryan elements among the region's population.

To this end, the SS kidnapped blond, blue-eyed children from their parents in occupied areas and sent them to Germany for adoption. Operating under the code name "Haymaking," this sinister campaign was carried out with particular viciousness in Poland and Russia. Thousands of children were cruelly taken from their families. Most of the children were placed in *Lebensborn* homes and later adopted by suitably Nordic couples, often by households in which the father was a member of the SS. This unconscionable criminality was planned also for Latvia and other occupied nations.

This was but one aspect of Himmler's *Lebensborn* (Fountain of life) program, designed to preserve, improve, and extend "pure" Aryan blood. In order to encourage the propagation of "good blood," Himmler also issued procreation orders to the SS. It mattered not if the children produced were illegitimate—only that the parents were of pure Aryan stock. Thirteen special institutions throughout Germany served as both "stud farms" for SS men and maternity homes for unwed German mothers.

Women and children lost their lives as victims of mass executions. This photograph shows a mother and her two children, as well as several hundred others, just before the mass shooting at Lubny, Ukraine, on October 16, 1941.

Jewish women and children were usually forced to surrender their belongings and strip off their clothes shortly before their executions. These items usually were stolen by the killers. At Lubny, *Sonderkommandos* murdered 1363 Jews, Communists, and partisans.

1941

October 28, 1941. • Jews of Sluzk, 60 miles south of Minsk, Belorussia, are annihilated by *Einsatzkommando* troops, half of whom are German, half Lithuanian.

• October 28, 1941: More elderly Jews from a convalescent home in Kalisz, Poland, are taken away in gassing vans. • 27,000 Jews assembled in Democracy Square in Kovno, Lithuania, must pass before an SS officer named Rauca, who signals life or death for each. 9200 of the Jews—4300 of them children—are sent to their deaths at pits at the nearby Ninth Fort; *See* October 30, 1941.

• October 30, 1941: Four thousand Jews are murdered at Nesvizh,

This vio-
lin once belonged to
a Roma Gypsy, Miodrag
Djordevic-Tukalia, from Yugoslavia.
German soldiers shot him in the town of
Kragujevac sometime between October 20 and 26,
1941, a week of mass shootings. Djordevic-Tukalia's son kept
the violin as a memento of his deceased father.

The Kovno Ghetto in Lithuania became one of the most infamous in Eastern Europe. This photograph shows the Ninth Fort, also known as Killing
Center No. 2, where about 50,000 Jews were executed. After their deaths,
the murderers pushed the victims into vast pits, which became mass graves
containing as many as 3000 corpses.

Naked and terrified, a young
Jewish woman begs for her life.
Already stripped of her clothes, she
is pushed toward a mass grave,
where she will be shot in the back
of the head or machine-gunned.
Because this photograph was
snapped head-on and at eye level,
it almost certainly was not taken surreptitiously. To the contrary, the photographer likely wished to make a
document—or perhaps a keep-
sake—of this interlude in the day's
work of his unit. One cannot help
but wonder about this woman's
fate: In their haste, the *Einsatzkommandos* sometimes failed to deliver
a fatal shot, leaving a few of their
victims to gasp for air and claw
their way through the corpses surrounding them.

Belorussia. • A 12-year-old boy who
escapes the Ninth Fort massacre of
October 28 returns to the Kovno
Ghetto and reveals what happened.

• November 1941: More than 15,000
Serbian Jews deported to a concen-
tration camp at Sajmiste, Yugoslavia,
are later killed in mobile gassing units
disguised as Red Cross vans. • A Jew-
ish ghetto is established at Brest-
Litovsk, Belorussia. • Thousands of
German-Jewish deportees arrive in
Minsk, Belorussia. • Newspapers in
London and New York report Nazi
murders of 52,000 Jews in Kiev,
Ukraine.

• November 1, 1941: Construction of
an extermination center begins at
Belzec, Poland. • A Jewish ghetto at
Grodno, Belorussia, is established.
• A Nazi-sanctioned concentration
camp opens at Hadjerat-M'Guil,
North Africa.

• November 5–6, 1941: Seventeen
thousand Jews are killed outside
Rovno, Ukraine.

Soviet troops reposition an antitank gun at the Battle of Moscow late in 1941. The Germans' superiority in tactics and armor resulted in huge initial losses of Soviet troops and territory. The main German objectives were Kiev, Leningrad, and Moscow, but the winter weather and desperate Russian resistance prevented the Germans from fully capturing any of the three cities.

The expressions on the faces of these Jewish women reflect the nightmarish conditions in the Minsk Ghetto in 1941. The city was ghettoized in July, and soon the Nazis began to murder its Jewish population en masse. About 12,000 Jews were killed on November 7, and 7000 more were murdered on November 20.

Workers from Kovel in the former Soviet Union embark on a freight train for an unknown destination. Millions of non-Jewish workers from all across Europe were deported to Germany as slave laborers. Without those laborers and Jewish workers, the German war effort could not have kept up as well as it did with the demands of the war economy.

1941

● **November 6, 1941:** Popular German film star Joachim Gottschalk kills his family and himself rather than submit to the deportation and probable deaths of his Jewish wife and child.

● **November 7, 1941:** Twelve thousand Jews are transported from Minsk, Belorussia, to burial pits in the

nearby Tuchinka Forest and murdered. ● In Bobruisk, Belorussia, 20,000 Jews are executed.

● **November 7-8, 1941:** More than 17,000 Jews are forced from Rovno, Ukraine, and murdered at burial pits in the Sosenki Forest, outside of town.

All three members of this family from Minsk, Belorussia, lived through the Holocaust. A Russian family protected the daughter, Alia, throughout the war. A German officer named Shultz risked his life to save the father and mother, along with other Jews. The righteous German soldier later joined the anti-Nazi underground.

The Germans drive 7000 Jews from the Minsk (Belorussia) Ghetto to a pit dug into the still-frigid soil outside the city. The Nazis murdered them with firearms. Not satisfied with killing the adults, the Germans tossed the children into the pit alive and suffocated them.

The Jews of Finland

The Jews of Finland found themselves in a bizarre situation with the outbreak of World War II. Despite the Nazis' war on Europe's Jews, Finland's alliance with Germany caused over 300 Finnish Jews to fight alongside German soldiers on the Eastern Front, while Jewish women served in the country's civil-defense corps.

Finland's Jewish community numbered only about 2000 (including almost 300 refugees from Germany and Austria), and antisemitism was practically nonexistent in the country. Finnish Jews had full rights as equal citizens. Most of the refugees were housed in labor camps, where they lived in barracks.

When Heinrich Himmler broached the subject of Finnish Jews, the country's prime minister, Johann Wilhelm Rangell, curtly replied that Finland had no "Jewish problem." Valuing Finland's military cooperation against the Soviet Union, the Nazis applied no further pressure.

In the autumn of 1942, however, eight Jewish refugees were handed over to the Gestapo. Transported to the extermination camp at Auschwitz, Poland, all but one of the refugees perished. Lengthy negotiations with the Swedish government secured the transfer of 160 other refugees to that neutral country. The remaining refugees, along with almost all Jewish-Finnish citizens, survived the war—except for a few Jewish soldiers who died in battle fighting for the German cause.

• **November 7–9, 1941:** Close to 5000 Jews are killed in Pogulanka, outside Dvinsk, Latvia.

• **November 8, 1941:** A Jewish ghetto at Lvov, Ukraine, is established.

• **November 13, 1941:** Warsaw diarist Chaim Kaplan writes that his wife has been stricken with typhus.

• **November 14, 1941:** Nine thousand Jews from Slonim, Belorussia, are murdered at Czepielow.

• **November 17, 1941:** Eight Warsaw, Poland, Jews, including six women, are executed for leaving the ghetto without permission. The executioners, pressed into service, are Polish policemen.

• **November 20, 1941:** Approximately 7000 Jews from Minsk, Belorussia, are killed at nearby Tuchinka.

• **November 23, 1941:** Thirty thousand Jews are killed at Odessa, Ukraine.

• **November 24, 1941:** A large "model ghetto"/concentration camp is estab-

Theresienstadt

On June 4, 1942, Pavel Friedmann, 21, finished a poem about the last butterfly he ever saw. "Butterflies," the Jewish writer concluded, "don't live in here, in the ghetto."

A few weeks earlier, the Germans had deported Friedmann to Terezín, Czechoslovakia (*Theresienstadt* in German), the walled military town where they began to ghettoize Czech Jews in the autumn of 1941. A year later 50,000 Jews were struggling to survive in Theresienstadt's deteriorating conditions.

Theresienstadt also became a concentration and transit camp for German and Western European Jews who were eventually deported to Auschwitz. In mid-1944 the Nazis temporarily beautified Theresienstadt to deceive an investigating committee from the International Red Cross and to make a propaganda film that pictured the ghetto as Hitler's gift to the Jews.  The facts were very different. Of the over 140,000 Jews who were sent to Theresienstadt, 33,000 died and 88,000 were deported and killed. Only about 19,000 survived. Pictured is a standard identity card.

Despite starvation, overcrowding, disease, and the constant dread of transports to the East, the Jewish leadership of Rabbi Leo Baeck and others emphasized educational and cultural activities. Friedmann died in Auschwitz on September 29, 1944, but his poem, "I Never Saw Another Butterfly," exemplifies the artistic expressions from Theresienstadt, which are among the most precious documents recovered from the Holocaust.

At Theresienstadt in Occupied Czechoslovakia, the Nazis established a "model" ghetto and concentration camp. This photograph shows the arrival of Jews in the camp. Theresienstadt became infamous as Europe's largest children's camp. All but a few hundred of the thousands of children interned there died. Nevertheless, the Nazis cynically exhibited the camp to the outside world, insisting that the inmates were treated well.

Jacob Edelstein was among the leading figures in Czechoslovakia's Zionist movement before the start of the war. He became the first chairman of the Theresienstadt Ghetto's Jewish Council. He used this position to resist efforts to deport the ghetto's Jews. Bravely, he falsified daily reports concerning the number of Jews in the ghetto. The Nazis deported him in December 1943 to Auschwitz, where he and his family were shot on June 20, 1944.

1941

lished at Theresienstadt, Czechoslovakia, 35 miles from Prague. To prepare for the imminent arrival of inmates, 342 young Jewish men from Prague are brought in as forced laborers.

● November 27, 1941: The first of 19 deportation trains leaves Germany for Riga, Latvia. In the Riga Ghetto, more than 10,600 Jews are rounded up and shot in the nearby Rumbula Forest.

● November 28, 1941: Hitler entertains Hajj Amin al-Husseini. The grand mufti of Jerusalem pledges to cooperate in the extermination of the Jews and offers to enlist Arabs to fight for Germany.

The gate of Theresienstadt's Small Fortress bore the Nazi slogan *ARBEIT MACHT FREI* ("Work Will Set You Free"). The Nazis, insisting that Jews were universally "work shy," cynically tried to create the impression that, if Jews worked hard enough, they could earn their freedom. No Jews ever "earned" freedom, though for some continued work allowed them to survive until liberation. More often, however, Jews were allowed to work only as long as they were needed, or until they were no longer physically capable of performing their tasks. At that point the charade would end and the workers would be put to death.

The Nazis tried to dupe the world into believing that Theresienstadt was a relatively pleasant, politically independent Jewish city. As part of this deception, they issued currency for the city. Of course, the Theresienstadt Ghetto and concentration camp remained under German control throughout their existences.

A band of Jewish partisans marches in a forest in Yugoslavia. Partisans often liked to be pictured with their weapons to portray their strength and determination. They needed every ounce of both, given the rugged nature of Yugoslavia's terrain and the obvious advantages of the Nazis.

• **December 1941: The Night and Fog Decree is issued by Hitler through Field Marshal Wilhelm Keitel. It allows German troops to execute any obstructive non-German civilians in occupied nations.** • *Generalplan Ost* **(General Plan for the East), directed by SS chief Heinrich Himmler, proposes the deportation of 31 million non-Germans in the conquered Eastern Territories to create** *Lebensraum* **("Living space") for German colonists.** • **The German Ministry of Occupied Eastern Territories decrees that the destruction of Jews shall continue irrespective of economic considerations; i.e., the allure of unpaid Jewish labor will be ignored.**

• **During the murder of 5000 Jews at Novogrudok, Belorussia, 200 Jews resist and kill 20 Nazis before being gunned down.** • **A death camp opens at Chelmno, Poland.** • **Ten thousand Jews deported from Odessa, Ukraine, are murdered at camps at Acmecetka, Bogdanovka, and Domanevka, Romania.** • **Mass murders of Jews in the Ukraine and Volhynia region of**

Hanna Lehrer, a Munich Jew, wears both her personal Jewish star around her neck and the mandated Yellow Star badge identifying her, isolating her, and alienating her from other Germans. Hanna was later sent to Riga, Latvia, where she was killed.

Late in 1941 about 80 Jews residing in Bielefeld, Germany, were rounded up along with hundreds of other German Jews for transport to the Riga-Kaiserwald concentration camp in Latvia. This camp specialized in murdering Jews by means of poison-gas vans. One of the SS's innovations was to load Jews into a poison-gas van and kill the Jewish occupants while the van was driving to a mass grave site. The dead Jews could then be conveniently dumped into the pit, which was covered over with dirt by other Jewish prisoners.

Vichy France leader Philippe Pétain (second from left) marches with top Nazi official Hermann Göring (fourth from left) in St. Florentin-Vergigny, France, in December 1941. The Vichy regime not only collaborated with the Germans, but went out of its way to round up Jews who were not French citizens and ship them off to death camps in Poland before the Germans asked them to. In the minds of many Vichy supporters, France may have lost to Germany but at least stood victorious over the Jews.

1941

Poland are slowed when the frozen ground prevents the digging of execution pits.

• Fur coats belonging to Jews in eastern Germany are confiscated by the Nazis. They'll be used by German soldiers on the Eastern Front. • The Jesuit journal *Civiltà Cattolica*, published in Rome under strict Vatican supervision, reminds Catholics that the Jews are supposedly those primarily responsible for murdering God and that the Jews repeat this crime by means of ritual murder "in every generation."

• December 1, 1941: SS Colonel Karl Jäger, commander of *Einsatzkommando* 3, reports to Berlin that 85

This card contains photographs of people exhibiting a "low level" of Germanic racial background. Photographs like these were used to demonstrate so-called un-German, or non-Aryan, physical characteristics. Nazi racial belief was that physical traits represented moral or spiritual qualities. Those who did not fit the standard were to be eliminated.

MAJOR GHETTOS IN BALTIC NATIONS, 1941–1943

Of the 350,000 Jews in the Baltics, most were shot in 1941 by the Nazis and collaborators from those countries. The Nazis established ghettos for the remaining Jews, but then executed or deported most of them by 1944.

Some ghettoized Jews had to perform work beneficial to the German war effort. Here, men and women in the Łódź (Poland) Ghetto sew *Wehrmacht* uniforms. Possessing a skill, such as being a tailor, often saved a Jew from deportation to the extermination camps. But, in the end, even the most skilled workers were deported to their deaths. Nazi hatred of Jews took precedence over any utility Jews may have had for the war effort.

percent of Lithuanian Jewry has been destroyed.

• December 5–8, 1941: Seven thousand Jews from Novogrudok, Belorussia, are forced to stand all day and night in frigid temperatures outside the municipal courthouse. Five thousand are taken away to their deaths on the 6th; the remaining 2000 are

impressed into forced labor at suburban Pereshike.

• December 6, 1941: The Soviets mount a million-man counteroffensive outside of Moscow.

• December 7, 1941: Carrier-based Japanese aircraft attack American naval bases in the Pacific, with heavy

assaults against Pearl Harbor, Hawaii, as well as Clark Field in the Philippines; *See* December 8, 1941.• The Nazis begin gas-van extermination operations at the Chelmno, Poland, death camp.

• December 7–9, 1941: 25,000 Latvian Jews are taken from the Riga Ghetto and murdered in the Rumbula

Arthur Seyss-Inquart was *Reichskommissar* for the Occupied Netherlands from 1940 to 1945. Although he was largely responsible for the devastation the Holocaust brought to the Netherlands, Seyss-Inquart is most famous for the role he played in Germany's annexation of Austria in 1938. Long a Nazi sympathizer, he became Austria's chancellor as a result of pressure from Hitler on March 11, 1938, welcoming a German invasion and incorporation into the Reich. Seyss-Inquart was hanged following trial at Nuremberg.

This map is entitled "Jewish Executions Carried Out by *Einsatzgruppe* A" and stamped "Secret Reich Matter." It shows the number of Jews executed in the Baltics and Belorussia by late 1941. The legend near the bottom states that "the estimated number of Jews still on hand [was] 128,000." The coffin is a symbol for the number of dead Jews in each designated area.

The Nazis went to extensive lengths to segregate the Jewish from the gentile population. In Lódź, Poland, for example, where the ghetto was divided by Zgierska Street, the Germans constructed a bridge linking the two sections of the ghetto. This way, the Nazis did not have to include this important thoroughfare within the confines of the Jewish sector of the city.

1941

Forest. Among the victims is a preeminent Jewish historian, 81-year-old Simon Dubnow.

• **December 8, 1941:** The United States, Great Britain, Australia, and New Zealand declare war on Japan. News of America's involvement in the war cheers many European Jews, who believe rescue will come soon; *See*

December 10, 1941. • **Four thousand Jews of Novogrudok, Belorussia, are killed.**

• **December 8–December 14, 1941:** The Nazis gas Jews at a forest near Chelmno, Poland. On the 8th alone, 2300 Jews are killed this way. Seven hundred victims are from Kolo, Poland.

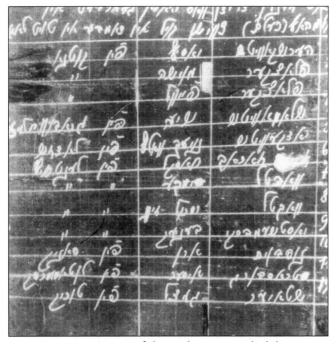

Many perpetrators of the Holocaust prided themselves on their record-keeping, even when, as on this slate of prisoners' names photographed at the Chelmno death camp, the notation was done quickly and impermanently. Such records were maintained to keep track of daily work details, new arrivals, deaths, and other camp data. Not surprisingly, inaccuracies were common, even on printed material.

SS General Arthur Greiser co-founded the *Stahlhelm*, a nationalist German veterans organization, after the First World War. An SS administrator in Poland following the outbreak of the Second World War, he deported thousands of Jewish and Christian Poles to create living space for Germans in Eastern Europe. A brutal Nazi, he was captured after the war, tried, and—after being paraded around Poznań in a cage—hanged in front of his former palace on June 20, 1946.

Chelmno

"It's hard to recognize," said Shimon Srebnik, "but it was here. They burned people here." Srebnik, 47, had returned to Chelmno, a place he first saw in the summer of 1944 when he was sent there from the Łódź Ghetto at the age of 13. The SS assigned Srebnik to a work detail. Shot and left for dead by the fleeing Nazis as Soviet troops approached in January 1945, Srebnik was one of the very few Jews who survived the killing center.

Situated in Poland, about 50 miles west of Łódź, Chelmno was the first Nazi extermination camp. More than 150,000 Jews and about 5000 Gypsies were murdered there. Chelmno's victims perished in special mobile gas vans that piped deadly engine exhaust fumes into the trucks' hermetically sealed interior compartments. Chelmno operated from December 1941 to March 1943. It reopened in the spring of 1944 during the liquidation of the Łódź Ghetto.

That September the Nazis tried to obliterate the evidence of mass murder by exhuming the mass graves and burning the remains. "A lot of people were burned here," Srebnik recalled. "Yes, this is the place. No one ever left here again."

● **December 9, 1941:** China declares war on Germany and Japan.

● **December 11, 1941:** Germany and Italy declare war on the United States. Germany, Italy, and Japan agree that none will pursue a separate peace.
• **The United States declares war on Germany and Italy, which provides hope to Europe's Jews. The U.S. will** concentrate nearly 90 percent of its military resources within the European Theater, to defeat the Nazis.
• **A Jewish ghetto is established at Lutsk, Ukraine.**

● **December 11–13, 1941:** More than 14,000 Jews are murdered by *Einsatzkommandos* in Simferopol, Ukraine.

● **December 13, 1941:** The last six Jews living in Warendorf, Germany, are deported to Riga, Latvia, and killed.

● **December 14, 1941:** A Jewish ghetto at Kharkov, Ukraine, is established. • In the Warsaw Ghetto, a German policeman opens fire on a Jewish funeral procession, killing two

German Churches and the Holocaust

The Christian churches of Germany remained publicly silent in the face of the Nazi annihilation of Europe's Jews. Unlike the protest of the Nazi "euthanasia" policy, which Catholic intervention succeeded in halting, there was no public outcry from the churches when Jews were "evacuated," and no official church condemnations were issued when news of atrocities in the East reached Germany.

Both the Protestant (or Evangelical) Church and the Catholic Church yielded to Nazi pressure that restricted many church functions, closed most religious schools, and sent the few who did preach anti-Nazi sermons to concentration camps. The majority of the clergy avoided dangerous topics, and church doors consequently remained open. There was also considerable sympathy among Catholic and Protestant clergy for Hitler's traditional nationalist and conservative values, and especially for the Nazis' anticommunist crusade.

Additionally, some leading figures of both churches maintained antagonistic attitudes toward Judaism and, in fact, harbored antisemitic sentiments that made them unwilling to protest the regime's treatment of the Jews. Both churches willingly handed over genealogical records that helped the Nazis determine Jewish ancestry as defined by the Nuremberg Laws.

Some Catholic Church leaders were publicly antisemitic. A pastoral letter written in 1941 by Archbishop Konrad Gröber blamed Jews for the death of Jesus, and implied that their current terrible fate was not only justified but was a "self-imposed curse."

In view of the continued Nazi persecution of the churches, Catholic leaders preached submission in order to ensure survival. Papal announcements deplored the persecution but extended only prayer to non-Aryan victims of the Nazis. Catholic bishops spoke out against the SS killings in the East, but most decried the murders only of "Christian" Poles and Slavs. Only a few clerics publicly denounced the extermination of the Jews.

Protestant Church leadership traditionally supported the authority of the state. Many clergy sympathized with Hitler's nationalism, and had long viewed the Jews as enemies of Christianity. Of course, the nazified segment of the Protestant Church, known as the *Deutsche Glaubensbewegung* (German Christians' Faith Movement), under Reich Bishop Lüdwig Müller, fully supported the regime's attack on Jews. With its mix of Christianity and Nordic paganism, this official "Reich Church" regarded racial "mongrelization" as immoral. Dissenting Protestants, organized as the *Bekennende Kirche* (Confessing Church), opposed Nazi interference in church affairs but were silenced by Nazi coercion after the imprisonment and "re-education" of 700 ministers.

One of the few German religious leaders who took up the Jews' cause was Pastor Heinrich Grüber, head of a Protestant organization that aided Jewish converts to Christianity. In 1940 Grüber was imprisoned for protesting the deportations of Jews. Notably, Protestant Bishop Theophil Wurm of Württemberg, in a 1943 memorandum to Nazi authorities, futilely demanded "an end to putting to death members of other nations and races."

1941

mourners and wounding five other people.

● **December 15, 1941:** On this first day of Chanukah, 15 Jews are shot to death in the courtyard of the Warsaw Ghetto prison. ● Latvian gentiles Yanis Lipke and Janis Briedys are able to smuggle ten Jews out of the Riga Ghetto. Lipke plans to construct a Jewish hiding place beneath his home.

● **Mid-December 1941:** Hitler appoints himself supreme commander of the German Armed Forces.

● **December 16, 1941:** Hans Frank, governor-general of Occupied Poland, notes in his diary that some

On December 7, 1941, the Japanese staged a surprise attack on the U.S. fleet that was stationed in Pearl Harbor, Hawaii. The assault brought the United States into not only the Pacific war but also the European war. American entry into the conflict raised the spirits of all the victims of Nazi aggression, including European Jews.

Not until Hitler declared war on the United States did these office workers at the America First head-quarters remove isolationist material. Formed in July 1940, the America First Committee was the major isola-tionist group of the time. Infiltrated by the Nazis and determined to prevent American entanglements in Europe, America First had ties with congres-sional isolationists and antisemites. The committee did not officially adopt antisemitism, although its mem-bership list contained such prominent antisemites as Henry and Clara Ford, Charles Coughlin, Gerald Smith, Gerald Winrod, William Pelley, and American Nazi leader Fritz Kuhn.

Eminent historian Simon Dubnow espoused Jewish cultural national-ism, or Autonomism. In various books, including the massive *World History of the Jewish People,* Dub-now described Jews of the diaspora as linked through the centuries by their unique cultural and spiritual lives, an achievement that he argued should culminate in auton-omy. Born in Belorussia, Dubnow moved to Berlin in 1922, but with Hitler's rise he left Germany in 1933 for Latvia. Confined in the Riga (Latvia) Ghetto, the 81-year-old historian was among those shot on December 8, 1941.

As part of an effort to attract Ger-man companies to the Warsaw Ghetto, German soldiers film Jewish women at work in a textile factory. Recognizing the need to bring money into the ghetto to pay for food and medical supplies, the *Judenrat* (Jewish Council) strove to provide the companies with skilled workers, an effort hampered by the unwillingness of the companies to pay even minimally acceptable wages.

In December 1941 mass executions of Jews from Odessa took place at Acmecetca and Dumanovca as well as at Bogdanovca, Romania *(pictured)*, where the killings were particularly gruesome. In the first phase of the Bogdanovca massacre, some 5000 elderly and ill Jews were herded into stables, which were covered in straw, drenched with gasoline, and set afire; the prisoners suffered agonizing deaths.

While some Jews were being burned alive at Bogdanovca, Romania, Romanian death squads took others into the forest to be executed. Made to undress completely in the bitter cold of December, men, women, and children were forced to kneel on the edge of a precipice. They were then shot, with their bodies falling into the valley below. This skull with its gaping hole is testimony to these forest executions, in which over 40,000 died by the end of December.

Half-clad Jewish women and a young girl about to be executed on the beach at Liepaja, Latvia, are forced to pose for a final photograph during a mid-December murder spree that took the lives of at least 2700 Jews. The executions were carried out by a Latvian SD guard platoon and the 21st Latvian Police Battalion, as well as men of the *Schutzpolizei* (German border police) under the supervision of Fritz Dietrich, a local SS commander. Dietrich saw to it that the executions were filmed to provide evidence that the primary perpetrators were Latvians.

1941

3,500,000 Jews live in the region under his control; *See* January 25, 1944.

• December 17, 1941: A Jewish physician named Dubski dies of spotted typhus while treating patients at a Gypsy camp near the Lódź (Poland) Ghetto; *See* December 29, 1941.

• December 21, 1941: Nazis display the corpses of several thousand Soviet prisoners of war on a road in Minsk, Belorussia.

• December 21–30, 1941: More than 40,000 Jews are murdered at Bogdanovka in the Transnistria region of Romania.

Fearful Jewish women and children huddle together in the cold and in fear on the beach at Liepaja, Latvia, where they await their deaths at the hands of Latvians and SS. They are about to be stripped of their clothing and shot to death. Jewish clothing is to be sent back to Germany to be used by German civilians. (One report from a German soldier's wife indicates that she was angry that a few of the items of Jewish clothing sent back to her had bloodstains on them.) At least 2700 Jews were killed in this *Aktion* of December 1941.

This Nazi film still shows something with which all too many Europeans, especially Jews, were familiar: the unexpected knock on the door in the middle of the night. The Germans burst in on their victims, thereby increasing their confusion and reducing the likelihood that they would resist. The tactic had the further advantage of keeping many of the arrests secret.

Thea Borzuk Slawner poses with her mother on the occasion of her second birthday party, which was celebrated behind the walls of the Warsaw Ghetto. Despite living in appalling conditions, Warsaw's Jews spared no effort to retain their humanity. Religious and family celebrations became symbols of Jewish resistance. Thea and her mother escaped the ghetto just prior to the 1943 uprising. They survived the war, living among gentiles under assumed names.

• **December 22, 1941:** The United States passes amendments to the Selective Service Act, making men ages 20 to 44 eligible for military service.

• **December 29, 1941:** A Jewish physician from Prague, Czechoslovakia, Dr. Karol Boetim, dies of spotted typhus while treating patients at a

Gypsy camp near the Lódź (Poland) Ghetto.

• **December 31, 1941:** Abba Kovner, the founder of the United Partisans Organization in Vilna, Lithuania, calls for armed Jewish resistance to the Nazis, proclaiming, "We must not go like sheep to the slaughter!"

• **December 1941–January 1942:** Six hundred Soviet prisoners of war are murdered in a gas-chamber experiment at Auschwitz.

• **Winter 1941–1942:** Sixteen thousand Jews are rounded up in Germany and deported to the Riga (Latvia) Ghetto.

1942

ON August 8, 1942, Dr. Gerhart Riegner, a 30-year-old refugee from Berlin, prepared an important telegraph message for Rabbi Stephen S. Wise, American Jewry's most influential leader, and Sidney Silverman, a member of the British Parliament. Based in Switzerland, Riegner represented the World Jewish Congress, an international advocacy organization that defended Jewish rights and interests. Through an anti-Nazi German industrialist named Eduard Schulte, he had received desolating information.

According to Schulte's intelligence, Nazi Germany aimed to resolve once and for all the "Jewish question in Europe." This goal required the deportation of 3.5 to four million Jews to the East, where they would be "at one blow exterminated." Furthermore, Schulte's report indicated that "prussic acid" might be used to gas the victims. These actions were "planned for autumn." The terse telegraphic text that Riegner wrote to convey Schulte's testimony ended with two brief points: Riegner was relaying this information "with all necessary reservation as exactitude cannot be controlled by us," but his intelligence source was considered to have "close connections with highest German authorities" and should be viewed as reliable.

Wartime secrecy required Riegner's message to go through government channels. Thus, on August 8 he contacted Howard Elting, an official at the American consulate in Geneva. Riegner made three requests. In addition to sending his message to Rabbi Wise, he wanted the American and other Allied governments to be informed of its contents, and he also urged, as Elting's summary of their conversation indicates, that "they be asked to try by every means to obtain confirmation or denial" of Riegner's information. With Elting confirming his good opinion of Riegner's seriousness and reliability, the "Riegner Cable" went to the U.S. State Department.

Owing to what the State Department called "the fantastic nature of the allegation," Riegner's message was not delivered to Rabbi Wise, who nevertheless learned of its contents at the end of August. Yet not until November—after the State Department had confirmed the Riegner Cable's information—could Wise break the news to the media, which he did. By that time, however, 1942—the deadliest year of the Holocaust—had claimed most of its human toll.

Uncertainty, if not disbelief or indifference, made it difficult for governments and individuals outside of Nazi-occupied Europe to grasp fully

Anxious faces peer through a train window as they await deportation from Westerbork, Holland.

1942

what Adolf Hitler and his followers intended for European Jewry in 1942. In Nazi offices, in Jewish ghettos, and at the killing centers that were becoming operational in Poland, the situation became much less ambiguous as it turned ever more deadly. In late November 1941, for example, Reinhard Heydrich issued invitations to important German government and SS officials for a meeting to be held on December 9. Heydrich's invitations contained copies of the document he had received from Hermann Göring on July 31, 1941, which authorized Heydrich to plan the "Final Solution" to the "Jewish question." The Japanese bombing of Pearl Harbor and the entry of the United States into World War II forced the postponement of the December meeting. But on January 20, 1942, Heydrich convened the Wannsee Conference at *Am Grossen Wannsee* 56/58, a comfortable lakeside villa in an affluent Berlin suburb.

Fifteen men, many with doctorates from German universities, attended the meeting. By this time, the slaughter of Jews at the hands of the *Einsatzgruppen* and, more recently, at the Chelmno death camp was already far along. Heydrich's invitees were not the uninitiated. Most knew that mass murder of Jews had become state policy. Thus, the purpose of the Wannsee Conference was not to launch the Final Solution but to coordinate full implementation. Heydrich's meeting would ensure that all of the leaders in attendance, and the bureaucracies they supervised, were on the same page.

SS Lieutenant-Colonel Adolf Eichmann, head of the office of Jewish Affairs and Evacuation, prepared the meeting's final record, which Heydrich and Gestapo chief Heinrich Müller carefully edited before approving the text for the 30 copies that were made. Only one of those copies, the 16th, survived the war. Containing another of the Holocaust's most alarming reports, its fatal points included Heydrich's announcement that through the "final settlement" of the Jewish problem, "Europe will be cleaned up from the West to the East." According to his calculations, some 11 million Jews—"from Ireland to the Urals and from the Arctic to the Mediterranean," as historian Christopher Browning puts the point—would be "involved in this Final Solution of the European problem." Group by group, Jews would be sent to transit ghettos and then "to the East." Elderly Jews would go to "an old-age ghetto." The able-bodied, "separated according to sexes," would be selected for hard labor, which would eliminate many by "natural causes." The survivors would "have to be treated accordingly" to prevent "a Jewish reconstruction."

A walkway through the electric fences of Auschwitz, where more than one million Jews were gassed.

Euphemistic though it was, the language of the Wannsee Conference report sanctioned the industrialization of death. Given what they previously knew, the participants in Heydrich's meeting could scarcely doubt that Nazi Germany's policy now entailed that every European Jew was sentenced to die, either by attrition, extermination through work, or outright murder.

How to do those things, given the vast scope envisioned for the Final Solution and thus the inadequacy of mass shooting, was not crystal clear. But in his Wannsee Conference remarks, Heydrich had spoken about "practical experience" that was being collected "in relation to the future Final

Solution of the Jewish problem." As 1942 developed, such experience was put to practical use in six major killing centers operational on Polish soil: Belzec, Sobibór, Treblinka, Majdanek, and Auschwitz-Birkenau as well as Chelmno. At each of those places, gas chambers—some using carbon monoxide, others using Zyklon B—destroyed Jewish lives.

One Wannsee Conference participant, Dr. Josef Bühler, state secretary of the *Generalgouvernement*—the German administrative unit in Occupied Poland that contained many Jewish ghettos in the districts of Galicia, Kraków, Lublin, Radom, and Warsaw—had urged that "the Jewish question in this territory be solved as quickly as possible." In fact, he argued, the Final Solution could well start there because transportation problems were minimal and most of the Jews in that part of Poland were no longer fit for work anyway. Bühler's wish did not come true immediately, but on July 19 SS chief Heinrich Himmler ordered the "resettlement" (extermination) of "the entire Jewish population of the *Generalgouvernement*" by the end of the year.

On July 22 Warsaw Ghetto Jewish Council leader Adam Czerniaków received German orders to provide a daily quota of 6000 Jews, including children, for deportation. Overwhelmed by the orders he had received, Czerniaków committed suicide in Warsaw on July 23. Nevertheless, the newly opened death camp at Treblinka destroyed its first transport of Warsaw Jews that very day. By mid-September more than 250,000 Warsaw deportees had been murdered at Treblinka.

Jewish ghetto leaders confronted one "choiceless choice" after another. On September 3, 1942, Mordechai Chaim Rumkowski, the Jewish Council leader in Lódź, Poland, was ordered "to send more than 20,000 Jews out of the ghetto." The quota, Rumkowski told a terrified crowd the next day, must consist of sick and elderly people and, even more devastating, children under the age of ten. Ever hopeful that salvation might come through work, Rumkowski cried, "Brothers and sisters, hand them over to me! Fathers and mothers, give me your children!... The part that can be saved is much larger than the part that must be given away." Other leaders of Jewish councils, notably Dr. Elchanan Elkes, who headed the Kovno Ghetto in Lithuania, actively supported forest-based partisan units and anti-Nazi underground activity in the ghettos.

However, neither those efforts, nor a declaration entitled "German Policy of Extermination of the Jewish Race," which the Allied governments issued on December 17, 1942, could do anything to lift the death sentence that Nazi Germany had pronounced on Europe's Jews. The Allies' declaration identified Nazi Germany's "intention to exterminate the Jewish people in Europe," condemned "in the strongest possible terms this bestial policy of cold-blooded extermination," and affirmed that the perpetrators "shall not escape retribution." Important though it was as the first and strongest public condemnation of atrocities against the Jews that was issued by the Allies during World War II, the fact remained that 1942 was the most lethal year in Jewish history: 2.7 million Jews had lost their lives.

This gas chamber in the main camp at Auschwitz operated throughout 1942, and used Zyklon B to murder thousands of Jews.

Hesia Strom was a member of the Kovno (Lithuania) Ghetto Resistance.

The wedding of Salomon Schrijver took place in the Jewish Quarter of Amsterdam in 1942. In spite of the Nazis' defeat of Holland, normal routines continued for Dutch Jews until preparations were made for their deportation. Beginning in January 1942, many Dutch Jews were concentrated in labor camps. The Nuremberg Laws were promulgated in March and Jews were ordered to wear the yellow badge in April.

Most photographic equipment in Łódź was confiscated by the Nazis in 1939. The limited photography that occurred was controlled by the ghetto administration. Photographer Mendel Grossman fulfilled official requests as part of the statistics department, but he also sought to preserve a record of ghetto life. Here he records a Jewish labor crew struggling to clear ice from the ghetto's streets.

Already shivering and suffering from frostbite, two Jewish prisoners endure the torture of sitting in the snow. Reduced to skin and bones from months or years of malnutrition, few had the wherewithal to withstand the bitter cold. One woman, Gerda Weissmann Klein, survived a winter death march only because her father, guided by intuition, had ordered her to wear her ski boots when deported from her native town of Bielitz, Poland—on a hot summer day in 1942.

1942

- **1942: A gas chamber (probably never used) and a crematorium are installed at the Dachau, Germany, concentration camp.** • **A concentration camp is established at Riga, Latvia.** • **A forced-labor camp for Jews is established at Vilna, Lithuania.** • **Delegates from the United States, Great Britain, and Occupied European nations' governments-**in-exile attend the St. James Palace Conference in London to discuss Nazi war crimes and possible Allied responses. Jews are not discussed as a unique category of victims. • **The Germans elevate collaborator Pierre Laval to premier of Vichy France.** • **Hajj Amin al-Husseini, grand mufti of Jerusalem, flees to Germany following an unsuccessful attempt by Arab**

Soup kitchens run by local and international Jewish agencies proliferated in Nazi-occupied Poland. Once Polish Jews were concentrated in ghettos, their food supplies were controlled by the Germans. With food allocations limited to only a fraction of that required to maintain life, Polish Jews were dependent on supplemental nourishment provided by soup kitchens. Pictured here are identification cards that enabled the bearers to receive rations from the Kielce Ghetto soup kitchen, which was operated by the local Jewish Council. The first card, valid for breakfast only, says "1600 morning meals served daily." The second, a dinner pass, says "2100 dinners served daily."

Exploitation or Extermination?

As the war expanded, Hitler urgently needed to stem the ever-growing labor shortage and increase production of war-related materiel. Of course, the Nazis could use Jews as slave labor, but did they want to put to work the same people they aimed to exterminate?

These incompatible aims produced inconsistent policies that ultimately attempted to do both. At the Wannsee Conference, Reinhard Heydrich speculated that "a great part" of the Jews "evacuated to the East" and conscripted for labor would "undoubtedly be eliminated by natural causes." Accordingly, in 1942 the Nazis sought to extract more productive labor from the Jews before they died.

Ghettos and labor camps then became for Jews mere transit stops on the road to death. Long hours of toil under inhuman conditions, coupled with brutal physical mistreatment, led to extremely high death rates. At Majdanek, 40 percent of those who died were victims of gassings and shootings, while 60 percent perished from the "natural causes" of work exhaustion, starvation, and disease.

Inmate labor, such as moving piles of rocks back and forth, often served no productive purpose. SS guards took sadistic satisfaction in forcing Jews to perform backbreaking work, often prodding their prisoners with a hail of blows or even electric shocks.

---

nationalists to undermine British control of Palestine, and to create a Muslim legion to fight alongside German troops.

• The American Council for Judaism, an anti-Zionist organization, is cofounded in New York by *New York Times* publisher Arthur Hays Sulzberger. • German Protestant theolo-

gian Karl Friedrich Stellbrink is arrested after disseminating letters of anti-Nazi Bishop Clemens August Graf von Galen; *See* November 10, 1943. • Hitler names Albert Speer minister for armaments and munitions. • Yitzhak Shamir succeeds Abraham Stern as head of the Zionist Stern Gang in Palestine after Stern is killed by British security forces. • The

Jewish Combat Organization, a resistance group, is formed in Warsaw, Poland. • Janusz Korczak, director of a Jewish orphanage in Warsaw, refuses an offer of freedom from his Polish friends and accompanies his young charges to Treblinka.

• The Antifascist Bloc, an amalgamation of Jewish Communists and Zion-

Three Jews from the city of Kharkov, Ukraine, are strung up by German soldiers for alleged participation in resistance activities. Kharkov was captured by the advancing German armies in late fall 1941. On December 14 the occupation forces created a Jewish ghetto. The forced concentration of the Jews in this town was short-lived, as the ghetto was liquidated on January 5, 1942.

The front page of *The Jewish Advertiser,* a bilingual publication of the Jewish religious community in Prague, Czechoslovakia, delineates the restrictions placed on Jews throughout Eastern Europe. This January 1942 issue contained information of activities forbidden to Jews, which were not known about in the West until these papers were smuggled out.

MAJOR GHETTOS IN OCCUPIED EUROPE, EAST OF *GENERALGOUVERNEMENT*, 1941–1942

Jews in the Soviet Union who were not massacred by *Einsatzgruppen* were confined to ghettos, of which Minsk (80,000) was the largest. Most of these ghettoized Jews would eventually be shot or deported to death camps.

1942

ist Socialists, begins publication of *Der Ruf (The Call),* an underground, anti-Nazi newspaper.

• At the Theresienstadt, Czechoslovakia, camp/ghetto, a half-Jewish Czech youth named Petr Ginz conceives *Vedem (In the Lead),* a secret camp "magazine" of poetry, humor, gardening tips, and the grim truth about

camp operations; *See* September 28, 1944. • German Catholic priest Max Josef Metzger writes a plea for a new German government. The letter will be intercepted by the Gestapo, precipitating his arrest; *See* April 1944.

• Early 1942: The United Nations establishes the United Nations War Crimes Commission to handle future

These Viennese Jews were deported to the East. The Nazis hoped to make Vienna "Jew free," and shipped the city's Jews to ghettos in Poland beginning in 1939. On January 11, 1942, German authorities deported approximately 1500 Viennese Jews to Riga, Latvia, many of whom died on the journey. One survivor of the deportation remembered that "there was no water. The coaches were sealed. . . . It was very cold, and we chipped off some ice from the windows to have water." The children and elderly who survived this ordeal were murdered upon reaching their destination.

Separated by a fence at the Łódź (Poland) Ghetto, a sorrowful mother bids her son farewell as he awaits deportation from the Central Prison on Czarniecki Street. Among the first 10,000 targeted for "resettlement" in January 1942 were those serving sentences in the prison. In order to convince deportees that they were being sent to a labor camp, overseers handed out bread and sausage, as well as warm clothing.

To encourage Łódź's Jews to participate in the deportations, the Germans distributed, according to the ghetto's chronicle, "twelve thousand pairs of warm underwear, earmuffs, gloves, stockings, socks, and clogs." This child is dressed for the frigid conditions to be experienced on the deportation trains.

prosecution of Nazi war criminals. • Christian Wirth, Nazi executions expert, hooks an armored-car diesel engine to the gas chambers at Belzec.

• January 1942: Mass killings of Jews using Zyklon B begin at Auschwitz-Birkenau. The bodies are buried in mass graves in a nearby meadow. • Nearly all of the remaining Jews in

Odessa, Ukraine, are deported to concentration camps. • A special medical commission visits the Gross-Rosen, Germany, concentration camp to select human subjects for medical experimentation. • In France, Joseph Darnand establishes the *Milice Française* (French Militia), a Fascist paramilitary organization.

• January 1, 1942: In the U.S., the Counter-Intelligence Corps (CIC) is established to investigate and arrest suspected Nazi war criminals. • The United Nations is formed in Washington, D.C., by 26 signatories who agree to work together to defeat the nations of the Tripartate Pact, and to work for a single, commonly shared resolution to the war. • The Germans

The Wannsee Conference

In November 1940 Reinhard Heydrich, head of the Reich Security Main Office, arranged for the *Nordhav SS* Foundation to buy an impressive lakeside villa at Wannsee, an affluent suburb of Berlin. It became a guest house for both SS officers and visiting police. The *Wannsee Haus (pictured)* is best known, however, for an important meeting that Heydrich convened there on January 20, 1942.

Mass shootings of Jews in the East had begun seven months earlier. At Chelmno, Poland, the gassing of Jews had started in early December. Thus, the Wannsee Conference did not initiate the "Final Solution"; rather, Heydrich used the meeting to orchestrate it.

High-ranking officials in the SS and key Reich ministries received Heydrich's invitations to the conference. Nearly all knew about the deportations and killings already in progress. Nevertheless, Heydrich expected objections to his agenda, which required eliminating European Jewry by murder or "extermination through work."

His worry was unnecessary. The participants stated their views about details—where the Final Solution should have priority, what to do with *Mischlinge* (part-Jewish offspring of mixed marriages), and whether to exempt skilled Jewish workers— but members were generally enthusiastic about Heydrich's basic plan.

Besides Heydrich and Adolf Eichmann, the SS officer who prepared the meeting records, 13 men attended the Wannsee Conference. Representing the Reich Ministry for the Occupied Eastern Territories (primarily Lithuania, Latvia, and Estonia) were Dr. Alfred Meyer, who held a Ph.D. in political science, and Dr. Georg Leibbrandt, whose study of theology, philosophy, history, and economics had also given him a doctorate.

Six others had advanced degrees in law. Coauthor of the 1935 Nuremberg Laws, Dr. Wilhelm Stuckart represented the Ministry of the Interior. Dr. Roland Freisler came from the Ministry of Justice. He would later preside over the *Volksgerichtshof* (People's Court), whose show trials would condemn nearly 1200 German dissidents to death.

Dr. Josef Bühler would argue that the *Generalgouvernement* in Occupied Poland, the territory he represented, should be the Final Solution's priority target. Gerhard Klopfer worked under Martin Bormann as director of the Nazi Party Chancellery's legal division, where he was especially concerned with Nazi racial policies. Dr. Karl Eberhard Schöngarth and Dr. Rudolf Lange served security and police interests in Poland and other Nazi-occupied territories in Eastern Europe.

The conference's other participants included Martin Luther, Friedrich Kritzinger, Otto Hofmann, Erich Neumann, and Heinrich Müller. The men who planned, ate, and drank at the *Wannsee Haus* on January 20, 1942, were neither uneducated nor uninitiated as outlines for the Final Solution were put on the table. When Hitler's Berlin speech of January 30 proclaimed that "the results of this war will be the total annihilation of the Jews," these men could nod in well-founded agreement.

1942

execute 23 Czechoslovakian workers for sabotage.

• January 5, 1942: The Jewish ghetto at Kharkov, Ukraine, is liquidated.

• January 7, 1942: Throughout the day at the Chelmno, Poland, death camp, Jewish deportees from nearby villages are systematically gassed in vans; German and Ukrainian workers pull gold teeth and fillings from the corpses' mouths. Germans undertake van gassings of 5000 Gypsies from Lódź, Poland.

• January 9, 1942: One thousand Jews are deported from the Theresienstadt, Czechoslovakia, camp/ghetto to Riga, Latvia.

Wannsee, outside Berlin, was a beautiful location, and the leaders of the Third Reich met there frequently, most importantly for the infamous January 1942 conference. This photo shows some of the leaders of the Third Reich's immense police apparatus. From the left they are: Kurt Daluege, head of the Order Police; Karl Wolff, chief of Heinrich Himmler's personal staff; Himmler, head of the SS; Captain Bonin of the Order Police; Field Marshal Erhard Milch; SD chief Reinhard Heydrich, who was put in charge of implementing the "Final Solution"; and Friedrich Wilhelm Krüger, chief of police in the *Generalgouvernement.*

Cold and ruthless, Reinhard Heydrich earned the nickname "The Hangman." When he hosted the Wannsee Conference, he made sure his guests were comfortable by providing them with refreshments. He then opened with a speech that discussed the deportation of *11 million* Jews—including those of England and Ireland—to the East, meaning instant death or extermination through work. Heydrich would be assassinated in the spring of 1942.

A stately mansion in the Berlin suburb of Wannsee, formerly the residence of a wealthy Jewish family, was expropriated by the Nazis. Once a site for lakeside summer gatherings, it hosted a meeting of senior government bureaucrats to plan the "Final Solution" to the "Jewish problem" on January 20, 1942. Chaired by Reinhard Heydrich, the meeting went so well that Heydrich downed a celebratory glass of cognac at its conclusion.

• **January 12, 1942:** The seeds of the postwar Nuremberg Trials are sown when China and nine European nations pass a resolution to try Axis leaders for war crimes "whether they have ordered them, perpetrated them or in any way participated in them."

• **January 13, 1942:** The first of 10,000 Jews selected by the Jewish Council of the Lódź (Poland) Ghetto report for labor. • The governments-in-exile of Belgium, Czechoslovakia, France, Greece, Holland, Luxembourg, Norway, Poland, and Yugoslavia condemn German atrocities against their citizens without specifically mentioning Jews. The British Foreign Office approves the declaration but doesn't mention Jews.

• **January 14, 1942:** The United States blacklists 1800 European companies, making it illegal for any American to continue or begin business transactions with them.

• **Mid-January 1942:** The first Jews are deported from Lódź, Poland, to the Chelmno extermination camp.

Martin Luther

Martin Luther's meteoric career advancement reveals the professional opportunities unleashed by the genocidal policies of the Third Reich. Though he never finished high school, Luther became an influential figure within the German Foreign Office.

Luther's entrance into the Foreign Office was facilitated by Joachim von Ribbentrop, Germany's foreign minister. A talented organizer who was extremely adept at Nazi Party infighting, Luther positioned the Foreign Office as a major player in the "Final Solution."

At the Wannsee Conference on January 20, 1942, Luther arranged for the Foreign Office to coordinate the deportation of European Jews. He clearly recognized that the Final Solution was a golden opportunity to expand his personal power base. Luther's unsuccessful efforts to oust Ribbentrop in 1943, however, landed him in the Sachsenhausen concentration camp. He died of heart failure shortly after the war.

From January 21 to 23, 1942, Hungarian and other troops murdered hundreds of Jews and other Serbs at Novi Sad, Yugoslavia. Bodies of the dead were stacked in the cemetery.

Germans executed many Soviet POWs, while many more were imprisoned and left to die. Indeed, as a group, Soviet POWs were singled out for persecution and death more frequently than any others, save Jews. The Nazis were encouraged to do this, in part, because the Soviet Union had declined to sign international agreements of 1907 and 1929 pertaining to the treatment of prisoners of war. Murderous hatred provided the remainder of the German motivation. This photograph shows the mass grave of 3000 Soviet prisoners of war about 12 miles outside of Leningrad. Hundreds of thousands of Soviet soldiers met similar fates at the hands of their German captors.

1942

• **January 16, 1942:** Red Army Major Senitsa Vershovsky is shot by an *Einsatzkommando* unit at Kremenchug, Ukraine, for protecting Jews.

• **January 17, 1942:** Walter von Reichenau, a *Wehrmacht* general who cooperated with *Einsatzgruppen* in Russia, dies of a heart attack.

• **January 19, 1942:** Soviet forces recapture Mozhaisk, the closest that German troops had come to Moscow. With this, the Soviet capital is saved from occupation.

• **January 20, 1942:** The Wannsee Conference of top Nazi leaders is held in the Berlin suburb of Wannsee; attending are Heydrich, Meyer, Leib-

This woman awaits execution in the Belzec death camp, as pleas for her life fall on deaf ears. About 600,000 people, virtually all of them Jews, died at Belzec.

Three nurses pose outside the Jewish hospital in Tarnów, Poland. The Nazis began to deport Tarnów's Jews to the Belzec death camp in 1942. On September 2, 1943, when the Nazis began the liquidation of the ghetto, the remaining population resisted. The Germans used force to put down the rebellion and deported the remaining Jews to Auschwitz and Plaszów.

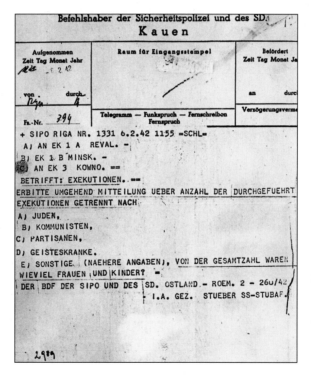

A 1942 telegram from the Riga, Latvia, office of *Sipo*, the *Sicherheitspolizei* (Security Police), testifies to the Nazis' methodical approach to killing. Sent to three *Einsatzkommandos* (special killing units), the telegram requests specific data regarding the number of people who have been executed. Specific numbers are requested for the following categories: Jews, Communists, partisans, and mentally ill, as well as women and children.

---

brandt, Stuckart, Neumann, Freisler, Bühler, Luther, Klopfer, Kritzinger, Hofmann, Müller, Eichmann, Schöngarth, and Lange. Discussion pertains to the number of European Jews still to be dealt with, the future of slave labor, the separation of Jewish men from Jewish women, mass deportations, and extermination: the "Final Solution." According to the protocol

of the meeting, five million Jews in the USSR are marked for death (including nearly three million in the Ukraine), 700,000 in the Unoccupied Zone of France, 5600 in Denmark, and 200 in Albania. Figures also are given for nations not yet under Nazi control, including England (330,000), Spain (6000), Switzerland (18,000), Sweden (18,000), and Turkey (55,500).

The total meeting time is less than 90 minutes.

• January 21, 1942: Jews in the Vilna (Lithuania) Ghetto establish the Unified Partisan Organization to resist Nazi terror.

• January 21–23, 1942: Hungarian Fascists drive 550 Jews and 292 Serbs

The saga of the ship *Struma* demonstrates the desperate measures Jews took to flee Nazi persecution and reach Palestine. Crammed with 769 Romanian Jews, the ill-equipped cattle boat left port in December 1941. It barely reached its first destination of Istanbul, Turkey, where the British refused visas to Palestine and the Turks would not permit the passengers to disembark. Desperate pleas proved fruitless, and the Turks at last towed the boat to open seas and ordered it to sail, even though it lacked both food and fuel. The final tragedy struck on February 24, 1942, when the boat was sunk by a torpedo, possibly fired mistakenly by a Russian submarine.

David Stoliar, now a rich businessman (far left), first heard of the existence of the *Struma* through the advertisement (above) in a Romanian newspaper. It seemed that the only problem in getting to Palestine was the limited number of places left. Stoliar bought a ticket (left). The *Struma*, grossly overcrowded, crawled into Istanbul. The British, unwilling to risk Arab hostility to further Jewish immigration at this crucial time, refused to clear the boat for Palestine. She was towed out of Turkish waters and was sunk, probably by torpedo, on February 24, 1942 (below). Jewish terrorists accused the British High Commissioner of murder (far left)

Extreme shortages of food encouraged the development of active black markets in the ghettos. The Nazis, who hoped that all of the ghettos' inhabitants would die of disease or starvation, naturally frowned on these activities. Those caught engaging in black-market commerce were summarily executed, including these four men who were publicly hanged in the Zdunska Wola (Poland) Ghetto.

Only one person, 19-year-old David Stoliar, survived the sinking of the *Struma*. Like other men living in Bucharest, Romania, Stoliar had been compelled to perform forced labor. Fearing for his son's well-being, his father bribed the authorities and bought him a ticket for the *Struma* in the hope that he would reach safety in Palestine. Hit by a torpedo, the ship sank before rescuers could reach it. Stoliar was rescued by Turks from a lighthouse, and after his recovery was granted an immigration visa by the British.

1942

to the Danube River at Novi Sad, Yugoslavia. They force them onto the ice, shoot the ice to break it up, and then shoot those who do not quickly drown.

• January 24, 1942: Four hundred Jewish intellectuals are arrested and subsequently murdered in Kolomyia, Ukraine.

• January 30, 1942: In a speech to the German public, Hitler commemorates the ninth anniversary of his taking power, declaring that the end result of the war will not be the destruction of the Aryans but will be the complete annihilation of the Jews. The speech is monitored in Washington, D.C., and London.

A Jewish man scales the Warsaw Ghetto wall with a large bag of contraband food to be dropped to the waiting ghetto residents. Often children were used to smuggle food in their clothing. The German penalty for smuggling was death. Yet despite this, some Jews and Polish gentiles took the risk because the benefits—money and food for themselves and their families—seemed to outweigh the consequences.

Vidkun Quisling

Vidkun Quisling, founder of the antisemitic political party *Nasjonal Samling* (NS, or National Unity), welcomed Germany's occupation of his own country on April 9, 1940. That evening his broadcast proclaimed a new Norwegian government. Quisling would be its prime minister.

This coup met Norwegian resistance, and did not entirely satisfy the Germans, who sidelined Quisling  in favor of Josef Terboven, the German administrator who would govern Norway brutally throughout the war. Meanwhile, Quisling's persistence served some German interests; for example, he recruited Norwegian troops for the German military. On February 1, 1942, Terboven permitted Quisling to become *Ministerpresident* of a "national government." Quisling supported the subsequent deportation of Norwegian Jews to Auschwitz.

A Norwegian firing squad executed Quisling on October 24, 1945. His legacy is that his name has become a standard noun: A "quisling" is a traitor.

The Jews of Zychlin, Poland, were deported in March 1942. About 3500 Jews lived in the town when the Germans occupied it in 1939. One month before the 1942 liquidation, German police stormed the ghetto and killed hundreds of Jewish residents. On March 3 the remaining Jews were assembled in the marketplace, loaded on carts, and deported to the Chelmno death camp.

• **February 1942: Thirty-three Jewish doctors in the Warsaw (Poland) Ghetto begin a study of the effects of starvation as they themselves slowly starve to death.** • **Jewish partisans in the Eastern Galicia region of Poland attack German troops in several locations.** • **Bricks and cut stone made by concentration-camp inmates are diverted from** future official monuments and buildings to construct badly needed German arms factories.

• **February 1, 1942: The SS *Wirtschafts-Verwaltungshauptamt* (Economic-Administrative Main Office; WVHA), led by Oswald Pohl, is established.**

• **February 13, 1942: At the Minsk (Belorussia) Ghetto, Nazis execute Jewish leaders deported from Hamburg, Germany, three months earlier.**

• **February 15, 1942: The first mass gassings of Jews at the Auschwitz, Poland, death camp begin.**

Albert Speer

As Reich minister for armaments and war production from 1942 to 1945, Albert Speer was an extremely important man within the Third Reich. His personal friendship with Hitler and his exceptional organizational skills propelled him from an assistant architect to a highly influential insider within the Nazi regime.

Hitler, who fancied himself a student of architecture, became Speer's personal mentor after witnessing his flair for visual pageantry. Speer per-  fected the Nazi style of public parades and Party rallies that characterized Hitler's regime. The megalomaniac passions of the two men were realized in the design plans for Berlin and Nuremberg, where the power and durability of the Third Reich were to be etched in stone.

Speer's managerial talents produced near-miracles for the German war machine. As minister of armaments, Speer kept the Army supplied in spite of massive Allied bombing. Unscrupulous in his use of slave labor, Speer is credited with prolonging the war for at least two years.

Speer parted company with Hitler in 1945 when he refused *der Führer's* order to destroy German industries. At the Nuremberg Trials, Speer professed to accept responsibility for his actions and was sentenced to 20 years' imprisonment. He was released in 1966. While in prison, Speer wrote his widely read book, *Inside the Third Reich*. He died in 1981.

This empty pit is about to receive the bodies of 5000 Jews of Minsk, Belorussia. They were slaughtered in March 1942 by Germans and Ukrainians. The pit was dug within the Minsk Ghetto on Ratomskaya Street.

One hundred thousand ghettoized Jews lived in Minsk, Belorussia, when mass shootings began in the city in 1941. In 1942 the Germans brought in gas vans, although the shootings continued as well. On March 2 the ghetto's nursery (or orphanage) was liquidated; the children were buried alive as SS officers tossed them candy. On March 31 the Germans raided the ghetto in an attempt to arrest Resistance leaders. As a result, much of the ghetto, including the synagogue pictured here, burned.

1942

● **February 19, 1942:** Jews at the Dvinsk, Latvia, concentration camp are forced to witness the execution of a Jewish woman who exchanged a piece of cloth with a non-Jewish inmate for a box of flour.

● **February 22, 1942:** Ten thousand Jews are deported from the Lódź (Poland) Ghetto to the Chelmno extermination camp, where they are gassed.

● **February 24, 1942:** The ship SS *Struma*, flying a neutral Panamanian flag and carrying Jewish refugees fleeing from Romania, is sunk in the Black Sea after Britain pressures Turkey to turn the ship back from Istanbul. More than 700 Jewish pas-

These Slovakian Jews, along with their luggage, are about to board a deportation train. Six thousand Jews from Slovakia, deported in March 1942, were among the first shipped to the Auschwitz death camp, where more than one million Jews ultimately perished.

Inmates at the Mauthausen concentration camp in Austria haul cartloads of dirt and stones for the construction of the "Russian Camp." Located outside the main prison camp, the Russian Camp housed Soviet POWs. The conditions within this installation were particularly harsh. The Russian camp had its own perimeter of barbed wire, and the inmates lived in rude huts close to Mauthausen's notorious rock quarry. A convenient thoroughfare connected the Russian camp to the main-camp gas chamber, morgue, and crematorium. Nazi guards were particularly harsh to Soviet noncommissioned officers who had escaped from other camps and been recaptured. Of the 5000 Soviet POWs who arrived in the first shipment in 1941, only about 80 were still living in March 1942.

A Jewish family loads a bicycle and a large bundle onto a railroad car during a deportation operation from Slovakia. Oblivious to their fate, tens of thousands of Slovakian Jews were deported during a four-month period from March to June 1942.

sengers attempting to save their lives by reaching Palestine are drowned. Only one passenger survives; *See March 5, 1942.*

• **March 1942:** This month, nearly 5000 Jews in the Warsaw Ghetto die of starvation. • 24,000 Jews from the Łódź (Poland) Ghetto are gassed at the Chelmno death camp. • The Nazis begin deportations from Central Europe to the death camp at Belzec, Poland. • In Norway, the *Hirdens Bedriftsvern*, a collaborationist, anti-Resistance unit, is created to protect Norwegian factories and infrastructure from saboteurs. • A Russian collaborationist group, Russian National People's Army, is established in Smolensk. • A brief article appears in the London press reporting that all Jews in Mariupol, Ukraine, have been killed.

• **March 1, 1942:** The Nazis begin the construction of a new death camp at Sobibór, Poland.

• **March 1–2, 1942:** Thousands of Belorussian Jews are transported to

MAJOR DEPORTATIONS OF JEWS TO BELZEC, 1942

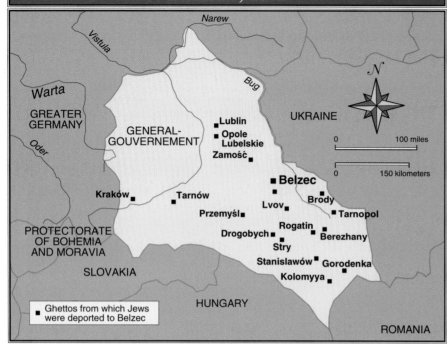

Narew
Vistula
Warta
GREATER GERMANY
Oder
GENERAL-GOUVERNEMENT
Bug
UKRAINE
■ Lublin
■ Opole Lubelskie
■ Zamość
0 — 100 miles
0 — 150 kilometers
■ Belzec
Kraków ■
Tarnów ■
Lvov ■
Brody ■
Przemyśl ■
■ Tarnopol
Rogatin ■
Drogobych ■
■ Berezhany
Stry ■
PROTECTORATE OF BOHEMIA AND MORAVIA
Stanislawów ■
■ Gorodenka
Kolomyya ■
SLOVAKIA
HUNGARY
■ Ghettos from which Jews were deported to Belzec
ROMANIA

The Belzec extermination camp was the site of 600,000 deaths. Most of the victims were Jews from southern Poland, but the Nazis also deported Jews from Germany, Austria, Bohemia, and Moravia to the killing center.

Organized into a column and with their meager belongings in sacks, Jews march into Belzec. The prisoners were deceived by their guards, who told them they had entered a transit camp from which they would be assigned to various labor camps. Instead, they were sent to the gas chambers.

Initially a labor camp, Belzec became an extermination facility in March 1942, with killings conducted first by carbon monoxide and then by Zyklon B. In spite of the orderly impression conveyed by this formation of SS guards, the killing process often went awry, inflicting horrendous suffering upon its victims. The guards jokingly referred to the killing site as the Hackenholt Foundation, named after *SS Hauptscharführer* Lorenz Hackenholt *(second row, far right)*, who ran the diesel motor that produced the carbon monoxide.

1942

Koidanav, Belorussia, where they are murdered.

• March 2, 1942: Six Jews at the Janówska, Ukraine, labor camp near Lvov are forced to spend the night outside; all six freeze to death. • Children from a Jewish nursery in the Minsk (Belorussia) Ghetto are thrown into a sandpit, tossed sweets, and then smothered to death. More than 5000 Jewish adults from Minsk are also killed.

• March 3, 1942: Belgian Jews are drafted for forced labor.

• March 5, 1942: In the wake of the February 24 *Struma* sinking, the British War Cabinet reaffirms its

As part of an effort to reduce partisan activity, the Nazis regularly performed mass executions. This one was carried out in the Ukrainian town of Drogobych. The atrocity was not the end of the suffering of Drogobych's Jews, however. From March to November 1942, about 7800 of the town's Jews died in the gas chambers at Belzec.

Although the British made a valiant effort to withdraw their forces after the April 1941 fall of Greece, not all could be rescued from there or from Crete, which fell shortly thereafter. Among those captured were 1400 Jewish soldiers from Palestine, who had volunteered to fight in the British Army. To keep up morale during the dark days of imprisonment in 1942, this group of *eretz Israel* soldiers, interned at a POW camp in upper Silesia, Germany, combined their talents to start an orchestra.

German successes in 1942 led to the near collapse of the Soviet Red Army. Casualties on both sides were enormous. Despite overwhelming odds, Soviet forces—motivated by a fierce patriotism—sought to hold the line and even push forward. Here, Soviet soldiers crouch behind modest revetments as they fire machine guns and rifles, and tend to their wounded.

decision not to allow "illegal" Jewish refugees admission to Palestine.

• **March 6, 1942:** During a meeting at the Head Office for Reich Security, Adolf Eichmann emphasizes the need for strict security during deportation and annihilation of Jews presently living in Germany, Austria, Moravia, and Bohemia.

• **March 14, 1942:** At Ilja, Poland, Jews sent to labor on a farm join Soviet partisans in a nearby forest. In reprisal, the Germans shoot old and sick Jews in the streets, then herd more than 900 Jews into a building that is set ablaze. All inside die.

• **March 15, 1942:** Trumpeting his *Wehrmacht*, Hitler predicts that the

Red Army will be "beaten in every direction in the summer."

• **March 16, 1942:** More than 1800 Jews from Pochep, Russia, are executed.

• **March 17, 1942:** Full-scale extermination begins at the Belzec death camp; deportees are accepted from

Aktion Reinhard Camps

About two million Jews inhabited the *Generalgouvernement* (Nazi-occupied Poland), which was divided into the districts of Warsaw, Radom, Kraków, Lublin, and Eastern Galicia. With that fact on his mind, Hans Frank, the head of the *Generalgouvernement*, assembled his top officials on December 16, 1941, and told them that Reinhard Heydrich, head of the Reich Security Main Office, was planning an important conference. Frank's deputy, Dr. Josef Bühler, would attend on Frank's behalf.

On January 20, 1942, Bühler was one of 15 Nazi leaders at the Wannsee Conference, which facilitated the "Final Solution." There he urged that the *Generalgouvernement*'s Jewish question should be "solved as quickly as possible."

To honor Heydrich, who had been assassinated by Czech Resistance fighters in the late spring of 1942, the SS used the code name *Aktion Reinhard* to refer to the destruction of the *Generalgouvernement*'s Jews. Even before the Wannsee Conference, however, plans for the mass murder were in motion. Directed by SS officers Odilo Globocnik and Christian Wirth, the scheme included construction of three camps whose fundamental purpose was to kill Jews. Staffed by SS and police, quickly trained Ukrainians, and former managers of Nazi Germany's so-called "euthanasia program," Belzec, Sobibór, and Treblinka would become death factories. More than 1.7 million Jews, most of them from the *Generalgouvernement*, were gassed during the 21 months of *Aktion Reinhard*, from March 1942 to November 1943.

Compactly designed, the camps' brick-and-lumber layout called for ordinary gasoline and diesel motors to produce carbon monoxide for the gas chambers. Four factors determined the camps' locations: large Jewish populations in the vicinity; nearby railroad lines to ensure transportation; isolated locales for security; and proximity to the *Generalgouvernement*'s eastern border to maintain the operation's "cover"—that the victims were being "resettled in the East."

Belzec, which opened on March 17, 1942, fit the criteria. It stood less than a half-mile from the rail station at a village on the main line between the cities of Lublin and Lvov. Belzec killed about 600,000 Jews. Sobibór, where full-scale killing started in the spring of 1942, also took advantage of a major railroad line, which brought some 250,000 Jews to its gas chambers. Treblinka, which was northeast of Warsaw, launched its mass exterminations on July 23, 1942. Linked to the Warsaw-Bialystok rail line, this remote camp, like the others, was also close to hundreds of trapped and starving Jewish communities. When Treblinka closed in the autumn of 1943, it had claimed between 700,000 and 900,000 Jewish lives.

Escape attempts took place in each camp, and uprisings erupted in Treblinka and Sobibór. However, few Jews survived any of these lethal places. The corpses, though, were many. They were initially buried in mass graves. Later they were burned, including those that were exhumed as the Germans tried to erase the evidence of their crimes.

1942

Poland and from as far away as the western provinces of Germany. By the end of 1942, 600,000 Jews will be murdered there.

• March 17–April 14, 1942: Nearly 30,000 Jews from the Lublin (Poland) Ghetto are deported to the Belzec death camp.

• March 19, 1942: Nazis arrest and deport to Auschwitz 50 Jews from Kraków, Poland, as part of an operation directed against Jewish intellectuals.

• Late March 1942: Fifteen thousand Jews are deported from Lvov, Ukraine, to Belzec.

THE SIX DEATH CAMPS OF POLAND, 1942

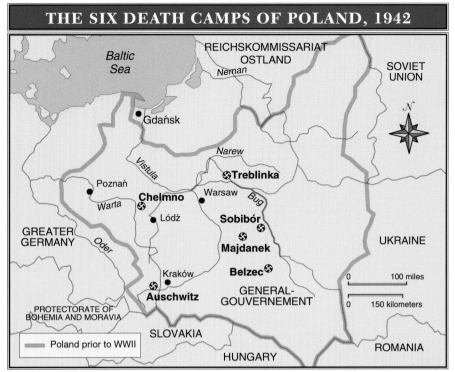

Ustasa soldiers pose with the severed head of one of their victims. The *Ustasa* (Insurgents) was a Fascist movement centered in Croatia. Relatively few in number before the war, the *Ustasa* members came to dominate Croatia after the Nazi conquest of Yugoslavia. Infamous for their cruelty, they murdered not only Jews but also Serbs, Gypsies, and their political opponents.

The Nazis killed 3.5 million Jews and tens of thousands of other people at their six death camps, all located in Occupied Poland. Workers at the Operation Reinhard camps (Treblinka, Belzec, and Sobibór) murdered 1.7 million Jews, the vast majority of whom were Polish. More than a million Jews died at Auschwitz.

Polish civilians from the town of Belchatów are deported to Germany for use as forced labor. As the war dragged on, the Germans experienced an ever-intensifying shortage of labor as increasing numbers of their young men were called up for military service to replace those who had been wounded and killed. From the point of view of Nazi racism, Polish gentiles were preferable to Jews, who were designated for extermination.

• **March 24, 1942:** The first deportations of Jews from Western Europe to Belzec begins.

• **March 26, 1942:** The first transport of Jews sent by Adolf Eichmann's office goes to Auschwitz. • The first transport of Jews (1000) from Slovakia is deported to Auschwitz.

• **March 27, 1942:** The first deportations of Jews from France to Auschwitz begin.

• **March 28, 1942:** Fritz Sauckel is named chief of manpower to expedite recruitment of slave labor.

• **March 31, 1942:** German troops raid the Minsk (Belorussia) Ghetto,

searching for and arresting Jewish Resistance leaders.

• **March-October 1942:** Approximately 60,000 Slovakian Jews are sent to death camps.

• **April 1942:** The Sobibór camp is nearly operational; gassings will begin in May. • Over 4400 Jews die of

Action Française (French Action) was a Fascist movement that emerged in France in 1899. Disillusioned with the chaos that characterized the Third Republic, the group began increasingly to admire Hitler and Italian dictator Benito Mussolini. At the cornerstone of the movement's political program was virulent antisemitism complemented by hatred of Freemasons, Protestants, and French residents of foreign origin. In the minds of *Action Française* members, these "enemies" had forced the group to fight a titanic battle for France's nationalistic and racial integrity. Supporters of *Action Française* played an important role in the Vichy France regime.

When the Schultz clothing firm opened in the Warsaw Ghetto in September 1941, it employed approximately 150 workers to produce uniforms for the German Army. By July 1942 there were nearly 4500 workers. The massive deportations during the summer months, however, led to a precipitous decline in the number of employees. The pictures shown here, a model of the complex and employees inspecting army uniforms, were part of an official album compiled by the firm's manager to demonstrate its importance and forestall its closure. The Schultz clothing company operated in Warsaw until early 1943, when the entire enterprise was transferred to the Trawniki, Poland, labor camp.

1942

starvation in the Warsaw Ghetto.
• The first transports of Jews arrive at the camp at Majdanek, Poland, which will begin gassing Jews later in the year. • The *London Sunday Times* runs but does not highlight a news item about the Nazi executions of 120,000 Romanian Jews. • German headquarters at Arras, France, is attacked by the French Resistance.

• In Russia, a collaborationist group, *Druzhina* (Bodyguard), is established and led by Soviet defector Lieutenant Colonel V. V. Gil.

• Early April 1942: Jews are mocked and hanged at Mlawa, Poland.

• April 1, 1942: 965 Slovakian Jews are deported to Auschwitz.

On April 3, 1942, 1200 Jews were deported from the Ukrainian town of Tlumacz to the death camp at Belzec, which began operation the previous month. They were among the approximately 600,000 Jews, most of them from Poland, who died in Belzec in 1942. Here the Jews are being assembled for deportation.

Edith Stein

Edith Stein used her faith and intellect to become a thorn in the side of the Third Reich. A German Jew who earned a doctorate in philosophy, she converted to Catholicism in 1922. Following a decade of teaching and writing, Stein was appointed to lecture at the German Institute for Scientific Pedagogy in 1932. She wrote to Pope Pius XI, asking him to issue an encyclical condemning Nazi racism. She was dismissed a year later because her parents were Jewish.

Shortly after, Stein relocated to Cologne, Germany, and became Sister Teresia Benedicta, a Carmelite nun. While at a convent in the Netherlands in 1942, Stein was arrested by the Gestapo. She was deported to Auschwitz, where she comforted many inmates. She was gassed there on August 8, 1942, ostensibly in retaliation for the anti-Nazi activities of Dutch Catholic bishops.

Stein was recognized as a saint by the Roman Catholic Church in 1998. A chapel stands in her honor at Auschwitz.

With his mistress, Eva Braun, at his side, the *Führer* admires the flowers and gifts presented in celebration of his 53rd birthday on April 20, 1942. Hitler enjoyed his birthday at his retreat, the Berghof in Berchtesgaden, surrounded by the Bavarian Alps. Secretive about Eva's presence in his life and disdainful of her girlish tastes, Hitler nonetheless enjoyed the sense of home and comfort she provided. She played hostess at countless tea parties and evening gatherings of his inner circle.

• **April 3, 1942:** This day's deportations from Augsburg, Germany, empty the town of Jews, ending a Jewish presence that was established in 1212. They are deported to the Belzec death camp.

• **April 5, 1942:** The Lutheran Church of Norway issues *"Kirken grunn"* ("Foundations of the Church"), a letter condemning Nazism and racism and protesting efforts of Vidkun Quisling, Norway's German puppet, to "nazify" Norway's churches.

• **April 11, 1942:** A German proclamation issued in Lvov, Ukraine, excoriates Polish civilians who assist Jews.
• Three thousand Jews from Zamość, Poland, are deported to the Belzec death camp.

• **April 16, 1942:** SS officials in the Ukraine inform authorities in Berlin that the Crimea is *judenrein* (purged of Jews).

• **April 17, 1942:** The Nazi government decrees that apartments occu-

These photographs offer differing perspectives on the April 1942 trial of 27 members of the French Resistance. While one photograph portrays the tribunal, composed of German military officers, another shows the heavily guarded defendants after the trial. The third photograph appears to show a timer for a bomb. Two of the defendants were Jewish; 25 of the 27 were sentenced to death. The verdicts were unhappy ones for the defendants, but hardly heralded the end of French opposition to the German-controlled puppet government. Collaborationist politician Pierre Laval reinstalled himself—with Hitler's support—as the chief of the Vichy government at about this time, which only spurred heightened Resistance activity.

1942

pied by Jews in Greater Germany must be identified as such.

• April 18, 1942: In the Warsaw Ghetto, 52 people on a wanted list are dragged from their beds and killed. This will become known as "The Night of Blood." • One thousand Jews who leave the Theresienstadt, Czechoslovakia, camp/ghetto

by train for a ghetto at Rejowiec, Poland, are diverted to the death camp at Sobibór. • Disgusted with the inability to take Leningrad, Hitler relieves Field Marshal Wilhelm von Leeb of command of German forces in north Russia.

• April 20, 1942: At a birthday banquet for Hitler in East Prussia, Her-

Joseph Goebbels's Propaganda Ministry churned out filmstrips that played upon traditional anti-Jewish stereotypes. This frame depicts a middle-aged Jewish man lounging leisurely with a younger gentile woman. The caption, "Jews have always been race defilers," plays on the myth that Jewish men seduced gentile women.

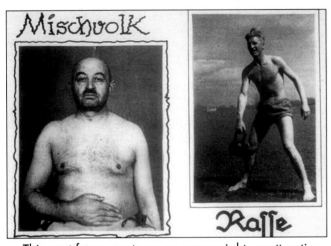

This next frame portrays an overweight, unattractive man of mixed race on the left and a healthy "Aryan" youth on the right. The image demonstrates the Nazi desire to keep the Aryan "race" pure.

Joseph Goebbels

Joseph Goebbels was the most ardent member of Hitler's inner circle. Cunning and amoral, he was a masterful manipulator whose control of German media rallied the populace to the cause of Nazism, and threw gasoline on the fires of antisemitism.

Paul Joseph Goebbels was born in the Rhineland in 1897 to parents of the lower middle class. Crippled by polio while a small boy, he devoted himself to the development of his intellect. He earned a doctorate in literature and philosophy in 1921 and soon joined the Nazi Party. A failed novelist with grandiose ideas, Goebbels was initially more fond of Nazi ideology than of Hitler. He soon fell under Hitler's spell,

however, and became, after Hitler himself, the No. 1 proponent of the "*Führer* myth" of infallibility. For his loyalty, Goebbels was named minister of propaganda when Hitler assumed power in 1933.

Goebbels prohibited Jewish publishing activity and demanded the demonization of Jews through Nazi propaganda: feature films, faked newsreels, phony documentaries, fabricated news stories, radio plays, and choreographed antisemitic demonstrations. Under his guidance, "Jew" became synonymous throughout the Reich with "enemy" and "vermin."

Goebbels and his wife, Magda, committed suicide in the *Führerbunker* on May 1, 1945, shortly after poisoning their six children.

---

mann Göring announces that he was responsible for the *Reichstag* fire of February 27, 1933, that set off Nazi reprisals against purported Communist subversion.

• April 24, 1942: Jews throughout Greater Germany are prohibited from taking public transport.

• April 26, 1942: The *Reichstag* grants Hitler full authority in executive, legislative, and judicial matters.

• April 27, 1942: One thousand Jews are deported from the Theresienstadt, Czechoslovakia, camp/ghetto to Izbica Lubelska, Poland; one, a woman who escapes after arrival, survives. Other Theresienstadt depor-

tees are sent to their deaths at the Sobibór and Belzec extermination camps. • Nazis execute 60 Jews in the Warsaw Ghetto. Among the victims are people suspected of being involved with the ghetto's underground newspaper.

• April 29, 1942: A German truck that refuels near the Lódź (Poland)

This filmstrip scene depicts Germany being "overrun" by Jews. The caption, "13 Jews daily," gives the impression that Germany was the destination of choice for European Jews on the move. Nothing, however, could have been further from the truth. The social climate was obviously inhospitable, and Nazi laws expressly prohibited Jews from entering the country.

Three deadly historical events are blamed on the Jews: the destruction of Haman at Purim, the terror of the French Revolution, and the horrors of Russia's Bolshevik Revolution. Under the direction of the Nazis, world history textbooks used in German schools were rewritten so that all negative historical developments were attributed to the Jews, while positive ones were linked to the Germans.

The Jewish spider entangles the capitals of Europe. Positioned directly on top of Berlin, the spider is poised to dominate the continent. The "international Jewish conspiracy" was a prominent theme in Nazi propaganda.

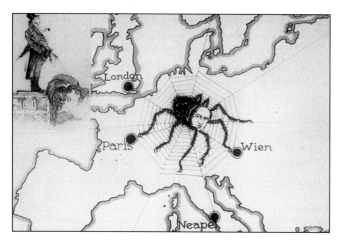

This frame shows the "spread" of Jews from Palestine after the birth of Christ. Nazi propaganda continually emphasized the supposed rootless nature of the Jew. As a diaspora people, Jews were portrayed as parasites who sucked the blood from nations in which they resided.

1942

Ghetto carries luggage belonging to "resettled" Jews who have already been murdered at the Chelmno death camp.

• **April 30, 1942:** The Jews of Pinsk, Poland, are ordered to establish a ghetto within one day. Twenty thousand Jews will move into it. • Twelve hundred Jews are killed in Diatlovo,

Belorussia. The Jews offer armed resistance, but it is futile.

• **May 1942:** More than 3600 Jews in the Warsaw Ghetto die of starvation. Nazis force their way into Jewish apartments in Warsaw, shoot and club the residents, and throw the bodies from windows. • A slave-labor camp opens near Minsk, Belorussia. • Small

This woman resided in Kerch in the Crimean Peninsula of the Soviet Union. The Jews of Crimea were murdered up through April 1942. That month the Germans declared the Crimea *judenrein* (cleansed of Jews).

> ## "No tiger can eat me, no shark can beat me. . . . Even the Devil would lose his teeth biting me. I feel it: I will get out of this place."
>
> —*Fritz Loehner–Beda, Jewish songwriter who was killed at Auschwitz*

The Mauthausen concentration camp, located near Linz in upper Austria, was renowned for its cruel working conditions. The camp included within its confines a stone quarry in which prisoners were assigned to backbreaking work. While pushing heavy carts or carrying stones weighing over 100 pounds, prisoners were forced to ascend the "staircase of death." Composed of 186 steps, the staircase meant death for any prisoner who lost his or her footing and fell under the loads. Later in the war Mauthausen prisoners were assigned to build underground tunnels for weapons production.

Political prisoners were among the first inmates of Mauthausen, including more than 7000 Spanish Republicans, some of whom are pictured. The Spanish Republicans had sought sanctuary in France but were deported by the French Vichy government. Hungarians, Poles, and Czechs—including many Jews—also were sent to Mauthausen. The cruel conditions of the camp were set by its commandant, Franz Ziereis, nicknamed "Babyface" by the prisoners.

groups of Jewish youths manage to escape into the woods outside Lida and Stolpce, towns in Belorussia. • Slovakian Jews and resident Jews at Chelm are deported to the nearby Sobibór death camp and gassed. In addition, more than 36,000 Polish Jews from communities located between the Vistula and Bug rivers are gassed at Sobibór.

• In the Eastern Galicia region of Poland, Jews aged 14 to 60 are driven to isolated spots and killed by hand grenades and machine guns after being forced to dig their own graves. Other victims of this *Aktion* include orphans, residents of old-age homes, and women in the streets. • Inmates at Auschwitz-Birkenau are put to work as slave laborers at the camp

itself and at a synthetic-oil and rubber plant at nearby Monowitz. • Jewish women at Auschwitz-Birkenau are selected for medical experiments. • A Jewish inmate at a labor camp at Schwenningen, Germany, is buried in earth up to his shoulders as punishment for having an attack of diarrhea outside a barracks; after more than ten hours in the ground, the man

Looted Art

As the German armies swept through Europe, they plundered the property of those they murdered. Hitler's stated intention was to "extract from these territories everything that is possible to extract."

Consequently, the Nazis shamelessly looted Europe's cultural treasures. Hermann Göring,  one of the biggest looters, scoured museums and private collections of wealthy deported Jews for works by famous masters. In his villa, he proudly displayed stolen masterpieces by Titian, Raphael, Rubens, and Rembrandt. Hitler's interest in Europe's art stemmed from his plan to turn Linz, the Austrian city of his youth, into the world's cultural capital. He envisioned displaying the world's greatest art treasures, such as the confiscated *Madonna and Child* by Michelangelo, in the world's biggest museum.

The pillaging of art reached astronomical proportions. Throughout Europe, the Nazis acquired more than 100,000 works. In France alone they appropriated almost 22,000 objects (including 5281 paintings) from 1940 to 1944, bringing them to Germany in 29 shipments that involved 137 freight cars. After the war, Allied officials attempted to return the treasures, a process complicated by the deaths of former Jewish owners. Some pieces are still unclaimed, and legal intervention continues to grapple with disputed ownership claims.

Prominent Soviet Jews, at the behest of their government, established the Jewish Antifascist Committee in April 1942. Its function was to rally Western Jews behind the Soviet Union's effort to resist the Nazi invasion. Pictured here, at a rally held in New York City's Polo Grounds, are writer Itzik Fefer *(center)* and the committee chairman, Shlomo Mikhoels *(right)*. The Jewish Antifascist Committee also attempted to document the experience of Soviet Jewry during the Holocaust, but Soviet dictator Joseph Stalin thwarted these efforts, eventually disbanding the committee in 1948.

A group of Gypsy (Sinti and Roma) prisoners awaits orders from the Germans at the Belzec death camp in Poland. The Nazis began construction of an extermination center at Belzec in November 1941. Hundreds, perhaps several thousand, Gypsies would eventually be gassed there.

1942

dies. • A slave-labor camp opens at Maly Trostinets, Belorussia.

• In Holland, a collaborationist auxiliary police unit, *Vrijwillige Hulp-Politie* (Volunteer Auxiliary Police), is established. It is charged with the roundup of Dutch Jews for deportation to the East. • Communist Jews in Paris initiate organized armed resistance to the Nazi occupiers.
• The Bund (Jewish Labor Organization of Poland) appeals to the Polish government-in-exile in London to persuade the Allied governments to warn the German government about the consequences of the murder of the Polish Jews. The Bund's appeal contains detailed information concerning the systematic mass murder

One method the Nazis used to discourage rebellion was the shooting of hostages, especially women and children, in retaliation for acts of resistance. Five women, about to fall victims to a firing squad, were among 100 Slovenians shot in the village of Celje in 1942. The Nazis believed that the shooting of women and children would be especially effective in discouraging resistance activity. Yet, even such atrocities did not completely halt the actions of the Yugoslavian partisans.

Jewish workers push a heavily loaded cart down a railroad line near Bor, Yugoslavia. Guarded by Hungarians but supervised by Germans, workers in the Bor camp labored day and night in the copper mines, producing the mineral vital to the manufacture of armaments. More and more slave laborers were needed to keep the German war machine going as the Germans battled on several fronts.

Their work done, the 30 troops of the German firing squad in Celje turn on their heels, leaving their five victims sprawled awkwardly in death. The bodies were removed on gurneys and taken to a mass grave for burial.

of Jews. It reports that 700,000 Polish Jews have already been executed.

• 2600 Libyan Jews are deported to a forced-labor camp at Giado, Libya, to build roads for the military. • More than 1750 Jews are deported from Tripoli, Libya, to forced-labor sites at the Libyan cities of Benghazi, Homs, and Derna. Hundreds perish from heat and hunger, and others die during Allied bombings after being forbidden to use air-raid shelters.

• Early May 1942: Jewish Council members at Bilgoraj, Poland, are executed after refusing to compile a list of candidates for deportation. • 260 Luxembourg Jews, some converted to Christianity, are sent to Chelmno.

• May 1, 1942: About 1000 Jews are murdered at Dvinsk, Latvia. Only about 450 Jews are left in Dvinsk, down from 16,000 from the previous year.

• May 4–8, 1942: Six Jews in Lódź, Poland, fearing deportation, commit suicide.

Holding the shield of David, Jewish men pose in a makeshift synagogue in the transit camp of Beaune-la-Rolande, France. The first targets of the Nazis in France, foreign Jews were evicted from their homes and sent to transit camps, prior to deportation to the death camps of the East. While enduring uncertainty and deprivation, Jews sought to maintain religious community.

Waffen-SS and SD officers force Jews to dig their graves before being shot. Such scenes were common in Russia in the months following the German invasion. Forcing the victims to dig their own graves not only lightened the workload for many of the perpetrators—many of whom were too drunk to dig—but was also a final humiliation for those about to be murdered.

A Gypsy woman leads a group of children along the unpaved streets of the Rivesaltes transit camp, located in the Pyrénées-Orientales region of France. The Gypsies were viewed as alien to the French national culture, and they were therefore included in the internment policies of the Vichy regime. Gypsies suffered terribly at the hands of their oppressors.

1942

● **May 4–15, 1942:** More than 10,000 Jews are deported from the Łódź (Poland) Ghetto to Chelmno.

● **May 5, 1942:** Jewish teachers and educators in the Warsaw Ghetto create a special day for children, during which they are treated to games, plays, and special rations of sweets.
● In the ghetto at Łódź, Poland, Prof. Jakob Edmund Speyer, a Jew from Frankfurt, Germany, who invented an important painkiller called Eukodal, dies of exhaustion.

● **May 9, 1942:** The Jews of Markuszow, Poland, led by Shlomo Goldwasser, Mordechai Kirshenbaum, and brothers Yaakov and Yerucham Gothelf, escape to nearby forests; *See*

In 1941 local Lithuanians and Germans carried out murderous campaigns against the Jews of Kovno. In contrast, 1942 was relatively quiet in Kovno. Although the Jews were deprived of adequate food supplies and were subjected to life in a ghetto, the Jewish Council operated a medical clinic, a soup kitchen, and a school. The council even managed to stage concerts and other cultural events.

A German and a local militiaman shoot Jews outside a Ukrainian village. The SS often received help from auxiliary forces to carry out the mass executions that were part of the "Final Solution." In the Ukraine, members of the local populace eagerly participated in these murderous campaigns. The relaxed men in this picture appear as if they are hunting birds, not human beings.

Hunger and Starvation

Besides shootings and gassings, the Nazis also killed Jews through natural means: slowly starving them to death. In ghettos such as Warsaw, Jews received food rations that were a fraction of normal requirements. Children and the elderly perished first. Bloated corpses littering streets became commonplace.

In the Lódź (Poland) Ghetto, journalist Joseph Zelikowicz witnessed thousands of people dragging themselves through streets, rummaging through piles of garbage to find "a piece of broken pot that can still be licked, or a rag that once wrapped food and can still be gnawed at."

Zelikowicz described bodies distorted by starvation, with "flabby stomachs, sunken breasts, hollows around their necks," and legs so badly swollen that "if you stick a finger in such a leg, you leave an impression, a sallow gray spot, as in half-baked bread."

In concentration camps, inmates also suffered starvation but were additionally forced to work to the point of exhaustion. Utterly desperate for food, prisoners in some camps even ate grass. Many became skeletal figures with dry, ashen skin, their cheekbones almost protruding, with elongated heads. Most also suffered from extreme, dehydrating diarrhea. Totally apathetic to life, for many relief came only through death.

October 1942. • American poet Ezra Pound, who is working for the Fascist Italian government, broadcasts from Italy: "You would do better to inoculate your children with typhus and syphilis" than allow more Jews into the United States. America, Pound continues, is ruled by Jews and their allies, who are "the dirtiest dirt from the bottom of the Jew's ash can."

• May 11–12, 1942: American Zionists participating in the Biltmore Conference at New York City's Biltmore Hotel demand that Jews be given sovereignty over Palestine. The demand is ignored by Britain, which controls Palestine.

• May 11, 1942: Alter Dworetsky, a member of the Jewish Council at Diatlovo, Belorussia, escapes to a nearby forest, only to be shot to death by Soviet partisans after refusing to hand over his pistol.

• May 14, 1942: Noted Jewish Viennese pianist Leopold Birkenfeld is murdered at the Chelmno death camp.

The Markuszów (Poland) Ghetto was liquidated on May 9, 1942, a day when the ghetto's remaining 1500 Jews were deported to the Sobibór death camp. This and other May deportations from ghettos in the region signaled the beginning of Sobibór's mass-extermination program. However, a few of Markuszow's Jews escaped to the Parczew Forest, located about 25 miles northeast of the city. There, men and women—ill-trained, poorly armed, and underfed—organized as partisans and resolved to take the measure of their persecutors.

Mordechai Chaim Rumkowski, "Eldest of the Jews" in Lódź, Poland, informs the ghetto population that the deportations have come to an end. In the two previous weeks, May 4 to 15, 10,915 people had been deported for "resettlement"— in reality, the Chelmno death camp. But the population remained suspicious, and rumors—unfortunately accurate—soon began to spread about renewed deportations in the near future.

From May 10 to 12, 1942, about 1500 Jews were sent from Sosnowiec, Poland, to Auschwitz, the first of several deportations from that city. In August 1943 the Nazis deported Sosnowiec's remaining 15,000 Jews to Auschwitz.

1942

• **May 18, 1942:** *The New York Times* reports that more than 100,000 Jews have been machine-gunned by Nazis in the Baltic countries, 100,000 in Poland, and some 200,000 in western Russia. • During a public protest of Nazi antisemitism staged in Berlin by Herbert Baum and his followers, portions of "The Soviet Paradise," a government-sponsored anti-Bolshevik exhibition, are set afire. Most members of Baum's group, as well as approximately 500 other Berlin Jews, are arrested.

• **May 22, 1942:** In an exercise conducted in a forest outside Mielec, Poland, Gestapo agents "cast" Jews as partisans, beat and mutilate them, and then kill them.

A poster advertises the anti-Bolshevik Nazi propaganda exhibit that was displayed in the Berlin *Lustgarten*. The exhibit, entitled The Soviet Paradise, was designed to demonstrate the superiority of Nazism over communism. The Nazi propaganda machine worked tirelessly throughout the war years to bolster the regime's military campaigns. The exhibit was particularly repugnant to the Baum Group since most of its members belonged to Communist and other left-wing organizations.

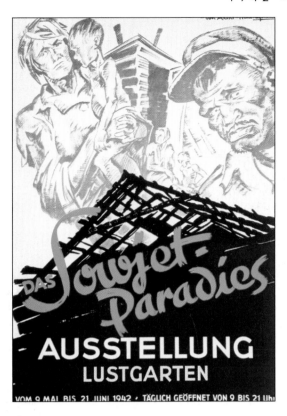

Baum Gruppe

Named after its leaders, Herbert and Marianne Baum, the *Baum Gruppe* (Baum Group) was diverse in its membership but unified in its opposition to the Nazis. Founded in 1937 and composed mainly of young Jewish Communists, the group also included fervent, left-wing Zionists. Most of the members were in their early 20s.

The Baum Group produced and distributed anti-Nazi pamphlets, arranged educational events for the increasingly isolated Jewish youth of Berlin, and offered moral support and camaraderie. In May 1942 members engaged in a daring anti-Nazi act, an attempt to burn down an anti-Bolshevik propaganda exhibit called *Das Sowjetparadies* (The Soviet Paradise).

Herbert, Marianne, and about 25 other members of the group were caught, tortured, and either killed or sent to concentration camps. Five hundred Berlin Jews not associated with the group also were arrested in reprisal and sent to camps or killed.

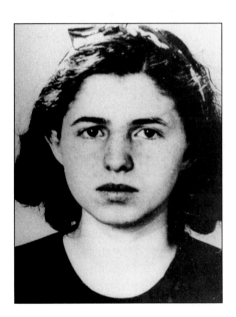

Hella Hirsch belonged to the Baum Group. On May 18, 1942, Hirsch and other members of the group set fire to an anti-Bolshevik exhibit on display in Berlin. The Gestapo arrested 500 Berlin Jews in reprisal for the attack, shooting 250 of them and sending the rest to the Sachsenhausen, Germany, concentration camp. Hirsch and the others in her immediate group, 12 altogether, were tried on December 9, 1942. Nine were given death sentences. Hirsch was sentenced to just three years in prison due to "extenuating circumstances."

• **May 26, 1942: Great Britain and the Soviet Union sign a mutual assistance treaty.**

• **May 27, 1942: Belgian Jews are ordered to wear the Yellow Star.**
• **Jozef Gabcik and Jan Kubis, British-trained Czech partisans armed with small arms and grenades, mortally wound Reinhard Heydrich, chief of** the Reich Security Police and SD, in an ambush of his car in Prague;** *See* June 4, 1942.

• **May 29, 1942: Vichy France forbids Jews access to all restaurants and cafes, libraries, sports grounds, squares, and other public places.**
• **Three thousand Jews led by Asher Czerkaski resist Germans at Radziwil-** low, Ukraine; 1500 are killed but the others melt into nearby forests.** • In the Warsaw Ghetto, an ill Jewish man is tossed through a window to the ground, where he is shot.**

• **May 30, 1942: Britain's first 1000-bomber raid on Germany (the target is Cologne) encourages Jews to hope that the war might soon be over.**

Munkaszolgálat

After the adoption of anti-Jewish laws in Hungary in 1938 and '39, Jews of military age were deemed "unreliable." Considered unfit to bear arms, tens of thousands of Jews were drafted into the *Munkaszolgálat* (Hungarian Labor Service System).

Instead of carrying guns, these Jews were given shovels and pickaxes. They worked construction and toiled in mines, and, during combat, performed such dangerous tasks as clearing mine fields.

Many Hungarian officers, viciously antisemitic, abused members of the *Munkaszolgálat*. They deprived Jews of their boots and rations and sometimes sadistically tortured them. They forced some Jews to participate in humiliating games of leapfrog and acrobatics. Other Jews, in the dead of winter, were doused with water and ordered not to move until the water iced up on their skin.

After Hungary declared war on the Soviet Union in June 1941, tens of thousands of *Munkaszolgálat* Jews lost their lives as casualties of war. Ironically, after the Nazis occupied Hungary on March 19, 1944, many Jews found refuge in *Munkaszolgálat*, where they performed the hard labor but avoided deportations.

A long line of Jews winds its way through the streets of Pabianice, Poland, on the way to deportation. In mid-May 1942 some 4500 Jews from the town were rounded up and deported to Chelmno, where they were executed. While the Jews of the town were sent to their deaths, the goods that they took with them to the death camp were sent back to warehouses in Pabianice.

Bending over their shovels and spades, Hungarian Jews till the muddy Ukrainian soil. Beginning in 1939, Hungarian Jews not serving in the military had been required to join labor battalions. This cruel and backbreaking work took on new danger when Jewish units were ordered to the Eastern Front. There they were mistreated by Axis military personnel and treated as the enemy when captured by the Soviets.

1942

• **June 1942: The World Jewish Congress, based in New York, announces at a press conference that Eastern Europe is being turned into "a vast slaughterhouse for Jews."** • **At the Belzec and Sobibór death camps, more than 23,000 Jews are gassed.** • **Auschwitz is ravaged by an epidemic of typhus.** • **Germans invade Jewish hospitals in Sosnowiec, Poland,** murdering newborns and tearing patients from operating tables. **Ambulatory patients are sent to Auschwitz and gassed.** • **A young Sosnowiec Jew named Harry Blumenfrucht endures two weeks of Nazi torture, refusing to name his co-conspirators in a scheme to steal weapons. His suffering ends when he is hanged.**

On May 19, 1942, the Nazis expelled 1420 Jews from the ghetto in Brzeziny Slaskie, Poland *(pictured)*. The Jews marched to the train station at nearby Galkówek, where they were loaded onto trains bound for the Lódz (Poland) Ghetto. Most of those who survived the deportation and their time in Lódz eventually died in the Chelmno death camp.

The Polish town of Wlodawa was one of the areas of Jewish resistance to the Nazi murderers. The town's Jewish population of about 9000 would eventually be deported to the Sobibór death camp. The men pictured here were engaged in forced labor in a sawmill.

A Nazi security officer photographs SS and Red Cross officials during a Red Cross visit to the Amersfoort concentration camp in the Netherlands. The SS carefully controlled outside access to the camps, and all visits were meticulously staged. Camps were decorated for the occasions and inmates received new clothing. Even musical events were presented, to show that the prisoners were living under agreeable conditions.

• Jews from Dabrowa Tarnowska, Poland, led by Rabbi Isaac and gathered in a Jewish cemetery, defy their Nazi captors when they hold hands, dance, and drink "to life." The enraged Germans shoot and disembowel the entire group. • Four thousand Jews in the Warsaw Ghetto die of starvation. • At Lutsk, Ukraine, Jewish resistance is led by Joel Szczerbat. • Three thousand Jews at Pilica, Poland, are deported to Belzec, but several hundred manage to escape before the journey is complete. • In Norway, Jews are given identity cards stamped with the letter "J." • In Yugoslavia, a collaborationist paramilitary force, *Heimwehr* (Home Defense), is established. • Mordecai Gebirtig, a Kraków carpenter whose songs of freedom are sung throughout Poland, is executed at Belzec.

• June 1, 1942: Polish Jews are deported from Hrubieszów to the Sobibór death camp. Another 500 will be deported the following week.
• Warsaw's underground newspaper, *Liberty Barricade*, published by the Polish Socialist Party, reveals Nazi

These children from the Polish town of Pitroków Kujawski were shipped to Chelmno, where they were murdered in the camp's gas vans. Though deportations from the nearby Lódź Ghetto to Chelmno began in January 1942, Lódź residents weren't aware of the death camp until summertime.

Even in its darkest days, the Lódź (Poland) Ghetto sought to provide for the children. Homes were found for those whose parents had been deported, and orphanages and hostels tried to provide children with nourishment and comfort. In this photograph, Yankev Chmielnicki and other ghetto children eat at the orphanage on Garbarska Street. The number of ghetto children was reduced dramatically in September 1942, when the authorities ordered the deportations of all children under the age of ten.

Work was the key to survival in the Lódź Ghetto, and most children worked. An accelerated course in tailoring was developed so that young people could learn a useful skill. By the end of 1942 even nine-year-olds were expected to work. All members of the ghetto were on call for assignments of forced labor. Here, a Jewish youth, the Star of David pinned to his back, washes the car of a German official.

1942

gassing activity at the Chelmno death camp. • I.G. Farben's Buna-Monowitz synthetic-rubber and oil works opens near Auschwitz.

• **June 1–6, 1942:** Seven thousand Jews from Kraków, Poland, are murdered at the Belzec extermination-camp.

• **June 2, 1942:** Viennese Jews are deported to the Minsk (Belorussia) Ghetto. One woman, Elsa Speigel, decides to leave her 5½-month-old son, Jona, behind. The baby will eventually be sent to the the camp/ghetto at Theresienstadt, Czechoslovakia, where he will survive the war. • **The BBC reports that 700,000 Jews have been exterminated. Its information**

Jews of Kraków, Poland, were ordered to clean out the homes of their brethren, who had recently been deported from the ghetto. The first round of deportations began at the end of May 1942 and continued until June 8. During the first wave of roundups, 6000 Jews were deported to the Belzec death camp and 300 were murdered on the spot. A second *Aktion* took place on October 27–28; 7000 Jews were deported and 600 were killed.

Appointed president of the Vichy Republic in 1942, Pierre Laval immediately became a willing tool of the Nazis. He approved and facilitated German efforts to round up and deport Jewish émigrés, including children. Laval expedited the deportation process by ordering French police to cooperate with Nazi authorities, sending some 25,000 Jews to the ghettos and concentration camps of the East during the summer months.

Kraków/Plaszów

Home to one of the oldest and most important Jewish communities in Europe, Kraków, Poland, was transformed by the Nazis into a place of terror. The city was occupied by the Germans in September 1939 and declared the capital of the *Generalgouvernement* of Poland. All anti-Jewish legislation for the region was issued from Kraków.

Terror campaigns against the Jews began in December 1940. Jewish property was seized, synagogues were burned, and thousands of Jews were expelled from their residences. A formal ghetto that measured 656 × 437 yards was established in March 1941. Jews from the neighboring communities were packed into the ghetto; by the end of the year, 18,000 Jews were

imprisoned in Kraków. The overcrowding and deplorable sanitary conditions caused many deaths. Those pictured were hanged for railway sabotage.

Deportations from Kraków to the Belzec and Auschwitz death camps began in May 1942 and continued until March 1943. On March 13, 1943, 2000 Jews were transferred to the Plaszów forced-labor camp. Located on the outskirts of Kraków, the Plaszów camp was run by the notorious Amon Goeth, a psychopathic killer who took pleasure in shooting Jews for sport from his balcony. The Kraków Ghetto and Plaszów labor camp provided the setting for the film *Schindler's List.*

comes from a report smuggled out of Poland by the Jewish Bund in Warsaw.

• June 3, 1942: Jews revolt in Breslau, Germany. • In Warsaw, Nazis shoot 110 Jews in a prison on Gesia Street. Ten Jewish policemen are among the victims.

• June 4, 1942: Reinhard Heydrich, chief of the Reich Security Police and SD, dies of blood poisoning caused by injuries suffered in the May 27 attack by Czech partisans; *See* June 9, 1942. • The U.S. declares war on Romania.

• June 5, 1942: The SS reports that 97,000 persons have been "processed" in mobile gas vans.

• June 5–6, 1942: During a roundup of Jews in Kraków, Poland, SS men brutally torment two men—one who has just one leg and another who had lost his eyesight while fighting for Germany in World War I.

• June 6, 1942: Adolf Eichmann insists via a telegram sent to Gestapo officials that residents of a mental

What Was Known in the West

In late May 1942, the London-based Polish government-in-exile got news from the Warsaw Jewish Bund. The communication emphasized several points: the Germans had murdered 700,000 Polish Jews; it identified the sites of the death camps and contained a list of the places in which *Aktionen* were carried out; and the Nazis planned to destroy all of Polish Jewry. On June 2 the British Broadcasting Corporation (BBC) reported the murder figure. The Bund's calculation, however, was too low. As the BBC aired the news that day, Poland's Jewish death toll actually approached two million.

A second BBC broadcast on June 26 gave more details about the Bund report. Three days later a World Jewish Congress press conference in London provided corroborating testimony. Public reports in June 1942 about the destruction of Polish Jewry became what scholar Deborah Lipstadt calls "a watershed in the dissemination of information regarding the Final Solution."

During the summer of 1942, U.S. President Franklin Roosevelt and British Prime Minister Winston Churchill vowed to hold the Nazis responsible for anti-Jewish atrocities. Meanwhile, downplaying special efforts to rescue Europe's Jews, the Allies' wartime policy contended that winning the war was the best, if not the only, way to save them. This attitude continued until the end of the war, despite late-1942 visits to Churchill and FDR by Jan Karski, a Polish gentile who had witnessed the horrors of the Warsaw Ghetto.

German troops force their way into a house during the invasion of the Soviet Union. The war against the Bolshevik foe did not differentiate between civilians and soldiers. As the German armies rapidly advanced east, toward Moscow, untold numbers of homes were destroyed and thousands upon thousands of civilians were killed.

A Jewish policeman from the Warsaw Ghetto removes a dead baby. Note the emaciated condition of the corpse. Jews lived in the ghetto on starvation rations, and the sick, young, and infirm were the first victims of famine and disease. Infants, many of whom were born dead, were particularly susceptible to these conditions.

1942

institution must be included in a planned mass deportation of Jews from Coblenz, Germany, to Lublin, Poland. • The Jewish ghetto at Kraków, Poland, is liquidated; 6000 Jews from the city are murdered at Belzec.

• June 7, 1942: A Jewish woman who has escaped from the Warsaw Ghetto into the city proper is dragged back to the ghetto and shot. • The Jewish Yellow Star is made mandatory in Occupied France.

• June 8, 1942: The Jewish Council at Pilica, Poland, warns that every able-bodied Jew must attempt to flee to nearby forests.

As appalling as conditions were in the Warsaw Ghetto, some of the city's Jews survived, often by hiding outside the ghetto in the homes of gentiles who were willing to conceal them. Here, Jacob, David, and Shalom Gutgeld pose with their Aunt Janke. Janke managed to get the three boys out of the ghetto, hiding them in the small apartment of a couple named the Roslans. Jacob and David survived the Holocaust, but Shalom died of scarlet fever.

This destitute girl, perhaps dead, lies on a street in the Warsaw Ghetto. Notice the people who casually walk by. Starvation became so common in Warsaw that several Jewish physicians undertook a self-study of the effects of famine that resulted from the horrible conditions imposed by the Germans. They considered the study an act of resistance performed to commemorate the dead. One of the doctors involved insisted that the study was proof that "not all of me shall die!"

Because of the scarcity of raw materials in the ghettos, it became increasingly difficult for Jews to continue to perform their jobs. Repeated conscriptions for forced labor only exacerbated the situation. This shoemaker was one of the few permitted to continue his trade in the Warsaw Ghetto. The Germans made exceptions of this sort in order to promote a feeling of normalcy in the ghetto and to convince the Jews that deportation to the East really meant resettlement.

• **June 9, 1942:** At Lidice, Czechoslovakia, Germans begin to murder over 190 men and boys in retaliation for the attack on Reinhard Heydrich. The Germans will murder another 47 men, women, and children at Lezaky, Czechoslovakia; *See* June 18, 1942.
• **When a Jewish mother at Pabianice, Poland,** fights fiercely for her baby during a deportation, the baby is taken from her and thrown out a window. • German police in Lódź, Poland, report to their superiors in Poznań that 95 Lódź Jews have been publicly hanged. • A gassing van is sent to Riga, Latvia, for the execution of Jews; *See* June 15, 1942.

• **June 10, 1942:** One thousand Jews are deported from Prague, Czechoslovakia, to the East, where they are murdered.

• **June 11, 1942:** Adolf Eichmann meets with representatives from France, Belgium, and Holland to discuss deportation plans for Jews.

• **June 11–12, 1942:** Ten thousand Jews from the Tarnów, Poland,

Hlinka guardsmen of the Slovakian nationalist party stand in front of a truck loaded with Jewish deportees at an assembly point in Kralovsky-Chlumec. Local police and guard units helped round up and deport the Jews to one of the six death facilities located in German-occupied Poland.

Heirs to a long tradition of anti-semitism, many Poles collaborated with the Nazis, betraying their Jewish friends and neighbors. Others feared the Nazi death sentence levied against any who hid Jews. Antisemitic attitudes had taken on a new cast in 1918 to 1920, when Poland struggled for independence from Russia, Prussia, and Austria, and began to establish a capitalist economy. The combination of nationalism and economic ambition cast Jews not merely as outsiders, but as competitors. In the years leading up to World War II, then, Polish Jews grew increasingly marginalized. Here, a Pole in the town of Swierze literally carries a Jewish woman to the Gestapo.

The Nazis often insisted upon adding insult to injury by tormenting Jews who were about to be deported to their deaths. Here, Nazi thugs humiliate an Orthodox Jew from the Czechoslovakian town of Stropkov by trimming his beard—an all too common occurrence. Such actions not only pained the victims, but also allowed the perpetrators to unleash their contempt for the centuries-old culture of European Jewry.

1942

Ghetto are murdered at the Belzec extermination camp.

• **June 12, 1942:** Jewish babies, children, and elderly of Khmel'nik, Ukraine, are shot in a nearby forest. • **Anne Frank turns 13 years old.**

• **June 13, 1942:** Three thousand Jews are deported from the Theresien-

stadt, Czechoslovakia, camp/ghetto to their deaths. • **British Ambassador to the Vatican Francis d'Arcy Osborne observes about Pope Pius XII that his "moral leadership is not assured by the unapplied recital of the Commandments."**

• **June 14, 1942:** Two thousand Jews break out of Dzisna, Belorussia.

Gestapo chief Reinhard Heydrich and his wife, Lina, attend a concert in Prague on May 26, 1942, the night before he was ambushed and mortally wounded by Czech partisans. Also the *Reichsprotektor* of Bohemia and Moravia, Heydrich was charged with rooting out and destroying the increasingly effective underground movement that operated along the Czech countryside. Toward this end, thousands of Czechs were arrested and hundreds killed.

Spain and the Holocaust

Although Spain's head of state, General Francisco Franco, sympathized with the Axis powers, his political policies saved an estimated 17,000 Jews from death camps. Franco refused to enter the war. Instead, he declared Spain a "nonbelligerent," and during the latter half of the war changed the country's status to "neutral."

Franco frustrated the SS by declaring descendants of Sephardic Jews eligible for Spanish citizenship, and thus entitled to asylum in Spanish embassies. Spain consequently became a main avenue of escape for Europe's Jews. Some hoped to find asylum within the country, but most intended to embark from Spanish ports for sanctuary overseas.

The fall of France in 1940 unleashed a flood of refugees seeking entry into Spain. Initially, the Spanish government willingly granted transit visas, but then authorities became more hesitant to open frontiers. Still, many refugees slipped across the northern border illegally, trekking over hazardous mountain routes. By the summer of 1942, Jewish aid organizations helped an estimated 7500 pass through Spain to continue their journeys.

Spanish authorities worked to discourage refugees from remaining in the country, and established internment camps for those who did. When border crossings increased again in 1943, refugees were permitted to live in Spanish cities.

Following the ambush of Reinhard Heydrich, the two assassins and other parachutists who participated in the operation took refuge in the crypt of St. Cyril and St. Methodius, located in Prague. Once their hiding place was discovered, German troops stormed the crypt. A gun battle ensued, and all of the partisans were killed.

• **June 15, 1942: Authorities in Riga, Latvia, request a second gassing van.**

• **June 16, 1942: The American *chargé d'affaires* in the Vatican, Harold Tittmann, reports to the State Department that Pope Pius XII is adopting "an ostrich-like policy towards atrocities that were obvious to everyone."**

• **June 18, 1942: Jozef Gabcik and Jan Kubis, British-trained Czech partisans who mortally wounded Reinhard Heydrich on May 27, are discovered with several other partisans inside Prague's Sts. Cyril and Methodius Church. The church is besieged by German troops and SS. All partisans perish.**

• **June 19, 1942: Jews revolt at Glebokie, Belorussia; 2500 are murdered in the Borek Forest.**

• **Summer 1942: The Third Reich achieves its high point of conquest and territory. • Three-year-old Jewish twins in Sosnowiec, Poland, Ida and Adam Paluch, are spirited away from Gestapo agents by their aunt and sent**

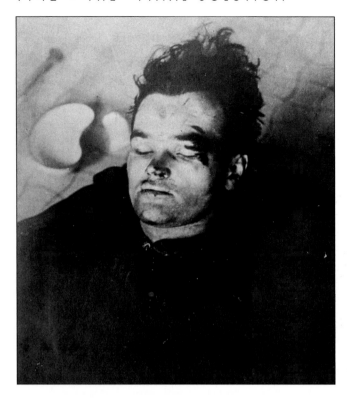

Jan Kubis, the man who threw the grenade that mortally wounded Reinhard Heydrich, was killed during the gun battle at St. Cyril's crypt. The killing of Kubis, however, did not quiet Hitler's fury. The German chancellor ordered a series of reprisal operations.

A typed radio message announced the havoc wreaked on the town of Lidice in retribution for the assassination of Heydrich. On the day prior to the destruction of Lidice, Hitler issued the following warning: "Nothing will prevent me from expelling millions of Czechs if they are not prepared for a peaceful life together." The massacre at Lidice sent a clear message to anyone thinking about opposing the Nazi regime. This poster was created by the U.S. Office of War Information.

News of Heydrich's death on June 4 enraged Hitler and prompted Nazi officials to enlist help to locate his killers. This bilingual poster advertised a reward of ten million Czech crowns for information leading to the capture of Heydrich's assassins.

1942

to live with separate Catholic families; *See* 1995.

• June 20–October 9, 1942: 13,776 Jews are deported from Vienna to Theresienstadt.

• June 24, 1942: Thousands of Lvov, Ukraine, Jews are killed at Janówska, Ukraine, and Piaski, Poland.

• June 25, 1942: An article in the *London Daily Telegraph* reports, "More than 700,000 Polish Jews have been slaughtered by the Germans in the greatest massacres in the world's history."

• June 26, 1942: The British broadcast information about the plight of Jews in Occupied Poland.

Hitler's fury over the Heydrich assassination was vented in Lidice. The Czech village was brutally destroyed in a murderous burst of revenge carried out by SS and police. On June 9–10, 1942, 199 of the village's adult males and 47 of its women were executed. The remaining women were imprisoned in the Ravensbrück concentration camp, and the children—only 16 of whom would survive the war—were sent to "educational" institutions. The murdered citizens of Lidice were laid out in rows before being buried in a mass grave.

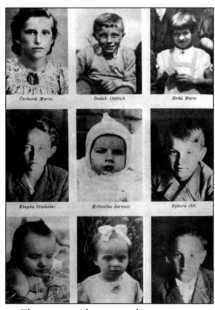

The reprisals carried out in retribution for the assassination of Heydrich were both swift and brutal. Pictured here are but a few of the children who were deported to the Ravensbrück and Mauthausen concentration camps. Most of these children did not survive the war.

Drancy

An unfinished apartment complex in the Paris suburb of Drancy was a transit camp for most Jews shipped from France to Auschwitz. From 1942 to 1944, more than 60 of the 79 trains that left for the East from France left from Drancy. About 67,000 of 75,000 Jews deported from French soil spent time at Drancy.

When Drancy opened on August 21, 1941, living conditions were abysmal. There were 1200 wooden bunk-bed frames for the first 4000 inmates. Forty to 50 internees crammed each room, and their diet consisted exclusively of cabbage soup. As a result, the mortality rate at Drancy was very high.

Ironically, material conditions improved when German officials took over camp administration from Vichy France officials in July 1943. The last deportation transport left Drancy on July 31, 1944.

• **June 28, 1942:** The Germans launch a summer offensive against the Red Army in the Don River basin of the Soviet Union.

• **June 29, 1942:** Armed Jewish resistance takes place at Slonim, Belorussia. Germans burn Jews to death; nearly 15,000 are killed.

• **June 30, 1942:** A second gas chamber begins functioning at Auschwitz-Birkenau. • A headline in the *London Daily Telegraph* reads: "MORE THAN 1,000,000 JEWS KILLED IN EUROPE."

• **June–July 1942:** *The New York Times* highlights articles on Christian victims of the Germans rather than on Jewish victims, even though the numbers of Jewish victims are immensely greater.

• **July 1942:** Hundreds of German Jews are deported to the ghetto/camp at Theresienstadt, Czechoslovakia. In Paderborn, Germany, all Jewish orphans are deported to Theresienstadt. • Seven trains of Jewish depor-

Police Battalion 101

As dawn broke on July 13, 1942, Major Wilhelm Trapp, 53, the beloved commander of German Reserve Police Battalion 101, addressed his men near Józefów, a village with 1800 Jews in the *Generalgouvernement* of Nazi-occupied Poland. Mostly middle-aged family men who had been in Poland less than three weeks, these members of the *Ordnungspolizei* (Order Police) heard the teary-eyed major explain that the battalion had orders to round up Józefów's Jews. They were to select the able-bodied males for labor, and then shoot everyone else—women, children, and the elderly.

Trapp's explanation included a significant option: Those *Ordnungspolizei* who could not perform the task did not have to kill. Murder, in other words, was not mandatory. About a dozen members of the 500-man battalion accepted this offer. The rest murdered 1500 of Józefów's Jews. By the end of 1943, Reserve Police Battalion 101 *(members pictured)*—in conjunction with other Order Police killing units—had shot 38,000 Jews and helped to deport another 45,000 to Treblinka.

Using postwar interrogation records, Holocaust scholar Christopher Browning's book *Ordinary Men: Reserve Police Battalion 101 and the Final Solution in Poland* documents this history and explores one of the Holocaust's most fundamental questions: How could apparently normal persons become mass murderers?

The Nazis made a concerted effort to recruit soldiers from occupied countries. At first they made this effort only among those peoples whom they considered "Aryan," such as these Norwegians who volunteered to fight against the Soviet Union. Eventually, they also recruited among the Slavic peoples of Eastern Europe, who were notorious for their antisemitism and who played an important role in perpetrating the Holocaust.

Many Europeans of "Aryan" heritage found the *Waffen-SS*, the combat arm of the SS, particularly attractive. These Belgian recruits had joined the most elite fighting force in Europe, one that emphasized the racial purity of its troops. Membership in the *Waffen-SS* was perceived as a way of obtaining influence after the war, when the Nazis planned to put their "New Order" into effect.

1942

tees leave Westerbork, Holland, for the Auschwitz death camp. • At Kleck, Belorussia, a few dozen Jews break out and join partisans. • Extermination activities at the Sobibór death camp are temporarily halted for railway construction and enlargement of the camp's gas chambers. • The Jewish community at Gorodenka, Ukraine, is wiped out. • The U.S. and

Britain agree on an Allied invasion of North Africa.

• July 2, 1942: The Jewish community from Ropczyce, Poland, is murdered at the Belzec death camp. • *The New York Times* reports the "slaughter of 700,000 Jews" in German-occupied Poland.

The summer of 1942 marked a dramatic turning point for the family of Anne Frank *(pictured)*. When Margot, Anne's older sister, was ordered to report for labor, Otto Frank decided to move his entire family into hiding. A secret attic in Amsterdam became their home for the next two years. That same year, for her birthday on June 12, Anne received a diary that would become her best friend. Writing to "Dear Kitty," Anne shared her secret fears, hopes, and dreams.

Children sometimes proved immune to the prejudices so prevalent among their parents. On June 7, 1942, at *Ecole rue Michel Bizot,* non-Jewish boys showed their solidarity with their Jewish classmates by wearing the yellow Star of David that was mandatory for Jews. This action, of course, made it impossible to tell the Jews from the non-Jews, making it more difficult for authorities to persecute the Jewish boys. Here, the courageous boys are pictured at a later date.

Men from all over Occupied Europe volunteered to serve in national regiments fighting on the side of the Germans. These Danish troops volunteered for a variety of reasons. Some hoped that service alongside the Germans would be an advantage after what they considered an inevitable German victory. Others fervently supported National Socialist ideology; they were attracted by the Nazis' glorification of the "Aryan race" and/or supported the Germans' antisemitic policies. Such motives were cleverly played upon by ideologically seductive recruitment posters and other Nazi propaganda devices that were common in occupied nations.

• **July 6, 1942:** The first issue of *Eynikeyt* (Unity), a Yiddish-language journal of the Soviet Jewish Antifascist Committee, is published. • Anne Frank and her family go into hiding in Amsterdam.

• **July 7, 1942:** SS chief Heinrich Himmler chairs a meeting of SS functionaries to discuss sterilization and other gynecological procedures and experiments on Jewish women held at Auschwitz. The procedures will be conducted without the women's knowledge; *See* July 10, 1942. • One thousand Jews from Rzeszów, Poland, are killed at the Rudna Forest. Fourteen thousand are deported to the Belzec death camp.

• **July 8, 1942:** Seven thousand Lvov, Ukraine, Jews are murdered at the Janówska, Ukraine, labor/extermination camp. • Jewish partisan Vitka Kempner and two others leave the Jewish ghetto at Vilna, Lithuania, carrying a land mine with which they hope to disable a German military train located five miles southeast; *See* July 9, 1942.

A German-Jewish girl wearing the Yellow Star and a numbered tag around her neck was photographed just prior to her deportation. The tag bears her name, date of birth, and convoy number, which indicates that she was deported to the Theresienstadt camp/ghetto in Czechoslovakia. Deportation of German Jews to Theresienstadt commenced in June 1942 and continued throughout the year. By December 33,554 German Jews had been deported to the "model ghetto," located near Prague.

A number of Jews are being buried in the Jewish cemetery in Siedlce, Poland. The Germans forced the local firemen, among them the man who took this photograph, Tadeusz Castelli, to bury the bodies.

Mordecai Gebirtig *(second from left)* sits with three of his colleagues from the Hebrew *Gymnasium* (secondary school) in Kraków, Poland. Gebirtig was a Yiddish folk poet who reflected the sentiments of Jews in Eastern Europe. During the Holocaust his poems expressed fear, hope, and anger, such as the poem *"A Tog fun Nekome,"* ("A Day of Revenge"). He died on June 4, 1942.

1942

- July 9, 1942: Jewish partisan Vitka Kempner returns to the Vilna Ghetto, having successfully planted a land mine and blown up the engine and ammunition cars of a German military train; *See* September 1943.

- July 10, 1942: At Auschwitz, 100 Jewish women are selected for experiments with sterilization.

- July 11, 1942: Nine thousand Jewish males from Salonika, Greece, are assigned to the *Organisation Todt* labor battalions.

- July 13–15, 1942: Several thousand Jews of Rovno, Ukraine, are rounded up and executed in the streets by *Einsatzgruppen*.

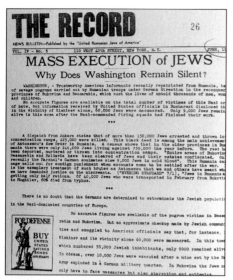

The news bulletin of the United Romanian Jews of America published reports of atrocities committed against Romanian Jewry as early as June 1942. Printed in New York City and distributed throughout the United States, the headline proclaimed the "Mass Execution of Jews" and queried the government's policy of silence. Pleas such as this were typical of Jewish organizations throughout the United States.

As his comrades look on, a German soldier offers food to a barefoot and hungry Croatian child. Axis military victory led to the division of Yugoslavia. Croatia became a Nazi puppet state, led by the *Ustasa*. The *Ustasa* persecuted any who opposed them, including Serbs, leaving those fortunate enough to survive hungry and homeless.

Deportations in France

The treatment of French Jews at the hands of the Nazis offers a poignant reminder of the fragile nature of democracy. Though French Jews were emancipated in 1790 and well integrated into the fabric of French society on the eve of World War II, their fate was altered dramatically in 1942.

Beginning in the summer Jews in France were rounded up and deported to the East, where they were executed. The roundups that began on July 16, 1942, targeted mostly stateless and foreign-born Jews, though British and American Jews were exempt from the operation. Those who were caught in the first wave were interned in the Paris sports arena known as the *Vélodrome d'Hiver*.

With 7000 people packed into the arena, a facility that lacked food, water, and sanitary facilities, the conditions were horrible. Internees were confined for several days before being deported. From the *Vélodrome d'Hiver*, Jews were deported to Drancy (a camp in the suburbs of Paris) or other temporary internment centers before being shipped to Auschwitz.

In all, at least 77,000 Jews from France were murdered during the Holocaust, including Henri Sznajderman and his mother *(both pictured)*. Most died at Auschwitz, while others were killed at Majdanek and Sobibór or while in detention.

• **July 14, 1942:** Thousands of Dutch Jews are arrested in Amsterdam and deported to Auschwitz, where many are gassed. • The Przemyśl, Poland, ghetto is sealed by the Nazis.

• **July 15, 1942:** The first deportation train leaves Holland (from the Westerbork transit camp) for Auschwitz.

• **July 16, 1942:** *La Grande Rafle* ("The Big Sweep") commences in Paris, as the German and Austrian Jews living in the city, about 13,000 total, are rounded up; *See* July 19, 1942.

• **July 17, 1942:** A Nazi delegation headed by SS chief Heinrich Himmler tours the death camp at Auschwitz,

where Himmler observes a mass gassing of inmates.

• **July 19, 1942:** Deportations to the Auschwitz death camp begin for Parisian Jews who have been held at Drancy, France, since July 16. • SS chief Heinrich Himmler orders that all Polish Jews in the *Generalgouvernement* be deported eastward by

Jewish Responses

Jews reacted to the Holocaust in a variety of ways. Some, fearing for their lives and the safety of their families, collaborated under duress with the Germans, serving in the ghettos' Jewish councils or as Jewish police. Some American Jews, in the face of critical levels of antisemitism in the U.S., were too afraid to put political pressure on their government. Other Jews refused to face the devastating realities of the "Final Solution."

European Jews, however, fell into a spectrum that ran from adherence to their Judaism at all costs to guerrilla warfare against the murderers. Disgusted with God's apparent silence, some Jews rejected their religious beliefs. Rabbi Irving Greenberg argued after the war that debate about the nature of God is ridiculous in the presence of a burning child; the only appropriate behavior is to jump in and pull the child out of the fire. Rabbi Emil Fackenheim discovered a new commandment: to survive as a Jew. Rabbi Yitzhak Nissenbaum in the Warsaw Ghetto admonished Jews to do their utmost to save their own lives.

In the ghettos, before the machine guns of the SS and *Einsatzgruppen*, and before and in the gas chambers themselves, Jews made personal decisions. Some went to their deaths stoically, others defiantly, still others confident in the unalterable tenets of their faith.

Radio correspondent William L. Shirer conveyed to millions of Americans the news of France's capitulation to Germany in June 1940. A perceptive observer of Nazism, and later the author of *The Rise and Fall of the Third Reich,* Shirer was one of the earliest voices to warn Americans of Hitler's demonic intentions. In December 1942 he joined other Americans of German descent in signing a Christmas declaration denouncing the "cold-blooded extermination of the Jews" and urging Germans to overthrow Hitler and his government.

These seven Poles were hanged by the German military in Plaszów for the crime of railway sabotage. The Germans liked to hang those who defied them, as a deterrent to the local population.

1942

December 31, 1942. •The Family Hostage Law is announced in Occupied France. Under its provisions, fugitive "terrorists" who do not surrender to German authorities can expect their male relatives to be killed, female relatives sent to work camps, and children sent to special schools for political reeducation.

• July 20, 1942: Germans murder 1000 Jews at Kleck, Belorussia; 400 flee into forests. Two from the latter group, Moshe Fish and Leva Gilchik (from nearby Kopyl), will form a partisan group; *See* January 1943.

• July 20–21, 1942: Jews are deported from Kowale Pańskie, Poland, to the Chelmno death camp.

"All right, give them something nice to chew on."

—Gassing command given at Auschwitz by Sergeant Major Otto Moll

The rear door to this gas chamber at Birkenau was labeled: "Harmful gas! Entering endangers your life!" The words were for those who ran the gas chambers, not its victims. The prisoners' entrance labeled the chambers as a shower and was inscribed with a message about the virtues of cleanliness.

The ovens for crematorium II in Auschwitz-Birkenau, like those in the first crematorium, were built by prison inmates. With a ready supply of labor and the confiscated wealth of European Jewry at their disposal, the Nazis had the necessary resources for their genocidal agenda.

Prisoners at Auschwitz were used to build the Birkenau killing center. This picture shows crematorium IV, under construction. Early on, the victims of the gas chambers were buried in pits. As the pace of the killing intensified, the bodies were burned, first in the pits themselves and later in the crematoria. Construction at Auschwitz-Birkenau was continuous from the winter of 1941 through the summer of 1944.

• **July 21, 1942:** Six hundred Jews remaining in Nieświez, Poland, battle their Nazi attackers. Many Jews and a few Nazis are killed, and some of the Jews who survive manage to flee into nearby forests.

• **July 22, 1942:** German authorities and Ukrainian and Latvian guards in SS uniforms surround the walls of the Warsaw Ghetto. Mass deportations of Jews from Warsaw to the Treblinka death camp begin; personnel at the camp railway station are told to expect a "shuttle service" of Jews.

• **July 23, 1942:** Adam Czerniaków, chairman of the Warsaw Ghetto's Jewish Council, commits suicide rather than acquiesce to German demands to prepare 6000 Jews each day for deportation. • SS Senior Colonel Viktor Brack advises Heinrich Himmler that all healthy Jews should be castrated or sterilized, and the remainder annihilated.

• **July 22–September 12, 1942:** 265,000 Jews are deported from War-

Among the guests at a 1942 Jewish marriage ceremony at Bochnia, Poland—located about 20 miles southeast of Kraków—were Jewish police officers and members of the *Judenrat*. Relations between the rank-and-file residents of any Jewish ghetto and fellow Jews who enjoyed privileged status and a modicum of power were typically strained. If the groom was not a policeman or *Judenrat* representative, this moment of solidarity was rare indeed.

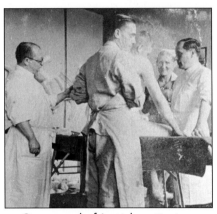

Composed of Jewish patients, mostly women, Block 10 at Auschwitz was the site of Nazi medical research. The barrack was known as "Clauberg's Block" after the physician, Carl Clauberg *(left),* who conducted much of the experimentation there. Clauberg was especially interested in infertility and sterilization research, areas that won him the personal backing of Heinrich Himmler, who wondered "how long it would take to sterilize a thousand Jewesses." Clauberg used injections, probably of the substance formalin, to cause obstructions in the fallopian tubes and prevent pregnancy.

Joseph Goebbels began publication of *Der Angriff (The Attack)* on July 4, 1927, as a propaganda sheet for the Nazi Party in Berlin. Goebbels relinquished editing duties after 1933 but remained publisher, and the newspaper became the official organ of the *Deutsche Arbeitsfront* (Labor Front). The paper continued to be an important propaganda tool in the hands of its new editors. The headline for July 4, 1942, reads, in part, "'Angriff' Interview with Dr. Goebbels."

1942

saw to the Treblinka death camp, where they are exterminated.

• **July 24, 1942:** Martin Luther, undersecretary of state at the German Foreign Ministry, alerts Nazi Foreign Minister Joachim von Ribbentrop that Italian authorities are resistant to the German plan to deport Jews from Italian-held regions of Croatia.

• **July 27, 1942:** The German government in the Occupied Eastern Territories warns that any Pole or Ukrainian who attempts to hide or assist a Jew will be "shot dead."

• **July 28, 1942:** SS chief Heinrich Himmler writes to a senior SS official that the Occupied Eastern Territories "are to become free of Jews." • Jew-

Complex challenges faced the *Judenrat* (Jewish Council) of a huge ghetto like Lódź. To support the needs of the ghetto, the *Judenrat* set up hospitals, schools, and soup kitchens. All required funding, which the council raised by taxing everything they could, beginning with wages. Here, Nazi Walter Genewein, financial director of the Lódź Ghetto administration, counts money into piles delegated to the ghetto's various needs and to special German demands.

Though not as strong as in other countries, antisemitism did occur in Italy. Here, an Italian soldier whips a Greek Jew in the city of Salonika. The Jews were assembled in Liberty Square. Forced to do calisthenics in the hot sun, the Jews were beaten if they slowed down.

The German offensive against the Soviet Union relied heavily upon surprise and speed. The first phases of the attack led to one Nazi victory after another, as Hitler threw masses of men and machines into the Eastern Front. The successes of the summer of 1941 were followed by even more spectacular victories the next summer, including the capture of the Crimea and its naval base at Sevastopol.

ish parents in Tarnów, Poland, are forced to watch as their children are shot by Gestapo agents. The parents and other adults are subsequently deported to the camp at Belzec for extermination. • In the Lódź (Poland) Ghetto, two male Jews, one just 16 years old, are hanged after escaping a work gang. • Young members of the Warsaw Ghetto establish *Zydowska*

Organizacja Bojowa (ZOB; Jewish Fighting Organization). At this time, the only weapon in the ghetto is a single pistol.

• July 28–31, 1942: About 30,000 Jews are killed in Minsk, Belorussia.

• July 29, 1942: The Nazis post notices in the Warsaw Ghetto offer-

ing extra food (mainly bread and jam) to Jews who go voluntarily to "resettlement."

• July 30, 1942: German industrialist Eduard Schulte, whose company has mines near Auschwitz, reveals to a Swiss colleague that Hitler and the German Reich have decided to round up the millions of Jews of Occupied

Parisian Jew Paulette Zelasneg, pictured at age six, wears her Yellow Star. On July 16, 1942, *La Grande Rafle* ("The Big Sweep") began in Paris, as foreign Jews living in the city were rounded up.

GERMAN ADMINISTRATION OF EASTERN EUROPE, 1942

The Germans renamed certain territories after occupying them. The Baltic states became *Reichskommissariat* Ostland. Greater Germany and the *Generalgouvernement* included western and eastern Poland, respectively.

With trains bringing thousands of fresh laborers to replace those who dropped from exhaustion and malnutrition, Monowitz-Buna developed into a vast industrial machine, with the huge chemical firm I.G. Farben at its hub. In the midst of industrialized inhumanity, prisoners struggled to remain human rather than to become animals. Primo Levi recounted that precisely "because the *Lager* (camp) was a great machine to reduce us to beasts, we must not become beasts; that even in this place one can survive, and therefore one must want to survive, to tell the story, to bear witness."

1942

Europe, concentrate them in the East, and murder them using prussic acid starting in the fall of 1942. The information is soon communicated to Swiss World Jewish Congress representative Gerhart Riegner.

• July 31, 1942: Governor Wilhelm Kube reports to Hinrich Lohse, *Reichskommissar* of the Baltic regions

and Belorussia, that "Jewry has been completely eliminated" in the Minsk area. • Bluma Rozenfeld, 19, leaps to her death from a fifth-floor window in the Lódź (Poland) Ghetto. • Israel Lichtenstein writes from the Warsaw Ghetto: "At present, together with me, both of us get ready to meet and receive death. I wish my little daughter to be remembered. Margalith,

SS chief Heinrich Himmler wipes sweat from his forehead during an inspection of Auschwitz III, or Monowitz-Buna. The camp was named after the village of Monowice and the word for synthetic rubber, *Buna,* which the I.G. Farben company sought to produce by using thousands of concentration-camp workers. Accompanying Himmler was *Bauleiter* (chief engineer) Faust of I.G. Farben. Due in part to Allied air attacks, no synthetic rubber was ever produced at Monowitz-Buna.

Inmates work in a chemical factory at the Auschwitz concentration camp. Manufacturers at the site utilized slave labor to staff their enterprises. Inmates greatly coveted positions of skilled labor. Italian author and Holocaust survivor Primo Levi attributed his survival to being a trained chemist. Levi's skills relieved him of the torturous heavy labor that consumed so many lives.

The Business of Killing

The concentration and death camps provided German industry with new opportunities for profit. The Nazi plan to build the camps, and especially to expand Auschwitz, led to huge building contracts. Once built, the camps provided a cheap source of labor for mining, production of synthetic fuels, and other enterprises.

The camp at Jawiszowice in southern Poland supplied workers for the coal mines of the Hermann Göring Works. In Austria, Mauthausen inmates labored in hellish conditions to mine granite for the Reich's ambitious building projects. Even the inmates' bodies furthered German industry. Women's hair from Auschwitz, Majdanek, and other camps was sent to various manufacturing 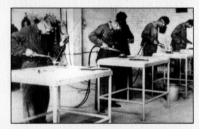 firms to be turned into felt or spun into thread to make socks for submarine crews. The workers pictured toiled at Auschwitz.

I.G. Farben, a massive chemical conglomerate, funded the construction of Monowitz-Buna to produce synthetic rubber, with some 10,000 prisoners from Auschwitz designated for the building project. Experiments with the lethal chemical Zyklon B resulted in the decision to build vast new gas chambers, requiring new furnaces to incinerate the bodies. J. A. Topf and Sons built furnaces for several camps. Meanwhile, the DEGESCH Company received the contract to supply the extermination camps with Zyklon B. Mass killing was definitely good for business.

---

twenty months old today.... I don't lament my own life nor that of my wife. I pity only the so little, nice and talented girl. She deserves to be remembered."

• Late July 1942: Germany decides not to disclose the whereabouts of Dutch deportees, saying only that they had been sent to "an unknown destination...somewhere in the East"—that is, to the Auschwitz extermination camp.

• August 1942: Throughout Europe, more than 400,000 Jews are murdered. • In Poland, Swedish diplomat Baron Göran von Otter is told by SS *Obersturmführer* Kurt Gerstein of Nazi killings of Jews in Poland.

• Deportations of Jews from France and Holland continue. • 5500 Jews are deported from Zagreb, Croatia, to Auschwitz, which is suffering a virulent epidemic of typhus. • 76,000 Jews from the Eastern Galicia region of Poland are deported to Belzec. Throughout the month 150,000 Jews are murdered there. • In the Volhynia region of Poland, 87,000 Jews are

Friedrich Wilhelm Krüger commanded the police and SS forces of the *Generalgouvernement*. On July 19, 1942, Krüger received an order from SS chief Heinrich Himmler that commanded him to assure "that the resettlement of the entire Jewish population of the *Generalgouvernement* be carried out and completed by December 31." Krüger willingly obeyed.

Seated next to Massachusetts Senator Henry Cabot Lodge, Rabbi Stephen Wise *(left)* prepares to address a rally of 18,000 people in Madison Square Garden. Speakers promised a day of reckoning for Nazi barbarity. A gifted orator, Wise worked tirelessly to call attention to the plight of peoples under Nazi oppression. When he learned of the implementation of the "Final Solution," he turned his energies to urging the Roosevelt administration to launch rescue efforts.

Helping Jews in any way was considered a crime. Here a boy and his mother in the Przemyśl (Poland) Ghetto attempt to sell some goods. The woman and child would eat if they sold something, but the likelihood of that was slim because local authorities arrested anyone who engaged in commercial trade with Jews.

1942

killed. • A heat wave and caterpillars destroy a cabbage crop cultivated by residents of the Łódź Ghetto. • In the Ukraine, some 500 Jewish families are shot to death by SS *Einsatzgruppen* and dumped in a mass grave near the town of Zagrodski.

• The Majdanek, Poland, camp is fitted with gas chambers. • Fifty thousand Jews are deported from Lvov, Ukraine, to the Belzec death camp.
• Catholic nun Edith Stein, born a Jew, is arrested in the Netherlands by the Gestapo; *See* August 8, 1942.
• The United States, British, and German governments save two and a half million Greek civilians from starvation. Great Britain and the United States agree to permit food to reach

The very young, the very old, and the sick—that is, all those who could not work—were the first Warsaw Jews to be deported to Treblinka. This July 1942 photograph shows an elderly man waiting to be helped to the deportation center. The appalling circumstances in the ghetto, coupled with the horrific conditions on the deportation trains, assured that many of those who began the journey died before they reached their destination. Almost all of the rest were murdered in the camp's gas chambers.

The first trainload of Jews arrived at Treblinka on July 23, 1942. From that day until the middle of August, between 5000 and 7000 victims arrived each day to be exterminated in the camp's gas chambers, which used diesel engines to produce lethal carbon monoxide gas. In total, about 800,000 perished in Treblinka, most of whom first passed through this train station.

Umschlagplatz

The tragic history of the Warsaw Jewish community resonates with the word *Umschlagplatz* (transfer point). During the massive deportations that began in July 1942, an average of 7000 Jews per day were forcibly marched to the *Umschlagplatz*, a way station on the route to the Treblinka extermination camp.

During the first ten days of the *Aktion*, 65,000 Jews were herded through the *Umschlagplatz* en route to their deaths. The violence of this operation surpassed anything the Nazis had previously perpetuated in Warsaw. The SS, German police, and their able-bodied and willing Latvian and Ukrainian helpers prowled the streets of Warsaw in search of their Jewish prey.

As long as the deportations continued, the Jews of Warsaw clearly understood that survival depended on avoiding the *Umschlagplatz*, the antechamber to death.

Greece after the Germans assure them that the food will not be confiscated. Great Britain ships 35,000 tons of food per month to Greece and the United States pays for it; the process is monitored by neutral nations and the International Red Cross. The agreement costs the Allies $30 million per year. In contrast, the Allies do not seek to help feed Europe's Jews.

• A Polish partisan named Trzcinski passes a hand grenade into a railcar carrying Jewish deportees to the Treblinka death camp. The grenade will be used later at the camp to wound a group of Ukrainian guards.

● **August 1–12, 1942: 81,000 Polish Jews from Warsaw are deported to the Treblinka death camp.**

● **August 2, 1942: Lota Hirszberg, 56, kills herself with sleeping powder in the Lódź Ghetto.**

● **August 3, 1942: Twelve thousand Jews from Przemyśl, Poland, are deported to the Belzec death camp.**
• The first portion of Emanuel Ringelblum's Warsaw diary, hidden in ten tin boxes and milk cans, is secretly

Adam Czerniaków's Diary

Adam Czerniaków, a balding engineer in his early 60s, headed the Warsaw Ghetto's *Judenrat* (Jewish Council) for nearly three years. He wrote almost daily in his diary, which eventually consisted of nine notebooks. The fifth notebook is missing, yet it remains unclear how any part of this important diary survived at all. Rosalia Pietkiewicz, a Warsaw Ghetto survivor, purchased it from an unidentified source in 1959. The original copy has been in Jerusalem at Yad Vashem since 1964.

Czerniaków's reports, many of which begin with the morning temperature, reveal him to be a modest man who worked against impossible odds to save Jewish lives. His last entry, dated July 23, 1942, states: "It is 3 o'clock. So far 4000 are ready to go. The orders are that there must be 9000 by 4 o'clock." The numbers refer to the daily quota of Jews that the Nazis required the *Judenrat* to assemble for "resettlement."

All but a relative few of the Warsaw Ghetto's Jews perished in the Holocaust. A majority were deported to Treblinka and gassed. Especially distressed by his inability to save the ghetto's children, Czerniaków committed suicide on July 23, soon after writing his diary's final entry.

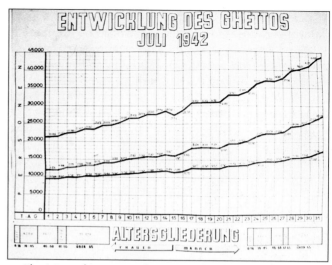

The Nazis kept meticulous records of the population in the Theresienstadt camp/ghetto. This July 1942 document charts the ghetto's human gender. July marked a significant transition at Theresienstadt: All gentiles were moved out to make room for trainloads of arriving Jews, many of them eminent persons, from Germany and Austria.

Yeheskel Atlas was a Polish physician and partisan commander. Atlas's entire family died in the Slonim (Belorussia) Ghetto in November 1941. He remained in the ghetto until July 1942, when he escaped into a partisan company. Atlas led a number of successful attacks against German installations, but he was mortally wounded in a battle at Wielka Wola, Poland.

1942

buried for safekeeping by a Warsaw schoolteacher named Israel Lichtenstein.

• **August 4, 1942:** The first deportations of Jews from Belgium to Auschwitz begin; the first day's deportees number 998. Throughout Belgium, non-Jewish Belgian households hide 25,000 Jews.

• **August 4–31, 1942:** More than 5600 Jews are deported from Belgium to Auschwitz.

• **August 5, 1942:** SS troops in Radom, Poland, shoot 600 older people and children as well as hundreds of other Jews found in hiding places. Six thousand Jews from the city's small ghetto and 2000 from the large

In July 1942 22,000 Jews from the area of Rzeszów, Poland, were sent to the Belzec death camp. Another 1000 Jews were brought to the nearby Rudna Forest and shot. Here, Jewish women undress before execution. The Germans usually required the Jews to disrobe so that their clothes could be sent back for use in Germany.

Jews of Nice sort through a pile of potatoes on the street. By 1942 many French Jews were reduced to poverty. The antisemitic policies of the Vichy government deprived many Jews of their livelihoods. When the deportation of Jews began in July 1942, the administrator of Nice was anxious to get rid of the nearly 8000 Jews who lived under his authority. In France, most Jews who were deported were foreign Jews.

This propaganda photograph presents a staged view of the living conditions in the barracks of the Dutch transit camp Westerbork. The plump pillows and crisp sheets that cover each bunk were calculated to assure the Red Cross that inmates were enjoying sanitary and comfortable conditions. Of course, nothing could have been further from the truth. Additional insult arose from the fact that renovations made to Westerbork in 1942—and probably these pristine barracks, as well—were financed by monies realized from the sale of confiscated Jewish property.

ghetto are deported to the Treblinka death camp. • The Jewish community at Pilica, Poland, is liquidated.

• **August 6, 1942: Three thousand Jews are murdered at Diatlovo, Belorussia. Six hundred escape, more than 100 of whom form a partisan unit led by Hirsch Kaplinski;** *See* **December 1942. • Fifteen thousand**

Jews from Warsaw are deported to the Treblinka death camp.

• **August 6–17, 1942: Twenty thousand Jews from Radom, Poland, are murdered at the Treblinka death camp.**

• **August 8, 1942: Jews of Szczebrzeszyn, Poland, go into hiding when**

Nazis order 2000 to assemble for deportation. By day's end, only a handful have been discovered. • Catholic nun Edith Stein is gassed at Auschwitz.

• **August 9, 1942: The Jewish Council of Zwierzyniec, Poland, ransoms its community with gold. Only 52 of the town's poorest Jews are seized for**

Janusz Korczak

Janusz Korczak, the pen name of Henryk Goldszmit, was a Polish-Jewish physician, writer, and educator. Korczak spent his entire professional life studying and caring for children.

Korczak *(pictured)* became the director of a Jewish orphanage in Warsaw in 1912. From this position he studied the psychological workings of the child brain and applied his findings to his educational ideas. With the outbreak of World War II, and the creation of the Warsaw Ghetto, Korczak dedicated himself to helping Jewish boys and girls.

As the economic conditions of the ghetto rapidly deteriorated, Korczak concentrated his efforts on securing food and shelter for the children. His ghetto diary painstakingly details his tireless efforts.

On August 5, 1942, the Nazis rounded up Korczak and his 200 children. Their three-mile march to the deportation trains was described by diarist Emanuel Ringelblum as follows: "This was not a march to the railway cars, this was an organized, wordless protest against the murder!... The children marched in rows of four, with Korczak leading them, looking straight ahead, and holding a child's hand on each side."

Nothing is known of Korczak's journey to Treblinka, where he, and the children, were gassed.

The fact that the Ukrainian town of Tluste had relatively few Jews did not mean that the Nazis would leave it unmolested. Their intention was to kill every last Jew in Europe, and 300 of Tluste's Jews were sent to the Belzec death camp in August 1942. Another 1000 were shipped to Belzec on October 5. This photograph shows the deportation to Belzec.

Two SS officers from Dachau, Germany, enjoy a break from their duties during a furlough at a local lake. Many camp officials successfully moved between their jobs as concentration-camp guards and life's normal routines. Time away from the camps was spent with families and, often, on vacation. The normalcy with which camp officials approached their jobs is one of the more perplexing facets of the Holocaust. The vast majority of individuals involved in the genocide of the Jews were "ordinary men."

1942

deportation. • 180 Jews escape to forests outside Mir, Belorussia. • The Jewish community at Radun, Belorussia, is liquidated. • Fifteen hundred Jews from Kremenets, Ukraine, are relocated to the Bialokrynitsa camp; *See* August 10, 1942.

• **August 10, 1942:** One thousand Jews deported by train from the

Theresienstadt, Czechoslovakia, camp/ghetto on August 4 are transferred to gassing vans at Maly Trostinets (near Minsk, Belorussia), executed, and dumped into open graves. • **Eight hundred Jews are murdered at Brzozów, Poland.** • **Six German and Ukrainian policemen are killed by Jews while attempting to enter the Jewish ghetto at Kremenets,**

Nazi occupation of the Netherlands brought suffering and hardship to the populace, including this young child. This photograph is part of a series documenting the German occupation taken by Emmy Andreisse, a member of the Dutch Resistance. Before the war she had studied photography and graphic design. During the war years she put her talents to work in "Hidden Camera," a project designed to photograph conditions in the Netherlands under the occupation.

Although Dachau was not technically a death camp, almost 32,000 people died there, victims of the Nazi terror apparatus. From the outset the Nazis found it difficult to dispose of the bodies of their thousands of victims. Bodies interred in mass graves often swelled so much during the summer months that they resurfaced and had to be reburied. Among the most effective solutions to this "problem" was the construction of crematoria in the major concentration camps. Dachau's crematorium *(pictured above and below)* housed several ovens for the burning of numerous bodies simultaneously. Still, the camp's inmates died in numbers too large for the ovens to incinerate every corpse.

Ukraine; *See* August 11, 1942. • The Yeheskel Atlas Jewish partisan company attacks a German garrison in Derechin, Belorussia. Forty-four German policemen are captured and executed.

• August 10–30, 1942: Fifty thousand Jews from Lvov, Ukraine, are murdered at the Belzec death camp.

• August 11, 1942: Jews resisting deportation from Kremenets, Ukraine, set the ghetto on fire. • In Belgium, 999 Jews, including 172 children, are deported to their deaths in the East.

• August 13, 1942: The Jewish communities at Mir, Belorussia, and Gorodok, Ukraine, are liquidated.

• Switzerland forces Jews (mostly French) already safe in Switzerland back across the border. The Swiss government will turn back 10,000 Jews to their deaths during the remainder of the war on the grounds that only political refugees can be admitted into Switzerland, not "racial refugees." The Swiss government does, however, welcome the gold that

Head of the *Judenrat* (Jewish Council) in Warsaw, Adam Czerniaków was caught between the dictates of his conscience and the demands imposed upon him by the Nazis. In late July 1942 new deportations were ordered with the goal of greatly reducing the ghetto. When Czerniaków learned that even the children and orphans would not be spared, he decided to take his own life, writing in his diary: "My heart trembles in sorrow and compassion. I can no longer bear all this."

Calling for "freedom and honor," this flyer from the White Rose organization urges German youth to rise up against Nazi tyranny. Devastated by the deaths of so many young men at the battle of Stalingrad, siblings Sophie and Hans Scholl and their circle of courageous friends struggled to change Germany's course. Using carefully hidden duplicating machines and varying the sources for paper and ink, they printed leaflets that were distributed at the University of Munich and at other universities throughout Germany.

"Newborn infants should have a prisoner number tattooed on their thighs immediately because the arm of an infant is too small."

—*SS guidelines at Auschwitz*

Swedish Prince Gustavus Adolphus visits Germany in 1942. Swedish policy was mildly pro-German until February 1943, when the German advance in Russia was stopped at Stalingrad—a crucial turning point in World War II. At that point, the Swedes and most Europeans felt that the Allies would win the war. As a result, Sweden decided to accept Jewish refugees. In October 1943 the country opened its doors to roughly 10,000 Danish Jews.

1942

the Germans extract from the mouths and fingers of the dead Jews.

• **August 13–27, 1942: 53,750 Jews from Warsaw are deported to the Treblinka death camp.** • United States State Department officials and the British Foreign Office decide that the Riegner Cable outlining details of the Holocaust be kept secret.

• **August 14, 1942: The entire Jewish community from Gorlice, Poland, is deported to the Belzec extermination camp.**

• **August 14-15, 1942: A woman named Rivka Yosselevska is one of just four Jews to survive a bloody burial-pit massacre outside Zagrodski, Poland, near Pinsk.**

Polish Jews in the Kremenets (Ukraine) Ghetto violently resisted the Nazi deportations. On September 9, 1942, 1500 Jews, among them the ghetto's leadership, were transported to a ghetto five miles away. Incensed, a young Jew shot and killed six Germans and Ukrainians who were part of the "liquidation squad," forcing the Nazis temporarily to retreat. The next day another ten Nazis were killed. On August 11, rather than accept deportation and certain death, the remaining Jews set the ghetto on fire. Among the buildings destroyed was the ghetto's synagogue, pictured here.

Serbia

On the heels of their invasion of Yugoslavia, the Nazis constructed concentration camps. Especially notorious was Sajmiste *(pictured)*, across the river from Belgrade in the town of Semlin. Sajmiste became a killing site for Serbian Jews, mostly women and children.

In retaliation for partisan attacks, the German Army shot 100 hostages for every soldier killed. Some 4000 to 5000 males, mostly Jews and Gypsies, were killed in reprisal for German losses. Their wives and children were transported to Sajmiste for detention, where they were housed in rough barracks awaiting deportation.

Seeking a way to rid themselves of Jews more efficiently and economically, German authorities in Serbia used a mobile killing van in the spring of 1942. Victims were told they were being relocated, but instead they were gassed and buried near Belgrade. In 1942 Nazi commanders crowed that Serbia was *judenrein* (cleansed of Jews).

Glimpsing freedom and safety ahead, Jewish refugees cross over the border into Switzerland. Few were so fortunate as this group since the Swiss, citing their need to protect their neutrality, turned a cold shoulder toward most refugees, especially Jews. One official referred to his country as a "crowded little lifeboat," and in 1942 the Swiss government instructed border officials to turn back refugees at the French border, essentially dealing death sentences to Jews.

• **August 15, 1942:** The Germans open Jawiszowice, a slave-labor camp located near Auschwitz. • One thousand Belgian Jews, including 172 children, are deported to their deaths in the East.

• **Mid-August 1942:** A healthy Jewish teenage boy is removed from a deportation train at the Belzec death camp,

stripped naked, hung upside down from gallows for three hours, and then killed as camp guards use sticks to force sand down his throat.

• **August 17, 1942:** 341 French-Jewish children from the ages of two to ten, as well as 323 girls up to the age of 16, are gassed at Auschwitz. Two of the victims are Suzanne Perl,

seven, and her sister Micheline, three.

• **August 17–18, 1942:** 2500 Jews from Drogobych, Ukraine, are murdered at the Belzec death camp.

• **August 18, 1942:** 998 Jews, including 287 children, are deported to the East from Belgium.

Judenräte

Established by Nazi orders, the *Judenrat* (Jewish Council) in Lithuania's Kovno Ghetto was called the *Ältestenrat* (Council of Elders). Its deputy secretary, Avraham Tory, kept a diary that illustrates how this council—led by Dr. Elchanan Elkes, a prominent physician—confronted dilemmas faced by hundreds of Jewish councils (*Judenräte*) in Nazi-occupied Europe.

Held responsible for implementing German directives, *Judenrat* leaders (such as the man pictured, from Bochnia, Poland) also tried to relieve community needs. The councils' conflicting responsibilities required many departments.

Tory's diary entry for August 4, 1942, states how identity cards must be used by nine different offices in the Kovno Ghetto: food administration, labor, social welfare, health, police, registration, housing, economic affairs, and education.

As the Nazis gradually "liquidated" Eastern Europe's ghettos during 1942 and 1943, the *Judenräte* led doomed communities. In autumn 1943 the Germans reclassified the Kovno Ghetto as a concentration camp. They abolished the *Ältestenrat* in April 1944. Kovno was home to about 37,000 Jews when the Nazis occupied the city on June 24, 1941. Only 2400 survived the war. After deportation, Dr. Elkes perished at Dachau on July 25, 1944.

The plan developed at the Wannsee Conference called for a sweeping of Jews from Western to Eastern Europe. In 1942 the deportations from Occupied Western Europe began in earnest. These Jews were shipped from the Westerbork transit camp in Holland to Auschwitz. This deportation, one of the first from Holland, took place from July to October 1942.

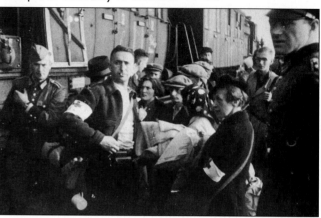

Beginning in July 1942 the Nazis undertook the deportations of Jews from the Warsaw Ghetto to the Treblinka death camp, where almost all of them were gassed as part of Operation Reinhard. These Jews were among the over 250,000 deported from Warsaw from July to September 1942. A further 13,000 would be deported to Treblinka in 1943.

1942

● **August 19, 1942: Nazis murder the children of the Rembertów (Poland) Ghetto.** The town's adult Jews, more than 1000, are assembled for deportation to the Treblinka death camp. About 300 of the people are ordered eastward along the road to Wesola. Before they walk a mile, the 300 are murdered. The 700 who remain are ordered to march south, and as the group passes the town of Anin, one woman melts into a crowd of non-Jewish Polish onlookers and escapes. Forty-five others are machine-gunned at Anin, ostensibly because they attempted escape. Hours later the marchers reach the ghetto at Falenica, where Jews already have been forcibly assembled; those who are discovered in hiding are shot.

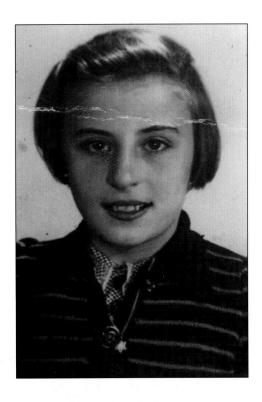

Children were useless from the Nazi point of view because they could not do heavy labor, so they were often among the first to be deported. Teenagers were also deported early because they were considered the most likely to partake in resistance. Pictured here are several Jewish adolescents from the ghetto in the Polish town of Bedzin, home to one of Eastern Europe's most active youth Resistance movements. The fervent desire for freedom held by many Bedzin youth worried the Nazis, particularly because these young men and women had consciously broken with Jewish tradition, and their actions were likely to be daring and unpredictable. The young Bedzin residents seen here may very well have been among the 5000 Jews deported to Auschwitz from Bedzin in August 1942.

Inside the ghetto, two Jews resist, using an axe to kill the first German who steps through the doors of their apartment.

• At the Belzec extermination camp, 700 to 800 Jews herded into a gas chamber wait in torment for nearly three hours until a balky diesel engine can be started and the chamber filled with deadly exhaust. SS gas/disinfectant expert but anti-Nazi Kurt Gerstein is on hand to observe; *See* August 20–24, 1942.

• August 19–23, 1942: Seventeen thousand Jews from Lutsk, Ukraine, are taken to Polanka Hill and executed.

• August 20, 1942: The ZOB (Jewish Fighting Organization) attempts to assassinate Joseph Szerynski, commander of the Jewish police in the Warsaw Ghetto. Later in the day, other ZOB members set fire to several Warsaw warehouses. • The Jewish community from Falenica, Poland, is liquidated at the Treblinka death camp.

German police execute four men in German-occupied Drogobych, Ukraine. In July 1941 Jews of Drogobych were driven by antisemitic locals to a cemetery and slaughtered. In August 1942 more than 500 Jews were murdered by German and Ukrainian police during the selection of Jews to be deported.

Winston Churchill and Joseph Stalin, the leaders of Great Britain and the Soviet Union, respectively, appear to be on the best of terms during their August meeting in Moscow. In reality, the two were suspicious and wary of one another. Engaged in an epic struggle with the Nazis in which millions of his countrymen were dying, Stalin pressed Churchill at this meeting to initiate a second front in France.

Officers from Germany's Secret Field Police, a branch of the *Abwehr* (Military Intelligence Service), pose for a photo in Gniezno, Poland. Headed by Admiral Wilhelm Canaris, the *Abwehr* was charged with gathering intelligence about the enemy. While some officers faithfully performed their counterintelligence duties, others found a home within the *Abwehr* for resistance activities, thanks to Canaris's growing opposition to Hitler.

1942

• **August 20–24, 1942: Nineteen thousand Jews of Kielce, Poland, are deported to the Treblinka death camp.** • **Gas/disinfectant expert Kurt Gerstein observes gas executions at the Treblinka, one day after witnessing similar deaths at Belzec.**

• **August 21, 1942: 3500 Jews from Mińsk Mazowiecki, Poland, are mur-** dered at Treblinka. • **The Jewish community at Ozorków, Poland, is murdered.**

• **August 22, 1942: Ten thousand Jews from Wieluń, Poland, are deported to the Chelmno death camp.** • **Ten thousand Jews from Siedlce, Poland, are murdered at the Treblinka death camp.** • **The Jewish**

Jewish children were sometimes hidden in Roman Catholic monasteries and convents. (Often church officials would not take them unless they did convert.) Pictured are Jewish children of the *Soeurs de Sainte Marie* convent school in the Belgian village of Wesembeek-Oppem. Included is Sara Lamhaut, who survived the war under the name Jeannine van Meerhaegen. Both of Sara's parents died at Auschwitz in 1943.

Father Bruno, a Belgian priest, saved several Jewish children from the Nazis. Among them were *(left to right)* Henri Zwierszewski, George Michaelson, Willy Michaelson, Henri Fuks, and Willy Sandorminski. Father Bruno risked his life to rescue these children. After the war Yad Vashem recognized him as "Righteous Among the Nations."

Jews of Belgium

The capitulation of Belgium to Germany on May 28, 1940, brought approximately 65,000 Jews under Nazi domination. Tragically, many of these Jews had previously fled from Germany and Austria, thinking they had found a safe haven. For most such Jews, the Nazi shadow of death could not be avoided.

At the beginning of the occupation, Jewish businesses and individuals were registered. In 1941 formal Jewish councils (*Judenräte*) were created. When Jews were ordered to wear yellow badges in May 1942, the lack of cooperation on the part of Belgian officials enabled many Jews to go into hiding.

Against a wave of opposition, the deportation of Jews from Belgium began in the summer of 1942. Public protests raised on behalf of the Jews, coupled with the intervention of Belgium's queen mother, forced the Nazis to focus their efforts on the thousands of foreign Jews living in Belgium. While many Belgian Jews went underground, others were deported from Belgian soil to the gas chambers at Auschwitz—more than 16,000 from August to October 1942.

By the time the killings at Auschwitz ended in October 1944, approximately 29,000 of the Jews who had been living in Belgium when the Germans captured the country were dead.

community from Losice, Poland, is liquidated at the Treblinka death camp.

• **August 24, 1942:** Jews are locked in a church at Lask, Poland, and killed. Among the victims are a mother and her baby, who is born inside the church. • At Zduńska Wola, Poland, 1100 Jews are herded to the local

Jewish cemetery, where all but about 100 are shot and beaten to death. Survivors are forced to bury the victims. • At the Treblinka death camp, a deranged, young Jewish woman is discovered hiding a small child beneath the bedsheet she wears. Camp guards shoot and kill both the woman and the child.

• **August 24–28, 1942:** Ten thousand Jews from Nowy Sacz, Poland, are deported to the Belzec extermination camp.

• **August 26, 1942:** After being unloaded at the Treblinka death camp, a Jew named Friedman uses a razor blade to cut the throat of a Ukrainian guard. SS guards retaliate by immedi-

Breendonck

The concentration camp at Breendonck, Belgium, was a primary internment point for Jews in Occupied Belgium. Located about 15 miles south of Antwerp, it was a moated fortress that dated from the early 1900s.

The Nazis turned Breendonck into a place of internment in the summer of 1940, adding cells, gallows, barracks, a torture chamber, a site to drown prisoners and another to bury them alive, and quarters for the camp's SS and *Wehrmacht* overseers. The prisoners' food and living conditions were execrable, and extreme physical cruelty was encouraged by the camp's head of forced labor, Artur Prauss.

On September 24, 1942, Rabbi Dr. Salomon Ullman—chief Jewish chaplain of the Belgian military since 1937—was sent to Breendonck as a warning to resisters. Ullman was released after 15 days; other Jewish detainees were not as fortunate. When deportations of Jews from Belgium began in 1942, many Jewish prisoners held at Breendonck were sent to the Jewish transit camp at Mechelen before being condemned to Auschwitz.

Breendonck's Belgian location and the harshness of its administrators "distinguish" it; Jews were never held there in great numbers, but all who were suffered terribly. Between 1940 and 1944 the number of Jewish prisoners never exceeded 200, and by 1942 Jews no longer comprised the majority of inmates. The camp was liberated in the summer of 1944.

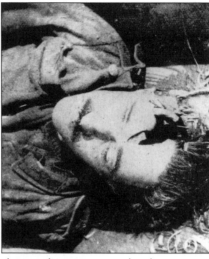

Jasenovac, the largest of the Croatian concentration and death camps, was established in autumn 1941. It became the final destination for some several hundred thousand Gypsies, Serbs, and Jews. As this man's battered and broken skull shows, the camp, run by the *Ustasa,* was especially barbaric. Thousands were murdered outright or simply starved to death as a result of the inhuman conditions. In 1942 some 12,000 Jewish and Serbian children were executed.

Founded in the 1920s, the Zionist organization *he-Halutz* (The Pioneer) taught young German and Austrian Jews the essentials of farming. After the Nazis gained power, the organization accelerated its training efforts. Once members qualified for labor permits as skilled farmers, they could obtain permission to join the fortunate few legally permitted to enter Palestine.

1942

ately opening fire on the other newly arrived deportees.

• **August 25–26, 1942:** Thousands of Jews from Miedzyrzec, Poland, are deported to the Treblinka death camp. • Nearly 1000 Belgian Jews, including 232 children, are deported to the East.

• **August 26, 1942:** 518 Jewish children deported from Paris are gassed at Auschwitz.

• **August 27, 1942:** Eight thousand Jews from Wieliczka, Poland, are killed at the Belzec death camp. • When a transport train carrying 6000 Jews from Miedzyrzec, Poland, arrives at the Treblinka extermination

The Nazis often ordered their victims to prepare bundles for their deportation journeys. In Drogobych, Ukraine, 3000 Jews were ordered to prepare for resettlement and subsequent work in the Pripet Marshes. Their bundles *(pictured)* never made it onto the train. The 3000 Jews were shipped not to the Pripet Marshes but to the gas chambers at Belzec.

This secretly taken photograph shows a transport train at the station at Siedlce, Poland. This station was along one of the major routes between Warsaw and Treblinka, and many of the Jews deported during the liquidation of the Warsaw Ghetto passed through the station. The Nazis tried to select out-of-the-way places for such activities in order to keep them secret from the local population. But invariably some civilians knew what was going on.

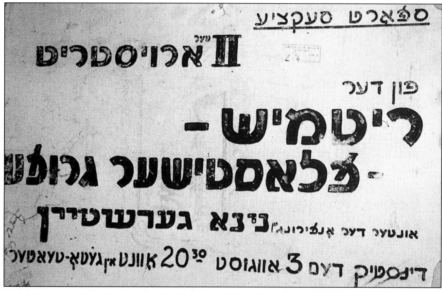

While some Jews, such as Abba Kovner, sought to organize an underground resistance within the Vilna (Lithuania) Ghetto, others engaged in a different kind of community resistance. Struggling to maintain the spirits of fearful ghetto residents, Jews in Vilna organized a variety of community cultural activities. This poster, from August 1942, invites the community to attend a performance of the rhythmics and plastic arts group directed by Nina Gerstein.

---

camp, guards discover that all 6000 have died of suffocation during the 75-mile journey. • Several thousand Jews from Chortkov, Poland, are assembled in the town square and forced to witness the murders of the community's children; *See* August 28, 1942. • The Soviet defense of Stalingrad stiffens as the German siege intensifies.

• **August 27–28, 1942:** Fourteen thousand Jews are killed at Sarny, Ukraine.

• **August 28, 1942:** World Jewish Congress (WJC) President Stephen S. Wise receives a cable from Swiss WJC representative Gerhart Riegner regarding the "Final Solution." Wise elects to suppress the information until it can be verified; *See* mid-November 1942. • Ten thousand Jews are murdered at Miedzyrzec, Poland. • Jews of Chortkov, Ukraine, are put into freight cars and transported to the death camp at Belzec. • German authorities order the arrests of Parisian priests who have sheltered Jews.

Franz Stangl

An Austrian policeman who rose to the rank of SS captain, Franz Stangl commanded two of the six Nazi extermination centers in Poland: Sobibór and Treblinka.

Under Stangl's supervision, Sobibór opened in early May 1942. By the end of July, about 100,000 Jews had been killed there. Meanwhile, Stangl went to Treblinka. Between 750,000 and 870,000 Jews were gassed there, most of them during Stangl's administration, which lasted from September of 1942 until the following August.

After the war Stangl fled to Brazil. In 1967 he was arrested, extradited to Germany, tried for his crimes, and sentenced to life imprisonment. Journalist Gitta Sereny interviewed him in 1971. "Do you think that that time in Poland taught you anything?" she asked Stangl on June 27. "Yes," he replied. "That everything human has its origin in human weakness." Less than 24 hours later, Stangl died of heart failure.

On August 25–26, 1942, Jews of Miedzyrzec Podlaski, Poland, were boarded onto cattle cars and deported to Treblinka. One of the jammed trains arrived with over 80 percent of the passengers dead from suffocation. Abraham Jacob Krzepicki, a Jew who worked in the Treblinka death factory, remembered one of the "survivors": "Among those living I found a baby, a year or a year and a half old, who had woken up and was crying loudly. I left him by the side. In the morning he was dead."

Elderly deportees from the German city of Wiesbaden await the train that will transport them to an unknown location in the East. The deportation of the 1006 "full-blooded" Wiesbaden Jews began in March 1942. In addition to these individuals, other Wiesbaden Jews were deported to the East via Frankfurt. Of the approximately 2800 members of the prewar Jewish community in Wiesbaden, only ten returned to their hometown after the war.

1942

• **August 29, 1942:** The Jewish community from Olesko, Ukraine, is deported to the Belzec death camp. • Occupation officials in the East inform Berlin that the "Jewish problem" has been "totally solved" in Serbia. Since German occupation, 14,500 of Serbia's 16,000 Jews have been murdered.

• **August 30, 1942:** Members of the Jewish community at Rabka, Poland, are murdered. • French Bishop Pierre-Marie Théas reminds his parishes that all human beings are created by the same God, Christians and Jews alike, and that "all men regardless of race or religion deserve respect from individuals and governments."

This poster is a painful commemoration of the fate of Polish Jewry during the first three years of the Nazi occupation. The Hebrew text reads, "Polish Jewry Day: September 1, 1939–September 1, 1942." No group in World War II Europe suffered as profoundly as Poland's Jews, who by their very numbers were marked by the Nazis as special targets. From the time that the German Army first occupied Poland in September 1939, Polish Jews were systematically herded into crowded ghettos, deprived of life's essentials, and subject to summary executions. Beginning in the spring of 1942, Polish Jews were deported to Nazi death facilities. Of the more than 3.3 million Polish Jews alive in September 1939, three million were dead by 1945.

EUROPE'S BORDERS AT THE HEIGHT OF NAZI POWER, 1942

By 1942 Germany had occupied most of Northern Europe, while most Southern European countries were ruled by pro-Nazi regimes. In the East, German forces advanced deep into the Soviet Union. In the second half of 1942, the Soviets began to push the Germans back.

An energetic *Führer* addresses a crowd in 1942. Such occasions grew increasingly rare soon after, as the Third Reich began to disintegrate. Failure to achieve victory on the Russian front and accelerated British bombings of German cities plunged Hitler into growing isolation and depression.

• **Late summer 1942:** SS officer Kurt Gerstein fails in his attempt to publicize his knowledge of the mass gassings of Jews. He is rebuffed in his approach to the German papal nuncio, Cesare Orsenigo.

• **September 1942:** Fourteen thousand Jews are taken to gravel pits at Piatydni, Ukraine, and machine-gunned. • Moshe Skoczylas and Michael Majtek form Jewish partisan units at Dzialoszyce, Poland. • German troops reach the Caucasus and begin exterminations of indigenous Jews. • SS chief Heinrich Himmler suggests that camp inmates be put to work in on-site arms factories. Armaments chief Albert Speer objects, offering a compromise accepted by Hitler: Himmler's inmates will be made available to Speer for labor in conventional arms factories.

• New York Congressman Emanuel Celler, a Jew, submits legislation to allow French Jews about to be deported to their deaths in Eastern Europe to immigrate to the United States. The bill is killed by the House

"Hier ist kein warum."
("Here there is no why.")

—Auschwitz guard to inmate Primo Levi, explaining his justification for preventing the thirsty Levi from sucking on an icicle; circa 1942

A prisoner at Auschwitz is left dangling on top of the barbed-wire fence after he was killed by machine-gun fire while attempting to escape. The body was left in full view for hours on end to serve as a deterrent. Prisoners were well aware that escape was nearly impossible. Armed guards and police dogs patrolled the camp, and much of the fence was electrified.

This flyer, issued by the chief of the SS and police in the Kraków district of Poland, announced that the deportation of the Jews in and around Sanok would begin on September 5, 1942. Lack of cooperation in any way would be punished by summary execution by firing squad. The deportation was a success from the point of view of the Nazis, as 8000 Jews from the Sanok region died in the Belzec death camp from September 5 to 10.

ZAWIADOMIENIE

Do przeprowadzenia zarządzonego przez SS nd Polizeiführera w Dystrykcie Krakowskim wy iedlenia żydów w okręgu sanockim, podaje si astępujące do wiadomości ogółu:

1. Od dnia, 5. 9. 1942 r. począwszy nastąp w okręgu sanockim wysiedlenie żydów.

2. Każdy, kto w jakiejkolwiek formie przeciw działać lub utrudniać będzie wysiedleniu alb przy przeciwdziałaniu udzieli pomocy, będzi rozstrzelany.

3. Każdy, kto podczas wysiedlania przyjmi lub przechowa żyda, będzie rozstrzelany.

4. Każdy, kto bez zezwolenia wejdzie do mie szkania wysiedlonego żyda, będzie jak plondrownik rozstrzelany.

5. W czasie wysiedlania zakazane jest przysta wanie na ulicach; okna należy trzyma zamknięte.

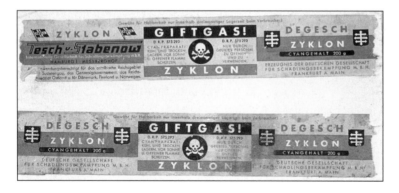

Zyklon B, the commercial name for hydrogen cyanide, was the Nazis' killing agent of choice. Zyklon B was first used to exterminate the mentally ill under the auspices of the T-4 program. In 1941 Soviet POWs held at Auschwitz were killed with the lethal gas, and by 1942 Zyklon B had become the preferred method for killing large numbers of people. Within minutes after being placed in a sealed room filled with hundreds of people, the gas would kill every occupant.

1942

Committee on Immigration. • As Jews are being deported from France to their deaths in the Third Reich, the Vichy Ministry of Information urges the press to remember "the true teaching of Saint Thomas and the Popes...the general and traditional teaching of the Catholic Church about the Jewish problem."

• Early September 1942: An SS guard on a deportation train headed for the Belzec death camp shoots and kills Jadzia Beer, a Polish girl from Jaworów, after her skirt becomes caught in a railcar window and she dangles helplessly from the window.

• September 1, 1942: Thousands of Jews from Stry, Ukraine, are mur-

The Holocaust in the Balkans

The story of the Holocaust in the Balkans is complex as well as tragic. While more than 550,000 Jews from Romania, Yugoslavia, Greece, and Bulgaria were killed, the circumstances surrounding their deaths and chances for individual survival varied from country to country.

The killing operations in Romania were particularly barbarous. German, Romanian, and Ukrainian forces swept through the Romanian territories of Bukovina and Bessarabia, slaughtering every Jew within their grasp. The city of Odessa in Transnistria (a Ukrainian territory acquired by Germany and Romania in 1941) was home to 180,000 Jews. In February 1942, however, it was proclaimed "cleansed of Jews."

In the traditional Romanian territories known as the Regat, the campaigns against the Jews followed a typical pattern: anti-Jewish violence, property seizures, and the creation of ghettos. A conflict between the Romanian government and the Germans, however, limited the number of Jews deported to Belzec. All told, upwards of 420,000 Romanian Jews perished during the Holocaust.

With the division of Yugoslavia in April 1941, Jews in the territory became governed by Hungary, Italy, Germany, Bulgaria, and the independent state of Croatia, led by the Fascist Ante Pavelić. After Pavelić's *Ustasa* movement gained power with the help of Hitler, the

Croats slaughtered more than a half-million Serbs (including the child pictured) and moved against the Jews as well. More than 80 percent of Yugoslavia's 80,000 Jews were murdered by the Nazis and the *Ustasa*.

The fate of Greek Jewry hinged on the Italians. When Italy capitulated to the Allies in September 1943, German troops occupied Greece. Although deportations to Auschwitz were delayed until March 1943, 80 percent of Greece's Jewish population was killed.

The only Balkan-Jewish communities that sidestepped the Nazi whirlwind were located in Bulgaria. Bulgarian government officials were generally antisemitic but opposed the murder of Jews, and thus resisted German demands to initiate deportation procedures. Ultimately, however, the Bulgarian government agreed to deport the approximately 9000 foreign Jews who lived in areas acquired from the division of Greece. However, aggressively public, pro-Jewish campaigns mounted by physicians, writers, attorneys, and members of the Orthodox clergy were effective in persuading the Bulgarian citizenry that the antisemitic, collaborationist plans of the Bogdan Filov government were wrong. Bulgarian officials confiscated the possessions of the nation's Jews, but 78 percent of Bulgaria's 65,000 Jews survived the war.

---

dered at the Belzec death camp.
• Security forces raid five hospitals in the Lódź (Poland) Ghetto, evacuating and slaughtering patients. Babies are thrown out of an upper-story windows, some bayoneted before they hit the ground. • A German shepherd that licks the face of a Jewish baby at the Treblinka extermination camp is savagely beaten by its SS master

before the guard tramples the baby to death. • Allied troops make significant gains in France and Italy, and Soviet troops reach Bulgaria.

● September 2, 1942: The 10,000 Jews of Dzialoszyce, Poland, are rounded up by Gestapo agents and by Polish and Ukrainian police, then terrorized while standing in the hot sun

all day. Two thousand residents are executed in the Dolles Jewish cemetery. The 8000 residents who remain are deported to the Belzec death camp. • In Oslo, Norway, Julius Samuel, the chief rabbi of Norway, refuses to go into hiding or to flee the country. He is arrested and interned in a camp at Berg, south of Oslo.

Jews in Britain and Australia

In the 1930s and 1940s, in order to keep Jews out of Palestine and because of the high degree of antisemitism in the Foreign and Colonial Offices, the British government ordered all aliens to register with the police. After France fell to the Germans, the British government ordered the internment of about 30,000 "enemy aliens" on British soil, most of whom were Jewish. About 8000 of them were deported to Canada and Australia. No matter that they were officially classified as the least dangerous of refugees; governments and native peoples treated the "enemy aliens" like pariahs.

Internment and deportations ceased only after several hundred deportees were killed when their ship, the *Arandora Star*, was torpedoed and sunk in July 1940. Jews on another ship, the *Dunera*, were abused by the crew.

The few Jews who arrived in Australia had to report to the police. They could not travel without police permission and could not own radios.

Mordechai Chaim Rumkowski *(left)*, head of the Lódź Jewish Council, confers with Hans Biebow, the German head of the ghetto administration. Rumkowski sought vainly throughout 1942 to limit deportations and to turn the ghetto into an irreplaceable factory. Unaware that deportees were sent directly to their deaths at Chelmno, Rumkowski prepared his deportation list, hoping to buy time for those remaining. By the end of September, over 70,000 people had been deported. The chronicler of the ghetto wrote on September 25: "There is [almost] no one in the ghetto over the age of 65 or under the age of 10."

On September 4, 1942, fears of a renewed deportation from Lódź came to pass when Jewish Council leader Mordechai Chaim Rumkowski announced that 25,000 Jews under the age of ten and over 65 must be resettled outside the ghetto. From September 5 to 12 alone, at least 14,000 Jews were deported in the infamous *Gehsperre* (ban on movement) action. The ghetto chronicle called this period "eight days that seem an eternity!" This photograph shows a woman and child—probably mother and daughter—kissing through the fence in the ghetto's prison.

1942

• **September 3, 1942: At Lachva, Belorussia, more than 800 Jews battle Nazis in a revolt led by Dov Lopatyn. Most of the rebels are killed. • The Geneva-based World Jewish Congress learns of deportations of French Jews. • Josef Kaplan, a leader of the ZOB (Jewish Fighting Organization), is arrested in Warsaw, joining another leader, Yisrael Zeltzer, in** detention. When another ZOB leader, Shmuel Braslav, is stopped in the street by German troops, he is shot dead after trying to pull a knife. Another ZOB leader, Reginka Justman, is shot after being stopped while carrying the ZOB's arms cache to a new hiding place; the arms are seized.

The Lódź Ghetto deportations often separated families—husbands from wives, parents from children. Saying goodbye to loved ones being deported was a traumatic experience. In the vast majority of cases, family members would never see each other again.

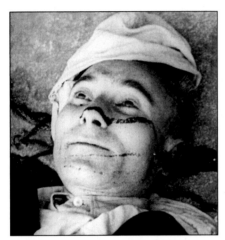

This man was among the many killed during the *Gehsperre* action in Lódź, even before the deportation to Chelmno. The action proceeded with unprecedented speed, beginning with the sick in the hospitals and moving on to the elderly and children. People were transported in five-ton trucks to the train station outside the ghetto, where they were shipped to the death camp in trains or trucks. Some were even forced to walk. Often friends and family did not know that someone had been deported until well after he or she was gone. Operation *Gehsperre* was part of a larger effort, Operation Reinhard, to kill all of the Jews in the *Generalgouvernement*.

Many of the victims of the *Gehsperre* deportations, from the Lódź Ghetto in September 1942, sought to escape their fate by fleeing. But those attempting to elude deportation were summarily shot. This photograph shows Jewish policemen—who had been promised that their children would be spared if they participated—rounding up women and children attempting to escape from the assembly point at the Jewish hospital on Drewnowska Street.

● **September 3–14, 1942: The *Times* of London runs articles describing the deportations of French Jews.**

● **September 4, 1942: Jews in Macedonia are required to wear the Yellow Star.**

● **September 4–12, 1942: Lódź (Poland) Ghetto's Jewish Council** leader, Chaim Rumkowski, acquiesces to Nazi demands for deportation of the community's children and adults who are over the age of 65. During the action, Germans fire randomly into crowds, execute individual Jews, and invade Jewish hospitals. They deport approximately 15,000 people.

● **September 5, 1942: Some 800 Jewish women at the Auschwitz-Birkenau death camp, weakened by hunger and overwork, are gassed. Later at the camp, 661 Jews taken from a Holland deportation train are gassed.**

● **September 6–7, 1942: More than 1000 Polish Jews are killed by Nazis in the streets of the Warsaw Ghetto.**

Most children had been deported from the Lódź (Poland) Ghetto by the end of September 1942. The ghetto struggled to find employment for those remaining and to find homes for the orphaned. The *Chronicle of the Lódź Ghetto* proudly reported that some 720 children had been placed with families by early December. In the latter part of 1942, a juvenile concentration camp was established for Polish (not Jewish) children, with Karl Ehrlich as commandant. Here he inspects his youthful prisoners.

William Joyce, a.k.a. "Lord Haw-Haw," was a British Fascist renowned for his Nazi propaganda broadcasts. A member of the British Union of Fascists since 1932, Joyce became disenchanted with the Union's "soft" anti-Jewish policies. In 1937 he co-founded the National Socialist League, an organization that wanted England to emulate the policies of Nazi Germany. Joyce moved to Germany in August 1939; from there he broadcast his radio program, "Germany Calling." Considered a traitor in Britain, Joyce was granted German citizenship. He was arrested by British authorities in May 1945 and put on trial for treason. He was convicted and executed in January 1946.

Leib Rotblatt was a member of the ZOB (Jewish Fighting Organization), which emerged in the Warsaw Ghetto during the summer of 1942. Members of the organization collected weapons throughout the summer in preparation for a final confrontation with the Nazis. Emanuel Ringelblum's words, written after the brutal *Aktion* of September 12, 1942, were prophetic for the ZOB. "Never shall the Germans move us from here with impunity," he wrote. "We will die, but the cruel invaders will pay with their blood for ours."

1942

● **September 6–21, 1942: Nearly 48,000 Jews from Warsaw are deported to the Treblinka extermination camp.**

● **September 7, 1942: At least 5000 Jews from Kolomyia, Ukraine, are deported to Belzec; 1000 are killed in the Kolomyia Ghetto itself.**

● **September 8, 1942: During a session of Britain's House of Commons, Prime Minister Winston Churchill remarks angrily about Nazi deportations of French Jews.**

● **September 9, 1942: Two thousand Jews are deported from the camp in Lublin, Poland, to Majdanek. • The *Times* of London reports on the Vichy**

A child in a *Ustasa* children's camp in Sisak, Croatia. The Independent State of Croatia, led by the *Ustasa* movement, implemented a full complement of anti-Jewish legislation modeled on the Nuremberg Laws. The first concentration camp in Croatia was established early in 1941. In many camps men, women, and children were strictly segregated.

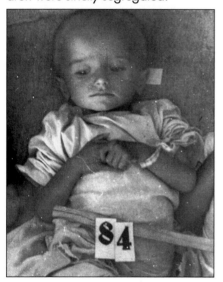

Hajj Amin al-Husseini

The Muslim grand mufti of Jerusalem, Hajj Amin al-Husseini *(pictured, left)* was a nationalist Palestinian religious leader. In the 1930s he organized Arab attacks against the British and Jews in Palestine and Iraq. Fleeing British authorities, Husseini was greeted with open arms by the Nazis in Berlin.

During World War II Husseini sympathized publicly and privately with the Nazis' antisemitism as well as with their anti-British policies. He spent most of the war in Berlin and reportedly visited several camps. Husseini obtained a promise from Hitler that after Germany conquered the Middle East, the Jews who resided there would suffer the same extermination as the European Jews.

Husseini recruited thousands of European Muslims for service in the *Waffen-SS*. He escaped trial for war crimes, and after 1946 he spent the rest of his life entertained in various Middle Eastern capitals.

Arab resentment against the British role in the Middle East increased as more European Jews sought a homeland in Palestine, requiring British troops to keep peace between Jews and Arabs. Nonetheless, some Jews and Arabs were sympathetic to the British and joined the fight against the Nazis and Fascists. Arab leader Fakhri al-Nashashibi even urged his followers to join the British Army. Here, a squad of Arabs belonging to the Palestine Regiment is shown on parade after completing six months of training.

(Occupied France) government's dismissal of General Robert de Saint-Vincent, military governor of Lyons, for his refusal to initiate mass arrests of Jews in his region of responsibility. The same edition of the *Times* reports on a German order for the arrest of Catholic priests who shelter Jews in the unoccupied zone of France.

• September 10–12, 1942: In Belgium, foreign Jews are seized in Antwerp. They are sent to a camp in Mechelen, Belgium, and then to forced labor in northern France.

• September 11, 1942: Meir Berliner, an Argentine Jew deported to the Treblinka death camp from Warsaw, stabs an SS officer, Max Bialas, to death with a penknife. In reprisal, Berliner and 150 other Treblinka inmates are executed. • At Stolin, Belorussia, Jewish resistance is led by Moses Glazer and Asher Shapira. • Five thousand Jews are deported from the Warsaw Ghetto to Treblinka. Among the deportees is noted author Hillel Zeitlin, age 71.

Jewish Combatants

Jews made significant contributions in the military effort to defeat Hitler. Estimates suggest that almost one and a half million Jewish soldiers fought against the Nazis as members of Allied military units.

Eminently motivated, Jews served in proportionately much greater numbers in every Allied country than their percentage of the total population. United States forces included 550,000 Jews from a total American-Jewish population of 5,500,000. That constituted a military representation of ten percent, when

Jews made up less than three percent of the total American population.

American Jews fought in every theater of the war, some flying bombing missions over Germany before the arrival of U.S. ground forces. About 8000 American Jews died in fighting, and thousands more were wounded.

In the Soviet Union, Jewish submarine Captain Israel Fisanovich stalked German shipping in the Arctic and sank many ships. Spirited Cossack commander General Lev Dovator contributed to the stalling of the German offensive in southern Ukraine, which had been pushing toward the oil fields of the Caucasus.

British Army units included about 30,000 Jewish volunteers from Palestine, 5000 of whom served in the Jewish Brigade, which saw action in Italy in 1944. It was the only unit in World War II to fight under the Jewish flag.

Ada Levi, a Jew, of Bologna, Italy, received forced-labor notification No. 307. It was signed by the prefect of Bologna, president of the Provincial Council, on September 14, 1942. Although the Italian government treated Jews better than the Germans—indeed, better than the Vichy French government—Jews were nevertheless required to provide labor.

Forced labor was a common characteristic of the German occupation of Poland. This labor pass of September 15, 1942, was awarded to Chaim Jakub Hallsweder by the *Judenrat* of Bochnia, Poland. Less than two months later, the Germans attacked the ghetto, killed dozens of Jews, and sent hundreds of others to the Belzec death camp.

1942

• **September 12, 1942:** More than 4800 Polish Jews are deported from Warsaw to the Treblinka extermination camp. A young Jew named Abraham Jakób Krzepicki escapes from Treblinka and makes his way to Warsaw, where ghetto historian Emanuel Ringelblum sees that Krzepicki's eyewitness camp testimony is taken down; *See December 1, 1950.* • The German Sixth Army and Fourth Panzer Army reach the suburbs of Stalingrad, Russia. They're primed to meet the Soviets in the Battle of Stalingrad.

• **September 13, 1942:** The Jewish community at Checiny, Poland, is deported.

Although the Rabbinate was abolished in the Lódź (Poland) Ghetto in September 1942, Jews continued to observe the religious holidays, and the chairman of the Jewish Council, Mordechai Chaim Rumkowski, took on the task of performing marriages. Here, the generations of the Lódź Ghetto join in observance of the High Holy Days as an elderly Jew, holding his prayer book and wearing a tallit, sits with a young man, perhaps his grandson.

Dietrich Bonhoeffer was a German Protestant theologian who actively opposed the Nazi regime. Along with Martin Niemöller and Karl Barth, Bonhoeffer founded the Christian Resistance movement known as the Confessing Church. Bonhoeffer's attempts to smuggle Jews to Switzerland in 1942 led to his imprisonment in the Flossenbürg concentration camp, where he was executed by hanging on April 9, 1945.

Sonderkommando prisoners burn bodies at Auschwitz. When there were too many corpses for the ovens and/or when the ovens failed, other means of disposing of Jewish corpses were used. The death camp at Sobibór had gas chambers but no crematoria ovens.

• **September 15–16, 1942:** Members of the Kalush, Ukraine, Jewish community are deported to the Belzec death camp.

• **September 15–21, 1942:** The Jewish community from Kamenka, Ukraine, is murdered at the Belzec death camp.

• **September 16, 1942:** Six thousand Jews from Jedrzejów, Poland, are murdered at the Treblinka death camp.

• **September 18, 1942:** Food rations are dramatically reduced for Jews throughout Greater Germany.
• Reich Minister of Justice Otto Thierack and SS chief Heinrich

Himmler agree that Jews and selected other camp inmates will be transferred to SS custody for *Vernichtung durch Arbeit* (extermination through work); i.e., hard labor until death.

• **September 21, 1942:** Open-pit burning of bodies begins at Auschwitz in place of burial. The decision is

System of Death

"Men to the left! Women to the right!" In his classic Holocaust memoir, *Night*, Elie Wiesel recalls that an SS man barked those orders as Hungarian Jews left the railroad cattle cars that transported them to Auschwitz-Birkenau in the spring of 1944. "Form fives!" Wiesel heard, as a selection began to determine who would go to the gas chambers.

Such commands were part of death-camp methodology, a system invented by Nazis who became specialists in the destruction of Jewish life. The killing centers at Chelmno, Belzec, Sobibór, Treblinka, and Majdanek, as well as Birkenau, combined to make 1942 the most catastrophic year of the Holocaust.

The destruction process varied from place to place, but the similarities increased the "Final Solution's" efficiency. As 1942 unfolded, packed rail transports regularly brought European Jews from ghettos and transit camps to the Nazi killing centers in Poland. When the trains reached their destinations, the dead had to be separated from the living. Next, those unable to walk were culled out and shot so that foot traffic on paths to the gas chambers could move more rapidly.

The more-or-less able-bodied were segregated by sex, which split up families. Babies and small children remained with their mothers. At Belzec, Sobibór, and Treblinka, no further selection took place (except for a few people who were selected to work in the camp). Within hours virtually all arrivals in those three camps were gassed after giving up valuables, clothes, and hair.

At Auschwitz *(pictured)*, which was a huge slave-labor camp as well as a killing center, the *Selektion* was more detailed. Under the supervision of SS physicians such as Dr. Josef Mengele, and depending on the camp's needs,

smaller or larger numbers of healthy men and women between the ages of 18 and 40 were singled out for "extermination through work." The new laborers were sheared, tattooed, registered, inadequately clothed, starved by meager food, sleep-deprived, sickened by deficient sanitation, condemned to exhausting labor, demoralized and sometimes tortured by their captors, and always endangered by further selections. During work hours, they confronted a brutal routine that racked body and spirit to the breaking point. Relatively few survived.

At Majdanek and Auschwitz, those who failed the selection for slave labor walked on toward death. After their clothes and valuables were stripped away and their hair was shorn, they were gassed. Before their bodies were burned, gold fillings were harvested. After cremation, ashes that were not dumped in ponds or rivers became fertilizer.

This process produced huge amounts of booty. The system ensured that nothing was wasted—except, of course, millions of Jewish lives.

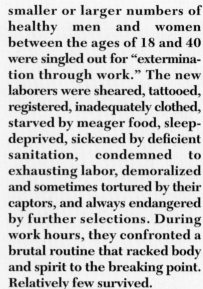

1942

made to dig up and burn those already buried (107,000 corpses) to prevent the fouling of ground water and to hide evidence of atrocities.

• September 22, 1942: The Jewish ghetto in Czestochowa, Poland, is liquidated; 40,000 residents are transported to the Treblinka death camp and killed. • The leading French Protestant, Pastor Marc Boegner, publicly protests the Jewish deportations. He personally attempts to convince Vichy France Premier Pierre Laval to end the roundups of Jewish children. After Boegner offers to have the children adopted, Laval tells him that "not one of them must remain in France."

This badge of a Jewish policeman in the Czestochowa (Poland) Ghetto was issued by the local Jewish Council. When the ghetto was liquidated in September 1942, nearly 40,000 Jews were deported to the Treblinka death camp. This massive operation spawned a resistance movement that engaged in successful operations against the German Army.

BEKANNTMACHUNG

Betrifft:
Beherbergung von geflüchteten Juden.

Es besteht Anlass zu folgendem Hinweis: Gemäss der 3. Verordnung über Aufenthaltsbeschränkungen im Generalgouvernement vom 15. 10. 1941 (VO. Bl. GG. S. 595) unterliegen Juden, die den jüdischen Wohnbezirk unbefugt verlassen, der Todesstrafe.

Gemäss der gleichen Vorschrift unterliegen Personen, die solchen Juden wissentlich Unterschlupf gewähren, Beköstigung verabfolgen oder Nahrungsmittel verkaufen, ebenfalls der Todesstrafe.

Die nichtjüdische Bevölkerung wird daher dringend gewarnt:

1.) Juden Unterschlupf zu gewähren,
2.) Juden Beköstigung zu verabfolgen,
3.) Juden Nahrungsmittel zu verkaufen.

Tschenstochau, den 24. 9. 42.

OGŁOSZENIE

Dotyczy:
przetrzymywania ukrywających się żydów.

Zachodzi potrzeba przypomnienia, że stosownie do § 3 Rozporządzenia o ograniczeniach pobytu w Gen. Gub. z dnia 15. X. 1941 roku (Dz. Rozp. dla GG. str. 595) żydzi, opuszczający dzielnicę żydowską bez zezwolenia, podlegają karze śmierci.

Według tego rozporządzenia, osobom, które takim żydom świadomie udzielają przytułku, dostarczają im jedzenia lub sprzedają artykuły żywnościowe, grozi również kara śmierci.

Niniejszym ostrzega się stanowczo ludność nieżydowską przed:

1.) udzielaniem żydom przytułku,
2.) dostarczaniem im jedzenia,
3.) sprzedawaniem im artykułów żywnościowych.

Częstochowa, dnia 24. 9. 42.

Der Stadthauptmann
Dr. Franke

The liquidation of the Czestochowa (Poland) Ghetto in September 1942 prompted the officials of the *Generalgouvernement* to issue a decree about harboring Jewish escapees. Jews who left the Jewish Quarter without permission were subject to the death penalty. In addition, persons who offered escaping Jews shelter, funds, or food were also subject to death. Given, however, that the Jewish population was already targeted for extermination, the stern warning was directed primarily at the gentile population.

In November 1942 more than 2000 of the Jews in Grodno, Belorussia, were removed from the ghetto and deported to Auschwitz. This was prompted, in part, by German impatience with the underground activity that flourished in and around Grodno. This photograph was snapped at the ghetto entrance, where German troops supervise Jews who have assembled with carts, bedrolls, furniture, and other items—all of which would be stolen from them upon arrival at Auschwitz.

● **Early autumn 1942:** New construction at the Treblinka death camp greatly increases its gas-chamber capacity.

● **Autumn 1942:** Workers at the Sobibór extermination camp begin to burn the bodies of the camp's victims.

● **September 23, 1942:** Hundreds of Jews from Slovakia and 641 from France are gassed at Auschwitz. • At the Treblinka death camp, 10,000 Jews from Szydlowiec, Poland, are killed. • British Home Secretary and Minister of Home Security Herbert Morrison opposes any further admission of Jewish immigrants into Britain. He fears this would encourage the French Vichy government to "dump" Jewish children into Britain.

● **September 24, 1942:** Ukrainian and German police begin firing into the Jewish ghetto at Tuchin, Ukraine. A Jewish revolt is led by Gecel Schwarzman (chairman of the *Judenrat*), Meir Himmelfarb (Schwarzman's deputy), and Tuwia Czuwak. Armed Jews

Kiddush ha-Hayyim

For centuries, many Jews responded to religious persecution with acts of martyrdom, choosing death rather than renouncing their faith through forced conversion. For centuries, Jews sacrificed their lives for their religion in an act of devotion know as *Kiddush ha-Shem* (Sanctification of the Name of God).

Although some Jews continued this ritualistic acceptance of fate during the Holocaust, there also emerged a new phenomenon, known as *Kiddush ha-Hayyim* (Sanctification of Life). As a response to the Nazis' genocidal programs, some Jewish religious leaders urged Jews to cling to life instead of willingly going to their deaths. Writing in the early months of the Warsaw Ghetto, Rabbi Yitzhak Nissenbaum declared: "This is the hour of *Kiddush ha-Hayyim* and not of *Kiddush ha-Shem* by death. Formerly, our enemies demanded our soul, and the Jew sacrificed his body in sanctifying God's Name. Now the enemy demands the body of the Jew. This makes it imperative for the Jew to defend it and protect it."

Kiddush ha-Hayyim was characterized by many different acts, from prayer to the covert publishing of newspapers to maintaining solidarity within the ghetto. In whatever ways they could, many Jews struggled to preserve their spiritual life and religious community. Rabbi Avraham Shalom Goldberg proclaimed, "Every Jew who remains alive sanctifies the Name of God among many."

This official letter from Reich Justice Minister Otto Thierack to Martin Bormann, Hitler's private secretary, expresses Thierack's favorable views on the extermination through labor policy—murdering concentration-camp inmates through neglect, abuse, and malnutrition. Among the groups targeted for extermination were Ukrainians, Poles, Gypsies, Jews, and Czechs. Thierack requests that Bormann approach Hitler for permission to carry out the discussed measures. Documents such as this demonstrate the centrality of Hitler to the Nazis' genocidal programs.

These Jews of Brody, Ukraine, many of them Orthodox, are being collected prior to their execution. In September 1942 more than 2000 Jews from Brody were deported to Belzec. Another 2500 were sent there in November. In May 1943 the Brody Ghetto was liquidated.

1942

return fire and others set the ghetto ablaze. Two thousand of the ghetto's 3000 residents escape to nearby forests; *See September 26–29, 1942.*
• German Foreign Office official Martin Luther passes on to subordinates the desire of Nazi Foreign Minister Joachim von Ribbentrop that deportations of Jews from across Europe be accelerated.

• September 25, 1942: Learning about the impending liquidation of their ghetto, some Jews of Korets, Ukraine, escape to the woods while others resist by setting the ghetto ablaze. Resistance is led by Moshe Gildenman. • Swiss police decree that race alone does not guarantee refugee status, thus preventing Jews from crossing the Swiss border to

Shmuel Kaplinski was a member of Vilna, Lithuania's United Partisan Organization, a wide-ranging alliance comprised of members from numerous youth groups. On September 23, 1942, Kaplinski helped 80 to 100 FPO members escape from the ghetto via the Vilna sewer system. Once outside of the ghetto, the group rendezvoused with the Kailis partisans, who operated in the nearby Rudninkai Forest.

An antisemitic and anti-Gaullist propaganda poster depicts French General Charles de Gaulle as the puppet of the Jews. The poster's headline reads, "The True Face of Free France." When combined with the portrait of the general standing in front of stereotypically portrayed Jews, these words clearly communicated the desired message. As leader of the Free French government-in-exile in London, de Gaulle's opposition to the Nazis was well established. The Nazi propaganda machine sought to discredit its opponents by linking them with "international Jewry."

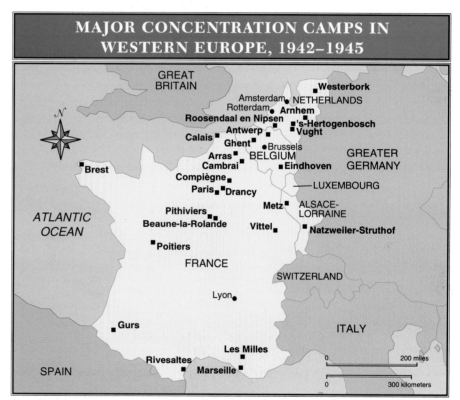

MAJOR CONCENTRATION CAMPS IN WESTERN EUROPE, 1942–1945

About 75,000 Jews in France (mostly foreign) were deported; others were confined to concentration camps. About 25,000 Belgian and 100,000 Dutch Jews were also deported, most to their deaths.

safety. • Seven hundred Romanian Jews, interned at Drancy, are deported to Auschwitz. • 475 French Jews are gassed at Auschwitz. One of the victims is ballet director René Blum, the brother of former French Prime Minister Léon Blum. • Abraham Gamzu, chairman of the Jewish Council at Kaluszyn, Poland, is executed after refusing to deliver Jews

for deportation. Six thousand of the town's residents are deported to the Treblinka death camp and later killed.

• September 26, 1942: SS Lieutenant General August Frank advises camp administrators that jewelry and other valuables seized from Jews should be sent to the German *Reichsbank*, and

that razors and other practical items should be cleaned and delivered to front-line troops for sale to them. Proceeds will go to the Reich. Further, confiscated household items are to be distributed to ethnic Germans. • Brussels Jewish leader Edward Rotbel is deported to Auschwitz. Several hundred Dutch Jews are gassed there; *See* October 9, 1942.

Hampered by the British White Paper of 1939, which severely restricted Jewish immigration to Palestine, members of the *Yishuv*, the organized Jewish community in Palestine, agonized as they learned of the deportations and deaths. Here, *Yishuv* members gather before the tomb of the prophet Zechariah on the Mount of Olives to mourn those who had died at the hands of the Nazis. The group recalled the prophet's words spoken in earlier times of persecution: "Behold, I will save my people from the east country and from the west country; and I will bring them to dwell in the midst of Jerusalem; and they shall be my people and I will be their God." (Zec 8:7–8, RSV).

This false identity card was issued to David Donoff in September 1942. The Donoff family engaged in forgery operations for the Jewish Resistance in France. All seven siblings of the Donoff family were members of a Resistance organization known as *Éclaireurs israélites de France*. Of the seven siblings, the two brothers were killed for participating in Resistance operations; the five sisters survived the war.

This obviously staged photograph shows Jews beating Jews in the Kolbuszowa (Poland) Ghetto. The Nazis used such propaganda photos to establish that Jews were animals who often turned on each other, just like the rats to which the Nazis often compared them. The implication was clear: If the Jews did not care about themselves, why should the German people care about them?

1942

● **September 26 and 28, 1942:** German railway officials meet in Berlin to plan track upgrades and additional trains in order to hasten deportations of Jews.

● **September 26–29, 1942:** Search parties of German and Ukrainian police capture 1000 of 2000 Jews who escaped from the Tuchin (Ukraine)

Ghetto on September 24. Some Jews are taken to Tuchin's Jewish cemetery and shot, while most are killed where they are found in the forest; *See* September 27, 1942.

● **September 27, 1942:** Three hundred cold and hungry women and children, part of the 1000 Jews still at large following a September 24

In July 1942 the Nazis began to deport foreign Jews living in Paris to Auschwitz. Of the first 1000 shipped to the death camp, only 17 survived the Holocaust. Many died on the journey, which took three days. One of the survivors recalled that the victims were "piled up in freight cars, unable to bend or to budge, sticking one to the other, breathless, crushed by one's neighbor's every move. This was already hell." Fourteen-year-old Denise Sternzus, pictured here, was deported from Paris to Auschwitz on September 25, 1942.

Oswald Pohl

SS General Oswald Pohl lived for loot and plunder. He was in charge of the SS Economic and Administrative Main Office. In that capacity, he controlled all of the slave labor in camps as well as the Third Reich's disposition of the possessions looted from Jewish victims of the "Final Solution," which were crucial to the German war effort.

Pohl supervised the construction of thousands of German concentration camps and extermination camps, which housed, worked, and worked to death more than 700,000 slave laborers. He was responsible for the exploitation of hair taken from Jewish victims, which were used for textiles, as well as the gold from Jewish teeth, rings, and eyeglass frames, which was passed on to the State Treasury.

After the war, Pohl was caught, tried, and convicted as a war criminal. He was hanged on June 8, 1951.

The Drancy internment camp outside of Paris was a halfway point between life and death for Jews arrested in France. During the July 1942 roundups, 13,000 foreign Jews living in Paris were arrested. A third of them were children, who were separated from their parents, mistreated, and murdered. Pictured here is a gendarmerie barracks that served to house Jews at Drancy.

---

escape from the ghetto at Tuchin, Ukraine, return to the city under German promises of safe repatriation. All 300 are shot. Of the 700 Tuchin Jews who remain at large, only about 20 will survive the war.

• September 29, 1942: 500 of nearly 800 Jews who attempt to escape Serniki, Poland, are killed by the Ger-

mans. Of 279 who reach nearby forests, 102 will perish before the end of the war.

• September 30, 1942: Hitler declares publicly that the war will mean the destruction of European Jewry.

• September 1942–January 1943: Polish Jews trapped in the Warsaw Ghetto

construct more than 600 fortified bunkers.

• October 1942: Jews are deported to Auschwitz from Holland and Belgium; to the Treblinka death camp from central Poland and the Theresienstadt, Czechoslovakia camp/ghetto; and to the Belzec death camp from the Eastern Galicia region of Poland. • In the

Kurt Daluege

Kurt Daluege was commander of the Police of the German Reich. He also became deputy protector of Bohemia and Moravia following Reinhard Heydrich's assassination. Short on intellectual abilities but a talented administrator, Daluege was a willing partner in the Nazis' "Final Solution."

Daluege, who joined the Nazi Party in 1922, became a member of the *Sturmabteilung* (SA) in 1926 and transferred to the SS in 1928. In January 1933 he was elected to the German *Reichstag.* As chief of the police department of the Prussian Ministry of the Interior, Daluege effectively transformed the Prussian police into a significant political instrument of the Nazi Party.

The activities for which Daluege is most infamous are the massacres carried out in Lidice, Czechoslovakia, in retaliation for Heydrich's assassination. For his crimes, Daluege was executed by the Czechs in October 1946.

On September 30, 1942, the Nazis deported these Jews from the Polish town of Zelechow. After marching to the Sobolewo railway station, the prisoners were loaded onto trains bound for Treblinka, where approximately 10,000 died in the camp's gas chambers on October 2. The Jews' worldly goods were confiscated by the Germans for use in the war effort.

As resources within the Warsaw Ghetto dwindled almost to nothing, contraband food and other items became unimaginably valuable. Whether consumed by oneself or used as barter, such items could mean the difference between life and death. The outraged Jewish teenager seen here is being relieved of illegal items (whether by a Jewish civilian or a Jewish policeman is unclear). In any case, the boy would have considered himself fortunate merely to have been stripped of his goods; at worst, he would have been executed.

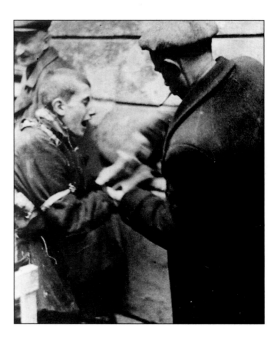

1942

Occupied Soviet Union, many Jews are killed in the streets, in forests, and in rock quarries. • At Novogrudok, Belorussia, 50 Jews escape from the Germans and join local resistance led by Tuvia Bielski. • Eighteen hundred Jews are seized at Radziwillów, Ukraine; 600 escape. All told this month, about 80,000 Soviet Jews are murdered at execution pits throughout the occupied regions of the Soviet Union.

• Fifteen deportation trains arrive at Auschwitz from Norway, Belgium, Holland, and Slovakia. • All Jewish property in Norway is confiscated. • Most Jewish escapees from the village of Markuszow, Poland, are destroyed by a German encirclement

Female members of the *Yishuv*, the Jewish community in Palestine, were encouraged to enlist in the women's Auxiliary Territorial Service unit of the British Armed Forces. The scope of World War II placed an enormous burden on Britain and other belligerents. The need for soldiers, munitions workers, nurses, doctors, and other personnel was seemingly limitless. Tremendous effort was expended to attract and recruit individuals from throughout the empire.

A bilingual poster in Hebrew and English entreated members of the *Yishuv*, the Jewish community in Palestine, to enlist in the British Armed Forces. The Hebrew text reads: "Follow in my footsteps." Throughout the Second World War, the British government attempted to enlist recruits from throughout its empire. In Palestine, however, the British had to be careful not to anger the Arab community.

A sheet of 12-*Pfennig* Hitler stamps reminds us of the ubiquitous image of the German chancellor. Hitler's presence was felt throughout German society. The Nazi propaganda machine tirelessly reinforced the link between the *Führer* and the nation. And that link was strong: The Third Reich that was Hitler's creation would not survive his demise.

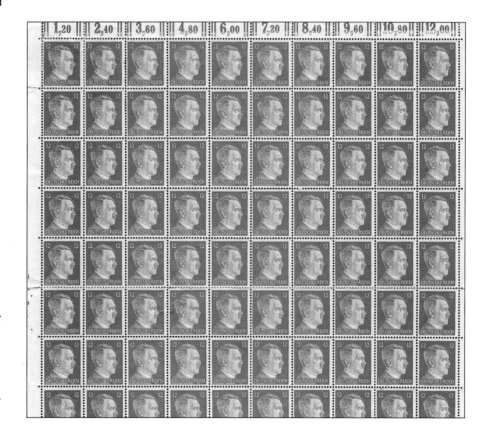

and subsequent armored and artillery attacks after five months of freedom in area forests. • As 3000 Jews are arrested at Pińczów, Poland, resistance is led by Michael Majtek and Zalman Fajnsztat. • Five thousand Jews are deported from Zawichost, Poland to Belzec. • British Vatican Ambassador Francis d'Arcy Osborne writes in his diary that Pope

Pius XII only occasionally denounces moral crimes. But such rare and vague declarations "do not have . . . lasting force and validity." Osborne points out that the Pope's "policy of silence in regard to such offences against the conscience of the world must necessarily involve a renunciation of moral leadership."

• Early October 1942: At a small labor camp at Budy, Poland, female German non-Jewish prisoners beat, mutilate, and kill dozens of captive Jewish women. When the massacre is over, Auschwitz commandant Rudolf Höss inspects the scene.

• October 1, 1942: The Chelmek slave-labor camp, located in Poland

Women Camp Guards

The SS included within its ranks female volunteers who guarded female inmates at the concentration and death camps. Relatively few in number, these women sometimes exceeded their male counterparts in cruelty.

Irma Grese, nicknamed the "Belle of Auschwitz," became a guard as a teenager and rose through the hierarchy to oversee nearly 20,000 women prisoners. Grese took special pleasure in watching the doctors at Auschwitz perform disfiguring surgeries on women.

The Ravensbrück, Germany, concentration camp for women contained a training camp to prepare women to become camp supervisors. Some 3500 women who trained at Ravensbrück served as guards there or at other camps. Hildegard Mende (*pictured*) worked at Theresienstadt. While a few guards exhibited kindness toward their prisoners, most followed the harsh camp rules, and beat and humiliated their prisoners. Few sought to intercede on inmates' behalf. Some guards even competed with one another in cruelty, believing that was the route to promotion and respect from their male superiors.

One prisoner reported that women were even worse than men in commanding their dogs to brutally attack inmates. Another prisoner attested that a female guard requested permission to watch the gassings at Auschwitz, a pastime she particularly enjoyed.

Extra food was, to say the least, a significant event in the daily lives of starved camp inmates. "Dividing the Bread in the Concentration Camp," a painting by Plaszów labor-camp survivor Joseph Bau, suggests the keen interest roused by unexpected windfalls.

One of the things that distinguished Orthodox Jewish men was their beards. Many, such as Rabbi Avraham Grodzensky (*pictured*), shaved their beards, violating Orthodox traditions. He likely shaved it because Othodox men were more likely to be chosen and abused, even on the streets.

1942

near Auschwitz-Birkenau, opens to house Jews draining swamps to provide water to the nearby Bata shoe factory. • In Luków, Poland, Jewish Council member David Lieberman is told by German authorities that money he has collected to ransom Lublin's Jews is useless, and deportations will continue, whereupon Lieberman tears the money to pieces and slaps the German official in the face. Ukrainian guards kill Lieberman immediately, and 4000 of the Jews Lieberman had hoped to protect are deported to the Treblinka extermination camp, where they are gassed.

• October 1–2, 1942: Hundreds of Jews escape the Ukrainian town of

The Jews of Biala Podlaska, Poland, are assembled prior to their deportation to a death camp. On June 10, 1942, 3000 Jews were shipped to Sobibór. A further 6200 were shipped to the death camp at Treblinka in September and October. Biala Podlaska had a horrific history under Nazi rule: In January 1940 800 Polish POWs had been marched from an internment camp on Lipowa Street toward Biala Podlaska. Because of winter cold and indiscriminate abuse and murder by the SS, only a few dozen of the POWs lived to reach the town.

The abandoned furniture of the Wloclawek (Poland) Ghetto is the sole reminder of those Jews who called this place home after the 3000 residents were deported on April 22, 1942. The stillness of the scene obscures the violence with which Jewish life in Wloclawek was tragically terminated.

Not all concentration-camp inmates were determined to survive. Devastated by the loss of loved ones, the inhuman conditions, and the barbarity they had witnessed, some chose to take their own lives. Others were ordered by their guards to run into the electrified fences—perhaps the case for the Dutch Jew pictured here. His life ended at the camp at Mauthausen, Austria, one of the harshest of the concentration camps.

Luboml but are quickly hunted down. In all, some 10,000 of the town's Jews are killed.

• October 2, 1942: At the Treblinka death camp, Jews from Zelechów, Poland, are murdered.

• October 3, 1942: The Polish ambassador to the Vatican details to Pope Pius XII (through a report through the secretariat of state) that the Germans have gassed thousands of Jews.

• October 4, 1942: Berlin orders that all Jews in concentration camps within Germany be deported to Auschwitz.

• October 6 and 9, 1942: Thousands of Jews from Miedzyrzec, Poland, are deported to the Treblinka death camp.

• October 9, 1942: In Brussels, Belgium, five of six leading members of the Belgian Jewish community are released from incarceration following the intervention of Cardinal Joseph-

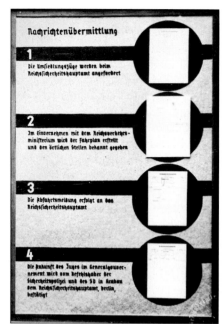

This chart outlines the appropriate forms of communication to be sent with each rail deportation of Jews. Coordinating the "Final Solution" was a tremendous logistical operation. Scheduling trains, selecting individuals for deportation, and determining where to send each shipment required a complex and sophisticated bureaucracy. It was important, therefore, to standardize the forms used to detail the shipping information that accompanied every train sent to a Nazi concentration camp or extermination center.

"One night we were awakened by terrifying cries. And we discovered, on the following day, from the men working the *Sonderkommando* . . . that on the preceding day, the gas supply having run out, they had thrown the children into the furnaces alive."

—*Marie Vaillant–Couturier, a French Resistance member imprisoned at Auschwitz*

Members of a *Sonderkommando* (special unit) burn the bodies of victims gassed at Auschwitz-Birkenau. Selected from among the prisoners, the *Sonderkommando* had to perform especially onerous tasks, including searching the dead for valuables, moving bodies to the crematoria or open pits, and cleaning the gas chambers. They received better housing and food, but these were short-lived privileges since the *Sonderkommando* members were gassed and replaced at regular intervals.

1942

Ernst van Roey and Belgium's Queen Elizabeth.

● October 11–12, 1942: Eleven thousand Jews from Ostrowiec-Swietokrzyski, Poland, are killed at the Treblinka death camp.

● October 15–21, 1942: An SS *Aktion* is undertaken against Jews of Piotr-ków Trybunalski, Poland. Many are shot in their homes and 22,000 are deported to the Treblinka death camp.

● October 15, 1942: 25,000 Jews of Brest-Litovsk, Belorussia, are murdered. Jewish resistance, led by Hana Ginsberg, attempts to fight back.

German Jews deported to the East had to leave their property behind. This photograph shows the auction of abandoned Jewish property in Hanau. The German government not only benefited from the profits brought by such sales, but, just as important from an ideological perspective, real estate was "Aryanized." The ability to purchase Jewish property at rock-bottom prices encouraged the local population to support the deportations.

Edwin Chwedyk was issued this identification bracelet, a leather strap with a metal tag and buckle, while imprisoned in the Majdanek concentration camp in Poland. After Chedwyk contracted typhoid, he was sent home; he died a short time later.

Odilo Globocnik

Odilo Globocnik headed Operation Reinhard, the plan to exterminate the Jews of the *Generalgouvernement*. Born in Trieste, Globocnik joined the Nazi Party in 1931, became a member of the SS in 1934, and was appointed SS and police leader for Poland's Lublin district by Heinrich Himmler in 1939. His scandalous past (illegal currency dealings) and virulent anti-semitism made him an ideal choice to head Operation Reinhard.

Globocnik founded the death camps at Belzec, Sobibór and Treblinka to facilitate the liquidation of Polish Jewry. His brutally efficient operations were so successful that the Nazis were able to shut down those camps in late 1942 and 1943.

Although Globocnik greatly enriched himself with the valuables stolen from the Jews, he too met an early death. Shortly after being captured by a British patrol in May 1945, Globocnik committed suicide by swallowing cyanide.

• **October 16, 1942:** The Nazis arrest more than 1000 Jews in Rome and deport them to Auschwitz.

• **October 17, 1942:** 1600 Jews from Buczacz, Ukraine, are murdered at the Belzec death camp. • 405 Jews held in the Buchenwald and Sachsenhausen, Germany, concentration camps are deported to Auschwitz.

Austrian-Jewish opera librettist Fritz Beda is among those deported from Buchenwald.

• **October 18, 1942:** Hitler issues *Kommandobefehl* ("Commando Order"), authorizing immediate execution of captured Allied Special Operations personnel, whether in or out of uniform.

• **October 20, 1942:** Twelve thousand Jews are murdered at Bar in the Transnistria region of the Ukraine.

• **October 22, 1942:** Icek and Fraidla Dobrzyńska, Jewish parents of two children who had been deported from Poland's Lódź Ghetto in September 1942, commit suicide.

Jewish Response in U.S.

When news reports about the mass murder of Eastern European Jews first reached the United States, the American Jewish community was ill prepared to deal with the impending tragedy. The lack of organizational cohesiveness and the disparate character of the American Jewish community prevented a unified response to the genocidal campaigns of the Nazis.

The U.S. Jewish defense organization, known as the American Jewish Committee, used quiet diplomacy to deal with the Nazi onslaught. As the crisis in Europe escalated, the committee joined with seven other organizations to form the Joint Emergency Committee on European Jewish Affairs. This group submitted a rescue proposal to the Bermuda Conference and sponsored mass meetings to publicize the murder of European Jews.

The creation of the American Jewish Conference in August 1943 was an attempt to promote Jewish unity and offer a unified response to the growing disaster in Europe. The conference's focus on postwar Jewish policy, however, limited the group's efficacy.

Pictured here are Chaim Weizmann *(left)*, Zionist activist and first president of the state of Israel, and Rabbi Stephen Wise, a founder of the American Zionist movement.

Several men, probably Jews, are executed in Lvov, Ukraine, in 1942. At the time of the German invasion of the Soviet Union, there were about 160,000 Jews in Lvov. When the Germans occupied the area, they turned the local Ukrainian population loose on local Jews, thousands of whom were tortured and killed even before the establishment of the ghetto. In December 1942 the Lvov Ghetto was liquidated, with most of its Jews sent to the Belzec extermination camp.

German Order Police humiliate Jews during an *Aktion* in Luków, Poland, in 1942. Almost 4000 Jews were murdered during the liquidation of the ghetto on May 2, 1943. Obvious Jewish symbols—such as prayer shawls, yarmulkes, and beards—made Jews seem "more Jewish" and left them especially vulnerable to German assault.

1942

● **October 23, 1942:** The Battle of El Alamein begins in Egypt; *See* November 2, 1942. • Algerian-Jewish resistance leader José Aboulker meets with American General Mark Clark in Morocco. Aboulker is given 800 Sten guns, 800 grenades, 400 handguns, and 50 portable radios; *See* November 8, 1942.

● **October 24, 1942:** 252 friends and relatives of persons from Lidice, Czechoslovakia, are murdered at the camp at Mauthausen, Austria, in reprisal for the assassination of Reinhard Heydrich.

● **October 25, 1942:** Male Jews in Norway are arrested and sent by sea to Szczecin, Poland, then by rail-

Although the Nazis employed threats and violence to destroy the underground press, courageous residents of the Warsaw Ghetto persevered. In this pamphlet illustration, a youthful Jewish fighter aims his gun at a Nazi officer. Hoping to instill defiance and fan the flames of resistance, the pamphlet proclaimed: "Nazis dare not travel alone in the streets."

The Ukrainian town of Mizoch contained a relatively small ghetto of 1700 Jews. But when the Germans attempted to liquidate the ghetto in mid-October 1942, they met a brief but determined resistance from the inhabitants. In the end the ghetto was successfully liquidated. Among those executed south of the nearby town of Rovno by Ukrainian and German police were these naked Jewish women, a few of whom were holding infants. Often, babies were not shot but were buried alive with their mothers.

Some victims of Nazi *Aktionen* survived the final shooting. This photo shows one of the German policemen shooting women who were still alive after the mass execution of Jews in Mizoch, Ukraine. It was not unusual for the perpetrators to take photos such as this one. A German policeman named Hille, who took this photo and others, gave them to a lawyer in Czechoslovakia, where Hille had settled after the war. In 1946 the Czech government seized the photos, which eventually became public.

car to Auschwitz; *See* November 25, 1942. • Germans demand that Oszmiana, Lithuania, give up 400 of its 1000 Jews. The selection of the victims is assigned to the Jewish police in the nearby city of Vilna. Vilna Ghetto leader Jacob Gens decides to hand over Oszmiana's elderly Jews in order to save the others.

• October 27, 1942: Three thousand Jews are deported from Opoczno, Poland, to the Treblinka death camp. A few who escape to forests nearby form a partisan group, the Lions.

• October 27–28, 1942: Seven thousand Kraków, Poland, Jews are deported to Belzec; 600 are killed in Kraków.

• October 28, 1942: The first transport from Theresienstadt, Czechoslovakia, arrives at Auschwitz. • Sixteen thousand Jews are murdered at Pinsk, Poland. • Mieczyslaw Gruber, a Jewish former soldier in the Polish Army, escapes with 17 others from a Nazi POW camp on Lipowa Street in Lublin. The group will later establish a partisan group in the forest north-

The deportation of the 22,000 Jews of Piotrków Trybunalski, Poland, began in the early morning hours of October 14, 1942. In the process 1000 Jews, most of them too sick to get out of bed, were shot. The remaining Jews were shipped to Treblinka, where those who did not die on the journey perished in the gas chambers.

Units of the regular military services often participated in deportations. Here, *Luftwaffe* troops round up a group of Orthodox Jews in the Polish town of Szczebrzeszyn. On October 21, 1942, Szczebrzeszyn's remaining Jews, about 1000 of them, were transported to Belzec. In addition, the Germans forced between 400 and 500 Jews from their hiding places and summarily shot them. The town's gentile population, threatened with death if they hid Jews and tempted by offers of rewards for handing them over, helped the Germans find Jews who had concealed themselves.

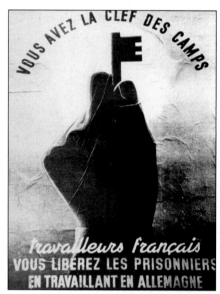

A German propaganda poster exhorts French workers to go to Germany. The appeal states: "You hold the key to the camps. French workers, you can liberate French prisoners (of war) by working in Germany." The message refers to the agreement between the Vichy government and Germany whereby a French POW would be released for every French laborer who volunteered to work in Germany.

1942

west of the city. • The SS issues a secret directive that mittens and stockings confiscated from Jewish children at death camps be gathered and sent to SS families.

• Jewish Warsaw Ghetto leaders ask Jan Karski, a Polish Catholic working for the underground, to tell the Polish and Allied governments: "We are helpless in the face of the German criminals.... The Germans are not trying to enslave us as they have other people; we are being systematically murdered.... Our entire people will be destroyed...."

• October 29, 1942: Written comments by Winston Churchill excoriating Germany for the systematic

These Jewish women and children, carefully guarded by Germans, board a train bound for the Treblinka death camp. They were among the 10,000 Jews from Miedzyrzec Podlaski deported to Treblinka during October 1942, a month that was among the bloodiest in the camp's history. Many of Miedzyrzec Podlaski's Jews died on the horrific train ride to Treblinka, rather than in the camp's gas chambers.

Ordnungsdienst

The *Ordnungsdienst* (order service) served as the police arm of the *Judenrat* (Jewish council) in the ghettos. Responsible for carrying out the orders of the council and of the German authorities, the *Ordnungsdienst* were loathed and feared by the ghetto population—even though they were Jews.

Ordnungsdienst personnel faced excruciating moral dilemmas. Initially charged with maintaining discipline in the ghetto, including guarding workers on labor details outside the ghetto, in time the order service was expected to enforce quarantines during typhus outbreaks and carry out deportations.

Failure to deliver the mandated number for deportation resulted in harsh repercussions for both the police and ghetto residents. As one Warsaw Ghetto policeman said as he tore a child from the mother's arms: "I have a wife and three children. If I don't deliver my five heads by five o'clock, they'll take my own children. Don't you see? I'm fighting for my own children!"

Rescued from Occupied France by Varian Fry, painter Marc Chagall, pictured here with his daughter, Ida, was among those modern artists whose work was condemned by the Nazis. When the Nazis gained power, Chagall's works were removed from museums and some were held up for censure in the enormous exhibit of "degenerate art" that was held in Munich in 1937. The Nazis considered Chagall's works, as well as those by Picasso and van Gogh, inappropriate for German collections.

---

extermination of European Jews are read at a London protest meeting chaired by the archbishop of Canterbury. • In Warsaw, resistance fighters with the Jewish Fighting Organization assassinate Jacob Lejkin, acting commander of the Warsaw Ghetto Jewish police, for his complicity in deportations of Jews. • 3230 thousand Jews from Sandomierz, Poland, are

murdered at the Belzec extermination camp.

• October 29–November 1, 1942: Nearly all of the Jews of Pinsk, Poland, are murdered.

• Late October 1942: Local peasants betray six members of the Jewish Fighting Organization near Kraków,

Poland, alerting German troops to the Jews' presence. • Three thousand Jews readied for deportation from eastern Poland to the Belzec death camp are stripped naked to prevent resistance.

• November 1942: Deportations of Jews from Holland and France continue. One thousand Jews are

Nazi Medical Experiments

Criminal and completely unethical medical experimentation carried out on human "guinea pigs" by German physicians mutilated and murdered more than 7000 men, women, and children. Victims were initially taken from Germany's general population (physically handicapped and mentally ill), then from the ranks of concentration-camp prisoners and POWs.

In 1927 the Kaiser Wilhelm Institute for Anthropology, Human Heredity and Eugenics was established in Berlin to develop German "race science." Under director Eugen Fischer, the institute formulated complex race theories, and encouraged the weeding out of Germany's "genetically unfit." Later, under Nazi rule, this philosophy culminated in forced sterilization and other, even more terrible research.

Nazi scientists were curious about the limits of human endurance as well as bodily reaction to a whole catalogue of remorseless physical insult. At Auschwitz, Dr. Horst Schumann removed the testicles of young men after subjecting the organs to burning X-rays. At the same camp, Dr. Eduard Wirths and gynecology professor Dr. Carl Clauberg studied women's wombs following injections of toxic chemicals.

Ravensbrück's Dr. Karl Gebhart inflicted leg fractures on healthy, young Polish women, and freely transplanted amputated limbs from prisoner victims to patients at the SS hospital. Dr. Sigmund Rascher was posted to Dachau, where he forced "patients" to swallow Polygal 10, a coagulant designed to inhibit blood loss. They were then shot at point-blank range.

Dr. Karl Brandt, chief of all German medical services, authorized tests of phosgene- and mustard-gas poisoning that were performed at Sachsenhausen by Drs. Walter Sonntag and Heinrich Baumkötter.

Dr. Arnold Dohmen infected Sachsenhausen prisoners with hepatitis; deadly gangrene bacilli came courtesy of Dr. Ernst Grawitz, head of SS health ser-

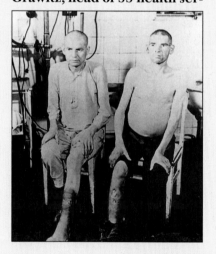

vices. At Buchenwald, Dr. Karl Genzken infected prisoners with typhus. Other physicians throughout the camp system induced yellow fever, smallpox, cholera, diphtheria, influenza, and tuberculosis. At the prompting of the *Luftwaffe*, physicians at Dachau and elsewhere killed prisoners while studying their reactions to extreme heat and cold; and to oxygen deprivation during painful experiments simulating high altitude.

Auschwitz's Dr. Josef Mengele—dubbed the "Angel of Death" by inmates—undertook particularly bizarre criminal research. He was fascinated by twins, and attempted to change victims' eye colors with chemical eyewashes; to surgically transform normal, living twins into Siamese twins; and to test comparative organ reaction after injecting chloroform directly into twins' hearts. When a one-year-old triplet fell into Mengele's hands, the child was "autopsied" while anesthetized but still alive.

Dwarfs and hunchbacks also captured Mengele's fancy. These unfortunates were studied and then murdered. The flesh of some was boiled from bones that were subsequently sent to the Anthropological Museum in Berlin. There, and at other such places, the Nazi "research" continued.

1942

deported to Auschwitz from the Drancy, France, transit camp. Nearly 5200 are deported there from the Netherlands. • The Nazis occupy Vichy (southern) France. • The Jewish *Sonderkommando* at Auschwitz-Birkenau nears completion of its task of exhuming and burning Jewish corpses buried at the camp. • The Jewish community in Vienna is offi-

cially dissolved. • The Yishuv (Jewish community in British-controlled Palestine) receives confirmation of the "Final Solution." • Klaus Barbie arrives in Lyons, France, to head a special commando in Section IV of the local Gestapo office. His instructions are to actively fight Jews, Communists, Freemasons, and members of the French Resistance.

Jewish inmates at the concentration camp in Berg, Norway, line up for roll call after being arrested on October 25, 1942. Almost all male Jews who were arrested during this phase of the deportation process were brought to this camp before being sent to Auschwitz. The main deportation of Norwegian Jewry was carried out on November 26, 1942.

Jews from the Tomaszów Mazowiecki Ghetto were transported to the Treblinka death camp, and were among the first Jews to die in the camp's new gas chambers. The new units had a capacity of 3800, an "improvement" over the three original chambers, which could hold 600 people at one time.

Jews from Chmielnik (Poland) were forced into a ghetto in March 1940. The subsequent overcrowding was exacerbated because Jews from beyond the region of Chmielnik were sent to the ghetto, as well. Here, Chmielnik Jews are loaded into open boxcars for deportation to Treblinka in the fall of 1942. Earlier in the year, from August 20 to 24, 21,000 of the region's Jews were shipped to Treblinka, where they died in the gas chambers.

• **November 1–6, 1942:** More than 170,000 Jews are killed within one week at the Belzec, Auschwitz, and Treblinka death camps.

• **November 2, 1942:** In the Lithuanian town of Marcinkańce, 370 Jews who refuse to board trains for deportation bolt for the ghetto boundaries. In the melée that follows, 360 Jews and many guards are killed. Between deaths and successful escapes, not one Jew is left to board the trains.

• In Zolochev, Ukraine, the chairman of the Jewish Council is murdered by Germans after refusing to sign a paper saying that the liquidation of the ghetto was necessitated by the spread of a typhus epidemic. 2500 Zolochev Jews, including poet S. J. Imber, are deported to Belzec.

• More than 100,000 Jews remaining in the towns and villages in the Bialystok region of Poland are arrested and deported to holding camps at Zambrów, Volkovysk, Kelbasin, and Bogusze before being sent to the Auschwitz and Treblinka death camps.

The Coveted Ausweis

The *Ausweis* (identification card) meant the difference between life and death, between remaining in the ghetto and being deported to the concentration or death camps.

The card indicated that the bearer was employed and therefore not simply a "useless" Jew. At least temporarily, it granted a margin of safety to oneself and members of one's family, sometimes forcing the permit holder to make impossible choices about whom to include. Gaining a valid *Ausweis* was not easy since Nazi authorities frequently changed the color of the cards, requiring new ones. Gaining a card sometimes required bribing the *Judenrat*, which distributed them, especially as the Germans increasingly limited the number of work permits.

In Vilna in October 1941, the Germans reduced the number of cards to 3000, allowing only 12,000 of the ghetto's 27,000 Jews to be saved. In the end, the Nazi quest to exterminate all Jews left no piece of paper a guarantee of safety.

Arms raised, a German tank officer surrenders to bayonet-ready soldiers of the British Eighth Army. The fierce battle in El Alamein, Egypt, was a turning point in the African campaign, as a rejuvenated Eighth Army, supplied with tanks from Britain and America, defeated the German *Afrika Korps*. For those in ghettos, the battle spelled hope of an eventual Allied victory over the Nazis and Fascists.

An antisemitic cartoon features members of a Jewish athletic club marching behind a banner that reads, "Meisel Sport Ima Talmud Federation." Blatant symbology links Jews to Freemasons and Communists. Propaganda such as this was created to reinforce the notion that Jews constituted a race, or national entity, that was fundamentally distinct from Germans. Given the German love of sport and attachment to local clubs, imagery such as this resonated with the local populace.

1942

• Six thousand Jews are deported from Siemiatycze, Poland. Resistance is led by Herschl Shabbes. • Wolfram Sievers, head of Germany's Ancestral Heritage Society, requests skeletons of 150 Jews. SS chief Heinrich Himmler okays a plan to establish a collection of Jewish skeletons and skulls at the Strasbourg Anatomical Institute in France, near the Natzweiler-Struthof concentration camp. • Allied forces at El Alamein, Egypt, send German General Erwin Rommel's troops into full retreat.

• November 3, 1942: Jewish communities of Bilgoraj, Poland, and Ostryna, Belorussia, are destroyed at the Belzec and Auschwitz death camps, respectively.

The Nazis began to deport Jews from the Plonsk (Poland) Ghetto on November 1, 1942. Rather than ship them to one of the Operation Reinhard death camps, the Germans sent them to a new death facility, Auschwitz, which would become the deadliest of the camps. Twelve thousand Plonsk Jews were killed at Auschwitz in this action.

This cap was worn by Karel Bruml during his time in Auschwitz. Bruml was first imprisoned in Theresienstadt, the "model" ghetto in Czechoslovakia. He was transported in 1942 to Auschwitz, where, because he was an artist by trade, he was forced to paint numbers on prison uniforms. A hierarchy existed within the camps: The lower one's number, the greater the privileges afforded to the prisoner. Bruml assigned himself this relatively low number.

A frame from a propaganda filmstrip depicts how relationships between Jews and non-Jews defile the "Aryan race." A major feature of Nazi ideology was racial purity. The Nuremberg Laws of 1935 explicitly prohibited interfaith marriages and outlawed sexual relations between Aryans and Jews. Joseph Goebbels's propaganda empire worked overtime to create graphic visual imagery that portrayed the dangers of "race defilement."

• **November 5, 1942: An SS man in Ciechanów, Poland, politely asks a Jewish woman to hand him her baby. When she complies, the trooper smashes the baby to the street headfirst, killing it. • Jewish men from Stopnica, Poland, are sent to a slave-labor camp at Skarzysko-Kamienna, while 400 old people and children are shot in the town cemetery. Three** thousand others are put on a forced march; many are shot along the way, and survivors are sent to Treblinka. • Peasants in Siedliszcze, Poland, gather scythes in anticipation of the day's roundup of Jews, for which they'll be paid for each Jew caught.

• Six hundred Jews from Borislav, Poland, are deported naked to prevent resistance. • 745 Jews, including 35 residents of the Rothschild Old Age Home, are deported from Paris to Auschwitz. After arrival, Jews awaiting entry into the gas chamber spy a truck loaded with corpses but continue on to their deaths.

• **November 5–11, 1942: 1060 Greece-born Jews in and around**

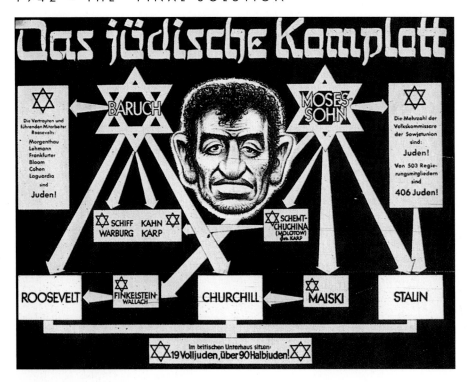

"The Jewish Plot" implicates the three powers aligned against Germany—the United States, Britain, and the Soviet Union—as pawns of the "international Jewish conspiracy." To the left of "Baruch" is a list of Jews labeled as "trusted" aides of U.S. President Franklin Roosevelt. To the right of "Moses-Sohn" is a caption that says, "The majority of leading officials within the Soviet Union are Jews! Out of 503 government officials, 406 are Jews!"

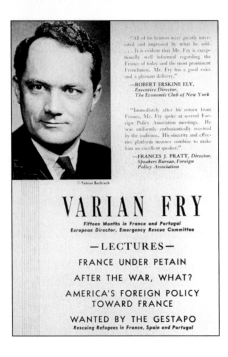

This 1942 poster advertising a lecture series in New York City by Varian Fry calls attention to France under the Nazis. An emissary of the New York-based Emergency Rescue Committee, Fry had been sent to France to arrange for the escape of some 200 prominent anti-Nazi artists and authors, many of them Jews. By the time he was expelled from France in September 1941, over a year after he entered, he had secured the release of more than 1000 people. At the bottom of this flyer on Fry are the words "WANTED BY THE GESTAPO."

An early and vocal opponent of the Nazis, Rabbi Abba Hillel Silver urged Americans to join in a boycott of German goods. He chaired the United Palestine Appeal before joining Rabbi Stephen Wise as co-chair of the American Zionist Emergency Council. Born in Lithuania and a rabbi for decades in Cleveland, Ohio, Silver parted company with Wise and others by arguing vociferously for the urgent need for a Jewish homeland in Palestine.

1942

Paris are seized and deported to Auschwitz.

• November 6–7, 1942: One thousand Jews in Drancy, France, spend the night on a railroad siding crammed into boxcars. After the train departs for Auschwitz, two Jews squeeze to safety after bars in a small window are loosened; *See* November 8, 1942.

• November 7–November 30, 1942: More than 50,000 Jews in Poland and the Ukraine are deported to death camps at Belzec, Treblinka, and Majdanek.

• November 8, 1942: The Jews from Drancy, France, arrive by train at Auschwitz, where 227 are assigned to forced labor and 773 are gassed.

A German soldier stands beside bodies of Jews murdered at the slave-labor camp at Skarzysko-Kamienna, Poland. Well after the ghettos in Occupied Poland were liquidated, the Nazis continued to ship prisoners to this work camp.

A sculpture by the American artist Gideon offers a moving image of human suffering. Gideon joined the Army at age 18 and spent much of the war in Europe. Exposure to pain and suffering profoundly affected the artist and had a marked influence on his work.

Jan Karski

A gentile courier for the Polish government-in-exile, Jan Karski took extraordinary risks to bring first-hand accounts of what was happening to Jews in Poland to the outside world.

Through contact with Menahem Kirschenbaum, a Zionist leader, and Leon Feiner, who represented the Bund, Karski—disguised as a Jew—gained entrance to the Warsaw Ghetto. His eyewitness accounts of the suffering made him a persuasive advocate. In another brave venture, Karski impersonated a guard and secretly entered a concentration or death camp. There he saw Jews being herded to their deaths inside boxcars filled with quicklime.

Karski delivered his reports to the Polish government-in-exile in London and met with British Prime Minister Winston Churchill. Driven by urgency, he traveled to Washington, where he asked President Franklin Roosevelt to act quickly to stop the murder of Jews.

• Allied Operation Torch landings take place on the Algerian coast and incidentally ensure the safety of 117,000 Algerian Jews. Algerian-Jewish resistance, armed by the United States, helps prevent a Vichy French response to the Allied landings. • In Tripoli, Libya, German occupiers press 2600 Jews into forced labor to build military roads.

• November 10, 1942: Six thousand Polish Jews who have been hiding in forests since the spring of 1942 surrender after the Germans promise safe passage to a new Jewish ghetto; *See* January 10, 1943.

• November 11, 1942: German and Italian troops occupy Vichy, France.
• Norwegian Protestant bishops in Oslo publicly protest deportations of Norwegian Jews. They state in a letter to Norwegian Prime Minister Vidkun Quisling: "God does not differentiate between people."

• November 15, 1942: The Soviet-based Jewish Antifascist Committee releases a report, "The Liquidation of the Jews in Warsaw." • In an action

Otto Thierack

First as president of the *Volksgerichtshof* (People's Court) and later as minister of justice, Otto Thierack used the law to subvert justice.

Thierack joined the Nazi Party in 1932 and became president of the People's Court of Berlin in 1936. As the nation's most feared judge, he handed down sentences with no appeal to those the Nazis declared enemies of the state. His slavish service to Nazi ideology earned him the post of minister of justice in 1942. That year, Thier-  **ack enacted Joseph Goebbels's proposal that various foreigners, especially Russians and Ukrainians, along with Jews and Gypsies, should be transferred to concentration camps and "exterminated through labor."**

A *Brigadeführer* in the SS, Thierack permitted Heinrich Himmler to remove Jews and other "asocials" from the jurisdiction of the courts and turn them over to the SS. Captured in 1945, Thierack hanged himself before his trial.

With the onset of World War II, the Nazi regime unleashed a barrage of propaganda that blamed the Jews for inciting world opinion against Germany. Traditional anti-Jewish stereotypes claiming that Jews controlled the media were exploited by the Nazis to demonstrate that the war was a product of international Jewry. Top-secret Gestapo reports suggest, however, that many Germans recognized the biases portrayed in governmental propaganda.

The German government developed extensive plans for the "Aryan" resettlement of Eastern Europe. On November 12, 1942, the *General-gouvernement* proclaimed the Zamość region the "First Resettlement Area" in Poland. As a result, about 110,000 Poles were forcibly removed from approximately 300 villages in the area. In the process, more than 30,000 Polish children, among them the one pictured here, were taken from their parents. While some of these children died in concentration camps, those deemed to have "Aryan" characteristics were given to German families to raise.

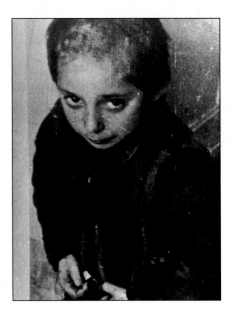

1942

led by Mayer List, two Jewish women partisans in Paris place two time bombs at a Nazi barracks window, which will kill several soldiers.

• **Mid-November 1942:** Official sources in Great Britain, the United States, and neutral nations confirm the validity of the Gerhart Riegner cable regarding the "Final Solution";

See August 28, 1942; November 24, 1942.

• **November 16, 1942:** German troops occupy Tunisia; *See* May 7, 1943.

• **November 19, 1942:** Soviet forces begin a counterattack against the Germans near Stalingrad, Russia.
• **Germans in Debica, Poland,**

In Nabeul, Tunisia, home to a thriving Jewish community of 2000 before the war, rabbis gather in prayer. As residents of a French protectorate, Tunisian Jews were made subject to Vichy racial laws, although they fared reasonably well due to the sympathetic governor-general, Jean-Pierre Estéva. Following the Allied assaults on Morocco and Algeria, German and Italian troops entered Tunisia in November 1942, bringing tolerance to an end. Tunisian Jews were subjected to forced labor, and some Jewish leaders were sent to their deaths in the extermination camps.

"November 15: A group of Jewish partisans, led by Mayer List, today placed two time bombs at the window of a German military barracks on *Rue de Vaugirard*, killing several Hitlerites while they were eating breakfast. In this action two Jewish women participated. They carried the bombs."

—*Diary entry by Parisian Jewish Resistance leader Abraham Liss; 1942*

Encircling a prisoner about to be tortured and killed, the orchestra from Janówska, a labor camp in the Ukraine, serenades him with, in Yiddish, *"Tango fun toyt"* ("Tango of Death"). The tune, composed by Jewish musicians ordered to do so by *SS-Untersturmführer* Wilhelm Rokita, also was played when the labor details left for work in the morning and when they returned—as well as during the selections of who would live and who would die.

announce that as of December 1, any Pole who assists Jews "will be punished by death."

• November 24, 1942: Rabbi Stephen S. Wise, a founder and president of the World Jewish Congress, announces at a press conference that the United States State Department has confirmed that Europe's Jews are being slaughtered by the Nazis. Wise estimates that the Germans have already murdered two million Jews, which is an understatement; *See* December 8, 1942.

• November 25, 1942: Jews in Piotrków Trybunalski, Poland, who are lured from hiding places by Nazi promises of no retribution, are taken to a synagogue, locked inside, and subjected to random gunfire by Ukrainians; *See* December 19, 1942.
• 532 Jewish women and children in Norway are arrested and deported to Auschwitz. More than 700 Norwegian Jews total have been sent to Auschwitz, although about 930 have been smuggled to Sweden.

Fate of Norwegian Jews

Numbering fewer than 2000 when Germany invaded Norway on April 9, 1940, Norway's Jews seemed an unlikely target for the "Final Solution" as 1942 began, because ships, which were scarce, would be required to send them to Nazi killing centers in Poland. That autumn, however, the German Navy made shipping available. On November 26, 532 Norwegian Jews—including children, the elderly, and ill persons taken from hospitals—were deported from Oslo aboard the *Donau.*

Rough seas delayed the dismally packed ship's arrival at the port of Stettin, Germany. The Norwegian Jews were then sent by rail to Auschwitz-Birkenau. They arrived at night on December 1. A selection process sent 346 of them to the gas chambers immediately. The remaining 186 were spared for labor, but within four months only about 20 were still alive. Fewer still survived the Holocaust.

In this relatively remote part of Europe, the Final Solution was quite thorough. In all, 763 Jews were deported from Norway. Only 24 returned. Nazi Germany and its collaborators killed about 45 percent of the Norwegian Jews. By comparison, 80 percent of Jews in both France and Italy survived.

This title page of the *Yugent-Shtime* (Yiddish for *Young Voice*) portrays a hand crushing the symbol of Nazi oppression, the swastika. Typed and duplicated in secret within the Warsaw Ghetto, the paper—the organ of the Bund's youth movement—reached hundreds of people. Its writers and readers faced death if caught.

The *Donau* steams with its cargo of Jews from Norway to Germany. In November 1942 the ship sailed with 532 Jews aboard, 346 of whom were killed as soon as they reached Auschwitz. Of the 763 Jews deported from Norway, on the *Donau* and on the *Monte Rosa,* only 24 survived the war. Meanwhile, some 900 Jews evaded deportation by fleeing to neutral Sweden. While the Norwegian church protested the deportations, puppet leader Vidkun Quisling aided the Nazis in making Norway "Jew free."

1942

● **November 27, 1942–August 1943:** More than 110,000 Poles are expelled from their homes in the fertile Zamość province so that the area can be resettled by ethnic Germans, SS troops, and Ukrainians. More than 300 villages are affected. Thousands of Polish children are deported from the area to Belzec and other death camps.

● **November–early December 1942:** Members of the ZOB in Kraków, Poland, disrupt rail lines and assassinate a German soldier, a German policeman, a German flier, two Gestapo agents, and a senior German clerk in the local Nazi administration.

● **December 1942:** Members of the Siemiatycze (Poland) Group of Jewish

Mordechai Tenenbaum was active in the Vilna, Warsaw, and Bialystok underground movements. Tenenbaum was convinced of the Nazis' genocidal intentions at a very early stage. He arrived in Bialystok, Poland, in November 1942, and eventually unified the various underground movements and acquired additional weapons. Tenenbaum's call to arms was preserved in the archive that he established to chronicle the demise of Bialystok Jewry: "Let us fall as heroes, and though we die, yet we shall live."

Showing the public hanging of a young man who tried to escape, this drawing represents the brutality of life in the Kovno (Lithuania) Ghetto. Mass killings in 1941 were followed by quieter days in 1942, a year free of large-scale *Aktionen* (deportations). Yet even in these "peaceful" days, the ghetto inhabitants daily encountered Nazi oppression. As this drawing from November 1942 shows, anyone who was caught breaking the ghetto's rules paid with his or her life.

The first "official" concentration camp in Germany, Dachau housed thousands of prisoners from throughout Europe. Overcrowding, disease, medical experiments, and unrelenting work led to a high death rate, necessitating the building of a new and larger crematorium, with four furnaces, in 1942. *Baracke X* (Barrack 10) also contained a gas chamber *(pictured)*. Disguised as a shower room, it was never put to use since the Nazis decided it was more efficient to send those judged mentally deficient or unable to work to killing sites, such as Auschwitz or Hartheim, Austria.

resisters kill a Polish peasant and his entire family as retribution for the peasant's capture and betrayal to the Nazis of three Jews. • Nazis lock 1000 Gypsies in a Lithuanian synagogue until the prisoners starve to death. • Ghetto resistance is organized at Czestochowa and Kielce, Poland. • At Brody, Ukraine, Jewish resistance is led by Solomon Halberszstadt, Jakub

Linder, and Samuel Weiler. • Concurrent Jewish resistance at Chortkov, Ukraine, is led by Heniek Nusbaum, Mundek Nusbaum, Reuven Rosenberg, and Meir Wasserman.

• Jewish Resistance leader Dr. Yeheskel Atlas, a young Polish physician, is mortally wounded by Nazi troops in a battle at Wielka Wola,

Poland. • The Jewish ghetto at Lvov, Ukraine, is liquidated. • The SS shuts down extermination activities at Belzec. • A forced-labor camp is established at Plaszów, Poland. • A *Sonderkommando* plan to escape from Auschwitz is discovered, and the inmates are gassed. • Partisan leader Hirsch Kaplinski, survivor of an August 1942 massacre of Jews at Diat-

MAJOR DEPORTATIONS OF JEWS TO AUSCHWITZ, 1941–1944

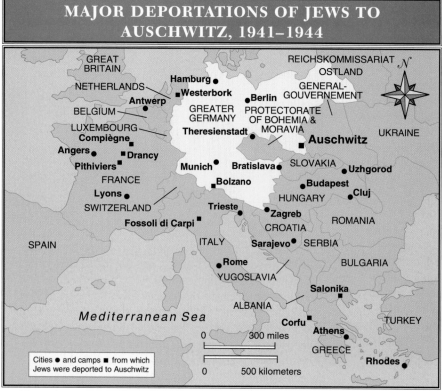

Cities ● and camps ■ from which Jews were deported to Auschwitz

More than one million Jews from all corners of Europe were deported to Auschwitz-Birkenau and killed. Nearly 440,000 Hungarian Jews died there in mid-1944 alone. Auschwitz also witnessed the deaths of about 70,000 non-Jewish Poles, 20,000 Gypsies, and 15,000 Soviet POWs.

Aharon Liebeskind was a leader of the Kraków, Poland, Jewish underground. Using the pseudonym Dolek, Liebeskind led the vocational training section of the Jewish Self-Help Society. He was also co-commander of the resistance group *He-Haluts ha-Lohem,* which attacked the Germans in December 1942. Liebeskind was killed in the subsequent hand-to-hand fighting.

Smiling prisoners at the transit camp at Drancy, France, carry large loaves of bread in early December 1942. This staged photo was taken to assure the Red Cross and Jewish organizations, as well as the French public, that inmates in the camp were being treated well. Until then, prisoners had suffered badly from malnutrition, surviving on only meager rations.

1942

lovo, Belorussia, is killed in combat during a German attack on the Lipiczany Forest.

• December 2, 1942: Jews in 30 countries hold a day of prayer and fasting for European Jews.

• December 3, 1942: Three young Jewish women who had escaped

from a labor camp in Poznań, Poland, are forcibly taken to the Łódź (Poland) Ghetto and shot. • One thousand Jews from Płońsk, Poland, are killed at Auschwitz. • Salomon Malkes, an official of the Łódź Ghetto, commits suicide after becoming despondent over the deportation of his mother.

The Nazis began the liquidation of the Lvov (Ukraine) Ghetto in December 1942. About 75,000 Jews had already been deported to Belzec before the final *Aktion* began. While the Nazis told the deported Jews that they would be put to work, the Jews realized a worse fate once they reached Belzec, which reeked of decaying flesh. "The majority knew everything," recalled one witness. "The smell betrayed it." In order to kill as many Jews as possible, as many as 800 people were crammed into a gas chamber that was only 192 square meters in size.

"Gestapo" Müller

With the nickname "Gestapo" Müller, Heinrich Müller embodied to many Germans the feared Secret State Police.

A decorated fighter pilot in the Great War, Müller afterward joined the Munich police department, becoming the department's authority on communism and left-wing movements. His zeal and knowledge of the Communist Party brought him recognition from Reinhard Heydrich, who advanced Müller's career within the Bavarian police. In 1936 Heydrich appointed him chief of Gestapo Division II and charged him with finding internal enemies of the Reich.

In 1939 Müller succeeded Heydrich as Gestapo chief, a position he held until the Nazis' defeat. A participant at the Wannsee Conference, Müller was deeply involved in the mass extermination of Jews. In October 1939 he commissioned Adolf Eichmann to begin the deportation of Austrian Jews to the Lublin-Nisko region.

Devoted to Hitler, Müller was relentless in tracking down those who had participated in the July 20, 1944, assassination attempt against the *Führer*. Müller was at Hitler's side during his last days in the Berlin bunker, but he disappeared at the end of the war. Thinly supported rumors maintained that Müller found sanctuary in South America or the Middle East.

• **December 4, 1942:** Zofia Kossak-Szczucka and Wanda Filipowicz establish Zegota, a secret name of the *Rada Pomocy Zydom* (Council for Aid to the Jews), a non-Jewish group based in Warsaw. Zegota is run jointly by Jews and non-Jews. • Three hundred citizens of Slonim, Belorussia, are killed. Another 500 escape to join local partisan groups.

• **December 6, 1942:** SS men lock 23 Christian Poles in a barn at Stary Ciepielow, Poland, and burn them alive on suspicion of aiding fugitive Jews.

• **December 6–10, 1942:** Nazis marshal troops, armored vehicles, and artillery to undertake a massive manhunt for more than 1000 fugitive Jews in the Parczew Forest in Poland; *See* December 7, 1942.

• **December 7, 1942:** German troops enter the Polish village of Bialka and murder 96 villagers suspected of shielding Jews fleeing the anti-Jewish *Aktion* in the nearby Parczew Forest. • United States State Department official G. Robert Borden Reams, an

Kurt Gerstein

Kurt Gerstein remains an enigma. A devout Christian with backgrounds in medicine and engineering, he joined the Nazi Party in 1933. Three years later he was dismissed for anti-Nazi activity and sentenced to a concentration camp.

After the murder of his sister-in-law during the "euthanasia" program, Gerstein wanted to learn the truth about such killings. He joined the *Waffen-SS* in 1941 and studied the effects of Zyklon B. Gerstein became head of the Technical Disinfection Department within the Institute of Hygiene.

However, when he was ordered to transport killing agent Zyklon B to camps, he witnessed the mass killings of Jews by carbon monoxide at Belzec. Horrified, Gerstein resolved to tell the world, approaching diplomats, church leaders, and even the papal nuncio in Berlin—but with little success.

Arrested by the French at the end of the war, Gerstein was imprisoned as a suspected war criminal. He died mysteriously, probably a suicide but perhaps at the hands of SS officers who feared his testimony.

Founder of the *Nationaal-Socialistische Beweging* (National Socialist Movement), engineer Anton Mussert sought to steer a middle path within the right wing in the Netherlands. He was grudgingly rewarded for his loyalty to the Reich in late 1942 when the Nazis appointed him "Leader of the Dutch People," a position of no real authority. Mussert was never fully trusted by the Nazi authorities, partly because he was opposed to Nazi measures against the Jews. At the same time, he was hated by his own people because he collaborated with the Nazis.

The Nazis murdered their victims in a variety of ways, not just by shooting and gassing. This Jewish man, an inmate at the Belzec extermination camp, was forced into an ice hole, where he froze to death. Many camp guards became notorious for their cruelty, trying to outdo each other in devising fiendish methods of killing their victims.

1942

"expert" on the Jews in the Division of European Affairs, advises that the United States government remain silent concerning details of the Holocaust. • British official John Cecil Sterndale Bennett is upset because Bulgarian Jewish children may be allowed into Palestine based on Jewish Agency appeals.

• December 8, 1942: Rabbi Stephen S. Wise, president of the World Jewish Congress, meets with other Jewish leaders and U.S. President Franklin Roosevelt to discuss the recently revealed plight of European Jews.

• December 9, 1942: German troops in Tunis, Tunisia, seize 128 Jews and march them to a labor camp. One

The Germans extended their antisemitic policies to the parts of North Africa under their control. These Tunisian Jews march off to engage in forced labor. Relatively few North African Jews perished in the Holocaust, however, because the Allies conquered the region before the Nazis had the opportunity to begin a systematic program of extermination.

Proudly posing in the regalia of an SS officer, Max Koegel found his career within the Nazi bureaucracy. Like many German soldiers after World War I, he had difficulty adjusting to civilian life. In 1926 Koegel served time in prison for bankruptcy and fraud, and in 1929 his frustrations led him to join the SS. He served on the staff of the Dachau concentration camp in 1933 and progressed from there through a variety of camp positions, including posts as the commandant of the Ravensbrück concentration camp and, beginning in 1942, the Majdanek death camp.

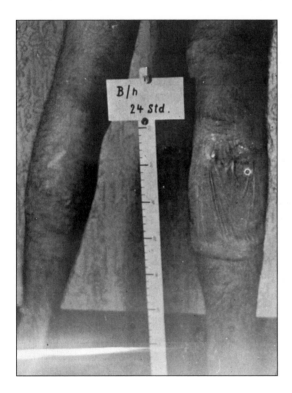

Considering their subjects only as research tools, not humans, Nazi medical experimenters put no ethical limits on their activities. As with the prisoner whose leg is pictured here, some inmates were injected with pus and toxic substances in order to generate infections on which various experimental medicines could be tested. Nazi researchers also amputated healthy limbs for transplant to soldiers who had been severely wounded. Few prisoners survived the experiments, either dying immediately or becoming so weakened and ill that they were soon consigned to the gas chambers.

young Jew who drops from exhaustion is shot and killed. • *Christian Century,* an American Protestant journal, attacks Rabbi Stephen Wise, claiming he has lied about the Holocaust in his recent press conference. *Christian Century* further argues that even if what Wise has to say is true, to make the facts of the Holocaust public serves no purpose.

• **December 10, 1942: A transport of Jews from Germany arrives at Auschwitz. • At Wola Przybyslawska, Poland, near the Parczew Forest, Nazis shoot seven Poles accused of aiding Jews. • The Polish ambassador to Britain informs Foreign Secretary Anthony Eden that the Polish government-in-exile can confirm that the German authorities are systematically** exterminating the entire Jewish population of Poland and the rest of Europe.

• **December 11, 1942: Jewish inmates of a labor camp at Lutsk, Ukraine, are informed by a Christian woman that the camp is about to be liquidiated. The Jews quickly plan a revolt;** *See* **December 12, 1942.**

In some occupied countries, Nazi racial policy found a warm welcome among scientists pursuing dubious research in eugenics. Here, just to the left of a large portrait of Vichy France leader Philippe Pétain, Louis Darquier de Pellepoix, head of the *Commissariat général aux questions juives* (Office for Jewish Affairs), delivers the inaugural address at the opening of the Institute for Anthroposociology. The Institute was dedicated to the study of eugenics and race. To Pellepoix's left stands racial scientist Count Georges Vacher de Lapouge, who, at the beginning of the century, had urged scientists to engage in breeding to improve the human race.

Admiral Jean François Darlan, commander-in-chief of the French Navy, served as prime minister in the Vichy government of Marshal Philippe Pétain from 1940 to 1942. After the reappointment of Pierre Laval as prime minister in April '42, Darlan resumed his position as head of the Navy. While in French North Africa, he played a dangerous game, urging the French Armed Forces not to resist the Allied invasion while at the same time continuing to represent the Vichy government. Regarded as a traitor by followers of both Pétain and Charles de Gaulle (the leader of the French government-in-exile), Darlan was assassinated by an opponent of the Vichy government, Olivier Bonnier de la Chapelle, in Algiers on December 24.

"A Crucified Jew on a Swastika," an ink drawing by Holocaust survivor Joseph Bau, is an unequivocal symbol of the Nazis' merciless solution to the "Jewish Question."

1942

• **December 12, 1942: Jewish prisoners at a labor camp in Lutsk, Ukraine, armed with knives, bricks, iron bars, acid, and several revolvers and sawed-off shotguns, revolt against Germans and Ukrainians. The uprising is crushed.**

• **December 13, 1942: German Propaganda Minister Joseph Goebbels complains in his diary about Italy's halfhearted persecution of Jews.**

• **December 15, 1942: Faked, upbeat postcard messages arrive at Jewish homes in Holland from friends and relatives interned at Auschwitz and the Theresienstadt, Czechoslovakia, camp/ghetto.**

The battle for Stalingrad became the turning point of the war, pitting the heretofore victorious, but overextended, German Army against exhausted Soviet forces *(pictured)* committed to defending the city at all costs. The struggle approached a bitter climax in the final days of 1942, as Red Army troops swept toward Stalingrad from the south and west. Hitler's dream of opening up the Soviet Union for German plunder and expansion was about to be dealt a crushing setback.

Gerd von Rundstedt was general field marshal and commander-in-chief of the Western Theater from 1942 to 1945. A veteran of the First World War, Rundstedt was relieved of his duties in 1938, when the leadership of the German Army was reorganized. He was reactivated during the Polish campaign, took part in operations in Western Europe in 1940, and returned east for the invasion of the Soviet Union in the summer of 1941. Although not a participant in the Generals' Plot to assassinate Hitler, Rundstedt was aware of the conspiracy and urged Field Marshal Erwin Rommel to participate.

Internment Camps in the U.S.

Paranoia and panic followed the Japanese bombing of Pearl Harbor, Hawaii, on December 7, 1941. Japanese Americans living in the western United States—including those born in the States—were rounded up at government decree, often with little warning, leaving behind their homes, businesses, and most of their belongings.

Some 110,000 people were imprisoned at ten camps, including Heart Mountain in Wyoming and Manzanar in the Owens Valley of California. Conditions at the camps were primitive and harsh. Manzanar, located west of Death Valley, was surrounded by barbed wire as well as guards on watchtowers. The crude barracks provided little relief during the intense heat of the summer or the bitter cold of the winter.

Isolated from their friends and relatives, demeaned and robbed of their rights, some committed suicide. Many young men sought to escape the camps and prove their loyalty by volunteering for service in the armed forces. Despite winning numerous medals for heroism in the European Theater, Japanese-American soldiers were told upon their return to American shores, "We don't serve Japs here." American-government reparations for these illegal internments did not begin in earnest until the 1990s.

• **December 16, 1942: A Jewish ghetto is established in Kharkov, Ukraine.** • **Germany decrees that German Gypsies must be deported to Auschwitz and destroyed.** Exceptions include former *Wehrmacht* soldiers, important war-industry workers, and those who are "socially adapted."

• **December 17, 1942: Pressure from members of Parliament, from Jewish groups in England, from the Anglican Church, from the British press, and from the Polish government-in-exile persuades the Allied governments to publish their first official recognition of atrocities in Poland.** The Allied nations—Great Britain, United States, Soviet Union, Belgium, Czechoslovakia, Greece, Luxembourg, Holland, Norway, Poland, Yugoslavia, and the French National Committee—officially condemn the Nazis' "bestial policy of cold-blooded extermination." They vow to punish those responsible. Several U.S. State Department officials try to block this declaration. All previous and following declarations neglect to mention Jews.

Stutthof

Stutthof, located in Poland about 20 miles east of Danzig, became the first camp established on Polish territory. Opened in September 1939, it began as a harsh labor camp for civilian POWs, who were later joined by Danes and others. In early 1942 Stutthof was transformed into a concentration camp and became the hub of a constellation of camps.

Jews from the Baltic states, Hungary, and other camps were sent to Stutthof in 1944. The majority were women. Many died from hard labor, starvation, and disease. Others were gassed or thrown alive into the crematorium.

As Soviet forces neared Stutthof in the winter of 1944–45, some Jews were sent on death marches; others died crossing the Baltic by boat. Many were so weak that they survived for only hours after their liberation in May 1945. About 65,000 people died at Stutthof.

Far from their homeland, Polish-Jewish refugees gather in a wooden shelter that functions as their synagogue on the Caribbean island of Jamaica. Fleeing persecution, they had reached Portugal, where the Joint Distribution Committee was able to arrange a journey for them and 150 others to Jamaica. Housed in a refugee camp, they awaited visas that would allow them to travel to the United States or various Latin American countries.

Richard Glücks was the direct supervisor of Rudolf Höss and other concentration-camp commandants. Besides selecting the site for Auschwitz, Glücks was responsible for the medical "services" rendered at the camp and the slave-labor operations that bolstered the German war efforts. He decided how many prisoners were selected for gassing and slave labor. He was last seen in a naval hospital near the Danish border; whether he committed suicide or was murdered by Jews seeking revenge has yet to be resolved.

1942

• Accepting the United States government position that the Jews being massacred by the Germans can be helped only by a total and unconditional Allied victory over Germany, the American press continues to treat the Holocaust as just another war story, and is unwilling to discuss the systematic annihilation of the Jews. Given the Allied governments' knowledge of the Holocaust at this time, waiting until the Allied Armed Forces have achieved a total victory over the Germans indicates that the Allied governments have accepted the probablility that the majority of European Jews will be killed before the Germans can be stopped. • Jewish inmates at the labor camp at Kruszyna, Poland, near Radom, attack guards

A scene from the Nazi documentary film *Between Vistula and Rhine* shows members of the SS engaged in a deportation operation in Warsaw. Notice that the image portrays the soldiers going about their duties calmly. The tremendous brutality that accompanied the roundups was not part of the propaganda films produced by the Nazis. The elimination of Polish Jewry was presented as a relocation operation, not programmatic genocide.

Even as conditions worsened within the Warsaw Ghetto, its intellectuals and artists, some seeking to perpetuate Hebrew and others Yiddish, struggled to keep culture alive. Writer, poet, and publisher Aaron Luboshitzki was a leader in the effort to further Hebrew literature. During a prolific career, he wrote textbooks, articles, poems, and plays, and established several publishing houses. He was killed by the Nazis in Warsaw in 1942.

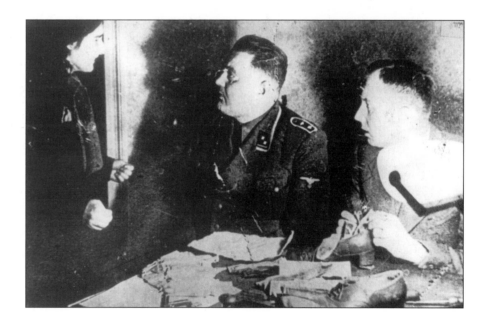

Agents from the Gestapo and *Sicherheitsdienst* (Security Police) interrogate a Jewish girl found with banknotes hidden in the heels of her shoes. Jews, deprived of their property and possessions, sought to tuck away whatever valuables they could as they prepared for deportation. Parents, fearful that they might be separated from their children, tried to give them money or gems so that they might better fend for themselves.

---

with knives and fists. Six prisoners are killed and four escape; *See* December 18, 1942.

• **December 18, 1942:** When Jewish forced laborers at Kruszyna, Poland, refuse to board trucks, more than 100 of them are shot. • British Ambassador to the Vatican Francis d'Arcy Osborne asserts that Pope Pius XII "does not

see that his silence is highly damning to the Holy See."

• **Late 1942:** Nineteen members of a Belorussian partisan group led by Tuvia Bielski are ambushed and killed by German soldiers.

• **December 19, 1942:** After three weeks trapped in a synagogue by hos-

tile Ukrainian troops, 42 Jewish men are marched to the Rakow Forest and ordered to dig ditches. They resist and are then shot. A few manage to escape. Later in the day, 560 more Jews are led from the synagogue to the forest and murdered.

• **December 22, 1942:** Nazi troops gathered at *Cyganeria*, a coffee-

The workers of the Lutsk, Ukraine, slave-labor camp were prepared for a revolt on December 12, 1942. Nazi troops who arrived to liquidate the camp were thrown back by Jewish workers, who were armed with axes, knives, acid, iron bars, bricks, and small arms. The Germans regrouped and tossed grenades at the carpentry shop for more than 12 hours. Finally, after the Nazis set the shop ablaze, about 50 of the resisters hanged themselves rather than die in the manner their antagonists intended. The resisters seen here are Lutsk-area partisans, whose own brand of defiance further preoccupied the Germans.

This women's band performed at the Vittel detention camp in France. Relatively good conditions prevailed there as long as the Gestapo sought to trade foreign nationals and Jews with valid foreign passports for German nationals held by the Allies. In spring 1944, however, Jews with valid papers from occupied and belligerent nations were shipped to the Drancy, France, transit camp. European Jews holding transit documents from Latin American countries (most of which were neutral) were sent to Auschwitz, in part because the countries that had issued the papers repudiated them.

Among the Vilna (Lithuania) Ghetto's most extraordinary accomplishments was its library. This poster from December 1942 celebrates the library's lending of its 100,000th book. Organized by the library's director, Hermann Kruk, the occasion celebrated the community's love of literature and commitment to learning even during these cruel times. Reading provided both entertainment and escape from the harshness of daily life in the ghetto.

1942

house in Kraków, Poland, are attacked by Jewish partisans. Several SS officers as well as two partisans, including partisan leader Aharon Liebeskind, are murdered during the attack.

• **December 24, 1942:** Germans mount a second hunt in Poland's Parczew Forest for fugitive Jews.

• French Admiral Francois Jean Darlan, a Vichy government political power and collaborator, is shot and fatally wounded by 20-year-old French royalist Fernand Bonnier de la Chapelle; *See* December 26, 1942.

• **December 25, 1942:** Four prisoners who escape from the Sobibór extermination camp are shot dead

The December 28, 1942, entry in the *Chronicle of the Łódź Ghetto* tersely reports: "Cold again." Here, young children and elderly Jews from the ghetto forage for bits of coal. For the inhabitants of the Łódź (Poland) Ghetto, the fierce and unrelenting chill caused even more deaths than did hunger. Within the ghetto, hopeful rumors of bread and sausage—even eggs—in honor of the Christmas holidays circulated among the populace, only to be proved untrue.

Abraham Stern, a Polish Jew who left to study at the Hebrew University in Palestine, founded the Fighters for the Freedom of Israel (FFI), a guerrilla organization designed both to promote Jewish emigration to Palestine and secure Israel's independence. Known to the British as the "Stern Gang," the FFI was widely regarded in Britain as one of the most active and extreme groups working for the establishment of a Jewish state.

The Vatican

Events in 1942 illustrate why the Holocaust provokes controversy about the Vatican and the Roman Catholic Church. The church's European network—bishops, diplomats, couriers, priests, and their parishioners—kept the Vatican and Pope Pius XII *(pictured)* informed about the fate of Europe's Jews. Nevertheless, responding to reports about deportations and mass killings that occured in 1941 and 1942, Vatican Secretary of State Cardinal Luigi Maglione regarded the news as unverified if not exaggerated.

Anxious for papal condemnation of Nazi Germany's treatment of the Jews, the Allies urged Pius XII to support a December 17,

1942, declaration entitled "German Policy of Extermination of the Jewish Race." The Vatican had protested atrocities in general, Cardinal Maglione replied. He went on to explain, however, that the Pope could not publicly condemn particular atrocities.

On December 24 Pius XII, in a veiled reference to Jews, lamented the "hundreds of thousands who through no fault of their own, and sometimes only because of their nation or race, have been consigned to death or slow decline."

Disputes about what the Vatican could or should have done during the Holocaust will be clarified but not resolved when its wartime archives are fully opened.

---

after they are betrayed by local villagers.

• December 26, 1942: Twenty-year-old French royalist Fernand Bonnier de la Chapelle is executed by Vichy firing squad two days after fatally wounding Vichy Admiral Francois Jean Darlan.

• December 28, 1942: Two Jews are shot for mutiny at the Stalowa Wola, Poland, slave-labor camp. • Dr. Carl Clauberg begins his sterilization experiments on women prisoners at Auschwitz.

• December 30, 1942: Pope Pius XII tells an American representative that he regards the atrocity stories about

Jews as exaggerations "for the purposes of propaganda."

• December 31, 1942: By this date, the German Reich has deported more than two million Jews to death camps. Hundreds of thousands more Jews have been murdered by *Einsatzgruppen* and police battalions.

1943

ALTHOUGH they rarely knew their Jewish victims' names, the Nazis intended that Zivia Lubetkin, Richard Glazar, and Thomas Blatt would not survive the "Final Solution." Nevertheless, they did, and after the Holocaust ended each wrote a book about resisting disaster in 1943.

Some 400,000 Jews had inhabited the crowded Warsaw Ghetto, but disease, starvation, and deportations to Treblinka—300,000 of them from July to September 1942—drastically reduced that number. Estimating that 40,000 Jews still lived there (the actual figure was closer to 55,000), SS chief Heinrich Himmler ordered the deportation of 8000 more when he visited the ghetto on January 9, 1943. However, the *Zydowska Organizacja Bojowa* (ZOB; Jewish Fighting Organization), led by 23-year-old Mordecai Anielewicz, launched armed resistance when the Germans implemented Himmler's order on January 18. Although more than 5000 Jews would be deported by January 22, Jewish resistance—it included hiding and refusal to report as well as violent struggle—prevented the ordered quota from being met and led the Germans to terminate the *Aktion*. The reprieve, however, was temporary.

Zivia Lubetkin helped to found the Jewish Fighting Organization, and participated in the Warsaw Ghetto's January uprising. "We fought with grenades, guns, iron rods and light bulbs filled with sulphuric acid," she recalled in her book, *In the Days of Destruction and Revolt*. "For a few minutes we were intoxicated by the thrill of the battle. We had actually witnessed the German conquerors of the world retreat in fright from a handful of young Jews equipped only with a few pistols and hand grenades."

Lubetkin knew the Germans would return. The only question was when. For the 50,000 Jews who remained in the ghetto, the decisive answer came on April 19, 1943, the eve of Passover. This time, General Jürgen Stroop's well-equipped German troops expected armed resistance upon entering the ghetto, and they got it. Outgunned by the Germans, the poorly armed Jewish fighters—about 700 to 750 strong—had no illusions about defeating Stroop. But Lubetkin saw the Germans fall back at first as the limited store of Jewish guns, grenades, and "Molotov cocktails" brought fear and death to the German invaders.

Again, the reprieve was temporary. "The enemy set fire to the ghetto," Lubetkin testified. "How can one describe the enormous suffering and terror of the Jews trapped in the flames?" Still, the ghetto fighters resisted.

Members of the Greenspan partisan group assemble in Poland's Parczew Forest.

1943

Not until May 16 could Stroop report that "the Jewish Quarter of Warsaw no longer exists." By then Lubetkin had escaped through the sewer system to Warsaw's "Aryan" side, where her resistance continued.

The significance of the Warsaw Ghetto uprising went beyond battle reports and casualty statistics. News about the uprising inspired Jewish resistance elsewhere, and increased Nazi uneasiness in the aftermath of the German Army's telling defeat on the Eastern Front at Stalingrad, Russia, late in January. As had been the case in the Warsaw Ghetto, however, Jewish resistance—heroic and spreading though it was—usually lacked the outside support necessary to produce more than moral victories.

While the Warsaw Ghetto uprising took place, a Czech Jew named Richard Glazar struggled to stay alive in Treblinka, a camp located 60 miles northeast of Warsaw. Born in 1920, he was sent to that killing center from the Theresienstadt, Czechoslovakia, camp/ghetto in early October 1942. Treblinka's gas chambers claimed more than 800,000 Jewish lives, but Glazar was among the very few who were spared for work. Like Lubetkin, he resisted and survived to tell his story in the book *Trap with a Green Fence.*

Commander Jürgen Stroop *(center)* keeps company with his troops during the Warsaw Ghetto uprising.

Glazar regularly saw the trains that delivered thousands of Jews to Treblinka. By the spring of 1943, he knew how far Nazi mass murder had reached, for the convoys brought Jews from distant Bulgaria and Greece. While Jews disappeared forever when they reached Treblinka, their possessions did not. Before the deportees were stripped, gassed, and burned, the Germans plundered their belongings. Glazar remembered the camp as "a huge junk store." Everything could be found in Treblinka, he wrote, "except life." Sorting the loot, wrote Glazar, became the routine work that kept him alive. He and his fellow prisoners understood that they were doomed if the sorting stopped.

Despite overwhelming odds, Jewish resistance did exist in Treblinka. Describing how the trains departing the death camp were loaded with loot, Glazar recalls one occasion when the inmates hid two escapees in the bundles so that the world could learn about the killing. Then, in late May 1943, Glazar saw "the most miserable of all the transports that have ever arrived in Treblinka." The people came from Warsaw. So meager were their remaining possessions that there was little to sort. But in another sense, Glazar emphasized, those last Warsaw transports were rich because they brought news about the ghetto uprising. That news made Glazar and his comrades believe that warnings from the Treblinka escapees had helped to incite the Warsaw uprising. In turn, the Warsaw uprising began to stir Treblinka's prisoners, in Glazar's words, to "give up hoping that you will be the last to escape this naked death. Show the world and yourselves. . . ."

At Treblinka, an inmate resistance group had planned since early spring to seize weapons from the SS armory, take control of the camp, destroy it, and flee to partisan groups in the forest. The date set for the Treblinka uprising was Monday, August 2. About 4:00 P.M., before the resistance leaders could gain full control of the arms cache, a suspicious SS officer was killed by a shot that alerted the camp guards and prematurely signaled the inmates to revolt. During exchanges of gunfire, some prisoners torched parts of the camp. As the escapees ran for their lives, most were gunned down from the camp's watchtowers or caught and killed later. On the day of the uprising, the camp held approximately 850 prisoners. Some 750 tried to escape. Glazar was one of about 70 who survived the Holocaust.

Crematorium IV at Auschwitz-Birkenau could burn almost 1500 bodies a day.

After the rebellion, the Germans forced the captured escapees to raze what was left of the Treblinka camp. Then those prisoners were shot, trees were planted, and the site was disguised as a farm. Jewish resistance had helped to shut down Treblinka, but only after the camp's work was essentially finished.

Meanwhile, southeast of Treblinka, three miles from the Bug River, the Sobibór death camp still operated. Between March and July 1943, 19 transports from the Netherlands brought 35,000 Dutch Jews to Sobibór's gas chambers, which killed about 250,000 Jews in all. The death traffic then diminished, with more than 13,000 Jews from liquidated ghettos in Vilna, Minsk, and Lida being gassed at Sobibór during the second half of September. The camp's inmates understood that the end of the transports meant the end of their lives, too.

In early September 1943, Sobibór's prisoner work force included about 650 Jews. As at Treblinka, some were skilled workers who maintained the camp, others sorted loot, and still others were condemned to gas chamber work crews and corpse disposal. Thomas Blatt was among the approximately 300 prisoners who escaped the camp during the uprising that broke out there on October 14, 1943. His 1996 book *Sobibór: The Forgotten Revolt* reports that just 48 of the Sobibór escapees survived to be liberated.

The uprising at Sobibór led the Germans to abandon plans to convert the death camp to a concentration camp. Instead, they decided to dismantle and disguise the site whose killing work had been virtually accomplished anyway. Like Treblinka, Sobibór became a farm. That result, however, was not the only outcome of the Sobibór uprising. Events in Warsaw, Treblinka, and Sobibór indicated that the Polish Jews increasingly realized there would be no "salvation through work." Stripped of hope for survival, they would resist until death. With the threat of such Jewish resistance in mind, Himmler accelerated the destruction of Jews who remained in Lublin-area labor camps at Trawniki and Poniatowa as well as in the Majdanek death camp.

Dejected German military officers face their Russian captors following the Battle of Stalingrad.

In the Lublin district on November 3, 1943, some 42,000 Jews were rounded up and shot. Historian Christopher Browning calls this massacre "the single largest German killing operation against Jews in the entire war." Its German code name was *Erntefest,* which means "harvest festival."

Conservative overall estimates show that the Holocaust took at least 500,000 Jewish lives in 1943. Through no fault of its own, that year's Jewish resistance—significant though it was, impressive though it remains—was unfortunately not enough to prevent disaster.

Rabbi Leo Baeck

Rabbi Leo Baeck was one of the preeminent rabbis and theologians of German Jewry. Ordained in 1897, Baeck served as a liberal rabbi in Berlin from 1912 until his deportation to the Theresienstadt, Czechoslovakia, camp/ghetto in early 1943.

When the Nazis created the Reich Representation of German Jews in 1933, Baeck was named its president. As chief representative of German Jewry, he refused to leave Germany, even when his safety and that of German Jewry was threatened.

After being deported to Theresienstadt, Baeck worked tirelessly to bolster the morale of many Jews, even those whom he knew were destined for Auschwitz. After the war Baeck settled in London, where he became the president of the Council of Jews from Germany. The Leo Baeck Institute, which is the primary research institution for the study of German Jewry, bears the name of this venerable man.

Duped into believing that they were headed for "resettlement" in the East, Jews bound for Auschwitz carried suitcases containing their most precious belongings. While the prisoners were often sent to their deaths upon arrival, their possessions were guarded, sorted, and stored before being shipped to Germany.

These Jews are being moved to the Grodno Ghetto in Belorussia. The ghetto was established shortly after the German invasion of Russia. In November 1941 25,000 Jews from Grodno and the surrounding area were forced into the ghetto. It was liquidated in January 1943, when the resident Jews were deported to their deaths at Treblinka. Even before the German occupation of this section of the Soviet Union, civilian antisemites had attacked Jews there.

1943

• 1943: Heinrich Himmler is named Reich minister of the interior. • Pope Pius XII announces that the Vatican can help oppressed peoples only via "our prayers." • A collaborationist party, *Nye Denmark* (New Denmark), is established. • *SS Galizien* (SS Galicia), a collaborationist Ukrainian volunteer SS unit, is established. • Jozef Tiso, prime minister of Slovakia and an ally to Adolf Hitler, briefly halts deportations of Slovakian Jews. • In France, French Jew Sabina Zlatin founds a children's home in Izieu, which shields some 100 Jewish children from the Nazis; *See* April 6, 1944. • The first issue of the antisemitic *Archiv für Judenfragen (Archive for Jewish Questions)* is published in Germany.

Inside the Warsaw Ghetto, a worker drags an emaciated body from the street. In January 1943 the Germans initiated a new deportation from the ghetto. For the first time, Jews resisted with force, using their few weapons to fight the Germans on the streets and in the ghetto's buildings. These skirmishes raised morale and provided vital experience for the decisive struggle that would begin a few months later.

Ragged children wait in front of a brick wall in the Warsaw Ghetto. By winter 1942–43, conditions within the ghetto were abominable. Pipes froze and raw sewage spewed into the streets. Typhus raged throughout the ghetto, and starvation rations were exacting a heavy toll on the Jewish populace. Upwards of 5000 people a month were dying, and those who clung to life were miserable beyond description.

"Streets full, full. . . . Selling. Begging each other. Crying. Hungry."

—*Jan Karski, witness to the Warsaw Ghetto*

Prisoners held at Dachau work in a nearby armaments factory. Perhaps a third of the slave laborers were Jewish; the remainder were political dissidents, clergymen, Gypsies, Jehovah's Witnesses, homosexuals, and Soviet POWs. The exploitation of slave labor and the extension of the war effort fueled the camp's growth. Dachau eventually included 36 subcamps that utilized 37,000 prisoners as forced laborers. The vast majority of these workers were engaged in armaments production.

• **January 1943: As the year begins, 10,000 Jews are performing forced labor in factories throughout Germany. • The last 27 Jews in Bilgoraj, Poland, are flushed from hiding and killed. • Nearly 870 children, invalids, and medical personnel are sent from Holland to Auschwitz. • A Soviet military victory on the River Don engulfs 50,000 Hungarian Jews utilized as** forced labor on the Eastern Front; more than 40,000 are killed in combat between German and Soviet forces. Many thousands more are captured and mistreated by both the Soviets and Axis POWs.

• An SS instruction sheet for implementation of death sentences at extermination camps decrees that executions by hanging are to be carried out by designated prisoners; payment will be three cigarettes. • **Jewish Resistance members in the Warsaw Ghetto begin to split into 22 groups. They construct shelters and bunkers and even create tunnels that lead to the gentile portion of the city. • Moshe Fish and Leva Gilchik, Jews who formed a partisan group in forests**

Nazi propaganda recognized no boundaries when it rallied the German *Volk* behind the war effort. In addition to the ever-present radio speeches and parades, postage stamps carried the message of military glory. The battle scenes depicted in these stamps reinforced the link between the German nation and the war.

Fritz Sauckel was Germany's plenipotentiary-general for labor mobilization from 1942 to 1945. As such, he secured slave laborers from the Soviet Union and other occupied territories and forcibly relocated more than five million people from their homes in occupied territories to Germany. Sauckel also bore responsibility for the extermination of tens of thousands of Jewish workers in Poland. Sauckel paid for his crimes with his life: He was hanged by the Allies on October 16, 1946.

Prisoners in Allach, a subcamp of Dachau in Germany, work in the *Bayerische Motoren Werke* (BMW) plane-engine factory. As the war progressed, camps provided an invaluable pool of labor for the German armaments industry. Private firms such as BMW could hire slave laborers at extremely low costs. In the 1990s business "arrangements" of this sort came back to haunt BMW and other still-extant German firms.

1943

outside Kleck, Poland, in July 1942, die in battle against German troops.

• A *Putsch* planned by some German generals at Stalingrad, Russia, and intended to overthrow Hitler never comes off. Leading German opponents of Hitler and the Nazis—mostly conservative political opponents—conspire to overthrow Hitler's Reich.

They feel that Hitler has overreached himself, and that the war has developed into a dangerous two-front endeavor. Despite their opposition to Hitler, his major German antagonists are antisemitic and still want the Jews to disappear. They conclude that the Jews are a "calamitous influence...on the nation," and that the Jews are "a danger to the German nation."

Pictured with French collaborator Marcel Déat is Joseph Darnand (right), one of the most hated of the French collaborators. Darnand led a French military organization that openly fought for the Germans. As head of the Legionnaire Law and Order Service (SOL), Darnand was responsible for security operations throughout Vichy France. The SOL tracked down and brutally tortured members of the French Resistance. When France was liberated in 1944, Darnand and 6000 followers fled to Germany.

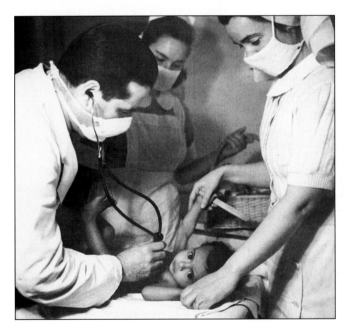

Choiceless Choices

"One wants to live," wrote Salmen Lewental. Those words are part of a notebook buried and found near the ruins of Birkenau's crematorium III. Selected for labor when he entered Auschwitz on December 10, 1942, Lewental was put in the *Sonderkommando* a month later and condemned to work in the gas chambers and crematoria. He lasted long enough to join the *Sonderkommando* uprising on October 7, 1944. The date of his death is unknown.

At one point in Lewental's notebook, he imagines someone asking him, "Why do you do such ignoble work?" Beyond answering that "one wants to live," there is no good reply, for what good choices did Lewental have?

Nazi power repeatedly forced defenseless people to make what Holocaust scholar Lawrence L. Langer calls "choiceless choices." Such choices, he says, do not "reflect options between life and death, but between one form of 'abnormal' response and another, both imposed by a situation that was in no way of the victim's own choosing."

Such was Lewental's miserable situation. He did not volunteer for the *Sonderkommando* any more than he chose deportation. Lewental was like millions of Holocaust victims. In Auschwitz, his "choices"—dying by suicide, dying by resisting, or dying as a *Sonderkommando*—were essentially "choiceless."

Doctors and nurses examine an infant refugee from Europe in the offices of the World International Zionist Organization in Tel Aviv, Palestine. Despite British efforts to limit Jewish immigration to Palestine, Jewish refugees steadily streamed into the region throughout 1943—many illegally.

• Germans murder 61,000 Jews at Auschwitz, Treblinka, and Belzec during this month alone. • The United States State Department, which knows much about the Holocaust, continues to block attempts to transfer Jewish children to America.

• January 1, 1943: Jews in the Netherlands are no longer allowed to have bank accounts. All Jewish money is put instead into a central account.

• January 3, 1943: Polish President Wladyslaw Raczkiewicz requests that Pope Pius XII publicly denounce German atrocities against the Jews. Pius remains silent concerning both the German slaughter of the Polish Jews and the German attacks against Polish Catholics.

• January 4, 1943: The SS administrative office instructs all concentration-camp commandants to send human hair taken from Jewish women to the firm of *Alex Zink, Filzfabrik AG* at Roth, Germany, near Nuremberg, for processing. • Young members of the

Auschwitz

"People lived and vanished overnight in this place," wrote Holocaust survivor Elie Wiesel. Polish people call that place Oświecim, but it is better known as Auschwitz, its German name. That place is synonymous with the Holocaust itself.

The town of Oświecim, whose prewar population of 12,000 included 5000 Jews, stands 40 miles west of Kraków in Upper Silesia, a southwestern Polish province that the Nazis annexed to the Third Reich. Situated on major railroad lines and near the confluence of the Sola and Vistula rivers, Oświecim was also the site of former Polish military barracks. They became the nucleus of Auschwitz, the Nazis' most notorious network of concentration, forced-labor, and death camps.

On April 27, 1940, Heinrich Himmler, head of the Nazi SS, ordered the establishment of a concentration camp at Oświecim. Under the command of Rudolf Höss, the early Auschwitz inmates were mostly Polish political prisoners. Soon, as its territory and population expanded, Auschwitz became several camps in one. On March 1, 1941, Himmler called for a second section—

Auschwitz II—and construction began in October. By the end of 1941, a third expansion was under way. Auschwitz III was known as Buna-Monowitz, taking its name from the Buna synthetic-rubber factory at Monowice, which slave laborers built for I.G. Farben, the German industrial firm.

When it came to the destruction of human life, no part of Auschwitz could compare to Auschwitz II, also known as Birkenau, the German name for Brzeźinka, the Polish village near the site. Located 1.5 miles from the *Stammlager* (Auschwitz I, the "main camp"), Auschwitz-Birkenau became the Third Reich's top killing center. By early summer 1943, it had four state-of-the-art gas chamber-crematoria installations, whose chief purpose was to murder

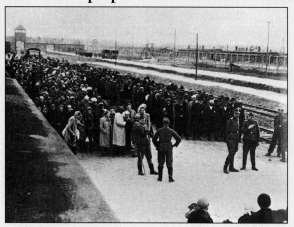

Jews and others on an assembly-line basis.

German engineers estimated that these four crematoria could incinerate 4415 bodies a day. That number, though, was less than the gas chambers' daily capacity. Thus, efforts were made to double the rate of corpse disposal by reducing the incineration time and increasing the number of bodies that could be burned at once. Pushed beyond capacity, Birkenau's killing machinery periodically malfunctioned. Nevertheless, it destroyed hundreds of thousands of Jews in 1943 and especially in 1944.

In all of its dimensions, Auschwitz spelled suffering and death. If not murdered in the gas chambers, prisoners died of starvation and disease. Slave laborers worked in hideous conditions until they perished. Deportees came from every European region and included German "undesirables," Soviet prisoners of war, Gypsies, Polish priests and nuns, French Resistance members, and—most of all—Jews. Between 1.1 and 1.5 million men, women, and children—90 percent of them Jewish—perished in that place.

1943

Jewish Fighting Organization are rounded up in Czestochowa, Poland. Its leader, Mendel Fiszlewicz, uses a hidden pistol to wound the German commander of the *Aktion*. Fiszlewicz and 25 other men are immediately shot, and 300 women and children from the group are deported to the Treblinka death camp and gassed.

• January 5, 1943: The Vught, Holland, concentration camp is established.

• January 5–7, 1943: Thousands of Jews are murdered at Lvov, Ukraine.

• January 6, 1943: The Jews of Lubaczow, Poland, are killed at the Belzec death camp. • Five hundred

Sister Marejanna Reszko was the head of the convent of St. Anthony in Ignacow, Poland. She rescued numerous Jewish girls by hiding them in her orphanage. When asked if one of her charges, Frida Aronson, was Jewish, her reply was that she did not care—she assisted all those who needed it.

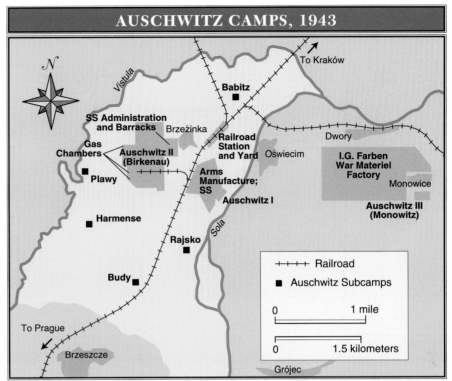

AUSCHWITZ CAMPS, 1943

Auschwitz was divided into three camps. Auschwitz I was primarily a concentration camp. At Auschwitz II (Birkenau), more than one million Jews fell dead in its five gas chambers. Auschwitz III (Monowitz) was an enormous industrial area, with chemical giant I.G. Farben relying on thousands of slave laborers.

Gentiles often collaborated with the Nazis in expropriating Jewish property, even in Holland. This moving van was part of the A. Puls company, owned by a Dutchman who willingly worked with the Nazis. Puls's vans appeared frequently in the Amsterdam Ghetto in order to haul away Jewish property. Such vans became so common that "Pulsen" became a slang term for stealing.

Jews hiding in Opoczno, Poland, are murdered by Germans after being coaxed out of hiding with a promise of rail transport to a neutral country.

• **January 7, 1943:** British Colonial Secretary Oliver Stanley informs the British War Cabinet that Germany's Eastern European allies have turned to a policy of expulsion of Jews as an alternative to exterminating them. He concludes that this change in policy makes it "all the more necessary" to limit the number of Jewish children accepted into Palestine.

• **January 7–24, 1943:** Twenty thousand Jews from Germany, Belgium, Holland, and Poland are gassed at Auschwitz.

• **January 9, 1943:** Germans apprehend, torture, and kill 20-year-old Jewish partisan Emma Radova. • The British magazine *New Statesman* urges that Jewish refugees be allowed at least temporarily into all nations, including 40,000 more into Palestine.

• **January 10, 1943:** In the *Generalgouvernement*, several thousand Jews

Meeting in Casablanca, Morocco, over several days in January 1943, U.S. President Franklin Roosevelt *(left)*, French General Charles de Gaulle *(center)*, and British Prime Minister Winston Churchill *(right)* set strategy for the next phases of the war in Europe. The leaders united in demanding Germany's unconditional surrender as a prerequisite for ending the fighting. British and American representatives were far less decisive a few months later when they met in Hamilton, Bermuda, to address the refugee crisis. There, they took no action to rescue Jews.

Miroslav Filipovic-Majstorovic was a ruthless killer who worked at the Jasenovać concentration camp in Croatia. A former priest and member of the Croatian Fascist organization *Ustasa*, Filipovic-Majstorovic killed countless prisoners with his bare hands. Approximately 600,000 people—including Serbs, Jews, Gypsies, and opponents of the *Ustasa* regime—were killed at Jasenovać.

Conductor Wolf Durmashkin poses with the Hebrew Ghetto Choir of Vilna, Lithuania. Durmashkin was a child prodigy and a leading musician in Warsaw. After the outbreak of war he went to Vilna, where he taught music at several Jewish schools. Once the ghetto was established, Durmashkin organized an orchestra, directed a Hebrew choir, and created a music school.

1943

who had left forest hiding places on November 10, 1942, after a Nazi promise of safe passage, are betrayed. Most are transported to Treblinka and gassed. The remainder are sent to labor camps at nearby Sandomierz and Skarzysko Kamienna. • Four hundred Jews who resist their German overseers at the Kopernik camp in Mińsk Mazowiecki,

Poland, are burned alive in their barracks.

• January 12–21, 1943: Twenty thousand Jews are deported from Zambrow, Poland, to Auschwitz.

• January 13, 1943: Fifteen hundred Jews are deported from Radom, Poland, to Treblinka.

Reichsbahn

Fahrplananordnung 586 was a train schedule that was dated August 25, 1942. During the Holocaust, thousands of these German documents coordinated railroad traffic to Nazi killing centers in Occupied Poland.

Scheduled to leave Luków, Poland, at 10:44 A.M. on August 28, *Fahrplananordnung* 586's "Resettlement Special Train" pulled 25 freight cars. Its scheduled arrival time at the Treblinka death camp was 2:52 P.M. The empty train left Treblinka at 5:22 P.M. By then, 2500 Jews—the train's cargo—had been gassed. This transport was not the largest to reach Treblinka.

The *Reichsbahn*, the German railroad network, played an essential part in the "Final Solution." Working with Adolf Eichmann and the SS, *Reichsbahn* officials organized the *Sonderzüge* (special trains) that sent Jews from all over Europe to their deaths at Belzec, Chelmno, Sobibór, Majdanek, Treblinka, and Auschwitz-Birkenau. Even amid the war's demands and shortages, these trains had high priority. They usually reached their destinations as scheduled.

Herded like cattle into freight cars—with 80 to 100 or more persons packed into a single wagon—the Jews were still ticketed as passengers on miserable journeys that could last for days. The SS used money and property seized from Jews to pay for fares—one-way.

Millions of Jews were deported to their deaths in cattle cars such as this. Up to 100 human beings were crammed into spaces that measured 31'6"×14'×13'2". The journey to a concentration camp was an unimaginably terrifying experience. Once the doors were sealed, the occupants were deprived of water and proper sanitation facilities. Thousands of people died en route and others went insane. On more than one occasion, parents and children engaged in lethal struggles for a crust of bread or a drink of water. The terror and disorientation were heightened by the fact that the Jews had no notion of where they were going.

• **January 14, 1943: When the Jewish Council and Jewish police in Lomza, Poland, refuse to provide the Gestapo with 40 Jews, Gestapo agents make the selections, and include two Council members. A further 8000 Lomza Jews are deported to Auschwitz.**

• **January 14–24, 1943. British Prime Minister Winston Churchill and** United States President Franklin Roosevelt meet at Casablanca, Morocco, to discuss the future Allied invasion of Western Europe. News of the meeting buoys the spirits of Jews, who hope the war may soon be over. Roosevelt, though, proposes to French North African official General Noguès and later to a leader of the Free French Forces, General Giraud, that the French government in North Africa should discriminate against local Jews just as Hitler did in the 1930s. Roosevelt specifically states, twice—once to Noguès and separately to Giraud—that "the number of Jews engaged in the practice of the professions . . . should be definitely limited to the percentage that the Jewish population in North Africa bears to the

For most Jews, the length of time spent in extermination camps was brutally abbreviated. The horrifying efficiency of the Nazi death apparatus is captured by "Entrance Through the Gate, Exit Through the Chimney," an ink drawing by Holocaust survivor Joseph Bau.

Léon Degrelle was the leader of the Belgian collaborationist group known as the Rexist movement. The Rexists were explicitly pro-Nazi. In 1943 Degrelle announced his plans to incorporate Belgium into the German empire. While Degrelle enhanced his power, the Rexists were largely excluded from political power. Moreover, many followers of the collaborationist movement became the targets of a ruthless assassination campaign carried out by the Belgian Resistance forces.

Cardinal Konrad Graf von Preysing, the bishop of Berlin during the Nazi era, viewed the Third Reich as a corrupt and pernicious regime. As early as May 1933, Preysing challenged the ideological tenets of Nazism and openly called for their repudiation. By January 1943 he was the only top German Catholic prelate who consistently opposed the German government's Jewish policies. Preysing threatened to resign his post if the other German bishops continued their collaborative behavior.

1943

whole of the North African population." President Roosevelt adds that limiting the number of Jews in the professions "would further eliminate the specific and understandable complaints which the Germans bore toward the Jews in Germany...."

• January 15, 1943: A non-Jewish Polish woman and her one-year-old child are shot at the Pilica River in Poland because the woman has aided Jews.
• Seventy-seven Jews leap from a deportation train traveling east from Belgium. Most are hunted down and killed by German and Flemish SS troops. • Thousands of Jews at the Zaslaw, Poland, concentration camp are deported to the Belzec death camp.

Rita Rosani was a member of the Italian Resistance and the only Italian female resister known to have been killed in combat. Born in Trieste, Rosani was a schoolteacher at the local Jewish school until 1943, when she joined the Resistance. She met her death on September 17, 1944, after fighting in several actions in the Verona region.

A vast pile of brushes, from women's hairbrushes to men's shaving brushes, attest to the Nazis' desire to rob those they executed of their most personal possessions. Hair became the raw material to stuff mattresses and weave cloth. Brushes were sold to consumers in Germany or distributed to soldiers at the front or in hospitals.

Joint Rescue Committee

Despite the odds, this committee of the Jewish Agency for Palestine was determined to obtain information concerning Jews imprisoned in Polish ghettos. The Joint Rescue Committee, based in Jerusalem, wanted to send these Jews food parcels. The members also wanted to help them, should they manage to escape from the Nazis, to obtain immigration certificates to Palestine.

Early leaders of the committee were Itzhak Gruenbaum *(pictured)*, Moshe Shapira, Eliyahu Dobkin, and Emil Schmorak. Gruenbaum felt that because the Nazis were so formidable, because the Allies were indifferent to the Jewish plight, and because no significant resources stood behind the committee that nothing the committee did could significantly help the Jews trapped in Nazi Europe. Instead, Gruenbaum believed they should focus on establishing Palestine as a home for the Jewish survivors after the war. By 1945 the committee was devoting all of its efforts to establishing a Jewish state in Palestine.

• **January 17, 1943: Berlin Bishop Konrad Graf von Preysing is the only top German Catholic prelate who consistently opposes the German government's Jewish policies. Preysing threatens Pope Pius XII, saying he will resign unless the collaborative behavior of the other German bishops ceases.**

• **January 18, 1943: Jewish deportees from Belgium arrive at Auschwitz, where 1087 are gassed. • After a four-month break, Germans resume deportations from the Warsaw Ghetto. Warsaw Jews react with their first acts of overt resistance, expressed in brutal street fighting. 1000 Jews are executed in the streets and 6000 are deported to the Treblinka death**

camp. An elderly, blind Jewish man is shot by an SS man because he is unable to walk without a guide.

• Nobel-prize winning Polish émigré poet Czeslaw Milosz—a righteous Christian—condemns antisemitism and nationalism as "ills that like cancer were consuming Poland." In his poem, *"Campo dei Fiori,"* Milosz laments from Warsaw in 1943—and

Ernst Kaltenbrunner

The successor to Reinhard Heydrich, Ernst Kaltenbrunner devoted himself to completing his predecessor's agenda of hate.

Born near Hitler's birthplace of Braunau, Austria, Kaltenbrunner enjoyed the advantages of wealth, earning a degree in law. A fierce antisemite, he joined the Austrian Nazi Party in 1932 and subsequently became a member of the SS. His Nazi activities led to imprisonment, but with the *Anschluss* (Germany's annexation of Austria) Kaltenbrunner was rewarded with an appointment as minister of state security. He cooperated with boy-

hood friend Adolf Eichmann to force the emigration of Austrian Jews. Following Heydrich's death in 1942, Heinrich Himmler promoted Kaltenbrunner to head the Reich Security Main Office in 1943.

An imposing figure with a huge facial scar, Kaltenbrunner preferred the shadows of anonymity. He hid in the Austrian Alps at the end of the war, but was captured and indicted. At the Nuremberg Trials, he pleaded ignorance and innocence. He could not escape, however, the fact that the position he held from 1943 to 1945 gave him extraordinary power to carry out the "Final Solution." Witnesses placed him at the Mauthausen gassings, and he was charged with ordering the executions of Allied POWs. Judged guilty, Kaltenbrunner was executed on October 16, 1946.

Head of the ghetto administration in Lódź, Poland, Hans Biebow *(left)* surveys the booty collected from the Jews under his charge. Biebow used his extensive powers for personal enrichment. He exploited Jewish labor and robbed Jews of their property. In order to maximize his profits, Biebow managed to keep the ghetto open until the summer of 1944.

As younger and older German males were conscripted into the armed forces, the Nazi authorities turned to the vast pool of labor from the conquered countries of the East to supply their needs. Here, female workers from the Soviet Union engage in forced labor at the Siemens factory in Berlin. They wear badges with the *OST* insignia, identifying them as *Ostarbeiter*, workers from the East.

1943

he's being literal, not figurative—that the carousel's carnival tunes and the laughing crowds in the Catholic area of Warsaw drown out the sounds of the Germans shooting Jews in the Warsaw Ghetto.

● **January 19, 1943:** As Nazis raid the Warsaw Ghetto for the second consecutive day, a crying child is acci-

dentally suffocated by his terrified mother.

● **January 19–22, 1943:** Six thousand Jews from Warsaw are murdered at the Treblinka death camp.

● **January 20, 1943:** In a letter to the Reich minister of transport, SS chief Heinrich Himmler requests addi-

Hans Nelson and Hildegard Neumann were among the Nazis stationed at the Theresienstadt, Czechoslovakia, camp/ghetto located just outside of Prague. Their wholesome, clean-cut appearances belie the nature of their work. As ghetto superintendents, the two contributed to the deaths of thousands of Jews imprisoned at Theresienstadt. Throughout the first half of 1943, Nelson and Neumann functioned as parts of an elaborate system that deported Jews from Germany, Austria, and the Protectorate to the camp/ghetto.

Krupp was among the many German corporations to make extensive use of the abundant supply of slave labor that the concentration-camp system provided. This airplane factory in Essen was just one of several major Krupp plants located throughout the Reich and the occupied territories. In September 1944 Krupp employed around 288,000 workers. During the Nuremberg Trials, the Allies accused Alfred Krupp, chief of the corporation, of profiting from the work of approximately 100,000 slaves, probably an underestimation.

tional trains so that the "removal of Jews" from across Europe can be speeded up.

• January 21, 1943: SS men in the Warsaw Ghetto fire into windows and toss grenades. The Jews resist and the Germans soon withdraw, leaving behind 12 dead.

• January 21-24, 1943: Two thousand Jews from the Theresienstadt, Czechoslovakia, camp/ghetto are deported to Auschwitz. Some 1760 are gassed on arrival, including patients from the Jewish mental hospital at Apeldoorn, Holland, as well as about 50 of the hospital's nurses who accompany the patients to lessen their terror.

• January 22, 1943: The Jewish ghetto at Grodno, Belorussia, is liquidated. • Jewish girls at the Auschwitz-Birkenau death camp light candles and sing songs for the Sabbath. • A death train that originated in Grodno, Poland, on January 17 erupts in violence at the Treblinka death camp when 1000 Jews armed with boards, knives, and razors attack guards. By

Huddling in small groups, Jews from Novo Moskovsk in the Ukraine are deported. Some 400 Jews from this town were transported to the death camps of Poland in spite of the *Wehrmacht*'s protests that trains were more urgently required for military purposes. Although the harsh winter weather halted the transports, they began again in mid-January 1943.

The German occupiers took advantage of French antisemitism to recruit Frenchmen to fight for the Nazi cause. While the Germans never got all of the aid they desired, the Vichy government was officially their ally and did supply a number of soldiers to the Nazis. These French legionnaires left to fight on the Russian front. One of them scratched the words "Death to the Jews."

Following their defeat at Stalingrad, Russia, German and Romanian soldiers wait to be sent to prisoner-of-war camps. Against the fierce cold, the soldiers huddle together for warmth and comfort as they march into what would be a cruel captivity. Few of those who entered the camps returned to their homelands; most died of disease and starvation.

1943

morning 10,000 Jews and guards who had been on the train are dead, killed by Treblinka SS troops armed with machine guns and grenades.

• **January 22-27, 1943:** During Operation Tiger in Marseilles, France, Nazis seize more than 4000 Jews for deportation. At nearby Les Accates, 29 Jewish children are seized at La

Rose Orphanage. Their guardian, Alice Salomon, insists on remaining with them; *See* March 23, 1943.

• **January 23, 1943:** Italian authorities refuse to cooperate with Germans in deportations of French Jews living in zones of France under Italian control. • British forces liberate Tripoli, Libya.

German Field Marshal Friedrich Paulus *(left)*, accompanied by two staff officers, walks toward Red Army headquarters to sign the formal surrender of the Sixth Army at Stalingrad, Russia. Paulus had begged Hitler to allow a retreat before it became too late, but the *Führer* refused to give up, leaving the exhausted and starving army surrounded by Soviet forces. "Fortress Stalingrad," as Hitler called the troops, could not withstand the fierce winter and the lack of supplies and reinforcements. Against orders and in the hopes of saving his remaining men, Paulus surrendered on February 3. While he and his senior staff survived, most of his men did not.

Blonde Poison

Still alive today, Stella Goldschlag was a German Jew who had Aryan looks. In her youth, the shapely blue-eyed blonde was a compulsive liar and renegade who desperately hated her Jewishness. Threatened, along with her parents, with deportation to the East and tortured by the Gestapo, Goldschlag was among a small number of Jews who collaborated with the Nazis and worked for the Gestapo. She received money, good food, and a temporary reprieve from deportation for her parents.

Using sex, her incredible memory, and her ruthlessness, Goldschlag's job was to root out the other so-called "U-boats"—Jews living underground in Berlin during the war—and to help the Gestapo arrest them. Those Jews would be sent off to extermination camps. On one weekend alone, Goldschlag helped the Gestapo catch 62 Jews. She was indeed the "Blonde Poison," seducing Jews to their deaths.

At the edge of a forest in Germany, *Schutzpolizei* (Protective Police) post a notice—perhaps a declaration of confiscation—on a Gypsy wagon. Gypsies were special targets of the Nazis, who saw them as a potential danger to the presumed purity of the "Aryan race." The essential mismatch of the Nazi/Gypsy relationship is clear in this tableau, as the husky, warmly dressed policemen, carried to the remote site in their modern automobile, confront the apprehensive Gypsy at his home, a wheeled relic of an earlier era.

• **January 27, 1943: The Eighth USAAF (United States Army Air Force) mounts the first all-American air raid on Germany, at Wilhelmshaven.**

• **January 28–31, 1943: Ten thousand Jews from Pruzhany, Belorussia, are deported to Auschwitz.**

• **January 29, 1943: Germans execute 15 Poles at the village of Wierzbica for aiding three Jews. One of the victims is a two-year-old girl.**

• **January 30, 1943: Ernst Kaltenbrunner is named by Hitler to succeed the late Reinhard Heydrich as chief of *Reichssicherheitshauptamt* (Reich Security Main Office).**

• **February 1943: As the month begins, 40,000 Jews are hiding in the forests of the Volhynia region of Poland. Before the year is out, 37,000 will perish from hunger and execution. • At Bialystok, Poland, eight SS men are killed by members of a Zionist youth movement resisting deportation. Members are captured and deported to the Treblinka death**

The Bielski Partisans

Of the estimated 20,000 to 30,000 Jews who fought in partisan groups in the forests of Eastern Europe, the group led by Tuvia Bielski (*pictured*) was the largest and the most renowned. Though members of his family were murdered by *Einsatzgruppen* in Novogrudok, Tuvia escaped to the forests of western Belorussia.

Together with his brothers Zusya, Asael, and Aharon, Tuvia secured arms and created a partisan group that grew to 30 members by summertime. This small band of Resistance

fighters dispatched couriers to the ghettos in the Novogrudok region to recruit fellow Jews to join their camp. Eventually, Bielski's camp contained hundreds of families.

The primary aim of the Bielski partisans was to protect Jewish lives. But they were also aggressive, launching raids against the Germans and exacting revenge on Belorussian police and farmers who helped the Nazis massacre Jews.

Frustrated by the activities of the Bielski group, the Germans offered a large reward for Tuvia's capture. However, the group successfully escaped by retreating deep into the forest. When the area was liberated in the summer of 1944, Bielski's band of partisans numbered 1200.

After the war, Tuvia immigrated to Palestine. He later settled in the United States with two surviving brothers.

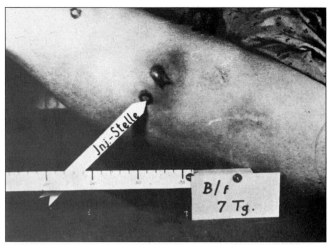

Within the walls of Auschwitz and other camps, humans replaced animals as subjects for experimentation. Unscrupulous surgeries were performed on inmates, both healthy and ill, and subjects were exposed to a variety of chemicals and viruses. Otherwise healthy prisoners were injected with typhus, tuberculosis, and malaria. This photo shows the results of a substance coded B/F, seven days after injection into a prisoner's forearm.

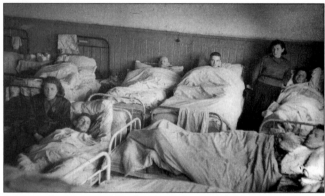

Jewish nurses and physicians struggled to care for the ill and injured within the ghettos. Pictured here are patients and family members in the Kovno (Lithuania) Ghetto. As trained medical personnel fell victim to disease and starvation, the ghetto's leadership sought to prepare new people to take their places. Secret medical training was offered in Warsaw and, most likely, Kovno.

1943

camp, where they attack guards and are killed. Their leader is Eliyahu Boraks. • The slave-labor camp at Chrzanów, Poland, is dissolved, with 1000 laborers sent to the death camp at Auschwitz. • The Nazis establish a Gypsy camp at Auschwitz-Birkenau. • A young Jewish woman at Treblinka, stripped naked by her captors, grabs a rifle from a Ukrainian guard and

kills two Germans and wounds a third before being subdued. She is subsequently tortured to death. • German authorities direct Hungary to provide 10,000 Jews for copper-mine slave labor at Bor, Yugoslavia; *See* September 1943.

• February 1, 1943: Nazis kill 1500 Jews at Minsk, Belorussia, bringing

Anna Wachalska, a gentile, lived in Warsaw at the time of the German invasion. She aided the Jewish Resistance throughout the Nazi occupation, even going so far as to give the identity of her deceased daughter, Stanislawa, to a young Jewish woman. Wachalska also worked closely with the Polish Socialist resistance, providing a link between it and the Jews of Warsaw. After the war she was named "Righteous Among the Nations" by the Yad Vashem.

The Nazis' genocidal policies in Eastern Europe involved more than just killing the people occupying Germany's "living space." In addition, tens of thousands of Germans emigrated to the newly conquered territories in order to make the lands the province of the German *Volk* (people). This illustration refers to the forced emigration of Poles who had to leave to make room for the Germans. The text reads: "Step by step the arrival [of German immigrants] follows the migration [of the Poles]. The Resettlement division of the Security Police prohibits any cessation of work within one's area of activity."

On October 29, 1942, in the midst of huge operations in Poland and the Soviet Union, the Germans deported 3000 Jews from Sandomierz, Poland, to the Belzec death camp. On November 10, 1942, those Jews not swept up in the local *Aktionen* were lured into a temporary ghetto at Sandomierz by German promises of safety from deportation. It was all a lie, as 6000 laborers at Sandomierz were killed in early 1943. In this photo, 20-year-old Yitzchak Goldman and seven other Jews are forced to pose for a German cameraman while laboring in front of a German office building.

the total number of Minsk victims since July 1941 to nearly 87,000.

• **February 2, 1943:** In a major turning point of the war, the encircled German Sixth Army surrenders to Soviet forces at Stalingrad, Russia. From this point on, most Europeans feel that the Germans will not win the war. • The Kolomyia (Ukraine)

Ghetto is liquidated; 2000 Jews are killed.

• **February 4, 1943:** In Lvov, Ukraine, German authorities assemble 12 surviving members of the ghetto's Jewish Council. When two do not appear and the others refuse to comply with German orders, four of the members are murdered. Six are sent to the labor

camp at Janówska, Ukraine, and the two who had refused to appear are later discovered in the non-Jewish section of Lvov and shot.

• **February 5, 1943:** At Bialystok, Poland, a Jew named Yitzhak Malmed resists deportation by throwing sulphuric acid into the face of a German police officer, who reacts by acciden-

Awaiting deportation to Auschwitz, a young girl squeezes her face into the narrow space between the train doors for a last look at her surroundings. Beginning in February 1943, trains left the Westerbork, Holland, camp every Tuesday morning. The trains carried to the East their cargo of 2000 to 3000 Jews each. Told they were being sent to do forced labor in Germany, most deportees suspected otherwise. Monday nights were filled with terror and dread, as people waited to see if they were among those to be deported.

E. Baskin, a radio operator for a Ukrainian partisan group, listens intently to a broadcast by the Soviet Information Bureau. Partisan units throughout Europe and particularly in the Soviet Union relied on radios to send and receive information. In addition, the ability to intercept German military broadcasts helped them to both evade capture and plan attacks against the enemy.

The inhumane living conditions created in the Polish ghettos and German concentration camps provoked some Jews to fight over crumbs of food and scraps of wood for heating. Here, Jews in Łódź battle for a few bits of wood. The dehumanization of European Jewry produced heart-wrenching incidents that would be unimaginable under normal conditions. Survivor/author Elie Wiesel relates the story of a boy who beat his father to death to secure a crust of bread.

1943

tally shooting and instantly killing a Gestapo officer standing nearby. Malmed escapes but surrenders later when the Germans threaten to execute 5000 Jews in retribution unless he turns himself in. He is publicly hanged. His body is displayed at the entrance to the Bialystok Ghetto as a warning to would-be activists.

• **February 5–12, 1943:** Following Jewish resistance, a combination of a street *Aktion* at Bialystok, Poland, and camp murders at Treblinka takes the lives of nearly 20,000 Jews.

• **February 6, 1943:** A marathon roll call at Auschwitz forces inmates to stand motionless in snow without food for over 13 hours. Many die on their

Standing before the annual general assembly, Ottó Komoly, president of the Zionist Federation, addresses the group in Budapest, Hungary. Komoly's most important role began in 1943, when he became one of the leaders of the effort to rescue Jews still alive in Poland and smuggle them to relative safety in Hungary. Although the German occupation brought those efforts to an end, Komoly's rescue work continued. He strove to save the Jews of Budapest from the Nazis and from fanatical members of Hungary's Fascist Arrow Cross Party.

This handmade metal box was carried by William Gruenstein throughout the Holocaust. The box was made by Josef Koplewicz while he and Gruenstein were enslaved in a Polish labor camp. After receiving the box, Gruenstein carved on the lid the names of Nazi concentration camps where he had been imprisoned. By clinging to this cherished piece of metal, his sole private possession, Gruenstein denied the Nazis' attempt to deprive him of his humanity and individuality.

Samuel Artur Zygelbojm

While some Jews chose suicide to end their suffering, others did it as a means of protest. Samuel Zygelbojm committed suicide to protest the world's indifference to Jews.

Zygelbojm served on the Warsaw Ghetto's first Jewish Council. He urged resistance when the Nazi authorities demanded that Warsaw's  Jews move into a ghetto ill-suited to their huge numbers. Hunted by the Gestapo, Zygelbojm fled to Belgium and eventually joined the Polish government-in-exile in London. He labored feverishly to secure Allied military support for the ghetto resistance, but to no avail. When he learned of the deaths of the ghetto resisters in 1943, including his wife and son, he killed himself.

In his farewell letter, Zygelbojm described his suicide as an act of protest "against the apathy with which the world regards and resigns itself to the slaughter of the Jewish people."

---

feet and many others who are too weak to dash back to the barracks at day's end are sent to the gas chamber.
• SS chief Heinrich Himmler receives a report about the quantities of items taken from Jews at Auschwitz and other camps in the Lublin area. Cited items include 155,000 women's coats, 132,000 men's shirts, and more than 6600 pounds of women's hair.

• **February 8, 1943:** The Red Army overruns a key German garrison at Kursk, Russia; *See* July 5, 1943.

• **February 8–26, 1943:** A German *Aktion* against Soviet partisans at Pripet Marshes, Ukraine, captures eight machine guns, 172 rifles, 14 pistols, 150 hand grenades, and eight land mines. German troops also make

off with more than 550 horses, 9578 head of cattle, 844 pigs, 5700 sheep, and 233 tons of grain. 2219 Jews are killed outright; 7378 receive "special treatment" (deportation and extermination). German losses in the action are two dead and 12 wounded.

• **February 10, 1943:** A cable devised by several U.S. State Department offi-

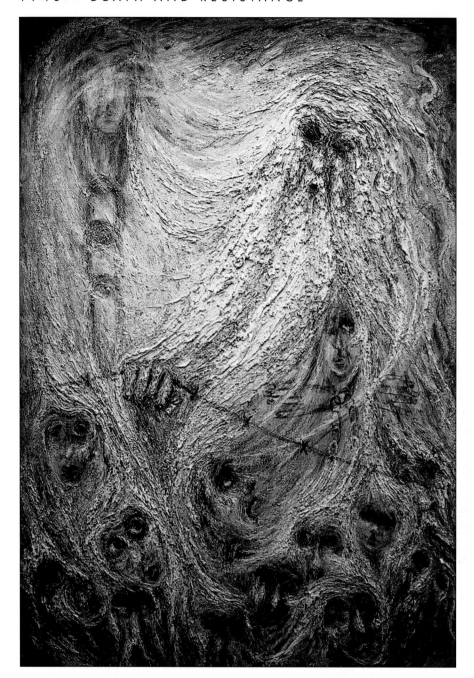

The American-born artist Gideon captured the horrors of war and the Nazi atrocities through the medium of art. His use of color, texture, and haunting images convey the pain and suffering of those caught up in the Nazi whirlwind. The tragic faces of the almost monochromatic art piece juxtaposed with the linked chain and barbed wire evoke the prison motif associated with Nazism. The vibrant colors of the second piece suggest the intense heat of the inferno that was Auschwitz.

1943

cials is sent to the U.S. legation in Bern, Switzerland. The cable suggests that the American consul in Bern should no longer transmit information about Jewish atrocities "to private persons in the United States." The cable is sent by Breckinridge Long, Ray Atherton, James Dunn, Elbridge Durbrow, and John Hickerson. Secretary of the Treasury Henry

Morgenthau's staff will later describe the cable of February 10 as "the most vicious document we have ever read," designed "by diabolical men" and intended to suppress information on the "Final Solution." "We don't shoot [Jews]. We let other people shoot them, and let them starve." Secretary Morgenthau observes that "when you get through with it, the [State Depart-

MAJOR DEPORTATIONS OF JEWS TO TREBLINKA, 1942–1943

More than 700,000 Jews perished at the Treblinka death camp. Most came from such major ghettos as Warsaw (250,000 in the summer of 1942) and Bialystok, while others endured (or died during) long train rides from Czechoslovakia, Greece, and other countries. Deportations to Treblinka ended in May 1943.

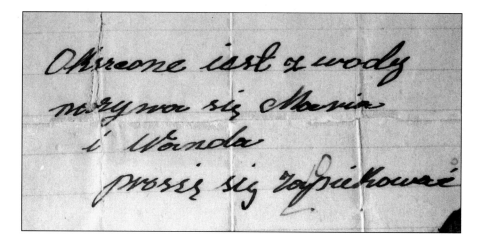

Shlomo Perel, a German Jew by birth, assumed the name Josef Perjell while a student at the Adolf Hitler school in Braunschweig. Hiding one's Jewish identity was a precarious proposition, especially for males living in a residential facility. Perel went to great lengths to hide his Jewishness, including an effort to reverse his circumcision, which was at the time clear physical evidence of Jewishness. Perel's exploits are brilliantly portrayed in the movie *Europa, Europa*.

This note, written by Christian woman Maria Dawelec, reads: "Baptized, Mania and Wanda. Please take care of them." Dawelec left the note along with two Jewish children in the backyard of a monastery. The real name of one of the children was Tamy Lavee. Lavee eventually would be sent to an orphanage in Lódź, Poland, where she would survive the war.

ment's] attitude to date is no different from Hitler's attitude." Secretary Morgenthau's assistant, Randolph Paul, describes the State Department officials involved in America's refugee policy as an "underground movement...to let the Jews be killed."

● **February 11, 1943:** Of 998 Jews deported from France on this date,

only ten will be alive at war's end two years later. Included among the 998 are 123 children under the age of 12, sent away without their parents. 802 are gassed immediately upon arrival at Auschwitz.

● **February 12, 1943:** Three French Jews escape an Auschwitz-bound train at the French frontier, but are

recaptured and forced to continue the journey.

● **February 13, 1943:** A Jewish partisan group active near Bialystok, Poland, and led by Eli Baumats attacks a German police detachment at Lipowy Most, Poland. ● Russian-born artist Aizik Feder, a onetime student of Matisse, is one of 1000

SS General Theodor Eicke was commandant of the Dachau concentration camp. Before his death in a plane crash on the Eastern Front on February 16, 1943, he founded and trained the SS Death's Head units and served as inspector general of concentration camps. Second only to Heinrich Himmler in his influence over the concentration–camp system, he ordered that the ironic phrase *Arbeit Macht Frei* (Work Will Set You Free) be posted in the concentration camps. He sought to make SS men hard and merciless; those who did not fit such criteria were to be sent off "to live in a monastery."

Peter Bergson (Hillel Kook) led a dissident group of Zionists known in the United States as the Emergency Committee to Save the Jewish People of Europe. During the war the Bergson group placed ads in newspapers and staged theatrical presentations to educate Americans about the "Final Solution." Their willingness to employ sensationalist tactics to rouse sympathy for Europe's Jews was deplored by the conservative leaders of the American Jewish community.

Rentabilitätsberechnung der SS über Ausnützung der Häftlinge in den Konzentrationslagern

Rentabilitätsberechnung

Täglicher Verleihlohn durchschnittlich RM 6,—

abzüglich Ernährung   RM —,60

durchschnittl. Lebensdauer 9 Mt. = 270 x RM 5,30 = RM 1431,—

abzüglich Bekl. Amort. RM —,10

Erlös aus rationeller Verwertung der Leiche:

     1. Zahngold   3. Wertsachen

     2. Kleidung   4. Geld

abzüglich Verbrennungskosten   RM 2,—

durchschnittlicher Nettogewinn   RM 200,—

Gesamtgewinn nach 9 Monaten   RM 1631,—

zuzüglich Erlös aus Knochen und Aschenverwertung.

This document calculates the value of work done by prisoners in a Nazi concentration camp. Detailed records weighed the cost of "maintaining" human life against the wealth produced by each individual, which suggests that the concentration camps were principally run as slave-labor operations. Yet, the Nazis' desire to exterminate all Jews often overrode even the most brute sort of economic practicality.

1943

Jews deported from Drancy, France, to the Auschwitz death camp. He is among the approximately 690 who are gassed upon arrival at the camp. • Amon Leopold Goeth becomes commandant of the Plaszów concentration camp. • The Jews of Djerba, Tunisia, are forced to pay ten million francs to the German authorities.

• *The New York Times* reports that the Romanian government is offering the Allies Romanian ships to transport 70,000 Jews anywhere the Allies wish. A departure tax to cover the transportation costs is all that is required. The U.S. State Department dismisses the offer. The British Foreign Office rejects the offer, fearing that it is a piece of blackmail that marks the

"Freedom."

—Word found on a scrap of paper left behind in the cell of White Rose resistance leader Sophie Scholl on the day of her execution; February 22, 1943

A gentile student living in Munich, Hans Scholl was shaken by the Nazi whirlwind of brutality that had swept up German Jews, Communists, and Social Democrats. In 1942 he told a family member, "It's time the Christians finally did something about it." With encouragement from a resister named Falk Harnaek, Hans founded a student resistance group called the White Rose. From a base at the University of Munich, Hans, his younger sister Sophie, and other White Rose members created vehemently anti-Nazi leaflets that were distributed at universities across Germany. He and Sophie were arrested at the University of Munich on February 18, 1943. They were sentenced to death, and were beheaded on February 22. In the courtroom after the verdict had been pronounced, Hans calmly said to his brother, Werner, "Remain strong—no compromises."

White Rose

Hans Scholl, a 25-year-old Christian medical student at the University of Munich, formed the White Rose resistance group with his 22-year-old sister, Sophie *(pictured)*, in 1942. The pair's goal was to create anti-Nazi pamphlets and disseminate them at universities across Germany. If caught, they would forfeit their lives.

Gestapo agents arrested the Scholls at the University of Munich early in 1943 after a janitor spotted Hans and Sophie emptying a suitcase full of anti-Nazi pamphlets into the university corridors. Although the Scholls revealed nothing to their interrogators, their White Rose compatriots—Professor Kurt Huber and students Christopher Probst, Willi Graf, and Alexander Schmorell—were soon arrested as well. Latter-day accounts of the Scholls' torture and captivity claim that the young people remained steadfastly brave—resigned to their fates but still committed to their cause.

The Scholls were tried by the *Volksgerichtshof* (People's Court), headed by the notorious Roland Freisler. Not surprisingly, the trial was a sham and the Scholls were sentenced to death by beheading.

According to her sister, Inge, Sophie Scholl lived her final hours with an odd sort of serenity. She left behind in her cell a scrap of paper upon which she had written the word "Freedom." She died on February 22, 1943. Hans followed. On his prison wall he had written, "To stand defiant before overwhelming power." Seconds before the executioner's axe fell, Hans Scholl shouted, "Long live freedom!"

---

start of Germany and her satellites in Southeastern Europe unloading all of their unwanted nationals (read Jews) on other countries (read the Allies). To Britain, Palestine is out of the question as a destination. The only way to help the Jews, the Allies maintain, is by an Allied victory; *See* February 16, 1943.

• **February 14–25, 1943: Americans and Germans clash at the Battle of Kasserine Pass, Tunisia.**

• **February 16, 1943: A small group of Palestinian Jews, the "Bergson Boys," agitate in the United States to try to help European Jews. Their strong activist stance upsets many main-line American Jewish organizations, who** fear that these tactics will stimulate American antisemitism—already at its highest level in history. The Boys run this full-page advertisement: "For Sale to Humanity/70,000 Jews/Guaranteed Human Beings at $50 a Piece." This advertisement in *The New York Times* offers Americans the opportunity to ransom 70,000 Romanian Jews; *See* March 9, 1943.

Germany's allies played an important role in the perpetration of the Holocaust. This agreement is signed by Bulgarian Commissar for Jewish Affairs Aleksander Belev and German Plenipotentiary *SS Haupsturm-führer* Theodor Dannecker. It is concerned with the deportation of 20,000 Jews from Thrace and Macedonia, newly annexed by Bulgaria, to Eastern Europe. Upon arriving in Occupied Europe, the Jews were murdered by the Nazis.

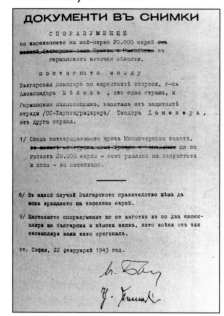

After their humiliating defeat at the hands of German forces in February 1943, U.S. forces, reinforced by the British troops of General Harold Alexander, rallied to retake the Kasserine Pass and block the German effort to capture Tébessa, Algeria. If the Germans had succeeded, they would have kept British and American troops from joining forces, a tactic key to winning the battle for Tunisia. Here, American soldiers salvage equipment.

Janine Putter, a refugee child from France, lights one of the memorial candles at a protest prayer service held in New York's Mecca Temple on February 22, 1943. More than 3000 children from 518 religious schools in the New York area attended the event to protest the treatment of children in Nazi-occupied Europe.

1943

• Theodor Eicke, inspector of concentration camps, dies in a plane crash.

• February 18, 1943: The anti-Nazi White Rose activities in Munich, Germany, culminate in the arrest of University of Munich students (and brother and sister) Hans and Sophie Scholl; *See* February 22, 1943.

• February 20, 1943: Crematorium II is completed at Auschwitz-Birkenau. It can burn 1440 bodies per day.

• February 22, 1943: White Rose student resistance leaders, the brother and sister Hans and Sophie Scholl, are beheaded in Munich, Germany; *See* Mid-July 1943. • The Jewish community at Stanisławów, Ukraine, is

Resistance against the German invaders was especially strong in the Soviet Union, where the Nazis pursued barbarous occupation policies. These five Soviets were hanged in Kharkov. The signs around their necks read, "Punishment for blowing up mines." Such acts of sabotage played a role in the turning of the tide on the Eastern Front and the eventual defeat of the Third Reich.

The Rosenstrasse Protest

One of the most effective acts of resistance against Nazi tyranny occurred in early 1943. Hundreds of male Jews married to gentile women were arrested and interned at the *Rosenstrasse* Jewish community center in the heart of old Berlin, but their wives' incessant demands for their release proved successful. This singular successful act of mass German protest against the deportation of German Jews raises a haunting question: What might have been achieved had more Germans acted in a similar manner?

The remarkable episode began when the last Jews remaining in Berlin were rounded up on February 27, 1943. Those married to German gentiles were brought to the *Rosenstrasse* facility. A "telephone chain" of interfaith couples spread the word on the whereabouts of their loved ones and, soon, anxious spouses arrived at *Rosenstrasse*. They demanded information about their husbands, brought them food, and insisted that the men be released.

Although the women were ordered to disperse and threatened with gunfire, they remained steadfast in their demands. The protest ended when Joseph Goebbels and others in the Nazi hierarchy grew fearful of domestic unrest, and released the Jewish men.

In March 1943 4000 Jews from Bulgarian-controlled Thrace in Greece were rounded up and sent to their deaths at Treblinka. A week later another 7000 Jews from nearby Macedonia in Yugoslavia were shipped to a tobacco company, whose buildings were converted into a concentration camp *(pictured)*. The Jews were kept there a few weeks, then sent to Treblinka. Few survived.

annihilated. • Bulgaria signs an agreement with Germany to allow deportations of 20,000 Jews from the former Yugoslav region of Macedonia and former Greek region of Thrace, both now controlled by Bulgaria. About 11,000 Jews will actually be deported (in March). • In Lyons, France, Italian military authorities order the local chief of police to nul-

lify a German order for the deportation of several hundred Jews to the Auschwitz extermination camp.

• February 23, 1943: The 16th (Lithuanian) Division of the Red Army, which includes many Jews, attacks a superior German force in the Ukraine.

• February 24, 1943: A ghetto is established in Salonika, Greece.

• February 27, 1943: SS troops begin to round up Jewish factory workers in Berlin to be sent to camps and killing centers in the East.

• February 27–early March 1943: Those Jewish workers rounded up in

Rescuers

Not nearly enough was done to rescue the Jews during the Holocaust. Yet, whereas governments, churches, and international conferences failed to stop the Nazis from murdering six million people, thousands of individuals did effectively act to save Jewish lives.

Ordinary people of all backgrounds defied the dangers to come to the aid of persecuted Jews. Rescue efforts were geographically diverse, and the degree of difficulty involved also varied. Rescuers' activities were influenced not only by the extent of Nazi control of an area, but by hostile or sympathetic attitudes of native populations. Moreover, not all rescuers acted from moral conviction. Some offered aid only in exchange for exorbitant fees.

Rescue operations in Occupied Western Europe, particularly in Denmark, Belgium, France, and Italy, succeeded in saving substantial portions of the respective nations' native Jewish communities. Danish citizens organized fishing-boat flotillas that helped almost all of the country's Jews escape to neutral Sweden. In France, a variety of groups and individuals rescued some 7000 children, smuggling many into Switzerland and Spain.

Involved were Protestant and Catholic church leaders and peasants as well as the Jewish child care organization *Ouvres de Secours aux Enfants* and the Jewish scouting organization *Éclaireurs israélites de France.* Director Germaine Le Henaff *(pictured)* hid several Jews in the *Chateau de la Guette* children's home.

The underground French organization *Circuit Garel* rescued many children from Nazi transit camps and hid them in foster homes. The villagers of Le Chambon-sur-Lignon in Vichy France provided safe haven for thousands of Jews until members of the Resistance could guide them into Switzerland.

In Eastern Europe, more direct German rule along with violently antisemitic attitudes created even greater obstacles to the rescue of Jews. Little organized aid was extended in Poland, although thousands of individu-

als helped Jews, particularly in Warsaw during 1942–43. The few groups offering support included the Catholic Scout movement as well as *Zegota* (Council for Aid to Jews). Some within the Polish Catholic Church urged rescue of Jews. In Lvov, Leopold Socha hid 21 Jews within the city's sewer system.

A number of international organizations, including the American Jewish Joint Distribution Committee, the World Jewish Congress, and the War Refugee Board, supported both overt and clandestine actions in order to save as many Jews as possible. They established secret contacts with Jewish communities in Occupied Europe, exchanged vital information, arranged crucial funding, organized emigration schemes, and abetted escape attempts.

Raoul Wallenberg, a member of the Swedish legation in Hungary, issued protective passports and secured life-saving shelter, food, and medicine for thousands of Hungarian Jews. Thousands of other quiet yet indispensable heroes—ranging from farmers and laborers to teachers and factory owners (such as Oskar Schindler)—fooled the Gestapo and concealed and protected Jews.

1943

Berlin who have Christian spouses are released after their spouses and children publicly protest their arrest at the Berlin Gestapo headquarters on *Rosenstrasse.* The release is ordered by Propaganda Minister Joseph Goebbels and later approved by Hitler himself, who seems to fear public disorder.

• March 1943: 850 Jews are deported from Poznań, Poland, to the Łódź (Poland) Ghetto. A few are assigned to work in a shoe factory but the rest are marked for death in the East. • In the Warsaw Ghetto, three orphaned children—12-year-old Matti Drobless, his 14-year-old sister, and his nine-year-old brother—escape through the city's sewer system. • Nearly 5700

Miriam Szyfman-Fainer and Moyshe Koyfman, members of the Bund, stroll through the streets of the Warsaw Ghetto. The Bund was a Jewish Socialist organization that had loose but cordial ties with the general Socialist movement in Poland. In the ghettos of Poland, members of the Bund were deeply involved in the Resistance movements. Szyfman-Fainer and Koyfman both perished in the Warsaw Ghetto uprising.

A parade of doomed souls stretches toward the gas chambers of Auschwitz-Birkenau. Exhausted by their endless journeys from distant towns and villages, trainloads of victims arrived to face Josef Mengele, whose flick of a finger meant life or death. French Resistance member Charlotte Delbo, imprisoned at Auschwitz, described the station as a place where arrival and departure became synonymous.

With barbed wire strung across its top, the Vilna gate separated the ghetto from the rest of the city. The Germans established two ghettos at Vilna in September 1941, but they moved within weeks to liquidate the smaller of the two, whose members did not have a *Schein* (work permit). For about a year, beginning in spring 1942, there were no major deportations, as the ghetto residents sought to ensure their survival by producing goods for the German war effort. This drawing by Z. Weiner dates from 1942–43.

Jews are deported from the Westerbork, Holland, transit camp to the Sobibór, Poland, death camp. • Thousands of Jews are shot at Minsk, Belorussia; 50 escape and join the "Revenge" partisan group. • The Bulgarian Army assists with Nazi deportations of Jews from Macedonia and Thrace to death camps in Poland. • Extermination activity is temporarily halted at the Chelmno, Poland, death camp; *See* June 23, 1944.

• March–July 1943: The SS mounts an ongoing effort at the Treblinka death camp to eliminate evidence of mass murder.

• Early March 1943: Jews of Thrace and Macedonia are arrested and transported by train and barge to the Treblinka death camp.

• March 1, 1943: One hundred Jews from Paderborn, Germany, are deported to Auschwitz. • A massive "Stop Hitler Now" rally takes place in New York City's Madison Square Garden.

The remaining Jews of Kolomyia, Ukraine, were slaughtered in March 1943. A few years earlier, the Hungarian governor had prevented local Ukrainians from murdering Jews, but liquidations began in 1942. This picture shows dozens of Jewish corpses lined up on the ground. A sympathetic Ukrainian appears to be contemplating the bodies in sorrow.

German soldiers force Jews in Marseilles, France, aboard freight cars for deportation to Drancy or Compiègne, France. Four thousand Jews were deported in the *Aktion* of March 1943. In 1942 Monsignor Jean Delay, the archbishop of Marseilles, said his government was justified in defending itself against Jews, who, in his words, had done much evil and should be punished severely.

Before United Nations flags and huge replicas of the Ten Commandments tablets, the Jewish pageant *We Will Never Die* opened in New York City on March 9, 1943. The show starred such Jewish-American actors as Edward G. Robinson, Paul Muni, and Sylvia Sidney. Ultimately, more than 100,000 Americans witnessed this pageant, including many government officials. The spectacle was sponsored by Palestinian Jews, called the Bergson Boys, who worked in the United States to communicate the plight of European Jews. They were unable, however, to change American policy.

1943

• **March 4, 1943: Noted painter Hermann Lismann is deported to the Majdanek death camp.**

• **March 5, 1943: About 1300 Jews are exterminated near the Khmel'nik (Ukraine) Ghetto. Shmuel Zalcman, chairman of the Khmel'nik Jewish Council, is dragged to his death behind a horse-drawn cart because** of his contacts with the local Jewish underground.

• **March 6, 1943: Twenty young Jews escape the ghetto at Swieciany, Ukraine, to nearby woods.**

• **March 7, 1943: The Jewish community at Radoszkowice, Belorussia, is destroyed.**

Dimitur Peshev, vice-president of the Bulgarian National Assembly, was one of the delegation deputies elected by the citizens of Kyustendil to appeal the order to evacuate the local Jewish population. The deputies presented a statement of protest to Parliament, but withdrew it after the king exerted pressure on them. Although Peshev's refusal to withdraw his signature resulted in his being dismissed from his government post, the deportation orders for the Kyustendil Jews were rescinded.

Even under the conditions that existed at Belzec, Jewish prisoners tried to maintain some remnant of their prewar religious practices. These kiddush cups, found in the camp, were used to celebrate the Sabbath. Such rituals were illegal in the camp, and the punishment for practicing them was death. Jews, however, still felt the need to practice their religious rites, especially under such trying circumstances.

Bulgaria and the Holocaust

Bulgaria is a Balkan nation on the Black Sea, bordered by Turkey, Romania, Yugoslavia, and Greece. In 1939 the Bulgarian government ordered foreign Jews out of the country, while the country's radio and press expressed antisemitic sentiments. In the same year, the British Foreign Office warned the Bulgarians that if Bulgarian Jews were shipped to Palestine, the British would "expect the Bulgarian government to take the immigrants back."

The Nazis pressured Bulgaria into allying with Germany during the Second World War—an alliance that frightened Bulgaria's 50,000 Sephardic Jews, who formed ten percent of the country's population. Pressured by the Germans, the Bulgarian government passed antisemitic laws that were supported by some trade and business groups as well as by right-wing  **and military organizations. Although antisemitism was common, the nation's clergy, monarchy, parliament, and workers prevented the German SS from deporting most Bulgarian Jews. Nevertheless, almost 12,000 Jews living in lands the Germans had awarded Bulgaria (Thrace and Macedonia) were rounded up and sent to their deaths at the Treblinka death camp.**

From September 1944 to April 1945, Bulgaria waged war against Germany. The Bulgarian Army, including Jews, fought Germans in Yugoslavia and Hungary.

● **March 8–13, 1943: Jews are part of a Red Army force that mounts a massive offensive against the Germans at Sokolov, Russia. Three hundred Jewish casualties, including 140 fatalities, are tallied by battle's end.**

● **March 9, 1943: The Bergson Boys pageant, "We Will Never Die," opens in New York City. More than 100,000** Americans witness the show, including many government officials.

● **March 10, 1943: The SS demands the deportation of all Bulgarian Jews to Poland, but the Bulgarian government resists thanks to the ambivalence of the nation's king as well as protests by clergy, farmers, and intellectuals. Despite the protests, some** Bulgarian Jews are exiled to labor camps at Radomir and Samovit, Bulgaria. However, none are deported, and Bulgaria's Jewish population will continue to increase throughout the remainder of the war.

● **March 13, 1943: A bomb plot is attempted against Hitler, but explosives disguised by General Henning**

American Jewish Organizations

Throughout the Second World War, American-Jewish organizations engaged in a relentless but relatively unsuccessful effort to save European Jewry. Their campaigns intensified in 1943 after reports of Hitler's genocidal programs were confirmed.

The mainstream American-Jewish organizations, led by Rabbi Stephen Wise, organized public demonstrations and lobbied government officials. The American Jewish Congress's "Stop Hitler Now" demonstration in New York City on March 1, 1943, attracted an estimated 75,000 people. The throng listened to speeches by leaders of the American Federation of Labor, the Congress of Industrial Organizations, and other non-Jewish associations.

A more radical group, the Committee for a Jewish Army (CJA), attempted to broker a rescue operation for Romanian Jews. The group took out ads in major newspapers, which claimed that the freedom of 70,000 Jews could be purchased for $50 apiece. Obvious shock value aside, the ad's intent was to show that rescue of Jews was a matter of Allied will.

On March 15, 1943, eight major Jewish organizations created the Joint Emergency Committee on European Affairs (JEC). The committee strived to expand the public-information campaign, to spur the United States Congress to support rescue operations, and to organize high-level conferences on behalf of European Jewry. President Franklin Roosevelt finally created the War Refugee Board, but not until January 1944—14 months after he had learned about the "Final Solution."

Henning von Tresckow was a major general in the German Army who joined the opposition movement against Hitler. While serving on the Russian front, Tresckow became convinced that the campaign was destined for failure and that Hitler had to be removed from power. He was involved in the failed attempt on Hitler's life in March 1943 that took place in Smolensk, Russia; a bomb made of plastic explosives and disguised as bottles of brandy failed to detonate after being placed aboard the *Führer*'s private plane. After the plot to kill Hitler in July 1944 also failed, Tresckow took his own life.

Accompanied by high-level German military officers, Jozef Tiso engages in friendly conversation with Hitler. As leader of Slovakia, Tiso allowed the deportation of Jews, although he had the power to intervene and did so in a few cases. Although some 25,000 Jews still resided in Slovakia, the deportations halted in March 1943, perhaps because the Nazis wished to focus on making other areas "Jew free"—or perhaps because many of the remaining Jews were skilled laborers useful to the Nazis.

1943

von Tresckow as bottles of brandy fail to explode aboard Hitler's private plane. • The SS establishes *Ostindustrie GmbH* (East Industry, Inc.) in Poland to organize and exploit slave labor in and around Lublin. The project is supervised by Odilo Globocnik.

• March 14, 1943: Two thousand Jews in Kraków, Poland, are assembled for deportation. Before the train leaves for Auschwitz, hundreds of small children and old people are murdered in the streets and in ditches outside of town. Patients at Kraków's Jewish hospital are murdered by Gestapo agents.

• March 15, 1943: Deportations of Jews in Salonika, Greece, to Ausch-

Surrounded by bags of goods, a Jewish woman in the Chelmno death camp sorts clothing from the transports, which will be shipped to warehouses near Lódź, Poland. Beginning in March 1943, transports to Chelmno ceased when the camp reached its goal of killing most of the Jews in Warthegau, the former Polish territory annexed to the Reich. The killings resumed about a year later when the decision was made to gas prisoners of the Lódź Ghetto.

Five German soldiers surround the corpses of two Russian civilians whom they have just executed. Although theoretically protected under the rules of war, civilians on the Eastern Front became frequent targets of the Germans. The Nazis exacted ruthless punishment on anyone suspected of being a partisan or aiding partisan activity.

Wilhelm Boger (far right) was generally considered the cruelest of the guards at Auschwitz. Witnesses at his trial claimed that his hands often became coated with the blood of the victims of his sadistic methods of torture. On the left is a model of the "Boger swing," an apparatus for torture that Boger called his "talking machine."

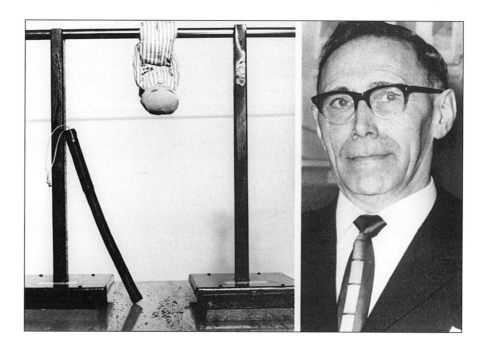

witz begin. The first group numbers 2800. • Trude Neumann, a former mental patient in a hospital near Vienna and daughter of Theodor Herzl, the founder of Zionism, dies of starvation at the camp/ghetto at Theresienstadt, Czechoslovakia.

• March 16, 1943: A much-feared SS trooper is murdered in Lvov,

Ukraine, by a Jewish man named Kotnowski; *See* March 17, 1943.

• March 17, 1943: More than 1200 Jews from Lvov, Ukraine, are killed at Piaski, Poland, as retribution for the March 16 murder of an SS trooper by a Jewish man. Eleven Jewish policemen are hanged in the ghetto, 1000 Jewish slave laborers are executed,

and an additional 200 Jews are murdered.

• March 18, 1943: The hiding place of Dr. Julian Charin, age 30, of Lapy, Ukraine, is betrayed to the Nazis, and Charin is shot. • At Auschwitz, 26-year-old underground fighter Lonka Kozibrodska dies of typhus.

Three elderly Jews walk arm-in-arm through the streets of Kraków, Poland, during the final liquidation of the ghetto. The deportations during 1942 had significantly reduced the number of ghetto inhabitants in Kraków and served as a prelude to the final liquidation that occurred in March 1943. That month 2000 Jews were transferred to the nearby Plaszów work camp, and 2300 more were deported to Auschwitz. Jewish Resistance groups helped hundreds of Kraków Jews escape to relative safety. Armed partisan groups were active in areas surrounding the city, and they engaged German troops in gun battles that helped indirectly to slow the pace of deportations.

The abandoned possessions of Jews recently deported from Kraków litter the streets of the ghetto. The liquidation of Kraków was a painfully brutal operation. In addition to the Jews who were deported to Plaszów, Poland, and Auschwitz, 700 Jews were shot on the spot.

This doll belonged to a child living in the Kraków (Poland) Ghetto. The doll's owner, Zofia Burowska, recovered it after the war from non-Jews who saved it for her. It was especially important to Zofia because it had been made specifically for her. Toys such as this doll were often the only links Jewish children had to a normal childhood.

1943

• **March 20, 1943: At Czestochowa, Poland, on the eve of Purim, more than 100 Jewish physicians, engineers, and lawyers as well as their families are taken to a cemetery by Nazis and shot. Victims include 56-year-old gynecologist Dr. Kruza Gruenwald, 30-year-old general practitioner Dr. Irena Horowicz, and 44-year-old neurologist Dr. Bernard Epstein.**

• **March 21, 1943: During the Jewish festival of Purim, 2300 Jews from Skopje, Yugoslavia, are deported to Auschwitz. • Eight members of the Jewish intelligentsia are taken from Piotrków, Poland, to a Jewish cemetery and shot, along with the cemetery's caretaker and his wife. The Germans engineer these killings to total ten, in a macabre reference to**

Janek Krauze fought with partisans in Czestochowa, Poland. The German *Aktion* against the ghetto's inhabitants in January 1943 inaugurated a series of resistance activities, both inside and outside the ghetto. Krauze was killed on March 19, 1943; the fighting continued on and off into the summer months. On June 25 the ZOB (Jewish Fighting Organization) mounted a campaign to resist the liquidation of the small ghetto area of Czestochowa.

MAJOR CONCENTRATION CAMPS IN BALTIC NATIONS, 1941–1945

Nazi *Einsatzgruppen* massacred most of the 350,000 Baltic Jews in 1941. Beginning in late 1942, tens of thousands of Jews from other European countries were sent to forced-labor camps in Estonia.

The deserted square and empty buildings testify to the recent *Aktion* (deportation) of Jews from Czestochowa, Poland. Almost 30,000 Jews, comprising 30 percent of the population, had once contributed to the hustle and bustle of this formerly lively town. During the war the city's ghetto became an assembly point to dispatch Jews sent there from throughout Europe. They were transported to labor camps and to the Treblinka death camp. At one time the ghetto held 48,000 Jews, but its numbers were greatly depleted by 1943.

the biblical story of the hanged ten sons of the Jew-hating Haman—a crucial character in the Purim story. • At Radom, Poland, Jewish physicians are removed from the ghetto and executed at nearby Szydlowiec.

• March 22, 1943: Crematorium IV opens at Auschwitz-Birkenau.

• March 23, 1943: Twenty-nine Jewish orphans at La Rose Orphanage in Les Accates, France, as well as Alice Salomon, the guardian who refused to leave them two months before, are gassed at the Sobibór death camp.
• Seventeen hundred Gypsies are murdered at Auschwitz. • In France, 4000 Jews are deported from Marseilles, interned briefly at Drancy,

France, then deported to Sobibór.
• William Temple, archbishop of Canterbury, states in the House of Lords that Britain should lift all quotas on Jewish immigration into Britain.

• March 25, 1943: One thousand Jews are deported from Marseilles, France, to the Sobibór death camp.
• The Jewish community from

William Temple, religious head of the Church of England, was one of a handful of British voices speaking out on behalf of the Jews. In March 1943 he moved in the House of Lords that Britain lift all quotas on Jewish immigration into their country. He also advocated warning the Germans that those responsible for war crimes would be held accountable once the war was over.

The bima from the destroyed synagogue in Lvov, Ukraine, remained largely intact after the liquidation of the ghetto. The ghetto officially became a labor camp in January 1943, but 10,000 Jews without employment cards were executed. A "cleansing" operation in March murdered 1500 more Jews and transported another 800 to a Nazi death camp. Armed resistance during the final liquidation compelled the Germans to destroy the ghetto building by building. Lvov's Greek Catholic Church expressed unhappiness with these events—not so much over the destruction of the Jews (the Church was of the opinion that Jewry was dedicated to the destruction of Christianity)—but because Ukrainian locals were encouraged to participate in the murders.

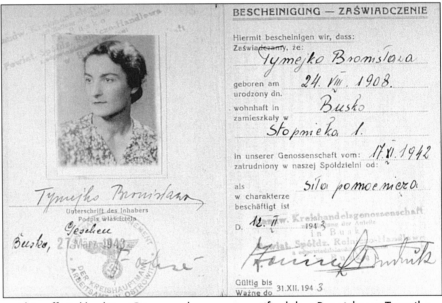

This official-looking German document certified that Bronislawa Tymejko (Laura Schwarzwald) was employed by the agricultural cooperative in Busko-Zdroj. False papers such as this enabled Polish Jews to live under assumed names and avoid deportation. Although conditions within the work cooperatives run by the Nazis were harsh, the laborers were not worked to death. False papers, therefore, were virtually a staff of life for Jews fortunate enough to obtain them.

1943

Zólkiew, Poland, is marched to the Borek Forest and executed. • An anonymous letter written by a non-Jewish German citizen, critical of Nazi ghetto-liquidation techniques, is forwarded to Hitler's Chancellery.

• Spring 1943: Nazi kill squads have so far murdered almost two million Jews in Eastern Europe. • The Ger-

mans force Jewish prisoners to burn the bodies of 600,000 Jews exterminated at Belzec.

• April 1943: A concentration camp is established at Bergen-Belsen, Germany. • Germans launch an offensive against Jewish partisans active in the Parczew Forest, Poland. • Resistance members derail a death train in Bel-

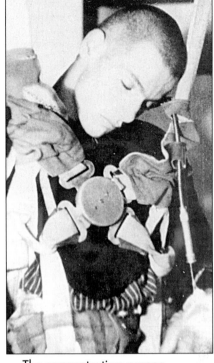

Over 75 percent of Dutch Jews were deported to Auschwitz, Sobibór, and other death camps. Few survived. Some Dutch citizens struggled to thwart the massive Nazi effort to exterminate the country's Jews. Among those efforts was the bombing of the Amsterdam population registry *(below)* on March 27, 1943. Several conspirators, including C. Hartogh *(left)*, plotted the destruction to impede the Nazis' deportation plans. Hartogh was executed a few months later.

The concentration camps provided Nazi doctors with a large pool of human guinea pigs for their "experiments," many of which had specifically military objectives. This man was the victim of an air-pressure experiment at the Dachau, Germany, concentration camp, the goal of which was to measure human endurance at extremely high altitudes. In the course of the experiment, the man was placed in a pressure chamber from which air was slowly removed. Thus, Nazi "scientists" could determine how high their pilots could safely fly.

gium. • Pope Pius XII complains that Jews are demanding and ungrateful. • Dr. Julian Chorazycki, a former captain in the Polish Army and a leader of inmate resistance at the Treblinka death camp, takes poison when the camp's deputy commandant spies currency Chorazycki had planned to use to buy small arms; *See* May 3, 1943.

• April 5, 1943: Three hundred Jews from Soly and Smorgon, Belorussia, are transported by rail westward to Vilna, Lithuania. En route, the captives shatter the railcars' wire-reinforced glass and attempt to flee, but are shot to death by guards. The survivors are later shot at Ponary, southwest of Vilna, by German and Lithuanian SS troops. About 4000

Jews from in and around Vilna are trucked to Ponary, slaughtered, and dumped into mass graves. Jews arriving at the Ponary station by rail from Oszmiana and Swieciany, Lithuania, resist with revolvers, knives, and their bare hands; a few dozen escape to Vilna and the rest are shot. During the massacre, a Lithuanian policeman is wounded by Jews and an SS ser-

The Bermuda Conference

Public outcry in the United States and Britain over the news that the Nazi regime was systematically murdering European Jewry provided the impetus for the Bermuda Conference of April 1943. Although ostensibly designed to solve the refugee problem caused by Hitler's genocidal policies, the conference is regarded as the pinnacle of Allied efforts to stonewall rescue operations.

Pre-conference negotiations limited the topics open to discussion in Bermuda, which virtually guaranteed the conference's failure. British and American officials decided beforehand to downplay the Jewish part of the problem and insist that Jews were only one of many victimized groups during the war. The decision demonstrated the unwillingness of Britain and the U.S. to seriously consider plans to rescue European Jews from the clutches of the Nazi regime. A myriad of additional problems doomed the entire enterprise.

Designed to deflect an aroused public opinion, the Bermuda Conference failed completely. In the words of Myron C. Taylor, the principal American representative at the Evian Conference of 1938, "The Bermuda Conference was wholly ineffective...and we knew it would be." The British and American governments' indifference to the tragic plight of European Jewry was plain for all to see.

Assistant Secretary of State Breckinridge Long exercised his influence within the State Department to prevent the U.S. from becoming a place of refuge for European Jews. Long's xenophobia influenced practically every move he made during the war: He led the State Department action to deny visas to political and intellectual refugees. He pushed for decreased immigration quotas. And he suggested Bermuda as the site for the refugee conference because of its inaccessibility.

Individuals from a range of professional backgrounds attended the ill-fated Bermuda Conference on refugees in April 1943. Standing *(from left to right)* are George Hall, the British parliamentary undersecretary in the Admiralty; Harold W. Dodds, president of Princeton University; Richard K. Law, British undersecretary for foreign affairs; Sol Bloom, chairman of the United States House Foreign Affairs Committee; and Osbert Peake, parliamentary undersecretary in the home office.

1943

geant is hospitalized after being stabbed in the back and in the head. • At the Treblinka death camp station, the final train bringing Jews from Macedonia arrives. All aboard are gassed immediately.

• April 7, 1943: Jewish resistance led by Michael Glanz occurs at Skalat, Ukraine.

• April 8–9, 1943: One thousand Jews are executed near Ternopol, Ukraine.

• April 13, 1943: In the Katyn Forest in the Soviet Union, the Germans discover more than 4000 corpses of Polish officers, some of them Jews. The officers were killed by the Soviets.

Bergen-Belsen, in Germany, opened in April 1943 as a transit camp. Hence, the majority of its early inmates were non-German Jews, and conditions there were less severe than in other camps. Nonetheless, as the war turned against Germany, and large numbers of prisoners reached the camp after death marches, conditions deteriorated. Around 50,000 died in Bergen-Belsen, approximately 14,000 of them after the camp's liberation.

Alfred Krupp was head of the famous German arms manufacturer from the early 1930s to the end of the war. This photograph shows him being taken into custody by American troops prior to being put on trial at Nuremberg. Under his oversight, the Krupp works made extensive use of the cruel and cost-effective slave labor provided by the Third Reich's system of concentration camps. He paid the government for his workers, who received no wages. Thousands died in the appalling conditions that characterized his factories.

These mountains of shoes were once the property of victims gassed at Auschwitz. The Nazis made a considerable effort to exploit their victims economically, and this included seizing any property that could be used in the war effort. At Auschwitz, confiscated property was kept in *Effektenkammern* (storerooms of movables). The inmates called the area "Canada" because of the sheer amount of loot stored there, which they associated with the riches of Canada.

• **April 14, 1943:** The slave-labor camp at Siedlce, Poland, is dissolved.
• **A paper,** *Program for the Rescue of Jews from Nazi Occupied Europe,* **is submitted to the Bermuda Conference by the Joint Emergency Committee for European Jewish Affairs;** *See* **April 19, 1943.** • **Gerhart Riegner, World Jewish Congress representative in Geneva, suggests that money**

be deposited in a Swiss account to be paid after the war to enable the 70,000 Romanian Jews previously offered to the Allies to immigrate to Palestine. This comes to be known as the Riegner Plan; *See* May 1943.

• **April 17-18, 1943:** Hitler meets with the Hungarian regent, Admiral Miklós Horthy, at the Klessheim Castle,

near Salzburg, Austria, to encourage the deportations of Hungarian Jews. Horthy refuses to acquiesce.

• **April 18, 1943:** Word leaks into the Warsaw Ghetto of German plans for the ghetto's destruction; *See* April 19, 1943. • Nearly 3500 Jews from six Polish towns are transported to Jaworow, Poland, and shot. Resisters

Harry Baur, one of the most esteemed actors of the French and German cinemas, was among the Nazis' victims. Born in 1880, Baur established an international reputation, starring in such films as *Les Miserables,* in which he played Jean Valjean, *The Life and Loves of Beethoven,* and *Crime and Punishment.* While some stars of both stage and film fled Europe for the United States, others were unable or unwilling to do so. Accused of being an Allied agent, Baur died on April 20, 1943, while in Nazi confinement.

Suitcases of Jews deported to Auschwitz-Birkenau, the camp's killing center, serve as a stark reminder that the victims had no notion of their impending doom. Orders for deportation came suddenly and swiftly. Jews hurriedly placed a few precious belongings in suitcases, wrote their names on the exteriors, and boarded trains to what they

thought would be relocation centers somewhere in Eastern Europe. Upon boarding, people were separated from their belongings and told the items would be returned when they disembarked. Sorting through the belongings of Jews deported to Auschwitz and other death camps was a major and profitable undertaking.

Gerard Kornmann hid Dutch Jews on two occasions. In the end, however, an informer betrayed him, and he was arrested and shipped to the Sachsenhausen, Germany, concentration camp via the Vught, Netherlands, transit camp. Following the Allied invasion of Western Europe, his captors shipped him to Lübeck, Germany. He was on the *Cap Arcona,* which was among the four boats that the British bombed, assuming that the passengers were German, on May 3, 1945. Kornmann died in the attack. The irony of all this is painfully obvious, yet Kornmann's ultimate fate can be traced back to the informer—possibly a neighbor or even a "friend"— who betrayed him to the occupying authorities. The possible reason can only be guessed at.

1943

who escape to nearby forests are led by Artur Henner and Henry Gleich; most will subsequently be killed by German troops.

• **April 19, 1943: The Warsaw Ghetto uprising begins.** More than 2000 soldiers—SS, regular Army, and foreign troops—invade the ghetto. They attempt to liquidate the ghetto (40,000 inhabitants) on the eve of Passover, but about 700 Jews revolt. The Jews arm themselves with about 17 rifles, 500 pistols, and several thousand grenades and Molotov cocktails. The Jewish underground will fight the Nazis until the middle of May. The Polish underground will give only minimal help because of antisemitism prevalent among many.

In April 1943 the Germans uncovered the bodies of more than 4000 Polish POWs in the Katyn Forest, killed in 1940, apparently by the NKVD, the Soviet secret police. The Soviets denied all responsibility, contending that the Germans were to blame. The Polish government-in-exile in London suspected the Soviets, and its insistence that a thorough inquiry be pursued led to a cessation of relations between the Russians and the London Poles. This provided a pretext for Joseph Stalin to establish a Communist government in Poland after the war.

The Katyn Massacre

In April 1943 members of the German Army discovered a mass grave in a heavily forested area just outside of Katyn, a remote Soviet village. An international commission of physicians identified the bodies—4143 discovered, but thousands more believed to be killed—as Polish officers and soldiers. According to the report issued by the German government, the men were captured by the Soviets during the 1939 Polish campaign; each was killed with a single shot to the nape of the neck just prior to the German invasion of Russia.

When the Polish government-in-exile in London concurred with the report, Soviet leader Joseph Stalin broke off relations with the civilian regime and claimed that the Germans had committed the murders. The Allies upheld Stalin's claim until 1952, when a United States congressional inquiry concluded that the Soviet secret police were responsible. In April 1990 the Soviet Union acknowledged its responsibility for the Katyn Massacre.

The Allies will neither publicize events nor try to help; See April 20, 1943.

• The Bermuda Conference of Great Britain and the U.S., held in Hamilton, Bermuda, takes no meaningful action to help Jews in Europe. Before the meeting, representatives of both countries had agreed not to discuss immigration of Jews to their nations nor to ship food to Jewish refugees in German-occupied Europe.

• April 20, 1943: In the Warsaw Ghetto, Germans set fire to houses block by block and shoot all who emerge from buildings, bunkers, and sewers. Many Jews travel across rooftops and continue to fight. Patients at Warsaw's Czyste Hospital are murdered by German troops; See April 25, 1943. • Popular French film star Harry Baur dies in Berlin after being tortured by the Gestapo.

• April 22, 1943: The Jews of Amersfoort, Holland, are deported.

• April 25, 1943: As fires set by Germans consume the Warsaw Ghetto, a

Warsaw Ghetto Uprising

Irena Kleppfisch, a child survivor of the Holocaust, is an important writer whose best known works include a poem called *"Bashert."* Its title, a Yiddish word, evokes senses of inevitability and fate. As it grieves and protests, *"Bashert"* does not mention the Holocaust directly, but that event shadows every line: "These words are dedicated to those who died.... These words are dedicated to those who survived."

Kleppfisch's father, Michael, was one of those who died. Israel Gutman, survivor and historian of the Warsaw Ghetto uprising, says that Michael Kleppfisch, "who played an important role in the manufacture of armaments in the ghetto," was killed on April 20, 1943. He died in hand-to-hand fighting against Brigadier General Jürgen Stroop's German forces, who had been directed to liquidate the ghetto.

In the summer of 1942, the Nazis removed 300,000 Jews from the Warsaw Ghetto. Most were sent to their deaths in Treblinka's gas chambers. Michael Kleppfisch and Gutman were members of a group of young Jewish men and women—they numbered 700 to 750—who trained and armed themselves as best as they could. They were determined to resist Nazi efforts to destroy the nearly 60,000 Jews who remained in the ghetto in the early spring of 1943.

In January of that year, SS chief Heinrich Himmler had ordered further deportations, but Jewish resistance impeded that effort. Aware that they would meet determined resistance, the Germans regrouped and returned on Monday, April

19, the eve of Passover, to finish the job. What ensued was, in Gutman's words, "the first urban uprising in German-occupied Europe, and, among the Jewish uprisings, the one that lasted the longest, from April 19 to May 16, 1943."

The poorly armed Jewish fighters, who also lacked military training and battle experience, were outnumbered three-to-one by Nazi forces, who had tanks and cannons. The Jews' "arsenal" consisted mainly of pistols, Molotov cocktails, and a few rifles, which had been smuggled into the ghetto or looted from Germans who were ambushed in January's resistance. Using hit-and-run tactics and taking advantage of bunker hiding places, the Jewish fighters kept the Nazis off balance during the uprising's early days. However, the Germans retaliated by burning the ghetto, building by building. Even then, Jewish resistance continued—doomed though it was. Not until May 8 did the Germans destroy the Jewish Fighting Organization's headquarters bunker at 18 Mila Street, a struggle in which Mordecai Anielewicz, the organization's commander, perished.

On May 16 Stroop declared victory, proclaiming that "the Jewish quarter of Warsaw no longer exists." The losses the Jewish fighters had inflicted on the Germans were militarily small—Stroop's report noted 16 dead and 85 wounded—but the Warsaw Ghetto uprising remains an immensely important example of heroic Jewish resistance against overwhelming odds.

1943

German Jew named Hoch desperately leaps from a fourth-floor window, breaking both arms and his spine; *See* Late April 1943.

• Late April 1943: Jewish resistance in the Warsaw Ghetto begins to falter as bunkers are broached by German troops. Artillery bombardment of the ghetto has foiled Jewish strategy of engaging Germans in costly hand-to-hand combat; *See* May 1943.

• April 27, 1943. Eminent American poet Ezra Pound continues his antisemitic broadcasts from Italy. He calls the Jews "rats," "bedbugs," "vermin," "worms," "bacilli," and "parasites" who constitute an overwhelming "power of putrefaction."

Members of the *Sicherheitsdienst* (SD) and other SS soldiers query a Hasidic Jew during the liquidation of the Warsaw Ghetto in April 1943. The interrogator may well have desired information about Jews in hiding. Ghetto *Judenrat* members and some other Warsaw Jews had hoped during 1941 and 1942 that, by developing the ghetto as a dependable source of labor, the majority of inhabitants might be saved. By the time of the uprising, however, Jewish assumptions of Nazi rationality had evaporated. If the soldiers seen here were determined to pry information from the assembled captives, they were likely disappointed.

A manhole cover from the Warsaw Ghetto offers tragic testimony to the fate of thousands of Jews. Jews engaged in resistance used sewers to escape and as avenues of transportation during the revolt. Sewers were also important links between Jewish Resistance fighters and the Polish underground, which operated on the Aryan side of Warsaw.

Ukrainian SS soldiers examine the bodies of Jews at the entrance to a destroyed apartment house in the Warsaw Ghetto. Auxiliary units from the Ukraine provided crucial manpower that was necessary to implement the Nazis' genocidal campaigns. The Ukrainian units were renowned for their brutal efficiency.

• **April 28, 1943:** An official SS telegram instructs the administration at Auschwitz to prepare 120 women for medical experiments.

• **April 29, 1943:** Near Kraków, Poland, Jewish women attack their male SS guards while being transferred from one prison to another. Two women escape but most of the others are killed. In Kraków proper, Jewish Resistance fighters incarcerated since December 1942 are trucked to the Plaszów, Poland, concentration camp. Most are killed after breaking out of the truck.

• **April 30, 1943:** Two thousand Jews deported from Wlodawa, Poland, to Sobibór attack the death camp's SS guards on arrival at the unloading ramp. All of the Jews are killed by SS machine guns and grenades.

• **May 1943:** *SS-Gruppenführer* Jürgen Stroop completes his official written chronicle of the liquidation of the Warsaw Ghetto: *The Stroop Report.*
• **Four trains carrying nearly 11,000 Jews arrive at Auschwitz from**

Before the liquidation of the Warsaw Ghetto, inhabitants feverishly constructed an elaborate series of bunkers and hideouts to evade their Nazi persecutors. Once the resistance operations began, the Nazis set fire to the ghetto in an attempt to force the Jews from their bunkers. In the above photo, a woman jumps from a balcony to escape the intense heat of the flames and avoid being burned alive.

1943

Salonika, Greece. • About 5000 Sephardic Jews are sent from Occupied Tunisia to labor camps near North African battle zones. • In Eastern Europe, the Red Army continues its westward advance. • Breckinridge Long and his supporters in the U.S. State Department, including Borden Reams and Robert Alexander, delay the license to transfer Jewish funds

intended to be used to allow the escape of 70,000 Jews from Romania (the Riegner Plan). These State Department officials worry that the Riegner Plan "might actually succeed."

• Abrasha Blum, an organizer of armed resistance in the Warsaw Ghetto and a member of the Coordi-

A Jewish man is removed from his hidden bunker during the Warsaw Ghetto uprising. Even after the ghetto was razed, Jews attempted to hide from the Nazis. To counter these efforts, SS commander Jürgen Stroop ordered his soldiers to employ whatever means necessary to flush the Jews from their hiding places. The troops used flamethrowers, gas, and grenades to achieve their goals.

Mordecai Anielewicz

Mordecai Anielewicz was the commander of the Warsaw Ghetto uprising. He personally led the attack against the Germans before being killed on May 8, 1943.

When Germany invaded Poland, Anielewicz became active in the underground movement. As the Nazi campaigns against the Jews turned genocidal, Anielewicz organized an armed resistance movement.

Returning to Warsaw in fall 1942, Anielewicz took command of the Jewish Fighting Organization (ZOB) and worked feverishly to secure weapons. During the mass deportations of January 1943, Anielewicz's group battled German troops in the streets. When a new wave of deportations began in April, Anielewicz and the ZOB launched a full-scale revolt. Shortly before his death, Anielewicz wrote: "My life's dream has come true. I have lived to see Jewish resistance in the ghetto in all its greatness and glory."

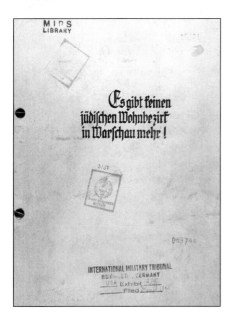

The *Stroop Report* was first published in 1960. The 75-page paper painstakingly describes the destruction of the Warsaw Ghetto and glorifies the author and commander Jürgen Stroop's role in the process. His daily entries and communiqués record the cold-blooded brutality he levied against Warsaw's Jews. On May 16, 1943, Stroop reported that the operation was complete and that "the Jewish Quarter of Warsaw is no more."

---

nating Committee of Jewish Organizations, is shot by Germans after enduring confinement and torture.

• **May 1, 1943:** Many members of the Brody, Ukraine, Jewish community are killed at the Majdanek death camp. • Jewish writers and artists, inspired by the Warsaw Ghetto uprising, gather in the Vilna (Lithuania)

Ghetto for an evening of poetry, with the hopeful theme "Spring in Yiddish Literature." • The Allies begin to push the Germans from Tunisia. • German Minister of Propaganda Joseph Goebbels, reacting to the Jewish Warsaw Ghetto revolt, notes in his diary: "Heavy engagements are being fought there which led even to the Jewish Supreme Command's issuing

daily communiques. Of course, this fun won't last very long. But it shows what is to be expected of the Jews when they are in possession of arms."

• **May 2, 1943:** Four thousand Jews from Miedzyrzec Podlaski, Poland, are murdered at the Treblinka death camp. • At Luków, Poland, 4000 Jews are killed.

Yitzhak Zuckerman

Born in Vilna, Lithuania, Yitzhak Zuckerman joined a Zionist youth movement, devoting himself to educating Jewish youth in Hebrew and Yiddish. Following the German invasion of Poland, he left for the Soviet-occupied area, but Zionist leaders later ordered him to return to continue his teaching and to develop a Jewish underground organization.

Zuckerman argued that educating the young was "meaningless...unless...an armed Jewish self-defense force would come into being." However, his pleas for armed resistance were initially rejected by the Warsaw Ghetto leaders. He became one of the founders of *Zydowska Organizacaja Bojowa* (ZOB; Jewish Fighting Organization) and was one of the heroic commanders of the Warsaw Ghetto revolt. Ordered to leave the ghetto to serve as a liaison to the Polish underground and to procure weapons, he returned through the sewers in the ghetto's last days to rescue survivors. Zuckerman died in 1981.

The razing of the Warsaw Ghetto enabled the Nazis to apprehend thousands of Resistance fighters. Most Jews hiding in bunkers, such as the two men in the photo above, were either killed or captured. The final hours and minutes of bunker-based resistance were frightening and savage: the cacophony of shouts and gunfire from above; footfalls that came increasingly closer; and the inevitable discovery, which culminated in suicidal firefights or rough hands that dragged the resisters blinking into the daylight. The Jews in the photo on the left have been removed from bunkers and now await their fate—probably deportation to Treblinka.

1943

• **May 3, 1943:** German troops in the "Aryan" section of Warsaw arrest and kill 21 women who are Jewish or suspected of being Jewish. • A Jewish man named Rakowski, an underground leader at the Treblinka death camp, is shot when currency intended to bribe Ukrainians to help him and a few others escape is discovered in his barrack.

• **May 4, 1943–May 25, 1943:** Four deportations of Jews from Holland to the death camps at Auschwitz and Sobibór total 8000 people.

• **May 6, 1943:** Hajj Amin al-Husseini, grand mufti of Jerusalem, suggests to the Bulgarian foreign minister that Bulgarian-Jewish children should be sent to Poland rather than to Pales-

Rubble from the Tlomacka Street synagogue in Warsaw, the so-called "Great Synagogue," is all that remained after Jürgen Stroop ordered its demolition in May 1943. The synagogue was located within the confines of the ghetto until November 1942, when the ghetto's size was greatly reduced. Even though the synagogue stood in the Aryan part of Warsaw when the ghetto was razed, Stroop ordered it destroyed in reprisal for the ghetto uprising.

On May 2, 1943, 3000 Jews of Miedzyrzec Podlaski, Poland—a transit ghetto—were deported to their deaths at Treblinka. Only 200 Jews, needed for forced labor, remained. Here, Jewish women, many carrying children, are brutally hustled into a waiting cattle car. During the previous August, thousands of Miedzyrzec Podlaski's Jews were sent to the death camp; 10,000 more were deported in October. Finally, in July 1943 the last 200 Jews were shot to death, making the town *Judenrein* (cleansed of Jews).

Although *Sonderkommandos* assisted the Nazis in order to spare their own lives (at least temporarily), they were often hated by those Jews doomed to die. Reportedly, a child of seven or eight told a Birkenau *Sonderkommando*: "Why, you are a Jew and you lead dear children to the gas—only in order to live? Is your life among the band of murderers really dearer to you than the lives of so many Jewish victims?"

tine. • In Tunisia, Allied forces launch a final offensive against Axis positions.

• **May 7, 1943:** Nearly 7000 Jews are killed in Novogrudok, Belorussia. • A group of Jewish fighters in the Warsaw Ghetto, led by Pawel Bruskin, is ambushed by German troops while traveling through the city's sewer system; *See* May 8, 1943. • Sephardic-

Jewish homes in Tunisia are ransacked and looted by departing German troops.

• **May 8, 1943:** German troops in the Warsaw Ghetto reach the headquarters of the Resistance. Leader Mordecai Anielewicz and about 100 of his followers are crushed, are suffocated, or die by their own hands during a

Nazi bombardment and gassing; *See* May 12, 1943.

• **May 9, 1943:** The Skalat, Ukraine, Jewish community is destroyed.

• **May 10, 1943:** Two Jews are successfully smuggled out of Dobele, Latvia, and hidden in a haystack.

Jürgen Stroop

General Jürgen Stroop gained notoriety for brutally suppressing the Warsaw Ghetto uprising of April-May 1943. In recognition of his services to the Third Reich, Stroop was awarded the Iron Cross First Class.

In April 1943 Stroop *(pictured, left)* was ordered to remove the remaining 56,000 Jews from Warsaw and to crush the revolt that had recently broken out. He approached the task with ruthless efficiency. More than 2000 SS and army units descended upon the ghetto and systematically destroyed it building by building. His detailed report of his activities attests to his cold-blooded callousness. On May 16 Stroop reported that the "operation" was complete and that "the Jewish Quarter of Warsaw is no more."

Stroop was sentenced to death by a Polish court of law and executed on September 8, 1951.

A Finnish battalion of the *Waffen-SS* returns home from action on the Soviet front. This *Freiwillige* (volunteer) unit was one of the many non-German groups that joined the *Waffen-SS*. Their anti-Russian attitudes were exploited by the Nazi regime for the benefit of both the war effort and facilitation of the "Final Solution."

A family interned in the Marzahn Gypsy camp in Germany awaits its fate. Large-scale deportations to Auschwitz began in February 1943, when a "family camp" for Gypsies was established at the Birkenau killing center. The appalling conditions condemned thousands to death, while Josef Mengele conducted ghastly "medical experiments" on Gypsy twins.

1943

• **May 12, 1943:** Seventeen-year-old Frania Beatus, active in the Warsaw Ghetto underground, commits suicide rather than surrender to the Nazis. • In London, Polish Jew Samuel Artur Zygelbojm, a key figure in the prewar Jewish Social Democrat Party, commits suicide following nearly a year of fruitless campaigning on behalf of Jews trapped in the War- saw Ghetto, including his wife and teenage son. His death is reported in the press, which pointedly omits the text of his suicide note, which condemns the Allies for their indifference to the Jews.

• **May 13, 1943:** Hans Frank, governor-general of Occupied Poland, sends SS Chief Heinrich Himmler a

This flower-shaped cloth brooch was handmade by a young girl from Warsaw who was incarcerated at the Bergen-Belsen, Germany, concentration camp. Fellow inmate Sala Spett received the brooch as a present from her husband and children in May 1943. The family members traded a slice of bread for the brooch, an act that meant a day's hunger.

"My sister Bracha, who was pregnant, wept in a loud voice. She was about 28. 'But my baby hasn't even been born yet, and never sinned. Why is he doomed?'"

—Survivor Zvi Szner

These Jewish women and their babies were photographed in the Rothschild maternity hospital in Paris. All but one of a group of 40, Fanny Kraus—who managed to escape with her child—were shipped to Auschwitz in May 1943. They were among the nearly 50,000 Jews deported to Eastern Europe from France through June 1943. Most of them died in the gas chambers of Auschwitz and Chelmno.

list of personal goods and valuables stolen from Jews. Among the booty are 25,000 fountain pens and 14,000 pairs of scissors. • German and Italian troops surrender in Tunisia.

• **May 15, 1943:** Jewish ghetto police in Rohatyn, Poland, plot to acquire weapons with which to defend themselves; *See* June 6, 1943.

• **May 16, 1943:** SS-*Brigadeführer* Jürgen Stroop reports the final liquidation of the Jewish ghetto at Warsaw, although some Jews remain in hiding; *See* June 3, 1943.

• **May 17, 1943:** 395 Jews are deported from Berlin to the extermination camp at Auschwitz.

• **May 18, 1943:** Nearly every resident of the Polish farming village of Szarajowka is shot or burned alive by the SS, *Wehrmacht* troops, and Gestapo agents. After the massacre, the village is razed.

• **May 19, 1943:** In the House of Commons, the courageous Eleanor Rathbone attacks the British govern-

I.G. Farben

German business quickly aligned itself with the Nazis and sealed a demonic pact with Heinrich Himmler and the SS. As the most powerful company in the Third Reich, I.G. Farben kept the German war machine rolling, enjoying huge profits in return.

From chemicals to explosives, I.G. Farben supplied the Nazis with a vast variety of products. As an incentive to build factories at Auschwitz, I.G. Farben received tax exemptions and the promise of an almost unending supply of slave labor. To seal the deal, the SS agreed to provide I.G. Farben with some 10,000 prisoners as construction workers. From I.G. Farben, the SS gained lucrative contracts that allowed Himmler and his cronies to pursue their own financial goals.

By mid-1944 I.G. Farben was Auschwitz's largest employer, with 11,000 slave laborers. Some worked in nearby mines, which supplied the coal for production of synthetic fuel and synthetic rubber. Others were directly engaged in the production of synthetic rubber, known as *Buna*, at the satellite camp Monowitz. The company was also willing to supply the Nazis' death machine: Through DEGESCH, a company it partially controlled, I.G. Farben provided Zyklon B for the Auschwitz gas chambers.

Female prisoners work in a factory owned by the AGFA company, one of the many companies that belonged to the I.G. Farben conglomerate. German industries that supported the Nazi regime's war effort benefited greatly from their access to forced labor. Hundreds of thousands of people were removed from their homes, relocated to Germany, and forced to work in German factories connected to the war effort.

British and American tank troops continued to score victories in Tunisia even though German troops, led by Field Marshal Erwin Rommel and General Jürgen von Arnim, fought fiercely. News of the huge defeat at Stalingrad, Russia, demoralized some German soldiers, who began to realize that the war might be lost. Here, a German prisoner, captured near Sejenane in northern Tunisia, holds his hands high as he is searched.

1943

ment for the defeatist attitudes expressed at the Bermuda Conference and notes that the Allies are responsible for the deaths of any Jews if they refuse to help. • SS chief Heinrich Himmler sends Reich Security Main Office chief Ernst Kaltenbrunner copies of *The Jewish Ritual Murder*, a book describing apocryphal Jewish religious rituals. Himmler plans to distribute copies throughout Romania, Hungary, and Bulgaria, and broadcast excerpts to England and the United States.

• May 21, 1943: Three thousand Jews driven from Brody, Ukraine, to a waiting transport train revolt, killing four Ukrainians and a few Germans. Many of the Jews break free after being put

Bernard Geron *(far right)* was a Jewish boy hidden with a Dutch family, the Dufours. The woman in the picture, the family's governess, knew that he was Jewish but kept his secret. Geron survived the war and was reunited with his father and brother; his mother had perished.

The teacher of a *heder* (Jewish religious school) interacts with students in the Jewish Quarter of Casablanca, Morocco. Most of Morocco's 200,000 Jews lived in the French-controlled part of the country. Early in the war, Moroccan Jews were the victims of violence perpetrated by French nationalists. Jews were attacked and many were deported to labor camps.

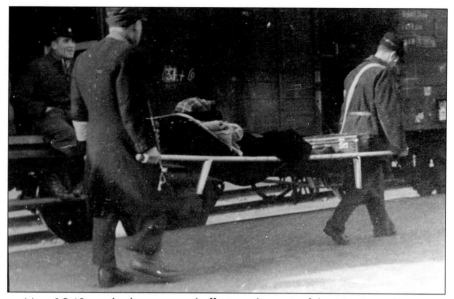

May 1943 marked a renewed effort on the part of the Nazis to deport Dutch Jews. Neither age nor disability provided a reprieve. Here, members of the *Ordedienst* (Jewish police), composed at its height of some 200 young Dutch and German men, carry an elderly woman to the train. Approximately 100,000 Jews passed through Westerbork, Netherlands, to the camps of the East, mostly Auschwitz and Sobibór.

on the train, only to be machine-gunned. The remainder are killed upon arrival at the Majdanek death camp. • Members of the Jewish community at Drogobych, Ukraine, are exterminated in the Bronica Forest.

• **May 23, 1943:** Nazi *Aktionen* kill thousands of Ukrainian Jews at Przemyslany and Lvov.

• **May 24, 1943:** A Jewish partisan group organized by Judith Nowogrodzka escapes from the Bialystok (Poland) Ghetto. The escape is led by Szymon Datner. • The Germans end their submarine attacks on Allied Atlantic convoys.

• **May 27, 1943:** The Jews of Sokal, Ukraine, are deported to the Belzec

death camp. • Three thousand Jews are killed at Tolstoye, Ukraine.

• **May 30, 1943:** Dr. Josef Mengele, an SS captain, arrives at the Auschwitz-Birkenau death camp to begin his medical duties.

• **May 31, 1943:** SS General Friedrich Wilhelm Krüger tells associates at a

A group of elderly Sephardic Jews gathers in the Jewish Quarter of Salonika, Greece. Such religious and social occasions would soon come to an end, as the Nazis began to enforce severe restrictions in 1943. The first deportations to Auschwitz followed in mid-March. By mid-August nearly 50,000 Jews had been sent to Auschwitz and Treblinka, with almost 80 percent killed there. Italian efforts to save Salonika's Jews were largely ineffectual; most of the Jews who avoided deportation did so only because they held passports issued earlier by Turkey, Italy, and a few other nations.

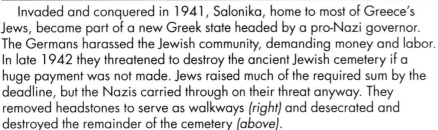

Invaded and conquered in 1941, Salonika, home to most of Greece's Jews, became part of a new Greek state headed by a pro-Nazi governor. The Germans harassed the Jewish community, demanding money and labor. In late 1942 they threatened to destroy the ancient Jewish cemetery if a huge payment was not made. Jews raised much of the required sum by the deadline, but the Nazis carried through on their threat anyway. They removed headstones to serve as walkways *(right)* and desecrated and destroyed the remainder of the cemetery *(above)*.

1943

meeting in Kraków, Poland, that, although the elimination of Jews is unpleasant, it is "necessary from the standpoint of European interests."
• A Nazi prison administrator in Minsk, Belorussia, reports that 516 German and Russian Jews have been killed in late May, their gold crowns and fillings taken from their mouths before their deaths.

• June 1943: Jews of Dalmatia, Serbia, are transferred to the island of Rab, which is off the coast of Croatia.

• Early June 1943: In a combination of street assaults and killings at Janówska, Ukraine, 10,000 Jews from Lvov lose their lives.

A glum Joseph Goebbels sits before the text of a radio broadcast to the German people. The German defeat at Stalingrad, Russia, and Allied victories in Tunisia made Goebbels's job increasingly difficult during 1943. Victory communiqués, which had been a staple of German national radio in the early years of the war, were now rare occurrences.

"So far as concerns us, we have burned our bridges behind us. We can no longer turn back, nor do we want to turn back. We shall go down in history as the greatest statesmen of all time, or as its greatest criminals."

—*Joseph Goebbels, writing in* Das Reich, *1943*

Following a reprisal at Pancero, Serbia, a German soldier blithely waves to the photographer as the victims twist nearby. Mindful of the need to maintain the upper hand in conquered territories, the Nazis reacted swiftly to local revolt. Executions—often indiscriminate—became commonplace.

Pictured here are weapons, including knives and pistols, from the Lvov (Ukraine) Ghetto. The Nazis discovered the weapons in June 1943 as they sought to clear the Lvov work camp of all remaining Jews. Although vastly outnumbered by the German and Ukrainian police units that surrounded the ghetto, the remaining Jews chose resistance, killing several of their captors and wounding more than a dozen.

• **June 1–6, 1943:** During liquidation of the ghetto at Sosnowiec, Poland, a spirited resistance is led by Zvi Dunski. Ill-armed Jews fight back as deportations proceed. • The Jewish ghetto at Buczacz, Ukraine, is liquidated. Some Jews resist and escape.

• **June 3, 1943:** German troops in the Warsaw Ghetto destroy a bunker on Walowa Street that conceals 150 Jews; *See* September 1943. • Near Michalowice, Poland, Germans kill two Polish farmers who have rescued and hidden three Jewish escapees in a barn.

• **June 5, 1943:** 1266 Jewish children under the age of 16 from Vught, Holland, are deported to the Sobibór death camp and gassed upon arrival.

• In Mińsk Mazowiecki, Poland, more than 100 Jewish workers at the Rudzki factory are shot.

• **June 6, 1943:** Jacob Gens, the leader of the Jewish Council in Vilna, argues that Vilna's Jews will have an improved chance of survival if they demonstrate their usefulness as workers. • Germans execute all 1000 Jews

Josef Mengele

The notorious "Angel of Death," Josef Mengele determined the fate of thousands of Jews shipped to Auschwitz. As chief doctor of the extermination camp, Mengele supervised the selections for the gas chambers and conducted horrific medical experiments.

Mengele, who received his medical degree from the University of Frankfurt am Main in 1938, joined the staff of the Institute of Hereditary Biology and Race Research, where he  specialized in the study of twins and race science. During the war years, Mengele joined the *Waffen-SS* and served as a medical officer in France and Russia. He was appointed chief doctor of Auschwitz in May 1943.

At Auschwitz, Mengele pursued his pseudoscientific research and personally selected victims from the steady stream of arrivals to the camp. People with deformities were immediately killed and sent to Mengele's lab for study. All twins became the subjects of his painful and grotesque experiments.

After the war Mengele was mistakenly released by U.S. authorities and eventually made his way to Buenos Aires, Argentina. Mengele was rumored to have drowned in 1978. An international team of forensics pathologists performed an autopsy on an exhumed body in 1985 and concluded that there was a high probability that it was indeed Mengele's last remains.

Natzweiler-Struthof, located near Strasbourg, France, was one of the smallest of the concentration camps. The inmates worked in the granite quarry and labored underground in arms production. In 1943 a gas chamber was built at the camp, paid for by the Institute of Anatomy at Strasbourg University. Jews and Gypsies were transferred from Auschwitz to serve as subjects for various grotesque experiments, after which they were gassed and cremated; the crematorium is seen here.

This drawing, sketched by an unknown inmate of Auschwitz, depicts SS doctor Josef Mengele selecting the sick and weak for extermination. Mengele, like the other doctors in the camp, played a vital role in the killing process by choosing who would die immediately and who would be worked to death. Today this sketch is in the Auschwitz Museum.

1943

still remaining in the Rohatyn (Poland) Ghetto after German authorities discover a plot of local Jewish policemen to purchase weapons.

• June 7, 1943: Dr. Klaus Clauberg reports from Auschwitz that the apparatus to sterilize 1000 Jewish women a day is being set in place.

• June 8, 1943: The Jewish community at Zbaraz, Ukraine, is destroyed.

• June 11, 1943: SS chief Heinrich Himmler orders stepped-up deportations of Jews from Polish ghettos to death camps.

• June 12, 1943: The Jewish community at Berezhany, Ukraine, is mur-

As Allied bombing continued to disable or destroy factories on German soil, German industrialists sought new locations where slave labor could keep production running. Following the bombing of the Krupp fuse plant in Essen in March 1943, a new Krupp factory was built at Auschwitz. These slave laborers do the dirty work.

With a benevolent Winston Churchill in the foreground and tanks and planes in the background, this recruiting poster calls upon members of the *Yishuv* (Jewish community in Palestine) to join the British effort to defeat the Axis powers. Although the British resisted creating a separate Jewish combat division, in 1940 they formed Jewish coastal artillery batteries and infantry companies as part of the British force in Palestine.

Hans Frank *(right)*, governor-general of Occupied Poland, hosts SS chief Heinrich Himmler at a dinner held at the *Wewel* castle in Kraków, Poland, in June 1943. Frank objected to Himmler's complete control of the "Jewish problem" in Poland and the decision to use the *Generalgouvernement* as a dumping ground for Jews. His protests to Hitler were to no avail, as Himmler's SS retained supreme authority over the "Final Solution."

dered. • In the Lódź (Poland) Ghetto, the chiefs of Jewish police are forced to witness Nazi executions of recaptured ghetto escapees: 23-year-old Hersch Fejgelis, 29-year-old Mordecai Standarowicz, and 31-year-old Abram Tandowski.

• June 15, 1943: A coal-mine labor camp at Jaworzno, Poland, near Auschwitz, opens. • SS Lieutenant-General Richard Glücks, chief of the Concentration Camp Inspectorate, orders that sensitive buildings at Auschwitz be relocated from prying eyes. • At the Janówska death pits at Lvov, Ukraine, hundreds of Jewish slave laborers are forced to exhume corpses of Jews, plunder them for jewelry and gold dental work, and then burn the corpses to destroy evidence of the killings.

• June 16, 1943: SS chief Heinrich Himmler allows a transfer of Jewish prisoners from the Auschwitz-Birkenau death camp to the Sachsenhausen, Germany, concentration camp for medical experiments involving jaundice. • Dr. Niuta Jurezkaya, a

These bodies await cremation in the ovens at the Mauthausen, Austria, concentration camp, where around 103,000 people died during the years 1938 to 1945. One survivor of Mauthausen, George E. King, said he often dreamt about escaping. "You go through this agonizing labor of trying to escape," he said about his dreams. "In these cases you are always moving in slow motion, as if you were up to your hips in mud. . . . You are making a maximum effort to run but you are just barely moving."

At the Mauthausen, Austria, concentration camp, *Kapos* and a German guard stand over the corpse of an inmate whom they have just beaten to death. According to eyewitnesses, the prisoner had stumbled from the barracks in need of medical treatment, behavior his captors found offensive and deserving of a painful and gruesome death.

This shirt was worn by the chief of a group of Romanian Gypsies known as the *Calderai*. Like other Gypsies, the owner, Gheorge Ciaoba, wore brightly colored clothes on special occasions. The shirt is from the years 1942 to 1945, during which the Nazis viciously persecuted the Gypsies, who were often (and easily) identified by their distinctive garments.

1943

physician who escaped from the Minsk (Belorussia) Ghetto to nearby forests, is recaptured, tortured, and shot. • In Berlin, 200 patients are deported from the city's Jewish hospital to the Theresienstadt, Czechoslovakia, camp/ghetto. • German authorities declare Berlin *Judenrein*—purged of Jews.

• **June 20, 1943: Five thousand Jews from Amsterdam are deported to Auschwitz.** • **The Ternopol (Ukraine) Ghetto is liquidated.**

• **June 21, 1943: SS chief Heinrich Himmler orders the liquidation of all Jewish ghettos in the Soviet Union.** • **The Jews remaining in the Lvov (Ukraine) Ghetto are hunted and**

The initial success of Operation Barbarossa generated huge numbers of Soviet prisoners-of-war, whom the Nazis treated as subhuman. Many were executed or died on long death marches; all suffered extreme hunger and deprivation. If their identities were discovered,

Jewish soldiers were singled out for death or sent to stalags and extermination camps such as Sobibór. This emaciated Jewish POW is identified by the Star of David he was forced to wear.

A footbridge over Paneriu Street connected the large and small ghettos of Kovno, Lithuania. In June 1943 the Kovno Ghetto was converted to a concentration camp, and the 4000 inhabitants were transferred to small camps situated outside Kovno. At the same time, a Resistance group known as the Jewish Fighting Organization was formed to facilitate the departure of Jews from the ghetto and train them for partisan activities.

Initiation at the Camps

Transition to life inside a Nazi concentration camp was a jarring and disorienting experience. From the moment one entered the *Lager*, life's every routine had to be renegotiated. Failure to adapt was lethal.

Deprived of food, water, and sanitary facilities for days on end, new arrivals were momentarily relieved when the doors to their rail wagons were thrown open and they were ordered to disembark. Their relief, however, was short-lived.

At some camps, SS officers dressed in crisply pressed black uniforms ordered new arrivals to move left or right, toward life or death. Guards welcomed prisoners with blows from their rifle butts and truncheons, while emaciated figures in striped uniforms herded the new prisoners to their destinations.

Once inside the camp, new arrivals were shaved, tattooed (in some camps), and discarded into a completely alien environment. To survive, prisoners had to forget that they had ever lived in a civilized society, and learn the ways of the *Lager*. They had to move with the crowd, avoid being singled out, and, whenever possible, secure an extra ration of food. Inmates had precious little time to learn the routines of their new surroundings. Within days they were transformed from human beings to nameless victims of the Nazi regime.

killed, including 350 of 500 discovered in the city's sewer system. • All Jewish workers at municipal factories in Drogobych, Ukraine, are killed. • German Professor August Hirt chooses 103 Jewish men and women at Auschwitz to be transported to the Natzweiler-Struthof camp near Strasbourg, France. There they are gassed. The soft tissues of their bod-

ies are removed, and their skeletons are strung up as exhibits in the Reich Anatomical Institute of Strasbourg for the study of the Jewish race; *See* October 25, 1943.

• June 23, 1943: Ukrainian police surround a Jewish school at Czortków, Ukraine, where 534 Jewish slave laborers are housed. The camp com-

mandant, Thomanek, shoots several prisoners and orders others carted off for execution. A local gentile, Jan Nakonieczmy, successfully hides five Jews in his tiny henhouse.

• June 25, 1943: Armed Jewish resistance occurs at Lvov, Ukraine, and at Czestochowa, Poland. • A new crematorium opens at Auschwitz-Birkenau.

The Technology of Death

Inaccessible to Western scholars until the USSR's collapse, File 17/9 of the Red Army's intelligence branch came to historian Gerald Fleming's attention in May 1993. It contained information about Kurt Prüfer, Fritz Sander, and other German engineers employed by *Topf und Söhne* (Topf and Sons), whose products included crematorium furnaces in Nazi camps at Buchenwald, Dachau, Mauthausen, Gross-Rosen, and Auschwitz-Birkenau.

In late 1944 the Germans destroyed equipment and records at Auschwitz-Birkenau, but that death factory was too big to cover up. When the Red Army liberated the camp two months later, the massive evidence contained, in Fleming's words, details about "the construction of the technology of mass death, complete with the precise costs of crematoria and calculations of the number of corpses each could incinerate in a day." Thus, beyond documenting the Red Army's arrest of Prüfer and Sander, File 17/9 contained transcripts of the interrogations that followed.

The construction of Auschwitz-Birkenau's four carefully planned gas chamber-crematorium units took considerable time, largely because of wartime building constraints. Topf was only one of 11 civilian companies needed to produce them. Utilizing prisoner labor, building began in the summer of 1942, but it was nearly a year before the last facility was operational. Each included an undressing room, a gas chamber, and a room containing Topf's incineration ovens. These lethal places were designed to dispatch thousands of Jews per day. Even so, Prüfer told his Red Army interrogators that "the [crematorium] bricks were damaged

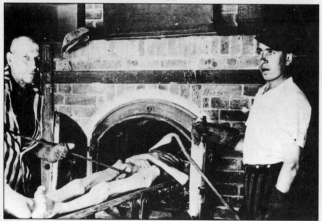

after six months because the strain on the furnaces was colossal."

"From 1940 to 1944," Prüfer stated, "20 crematoria for concentration camps were built under my direction." His work took him to Auschwitz five times, and he knew that "innocent human beings were being liquidated" there. So did one of Prüfer's superiors, Sander, a crematorium ventilation specialist whose work for Topf took him to Auschwitz three times. Red Army interviews show that Sander submitted plans in late 1942 for a crematorium with even greater capacity. Although never built, it would have used "the conveyor-belt principle," he explained. "That is to say, the corpses must be brought to the incineration furnaces without interruption." His duty, Sander claimed on March 7, 1946, had been to use his "specialist knowledge... to help Germany win the war, just as an aircraft-construction engineer builds airplanes in wartime, which are also connected with the destruction of human beings."

Less than three weeks later, Sander died in Red Army custody, the victim of a heart attack. Sentenced to "25 years deprivation of liberty," Prüfer died of a brain hemorrhage on October 24, 1952.

1943

• June 29, 1943: South of Warsaw, five Poles are shot for hiding four Jews. The latter also are shot. • At the Biala-Waka labor camp near Vilna, Lithuania, 67 inmates are shot as reprisal for the escape of six Jews to a nearby forest.

• Late June 1943: Elderly residents of a Jewish nursing home are de-ported to the Theresienstadt, Czechoslovakia, camp/ghetto.

• July 1943: In an American radio broadcast, Jewish Congressman Emanuel Celler excoriates the U.S. government for its continuing silence on Nazi treatment of European Jews. • The American Women's International League for Peace and Freedom

These Amsterdam Jews are being rounded up for deportation to Auschwitz in 1943. Numerous Dutch citizens befriended the 110,000 Jews and 30,000 immigrant Jews residing in Holland. However, many Dutch in the government and on the police force collaborated with the Germans. The last roundup, which netted 5000 Jews, took place in September 1943.

Beautiful grand pianos were among the many items the Nazis confiscated from the Jews of Prague, Czechoslovakia, and other locations. The genocide perpetrated against European Jewry was accompanied by the systematic expropriation of Jewish wealth. Anything perceived to be of value was taken, registered, and shipped to an appropriate warehouse.

Warily gazing out at the photographer, Dutch children in the Kallenburg district of Amsterdam huddle together for warmth and comfort. As the years of Nazi occupation wore on, conditions worsened for all civilians, and especially for the most vulnerable, children and the elderly. Photographer Emmy Andreisse, a member of the Dutch Resistance, recorded conditions in the Netherlands under the occupation.

estimates that millions of Jews have already been murdered by the Germans in Poland, and that the American government and people share in the guilt for these atrocities because they are complacent cowards covered "with a thick layer of prejudice."

• July 5, 1943: The Germans launch a major armored offensive at Kursk,

Russia, initiating the largest tank battle in history; *See* July 23, 1943.
• Heinrich Himmler orders that Sobibór, a death camp, be made a concentration camp.

• July 6, 1943: More than 2400 Jews are deported from Holland to Sobibór.

• July 10, 1943: Allies land in Sicily.
• Thousands of Jews from Lvov, Ukraine, are murdered at Kamenka-Bugskaya.

• July 11, 1943: Martin Bormann, Hitler's secretary, issues a top-level directive on Hitler's behalf, instructing that public discussion of Jews must not mention "a future overall

With gun held at the ready, Vitka Kempner *(right)* stands with fellow partisans Zelda Treger and Raizel Kartshak. Even among the partisans, Kempner was regarded as exceptionally daring. In early July 1943 she sneaked out of the Vilna (Lithuania) Ghetto with a homemade bomb, which she used to blow up a German munitions train. Although wounded, she walked three days and nights to return to the ghetto. She later carried on her heroic activities from the forests, helping Jewish slave laborers to escape from Keilis, near Vilna, and joining with other partisans to destroy a factory.

The Nazis hang 20 prisoners in the Buchenwald, Germany, camp, a reprisal for the killing of a German guard. As usual, the entire camp was forced to view the executions. The Nazis hoped that the inmates would conclude that such resistance would never go unpunished, and that the innocent would suffer along with the perpetrators.

The pro-Axis grand mufti of Jerusalem, Hajj Amin al-Husseini, inspects the rifle of a Bosnian-Moslem *Waffen-SS* volunteer. As a leader of Arabs and Moslems, al-Husseini saw the Axis powers as the means to gain Arab independence and to destroy the Jews. Although he failed to achieve his dream of an independent Arab legion, he was more successful in persuading some 20,000 Bosnian Moslems to join volunteer units called the *Handjar* (Sword). Incorporated into the *Waffen-SS,* these troops proved effective in hunting Jews and partisans.

1943

solution," but only that Jews are being assembled for labor.

• **July 14–17, 1943:** The "Krasnodar Trial" of 13 alleged Soviet collaborators opens in the Caucasus region of Russia. Eight are sentenced to death; three are sentenced to 20 years' imprisonment; two are acquitted.

• **Mid-July 1943:** Germans execute Professor Kurt Huber, an anti-Nazi activist and part of the Munich-based White Rose student resistance group.

• **July 16, 1943:** At Vilna, Lithuania, police invade a meeting between members of the United Partisan Organization and Jacob Gens, head of the Vilna Jewish Council, and seize

The notorious Amon Goeth, SS captain and commandant of the Plaszów, Poland, work camp, waits on his villa balcony for an opportunity to shoot a Jewish prisoner—*any* prisoner. Such "sport" was unique among camp commanders and ultimately cost Goeth his life, for he was tried by the Poles after the war and executed in Kraków. The commandant's passion for his demonic pastime was portrayed in the film *Schindler's List.*

By the time Treblinka was shut down in July 1943, its gas chambers had taken the lives of at least 750,000 people, mostly Jews from Poland. Following Heinrich Himmler's visit to the camp in March 1943, the Nazis exhumed hundreds of thousands of bodies that had been buried. Huge pyres were built, and the bodies were burned to obliterate the evidence of the mass murder that had occurred. These bones bear silent testimony to the Nazis' failure to achieve their goal.

Aktion 1005

In 1942, when the Allies caught wind of the Nazis' mass murders—and when hundreds of thousands of hastily buried bodies posed a serious health hazard—the Nazis planned their most gruesome operation of all: Revisit the mass graves, dig up the corpses, and burn them.

This *Aktion* 1005 was headed by Paul Blobel, the mastermind of the Babi Yar massacre. Each *Sonderkommando* 1005 was supervised by members of the Security Service, Security Police, and regular German police. Nazi prisoners, mostly Jews, did the dirty work. Beginning in June 1942, the *Sonderkommandos* burned the corpses that had been dumped at the Nazi death camps. Starting in June 1943, they ventured to the mass graves of Poland and the Occupied Soviet Union.

The prisoners were divided into three groups. The first opened the graves and exhumed the bodies. The second group arranged the corpses on pyres for burning. The bodies were alternated with wood logs, doused with fuel, and lit. The third group sifted and scattered the ashes and crushed the bones.

The Nazis covered up many, though not all, of their mass burials. As for the *Sonderkommando* 1005 prisoners, most were killed after they completed their work. Dozens of others survived after revolting and running away.

---

its leader, Yitzhak Wittenberg. Outside, Jewish partisans attack the police and free Wittenberg; *See* July 17, 1943. • Theophil Wurm, bishop of the Evangelical Church in Württemberg, Germany, sends a letter to Berlin in which he asks that the persecution of "members of other nations and races" be halted immediately.

• **July 17, 1943: Partisan leader Yitzhak Wittenberg surrenders to the Gestapo to prevent the razing of the Vilna (Lithuania) Ghetto.**

• **July 18, 1943: Two hundred slave laborers are murdered at Miedzyrzec, Poland. • One thousand Jews are deported to Auschwitz from Paris.**

• **July 19, 1943: Germans use 3500 Jewish slave laborers to undertake a massive search for valuables in the remains of the Warsaw Ghetto.**

• **July 20, 1943: Five hundred slave laborers are murdered at Czestochowa, Poland. • 2209 Jews are deported from Holland to Sobibór. • Two Jews escape from Sobibór.**

Music for the Doomed

In Germany and occupied countries, the Nazis silenced Jewish musicians. Yet they turned to Jews to mask with music the anguished cries from the camps, creating what the prisoners termed *"Symphonia diabolica"* ("Devil's Symphony").

At each of the death camps, orchestras played cheerful and comforting tunes as the trains rolled in with their exhausted human cargo. Deportees' suspicions and fears were allayed when they heard the familiar music of civilized society.

At Auschwitz, which had six orchestras, and at other camps, orchestras played as inmates went to work (for the entertainment of the SS) as well as at selections and executions. At the camp at Janówska, Ukraine, the Nazis ordered the composition of a special tune, the *"Tango fun toyt"* ("Tango of Death"), to usher prisoners to their deaths.

The new leaders of the Polish government-in-exile, Prime Minister Stanislaw Mikolajczyk *(right, in uniform)* and President Wladyslaw Raczkiewicz *(in suit),* receive a report from their officers. Initially established in Paris, the government-in-exile moved to London in July 1940. From there officials broadcast radio messages of hope back to Poland. They also used couriers like Jan Karski to learn as much as possible of what was occurring in Poland, and they tried to support the Resistance with arms and intelligence information.

The drawings of Walter Spitzer dramatically portray the horrors of the Holocaust. In the first illustration, the dead and the skeletal living are intertwined. Arms and legs dangle over the side of the wagon as it makes its last journey. In the second drawing, emaciated bodies in a variety of positions testify to the living hell of life in the camp.

1943

• **July 22, 1943:** Because the U.S. State Department continues to delay any action on the Riegner Plan to save 70,000 Jews, American Rabbi Stephen Wise pleads with President Franklin Roosevelt to support the plan. Roosevelt allows the plan to be killed because of "strenuous British objections."

• **July 23, 1943:** Forty-year-old Mandel Langer, active as an anti-Nazi saboteur since the end of 1942, is captured and executed in Toulouse, France. • The German armored offensive at Kursk, Russia, the largest tank battle in history, fails.

• **July 24, 1943:** Twenty-one young Jewish partisans in Vilna, Lithuania,

A longtime Nazi, Odilo Globoc-nik joined the Party in Austria in 1931. Before the *Anschluss* (annex-ation), he worked to increase the Party's numbers and influence. Fol-lowing the *Anschluss,* Globocnik's obedient service in the SS earned him the position of *Gauleiter* of Vienna, an office from which he was later fired due to corruption. Putting Globocnik's ambition and slavish obedience to use, Heinrich Himmler pardoned him and placed him in charge of the Lublin region of Poland. Globocnik oversaw the building of Majdanek, Belzec, Sobibór, and Treblinka, and con-trolled forced labor and extermina-tion until August 1943.

As part of a widespread effort by Nazi scientists to increase the "Aryan" birthrate, Dr. Josef Men-gele conducted research on twins. Twins plucked by Mengele's assis-tants from the incoming trains were endlessly measured and compared. Some died simply from loss of blood following day after day of experi-mentation. Others died through even more terrible procedures such as spinal surgery and supremely cruel operations that joined twins together. The Guttmann twins, Rene and Renate, pictured here with their mother, were deported first to There-sienstadt and then to Auschwitz, where Mrs. Guttmann died in the gas chambers. The twins survived Mengele's experiments and eventu-ally were reunited after the war in the United States. It should be noted that because Mengele killed his sub-jects (via injection) when he felt they had served their purposes, very little firsthand information about his "twin" research exists. The Guttmann siblings, and a relatively few other subjects who managed to avoid death, provided Allied investigators with invaluable information about Mengele's perverse crimes.

A barracks at the Auschwitz concentration camp is lined with triple-tiered wood bunk beds, on which inmates slept. Each level was shared by more than one person and often lined with little more than a thin blanket. Survivors describe the sleep routines with mixed feelings. Whereas most viewed their bunks as refuge from the day's precarious and dangerous existence, the nights were also filled with terror. The nocturnal ragings of drunk *Kapos,* ceaseless struggles with bunkmates, and the relentless trips to latrines and chamber pots punctuate the memories of survivors.

join with Soviet partisans behind Ger-man lines. North of Vilna, nine of the Jews are killed in an ambush at the Mickun bridge. Three days later, 32 relatives of the nine dead partisans are seized by the Gestapo at Vilna, taken to nearby gravel pits at Ponary, and executed. Bruno Kittel, head of the Gestapo in Vilna, announces that the entire family of any Jew who

escapes the ghetto to the forest will be executed. If an escapee has no family or roommates, all residents of his building will be executed. Further, if any ten-man Jewish labor gang comes back short, the remaining gang laborers will be executed.

• The Spanish government intervenes on behalf of 367 Sephardic Jews in

Salonika, Greece, seeing that they are spared deportation to Auschwitz and sent instead to safety in Spain.
• Britain's Royal Air Force begins raids against Hamburg, Germany.

• July 25, 1943: Italian dictator Ben-ito Mussolini resigns under pressure and is arrested. • A young Jew in the Janówska, Ukraine, labor camp near

Heinz Birnbaum *(top left)* and *(clockwise)* Werner Steinbrink, Lotte Rotholz, and Edith Fraenkel were members of the resistance movement known as the Baum *Gruppe* (group). The fallout from the group's attack on the anti-Bolshevik art exhibit in May 1942 eventually led to the deaths of almost all of the members, including these four. Birnbaum, it is believed, was hanged. Steinbrink was apprehended after the arson attack on the exhibit and was executed on August 18, 1942. Rotholz died in Auschwitz. Fraenkel was deported to the Theresienstadt, Czechoslovakia, camp/ghetto and moved later to Auschwitz, where she died in 1944.

1943

Lvov, apparently pleased by Mussolini's downfall, angers a Gestapo agent, who orders the youth hung upside down, his penis amputated and placed in his mouth, and his stomach kicked until he dies.

• July 27, 1943: Germans murder 17 Jews discovered hiding in the rubble of the Warsaw Ghetto.

• July 28, 1943: Jan Karski, a Catholic-Polish underground fighter who had visited the Warsaw Ghetto and the Belzec death camp, arrives in the United States to tell American leaders what he has seen. His interview with President Franklin Roosevelt indicates that the President already knows much about the Holocaust.

The Bedzin (Poland) Ghetto, like hundreds of others, was eventually liquidated. This photograph, taken after the destruction of August 1, 1943, shows furniture and other items strewn chaotically about. Standing at the left is a smiling German police officer who is undoubtedly pleased by the annihilation of the Polish-Jewish community.

Fryda Litwak was born in Lvov, Ukraine, in 1916. She was one of thousands of Jews who survived the Holocaust by posing as an Aryan, in her case under the name of Zofia Wolenska. Constantly living in fear of exposure and the certain death it would bring, she found a job with a pharmacist in Radom, Poland. Later she even went to Germany to work. Although she escaped the Nazis, she died in the final months of the war, possibly the victim of Allied bombs.

Janówska

Located on Janówska Street, leading from Lvov, Ukraine, the Janówska concentration camp was notorious for brutality serenaded by music.

In fall 1941 the *Deutsche Ausrüstungswerke* (German Equipment Works), a section of the SS, moved ghetto prisoners to Janówska to produce war materiel. Housed in inhuman conditions, inmates were made to perform grueling physical tests to prove their stamina. The few who survived worked another day. The many who did not were taken *na Piaski* (to the sands), a sand quarry, and shot.

In March 1942 Janówska became a transit camp for Jews en route from Eastern Galicia to the extermination camp at Belzec, and in 1943 Janówska itself became a killing site. At the whim of SS officer Wilhelm Rokita, a former violinist, death was set to music. The inmate orchestra was ordered to compose and then to play the *"Tango fun toyt"* ("Tango of Death") as accompaniment to selections and executions.

• **Late July:** Members of the *Sonderkommando* at the Belzec death camp are sent north to the extermination camp at Sobibór, where the inmates revolt upon arrival and are shot.

• **August 1943:** Inmates revolt at the slave-labor camp at Sasow, Poland. • Armed resistance occurs at the slave-labor camp at Lackie Wielkie,

Poland. • Following armed resistance at the Jaktorów, Poland, slave-labor camp, the camp is liquidated and the inmates killed. • Frumka Plotnicka, who has repeatedly risked her life by slipping out of and back into the Warsaw Ghetto with news and contraband, is cornered by Nazis in a cellar in Bedzin, Poland, and shot. • A Jewish revolt at the Konin, Poland, slave-

labor camp, led by Rabbi Joshua Aaronson, culminates in the killing of nearly all rioters. • Beneath the limestone of the Harz Mountains in Germany, slave-labor construction begins on Nordhausen, an underground weapons plant.

• **August 1, 1943:** The Jewish ghettos at Bedzin and Sosnowiec, Poland, are

Deportation of European Jews

Trains from Westerbork, a transit camp in northeastern Holland, deported more than 100,000 of the Netherlands' 140,000 Jews to the death camps at Sobibór and Auschwitz. On August 24, 1943, a 29-year-old Dutch Jew named Etty Hillesum wrote a clandestine letter describing one of those deportations: "My God," she wrote, "are the doors really being shut now?... Through small openings at the top we can see heads and hands, hands that will wave to us later when the train leaves.... The train gives a piercing whistle, and 1020 Jews leave Holland."

Prior to the autumn of 1938, Nazi Germany pressured Jews to emigrate. As military conquest brought new territory and millions of Jews under Nazi domination, solutions to the "Jewish question" required a more aggressive policy. During the first 18 months of World War II, deportation was part of a Nazi plan to eliminate Jews from Hitler's expanding Third Reich by sending them to ghettos or restricted areas in the East. With the 1941 *Einsatzgruppen* massacres and decisions to solve the "Jewish question" by mass murder, the meaning of deportation changed. No longer the goal, deportation became the means for sending Jews to killing centers at Chelmno, Belzec, Sobibór, Treblinka, Majdanek, and especially Auschwitz-Birkenau.

With essential support from the German Transport Ministry and its railroad bureaucracy, Adolf Eichmann and his staff in Section IV B 4 of the Reich Security Main Office managed this continent-wide operation. From far-flung European stations, trains shipped almost three million Jews to the killing centers. "Passengers" had to pay one-way fares, then often were transported as cargo in crowded freight wagons.

In 1942 deportations devastated Polish Jewry, but the network extended far and wide. In March it snared Slovakian Jews.

In July mass deportations of Jews from France and Belgium, as well as the Netherlands, were under way. Deportation by sea and rail decimated Norway's small Jewish population in November.

Deportation continued in 1943, the year in which new gas chambers and crematoria became operational at Auschwitz-Birkenau. Danuta Czech's *Auschwitz Chronicle* records the gassing of 873 Jews from Berlin on January 13. On February 6 1868 deportees from the Bialystok (Poland) Ghetto were gassed on arrival. Six weeks later 2191 Jews from Salonika, Greece, were killed in the gas chambers. On and on it went.

Etty Hillesum and her family were deported from Westerbork on September 7, 1943. They probably reached Auschwitz on September 9. Her parents were gassed immediately. On November 30, 1943, the prisoner population at the Auschwitz complex consisted of 54,446 men and 33,846 women. Of that number, 9273 men and 8487 women were reported as sick and unable to work. A Red Cross report lists November 30, 1943, as the date of Etty Hillesum's death.

1943

liquidated. Most of the Jews are deported to Auschwitz. Jews offer armed resistance.

• August 2, 1943: Jewish inmates at the Treblinka death camp, armed with small numbers of pistols, rifles, and hand grenades as well as gasoline, stage a violent revolt that allows the escape of 350 to 400 of the camp's 700 inmates. All but 100 are hunted down and murdered. Leaders of the revolt include Dr. Julian Chorazycki, Alfred Marceli Galewski, and Zelo Bloch.

• August 3, 1943: Jewish Fighting Organization members in the ghetto at Bedzin, Poland, mount an unsuccessful resistance to the Nazis. Local

Abraham Kolski *(left)* is seen here with Erich Lachman and a man named Brenner. The three men participated in the Treblinka uprising of August 2, 1943, and successfully found refuge in the nearby forest. A short time later, all three were taken in by a gentile family, which hid them until Poland was liberated.

JEWISH REVOLTS IN GHETTOS AND CONCENTRATION CAMPS, 1941–1944

Despite insurmountable odds, Jews nevertheless revolted in ghettos (most notably Warsaw and Bialystok), concentration camps, and death camps. Jews set the Treblinka camp on fire (August 2, 1943), killed 11 SS guards at Sobibór (October 14, 1943), and blew up one of the crematoria at Auschwitz (October 7, 1944).

The Treblinka death facility smolders in the distance following the uprising. The revolt was engineered by a small group of Czech-Jewish prisoners. During the uprising, some SS guards were killed and a few of the participants managed to escape to the surrounding forests. Even though the gas chambers were damaged, they continued to function after the revolt. The camp remained in operation for two additional months.

JFO leader Baruch Graftek and his fellow fighters are killed.

• **August 6, 1943:** One thousand Jews in Vilna, Lithuania, are deported to Klooga, Estonia, as the Germans begin to liquidate the Vilna Ghetto.
• French Jew Albert Kohan is smuggled from France to Great Britain to make contact with London-based rep-

resentatives of the French underground.

• **August 7, 1943:** The last trainload of Jews from Salonika, Greece, leaves for Auschwitz with 1800 detainees. Most will be killed at the camp. By this date, most of Salonika's prewar Jewish population (estimated at 56,000) has been murdered.

• **August 10, 1943:** Twenty-seven Jewish women seized by Nazis in the "Aryan" section of Warsaw are executed.

• **August 15, 1943:** Nearly 1000 French Jews of Polish birth are deported to a slave-labor camp on Alderney, one of the British Channel Islands seized in 1940 by Germany,

Bialystok

The northeastern Polish city of Bialystok was first occupied by the Germans on September 15, 1939. It was turned over to the Soviet Union, which held it for the next 21 months, and then reoccupied by the Germans on June 27, 1941. The creation of the ghetto in August 1941 sealed off Bialystok's 50,000 Jews. Because the ghetto needed workers for its factories and workshops, the Jews felt their lives would be spared.

The *Aktion* of February 1943, however, quickly dispelled any thoughts of long-term security. Two thousand Jews were murdered in the streets of Bialystok, and 10,000 others were sent to their deaths at the Treblinka extermination camp.

The liquidation orders of August 1943 spurred the ghetto's Resistance groups into action. The fighting lasted from August 16 to 20. With few arms at their disposal, the Resistance fighters were overwhelmed by the numerically superior and better-equipped German forces. Almost all of the fighters were killed by the Germans. Only a few hundred of Bialystok's Jews survived the war.

The Katzowicz brothers fought in the Bialystok (Poland) Ghetto uprising of August 1943. The city had numerous underground factions, and not until 1943 did they put politics aside and unite in common purpose. During the five days of battle, more than 1500 Jewish fighters gave their lives.

Haika Grossman, a Jew, was an underground activist. As a youth she joined a Zionist youth movement in Bialystok, Poland, and she later helped organize underground resistance there following the German occupation. Grossman posed as a Polish gentile during her many missions to other ghettos on behalf of the Jewish underground. She also participated in the Bialystok Ghetto revolt in August 1943.

1943

and are put to work building fortifications.

● **August 16, 1943:** Inmates revolt at the slave-labor camp at Krychów, Poland.

● **August 16–20, 1943:** Nazi troops enter the Jewish ghetto at Bialystok, Poland, to destroy the more than 30,000 Jews inside. Hundreds of Resistance fighters, led by Mordechai Tenenbaum-Tamaroff and Daniel Moszkowicz—who battle back with small arms, axes, and bayonets—are annihilated. Those who survive are transported to death camps, where 25,000 are killed; *See* August 17, 1943.

Peering into the distance, a man—probably a Jewish partisan—stands guard in Poland. In August 1943 the Nazis moved to liquidate the Bialystok (Poland) Ghetto, deporting the remaining 30,000 Jews. Recognizing that the end was near, some Jews—led by Mordechai Tenenbaum and Daniel Moszkowicz—staged a valiant, fierce struggle of defiance. Others sought to prolong resistance by fleeing to the forests, where they joined the *Forois* and other partisan groups.

This was one of the hundreds of mass graves dug near the Chelmno death camp. From 1941 to 1944, Chelmno gassed 150,000 to 320,000 people (estimates vary greatly), most of whom were Polish Jews. The Nazis stopped deportations to Chelmno in 1943 because the camp's gas-van extermination process was, in their minds, too slow. However, they reopened the camp in April 1944 to receive and kill the Jews of Lódź, Poland.

Originally established by the Dutch in 1939 as a detention center for illegal Jewish immigrants, Westerbork under the Nazis became the transit hub in the deportation of Dutch Jews. While the majority spent only a few days at the camp, a minority became permanent residents, receiving work cards like the one pictured here. Most of the employed prisoners worked in the camp hospital and dispensary.

• **August 17, 1943:** Some 1200 children are taken from the Jewish ghetto at Bialystok, Poland, to the Theresienstadt, Czechoslovakia, camp/ghetto and later to Auschwitz, where they will be killed. • The Allies defeat Axis forces in Sicily.

• **August 19, 1943:** The Treblinka death camp receives its final trainload of Jewish deportees. They come from Bialystok, Poland.

• **August 20, 1943:** Three thousand Jews are executed during a revolt at Glebokie, Belorussia.

• **August 23, 1943:** The Red Army captures Kharkov, Ukraine.

• **August 24, 1943:** Five thousand Jews from Bialystok, Poland, are killed at Auschwitz, Treblinka, and Majdanek.

• **August 25, 1943:** SS troops at the Janówska, Ukraine, labor camp select 24 attractive Jewish women aged 17 to 20 and take them to a night-long SS bacchanalia; *See* August 26, 1943.

Partisans from Rovno in the Volhynia area of Poland prepare to join their comrades in the fight against their oppressors. As the Nazis planned a final *Aktion,* some Jews escaped and fled to the surrounding forests. Operating within Volhynia, Moshe Gildenman, known as "Uncle Misha," organized an effective partisan unit that inflicted losses on German and Ukrainian troops.

The Nazis made widespread use of forced labor in high-tech industries, such as the manufacture of the V-2 rockets that rained down on Britain and Belgium during the final months of the war. These workers are engaged in the construction of a vast system of underground tunnels to house the rocket works. Unlike many of the Reich's millions of slaves, the primary danger to these inmates—who were housed in the open outside the tunnels—came from the threat posed by Allied bombing.

Two Jewish partisans, weapons at the ready, prepare for battle. Heeding the call of Abba Kovner to fight rather than to surrender to their oppressors, young people from the ghettos of Vilna and Kovno, Lithuania, tried to escape and join the partisans. Most groups were poorly armed and sometimes faced hostility from antisemitic partisans who hated the Nazis for reasons other than the persecution of Jews. Fired by a desire for revenge, Jews formed partisan groups like *Ha-Nokem,* founded by Vilna Jews, and *Kadima,* started by Jews from Kovno.

1943

• **August 26, 1943:** The Jewish community from Zawiercie, Poland, is destroyed at Auschwitz. • A young Jewish woman, one of 24 who was an unwilling guest at an SS "party" at the Janówska, Ukraine, labor camp the previous night, is shot during an escape attempt. The remaining 23 women are subsequently murdered.

• **August 27, 1943:** All the Jews working at a cement factory at Drogobych, Ukraine, near the Janówska labor camp, are murdered. One of the victims is Dr. Mojzesz Bay, a 36-year-old graduate of the Sorbonne.

• **August 28, 1943:** Germany imposes martial law on Denmark and abolishes the Danish-German agreement of

This is a page from the scrapbook of Kurt Franz, deputy commandant of the Treblinka death camp. After arriving there in the late summer of 1942, Franz began to keep an extensive photographic record of events in the camp. He later wrote, "Everywhere there were corpses. I remember that these corpses were already bloated." Franz was among the Treblinka personnel tried between October 1964 and August 1965. He was sentenced to life in prison.

A Jewish volunteer in a coastal artillery battery holds a shell on which is inscribed in Hebrew: "A gift for Hitler." Formed in 1940, these units served as part of the British force in Palestine. As news of the death camps reached Palestine, the desire for revenge grew among Jewish troops. Ultimately, the British agreed to form the Jewish Brigade Group.

American Jewish Conference

The American Jewish Conference was organized in 1943 by the American Zionist movement. Recognizing that war often results in great political change, many American Jews believed that the time to lobby for the creation of a Jewish state in Palestine was when the Second World War and the Holocaust had ended. Almost every American-Jewish organization was represented in the 1943 convention of more than 500 delegates.

Because the conference seemed more interested in establishing a Jewish state than in focusing on the rescue of European Jews, several Jewish organizations—especially the American Jewish Committee—criticized the conference's lack of emphasis on rescuing Holocaust victims. Moreover, the conference—established by Henry Monsky (pictured)—failed in its attempt to influence the U.S. government on the Palestine issue. Not until January 1945 did the conference urge rescue and aid for the Jews of Europe.

The conference was a harbinger of wide American-Jewish commitment to the establishment of Israel. In September 1945 a Roper poll indicated that 80 percent of American Jews favored the Zionist position. The most significant achievement of the conference was helping to swing American non-Jewish and political opinion in favor of the creation of a postwar home for the Jews of Europe.

April 9, 1940, which prevented German molestation of Jews.

• Late August 1943: Forty-seven Jewish women and 50 Jewish men are executed after being discovered in the "Aryan" section of Warsaw.

• September 1943: Germans send a Polish labor battalion into the ruins of

the Warsaw Ghetto to flatten any walls and other structures still standing following the German assault of the previous spring. Most survivors of the April-May "liquidation" die during this demolition. • The American Council for Judaism declares that Jewishness exists in a religious sense only, and that attempts to establish a Jewish homeland would be disloyal to

the homeland nations of individual Jews. • Jews at the Sobibór death camp attack SS guards with stones and bottles. All attackers are killed.
• Jewish women and children, as well as the elderly and the sick, left on the island of Rab after deportation from Dalmatia, Serbia, are transferred to a concentration camp at Zemun, Yugoslavia, and killed. Others remain

Art as Resistance

In the midst of degradation and despair, concentration-camp prisoners refused to allow their creativity to be stifled and destroyed. Even as they struggled to survive, prisoners used whatever scraps of paper and stubs of pencils they could find to express themselves. Through poetry and art, they affirmed their own existence and documented the horrors they feared might be forgotten.

In Theresienstadt, the model camp/ghetto the Nazis established near Prague, Czechoslovakia, artists such as Felix Bloch produced "official" art on command while secretly creating works that portrayed Jewish existence as it was. Teacher Friedl Dicker-Brandeis nurtured the talents of her young Theresienstadt charges, enabling them through art to transform the dark and dangerous world of the Nazis into a realm of light and love. The drawings the children left behind portray images of butterflies and birds, sailboats and family gatherings. But they also record the trauma of daily life, ghetto guards, and train departures to the death camps.

One child's poem voices the longing reflected in the drawings of many: "I'd like to go away alone/Where there are other, nicer people/Somewhere into the far unknown/There, where no one kills another."

Ignacy Isaac Schwarzbart was a Zionist member of the Polish Parliament and the Polish government-in-exile. He published a Jewish newspaper, *The Future,* in London, documenting the German Holocaust against Jews in Poland. Like all such information going to the Allies, his newspaper had little effect on Allied disinclination to rally aid for Jews. Schwarzbart opposed bombing Auschwitz, fearing that too many Jews would lose their lives to Allied attacks.

The Jewish synagogue in Zagreb, Croatia, was demolished in 1943. The onslaught against Croatian Jewry that began in 1941 with the German invasion of the Soviet Union continued into 1943. Deportations from Zagreb were personally ordered by Heinrich Himmler in May 1943, and the vast majority of Croatian Jews who were sent to Auschwitz never emerged. Most Croatian Jews who died, however, were killed not by the Nazis but by the country's ruthless *Ustasa* regime.

1943

on the island and are protected by partisans.

• Hundreds of Jews escape from Vilna, Lithuania, and head east toward the Soviet front line. • Vilna-based partisan Vitka Kempner blows up an electrical transformer located in the city. A day later, she enters the labor camp at Keilis, near Vilna, and smuggles several dozen prisoners to safety. Still later, she travels with five other partisans to Olkiniki, Poland, where she helps torch a turpentine factory. • In Paris, three Jewish partisans ambush and assassinate Karl Ritter, aide to Nazi slave-labor chief Fritz Sauckel. • After refusing for months, the Hungarian government accedes to German demands for Jews

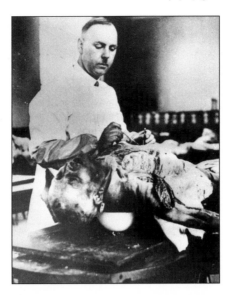

Dr. August Hirt, director of the Strasbourg Anatomical Institute in France, works on the cadaver of a Jewish person. As part of the Nazi quest to prove Aryan racial superiority, Hirt aimed to establish a vast collection of skeletons from all peoples. In 1943 the collection still lacked sufficient Jewish examples. Thus, at Hirt's request, 86 Jews from Auschwitz, whose bone structure exemplified the desired characteristics, were sent to Natzweiler-Struthof, where they were gassed. Their bodies were then sent to Hirt in Strasbourg, where the corpses were reduced to skeletons.

As the architect of the Nazi program of genocide, Heinrich Himmler spent much of 1943 implementing the "Final Solution." Named minister of the interior in August, Himmler utilized his control over the courts and civil service to advance the racial reordering of Europe, and paid particular attention to the fates of the 600,000 Jews he estimated to be in France. During an October speech to SS *Gruppenführers* (major generals) at Posen, Germany, Himmler declared that the Nazis had a "moral right" and a "duty" to exterminate the Jews. He proudly hailed the SS role in that process. Oddly, although Himmler told the group that the Final Solution was "an unwritten and never to be written page in [SS] history," he took pains to ensure that his speech was tape-recorded.

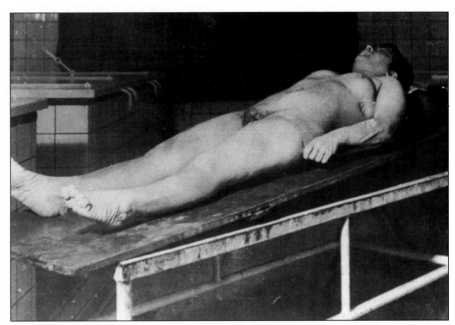

In August 1943 30 women were taken from Block 10 at Auschwitz-Birkenau and gassed at Natzweiler-Struthof, with their corpses then shipped to the Strasbourg Anatomical Institute for study. Conducted under the auspices of the *Ahnenerbe* (ancestral heritage) office of the SS, Dr. August Hirt's research was intended to yield an anthropological classification system. He intended to separate inferior from superior races and prove Aryan superiority.

to be used as slave labor at copper mines at Bor, Yugoslavia. • A concentration camp for Soviet POWs is established at Vaivara, Estonia; *See* June 28, 1944.

• September 2, 1943: One thousand Jews are deported from Paris to Auschwitz. • Ten thousand Jews from Tarnów, Poland, are deported to

Auschwitz and the Plaszów slave-labor camp. • At Treblinka, 13 Jews use a crowbar to kill a Ukrainian SS guard. The uprising's 18-year-old Polish leader, Seweryn Klajnman, puts on the dead man's uniform and marches the other 12 prisoners, who are already on a work detail outside of camp, farther away from the camp.

• September 2–3, 1943: Thirty-five hundred Jews are deported from Przemyśl, Poland, to Auschwitz.

• September 3-8, 1943: The Allies invade the Italian peninsula. Italy surrenders to the Allies. The new Italian leader, Marshal Pietro Badoglio, signs an armistice with the Allies.

Jewish intellectuals were particularly offensive in the eyes of the Nazis. They not only played a vital role in preserving Jewish culture, but were also, from the point of view of Nazi ideology, responsible for the totally negative effects of Jewish influence upon German culture. The Nazis believed that the Jews were responsible for every intellectual movement of which they disapproved. This included, most importantly, all forms of cultural modernism. These Viennese-Jewish intellectuals, imprisoned in the Mauthausen, Austria, concentration camp, paid a heavy price for this Nazi prejudice.

This cartoon, depicting a Jew praying at an altar of wealth, appeared in an antisemitic Hungarian publication. The elevated position of the money in relation to the Torah scroll, Judaism's most holy book, suggests that material values had replaced Jewish spiritual and ethical teachings. The juxtaposition of money and Jews was a favorite theme of Nazi propaganda. The cartoon's artist, Philipp Rupprecht, signed his work "FIPS," and was a frequent front-page contributor to Julius Streicher's crude antisemitic newspaper, *Der Stürmer*.

Allied troops march across a pontoon bridge over the Volturno River in Italy. The Fifth Army followed in their footsteps, pursuing the Germans as they retreated over the Apennine Mountains. Although progress was slow and casualties were heavy, the Fifth Army slowly made its way north until the winter snows brought progress to a halt near the Rapido River.

1943

• September 5-6, 1943: An old shoe warehouse in the Łódź (Poland) Ghetto takes delivery of 12 freight cars filled with shoes stolen from murdered Jews; *See* September 13, 1943.

• September 8, 1943: 5006 Jews deported from the Theresienstadt, Czechoslovakia, camp/ghetto arrive at Auschwitz. • Italian forces surrender to Germany in Rhodes. German troops occupy Athens.

• September 10, 1943: Jewish youths attack German troops at Miedzyrzec, Poland, killing two. Five Jews are shot. • A tea party attended by the widow of Wilhelm H. Solf (former colonial minister under German

Human skeletons cover the ground outside the crematorium at the Majdanek camp in Poland. Approximately 145,000 people died in the seven gas chambers, which began operating, utilizing Zyklon B, in 1942. Many others died from starvation, dysentery, or shootings. The small crematorium proved incapable of handling the great influx of bodies, and so a large new one was constructed in September 1943.

This mountain of shoes at the Majdanek death camp testifies to the number of people who walked through the gates of the camp to their deaths. While prisoners hobbled in ill-fitting clogs, tons of shoes accumulated in the storerooms of the death camps. At Auschwitz-Birkenau, women were assigned to the *Schuhkommando.* They performed tedious labor, separating soles from uppers and rubber from leather, with the pieces shipped to Germany. One woman, Giuliani Tedeschi, described the work as "drowning in a sea of shoes."

Majdanek

Majdanek, a concentration and death camp near Lublin, Poland, became operational in October 1941. Before Soviet troops liberated the camp on July 24, 1944, nearly 500,000 persons from 28 countries were imprisoned there. Majdanek's death toll reached 360,000—mostly Soviet POWs, Poles, and Jews. Sixty percent died from starvation, disease, and exhausting labor. The others were executed, often on arrival. Those victims included thousands of Jews who were murdered in Majdanek's seven gas chambers.

In late October 1943, prisoners were ordered to dig three huge trenches in the camp's southern sector. These preparations were for *Erntefest* (Harvest Festival). At Majdanek's morning roll call on November 3, Jews were separated from the other prisoners, sent to the trenches, and shot. Dance music blared from the camp's loudspeakers to drown out the screams and machine-gun fire. The murders continued until nightfall. "Bloody Wednesday" left 18,000 Jews dead in Majdanek's trenches.

Intended to prevent Jewish prisoner revolts, *Erntefest* went beyond Majdanek. Jewish prisoners at other camps in the Lublin district—8000 to 10,000 at Trawniki and 15,000 at Poniatowa—also were shot on November 3. It remained Majdanek's distinction, however, to be the most deadly site of the Germans' largest one-day killing operation against the Jews.

Emperor Wilhelm II), her daughter Grafin Ballestrem, and other members of the anti-Hitler German Resistance is infiltrated by a Dr. Reckse, a Gestapo informant; *See* January 1944.
• Germans occupy Rome.

• **September 11, 1943:** One thousand Jews discovered hiding in Przemyśl, Poland, are murdered.

• **September 11–14, 1943:** The Jewish community at Minsk, Belorussia, is liquidated.

• **September 13, 1943:** In the Łódź (Poland) Ghetto, Icek Bekerman is hanged for taking leather scraps for use as shoelaces. The ghetto carpentry shop is ordered to construct the gallows.

• **September 14, 1943:** Jacob Gens, *Judenrat* leader at the Vilna (Lithuania) Ghetto, is shot by Nazis.

• **Mid-September 1943:** At the Sobibór death camp, members of the corpse-burning detail have built an escape tunnel intended to lead them into the camp minefield. Most of the 150 members of the detail are killed.

Abba Kovner

In 1941 23-year-old artist Abba Kovner was one of the leaders of *Ha-Shomer ha-Tsa'ir*, a Socialist Zionist youth organization, in Vilna, Lithuania. As the Nazis increased their roundups of Jews, Kovner and others hid in a Dominican convent. When he learned of the killings in the Ponary Forest, Kovner realized the full scope of the Nazi plan—and vowed to fight back. On January 1, 1942, Kovner warned his people that deportation meant death. He issued a stirring call to Jewish youth to flee and fight, not "to go as sheep to the slaughter." Kovner helped organize a united partisan resistance, and with the death of Yitzhak Wittenberg, he became the commander of the United Partisan Organization (FPO). As the Nazis emptied the Vilna Ghetto of its last Jews in September 1943, Kovner led the escape of his fighters into the Rudninkai Forest, where, as the "Avenger" battalion, they fought on. Kovner lived until 1988.

Enjoying a reprieve from work, a platoon of forced-labor workers gathers for a photograph. Although mostly garbed in civilian clothing, these members of an Hungarian labor battalion all wear military caps. While Heinrich Himmler and the SS sought to kill all of Europe's Jews, Albert Speer, as head of the German war economy, maneuvered to secure as many workers as possible to rebuild factories and produce desperately needed war materiel.

The demolition of this Luxembourg synagogue was completed in the fall of 1943 after a two-year delay. The order to destroy the Jewish house of worship was issued in May 1941. No local contractor was willing to do the job, so the Nazis hired two Italians to complete the task. Approximately 3500 Jews lived in Luxembourg at the beginning of World War II. The tiny nation was declared *Judenrein* (cleansed of Jews) after the last Jewish transport left the country on September 28, 1943.

1943

• September 16, 1943: More than 37,000 Italian Jews come under German rule.

• September 18, 1943: Two thousand Jews in Minsk, Belorussia, are deported to the Sobibór death camp; 80 are selected for forced labor and the rest are gassed.

• September 18–19, 1943: The Jews of Lida, Belorussia, are deported to the Majdanek death camp.

• September 20, 1943: One thousand Jewish inmates of the camp at Szebnie, Poland, are trucked to a nearby field and executed with machine guns. The bodies are burned and the bones thrown into the Jasiolka River.

Surrounded by German parachutists, a slimmed-down Benito Mussolini rejoices in being freed from captivity. With the landings in Sicily and the momentum swinging to the Allied side, Italian King Victor Emmanuel III dismissed Mussolini as premier in July and placed him in military detention. Unwilling to lose his Fascist partner or allow Mussolini's government to fall, Hitler ordered a daring rescue. Mussolini became the puppet head of a Fascist republic based in northern Italy and controlled directly by Germany.

A German honor guard flanks the flag-draped casket of Wilhelm Kube, *Generalkommissar* of Belorussia. A long-time Nazi, Kube *(above, right)* founded the *Glaubensweg deutscher Christen* (Movement of German-Christian Believers), which sought the "Aryanization" of Christianity. He served as a Nazi member of the *Reichstag* and in various posts, including governor of Brandenburg-Berlin. In 1941 he was appointed to his post in Belorussia. On September 22, 1943, a bomb, placed under his bed by his maid, a member of the Resistance, killed Kube as he slept.

• Jacob Kapler, a Jew assigned to the body-burning detail at the Babi Yar, Ukraine, mass-murder site, finds a key that fits the padlock on a bunker in which he and other laborers are locked each night; *See* September 29, 1943.

• Late summer 1943: Forty Jews hiding in forests near Koniecpol, Poland, are attacked by Poles. Many of the Jews are killed.

• September 22, 1943: Wilhelm Kube, the *Generalkommissar* of Belorussia, is assassinated by a bomb placed beneath his bed by a Soviet partisan who had been assigned to work as his maid.

• September 24, 1943: Nazis complete the liquidation of the Jewish ghetto at Vilna.

• September 25, 1943: The Red Army captures Smolensk, Russia. • Only about 2000 Jews, scattered among four labor camps, remain in Vilna, Lithuania. • Eliahu Barzilai, the chief rabbi of Athens, Greece, disguises

Riga was Latvia's largest Jewish center. With the German occupation of Latvia in July 1941, thousands of Jews were murdered and 30,000 sealed off in the Riga Ghetto. In late 1941 the eminent Jewish historian Simon Dubnow was murdered along with most of the city's surviving Jews. Repopulated by German Jews, the Riga Ghetto was finally destroyed in November 1943.

Even music was subverted by the Nazis. To calm arrivals and delude them into thinking that they were in a safe haven, the Auschwitz-Birkenau camp orchestra played cheerful and familiar melodies as people descended from the trains. Music also provided a macabre accompaniment to death, as shown in this photo from Mauthausen. Prisoners are marched to the gallows while accompanied by the violins and accordion of the camp orchestra. The inmates referred to this as the *Symphonia Diabolica,* the Devil's Symphony.

> "From time to time we see people working on the tracks... many of them in POW uniforms. We ask them where, what is the probable target of our trip. They shrug their shoulders. One of them points to the sky. We fail to understand the hint."
>
> —*Survivor Anneliese Borinsky*

1943

himself as a peasant and escapes from the city.

• September 26, 1943: At the Novogrudok, Belorussia, labor camp, Jews complete secret work on a tunnel dug under the wire. Of the 220 Jews who use the tunnel to attempt escape, 120 are killed or captured.

• September 28-29, 1943: Five thousand Jews from Amsterdam are deported to the Westerbork, Holland, transit camp. • The Jewish community from Split, Yugoslavia, is killed at the Sajmiste, Yugoslavia, concentration camp. • Roman Jews deliver 50 kilograms of gold to the Gestapo in Rome, as ordered. Pope Pius XII had offered to lend the Italian Jews 15

A Belgian priest proudly stands between two girls at their First Communion. The girl on the right, Marie-Rose, is a Jewish girl in hiding during the war. Belgians protested the deportation of Jews. While some Belgians, especially those in the police forces, collaborated in the deportations, others, including priests and nuns, protected and hid Jews. The facts that Belgium was a democracy, and that Jews, by and large, had been assimilated into the nation's economic and even political mainstreams, helped to encourage the sort of assistance received by young Marie-Rose.

While some 4000 Belgian-Jewish children were kept safe in hiding throughout the war, others were not so fortunate. An estimated 65,000 Jews were living in Belgium at the time of the Nazi invasion. The first deportation of Jews began in July 1942; they were sent via Malines to Auschwitz. Eventually, some 25,000 Jews were deported to their deaths, including all of these children.

kilograms of gold if they could not collect the full amount themselves.

• **September 29, 1943:** More than 320 Jews and Soviet POWs on work detail at the Babi Yar, Ukraine, mass-murder site attempt a mass escape. Nearly all are shot down almost immediately, but about 14 find hiding places; *See* November 6, 1943.

• **September 30, 1943:** The Krupp arms factory at Mariupol, Ukraine, is dismantled and relocated west to Fünfteichen, Silesia, Poland, where it is staffed by Jewish slave laborers.

• **September 1943–April 1944:** Jewish slave laborers exhume at least 68,000 corpses of murdered Jews and Soviet POWs at the Ponary, Lithuania,

killing ground, near Vilna; *See* April 15, 1944.

• **Autumn 1943:** Technicians representing Topf and Sons, the German manufacturer/installer of crematoria furnaces at Auschwitz-Birkenau, study the combustibility of corpses mated to various grades of coke.

• British and American bombing of

Sexual Abuse in Camps

Sexual abuse in the camps took many forms. Barbaric medical experiments conducted by Nazi doctors robbed men and women of their sexual organs. At Auschwitz, women spared from the gas chambers upon arrival were forced to parade their nakedness in the showers before leering SS guards, who delighted in poking their breasts.

Within the camps, rumors abounded that attractive young women were forced into brothels. At Buchenwald, some political prisoners, known for their ethical and religious principles, were compelled by the SS to visit the camp brothel, populated by non-Jewish "volunteers" from the Ravensbrück concentration camp for women. Irma Grese, the sadistic SS supervisor at Auschwitz-Birkenau, was rumored to have had homosexual relations with prisoners whom she then sent to the gas chambers. To save their lives, starving women at Birkenau sometimes bartered sex for food from male prisoners.

While Nazi racial ideology prohibited relations between Jews and "Aryans," there were some instances of rape. The Nazis, though, were not the only ones who committed sexual abuse. Buchenwald survivors report that Polish and Russian boys, some as young as 12, were forced into homosexual acts by sexually rapacious prisoners. Victims of sexual abuse have largely kept silent, leaving this aspect of camp life shrouded in ambiguity.

The Jewish Agency, established by the League of Nations in the 1920s, published material on the "Massacre of a People" in the *Jewish Frontier* in October 1943. The Jewish Agency brought orphans to Palestine, advocated bombing railways leading to Auschwitz, and urged the Allies to save Jews from concentration camps.

A Swiss volunteer named Abbe Gross *(left)* reaches through a barbed-wire fence surrounding the Gurs transit camp to share a cigarette with a prisoner. Located in the Pyrénées region of France, Gurs was a makeshift detention center that held thousands of Jews before they were deported to Auschwitz. Flimsy shelters, dirt roads that turned to mud when it rained, and starvation rations made for extremely unpleasant conditions for those imprisoned at Gurs.

1943

Germany, most notably the heavily industrialized Ruhr region, increases in intensity. • Jews in Wlodawa, Poland, attack the Turno Estate, a onetime Jewish farm that has since fallen into German hands. The Jews set the buildings on the estate ablaze. A Jew named Yankel, who has lived in a hole in the floor of the estate's barn for about a year, dies just hours after being taken to safety by the attacking Jews.

• October 1943: The Jewish ghetto at Chernovtsy, Romania, is liquidated.
• SS chief Heinrich Himmler delivers a speech at a "Final Solution" conference. • Just before their murders, several Jewish women use their bare hands to attack SS troops at Auschwitz.

Moshe Gildenman, also known as "Uncle Misha," commanded a partisan unit in the Ukraine. After the Nazis killed his wife and daughter on May 21, 1942, Gildenman and his surviving son formed a rebel group that attacked German farms and Ukrainian police centers. When his unit was incorporated into a general partisan group in 1943, Moshe volunteered for the Soviet Army. He emigrated to Israel in 1950 and died in 1958.

Near Minsk, Belorussia, a German soldier aims his pistol at a Jew, perhaps suspecting him to be a partisan. Following the deportation of 4000 Jews from Minsk in October 1943, only the few Jews who had managed to hide remained in the ghetto. Beginning in spring 1942 many had fled the ghetto for the surrounding forests, where they joined partisan groups such as the *Shalom Zorin* unit, which eventually included 800 fighters.

Seeking to prevent people from fleeing the Minsk (Belorussia) Ghetto for the forests, this bilingual sign warns against climbing through a fence. Although the penalty was death, many in the ghetto took the risk. Guided by daring children, some as young as 11, entire families sought safety in the forest, where many joined the family camp and partisan unit of *Shalom Zorin*.

• October 2, 1943: The Danish people rescue about 7000 Jews, only 500 of whom are captured by the Germans. The 500 seized by the Germans are sent to the Theresienstadt, Czechoslovakia, camp/ghetto; all but 77 will survive the war. The Danish government will persistently check on the health and welfare of the Jews who were sent to Theresienstadt, enabling almost all of them to survive to war's end. • The first Jewish Palestinian paratroopers land in the Balkans. These Jews agree first to help organized non-Jewish underground units on behalf of the British war effort. Only then, unsupported, will the British allow them to aid other Jews.

• October 2–3, 1943: In Holland, the families of Jewish men drafted for forced labor are sent to the Westerbork, Holland, concentration camp.

• October 3, 1943: On a routine barracks inspection at the Auschwitz-Birkenau death camp, an SS doctor judges 139 inmates unfit to work. These inmates are promptly gassed.

Jews in Hiding

Throughout Europe, in attics and basements, in secret cupboards so small they could barely crouch, Jews struggled to hide themselves from their Nazi persecutors. Sometimes they were hidden by gentile friends; sometimes by complete strangers.

In Amsterdam, the Frank family, along with several others, hid for months in a secret annex, supplied with the essentials of life by Miep Gies. Dutch woman Dieuwke Hofstede *(pictured)* opened her doors to Henny Kalkstein *(right)*. Convents and monasteries also hid Jewish children. In the northern Italian town of Assisi, Father Rufino Niccacci supplied Jews with forged identity papers and helped them to find homes and work. In France, the entire village of Le Chambon-sur-Lignon, guided by its pastor, André Trocmé, was committed to hiding/protecting Jewish refugees.

In Eastern Europe, finding a hiding place was extremely difficult. Although many Poles were antisemitic and many others feared the consequences of aiding Jews, some Poles responded to the cries for help. Irene Gut Oppyke hid 12 Jews in the house of a German officer for whom she worked as a housekeeper. In Wlodawa, Poland, a Jewish man named Yankel lived for a year in a hole in the floor of a barn. The farm itself was occupied by German soldiers.

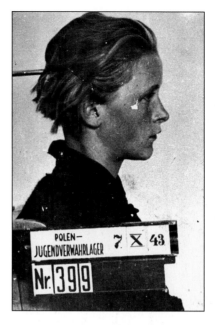

Pictured is a child prisoner of the *Jugendschutzlager* (Youth "Protection" Camp), located in the Lódź (Poland) Ghetto. The *Jugendschutzlager,* for non-Jewish Poles, was established in December 1942. About 10,000 children passed through its gates; most were subsequently killed at Chelmno and Auschwitz.

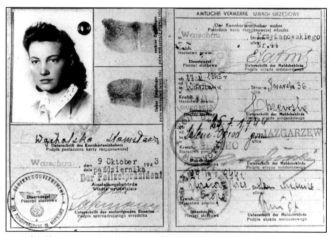

Vladka Meed, who used this false identification card of Stanislawa Wachalska to live on the Aryan side of Warsaw, utilized her position on behalf of the ghetto's Resistance movement. Besides procuring guns for the ZOB fighters, she helped smuggle Jews out of the ghetto and found shelter for them. The heroics of Meed and others like her were critical to the success of Resistance movements in Warsaw and other Polish ghettos.

1943

• **October 4, 1943:** In an address to senior SS officers, SS chief Heinrich Himmler notes that killing is hard but necessary, and that killing the Jews will never be spoken of publicly.

• **October 6, 1943:** A Jew posing as a Catholic, Helen Manaster is called out of the delivery room in the Kraków, Poland, hospital while in labor pains to face two Gestapo agents. She keeps her calm and the Gestapo agents tell her to go back to bed.

• **October 7, 1943:** A Jewish partisan unit active near Vilna, Lithuania, destroys more than 50 telegraph poles lining the road from Vilna to Grodno. • In an official report, the

Josef Glazman was the deputy commander of the Vilna (Lithuania) Ghetto police and the leader of the *Betar* youth group. His negotiations with the leaders of Jewish youth groups produced a unified Resistance faction known as the FPO (United Partisans Organization). Glazman was responsible for gathering intelligence about the German and Lithuanian forces, training new recruits, and organizing housing within the ghetto. He was killed in a gunfight with the Germans in the Naroch Forest in October 1943.

When the war turned against the Germans, they began a concerted effort to conceal their crimes. Hence, *Sonderkommandos,* most of them Jews, were ordered to begin the grisly task of exhuming the bodies of Nazi Germany's millions of victims and disposing of the remains. This photograph shows a bone-crushing machine that was used to grind up the body parts that could not be burned. The man on the right, with the surname of Korn, burned about 46,000 corpses, including that of his wife, during the three months he worked as a *Sonderkommando.*

Prisoners from the Buchenwald, Germany, concentration camp staffed this assembly line at the *Gustloff Werke* II munitions plant. The *Gustloff Werke* facility was built in 1943 and was one of the main armaments factories at Buchenwald. The armaments complex was staffed by 3600 prisoners. The particularly sadistic treatment of the prisoners at the hands of their Nazi guards resulted in a very high death rate.

German chief of police in Poland recommends that Poles who aid Jews should be dealt with without benefit of trial. • One thousand Jews are deported from Paris to their deaths at Auschwitz.

• October 8, 1943: On the eve of the Jewish Day of Atonement, several thousand ill or weak Jewish men are

gassed at Auschwitz. • Three thousand Italian prisoners of war are murdered by the SS and Ukrainian guards at La Risiera di San Sabba, Italy, south of Trieste. Of 1920 Jews in Trieste, 620 are murdered by the SS.

• October 10, 1943: A non-Jewish Latvian named Yanis Lipke rescues three Jews in Riga by offering ghetto

guards two packs of cigarettes for "some Yids to work in my kitchen garden"; *See* October 11, 1943. • At the Sobibór death camp, a revolt is planned by Jewish laborers and Jewish Red Army POWs; *See* October 13, 1943.

• October 11, 1943: One day after rescuing three Jews from the Riga

An Italian soldier and Italian sailor hug as they celebrate the announcement that Italy has declared war on Germany. For many soldiers, their rejoicing would be short-lived. Italy's new government, headed by Marshal Pietro Badoglio, surrendered to the Allies on September 8, and five weeks later King Victor Emmanuel III took the next step, declaring war on Germany. As a result, hundreds of thousands of Italian soldiers in the regions controlled by German troops were disarmed by the Germans and sent to internment camps. Thousands perished.

Danish fishermen ferry a boatload of Jewish fugitives across a narrow sound to neutral Sweden during the nationwide rescue operation. News of impending deportations of Jews spawned a rapid response by the Danes, who worked feverishly to save Jewish citizens. Boats of every size and shape were used to transport the Jews from Denmark to Sweden, away from the grasp of the Nazis.

A Jew, recently apprehended by a Danish Nazi *(center, in black raincoat and hat)*, is rescued by his fellow Danes. As the Nazi escorted the Jew through the streets, an angry crowd forced him to surrender his prisoner to the Danish police. Once safely inside the police station, the gendarmes helped the Jew escape. The Danish police consistently refused to cooperate with the German occupation authorities.

1943

(Latvia) Ghetto by asking guards for Jews to labor on his property, Yanis Lipke rescues additional Jews with the same ruse. • At the Sobibór death camp, new arrivals panic and run toward barbed wire, only to be machine-gunned by guards.

• October 13, 1943: Italy declares war on Germany. • Hatchets, knives,

and warm clothing are secretly distributed among inmates at the Sobibór death camp; *See* October 14, 1943.

• October 14, 1943: Leon Feldhendler and Jewish Soviet officer Aleksandr Pechersky, interned at the Sobibór death camp since September, instigate an inmate revolt and

This group portrait of Danish-Jewish children was taken in a children's home in Sweden after their escape from Denmark. The rescue of Danish Jewry was one of the few positive stories in the tragic annals of the Holocaust. These Jewish children unknowingly defied all odds by surviving the genocidal intentions of the Nazis.

A Swedish policeman accompanies a newly arrived Danish-Jewish refugee to the welfare office in Rebslagergade, Sweden. Swedish participation was critical to the success of the rescue operation. Not only did the government proclaim its willingness to accept all Jewish refugees from Denmark, but the Swedish Red Cross helped save the approximately 500 Danish Jews who were deported to the Theresienstadt camp/ghetto in Czechoslovakia.

Denmark's Rescue of Jews

The heroic actions of the Danish people during the autumn of 1943 saved nearly all of Denmark's Jews from certain death in Nazi concentration camps.

After the Germans occupied the country in 1940, the Danish government resisted Nazi pressure to hand over its Jews. In 1943, however, the Danes intensified resistance, prompting a harsh Nazi reaction. Imposing martial law, the Germans in October began to arrest and deport Danish Jews. Reacting spontaneously, Danes alerted and hid the Jews, helping them to the coast and organizing secret passage across the sea to Sweden (pictured).  The unassuming Danish rescuers included police, fishermen, and members of church and social organizations.

Over the course of three weeks, the Danish people transported more than 7200 Jews and almost 700 of their non-Jewish relatives to safety aboard Danish fishing vessels. The Nazis did capture 464 Jews, whom they sent to the Theresienstadt, Czechoslovakia, camp/ghetto. Aid continued, nonetheless, as the Danish public sent food parcels to their Jewish countrymen imprisoned in Theresienstadt. Just before the conclusion of the war, in spring 1945, negotiations rescued most of these Jews through an agreement that transferred many Scandinavian nationals from concentration camps to Sweden.

escape, during which 11 German SS guards and two or three Ukrainian SS guards are killed. Two hundred of 600 Jews in the camp are killed by gunfire and exploding mines; among them is 33-year-old Dutch painter Max Van Dam. Of the 300 who escape, only 100 are recaptured; many of the remaining 200 escapees join Soviet partisan forces. Of these,

only 50 to 70, including Pechersky, will survive the war; See October 16, 1943.

• October 16, 1943: Two days after a violent Jewish revolt at the Sobibór death camp, SS chief Heinrich Himmler orders the camp destroyed.
• Germans looking for Jews in Rome conduct house-to-house searches.

About 1000 Jews are briefly held at Rome's Collegio Militare, then deported to Auschwitz. 477 Jews are sheltered in the Vatican, and another 4238 find sanctuary in convents and monasteries throughout Rome. Nevertheless, by this date more than 8300 Italian Jews have been deported to Auschwitz.

Zyklon B

At six-week intervals in 1943, a truck dispatched from Auschwitz traveled to Dessau, Germany. It returned with hermetically sealed tin canisters of Zyklon B, the commercial name for the bluish hydrogen cyanide pellets that asphyxiated more than a million Jews in the Auschwitz killing center.

A powerful pesticide developed during World War I, Zyklon B was used to combat contagious disease by fumigating lice-infested buildings. At first it served those purposes at Auschwitz, where overcrowding, malnutrition,

and poor sanitation made dysentery, typhoid fever, and especially typhus constant threats. By late summer 1941, however, the Nazis experimented with Zyklon B on Soviet POWs. They found that the compound's vaporizing pellets offered a particularly reliable and efficient way to advance the "Final Solution."

Two German companies—DEGESCH, a subsidiary of I.G. Farben, and Tesch and Stabenow Company—profited immensely by supplying Zyklon B to the SS. They even modified it for Auschwitz by removing the special odor that ordinarily warned people about their product's deadly presence.

In 1942 Auschwitz used 8.2 tons of Zyklon B. The tonnage for 1943 was 13.4. Most of it was poured through small rooftop openings into gas chambers packed with Jews. Once exposed to air, the pellets produced lethal gas. Minutes later, after panic-filled screams, the human victims were dead.

Stanislaw Szmajzner, 16, participated in and helped to organize the revolt at the Sobibór death camp in October 1943. After the uprising, Szmajzner was one of the prisoners who successfully escaped and joined forces with Russian partisans. He was one of three members of his particular group to survive the war.

Ernst von Weizsäcker was a career diplomat who loyally served the Nazi regime. His career followed the path of his mentor, Foreign Minister Joachim von Ribbentrop. Weizsäcker served as chief state secretary from the time that Ribbentrop was appointed foreign minister until 1943, when he was named as the ambassador to the Vatican.

1943

• German Ambassador to the Vatican Ernst von Weizsäcker compliments the Holy See for its "perfect even-handedness" in treating Germany and the Allies. When Weizsäcker asks what Pope Pius XII will do if the German government persists in its present Jewish policy in Italy, Vatican Secretary of State Maglione replies that "the Holy See would not want to be put in the position of having to utter a word of disapproval." The Pope is being "cautious so as not to give the German people the impression that [he] has done or has wished to do even the smallest thing against Germany during this terrible war."

• October 17, 1943: A Jewish partisan unit commanded by Abba Kovner

In a family portrait reflecting happier times, Leone Biondi and Virginia Piperno are photographed with three of their six children. October 1943 marked a new stage in German control over Italian affairs following the German occupation of northern Italy. Orders were issued to round up and deport the Jews of Rome, and on October 18 approximately 1000 were sent to Auschwitz. Thanks to the intervention of their Italian friends and neighbors, many Jews were able to hide and to escape capture, some in Catholic churches and monasteries. The Biondis were not so fortunate; the entire family perished at Auschwitz.

Gertruda Babilinska worked for 15 years for a Jewish family. She is shown here with one of the family's children, Michael Stolovitzky. Babilinska refused to abandon the family after the onset of the German occupation. After Mr. Stolovitzky was shipped to Auschwitz and his daughter died, Bablinska helped Mrs. Stolovitzky and Michael escape, first to Warsaw and then to Vilna. There, she rented an apartment in which she hid Michael. Because Michael's mother also died, Babilinska was responsible for Michael's well-being after the war. The pair emigrated to Israel, where Bablinska provided him with a Jewish upbringing.

While Jewish leaders in the Italian cities of Florence and Venice warned Jews to go into hiding, leaders in Rome reacted slowly to the news of possible deportations. Lists and addresses were not destroyed, leaving many families vulnerable to immediate capture. Among those deported were Franza and Enrica Spizzichino, ages seven and ten, respectively, who pose here on a bicycle in a Roman piazza. The girls, their parents, and their brother Mario were hunted down and deported to Auschwitz, where they were killed upon arrival.

destroys two rail engines and two bridges near Vilna, Lithuania. • German Ambassador to the Vatican Ernst von Weizsäcker writes to the German Foreign Ministry that the College of Cardinals has been "particularly dismayed" since the roundup of Jews in Rome is occurring "below the very windows of the Pope." He notes that the Pope continues to do everything

he can "not to burden relations with the German government and German agencies in Rome."

• October 20, 1943: The United Nations War Crimes Commission is established; *See* October 26, 1943.

• October 21, 1943: During the final *Aktion* in Minsk, Belorussia, about

2000 Jews are murdered at Maly Trostinets.

• October 23, 1943: Eighteen hundred Polish Jews formerly held at Bergen-Belsen, Germany, arrive at Auschwitz, where the women revolt outside the gas chambers, killing one SS guard and wounding two. SS reinforcements use gas grenades and

Jewish Resistance

Facing overwhelming odds, many Jews courageously defied the Nazis while significant numbers actively fought against them. Jewish resistance to the Nazis indeed took many different forms.

For many Jews, "spiritual resistance" was often their only means of defiance within the ghettos and camps of Eastern Europe. Jews cherished any means through which self-dignity and cultural heritage could be saved. They stubbornly resisted the Nazis' dehumanizing policies by performing illegal religious ceremonies, orchestra concerts, or theater productions. They conducted Hebrew language classes, published newspapers, and documented life in ghettos and camps by producing pictorial records and maintaining diaries and archives.

Jews established active underground networks that smuggled food, clothing, and medicine, thereby allowing those who had been trapped to prolong their existences. By not succumbing to the Nazis, but instead intensely clinging to life under the most extreme conditions, Jews demonstrated their "sanctification of life," their will to survive. In some camps, Jews initiated work slowdowns and other overt acts of nonviolent noncompli-

ance. Jewish leaders and council elders who refused to follow Nazi directives paid with their lives for their defiance.

Against overwhelming odds and in extremely difficult circumstances, Jews also took up armed resistance in ghettos and camps, and fought the Nazis as members of partisan units. Revolts occurred in more than 40 ghettos. The Warsaw uprising of 1943, although crushed by the

Germans, had symbolic importance. It inflicted considerable casualties on the Germans, proved that Jews were not passive victims, and inspired underground organizations and individuals in other ghettos and camps.

Despite the possibility of severe retribution—and in spite of fences, guard towers, machine guns, search lights, and vicious dogs—uprisings broke out in four death camps and several concentration camps. Highly symbolic inmate destruction of crematoria at Auschwitz was a

brave and desperate act that, unfortunately, did not save many lives. Most rebels were killed.

Tens of thousands of Jews fought the Nazis in partisan actions. As urban guerrillas and saboteurs—or wilderness assassins hiding in mountains, woods, and marshes—they inflicted considerable damage on German operations. In Eastern Poland and Western Russia, Soviet soldiers parachuting into the region commanded units of Jewish volunteers. A Lithuanian Jewish brigade operated in the dense forests near Vilna. In Belorussia, the Bielski brothers led a Jewish combat group roaming the Naliboki Forest. The men pictured operated in Belorussia's Rudninkai Forest.

In Yugoslavia, Tito's national liberation army included 4000 Jews. Almost all members of the Jewish Rab battalion died in battle in the Balkans. More than 1500 Jewish fighters joined the ill-fated rising in Slovakia in 1944. In France, the amalgamated Jewish Fighting Organization aided the Normandy invasion by undertaking 1900 armed actions and numerous sabotage attacks on railroads, factories, and bridges. Half of its 2000 members perished. A Jewish *Maquis* unit, however, reputedly killed over 1000 Nazis.

1943

machine-gun fire to subdue and kill the resisters. • In Lithuania, a Jewish partisan unit destroys telegraph and telephone lines along the Vilna-to-Lida railway.

• October 25, 1943: Members of the Jewish community at Dvinsk, Latvia, are deported to the concentration camp at Riga-Kaiserwald, Latvia.

• The Germans begin the liquidation of the corpse-burning squad at the Janówska, Ukraine, labor camp. • SS chief Heinrich Himmler orders the destruction of the collection of Jewish skulls and skeletons at the Reich Anatomical Institute at Strasbourg; *See* June 21, 1943. • Dnepropetrovsk, Ukraine, is liberated by the Red Army.

With hands raised high above their heads, suspected resisters are guarded by a revolver-toting member of the *milice* (French militia). The militia operated as the police arm of the Vichy government and as undercover agents in pursuing the members of the *Maquis,* the French Resistance. Numbering some 29,000 volunteers by fall 1943, the *milice* increasingly turned to assassination in its pursuit of power.

MAJOR JEWISH RESISTANCE GROUPS IN EASTERN EUROPE, 1942–1944

Upwards of 20,000 Jews comprised partisan groups in the forests of Eastern Europe, most having escaped from nearby ghettos. Partisans struggled to survive while planning surprise attacks with their limited arsenal of weapons.

A gruesome mound of burnt bodies testifies to the mass murder that occurred at Maly Trostinets, near Minsk in Belorussia. With the liquidation of the Minsk Ghetto in late October 1943, more than 2000 Jews were transported to Maly Trostinets to meet their deaths. In all, tens of thousands of Jews were executed at this site.

• **October 26, 1943:** Three thousand Jews are deported from Kovno, Lithuania, to the slave-labor camp at Klooga, Estonia. • The United Nations War Crimes Commission, composed of 15 Allied nations (the Soviet Union is not among the participants), has its first meeting, in London.

• **October 30, 1943:** Dr. Zelik Levinbok, a Jewish doctor interned at the Koldichevo camp in Belorussia, escapes with his wife and eight-year-old son.

• **November 1943:** Nazis raze the death camp at Treblinka. • A Hebrew teacher named Szosznik leads inmate resistance at the Majdanek death camp. Hundreds are killed, ten escape. • The corpse-burning squad revolts at Borki, Poland. Fifty are killed and three survive. • The first deaths occur at the Fünfteichen, Silesia, Poland, slave-labor camp. • The death camp at Sobibór is demolished.

• State Department official Breckinridge Long's campaign against Jewish

493

In November 1943 Joseph Stalin, Franklin Roosevelt, and Winston Churchill met at Tehran, Iran. They discussed military tactics and the formation of an international organization to peacefully settle disputes between nations. Stalin particularly wanted the opening of a second front to help divert German pressure from his Red Army. Pictured *(from left to right)* are Soviet Foreign Minister Viacheslav Molotov, U.S. Envoy W. Averell Harriman, Churchill, and Stalin.

Ivan Vranetic concealed dozens of Jews from the Nazis in Yugoslavia. He sheltered the Jews in barns and, on occasion, his own home. But since his village, Topusko, was so close to the German border, German soldiers often searched it for concealed Jews. When this happened, Vranetic had the Jews hide in the nearby forest. After the war Yad Vashem named him a "Man of Honor." Today Vranetic resides in Israel.

This finely crafted violin once belonged to Henry Rosner, a prisoner at the Plaszów, Poland, forced-labor camp that was commanded by the infamous Amon Goeth. Rosner and his brother, Poldek, an accordionist, entertained Goeth and his frequent guest, Oskar Schindler, at numerous dinner parties. Schindler's fondness for Rosner's music compelled him to add the entire Rosner family to the list of 1100 workers for his Brinnlitz munitions plant. Although the violin never made it to the factory, Rosner was reunited with his beloved instrument—and his wife—after the war.

1943

immigration reaches its apex when he falsely testifies before the House Foreign Affairs Committee. He informs the committee that the United States has admitted 580,000 refugees since 1933. He implies that most are Jews and that they remain in the United States. But the fact is that fewer than 200,000 remain in the United States; many have emigrated from the United States to other countries, and many of the refugees were non-Jews. Long's figures apply only to the number of visas issued by the United States. The net number of German refugees who stay in the United States is only 51,960. Between the attack on Pearl Harbor and the end of the war, only 21,000 additional refugees are admitted to the U.S.

A scale model of crematorium II at Auschwitz-Birkenau, built and sculpted in 1991 by artist Mieczyslaw Stobierski, depicts the processing of victims. Individuals responsible for removing the bodies from the gas chambers, transporting them to the ovens, and burning the corpses were known as *Sonderkommandos*. Those selected for these ghastly tasks were given extra rations and were treated better than the average inmate. Every three or four months, the *Sonderkommandos* were sent to the gas chambers and processed precisely like the thousands of victims whom they had personally handled.

Karl Lowenstein, a Jew, was the head of the ghetto guard in Theresienstadt, the "model camp" near Prague, Czechoslovakia. Lowenstein enjoyed considerable power within the camp as the commander of some 400 young men. He clashed frequently with the ghetto's council over the privileges accorded to him and his men. Ultimately, Lowenstein's abuse of power led to his dismissal and imprisonment by the Nazi camp administration.

Oneg Shabbat

Driven by the urgency to document the inhumanity of the Nazi attack on the Jews of Warsaw, Jewish historian Emanuel Ringelblum *(pictured, left)* initiated an effort to collect and preserve a documentary record of life within the walls of the ghetto. Under his leadership, a small group of writers, journalists, teachers, and students of history formed *Oneg Shabbat* (Sabbath Delight).

This underground operation, code-named after the group's clandestine meetings on the Sabbath, created a secret archive chronicling the Jewish experience. Ringelblum's team encouraged the writing of memoirs and diaries. It collected underground materials such as ghetto newspapers, posters, announcements, photographs, and reports and statistics on the ghetto. The team also recorded testimonials of refugees arriving in Warsaw from other ghettos and camps. Ringelblum himself kept a diary of events.

Oneg Shabbat archivists attempted to transmit documentary evidence to the West, although they stored most archival materials in three sealed milk cans, buried in separate locations. One can was discovered in 1946, another in 1950. The third, reportedly containing information on the resistance, has still not been found. Most members of the organization did not survive the deportations of 1942. Ringelblum hid in non-Jewish Warsaw until arrested on March 7, 1944, whereupon he and his family were executed.

• **November 1, 1943:** Joseph Stalin, Franklin Roosevelt, and Winston Churchill sign the Moscow Declaration. Because of British suspicions that the Jews and Poles are exaggerating German atrocities, the declaration omits references to gas chambers. Also, while promising postwar justice for murderers, it does not mention Jews.

• **November 3, 1943:** Three hundred Jews at Borki, Poland, near Chelm, are put to work exhuming 30,000 corpses, mostly of Red Army POWs taken prisoner and murdered late in 1941. The bodies are burned on massive pyres. • Jacob Katz, a Jewish cleaner at the Budzyn, Poland, concentration camp, rescues seven elderly Jews by hiding them beneath

mattresses. • Riccardo Pacifici, rabbi of Genoa, Italy, is deported to Auschwitz along with 200 members of his congregation and 100 Jewish refugees from Northern Europe. • Anti-Nazi Catholic priest Bernhard Lichtenberg dies on his way to internment at the Dachau, Germany, concentration camp.

Bernard Lichtenberg, the provost of St. Hedwig's Cathedral in Berlin, was one of the few German clergymen to speak out against the Nazi regime. He joined Archbishop Clemens August Graf von Galen of Münster in opposing the "euthanasia" measures and openly prayed for the well-being of Jews. Arrested by the Gestapo, Lichtenberg boldly proclaimed that he wished to join the Jews who had been deported. His two years of imprisonment ruined his health, but that did not deter the Nazis from sending him to Dachau after his release from prison.

U.S. President Franklin Roosevelt signs the UNRRA agreement in November 1943. The UNRRA was the United Nations Relief and Rehabilitation Agency. The agency was sponsored by the Allies but, during its five-year life span, was funded mostly by money from the United States. Headed by former New York City Mayor Fiorello La Guardia, the UNRRA was of great help to non-Jews and, secondarily, to Jews living in displaced-persons camps.

MAJOR JEWISH RESISTANCE GROUPS IN WESTERN EUROPE, 1942–1944

The "Jewish Army," a French partisan group, operated from 1942 to 1944. The group smuggled French Jews into neutral Spain, procured money to aid Jews in hiding, and participated in 1944 uprisings in Paris, Toulouse, and Lyon.

1943

• **November 3-4, 1943: The Germans undertake *Erntefest* (Harvest Festival), a planned massacre of Jews of three camps in the Lublin, Poland, area. About 18,000 are murdered at Majdanek, 10,000 at Trawniki, and 15,000 at Poniatowa. At Poniatowa, Jews who resist are burned alive in a barrack.**

• **November 4, 1943: The Germans put down an inmate revolt at the slave-labor camp at Szebnie, Poland. The camp is liquidated; about 3000 Jews are deported to Auschwitz.**

• **November 6, 1943: Five weeks after escaping from a work detail at the Babi Yar, Ukraine, mass-murder site, about 14 Jews and Soviet POWs come**

Pictured is the cemetery at Hadamar, Germany, where one of the largest extermination centers of the "euthanasia" program was located. The bodies of the victims—who had received lethal injections, were gassed, or were simply allowed to die from starvation—were usually cremated. Next of kin were informed that they had died of a contagious disease. During 1942 and 1943, many of the leading figures from the euthanasia program brought their "talents" to the death camps of Eastern Europe.

General Field Marshal Wilhelm Keitel was the chief of staff of the German High Command. As Hitler's closest military adviser, Keitel never questioned Hitler's plans and remained silent when he disagreed with the *Führer.* Many of the notorious orders issued for genocidal operations in Eastern Europe bear Keitel's signature. Keitel was convicted by the International Military Tribunal at Nuremberg, Germany, of conspiracy, crimes against peace, and crimes against humanity. After his request to be shot as a soldier was denied, General Keitel was hanged on October 16, 1946.

German Resistance

Many different faces composed the German resistance. Military men and pastors, diplomats and jurists, and political leaders of vastly different persuasions united in the conviction that Nazi rule must end.

Not all agreed on the means to that goal. In Munich, the White Rose organization of students Hans and Sophie Scholl printed leaflets opposing Hitler. This action led to their capture and execution. The Kreisau Circle of Helmuth James Graf von Moltke *(pictured)* **planned for a new Germany guided by Christian principles. Their planning for a future free of Nazism resulted in their deaths.**

The military group led by charismatic Colonel Claus von Stauffenberg plotted to assassinate Hitler with a bomb and establish a government that would make peace with the Allies. Their plot nearly succeeded, but Hitler survived. The conspirators and any associated with them, including Lutheran pastor Dietrich von Bonhoeffer, were killed. Some were shot; others were tortured and then sent to the Plötzensee Prison, where they were hung from meat hooks until they slowly strangled to death.

From all strata of society, Germans of conscience and conviction opposed Nazi tyranny and obstructed the growing persecution of the Jews. For many, challenging authority cost them their lives.

out of hiding to greet the Red Army as it liberates Kiev, Ukraine.

• **November 9, 1943:** Two hundred Jews from Venice, Italy, are deported to Auschwitz. Four hundred Jews from Florence and Bologna, Italy, are deported to Auschwitz. • At the Theresienstadt, Czechoslovakia, camp/ghetto, Council of Elders head Jacob Edelstein and three other Jews are accused of saving 55 of the ghetto's Jews from deportation by falsifying population reports. • U.S. Senator Guy Gillette and Representatives Will Rogers and Joseph Baldwin introduce a resolution into Congress calling upon the president to establish "a commission of diplomatic, economic, and military experts to formulate and effectuate a plan of action to save the surviving Jewish people of Europe." This resolution will serve as the basis of the War Refugee Board (WRB). • The United Nations Relief and Rehabilitation Administration (UNRRA) is founded.

• **November 10, 1943:** Anti-Nazi, German Protestant theologian Karl

Kurt Waldheim

The career of Kurt Waldheim demonstrates the ease in which some individuals moved between civil society and Nazism. When the United States Justice Department put him on its Watch List as a suspected war criminal in 1987, the shroud of secrecy Waldheim had placed over his past quickly unraveled.

Kurt Waldheim entered law school at the University of Vienna in 1937. Following the *Anschluss*, he joined the Nazi Students' Association and became a Storm Trooper. Waldheim participated in the French and Russian campaigns as a *Wehrmacht* soldier and was wounded in December 1941.

Waldheim's service in the Balkans from 1942 to 1945 provided him with direct knowledge of the atrocities committed against Yugoslav partisans. Although he personally did not participate in the killings, an Austrian commission investigating his role ruled that he was close to persons who issued and carried out atrocities and that he did nothing to disrupt them.

After the war Waldheim immediately distanced himself from his Nazi past. He joined the Austrian diplomatic service in 1945, served as foreign minister from 1968 to 1970, and was named the secretary general of the United Nations in 1971. Although publicly discredited, Waldheim has yet to openly confront his past.

This circular encourages Palestinians to make contributions to rescue efforts of European Jews. An excerpt of the text: "Children of Israel, listen! Listen to the voice that cries out for help. Remember our brothers at every moment, when you study and when you rest, when you eat and when you play. Join together as one individual to rescue and support [our brothers]."

Jews seeking to emigrate to Palestine without permission had to evade a British Navy intent on preventing their entry. In late November 1943, Jews aboard three ships seeking to enter Palestine were detained and sent to a camp on the island of Mauritius. Committed to caring for their own, the detainees established a hospital. The nurses and doctors faced many challenges, including an outbreak of typhus.

1943

Friedrich Stellbrink is executed at Hamburg, Germany. • Arthur Liebehenschel replaces Rudolf Höss as commandant of Auschwitz.

• November 11, 1943: At the Theresienstadt, Czechoslovakia, camp/ghetto, on the 25th anniversary of Germany's defeat in World War I, the Germans assemble all 47,000 Jews in a large square for an ill-organized census. It lasts for 18 hours in a chilly rain. Some of the Jews die during the census or soon after.

• November 13, 1943: A Jew named Fritz Lustig makes an unsuccessful attempt to escape from the Auschwitz-Birkenau death camp.

A free-standing crematorium stands outside the barbed-wire fence of Vught, Netherlands. While Vught was not an extermination camp, many prisoners died while they were incarcerated, especially during the period from October 1943 to January 1944, when the camp was run by *SS-Sturmbannführer* Adam Grünewald. A pile of human ashes lies in front of the oven.

A concrete wall topped with broken glass and steel spikes surrounds part of the Vught concentration camp, the main transit station for Jews in the southern portion of the Netherlands. Vught was established in December 1942 and received its first Jewish prisoners the next month. While conditions inside the camp were not as bad as those in Eastern Europe, the fact remains that Vught functioned as a transfer station to Westerbork, an important way station on the one-way journey to Auschwitz.

Reich Minister Richard Walther Darré greets Hitler in 1943. Darré's background in agriculture and economics propelled him to the head of the Race and Settlement Office (RuSHA) and the head of the Office for Agricultural Policy. He was dismissed from his posts for criticizing how Hitler and Himmler handled the war, and was consequently banished to his hunting lodge in Schorfheide, Germany.

• **November 14, 1943: Jews from Ferrara, Italy, are deported to Auschwitz.**

• **November 16, 1943: Ill Jewish slave laborers at the Skarzysko-Kamienna, Poland, ammunition factory, who are lured from their barracks by Ukrainian guards and SS men promising soup, are gunned down or loaded** onto trucks and taken to an execution site elsewhere in the camp.

• **November 17, 1943: 995 Dutch Jews arrive at Auschwitz; 531, including 166 children, are immediately gassed.** • **Romanian dictator Ion Antonescu orders his Cabinet to resist German efforts to exterminate Jews in the Transnistria region.**

• **November 19, 1943: Prisoners from** *Sonderkommando* **1005, a corpse-burning unit, revolt at the Janówska, Ukraine, slave-labor camp near Lvov. A leader of the uprising, Leon Weliczker, is one of the few who survive.**
• **One thousand Jews are shot at the Jewish cemetery outside Sandomierz, Poland.**

"There were rats as big as cats running about and gnawing the corpses and even attacking the dying, who had not enough strength left to chase them away.... [Inside,] the straw mattresses were dirty and were changed only when absolutely rotten. The bedding was so full of lice that one could see them swarming like ants."

—*Marie Vaillant-Couturier, a French Resistance member imprisoned at Auschwitz*

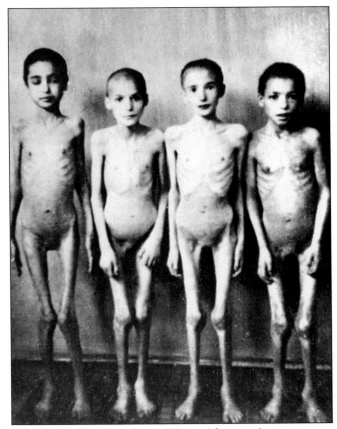

Emaciated Gypsy boys selected for cruel surgery to remove their penises and testicles are catalogued by the Auschwitz camera. Hitler was keenly interested in sterilization of "undesirables" as a way to control unwanted population growth. A side benefit from Hitler's perspective was that sterilized subjects could be useful as laborers for the Reich. Nazi camp physicians undertook the surgeries and other procedures with vigor. Besides being profoundly unethical, medical experimentation of this sort was often clumsy and not even remotely grounded in legitimate science. Instead, Auschwitz's Dr. Josef Mengele and other camp surgeons were motivated by an amoral "what if?" mentality; that is, by a deadly curiosity about what would happen to a human being if a particular procedure were performed. To such doctors, human suffering was irrelevant.

The main section of the synagogue in Kraków, Poland, was destroyed in the winter of 1943–44. Plaszów camp commander Amon Goeth callously ordered its destruction to make room for a new railroad line. Train connections were crucial for the Nazi war effort, and thousands of kilometers of track were laid to facilitate the movement of raw materials and war-related materiel.

1943

• **November 22, 1943:** More than 1000 Jewish patients at a Berlin mental hospital are deported to Auschwitz.

• **November 23, 1943:** 150 Jewish partisans escape Occupied Kovno, Lithuania, and head eastward into the Rudninkai Forest.

• **November 28–December 1, 1943:** Allied leaders Winston Churchill, Franklin Roosevelt, and Joseph Stalin meet in Tehran, Iran. They discuss a British/American invasion against the Germans from the west.

• **November 30, 1943:** Italy's Interior Ministry orders the concentration of all Italian Jews in camps.

"Life" in the Camps

The Nazis subjected concentration-camp prisoners to abysmal, dehumanizing conditions that weakened the body and broke the spirit. Inmates endured woefully inadequate nutrition, unpotable water, overcrowded and lice-infested barracks, unsanitary washing and toilet facilities, endless hours of exhausting labor, and—sometimes—sadistic punishments.

An inmate's day began frightfully early. Fearing beatings from cursing guards, weary prisoners feverishly scrambled out of bunks, hurriedly reshaping bedding. Rushing to filthy lavatories and jostling with hundreds trying to wash from the few faucets, inmates then waited in line for "breakfast," which was often bitter coffee and a piece of bread.

After a prolonged roll call, work squads formed. In some camps, work-group members were obliged to sing while marching out of camp; the camp orchestra accompanied them. Some prisoners marched up to ten miles to reach work sites. Others performed torturous, unproductive work within camp confines. In the evening, after arduous 11- or 12-hour work days, prisoners again endured a head count, standing at attention for hours, followed by "supper" and lights out at 9 P.M.

Always overcrowded in barracks that often had no heating, prisoners found sleep difficult. Packed to capacity in three-tiered wooden bunks, two or three people lay in space for one—sometimes on straw mattresses, often simply on bare board; not always with blankets. Sanitary facilities consisted of urinals and latrines that were nothing more than rows of holes cut in concrete slabs above waste pipes. Washrooms held earthenware gutters with several taps drawing polluted well water.

Prisoners were constantly hungry—literally starving. During mornings and evenings, the coffee was sometimes accompanied by sour, hard bread. If inmates were lucky, supper offered a few grams of stale or moldy sausage,

cheese, or jam. At noon a foul-tasting, watery turnip soup—containing only traces of potatoes and barley—provided 300 to 400 calories. Often forced to eat outside in even frigid weather, prisoners had to drink the soup directly from bowls. Many prisoners resorted to rummaging through refuse bins next to camp kitchens, contracting dysentery from eating raw peelings or rotten cabbage. Some inmates stole or traded for food, risking severe punishment.

Summary beatings became routine. Every SS man enjoyed the right to beat, or even kill, any prisoner. Floggings took place usually during roll call. Prisoners lay on special benches, unable to move their legs, and absorbed dozens of lashes from sticks or whips.

In an extremely painful punishment called the "pillar," prisoners' hands were tied behind their backs. They were then suspended from a ceiling beam or tree by rope tied to their wrists. Equally cruel was confinement in the "standing cell." Four prisoners were jammed for days into a completely dark space of about one square yard, unable to lie down, with only a two-inch opening for air. Prisoners caught trying to escape were hanged in plain view of other inmates.

• **Early December 1943:** United States Secretary of the Treasury Henry Morgenthau instructs assistants Randolph Paul and John W. Pehle to investigate the State Department's handling of the Jewish refugee issue.

• **December 2, 1943:** 100 Jews from Vienna arrive at Auschwitz.

• **December 12, 1943:** The chairman of the Jewish Council in Wlodzimierz Wolynski, Poland, the site of street massacres in 1942, assures the remaining ghetto residents that they will be safe; *See* December 13, 1943.

• **December 13, 1943:** The Jewish community at Wlodzimierz Wolynski, Poland, is liquidated. • In Greece,

Nazis murder all males over age 14 in the village of Kalávrita.

• **December 17, 1943:** Jews are executed at Kovno, Lithuania, as reprisal for an escape of several Jews from the ghetto.

• **December 21, 1943:** Hersz Kurcweig, a Jew, and Stanislaw Dorosie-

Partisan Life

During the Second World War, tens of thousands of men and women joined partisan forces that operated primarily in Eastern Europe and the Balkans. Whether they operated alone, teamed with family members, or belonged to secular nationalist units, partisan fighters lived a precarious and dangerous existence.

Many partisans based themselves in the forested regions of Eastern Europe, surviving on captured and foraged food. The need to avoid detection prevented them from building permanent structures. They sheltered in dugouts or slept under the cover of branches and leaves. The long winter nights were especially brutal, for fires were a luxury that clandestine partisan fighters could not afford.

Partisan life differed for Jews and gentiles. Whereas gentile partisans could vanish from the scene by seeking shelter from local residents, very few Eastern Europeans willingly sheltered and fed Jewish partisans. Having escaped life in a ghetto to become a partisan, Jews had no neutral area where they could live unmolested by the Nazi authorities. Jewish partisans were hunted by the Nazis and often hated by the local inhabitants.

Rabbi Stephen S. Wise *(left)* converses with U.S. Representative Sol Bloom of New York during a hearing of the House Foreign Relations Committee. Wise's tireless efforts on behalf of European Jewry brought little relief for his persecuted brethren. At this December 1943 hearing, Rabbi Wise reiterated a six-point program that he had introduced eight months earlier at the Bermuda Conference. Those points called upon Britain to open Palestine to Jewish immigration. British opposition prevented the idea from ever being seriously considered.

The SS staff of the Neuengamme, Germany, concentration camp celebrates Christmas with their families in what is believed to be 1943 or '44. The war and the "Final Solution" did not prevent the camp staff from taking time from their duties to share the spirit of the season. Throughout the war, the SS strove to maintain normal routines for camp guards and their families.

1943

wicz, a non-Jew, escape from Auschwitz after killing an SS guard.

• December 22, 1943: The Gestapo discovers 62 Jews hiding in a cellar of a building on Krolewska Street in Warsaw. All are murdered. • United States Secretary of the Treasury Henry Morgenthau confronts U.S. Assistant Secretary of State Breckin-

ridge Long, telling him to his face that "the impression is all around that you, particularly, are antisemitic!"

• December 23, 1943: The Jewish community at Pinsk, Poland, is liquidated. • U.S. Secretary of the Treasury Henry Morgenthau is informed by his staff that, "when you get through with it, the [State Depart-

This December 1943 photograph shows Bosnian SS volunteers, called *Handoza*. These troopers are standing at attention, looking professional—if not as intimidating as their German counterparts. The uniform of each is adorned with the swastika, German eagle, and SS *Totenkopf* (Death's Head).

Edward R. Murrow was a distinguished American war correspondent with CBS radio who reported on Germany's extermination policy against Jews. Murrow had already brought reliable and dramatic eyewitness reports to America of German events: the prewar occupation of Austria, the Munich Conference, the German takeover of Czechoslovakia, and the wartime Battle of Britain. His courageous reporting was an exception to the American media's often cynical reaction to Holocaust reports.

The Nazi propaganda effort stretched beyond the shores of Europe to America. Allegedly broadcasting from Iowa, the Nazi radio station "Station Debunk" urged pacifism and condemned the policies of President Franklin Roosevelt. To build public support for the American war effort, well-known writers and broadcasters joined forces against Axis propaganda. Rex Stout *(pictured)*, best known as the author of the Nero Wolfe detective stories, hosted the CBS radio program *The Secret Weapon* and served as spokesman for *The Voice of Freedom*.

The Ninth Fort was a prison and killing site in Kovno, Lithuania, where at least 9000 Jews were murdered by Germans and Lithuanians in October 1941. This young Jewish man, Abe Diskont, was one of 64 prisoners who escaped from the Ninth Fort on Christmas Eve, 1943. He later joined partisans and died in battle against the Germans in 1944.

ment's] attitude to date is no different from Hitler's attitude."

• **December 24, 1943:** Of 64 Jews who escape the Ninth Fort near Kovno, Lithuania, 32 are quickly recaptured, five are shot down, and eight more are captured near the Kovno Ghetto. Nineteen enter the ghetto, but one, Rabbi Gabriel Shus-

terman, dies of frostbite. • At Borki, Poland, 60 Jews working on an exhumation squad attempt to escape through a tunnel, but few of them are successful.

• **December 25, 1943:** Trucks carrying naked Jewish women make regular trips to the gas chamber at Auschwitz-Birkenau. Any woman who

leaps from a truck is immediately shot down.

• **Late 1943:** SS chief Heinrich Himmler orders that the extermination camp at Belzec be razed, as has been done at the Sobibór and Treblinka death camps. At all three camps, the land is to be plowed under and settled by Ukrainians.

1944

AFTER tremendous research, Holocaust scholar Danuta Czech compiled *Auschwitz Chronicle 1939–1945.* Her 855-page book documents in overwhelming detail the destruction of more than one million men, women, and children—90 percent of them Jews—who were killed at the infamous death camp.

Czech's entry for May 24, 1944, refers to 2000 Jewish prisoners who were deported to Auschwitz from Hungary. They received individual identification numbers: A-5729 through A-7728. One of those numbers—A-7713—was tattooed on the left arm of a Jewish teenager from Sighet, a Romanian town of 26,000 people that came under Hungarian control in 1940. That boy, Elie Wiesel, survived Auschwitz, became an important writer, and received the Nobel Peace Prize in 1986. "At Auschwitz," Wiesel has said, "not only man died, but also the idea of man.... It was its own heart the world incinerated at Auschwitz."

Wiesel is the author of *Night,* one of the two most widely read books about the Holocaust. Recalling the horrific months he spent in Auschwitz during 1944, the memoir states that Wiesel and his father, mother, and little sister, Tzipora, were deported from Sighet on a Sunday. Their train was one of four that sent Sighet's Jews to Auschwitz from May 16 to May 22. The Sighet transports were part of a massive deportation of Jews from Hungary, whose large Jewish population, 725,000 as of 1941, had been spared the worst of the Holocaust's devastation.

The situation changed drastically on March 19, when German forces occupied Hungary to prevent their faltering collaborators from negotiating an armistice with the Allies. More than 60,000 Jews living in Hungary had been killed before the German occupation.

Adolf Eichmann supervised the onslaught. In a few weeks, with time running against the Nazis as their military effort on the Eastern Front deteriorated, all of Hungary's Jews except those in Budapest were ghettoized. Their property was expropriated and deportations were under way. From May 15 to July 9, more than 140 trains carried 437,000 Jews from Hungary to Auschwitz. The vast majority, including Wiesel's mother and little sister, were gassed.

Far away from Auschwitz on May 25, one day after Wiesel was given his Auschwitz tattoo, another Jewish teenager, Anne Frank, wrote in her diary. This young author never met Wiesel, but she was thinking of people like

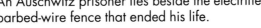

An Auschwitz prisoner lies beside the electrified barbed-wire fence that ended his life.

1944

him and his family when she observed that "the world has been turned upside down. The most decent people are being sent to concentration camps, prisons and lonely cells, while the lowest of the low rule over young and old, rich and poor." Soon Frank's words would apply to her and her family. But as Elie Wiesel and the Jews from Sighet reached Auschwitz and the smell of burning flesh, Anne Frank slept in her Amsterdam hiding place at Prinsengracht 263.

Born on June 12, 1929, about nine months after Wiesel, Anne Frank and her family left their native Germany for Holland soon after the Nazis took power in 1933. Her relatively carefree life changed on May 10, 1940, when Germany invaded and occupied the Netherlands. By early June 1942, conditions for Dutch Jews had drastically worsened. With the help of friends such as Miep Gies, the Franks entered their hiding place. About one-fourth of the 25,000 Dutch Jews who went into hiding were eventually arrested and deported. The Franks were betrayed (the identity of this person remains unknown) and arrested by the SD (Security Service) on August 4, 1944. A month later, on September 3, Anne Frank and her family were among the 1019 Jewish prisoners forced to board the last Auschwitz-bound transport that left Westerbork, the Dutch transit camp from which about 107,000 Jews had been deported since July 1942.

The *Auschwitz Chronicle* states that 549 Jews in the Franks' transport from Westerbork were gassed on arrival at Auschwitz. Anne Frank was spared and sent to the women's camp at Auschwitz-Birkenau. On October 28, 1944, she was among 1308 Jewish women who were transferred from Auschwitz to Bergen-Belsen, a concentration camp inside Germany, where she perished from typhus in March 1945.

Hungarian Jews wait at a collection point in Auschwitz-Birkenau in 1944 before being gassed.

Anne Frank began writing in her diary on June 14, 1942, two days after her father, Otto, gave it to her as a 13th-birthday present. Saved by Gies, the diary has become the most widely read book about the Holocaust. Its last entry is dated August 1, 1944. Less than three weeks earlier, on July 15, Anne had written the diary's best-known words. She knew that the world was turning into "a wilderness," and she could hear "the approaching thunder that, one day, will destroy us, too." But nevertheless, she wrote, "I still believe, in spite of everything, that people are truly good at heart."

It was hard to share Anne Frank's belief about human goodness in 1944. The end of the Third Reich was coming, but the Nazis were determined to win their war against the Jews. Auschwitz remained what Elie Wiesel called it: "the place of eternal night . . . the grave of man's heart."

On June 6, while Anne Frank heard BBC broadcasts about D-Day, the Allies' massive invasion of Normandy, transports continued to send thousands of Hungarian Jews to Auschwitz. On July 20 German officers made an unsuccessful attempt on Adolf Hitler's life, but that same day Auschwitz became the destination for 2000 Jews deported from Greece. Early the next week, Soviet troops liberated the killing center at Majdanek, Poland, as well as the Polish city of Lublin, but only a relative handful of Jews were left from Lublin's prewar Jewish population of 40,000.

On August 20 Elie Wiesel witnessed the American bombardment of the I.G. Farben chemical plant near Monowitz-Buna, the part of the Auschwitz complex to which he and his father, Shlomo, had been sent to do slave labor. Accompanied by Mustang fighters, 127 American bombers dropped 1336 500-pound bombs on the factory. Less than five miles away, the killing center at Auschwitz-Birkenau was untouched. Postwar analysis of aerial photographs from a September 13 raid on I.G. Farben indicates that 65 cars stood on the Birkenau railroad track while a line of people—perhaps 1500 of them—appeared to be moving toward gas chambers.

The Allies bombed numerous targets in Occupied Europe, but were criticized for not bombing Auschwitz.

Controversy still swirls about whether the Allies should have bombed Auschwitz or the railroads leading to that killing center. Holocaust scholar David Wyman has argued that, as early as May 1944, the U.S. Army air forces could have bombed Auschwitz and the approaching rail lines. Pleas for such raids were made throughout 1944. The U.S. War Department's spokesman, Assistant Secretary of War John J. McCloy, stated on August 14 that "after a study it became apparent that such an operation could be executed only by the diversion of considerable air support essential to the success of our forces now engaged in decisive operations elsewhere and would in any case be of such doubtful efficacy that it would not warrant the use of our resources. There has been considerable opinion to the effect that such an effort, even if practicable, might provoke more vindictive action by the Germans."

Auschwitz-Birkenau was not bombed. Less than two weeks after McCloy's statement, the Allies liberated Paris, but not before the Nazis raided Jewish children's homes in the Paris area and deported 250 Jewish girls and boys to Auschwitz. On September 3–4 the Allies freed the Belgian cities of Brussels and Antwerp. By then the Franks were on their way to Auschwitz.

While the transport carrying the Frank family traveled east, about 200,000 Hungarian Jews remained in Budapest. On October 15, shortly after the SS quelled an October 7 prisoner uprising in Auschwitz-Birkenau, the Arrow Cross, a fanatically antisemitic Hungarian Fascist party that enjoyed German backing, launched a reign of terror against Budapest's Jews. Gassing operations at Auschwitz were winding down, but in the autumn of 1944 forced labor, death marches, and wanton shootings took the lives of tens of thousands of Budapest's Jews. Thousands more were murdered along the banks of the Danube by the Arrow Cross, who then threw the bodies into the river. Swedish diplomat Raoul Wallenberg used "protective passports" and protected houses to rescue thousands of Budapest's Jews. When Soviet forces liberated the city in early 1945, 120,000 Jews remained alive.

In her now-famous diary entry for July 15, 1944, Anne Frank said that she felt "the suffering of millions." Yet, she continued, "when I look up at the sky, I somehow feel that everything will change for the better, that this cruelty too shall end, that peace and tranquility will return once more." The end of the Holocaust was indeed at hand, but would not come in 1944. The death toll of European Jewry that year exceeded 600,000.

André Trocmé, pastor in the French village of Le Chambon, provided refuge to hundreds of Jews seeking safety.

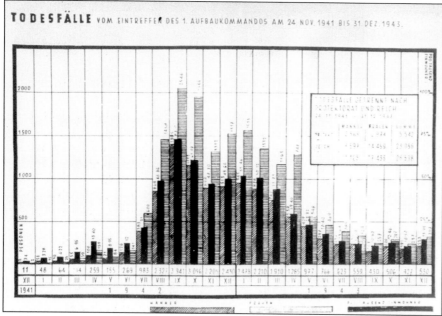

TODESFÄLLE VOM EINTREFFEN DES 1. AUFBAUKOMMANDOS AM 24. NOV. 1941 BIS 31. DEZ. 1943.

Many camps and ghettos kept detailed records of the number of deaths that occurred at those sites. This chart, from January 1, 1944, shows the number of deaths in Theresienstadt—the "model" ghetto and concentration camp in Czechoslovakia—between November 24, 1941 (when construction of the camp began), through the end of 1943. About 33,000 people died in Theresienstadt. In addition, almost 88,000 of the camp's inmates were deported to their deaths in the gas chambers of Auschwitz.

The Jewish Sara Lamhaut *(left)*, under the assumed name of Jeannine van Meerhaegen, prepares for her Catholic First Communion. Sara's parents, Icek Leib and Chana Laja Goldwasser, fought with the Belgian partisans until they were denounced, arrested, and eventually sent to their deaths at Auschwitz. Hidden in various convents, including that of *Soeurs de Sainte Marie,* near Brussels, Sara survived the war to be reunited with friends of her parents, who became her guardians. Working together, the Jewish underground and the Belgian Catholic Church succeeded in hiding some 4000 Belgian-Jewish children.

A close friend of President Franklin Roosevelt, Henry Morgenthau, Jr., was secretary of the Department of Treasury and the highest-ranking Jewish member of the administration. In early 1944 Morgenthau received a document from several of his subordinates entitled "Report to the Secretary on the Acquiescence of This Government in the Murder of the Jews." Taking the report to the President, Morgenthau set the wheels in motion to establish the War Refugee Board, responsible for saving some 200,000 lives in the closing months of the war.

1944

• **1944: The Nazi extermination industry is at its peak and is staffed by 47,000 well-trained, full-time people.** • **Worker life expectancy at I.G. Farben's *Bunawerk* (Buna works) synthetic-rubber and oil plant at Auschwitz, Poland, is three to four months. In coal mines: one month.** • **King Gustav of Sweden and Pope Pius XII pressure Hungary to halt** deportations of Jews. • *Axis Rule in Occupied Europe*, a book by jurist Raphael Lemkin, describes Nazi rule and the murder of Jews as a return to barbarism. Lemkin coins the word "genocide," from the Greek *genos* (nation/people) and *cide* (to kill).

• **Early 1944: The Nazi Propaganda Ministry releases a film, *The Führer***

JEWISH BRIGADE GROUP

In English and Hebrew, this poster urges members of the *Yishuv* (the Jewish community in Palestine) to join the Jewish Brigade. From the start of the war, Jews in Palestine had joined the British Army. But news of the mass killings fueled a desire for a separate unit, serving under a Zionist standard, to fight the Axis forces in Europe.

Ona Simaite was named "Righteous Among the Nations" by Yad Vashem. A librarian in Vilna, Lithuania, she regularly traveled into the city's Jewish ghetto, supposedly in search of unreturned library books. In reality she was taking food and other provisions to the ghetto's inhabitants, as well as helping the underground. Captured by the Nazis in 1944, she refused to surrender any information to her captors despite enduring horrific torture. Eventually the Nazis sent her to a camp in France, where the Allies liberated her.

War Refugee Board

International efforts to rescue Europe's Jews improved with the January 1944 creation of the U.S. War Refugee Board (WRB). After hedging for more than a year, President Franklin Roosevelt finally responded to public pressure and ordered the establishment of the board. He told the WRB to take "all measures within its power to rescue the victims of enemy oppression in imminent danger of death."

Neither the president nor the State Department, however, was committed to the WRB, and they provided inadequate financial sup-

port for its activities. Most funding was solicited from private Jewish organizations.

Led by John Pehle (*pictured*), the War Refugee Board coordinated rescue efforts through a small number of operatives stationed overseas. Their rescue strategies included planning evacuations of Jews from Nazi-occupied areas; finding suitable relocation sites; preventing anticipated deportations; and mailing emergency supplies to prisoners in Nazi camps. In August 1944 the WRB succeeded in bringing 982 refugees from Italy, 874 Jewish, to safety in the United States. The WRB focused much of its work during 1944 on rescuing Hungarian Jews threatened by Nazi deportation as well as brutalization at the hands of Hungary's Arrow Cross. Despite valiant efforts, and saving probably more than 200,000 lives, the work of the WRB, in the estimation of its director, was still "too little, too late."

Gives the Jews a Town, a largely fabricated look at the alleged good life enjoyed by Jews in the camp/ghetto at Theresienstadt, Czechoslovakia.

● January 10, 1944: Professor Victor Basch and his wife are executed near Lyons, France, as reprisal for the death of a French collaborator killed by French partisans.

● January 12, 1944: Frau Hanna Solf, the widow of Wilhelm Solf (former German ambassador to Tokyo) and her daughter, Lagi Gräfin von Ballestrem—both of them members of the anti-Nazi German Resistance— are arrested four months after attending a Resistance tea party that was infiltrated by a Gestapo informer.

● January 13, 1944: Two United States Treasury Department officials—Josiah DuBois and Randolph Paul—threaten to resign and make public the report on their investigation into the State Department's scandalous activities in regard to the Jews. The report is originally entitled "Report to the Secretary [of the Treasury] on the Acquiescence of This Government in the

The Village That Cared

During the winter of 1940–41, Magda Trocmé answered a knock at her door. There stood a frightened woman who identified herself as a German Jew. She had heard that help might be found in Le Chambon. Magda Trocmé said, "Come in."

Le Chambon is a mountain village in south-central France. Many of the villagers were descendants of Huguenots, who had fled to the high plateau so they could practice their Protestant Christianity without fear of punishment. The residents' long-standing distrust of authority and tradition of listening to Christian conscience inspired them to help the Jews.

Five thousand persecuted Jews found refuge in Le Chambon, but the village's response did not take place overnight. The seeds of the people's bravery and selflessness had been growing for years because André Trocmé, the community's Protestant minister, had preached Christianity's basic lessons: peace, understanding, and love. His was a message of nonviolence, but a nonviolence that rejected inaction and deplored injustice. The people of Le Chambon responded.

Though hiding Jews was a crime punishable by death, the people of Le Chambon opened their doors. "None of us thought that we were heroes," Magda Trocmé said. "We were just people trying to do our best."

British troops arrive on the beach of Anzio, Italy, on January 22, 1944. After absorbing fierce German resistance at Anzio, Monte Cassino, and the fortified Gustav Line, Allied forces pressed northward. Rome fell on June 4 and Florence was taken in mid-August. In an intriguing twist, August also marked the beginning of the Italian campaign against Germany, its erstwhile—and now irreversibly imperiled—ally. The Allied drive into Italy and the June 6 Allied cross-Channel assault on Normandy, France, were the beginning of the end of the Third Reich.

Those who did not die from Nazi medical experimentation often carried the effects with them forever. This woman, imprisoned during the war in the Ravensbrück, Germany, concentration camp, shows the results of an operation to remove the calf muscle of her right leg. Part of a project led by Dr. Karl Gebhardt, the experimenters even amputated limbs of prisoners for the supposed benefit of injured soldiers. Almost half of the 24 women who endured these particular experiments died.

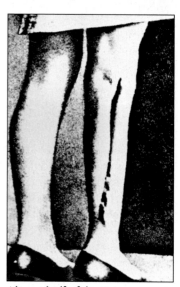

1944

Murder of the Jews." The report indicts officials of the State Department for their "willful attempts to prevent action from being taken to rescue Jews from Hitler."

• January 18, 1944: Three hundred Jews hiding in forests near Buczacz, Ukraine, are surrounded by Nazi tanks and killed.

• January 20, 1944: 1155 Jews are deported from the Drancy, France, transit camp to Auschwitz.

• January 22, 1944: Under pressure, U.S. President Franklin Roosevelt creates the War Refugee Board.

• January 25, 1944: Hans Frank, governor-general of Occupied

Religious conviction led many Jehovah's Witnesses to shun obedience to the Nazi government. In the dark days of the war in 1943, office worker Mary Smigiel, seen here, became a Jehovah's Witness in Gdynia, Poland. Believing that only Jehovah was to be praised and honored, Smigiel refused her German boss's demand that she type *"Heil Hitler"* on all correspondence. Her disobedience was reported, and she was sent to the Stutthof, Poland, labor camp. She survived the war, married, and eventually settled in the United States.

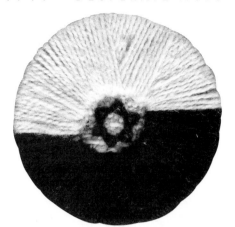

Even in the horrific conditions prevailing in the concentration camps, inmates sought to preserve some semblance of humanity. This woolen pin, made by an inmate at the Bergen-Belsen, Germany, camp, was presented to Ruth Wiener as a birthday gift.

For some Jews in the Occupied Netherlands, simply to hide from the Nazis was a gambit that worked—as it did for this elderly couple, Coen and Ella van Eekeres-Jünge, who hid in this tiny Amsterdam basement. Discomfort and inconvenience were the least of the perils associated with hiding; the primary residents of the building had to be completely committed to the safety of their Jewish guests and cognizant of the grave risks to themselves. Also, they had to be wary of antisemitic neighbors and even relatives, as well as the inevitable snooping of Nazi authorities.

Poland, notes in his diary that approximately 100,000 Jews remain in the region under his control, down by 3,400,000 from the end of 1941.

• **January 29, 1944: A Nazi court in Kraków, Poland, sentences five Poles to death for aiding Jews. One of the accused, Kazimierz Jozefek, is hanged in the public square.**

• **January 30, 1944: 700 Jews are deported from Milan, Italy, to Auschwitz.**

• **February 1944: Adam Goetz, a Hamburg engineer instrumental in the development of dirigibles, dies in the Lódź (Poland) Ghetto. • Jewish Resistance leader Moise Fingercwajg, age 20, is executed in France.**

• **February 4, 1944: 365 Jews from Salonika, Greece, who are under the protection of the Spanish government, leave the concentration camp at Bergen-Belsen, Germany, for Spain and safety.**

• **February 8, 1944: 1015 Jews are deported from Holland to Auschwitz. Among the deportees are children**

In January 1944 SS functionary Adolf Eichmann distributed this secret telegram to all heads of the *Sicherheitspolizei* and *Sicherheitsdienst* in Brussels, Belgium. In it he ordered all Argentinean Jews residing in Belgium to the Bergen-Belsen, Germany, concentration camp. During the war, many Jews were protected by the Argentinean documents they carried. After the war, many Nazis and some Jewish survivors ended up in Argentina.

Deportations of Dutch Jews began in 1942 and were largely complete two years later. Most of the deportees were sent to Westerbork, and from there to Auschwitz or Sobibór. Few Jewish citizens of the Netherlands remained in the country in 1944, and their options were limited: hide; pay outrageous sums to local extortionists who promised to delay or cancel deportation orders; or resist. Here, members of the Dutch underground secrete a rifle and 9mm ammunition beneath a bathroom floor.

With his body held taut by two *Kapos*, a camp prisoner awaits the sting of the lash on his bare back. Even the slightest offense could lead to harsh penalties. Punishment, like this whipping, could so weaken an inmate that he could no longer work, and failure to work meant death. This drawing by Hungarian artist Gyorgy Kadar, who survived five camps, powerfully conveys the inmate's suffering and anguish.

1944

sick with scarlet fever and diphtheria; *See* February 10, 1944.

● **February 10, 1944: Of 1015 Jews** on a deportation train that arrives at Auschwitz from Holland, 800—including all of the children—are immediately gassed. 1229 Jews are deported from Westerbork, Holland, to Auschwitz.

● **February 14, 1944:** *Reichsmarschall* **Hermann Göring wires Minister of Armaments and Munitions Albert Speer. He asks for as many concentration-camp inmates as possible for use as slave laborers in air-armament factories.**

● **February 20–25, 1944: In the Big Week (Operation Argument), Ameri-**

Nahum Gold-mann helped create the World Jewish Congress (WJC) in 1936. The organization, headquartered in the United States, sought "to assure the survival and to foster the unity of the Jewish people." The Holocaust only deepened Goldmann's conviction that a Jewish state must be established in Palestine.

Konzentrationslager
Abteilung II

Erklärung.

Ich, - der - die _____

geboren am: _____ in: _____

gebe hiermit folgende Erklärung ab:

1. Ich habe erkannt, dass die Internationale Bibelforschervereinigung eine Irrlehre verbreitet und unter dem Deckmantel religiöser Betätigung lediglich staatsfeindliche Ziele verfolgt.

2. Ich habe mich deshalb voll und ganz von dieser Organisation abgewandt, und mich auch innerlich von dieser Sekte freigemacht.

3. Ich versichere hiermit, dass ich mich nie wieder für die Internationale Bibelforschervereinigung betätigen werde. Personen, die für die Irrlehre der Bibelforscher an mich werbend herantreten oder in anderer Weise ihre Einstellung als Bibelforscher bekunden, werde ich unverzüglich zur Anzeige bringen. Sollten mir Bibelforscherschriften zugesandt werden, so werde ich diese umgehend bei der nächsten Polizeidienststelle abgeben.

4. Ich will künftig die Gesetze des Staates achten, insbesondere im Falle eines Krieges mein Vaterland mit der Waffe in der Hand verteidigen und mich voll und ganz in die Volksgemeinschaft eingliedern.

5. Mir ist eröffnet worden, dass ich mit meiner erneuten Inschutzhaftnahme zu rechnen habe, wenn ich meiner heute abgegebenen Erklärung zuwiderhandle.

_____ , den _____

Unterschrift.

KL/47/4. 43 5000

Unlike many of the Nazis' victims who had no hope of freedom, members of the Jehovah's Witnesses needed only to sign an *Erklärung* (declaration) to be released from Dachau or other concentration camps. Although the Nazis sought to separate the Witnesses from one another and break their spirit, most remained steadfast, unwilling to pledge their loyalty to Hitler. Jehovah's Witnesses saw the persecution as a sign of the approaching final judgment.

Pierre Marie Benoît

While many churchmen chose silence and safety during the Holocaust, an heroic few remembered the admonition to love one's neighbor, whether Jew or Christian. A Capuchin monk of the Franciscan order, Father Pierre Marie Benoît rescued Jews first within his native France and later in Rome.

From the safety of his Marseilles, France, monastery, Father Benoît witnessed the roundups of non-French Jews destined for concentration camps. Like Protestant Pastor André Trocmé, Benoît believed that effective action was possible. His monastery became a center of rescue activity for Jews seeking to escape to neutral Switzerland or Spain.

Following the Nazi occupation of Vichy France, Benoît prepared a bold rescue effort in concert with French and Italian authorities to save the 30,000 Jews living in Nice and send them to safety in North Africa. This plan was thwarted by the Nazi occupation of northern Italy. Such obstacles spurred Benoît to initiate new rescue efforts, focusing on the Jews of Rome. Working with Jewish organizations and using a false name, Benoît saved over 100 Jews by supplying them with counterfeit identity papers and by persuading various embassies to help in his endeavor. Following the war, Benoît was named "Righteous Among the Nations" by the Yad Vashem.

---

can air units successfully engage German flyers in order to draw the *Luftwaffe* into a battle of attrition it cannot win. The Allies establish air superiority over Western Europe before D-Day.

• **February 24, 1944:** Anticipating escapes, the SS deports 200 *Sonderkommando* prisoners from Auschwitz to the death camp at Majdanek, Poland, where all 200 are shot.

• **March 1944:** German forces invade and occupy Hungary. The kitchen-utensil factory of industrialist Oskar Schindler is nearby, and Schindler repeatedly intercedes with local authorities to prevent the arrests and deportations of his Jewish employees; *See* Summer 1944. • Three hundred Jewish orphans from the Transnistria region of Romania are given safe passage to Palestine. • Jews on the island of Rab, off the coast of Dalmatia, Serbia, are arrested and deported to Auschwitz. • Germans begin to evacuate Jewish concentration-camp inmates to the west as the Soviets advance from the east. The Reich

Gisi Fleischmann

Sent in a train car listed as *"Rückkehr unerwünscht,"* ("Return Not Desired"), Zionist activist Gisi Fleischmann numbered among the last Jews transported to Auschwitz. She who had saved so many lives could not save her own.

Working in Bratislava, Slovakia, Fleischmann headed the *Aliya* (immigration section) of the Jewish Center, arranging for Jewish emigration to Palestine. As a leader of the "Working Group," she saved lives by bribing Nazi officials with private funds raised in the United States. When deportations ceased in Slovakia in October 1942, Fleischmann helped develop the "Europa Plan," to barter Jews for goods needed by the Germans, while also continuing to run an underground railroad to rescue Polish Jews who were fleeing the ghettos.

Even as the SS closed the net around her in Bratislava, Fleischmann continued her rescue work, refusing the possibility of a hiding place. She was gassed on October 18, 1944.

In English and Hebrew, this poster appeals to readers for donations to rescue Jews from Nazi-controlled Europe. Published by the Hebrew Sheltering and Immigrant Aid Society (HIAS), the poster urged people to help Jews flee death and find sanctuary in the United States. Knowing that millions were threatened, HIAS worked with other organizations in frantic efforts to arrange ocean passage for as many Jews as possible. HIAS activists were particularly interested in safe passage for Jewish children, and continued that crusade after the war as advocates for Jews in European DP camps. HIAS was part of a larger relief and immigration organization, HICEM, which had been founded in 1927.

With the inflated title of *Reichsgesundheitsführer* (Reich Health Leader), Leonardo Conti led the Nazi health program. In that role, he ordered the murder of adult mental patients. To inspire other physicians to follow his lead, Conti gave the first lethal injections himself. An early member of the Nazi Party, Conti founded the *Ärztebund* (National Socialist Physicians' League) before Hitler named him the nation's chief physician in 1939. Captured at the end of the war and held for trial in Nuremberg, he chose suicide rather than answer for the thousands of "mercy killings" he had ordered.

1944

orders the destruction of camp documents and corpses.

● **March 4, 1944:** Four Jewish women discovered in the "Aryan" section of Warsaw are murdered by Germans. Also killed are 80 non-Jewish Poles. The bodies of the dead, as well as people who are still living, are torched.

● **March 5, 1944:** Max Jacob, 60, a baptized Catholic forced to wear the Yellow Star, dies at Drancy, France, of bronchial pneumonia while awaiting deportation. Jacob, a godson of Pablo Picasso, was a noted poet.

● **March 7, 1944:** Polish historian and Warsaw Ghetto archivist Emanuel Ringelblum is among 38 Jews cap-

Mobilized for all-out war, the Red Army utilized women—including these Polish members of the Kosciuszko Division—as combatants. By February 1944 Soviet forces had driven the Germans from portions of Poland, and continued their westward advance. But the drive to liberate Eastern Europe necessarily came in stages, over great periods of time. The justifiably triumphant smiles of these soldiers aside, countless prisoners of the Holocaust were still to die, and many Polish Jews who survived discovered that antisemitism had not been banished from their homeland.

Paul Célan, born in Romania in 1920, composed haunting poetry about the Holocaust. During the Nazi occupation, his parents were deported to Transnistria, where his father died from typhus and his mother was shot. Célan spent 18 months in a labor camp. His experiences there and the deaths of his parents shaped his most famous poem, "Death Fugue." The poem evokes images of unceasing suffering, such as the words "black milk of daybreak we drink it at dusk."

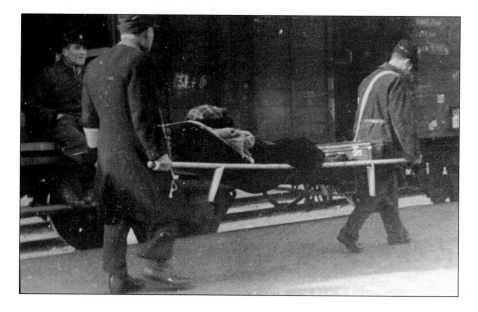

At the Westerbork, Holland, camp, Jewish policemen carry an elderly woman to a train bound for Auschwitz. On February 10, 1944, a train containing approximately 1000 Westerbork inmates arrived at the death camp. Of that group, about 800 were gassed. The rest were put to work, their deaths merely postponed.

tured by the Gestapo in a bunker in the "Aryan" section of Warsaw. Ringelblum and his family are tortured and killed. • Poet David Vogel is deported from Drancy, France, to Auschwitz. Children on the same transport include 17-year-old Henriette Hess and her nine-year-old brother, Roger. Both are deported without their parents.

• 3800 Czech Jews are gassed at Auschwitz just days after a stage-managed camp tour for the benefit of a visiting Red Cross delegation, during which camp administrators offered assurances of inmate safety. During the gassing, those Jews who resist with bare hands are driven into the gas chamber with rifle butts and flamethrowers. They die singing the

Czech national anthem and "Hatikvah," later the national anthem of Israel. Eleven pairs of twins are spared for "research" experiments by Dr. Josef Mengele. • Fifteen hundred Jews are deported from Drancy, France, to Auschwitz. • Anne Frank observes that "he who has courage and faith will never perish in misery!"

The Holocaust in Greece

The devastation of Greek Jewry is one of the bleakest chapters of the Holocaust. Of the more than 58,000 Jews who were deported from Greece from March 1943 to July 1944, fewer than 2000 returned.

The murder of Greek Jews went through three stages. In March 1943 the Jews of Thrace *(pictured)* and Macedonia, two Greek regions annexed by Bulgaria, were deported to Treblinka. About 4200 Jews were gassed when they arrived.

In the second stage, Jews living in the German-occupied zones of Greece were isolated in ghettos located in Salonika, and later transported to Auschwitz. Approximately 45,000 Jews were deported during the months of March through August 1943. About 34,000 were gassed immediately and more than 12,000 were selected for forced labor.

The final stage of the murderous campaigns against Greek Jewry took place after the September 1943 surrender of Italy. Deportations from Athens and many smaller mainland towns carried more than 9000 Jews to their deaths at Auschwitz.

Some Greek Jews resisted the Nazi oppressors. Greek prisoners helped blow up crematorium III at Auschwitz, and one man, Albert Errera, escaped after wounding his guards.

About 60,000 of Greece's 75,000 Jews were deported to their deaths. These Jews from northern Greece were rounded up in March 1944. For a time, Jews in sections of Greece under Italian occupation were protected by the Italian Army. However, the Germans ultimately occupied those areas, too. Most Jews were deported to their deaths in Poland.

The Kovno (Lithuania) Ghetto orphanage was disguised as a children's ward of the ghetto hospital. Orphaned children were among the first targets of the Germans. In October 1941 the Germans sealed the ghetto and murdered 9000 Jews, nearly half of them children. The "Children's Action" of March 27–28, 1944, resulted in the deaths of 1300 Jews.

1944

• **March 15–April 2, 1944:** The Germans undertake a sweeping search for Jews on mainland Greece for deportation to Auschwitz.

• **March 19, 1944:** German control is imposed in Hungary, putting 725,000 more Jews directly into German hands. *Sonderkommando Eichmann* SS units, charged with purging Hungary of Jews, begin deportations.

• Two hundred Jewish doctors and lawyers randomly selected from a telephone directory in Hungary are deported to the concentration camp at Mauthausen, Austria. • The Majdanek death camp is evacuated as Soviet troops approach. Sick prisoners are transported to Auschwitz and gassed.

By March 1943 almost all of the Jews living in the *Generalgouvernement* had been killed. Thus, Heinrich Himmler decided to wind down Operation Reinhard (the extermination of Jews in the area), which officially ended on October 19, 1943. In August the last 25,000 Jews living in the Bialystok Ghetto were transported to Treblinka, where they were murdered. The Nazis closed the camp in the fall, then razed it in order to cover up their crimes. When the Soviets arrived in the region in July 1944, they discovered that a Ukrainian peasant family had moved into a house *(pictured)* that had been built on the camp's grounds by the SS. The Red Army forced the Ukrainians to move and then burned the house.

Saly Mayer was a Swiss businessman and president of the *Schweizerischer Israelitischer Gemeindebund* (Federation of Swiss-Jewish Communities) from 1936 until 1942. He walked the tightrope of negotiating with the Nazis to save Hungarian Jews while refusing the Nazis' requests for resources that would have prolonged the war. In 1940 he became the representative of the Jewish Distribution Committee (JDC) in Switzerland. In that position, he sought to funnel Swiss-Jewish funds to support Jews in occupied countries and to bargain for their release.

From its headquarters in an imposing building on the corner of a Paris street, the *Milice* (French militia) was a pro-Nazi paramilitary unit founded in January 1943 at the initiative of Joseph Darnand. It functioned partly as a counterpart to the SS. Charged with internal security in Nazi-occupied France, the militia concentrated on ferreting out Jews and members of the French Resistance.

• **Spring 1944: The camp system near Stutthof, Germany, is enlarged to include 74 satellite camps.**

• **March 22, 1944: Led by Shlomo Kushnir, nearly 100 Jews escape the labor camp at Koldichevo, Belorussia. Rebels leave behind an explosive charge, which kills ten SS guards. Most escapees avoid capture and join** the Bielski resistance group in the Naliboki Forest. Kushnir commits suicide after being captured.

• **March 23, 1944: In the Bialystok region of Poland, a Jewish partisan group led by Andrei Tsymbal destroys a German military train transporting armored cars to the Eastern Front.**
• **Nearly 6500 Jews from Greece,** including 1687 from Jannina, are deported to Auschwitz.

• **March 24, 1944: Eight hundred Jews from Athens, Greece, are murdered at Auschwitz.** • **Near the catacombs outside Ardea, Italy, near Rome, Germans kill 335 civilians in the Ardeatine Caves as reprisal for anti-Nazi resistance; more than 250 of**

In his official photograph, Hans Frank appears to be a commanding presence in the Nazi hierarchy. After March 1942, however, Frank no longer wielded any real power, although he retained his title as head of the *Generalgouvernement,* the conquered areas of Poland not incorporated into the Reich. True authority in the *Generalgouvernement* rested with the SS. Early in 1944 Frank proudly noted in his diary that only 100,000 Jews remained in his region, down from 3.5 million in 1941.

Newly married, Donna Habib and Peppo Levi pose for a traditional wedding picture. Following the surrender of Italy, Greek Jews, among them this young couple from Rhodes, faced new threats. Their wedded bliss would come to an abrupt end a month later when they, along with some 1700 other Jews from Rhodes, were sent to Auschwitz. Most of that group went directly to the gas chambers, although about 400 were selected for slave labor.

Pictured *(from left to right)* in the office of U.S. Secretary of State Cordell Hull are Hull, Secretary of the Treasury Henry Morgenthau, Jr., and Secretary of War Henry L. Stimson. The three Cabinet members met on March 21, 1944, at the third meeting of the War Refugee Board. The board was commissioned by executive order of President Franklin Roosevelt in January 1944 and given authority to develop policies to rescue the victims of Nazi aggression.

1944

the victims are Catholic, 78 are Jewish. • U.S. President Franklin Roosevelt warns perpetrators of war crimes that they will not escape punishment.

• March 27, 1944: 1000 Jews are deported from Drancy, France, to Auschwitz.

• March 27–28, 1944: In the Zezmariai, Lithuania, camp and in nearby Kovno, all Jewish children are rounded up and murdered. Among the few survivors is five-year-old Zahar Kaplanas, who is smuggled to safety in a sack carried by a Lithuanian gentile. One woman, told by a German that she may keep just one of her three children, cannot choose

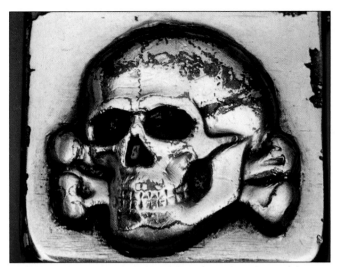

This SS Death's Head emblem found at the Dachau, Germany, concentration camp exemplifies the deadly cruelty of those who chose to wear it. In the last months of the war, Dachau expanded with thousands of inmates from the camps of the East. Disease and death ruled the camp, turning skulls and bones into the dominating reality of the camp.

One of the most articulate and forceful voices in the Jewish community, Rabbi Abba Hillel Silver immigrated to the United States from Lithuania at the age of nine. After his ordination from Hebrew Union College in 1915, Silver accepted a call to a congregation in Cleveland, Ohio, where he remained for his entire career. A Zionist, Silver was a fervent and vocal spokesman for a Jewish homeland. In 1938 he became head of the United Palestine Appeal. Later, with Rabbi Stephen Wise, he became co-chair of the American Zionist Emergency Council.

Massacre at the Caves

The Ardeatine Caves just outside of Rome were the site of the murder of 335 Italian hostages, 78 of whom were Jews. The slaughter was in retaliation for a partisan attack that had resulted in the deaths of 33 German troops on Via Rasella in Rome. Lieutenant Colonel Herbert Kappler ordered the massacre on March 24, 1944.

Five months earlier, on October 16, 1943 ("Black Saturday"), Kappler had ordered the roundup of Roman Jews. More than 1000 were deported to Auschwitz, where over 800 were murdered. After the war, Kappler was tried by an Italian military court and sentenced to life imprisonment. He escaped in the trunk of his wife's car in 1977 but died shortly thereafter in Germany.

SS Captain Erik Priebke, who led the Caves massacres, was extradited from Argentina to Italy in 1996. An Italian court martial tried but refused to convict him of war crimes, arguing that he was only following orders and that the statute of limitations had run out. Retried by another Italian court martial in 1996, Priebke was sentenced to five years but served only six months.

and watches as all three of them are trucked away.

• March 31, 1944: SS functionary Adolf Eichmann assures leading Hungarian Jews that German-Jewish relations will be normalized after the war.

• April 1944: At burial pits at Ponary, Lithuania, Isaac Dogim, one of the Jews ordered to exhume and burn the corpses of murdered Jews, uncovers the moldering bodies of his wife, his three sisters, and his three nieces.
• Former Pripet Marshes, Ukraine, partisan leader Berl Lopatyn, by now a member of the Soviet Army, is killed while negotiating a minefield. • Nine hundred Jewish orphans from the Transnistria region of Romania are given safe passage to Palestine. • Max Josef Metzger, a German-Catholic priest whose 1942 plea for a new German government had been intercepted by the Gestapo, is executed at Brandenburg, Germany. • A synthetic fuel plant at Blechhammer, Poland, staffed with 5500 Jewish slave laborers when it opened in 1942, now has just 4000 left alive. This month,

Itzhak Katzenelson

Among those killed in the gas chambers of Auschwitz in the spring of 1944 were poet Itzhak Katzenelson and his 18-year-old son, Zvi. In happier days in Poland, Katzenelson had been a prolific writer in both Yiddish and Hebrew in several genres, from theatrical comedies to children's books. Under the German occupation, first in Łódź, Poland, and then in Warsaw, Katzenel-

son rallied the ghetto community through works that expressed tenacity in the face of overwhelming hardship, including the deportation of his own wife and two of his children to Treblinka.

During the Warsaw Ghetto uprising, Katzenelson and his son, protected by forged Honduran documents, were sent to the Vittel concentration camp in France as part of a proposed prisoner exchange with the Allies. The horror Katzenelson had witnessed compelled him to keep writing. In his diary he testified to the courage of the ghetto deportees and the heroism of the Warsaw Ghetto fighters. His poems from Vittel express the wrenching premonition that the exchange would fail and he and his son would perish. In "The Song of the Murdered Jewish People," Katzenelson agonizes: "Such blessed harvest at one stroke—a people gathered in entire."

Katzenelson died with his son at German hands in April 1944.

Holding their baby, a young Jewish couple in North Africa prepares to board the ship that will take them to a new life in Palestine. From various points of origin, including Portugal, ships organized by Jewish rescue agencies took Jews from North Africa to Palestine. Yet, even with the arrival of American troops, Jews in places such as Casablanca, Morocco, continued to experience arrest and abuse, sometimes at the hands of right-wing and antisemitic French authorities.

Walter Schellenberg achieved new prominence and power in 1944 as head of the combined SS and *Wehrmacht* security services. His appointment followed the dissolution of the *Abwehr* and the arrest of its leader, Admiral Wilhelm Canaris. A one-time aide to Heinrich

Himmler, Schellenberg performed various responsibilities throughout the war, including leading RSHA *Amt VI*, which was responsible for intelligence gathering in foreign countries. His new appointment in 1944 placed him second in command only to Himmler within the SS.

1944

Blechhammer is designated Auschwitz IV.

• April 4, 1944: The first United States air-reconnaissance photos of Auschwitz are taken.

• April 5, 1944: Of 835 Jews deported from Fossoli, Italy, to Auschwitz, 692 are gassed on arrival. Victims include

71-year-old Sara Klein and five-year-old Rosetta Scaramella.

• April 6, 1944: Three thousand German troops fan out across the "Aryan" section of Warsaw, Poland, to root out fugitive Jews. Seventy men and 30 women are arrested and will be murdered. • A Gestapo unit headed by Klaus Barbie searches the Children's

"I saw many internees cling to their human dignity to the very end. The Nazis succeeded in degrading them physically, but they could not debase them morally. Because of these few, I have not entirely lost my faith in mankind. If, even in the jungle of Birkenau, all were not necessarily inhuman to their fellowman, then there is hope indeed."

—*Olga Lengyel*, Five Chimneys:
The Story of Auschwitz

Max Josef Metzger was a Catholic priest, and a pacifist. A World War I German Army chaplain, he founded and headed the Peace Alliance of German Catholics. During the war he called for a non-Nazi government for Germany. Arrested and condemned for high treason by the vehemently pro-Nazi People's Court, he was executed in April 1944.

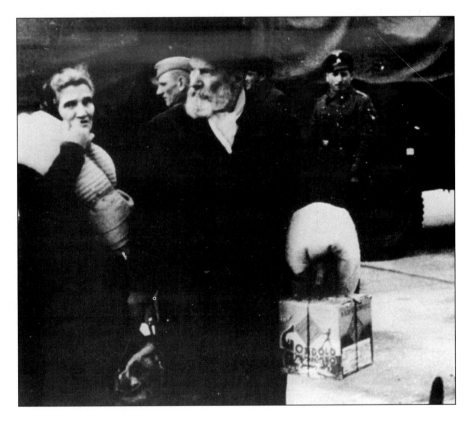

On April 13, 1944, one of the final deportations of Jews from the Drancy, France, transit camp left for Auschwitz. Fifteen hundred prisoners arrived in Auschwitz on April 16, including the Brin family *(pictured)*. All but 388 perished in the gas chambers.

Home at Izieu, France, near the Swiss border, and arrests ten nurses and 43 Jewish children. Most are transported to Drancy, France, and then to Auschwitz. One of the children taken to Auschwitz, 11-year-old Liliane Berenstein, writes a letter to God in which she pleads for the return of her parents.

• **April 8, 1944:** On this first night of Passover, Polish rabbi Mosze Friedman, newly arrived at Auschwitz, grabs an SS lieutenant and excoriates him for his crimes, promising the eternal existence of the Jews and the imminent destruction of Nazism.

• **April 10, 1944:** Two Slovakian Jews, Alfred Wetzler, age 26, and Rudolf

Vrba, age 19, escape from Auschwitz. The pair will later provide the Allies with the first eyewitness accounts of the "Final Solution," as well as a warning about the Nazis' intention to exterminate Hungarian Jewry. • The Red Army captures Odessa, Ukraine.

• **April 13, 1944:** 1500 Jews are deported from Drancy, France, to

The process of ghettoization and deportation proceeded remarkably quickly in Hungary, and Jews were usually shipped out just a few days after being forced into ghettos. This photograph shows Moritz Goldstein and his son Endre in the ghetto in Debrecen. Moritz and his wife, Matilde, had four sons, only one of whom, Ernst, survived the war. He immigrated to the United States in 1946.

MAJOR GHETTOS IN HUNGARY, 1944

After Germany occupied Hungary on March 19, 1944, the country's Jews (except those in Budapest) were ordered into ghettos. From May 15 to July 9, more than 430,000 Hungarian Jews were deported, mostly to the gas chambers of Auschwitz.

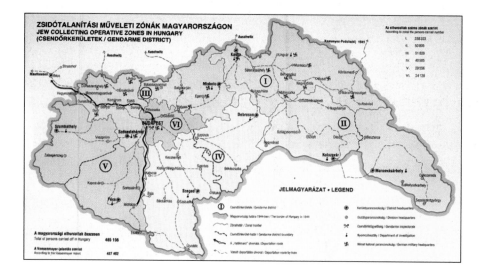

On March 19, 1944, the Nazis occupied Hungary and began to draw up plans for the annihilation of that country's 725,000 Jews, who had been largely unmolested until then. Most of these Jews were deported to Auschwitz, the largest of the death camps. This map shows the police districts into which the Nazis divided Hungary for the purpose of efficiently transporting the nation's Jews.

1944

Auschwitz. One survivor of this group, 16-year-old Simone Jacob, will grow up to become France's minister of health (as Simone Veil) and, in 1979, president of the European Parliament at Strasbourg, France.

● April 15, 1944: Jewish slave laborers forced to exhume corpses of murdered Jews and Soviet POWs at the Ponary, Lithuania, killing ground, near Vilna, mount an escape attempt. Of the 40 who manage to enter a secret tunnel dug into the side of the burial pit, 15 reach nearby woods. Most of these join partisan groups; *See* April 20, 1944. ● In Hungary, tens of thousands of Jews are forced from their homes and into ghettos.

Men and women of the Polish Resistance share a moment of camaraderie before returning to the fight. Using guerrilla tactics, these fighters aided the Russian Army by harrassing German troops in the area of Vilna, Lithuania. Some Jews, operating from the Rudninkai Forest and other secret locations, participated in the Resistance, preparing the way for the liberation of Vilna in July.

Hermann Göring had been among the most influential figures in Nazi Germany, but by 1944 he was hopelessly addicted to heroin and his influence was on the decline. He had also ballooned to over 300 pounds. Hitler, who blamed Göring for the war turning against Germany, often refused to even meet with him. Most of his earlier clout had been lost to Joseph Goebbels, Heinrich Himmler, and Martin Bormann.

Joseph Darnand was a veteran of World War I and had long been associated with right-wing antisemitic groups in France. He founded the *Service d'order légionnaire* (SOL), a collaborationist paramilitary group with about 15,000 members. Darnand eventually became leader of the militia in Vichy France, and hence was in charge of maintaining law and order there. Here he is shown at an April 16, 1944, rally in Paris designed to encourage collaboration among the city's population.

• **April 20, 1944:** Twenty-nine Jewish slave laborers left behind after a partially successful escape from Ponary, Lithuania, are shot by SS overseers.

• **April 22, 1944:** Fifty children are among 250 Jews and Soviet POWs laboring at a Siemens Schuckert electrical-instruments plant at Bobrek, Poland.

• **April 28, 1944:** Adolf Eichmann dispatches the first 1500 Jewish slave laborers from Hungary to arms factories in and near Auschwitz.

• **April 29, 1944:** The first deportation of Hungarian Jews to Auschwitz occurs at Kistarcsa. • 1004 Jews are deported from the Drancy, France, transit camp to Auschwitz, including

Yiddish poet Itzhak Katzenelson and his eldest son.

• **April 30, 1944:** Two thousand able-bodied Jews are deported from Topolya, Hungary, to Auschwitz.

• **May 1944:** Christian Wirth, *SS-Sturmbannführer* and commandant of the Belzec, Poland, death camp, is

Carefully arranged and stored, these sets of china had once been the pride of Jewish families in Prague, Czechoslovakia. They formed part of a massive collection of goods, including books and furniture, plundered by the Nazis from one of Europe's most renowned Jewish communities, and intended as part of a collection in the proposed Central Museum of the Extinguished Jewish Race. Sadly, the goods outlived many of their owners.

SS Major Christian Wirth initiated the use of poison gas to kill "euthanasia" victims. He administered the Belzec, Treblinka, and Sobibór death camps. At Belzec, he held up a large can full of teeth taken from murdered Jews. "See for yourself the weight of that gold!" he boasted. "It's only from yesterday and the day before. You can't imagine what we find every day—dollars, diamonds, gold!" Later in the war he was put in charge of the Italian concentration camp *La Risiera di San Sabba,* where he arranged 22 transports of deportees to Auschwitz. He was killed by Italian partisans near Fiume, Yugoslavia, in May 1944.

Three Jewish men move an elderly Jewish woman to a gas chamber at Auschwitz. The men probably did this in order to avoid a violent response from the SS guards pictured in the background. Many Jews clung to the hope, right up to the end, that what they had heard about Auschwitz was untrue.

1944

assassinated by partisans in Fiume, Yugoslavia. • Many Jews are among the Polish and Allied troops at the Monte Cassino abbey in Cassino, Italy. • The Jewish ghetto at Lódź, Poland, is liquidated. • As mass deportations of Jews from Hungary to death camps begin, hundreds of Hungarian Jews at Sátoraljaújhely and Miskolc are shot after refusing to board trains destined for Auschwitz. • 33,000 Jews from Munkács, Hungary, are killed at Auschwitz.

• May 3, 1944: At Gleiwitz, Poland, near Auschwitz, Germans open a slave-labor plant for production of "black smoke" for use in smoke screens.

Dwarfed by the mountain of shoes before them, women inmates at Auschwitz sort the footwear into piles according to size. Often the shoes would exist longer than the women who sorted them. After initial sorting, the shoes would be moved to "Canada," the storage depot. Then the women of the *Schuhkommando* (shoe detail) set to work, separating uppers from soles and leather from rubber. Most of the material was sent to Germany.

The *Aufräumungskommandos* (cleaning commandos), most of whom were Jews, were given the ghoulish task of sorting through the belongings of the victims of Auschwitz's gas chambers. The camp's inmates referred to the several dozen barracks in which this material was stored as "Canada," associating them with the riches of that country.

"Canada"

While their victims perished in the gas chambers of Auschwitz-Birkenau, the Nazis plundered the personal belongings of the dead. In a special section of the Birkenau camp, work details of mainly Jewish women sorted the collected loot. This part of the camp became known as "Canada," sardonically likened to a country known for its riches and abundance.

Day- and night-shift prisoner "commandos" systematically sorted and classified clothing, luggage, blankets, utensils, valuables, and food. Some prisoners sorted shoes, some only men's clothing. They separated suitcases, blankets, and even baby carriages and tossed them into huge piles. In the building known as the "feed barrack," great mounds of foodstuffs such as Hungarian salamis and Dutch cheese became moldy and rotten.

Eager to find money and jewelry, the SS ordered prisoners to squeeze toothpaste into buckets in their search for hidden diamonds. Even such personal items as hair ribbons, watches, eyeglasses, and dentures were collected. Sorted booty was loaded onto trains and trucks and hauled to Germany. Forced to evacuate the camp in early 1945, the Nazis left behind 349,820 men's suits, 836,255 women's outfits, and approximately 38,000 pairs of men's shoes.

• **May 13, 1944:** The Red Army captures Sevastopol, Ukraine. • Throughout the Nazi camp system, inmate tattoo numbers gain a new series, prefaced with the letter "A." The intention is to conceal the number of prisoners at Auschwitz.

• **May 15, 1944:** Germans begin deportations of Hungarian Jews to Auschwitz from Ruthenia and northern Transylvania. • 878 Jews are deported from Drancy, France, to the Revel, Estonia, slave-labor camp.

• **May 15–July 9, 1944:** More than 430,000 Jews are deported to Auschwitz. Up to 100 are crammed into individual boxcars, with a single water bucket and a single bucket for waste. Suicide and insanity are rampant during transports.

• **May 18, 1944:** Jewish partisan leader Aleksander Skotnicki is killed as his unit battles the armored SS Viking Division near the Parczew Forest in Poland. • A deportation train from Paris arrives at Kovno, Lithuania; *See* May 19, 1944.

The Destruction of Hungarian Jews

"I was born in May. I died in May," Isabella Leitner writes in a Holocaust memoir called *Fragments of Isabella*. "We started the journey of ugliness on May 29th. We headed for Auschwitz. We arrived on May 31st."

Even in early 1944, Hungary's 725,000 Jews seemed to be relatively safe. The leaders of this last great European Jewish community had reports about the fate of Jews under Nazi occupation, and Hungarian Jewry did live in a precarious situation given that country's alliance with Hitler. But compared to the situation of other Jewish communities, most of which had been annihilated by 1944, Hungarian Jews seemed fortunate. Indeed, until March 19, 1944, when the Germans occupied the territory of their faltering ally, many of Hungary's Jews suffered from what writer Ida Fink, another Holocaust survivor, called "the poverty of imagination." They did not believe that what had happened to the Jews in Nazi-occupied Europe would happen to them.

Nevertheless, the nightmare began in April 1944. First Hungarian Jews were ghettoized, and then on April 29–30 two transports, carrying a total of 3800 men and women, departed Hungary. They reached Auschwitz on May 2. The "selection" spared 486 men and 616 women for labor. The remaining 2698

were gassed. By mid-July 147 trains had deported more than 430,000 Hungarian Jews to Auschwitz. More than 75 percent were killed on arrival. Before Hungary's liberation in early 1945, more than 560,000 Hungarian Jews were dead.

Isabella Leitner's 20th birthday was on Sunday, May 28, 1944. Her "celebration" included prepara-

tion for the next day's deportation. That journey took Leitner, her four sisters, her brother, and her mother—along with hundreds of other Hungarian Jews—from the ghetto at Kisvárda to Auschwitz. Her mother and youngest sister were killed on arrival. Another sister perished in Bergen-Belsen, but Isabella and her other siblings survived. Eventually she was reunited with her father, too. In desperation he had gone to the United States in an effort to save his family by obtaining visas for them. He was spared the Nazi horrors, but for the rest of his life he felt that he had not done enough to save his family.

After her liberation and arrival in the United States, Leitner was unable to leave behind her "other life" in the ghetto, on the train, in the camps. "You have one vision of life," she says during an oral history interview, "and I have two." Speaking for many Holocaust survivors, she adds that "we have these . . . these double lives. We can't cancel out. It just won't go away. . . it's very hard."

1944

• Deportations from Theresienstadt, Czechoslovakia, to Auschwitz end with the transport of 2500 Jews.

• May 19, 1944: Jews deported from Paris to Kovno, Lithuania, are machine-gunned by guards in a fenced enclosure after some of the prisoners attack SS troops. • The Germans transport Hungarian Jew

Joel Brand to Turkey with a proposal from Adolf Eichmann that the Western Allies exchange 10,000 trucks for one million Eastern European Jews. Eichmann calls it "blood for trucks." Arrested by the British, Brand is sent to Lord Moyne (resident minister of state in the Middle East), who comments: "What shall I do with those million Jews?"

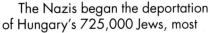

The Nazis began the deportation of Hungary's 725,000 Jews, most of them to Auschwitz, in the spring of 1944. These three photographs show Hungarian Jews in Auschwitz-Birkenau. The first picture is of a group of Orthodox men; the man on the left is Rabbi Naftali Zvi Weiss from the town of Bilke. The second photograph, possibly of an extended family, shows Jews awaiting their fate. The third photo shows a woman and her three grandchildren on their way to the gas chamber in May 1944. The people in these photos were among the first of about 400,000 Hungarian Jews to perish in Auschwitz.

● **May 21, 1944:** The Gestapo imprisons all 260 Jews of Canea, Crete, at Rethymnon, Crete.

● **May 22–27, 1944:** Jews readied for rail transport from Munkács, Ukraine, and from the Hungarian town of Sátoraljaújhely resist being loaded. Some are shot.

● **May 25, 1944:** At Auschwitz, Hungarian Jews being led to the gas chamber scatter but are shot down by the SS; *See* May 28, 1944.

● **May 27, 1944:** Two Jews, Arnost Rosin of Czechoslovakia and Czeslaw Mordowicz of Poland, escape from Auschwitz.

● **May 28, 1944:** In a repeat of an incident of May 25, Jews being led to the gas chamber at Auschwitz run for nearby woods but are shot down.

● **May 29, 1944:** Several thousand Jews from Baja, Hungary, arrive at the German frontier after a 3½-day rail journey; 55 are dead and about 200 are insane.

"**Around us, everyone was weeping. Someone began to recite the *Kaddish*, the prayer for the dead. I do not know if it has ever happened before, in the long history of the Jews, that people have ever recited the prayer for the dead for themselves.**"

—Holocaust chronicler Elie Wiesel, recalling what he experienced as a teenager fresh off the transport train at Auschwitz in the spring of 1944

Two children clutch their father's hand while their mother, balancing on crutches, struggles to keep up during the deportation of Jews from the Sighet (Hungary) Ghetto. From May 16 to 22, 1944, most of the nearly 8600 Jews who had been crowded into the town's ghetto were deported to Auschwitz. Among those sent from Sighet to Auschwitz was 14-year-old Elie Wiesel, who would later write of his experiences in *Night*.

The little Hungarian town of Köszeg had only 80 Jews when a ghetto was created there on May 11, 1944. The total population of the ghetto, which incorporated Jews from surrounding towns, was only 103. This photograph shows the loading of the ghetto's population onto transport trains bound for Auschwitz. Note the participation of troops from Hungary's Fascist organization, the Arrow Cross, in the deportation. The organization's members, many of whom were poor and uneducated, participated vigorously in deportations.

1944

• **Late May 1944: At the Auschwitz rail junction, German soldiers who encounter a sealed deportation train carrying Hungarian Jews to the Birkenau death camp defy threats of SS guards and give water and food to pleading prisoners. • An SS man who has fallen in love with a Jewish girl manages for months to shunt her away from the gas chambers, but** when the romance is discovered both are executed.

• **May 31, 1944: SS Brigadier General Edmund Veesenmayer reports to Berlin that 204,312 Jews have been deported from Hungary. • Near the German border, a Hungarian deportation train stops for the removal of 42 corpses.**

Hannah Szenes relaxes in her native Budapest, Hungary, before the war. Very gifted, Hannah excelled in her studies before immigrating to Palestine, where she joined a *kibbutz*. Her diaries and poems reflect a love of life exceeded only by her fierce commitment to the Jewish people. One of a daring band of parachutists sent into Yugoslavia to rescue Allied pilots and further Jewish resistance, she was captured after crossing into Hungary. Tortured, she refused to reveal radio codes. Her poem "Blessed Is the Match" became an emblem of her own heroic self-sacrifice. It included the line "Blessed is the match consumed in kindling flame."

Immigrating to Palestine from her native Slovakia in 1939, Haviva Reik joined the *Hagana* (Jewish military organization) to fight the Nazis. Following that service, Reik volunteered for the even more dangerous duty of parachutist, hoping that she could return to her native land to rescue her fellow Jews. Landing near Banská Bystrica, Slovakia, on September 21, 1944, she sought to reach leaders of the Jewish Resistance in Bratislava. Fierce fighting impeded her mission, and Reik, her fellow parachutists, and local partisans retreated to the mountains. Captured by the SS, she was fatally shot on November 20.

Palestinian Paratroopers

About 250 Palestinian Jews volunteered to serve as paratroopers in the British Army—a highly dangerous mission. The ones selected were chosen from the best and brightest Eastern European Jews, those who could speak Balkan languages and were familiar with Balkan customs and geography.

After training, 32 Jews parachuted into the Balkans, Austria, and France to spy for the British. Once the Jews finished their Allied missions, the British permitted them to help their Jewish coreligionists.

Although the British were at first opposed to the training of Palestinian Jews to fight, the British deputy minister of state in Cairo, Lord Walter Moyne, finally agreed to their training. Cynically, he recognized that parachuting the bravest Jews on suicide missions in Eastern Europe would permanently remove them from Palestine.

One of the most famous Palestinian-Jewish paratroopers was Hannah Szenes, a Hungarian-born poet. Like most others, she successfully completed her mission for the British. But once her task for them was completed, she was caught and executed by the Germans. Another of the group, Enzo Sereni, was trained by the British and dropped into northern Italy in May 1944. Wearing the uniform of a British captain, he was captured and sent to the Dachau, Germany, concentration camp, where he was a leading figure among the prisoners.

• **June 1944:** An American public opinion poll indicates that 57 percent of Americans anticipate "a widespread campaign in this country" against Jews. • **13,500 Jews are deported from Miskolc, Hungary, to Auschwitz.**

• **June 1, 1944:** With 55,000 unused United States quota slots from Occupied Europe, President Franklin Roosevelt agrees to allow only 1000 Jewish refugees into the United States. They will be housed at Fort Ontario in Oswego, New York.

• **June 2, 1944:** Itzhak Gruenbaum, the chairman of the Rescue Committee of the Jewish Agency, requests the bombing of rail lines that lead to Auschwitz. • The Allies begin a bombing operation (Operation Frantic) in the Balkans, the goal of which is to distract the Germans from upcoming Allied landings in France. Bombing routes overfly the railway lines leading from Hungary to Auschwitz. The operation lasts for four months, during the deportation of tens of thousands of Hungarian Jews to

Joel Brand was a Jewish leader of the Relief and Rescue Committee in Hungary. Approached by Adolf Eichmann with an apparently phony deal to exchange the lives of Hungarian Jews for 10,000 Allied trucks, Brand attempted to communicate this offer to the Allies, who rejected it and arrested Brand. Released in 1944, Brand joined the Stern Group in Palestine, where he participated in violent anti-British and anti-Jewish Agency activities. He died in 1964.

In 1943 France's Vichy government created the *Milice,* a collaborationist paramilitary organization headed by Joseph Darnand, which sought both to maintain order in France, remold it in the Nazi image, and fight enemies of the Vichy regime. Most of its members, including special groups for women and children, came from the *Service d'order légionnaire,* a war veterans group dedicated to protecting the Vichy regime. This photograph shows *Milice* troops marching members of the Resistance into an internment camp on June 2, 1944.

Jews for Trucks

During the height of the deportations from Hungary in 1944, a German "plan" emerged to ransom Jews for trucks. Even Heinrich Himmler, the primary architect of the "Final Solution," was not averse to ransom. A proposal was introduced to exchange one million Jews for 10,000 trucks and hundreds of tons of tea, coffee, and soap.

The negotiations, such as they were, included Joel Brand, a Jew; members of the War Refugee Board; and the British Foreign Office. The Allies did not seriously consider the proposal. Not only did they not trust Himmler, but the British thought the release of so many Jews would lead to pressure for their immigration to Palestine, which Britain was trying to limit. The Soviets opposed the plan because the Nazis would have used the trucks against them. During the negotiations, more than 1600 Hungarian Jews (including those pictured) were given their freedom, finding safety in Switzerland.

1944

Auschwitz. The railway lines carrying the Jews are never targeted.

• June 4, 1944: The Allies liberate Rome.

• June 6, 1944: Allied forces land on the beaches of Normandy, France, in the first phase of the Western Allies' liberation of Europe. When German authorities become aware that news of the Allied invasion is circulating though the Jewish ghetto at Lódź, Poland, a search is mounted for illegal radios. Six Jews are arrested. • All 1800 Jews on the island of Corfu, west of Greece, are arrested by the Gestapo and deported to Auschwitz, where 1600 are gassed and the remaining 200 assigned to forced labor. • A Ger-

American soldiers hurry German prisoners of war, with hands held high and field equipment still strapped to their backs, out of the range of sniper fire, as the Allies advance through Cisterna in Italy. The long Italian campaign yielded major victories for the Allies in early 1944. American troops entered Rome on June 4 under the command of General Mark Clark.

American troops and tanks enter Rome on June 4, 1944. Both sides agreed that Rome was an open city, thus preserving the great capital from further destruction. The Italian campaign was intended as a shortcut for Allied forces into Germany, but it resulted in a long, bitter, hard-fought operation against a stubborn, well-entrenched, and brilliantly led German resistance. Eight thousand Jews had hid in Rome, but in October 1943 the Germans rounded up a thousand Jews "under the Pope's nose" and transported them to their deaths at Auschwitz.

Dutch Jews are deported in early June 1944. From March to September 1944, the Nazis deported several hundred Dutch Jews each month, with 1019 aboard the final train (which included Anne Frank) in September. Of the 107,000 Jews deported from the Netherlands, only 5200 survived the Holocaust.

man deportation ship with approximately 260 Canean Jews aboard is sunk off the coast of Crete. Latter-day accounts conflict as to the details: In one version, the ship carried the corpses of Jews murdered by Nazis, who set the ship afloat and sank it to destroy evidence of the crime. In another, the ship was bound for Auschwitz but was torpedoed and

sunk by a British submarine. Besides Jewish people, the ship may have carried 300 Italian POWs and 400 Greek civilians.

• June 7, 1944: The first phase of the deportation and mass murder of the Hungarian Jews is complete. Nearly 290,000 Jews have been killed in 23 days.

• June 9, 1944: Jewish-Hungarian poet and Jewish-Palestinian paratrooper Hannah Szenes is arrested in Hungary after completing her mission for the British in Yugoslavia. She was attempting to help the Hungarian Jews who were being transported to Auschwitz.

Living in Filth

The Germans attempted to destroy Jewish hearts, souls, minds, and bodies in many ways, often involving excrement. This was an aspect of German policy: Degrade the Jews by forcing them to live and die in an environment that was dominated by filth. Troops locked deportees in freight cars with no provisions for excretion.

Camp barracks were running rivers of filth, filled with dirt, vomit, disease, and excrement. At the Bergen-Belsen, Germany, camp, one latrine served 30,000 women prisoners. Prisoners at almost all camps caught typhus and/or dysentery, both of which caused diarrhea. Many prisoners tied string around the bottom of their trousers to catch their excrement, thus saving themselves from being beaten or killed for taking time to try to get to a latrine. Reska Weiss wrote of prisoners who were "not even animals, but putrefying corpses moving on two legs."

American, British, Canadian, and other Allied troops landed at Normandy, France, on June 6, 1944. The invasion forced Germany into a two-front war (with the Soviets attacking from the east), a war Germany could not win. Although held up for weeks in the difficult Norman terrain, the Allies eventually broke through. They then swept quickly across France and approached Germany's borders by December. As the Allies gradually conquered territory, they encountered and liberated concentration camps.

On the eve of the June 6 D-Day invasion, Jewish men gather on the steps of the synagogue at the Brooklyn (New York) Hebrew Home and Hospital for the Aged. Wearing prayer shawls and blowing the *shofar* (ram's horn) to call people to gather for prayer, these elderly Jews pleaded for a speedy Allied victory that would end the Nazi reign and bring an end to the suffering of the Jews of Europe.

1944

• **June 10, 1944:** In the French village of Oradour-sur-Glane, Germans kill 642 residents as revenge for the killing of an SS officer by a Resistance sniper. Women and children are burned alive in a church and the men are machine-gunned. Of the 642 victims, seven are Jewish refugees who had escaped deportation to Auschwitz by living with sympathetic Oradour-sur-Glane villagers. Included among the dead is eight-year-old Serge Bergman.

• **June 11–16, 1944:** Germans ship an additional 50,805 Hungarian Jews to Auschwitz.

• **June 14, 1944:** Two thousand Jews are deported from Corfu, Greece,

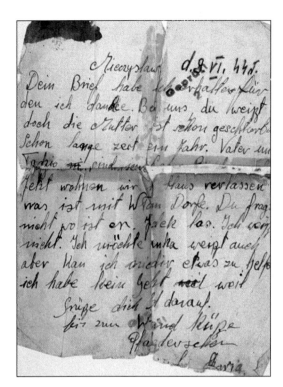

Separated from one another, family members sought ways to maintain contact and learn news. Much of the news, however, was heartbreaking. Pictured here is a letter from Marian Watnicki to his brother, Mietek, in Auschwitz. Marian tells Mietek that while some family members are in a concentration camp, others are dead or missing. Imprisoned as a political prisoner, Mietek prevented his captors from discovering that he was a Jew.

Sylvester Stadler commanded the SS regiment *Der Führer*, which murdered 634 people, including Jews, in the French village of Oradour-sur-Glane. They were assembled in the town's church and then butchered. The massacre was in retaliation for the shooting of an SS officer by the Resistance.

These 38 schoolgirls were among the 634 victims murdered by the SS regiment *Der Führer* on June 10, 1944, at Oradour-sur-Glane, France. The Nazis usually killed women and children in their reprisals, believing that would make a more effective impression upon the Resistance.

to Auschwitz. • Jewish Resistance fighter Leon Sakkis is killed by German machine-gun fire while aiding a wounded comrade in Thessaly, Greece.

• June 16, 1944: Residents of the Jewish ghetto at Lódź, Poland, are notified of "voluntary registration for labor outside the ghetto." In truth,

there is no work but only death at the Chelmno, Poland, extermination camp, where the Germans plan to murder 3000 Jews a week for three weeks. • In France, Jewish historian Marc Bloch, a leader of the resistance group *Francs-Tireurs et Partisans*, is executed by German troops. • German forces begin to pull back from the Douve River.

• June 17–24, 1944: The Jews of Budapest, Hungary, are confined to specially marked "Jewish buildings."

• Summer 1944: More than 500 Jews are being secretly protected by industrialist Oskar Schindler.

• June 22, 1944: The Red Army launches a 300-mile-long offensive

One result of the liberation of France was that those who had collaborated with the Germans were arrested. Some were prosecuted while others were unceremoniously executed by the Resistance. The first photograph shows the rounding up of collaborators in an unidentified French town. The second shows the execution, by firing squad, in Grenoble, of a young man found guilty of collaboration. He was one of six of the town's citizens shot that day.

False papers were vitally important to Jews who hid among the non-Jewish population. This French identity card, held by Lina Donoff, identified her as Denise Alice Josephine Rochard. Lina's mother made the card in order to protect her daughter from deportation. False documents of this sort were not uncommon, and often provided the protection the bearers desired. This, of course, exposes the absurdity of the Nazi insistence that physical characteristics make Jews instantly recognizable.

1944

along the Baltic and Belorussian fronts. The initial target is Vitebsk, Belorussia, located on the Riga-Moscow rail line. • The SS closes the concentration camp at Riga-Kaiserwald, Latvia.

• June 23, 1944: Operations resume at the Chelmno death camp. • The Allies learn that more than 430,000

Hungarian Jews have been deported to Auschwitz and murdered since May. There are about 300,000 Jews left alive in Hungary. • A Red Cross delegation visits the camp/ghetto at Theresienstadt, Czechoslovakia, and is apparently fooled by the camp's superficially benign atmosphere. However, the Red Cross almost simultaneously sends an official protest to

America and the Jews

On June 6, 1944, American soldiers hastened the end of World War II in Europe by joining British and Canadian troops in the D-Day invasion at Normandy, France. Only the defeat of Nazi Germany would stop the Holocaust, and the United States played a vital part in crushing the Third Reich. Nevertheless, the U.S. government never made the saving of European Jewry a top priority.

Germany did not declare war on the United States until December 11, 1941. By then the murderous *Einsatzgruppen* had shot hundreds of thousands of Eastern European Jews, gassing operations had started at Chelmno, Poland, and the Nazis had killed nearly one million Jews since the beginning of 1941. Calling the "wholesale systematic murder of the Jews" one of the "blackest crimes of all history," U.S. President Franklin Roosevelt *(pictured)* promised on March 24, 1944, that the perpetrators would not "go unpunished." Still, the plight of Europe's Jews was never considered a decisive reason for America's involvement in the war.

On a plaque accompanying New York's Statue of Liberty are the words of Emma Lazarus, an American-Jewish poet:

Give me your tired, your poor,
Your huddled masses yearning
to breathe free,
The wretched refuse of your
teeming shore.

Despite these words, strong anti-immigration, antisemitic, and, at times, isolationist currents surged through American life. During the 3½ years that the United States waged war against Nazi Germany, State Department policies allowed only 21,000 refugees to enter the country, just ten percent of those who could have been legally admitted under the already restrictive quotas. Not until the summer of 1944 did the United States make special provisions to bring Jewish refugees to America, and even these were inadequate.

Roosevelt issued instructions that the group should "include a reasonable proportion of various categories of persecuted peoples." On June 9, 1944, he announced that 1000 refugees outside the immigration quota could be accommodated temporarily in an "Emergency Refugee Shelter" at Fort Ontario, an obsolete army facility 35 miles northwest of Syracuse, New York. The actual arrivals numbered 982, 89 percent of them Jewish.

American attitudes toward this token gesture were mixed, for antisemitism was widespread in the United States. From 1938 to 1941, national public-opinion polls indicated that one-third to one-half of the American people felt that Jews had "too much power in the United States." After 1941, and throughout America's war years, agreement with that proposition rose above 50 percent. While Americans fought the war that defeated Nazi Germany and ended the Holocaust, 15 to 24 percent of American survey respondents said that Jews were "a menace to America."

Hungary about deportations of Hungarian Jews.

• June 24, 1944: The United States Military Air Operations declares that bombing rail lines to Auschwitz is "impracticable" because it could be achieved only by diverting air support from "decisive operations" in progress; i.e., bombing German synthetic-oil plants. The fact is that many of these plants are located near Auschwitz. • Lovers Edward Galinski, a Polish gentile, and Mala Zimetbaum, a Jew, escape from Auschwitz-Birkenau in purloined SS uniforms and remain at liberty for two weeks.

• June 25, 1944: Pope Pius XII sends a telegram to Admiral Miklós Horthy, regent of Hungary, asking him to stop the deportation "to an unknown destination" of Hungarians because of their race. The Pope does not use the word "Jew" in his messages.

• June 27, 1944: Jewish Resistance leader David "Dodo" Donoff, 24, is executed near Lyons, France.

Theresienstadt

On June 4, 1942, Pavel Friedmann, 21, finished a poem about the last butterfly he ever saw. "Butterflies," the Jewish writer concluded, "don't live in here, in the ghetto."

A few weeks earlier, the Germans had deported Friedmann to Terezín (Theresienstadt in German), the walled military town in Czechoslovakia where they began to ghettoize Czech Jews in the autumn of 1941. A year later 50,000 Jews were struggling to survive in Theresienstadt's deteriorating conditions.

Theresienstadt also became a concentration and transit camp for German and Western European Jews who were eventually deported to Auschwitz. In mid-1944 the Nazis temporarily beautified Theresienstadt to

deceive the visiting Red Cross and to make a propaganda film that pictured the ghetto as Hitler's gift to the Jews. The facts were very different. Of the more than 140,000 Jews who were sent to Theresienstadt, over 33,000 died and about 88,000 were deported and killed. Only about 20,000 survived.

Theresienstadt's Jews included many prominent artists, writers, scientists, musicians, scholars, and teachers from Czechoslovakia, Germany, and Austria. While in Theresienstadt, children and young people wrote poetry about their feelings and drew pictures about their experiences. Pavel Friedmann died in Auschwitz on September 29, 1944, but his poem, "I Never Saw Another Butterfly," exemplifies the artistic expressions from Theresienstadt.

These children, who seem to have been treated well, were photographed in a park in Theresienstadt. The Nazis established this "model" ghetto and concentration camp in Czechoslovakia partly as a propaganda ploy to create the impression that the Nazi camps were pleasant places. It was the only camp that the Nazis permitted foreigners to visit, including representatives of the International Red Cross. Of the 15,000 children who were interned at the camp, only about 100 survived the war.

This photo from the German propaganda film about Theresienstadt, *The Führer Gives the Jews a Town*, shows women and children reading in their barracks early in 1944. Several social agencies, including the Red Cross, were escorted through Theresienstadt. The Nazis insisted that the Jews were living well, even though most of the inmates would be executed. Of the 140,000 prisoners who passed through Theresienstadt, 90,000 were shipped to death camps, primarily Auschwitz.

1944

• **June 28, 1944:** As the Red Army approaches the concentration camp at Maly Trostinets, Belorussia, near Minsk, regular SS troops replace the non-German SS-auxiliary guards. All surviving prisoners—Jews and non-Jewish Russian civilians—are herded into a barracks that is set ablaze. Any prisoners who manage to exit the burning building are shot. About 20 Jews who had come to Maly Trostinets from the camp/ghetto at Theresienstadt, Czechoslovakia, escape to the woods; *See* July 4, 1944. • The concentration camp for Soviet POWs at Vaivara, Estonia, is closed.

• **June 30, 1944:** The crematoria at Auschwitz are working at full capacity when 2044 Jews from Corfu and

Marc Bloch, an eminent French-Jewish historian, authored *Strange Defeat*, an analysis of the causes of the fall of France in 1940. He also served as a partisan leader at Lyon, where he was arrested, tortured, and shot on June 16, 1944, ten days after the Allied invasion of Normandy.

Attesting to the meticulous record keeping of the Nazi doctors, this document from late June 1944 accompanied the head of a corpse of a 12-year-old Gypsy child. Signed by Josef Mengele and sent from the infirmary of the Gypsy camp at Auschwitz, it directed that the head be given further examination.

In June 1944 Jews remaining in Budapest, Hungary, were forced to move to houses marked with a Jewish star. Starting on November 8, 1944, about 70,000 Hungarian Jews were forced by the SS and the Hungarian Fascist Arrow Cross to march from Budapest to the Austrian border. Thousands of Budapest Jews died on the death marches.

Athens, Greece, arrive. At day's end, lightning rods on crematoria chimneys are warped from the heat generated by the furnaces.

• July 1944: Jewish-Soviet partisans from Poland and Lithuania are active behind the lines at Lublin, Poland, and Kovno, Vilna, and Siauliai, Lithuania, as Soviet troops approach from the east. • The Red Army liberates Lvov, Ukraine. • The SS completes the evacuation of the death camp at Majdanek. • The SS evacuates the concentration camp at Kovno, Lithuania. • Jewish-American Lieutenant Colonel Murray C. Bernays is assigned by the U.S. Army Civil Affairs Division to collect evidence of war crimes committed against American servicemen. Bernays begins to formulate his concept of Nazism as a criminal conspiracy, which will be central to the Nuremberg Tribunal of 1945–46. • Neutral Switzerland ends long-standing, restrictive Jewish-immigration standards and admits all Jewish refugees who wish and are able to enter.

Pictured here are leaders of the Vilna FPO (*Fareynitke Partisaner Organzatsye*; United Partisan Organization). The FPO tried but failed to prepare the Vilna (Lithuania) Ghetto for liberation, and the group's members were forced to fall back to nearby forests and mount resistance from there.

Alfred Rosenberg, a chief Nazi theorist, was Reich minister for the Occupied Eastern Territories, and a vocal proponent of the superiority of Aryan and German blood. After writing many racist tracts—often purchased by Germans but seldom read—Rosenberg headed the Nazi Institute for the Study of the Jewish Question, and planned to chair an international anti-Jewish congress in July 1944.

The first Polish children arrived at Auschwitz in June 1940, but it was in the latter half of 1944 that the greatest number came. Here, a group of Polish children looks out from behind a barbed-wire fence at Auschwitz. Polish and Russian children judged to possess "Aryan" physical qualities—blond hair and blue eyes—were forcibly taken from their parents and sent to offices of the Resettlement Bureau for placement. Thousands of Polish boys and girls were imprisoned in Auschwitz before being transferred to Germany during the *Heuaktion* (Hay Action).

1944

• **July 2–3, 1944:** Three thousand Jews from Vilna—factory laborers and the town's last remaining Jews—are executed by the SS at nearby Ponary.

• **July 3, 1944:** The Red Army captures Minsk, Belorussia. • The British War Cabinet agrees to examine Zionist leader Chaim Weizmann's request for the formation of a Jewish Brigade to fight in the British Army, with the white and blue Star of David as its standard.

• **July 4, 1944:** Red Army units reach the Maly Trostinets, Belorussia, concentration camp. About 20 Jews who escaped to the woods six days earlier are seized by Red Army soldiers; *See*

The gallows at Vught, Holland, dominate the landscape, symbolic of the harsh turn the transit and work camp took in 1943 when *SS-Sturmbannführer* Adam Grünewald became commandant. Belgian and Dutch partisans were hanged from the gallows. The number of prisoners at Vught steadily decreased from mid–1943 as the Nazis sought to kill all Jews interned there. From a high of 8684 Jewish prisoners in early May 1943, the camp's Jewish population stood at less than 500 by the early summer of 1944. Most of Vught's Jews were deported through Westerbork to their deaths at Auschwitz and Sobibór.

The Red Cross

Despite its commitment to humanitarian initiatives worldwide, the Switzerland-based International Committee of the Red Cross (ICRC) made only sporadic efforts to aid Europe's Jews during World War II. Red Cross officials feared that public condemnation of Nazi atrocities could backfire and jeopardize the organization's relief work on behalf of POWs and civilian internees.

The ICRC was convinced it could do little to actually rescue Jews. Unable to even learn the fate of most deportees, the ICRC tried to relieve suffering by sending a few parcels of food, clothing, and medicine to camp inmates whose whereabouts were known. The shipments failed to reach those in greatest need. The Nazis blocked most Red Cross attempts to visit concentration and extermination camps. Only after increased pressure in 1944 did the Nazis grudgingly allow the Red Cross to inspect the Theresienstadt, Czechoslovakia, camp/ghetto. The "inspection," however, was a charade, as the Nazis briefly turned the prison into a comfortable "model" ghetto. Deceived Red Cross inspectors wrote a favorable report of conditions.

The ICRC more effectively protected Jews through the work of its representative in Budapest, Friedrich Born, who participated in international efforts to halt the deportations from Hungary in 1944. More than 50 years after the Holocaust, International Red Cross officials acknowledged that more should and could have been done, and that the organization's meager efforts constituted a "moral failure."

1946. • One thousand Jewish women are sent from Auschwitz to Hamburg, Germany, to pull down the remains of structures damaged during Allied bombing raids. • 250 inmates, most of them French Jews, from the Alderney camp on the Occupied Channel Islands are killed by fire from British warships while being transported to the mainland.

• July 4–5, 1944: 2565 Jews from Pápa, Hungary, are sent to Auschwitz just as the Hungarian government is poised to defy Germany and halt the deportation. Only 30 of Pápa's 2800 Jews will survive the war.

• July 7, 1944: British Prime Minister Winston Churchill informs Foreign Secretary Anthony Eden that he is in favor of the Royal Air Force bombing Auschwitz. From July 7, 1944, to January 19, 1945, the Allies will bomb industrial targets near Auschwitz at least four times, including one resulting in the accidental bombing of Auschwitz.

• July 8, 1944: The Hungarian government declares to Berlin that it

Reflecting the cruelty of life even at the Vught, Holland, work camp, this dissection table was used in the autopsies of prisoners. For some inmates, particularly those working for the Philips Company (which produced electrical components), the camp offered a better chance for survival since Philips sought to protect its workers and see that they received adequate food. Pneumonia and scarlet fever were among the illnesses that spread rapidly in the camp as conditions worsened.

The Hitler Bomb Plot

On July 20, 1944, Colonel Claus von Stauffenberg detonated a bomb near Adolf Hitler that damaged Hitler's eardrums, injured his right arm, and burned the *Führer*, but did not kill him. The failure to eliminate Hitler unleashed an immediate and murderous response.

The conspirators in the assassination attempt included important individuals within the German military establishment. They sought to end Hitler's "incompetent, unscrupulous leadership." Stauffenberg's direct access to Hitler made him the most likely candidate to assassinate the German leader.

After the bomb was detonated, the conspirators believed that they had successfully killed Hitler. They moved to take over the War Ministry in Berlin and issue orders to arrest leading Nazis and members of the SS. Hitler's miraculous survival, however, preempted plans to topple the Nazi regime.

Hitler's vengeance was rapid and severe. Participants in the attempted coup were arrested and hanged by wire, dying the most painful of deaths. The executions were filmed for Hitler, who reportedly enjoyed watching the men twist in agony. More than 7000 additional individuals were captured by the Gestapo, 200 of whom were executed.

German officer Claus von Stauffenberg planted the bomb intended to kill Adolf Hitler. Stauffenberg, who came from a prestigious aristocratic family, was a badly wounded war hero. But like most of the conservative Germans involved in the July 20, 1944, plan, he believed that Hitler had "gone too far." He was executed by firing squad hours after the plot had failed.

1944

intends to stop deportations of Jews within its borders. Some 300,000 Jews (including more than 170,000 in and around Budapest) are saved, though more than 430,000 have already been murdered. • Marianne Cohn, a Jewish woman active in aiding Jews' escapes to Switzerland through France, is executed by Germans at Ville-Le-Grande, France.

• **July 8–13, 1944: Red Army troops and Jewish partisans kill about 8000 German soldiers at Vilna.**

• **July 9, 1944: Swedish diplomat Raoul Wallenberg arrives in Budapest with a list of more than 600 Hungarian Jews for whom Swedish visas are available. With the help of other diplomats in Hungary, outside finan-**

Hitler, his right hand trembling following the explosion, inspects the aftermath of the July 20 bombing. To Hitler's right stands his ally, Benito Mussolini, the Italian dictator who had fallen from power and was rescued from imprisonment on Hitler's orders. Between them is Paul Schmidt, diplomat and Hitler's personal interpreter. Schmidt later wrote a memoir describing Hitler's personality.

Ludwig Beck served as chief of the German Army's General Staff. Initially welcoming Hitler's takeover of the German government, Beck feared a protracted war and resigned as chief of staff in 1938. Afterward, he participated in the "Wednesday Club" of intellectuals, economists, and politicians opposed to Hitler. One of the leading July 20 plotters, Beck was considered a likely candidate to replace Hitler as German chief of state. Before he could be arrested, he unsuccessfully tried to commit suicide. A soldier with the Guard Battalion finished him off.

Carl Friedrich Goerdeler, a former mayor of Leipzig, Germany, and former Nazi official, was involved in the plot to assassinate Hitler. Goerdeler, a unifying force among the July conspirators, was intended to become German chancellor, replacing Hitler, had the conspiracy succeeded. He was arrested, tried before the People's Court, and executed in February 1945.

cial support, and his own courage and imagination, Wallenberg will save tens of thousands of Hungarian Jews.

• July 10, 1944: Thirty Jews are shot after being discovered in the "Aryan" section of Warsaw.

• July 12, 1944: Many of the 8000 Jews remaining in the Kovno (Lithua-nia) Ghetto are killed, and the ghetto is burned. Nearby, a Lithuanian carpenter named Jan Pauvlavicius shields at least eight Kovno Jews in a hiding place he has constructed in his cellar.

• July 14, 1944: Hungarian Jews held at the Revel, Estonia, slave-labor camp are shot in a nearby forest.

• Germans murder hundreds of POWs and Jewish partisans at Vercors, France. • Forty-two Jews laboring in workshops at the Pawiak prison in Warsaw are executed by Germans anticipating a Red Army assault.

• July 15, 1944: The Germans deport 7000 Jews assembled in the ghetto at Siauliai, Lithuania, to the Stutthof,

General Friedrich Olbricht was chief of the General Army office in the Army High Command. A religious man who loved Germany, Olbricht initiated and organized the July 1944 bomb plot against Hitler. On July 15, the original date chosen for the attempt on the *Führer*'s life, Olbricht tipped his hand when he prematurely ordered troops to march on Berlin. He was reprimanded for that action, and was arrested when the plot was unsuccessfully carried out on July 20. Olbricht was executed by firing squad just hours later, along with co-conspirator Claus von Stauffenberg.

Otto Mueller was among Germany's most influential Roman Catholic theologians. He established the Ketteler House, which became the heart of Catholic anti-Nazi activities in the city of Cologne. This put him at odds with factions in the Catholic Church that hated and feared the social forces supposedly personified by Jews: liberalism, socialism, and worst of all communism. The relationship of the German Catholic Church to the Hitler government started off as ambivalent (rather than hostile) in 1933, and stayed that way. Nevertheless, Mueller continued his efforts and became well known to the Nazi authorities. He was arrested after the failed July 20, 1944, coup against Hitler and died in prison.

Roland Freisler *(center)* was president of the *Volksgericht* (People's Court) from 1942 to 1945. Here he opens the trial of the July 20 plot conspirators. A longtime Nazi, Freisler was a fanatic anti-Bolshevik, having been captured by the Russians during World War I and imprisoned for five years in Siberia. He was infamous for berating prisoners on trial before him. Freisler was killed by an Allied bomb on February 3, 1945, as he presided over the trial of a conspirator in the July 20 plot.

1944

Germany, concentration camp. One hundred Jews who are left behind are killed where they stand; *See* July 27, 1944.

• July 19, 1944: Twelve hundred Hungarian Jews from Kistarcsa are trucked to Rákoscsaba, Hungary, then loaded onto trains bound for Auschwitz. • Angelo Roncalli, the

future Pope John XXIII, appeals to Admiral Miklós Horthy on behalf of 5000 Hungarian Jews with Palestinian visas. Roncalli provides baptismal certificates for Jews in hiding.

• July 20, 1944: Select members of the German High Command and political conservatives mount an unsuccessful bomb-plot assassination

"There is no doubt that this is probably the greatest and most horrible crime ever committed in the whole history of the world."

—British Prime Minister Winston Churchill, on extermination-camp atrocities; summer 1944

The Majdanek death camp in eastern Poland was the first of the camps liberated by the Allies, on July 23, 1944. Pictured are corpses in Majdanek that the Germans had exhumed, hoping to burn them before the Russians arrived. Often, as was the case here, the Soviet offensives advanced so quickly that the Red Army showed up before the Germans could complete their grisly task.

The Nazis often used incinerators, such as these in Majdanek, to burn the bodies of their victims. In the end, however, the number of victims was too great even for this relatively "efficient" method of corpse disposal. The Allies found hundreds of thousands of cadavers in the camps that they liberated.

In Theresienstadt, the Nazis' "model" ghetto and concentration camp in Czechoslovakia, extensive attempts were made to create the illusion of normalcy. Pictured in this still from a German propaganda film is the "Ghetto Swingers" orchestra. Although the "Swingers" undoubtedly were not as carefree as this image suggests, Theresienstadt did have a lively musical community that produced some notable works, such as the Victor Ullman/Peter Kien opera *Der Kaiser von Atlantis (The Emperor of Atlantis);* Ullman's Piano Sonata no. 6, opus 49; and Hans Karasa's opera for children, *Bundibar.*

attempt on Hitler at the *Führer's* "Wolf's Lair" in Rastenburg, Germany. Protected from the bomb by a massive wooden table, Hitler is shaken and temporarily deafened but is not seriously injured. Most of the conspiring soldiers and their supporters are conservatives who believe that Hitler is leading Germany to complete ruin by continuing to prosecute the war in the face of insurmountable odds. • German troops commence deportations of Jews from the Italian (later Greek) islands of Rhodes and Kos.

• **July 21, 1944:** Soviet troops speed toward Brest-Litovsk, Belorussia, and Lublin, Poland.

• **July 22, 1944:** Survivors of a July 13 mass execution of Jewish slave laborers at Bialystok, Poland, reach Red Army lines after crawling for nine nights. • German troops withdraw from Parczew Forest, Poland, the site of numerous Nazi searches for Jewish fugitives and partisans. • The Red Army occupies Chelm, Poland, east of Lublin.

Partially burnt corpses tell the gruesome story of Maly Trostinets, a village near Minsk in Belorussia, where the final deportees from the Minsk Ghetto met their deaths. With the approach of Soviet forces, the Germans hastily executed prisoners who had been utilized to destroy the evidence of thousands of other deaths. The prisoners, both Jews and non-Jewish Russian civilians, were herded into a barracks, which was set afire. In spite of the Nazis' efforts, a few Jews survived to tell the story of the mass killings at Maly Trostinets and at the neighboring village of Bolshoi Trostinets.

Russian soldiers and Polish civilians, including a nun, are overcome by grief and horror as they stand among the ruins of the Majdanek death camp. Camp administrators, fearing they would be captured and the purpose of the camp revealed, hastily fled in July 1944 before the advancing Russian Army arrived, taking along about 1000 prisoners. They set fire to the camp, hoping to destroy the evidence of their crimes, but failed to obliterate the gas chambers, which were testimony to the camp's ghastly purpose.

This mound of bones provides grisly evidence of the death toll at Majdanek. Over its years of operation as a concentration and death camp, around 500,000 inmates were imprisoned there, 360,000 of whom, mostly Jews, died by gas, hanging, starvation, disease, or overwork. When the Red Army liberated the camp, they found about 500 inmates still alive.

1944

• **July 23, 1944:** Soviet troops liberate the abandoned death camp at Majdanek, where about 500 inmates are alive. • The Nazis deport 1700 Jews from Rhodes, Italy, to Auschwitz.

• **July 24, 1944:** 258 Jewish orphans from Paris and the surrounding area are seized. • At Bourges, France, Gestapo agents and militiamen massacre 28 Jewish men and eight Jewish women active in the Resistance. Some victims are thrown alive into a well.
• **The German Army adopts the Nazi salute, abandoning the standard military salute.**

• **July 25, 1944:** Three tankers carrying more than 1600 Jews from the Italian-held island of Rhodes stop at

On November 9, 1942, 4000 Jews from Lublin, Poland, were the first to die in Majdanek's gas chambers. Like Auschwitz, Majdanek's death factory made use of the pesticide Zyklon B to murder its victims. Here, in 1944, a pair of the camp's personnel holds canisters of the crystals, which could turn into a deadly gas at room temperature. These two Germans would later be executed for the crimes they committed at the camp.

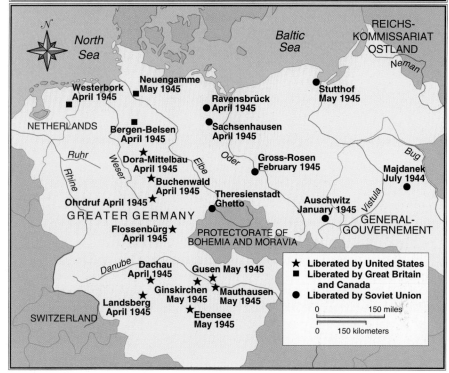

LIBERATION OF MAJOR CONCENTRATION CAMPS, 1944–1945

As Allied troops pushed toward Germany, they encountered Nazi concentration camps and liberated their prisoners. The Soviets first discovered atrocities at Majdanek, near Lublin, Poland, on July 23, 1944, while U.S. troops first witnessed the Holocaust at Ohrdruf, Germany, on April 4, 1945.

Although many people in Germany and Occupied Europe knew what was happening to the Jews, the Nazis made an effort to conceal their crimes. Outsiders, for example, were discouraged from going near the camps, and it was almost impossible to visit one. This sign at Majdanek, written in both German and Polish, reads: "Attention! Camp grounds. Stop! No photography! You will be shot without warning!"

the island of Kos, where 94 additional Jews are forced aboard; *See* July 30, 1944. • Thirty-one faked postcards from deportees arrive at the Lódź (Poland) Ghetto. The writers claim to have been happily resettled, when in reality they have been gassed at Chelmno. • Hitler names Joseph Goebbels Reich minister for total war. • Lord Walter Moyne, chief British

official in the Middle East, finally approves British military training for Jewish Palestinians who are being sent on suicide missions into Occupied Europe. He writes: "The scheme would remove from Palestine a number of active and resourceful Jews.... The chances of many of them returning in the future to give trouble in Palestine seem slight."

• July 27, 1944: Siauliai, Lithuania, is liberated by the Red Army, 12 days after German deportations of 7000 local Jews and the murder of 100 left behind. • Dvinsk, Latvia, is liberated by the Soviet Union. • The *Wehrmacht* retreats from Lvov, Ukraine. Only a few of the city's Jews, many of them hiding in sewers, have lived through the German occupation.

The Nazis sought not only to exterminate every last Jew in Europe, but also to erase most evidence that the Jews ever existed. This photograph shows two Red Army soldiers inspecting a partially burned Torah scroll, a remnant of the culture the Third Reich sought to destroy. The scroll was found when Soviet troops liberated the Majdanek death camp.

A few weeks after D-Day, Secretary of War Henry L. Stimson proudly points to Allied progress into Nazi-held territory. After visiting several war fronts, Stimson informed the American people in his radio address that victory was in sight, although the enemy was still fighting fiercely. Just *how* fiercely even Stimson probably could not conceive: Although D-Day did indeed mark the beginning of the Allied march toward the Fatherland, German troops would resist for another 11 torturous months. Egged on by Hitler, the retreating *Waffen-SS* and *Wehrmacht* often destroyed what they could not defend, depriving the Allies of housing and fuel and other materiel.

One of about 20,000 Gypsies registered in Auschwitz-Birkenau, a young woman is photographed in various mug shots. The Nazis' treatment of the young woman was determined in part by whether or not she was of "pure" or "mixed" blood. Those who were considered *Mischlinge* (mixed blood) ironically suffered more than those who were "pure" Gypsies, who were originally considered Aryans. Those housed in the family camp, perhaps this young woman among them, were sent to their deaths in the summer of 1944.

1944

• **July 28, 1944:** The Red Army captures Brest-Litovsk, Belorussia.

• **July 29, 1944:** 3520 Jews are forced on a death march westward from Warsaw. More than 200 die.

• **July 30, 1944:** Three tankers, carrying some 1750 Jews from the Italian-held islands of Kos and Rhodes,

arrive at Piraeus, Greece, where the Jews are bullied onto trucks and driven to the Haidar detention camp near Athens. • More than 100 Jews are deported from Toulouse, France, to Auschwitz.

• **July 31, 1944:** Among 1300 Jews deported from Drancy, France (northwest of Paris), to Auschwitz are

This drawing by Holocaust survivor Gyorgy Kadar conveys the extremes of life in the concentration camps: Emaciated and downcast prisoners contrast with the well-fed and arrogant camp guard. While some guards did not overtly abuse the inmates, others used their positions of power to inflict sadistic punishments and humiliations on the men and women under their control. Behavior of this sort, although fueled by antisemitism and fanned by years of war, arose also from some dark crevice of the human consciousness where brute force, a lust for dominance, and complete disdain for the dignity and lives of a powerless "enemy" had taken root.

British Policy in Palestine

British policy in Palestine during World War II was predicated on the White Paper, published in May 1939. This official government document reversed Britain's long-standing support for a Jewish state and placed stringent regulations on land transfers in Palestine. The provision of the White Paper that had the greatest impact on European Jewry was the limit placed on Jewish immigration.

Fearful of escalating violence in Palestine, the British government capped Jewish immigration at 75,000 people over a five-year period. After five years, further immigration was contingent on Arab approval. Although Britain paid lip-service to the notion of providing Europe's Jews with a place of refuge, it never pursued a deliberate policy that would allow such a haven to be created in the Middle East.

During the first two years of the war, Britain barred the escape routes for Jewish refugees. Boatloads of people fleeing Nazi persecution were refused entry into Palestine and returned to the perilous lands from which they came. British Foreign Minister Anthony Eden was particularly adamant in his refusal to designate Palestine as a place of refuge for Jews. At least indirectly, the British contributed to the deaths of tens of thousands of Jews.

---

258 Jewish orphans seized in and around Paris on July 24. Upon arrival at the camp, all 500 children and 300 adults are gassed. This is the last transport of Jews from the Drancy camp to Auschwitz. In total, 73,853 Jews have been shipped from Drancy to their deaths at Auschwitz and Sobibór.

• Late July 1944: French Jew Maurice Löwenberg, founder of the National Liberation Movement resistance group, is tortured to death by the Gestapo. • SS General Richard Baer becomes the new Auschwitz commandant. • 46,000 Jewish inmates are gassed and cremated at Auschwitz.

• August 1944: Religiously nonobservant Jews freed in Berlin early in 1943 are rearrested and deported to Auschwitz. • Auschwitz III (a synthetic-rubber plant) is bombed by Allied air forces based in Italy. • Jewish uprisings occur at Castres and Mazamet, France. • By this date, only 4000 Gypsies remain alive in Greater Germany.

Anne Frank and the Jews of Holland

Of the 140,000 Jews living in Holland when that country fell to the Nazis in May 1940, 75 percent ultimately perished. Only about 5200 of the more than 100,000 deported to the East survived the war.

The Jewish population of Holland also included more than 14,000 Jews from Germany who, in trying to escape the Nazis, had fled across the border. Among them was 11-year-old Anne Frank and her family, living in Amsterdam. The Franks, who had left Germany in 1933, suddenly found themselves trapped with the Nazi takeover of Holland. When roundups and deportations began in 1942, the Franks went into hiding. For two years Anne and her sister, mother, and father lived secretly in a tiny attic space they shared with four others. They relied on non-Jewish friends, who risked their own safety to supply them with food.

In a diary she received for her 13th birthday, Anne recorded the emotions, fears, and daily difficulties of the group's harrowing existence. In August 1944, however, an anonymous informant revealed their location to the police. The SS arrested all eight Jews and transported them to the Westerbork transit camp; from there the prisoners were shipped to Auschwitz. Anne's mother, Edith, perished at Auschwitz in January 1945. After contracting typhus, Anne and her sister, Margot, died at Bergen-Belsen in March 1945. Her father, Otto, survived, and later published Anne's remarkable and now famous diary.

This is the house at 263 Prinsengracht in which Anne Frank and her family hid for about two years. But in the end, an informer told local authorities about the Jews hiding in the house. On August 4, 1944, the SS and Security Police arrested the eight people concealed in the house's "secret annex." They also arrested two of the people who had been aiding them, Victor Kugler and Johannes Kleiman. Anne was transported to Auschwitz on September 3 and was eventually shipped to the camp at Bergen-Belsen, Germany. She died there in the early spring of 1945, just a few weeks before the British liberated the camp.

The staircase leading to Anne Frank's "secret annex" was hidden behind a bookcase. Hiding Jews from the Nazis was an extremely difficult, and dangerous, undertaking, and elaborate measures often had to be taken in order to assure successful concealment.

1944

• **August 1, 1944:** The Red Army liberates Kovno, Lithuania. During the liberation, non-Jewish residents murder local carpenter Jan Pauvlavicius for having shielded Jews three weeks earlier. • In Pisa, Italy, Catholic philanthropist Giuseppe Pardo Roques, four gentiles, and seven Jews he had sheltered are murdered by Nazis.

• **August 1–October 4, 1944:** The Polish underground and 1000 Jews revolt against the Germans in Warsaw. *The New York Times* carries long stories on this uprising almost every day, several of them on the front page. The Allies make great efforts to assist the Poles, even when the Allies know that to fly war materiel into Warsaw will result in heavy air losses

Pictured is probably the most famous diary in history—Anne Frank's. The adolescent girl kept the diary from June 12, 1942, until August 1, 1944. The diary, published for the first time in 1947, records not only the family's extraordinary experiences during its years of concealment, but also the inner life of a truly remarkable young girl. On July 15, 1944, she wrote: "[I]n spite of everything, I still believe that people are really good at heart."

"We Jews mustn't show our feelings, must be brave and strong, must accept all inconveniences and not grumble, must do what is within our power and trust in God. Sometime this terrible war will be over. Surely the time will come when we are people again, and not just Jews...."

—Anne Frank

Anne Frank was, in many ways, a typical girl who attempted to cling to something resembling a normal life. On this wall in her room, she tacked pictures of movie stars as well as postcards depicting an outside world that she was forbidden to frequent.

and in German seizure of most of the materiel that lands. About 100 bombers are diverted from other war action for two months, interrupting the Allied strategic bombing campaign against Germany.

• August 2, 1944: 2897 Gypsies are murdered at Auschwitz.

• August 2–August 30, 1944: At least 60,000 Jews are deported from the Lódź (Poland) Ghetto to Auschwitz.

• August 4, 1944: Jews are evacuated by death train from Warsaw to the Dachau, Germany, concentration camp; See August 9, 1944. • In Amsterdam, acting on a tip from a neighborhood informer, an SS sergeant—an Austrian named Karl Silberbauer—and five members of the Dutch Security Police invade the secret-annex hiding place of teenage diarist Anne Frank and her family at 263 Prinsengracht. All are arrested; See September 3–5, 1944.

• August 5, 1944: Polish forces liberate their country's Gesiowka camp

A long line of Jews stretches from the Lódź (Poland) Ghetto toward the train station for deportation to Auschwitz. On August 7, 1944, Hans Biebow, the administrator of the ghetto, stood before the assembled Jews and proclaimed the "transfer of the ghetto" for work duty in munitions factories and other war industries. To further the deception and calm fears, Biebow even urged deportees to take along their utensils, pots, and pans so they could resume family life at their destination.

In France, the joy of liberation was followed by an outpouring of anger toward the Nazis and those who had collaborated with them. In Laval, this woman, accused of aiding the Germans, is forced by members of the Resistance and the local populace to march through the town, wearing a large swastika on her clothing.

Joop Westerweel (pictured), a Dutch gentile, along with Joachim Simon, a Jew, oversaw an underground operation based in Holland. They saved Dutch Jews by smuggling them over the French border and on to neutral Spain. From there, many of these refugees sailed across the Atlantic to safety in the Americas. The Nazis ultimately captured Westerweel and executed him on August 11, 1944, bringing a halt to this successful operation.

1944

and free 324 Jewish men and 24 Jewish women.

• August 6, 1944: As the Soviet Red Army advances westward, the SS begins to drive Eastern Poland's concentration-camp inmates to the concentration camp at Stutthof, Germany.

• August 6–8, 1944: Forty-four Jews held at the Kaiserwald camp near Riga, Latvia, are loaded onto boats for a two-day journey along the Baltic coast to Stutthof, Germany.

• August 9, 1944: A Warsaw death train en route to Dachau, Germany, since August 4 arrives at the camp; 2000 of 3600 on board have died.

German tanks roll through the streets of Banská Bystrica, Slovakia, while German and pro-Nazi Hungarian soldiers line the street. Deportations of Jews, which had been halted in October 1942, were renewed following the failed uprising in the fall of 1944 against the Hlinka Guard and the Nazis. While some Jews managed to hide, others were discovered and killed. More than 13,000 were sent to Auschwitz and other camps.

Completing their long odyssey to freedom, Jews from the "Kasztner train" arrive in Switzerland. Named after Rezso Kasztner, one of the leaders of the Relief and Rescue Committee of Budapest, the trip had been organized by the committee after long negotiations with the Nazis as part of a proposed "Jews for trucks" deal. Although the arrangement to exchange trucks and other goods for the lives of Hungary's Jews fell through, the committee succeeded in bringing this group of 1684 Jews to safety.

Jewish Antifascist Committee

Established in Moscow in April 1942, the *Evreiski Antifashistski Komitet* **(Jewish Antifascist Committee) was approved by Soviet leader Joseph Stalin because it tried to gain worldwide Jewish support for the Soviet Union during the war. The committee distributed anti-Fascist propaganda and also addressed specific Jewish needs.**

Its Yiddish magazine, *Eynikeyt (Unity),* **recounted Nazi atrocities during the Holocaust and offered information about Jewish life in the Soviet Union during and after the Holocaust. Prominent leaders were Yiddish literary and intellectual figures, such as Bernard Mark, a Jewish historian; Ilya Grigoryevich Ehrenburg, author of the** *The Black Book of Soviet Jewry,* **which detailed Nazi atrocities against Soviet Jews; Shlomo Mikhoels, director of the Moscow State Jewish Theater; and Peretz Markish** *(pictured)*, **a prominent writer.**

The committee was destroyed in 1948 with Stalin's purge and murder of Jewish intellectuals. Many of them were still among the committee's leadership, including Mikhoels and Fefer.

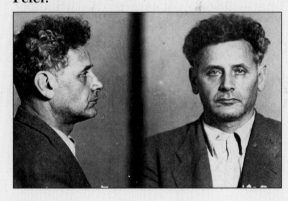

● **August 15–August 25, 1944:** A general uprising breaks out in Paris, which is liberated by the Allies on August 25.

● **August 16, 1944:** A deportation train carrying Jews from the Italian-held islands of Rhodes and Kos arrives at Auschwitz.

● **August 17, 1944:** The last deportation from Drancy, France, leaves for Buchenwald bearing 51 Jews.

● **August 20, 1944:** The United States Army Air Force bombs Auschwitz III (oil and rubber plant), three miles from Auschwitz I (main camp) and five miles from Birkenau, the Auschwitz death camp. 127 bombers escorted by 100 fighters (who face only 19 German planes) drop more than 1300 500-pound bombs. Only one bomber is shot down.

● **August 22, 1944:** The Gestapo undertakes a terror campaign, Operation Thunderstorm, against anti-Nazi German functionaries. Five thousand people are arrested • **261**

Fort Ontario

Beginning in August 1944, Fort Ontario in Oswego, New York, provided a haven to 982 refugees, mostly Jews, from 17 countries. Liberated by the Allies in southern Italy, they received sanctuary in the "free port" on the condition they return to their homelands at the end of the war. Inmate numbers were limited to allay fears that the U.S. might be overwhelmed by a tide of penniless Jewish refugees at war's end.

Confined to the camp, many people despaired. One mother, with two sons who had emigrated earlier and were fighting in the U.S. Army, faced the heartbreaking predicament of never seeing them if she were to be repatriated. First Lady Eleanor Roosevelt was deeply touched by the refugees' plight, but noted "that people in wartime are not logical, and Congress acts in the way people at home want them to act."

With tags attached to their clothing, refugees arrive at the Fort Ontario camp in Oswego, New York. Opened in 1944, the camp served as a temporary refuge for nearly 1000 European Jews, along with a few non-Jews. With little initial hope of staying in the United States after the war ended, the refugees suffered from low morale and anxiety about their future. In December 1945 President Harry Truman eased restrictions, allowing the refugees to remain in the U.S. if they wished.

Yohovet and Abraham Alcana, Sephardic Jews from the island of Rhodes, pose solemnly for the photographer. Nazi efforts to eradicate the island's Jews accelerated in the summer of 1944 when Adolf Eichmann sent his assistant, Anton Burger, to the island. Jews were assembled at various points and sent by ship to Athens, where they were imprisoned before being sent to Auschwitz. Abraham, age 70, and Yohovet, age 60, were among those whom the Nazis deemed too old for work. They were consigned to the gas chambers upon their arrival at Auschwitz.

1944

United States bombers raiding German oil refineries pass within 40 miles of Auschwitz.

• August 23, 1944: The regime of Romanian dictator Ion Antonescu is overthrown. Romania joins the Allies.

• August 24, 1944: Three thousand slave laborers are killed at Mielec,

Poland. • A Jewish survivor in liberated Lvov, Ukraine, notes in her diary that only three percent of the region's Jews remain alive.

• August 25, 1944: German forces surrender in Paris. Large numbers of Jews join Free French forces in the battle to liberate Lyons. • Adolf Eichmann and his staff leave Hungary,

Among the things that made Auschwitz the most horrific of the camps was the infamous selection process that took place upon the prisoners' arrival. This photograph shows an SS man deciding who will die immediately in the gas chambers and who will work himself or herself to death as a slave of the "master race." Children and pregnant women, who represented the future of the Jewish "race," were universally selected for the gas chambers.

Photographing what happened in the death camps was forbidden and an extremely dangerous undertaking. But members of the Resistance considered it a top priority to record what happened, so that no one could doubt accounts of what the Nazis had done to Europe's Jews. This photograph of a group of women being driven to the gas chambers of an Auschwitz crematorium was taken by a member of the Resistance. All of these women died shortly after the photo was taken.

Inmates at concentration and death camps experienced "communal living" at its most harsh and demeaning. The barest suggestion of privacy, which might have given prisoners a shred of hope or dignity, was an impossibility by virtue of the camps' very designs. This open row of latrines at Auschwitz, as elsewhere, prompted inmates to perform their bodily functions as quickly as possible, particularly since some guards turned these interludes into opportunities for particularly vile humiliations.

effectively ending Nazi deportations of Hungarian Jews.

• **August 28, 1944:** The slave-labor camps at Narva, Revel, and Klooga on the Estonian coast are evacuated south by sea to the camp at Stutthof, Germany, as Soviet troops approach from the east.

• **August 29, 1944:** More than 800 Jews earmarked for forced labor are transported from Auschwitz to the Sachsenhausen, Germany, labor camp for assignment to nearby factories. Elsewhere in Germany, about 72 ill or pregnant Jews are taken from a labor camp near Leipzig and transported to gas chambers at Auschwitz.

• **August 31–September 3, 1944:** Jews formerly interned at the Nováky labor camp fight in a Slovakian uprising against the Germans. In all, more than 1500 Jews join 16,000 Slovak soldiers and partisans. One partisan battalion commander, a Jewish woman named Edita Katz, covers the retreat of her men with a machine gun and hand grenades until she is

Why Wasn't Auschwitz Bombed?

On August 9, 1944, U.S. Assistant Secretary of War John J. McCloy was sent a message from Ernst Frischer, a Jewish member of the London-exiled Czechoslovak State Council. Frischer wanted Auschwitz bombed. In Allied and Jewish circles alike, opinion was divided about the feasibility of such action, but Frischer's plea was neither the first nor the last of its kind.

McCloy acknowledged the request's "humanitarian motives" but rejected it nonetheless. "A study," McCloy claimed, showed that bombing Auschwitz would require "the diversion of considerable air support." Bombing would be of "doubtful efficacy" and "might provoke even more vindictive action by the Germans."

McCloy's less than straightforward arguments camouflaged the confidential policy prepared by the War Department in January: American military forces would not be "employed for the purpose of rescuing victims of enemy oppression unless such rescues are the direct result of military operations conducted with the objective of defeating the armed forces of the enemy."

In June 1944 the Allies began to consider bombing the synthetic-oil and rubber factories connected to Auschwitz. Subsequent aerial reconnaissance photographs show the Auschwitz complex. During a raid on August 20, American planes dropped 1336 500-pound bombs on factory areas less than five miles from the camp's gas chambers.

Controversy remains about the reluctance to bomb Auschwitz. It now seems clear, however, that bombing in the spring and summer of 1944 would have saved many lives.

Russian soldiers are joyously received by Romanians in Bucharest in August 1944. But liberation was too late for hundreds of thousands of Romanian Jews who were butchered by native antisemites and German *Einsatzgruppen*. In all, upwards of 420,000 Jews of Romania perished under Nazi rule.

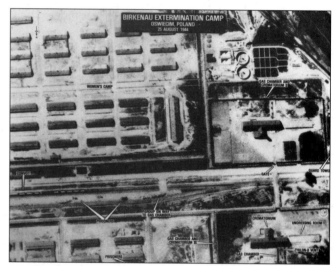

Allied reconnaissance aircraft regularly flew over and photographed the Auschwitz-Birkenau death camp. Crematoria and gas chamber units as well as numerous barracks and guard towers are clearly visible. Even some of the prisoners can be seen, as can the tracks that brought the trainloads of victims to the camp. The Allies, who decided that the best way to put an end to the atrocities committed at Auschwitz was to win the war quickly, made no effort to bomb the camp.

1944

killed by Germans and the Hlinka Guard. Another Jewish partisan, Tibor Cifea, is shot by Germans and left hanging for three days.

• September 1944: Five thousand women and 500 men are evacuated from Auschwitz north to Stutthof, Germany. Three thousand interned women are evacuated from Auschwitz northwest to Neuengamme, Germany. • Following American bomber hits on factories at Auschwitz, the SS gives wounded inmates excellent medical attention as well as flowers and chocolate—a propaganda ploy for the benefit of German media. Once recovered, the inmates are exterminated. • The Gestapo and SS men in Przemyśl, Poland, execute

Despondent officers of the *Wehrmacht* sit in the hallway of the Hotel Majestic, their former headquarters, in Paris. The German commander of Paris, General Dietrich von Choltitz, ignored Hitler's order to destroy the city, reasoning that to do so would be valueless as well as destructive. After some fighting, his army surrendered to the first French forces to enter Paris, the Second Armored Division commanded by General Jacques Leclerc, on August 25, 1944. Four years of German rule in France ended with the *Wehrmacht* outmaneuvered, outgunned, and in full retreat.

Celebrating the long-awaited liberation of Paris on August 25, 1944, jubilant young women embrace an Allied soldier. Speaking to the citizens of the capital, General Charles de Gaulle, leader of the Free French forces, proudly proclaimed: "Paris broken, Paris martyred, but Paris liberated by her own people."

General Charles de Gaulle leads the victory parade from the *Arc de Triomphe* down the *Champs Élysées* in Paris on August 26, 1944. A towering symbol of the French will to defeat the Nazis, de Gaulle became premier of the Provisional French government at the end of the month.

eight members of a non-Jewish Polish family and a little Jewish girl after discovering the group playing together in a courtyard. • Winston Churchill, a supporter from the start, finally orders the creation of a Jewish Brigade of Palestinian Jews in the British Army. Foreign Secretary Anthony Eden continues to object.

• Early September 1944: At Auschwitz, inmate Gisella Perl observes an elderly Dutch Jew hand a work-gang foreman a pouch of diamonds in exchange for a few uncooked potatoes. With trembling hands, the man immediately eats the potatoes.

• September 2, 1944: Approximately 2000 Jews deported from Plaszów,

Poland, are gassed to death at Auschwitz.

• September 3, 1944: Brussels, Belgium, is liberated by Allied troops.
• The Allies begin air evacuations of Jews from partisan-held regions of Yugoslavia to Allied-occupied Italy.
• A senior Italian police officer named Giovanni Palatucci, arrested

In August 1944 the by-now largely non-Jewish Polish underground revolted against German troops in the city of Warsaw. Some early triumphs, such as the capture of German soldiers *(top left)*, were psychologically important, and the Poles were further buoyed by the nearness of Soviet troops. But instead of sending his forces into Warsaw as soon as possible, Soviet leader Joseph Stalin ordered his troops to wait outside the city, until the Germans had crushed the uprising. However, in September Stalin did allow British and American planes to use Soviet airfields to drop badly needed food and materiel to the beleaguered Poles. Much of what was air-dropped fell into German hands, and Stalin suspended Allied use of Russian airfields after only a week. Other Allied flights originating from Foggia, Italy, ironically flew within sight of Jews and others interned at Auschwitz. By October *(top right and above)* the Warsaw revolt had been put down.

1944

in the German-held Yugoslavian city of Fiume for aiding Jews, is sent to the concentration camp at Dachau, Germany, where he dies.

• September 3–5, 1944: Anne Frank is among 1019 Jews deported on the last transport from the Westerbork, Holland, camp to Auschwitz; *See* September 6, 1944.

• September 4, 1944: At Lugos, Hungary, hundreds of Jews are massacred by Hungarian Fascists. • The Allies capture the Belgian port of Antwerp.

• September 5, 1944: False rumors of imminent liberation in Holland cause Dutch Nazis to flee. The day becomes known as *Dolle Dinsdag* (Mad Tuesday). • The SS closes the concentra-

This *Schutzpass* (letter of protection) was issued to Hungarian Jew Lili Katz by Swedish representatives in Budapest. The *Schutzpass* protected the bearer from deportation to almost certain death in one of the camps. Note the "W" in the bottom left-hand corner, denoting that it had been issued by Raoul Wallenberg.

Klaus Barbie

As chief of the Gestapo in Lyons, France, Klaus Barbie was a committed Nazi, ruthlessly fulfilling his duties right to the end.

Barbie oversaw the last transport of Jews from Lyons to Auschwitz in early August 1944, just weeks before the city was liberated by the Allies. Only a few months before, in April, Barbie had sent 41 Jewish children from Izieu, France, to the camp. Barbie's tenacity in deporting Jews was matched only by his ferocity in hunting down members of the French Resistance. On his orders, for example, Resistance leader Jean Moulin was captured and tortured.

Following the war, Barbie fled to Bolivia, where, under an assumed name, he sought to escape judgment for his crimes. After years of effort by Jewish organizations, he was extradited to France. Barbie, the "Butcher of Lyons," was tried in 1987 on the charge of crimes against humanity. He was sentenced to life in prison, where he died in 1991.

The Allies made a concerted effort to accumulate evidence of German crimes against humanity. Here, Russian investigators at Treblinka, Poland, examine the exhumed bodies of some of the camp's victims. Try as they might, the Nazis could not cover up their horrific crimes, and pictures such as this one served as evidence at Nuremberg and other war-crimes trials.

tion camp at s' Hertogenbosch, the Netherlands.

• September 6, 1944: Zalman Gradowski, a *Sonderkommando* laborer at Auschwitz, buries a diary of camp life he has kept since arriving at the camp in February 1943. • An *Einsatzkommando* unit commanded by SS Captain Hauser enters Topolcany,

Slovakia, to quell a Jewish uprising. Many leaders of the local Jewish community are arrested and killed, including former Deputy Mayor Karl Pollak, his wife, and Moritz Hochberger, who are set upon by SS troopers. • Of the people with Anne Frank on a transport to Auschwitz, 549 Dutch Jews are gassed. Anne is saved for the time being because she is 15

years old. If she were 14, she would be immediately killed. Like all prisoners, she is tattooed and her head is shaved; *See* October 30, 1944.

• September 7, 1944: Hungarian authorities permit Ottó Komoly, a Jew, to rent buildings in Budapest to be used for the protection of Jewish children. Komoly will ultimately pro-

Children and the Holocaust

The Nazis' cold-blooded and vicious treatment of Jewish children during the Holocaust enters the realm of pure evil. Not only did the Nazi butchers and their accomplices kill more than one million Jewish children, they subjected countless others to situations that no human being, yet alone a child, should experience.

The creation of ghettos in Poland marked a profound change in the lives of Jewish children. Every defining feature of childhood, from innocence to freedom to security, was absent from their lives. The disintegration of the nuclear family within the ghettos meant that parents could no longer provide for or protect their children. Tens of thousands of Jews fell victim to hunger and disease. A contemporary observer exclaimed that the most painful changes affected the faces of children. They were "worn down to the bones by misery, lack of food, vitamins, air and exercise; [their faces were] disfigured by overwhelming worries, anxieties, mishaps, sufferings, and illness."

As epidemics raged through the ghettos and parents were deported to their deaths, thousands of children were orphaned. Half-naked, unwashed youngsters lay listlessly on the floors of the overcrowded orphanages.

The lack of sanitary facilities, proper nutrition, and adequate shelter drove many to the streets. According to Chaim Kaplan of the Warsaw Ghetto, every morning one "would see their little bodies frozen to death in the ghetto streets." A welfare report written in February 1942 summarized the children's situation as follows: "Hunger, sickness and want are their constant companions, and death is the only visitor in their homes."

The unending terror of Nazi policy wreaked havoc on the lives of Jewish children. Most lived their tragically short lives

without playing in a park or swimming pool. Worse yet, the closure of schools within the ghettos robbed youngsters of the intellectual stimulation fundamental to childhood.

Once the "Final Solution" began in 1941, only Jews who could work were kept alive. Since children served no productive role, most were killed immediately when they arrived at the camps. Youngsters who could pass as adults survived the notorious selection process. Regardless, the extermination centers consumed Jewish children remorselessly. Preadolescents accompanied their mothers into the gas chambers, while babies were often tossed into pits filled with burning corpses.

Young people who survived the selection process became slave laborers. As such they were starved, beaten, and worked to death. In the words of Jack Rubinfeld, a childhood survivor of the camps, "I had to grit my teeth and bear it, and try to show that I was tough, that I was just like the adults."

The Nazi terror system brutally eliminated the concept of childhood for millions of Jews. Those who survived, including Aljoscha Lebedew (*pictured*), lived with the horrors for the rest of their lives.

1944

tect 5000 children in 35 buildings; *See Early 1945.*

• September 9, 1944: SS men guarding quarry workers at the Mauthausen, Austria, camp torture and murder 39 Dutch, seven Britons, and an American secret agent. • Since the beginning of deportations from the Jewish ghetto at Lódź, Poland, to the Chelmno death camp on June 23, 1944, 775 wristwatches and 550 pocket watches have been stolen from Jews before their deaths.

• September 10, 1944: Fifty-two Jews are captured in Topolcany, Slovakia, and ordered by *Einsatzkommando* and Slovak auxiliary units to dig their own burial pit before being

On July 8, 1944, three weeks before the Soviets liberated the Kovno (Lithuania) Ghetto, the Nazis forced Jews from underground bunkers with dogs, smoke grenades, and firebombs. Two thousand Jews died, while 4000 others were sent to camps in Germany. The Germans were very successful in Lithuania because elements at all levels of Lithuanian society collaborated with the Germans to "rid the nation" of the Jewish "vermin."

The Ninth Fort, part of the original defense system of Kovno, Lithuania, was the site where Germans and Lithuanians murdered nearly 10,000 Jews in October 1941. Later, tens of thousands of other Jews from all over Europe also were killed there. This photograph reveals graffiti left by Jews about to be murdered. Some messages were simple memorials. Others asked for revenge. Still others noted that Jews were "dying for our Jewish nation with pride."

U.S. Army troops and supplies land at a beach in southern France in support of the Allied invasion of the area on August 30, 1944. This attack coincided with the ongoing Normandy assault in northern France. The invasion of the south incidentally liberated Jews hiding in the Vichy-controlled area, but it did not have a major impact on the Holocaust since most Jews were located in Eastern Europe.

executed. Six children are among the victims, including a three-month-old baby.

• September 12, 1944: Jewish slave laborers work near Lieberose, Germany, to build a vacation complex for German officers; *See* December 1944.

• September 13, 1944: Ineffective Soviet air drops of supplies are made to Warsaw resistance fighters.

• September 15, 1944: Nancy, France, is liberated by Allied troops.

• September 16, 1944: Bulgaria declares war on Germany following a Communist coup.

• September 17, 1944: The Germans begin the evacuation of the forced-labor copper-mine camp at Bor, Hungary. Sixty of these laborers are shot to death during the march and 600 are shot after arriving at their destination, the kiln of a brickworks at Cservenka, Hungary. • Near Verona, Italy, 23-year-old Rita Rosani, the Jewish leader of an Italian partisan

Two women in Strasbourg, France, read the first French newspaper they have seen since the German occupation began. The sign on the wall behind them, stenciled in German, reads: "Jews, Democrats, and Bolsheviks are the grave-diggers of humanity. Therefore, we will fight on to the final victory."

Marion Kaufmann *(background, center)* stands in the midst of the Gypsy family that concealed and protected her in September 1944. Marion endured years of fear, hiding, and escape beginning in 1942, when she and her mother fled to southern Germany. They were helped by Christians to escape into the Netherlands, only to discover that the Nazis had occupied that country. Separated from her mother, who hid for over a year in a haystack, Marion was sheltered by the underground until liberated by Canadian troops.

American soldiers enjoy a song as they ride the merry-go-round in Verviers, Belgium. For Belgian Jews, life was not so joyful, and liberation from the Nazis was only the first step in a long reconstruction of their lives. Survivors struggled to locate family members and to regain confiscated property. In the months after liberation, Jewish chaplains in the Allied armies and members of the Jewish Brigade helped survivors to secure the basics of life and search for lost loved ones.

1944

group, is killed in a battle with German troops.

• September 18, 1944: Fourteen hundred Jewish boys at Auschwitz are taken from their barracks to the children's block and are later gassed.

• September 19–23, 1944: The SS murders 2400 Jews and 100 Soviet POWs at the Klooga, Estonia, labor camp as Soviet forces draw closer. Only 85 inmates survive.

• September 22, 1944: Arad, Romania, is liberated by Soviet troops.

• September 24, 1944: As deportations to Auschwitz slow, Nazis gas 200 inmate *Sonderkommandos*. The bod-

A Jewish policeman shakes the hand of one of more than 1000 Jews who are about to leave the Westerbork, Holland, concentration camp in early September 1944. Of the 1019 Westerbork prisoners who arrived in Auschwitz in early September, 549 were immediately sent to the gas chambers. Among those admitted to the camp on that day was Anne Frank, young author of the famous diary. Killings would continue at Auschwitz for another five months, a fact that is particularly terrible because Allied aircraft had gained the ability to bomb the camp complex in the autumn of 1943.

Westerbork

Established near the German border by the Dutch government, Westerbork originally served as a camp for Jewish refugees. With their occupation of the Netherlands in May 1940, the Nazis turned Westerbork into a transit camp with a constantly changing population, while at the same time maintaining a core camp with a stable population of workers.

Beginning in July 1942, Westerbork became a way station for over 100,000 Dutch Jews dispatched to the death camps of the East. The barracks served as the last home for thousands of families, including that of Anne Frank. Usually on Tuesdays, thousands of men and women were crowded into cattle cars for their last journey. No one was exempt. After watching the hellish process of deportation, Etty Hillesum, who would herself soon be sent to Auschwitz, reported that "one more piece of our camp has been amputated."

The Vittel transit camp played a vital role in the murder of France's Jews. Thousands, many of them not French citizens, passed through the camp on their way to larger French concentration camps or to Auschwitz for extermination. The people pictured here were among the 2087 prisoners at Vittel when it was liberated by Allied armies on September 12, 1944.

ies are cremated later in the day. Total number of *Sonderkommandos* now remaining at the camp: 661.

• **September 26, 1944:** On this day of Yom Kippur, 1000 young boys are assembled at Auschwitz in the presence of Dr. Josef Mengele. Any boy whose head does not reach a board Mengele has nailed to a post is set aside for gassing; *See* September 28, 1944.

• **September 28, 1944:** Boys deemed too short by Auschwitz's Dr. Josef Mengele are gassed. • The Nazis resume deportations from the Theresienstadt, Czechoslovakia, camp/ghetto to Auschwitz after a four-month hiatus. Among the 2499 prisoners deported on this day is teenager Petr Ginz, a Czech of Jewish background who was the guiding light behind *Vedem* (*In the Lead*), a secret "magazine" created and distributed throughout Theresienstadt. More than 1000 of these 2499 prisoners are gassed immediately. • Josef Bürckel, Reich commissar of Austria, and his wife commit suicide. • The

Forced and Slave Labor

As the war dragged on, the Nazis' manpower needs became ever greater. The available German labor pool, however, became seriously depleted. By 1944, with increasingly more German men taken out of the work force and drafted into the Army, the need for laborers became acute.

Reluctant to force women (those pictured toiled at the Ravensbrück, Germany, camp) into work for war industries, the Nazis tried to fill the growing gap by recruiting foreign laborers. These came from the ranks of the civilian population in occupied countries, from prisoners of war, and from Jews imprisoned in ghettos and labor camps. Quotas established in early 1944 required an immense mobilization of millions of additional laborers for the war effort. By the end of the year, more than nine million foreign civilians and POWs labored in the Reich. For the entire length of the war, this number totaled at least 12 million. The Nazis conscripted foreign workers (*Fremdarbeiter*) for forced labor in both agriculture and industry, while Jews in concentration camps toiled exclusively as slave labor for German industry.

A forced-labor decree enacted in 1942 allowed Fritz Sauckel, plenipotentiary for Labor Allocation, to ruthlessly round up "recruits." His agents plucked people off city streets, from town squares, and out of churches and movie houses for forced deportation to Germany. Guided by racial principles, the treatment and working conditions of these foreign workers varied. Nazi policy regarded Eastern European workers as inferior "subhumans," subjecting them to stringent controls, harsh penalties, and strenuous

physical labor. Forced to wear identifying patches, Poles and Russians received extremely low wages, could not socialize with Germans, and were confined to their quarters after work. By contrast, Western European workers received higher wages and much better treatment.

Much worse, however, was the condition of Jews in Occupied Poland, who were exploited by the Nazis as slave labor in ghettos and specially constructed labor camps. Under SS jurisdiction, the camps produced a high death toll as inmates toiled through 12-hour work days while deprived of adequate food and shelter. A number of German industries exploited the readily available, cheap slave labor by locating factory compounds near or even in concentration camps.

The factories in the Auschwitz region expanded during the first half of 1944, and made use of POWs in addition to Jews. The Krupp Works utilized slave labor to make steel. The munitions manufacturing firm *Rheinmetall*, of Düsseldorf, set up production at Buchenwald. I.G. Farben, the giant chemical cartel that produced dyes, explosives, synthetic rubber, and numerous war-related products, established an extensive subcamp system near Auschwitz. This included the Buna Works, where slave labor manufactured synthetic rubber and coal oil.

The labor camp at Myslowice provided 1300 slaves for work in the Fürstengrube coal mines. At Sosnowiec, prisoners made gun barrels and shells for the *Ost-Maschinenbau Gesellschaft* works. The Siemens-Schukert works used children to manufacture electrical parts for airplanes and submarines. Workers were easily replaced when worn out and no longer fit for labor.

1944

camp at Klooga, Estonia, is liberated by the Soviets.

• September 29, 1944: Fifteen hundred prisoners are deported from the Theresienstadt, Czechoslovakia, camp/ghetto to Auschwitz. 750 are gassed upon arrival. • German trade unionist Wilhelm Leuschner is hanged by Nazis. • Jews gather in liberated Kiev, Ukraine, to commemorate the third anniversary of the Nazi massacre of Jews at Babi Yar, Ukraine.

• October 1944: About 15,000 Jews are deported from the Theresienstadt, Czechoslovakia, camp/ghetto to Auschwitz. • The Germans initiate death marches of prisoners from

The concentration camp at Klooga, Estonia, located in the northern part of the country, was established in 1943. On September 19, 1944, as Soviet forces approached the camp, the Nazis fell back on what was becoming a standard response to imminent liberation: hurried, calculated murder. Inmates were taken in groups into nearby woods and executed. About 2400 of the camp's Jewish inmates and approximately 100 Soviet prisoners of war were killed this way. Among the victims were a pregnant woman *(above)* and her unborn child. When the Red Army liberated the camp on September 28, only 85 inmates were found alive, including the four Russians pictured *(below)*.

An energetic Nazi organizer in the Saar-Palatinate since 1925, Josef Bürckel rose through the ranks to become *Gauleiter* (Nazi Party leader) for the region. Following the *Anschluss* (Annexation) of Austria in 1938, Bürckel became *Gauleiter* of Vienna and *Reichstatthalter* (governor) of Austria. He worked diligently to further unification with Germany, including promoting anti-Jewish decrees and seizing Jewish property. He died, probably by his own hand, on September 28, 1944.

Auschwitz to camps in Germany, including Dachau, Bergen-Belsen, and Sachsenhausen. • At the Stutthof, Germany, concentration camp, executions of Jewish prisoners begin. Initial killings are carried out by assembling inmates with their backs to an infirmary wall with the stated purpose of medical examinations. Slits in the wall behind the heads of each inmate

allow a pistol shot to be fired into their brains from the adjoining room. • Some 150 twins, most of them children, remain in Dr. Mengele's medical block at Auschwitz-Birkenau.

• October 4, 1944: All women and children on a train traveling from Theresienstadt, Czechoslovakia, to Auschwitz are gassed upon arrival.

• October 6, 1944: The Red Army enters Hungary.

• October 6–7, 1944: *Sonderkommando* Jews from Poland, Hungary, and Greece, who are forced to transport gassed corpses to crematoria at Auschwitz, attack SS guards with hammers, stones, picks, crowbars, and axes. They also blow up one of

Slovak National Uprising

After the Germans seized Czechoslovakia in 1938, they created a conquered territory called the Protectorate of Bohemia and Moravia, and a rump state allied to Germany called Slovakia. Slovakia's government was a totalitarian dictatorship led by Dr. Jozef Tiso, a Catholic priest. Tiso collaborated in the German campaign to deport two-thirds of Slovakia's 90,000 Jews to Auschwitz.

In August 1944 several groups, including the Czech government-in-exile and the Communist Party, called for a national revolt. Sixteen thousand members of the Slovak national army responded—as did large numbers of partisans and Jews from labor camps. In one bloody battle, a Jewish unit from the Nováky labor camp fought gallantly against the Nazis before being overrun.

The revolt was put down by the Nazis on October 27, 1944. More than 1500 Jews had participated in the uprising.

A smiling Petr Ginz is pictured with his parents and sister. A teenager when he was sent to the Theresienstadt, Czechoslovakia, camp/ghetto, Petr joined with other talented boys, led by Professor Valter Eisinger, to publish a secret "magazine" called *Vedem (In the Lead)*. Risking their lives, they painstakingly copied drawings, poetry, and stories by hand at night in their barracks. They then distributed the magazine throughout the ghetto. In September 1944 Petr was one of 2499 prisoners deported to the gas chambers at Auschwitz.

Unshakable in his opposition to the Nazis, Wilhelm Leuschner paid with his life for the failure of the July 1944 assassination attempt on Hitler. Along with Julius Leber, Leuschner led the Socialist opposition to the Nazis and later joined the Kreisau Circle of resistance. His fellow resisters nominated him to serve as vice-chancellor in the government they would establish after Hitler's removal from power. Following the botched plot, he was subjected to a rigged trial in the People's Court and sentenced to death by hanging, which occurred on September 29, 1944.

1944

the four crematoria with explosives smuggled into the camp from a nearby munitions factory. Russian POWs throw an SS man alive into a crematorium furnace. The SS fights back with machine guns, hand grenades, and dogs. 250 Jews are shot outside the camp wire. An additional 12 who escape will later be found and executed; *See* October 9, 1944.

• October 9, 1944: The SS arrests three Jewish women at the Auschwitz munitions factory for complicity in the smuggling of explosives used in the uprising of October 6–7; *See* October 10, 1944.

• October 10, 1944: Four additional women involved in smuggling explosives used in the October 6–7 uprising

Oskar Schindler poses with his horse at "Emalia," his enamelware factory. Known for his cosmopolitan tastes and love of luxury, Schindler also recognized the need surrounding him, reaching out in small gestures of humanity to his workers. Leon Leyson, then a boy working in the factory, vividly recalls how Schindler repeatedly intervened to save him and his family, even remembering to order an extra ration of soup for the hungry boy.

The secretarial staff of Oskar Schindler's enamelware factory in Kraków assembles for a group photograph. Intensely loyal to the people who worked for him, Schindler risked his own life to rescue his 300 female workers when they were mistakenly sent on a train to Auschwitz, instead of to safety in Brünnlitz in the Sudetenland, where Schindler had opened his new factory.

This factory at 4 Lipowa Street in Kraków, Poland, provided a refuge for those Jews fortunate enough to work for Oskar Schindler, a Sudeten German and Nazi Party member. Using cheap Jewish labor, Schindler succeeded in making a fortune, but later expended his enormous wealth to protect his laborers from deportation and death. In October 1944, as the Nazis accelerated their destruction of Kraków's Jews, Schindler bribed Nazi authorities to allow him to move his factory and some 1100 workers to safety in Brünnlitz in the Sudetenland.

---

at Auschwitz are arrested, including an inmate named Roza Robota. Fourteen men from the camp's *Sonderkommando* unit also are arrested. The sole surviving conspirator, a Greek Jew named Isaac Venezia, will later die of starvation after Auschwitz inmates are evacuated by their captors to Ebensee, Austria; *See* January 6, 1945.

• October 13, 1944: Soviet troops liberate Riga, Latvia.

• October 14, 1944: In Hungary, the Horthy government promises to release imprisoned Jewish-Palestinian paratroopers; *See* October 15, 1944.

• October 15, 1944: The Hungarian Fascist group Arrow Cross is installed

in power by the Nazis following a request to the Allies by Hungarian leader Admiral Miklós Horthy for armistice terms. A Hungarian Nazi, Ferenc Szálasi, is installed as regent.

• October 16–26, 1944: Germans and members of the Fascist Nyilas group prohibit Jews in Budapest, Hungary, from leaving their homes. Many Jew-

Häftlingsart	Insgesamt	-20	20-30	30-40	40-50	50-60	60-70	70-80
Schutzhäftlinge arisch	11867	3587	4878	3472	1765	146	19	-
Bibelforscher	5	-	1	-	3	1	-	-
Homosexuelle	13	-	1	6	4	2	-	-
aus der Wehrmacht	18	-	14	4	-	-	-	-
Geistliche	7	-	-	3	3	1	-	-
Rotspanier	6	-	1	3	2	-	-	-
Ausl. Zivilarbeiter	1988	444	953	437	152	1	1	-
Juden	3720	508	1258	1334	565	49	6	-
Asoziale	211	29	68	52	41	8	3	-
Berufsverbrecher	342	7	127	103	83	17	5	-
Sich.-Verw.	28	2	9	14	3	-	-	-
Zigeuner	74	3	21	35	14	1	-	-
Kriegsgefangene	207	5	105	97	2	1	-	-
Gesamtstärke	18486	2593	7436	5550	2644	227	34	-

By the fall of 1944 the German situation in Poland was crumbling rapidly, as Soviet forces advanced westward through the country toward Germany. And so the Nazis, who had enjoyed absolute mastery over Poland's residents not long before, now found themselves fighting a defensive war with a foregone conclusion. The horror, of course, is that this turn of events came too late to prevent the extermination of three million of Poland's 3.3 million Jews. Here, Polish fighters armed with submachine guns take aim at Nazi troops at Praga, a Warsaw suburb.

Natzweiler-Struthof was located in the Alsace region of France. Physically notable for stone and slate quarries, as well as subterranean factories built by inmates, Natzweiler was a concentration camp at which prisoners were worked to death. The camp's activities were expansive enough, in fact, to support numerous satellite camps; the whole complex exploited at least 20,000 people. The document seen here was found at Natzweiler in the autumn of 1944. Ledger-style, it subdivides male prisoners by age and type, and shows a complex mix: socialists, priests, criminals, Gypsies, POWs, anarchists, foreign civil workers, Spaniards, Jehovah's Witnesses, homosexuals, soldiers, "Aryans," and, inevitably, Jews.

A Jewish Brigade soldier teaches children Hebrew at the *Rinshonim hachshara* (agricultural training farm) in Bari, Italy, near the Adriatic Sea. The first of the training farms in Italy, Bari and those that followed sought to prepare refugees and survivors for a new future in Palestine. Reaching Italy in November 1944, the soldiers of the Brigade would take part in the final Allied offensive the following spring.

1944

ish slave laborers are killed by Nyilas members on a bridge linking Buda with Pest.

• October 17, 1944: SS functionary Adolf Eichmann returns to Budapest, Hungary, to secure 50,000 healthy Jews, who will be marched to Germany for forced labor; *See* October 20, 1944. • Dr. Josef Mengele super-

vises further gas-chamber selections of inmates at Auschwitz.

• October 18, 1944: Seven hundred Plaszów, Poland, camp deportees are sent from the Gross-Rosen, Germany, camp to Brünnlitz in the Sudetenland. Oskar Schindler, owner of a newly opened munitions factory in Brünnlitz, persuades the SS to give

Women and the Holocaust

The murderers are loose! They search the world

All through the night, oh God, all through the night.

Gertrud Kolmar, a brilliant Jewish writer, included those words in a poem she called "Murder." The exact date of her death in Auschwitz—she was deported from Berlin during the winter of 1943—is unknown, but her cry lives on. Its anguish laments the ruthless murders of millions of women, Jews foremost among them, in the "Final Solution."

German deportation and death lists often included gender identification. Women and men were segregated in concentration and death camps, and early on Jewish women were treated better than Jewish men. However, once World War II began in 1939 and the Final Solution was under way in 1942, Jewish women were increasingly at risk.

German authorities considered elderly Jewish women useless to the war effort. They were therefore sentenced to death by starvation, disease, shooting, or gas. Of more troubling concern were Jewish women of child-bearing age. On one hand, their work for the Third Reich could be productive. On the other, their menace was especially acute because they could produce Jewish children. The Final Solution had to prevent that outcome.

Hundreds of thousands of Jewish women were killed at Treblinka. Hundreds of thousands more were worked to death or gassed at Auschwitz. Still others were subjected to forced labor, brutal medical experiments, and death at Ravensbrück, a concentration camp for women that opened near Fürstenberg, about 50 miles north of Berlin, in May 1939. Designed to hold several thousand prisoners, its population soared to more than 40,000 in 1944.

Women from over 20 countries were among the more than 100,000 who were imprisoned in Ravensbrück at various times. About 13.5 and 5.5 percent of that number were Jews and Gypsies, respectively. Death claimed about 92,000 of the camp's total prisoner population. About 6000 people were gassed in the camp's final months, when the Germans selected Ravensbrück as a destination for prisoners evacuated from camps in the East, as the Red Army forced Germany's retreat. No other concentration camp in Germany had such a high percentage of murdered prisoners.

Holocaust scholar Myrna Goldenberg aptly sums up the situation: The hell may have been the same for women and men during the Holocaust, but the gender-related horrors were different. The last words of her poem "The Woman Poet"—"do you hear me feel?"—suggest that Gertrud Kolmar would agree.

---

him all 700 Jews for use as workers. Schindler also makes arrangements to have 300 Jewish women transferred from Auschwitz to his factory; *See* January 21–29, 1945.

● October 18 or 19, 1944: Gisi Fleischmann, prewar head of the women's Zionist movement in Slovakia, is gassed at Auschwitz.

● October 20, 1944: Nazi administrators at Auschwitz burn documents related to prisoners and their fates.
● Nazis initiate death-march deportations of Jews from Budapest, Hungary, to Germany. ● 22,000 Budapest Jews are entrained for deportation to Auschwitz. ● Six hundred Jewish boys from a group of 650 locked in a barracks at Auschwitz-Birkenau are to be gassed. Many race about the camp, naked and panicked, before being clubbed by the SS guards who pursue them. The 50 survivors are put to work unloading potatoes from railcars. ● Men of the Polish Home Army attack Jewish houses in the freshly liberated village of Ejszyszki. The village's Jews subsequently retaliate against the Poles. ● Nazis put 25,000

Roza Robota

In the annals of Holocaust heroism, Roza Robota holds a special place. An activist in the Zionist underground of Poland, she was deported to Auschwitz in 1942. Her strong spirit was not broken by the horrors of Auschwitz-Birkenau, and she became a link between the women's  camp and the resistance that was forming within the men's camp. Detailed to a factory manufacturing bombs, she and several other brave women began to smuggle out small quantities of gunpowder with which the underground planned to blow up a Birkenau crematorium in October 1944. Caught and questioned, along with three other women working in the factory, Roza refused to divulge any information, even under prolonged torture.

Her execution by hanging before the camp population was intended to extinguish any fires of resistance. Roza left her comrades with a different memory, as she yelled *"Nekama!"* ("Revenge!") just before her death.

Ala Gertner, one of the heroines of the 1944 *Sonderkommando* uprising in Auschwitz-Birkenau, strikes a stylish pose in this photograph from happier days in prewar Bedzin, Poland. Deported with her husband to Auschwitz, she was assigned to work in the Union Munitions factory. There she and two of her fellow workers managed to steal and hide the explosives the *Sonderkommando* used to blow up the crematorium on October 7. Arrested, held in a bunker, and tortured, she died without betraying her accomplices.

Admiral Miklós Horthy led Hungary's authoritarian government during much of the war. Although he was an antisemite, the Germans considered Horthy soft on Jewish issues. For example, he opposed the ghettoization of Hungary's Jews. Finally, when he began armistice overtures to the Soviets in the fall of 1944, the German-backed Arrow Cross movement overthrew his government, establishing a Fascist and viciously antisemitic dictatorship.

1944

Hungarian Jewish men and 10,000 Jewish women to work digging anti-tank trenches in the path of the advancing Red Army.

• October 21, 1944: Aachen, Germany, is captured by U.S. troops. This is the first German city to fall to an Allied army.

• October 23, 1944: In Budapest, Swedish consul Raoul Wallenberg and Swiss consul Carl Lutz continue to issue protective documents to Jews, partly in response to a decree that Jews in Hungary who are of foreign nationalities or those holding foreign passports will be exempt from forced labor.

Among the primary goals of Hungary's new Arrow Cross government was to cooperate with the Germans in their efforts to exterminate Hungary's Jews. Pictured here are the leaders of the Arrow Cross movement at a rally held at the time of the coup that toppled the Horthy government. Note the similarity between the Arrow Cross and Nazi salutes as well as similarly declarative insignia and symbology.

On October 15, 1944, the Hungarian Fascist organization Arrow Cross staged a coup, with German support, against the government of Admiral Miklós Horthy, whom the Arrow Cross branded as "a hireling of the Jews and a traitor to his country." The Nazis supported the new government because of the violent antisemitism of its leadership. This photograph shows the swearing in of Ferenc Szálasi, chief of the Arrow Cross movement, as Hungary's new leader.

After the October 15 coup, the Arrow Cross government gave free rein to the Hungarian people's long-standing hatred of Jews. Here we see Arrow Cross members beating Jews in Budapest's Kalman Tisza's square. A series of violent actions against Budapest's Jewish population characterized the days after the Arrow Cross takeover. The SS and Arrow Cross rounded up thousands of Jews. However, international protests forced the Hungarian government to release the Jews, who escaped (at least temporarily) almost certain death.

• **October 26, 1944:** Munkács, Hungary, is liberated by Soviet troops.

• **October 27, 1944:** Nazis tramping through the Warsaw Ghetto discover a hidden bunker. They kill the seven Jews inside after the Jews open fire.

• **October 28, 1944:** A train from Bolzano, Italy, reaches Auschwitz with 301 prisoners. Of these, 137 are immediately gassed.

• **October 30, 1944:** The final deportation train from Theresienstadt, Czechoslovakia, to Auschwitz arrives at the camp. Of the 2038 prisoners on board, 1689 are immediately gassed.
• The Germans transfer Anne Frank to Bergen-Belsen; *See* March 1945.

• **Late October 1944:** Eighteen-year-old Jehovah's Witness Jonathan Stark is hanged by Nazis at Sachsenhausen, Germany, where he had been interned because of his refusal to swear an oath of loyalty to Hitler.

• **November 1944:** Twelve thousand Jews from Stutthof, Germany, including 4000 women, undertake a forced

Raoul Wallenberg

The determined, energetic efforts of young Swedish diplomat Raoul Wallenberg saved thousands of Hungarian Jews from certain death in the gas chambers of Auschwitz.

Sent to Budapest by the Swedish Foreign Ministry, Wallenberg worked to save the city's remaining 200,000 Jews from planned deportations in July 1944. He issued thousands of special Swedish Embassy-stamped "protective passports" to Hungarian Jews. Armed with funds supplied by the War Refugee Board, Wallenberg also bought property in Budapest, which he turned into "safe houses" for those

rescued from transports. In organizing a network of hundreds of young Jewish agents, he managed the distribution of food and medicine to Jews taking refuge in those shelters.

Using bluff and diplomatic credentials, Wallenberg even pressured the SS into turning over to him some prisoners already on board deportation trains. As Adolf Eichmann initiated the death marches of thousands of Jews toward the Austrian border, Wallenberg pursued the departing columns, winning the release of many of those in possession of the Swedish passports. In early 1945, as the Soviet Army neared Budapest, he dissuaded the SS commander from carrying out an ordered massacre of Jews still in the city.

After Budapest's liberation, Wallenberg disappeared, presumably arrested by the Soviets on espionage charges. His fate remains a mystery.

Head bowed in defeat, the commander of the German garrison in Aachen, Germany, Colonel Gerhard Wilck, accompanied by three of his officers, sits in a U.S. Army jeep after his capture. Although months of fighting, including the Battle of the Bulge, lay ahead, the German defeat now appeared to be only a matter of time as the Western Allies pushed toward the Rhine and the Soviets moved into East Prussia. With the capture of Aachen on October 21, American troops stood for the first time on German soil.

Chaim Weizmann makes an address in Tel Aviv, Palestine, to an audience of Jewish Brigade volunteers. Weizmann was the leader of the World Zionist Organization, the goal of which was to encourage Jews to emigrate to Palestine and establish a Jewish state there. Having fled antisemitism in both Russia and Germany, where he had been a chemistry professor, Weizmann became the first president of the state of Israel, in February 1949.

1944

death march southwest into Germany. Hundreds are killed or die of exhaustion along the 500-plus-mile route.
• The final 400 slave laborers in Piotrków, Poland, are force-marched to Bergen-Belsen, Germany; Buchenwald, Germany; Mauthausen, Austria; and other concentration camps.
• Jewish parachutists recruited by the British in Palestine are dropped

behind German lines. • A non-Jewish Polish physician, Stanislaw Switala, shelters seven former leaders of the Jewish Fighting Organization, including Yitzhak Zuckerman and Tuvia Borzykowski, in his hospital. • The Hungarian government agrees to establish an international Jewish ghetto in Budapest, where Jews in 72 buildings will be protected under

This photograph, snapped from Raoul Wallenberg's automobile, shows a group of Budapest Jews rescued from deportation to a death camp. When they arrived at the train station for their fateful journey, the Jews were given *Schutzpassen* by Wallenberg's Swedish diplomatic delegation. Here, they return to the international ghetto in Budapest, populated by non-Hungarian Jews.

Eliyahu Dobkin, a member of the Jewish Agency Executive, towers over his young charges as they prepare to sail from Lisbon, Portugal, to Palestine aboard the Portuguese ship *Guine*. Smuggled out of France by the French underground, these children had already survived enormous peril. In spite of overwhelming obstacles, the Jewish Agency Executive managed to secure ships and bring more than 3500 refugees to Palestine by the end of 1944.

Jews assemble on the platform of Budapest's *Jósefváros* station. Raoul Wallenberg can be seen on the right, with his hands behind his back. These Jews are being issued Swedish *Schutzpassen*, which will save them from deportation. Many were saved, but many more were not. Even holders of passes issued by Wallenberg and other "neutral" diplomats were not necessarily safe, as Arrow Cross thugs honored or ignored the paperwork as the mood struck them.

Swiss authority; *See* December 31, 1944.

• November 3, 1944: A trainload of Jews from the labor camp at Sered, Slovakia, arrives at Auschwitz. Because the camp's gas chambers are being dismantled, the 990 Jews on board are sent to work or to barracks rather than to their deaths.

• November 4, 1944: Szolnok, Hungary, is liberated by Soviet troops.
• After being forced to dig their own graves, hundreds of Jews from the copper-mine labor camp at Bor, Hungary, are shot or beaten to death at Györ, Hungary. Among the victims is a noted poet named Miklós Radnóti, age 35.

• November 6, 1944: Hungary's Arrow Cross murders 19 Jews in Budapest and drives close to 30,000 toward the old Austrian border.

• November 7, 1944: Zionist poet Hannah Szenes is executed by the Arrow Cross in Budapest, Hungary, after parachuting into the country on a resistance mission for the British.

Raphael Lemkin

Polish jurist Raphael Lemkin coined the term "genocide" to describe the Nazis' systematic extermination of European Jewry. The word first appeared in his 1944 publication *Axis Rule in Occupied Europe, Laws of Occupation-Analysis of Government, Proposals for Redress*.

Lemkin was born into a Jewish family in rural Eastern Galicia and educated at the University of Lvov. After Hitler came to power, Lemkin's interest in crimes of mass murder and the persecution of minorities increased. He compiled his pathbreaking analysis of Nazi racial legislation while living in Sweden. He published it in 1944 after he arrived in the United States via a circuitous route that took him through Sweden, the USSR, Japan, and Canada.

After the war, Lemkin helped the United States prosecute Nazi war criminals at Nuremberg and other war-crimes trials.

As assistant secretary of war, John J. McCloy was a crucial voice in setting U.S. military priorities. McCloy was repeatedly asked by the War Refugee Board, the Emergency Committee to Save the Jewish People of Europe, and other groups to order the bombing of the railroad lines leading to Auschwitz and the gas chambers in the camp. McCloy refused the request, claiming erroneously that the target was outside the range of U.S. and British bombers.

Using his diplomatic status as a weapon for good, Carl Lutz intervened to save the lives of thousands of Jews in Budapest, Hungary, from 1942 to 1945. As Swiss consul responsible for granting visas, he issued some 50,000 Swiss passports, placing Jews under the protection of the Swiss government. Risking assassination at the hands of the SS, Lutz labored to save as many lives as possible in the last months of the war. He eventually attached himself to the November 1944 death march of 70,000 Jews, saving some by granting them Salvadorean certificates of citizenship.

1944

• **November 8, 1944: Germans initiate a death march of Jews from Budapest to the Austrian border. Raoul Wallenberg's intervention saves tens of thousands of Jews.** • **The Stern Gang resistance group assassinates Lord Walter Moyne, Britain's minister of state in the Middle East.** • **John W. Pehle, head of the War Refugee Board who has delayed for months a** request that Auschwitz be bombed, changes his mind. He argues that bombing would destroy the gas chambers as well as German factories and soldiers in the area, encourage resistance, and free prisoners. Assistant Secretary of War John J. McCloy rejects Pehle's reasoning, erroneously arguing that bombing Auschwitz will hinder the war effort.

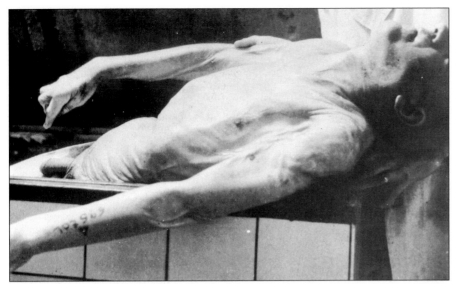

At the Strasbourg University Institute of Anatomy in France, Dr. August Hirt led a special program to display 86 Jewish skeletons for "educational" purposes. The Jews had been specially chosen at Auschwitz and shipped to Struthof, France, to be gassed. Their corpses were immersed in vats of alcohol for more than a year before Hirt's group had the opportunity to strip the flesh from the bones. Directors of the institute attempted at the last minute to destroy the evidence, but the Allies arrived too quickly.

A child at the Neuengamme concentration camp raises her arm to show the scar following the removal of her lymph nodes, part of a Nazi experiment to gauge the effects of tuberculosis on the immune system. Most inmates at Neuengamme, located near Hamburg, Germany, labored in armaments manufacture. A few, about 100 adults and 20 children sent from Auschwitz, were chosen to participate in medical experiments. On the orders of Dr. Kurt Heissmeyer, the children were infected with tuberculosis. When Germany's impending defeat became obvious, most were killed so they could not testify to the horrors they had experienced.

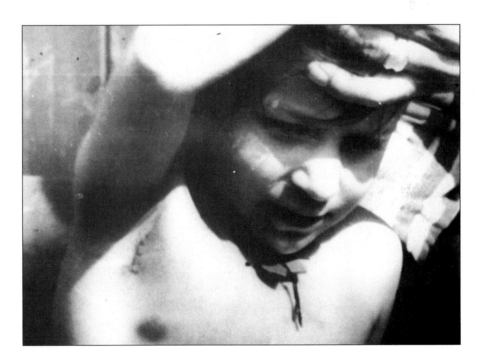

• **November 14, 1944: Catholic labor leader and Resistance member Bernhard Letterhaus is hanged by the Germans.**

• **November 18, 1944: Jewish-Palestinian paratrooper Enzo Sereni is executed by Germans at Dachau, Germany.**

• **November 20, 1944: Jewish-Palestinian paratroopers Haviva Reik, Rafael Reiss, and Zvi Ben-Yaakov are executed in Czechoslovakia.**

• **November 21, 1944: Saarburg, Germany, is taken by Allied troops.**

• **November 22, 1944: Protectors of Jews in Budapest, Hungary, meet** with Swedish diplomat Raoul Wallenberg at the city's Swedish legation; *See* November 23–27, 1944. • **Mulhouse, France, is liberated by Allied troops.**

• **November 23–27, 1944: Swiss consulate officials Leopold Breszlauer and Ladislaus Kluger issue about 300 protective documents to Hungarian**

Since so many Germans were at the front or had been killed in the war, the Nazis increasingly relied on slave labor for production. This was the case, as this photograph indicates, in even high-tech operations. These prisoners, at the underground weapons plant at the Dora-Mittelbau complex near Nordhausen, Germany, perform highly complex work that would go into the construction of the V–2 terror rocket.

The Germans became increasingly desperate as it became clear to them that their war was lost. Germany's leaders placed a great deal of faith in newly conceived "Vengeance" weapons that they believed would turn the tide of the war. These photos picture the infamous V–2 rocket, designed to wreak havoc on London. While hundreds of V–1s and V–2s rained down upon London late in the war, they had little military effect; still, the rockets unnerved many Britons and killed about 5500.

1944

Jews gathered at the Hungarian-Austrian border.

● November 25, 1944: A prisoner demolition of Auschwitz's crematorium II begins. Pipes and ventilation motors are separated and sent to camps at Mauthausen, Austria, and Gross-Rosen, Germany.

● November 27, 1944: "The Trial and Punishment of European War Criminals," a report by U.S. Secretary of War Henry Stimson and Secretary of State Cordell Hull, is submitted to President Franklin Roosevelt.

● December 1944: After three months' work at Lieberose, Germany, Nazis suspend slave labor on a vaca-

As this picture shows, the Nazis developed an elaborate system for disposal of the bodies of their victims. This American soldier and a member of the French Resistance inspect the crematorium at the liberated camp at Natzweiler-Struthof, France, on December 2, 1944. Notice the tongs, which were used to manipulate the corpses as they were placed in the ovens.

Dora-Mittelbau/Nordhausen

Constructed as a subcamp of the Buchenwald concentration camp, Dora-Mittelbau, located near the town of Nordhausen in eastern Germany, became an independent camp in the fall of 1944. Beginning in 1943, thousands of prisoners were assigned to Dora to expand the tunnels of an old salt mine buried deep in the Harz Mountains. They built an underground factory that produced the secret V–1 and V–2 rockets. Human life meant nothing in the Nazis' quest to turn the tide of war and avoid defeat.

Even by concentration-camp standards, prisoners in Dora were treated brutally by their captors. They spent their lives with no glimpse of the sun and with no sanitary facilities, laboring until they dropped. Bodies, covered in lice and often weighing only 80 pounds, were returned to Buchenwald for burning at the rate of about 1000 a month.

Once completed, the factory that manufactured the rockets—the state-owned *Mittelwerk GmbH*—used thousands of prisoners as laborers, including many Jews. They too labored under dismal conditions, drinking their water from leaks in the pipes. Fear of sabotage provided the pretext for guards to employ extraordinary sadism, hanging prisoners or torturing them on a whim. Untold thousands died at Dora and on death marches from the camp in the closing days of the war.

Even after a body is cremated, ashes remain. This presented a problem for the perpetrators of the Holocaust, especially when one considers the sheer number of their victims. Pictured here is a member of the French Resistance, who inspects some of the urns that the Nazis used to bury their victims' ashes in the Natzweiler-Struthof camp.

tion complex for German officers. They instead evacuate the Jewish workers 100 miles on foot northwest to the concentration camp at Sachsenhausen, Germany. Of 3500 who begin the march, only 900 arrive at the destination. Several hundred sick inmates who are unable to begin the march are shot in their beds. • Liberated France has a "Week of the

Absent" to commemorate innocents still in the hands of the Nazis. • American pollster Elmo Roper warns that antisemitism has infected the U.S., most strongly in and around cities.

• December 11, 1944: Jewish slave laborers at Auschwitz III (Monowitz-Buna) quietly celebrate Chanukah.

• December 16, 1944: Along a 40-mile front in Luxembourg's Ardennes Forest, 300,000 German troops comprising the Fifth and Sixth Panzer armies launch a surprise offensive against the American First and Ninth armies. Inexperienced, front-line American troops are overwhelmed as the Germans gamble everything in a bid to seize the strategic port of

The Jewish Brigade

The Jewish Brigade was a British Army regiment comprised exclusively of Jewish volunteers from Palestine. Officially established in September 1944, the group fought in the Italian Theater of the war and later assisted illegal Jewish-immigration efforts to Palestine.

The forerunner of the Jewish Brigade, the Palestine Regiment, was created in August 1942. It consisted of four battalions: three Jewish and one Arab. Pressure exerted by the World Zionist Organization, as well as support from Winston Churchill and Franklin Roosevelt, resulted in the creation of the independent Jewish Brigade. Led by Brigadier Ernest Benjamin, the brigade employed the Zionist flag as its standard. Five thousand Palestinian Jews served in the brigade.

The idea of creating a Jewish regiment was initially dismissed by the British for fear of antagonizing the Arab populace in Palestine. Wartime contingencies, however, compelled the British government and military establishment to change their minds.

This American GI, among those who liberated the Natzweiler-Struthof camp, inspects the markings on a prisoner's clothing. The letters "NN" stand for *Nacht und Nebel* (night and fog). The Night and Fog decree, issued by Hitler on December 2, 1941, was intended for use against sabotage organizations and those guilty of espionage. They were to be executed upon capture or, if that did not prove practicable, deported to the Reich for trial. Most such prisoners were first sent to Natzweiler.

Still in civilian dress, a group of recruits joins the Jewish Brigade at Meir Park in Tel Aviv, Palestine. Wearing armbands designating them as "volunteers," they seek to join Jewish forces already sent from Palestine a month earlier to fight in the Italian campaign. Some members of the *Armée Juive*, the Jewish Resistance in France, had already fled across the Pyrenees to Spain the previous year, intent on making their way to Palestine to continue the fight for freedom.

1944

Antwerp, Belgium. Because of early German gains that create a bulging salient in the American lines, the action comes to be known as the "Battle of the Bulge"; *See* December 26, 1944.

• December 17, 1944: Eighty-six American prisoners of war are murdered by SS troops at Malmédy, Belgium.

• Winter 1944: Hundreds of ill and starving Jewish women die slowly in segregated tents at the Stutthof, Germany, concentration camp. • In France, a clandestine collaborationist agency, *Organisation Technique* (Technical Service), is established.

• December 26, 1944: The Germans' last-ditch offensive of the war, insti-

These signs pointing toward Malmédy and Saint-Vith, Belgium, testify to another barbaric episode in the war. In a last desperate ploy to avoid defeat, Hitler sent as many men and tanks as he could muster against the Western Allies in the Ardennes in mid-December. Near Saint-Vith, the Sixth SS Panzer Army encountered fierce American resistance, which halted its progress. In frustration and in blatant violation of the rules of war, soldiers in the First Panzer Division at Malmédy turned their guns on the Americans they had captured, killing 86.

Hands lifted in surrender, American soldiers march before their German captors. The last great German offensive of the war was designed to split in two the Allied armies on the Western Front. Helped by foggy weather, which kept American and British planes grounded, the Germans were initially successful. But their advance ended when reinforcements arrived for the Allies and planes could resume their bombing of German supply lines.

Bodies of German soldiers lie strewn over the battlefield of Bastogne, Belgium, the site of one of the fiercest confrontations of the Battle of the Bulge. Reinforced by paratroopers, the Allied forces refused to surrender even though they were encircled and outnumbered. When the clouds lifted, Allied planes dropped supplies, and Bastogne was relieved the day after Christmas.

gated against American troops at Luxembourg's Ardennes Forest on December 16, stalls following ten days of impressive gains. The offensive's ultimate goal, the seizure of Antwerp, Belgium, is not achieved. Nearly a quarter of a million German troops have been killed, wounded, or captured, and more than 1400 German tanks and heavy assault guns have been lost. From this point, Germany's war will be strictly defensive.

• December 28, 1944: Members of Hungary's Arrow Cross abduct 28 Jews in a Budapest hospital. They will murder them two days later.

• December 31, 1944: Hungarian Arrow Cross members storm a Swiss-sponsored "safe house" in Budapest and attack residents with machine guns and hand grenades. Three Jews are killed but the rest are saved by a Hungarian military unit; *See* January 11–14, 1945.

• 1944–47: Civil war in the increasingly Sovietized Poland incidentally kills thousands of Jews.

1945

NEITHER Adolf Hitler nor Franklin Roosevelt lived to see the end of World War II and the Holocaust. On May 7, 1945, at Rheims, France, General Alfred Jodl signed Nazi Germany's unconditional surrender. One week earlier, on April 30, the *Führer* and Eva Braun—whom Hitler had married the night before—committed suicide in his Berlin bunker. On April 12, less than three weeks before Hitler's death, a brain hemorrhage had taken the American president's life.

The Nazis had begun evacuating Jewish prisoners from Auschwitz on January 17, partly to cover evidence of the "Final Solution," partly to preserve slave labor, and also to prolong the policies of mass death. Without food or shelter during the bitter winter, some 60,000 Jews were force-marched toward concentration camps in the German interior. The death rates were immense. Once the prisoners reached camps such as Buchenwald or Bergen-Belsen, hopeless conditions awaited them.

While advancing Soviet forces reached Nazi camps in Eastern Europe—including Stutthof, Gross-Rosen, and Sachsenhausen—American and British troops came upon other concentration camps. On April 4, 1945, Ohrdruf, a Buchenwald satellite, became the first camp liberated by American troops. On April 12, the day that President Roosevelt died, American Generals Omar Bradley, George Patton, and Dwight Eisenhower saw Ohrdruf themselves. Eisenhower wrote that the scenes of brutality and starvation "beggar description." Ohrdruf was not the worst of the Nazi camps. American and British liberators encountered greater devastation on April 9 at Dora-Mittelbau and its satellite camps, where thousands of prisoners had slaved in unbearable underground conditions to manufacture V–2 missiles.

On April 11 American forces freed Buchenwald. One of the oldest concentration camps in the Nazi system, it held more than 238,000 prisoners during its eight-year existence, 43,000 of whom died or were killed. Four days later British troops liberated Bergen-Belsen, where they found 13,000 corpses and 58,000 prisoners—mostly Jews—still alive but in critical condition. Unable to recover from the abuse they had received, about 10,000 inmates perished in the next few weeks.

On May 5 American troops reached the Mauthausen concentration camp in Austria. Operational for seven years, Mauthausen had contained a total of nearly 200,000 prisoners. Few were alive at Mauthausen at liberation.

Two liberated Dachau prisoners stand over a camp guard named Weiss, who is reduced to helplessness without his weapons of punishment.

579

1945

The camp's death toll was 119,000. On May 8 the Allies celebrated V-E Day (Victory in Europe Day)—the war in Europe was officially over. That same day, Soviet troops liberated the camp/ghetto at Theresienstadt, Czechoslovakia, and found 19,000 prisoners alive. Another 121,000 had died.

On May 2 Roosevelt's successor, President Harry S. Truman, signed Executive Order 9547, appointing Justice Robert H. Jackson of the U.S. Supreme Court as chief U.S. counsel to the United Nations War Crimes Commission (UNWCC). The American, British, and Soviet governments had established the UNWCC on October 20, 1942, to ensure that Nazi war criminals would be brought to justice once the war ended. Truman's order also made Jackson the chief U.S. prosecutor at the planned international war-crimes trial, which opened officially at Nuremberg, Germany, on November 20.

On April 25, 1945, members of the U.S. First Army's 69th Infantry Division *(left)* and advance units of the Red Army's 58th Guards Division met at Torgau, Germany, on the Elbe River. The historic linkup cut Nazi Germany in two.

The war's devastation included an estimated 11 million people who remained uprooted from their home countries. Among them were former German prisoners of war, released slave laborers, and concentration-camp survivors (a large number of whom were Jewish). Confronting the immense task of helping these needy people, the Allies classified the refugees as "displaced persons" (DPs) and made the United Nations Relief and Rehabilitation Administration (UNRRA) responsible for them. At first, the UNRRA lacked sufficient personnel for this task, so much of the work involved in aiding the DPs fell to Allied military units.

In the spring of 1945, about seven million DPs were in Occupied Germany. Gradually most went home, but more than a million were unwilling or unable to return to their native lands. They included about 50,000 Jews, as well as hundreds of Roma and Sinti (Gypsies) recently liberated from the concentration camps. Some non-Jews feared retaliation for their Nazi collaboration. Others feared persecution by Communist states.

Jewish Holocaust survivors typically faced different dilemmas, as they could not return to their former homes because those homes no longer existed. The few Eastern European Jews who went home often experienced renewed antisemitism and found their property in the unfriendly hands of former neighbors.

Liberation left the Jewish survivors less than free. Most were in poor health and plagued by horrific memories and nightmares. Jews found some relatives and friends alive, but more often they were struck with the news that loved ones had perished.

Most Jews who wanted to escape postwar Europe completely in 1945 were not able to. Britain allowed merely a trickle of legal Jewish immigration to Palestine; illegal immigration was vigorously checked. Jewish refugees hoping to reach other countries, including the United States, usually found restrictions rather than open doors. In 1945 most Jewish Holocaust survivors had little choice but to stay in the hundreds of DP camps, which had been quickly established at such sites as former German Army barracks, prisoner-of-war camps, and even concentration camps such as Bergen-Belsen and Dachau.

As the months passed, the American Jewish Joint Distribution Committee (JDC), the Organization for Rehabilitation through Training (ORT), and other Jewish relief agencies began work to improve living conditions and to provide education and occupational training for the Jewish survivors in the DP camps. In spite of extremely difficult physical and psychological conditions, Jewish life began to renew itself. Survivors married and new families formed.

Nevertheless, the DP camps were never healthy places. On June 22, 1945, after receiving reports about the poor conditions in these camps, President Truman appointed Earl G. Harrison, dean of the University of Pennsylvania Law School, to head an investigative commission, underscoring that Harrison should pay specific attention to the circumstances of Jewish DPs. During July 1945 Harrison's delegation visited more than 30 DP camps. His report to Truman contained a grim evaluation: "Beyond knowing that they are no longer in danger of the gas chambers, torture and other forms of violent death," he wrote, the Jewish DPs could see so little change in their situations that they were left to "wonder and frequently ask what 'liberation' means."

Harrison's report increased pressure to admit Jews to Palestine. On December 22 President Truman authorized that DPs of "all faiths, creeds and nationalities" in the U.S. occupation zones be allowed into the United States (albeit within quota limits). The DP camps gradually improved as well, but during much of 1945 their conditions fitted Harrison's description. Barbed wire enclosed some of the DP camps. Food was meager, movement restricted, quarters overcrowded, and sanitation inadequate. Housed with non-Jewish DPs, including at times Nazi collaborators and former enemy prisoners, the "liberated" Jews were still targets of antisemitic outbursts. Not until late 1945 did some DP camps become specifically Jewish camps, where the needs of the Jewish survivors could be better served.

"As matters now stand," Harrison stated in his DP camp report during the summer of 1945, the Allies "appear to be treating the Jews as the Nazis treated them, except that we do not exterminate them." Harrison's harsh assessment was overstated, of course. Until Germany surrendered, the Nazis continued to torture and destroy Jews and loot their property in the process.

More than 35 million people, civilian and military, lost their lives in the European Theater of World War II. The dead included nearly six million Jews and millions from other populations—Gypsies, Poles, Soviets, Slavs, Jehovah's Witnesses, homosexuals, mentally handicapped—singled out for Holocaust-related persecution and murder.

The chaos at the end of World War II makes it impossible to state exactly how many Jews were liberated from the Nazi concentration camps. But by the early 1950s, some 250,000 Jewish survivors of the Holocaust had lived in the Allies' postwar DP camps while waiting to emigrate. Eventually, they found new homes: 142,000 went to Israel, 72,000 to the United States, 16,000 to Canada, 8000 to Belgium, 2000 to France, 1000 to Britain, and about 10,000 to Latin America and elsewhere.

Three Ebensee, Austria, survivors suck on sugar cubes, hoping to gain enough organic strength to eat solid food.

Children celebrate Chanukah at the displaced-persons camp in Zeilsheim, Germany.

581

An American GI stands guard over Germans captured in the Ardennes offensive. Although the German counteroffensive, led by eight panzer divisions, caught the Allies by surprise and scored some initial success, it came to a rapid halt under improved weather and combined pressure from British and American forces. By January 1945 the Germans began their retreat into the Reich, bringing any hope of victory to an end.

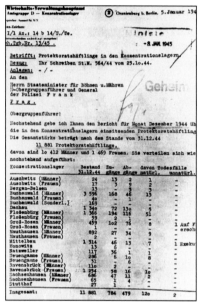

This January 1945 report lists the total number of prisoners, originally from the Protectorate of Bohemia and Moravia, held in a variety of Nazi camps. The report was prepared under the aegis of Karl Hermann Frank, who succeeded Reinhard Heydrich as *Reichsprotektor* of Bohemia and Moravia. Frank was captured by the Americans after the war and was extradited to Czechoslovakia. He was tried and executed in 1946.

Red Army Commander Georgi K. Zhukov *(right)* discusses the upcoming Soviet assault against Berlin. The Red drive on the German capital was the culmination of what Hitler's advisers had feared most: a two-front war. Now, on the eve of the final Allied push, American and British forces closed on Germany from the west; the Soviets from the east. Although General George Patton and some others on the American general staff prodded General Dwight Eisenhower to race to beat the Soviets to Berlin, Eisenhower correctly reasoned that to do so would gain the U.S. nothing politically and that, more significantly, an American assault on the city would mean the deaths of thousands of GIs. Patton was thus ordered to halt at the Elbe River, allowing the Soviets their much-anticipated—and costly—revenge.

1945

• **1945: German Admiral Wilhelm Canaris is executed by the Nazis after being implicated in anti-Nazi resistance. • Richard Glücks, inspector of concentration camps, dies, probably by his own hand. • Italy grants citizenship to Jews.**

• **Early 1945: Ottó Komoly, a Hungarian Jew who has protected about 5000**

Jewish children in rented buildings since September 1944, is murdered by Hungary's Arrow Cross. • German-Jewish poetess Hilde Monte is shot and killed by SS border guards while attempting to enter Germany from Switzerland.

• **January 1945: The overcrowding of slave-labor camp evacuees inside**

Soviet troops march through the ruins of Warsaw in January 1945. Little survived of Jewish Warsaw, and few survived to rebuild what had once been a flourishing Jewish community. From the rubble, some Jews emerged from hiding, their joy mixed with anguish over the loss of so many loved ones.

By the time Czestochowa, Poland, was liberated by the Red Army in January 1945, what was once a thickly populated ghetto had been nearly eradicated by fleeing Nazis. Not long before this January photo of Soviet soldiers posing with a few of the town's 5000 Jewish survivors, many Jews in the area had perished from a typhus epidemic, been shipped to their deaths at Buchenwald and Ravensbrück, or been sent as slaves to HASAG Pelzery, a nearby munitions factory.

Zivia Lubetkin

A true heroine of the Resistance, Zivia Lubetkin fought valiantly in the Warsaw Ghetto revolt. Only after the Germans set the ghetto afire in May 1943 did she flee through the sewers to the "Aryan" side of Warsaw, having fulfilled her vow to remain to the end.

An activist in the Zionist youth movement before the war, Lubetkin represented  the *Dror He-Halutz* party in the Antifascist Bloc, formed in 1942 to battle the Nazis and support the Soviet Army. The next year she joined with Yitzhak Zuckerman, whom she would marry after the war, and others to found the *Zydowska Organizacja Bojowa* (ZOB; Jewish Fighting Organization). Hidden by a physician after the fall of the ghetto, Lubetkin witnessed the relief that accompanied the arrival of Soviet forces on January 17, 1945. She recounts that she and her comrades nevertheless remained "crushed and dejected," knowing that few Jews had lived to witness this day.

Germany becomes critical. Five thousand Jews from the Skarzysko Kamienna slave-labor camp are evacuated westward. Camps near Danzig and Königsberg are evacuated. • Helmuth James Graf von Moltke, an anti-Nazi Resistance leader and former legal advisor to the German High Command, is executed at the Plötzensee Prison in Berlin. • The Central Reg-

istry of War Criminals and Security Suspects (CROWCASS), an inter-Allied investigative group, is created by the Supreme Headquarters, Allied Expeditionary Force (SHAEF). Its mission is to identify and prosecute Nazi war criminals.

• January–March 1945: 2163 Spanish Republicans, who had fought against

Nazi-backed forces during the Spanish Civil War, are worked to death or murdered outright at stone quarries at the Mauthausen, Austria, labor camp.

• January 1–16, 1945: The leading edge of the German Ardennes offensive is halted by the Allies, ending the so-called Battle of the Bulge, the last great German offensive of the war.

In January 1945 the Red Army liberated the deadliest of the Third Reich's death camps, Auschwitz-Birkenau, where an estimated 1.1 million had died, most of them in the camp's gas chambers. These children were among the few who survived imprisonment in Birkenau.

A Red Army soldier films a destroyed crematorium at Auschwitz. The dismantling of crematoria at Birkenau happened in phases. Crematorium IV was destroyed in the *Sonderkommando* uprising of October 7, 1944, while rebellious Jews demolished II on November 25. The remants of II, III and the still operational V were blown up by the Nazis in late January 1945.

I sit with my dolls by the stove and dream.
I dream that my father came back.
I dream that my father is still alive.
How good it is to have a father.
I do not know where my father is.

—*Anonymous*, A Treasury of Jewish Poetry

1945

• **January 4, 1945:** Fritz Elsas, the Jewish mayor of Berlin until his arrest for alleged resistance activities in 1933, is executed at Sachsenhausen, Germany, after 12 years of imprisonment.

• **January 6, 1945:** Roza Robota and three other Jewish women implicated in the smuggling of explosives used in

the October 7, 1944, uprising at Auschwitz are hanged. • Hungarian authorities accede to Raoul Wallenberg's request that 5000 Jews be transferred to Swiss-sponsored safe homes in Budapest. • Anne Frank's mother, Edith, dies at Auschwitz.

• **January 11–14, 1945:** Hungarian Fascist Nyilas thugs enter "protected"

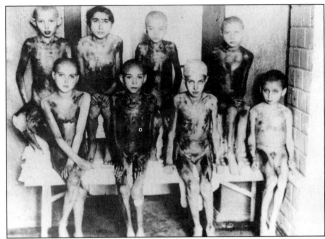

The Soviets, who had seen much suffering during the course of the war, were nonetheless horrified by what they discovered at Auschwitz. These Red Army troops stand among the tens of thousands of pairs of shoes confiscated from the victims of the camp.

These children, liberated from Auschwitz by the Soviet Army, had been subjected to savage "medical" experiments that they were fortunate to survive. Auschwitz doctor Horst Schumann sterilized men, women, and children by exposing them to extreme doses of radiation. He burned most of them so badly that they were deemed unfit for work and sent to the gas chambers. It is uncertain precisely what experiments these children underwent.

These children at Auschwitz, liberated by the Soviet Army on January 27, 1945, show their tattooed arms to the photographer. Everyone imprisoned in Auschwitz had his or her arm tattooed with an identification number. This served two purposes. First, it allowed camp officials to keep track of the thousands of prisoners in the camp. Second, making the inmates into nameless units served to dehumanize them, both crushing the spirit of the prisoners and making it easier for their guards to avoid facing the humanity of their charges.

Jewish houses throughout Budapest, murdering dozens of residents. The bodies of many are hurled into the Danube River. Elsewhere in Budapest, Nyilas members surround the Jewish Orthodox Hospital. They torture 92 patients, doctors, and nurses, killing everyone except a single nurse.

• January 12, 1945: Anti-Nazi German nurse Gertrud Seele is executed at the Plötzensee Prison in Berlin.

• January 12–14, 1945: A Soviet breakthrough is achieved on the Vistula River.

• January 14, 1945: The SS evacuates the remaining prisoners from the concentration camp at Plaszów, Poland.

• January 15, 1945: The concentration camp at Plaszów, Poland, is liberated by the Red Army. • 152 Jewish women at the Brodnica labor camp near Stutthof, Poland, are murdered by their overseers. A few escape.

Death Marches

By the summer of 1944, the Allies were closing in on the Third Reich, which still held 750,000 persons in its huge but increasingly vulnerable concentration-camp network. Fierce fighting would continue until Germany's surrender in May 1945. But in early November 1944, deteriorating military circumstances led the Nazis to stop gassing operations at Auschwitz-Birkenau and attempt to cover up the mass murder they had committed there. As for the prisoners who remained in the concentration camps, the Nazis knew that this labor source—and also the devastating testimony these men and women could deliver—would fall into the Allies' hands if the prisoners were not evacuated.

Earlier the Nazis had transported Jews and other prisoners in trucks and railroad cars, but forced marches also took place throughout the war. Especially during 1944 and 1945, with other forms of transport scarcer than ever, the Nazis ordered marches over long distances to keep concentration-camp prisoners beyond the Allies' reach and to relocate them for labor purposes. As the weeks and months passed, these *Todesmärsche* (death marches) became increasingly brutal, deadly, and senseless. Starved, ill, wounded, and exposed to bitter winter weather, the tormented marching prisoners were kept under guard, shot if they faltered, or left to die where they lay if felled by exhaustion. In the war's final months, when it was clear that Hitler's Germany was doomed, the Nazis continued to march the hapless prisoners aimlessly and mercilessly from one place to another.

Beginning in mid-January 1945, as the Soviet Army liberated Warsaw and Kraków, Poland, about 66,000 prisoners were evacuated on foot from Auschwitz. More than 15,000 died on the way to Gleiwitz and Wlodzislaw, Poland, where those who remained alive were jammed onto uncovered railroad cars. Without food or water, many

more perished during the long and frigid journey that took the prisoners west to such concentration camps as Sachsenhausen, Gross-Rosen, Dachau, Buchenwald, and Mauthausen.

In late January 1945, another 50,000 Jews were evacuated on foot from the Stutthof camp system, which was situated along the Baltic Sea near Danzig. About 5000 of them trudged to the Baltic shore, where they were forced into the water and shot. The remainder headed for Lauenburg in eastern Germany; but when advancing Soviet units cut off the route, the prisoners were marched back to Stutthof. By late April 1945 Soviet ground forces surrounded Stutthof. Once again the prisoners were marched to the sea, where hundreds more were shot. Sea evacuation sent about 4000 prisoners to Germany, though many drowned on the way. About 25,000 prisoners died during the Stutthof death marches.

All told, between 250,000 and 375,000 prisoners, most of them Jewish, perished during the death marches ordered by Nazi Germany during the throes of its defeat.

1945

• January 16, 1945: Soviet troops enter Czestochowa, Poland, shortly after the last slave laborers have been evacuated.

• January 17, 1945: The Red Army enters Warsaw, Poland, as well as Pest, Hungary. • Final roll call is taken at Auschwitz: 11,102 Jews remain at Birkenau; 10,381 women in the Birkenau women's camp; 10,030 at the Auschwitz main camp; 10,233 at the Monowitz satellite camp; and about 22,800 in the remaining factories in the surrounding region; *See* January 18–March 1945.
• In Budapest, 119,000 Jews are freed by Soviet troops. • The Soviets arrest Raoul Wallenberg, whom they cynically suspect is using his humanitar-

As Allied troops approached the Klooga, Estonia, concentration camp in January 1945, guards hurriedly murdered Soviet men, women, and children interned there, and carefully arranged the corpses on pyres that the victims themselves had been forced to construct. Note the alternating arrangement of bodies and logs, for maximum burn effect.

The final meeting of the "Big Three," Winston Churchill, Franklin Roosevelt, and Joseph Stalin, took place at Yalta, Ukraine, in February 1945. At this conference the three Allied powers made plans regarding the composition of postwar Europe, including finalizing arrangements for the occupation of postwar Germany. The Soviet Union also agreed to enter the war against Japan once the conflict in Europe was over.

The Soviets liberated Budapest, Hungary, in January and February 1945. Upon arrival, the Red Army discovered thousands of Jews who had been murdered by the Nazis. Although it became quite common for the Allied armies to uncover grisly evidence of the crimes committed by the Germans, even the most battle-hardened soldiers could not view such scenes impassively.

A Star of David marks a safe house on *Kossuth Platz* in Budapest, Hungary. In the last months of the war, diplomats—especially the Swedes and the Swiss—sought to protect as many Jews as possible from the rampant violence unleashed by the Arrow Cross, the Hungarian Fascists. When the city fell to the Soviets early in 1945, some 120,000 Jews survived to be liberated, among them 25,000 in safe houses.

These four French women were accused of collaborating with the Germans while France was occupied during the war. After the war, revenge was exacted upon female collaborators through such acts of public humiliation as shaving their heads and undressing them. Male collaborators were often treated even more harshly—sentenced to prison or executed. Yet many important collaborators escaped punishment for years, being protected by influential French government and Catholic Church officials.

Allied troops moving eastward knew that the Rhine River was the last great natural barrier to Germany's heartland. The U.S. Ninth Armored Division crossed the river at a bridge the Germans had left intact, at Remagen, on March 7, 1945, inflicting upon Germany a crushing strategic and psychological defeat. Two days later the bulk of the U.S. Third Army reached the Rhine, bringing up the curtain on the penultimate military act of World War II in Europe.

This March 1945 photograph is one of the last images of the living Adolf Hitler. Still suffering the effects of physical injury from the July 1944 assassination attempt and loaded with recklessly prescribed drugs, he greeted members of the Hitler Youth in Berlin as the Red Army moved virtually unchecked toward the city. Amidst an atmosphere of suffering, chaos, and anger, the naive Hitler Youth was among the few Nazi groups to remain wholly loyal to the *Führer*.

1945

ian efforts for the Jews to cover his collaboration with the Germans or the Western Allies (the War Refugee Board was sponsoring him); *See* 1947.

• SS guards at the Chelmno, Poland, death camp play "William Tell" by shooting at bottles placed on the heads of Jewish inmates who have been engaged in demolishing the camp's crematoria. In the evening, the remaining Jews are led from their barracks in groups of five and shot. One of the prisoners, Mordechai Zurawski, stabs an SS guard and escapes despite suffering a gunshot wound to the foot. A second inmate, Shimon Srebnik, also survives after being shot through the neck and mouth and left for dead. Forty-seven

Among the last victims of Bergen-Belsen in the spring of 1945 were 15-year-old Anne Frank *(pictured)* and her sister, Margot. Arriving from Auschwitz in October 1944, the sisters clung to each other and struggled to survive in the midst of the increasingly deteriorating conditions of the camp. Typhus claimed Margot first, and a frail Anne died of the disease a few days after.

Soviet soldiers trample a Nazi flag as they march westward early in 1945. Under such skilled leaders as Marshals Konstantin K. Rokossovky and Ivan S. Konev, the Soviet Army swept from one victory to another. In spite of sometimes ferocious German resistance, the Soviets captured Warsaw and Gdansk in Poland as they pushed toward their ultimate goal of crossing the Oder River to capture Berlin.

ALLIED PUSH ON GERMANY, 1944–1945

After their epic victory over German forces at the Battle of Stalingrad in the winter of 1942–43, the Soviets moved steadily westward until capturing Berlin on May 2, 1945. Following the Normandy invasion on June 6, 1944, the Western Allies unleashed more than two million troops, who pushed eastward over the next 11 months.

other Jewish prisoners at Chelmno, aware that the SS will shoot them before fleeing west ahead of the Soviets, take refuge in a building that is then set afire by the SS. Jews who run from the blaze are machine-gunned; only one of the original 47 survives. The SS abandons the Chelmno camp later in the day.

• January 18–March 1945: Acting on orders from Berlin, the SS begins a massive, on-foot evacuation of all prisoners and slave laborers at the Auschwitz, Birkenau, and Monowitz camps and from the Auschwitz region (Upper Silesia, Poland). Of the thousands of marchers, most die from exposure, exhaustion, and abuse on their way to their destinations. Boys

evacuated from Birkenau march toward Mauthausen, Austria. Many of the boys are on "cart commando" duty; i.e., harnessed to enormous carts in groups of 20.

• January 20, 1945: 4200 Jews are shot at Auschwitz. • The Red Army moves into East Prussia.

The death marches were, in many instances, extremely public. This group of weakened prisoners from Dachau was photographed marching through a tiny Bavarian village on its way through Wolfratshausen. Many of these prisoners cover their heads in order to protect themselves from the damp, chilly weather.

SS leader Heinrich Himmler *(right)* shares a moment of conversation with his personal physician and masseur, Felix Kersten. In the final days of the war, Kersten, who treated several of the Nazi leaders, served as an intermediary between representatives of the World Jewish Congress and the head of the SS. At two meetings held at Kersten's estate outside of Berlin, Himmler eventually agreed to free about 10,000 women held at the Ravensbrück, Germany, concentration camp.

The Allied High Command was interested in what had occurred in the camps, and officers regularly toured them to gain information regarding Nazi crimes. Here, Generals George Patton, Omar Bradley, and Dwight Eisenhower *(left to right)* visit the Ohrdruf, Germany, camp—the first camp liberated by the Americans—on April 4, 1945. A former prisoner demonstrates SS torture techniques for them.

1945

• **January 21–29, 1945:** Ninety-six Hungarian Jews interned at Auschwitz and working at a quarry at Golleschau, Germany, are sealed inside a pair of cattle cars labeled "Property of the SS." Half of the prisoners freeze to death as the train travels aimlessly for days. At Zwittau, Germany, the cattle cars are detached from the train and left at the station. Manufacturer

Oskar Schindler alters the bill of lading to read "Final Destination—Schindler Factory, Brünnlitz." After unsealing the cars at his factory, Schindler frees the Jews; *See* April 26, 1945.

• **January 23, 1945:** Soviet forces close on Auschwitz.

"We had known. The world had vaguely heard. But until now no one of us had looked on this. Even this morning we had not imagined we would look on this. It was as though we had penetrated at last to the center of the black heart, to the very crawling inside of the vicious heart."

—*Writer Meyer Levin, on the liberation of Ohrdruf*

The SS shot these Polish inmates in a mass execution at Ohrdruf, Germany. As so often happened, the Germans killed their prisoners rather than see them fall into the hands of the Allies. American General Omar Bradley said of the atrocities at Ohrdruf: "The smell of death overwhelmed us even before we passed through the stockade. More than 3200 naked, emaciated bodies had been flung into shallow graves. Others lay in the streets where they had fallen. Lice crawled over the yellowed skin of their sharp, bony frames."

Liberation of Ohrdruf

The labor camp Ohrdruf, near Gotha, Germany, occupies a distinct place in history. The first camp liberated by the Western Allies, Ohrdruf provided American troops with proof of Nazi barbarity.

At Ohrdruf, thousands of slave laborers had worked frantically under brutal conditions to prepare an underground communications center for the German Army. On April 4, 1945, American soldiers entering Ohrdruf *(pictured)* found mass graves containing thousands of corpses. Some prisoners had been executed and hastily buried only four days before the Americans entered the camp. The troops also encountered a few living witnesses, men who had escaped from the camp shortly before the Nazis began shooting the remaining prisoners.

Eight days after the camp was liberated, U.S. Generals Dwight Eisenhower, Omar Bradley, and George Patton, men deeply familiar with the mayhem of war, visited the camp. An angered Eisenhower encouraged the press to tour the camp and inform the world of the atrocities committed there.

• **January 25, 1945:** The SS evacuates the concentration camp at Stutthof, Poland.

• **January 26, 1945:** One thousand Jewish women interned at the Neusalz, Poland, slave-labor camp are set on a month-and-a-half-long forced march to the concentration camp at Flossenbürg, Germany, about 200 miles to the southwest. Along the way, 800 are beaten and shot; *See* February 15, 1945.

• **January 27, 1945:** Soviet troops liberate Auschwitz and find 7000 living inmates, including Anne Frank's father, Otto. They also discover more than 830,000 women's coats and dresses, nearly 348,000 men's suits, and seven tons of human hair.

• Memel, Lithuania, is liberated by Soviet troops.

• **Late January 1945:** A forced march of several thousand Jews is undertaken from the Danzig/Königsberg region of Germany to the coastal city of Palmnicken. At least 700 marchers are shot along the way and, with the

591

Folke Bernadotte

In the closing days of the war, Count Folke Bernadotte, vice-president of the Swedish Red Cross, used his diplomatic skill to rescue Jews from the clutches of the Nazis. His negotiating efforts saved the lives of 423 Danish Jews imprisoned at Theresienstadt, Czechoslovakia. In a daring wartime operation, the Jews were not only rescued from death but delivered by a convoy of buses to safety in Denmark.

To save Jewish lives, Bernadotte met several times with Heinrich Himmler. While Bernadotte negotiated to save Jews from slaughter, Himmler used them as a bargaining chip in his quest to conclude a separate peace with the Western Allies, a ploy the Allies would firmly reject. Bernadotte's negotiations with Himmler resulted in freedom for some 14,000 women imprisoned in the Ravensbrück, Germany, concentration camp. The women were transferred to Denmark, then to Sweden.

A page from the Hadamar Institute's death register. The institute was one of the six major facilities in the German "euthanasia" program. The document indicates each victim's date of arrival, family and given names, date of birth, date of death, cause of death, and age at death.

No one is exactly sure how many concentration and work camps the Nazis established. Many camps had numerous subcamps in which inmates could be housed while they participated in temporary work assignments. This survivor was discovered in the Vaihingen camp, a subcamp of Natzweiler in Germany.

1945

exception of a few who escape, the remainder are machine-gunned by the SS at the edge of the Baltic Sea. • 29,000 Jews, mostly women, are evacuated on forced marches from Danzig, Poland, and Stutthof, Poland. Only 3000 survive. • Thousands of Jews are sent on a death march from the Lamsdorf camp near Breslau, Germany, westward toward

Thuringia, Germany. Hundreds die or are killed on the way.

• February 1945: Ukrainian nationalists hunt down and murder Jews throughout the Ukraine. • Allied forces close on Cologne, Germany.

• February 3, 1945: 3500 prisoners from Gross-Rosen, Germany, are

U.S. Army soldiers gather around one of the numerous piles of corpses at the Buchenwald, Germany, concentration camp. The smell of rotting flesh was nauseating. U.S. GI John Glustrom said: "My first impression of [Buchenwald] was of the odor. The stench was all over the place, and there were a bunch of very bewildered, lost individuals who came to me pathetically at the door in their unkempt uniforms to see what we were doing and what was going to be done about them."

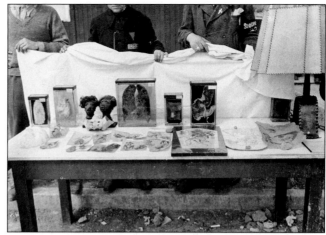

The human remains on this table, including two shrunken heads and a lampshade allegedly made from human skin, were taken from a laboratory run by Buchenwald's SS guards. The commandant's wife, Ilse Koch, kept a collection of tattooed human skin. The two heads were those of Polish prisoners who had escaped and were recaptured.

Food rations at Buchenwald, which had never been sufficient for the heavy work required of the prisoners, shrank throughout the war. In March 1945, for example, inmates received 250 grams (a little over a half-pound) of horse meat *per week*. Prisoners sometimes stole food from the well-fed dogs that helped guard the camp. At the time of liberation, surviving prisoners raided a supply of dog biscuits kept in the camp's kennel. The man closest to the camera, a Hungarian Jew, was so thin that one can see his spine from above. Victims of such severe cases of starvation and malnutrition had little chance of survival.

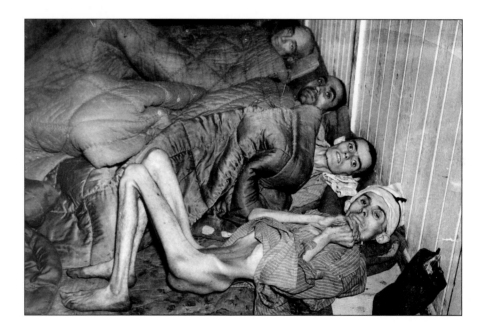

marched southwest to the concentration camp at Flossenbürg, Germany, nearly 200 miles away. Five hundred will die on the way. Two thousand more are evacuated by train to the labor camp at Ebensee, Austria, near Mauthausen; 49 will die on the journey and another 182 will perish at the camp. • An American bomb crashes onto the *Volksgerichtshof* (People's Court) building in Berlin, killing fanatic Nazi judge Roland Freisler and interrupting the sentencing of anti-Nazi German Resistance members Frau Solf and her daughter, Gräfin Ballestrem; *See* September 10, 1943; April 23, 1945.

• February 4, 1945: An Allied conference at Yalta, Ukraine, establishes respective spheres of influence that will take effect at war's end.

• February 8, 1945: Soviet troops are 30 miles east of Dresden, Germany.

• February 13, 1945: German troops surrender Budapest, Hungary. • The SS evacuates the concentration camp at Gross-Rosen, Germany.

As the Nazi extermination camps in Poland were emptied of prisoners late in the war, Buchenwald and other established concentration camps to the west became receiving centers for many thousands of Jews. Twenty thousand arrived at Buchenwald between May 1944 and March 1945. Here, a young war orphan sits astride the running board of a truck belonging to the United Nations Relief and Rehabilitation Administration. As they liberated Buchenwald, American soldiers found about 900 children, including this five-year-old. Along with children from Poland, Russia, and other countries, he awaits transportation to Switzerland.

In April 1945 Heinrich Himmler, frightened at last by the Allied advance, ordered a halt to evacuations of concentration camps in the enemy's paths, and insisted that the camps be left intact for the liberators. Some guards were caught unprepared and had no time to escape before Allied troops arrived. Here, a Russian prisoner points out a Buchenwald guard who had brutally beaten prisoners.

1945

• **February 15, 1945:** The Red Army liberates the slave-labor camp at Neusalz, Poland; *See* March 19, 1945.

• **February 17, 1945:** Seven Jews, including a small orphan girl, are murdered by a Pole in Sokoly, Poland.

• **February 18, 1945:** Five hundred Jews married to Christians are seized throughout Germany and deported to the Theresienstadt, Czechoslovakia, camp/ghetto.

• **February 23, 1945:** Nazis evacuate the Jews from the concentration camp at Schwarzheide, Germany. The 300 weakest prisoners are sent in open wagons to the concentration camp at Bergen-Belsen, Germany.

German civilians dig graves at Buchenwald. Whenever possible, the Allies forced the local population to bury the corpses left to rot in the camps. This both relieved Allied soldiers of performing the grisly task and made the Germans personally confront the crimes committed by their countrymen.

These male prisoners freed from Buchenwald all suffered from maladies of the legs and feet. These problems were the product of working under horrific conditions with little to eat, not to mention shoes that did not fit—if the prisoners had shoes at all.

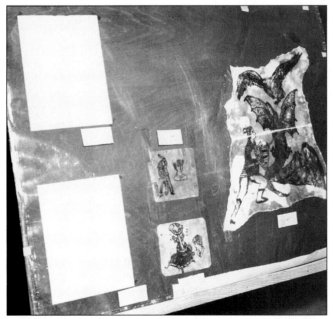

This exhibit of tattooed human skin was presented as evidence of German atrocities during a trial of SS members at Dachau, Germany. The victims had been prisoners at Buchenwald, and their tattoos had attracted the attention of Ilse Koch, the "Bitch of Buchenwald." She allegedly used their tattooed skin to make lampshades.

Young Jews travel to Palestine after being released from Buchenwald. The Americans liberated Buchenwald on April 11, 1945, freeing 21,000 inmates, including 4000 Jews. Most were sent to displaced-persons camps, while others tried to enter Palestine—either legally or illegally.

Residents of Washington, D.C., seek solace from one another on April 12, 1945, as they absorb the news of the death of President Franklin Roosevelt. His little-known successor, Harry Truman, struggled to fill the shoes of the beloved president. Concerned about Jews liberated from the Nazi camps and now confined to displaced-persons camps, Truman pressured the British to allow more Jews to immigrate to Palestine. He also lobbied Congress to permit more displaced persons to enter the U.S. Truman's efforts faced opposition from segments of the public, the State Department, and some congressmen, including Senator Patrick McCarran, the powerful chair of the Senate Judiciary Committee.

Several Jewish Allied soldiers celebrate a Passover Seder in 1945 at Lake Como in Italy. The Passover annually celebrates the liberation of the Jews from slavery in ancient Egypt. This Passover was especially meaningful for European Jews, since it was the first time in a dozen years that they were not "enslaved" by the Nazis and their collaborators.

This necklace in the shape of the Star of David was fashioned by a young Jewish girl—a slave laborer—from bits of colored conduit wire. If she had been discovered with the necklace, she would have been executed. A Nazi transport train that carried her and other laborers (including her ailing sister) was mistakenly attacked and crippled by U.S. planes near Munich. The German troopers fled, leaving the prisoners to the care of a U.S. Army reconnaissance unit. So grateful was the girl that she gave the necklace as a gift to her rescuer, a GI named Marvin Dorf.

1945

• **Early March 1945: Fifteen-year-old Anne Frank dies at the Bergen-Belsen, Germany, concentration camp.** • **Arthur Nebe,** *Einsatzgruppe* **B commander in Belorussia, is executed by the Nazis because of his involvement in the plot against Hitler.**

• **March–April 1945: Two thousand inmates from the Kőszeg, Hungary,** slave-labor camp are marched for weeks through rugged Hungarian and Austrian countrysides.

• **March 3, 1945: An evacuation train from Gross-Rosen, Germany, arrives at the Ebensee, Austria, camp with more than 2000 Jews. More than 180 are killed almost immediately.**

Liberation of the Camps

On V-E Day, May 8, 1945, men and women danced in the streets of American cities to celebrate the Allies' victory over Nazi Germany. An ocean and a continent away, a more somber victory ceremony took place at Mauthausen. This Nazi concentration camp stood about 12 miles southeast of the Austrian city of Linz, Adolf Hitler's hometown as a teenager—a place, he wrote in *Mein Kampf*, where his "happiest days" had been spent.

There were no "happiest days" at Mauthausen. Established in May 1938, this especially harsh camp was distinctive for the brutal work and sadism associated with its stone quarry. During the war years, Mauthausen and its more than 60 subcamps—Gusen, Gunskirchen, and Ebensee among them—became an industrial empire controlled by the SS. Of the 199,404 prisoners who passed through the camp at Mauthausen, about 119,000 perished, including 38,120 Jews.

Soviet troops liberated Majdanek and Auschwitz, death camps on Polish soil, during July 1944 and January 1945, respectively. In the West, units of the U.S. Army freed Buchenwald *(pictured)* and Dachau, concentration camps in Germany, on April 11 and April 29, 1945, while the British and Canadians reached Bergen-Belsen, Germany, on April 15. At every camp, the liberators found carnage so vast that even battle-scarred veterans were shocked by what they saw.

Members of the U.S. Army's 71st Infantry and 11th Armored divisions discovered some of the worst horrors. The 71st liberated Gunskirchen, a Mauthausen satellite, on May 5. The 11th took the city of Linz and freed the Gusen concentration camp on May 5. Its tanks reached the Mauthausen camp itself at 11:30 A.M. on May 5, about 50 hours before Nazi Germany surrendered unconditionally.

Captain J. D. Pletcher particularly remembered the odor when he entered Gunskirchen. "The smell," he said, "nauseated many of the Americans who went there. It was a smell I'll never forget, completely different from anything I've ever encountered. It could almost be seen and hung over the camp like a fog of death." Mauthausen and its satellite camps, he said, were places of "foul bodily odors, smoldering trash fires," and "mud mixed with feces and urine." Liberation could not prevent former prisoners from death. For days, dehydration, starvation, disease, and exhaustion continued to take their toll.

Liberation came late for Mauthausen and its subcamps—much too late for the vast majority of their defenseless victims—but those places were not the last Holocaust sites to be set free. Not until May 9 did Soviet troops reach the Theresienstadt, Czechoslovakia, camp/ghetto, where they found 19,000 prisoners alive. Polish and Soviet units freed the camp at Stutthof, Poland, on the 8th. Even after Nazi Germany's surrender, a fog of death continued to hang over the liberated camps, as it does at those sites to this day.

• **March 5, 1945:** The U.S. Ninth Army reaches the Rhine River south of Düsseldorf, Germany.

• **March 7, 1945:** The U.S. First Army crosses the Rhine River at Remagen, Germany.

• **March 12, 1945:** SS chief Heinrich Himmler and his personal physician, Dr. Felix Kersten, sign the Himmler-Kersten Agreement, which provides for the handling of concentration camps as Allied troops approach. Notably, the document calls for an end to the killing of Jewish inmates.

• **March 19, 1945:** Yugoslav partisans launch an offensive at Trieste, Italy.
• Adolf Hitler issues the *Nero-Befehl* (Nero Order), a scorched-earth directive intended to leave only a ruined Germany for advancing troops. • Two hundred survivors out of 1000 Jewish women who began a forced march from the Neusalz, Poland, slave-labor camp on January 26 are evacuated by train to the concentration camp at Bergen-Belsen, Germany; *See* March 24, 1945.

American soldiers stride among the thousands of corpses that German guards had left to rot at the Nordhausen, Germany, concentration camp. As was often the case, the first thing that American GI C. W. Doughty noticed about the camp was the stench. "Oh, the odors," he said. "Well, there is no way to describe the odors.... Many of the boys I am talking about now—these were tough soldiers, there were combat men who had been all the way through the invasion—were ill and vomiting, throwing up, just [at] the sight of this...."

The end of the war provided survivors, at last, with the opportunity to grieve for those whom they had lost to the Nazi death factories. Scenes such as this one from Nordhausen were quite common. This Polish boy mourns his dead grandmother while his father prays over her body.

Two former slave laborers clasp hands in victory beside a partially completed V–2 bomb they had built in a factory near Nordhausen. The hard labor, cruel working conditions, and near-starvation diet killed many of the factory's Russian, Polish, and French workers. The Americans who liberated the factory discovered a room with 20 bodies awaiting cremation.

1945

- **March 20, 1945: An Allied air raid kills Jewish women in a camp at Tiefstack, Germany, near Hamburg.**

- **March 21, 1945: Red Army troops enter the Pruszcz, Poland, camp near Stutthof. Only about 200 women prisoners, out of an original 1100, remain alive.**

- **Spring 1945: The SS hatches a scheme to poison all inmates of the Dachau, Germany, concentration camp before Allied liberation. The idea is not pursued.**

- **March 24, 1945: A train carrying 200 Jewish women, exhausted from a death march from Neusalz, Poland, arrives at Bergen-Belsen, Germany.**

Forsaken humanity: The painter Gideon impressionistically captures the surreal horrors that greeted Allied troops who liberated concentration camps as they drove eastward.

The dirty bandages on the face of this Bergen-Belsen survivor provide evidence of the abuse she received during her imprisonment. Many of the camp's "survivors" continued to die even after the camp's liberation. A British soldier remembered that many of the former inmates "collapsed as they walked and fell dead." About 14,000 prisoners died from April 15 to June 20.

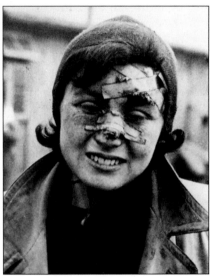

When the British liberated the Bergen-Belsen, Germany, concentration camp on April 15, 1945, they discovered tens of thousands of unburied bodies abandoned by the Germans. The British had no choice but to bury the corpses in mass graves. Curtis Mitchell, an American who visited the camp at this time, described the Germans who were forced to load the bodies into trucks in preparation for mass burial as behaving "just as if they were dumping garbage."

• **March 29, 1945: The Red Army takes Danzig.**

• **March 30, 1945: Jewish women being led to their deaths at the Ravensbrück, Germany, camp grapple with their SS guards. Nine of the women escape but are recaptured and murdered with the rest. • Soviet troops enter Austria.**

• **April 1945: In a transparent attempt to save himself, Heinrich Himmler tells Norbert Masur, a representative of the Geneva-based World Jewish Congress, that Jews and National Socialists should "bury the hatchet";** *See* **April 20, 1945. • Because there is no longer a way for prisoners at Mauthausen, Austria, to wash, lice infestation there is out of control.**

• **Early April 1945: The SS evacuates thousands of Jews—mostly on foot— as Allied and Soviet forces press in from the east and west. Evacuees are taken to camps at Bergen-Belsen, Germany; Dachau, Germany; Ebensee, Austria; Leitmeritz, Czechoslovakia; and Theresienstadt, Czechoslovakia. The operation is rife with daily beatings and murders as well as**

Bergen-Belsen

The notorious Bergen-Belsen concentration camp, near Celle in northern Germany, began operations early in 1943. It was designed to house approximately 10,000 Jewish prisoners. The collapse of the German war effort and the consequent closure of camps throughout Eastern Europe forced tens of thousands of inmates to Bergen-Belsen. When the camp was liberated on April 15, 1945, by the British Army, more than 60,000 emaciated and diseased human beings occupied the grounds.

The vile living conditions at Bergen-Belsen were similar to those at the camps of Eastern Europe: Food, shelter, and sanitary facilities were entirely inadequate. The declining health of the inmates resulted in  thousands being murdered by lethal injections during the summer of 1944.

As Bergen-Belsen's camp population swelled in 1945, the situation deteriorated rapidly. Camp officials and the facilities were simply overwhelmed. All efforts to organize and feed the prisoners broke down completely. When British soldiers arrived in April, they were greeted by an unimaginably grisly scene. Corpses were rotting on the ground. Barracks built to house 100 prisoners were stuffed with more than 1000 typhus-ridden, excrement-covered people. Death by disease and starvation claimed 14,000 lives between April 15 and June 20, 1945.

Josef Kramer, glum and in shackles, was the commandant of Bergen-Belsen at the end of the war. In 1944 he had served as chief of Auschwitz II, the death camp, during the annihilation of Hungary's Jews. He admitted that he had personally gassed prisoners while serving as the commandant of the Natzweiler, Germany, camp. On November 17, 1945, he was sentenced to death for his crimes.

Inmates in the camps were forced to live under incredibly filthy conditions that often led to disease and infestation by parasites. These children at Bergen-Belsen take their first baths in months.

1945

deaths from starvation and typhus. Thirteen hundred Jews are evacuated on foot from Vienna; only 700 will reach their destination, the Gusen, Austria, camp, alive.

• April 1, 1945: The SS initiates death marches to evacuate the concentration camps at Dora-Mittelbau and Kochendorf, Germany.

• April 3, 1945: All 497 members of a slave-labor group at Bratislava, Slovakia, are shot and killed by their captors. • The Nazis evacuate the concentration/slave-labor camp at Nordhausen, Germany; *See* April 11, 1945.

• April 4, 1945: The U.S. 4th Armored Division liberates the concentration

> **"One woman came up to a soldier who was guarding the milk store and doling the milk out to children, and begged for milk for her baby. The man took the baby and saw that it had been dead for days, black in the face and shriveled up. The woman went on begging for milk. So he poured some on the dead lips. The mother then started to croon with joy and carried the baby off in triumph. She stumbled and fell dead in a few yards."**
>
> *—American reporter Patrick Gordon at Allied liberation of Bergen-Belsen; April 1945*

Known as "the SS woman without uniform," Hilde Lobauer embodied evil to the prisoners of Bergen-Belsen. A political prisoner of the Nazis, Lobauer chose to side with her captors, indulging her penchant for cruelty with a leather whip and a cane. Her sadism earned her a promotion to internee in charge of a section of the camp. Following the war, she was tried at Nuremberg and sentenced to ten years in prison, though she was released in July 1950.

This survivor of Bergen-Belsen was found in agony at liberation. Internment in Hitler's camps had long-term—often calamitous—psychological and physical effects upon survivors.

By April 1945 the camp system at Bergen-Belsen had broken down completely beneath a flood of new inmates (for example, 28,000 arrivals in just ten days, April 3–14). Food rations were cut off, roll ceased to be called, and prisoners were left to their own devices. And yet some staff members remained at Bergen-Belsen to the end, such as these female SS guards, who had earned reputations for being as cruel as their male counterparts. Thousands of average Germans became active perpetrators of the Holocaust.

Jewish women liberated from concentration camps under the Bernadotte Agreement arrive in Malmö, Sweden. One woman reacts with joy in response to the kind person who has offered her a glass of milk. Count Folke Bernadotte arranged the Swedish rescue of nearly 30,000 survivors, mostly from the Ravensbrück concentration camp.

Most smaller camps employed diesel-powered engines to create the gas used to murder their victims, but the Nazis often improvised (above) to carry out their grisly tasks.

U.S. troops discovered these charred bodies when they entered the camp at Thekla, Germany. Margaret Bourke-White, a correspondent for *Life* magazine, described one of the corpses, that of a professor from Poland, with these words: "The shriveled lower half of his body lay in cinders... with his charred crutch close by, but the fine intellectual bald head thrust through to the outside [of the camp's fence] was still unmarred, with even the spectacles in place. He must have been much loved; the survivors shed many tears over him."

1945

camp at Ohrdruf, Germany, the site of more than 4000 deaths during the previous three months. Victims were Jews, Poles, and Soviet POWs. Hundreds shot just before liberation had been working to build an enormous underground radio and telephone communications center. Very few inmates remain alive at liberation.

• Jews toiling in quarries at Gotha, Germany, are murdered by their Nazi overseers.

• April 8, 1945: Jewish inmates are marched out of the concentration camp at Buchenwald, Germany, to the camp at Flossenbürg, Germany, 100 miles to the southeast. Non-Jewish prisoners are left behind to await the advancing Americans. A few

The Allies often ordered the local population to exhume the bodies of prisoners killed in concentration camps or on death marches for proper burial, especially in cases such as this one in Helmbrechts, Germany, where female slave laborers from Eastern Europe had been buried in locations that were not well hidden.

These recently rescued Jewish women had been slave laborers in a munitions factory in Kaunitz, Germany. The yellow crosses painted on their clothing had made them easily identifiable to the local German population, thereby decreasing the possibility of escape.

Allies Interpret the Holocaust

The liberation of the concentration camps in Germany unleashed a torrent of information regarding the Nazis' treatment of the Jews. News reports focused on the mountains of corpses (including those pictured at Gotha, Germany), the horror and stench of the camps, and the surreal, skeletal figures who remained alive. Although news stories about the systematic mass  murder of European Jewry had appeared in the Western media since 1942, virtually nobody had imagined the scenes that lurked behind the barbed-wire fences of Nazi camps.

Reporting from Buchenwald, CBS radio correspondent Edward R. Murrow offered the following description: "There surged around me an evil-smelling stink. Men and boys reached out to touch me. They were in rags and the remnants of uniforms. Death already had marked many of them, but they were smiling with their eyes.... Murder had been done at Buchenwald. God alone knows how many men and boys died there during the last 12 years."

Well-intentioned reports such as this led people to mistakenly believe that the genocidal programs of the Nazis had taken place in Germany only. Many years elapsed before the full details of the "Final Solution" were pieced together and people were able to more accurately interpret the events of the Holocaust.

Jews are able to hide and avoid the march; *See* April 11, 1945.

• **April 9, 1945:** The concentration camp at Dora-Mittelbau, Germany, is liberated by the U.S. Army. Very few inmates remain alive.

• **April 10, 1945:** SS functionary Adolf Eichmann visits the Theresienstadt,

Czechoslovakia, camp/ghetto to gloat over the many Jews who have perished there.

• **April 11, 1945:** American troops liberate the concentration camp at Buchenwald, Germany; 21,000 inmates are still alive. In the Pathology Block (Block 2), GIs discover tanned and tattooed human skin.

• The U.S. 104th Infantry and 3rd Armored divisions liberate the concentration/slave-labor camp at Nordhausen, Germany. • Inmates at the Aschersleben, Germany, camp are evacuated by the SS to Theresienstadt, Czechoslovakia.

• **April 12, 1945:** U.S. Generals Dwight Eisenhower, George Patton,

The diets that camp inmates received had profound long-term effects upon their digestive systems. Among the results of prolonged malnutrition were severe cases of dysentery, many of which proved fatal even after liberation. Here, a young Czech man suffering from a serious case of the disease is helped by two other survivors of the Flossenbürg camp.

The Flossenbürg, Germany, work camp, where prisoners labored in a stone quarry and in the manufacture of arms and munitions, had functioned since 1938. Camp personnel evacuated prisoners from the facility on April 20, 1945, setting the inmates forth on an eight-day death march toward Dachau. American troops reached Flossenbürg and liberated the few inmates who remained on April 23. Hastily buried bodies of prisoners who had perished or been murdered lined the route of the march. General George Patton was appalled by the deaths and the makeshift graves that would have to be exhumed. He issued a blunt command: "I want no American soldier digging for these bodies. Round up the town *Bürgermeister* and whatever civilians are available and have them commence digging." The German women seen here were among those conscripted for that duty.

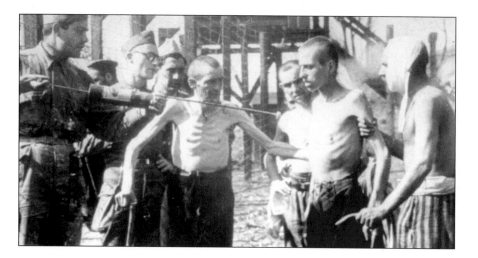

Lice and fleas were among the banes of existence for concentration-camp inmates. Not only did these vermin make camp life even more unbearable, but they also carried disease. Hence, the Allies made a concerted effort to help former prisoners to end infestations. Here, an American soldier disinfects survivors of the Flossenbürg, Germany, camp.

1945

and Omar Bradley visit the camp at Ohrdruf, Germany, and view corpses and other evidence of Nazi atrocities.
• SS troops evacuate inmates of the camp at Schönebeck, Germany, to Theresienstadt, Czechoslovakia.
• U.S. President Franklin Roosevelt dies. Vice-president Harry S. Truman becomes president.

• April 13, 1945: Soviet troops enter Vienna. • Death marchers from the small labor camp of Rottleberode, a subcamp of Dora-Mittelbau, are driven to the outskirts of Gardelegen, Germany, which they had reached two days before. The just over 1000 prisoners are herded by SS guards and members of the local militia into a barn, which has been prepared as

This jacket belonged to William Luksenburg, a Holocaust survivor. After his parents were deported to Auschwitz in 1942, Luksenburg was sent to one of Auschwitz's satellite camps. By January 1945 he had been shipped to Flossenbürg and then Regensburg, Germany, where he worked on the railroad. As the end of the war drew near, Luksenburg survived a death march. An American soldier who found Luksenburg's jacket and buried it to avoid the spread of disease dug it up four months later and kept it as a "souvenir."

Nazi exploitation of their victims extended beyond plundered hair and dental gold. It included even the ashes of the murdered. At some camps, random ashes were collected in urns and *sold* to grieving survivors as the remains of specific loved ones. This urn and barrel of ash were discovered at the Flossenbürg, Germany, concentration camp, where commandant Hans Vogel made tidy sums from the deception.

These Polish women partisan soldiers had been captured by the Germans in the battle for Warsaw in the fall of 1944. The women were liberated from German prisoner-of-war camps by Polish troops near Emden, Germany. Some of the liberators found their wives here. The Germans recognized some rights for West European soldiers who became POWs. The Nazis treated gentile partisans less well, and accorded no rights at all to Jewish civilians.

an execution site. As the last prisoners are pushed into the barn, the SS guards throw torches onto the gasoline-soaked straw and lock the doors. Those prisoners who are not killed by the smoke and fire are shot by the SS as they try to escape. Only a few of the prisoners survive; *See* April 14, 1945.

• April 14, 1945: Swedish diplomat Count Folke Bernadotte negotiates the repatriation of 423 Danish Jews held at the Theresienstadt, Czechoslovakia, camp/ghetto. • American troops reach Gardelegen, Germany, and discover the charred corpses from the previous day's massacre of Jews.

• April 15, 1945: British troops reach the Bergen-Belsen, Germany, concentration camp and find 60,000 survivors and 27,000 unburied corpses. Following liberation, starvation and typhus will claim about 500 inmates every day for ten days; *See* April 15–17, 1945. • British troops close on Bremen and Hamburg, Germany. • Soviet forces are 35 miles east of

African-Americans at the Camps

The Allies' liberation of the disease-infested and horribly over-crowded concentration camps in Germany was a bittersweet experience. For African-American soldiers, seeing victims of racism—dead, dying, or suffering—was a frightening reminder of the potential consequences of prejudice.

While nothing could have prepared anyone for what lay behind the gates of Dachau and Buchenwald, African-American soldiers seemed particularly affected by what they witnessed. Bob Bender, a survivor liberated from Buchenwald, recalls the "black soldiers of the U.S. Third Army, tall and strong, crying like babies, carrying the emaciated bodies of the liberated prisoners."

Awestruck by what he had seen at Buchenwald, Leon Bass of the 183rd Combat Engineer Battalion of the U.S. Third Army offered this powerful observation: "I came into that camp an angry black soldier. Angry at my country and justifiably so. Angry because they were treating me as though I was not good enough. But [that day] I came to the realization that human suffering is not relegated to me and mine. I now knew that human suffering could touch us all.... [What I saw] in Buchenwald was the face of evil...it was racism."

These children, survivors of the Bergen-Belsen, Germany, camp, play with toys seized from surrounding towns by Allied soldiers. With about six million Jews murdered during World War II, it is probable that most of these children were orphans who had no place to go. Such scenes were not unusual; a large percentage of the inhabitants of the displaced-person camps were children and adolescents.

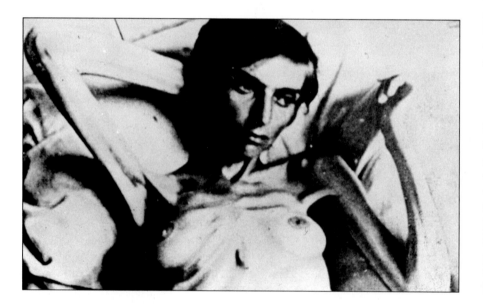

As the end of the war drew near, the Nazis moved tens of thousands of prisoners to camps in the heart of Germany. This skeletal young woman, who had been in the women's camp in Ravensbrück, Germany, was among thousands of inmates shipped to Sachsenhausen in the spring of 1945. Thousands of prisoners died on these journeys, which have justifiably become known as "death marches."

1945

Berlin and 60 miles east of Dresden, Germany. • At Ravensbrück and Sachsenhausen, Germany, 57,000 inmates—17,000 of them women—are marched westward by the SS. Once under way, many will be shot and/or die of exhaustion, and others, including 21-year-old Mila Racine, will be killed during Allied bomb attacks aimed at nearby targets. • A

deportation train from Vienna, the final one organized by Adolf Eichmann's staff, arrives at the Theresienstadt, Czechoslovakia, camp/ghetto with 109 Jews.

• April 15–17, 1945: A small contingent of British troops at the Bergen-Belsen, Germany, camp is unable to prevent Hungarian SS guards from

Benito Mussolini was arrested by Communist partisans in April 1945 as he tried to flee to Austria disguised as a German soldier. The partisans shot him on April 28. Subsequently, his body, along with that of his mistress—Clara Petacci—and five other close confidants, was hanged in Milan, Italy's *Piazzale Loreto* and mutilated by an angry mob. Ironically, Mussolini ignored the advice of his son and others when he refused to fly out of the country to temporary safety. Petacci, too, was foolishly stubborn, and refused to abandon *Il Duce.*

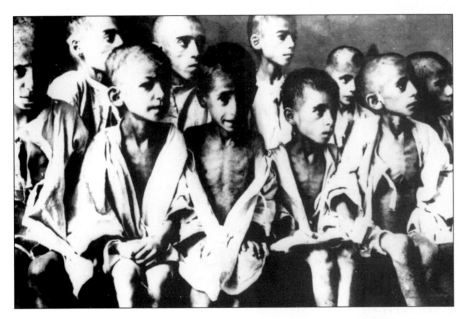

These emaciated children survived the Ravensbrück, Germany, concentration camp. Though Ravensbrück imprisoned mostly women, it also included a children's camp at Uckermark and a separate section for men. In December 1944 and January 1945, Uckermark was recognized as a selection and extermination camp for Ravensbrück. At the end of January, a large selection took place; old, sick, or weak women were taken to Uckermark and murdered, many by gassing. These selections continued into spring, leading to the deaths of at least 5000 women.

A sparse complement of guards leads numerous prisoners in a death march from the Dachau, Germany, concentration camp on April 29, 1945. This photograph, surreptitiously taken by a German civilian, shows the emaciated prisoners as they march through the Bavarian countryside down the *Nördlichen Münchner Strasse* in Grünwald. Few civilians tried to help the suffering marchers.

These physically and psychologically abused men were among those liberated from the Dachau, Germany, concentration camp by the U.S. Army on April 29, 1945. One American soldier said the camp's inmates "were skin and bones." Many of the survivors had lived for months on starvation rations. A large percentage of them died even after being liberated.

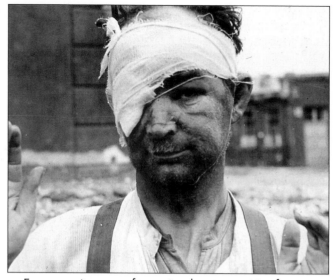

Former prisoners often seized opportunities for revenge against camp guards. This German, previously a guard at Dachau, was beaten by inmates who, against the odds, had survived his cruelty.

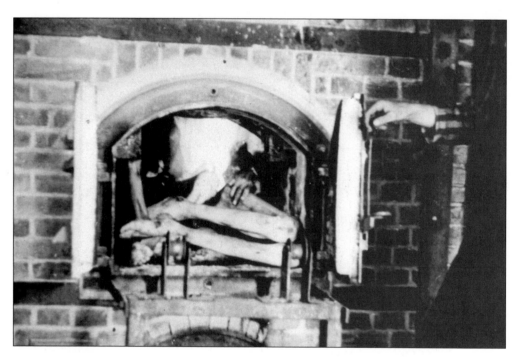

Thirty minutes after the camp's liberation, a human body continues to burn in one of Dachau's crematorium ovens. As the death toll mounted, the Nazis kept Dachau's ovens operating night and day. Still, it was not nearly enough to dispose of the bodies of the hundreds who were dying each day.

1945

murdering 72 Jewish and 11 non-Jewish prisoners.

• April 16, 1945: The Red Army launches its final assault on Berlin. • French forces enter Nuremberg, Germany, onetime site of mammoth Nazi Party rallies. • The camp at Johanngeorgenstadt, Germany, is evacuated to Theresienstadt, Czecho-slovakia. More than 60 inmates from this group are killed in the village of Buchau, Czechoslovakia.

• April 18, 1945: Nazis initiate a death march of prisoners from Schwarzheide, Germany, to Theresienstadt, Czechoslovakia; *See* May 6, 1945.

Two British soldiers guard the infamous Alex Bernard Hans Piorkowski, former commandant of Dachau. While relatively few of the inmates at Dachau were gassed, Piorkowski assured that conditions there were so appalling that inmates died by the thousands of starvation, disease, and abuse (including outright execution) at the hands of the camp's personnel.

Jack Hallett, an American soldier who helped liberate Dachau, noted that the "first thing I saw was a stack of bodies—oh, 20 feet long and about, oh, as high as a man could reach. . . . And the thing I'll never forget was the fact that closer inspection found people whose eyes were still blinking maybe three or four deep inside the stack." A particularly haunting aspect of the terrible scene photographed here is the clothed young woman among the dozens of shaven, naked male bodies.

One of the first things the Allies did was assure that survivors got enough to eat. Here, a truckload of bread is distributed to survivors at Dachau. Tragically, many former prisoners, after months of malnourishment, overate to the point of death. They had gone so long without food that the heavy eating overloaded their digestive systems and killed them.

• April 19, 1945: Leipzig, Germany, is captured by American forces.

• April 20, 1945: SS chief Heinrich Himmler meets with Swedish diplomat Norbert Masur to arrange for 7000 women, about one-half of them Jewish, to be transported from the Ravensbrück, Germany, camp to neutral Sweden. The scheme is Himmler's transparent bid to improve his position with the Allies. • The SS evacuates the concentration camp at Flossenbürg, Germany; See April 23, 1945.

• April 22, 1945: Six hundred Jewish and Serbian prisoners at Jasenovac, Croatia, revolt against their guards. 520 prisoners are killed by machine-gun fire and grenades. The other 80, including 20 Jews, escape.

• April 23, 1945: The concentration camp at Flossenbürg, Germany, is liberated by the U.S. Army; 2000 inmates remain alive. • The SS evacuates the concentration camp at Ravensbrück, Germany. • German anti-Nazi Resistance members Frau

When Dachau was liberated on April 29, 1945, an unknown number of American GIs lined 16 SS camp guards against a coalyard wall in the adjacent SS training camp *(left)* and executed them. Additional executions took place at Dachau's railyard; a guard tower; and at Würm creek. In all, 37-39 SS personnel were dispatched that day. These actions were "unauthorized," and did not reflect U.S. Army policy toward captured SS.

As Soviet troops closed in on Berlin, Eva Braun returned to the city to stand at the side of her *Führer.* On April 29, in a simple civil ceremony in the bunker, they wed. Joseph Goebbels and Martin Bormann served as witnesses, and the ceremony was followed by a small celebration. The next day the newlyweds committed suicide, Eva by cyanide and Hitler probably by cyanide and gun.

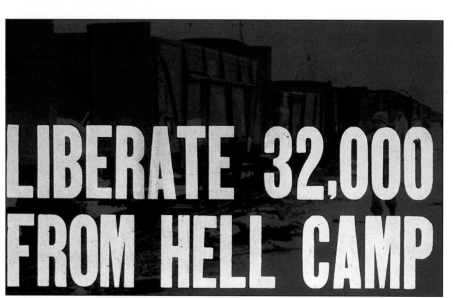

LIBERATE 32,000 FROM HELL CAMP

A stark headline from the April 30, 1945, edition of the *Chicago Herald,* overlaid on an Allied photograph of a Dachau death train. To Americans, who had been told little about the Holocaust by their leaders, such scenes and headlines were nearly incomprehensible.

1945

Solf and her daughter are released from Moabit Prison due to bureaucratic oversight; *See* September 10, 1943; February 3, 1945.

• April 25, 1945: American troops advancing from the west and Soviet troops advancing from the east meet at Torgau, Germany. • French forces in southern Germany reach four sites

of mass murder: Schömberg (1771 victims), Schörzingen (549), Spaichingen (111), and Tuttlingen (86). • In the final evacuation of prisoners from Stutthof, Poland, 200 Jewish women are taken to a beach and shot. The remaining 4000 prisoners, 1500 Jews among them, are loaded on five barges and sent across the Baltic toward the German-Danish coast.

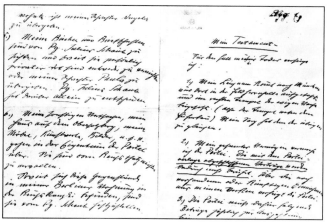

This handwritten document, entitled *Mein Testament* (My Testament), spelled out Adolf Hitler's last wishes. Hitler actually composed two documents. One was a political testament naming Admiral Karl Dönitz as his successor and dismissing "traitors" such as Heinrich Himmler and Hermann Göring from the Party. The other was a personal will, stipulating that mementos were to go to his loyal secretaries. He verbally ordered that his and Eva's bodies were to be burned so that the Soviets would have no remains over which to gloat.

Hitler's faithful subordinates, including his driver, Erich Kempka, and the commander of the SS guards, Hans Rattenhuber, followed the last order of the *Führer:* They took his body and that of Eva Braun to the courtyard above the bunker, doused both with gasoline, and set them aflame. Debate would swirl afterward over whether or not the remains the Soviets found and placed in this casket were in fact those of Adolf Hitler.

Hitler's Last Days

The collapse of the German war effort and the steady advance of the Allied armies drove major agencies of the Nazi government into a subterranean network of underground bunkers. Adolf Hitler spent the final weeks of his life in a dank, 18-room bunker located directly under the Reich Chancellery in Berlin.

As the Red Army closed in, the *Führer* was a shadow of his former self. His body was stooped and emaciated, and he could not prevent his hands and voice from shaking. He suffered violent mood swings and forcefully rejected an opportunity to escape Berlin by plane.

Before Hitler's demise, he expelled Hermann Göring and Heinrich Himmler from the Nazi Party. He married his longtime mistress, Eva Braun, and dictated his last will and testament. The final sentence of his political testament reads: "Above all, I obligate the leaders of the nation and their following to a strict observance of the racial laws, and to a merciless resistance to the poisoner of all peoples, international Jewry."

On April 30, 1945, sometime between 3:00 and 4:00 P.M., Hitler put a pistol to his head, bit into a cyanide capsule, and shot himself. Braun, too, committed suicide. The German POW seen below apparently felt little sorrow.

More than 2000 drown or are shot by the Germans. • At Cuneo, Italy, the Gestapo arrests and murders six Jews.

• **April 26, 1945:** The Red Army captures Brno, Czechoslovakia, freeing Oskar Schindler's Jews.

• **April 26–May 3, 1945:** Survivors of the concentration camp at Stutthof, Poland, are evacuated by sea to Lübeck, Germany, a journey of more than 300 miles. Hundreds perish during the seven-day voyage.

• **April 27, 1945:** Of 2775 deathmarchers moving east from Rehmsdorf, Germany (near Buchenwald), 1000 are killed by grenades and machine-gun fire from SS guards at Marienbad, Czechoslovakia, for attempting to flee. Twelve hundred more will be killed on the march and another 500 will be murdered after arriving at Theresienstadt, Czechoslovakia. Of the 2775 marchers, just 75 will survive. • The concentration camp at Sachsenhausen, Germany, is liberated by the Red Army; 3000 inmates remain alive. • The camp at

Charlotte Delbo

Released from the Ravensbrück, Germany, concentration camp on April 23, 1945, Charlotte Delbo translated her experience into a literature of witness.

When the Germans invaded her native France, Delbo was far away, on tour with a theater company in Brazil. When she returned to her homeland, she joined her husband, Georges Dudach, in the Resistance. Dudach was arrested in March 1942 and shot that May. Delbo was sent to Auschwitz and Ravensbrück. While imprisoned at the former, Delbo wrote that she and the other women there were "larvae" whose blankets were "shrouds."

After the war Delbo returned to France, giving powerful voice to the lives of those who had perished. Of her day of freedom from Ravensbrück, she wrote: "I know why the flowers, the sky, the sun were beautiful, and human voices deeply moving. The earth was beautiful in having been found again." Yet for Delbo, the earth as she had known it could never be found again. For her, it was impossible to return "from a world beyond knowledge."

The death marches undertaken in earnest from concentration camps in 1944 and 1945 left behind pathetic trails of victims—people who died, were murdered, and, sometimes, hastily buried. This grave site near Namerring, Germany, was exhumed by American GIs.

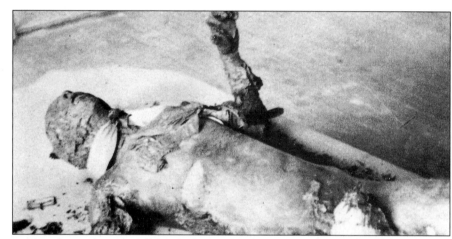

The charred remains of Joseph Goebbels testify to his fanatical devotion to Hitler. Goebbels's wife, Magda, shared his fanaticism, declaring that their children were "too good for the life that will come after us." On May 1, 1945, she requested an SS doctor to give fatal injections of morphine to her six children, Helga, Hilde, Helmut, Holde, Hedde, and Heide. Goebbels and his wife then poisoned themselves with cyanide. Subordinates later burned the couple's bodies.

1945

Kaufering, Germany, is liberated by the U.S. Army. Very few inmates remain alive.

• April 28, 1945: The SS works with the Red Cross to safely transport 150 Jewish women from the concentration camp at Ravensbrück, Germany, to neutral Sweden. On the way, five of the women are killed during an Allied air raid. • Deposed Italian dictator Benito Mussolini is captured and executed by Italian partisans at Dongo, Italy; See April 29, 1945. • Heinrich Müller, Gestapo chief from 1934 to 1945, is seen for the last time, in Hitler's bunker.

• April 29, 1945: Hitler designates Admiral Karl Dönitz to succeed him

The Allies often forced captured German soldiers to exhume victims of the Holocaust so that their corpses could be buried under more sanitary conditions. Here, several German POWs unearth a mass grave at Kaufering III. The Kaufering camps, 11 in all, were subsidiaries of the Dachau, Germany, camp. The Nazis intended for prisoners to build fighter-aircraft factories, a program that never developed. Thousands of Kaufering inmates died from disease, overwork, malnutrition, or execution, and their bodies were dumped like garbage.

Anton Mussert *(with hat)* was the leader of the *Nationaal-Socialistische Beweging der Nederlanden* (Dutch Nazi Party). Although a firm supporter of the Nazis, he had very little influence over events during the long years of occupation. Hitler had no respect for him. On May 7, 1945, he was arrested by the Dutch Resistance. Mussert was executed exactly one year later.

On April 29, 1945, Hitler chose Admiral Karl Dönitz *(pictured)* as his successor, naming him president and supreme commander of what remained of Germany's armed forces. The *Führer* was convinced that the SS, the *Wehrmacht,* and the *Luftwaffe* had betrayed him. Only the German Navy, which had long ceased to be a factor in the war, seemed to Hitler to be untainted. Further, Heinrich Himmler and Hermann Göring had broken with the regime and attempted to strike separate deals with the Allies in futile attempts to save their skins. So Dönitz succeeded Hitler mainly by default. During the 23 days that President Dönitz led Germany, he perpetuated Hitler's anti-Soviet policies. Found guilty at Nuremberg on counts of waging aggressive war and war crimes, Dönitz was sentenced to ten years' imprisonment.

as *Führer* and Reich president. Propaganda Minister Joseph Goebbels is named Reich chancellor. • While trapped with intimates in his bunker beneath Berlin, Hitler dictates his final political testament. The document blames the Jews and their "collaborators" for the war and all of Germany's problems. Hitler ends by warning Germany: "Above all, I charge the leaders of the nation and those under them to scrupulous observance of the laws of race and to merciless opposition to the universal poisoner of all peoples, international Jewry." • Via a Radio Stockholm broadcast, Hitler learns of the April 28 execution of Italian dictator Benito Mussolini.

• Mussolini's corpse, and that of his mistress, Clara Petacci, are strung upside down in Milan's *Piazza Loreto* and mutilated by an angry mob. • The U.S. 42nd and 45th Infantry Divisions liberate the concentration camp at Dachau, Germany, and find 32,000 living inmates and 50 railroad cars piled with emaciated corpses. • At Allach, Germany, near Munich, many

Celebrating their hard-fought victory, a soldier raises a Soviet flag from the roof of the Reich Chancellery, the seat of Nazi power, now occupied by the Soviet Army. Under the leadership of war-hardened Generals Zhukov and Konev, the Soviet Army swept into the city. Frightened citizens of Berlin, fearing retribution, sought to flee the devastated capital.

With a bronze bust of Adolf Hitler tucked under his arm, a Soviet soldier celebrates the taking of the Berlin Reich Chancellery building. The last German forces, mostly old men and young boys of the Hitler Youth, could do little to hold back the vast Soviet Army. Berlin fell on May 2, and on May 7, at a schoolhouse near Reims, France, the German forces unconditionally surrendered. Nearly six years of European war—and death and devastation without parallel in history—had ended.

1945

Jewish refugees die of overeating following the arrival of supplies brought by American troops. • The Neuengamme, Germany, concentration camp is liberated by Britain's Royal Army. Very few inmates remain alive. • 123 SS guards captured at the Dachau, Germany, concentration camp are summarily executed by outraged American troops.

• April 30, 1945: Hitler and his bride, Eva Braun, commit suicide in Hitler's bunker below Berlin. • Hitler's valet and other intimates ascended with the bodies to the Chancellery garden. The corpses were doused with gas and set ablaze. • Allied troops capture Munich, Germany. • The Soviet Army captures the *Reichstag* building in Berlin. • Soviet troops liberate the

The Allies often made practical—and ironic—use of the former concentration camps to house German prisoners of war. This British soldier stands watch over German POWs being held in what had been the Neuengamme concentration camp.

SS troops in Copenhagen, Denmark, turn over their weapons before surrendering. The long years of conflict had taken their toll. Recognizing that the war was lost, these soldiers respond with joy to the order to proceed to the British lines, knowing that they had survived a war that many of their comrades had not.

Liberation was welcomed by every prisoner—although those who had collaborated with the Nazis had qualms about their altered situations. This Polish slave laborer (left) who relaxed on May 4, 1945, with a young companion, in quarters that had been occupied by the adjutant of the Flossenbürg, Germany, concentration camp, was later accused of being a *Kapo* who had mistreated the camp's Jewish prisoners.

Symbolic victories over their erstwhile captors were often important to camp prisoners. Here, for example, some of the former prisoners of the concentration camp at Mauthausen, Austria, tear down the Nazi eagle and swastika over the camp's main gate. Former inmates had suffered Nazi terror in horrifyingly unique ways, and were eager to destroy physical reminders of the Third Reich. It was left to some Allied soldiers, who encountered German troops mainly as battlefield adversaries, to regard Nazi artifacts as souvenirs to be gathered and kept.

A German *Reichsbank* official and U.S. Third Army troops examine bags of European currency hidden deep within a salt mine. This hiding place, one of many maintained by the Nazis, also yielded an estimated 100 tons of gold bullion and several art treasures. Nazi policy sanctioned the looting of billions of dollars worth of gold and other goods from Jewish and Christian owners. Most of the gold came from the national banks of occupied nations, but some derived from the gold teeth and personal possessions of exterminated victims of the Holocaust. We now know that governments and national banks of some neutral nations, especially Switzerland, helped launder looted gold, aiding the German war effort.

U.S. Seventh Army soldiers carry a few of the priceless paintings discovered in Neuschwanstein Castle in Bavaria. This loot had been earmarked for an art gallery at Linz, Austria, where Hitler had spent much of his childhood. The pieces were collected on the orders of Hermann Göring, Nazi Germany's leading art thief.

The Nazis elevated looting to the level of a dark art form, appropriating virtually everything of value that fell within their grasp. As the Reich crumbled early in 1945, the Allies discovered increasing numbers of Nazi caches of valuables. Here, First Lieutenant James Rorimer of the U.S. Seventh Army examines a tray of stolen antique jewelry, gold snuff boxes, and other items uncovered at Bavaria's Neuschwanstein Castle.

1945

Ravensbrück, Germany, camp, where about 2000 inmates remain alive. In two years, 30,000 Jews and non-Jews, most of them women and children, have died there.

• Late April 1945: Photographic images of the concentration camp at Bergen-Belsen, Germany, are widely circulated in Great Britain.

• May 1945: After 68 months of war, just one of every ten of Poland's prewar Jewish population of 3.3 million is alive. • Thirty thousand prisoners transported from Mauthausen, Austria, and Warsaw revolt at the labor camp at Ebensee, Austria. When they are ordered into a tunnel packed with explosives, they refuse to budge, confusing the SS

Walking on makeshift artificial legs, crippled Russian and Polish prisoners accompany an American armored car at Mauthausen. These prisoners had escaped the executions of disabled prisoners that occurred in the last days of the camp. Many were double amputees, with little hope of returning to the lives and jobs they had before the war.

Germany Surrenders

Germany's unconditional surrender on May 8, 1945, marked an ignominious end to the Third Reich. The regime had lasted a mere 12 years, not the one thousand that Hitler had promised. Yet in those 12 years, more than 35 million people had lost their lives because of Nazi aggression.

Adolf Hitler committed suicide on April 30, 1945. Admiral Karl Dönitz, Hitler's designated successor, recognized that Germany's situation was hopeless. Thus, on May 7, he sent Field Marshal Alfred Jodl and other senior generals to U.S. General Dwight Eisenhower's headquarters to sign  the terms of surrender. Appalled at what he had seen in the concentration camps, Eisenhower refused to accord the enemy the honor of attending the ceremony in person, instead sending emissaries from the British, French, and Soviet armies. A day later, the ceremony was repeated in Berlin, with Soviet General Georgi Zhukov accepting the surrender from German Field Marshal Wilhelm Keitel (pictured). May 8, 1945, has gone down in history as "V-E Day"—Victory in Europe.

German Colonel General Alfred Jodl (center), Major General Wilhelm Oxenius (left), and Admiral Hans von Friedeburg sign the papers indicating that Germany has surrendered unconditionally. Friedeburg would soon kill himself, and Jodl would be hanged after his conviction by the International Military Tribunal.

and *Volksdeutsche* guards, all of whom are mindful of the advancing Allies and the likelihood of war-crimes trials. The prisoners' defiance is successful and they are left unharmed. • Reich Minister of Education Bernhard Rust commits suicide. • *SS-Obergruppenführer* Hans-Adolf Prützmann, deeply involved in the September 1941 Babi Yar massacre,

commits suicide. • Martin Luther, the former deputy to Reich Foreign Minister Joachim von Ribbentrop, dies of heart failure.

• Early May 1945: Martin Bormann, Hitler's influential secretary, is likely killed by Soviet troops as he attempts to flee Berlin on foot. Rumors of his survival will continue for years.

• May 1, 1945: Nazi Minister of Propaganda Joseph Goebbels and his wife, Magda, commit suicide in the *Führerbunker* after fatally poisoning their six children. • A Jew in a group of laborers from the camp at Sonneberg, Germany, chants and dances with joy upon word of Hitler's death. A German guard calmly shoots the man dead. • The concentration camp

On May 3, a few days after Hitler's suicide, the Czechs of Prague rose against their German overlords. *Wehrmacht* troops inside the city threw back the civilian resisters for three days. Then, on May 6, the collaborationist Russian National Liberation Army commanded by General Andrei Vlasov turned on its German comrades, assuring that the German forces could not hold the city. German troops inside Prague began a retreat, and on May 9 the city was entered by Soviet forces. Many Czechs were wounded *(below)* and about 2000 gave their lives during the uprising.

On May 6, 1945, the U.S. Third Army liberated a camp at Ebensee in Austria. These survivors had obviously suffered from months, if not years, of starvation rations. One soldier remembered that "the living that were walking around were so gaunt; their heads were shaven; they had sores on their bodies. Some were walking about naked in a daze. Others had blankets wrapped around them, held together by a belt, and their facial features were normal size but everything else was completely out of proportion."

Like millions across Europe and North America, Americans celebrate V-E (Victory in Europe) Day on May 8, 1945, in Times Square in New York City. Behind them is a banner advertising the screening of the U.S. Army Signal Corps films about German atrocities.

1945

at Stutthof, Poland, is liberated by the Red Army. Just 120 inmates remain alive.

• **May 2, 1945:** Berlin is occupied by Soviet forces. • German troops in Berlin surrender. • German armies in Italy surrender. • The SS guards at the Neustadt-Glowen, Germany, labor camp near Lübeck fail to report for morning roll call, giving freedom to Jewish women who have been brought from Ravensbrück and Breslau, Germany, to dig defensive trenches and anti-tank ditches.

• **May 3, 1945:** Approximately 9400 Jewish prisoners who had been evacuated from Neuengamme and marched to Lübeck, Germany, are

Jews all over the world naturally greeted the defeat of Nazi Germany with joy. These Palestinian Jews took to the streets of Jerusalem to celebrate the end of the war in Europe. The banner reads: "The people of Israel remember their huge losses. They will not be silent and will not rest until independence is established in their homeland." The Holocaust provided an important impetus for the founding of the state of Israel in 1948.

This American Army truck parked at Nordhausen, Germany, is adorned with the date of V-E Day, May 8, 1945. Germany had surrendered on May 7—a significant day for these GIs, and no less significant for the rail-thin survivor of slave labor who stands with them. May 8 also brought the end of German resistance in Latvia and, in a real coup for the Allies, the capture in Austria of top Nazi Hermann Göring.

The end of World War II—announced here by a variety of Palestinian newspapers—was received with joy by the victors; with confusion and a sort of relief by the vanquished. Perhaps no nation, though, felt the uncertainty and difficulty of what was to follow more than Palestine, where the British strictly controlled immigration, and where Jews lobbied fervently for a Jewish homeland.

loaded by their overseers onto two ships, the *Thielbeck* and the *Cap Arcona*, apparently for no other purpose but a Nazi hope that the Jews would die while on board. British planes, unaware that the ships are not hostile, attack. Both ships sink in the Lübeck harbor within 15 minutes. Survivors who attempt to swim to shore are fired upon by waiting

members of the Hitler Youth, *Volkstrum*, and the SS. Of the 9400 prisoners, only about 2400 survive. • With Germany near defeat, the Czech Resistance rises in revolt and battles the German Army in Prague. *See May 9, 1945.*

• May 4, 1945: Salzburg, Austria, is occupied by Allied forces. • German

forces surrender in the Netherlands, northern Germany, and Denmark.
• Red Army troops liberate the camp at Oranienburg, Germany, where 5000 inmates remain alive. • The International Red Cross takes over the administration of the camp/ghetto at Theresienstadt, Czechoslovakia. The last of the camp's SS men flee. • The U.S. 82nd Airborne Divi-

Odessa

In the days of confusion after the war, many Nazis—from senior SS officials to concentration-camp guards—escaped justice by fleeing Europe. How war criminals such as Adolf Eichmann, Josef Mengele, and Franz Stangl reached safety in South America remains shrouded in mystery. The name "Odessa" has been used to refer to a secret network of organizations that facilitated the escape of Nazis and furnished them with new identities.

Speculation abounds about the leadership and finances of these secret organizations, but no doubt exists that Nazis received help of various kinds, from forged passports to tickets and money, sometimes from those who knew their identities, sometimes from those who were duped. In South America, sympathetic dictators refused requests for extradition, sometimes leaving kidnaping as the only means to bring a Nazi criminal to justice. This was the case with Eichmann, who was seized in Argentina by Israeli secret-service agents and transported to Israel to stand trial.

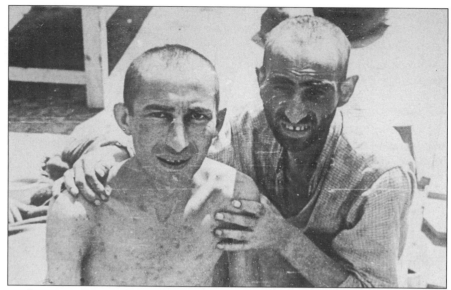

The Nazis originally created Theresienstadt in Czechoslovakia as a model ghetto/camp complex to dupe the outside world into believing that the regime was not treating Jews badly. But the camp soon became one of the most horrible in Europe. These two skeletal men survived Theresienstadt.

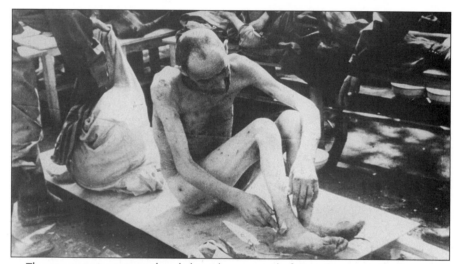

Those camp inmates who did not have poorly fitting footwear had none at all, and prisoners constantly confronted maladies of their feet and legs. This man, a survivor of Theresienstadt, is taking care of the abscesses on his legs and feet. Such debilitating foot problems often led to a prisoner's demise, since inability to work meant death.

1945

sion liberates the concentration camp at Wöebbelin, Germany.

• May 5, 1945: The U.S. 11th Armored Division liberates the concentration camp at Mauthausen, Austria. 110,000 survivors are found, including 28,000 Jews. Bodies of 10,000 inmates are discovered in a mass grave. In the days following lib-

eration, more than 3000 inmates will die. • The camp at Gusen, Austria, near Mauthausen, is liberated by the U.S. Army; 2000 inmates remain alive. • German troops surrender in Norway. • The presiding bishop of the German-Catholic bishops' conference instructs his priests to say a mass in Hitler's memory. • The U.S. 71st Infantry Division liberates the camp

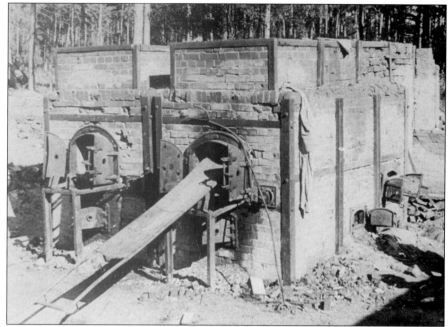

Eventually, of course, survivors left the camps, either to return home or to emigrate. The Holocaust had displaced millions, especially in Eastern Europe. These women were photographed as they left the labor camp in Theresienstadt.

These outdoor ovens were located at the concentration camp at Stutthof, Poland. Usually they would have been housed in a crematorium building, but in this case Nazi engineers improvised, probably to maintain the pace of cremations. Killing several million people was a very expensive undertaking, a cruelly practical consideration of which the Nazis were keenly aware.

By June 1944, Zyklon B was the preferred method for gassing con-centration-camp prisoners at Stut-thof. It was an easy, relatively economical way to kill many people quickly. These cans of the deadly pesticide were captured by Soviet troops at Stutthof before they could be put to use.

Two Soviet soldiers and three civilians stand near a mountain of victims' shoes at the Gross-Rosen camp in Germany. At its height, the Gross-Rosen complex included 77 satellite camps and at least 80,000 prisoners, most of whom performed slave labor. The Nazis evacuated the camp in February 1945, shipping out prisoners on wagons or death marches.

As Allied forces fought their way closer to concentration camps, German troops and collaborators, SS men assigned to the "care" of Jews and other prisoners were taken captive in ever-increasing numbers. The men seen here were photographed after they fell into Allied hands. Clockwise from top left they are Leonhard Eichberger, a death-march SS guard; Michael Redwitz, SS guard; Konrad Belsh, death-march SS guard; and Jean Scheibel, a guard, possibly not with the SS.

1945

at Gunskirchen, Austria, where 18,000 inmates remain alive. Hungarian author and journalist Geza Havas, force-marched to the camp from Mauthausen, dies a few hours before the Americans arrive. • At the Ebensee, Austria, concentration camp, a brutal German *Kapo* (foreman) pleads with inmates not to turn him over to approaching Americans as a war criminal. He is attacked by three Jewish boys and killed. Other Germans at Ebensee meet similar fates. Late in the day, a white flag is raised above the Ebensee guard tower.

• May 6, 1945: A death march from Schwarzheide, Germany, to Theresienstadt, Czechoslovakia, that began

Camp guards often executed inmates as the Allied armies approached. Here, commandant Eichelsdörfer of the Kaufering III concentration camp at Landsberg, Germany, is forced by American liberators to stand amidst the emaciated corpses of hundreds of

the camp's victims, many of whom had been shot as the Americans drew near. Kaufering III was a subcamp of Dachau.

Camp survivors often sought revenge against their former captors, especially those who had been particularly vicious. Here, at the camp at Gusen, Austria, a small crowd of liberated prisoners and American soldiers scrutinizes the dead body of a camp guard, who was killed by some of his former charges.

Victims and Statistics

On June 28, 1941, German forces conquered the Belorussian city of Minsk. The Germans had killed thousands of its 80,000 ghettoized Jews by mid-autumn, but Masha Bruskina, a 17-year-old girl, was among the Jews who resisted. The Germans caught her, and she was hanged on October 26. Starvation, forced labor, shooting, gassing . . . Nazi Germany destroyed European Jews and millions of non-Jews in many ways, but each person perished one by one.

Individual deaths multiplied into mind-boggling statistics. One leading Holocaust scholar, Raul Hilberg, estimates that 5.1 million Jews perished in the Holocaust. Most scholars now believe that the Jewish death total approached six million. Israel Gutman and Robert Rozett, for example, put Jewish losses between 5,596,000 and 5,860,000. German scholar Wolfgang Benz lists the figure at 6.1 million. The estimates of deaths vary widely for several reasons: the years and geographical boundaries used to determine prewar census data, the margins of error in death reports from German and Jewish sources, the difficulties of comparing prewar and postwar populations, and the fact that the Germans and their collaborators did not record the death of every victim.

Every reliable judgment finds that nearly two-thirds of the European Jews—and one-third of the Jews in the world—were killed in the Holocaust. Hitler intended to obliterate all Jewish life—root and branch. The staggering number of those who indeed met their deaths demonstrates how close he came.

on April 18 halts at Leitmeritz, Czechoslovakia. • The U.S. 11th Armored Division liberates the concentration camp at Ebensee, Austria. Nearly 10,000 bodies are discovered in an enormous communal grave. 3500 inmates remain alive; however, many of these survivors die from overindulging in food innocently offered to them by the Americans.

• May 7, 1945: Germany signs an unconditional surrender at U.S. General Dwight D. Eisenhower's headquarters at Rheims, France. The fighting in Europe is to end at 11:01 P.M. on May 9; See May 8, 1945. • Breslau, Germany, is captured by Soviet troops after an 82-day siege. • Dutch Nazi leader and collaborator Anton Mussert is arrested. • Hungarian novelist Andor

Endre Gelleri, age 38, dies at the Mauthausen, Austria, slave-labor camp two days after liberation.

• May 8, 1945: V-E (Victory in Europe) Day: The Allies accept the unconditional surrender of Germany. • The Red Army liberates the concentration camp at Gross-Rosen, Germany. • Allies capture Hermann Göring.

Aliya Bet

Aliya Bet refers to the illegal migration of Jews to Palestine before the creation of the state of Israel in 1948. Approximately 25 percent of the 530,000 Jewish immigrants who entered Palestine before 1948 did so by way of *Aliya Bet.*

While some Jews who illegally entered Palestine took the trip on their own initiative, many journeys were arranged by Zionist organizations. The majority of immigrants traveled by boat, although some took an overland route from Eastern Europe. Some Jews simply remained in Palestine after entering as tourists. Regardless of the method employed, illegal Jewish immigration was challenged by the British (who governed Palestine) at every juncture. More than 50,000 people were caught *(above)* and deported to detention camps in Cyprus.

After the war, Zionists worked feverishly to relocate survivors of the Holocaust from Europe's displaced-persons camps to Palestine. The high visibility of *Aliya Bet* and the international pressure it brought to bear were instrumental in the creation of a Jewish state.

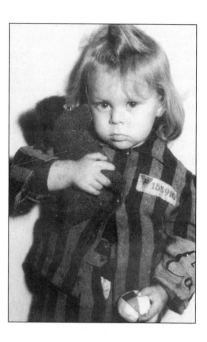

It was impossible to have a normal childhood in a concentration camp, but parents and other adults often sought to provide some sense of normality for the children imprisoned in the camps. This little girl, photographed in Prague, Czechoslovakia, wears her camp uniform while holding a stuffed animal and a ball, toys she undoubtedly held dear.

The Nazis, as part of their effort to give their crimes an aura of legality, were fanatics about paperwork. These deportation notices, discovered in Prague, sent thousands of Czechs to their deaths. These papers also helped convince victims that they were indeed going to be resettled in the East rather than shipped to extermination camps.

1945

• **May 9, 1945: The camp/ghetto at Theresienstadt, Czechoslovakia, is liberated by Soviet forces.** • **Friedrich Krüger, an *SS-Obergruppenführer* responsible for mass exterminations of Polish Jews, commits suicide.** • **Soviet troops and members of the Czech Resistance defeat German forces in Prague, the last European capital to be liberated.** • **The Russian** Army of Liberation, a collaborationist, anti-Communist Soviet force of 20,000 that elected to battle alongside the SS, turns against its German "allies" in Prague. Army of Liberation commander Andrei Vlasov, with help provided by General Sergei Bunyachenko, holds off German reinforcements in heavy street fighting.

Nazi doctors took unconscionable advantage of the human guinea pigs at their disposal. This woman, a concentration-camp survivor, was the victim of horrific "experimental" operations upon her breasts. Possibly, the doctors were testing a new treatment for cancer or were interested in various aspects of the woman's reproductive system.

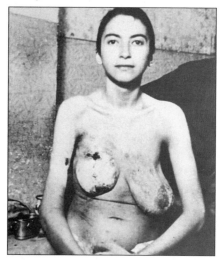

The chief rabbi of Rome, Dr. David Prato *(left)*, discusses the problems of displaced European Jews in Italy with the chief rabbi of Jerusalem, Isaac Herman Herzog, and a representative of the European headquarters of the American Joint Distribution Committee, Arthur Greenleigh. Although only 40 percent of the displaced persons who migrated to the U.S. after the war were Jews, Americans assumed that Jews comprised the vast majority and, in general, opposed this immigration. But once it became clear that most Jewish displaced persons wanted to go to Israel, American opinion began to favor Jewish emigration from Europe. A blunt analysis of this situation was made by postwar British Foreign Minister Ernest Bevin: The Americans were enthusiastic about opening Palestine to the Jews because they didn't want to have many of them in New York.

Heinrich Himmler, the chief of the SS, had attempted to sell Jews to save his own neck during the final months of the war. At the end of the war he was among the most-wanted war criminals in Occupied Germany. He attempted to avoid arrest by shaving his mustache, donning an eyepatch and a *Wehrmacht* uniform, and traveling under the pseudonym Heinrich Hitzinger. Nonetheless, he was arrested on May 23, 1945, only to commit suicide almost immediately by biting down on a small glass vial of cyanide he had secreted in his mouth.

● **May 10, 1945:** ● SS General Richard Glücks, head of the Reich concentration camp inspectorate, is found dead at the Flensburg naval hospital. The cause of death—suicide or murder—is unclear. ● German forces in Czechoslovakia surrender. ● Norwegian traitor Vidkun Quisling is arrested; *See* October 24, 1945.

● **May 11, 1945:** Josef Terboven, the Reich commissioner for Norway who deported many Norwegian Jews to Germany, commits suicide with dynamite.

● **May 19, 1945:** Philip Bouhler, Hitler's assistant and supervisor (1939–1941) of "mercy killings" of the hopelessly ill and insane, commits

suicide with his wife as American troops attempt to arrest him.

● **May 20–27, 1945:** Four Polish Jews who return to their hometown of Dzialoszyce are murdered by Poles.

● **May 21, 1945:** Many liberated survivors continue to live at the Dachau concentration camp. ● Odilo Globoc-

Rivka Tusko-laska, a survivor of Auschwitz, was among the inhabitants of Kibbutz (communal farm) Buchenwald, which was founded in June 1945 near the town of Geringshof, Germany, in the American zone of occupation. The members of the *kibbutz* immigrated to Palestine in 1946, where they joined the Kibbutz Afikim, but later established their own *kibbutz*, Netzer Sereni.

Residents of the Kibbutz Buchenwald, founded by survivors of the infamous Buchenwald, Germany, concentration camp, dance the *hora*. This *kibbutz*, founded on German soil, was designed to prepare its members —through agricultural training—for immigration to Palestine. Kibbutz Buchenwald was dissolved in 1947 when its inhabitants immigrated to Palestine on the boat *Tel Chai*.

German prisoners of war held in American hands were well treated —a situation in marked contrast to the horrors perpetrated by Nazis against Soviet POWs and helpless Jews and other civilians. These yet-to-be-repatriated German POWs were assembled at New York's Halloran General Hospital on the morning of June 26, 1945, to view films of German atrocities. Reactions ranged from keen interest to outright shame and grief.

1945

nik, *SS-Gruppenführer* and founder of the death camps at Belzec, Majdanek, and Sobibór, commits suicide shortly after being taken prisoner by the British.

• **May 22, 1945:** Polish freebooters stop a train in the Bialystok region of Poland and beat and abduct a Jew named Mejer Sznajder.

• **May 23, 1945:** A clumsily disguised Heinrich Himmler is recognized and arrested by a British patrol at Bremervörde, Germany. During a preliminary interrogation later in the day at Lüneburg Heath, Germany, the SS chief surprises his captors by abruptly committing suicide with a cyanide capsule hidden in his mouth.

In July 1945 the Swedish government agreed to provide medical care for 10,000 infirm concentration-camp survivors. The former prisoners were first sent to the Swedish Transit Hospital at Lübeck, Germany, and then were transported to Sweden. This patient, among others, was too ill to travel and had to remain at the hospital. A United Nations Relief and Rehabilitation Association official is interviewing him about his possible return to Poland.

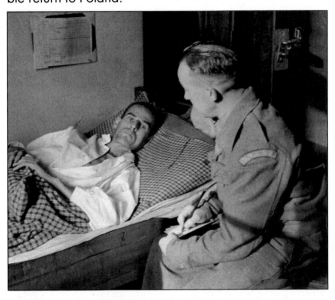

Elie Wiesel

As a Jewish teenager in 1944, Elie Wiesel was deported with his family from Transylvania to Auschwitz-Birkenau. Though his mother and sister were gassed, Elie was liberated from the Buchenwald concentration camp in 1945. Questioning the silence of both the Allies and of the Jewish God before the apocalypse that was the Holocaust, Wiesel wrote a memoir of his Holocaust experiences, *And the World Stood Silent*, which was later retitled *Night*.

Winner of the 1986 Nobel Peace Prize, Wiesel has movingly portrayed Jewish life and spirit in countless essays and more than 20 books. He has pointed out that "while not all victims [of the Holocaust] were Jews, all Jews were victims."

Jolting the conscience of the world, he publicly questioned U.S. President Ronald Reagan's decision to visit the Bitburg, Germany, cemetery, where SS members were buried: "Mr. President," he declared, "your place is with the victims, not the SS." Wiesel continues to write and speak about the moral indecency of silence and the necessity of human dignity.

An American GI stands at the "Temple of Honor," a memorial of "Nazi martyrs" in Munich, Germany. The stately monument memorialized deceased National Socialists, whereas their victims' corpses, mostly those of Jews, were dumped in nameless mass graves or burned in ovens. The only memorial to the Nazis' victims was the fleeting smoke that rose to the sky.

• **June 1945: Displaced Jews at the Buchenwald, Germany, displaced-persons camp establish Kibbutz Buchenwald, an agricultural training center designed to help young Jews succeed at *kibbutz* (communal) life.**

• **Public-opinion polls indicate that Americans consider Jews a far greater threat to America than they consider German or Japanese Americans.**

• **Mid-1945: Kibbutz Nili is established on the former estate of Julius Streicher, near Pleikershof, Germany, to train Jewish displaced persons in agriculture and provide schooling for Jewish boys and girls.**

• **June 14, 1945: Nazi Foreign Minister Joachim von Ribbentrop is arrested by the British.**

• **June 30–July 14, 1945: "Lest We Forget," an exhibition of death-camp photography organized by the *St. Louis Post-Dispatch* and the Washington *Evening Star*, tours Boston, Massachusetts, and the Midwest. It is viewed by nearly 90,000 Americans.**

• **July 25, 1945: "Euthanasia" advocate Kurt Gerstein, the former head**

Primo Levi

The writings of Primo Levi, an Italian Jew who survived the Holocaust, comprise one of the most articulate analyses of life in Nazi concentration camps.

Born in Turin, Italy, and trained as a chemist, Levi fled to the mountains when the Italian government of Pietro Badoglio surrendered to the Allies in 1943, prompting the Germans to occupy much of the country. After being captured by a Fascist militia, Levi was imprisoned in the Fossoli, Italy, transit camp and then sent to Auschwitz-Birkenau in February 1944.

The ten months that Levi spent in Birkenau provide the context for his memoir, *Survival in Auschwitz: The Nazi Assault on Humanity*. This poignant book describes the notorious death camp as a "biological and social experiment of gigantic dimensions."

Levi's suicide in 1987 serves as a painful reminder of the long-term impact of the Holocaust.

Pierre Laval, the former collaborationist premier of Vichy France, testifies at the trial of Marshal Philippe Pétain *(seated, right),* who was charged with high treason. Pétain was convicted and sentenced to death, but his sentence was commuted by General Charles de Gaulle to exile on the island of Yeu. Two months later it was Laval's turn to stand before the court, in a hasty trial in which no defense witnesses were called and at which he was speedily convicted. Although Laval pleaded his innocence, he was executed on October 9, 1945.

In August 1945 the leadership of the Zionist movement held the World Zionist Conference in London. In the first row, from left to right, are Yitzhak Zuckerman, Haika Grosman, Emil Sommerstein, and an unidentified man. In the second row are Abba Hillel Silver, Moshe Sharett, and Nahum Goldmann. Third row: Moshe Sneh, Itzhak Gruenbaum, and an unidentified man. Participants at the conference protested Britain's refusal to permit more Jews to immigrate to Palestine. In Palestine, the impatience of the Jewish population led to an increase in violent attacks upon the British.

1945

of the *Waffen-SS* Institute of Hygiene in Berlin, hangs himself in prison.

• July 30, 1945: The administration of Germany is assumed by the Allied Control Council; *See* October 10, 1945.

• July 31, 1945: French collaborationist politician Pierre Laval is

arrested in Austria; *See* October 9, 1945.

• August 1945: The 22nd World Zionist Congress demands immediate admission of 100,000 Jewish refugees to Eretz-Israel. Britain refuses, prompting violent revolts by the Jewish underground in Palestine, carried out by *Hagana, Palmah, Lohame*

Vidkun Quisling led the National Socialist movement in Norway, helping to establish the German occupation of his country in 1940. Over the next five years, thousands of Norwegian patriots died resisting the Nazi occupation. On June 19, 1945, Quisling was forced to view some of the mass graves of those murdered during the occupation. On October 24 the traitor Quisling paid for his crimes when he was executed.

British Lieutenant General Sir Frederick Morgan, seen here, was appointed to the United Nations Relief and Rehabilitation Administration (UNRRA) directorate late in the summer of 1945, some two years after the organization's creation. Although the end of the war had been anticipated long before hostilities ceased, UNRRA was initially overwhelmed by the vast numbers of displaced persons who were housed in DP camps, or who wandered former battlegrounds and captive nations.

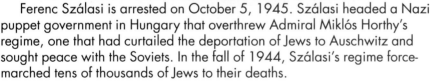
Ferenc Szálasi is arrested on October 5, 1945. Szálasi headed a Nazi puppet government in Hungary that overthrew Admiral Miklós Horthy's regime, one that had curtailed the deportation of Jews to Auschwitz and sought peace with the Soviets. In the fall of 1944, Szálasi's regime force-marched tens of thousands of Jews to their deaths.

Herut Israel (Stern Gang), and *Irgun Zva'i Leumi* (IZL; National Military Organization).

• **August 6, 1945: An American B-29 drops an atomic bomb on Hiroshima, Japan.**

• **August 8, 1945: The Allies meet to develop a charter for an International** Military Tribunal to try German war criminals. • **The Soviets declare war on Japan, to take effect on August 9.**

• **August 9, 1945: An American B-29 drops an atomic bomb on Nagasaki, Japan.**

• **August 11, 1945: Anti-Jewish riots erupt in Kraków, Poland.**

• **August 27, 1945: Hermann Göring is the first Nuremberg defendant to be interrogated intensively by the Allies.**

• **Autumn 1945: Reich chief physician Leonardo Conti, who killed hundreds of Germans of "unsound mind," commits suicide.**

Displaced Persons

Following Nazi Germany's surrender on May 8, 1945, an estimated 11 million Europeans—specifically non-German and non-Austrian nationals—remained uprooted from their home countries. They were classified as "displaced persons" (DPs) by the Allies and the United Nations Relief and Rehabilitation Administration (UNRRA), which had been founded on November 9, 1943, to deal with anticipated DP issues.

Seven million of the DPs were in Germany. During the war, the majority of these people had been brought to Germany to work for the Third Reich. About 800,000 Poles alone had been conscripted for labor by the Nazis. Still others, including approximately 200,000 Jews, were recently liberated inmates who had survived Nazi camps and death marches.

By the end of 1945, more than six million DPs had gone back to their native lands, but between 1.5 and two million of them refused repatriation. The non-Jews who did not want to return home were mostly Poles, Estonians, Latvians, Lithuanians, Ukrainians, and Yugoslavians. In some cases they feared political reprisals for their Nazi collaboration; in other cases they dreaded persecution by Eastern Europe's Communist regimes.

For Jews, returning home was scarcely an option. Their families had been annihilated, their communities destroyed, their property confiscated. If these Jews did try to go home again, their arrival was often greeted with hostility and physical violence from former neighbors.

For the most part, the concept of "home" no longer existed for Jewish DPs. Instead, they found themselves in grim DP camps on German soil (such as the one pictured at Zeilsheim). Most of these places were enclosed by barbed wire, overcrowded, and situated in former labor or concentration camps. Many Jews were harassed or assaulted by former Nazi collaborators. Jews hoped for immigration opportunities that would take them to destinations such as Palestine or the United States, but until then they endured daily drudgery and tension.

Jewish chaplains in the U.S. Army, such as Rabbi Judah Nadich and especially Rabbi Abraham Klausner, worked tirelessly on behalf of Jewish DPs. They successfully encouraged the Allied authorities to establish all-Jewish DP camps, where conditions for the Jewish DPs improved. Feldafing, which housed about 3700 people, was the first of these places. Jewish DP camps at Landsberg and Föhrenwald sheltered another 5000 Jews each. In the American zone of occupation, a dozen DP camps were maintained exclusively for Jews by the end of 1945.

By 1952 most of the Jewish DP camps had closed, although the one at Föhrenwald operated under the supervision of the democratic Federal Republic of Germany until early 1957. Before the Jewish DP camps finally were emptied, nearly 250,000 Jews had lived in them.

1945

- September 1945: *Ichud* (Unity), a Jewish political organization, is established by the leadership of the Landsberg displaced-persons (DP) camp. It initially acts as an intermediary between DPs and the United States Army in negotiations for DP immigration to Palestine. • The policy regarding displaced persons in the American Zone of Occupation is changed following a report of abuses against DPs.

- September 1, 1945: Yaakov Waldman, a survivor of a 1942 death march, is murdered by Poles in Turek, Poland.

- September 2, 1945: Japan surrenders, ending World War II.

Women in a DP camp in Germany participate in sewing lessons run by the Organization for Rehabilitation through Training (ORT). The ORT offered vocational training to European Jews beginning in 1940, and also sponsored courses that, if discovered, would have incurred Nazi displeasure: medicine, graphic arts, architecture, and other arts. By war's end, the ORT turned its energies to the more immediate needs of Europe's DPs. It was one of various groups, some with financial support from the American Joint Distribution Committee, that sought to train survivors in the skills they would need to find jobs and support themselves in the postwar world.

This sign for the Jewish Agency for Palestine hung on the agency's office door in the Zeilsheim, Germany, displaced-persons camp. The Jewish Agency had been promoting the emigration of Jews to Palestine, both legally and illegally, since the 1930s. The British estimated that approximately 58,000 European Jews arrived in Palestine between 1940 and 1945, a significant number of them unlawfully.

Some Jewish immigrants arrived in Palestine legally. Among them was this man, a passenger on the ship *Transylvania*. He's being interviewed by journalists upon his arrival in Haifa on October 26, 1945. It was estimated that from January 1, 1946, to May 15, 1948, 48,451 Jews immigrated to Palestine—30,000 illegally.

A significant portion of SS camp personnel did not elude the Allies, and guards at the Dachau, Germany, concentration camp were no exception. Dachau had been liberated by American forces in April 1945, and in mid-November a month-long trial of 40 former camp staff members began. Thirty-six defendants were sentenced to death. Seen here is the main entrance to the court, which was established on the camp's grounds.

Because of the Holocaust, many Jews, especially children, had lost contact with their cultural heritage. Hence, it was important to Jews to educate young survivors about Judaism. This photograph shows a Hebrew lesson in the Zeilsheim, Germany, displaced-persons camp. The board gives a hopeful—and determined—message: "The Jews will immigrate to the land of Israel."

Dr. Hans Marx, Dr. Otto Stahmer, and Dr. Fritz Sauter (pictured; specific identifications not possible) were among the defense counsels at the Nuremberg Trials. Depending on whom they were defending, they argued that either their clients were "only following orders" or did not know about the crimes the Nazi regime had committed. Some defense lawyers even argued that the tribunal had no jurisdiction over their clients. The clients of these attorneys—Julius Streicher, Hermann Göring, and Rudolf Hess—were all convicted.

1945

• **September 17–November 17, 1945:** Forty-eight former members of the administration of the concentration camp at Bergen-Belsen, Germany, are tried at Lüneberg, Germany. Eleven are sentenced to death and executed and 23 are imprisoned.

• **September 20, 1945:** The Jewish Agency for Palestine makes its first claim for restitution from Germany for crimes Nazis committed against Jews.

• **Late September 1945:** Of 100,000 captured Nazi documents, the Allies select about 4000 as having evidentiary value to the War Crimes Tribunal.

Life was extremely precarious for Holocaust survivors after their liberation. Most had no place to live, no families left, and nothing to eat. Without a massive relief effort, many more of them would have died. Among the organizations that played an important role in aiding Holocaust survivors were the Red Cross and the American Jewish Joint Distribution Committee (JDC). This photograph, taken in Vienna, shows Harry Weinsaft, a member of the JDC, distributing Red Cross parcels to displaced Jews.

Russian men, women, and children stroll along the path of a displaced-persons camp in Allach, near Munich, Germany. Laundry hanging to dry testifies to their efforts to establish a pattern of normal life. At the end of the war, seven to nine million displaced persons were scattered throughout Europe, most of them uncertain about what the future would hold.

Joint Distribution Committee

The American Jewish Joint Distribution Committee (JDC) was the primary vehicle for relief operations carried out by American Jewry both during and after the war. While the JDC never mounted a mass rescue operation in Europe, its efforts on behalf of European Jewry were particularly important after World War II.

During the Holocaust, the JDC's relief activities increased the survival chances for many Jews. Its funds provided aid for European orphanages, hospitals, and public kitchens.  Money from the JDC also helped Jews obtain false identity papers and send food parcels to those in concentration camps and ghettos.

After the war, the committee intensified its efforts. Together with other organizations, the JDC provided tremendous support for Jews living in Europe's displaced-persons camps. The JDC spent $280 million from 1946 to 1950 on food, clothing, books, school supplies, and other necessities. In the photo seen here, JDC officials discuss a map of the organization's activities in the U.S. Zone of Germany.

With the founding of the Israeli State, the JDC helped bring refugees to Israel and established vocational training centers. That Israel overcame early obstacles and gave Holocaust survivors opportunities to rebuild their lives was due in no small part to the focus and dedication of the JDC.

• **October 1945:** At Boleslawiec, Poland, eight Jews are murdered by an antisemitic Polish underground group. • Pastor Martin Niemöller, German resister and founder of the Confessional Church, issues the *Stuttgart Confession of Guilt*, which maintains the collective guilt of the German people for the Hitler regime.

• **October 6, 1945:** Important German detainees at Nuremberg are informed for the first time that they are to be the defendants in an international trial.

• **October 9, 1945:** After his trial in Paris, French collaborationist politician Pierre Laval is executed by firing squad.

• **October 10, 1945:** The NSDAP is abolished, some 25 years after originating in Munich, Germany.

• **October 24, 1945:** Norwegian traitor Vidkun Quisling is executed at Oslo, Norway. • Nazi trade-union chief Robert Ley hangs himself in his prison cell at Nuremberg.

War-Crimes Trials

More than 35 million people—most of them civilians—were killed in Europe during World War II. What treatment should be meted out to the Nazi leaders who had unleashed genocidal violence? The Allies weighed these questions at Nuremberg, Germany, the site of a series of war-crimes trials.

On November 20, 1945, U.S. Supreme Court Justice Robert H. Jackson began the prosecution at Nuremberg. "The most savage and numerous crimes planned and committed by the Nazis," he emphasized, "were those against the Jews." Hitler, Heinrich Himmler, and other major Nazi figures did not hear his words. They had escaped trial by committing suicide. Twenty-two other Nazis were in the dock, however, when the International Military Tribunal (IMT), consisting of judges from the Allied powers—Great Britain, France, the USSR, and the United States—began its work.

The Nazi defendants included Martin Bormann, Nazi Party secretary and chief aide to Hitler, who was tried *in absentia* (he had not been found and was believed to be dead); Hermann Göring (*pictured, left*), who had authorized Reinhard Heydrich to prepare the "Final Solution"; Ernst Kaltenbrunner, head of the Security Police; Hans Frank, the Nazi governor of Occupied Poland; and Julius Streicher, a leading antisemitic propagandist.

Jackson's opening statement notwithstanding, the indictments against these men did not refer explicitly to crimes against Jewry. Instead, each of the Nuremberg defendants was tried on one or more of the following charges: (1) crimes against peace, (2) war crimes, (3) crimes against humanity, and (4) conspiracy to commit any of these crimes.

The IMT acquitted three of the defendants. Twelve others—including Bormann, Göring, Kaltenbrunner, Frank, and Streicher—were sentenced to death by hanging. Seven more, including Albert Speer and others who

had used concentration-camp prisoners as slave laborers, received prison terms.

Under U.S. jurisdiction, 12 more trials were held at Nuremberg from October 1946 to April 1949. Indictments against Nazi war criminals led to trials in a variety of other courts, too. Nevertheless, only a fraction of the thousands directly involved in war crimes and the Holocaust were brought to justice.

That shortcoming, however, does not diminish the essential contributions that those postwar trials made. They documented much that had happened, and their proceedings became a public record that continues to bear witness to the Holocaust. In addition, the trials established important principles: Leaders can be held legally responsible for crimes committed in carrying out their government's policies, and individuals cannot defend themselves by simply claiming that they had only obeyed orders.

In the aftermath of the trials, the United Nations adopted a Convention for the Prevention of Crimes of Genocide as well as a Universal Declaration of Human Rights.

1945

- October 25, 1945: Jews are attacked in Sosnowiec, Poland.

- November 15–December 14, 1945: Forty former members of the Dachau, Germany, camp administration are tried. Thirty-seven are sentenced to death, with some sentenced *in absentia*.

- November 19, 1945: Anti-Jewish riots erupt in Lublin, Poland.

- November 20, 1945: The Nuremberg Trials of suspected top-level Nazi war criminals open. Defendants include Hermann Göring, Alfred Rosenberg, Rudolph Hess, and Julius Streicher.

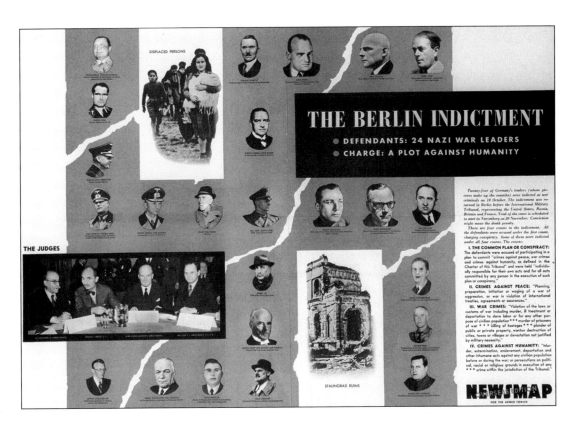

THE BERLIN INDICTMENT
- DEFENDANTS: 24 NAZI WAR LEADERS
- CHARGE: A PLOT AGAINST HUMANITY

This poster was designed to inform American GIs about the indictment of the alleged Nazi war criminals. The German leaders were accused of any combination of three crimes: crimes against humanity, planning aggressive war, and war crimes. Since the Nuremberg Trials were without precedent, the Allies believed that it was very important to explain their purpose to their own citizens and soldiers, and also to the people of Germany.

The defendants, sitting in the dock at Nuremberg, hear the reading of the indictment against them. High-ranking Nazis include *(beginning in the front row, far left)* Hermann Göring, Rudolf Hess, Joachim von Ribbentrop, and Wilhelm Keitel. This monumental war-crimes tribunal is quite likely "the trial of the century."

Julius Streicher is questioned during his trial at Nuremberg. An infamous antisemite, Streicher published the pornographic rag *Der Stürmer*. His personality was so repulsive that no one inside the Nazi movement took him seriously, and he had little influence over the course of events during the Nazi years. Nonetheless, the Allies held him responsible for fomenting the hatred of Jews that made the Holocaust possible, and he was convicted of crimes against humanity. Streicher was hanged in Nuremberg on October 16, 1946. His last words were "*Heil* Hitler!"

Robert H. Jackson

Head of the prosecutorial team at the Nuremberg International Military Tribunal, American Robert H. Jackson brought a wealth of judicial experience to his duties. Widely respected for his integrity, Jackson served in the Roosevelt administration—first as solicitor general and later as attorney general—before being appointed to the Supreme Court. President Harry Truman chose him to represent the U.S. in the trials, granting him the rank of lieutenant-general in the Army.

An eloquent spokesman for those who had suffered under Nazi rule, Jackson argued that the plaintiff in the case against the Nazi leaders was no single nation, nor even the Allies jointly. The complainant was, in fact, "civilization." In his closing speech at the trial, Jackson argued that a verdict of innocence would be tantamount to proclaiming that "there has been no war, there are no slain, there has been no crime."

An American military policeman looks into the cell of Hermann Göring, the most prominent prisoner at the Nuremberg city jail. Because the Allies feared that the indicted Nazi leaders would try to cheat the hangman by doing themselves in, the prisoners were under a constant suicide watch. Hitler, Joseph Goebbels, and Heinrich Himmler had all killed themselves rather than face justice. Göring would indeed commit suicide, on October 14, 1946, with cyanide that he had skillfully concealed for months, or that was slipped to him by persons unknown.

In November 1945 at Nuremberg, in a cell beneath the dining room of American war-crimes investigators, German Colonel Joachim Peiper could smell Thanksgiving dinner. Peiper had been accused of failing to prevent the massacre of 86 unarmed American servicemen captured at Malmédy, Belgium, in 1944. Because prisoner rations at Nuremberg were modest, Peiper let it be known he would work for whatever Thanksgiving food might be left over. The American officers agreed—on the condition that Peiper don a suit and work as their waiter. Here, the humbled colonel serves his captors. Peiper was rewarded with leftovers, but was transferred the next day to the Allied facility at Dachau, Germany, for further interrogation. Although sentenced to death in 1946, Peiper was released from prison ten years later.

1945

• **December 1945: Antisemitic Poles murder 11 Jews in the town of Kosow-Lacki, Poland,** which is located less than six miles from the site of the Treblinka extermination camp. • **Oliver Cox, an American sociologist, concludes that Christians in the United States regard the Jew as "our irreconcilable enemy within the gates, the antithesis of our God, the disturber of our way of life and of our social aspirations."

• **December 22, 1945: The American Displaced Persons Act makes it easier for Nazi war criminals to immigrate to the United States.** It particularly benefits Baltics, Ukrainians, and ethnic Germans—many of whom had engaged in a "high level of collabo-

Nazi physician Dr. Claus Schilling stands trial at the Dachau concentration camp near Munich, Germany. Charged with infecting over 1000 prisoners with malaria, Dr. Schilling was found guilty and condemned to death. He pleaded with the court to recognize his "great labor." "It would be a terrible loss if I could not finish this work," he said. "I need only a table and a chair and a typewriter. It would be an enormous help for science, for my colleagues, and a good part to rehabilitate myself." His voice then broke and he cried.

Among the numerous instances of illegal immigration to Palestine was that involving the ship *Hannah Szenes*, pictured here. The ship left Vado, Italy, on December 14, 1945, and managed to evade British patrol boats until running aground north of Haifa, Palestine, at Nahariya. The banner says: "This boat *Hannah Szenes* had disembarked immigrants here with the help of the Jewish Resistance movement. May this boat remain as a memorial to six million brothers and sisters who died in Europe, and as a token of shame of the British government."

In December 1945 a United Nations Relief and Rehabilitation Association worker in Klagenfurt, Austria, tallies the numbers and nationalities of displaced persons entering the country. DP camps in Austria were overcrowded, and many of the residents refused to perform work that would aid the rebuilding of the Austrian economy. Most of the refugees who found themselves in Austria wished to immigrate to Palestine—a reasonable desire that, nevertheless, was sharply opposed by the British government.

---

ration" with the Germans. The act discriminates against Jewish refugees. When the bill is debated, many congressmen and members of the Departments of State, Justice, and Interior express their anti-Jewish feelings indirectly and in private.

• **1945–1950: Between 250,000 and 300,000 Jews survive German concen-** tration-camp incarceration. About six million Jews have perished. About 1.6 million nonincarcerated European Jews also survive. During this period, Jews emigrate from Europe *en masse*: 142,000 to Palestine/Israel; 72,000 to the U.S.; 16,000 to Canada; 8000 to Belgium; and about 10,000 to other countries. Reactions of governments to the illegal, 1945–47 emigrations vary: the Soviets are mainly disinterested; Great Britain, irrationally jealous of its Palestine Mandate, remains fiercely negative; the U.S. armed forces, mindful that pro-Jewish sentiment is taking hold at home, allow the illegal emigration to go forward unhindered.

1946

As a snowstorm gathered on a late November day in 1946, a Jewish woman named Gerda Weissmann Klein headed home after finishing her grocery shopping in Buffalo, New York. Grocery shopping was important to her. Words and pictures on product labels were helping her learn English. Shelves stocked with food reassured her; their apparently unending abundance meant that she would never again be consumed by hunger.

After unpacking her groceries, Gerda took the bread she had purchased, sat by a window in her living room, and—as she watched the storm swirl—began to eat the loaf. Fresh though it was, the bread became salty and soggy, as tears fell upon her meal.

Holocaust survivor Gerda Klein, whose remarkable story became the subject of an Academy Award-winning documentary called *One Survivor Remembers*, recounts this episode in her memoir, *All But My Life*. As she ate, memory told her what was wrong. "During the long years of deprivation," she recalled, "I had dreamed of eating my fill in a warm place, in peace, but I never thought that I would eat my bread alone."

Married to Kurt Klein, a former U.S. Army lieutenant, Gerda was not alone in late November 1946—and yet she was. Born in 1924, Gerda Weissmann had witnessed the German occupation of her hometown, Bielitz, Poland, in 1939. She had spent years in Nazi forced-labor camps and endured brutal death marches in 1945 before American troops, among them Kurt Klein, liberated her in early May at Volary, Czechoslovakia.

After Kurt and Gerda met in Volary and fell in love, they married. They moved to Buffalo in September 1946 and began a long and successful life together. Nevertheless, what Gerda calls "a stabbing memory" or, in particular, "a pervasive loneliness" still afflicted her, for she had lost most of her family and many friends in the Holocaust.

While Gerda Klein coped with her pain, U.S. Brigadier General Telford Taylor tried to bring the Nazi perpetrators to justice. A skilled lawyer, Taylor had been part of the legal team assembled the year before by Robert H. Jackson, the U.S. Supreme Court justice who served as the chief American prosecutor at the International Military Tribunal (IMT). Including representatives from France, Great Britain, and the Soviet Union as well as the United States, the IMT had spent 12 months pursuing justice against 24 of the most significant Nazi leaders.

This Jewish Holocaust survivor, former prisoner B-12077, found fruitful work in Palestine.

1946

During trials held in the German city of Nuremberg, the IMT brought four charges against the defendants: (1) crimes against peace, (2) war crimes, (3) crimes against humanity, and (4) conspiracy to commit any of the aforementioned crimes. Making no mention of the Holocaust or the Shoah—such terms were not yet widespread—these indictments did not identify specifically what had happened to the Jews or to other civilian populations targeted by the Nazis and their collaborators. Yet, Article 6 of the IMT's charter did define crimes against humanity to include "murder, extermination, enslavement, deportation, and other inhumane acts committed against any civilian population, before or during the war, or persecutions on political, racial or religious grounds. . . ."

Taylor led the prosecution's case against the German High Command—the generals and admirals who directed Nazi Germany's military conquests. Those conquests put vast numbers of European Jews under Nazi domination and enabled the *Einsatzgruppen,* the SS, and the German Army itself to carry out a "war against the Jews." Taylor's explicit task was not to show that members of the German High Command were also Holocaust perpetrators; his aim was to document that Nazi Germany's military professionals had waged war in criminal ways.

When the verdicts were announced on October 1, 1946, 19 of the Nuremberg defendants—including Martin Bormann, head of the Nazi Party Chancellery, who was tried *in absentia*—were found guilty. Three men were acquitted: Hjalmar Schacht, former minister of economics; Franz von Papen, first vice-chancellor of the Nazi government; and Hans Fritzsche, chief of the Propaganda Ministry's Radio Division. Taylor achieved his goal, however, when the guilty verdicts included Nazi military leaders Wilhelm Keitel, chief of staff of the *Wehrmacht* High Command, and Alfred Jodl, chief of the *Wehrmacht* Operations Staff.

Seven defendants received prison sentences that ranged from ten years to life. Twelve defendants—Keitel and Jodl among them—were condemned to death by hanging. Ten executions took place in the early hours of October 16, 1946. Having been tried *in absentia,* Bormann was missing from the group of the condemned. Shortly before Hermann Göring, the commander-in-chief of the *Luftwaffe,* was to be hanged, he escaped the gallows when he killed himself by swallowing cyanide.

The pursuit of justice at Nuremberg did not end when the IMT concluded its work in the autumn of 1946. Thousands of Nazi war-crimes trials took place in numerous countries before and after those conducted by the IMT. The Subsequent Nuremberg Proceedings began in December 1946. Lasting until April 1949, they consisted of 12 trials under American jurisdiction. Now chief counsel for the prosecution, Telford Taylor played a key part in those proceedings, which ultimately focused on 185 Nazi doctors, jurists, industrialists, military and SS leaders (including *Einsatzgruppen* personnel), and other professionals and government officials. Their indictments specified crimes ranging from abusive medical experimentation and participation in Nazi Germany's "euthanasia" program to exploitation of slave labor, the administration of concentration camps, and mass murder.

Andrew Klein *(right)*, a survivor of Auschwitz, is greeted in New York by his brother, William.

Of the 142 defendants who were found guilty, 25 received death sentences but only 12 were carried out. One who was executed was Otto Ohlendorf, leader of *Einsatzgruppe* D. In 1941–42, this killing squadron, which was attached to Nazi Germany's 11th Army, murdered 90,000 men, women, and children, mostly Jews, in the Ukraine, the Crimea, and other regions in the southern sector of the war's Eastern Front. In his testimony as a prosecution witness during the initial Nuremberg Trial, Ohlendorf had stated that it was "inconceivable that a subordinate leader should not carry out orders given by the leaders of the state."

Those accused of war crimes were often extradited. This airplane contained numerous accused war criminals being flown to Poland.

Sentenced to death in April 1948, Ohlendorf spent more than three years in detention before he was hanged in Landsberg Prison on June 8, 1951. By that time, however, more than half of the 142 convicted defendants from the Subsequent Nuremberg Proceedings had been set free, and others had their sentences reduced as the new political climate of the Cold War brought pressure to strengthen West Germany as a check against Soviet expansion. Many of the ex-convicts, especially the industrialists and other professionals, resumed their careers and received retirement pensions.

Even if all of the sentences meted out to Nazi war criminals had been fully carried out, the pursuit of justice through legal proceedings could not begin to prosecute and punish all those who were responsible for the stabbing memories and pervasive loneliness experienced by survivors such as Gerda Weissmann Klein. Nor could the pursuit of justice do anything to bring back the millions who had been murdered during the Holocaust.

Nevertheless, the trials that took place in 1946 and thereafter remain significant for reasons that Telford Taylor emphasized on December 9 of that year, when he made the prosecution's opening statement in the "doctors' trial," the first of the so-called Subsequent Nuremberg Proceedings. "It is our deep obligation to all peoples of the world," he said, "to show why and how these things happened. It is incumbent upon us to set forth with conspicuous clarity the ideas and motives which moved these defendants to treat their fellow men as less than beasts." He then quoted Justice Jackson, saying, "'The wrongs which we seek to condemn and punish have been so calculated, so malignant, and so devastating that civilization cannot tolerate their being ignored because it cannot survive their being repeated.'"

As Taylor spoke those words, Gerda Klein's life in Buffalo, New York, went on. Nearly half a century later, she returned to Volary, Czechoslovakia, the site of her liberation. "I paused," she wrote in *All But My Life*, "at the graves of my beloved friends who were never privileged to know the joy of freedom, the security of a loaf of bread, or the supreme happiness of holding a child in their arms." Her memory of the Holocaust's dead, she adds, "brought up the unanswerable question that has haunted me ever since the day I left them there: Why?"

Because no pursuit of justice can ever put it to rest, that question—Why?—will continue to cry out whenever the Holocaust is remembered.

Dorothy Levy of the American Joint Distribution Committee holds a girl in the Berlin-Duppel camp for displaced Jews.

Zionism

The nationalist movement of the Jewish people is known as Zionism. The initial goal of the Zionist movement was to create a national homeland for Jews. Although progress toward this goal was made before 1939, the drive to create a Jewish nation assumed greater urgency after the Holocaust.

Throughout the war, Jewish immigration to Palestine was strictly limited by Britain, which held the mandate on the territory. Zionists in Europe, however, worked frantically to smuggle Jews into Palestine, and thousands of Jewish refugees successfully evaded capture by the British.

After the war, Zionist activists canvassed the displaced-persons camps, most of which were established in Germany to house Jewish refugees. The activists encouraged survivors of the Holocaust, such as the couple pictured,

to immigrate to Palestine. They persuasively argued that only a Jewish nation could guarantee the safety of the Jewish people. Great Britain still refused to open the gates of immigration to Jewish refugees, and they returned most of the 65 refugee ships to Europe. The plight of Jews being turned back from the shores of Palestine contributed to a growing consensus among the world powers that Palestine should become a Jewish state. Subsequent Jewish-Zionist activism, and United Nations support, led to the establishment of Israel in 1948.

Heinrich Himmler's wife, Marga (right), and daughter, Gudrun (left), were arrested after the war. Placing the families of leading Nazis in custody was a common practice after the war. Although most were never charged with crimes, the Allies suspected that they might know the location of their fathers or husbands, whom the Allies hoped to capture. Marga probably knew little about Heinrich since he paid scant attention to her. He had a mistress 20 years his junior who bore two of his children.

In many instances the Allies were forced to use former concentration camps as DP camps after the war. Residents of the DP camps often turned to arts and crafts to keep themselves occupied. This photograph shows a Rosh Hashana card that Josef Lipnicki made in the Bergen-Belsen, Germany, DP camp.

1946

• 1946: German geo-politician Karl Haushofer, whose theory of physical space as a vital component of a nation's political power was appropriated and distorted by the Nazis, commits suicide. • Former Reich Minister of Justice Otto Thierack commits suicide in Nuremberg, Germany, before going to trial for war crimes. • Vojtech Tuka, former prime minister of Slovakia, dies of natural causes before his scheduled execution for deportations of Jews to death camps. • In affidavits, 96,000 former SS men swear they had no knowledge of atrocities committed against Jews and others.

• Jews who had escaped the concentration camp at Maly Trostinets, Belorussia, six days before its liberation

One of the major goals of the Nazis was to completely destroy the culture of Europe's Jews, and survivors were determined not to see Hitler gain a victory on this score. Here, children in the Landsberg, Germany, DP camp study from a Hebrew religious text. Most of these DP children had never received such instruction, because the Nazis forbade it and executed those who attempted to teach others about Judaism.

Ferenc Szálasi, in death. As leader of the Arrow Cross movement, he led a Fascist government in Hungary during the last year of the war. He staged a coup against Admiral Miklós Horthy's government when it attempted to make peace with the Soviets in the fall of 1944. As a close ally of the Germans, Szálasi's government viciously persecuted Hungary's Jewish population. Szálasi was executed on March 12, 1946.

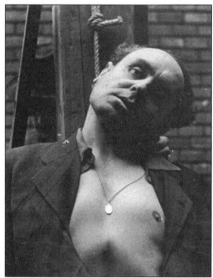

Large numbers of displaced persons settled in the United States under President Harry Truman's December 1945 immigration order. Here a displaced person, a passenger on the SS *Marine Flasher,* arrives in New York City. Like many other postwar immigrants, this woman apparently had family and friends who already lived in the United States. Such contacts helped the new arrivals acclimate to their new country.

by the Red Army in June 1944 are released from Soviet-sanctioned confinement in a camp in Siberia. • The Allies and Switzerland agree on the return of assets looted by the Nazis from treasuries of conquered nations. No provision is made for the return of assets looted from individuals; *See* May 1996.

• February 3, 1946: Friedrich Jeckeln, former *SS-Obergruppenführer* of the Soviet Union and the Baltic Republics, is hanged in the former Riga (Latvia) Ghetto after being convicted of war crimes.

• February 5, 1946: Polish antisemites murder four Jews in the Parczew Forest in Poland.

• March 1946: Survivors of a Jewish concentration-camp orchestra perform classical selections and songs from the ghettos for members of the Nuremberg Tribunal, at the Nuremberg Opera House.

• March 12, 1946: Ferenc Szálasi, the former head of the Nazi-controlled puppet government in

Fiorello LaGuardia, former mayor of New York City, led the United Nations' effort to deal with Europe's massive displaced-persons problem as the director general of the UNRRA. Here he makes a speech in the DP camp at Berlin-Schlachtensee. LaGuardia, whose mother was of Jewish descent, made his presentation in Yiddish, something his audience undoubtedly appreciated.

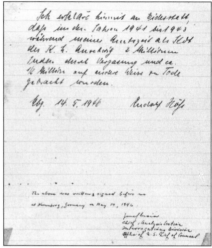

This document, written by the camp's commandant, Rudolf Höss, dated May 14, 1946, attests to the number of Jews murdered at Auschwitz. It reads: "I declare herewith under oath that in the years 1941 to 1943 during my tenure in office as commandant of Auschwitz concentration camp 2 million Jews were put to death by gassing and about ½ million by other means." Historians have since concluded that the number of victims at Auschwitz was actually between 1.1 million and 1.6 million.

For years the Nazis had forbidden the practice of the rituals that is a vital aspect of Judaism. Many of these involved a communal meal, especially the Passover Seder. Here children in the Landsberg, Germany, DP camp join in the Seder. For many of them, this was the first time they particpated in this important ceremony.

1946

Hungary, is executed after being convicted of war crimes; *See* March 22, 1946.

• **March 14, 1946:** Polish thugs in Warsaw stop an official car that is flying the British flag. They remove and shoot four riders they suspect are Jews.

• **March 19, 1946:** Chaim Hirszman, one of only two survivors of the Belzec death camp, is murdered by Polish antisemites in Lublin, Poland, after a day of testimony about the horrors he had witnessed.

• **March 22, 1946:** Döme Szojay, former prime minister of the Nazi-controlled puppet government in

After their liberation, European Jews were determined to stand up to any and all forms of persecution, which was distressingly common in postwar Europe, especially in Poland. These Jews march in support of Polish-Jewish partnership, calling for both groups to work together to rebuild their country after the terrible years of Nazi occupation. About 2.8 million Polish Jews had died during the Holocaust.

DISPLACED-PERSONS CAMPS, 1945-1946

No part of Occupied Europe or the Greater German Reich remained untouched by the Holocaust and its aftermath. These children, most likely orphaned during the war years, were assigned to a displaced-persons camp in Salzburg, Austria. Children whose parents had perished had nowhere to go after the war. They waited to be adopted by caring families.

After the war, more than 1.5 million Europeans—including a quarter-million Jews—either didn't want to return home or had no place to go. They stayed temporarily in displaced-persons camps, which were managed by the Allied countries. By 1951, more than two-thirds of the Jewish DPs had emigrated to Israel.

Hungary, is executed after being convicted of war crimes.

• **March 28, 1946:** Jewish leaders traveling from Kraków to Lódź, Poland, are tortured and murdered by Polish antisemites.

• **April 21, 1946:** Five Jews, each of them a concentration-camp survivor, motoring near Nowy Targ, Poland, are stopped at a mock police checkpoint and shot to death. The oldest victim is 35, one is 25, and the remaining three are 22; *See April 24, 1946.*

• **April 24, 1946:** Five thousand Jews attending a funeral for five Jews murdered by Poles at Nowy Targ, Poland,

three days earlier are abused from rooftops and windows by antisemitic taunts; *See April 30, 1946.*

• **April 30, 1946:** Seven Jews are murdered by antisemitic Poles at Nowy Targ, Poland, very near to where five Jews were killed on April 21; *See May 2, 1946.*

As horrible as the Nazi camps had been, life went on for the inmates who survived. This photograph shows several couples, each of whom fell in love in one of Hitler's camps, getting married in a group ceremony held in Stockholm, Sweden, on June 14, 1946. This was merely the first of thousands of marriages among DPs, many of whom had lost their first spouses during the Holocaust.

The ship *Josiah Wedgewood* attempted to take illegal immigrants to Palestine. However, it was overtaken by the British ship HMS *Venus,* and its passengers were taken to the detention camp at Athlit, Palestine. Here, some of *Josiah Wedgewood*'s passengers dance the *hora* on the ship's deck.

The ship *Haviva Reik,* which had been transporting illegal immigrants to Palestine, was captured by the British destroyer *Saumarez* in June 1946. The British towed the ship into the harbor at Haifa, Palestine, after which its passengers were interned in the

detention camp at Athlit, Palestine. As the ship entered the harbor, the passengers, singing the Jewish national anthem, unfurled a banner that stated, in Hebrew, "Keep the gates open—we are not the last."

1946

- **May 1946:** Former Jewish partisan leader and Red Army officer Eliyahu Lipszowicz is murdered by an antisemitic Pole at Legnica, Poland.
- Oswald Pohl, a former SS general in charge of camp works projects and the disposition of valuables stolen from inmates, is discovered in hiding and arrested.

- **May 1, 1946:** The recommendation of the Anglo-American Committee of Inquiry that 100,000 Jewish displaced persons should be allowed to enter Palestine is refused by the British government, which holds the mandate on Palestine.

- **May 2, 1946:** A funeral service is held in Kraków, Poland, for seven

Jewish Holocaust survivors who sought to enter Palestine illegally and who were captured by the British were detained in several DP camps. Thousands of these Jews were sent to Cyprus, seen here, where they were forced to endure poor, limited food; shortages of water; overcrowding; and inadequate sanitation. The bitter irony of the whole situation was not lost on the world's Jews.

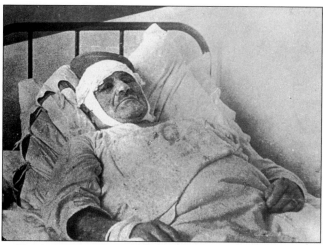

This man was among the survivors of the Kielce pogrom. While recovering in the hospital, he said: "I was in Oświecim [Auschwitz] for three years. It was awful there; but here in Kielce it was even worse. Everything was breathing hatred. The corpses of murdered people were massacred, trampled upon." The end of the Holocaust, obviously, had not brought an end to antisemitism in Europe.

Kielce Pogrom

Prejudice and hatred toward Jews did not end with the Nazis' defeat. Few Polish Jews survived the Nazis' death camps, and yet even those few who did were often greeted with violent hostility when they returned to their homes.

Before the war, the city of Kielce in southeast Poland had included some 15,000 Jews among a population of about 60,000. In 1946 about 200 Jews were living in Kielce, most of them waiting to immigrate to Palestine. For some Poles in the town, any Jewish presence was unwelcome.

The embers of hatred burst into flames when a Christian child disappeared. Townspeople accused the Jews of ritual murder, claiming that the Christian child had been abducted so that his blood could be used in a satanic ritual. A wave of deadly antisemitic violence was unleashed before the child (who had been staying with a friend) was found. Forty-two Jews were killed, dozens of others, including those pictured, were injured. The attackers included police and even a Catholic priest.

As the story of the killings spread, Jews fled in terror, shocked to have survived the Nazis' death camps only to return to their homes to be murdered by antisemitic Poles.

Jews who were murdered on April 30 by antisemitic thugs at Nowy Targ, Poland.

• May 7, 1946: Dutch Nazi leader and collaborator Anton Mussert is hanged, one year to the day of his arrest, after being convicted of war crimes.

• May 25, 1946: Switzerland signs the Washington Agreement, under which the Swiss government will voluntarily contribute $58.1 million in gold to an Allied commission established to help rebuild Europe. The Allies are aware that this payment will come from Swiss stores of looted gold taken from Jews and other victims of Nazi persecution. Regardless, the Allies agree

not to press the Swiss for additional claims. At this time, Switzerland holds between $300 and $400 million in looted gold; *See* 1951.

• May 29–June 1, 1946: Ten former members of the Natzweiler, Germany, camp are tried at Rastadt, Germany. One is sentenced to death and five to imprisonment; four are acquitted.

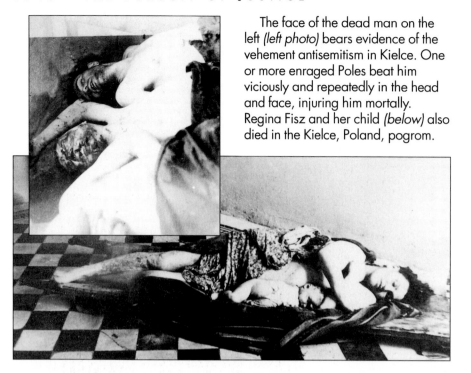

The face of the dead man on the left *(left photo)* bears evidence of the vehement antisemitism in Kielce. One or more enraged Poles beat him viciously and repeatedly in the head and face, injuring him mortally. Regina Fisz and her child *(below)* also died in the Kielce, Poland, pogrom.

Driven to desperation by British stonewalling on the issue of a Jewish state, Jewish nationalist groups in Palestine campaigned to evict the British and establish the nation of Israel. On July 22, 1946, the *Irgun Tseva'i Le'ummi* (National Military Organization), founded by dissident *Hagana* members, blew up Jerusalem's King David Hotel, the headquarters of the British government and military in Palestine. Seventy-six Jews, Arabs, and Britons were killed, and dozens of people were injured. The *Irgun* subsequently claimed that sufficient warning to evacuate had been given; the British denied this. Regardless, the bombing hardened British resolve to block the foundation of a Jewish state.

During the Holocaust, the Nazis destroyed thousands of Torah scrolls across Occupied Europe. Hence, after the war many Hebrew congregations had no Torah scrolls, an important component of Jewish ritual. Arthur Greenleigh *(in uniform)*, a representative of the Joint Distribution Committee, is shown here at a ceremony in which he presented 33 scrolls, donated by American Jews, to the Jewish community of France.

1946

• **June 1946:** Following the murder of two Jews in Biala Podlaska, Poland, the town's remaining Jews leave the country.

• **June 1, 1946:** Ion Antonescu, the antisemitic former dictator of Romania, is executed after being convicted of war crimes. Mihai Antonescu, the antisemitic former deputy prime min-

ister of Romania, is executed after being convicted of war crimes.

• **July 4, 1946:** Following the disappearance of a Christian child at Kielce, Poland, a violent pogrom breaks out against the city's Jews. A mob storms the Jewish community center and murders 42 Jews, including two children. (The missing Christian boy is

These Jewish displaced persons were members of a sports team that competed in the Zeilsheim, Germany, DP camp. Such teams, as well as nonsports clubs, helped Jews rebuild their social and cultural lives, which the Holocaust had largely destroyed. However, a presidential inquiry authorized by Harry Truman late in 1945 revealed that the conditions under which displaced Jews were detained were inexcusably harsh. Sports clubs and other in-camp groups could not compensate for the fact that "[h]ousing, medical, and recreational facilities were inadequate," and that "nothing was being done to improve the quality of life. . . . "

Jews suspected of terrorism by the British crowd against the barbed wire imprisoning them at the Latrun, Palestine, detention camp. Intent upon thwarting the Jewish push for a homeland, British authorities took strong measures, turning back ships, such as the *Exodus,* and imprisoning any people suspected of belonging to the *Mossad,* the Jewish intelligence organization.

The leaders of many ghettos were determined to keep a record of what was happening to Europe's Jews under Nazi occupation. Emanuel Ringelblum, as the Warsaw Ghetto's historian, kept copious records in secret, burying them in milk cans so that future generations would know about the Holocaust. Pictured is a place where some of Ringelblum's records were unearthed. Several cans remain undiscovered.

discovered unharmed in a nearby village.) Other anti-Jewish pogroms break out across Poland. Following the violence, 100,000 Polish Jews will leave their nation for Palestine, the United States, Latin America, Australia, Great Britain, and Western Europe.

● **July 11, 1946: A Polish primate, Cardinal August Hlond, blames** the Jews of Kielce, Poland, for the murderous pogrom against them on July 4.

● **July 20, 1946: Arthur Greiser, former *Gauleiter* of the Warthegau region in Poland, is hanged at Poznań, Poland, after being convicted of war crimes.**

● **July 22, 1946: Jewish guerrillas of *Irgun Tseva'i Le'ummi* (IZL; National Military Organization) explode a bomb at Jerusalem's King David Hotel, the headquarters of the British administrators of Palestine.**

● **July 26, 1946: A prosecution summation is presented by Robert H. Jackson at Nuremberg.**

Wilhelm Keitel

Wilhelm Keitel was the chief of staff of the High Command of the German Armed Forces from 1938 until the collapse of the Nazi empire. His complete subservience to Hitler and willingness to condone mass murder are the primary reasons why Keitel was sentenced to death by the Nuremberg Tribunal in October 1946.

A professional soldier  **who was wounded in the First World War, Keitel rose through the ranks during the 1920s and 1930s, and was appointed to the top position in the German military in February 1938. He assumed the rank of general field marshal in July 1940.**

Keitel's obsequious loyalty to Hitler and patent inability to criticize him influenced other officers to blindly obey the *Führer*. More disastrous, however, were Keitel's orders that sanctioned mass murder, most notoriously the deadly "Night and Fog" decree of December 1941.

The Allied prosecutors made use of the extensive records left behind by the Hitler regime to convict its leaders at Nuremberg. Prosecutors provided massive documentary evidence to the court, which carried more weight than witness testimony. This photograph shows only a tiny portion of the physical evidence presented. Pictured are a map, some photographs, and a few artifacts suggestive of atrocities.

Rudolf Hess was Hitler's secretary until being captured after flying to Great Britain on a self-appointed "peace mission" in 1941. At Nuremberg, he feigned insanity during much of the proceedings. He pretended that he was unaware of what was going on, had lost his memory, and was hence unfit to stand trial. Nuremberg courtroom artist Ed Vebell, on assignment for the U.S. Army newspaper *Stars and Stripes,* wrote: "Hess looked very hollow-cheeked and thin-necked. He seemed to ignore the proceedings and kept his head down—absorbed in a book." Hess was convicted of crimes against peace. The judges sentenced him to life in prison. He spent his remaining 43 years in Spandau Prison, and for the final 23 years he was the only prisoner in the institution. He committed suicide in 1987 at age 93.

1946

- **August 13, 1946: British authorities open detention camps on the island of Cyprus to hold Jewish refugees who have been prevented from entering Palestine due to British restrictions on immigration.**

- **September 1946: Paul Touvier, a former right-wing Vichy sympathizer and an adversary of French partisans,** is sentenced to death *in absentia* for treason.

- **September 18, 1946: One portion of Emanuel Ringelblum's Warsaw Ghetto diary, which was secretly buried by Ringelblum, is discovered in a ruined house at 68 Nowolipki Street in Warsaw; *See* December 1, 1950.**

"[Germany] allowed itself to be robbed of its conscience and its very soul. Evil masters came who awakened its primitive passions and made possible the atrocities which I have described to you. In truth, the crime of these men is that they caused the German people to retrogress more than 12 centuries."

—*French prosecutor Charles Dubost, in a statement before the Nuremberg Tribunal; 1946*

The International Military Tribunal at Nuremberg passed judgment on major German war criminals on September 30 and October 1, 1946. Most of the defendants claimed to have been mere subordinates forced to follow orders; only glib armaments minister Albert Speer admitted to wrongdoing. Of the 22 men who were tried at this first and most significant of the war-crimes tribunals (Martin Bormann was tried *in absentia*), 12 were condemned to death by hanging and seven received prison sentences ranging from ten years to life. (Rudolf Hess, who was sentenced to life, was not in the dock when this photo was taken.)

Nuremberg was a beautiful medieval city that the Nazis greatly admired for its "Germanness." They even chose it as the location for their annual Party rallies. For these reasons, the Allies selected Nuremberg as the site for the trial of the major war criminals of the Third Reich. This photo shows some of the city's medieval splendor, including the Palace of Justice, where the trials took place. Although the Palace of Justice stood intact, much of Nuremberg did not, for the city had been heavily bombed during the latter part of the war. Many landmarks of which the Nazis were particularly proud—some dating back to 1140—were shattered.

• **October 1, 1946:** The verdicts of the first Nuremberg trial are announced. Acquitted: Fritzsche; Schacht; Papen. Guilty: Hess, Speer, Raeder, Dönitz, Kaltenbrunner, Streicher, Frank, Funk, Schirach, Ribbentrop, Rosenberg, Göring, Frick, Sauckel, Seyss-Inquart, Jodl, Keitel, Bormann (*in absentia*).

• **October 11, 1946:** Nuremberg defense attorneys are informed by the Tribunal that the appeals of all convicted defendants have been denied.

• **October 15, 1946:** Hours before his scheduled execution by hanging, Hermann Göring commits suicide in his cell at Nuremberg by biting down on a capsule of cyanide, which may have been secreted inside his pipe.

• **October 16, 1946:** Following convictions for war crimes, these men are hanged at Nuremberg Prison: former Nazi Foreign Minister Joachim von Ribbentrop; former *Der Stürmer* editor Julius Streicher; Nazi jurist Wilhelm Frick; Nazi "philosopher" Alfred

After being convicted of war crimes by the Nuremberg Tribunal, Hermann Göring used cyanide to commit suicide in his closely watched cell on October 15, 1946, just two hours before his scheduled execution by hanging. Whether he had carried the capsule on his person for months or whether it was passed to him at the 11th hour remains unknown.

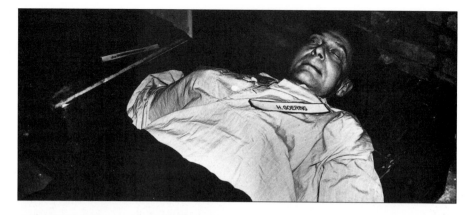

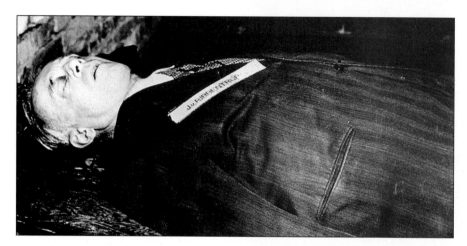

Charged with war crimes, as well as crimes against humanity and against peace, Joachim von Ribbentrop was found guilty on all counts by the Nuremberg War Tribunal. On October 16, 1946, he was the first of the Nazi leaders to mount the gallows to his death. Ribbentrop served Hitler faithfully, but his influence in the government declined during the war when diplomacy was no longer vital to Hitler's aims.

In addition to helping the Nazis annex Austria, Arthur Seyss-Inquart was also *Reichskommissar* of the Netherlands. The quintessential opportunist, he spent much of his Nazi career hurrying to do as much damage to as many Jews as possible—all with the goal of winning Hitler's approval. Seyss-Inquart was convicted of war crimes at Nuremberg and sentenced to death. This photo, from October 16, 1946, was taken following his execution by hanging.

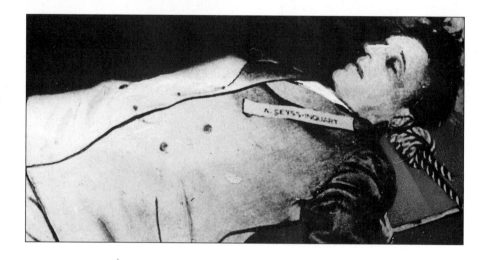

1946

Rosenberg; Nazi forced-labor chief Fritz Sauckel; Arthur Seyss-Inquart, former Reich commissioner of Occupied Netherlands; Hans Frank, former governor-general of Poland; Alfred Jodl, former *Generaloberst der Wehrmacht* and chief of the operations staff of OKW (High Command of the Armed Forces); Ernst Kaltenbrunner, former *SS-Obergruppenführer* and

RSHA chief; and Wilhelm Keitel, former field marshal and chief of OKW. The bodies of the executed, plus Hermann Göring's, are burned in the ovens of the former concentration camp at Dachau, Germany. The ashes are scattered late in the day in the Iser River.

• October 20, 1946: Kurt Daluege, former *SS-Obergruppenführer* and

The young man with the bandaged head was a passenger on the ship *Knesset Israel,* which transported illegal Jewish immigrants to Israel. The British made a concerted effort to stop such unauthorized settlement, and several British warships overtook *Knesset Israel.* In the course of the boarding of the ship, two young Jewish men were killed by gunfire and 57 were sent to the hospital with injuries. The British sent *Knesset Israel*'s passengers to a detention camp on the island of Cyprus.

Nazi physicians had committed horrific crimes against camp inmates, and the Allies were determined to hold them responsible. In 1946–47, 23 doctors stood trial in Nuremberg for crimes against humanity. The four women pictured here, all victims of Nazi medical "experiments," arrived in Nuremberg on December 15, 1946, in order to testify against the accused. The German medical profession struggled to recover from the horrors perpetrated by some of its members.

The Uniqueness of the Holocaust

Genocide involves state-organized destruction of a people because of what political scientist R. J. Rummel calls "their indelible group membership (race, ethnicity, religion, language)." Nazi Germany's destruction of European Jewry was clearly genocide; however, was the Holocaust unique?

Arguments for the Holocaust's uniqueness do not depend primarily on the number of Jewish victims or the way in which they were killed. Rather, as scholar Steven T. Katz maintains, the uniqueness claim rests on "the fact that never before has a state set out, as a matter of intentional principle and actualized policy, to annihilate physically every man, woman, and child belonging to a specific people.... Only in the case of Jewry under the Third Reich was such all-inclusive, noncompromising, unmitigated murder intended."

The uniqueness claim sparks debate. Some scholars contend, for example, that Nazi Germany's targeting of the Sinti and Roma (Gypsies) did not differ substantially from the fate intended for the Jews. Others fear that the uniqueness claim banishes other genocides to undeserved second-class status. Inquiry about these issues will not stop any time soon, but Holocaust scholar Yehuda Bauer, who defends the Holocaust's uniqueness, offers an important reminder: "Events happen because they are possible. If they were possible once, they are possible again. In that sense, the Holocaust is not unique, but a warning for the future."

deputy *Reichsprotektor* of Bohemia and Moravia, is hanged in Prague, Czechoslovakia, after being convicted of war crimes.

• October 25, 1946: Twenty-three former Nazi doctors are tried at Nuremberg on charges of conducting unethical experiments on camp inmates. The various experiments

included the drinking of seawater, bone grafting, exposure to mustard gas, and other atrocities. This is the so-called "doctors' trial"; *See* August 20, 1947.

• November 13, 1946–April 17, 1947: Former *Luftwaffe* Field Marshal Erhard Milch is tried at Nuremberg.

• December 11, 1946: The United Nations General Assembly confirms the judgments of the Nuremberg Tribunal.

• 1946–49: In 12 separate tribunals, an additional 185 alleged Nazi war criminals are prosecuted at Nuremberg.

EPILOGUE

THE day stops when the sirens scream at eight o'clock. Two minutes later an Israeli morning goes on as usual, but not entirely. It is *Yom ha-Sho'ah,* the April day that commemorates the Holocaust. Observances are held in many countries now, but this annual remembrance was first established in 1951 by the *Knesset,* Israel's parliament.

The Jewish lunar calendar puts *Yom ha-Sho'ah* on the 27th day of the month of *Nisan,* the anniversary of the beginning of the Warsaw Ghetto uprising, April 19, 1943. Not long after *Yom ha-Sho'ah, Yom Atzmaut* (Israeli Independence Day) is celebrated on *Iyyar* 5, the anniversary of the day when Israeli statehood was announced: May 14, 1948. The two days' close proximity is not accidental. It suggests that from the ruin and resistance of the Warsaw Ghetto, from the destruction and defiance of the Holocaust, Jewish life finds renewed vitality in Israel.

Nevertheless, screaming as they do before the celebration of Israeli independence, the sirens sound multiple warnings: Be vigilant; do not take Israel's existence for granted. Be realistic; do not assume that the Holocaust will never be forgotten, let alone that genocide is a thing of the past. Be undeceived; do not suppose that Israel's existence "makes up" for the Holocaust. Be careful; do not imagine, at least not easily, that the state of Israel reaf-

> **"As you view the history of our time, turn and look at the piles of bodies, pause for a short moment, and imagine that this poor residue of flesh and bones is your father, your child, your wife, is the one you love. See yourself and those nearest to you, to whom you are devoted heart and soul, thrown naked into the dirt, tortured, starving, killed."**
>
> *—Resister and author Eugen Kogon*

firms the covenant between God and the Jewish people. Be clearheaded; do not preempt the Holocaust by making its evil instrumental, the means that somehow produced a "greater good."

The sirens' scream should not diminish joy about the state of Israel, pride in its accomplishments, or hope for the Israeli future, including a secure peace with often hostile Arab neighbors. Nor should the sirens' scream mean that Jewish identity is synonymous with victimhood. Least of all should *Yom ha-Sho'ah*'s sirens deny that post-Holocaust Jewish life is thriving. To the contrary, the sirens can and should be heard, at least in part, as expressions of courage and confidence that Jewish life is here to stay—strong, vibrant, and, at its best, what the biblical prophet Isaiah called "a light to the nations."

A Kingly Dream

The modern state of Israel celebrated its 50th anniversary in 1998. Yearnings for a Jewish state, however, are much older. In the late 1800s, Austrian-Jewish leader Nathan Birnbaum led a Jewish nationalist group known as *Hovevei Tziyon* (Lovers of Zion). He gets credit for introducing the term *Zionism* in 1893. Since that time, Zionism has been, in part, a response to antisemitism.

A few months after Israel's independence, Jewish amputees stand outside a theater in Tel Aviv. The Hollywood film *The Best Years of Our Lives* focuses on Americans returning home after the war.

The illegal immigrant ship *Theodor Herzl* arrived in Haifa, Palestine, in 1947. The banner reads: "The Germans destroyed our families. . . . Don't you destroy our hopes."

It also expresses an affirmation of distinctively Jewish culture and a nationalistic commitment to found and sustain a Jewish homeland by political means. Historically, Zionist aspirations have reflected varied political, cultural, and religious persuasions. Some Zionists have been politically on the left, others on the right; some secular, others religious; some more militant, others less so. However, their common cause has been to support and defend a state for Jews in territory earlier called Palestine and even earlier, in biblical times, possessed by the Jews themselves.

The notion of a Jewish state was described in 1896 by Zionist leader Theodor Herzl as a "kingly dream." That dream did become a reality, but not before nightmares occured that Herzl neither lived to experience nor ever imagined.

A biblical term, *aliyah*, meaning "ascent," designates an uphill journey to Jerusalem; it is used generally to refer to immigration to Israel. Between 1882 and 1903, about 30,000 Jews immigrated to Palestine, which more than doubled the region's Jewish population. That number was small, however, in contrast to the 500,000 Jews from Eastern Europe and Russia who entered the United States during the same period.

Another 35,000 Jews went to Palestine in the Second Aliyah (1904–1914), again representing a small fraction of the 1.5 million Jews who fled Eastern Europe's relentless pogroms during those ten years. By 1914, Palestine was home to half a million Arabs and 85,000 Jews.

Deep British economic and strategic interests in the Middle East, particularly control of the Suez Canal, led to Britain's Balfour Declaration, named after Foreign Secretary Arthur James Balfour. It made clear that the British government favored "the establishment in Palestine of a national home for the Jewish people, and will use their best endeavors to facilitate the achievement of this object, it being clearly understood that nothing shall be done which may prejudice the civil and religious rights of existing non-Jewish communities in Palestine, or the rights and political status enjoyed by Jews in any other country."

The Balfour Declaration appeared shortly after British troops invaded Palestine in October 1917. By the next September, the entire region was under British control. Under postwar terms established by the newly formed League of Nations, Palestine became a British mandate. The British were then left to oversee a Palestine whose majority Arab population was not pleased to find that Palestine's minority Jewish population was increasingly committed to work for the Balfour Declaration's promised statehood.

Britain welcomed Jewish immigration to Palestine until Arab-

A British soldier forces Jewish children to disembark from the *Exodus 1947* in July 1947.

• **1947: Jozef Tiso, former prime minister of Slovakia and an ally to Adolf Hitler, is tried and executed in Czechoslovakia. • Swedish diplomat Raoul Wallenberg dies in a Soviet prison (according to a 1956 Soviet report). • Belgian government minister Jean Terfve, a Communist, pushes through a law to commemorate Jewish victims of Nazi persecution.**

• **January 4–December 4, 1947: The trial of 15 Nazi judges takes place at Nuremberg, Germany. Four are sentenced to life in prison, four to ten years, one to seven years, and one to five years. Four are acquitted and one is released because of ill health.**

• **January 13–November 3, 1947: Eighteen former members of Nazi**

Germany's *Wirtschafts- und Verwaltungshauptamt* (Economy and Administration Main Office) are tried at Nuremberg. Four are sentenced to death and 11 to imprisonment; three are acquitted.

• **February 8–December 22, 1947: Six German industrialists, including Friedrich Flick, are tried at Nurem-**

Jewish riots in May 1921. Immigration then was temporarily suspended, but the British colonial secretary, Winston Churchill, issued a government White Paper that reaffirmed the Balfour Declaration. The White Paper stated that Palestine would not become completely Jewish territory, and linked Jewish immigration to the land's capacity to support it economically.

Although the British made no rush to encourage Israeli statehood, Jewish immigration to Palestine increased steadily. By the late 1930s, the Jewish presence was strong, and the Arab population had grown as well. Agitation for an Arab Palestinian state echoed the calls for a Jewish state. Britain's attempt to quell unrest was the White Paper of 1939, issued in May. The White Paper's controversial provisions included the following: (1) After ten years, the British would set up an independent, binational Palestinian state in which Jews and Arabs would share governmental power proportionately to their population. (2) Over the next five years, 75,000 Jews would be permitted to enter Palestine; after that time, immigration would depend on Arab agreement. (3) Land purchases by Jews would be sharply curtailed.

When World War II began less than four months later, not only

had Theodor Herzl's dream of a Jewish state been put in suspended animation, but the doors to a haven from the antisemitism he feared were being slammed shut. From 1939 to 1945, only about 50,000 Jews were able to enter Palestine. Approximately 16,000 of them were smuggled in by sea, thanks to militant Jewish groups who defied British attempts to keep the refugees out.

Later, postwar passion for a Jewish homeland in Palestine incited Jewish underground

With grenade at the ready, a young woman in the *Hagana,* the Jewish underground, trains for battle on Mt. Scopus, near Jerusalem, in 1948.

Jewish Immigration to Palestine

Of the 250,000 Jews who became displaced persons at the end of the war, few wished to make Europe their home. Confined to DP camps, they desired to begin their new lives elsewhere.

Most Jews hoped to immigrate to Palestine. Yet, as was the case during the war, their escape was impeded by the immigration quotas set by the British, who held the mandate on Palestine. Through the illegal activities of the *Mossad*, the Jewish underground organization, the Jews were able to undertake clandestine voyages to Palestine from 1945 to 1948.

Making their way over mountains and under cover of night to Europe's coasts, Jewish families then crowded onto rickety ships that attempted to dodge the British blockade. Discovery meant arrest. Despite the risks, 64 ships delivered over 70,000 people to Palestine beaches. Another 50,000 were stopped and taken to British detention camps on the island of Cyprus.

Unable to halt the exodus of Europe's Jews, the British finally gave in. The 1948 establishment of Israel allowed the mass immigration of about two-thirds of the displaced persons. The remaining refugees chose to make their homes elsewhere, with about 70,000 going to the United States once quota limitations were eased in 1948 and 1950.

berg. Three are sentenced to prison; three are acquitted.

● **March 29, 1947: Former Auschwitz commandant Rudolf Höss is sentenced to death following his trial at Warsaw, Poland;** *See* **April 16, 1947.**
● **Nazi hunter Simon Wiesenthal founds a Documentation Center of Nazi war criminals in Linz, Austria.**

● **April 16, 1947: Former Auschwitz commandant Rudolf Höss is hanged at Auschwitz.**

● **May 8, 1947–July 30, 1948: Twenty-four members of I.G. Farben's board of directors are tried at Nuremberg. Thirteen are sentenced to imprisonment; ten are acquitted and one is not tried due to poor health.**

● **May 10, 1947–February 19, 1948: Twelve former senior *Wehrmacht* officers are tried at Nuremberg in the so-called "hostage trial." Of these, eight are sentenced to prison, two are acquitted, one commits suicide, and one is released because of ill health.**

● **July 1, 1947–March 10, 1948: The trial of 14 former SS leaders takes**

Jewish Underground in Palestine

The *Hagana* (Defense Force) was founded in 1920 to fight off Arab attacks on Palestinian Jews. Accepting women as equals, *Hagana* members fought for the British during World War II. The *Irgun* (National Military Organization) was founded in 1931 by dissident *Hagana* members who felt the need to open up Palestine despite British opposition to help save European Jews.

Throughout the Holocaust, the *Irgun* assisted the *Aliya Bet*, or "illegal" Jewish immigration, of European Jews into Palestine, as well as helping the British in anti-Nazi warfare. But once the war was nearly won, the *Irgun* began to attack British military targets in Palestine on the grounds that Britain's Jewish policy was overly restrictive, antisemitic, and in collaboration with the Germans. The aggressive Stern Group recognized that the British were generally anti-Jewish and pro-Arab and fought the British as well as the Germans.

groups to attempt to expel the British by violence. Groups included the *Irgun,* led by Menachem Begin, and *Lehi,* led by Yitzhak Shamir (both eventually Israeli prime ministers). British crackdowns kept these minority movements more or less in check, but the insurrection intensified the struggle for Israeli statehood.

This brief account of some 50 years of Palestine's history suggests a bit of the Jewish struggle for a homeland, and also prompts a serious question: Did the Jews in Palestine do as much as they could to thwart the Holocaust? Debate persists. Some arguments criticize

Hagana youths, members of the Jewish underground, and their dogs guard a Jewish settlement in the Negev against a possible Arab attack in 1948.

Menachem Begin was Israel's prime minister from 1977 to 1983. As a youth in 1930s Warsaw, he was an active Zionist, and traveled to Palestine with the Polish Army-in-exile in 1942. Begin was a leader of the militant *Irgun* group from 1943 until 1948.

the British for refusing to support Jewish-led military efforts. Others assert that the Jewish leadership in Palestine was too passive and compliant toward British policy. Whatever the truth—and it may be a combination of both positions—the inescapable fact is this: Antisemitic trends in Europe grew increasingly powerful throughout the 1930s, leading eventually to the systematic murder of six million Jews. Survivor reflection on that crime began to be widely published following the war.

The Shock of Knowledge

I've spoken with death
and so
I know
the futility of things we learn
a discovery I made at the cost
of a suffering

---

place in Nuremberg. Thirteen are sentenced to prison; one is acquitted.

● July 3, 1947–April 10, 1948: Twenty-four senior SS and SD officers are tried at Nuremberg. Fourteen are sentenced to death.

● July 12, 1947: Jews in Nathanya, Palestine, beat and kidnap two mem-

bers of a British Army intelligence unit, instigating temporary martial law by the British in the area.

● July 18, 1947: Spandau Prison in West Berlin accepts the following Nazi war criminals sentenced to internment: Baldur von Schirach (*See* 1966), Karl Dönitz, Konstantin Freiherr von Neurath, Erich Raeder,

Albert Speer (*See* 1966), Walther Funk, and Rudolf Hess (*See* August 17, 1987).

● August 14, 1947: German Prince Josias Erbprinz von Waldeck-Pyrmont, the first member of the old German nobility to be recruited by the SS, is convicted of war crimes and sentenced to life imprisonment.

so intense
I keep on wondering
whether it was worth it.
　　　　—*Charlotte Delbo,*
　　　　Auschwitz and After

Useless knowledge. That's what Charlotte Delbo said her experience in Auschwitz and Ravensbrück gave her. She was not Jewish. Nevertheless, Delbo was sent to Auschwitz in 1943. Of the 230 Frenchwomen in her convoy, she was one of the 49 who survived. Delbo saw what happened to the Jews, her French comrades, and herself. An Auschwitz fate, however, did not have to be hers.

Kazet Theatre, a survivor theater troupe, performs *The Death Colony* at the Bergen-Belsen DP camp. The troupe played before DP audiences throughout Europe in 1947.

When the Germans occupied her native France in June 1940, Delbo was on tour in South America with a theater company. Against the advice of friends, she returned to France in 1941, rejoining her husband, Georges Dudach, and working with him in the Resistance.

Arrested by collaborating French police on March 2, 1942, the couple was handed over to the Germans, who imprisoned the two separately. Delbo had a brief visit with her husband just before a firing squad executed him on May 23. A prisoner in France until her deportation, Delbo describes her Auschwitz arrival in January 1943 as follows: "The doors of the cattle cars were pushed open, revealing the edge of an icy plain. It was a place from before geography. Where were we? We were to find out—later, at least two months hence; we, that is those of us who were still alive two months later—that this place was called Auschwitz. We couldn't have given it a name."

Those words come from Delbo's superb trilogy, *Auschwitz et après* (*Auschwitz and After*), whose anguished visual descriptions and profound reflections on memory make it an unrivaled Holocaust

This bronze monument, "Memorial to the Victims in Camps," was sculpted by Nandor Glid and stands on the grounds of Yad Vashem in Jerusalem.

testimony. Its three parts begin with *Aucun de nous ne reviendra* (*None of Us Will Return*), which she wrote in 1946 after she had been released to the Red Cross from Ravensbrück, a Nazi camp for women. She recuperated in Sweden and then returned to France. Delbo waited nearly 20 years, however, before she allowed *None of Us Will Return* to be published in 1965. Parts of *Une connaissance inutile* (*Useless Knowledge*) were also written shortly after Delbo's return to France, but this second volume in the trilogy did not appear until 1970. Its sequel, *Mesure de nos jours* (*The Measure of Our Days*), soon followed.

"Auschwitz," Delbo said in *La mémoire et les jours* (*Days and Memory*), "is so deeply etched in my memory that I cannot forget one moment of it." True, in the

---

● **August 16, 1947–July 31, 1948: The Krupp Trial of 12 senior Krupp executives takes place. Eleven are sentenced to prison; one is acquitted. All sentences will eventually be commuted to time served.**

● **August 20, 1947: The "doctors' trial" at Nuremberg concludes. Sixteen of 23 physician/defendants are**

found guilty. Seven are sentenced to death, five to life imprisonment, two to 20 years' imprisonment, one to 15 years' imprisonment, and one to ten years' imprisonment. The remaining seven are acquitted.

● **Late August 1947: The Nuremberg Code, a ten-point statement of rules designed to protect the human rights**

of research subjects, is issued following the doctors' trial.

● **September 8, 1947: British troops in Palestine use tear gas to prevent the landing of the Jewish-refugee ship *Exodus*.**

● **November 3, 1947: The trial of Oswald Pohl, SS general in charge of**

Holocaust Justice and the Cold War

Even before the celebration of Victory in Europe Day, tensions were escalating between the Western Allies and the Soviet Union. The division of Europe into "spheres of influence" exacerbated the rivalry, leading to decades of "Cold War."

The race to create powerful nuclear weapons, enter space, and ensure the success of postwar economies at times outpaced the quest for justice. Some executives of I.G. Farben, tried as war criminals but seen as integral to West German economic success, received only short prison sentences, even though I.G. Farben had been the biggest wartime employer of concentration-camp labor at Auschwitz. Friedrich Flick *(pictured)*, head of the conglomerate *Mitteldeutsche Stahlwerke*, a coal and steel producer that had made extensive use of slave labor during the war, served only a few years in prison before resuming a career so successful that he became the richest man in Germany.

Scientists whose expertise was judged vital to the space program or the nuclear arms race were not held responsible for the use of slave labor in their wartime projects; NASA moon-rocket pioneer Wernher von Braun was one of these. In the postwar world, the quest for justice was tempered by the overarching desire to win the Cold War.

months and years *after* Auschwitz, she relearned what she had forgotten from *before* her ordeal. *Here* in the France to which she returned, she could do what was never possible *there*—such as use a toothbrush. *Now* she could do what was unthinkable *then*—such as calmly eat with a knife and fork. And yet, as she apparently became once more the person she had been before her intervening imprisonment in Auschwitz—charming, cultivated, civilized—she could hardly experience the smell of rain without recalling that "in Birkenau, rain heightened the odor of diarrhea." What happened in Auschwitz did little *then* or *now*, she testified, to unify, edify, or dignify life. For the most part, what happened in the Holocaust for-

ever divided, besieged, and diminished life instead.

Delbo did not mean to suggest that post-Holocaust life is necessarily hopeless. "Useless" though her knowledge might be in one sense, Delbo used it to show how dangerous it would be to forget that there was a time when Auschwitz was "the largest station in the world for arrivals and for departures." Scholar Lawrence L. Langer, too, does not say that knowledge of the Holocaust is simply useless. To the contrary, he argues that to encounter the Holocaust through serious study is as important as it is difficult, for such work, he says, "gives us access to the central event of our time, and perhaps of the modern era."

Delbo loathed abstraction, rejected sentimentality, and despised dishonesty even more. She wrote accordingly. "The sound of fifty blows on a man's back," she said, "is interminable."

Allies liberate Holocaust survivors, early 1945

An American stamp commemorates the 50th anniversary of the Allied liberation of the concentration camps in 1945.

---

camp works projects and the disposition of stolen valuables, concludes.

• **November 4, 1947–April 13, 1949:** Twenty-one former senior Nazi diplomats and government officials are tried at Nuremberg. Nineteen are sentenced to imprisonment; two are acquitted. All sentences will eventually be commuted to time served.

• **November 28, 1947–October 28, 1948:** Fourteen former members of the *Wehrmacht* High Command (OKW) are tried at Nuremberg. Twelve are sentenced to prison; two are acquitted. All sentences will eventually be commuted to time served.

• **November 29, 1947:** The United Nations votes in favor of a partition of Palestine that will create a Jewish state. Palestinian Arabs strongly oppose this.

• **December 1947:** Forty former members of the Auschwitz administration are tried at Kraków, Poland. Twenty-three are sentenced to death, 16 to imprisonment. One verdict is unknown.

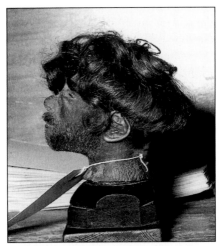

This shrunken head, found at the Buchenwald concentration camp, is a gruesome reminder of Nazi cruelty.

In Auschwitz, Delbo added, "not one of us utters, 'I'm hungry. I'm thirsty. I'm cold.'" Those things went without saying; to use such expressions in Auschwitz was absurd. Simple but pointed, Delbo's words show that the Nazis created an environment calculated to induce hunger, thirst, and misery so unrelenting that the most common expressions of need were reduced to silence under the blue sky's indifference.

Dying, Delbo continues, might bring a giddy instant in which one could feel "it is over, no more suffering and struggling, or requiring the impossible from a heart at the end of its resources . . . a bliss one did not know existed." The very lack of reverence for death, however, brought Delbo back to life—

but only partly: "I wish to die but not to be carried on the small stretcher. Not to be carried by on the short stretcher with hanging legs and head, and naked under a tattered blanket. I do not wish to be carried on the small stretcher." Because Auschwitz reduced the reasons for living to that extent, Delbo concluded that "it is far better to know nothing if you wish to go on living."

As for love, after Auschwitz it is no longer so tragically triumphant as conventional wisdom would have it. The phrase "better to have loved and lost than never to have loved at all" does not apply here. To an overwhelming degree, Delbo suggests, the Nazis defeated love. Granted a last meeting with her husband before he was killed, she reports that they found their separation compounded by the only act of love that seemed possible: mutual deception, pretending to each other not to know the fate awaiting them.

In Auschwitz, love could not be remembered well. There, memory itself was a luxury that energy scarcely permitted. When it did loom up, Delbo laments, memory often added pain too great for those already living beyond their emotional means.

And so for Delbo, as for every other survivor, came complex, searching questions. What Delbo called useless knowledge left her to wonder if her survival was worth it. Her brutally honest and profoundly melancholy testimony is not the same as that of others— Jews or non-Jews—who endured the Nazi camps. However, it amplifies one of the Holocaust's key repercussions, an impact or reverberation that deserves thoughtful attention: Especially after Auschwitz, care must be taken to resist utilizing the Holocaust as a sort of philosophical lever to affirm pre-Holocaust ideals and religious faith.

Delbo and others who survived knew that, although they did not physically perish at the hands of the Nazis and the Nazi collaborators, they were almost literally *removed from the world*—taken to

The last Jew in Vilkaviskis, Lithuania, stands in the town's Jewish cemetery, which he restored after the war.

• **December 2, 1947: Maria Mandel, chief SS supervisor for the women's camp at Auschwitz-Birkenau, is hanged in Kraków, Poland.**

• **1948: Pope Pius XII requests mercy for all Nazi war criminals condemned to death. His appeal is turned down by Deputy Military Governor General Lucius Clay.**

• **January 1948: In a staged auto accident, Shlomo Mikhoels, director of the Jewish State Theater in Moscow and the chair of the Jewish Antifascist Committee, is murdered by the Soviet secret police, the NKVD.**

• **April 1948: Franz W. Six, former *SS-Brigadeführer* and commander of *Einsatzgruppe* B, is sentenced to 20**

years' imprisonment for war crimes; *See* 1955.

• **April 28, 1948: Albert Forster, former *Gauleiter* of Danzig, Poland, is executed in that city after being convicted of war crimes.**

• **May 14, 1948: Britain's mandate to govern Palestine expires. Palestine is**

Immigration to the United States gave many Jewish child survivors of the Holocaust fresh starts, but nothing could compensate for their losses.

places where normal expectations and codes of conduct were turned upside-down, ripped apart, trampled into the ground. Many survivors continue to feel that sense of estrangement from the world, and to find it difficult, if not impossible, to celebrate anything resembling a human "triumph" over the Holocaust's destructiveness. Yet that same estrangement may be able to evoke responses at the deepest levels of human concern. As Lawrence Langer reminds us, there is profound horror in "a baby torn in two or a woman buried alive." Still, if we develop and maintain a deeply grounded awareness of the Holocaust, we may yet prevent despair and death from having the last

word. The state of Israel illustrates that possibility.

Destiny and Struggle

Spring 1945. Hitler was dead, the Third Reich in ruins. Many non-Jews across the globe assumed the horror had ended, but that was true only to a degree. The state-orchestrated terror and extermination had been forced to a halt, but antisemitism still was rife throughout continental Europe. Former SS and other low-level perpetrators roamed about freely, and the whereabouts of some top-level or high-profile Nazis were unknown. There seemed to be little sympathy in Great Britain and the Americas for Jewish concerns. Jews had no illusions about their lot. Murderous antisemitic pogroms in Poland in 1946 only

drove home the truth: If Jews were to live in security, they would have to make their own way—forge their own nation.

For Jews at the end of World War II and immediately thereafter, the goal for tens of thousands of Holocaust survivors was emigration to Palestine, where they hoped to join the Jews of Palestine in building an independent Jewish homeland. The British, however, still controlled Jewish immigration. Fearing that a flood of Jewish refugees would alienate the Arab world, the British remained unwilling to permit large-scale Jewish entry. They permitted a meager legal quota of 1500 Jews per month and clamped down on "illegal" immigration. Nevertheless, between 1944 and 1948, more than 200,000 Jews

Left: Jewish leaders *(left to right)* Nahum Goldmann, David Horowitz, Emanuel Neumann, and Rabbi Wolf Gold examine a map on November 12, 1947. It shows the United Nations' proposal for Palestine's partition. *Right:* On November 29, 1947, the UN approved a plan for the partition of Palestine, which included provisions for the creation of a Jewish state. Members of *Yishuv* (the Jewish community of Palestine) celebrate the news.

divided into the state of Israel and the Kingdom of Jordan. The Jewish National Council proclaims the independent state of Israel. U.S. recognition follows within hours; *See* May 15, 1948.

● **May 15, 1948:** Egyptian and Jordanian forces invade the one-day-old state of Israel; *See* January 7, 1949.

● **June 2, 1948:** Viktor Brack, former *SS-Oberführer* and organizer of "euthanasia" *Aktion* T-4, is hanged at Germany's Landsberg Prison after being convicted of war crimes. Karl Brandt, Adolf Hitler's physician and *SS-Gruppenführer*, involved in illegal medical experiments, also is hanged at Landsberg Prison after being convicted of war crimes.

● **September 30, 1948:** The United Nations Relief and Rehabilitation Agency closes.

● **November 1948:** During a purge of Soviet-Jewish culture, Soviet leader Joseph Stalin suspends publication of the Yiddish-language journal *Eynikeyt* (*Unity*).

tried to flee to Palestine, crossing borders any way they could. About 69,000 Jews made the journey by sea on 65 boats from August 1945 to May 1948. Only some of these

ships ran the British blockade successfully. About 51,000 of the Jewish refugees spent up to two years in British detention camps on the Mediterranean island of Cyprus.

As Jewish insistence mounted, international pressure also encouraged the establishment of a Jewish homeland. In Tel Aviv on May 14, 1948, several months after the

POSTWAR JEWISH POPULATIONS, 1950

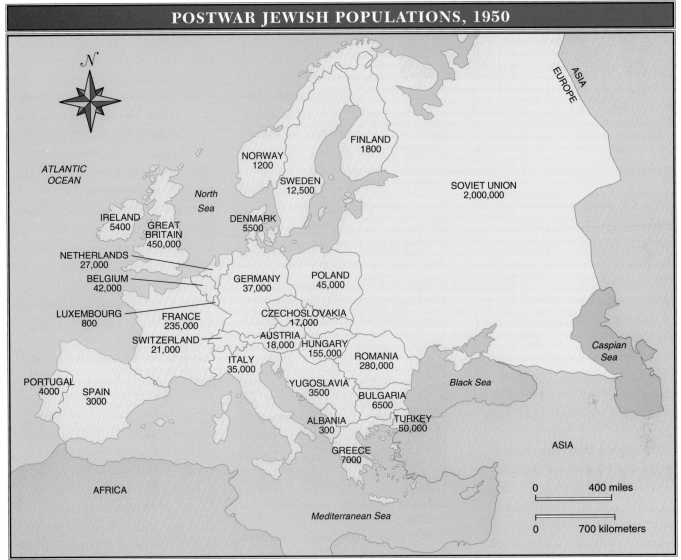

Europe's Jewish population fell from about 9.5 million in 1933 to 3.5 million in 1950. Poland's Jewish population fell from three million to 45,000. By 1950, upwards of 200,000 European Jews had immigrated to Palestine/Israel and 72,000 had moved to the United States.

● **December 1948:** The United Nations convenes a Genocide Convention, which calls on member states to react with firmness against groups committed to the destruction of people on racial, ethnic, religious, or national grounds. The United States delegation, keenly aware of the forced segregation within the U.S., declines to ratify the convention.

● **1949:** Only 300 of the 9600 people sentenced to confinement by the Nuremberg Tribunal and subsequent trials remain imprisoned. ● Auschwitz-Birkenau physician/torturer Josef Mengele adopts a pseudonym and settles in South America. ● Jew-baiting Nazi Hermann Esser, author of *The Jewish World Pest* (1939), is stripped of his property and civil

rights by a German denazification court and sentenced in absentia to five years' forced labor. ● Lutz Schwerin von Krosigk, former Reich minister of finance, is sentenced at Nuremberg to ten years' imprisonment. ● Western preoccupation with the nascent Cold War diminishes enthusiasm for further large-scale prosecution of alleged Nazi war criminals.

In February 1948 Arabs likely slipped through lax British security and detonated a bomb that reduced the Jewish District of Jerusalem to the rubble seen here. Three months later, on May 15, the day-old state of Israel was at war following attacks by Egypt and Jordan.

United Nations voted to divide Palestine into Jewish and Arab states and the British had begun their withdrawal from Palestine, David Ben-Gurion proclaimed Israel's independence. The census taken six months later found that the new nation's population numbered 782,000. Of that number, 713,000 were Jews, including Holocaust survivors whose numbers would approach 140,000 by the end of the decade.

Statehood, however, did not guarantee Israeli security. The new nation was declared on May 14, 1948, and on May 15 Israel was invaded by Arab forces; a cease-fire followed eight months later. The 1948–49 clash was the first in a series of wars with hostile Arab neighbors—most significantly the Six-Day War in June 1967 and the 1973 Yom Kippur War, both of which resulted in tremendous Israeli victories and territorial gains. Still, while the prospects for lasting peace in the region have improved, they are by no means assured. The vexing issue of an independent state for Palestinian Arabs, which would be established in the West Bank and Gaza Strip, remains in suspense as the 21st century begins.

Would the state of Israel have existed if the Holocaust never happened? Some arguments hold that a Jewish homeland might have existed even sooner if World

Israel soundly defeated Arab attackers in the Six-Day War in 1967. The triumph enlarged Israel's borders, created a new image of Israeli strength and power in the region, and engendered self-confidence and pride among Jews.

War II and the Holocaust had not intervened. Other arguments, whose framers are skeptical about "what-if?" speculation, stress that the existence of the state of Israel is bound up inextricably with Holocaust history. And as the sirens' scream warns, some would add, Israel can never relax its vigilance.

Israel's existence invites another "what if?" question—one grounded in Theodor Herzl's dream that an independent Jewish state was the only viable answer to the "Jewish question." The question asks: If the Jews had possessed a state of their own at the beginning of the 20th century, would the Holocaust have taken place? Perhaps not, but this question, too, invites deep speculation. Is it possible that the Nazis would have/could have deported all nine million European Jews to a Jewish Palestine, and that the territory could have handled such an enormous influx of humanity? Such a scenario strains credulity at every turn.

That said, the question nevertheless calls attention to key issues. Statelessness can mean helplessness and hopelessness. Defenselessness is unsound strategic policy. National power does make one's opponents think twice before tampering with it, and anyone who tampers with Israel's security, or with Jewish

---

• **January 7, 1949: A cease-fire ends Arab-Israeli hostilities that began in May 1948. In the settlement, Israel increases its territory by 50 percent.**

• **May 11, 1949: Israel is admitted to the United Nations.**

• **May 23, 1949: The Federal Republic of Germany (West Germany) is** established as a parliamentary democracy.

• **October 7, 1949: Communist East German states establish a centralized constitution and come together as the Democratic Republic of Germany.**

• **1949–1952: Acting under encouragement from Soviet leader Joseph** Stalin, puppet-state courts mount show trials of Jews in Hungary and Czechoslovakia.

• **1950: Responsibility for prosecution of the remaining Nazi war criminals is handed by the Allies to West Germany. • Erich Koch, former high commissioner for the Ukraine, is extradited to Poland for his complic-**

The village of Ma'alot in Galilee became a target of Palestinian terrorists in May 1974. Twenty schoolchildren were killed. Here, Galil Maimon carries his injured sister, Zipora, to safety.

well-being anywhere in the world, should not expect to do so with impunity. These political considerations are among some of the Holocaust's most important repercussions.

Issues of Guilt

Few events have affected Jewish and Israeli identity more than the Holocaust. Holocaust repercussions affect German identity in related ways. No April sirens' scream brings Germany to a silent halt in observance of the destruction of European Jewry, but that nation's history is inescapably tied to Holocaust history.

As a new century begins, Berlin will be the site of a new memorial, one whose birth pangs have been

painfully difficult. It will be Germany's Memorial to the Murdered Jews of Europe. For some time there have been Holocaust memorial sites on German soil; the former concentration camps at Buchenwald, Dachau, Ravensbrück, and Sachsenhausen are a few examples. But the Berlin memorial, which will be located in the heart of the nation's capital, represents a special national acknowledgment of Germany's historic responsibility for the Holocaust.

In June 1998 a five-member *Findungskommission* recommended a design submitted by

American architect Peter Eisenman, which features what has been called an expansive field of waving pillars. The design, widely praised in the German press, had been accepted by Helmut Kohl, who was chancellor at the time. However, resistance led by Kohl's political opposition put final decisions on hold until after Germany's September 1998 elections. Those elections made Gerhard Schröder the new chancellor. Michael Naumann, Schroeder's culture minister, opposed the idea of a national Holocaust memorial, but negotiations between Naumann, Eisenman, and the

Establishment of Israel

Zionists' long, cherished goal of creating a Jewish homeland in Palestine was finally achieved on May 14, 1948, when David Ben-Gurion (*standing, below*) proclaimed the existence of the state of Israel. Jewish loss of life during the Holocaust directly contributed to the overwhelming support of the international community for the creation of a sovereign Jewish nation.

On November 29, 1947, the United Nations voted to partition Palestine into two states, one Jewish and the other Arab. While Arab nationalists completely rejected the plan, leaders of the Jewish community in Palestine ultimately accepted the partition.

When Prime Minister Ben-Gurion announced the creation of the state of Israel within the boundaries allotted to it by the partition plan, armies from Arab states almost immediately invaded the newly created nation.

ity in the deaths of millions, including 72,000 Poles. His subsequent death sentence is commuted to life in prison because of his poor health. • Israel passes the "Law of Judging Nazi Criminals and Their Helpers," opening the way for trials in Israel of former Nazis. • SS functionary Adolf Eichmann escapes to Argentina with help of "Odessa" operatives, former

SS officers whose goal is to aid such escapes.

• **June 1950: The American Displaced Persons Act of 1948 is modified by Congress to allow equitable Jewish immigration to the U.S. The original act had favored Jews whose homelands were under Soviet rule after the war.**

• **December 1, 1950: The second of three secretly buried parts of the *Oneg Shabbat* archive, organized by Emanuel Ringelblum and including his personal diary, is discovered in Warsaw beneath what had been 68 Nowolipki Street. Contents include eyewitness testimony of the Treblinka death camp, given by Abraham Jacob Krzepicki, a young escapee.**

Israel and the Holocaust

The Jews of Palestine not only welcomed the European Jews of the Holocaust—they also fought to save their lives. Palestine was the only place on earth where a large proportion of the population would welcome European Jews during the war.

Zionism, a movement created by Theodor Herzl in the 1890s, held that Europe was not safe for Jews and that they must have a national homeland in Palestine. He encouraged legal and illegal immigration into Palestine, whose mandate was held by Great Britain.

David Ben-Gurion was the chair of the Zionist Executive and the Jewish Agency for Palestine. In the first years of the war, he sought American-Jewish support for both the European Jews and for a Jewish state in Palestine. He urged that German cities be bombed in retaliation for atrocities against Jews, although he considered mass demonstrations in the Allied nations as wastes of time because he saw that the Allies were not helping the Jews.

After the Holocaust, almost a million European Jewish refugees

were welcomed into Palestine and Israel, the Jewish state that was established in 1948. Pictured are arriving Jews on board the *Negev* in 1948. This unique nation, which awards automatic citizenship to all Jews who migrate there to live, was established and fought for as a place where Jews at last would be safe.

Ironically, Jews are still very much at risk in Israel. The enormous impact of the Holocaust on the Israeli mind-set has conditioned Israeli life and politics for decades. Surrounded by many hostile Arab governments, and residing in a topography that cannot be easily defended, the Israelis

have focused heavily on security needs, which has resulted in a necessarily aggressive foreign policy.

Although Israel's cultural, intellectual, and political lives reflect a broad spectrum of issues, always looming over the nation is the specter of a repeat of the Holocaust. Profound Jewish thinker Richard Rubenstein has described the stern resolve of Holocaust survivors who immigrated to Israel, which in turn allows us a crucial insight into the Israeli mind: "We may die on the sands of Palestine, but we will never again accommodate ourselves to your good graces or your prejudices. There may some day be another *Massada* in which every Jew fights to the last man before being overwhelmed by his enemies."

"There will never be another Auschwitz," he continued. "Jews will never again trust in your humanity only to endure the most degrading of impersonal deaths. We have folded our tents. We will be wanderers no longer. We will no longer live among you. For better or worse, we are going home."

• 1951: Hans Schmidt, a former Buchenwald guard, is the last war criminal to be executed by the Allies.
• Writer Ernst von Salomon publishes *Der Fragebogen* (*The Questionnaire*), which attempts to diminish German war guilt by "answering" an Allied questionnaire distributed in Germany in 1945. The latter was intended to weed out ardent Nazis and prevent

them from holding posts in postwar governments. • A U.S. bank, National City, colludes with the U.S. Federal Reserve to accept $30 million worth of looted Nazi gold, which has been laundered in Switzerland, as collateral for a loan to Spain. The gold bars, bearing the Nazi swastika, are melted down and issued as U.S. Assay Office bars; *See* November 1, 1997.

• Otmar von Verschuer receives an appointment to teach human genetics at the University of Münster in West Germany. As Josef Mengele's mentor, he received human specimens and reports from Auschwitz. • The Conference on Jewish Material Claims Against Germany is established in New York as an umbrella organization to handle German reparations to Jews.

Findungskommision led to workable modifications. The memorial's original design has been scaled down, and the memorial site will be complemented by a Holocaust interpretive center and research library.

As the memorial project moved toward implementation in 1999, two other noteworthy items appeared in that spring's German news. Both have at least implicit connections with the Memorial to the Murdered Jews of Europe. First, an Associated Press story—dateline May 22, Cologne, Germany—reported clashes between left- and right-wing political groups. Police kept the adversaries at a distance for a time, but when an estimated 200 supporters of the National Party, a radical rightist faction, began the demon-

On January 20, 1999, Michael Naumann—German Chancellor Gerhard Schroeder's cultural minister—explains the model of a proposed plan for a Holocaust memorial to be constructed in the heart of Berlin.

stration that court approval allowed them, about 400 of their left-wing opponents eluded police control and began to pelt the demonstrators with bottles, rocks, eggs, and tomatoes. During the fracas, nearby car and shop windows were smashed, combatants on both sides received minor injuries, and the police took 26 persons into custody.

Had the matter amounted to no more than this, international press coverage would have been unlikely, but the reasons behind this German clash were, in fact, newsworthy. Part of Germany's postwar identity has involved the belief that, whatever the evil Hitler and his Nazis did, the *Wehrmacht* (the World War II-era German Army) had fought with honor that the Holocaust could not besmirch. Many Germans knew better, but impressions about the Army's nobility persisted in the public mind. Then, in March 1995, an exhibition titled *Vernichtungskrieg: Verbrechen der Wehrmacht, 1941–1944* (War of Annihilation: Crimes of the *Wehrmacht*) began to appear in German and Austrian venues. This exhibition

"War of Annihilation: Crimes of the *Wehrmacht*," a controversial traveling exhibition, shattered the widely held view that the German Army fought nobly during the war and was untainted by Nazi atrocities.

of photographs and documents confirmed that the *Wehrmacht* implemented genocidal policies directed at Jews and Gypsies. The Army also engaged in mass killings of defenseless Slavic people in Poland, Serbia, and the Soviet Union, and it was responsibile for the deaths of more than three million Soviet prisoners of war. This controversial exhibition, viewed by more than 820,000 people in 32 cities as of late spring 1999, provoked considerable dissenting protests. Before the Cologne disturbance clashes between left- and right-wing groups took place in the southwestern German city of Saarbrücken. There, more than 100 leftists, defenders of the exhibit, were arrested when they contested rightist protests against the exhibit's depiction of *Wehrmacht* atrocities.

• **January 1951: Protesters in Jerusalem riot against a West German offer of monetary reparations to Israel and Jews for the Holocaust. Many Israelis don't want to reach an agreement of any kind with Germany; *See* September 27, 1951.**

• **January 12, 1951: The United Nations-sponsored Genocide Conven-** tion treaty, under terms of Article 56 of the U.N. charter, bans torture, murder, deportation, and persecution of a group for racial, religious, or political reasons.

• **April 12, 1951: A commemorative *Yom ha-Sho'ah* (Holocaust Day) is enacted into law by Israel's *Knesset* (parliament).**

• **June 8, 1951: After being convicted of war crimes, the following former Nazis are hanged at Landsberg Prison: Oswald Pohl, a former SS general in charge of camp works projects and disposition of valuables stolen from inmates; Paul Blobel, former SS-*Standartenführer* and the head of *Sonderkommando* 1005; and Otto Ohlendorf, former SS-*Gruppen-***

The presumed moral purity of the *Wehrmacht* was important to postwar Germans. The army's complicity in numerous atrocities became apparent later, and showed that the 1947 trials of General Wilhelm List *(above, center)* and other military leaders were appropriate.

News from Germany on May 21, 1999, contained another Holocaust-related story that was noteworthy. It dealt with an ethnic German named Alfons Goetzfried. In 1991 Goetzfried had immigrated to Germany from his native Ukraine as the Soviet Union disintegrated. His move did not succeed, however, in leaving his wartime past behind. The crucial chapter in Goetzfried's story turned out to be that he had been a member of the Gestapo and a participant in the 1943 murder of

17,000 Jews in Poland. Brought to trial in Germany, he was found guilty of war crimes by a state court in Stuttgart.

The prosecutor argued for a 13-year prison sentence, which the court denied. Even if the prosecutor's argument had prevailed, it is unclear that Goetzfried's situation would have ended up much differently. After sentencing him to ten years, the court then released Goetzfried on the grounds that he had previously spent 13 postwar years imprisoned in a Soviet labor camp in Siberia. Goetzfried's prosecutors stated that this trial might be the last of Germany's Nazi-era war-crimes trials. For just as Holocaust survivors are aging and dying, the same is true of war-crimes suspects and the witnesses who could testify against them.

Germany's Struggle with Its Past

The murderous legacy of Nazism has cast a long and foreboding shadow over the German nation. Questions of collective guilt and responsibility for the crimes of National Socialism permeate the fabric of German society. Although more than 50 years separate the present day from the end of World War II, Germany still struggles to come to terms with its past.

Until the 1960s, discussions of National Socialism were virtually absent from German textbooks. Although questions about culpability for the Holocaust are now cautiously broached in Germany, every effort to memorialize the Holocaust ignites a national debate.

On an individual level, German intellectuals have wrestled endlessly about German guilt. Whereas the German philosopher Karl Jaspers rejected the thesis of collective guilt, German theologian Martin Niemöller openly acknowledged it.

In his confession "I Am Guilty," Niemöller wrote: "We are most certainly not without guilt; and I ask myself over and over again what would have happened if 14,000 evangelical ministers all over Germany had defended the truth with their very lives in the year 1933 or 1934.... I can imagine that we should have saved 30 to 40 million lives."

Following the war, Dr. Josef Mengele, the sadistic chief physician at Auschwitz, found haven in South America. This wanted poster was released by the Simon Wiesenthal Center in 1985.

---

führer and commander of *Einsatzgruppe* D.

● **July 23, 1951:** Philippe Pétain, head of the collaborationist Vichy government in France, dies in exile on the island of Yeu at age 96.

● **September 8, 1951:** Jürgen Stroop, former *SS-Gruppenführer* in charge

of the 1943 liquidation of the Warsaw Ghetto, is hanged at Warsaw after being convicted of war crimes.

● **September 27, 1951:** West German Chancellor Konrad Adenauer formally apologizes for Nazi persecution of Jews and reiterates his nation's offer of reparations; *See* January 1951; September 10, 1952.

● **1952:** The first Criminal Senate of the German Federal Court rules that the official acts of the Nazi regime are invalid because they violate all standards of legality and morality.

● **February 1952:** The Federal Reserve Bank of New York obtains gold plates, buttons, coins, and smoking-pipe ornaments that were appar-

Germany is not the only country that has needed to deal with people who destroyed Jewish life during the Holocaust. In the United States, for example, the Department of Justice established its Nazi-hunting Office of Special Investigations (OSI) for that purpose in 1979. Since that time, 61 ex-Nazis have been stripped of U.S. citizenship and 49 have been removed from the United States. The OSI's "watch list" program has prevented entry to 150 suspected Nazi war criminals, and in 1999 the OSI had more than 250 persons under investigation.

Intense scrutiny has been directed, in particular, against Ukrainian-born John Demjanjuk, a retired auto worker from Cleveland, Ohio, who had immigrated to the United States in 1951 and became a naturalized citizen in 1958. In 1986 Demjanjuk was extradited to Israel, where he stood trial for crimes against humanity. He was cleared, however, when evidence from the Soviet Union cast doubt that he was the infamous Treblinka gas-chamber operator known as "Ivan the Terrible." The U.S. Justice Department initiated proceedings in a federal court on May 19, 1999, to strip Demjanjuk of his U.S. citizenship. Demjanjuk may not have been at Treblinka, but

Top left: Beate Klarsfeld was one of the more prominent and dedicated "Nazi hunters" to emerge postwar. Here she greets Israeli Prime Minister Yitzhak Rabin in July 1975. *Top right:* Ukrainian-born John Demjanjuk, suspected of being "Ivan the Terrible," the infamous Treblinka gas-chamber operator, was released by prosecutors because of a lack of evidence. However, the U.S. Justice Department linked him to other death camps. *Bottom right:* In March 1998 former SS officer Erik Priebke received a life sentence for ordering the massacre of 335 Italian civilians, including 75 Jews, at the Ardeatine Caves outside of Rome in 1944. He subsequently appealed his case.

the Justice Department charged that he was, among other things, an armed guard at Sobibór and Majdanek, two notorious Nazi death and concentration camps on Polish soil where hundreds of thousands of Jews were murdered during the Holocaust. The U.S. criminal code has lacked provisions relating explicitly to war crimes. However, falsification of information pertaining to citizenship applications has been used in the United States as a basis to remove citizenship and facilitate

deportation for war-crimes suspects. If the government's case against Demjanjuk is successful— it was pending at the time of this writing—he will likely be deported to his native Ukraine.

Controversial Scholarship

Meanwhile, Germany's Memorial to the Murdered Jews of Europe appears as the perpetrators' generation disappears. As the clashes in Cologne and Saarbrücken illustrate, however, repercussions with regard to post-

---

ently stolen from victims of Nazi persecution in Europe. The Federal Reserve later melted down these items and turned them into gold bars, which were turned over to European central banks; *See* December 1997.

● **September 10, 1952: Israel and West Germany sign the Luxembourg Treaty:** West Germany will pay reparations to Israel and Jewish organizations for Nazi genocide. Of an $820 million payment, $750 million will go to the Israeli government; *See* 1990.

● **November 9, 1952:** Chaim Weizmann, first president of Israel, dies.

● **1953:** The Israeli parliament declares a Day of Holocaust Heroism.

● *I. A. Topf und Söhne* (I. A. Topf & Sons), manufacturer of gas chambers and crematoria during the war, is granted a patent for a method of fueling furnaces with animal fat.

● **1955:** Franz W. Six, former *SS-Brigadeführer* and commander of *Einsatzgruppe* B, is released from prison after serving seven years of a

Fugitive Nazis in the Americas

Not all Nazis followed the path of Joseph Goebbels, who chose suicide rather than face life without the *Führer*. Many others, including some directly responsible for implementing the "Final Solution," fled Germany in the hope of eluding judgment.

Helped by secret networks of Nazi sympathizers, Adolf Eichmann, Franz Stangl, and Josef Mengele, along with untold others, escaped to South America. Eichmann, the SS "Jewish expert," fled to Argentina, but was eventually located and spirited out of the country by Israeli security agents. Stangl, commandant of the Sobibór and Treblinka death camps, escaped first to Syria with the aid of a sympathetic Catholic bishop and then journeyed to Brazil. For 16 years he lived there with his family, using his own name and working in a Volkswagen factory, until war-crimes investigators finally extradited him for trial in Germany.

Josef Mengele, the Auschwitz doctor known as the "Angel of Death," found asylum in Argentina. Facing extradition, he hid in Brazil and Paraguay, managing to avoid capture. He died a free man in 1978. Others, including concentration- and death-camp guards, joined the swell of refugees who immigrated to the United States, building new lives and escaping prosecution for their crimes. In the summer of 1998, Argentina signed an accord with Germany, Israel, and the United States to share information about Nazis still at large in Argentina.

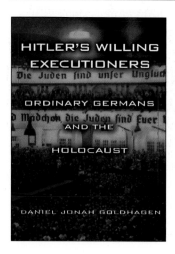

In *Hitler's Willing Executioners: Ordinary Germans and the Holocaust,* Daniel Goldhagen argues that widespread and deeply ingrained antisemitism caused average Germans to become "willing" killers of Jews.

Holocaust German identity are not likely to be silenced any time soon. The Berlin memorial, which will testify to the immensity of the "Final Solution," also suggests that German responsibility for the destruction of the European Jews was widespread. It included people such as Alfons Goetzfried and his Gestapo colleagues; it also implicated the *Wehrmacht*. At least for one scholar, Daniel Jonah Goldhagen, a young Harvard University professor of government, German responsibility was so vast that it became appropriate to let the title of his best-selling 1996 book—*Hitler's Willing Executioners: Ordinary Germans and the Holocaust*—identify Germans generally. Half a century after the Holocaust ended, no writing about the Holocaust—not even the most determined efforts of the pseudo-scholars who deny that the Holocaust took place—provoked greater controversy about German identity than his.

Even when they are about immensely important subjects such as the Holocaust, 600-page history books rarely get the attention received by *Hitler's Willing Executioners*. Finding his conclusions at odds with their own, most Holocaust scholars in the United States, Europe, and Israel have not given Goldhagen marks to

20-year sentence for war crimes.
• French film director Alain Resnais releases *Nuit et Brouillard (Night and Fog),* a powerful short documentary about Nazi concentration- and death-camp atrocities. Its major flaw is the omission of the fact that the Jews were the central victims of the Holocaust. • *Jud Süss,* the most notorious antisemitic feature film to be pro-

duced in Germany during the Hitler era, is dubbed into Arabic and distributed in the Arab states by Sovexport, a Soviet government agency.

• 1956: Polish film director Andrzej Wajda releases *Kanal,* a harrowing drama about fugitive Jews hiding beneath the streets in the Warsaw sewer system in September 1944.

• October 29, 1956: In response to Egypt's July 26 nationalization of the Suez Canal, Israel attacks Egypt's Sinai peninsula and drives toward the canal.

• November 6, 1956: A U.S.-forced cease-fire ends Arab-Israeli hostilities and preserves free use of the Suez Canal.

Himmler's SS troopers believed they were uniquely special, when in fact most of them, including these former Auschwitz guards who are pictured at their trial, were dull men devoid of scruples and conscience.

match the high sales figures that his book enjoyed. For mainly good reasons, the leading scholars whom Goldhagen vied to supplant found his methodology suspect and the tone of his writing arrogant and disdainful of even the best work in Holocaust studies. They considered his research results to be either far less original than Goldhagen claimed or perniciously incorrect to the point of being destructive because they reignited undeserved prejudices against Germans and Jews alike.

What did Goldhagen—this young academic of a postwar generation—say to provoke such critical reactions? Note, first, that *Hitler's Willing Executioners* was preceded by the work of Christopher Browning, a distinguished historian who published a 1992 work that has achieved classic status in Holocaust studies. Browning called his book *Ordinary Men*. It analyzed the postwar judicial interrogations of 210 members of Reserve Police Battalion 101, a 500-man killing squadron of the German Order Police that was responsible for 83,000 Jewish deaths in Poland during the Holocaust.

Goldhagen targeted Browning's book when he chose *Ordinary Germans and the Holocaust* as the subtitle for *Hitler's Willing Executioners*. Having probed the same archival material about Reserve Police Battalion 101 that Browning had investigated, Goldhagen believed that Browning mishandled and misinterpreted the data. Specifically, Goldhagen contended that Browning underestimated the extent and depth of antisemitism in Germany and played down its tenacious grip and deadly influence on the German people. Furthermore, Goldhagen charged that Browning inadequately explained the killing behavior of the men in Reserve Police Battalion 101 by citing conformity to peer pressure, blind acceptance of current political norms, and careerism as among its chief motivational causes.

Browning's interpretation did stress that the reserve policemen, German though they were and antisemitic though they may have been, were of special significance because they were also very ordinary human beings. He maintained that the story of Reserve Police Battalion 101 should cause, at the very least, discomfort for men and women everywhere. For as post-Holocaust history shows, people in other times and places—people like *us*—are also capable of complicity in genocide. Goldhagen was not impressed, let alone persuaded. He found fault with Browning's book because it missed what he regarded as the essential point about the Holocaust: Only

These former Auschwitz guards, put on trial in Poland in 1947, had once been "typical" German women. Power appealed to them, and they found fulfillment in the barracks and gas chambers.

• **1957: Fritz Katzmann**, former *SS-Gruppenführer* responsible for the extermination of Jews in the Galicia region of Poland, dies after evading prosecution for 12 years. • The last operating displaced-persons camp, located in Belgium, closes.

• **1958:** The *Einsatzkommando* trial in the Soviet Union documents the Nazis' genocidal actions during their occupation of Lithuania. Ninety-four percent of Lithuanian Jewry—about 220,000 people—were murdered during the Holocaust. • The West German government establishes the Central Office for the Investigation of National Socialist (Nazi) Crimes.

• **1959: Karl Jäger**, former *SS-Standartenführer* and head of *Einsatzkommando* 3, is arrested, but he commits suicide before his trial. • **Ante Pavelić**, founder of the Fascist *Ustasa* terrorist organization in Croatia, and the man behind the murders of tens of thousands of Jews and hundreds of thousands of Serbs, dies two years after a terrorist attempt on his life. • Ameri-

the deep-seated racist antisemitism that infested the German people could motivate, and thus account for, the behavior of particular Germans who committed the atrocities that advanced the Final Solution.

Making his case, however, obliged Goldhagen to do more than disagree with Browning's interpretation of the archival records about Reserve Police Battalion 101. He had to show, first, that "Germans' antisemitic beliefs about Jews were the central causal agent of the Holocaust." The claim required him not only to trace the history of German antisemitism but also to document how that history involved authority and power fatal enough to account for the Holocaust's enormous destruction. In addition, Goldhagen's case hinged on

In 1959 the Cologne, Germany, synagogue was rebuilt and reconsecrated. Soon, swastikas and the words *Juden raus* (Jews, get out) defiled its walls.

demonstrating that "ordinary Germans"—not just rabidly antisemitic Nazis who had political power—either willingly engaged in the slaughter or were so willing to let it go forward that they would not have hesitated to kill if called upon to do so. In short, Goldhagen had to show that the Holocaust, contrary to Browning's "ordinary men" hypothesis, was essentially the willful act of "ordinary Germans," who were much more lethally antisemitic than previous scholarship admitted.

To establish these positions, Goldhagen's book was organized around two arguments. Beginning with the history of German antisemitism, Goldhagen aimed to show how, in particular, a potentially lethal anti-Jewish racism had a powerful influence in pre-Nazi Germany. Then he focused on the actual German perpetrators of the Holocaust, studying specifically the personnel and work of killing squadrons such as Reserve Police Battalion 101. He also examined the parts played by other "ordinary Germans" in the huge system of concentration, labor,

Hannah Arendt, a brilliant German-Jewish philosopher—and a former mistress of Nazi sympathizer Martin Heidegger—immigrated to the United States. She later wrote *The Origins of Totalitarianism.*

and death camps that was, as he correctly stated, "the emblematic institution of Germany during its Nazi period." To these perspectives, he added detail, as hideous as it is valuable, about a less well-known aspect of the Holocaust, namely the brutal "death marches" that took place from late 1939 until the end of World War II.

First, according to Goldhagen, ordinary Germans were antisemitic. Their antisemitism entailed elimination of the Jews. Therefore, ordinary Germans were prepared to be willing executioners.

Second, far from being reluctant murderers, some Germans actually became willing execution-

---

can film director George Stevens releases *The Diary of Anne Frank*, a dramatization based on the biographical play concerning the young Dutch Jew Anne Frank, her family, and the secret room in Amsterdam in which they hid from the Nazis. The film, as the play before it, de-Judaizes Anne and her family. Her father, Otto, approves of this because he feels, cor-

rectly, that the public is not ready to accept a film that is "too Jewish."

• 1960: Former SS member Wernher von Braun, a leading German scientist who was instrumental in designing the V–2 terror rocket, is appointed the head of the George C. Marshall Space Flight Center in Huntsville, Alabama. • *Hitler's Zweites Buch*

(*Hitler's Second Book*) is published in Stuttgart, West Germany. The book is attributed to Adolf Hitler and is purported to be a sequel to *Mein Kampf*; authorship remains in doubt.

• May 23, 1960: Israeli Prime Minister David Ben-Gurion announces that Adolf Eichmann was located in Argentina by the Israeli Secret Serers of the European Jews. Typically, those same Germans were a representative cross-section of the German population. Therefore, with exceptions that only prove the rule, ordinary Germans stand indicted for the destruction of the European Jews.

Goldhagen's evidence for these claims derived initially from his appraisal of German antisemitism. According to his reading of that history, venomous forms of cultural and racist antisemitism became the ethical standard in Germany in the 19th and 20th centuries, well before Hitler and the Nazi Party gained power in 1933. Such antisemitism called for the elimination of Jews and Jewish influence in Germany. In one way or another, then, the majority of the German populace was prepared to destroy Jews.

When the Nazis came to power, they advocated an overtly *exterminationist* antisemitism. Crucial to Goldhagen's argument was his claim that this exterminationist ideology was only a variation on the already *eliminationist* antisemitism that had existed in Germany for some time. During the Nazi period, 1933 to 1945, German perpetrators of the Holocaust willingly persecuted and destroyed Jews because they shared the Nazis' antisemitic per-

spective. This perspective held that the annihilation of the Jews was necessary and just, for the Jews were a deadly pestilence threatening the racial superiority and political prerogatives that properly belonged to Germans.

Given legitimacy by the Nazi regime, the German killers, according to Goldhagen, were not an extraordinary minority. Instead they were representative of the German populace. Goldhagen's logic entailed this relationship to

Nazi Hunters

Following the war, a quest was undertaken to locate Nazis who had fled and bring them to justice. Two men, Simon Wiesenthal and Serge Klarsfeld, became the two most successful Nazi hunters.

Wiesenthal *(pictured)*, who survived several camps including Buchenwald and Mauthausen, founded the Jewish Historical Documentation Center in Linz, Austria, to locate, extradite, and try Nazi war criminals. He later moved his investigative activities to Vienna. His tireless efforts brought Franz Stangl, commandant of Sobibór and Treblinka, and other Nazis to the bar of justice.

Klarsfeld experienced the Holocaust as a child. Born in Bucharest, Romania, he and his family fled to Nice, France, where they hid from the Nazis. He, his mother, and his sister avoided the Nazis' dragnet, but his father was captured and killed in Auschwitz. The efforts of Klarsfeld and his wife, Beate, led to the capture of Klaus Barbie, the "Butcher of Lyons." Extradited from Bolivia, Barbie was tried in France and sentenced to life in prison.

Intent on preventing Nazis from living out their lives in peaceful obscurity, Wiesenthal and the Klarsfelds have dedicated themselves to shining the light of public scrutiny on war criminals and those who would offer them sanctuary.

The second part of Emanuel Ringelblum's *Oneg Shabbat* archive, which documented events in the Warsaw Ghetto, was discovered in 1950. The third and final part has never been found.

---

vice and has arrived in Israel to stand trial as a war criminal; *See* April 11–August 14, 1961.

• **1961: A wall erected at the edge of the Babi Yar, Ukraine, killing ground collapses, dumping mud, water, and human remains into the streets of Kiev. Twenty-four people are killed in subsequent fires and in flooded**

buildings and tram cars. • **Israel dedicates the Hall of Remembrance, a Holocaust commemoration.** • **Nazi hunter Simon Wiesenthal reopens a Documentation Center of Nazi war criminals in Vienna.** • *The Origins of the Second World War,* **a book by revisionist British historian A.J.P. Taylor, is published. The book attempts to spread the blame for**

World War II beyond Hitler to Allied leaders.

• **April 11–August 14, 1961: In Israel, the trial of Adolf Eichmann takes place. He is found guilty and sentenced to death;** *See* May 1962.

• **1962: Hans Globke, state-secretary of West Germany and onetime spear-**

The Eichmann Trial

The trial of Adolf Eichmann in 1961 was a transformative event in the scholarly investigation of the Holocaust. Before the trial, the details of the Nazi genocide had seldom been evaluated systematically, and survivors were reluctant to openly reflect upon their experiences.

Kidnaped by Israeli agents in Argentina in 1960, Eichmann was brought to Israel to stand trial. Not only did the trial establish Eichmann's guilt, but it also presented the details of the "Final Solution" as they unfolded in Europe from 1933 until 1945.

One of the most shocking revelations that resulted from the trial was the discovery that Eichmann, a primary agent in the killing of millions of Jews, was a relatively ordinary human being. He was not a zealous Nazi, only a bureaucrat doing his job. Adolf Eichmann was executed by hanging at midnight on May 31–June 1, 1962. His body was cremated and his ashes spread over the sea, beyond the territorial waters of Israel.

mean that the majority of Germans were not only willing to let the Holocaust happen, but probably would have participated directly in the killing if called upon to do so.

Confident of the superiority of his own judgment, Goldhagen contended that few puzzles remain about the Holocaust's causes. Although explaining how the Holocaust happened remains a long story, he believed that there was no need to dwell on most of the complexities that decades of causal analysis of the Holocaust has produced. As Goldhagen saw

it, the Holocaust had one cause that outweighed the others. Direct and straightforward, it involved the motivation without which the Holocaust was unthinkable: namely, the Germans' antisemitic beliefs about Jews. Remove that factor and the Holocaust that actually happened would not have taken place. On the other hand, to realize the Final Solution, the antisemitism of Goldhagen's ordinary Germans did need the catalyst that Hitler and the Nazi Party provided. Nevertheless, by themselves Hitler and the Nazi Party alone could not have made the

Holocaust happen as it did. The actual Holocaust required willing, ordinary Germans to bring it about.

Fanatically antisemitic as they were, Goldhagen suggests, Hitler and the Nazi Party had a reciprocal relationship with ordinary Germans when it came to the "Jewish question." In Hitler and the Nazi Party, ordinary Germans got the organization, determination, and legitimation to act on their latent, if not active, will to destroy European Jewry. In ordinary Germans, Hitler and the Nazi Party found a people who were well prepared to carry out the plan for a Third Reich that would be *judenrein* ("cleansed of Jews"). Thus, when Goldhagen reckoned with the actuality of the Holocaust, his book became much more than an explanation of how he thought the Holocaust took place. With his view that the Germans' antisemitic motivation was the most crucial condition—necessary though not alone sufficient—for the Holocaust, Goldhagen indicted "ordinary Germans," a category as broad as it was undiscriminating, and rendered a sweeping verdict of collective German guilt.

Goldhagen's book has its merits. They exist primarily in his expansion of some details about the Final Solution, but not in the

head of antisemitic legislation in Hitler's Germany, proposes legislation to rectify the exploitation of Jews by German corporations. West German industry rejects Globke's plan.
• The Avenue of the Righteous is inaugurated at the Yad Vashem memorial in Jerusalem, where trees are planted to honor non-Jews who helped Jews during the Holocaust.

• May 1962: Adolf Eichmann's appeal of his death sentence is rejected; *See* May 31, 1962.

• May 31, 1962: Adolf Eichmann is hanged in Israel.

• December 20, 1963–August 20, 1965: The trial of 21 leading SS officers who worked at the Auschwitz

extermination camp is held at Frankfurt am Main, West Germany. Verdicts range from acquittal to life.

• 1964: To date, approximately 65,000 Nazi war criminals have been tried and sentenced.

• 1965: The Vatican acknowledges that the Catholic Church must bear

book's specious promise to achieve a groundbreaking analysis that meets a need—more imagined than real—for "radical revision" of nearly all previous scholarship on the Holocaust. Nowhere is this appraisal of his book more apt than in regard to his claim that "German's antisemitic beliefs about Jews were the central causal agent of the Holocaust."

Goldhagen wrongly implied that scholars such as Raul Hilberg, Yehuda Bauer, and Christopher Browning "denied or obscured" the importance of German antisemitism. What they and other leading Holocaust scholars have done, however, is to avoid the

Adolf Eichmann would seem to be one of Daniel Goldhagen's "ordinary Germans." Eichmann's motivations, though, were more complex than Goldhagen believed.

oversimplifications that make and break Goldhagen's book. Antisemitism, for example, was a major current in pre-Nazi times. Nevertheless, while Goldhagen's work filled in empirical details about that ugly picture, pre-Nazi antisemitism in Germany was not primarily the essentially lethal variety that Goldhagen required to make his claims hold. Conveniently dismissing any evidence to the contrary as insufficient or inadequate, failing to do the comparative work that should have modified his extreme views about German antisemitism by placing it in a larger European context, Goldhagen relied too much on an assumed German uniformity to buttress his case.

At times Goldhagen emphasized that his "ordinary Germans" must not be caricatured as a slavish, order-obeying people and that their freedom of choice should be recognized as crucial if they are to be held responsible for their Holocaust-related actions. But then, to cite one of Christopher Browning's succinct rebuttals, Goldhagen ignored his own principles by describing ordinary Germans as basically "undifferentiated, unchanging, possessed by a single, monolithic cognitive outlook," especially as far as Jews were concerned before and during

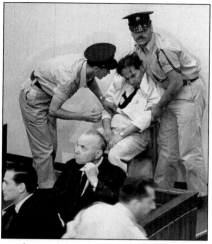

The Eichmann trial was an emotional experience for many Holocaust survivors. Here, Yehiel Koydzenik faints after testifying against the defendant.

the Holocaust.

The verdict on how Goldhagen's book stands the test of time has not yet been reached. Meanwhile, in deliberately provocative ways, he raised significantly debatable issues about the Germans' identity and the Holocaust. Complemented and complicated by episodes such as the Goetzfried trial, clashes surrounding the *Wehrmacht*'s history, and the future of the Berlin memorial, the repercussions of those issues remain to be defined and fully felt as the 21st century arrives. But of this we can be confident: The integrity of German identity depends on what political philosopher Hannah Arendt (a German-

---

some responsibility for antisemitism, and attempts to end it within the Church.

● **1966:** Albert Speer, former minister of armaments and war production for Nazi Germany, is released from Spandau Prison; *See* 1970. ● Baldur von Schirach, former head of the Hitler Youth, is released from Spandau.

● **June 5–10, 1967:** Responding to Syrian border raids and Egyptian troop movements and fearing an Arab attack, Israel strikes against Syria, Jordan, and Egypt, gaining victory in six days and expanding its territory by 200 percent. The conflict comes to be known as the Six-Day War. Israel now administers all former Palestinian territory that had been under British

mandate from 1922–1948; *See* October 6, 1973.

● **1967–1968:** The Communist Polish government spearheads an antisemitic campaign against Zionism.

● **1969:** The German penal code strikes out Paragraph 175, which made male homosexuality illegal and

born Jewish refugee from the Third Reich) called "examining and bearing consciously" the burdens of 20th-century history. Nothing less should be said of the identity we share as human beings after Auschwitz.

Christian Culpability

The Holocaust's repercussions leave few traditions, institutions, or governments untouched and unscathed. Christian churches of all denominations are obliged to examine and bear consciously the burdens of Holocaust history. At least they must do so if they are to have much credibility after the Holocaust. On the whole, the Christian community's response in those dark times—which was perhaps an inevitable result of Chris-

tianity's centuries-old anti-Jewish tradition—was less than sterling. Yes, a Christian minority protested and resisted what the Nazis were doing, but even their defiance was rarely practiced explicitly on behalf of beleaguered Jews. Some Christians rescued Jews, but not enough of them to eliminate the shame that sensitive Christians feel when they recognize what could and should have been done but was not.

The Holocaust's aftershocks place challenging opportunities before Christian churches, as well as difficult questions. How will the churches confront their Holocaust history? How will encounters with that history affect what they say and do, especially as the Holocaust recedes further into the past, where its chances of being forgotten are bound to increase? In particular, there are questions about what the churches should say and do—or not say and not do—to help ensure that the Holocaust is remembered and never rationalized or minimalized.

Christian churches come in many shapes and sizes, but in the West none is larger, older, more visible, or

A demonstration in Rome commemorates the sixth anniversary of the Ardeatine massacres of 1944, where the Germans murdered Italian hostages, both Christian and Jewish.

administered more hierarchically than the Roman Catholic Church. As far as Christianity is concerned, Holocaust repercussions inescapably arrive at the Vatican's doorstep. Especially under Pope John Paul II, the Polish pontiff who was installed on October 16, 1978, the Roman Catholic Church's handling of its Holocaust repercussions has been constructive on some occasions, unsuccessful on others, but nearly always stormy. The Holocaust's impact, as some recent events illustrate, will reverberate through the Church indefinitely.

On the evening of April 7, 1994, with Pope John Paul II as their host, 7500 people flocked to the

April 7, 1994, marked the Vatican's first official endeavor to memorialize the Jewish victims of Nazi aggression. Among the guests at the Papal Concert to Commemorate the Holocaust were more than 200 Holocaust survivors.

---

which helped to facilitate Nazi persecution of homosexuals.

• 1970: *Inside the Third Reich*, a memoir by Albert Speer, former Reich minister of armaments and war production, is published. • West German Chancellor Willy Brandt leads a pilgrimage of contrite Germans to the site of the Warsaw Ghetto.

• December 22, 1970: Franz Stangl, commandant of the Sobibór and Treblinka death camps, is sentenced to life in prison. He had escaped to Syria, moved to Brazil, and then was extradited to Germany in 1967.

• 1971: A note found in Argentine government files pertaining to fugitive Nazis in Argentina states that

more than 100 pages of file material have been removed.

• 1972: Argentine officials insist that only one fugitive Nazi—Adolf Eichmann—traveled to Argentina following the war. Jewish officials place the actual number at 60,000, of whom at least 1000 were SS members; *See* July 1997.

huge *Sala Nervi* (the Paul VI Hall, which stands next to St. Peter's Basilica in the Vatican) to attend what was called the Papal Concert to Commemorate the Holocaust. Television broadcasts in 50 countries enabled millions more to witness it. In Rome, the impressive interfaith assembly included numerous cardinals and rabbis—among them Rav Elio Toaff, the chief rabbi of Rome—as well as ambassadors and more than 200 Holocaust survivors from 12 countries. In a preconcert meeting with the survivors, John Paul II

German schoolchildren, provocatively photographed through a Christian "frame," mill about the main entrance of the former Sachsenhausen, Germany, concentration camp in 1999.

expressed hope that "the music which we shall listen to together shall reconfirm our resolve to consolidate the good relations between Christians and Jews so that with the help of almighty God, we can work together to prevent the repetition of such heinous evil."

Preparations for the concert had been under way since 1991, when the idea for it was conceived by Gilbert Levine. An American Jew, Levine had met Pope John Paul II three years earlier after being appointed music director for the Philharmonic Orchestra of Kraków, the Polish city not far from Auschwitz that is the Pope's hometown. In addition to conducting the Royal Philharmonic Orchestra, which flew from London for the concert, Levine wrote the program notes for the Justice Records CD that followed. They state that John Paul II's leadership—it included helping to select the music—did much to amicably confront difficult issues. The concert was held on "a night of firsts." Those "firsts" reveal the concert to have been truly historic. They also show how moving—in disturbing and disquieting senses—it remains.

April 7, 1994: Consider how long and late the "firsts" were in coming. According to Levine, the chief rabbi of Rome was invited for the first time to co-officiate at a public function in the Vatican. For the first time, Jews and Catholics prayed together, each

The antisemitic forgery, *Protocols of the Elders of Zion,* was published by antisemites all over the world before and after the Holocaust. This is a Spanish edition, published in 1963.

group in its own way, in such a setting. For the first time, a Jewish cantor, Howard Nevison, sang in the Vatican. For the first time, the 500-year-old Vatican Capella Giulia Choir sang a Hebrew text in performance. For the first time, the Vatican officially commemorated the Holocaust. Levine also cites the report of a Vatican official who said that the concert revealed "the best relations between Catholics and Jews in 2000 years." Accurately, Levine judged that "the Pope himself, the leader of 900 million Catholics worldwide, spoke out clearly on

---

• **1973: Only two American universities offer courses on the Holocaust;** *See* **1979.**

• **October 6, 1973: Egyptian and Syrian forces launch a surprise attack against Israel, hoping to regain territory lost in the Six-Day War of 1967. Early success ends with their defeat.**

• **November 26, 1975–June 30, 1981: Sixteen former members of the administration at the Majdanek, Poland, death camp are tried at Düsseldorf, Germany. Nine are sentenced to prison with terms ranging from three years to life; four are acquitted; two are deemed unfit to stand trial; one dies during proceedings.**

• **1977: The Canadian government declares that investigations of former Nazis living in Canada are not viable;** *See* **September 1987. • At Northwestern University in Illinois, engineering professor Arthur R. Butz publishes a revisionist Holocaust "history,"** *The Hoax of the Twentieth Century*; *See* **December 1996.**

April 7, 1994." Doing so was not a "first" for John Paul II, but it remains dishearteningly sad that history, and particularly Christianity's role in it, resulted in the need for the Papal Concert to Commemorate the Holocaust.

The need for the concert had much to do with Auschwitz, which Charlotte Delbo called "the center of Europe." More than once during John Paul II's reign, Auschwitz has been a flashpoint for Holocaust repercussions that affect Christian-Jewish relations. Thus, it is significant to note that in May 1999 the Sejm, Poland's parliament, passed legislation to restrict inappropriate development and public gatherings within a 100-meter perimeter of former Nazi concentration and death camps on Polish soil. Religious symbolism, specifically Christian crosses, at Auschwitz prompted this action.

Crosses at Auschwitz

Signifying the crucifixion of Jesus, the cross is a potent symbol—dear, even sacred, to Christians but not to Jews, who often have been persecuted under its domination. At Auschwitz, the cross has been more than potent; it has been a volatile symbol, one that has strained relations between Poland and Israel as well as

Polish-Catholic women pray before crosses erected just outside Auschwitz. Although tens of thousands of Poles died at Auschwitz, the presence of the Christian symbol offended many Jews.

between Christian and Jewish groups worldwide. In July 1998 a right-wing group of Polish Roman Catholics, determined to maintain Christian symbols at the former Nazi death camp in spite of strong opposition from Jews, planted more than 50 crosses outside Auschwitz I, the original part of the camp complex. By September the crosses numbered more than 300. The crosses were located at a site where the Nazis had once executed 152 Poles. At this same site another very large, 26-foot cross, visible from the camp's interior,

During a January 25, 1995, demonstration, Jewish activists protested the "Christianization of the Holocaust"—specifically, crosses on the grounds erected by Polish Catholics that commemorated Catholic victims.

had been erected more than ten years earlier. This particularly large cross had been relocated from Auschwitz-Birkenau, the camp's major killing center, where the symbol was initially used on June 7, 1979, when Pope John Paul II celebrated mass there during his first papal visit to his native Poland. Fearing that the more recent placement of this particular cross was jeopardized—its presence infuriated many Jews—the Catholic protesters planted a field of crosses in response. Poland's Catholic bishops condemned this response and urged that all but the large papal cross be removed.

Poland has long been a predominantly Roman Catholic country. Large numbers of Polish Catholics—including several thousand priests—were murdered by the Nazis. Christian Poles numbering in the tens of thousands had their lives taken from them at Auschwitz. At the same time, Auschwitz is often rightly called the largest Jewish cemetery in the world, for 90 percent of the more than one million persons who perished there were Jews. Understandably, the presence of Christian crosses or their removal has strained Jewish-Catholic relations, and especially those between Jews and Polish Catholics. During the winter of 1997–98, religious symbols—Stars of David as well as Christian crosses—were removed from a field at Auschwitz-Birkenau, where many could be seen in an area where the Nazis had created mass graves and dumped the ashes from Birkenau's crematoria. But the summer events that followed showed that the controversy surrounding religious symbolism had not been settled.

Even as the Polish Parliament's legislation to create a protected zone around former Nazi camps in Poland took effect on May 25,

1999, Auschwitz was still the scene of responses that were—almost literally—explosive. At dawn on May 28, Polish Army troops removed several hundred crosses near Auschwitz I. Meanwhile, Kazimierz Switon, a radical Catholic activist who complained that Jewish influence in Poland was too great, had been living in a tent on the site. He was supervising construction of a wooden hut that a retired priest had consecrated as a chapel on May 16, an

This Holocaust memorial was unveiled in Skokie, Illinois, home of many survivors. The film *Skokie* recounted reaction to an infamous 1977 neo-Nazi demonstration in the town.

Righteous Among the Nations

Through the dark nights of the Holocaust shone the luminous examples of the "Righteous Among the Nations," a title derived from the Talmud to describe those who risked their own lives to save the lives of others, sometimes complete strangers.

Individuals such as Oskar Schindler (seen below at a 1962 ceremony at Yad Vashem) and even entire nations such as Denmark risked safety and security to save those persecuted by the Nazis. Some hid Jews within their homes for months at a time. Others helped Jews cross the border into neutral Switzerland. Still others used their diplomatic status to issue transit visas or even to grant citizenship.

Since 1953 these "Righteous Among the Nations" have been honored at Yad Vashem in Israel, with a tree planted in honor of

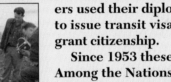

each as living testimony to their heroism. Risking torture and death, these righteous few bear witness that the small voice of conscience could still be heard over the Nazi rhetoric of racism. The "Righteous Among the Nations" saved not only individual lives, but, as the Talmud says, "the entire universe." By their courage and compassion, they preserved humanity in the midst of evil.

Holocaust, up from just two in 1973; *See* February 1997.

● **October 1980: The U.S. Congress unanimously passes the law creating the United States Holocaust Memorial Council, which will sponsor fundraising events for the United States Holocaust Memorial Museum.**

● **Late autumn 1980: Polish schoolchildren planting a tree near the site of the former Auschwitz-Birkenau death camp uncover a secret inmate diary inside a buried thermos.**

● **1981: American Jewish Holocaust survivors establish a national registry to document the lives of survivors who immigrated to the U.S.**

● **June 1981: More than 6000 Holocaust survivors gather in Jerusalem.**

● **1982: A Hollywood film version of *Sophie's Choice*, William Styron's novel of a Christian survivor of the Holocaust, is released.**

● **1984: Catholic nuns establish a Carmelite Convent, with one building**

Fifty years after the fact, the Nazis' gross criminality caused ill feelings between Catholics and Jews. Seen here in a 1947 trial photo is one of the wartime criminals, Auschwitz guard Vladimir Bilan.

action the Roman Catholic Church rejected. Switon's work at the site included something else. He booby-trapped the "chapel" with plastic explosives to prevent the demolition that local authorities had ordered. As police cleared the crosses—the large, 26-foot one was left standing—they also detained Switon and carefully detonated the explosives. Among those relieved by the defusing of the situation were many Roman Catholic leaders in Poland, who feared that the controversy at Auschwitz would sour Pope John Paul II's visit to his Polish home-

land. That visit, which began less than ten days later on June 5, included the beatification of 108 Polish Catholics who were murdered—some of them at Auschwitz—by the Nazis during World War II. Among the 108 were nuns and priests who helped rescue Jews during the Holocaust.

Will the removal of the crosses and the disarming of Switon's explosives be the last episode in Christian-Jewish conflict about Auschwitz? That is far from clear and even unlikely. A case in point involves a building at Auschwitz-Birkenau. Just outside the barbed-wire perimeter, situated across a narrow road, there is a former Nazi facility that is clearly identified on Auschwitz-Birkenau maps as the "new commandant's office." This structure was transformed into a Catholic church early in the 1980s. Among other functions, it commemorates Edith Stein, a German Jew who converted to Catholicism in 1922, became a nun as well as a distinguished philosopher, and was deported in 1942 from the Netherlands to Birkenau, where she was gassed. Although her deportation was provoked by Dutch Catholic dissent against Nazi antisemitism, Stein was not murdered primarily because she was Catholic but because, according to the Nazis'

racial definitions, she was Jewish. The Vatican's 1998 decision to canonize her as a saint was greeted with considerable disagreement, especially but not exclusively among Jews. Meanwhile, little protest about the Birkenau church took place when its doors first opened, but controversy about it has swirled since, and history suggests that it might do so again.

On August 1, 1984, a small group of nuns from the Order of Our Lady of Mount Carmel moved into the *Theatergebäude* (Old Theater building) at the site of Auschwitz I. The yard of this building would eventually be the place where the large papal cross

Post-Holocaust controversies aside, it is clear that the killers, such as Auschwitz commandant Rudolf Höss, were people of no real character or stature.

erected on the grounds of the former death camp at Auschwitz. Jews object because the nuns' activities will celebrate Christian martyrs on a site where more than one million Jews perished.

• **March 27, 1984: The United States deports Arthur Rudolph.** A Nazi scientist and engineer at Peenemünde,

Germany, Rudolph was brought to America as part of "Project Paperclip." His citizenship is revoked after his wartime activities are exposed.

• **1985:** *Shoah*, director Claude Lanzmann's 8½-hour Holocaust documentary film, is released. • Soviet film director Elem Klimov releases *Come and See*, a profoundly disturbing

drama about *Einsatzgruppen* activity in Russia in 1943. • Revisionist "historian" Ernst Zundel is tried in Toronto, Canada, for publishing an antisemitic pamphlet entitled *Did Six Million Really Die?* Zundel is found guilty of spreading false information and is sentenced to 15 months in prison.

appeared and the site of the many crosses erected in the summer of 1998. The Carmelite nuns had occupied the Old Theater building with the approval of Polish authorities and Catholic Church officials, but apparently without any dialogue with members of the Jewish community either within or outside of Poland.

By the following spring, an international Jewish outcry brought the "Auschwitz convent controversy" into full swing. Central to the debate was the precise location of the Old Theater. It stood outside the wall that encloses Auschwitz I, and some of the nuns' defenders argued that the building—it predated World War I—was not, strictly speaking, part of the camp. That argument was not convincing. Other facilities were also outside the wall— the commandant's house, a railroad siding where prisoners were unloaded, and an execution site. They could hardly be excluded from the camp. Furthermore, the Old Theater's multiple uses indicated that it had indeed been part of the Auschwitz complex. It had served as a storehouse not only for loot taken from those who were gassed but also for the Zyklon B that was used to murder Auschwitz's primarily Jewish victims.

Difficult negotiations between Jewish and Catholic leaders led to an agreement on February 22, 1987, which provided that the Auschwitz convent would be relocated outside the camp within two years. The same agreement also stated that there would be "no permanent Catholic place of worship on the site of the Auschwitz and Birkenau camps." By no means, however, did this agreement put matters to rest. Controversy escalated when the February 1989 deadline for relocating the nuns came and went without their departure. It got uglier that July, when Jewish demonstrators took their protest to the convent grounds and Polish workers responded violently. Following acrimonious debate, ground was broken for a new facility that would house the nuns close by but clearly at a distance from the Auschwitz grounds. In 1993, the Old Theater was vacated, and the nuns decamped to new quarters.

Overwhelmingly, Jews were offended by the Carmelite convent and Christian crosses at Auschwitz because their presence seemed to be "Christianizing" steps that robbed the Holocaust

Nothing is black and white, least of all the nature of the Catholic Church's responses to the Holocaust. Church efforts brought Dana Szefflan *(holding child)* to Canada in 1948.

and, in particular, Auschwitz of its Jewish particularity and uniqueness. For their part, the Polish Catholics who defended the convent and the crosses contended that they had a right and an obligation to memorialize their brothers and sisters who also perished in large numbers at Auschwitz, a place that many Poles regard as symbolic of Poland's martyrdom during World War II. The Roman Catholic Church at Birkenau,

Holocaust memorials bring a measure of healing to survivors and their families. These testaments, such as this one at Theresienstadt, are open to all, and encourage understanding.

Holocaust Memorialization

Since the end of World War II, hundreds of memorial institutions, monuments, and museums devoted to the Holocaust have been built in Israel, Europe, and the United States. Although every Holocaust memorial honors the millions of lives mercilessly destroyed by the Nazi regime, the subtext of the sites varies from location to location.

The memorials constructed at the death camps in Poland encompass the killing of the Jews under the broader theme of "Polish national remembrance." Neither the memorial that was established at Majdanek by the Soviet liberators nor the state memorial that was built at the Auschwitz extermination camp emphasizes Jewish victimization. Both sites take a broader view, memorializing all victims of National Socialism.

As in Poland, the memorials and museums in Germany also reflect on the collective entity of victims. The facility built at Dachau, Germany, has separate memorials for Protestants, Catholics, and Jews. The Berlin monument seen here commemorates gentile German women who defied the Gestapo; a Jewish-oriented Berlin monument is planned.

The memorialization of the Holocaust in both the United States and Israel differs significantly from that of Europe. The sites in the U.S. and Israel typically offer extended views of Jewish history, providing detailed accounts of Jewish life in Europe before the war. They also reflect on the renaissance of Jewish life after the Holocaust. In the United States, Holocaust memorials often emphasize the importance of liberty and pluralism to the security of the American Jewish community.

The national Holocaust memorial of the Jewish people in Israel, called Yad Vashem, was established by the Israeli *Knesset* (Parliament) in 1953. The Yad Vashem complex consists of museums and monuments as well as research, teaching, and resource centers. *Yad Vashem*, which means a mountain and a name, is taken from the biblical verse Isaiah 56:5: "I will give, in my house and within my walls, a monument... that shall not be cut off." Many Israeli sites focus on the range of resistance activities undertaken by Jews and the martyrdom of the Jewish people.

The United States Holocaust Memorial Museum was established in Washington, D.C., in 1993. More than any other museum, it uses a full spectrum of media to "recreate" the experience of the Holocaust. Visitors read stories on plaques, view photos and film coverage, listen to hate-filled Nazi speeches, watch videotaped testimony of survivors, and use computers to research topics of their choice.

Every year new Holocaust museums and memorials are planned and built. Each site offers testimony to the enormous importance attached to the Holocaust. They also provide insight into the self-perceptions of the people and nations who construct them.

● **February 16, 1987–April 18, 1988:** John Demjanjuk, accused of being the Treblinka death camp's "Ivan the Terrible," is tried in Jerusalem and found guilty; *See* Late 1993.

● **April 11, 1987:** Primo Levi, an Italian-Jewish partisan who wrote numerous books about his camp experiences, takes his life.

● **May 11–July 4, 1987:** Former SD/SS officer Klaus Barbie is tried in Lyons, France, for war crimes and sentenced to life imprisonment.

● **August 17, 1987:** Former Deputy *Führer* Rudolf Hess, imprisoned by the Allies since 1941 and interned at Spandau Prison since 1946, dies, an apparent suicide, at age 93.

● **September 1987:** Canadian law is changed to allow the prosecution of former Nazis currently living in Canada.

● **1988:** The U.S. Office of Special Investigations (OSI) maintains active investigations of 600 suspected former Nazis living in America.

This Warsaw memorial plaque—with words in Polish, Yiddish, and Hebrew—commemorates the hundreds of thousands of Jews deported from the Warsaw Ghetto to the Treblinka death camp.

which Jewish visitors to Birkenau can scarcely miss seeing, remains a potential tinderbox.

At least three other major Holocaust repercussions will affect Jewish-Christian relations in the 21st century. First, in March 1998 the Holy See's Commission for Religious Relations with the Jews released "We Remember: A Reflection on the *Shoah,*" a document that was widely expected to be the Church's long-awaited statement about the Vatican's posture during the Holocaust. Especially in Jewish circles, it received a lukewarm reception. Two points made the document particularly vulnerable: (1) It unconvincingly separated Nazi antisemitism from Christian anti-Judaism. Differences exist between the two, but "We Remember" stressed them too much while emphasizing their connections too little. (2) "We Remember" acknowledged that Christian conduct during the Holocaust "was not that which might have been expected from Christ's followers" and went on to say that "for Christians, this heavy burden of conscience of their brothers and sisters during the Second World War must be a call to penitence."

Many Jews and Christians felt that such language misplaced responsibility for Christian failure, for "We Remember" had little, if anything, to say—implicitly or explicitly—about the shortcomings of Roman Catholic leadership during the Holocaust. It created the dubious impression that the rank and file, more than its Catholic leaders, were responsible for Christian failings. The Commission for Religious Relations did not improve its credibility by emphasizing that Pope Pius XII, whose highly controversial reign—starting in 1939—covered the crucial Holocaust years, had been thanked by Jewish communities and leaders during and after the war for all that he and his representatives had done "to save hundreds of thousands of Jewish lives."

Fairly or unfairly, Pius XII has become a lightning rod for echoes of the Holocaust. He has been sharply and persistently criticized for failing to do what he could and should have done to intervene on behalf of Jews during the Holocaust. As "We Remember" indicates, his reputation has also been defended—so much so, in fact, that he may be canonized as a saint in the 21st century. In the spring of 1999, Jewish criticism of that possibility included the charge that sainthood for Pius XII would do

This is a minute portion of a wall in Prague's Pinkas synagogue. It memorializes the 77,000 Czechoslovakian Jews who perished in the Nazis' concentration and death camps.

● **March–April 1988: American Fred Leuchter writes a poorly conceived, pseudoscientific paper that will be published by revisionist British historian David Irving as *The Leuchter Report.* The paper claims that the Auschwitz chambers were never used for gas executions and that the camp crematoria could never have processed the number of bodies gener-** ally accepted to have passed through them.

● **1990: The Soviet Union collapses and breaks into numerous independent states. ● East and West Germany are reunited, creating one democratic Germany. The former East Germany agrees to the principles of the Luxembourg Treaty of 1952.**

● **1992: Following the reunification of Germany, the nation is swept by antisemitic violence. At the former Sachsenhausen concentration camp, a neo-Nazi firebomb attack destroys a major section of preserved barracks buildings.**

● **1993: French President François Mitterand publicly condemns the**

nothing less than desecrate the memory of the Holocaust. Catholic defenders of Pius XII take strong exception to views of that sort. The result is that stresses and strains in Jewish-Roman Catholic relations are likely to be exacerbated if steps toward sainthood for Pius XII are taken any time soon.

Whether those tensions can be relaxed depends in part on one more vexing issue, which focuses on the Vatican's archives and especially its holdings from the reign of Pius XII. As the 21st century arrives, a flood of new archival material has appeared, much of it coming into Western view from

A memorial was dedicated to the mostly Jewish victims of the massacre at Babi Yar, near Kiev in Ukraine, where the Germans murdered tens of thousands of innocents.

Soviet and Eastern European archives that became accessible only at the end of the Cold War. Among the recently available documents, for example, is a calendar/diary that SS leader Heinrich Himmler kept. Portions of self-serving memoirs by Adolf Eichmann also have surfaced. These new archival findings, which are in relatively early stages of scholarly assessment, will further detail and perhaps importantly revise the best understandings of the Holocaust that we have thus far. Be that as it may, the Vatican's Holocaust-era archives have yet to be fully opened to Holocaust scholars. As long as that situation remains, our understanding of Pius XII and Vatican policies during the Nazi period will remain ambiguous at best. How the Vatican's Holocaust-related opportunities—past, present, and future—are assessed, bungled, or put to sensible use will continue to be an area where Holocaust repercussions are sure to be keenly felt.

This is the Holocaust memorial at Majdanek, one of the six major death camps located in Poland.

Survivor Legacies

While no "official" definition exists and not every victim or survivor of the Holocaust was Jewish, Holocaust survivors are primarily those children, women, and men who were defined as Jews by Nazi Germany, lived under the rule or occupation of Nazi Germany and its collaborators, and yet eluded the total annihilation that Nazi policy intended for Jews in Europe and even worldwide. Every Holocaust survivor's experience is distinctive because survival involved different circumstances, times, and places. Some escaped Nazi persecution before World War II began in 1939 or before the "Final Solution" became Nazi Germany's official policy in 1941. Others endured the war years and the Final Solution itself, somehow making their way through impov-

---

French Vichy government of World War II. • Film director Steven Spielberg releases *Schindler's List*, the story of German industrialist Oskar Schindler

• April 1993: The United States Holocaust Memorial Museum opens in Washington, D.C.

• Late 1993: American resident John Demjanjuk, convicted in Jerusalem in 1988 of war crimes, is released from prison by the Israeli Supreme Court because of insufficient evidence.

• 1994: Britain's war-crimes investigation unit is shut down following the unsuccessful prosecution of a suspected former Nazi war criminal.

• Argentina lifts its ban on extradition of criminals convicted *in absentia* by other countries. • Hollywood film director Steven Spielberg founds the Shoah Foundation, a nonprofit concern dedicated to videotaping interviews with Holocaust survivors, rescuers, and witnesses. • Sabine Zlatin, who founded the Children's Home of Izieu in France in 1944,

erished ghettos, labor brigades, deportations, lethal camps, and death marches. Still others managed to survive by disguising themselves, hiding, or working in resistance groups.

As the 21st century begins, Holocaust scholar Michael Berenbaum estimates that no more than 300,000 Jews who lived under the rule or occupation of Nazi Germany and its collaborators after late June 1941 are still alive. This aging population is rapidly disappearing. By the middle of the 21st century, it will no longer exist. Berenbaum is well situated to know this demography because he headed the most ambitious campaign to gather the survivors' oral testimonies. Such work has been going on for some time, but no

project has been as extensive as the one at the Los Angeles-based Survivors of the Shoah Visual History Foundation.

Moved by his experience in producing *Schindler's List* (1993), the Academy Award-winning film that did so much to call attention to the Holocaust, Steven Spielberg established the Shoah Foundation in 1994. Its workers have created one of the survivors' most impressive legacies: the videotaping of more than 50,000 interviews as of May 1999. Conducted in 32 different languages, the interviews have been given by survivors from 57 countries. Their combined testimonies are preserved on more than 32,000 miles of videotape. It would take more than 13 years of continuous viewing to see and hear them all. The voices of Jewish survivors properly dominate the Shoah Foundation's interviews. Yet its outreach also includes interviews with non-Jews: persecuted groups such as Gypsies, Jehovah's Witnesses,

Oskar Schindler at Yad Vashem in Jerusalem. After his death, his former wife denigrated his status as a Righteous Christian. The fact remains that he was instrumental in saving hundreds of Jews.

political dissidents, and homosexuals as well as camp liberators and bystanders who were in a position to see what was going on during the Holocaust.

Nobody can watch 13 years of Holocaust testimony. The Shoah Foundation's challenge, then, is to put this priceless legacy into more retrievable forms that can be used for research and education. In addition to special precautions that must be taken to preserve the tapes themselves, cataloguers will work for several years to index the testimonies, which scholars will be able to access through designated research centers and analyze carefully with the help of high-speed,

"Memorial to the Deportees" was established at Yad Vashem in remembrance of the millions of Jews who were shipped in cattle cars to Nazi extermination camps in Eastern Europe.

opens a memorial museum for the children near the site of the home; *See* April 6, 1944.

● **March 17–April 19, 1994:** Paul Touvier, a former right-wing Vichy sympathizer, is tried and sentenced to life imprisonment for the 1944 murders of seven Jews.

● **July 16, 1994:** For the first time, France officially remembers the wartime deportations of 76,000 Jews from the nation.

● **1995:** Jewish twins Ida and Adam Paluch are reunited 53 years after being separated following a Gestapo attempt to abduct them from their home in Sosnowiec, Poland, in the

summer of 1942. The children were spirited away by their aunt and sent to separate Catholic homes at age three.

● **Summer 1995:** The International Committee of the Red Cross makes a formal apology for its passivity during the Holocaust, calling it a "moral failure."

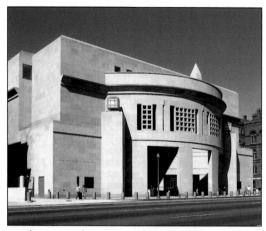

The United States Holocaust Memorial Museum in Washington memorializes the murdered millions. Visitors feel the impact of the Holocaust through photographs, words, artifacts, artwork, film, and videotaped testimony.

digital retrieval systems. In addition, the Shoah Foundation has developed CD-ROM material for use in school classrooms and films, including an Academy Award-winning documentary, *The Last Days* (1998), which featured five Hungarian Jews who were targeted during the Final Solution's last phase in 1944. The documentary confirms Charlotte Delbo's judgment when she said: "We were clinging to a hope made up of so many fragile pieces that not one of them could have resisted close scrutiny had we kept a modicum of common sense. To have lost that common sense, and persisted in the madness of hope, saved some of us. Their number is so small that it proves nothing."

In addition to the Shoah Foundation, repositories for survivor interviews can be found in several other places, including Yad Vashem, the Israeli Holocaust memorial and research center in Jerusalem; the Fortunoff Video Archive for Holocaust Testimonies at Yale University; and the United States Holocaust Memorial Museum in Washington, D.C. The USHMM opened in April 1993. On April 8, 1999, two weeks short of its sixth anniversary, the visitor total reached 12 million, including 8.6 million non-Jews. Typically, the survivors speak about their lives before, during, and after the Holocaust.

After Auschwitz, the human mind wants to make sense of the emotional turmoil provoked by Holocaust testimonies. The yearning runs deep for justice to prevail, wholeness to be restored, moral expectations to be vindicated, and the human spirit to be triumphant. But the testimonies show that what Holocaust survivor Ida Fink called "the ruins of memory"—they

include starvation, beatings, devastating illness, gassings, the smoke and smell of burning flesh, cannibalism—leave such optimism in scarce supply.

One survivor whose testimony can be found in Yale's Fortunoff Archive remembers seeing the sun at Auschwitz. "I saw the sun come up," she says, "because we had to get up at four in the morning. But it was never beautiful to me. I never saw it shine. It was just the beginning of a horrible day." Grieving both for her losses at Auschwitz and for how little her post-Holocaust hope—that the Holocaust's history would teach people to be more humane—has been fulfilled, another woman says of her survival, "I don't know if it was worth it."

In 1999 German Chancellor Gerhard Schroeder and U.S. film director Steven Spielberg discuss incorporating elements of Spielberg's "Shoah Foundation," which videotapes survivor testimonies, into the planned Holocaust memorial in Berlin.

• **Winter 1995: Bayer, a subsidiary of I.G. Farben, apologizes for the pain, suffering, and exploitation the company perpetrated.**

• **1996: A commercial developer based near Oswiecim (Auschwitz), Poland, shelves plans to build a mini-mall across from the Auschwitz Museum after being stung by world-**

wide condemnation of his scheme.
• **Argentine researchers discover the first hard evidence linking former Argentina President Juan Peron and his wife, Eva, to the secret entry of at least dozens of fugitive Nazis into Argentina following the war. Top Peron aides engaged Argentina-born SS captain Horst Fuldner to coordinate the program.**

• **April 1996: American book publisher St. Martin's cancels publication of *Goebbels*, a biography by revisionist British historian David Irving. The book argues that Hitler neither intended to commit the Holocaust nor had knowledge of it.**

• **May 1996: Swiss bankers and the World Jewish Congress establish an**

Lingering Questions

"What happened, happened," said philosopher Jean Améry, a survivor of Auschwitz. "But *that* it happened," he added, "cannot be so easily accepted." The Holocaust cannot be "accepted" because so many questions linger in its wake. *How? Why?* Those two small words ask the most persistent questions: How did the Holocaust happen? Why did it occur?

Holocaust scholar Raul Hilberg resisted "big questions" because he feared "small answers." Most Holocaust scholars find that "the devil is in the details." They do not jump to sweeping generalizations that "explain" the Holocaust. Instead, they gather, sift, and sort the evidence. They preserve and study documents, retrieve and evaluate testimony; they develop, analyze, and criticize the narratives that tell *what* happened.

As the 21st century begins, scholarly research focuses on questions such as: Precisely when did the Nazis decide to destroy European Jewry completely? What parts did Hitler, Himmler, Heydrich, and other key Nazi leaders play in the "Final Solution"? And were the perpetrators "ordinary" people or "willing executioners" of a specifically German kind? What is the significance of Jewish resistance during the Holocaust? How should oral histories from survivors be used in Holocaust research? How will memory of the Holocaust best be preserved as that event recedes further into the past and the survivors are no longer alive? Can the fundamental challenges that the Holocaust creates for Judaism and Christianity be credibly met? What can literature and art teach us about the Holocaust? In what ways is the Holocaust unique?

Although understanding emerges through inquiry about such issues, the resulting insights do not silence the questions *How?* and *Why?* How the Holocaust happened depends on why people acted as they did. Why people do the things they do is a question that historians can answer partly, but historical inquiry alone cannot master the range of human feeling, intention, reflection, and choice that enters into desires, motivations, yearnings, aims, hopes, and decisions. "Why did the Holocaust happen?" is a question that lingers even after our knowledge about how it happened has increased.

Why? also lingers because, as historian Saul Friedländer has pointed out, the smallest details raise the largest "whys." Those details—they involve the systematic murder of nearly six million Jews—show that Holocaust history is not history-as-usual. The Holocaust stretches comprehension beyond its limits. The more we learn about the Holocaust, the more devastating it turns out to be. Far from being satisfied, *Why?* lingers—silently if not openly—with unsatisfied intensity. Jean Améry was right: "What happened, happened. But *that* it happened cannot be so easily accepted."

Having listened to as many Holocaust testimonies as anyone, Lawrence Langer reports that such anguish is by no means all that survivors report. Many talk about their determination to survive, including some who "knew" they would come out alive. Others accent their defiance against German brutality. There are also many who stress how important it has been for them to make their lives worthwhile and to retain hope after Auschwitz. "We lost," says one survivor, "and yet we won, we're going on."

What was lost includes more than a million Jewish children who were killed and, in addition, the countless girls and boys who might have been born if their potential

---

investigative panel to look into probable Swiss misappropriation of Jewish funds during and after World War II. It also investigates wartime Switzerland's turning away of approximately 30,000 Jewish refugees from its borders; *See* September 1996.

● **May 8, 1996:** Ten of approximately 400 human brains, mostly those of children, kept in formaldehyde jars for more than 50 years, are buried in Hamburg, Germany. The brains are the remains of mental patients judged genetically "unfit" by Nazi physicians and geneticists. Before being murdered, the victims were subjected to immoral medical experiments at the Alsterdorfer Institute, a Hamburg mental hospital. Identification of the remains began when a Hamburg woman watching a television report on the brains saw her sister's name on one of the jars.

● **September 1996:** A report by London's *Jewish Chronicle* claims that $4 billion ($65 billion in 1996 dollars) looted by the Nazis from Jews and others during World War II was

mothers and fathers had not been murdered. Still, the "going on" is real, too. It includes children, grandchildren, and other descendants of the survivors. These flesh-and-blood survivor legacies already number in the millions. If the Holocaust is to be well remembered, *their* testimony will be important, too.

This monument to Raoul Wallenberg, who had rescued thousands of Jews, was to be erected in a Budapest, Hungary, park. But the Communist government hauled it away before it could be dedicated.

Loss and Restitution

Scholars know that keeping up with the Holocaust's history requires keeping an eye on late-breaking news. The survivors' legacy provides startling examples. In 1990 no one could have predicted that Steven Spielberg would launch the Shoah Foundation. In 1995, 50 years after the Holocaust ended, few expected that the 20th century would end with major, highly publicized international attempts to recover the huge amounts of money and property that had been expropriated from Holocaust victims. Yet no repercussions of the Holocaust have received more turn-of-the-century headlines than the complex issues surrounding the question of whether anything approximating just restitution for stolen property and slave labor can be accomplished before the survivors are gone. Along with the payments for slave labor that legal proceedings may award, the immense amounts and values of the property involved—bank accounts, stock holdings, insurance policies, stolen land, houses, buildings, businesses, jewelry, and artworks, to mention just

U.S. lawyer Edward Fagan and his client, Estelle Sapir, plaintiff in a class-action suit against European banks, discuss the Nazi gold case with reporters. "It's not about money," said Sapir, "it's about justice."

some examples—bear witness all over again about the vastness of Nazi Germany's "Final Solution" and the economic greed that helped to motivate it.

To explore a few facets of this complex repercussion of the Holocaust, consider a Jewish woman named Estelle Sapir, who died of cardiac arrest in New York City on April 13, 1999, at the age of 72. This Holocaust survivor was born in Warsaw, Poland, where her father, Josef, was a wealthy investment banker. In 1938, while Nazi Germany prepared for war, Josef Sapir began to deposit his assets in Credit Suisse, a Swiss bank where he believed they would be safe. His planning seemed to be especially prudent—it included making deposits in more than one Swiss

---

diverted to Swiss banks. The sum is about 20 times the amount previously acknowledged by the Swiss; *See* December 1996.

• **October 23, 1996:** Swiss historian Peter Hug reveals documents proving that unclaimed bank accounts of Holocaust victims were used by the Swiss government to help settle Switzer-

land's postwar compensation disputes with Poland and Hungary. Swiss authorities announce the formation of two panels to investigate the allegations; *See* February 12, 1997.

• **October 29, 1996:** The government of Switzerland promises to address by December 4 allegations that it appropriated the wealth of Holocaust vic-

tims in order to compensate Swiss citizens for property seized by the Nazis in Eastern Europe. • Art, coins, and other items looted by Nazis from the homes of Austrian Jews are sold at a benefit auction in Vienna. It is the intent of the auction organizers to keep the items in the Jewish community. By day's end, the auction grosses $13.2 million, with proceeds going to

bank—when he and his family fled the Nazis by going to France. For Jewish refugees, however, France was less than a safe haven. The Sapirs were eventually rounded up and placed in a concentration camp. Josef Sapir was deported to Poland; he was killed at Majdanek in 1943. Estelle avoided her father's fate, became active in the Resistance, and took care to remember one of the last things her father had told her: Remember, he urged her, Credit Suisse holds the family money— $82,000 of it (as valued in the 1940s). If Estelle survived, he made her promise, she must claim the Sapir money from Credit Suisse—and the other banks he had frequently identified—so the family could go on.

Reunited with her mother in Paris after the war, Estelle tried to

In postwar DP camps *(above)*, scrip replaced real currency. Years later it was revealed that Swiss banks and other institutions had benefited from the Nazi theft of Jewish assets.

When American GIs needed housing, DPs were the first to be relocated *(above)*. When European financial institutions wished to profit from "unclaimed" depositor assets after the war, Jewish property was chosen.

keep her promise by claiming her father's Swiss bank accounts. The officials at Credit Suisse were not helpful. No funds would be released without her father's death certificate. The Nazis killed Jews and counted the deaths at Majdanek, but they issued no death certificates. Estelle did have other evidence about her father, including Nazi records documenting Josef's deportation to Majdanek on March 6, 1943. For the Swiss banks, this documentation was insufficient. Persistently, Sapir kept trying to recover her family's assets. When 20 trips to Credit Suisse from Paris from 1946 to

German Reparations

In 1952 the democratic Federal Republic of Germany (West Germany) agreed to pay reparations to the state of Israel and to make restitution to Jewish people throughout the world for the crimes committed by the Third Reich. Since that time, billions of dollars have flowed into the Israeli economy, the budgets of Jewish organizations, and directly to individuals.

Claims for the restitution of Jewish property and indemnification were made as early as 1945. However, it was German Chancellor Konrad Adenauer's official proclamation in support of these claims that paved the way for the program that began eight years later.

Israel's first merchant fleet and its highly modernized agricultural industry were bankrolled by the German government. Hundreds of Jewish communities and organizations in Europe and other locations were rehabilitated with funds that flowed from West Germany. Moreover, restitution was made to thousands of people who were persecuted by the Nazis.

---

aid Holocaust survivors and their heirs.

● **November 1996: Volkswagen AG is embarrassed by a 1055-page history commissioned by the company. The book reveals details of Volkswagen's wartime use of Russian POWs and Jewish concentration-camp inmates as slave laborers.**

● **December 1996: Northwestern University engineering professor and historical revisionist Arthur R. Butz, who calls the Holocaust "the extermination legend," is at the center of controversy because the university provides him with free Internet access via the school's Web server, through which Butz presents his ideas to an enormous audience. A Jewish**

professor who criticizes the university's position during classtime is dismissed.

● **December 16, 1996: Five Swedish members of the National Socialist Front are sentenced to two months' imprisonment for participating in a ceremony at Trollhättan to commemorate the 1987 death of Rudolf Hess.**

At a May 1996 news conference in New York City, Avraham Burg *(left)*, chairman of the Jewish Agency, announces a landmark agreement with the Swiss Banking Association to investigate dormant assets deposited decades ago by Holocaust victims.

1957 accomplished nothing, she gave up her quest, left Europe for New York in 1969, and took up residence in a one-room apartment in Queens. She never married and spent 27 years working in a drug store before she retired. Then Sapir heard a news report.

Early in 1996, at the urging of the World Jewish Congress, U.S. Senator Alfonse D'Amato, head of the U.S. Senate's banking committee at the time, was launching an inquiry about the billions of dollars in accounts that Jews had established for safekeeping in Swiss banks. Sapir contacted D'Amato. After telling him her story the next day, she became the lead plaintiff in a class-action suit to require Swiss banks to restore—with rightful interest—Jewish assets to their owners or heirs. In May 1998 Sapir became the first Holocaust survivor to receive a settlement from a Swiss bank. When Credit Suisse made the payment—reported to be between $300,000 and $500,000—its press announcement from Zurich stated that the bank had done so after extensive research showed that Josef Sapir did indeed have prewar business links to Credit Suisse. By August 1998 Credit Suisse and UBS, another major Swiss bank, announced that funds totaling $1.25 billion would be available for other settlements. As for Estelle Sapir, her comment to the press was, "It's not about money. It's about justice." Less than a year later, Sapir, the lone surviving member of her family, was dead.

The Holocaust continues to defeat justice. Money provides tangible compensation, but there is no recompense for the Final Solution, even if Germany has already paid tens of billions of dollars in reparations and aid to Jewish groups, the state of Israel, and Holocaust victims. The irreplaceable cannot be replaced, even if 16 German companies announce, as they did in 1999, that they have created a fund of $1.7 billion to compensate former slave laborers, Jewish and non-Jewish, whose work during the Nazi period served those companies and benefited the Third Reich's genocidal policies. Those German companies include DaimlerChrysler, Deutsche Bank, Siemens, Volkswagen, Hoechst, Dresdner Bank,

In August 1998 Senator Alfonse D'Amato of New York announced that the Italian insurance company Generali had agreed to pay $100 million to Holocaust survivors and victims' heirs.

• **U.S., British, and French officials agree to halt distribution of $68 million in Nazi gold bars—much of it made from gold stolen from Jews (gold rings, watches, and dental work)—that have been stored in the vaults of the Federal Reserve Bank in New York City and in the Bank of England.** • **French art historians investigate claims that fine art looted** by Germans from Jews and other owners is hanging in the *Louvre* and other French museums. Many U.S. fine-arts museums may also contain art stolen by the Germans. • Jewish leaders ask the Canadian government to investigate claims that former SS men are living in Canada and receiving German war pensions.

• **February 1997: The University of Vienna announces it will investigate allegations that bodies of Holocaust victims were used as sources for illustrations in a highly regarded medical book, *Topographical Anatomy of the Human Being*, compiled by Eduard Pernkopf, a Nazi who headed the university's medical faculty after 1938.** • **A declassified letter stored in the**

I.G. Farben *(diagrammed above)* was Germany's largest chemical company. Like other high-profile German businesses, it paid the SS for slave laborers. In the 1990s, Volkswagen, Siemens, BMW, and others reacted to scrutiny by announcing compensatory fund programs for victims and their families.

Krupp, Allianz, BASF, Bayer, BMW, and Degussa.

The more one learns about the Holocaust, the more devastating it becomes. Until the late 1990s, for example, it was not widely known that Germany's Deutsche Bank provided lines of credit to help finance construction at Auschwitz. The extensive use of slave labor by German industry in Nazi Germany remains a Holocaust chapter that is still to be fully disclosed. In 1944, for example, 750,000 concentration-camp inmates—about half of them Jews—slaved for German companies. Millions of other conscripted workers, many of them unwillingly deported to

Germany and forced to live in cruel circumstances, also served German firms that remain respected for their efficiency and the quality of their products. Essayist Roger Rosenblatt's April 1999 *Time* article, "Paying for Auschwitz," makes a telling point about the Holocaust's prevailing injustice: "All moral thought," he observes, "is grounded in the possibility of correction. Yet here is a wrong that will never be set right, and people are left groping for something to take the place of the irreplaceable."

U.S. Undersecretary of State Stuart Eizenstat has no illusions about replacing the irreplaceable. However, he has done a great deal to coordinate international efforts to adjudicate claims about Holocaust-era assets that dominated much of the

Holocaust-related news on the eve of the 21st century. On May 20, 1999, for example, Eizenstat presented a 1200-page report of the proceedings from a most important conference on Holocaust-era assets, which was held at the U.S. Department of State from November 30 to December 3, 1998. The conference brought together representatives from 44 countries, including leaders of 13 nongovernmental organizations, art museums, and auction houses. Subsequently, work on related matters has continued, and it will not be finished easily or immediately. Issues about forced and slave labor, for instance, created the agenda for a meeting convened by Eizenstat and German Chancellery Minister Bodo Hombach on May 12, 1999. But the conference in Washington late in 1998 created momentum for ongoing

In March 1949 the DEGESCH corporation, which made the Zyklon B gas used in gas chambers, was tried in Frankfurt, Germany. Here, Protestant leader Martin Niemöller testifies against the firm.

United States National Archives reveals that a fragment of a Nazi rocket that exploded in Belgium is stamped with the words "Made in Sweden"—a violation of Sweden's wartime neutrality. • More than 1600 American universities offer courses in Holocaust study, up from 206 in 1979 and two in 1973.

• February 12, 1997: Switzerland, stung by allegations that the wartime government accepted and laundered funds from Nazi Germany that had been looted from Jews, agrees to create a $71 million fund for Holocaust survivors and their heirs.

• February 20, 1997: The Polish Parliament votes to return Jewish com-

munal property nationalized at the close of World War II. Property includes about 2000 synagogues, schools, and other buildings, as well as about 1000 cemeteries.

• March 1997: Jewish and Polish leaders sign a $93.5 million agreement to preserve and expand the Auschwitz Museum at the site of Nazi

Although Krupp, Germany's largest arms manufacturer, was ordered dissolved following a postwar trial *(above)*, the order was never carried out. Intense public pressure 50 years later prompted Krupp to offer financial restitution to Jewish and other slave laborers it had abused.

negotiations as well as setting objectives and principles to govern them.

One goal of the 1998 Washington Conference was to deal with Nazi-confiscated art treasures. During the past 50 years, much of that art has been sold and resold. Some of it has been purchased and displayed by world-renowned art museums, which may or may not have known the full history of these valuable works. Tracking the history of the artworks, and then returning them to the rightful owners, is a large and complicated task. As much as 20 percent of

Europe's major artworks was confiscated by the Nazis.

Philip Saunders, a specialist in stolen art, estimated in 1997 that 100,000 pieces of valuable art are "still missing from the Nazi occupation." Reflecting the diverse areas to which Jews fled from Nazism, claimants come from far and wide—Israel, Canada, Australia, and the United States as well as European countries. They range from individuals who are trying to find art that was displayed in their former homes to art collectors who had loaned

pieces to museums and galleries that fell prey to Nazi theft. In some cases, documentary evidence overwhelmingly supports the claimants. In other instances, just as Estelle Sapir could produce no Majdanek death certificate for her father when she approached Credit Suisse, the original owners of the confiscated art may know that a piece of art is theirs when they see it, and yet the difficulty of documenting ownership remains.

Artworks account for only a part of the household assets stolen by the Nazis. When Soviet forces reached Auschwitz in January 1945, they found six storerooms that contained hundreds of thousands of men's suits and women's coats. Property of this kind—furniture, furs, family heirlooms—may be "too small" to be considered by Holocaust-era assets negotiations 50 years later. But when one considers that the Nazis killed nearly six million Jews, uprooting millions more and turning them into refugees, and that the expropriation of Jewish property was an essential ingredient in Nazi policy, then the amount of lost household assets—small and large—becomes utterly mind-boggling.

As the 20th century ended, valiant efforts were made to advance restitution, which is unavoidably destined to be woe-

---

Germany's most notorious extermination camp.

• May 19, 1997: Long-secret documents released by Britain's Public Record Office prove that the mass extermination of Jews began as early as June 1941—several months before the date commonly thought to mark the beginning of the "Final Solution."

• July 1997: Argentina establishes a government commission to determine the number of Nazi war criminals who fled to Argentina following the war, and what kinds of Nazi loot were brought into the country.

• August 20–23, 1997: In reports published by the Swedish newspaper *Dagens Nyheter*, journalist Maciej

Zaremba asserts that the Swedish government sterilized approximately 60,000 Swedish women during the war years to rid Swedish society of "inferior" racial types, and to foster proliferation of Aryan physical attributes.

• August 24, 1997: The World Jewish Congress rejects Germany's offer of

fully incomplete because the losses are so great and too much time has passed to adequately identify, sift, and sort the myriad claims. The restitution effort is a noble one that seeks to bring at least a modicum of closure to the Holocaust. Unfortunately, the Holocaust eludes closure, for the inventory of its damages shows that there are always *more*, many more. For generations to come, undeserving people in Europe and around the world will be the will-

A 1996 auction in Vienna was organized around "heirless" artworks plundered by the Nazis from Jewish families. About 8000 objects, including Old Masters paintings, were auctioned, with proceeds going to needy Austrian-Jewish Holocaust survivors.

ful or unwitting beneficiaries of Nazi theft from Jews and also from other persons and institutions in Nazi-occupied countries. For example, the Nazis stole huge amounts of monetary gold, often stockpiling it in the banks of neutral countries such as Turkey, Spain, Portugal, and Sweden, as well as Switzerland. The "Nazi gold" also included substantial quantities of nonmonetary gold—dental fillings and crowns, for instance, that were "harvested" from the Nazis' death-camp victims. Those assets did not lie dormant. They created unearned benefits that went here or there but not to the rightful owners.

Property owned by Jewish groups—synagogues and schools, for instance—constitutes another area where theft took place and the issues of restitution loom large. This is partly true because only vestiges of those communities remain, especially in Poland and other Eastern European countries that experienced not only Nazi occupation but Soviet domination and Communist regimes during the Cold War. Then, as the story of a Jewish woman named Marta Drucker Cornell illustrates, there are huge problems to tackle that involve insurance.

In 1945 Marta Drucker was 17. Except for her 80-year-old grand-

Empowered at last: In 1959 Simone Veil, a French Jew and a survivor of Auschwitz, became president of the European Council.

mother, she was the only survivor of her middle-class Czech family. After more than three years in Nazi concentration camps, she had her life but little else. One of her few possessions was a postcard-sized piece of paper on which her father, Dr. Leopold Drucker, had written numbers whose meaning she did not know. With the help of a friend of her father's—he turned out to be Dr. Drucker's insurance agent—she learned that the numbers referred to her father's life insurance policies. Much as Estelle Sapir tried to retrieve her family's money from Swiss banks, Marta Drucker worked to get her family's insurance monies. The responses she got from the insurance firms were no different from the ones Sapir received from the

one-time reparations payments to Holocaust survivors living in Eastern Europe. WJC secretary general Israel Singer insists that these survivors be granted monthly pensions.

● **September 9, 1997:** The London-based Holocaust Educational Trust reports that British-based banks may be holding as much as $1.1 billion in

dormant accounts opened by victims of the Holocaust.

● **October 1997:** Accused former Nazi collaborator Maurice Papon goes on trial in France, for the deportations and subsequent deaths of hundreds of French, including children.

● **November 1, 1997:** Swiss documents are made public, showing that a U.S. bank, National City (later Citibank), knowingly accepted about $30 million of looted Nazi gold as collateral for a loan to Spain. National City, working with the approval of the U.S. Treasury Department, accepted the gold after it had been laundered by Swiss banks; *See* 1951.

banks. Drucker's pursuit was frustrated at every turn. The insurance companies would not honor her claims. On one occasion, she was told that her father had failed to make the premium payments that would have kept the policies in force. Other "explanations" for rejecting the claims filed by Drucker and claimants like her ranged from "the insurance company no longer exists," "the relevant records were destroyed by the war," or "the Communists nationalized the company" to "nothing can be done without a death certificate."

Thinking her cause was lost, Drucker immigrated to the United States in 1964. In 1997 she traveled to Washington, D.C., where she told her story to a group of insurance regulators. The regulators were committed to helping her and the many other Holocaust survivors and heirs who were seeking restitution from major insurers such as Allianz, Winterthur, and Generali for $1 billion of unpaid insurance claims.

Stuart Eizenstat's report indicated that "the issue of Holocaust-era insurance claims was one of the most complex and difficult challenges facing the Washington Conference." The report announced that "a fast track for payments to Holocaust survivors" is being pursued, but few would contest his judgment when he added that "there's more to be done."

U.S. Undersecretary of Commerce Stuart Eizenstat publicizes a massive report in May 1997, which harshly condemns Switzerland for dealing in Nazi gold during WWII.

Never Forget

The Washington Conference also stressed that more needs to be done for research, education, and remembrance about the Holocaust. "It's important," Eizenstat underscored in his report, "that the last word on the Holocaust for this century not be money alone." Restitution plans include using portions of the heirless assets for international educational initiatives that make increased Holocaust awareness a priority.

Without significant education, the Holocaust will be forgotten. If the Holocaust is forgotten, the survivors' testimony, even if it has been recorded, will be silenced, endangered, possibly even

These Sinti (Gypsy) survivors went on a hunger strike at Dachau, Germany, in 1980. They demanded moral rehabilitation for their suffering during the Holocaust.

• **November 9, 1997: A Holocaust memorial museum opens at Sachsenhausen, Germany, site of a Nazi-era concentration camp.**

• **November 13, 1997: Spurred by Jewish protest, Germany's parliament votes to stop government disability checks for suspected Nazi war criminals. Some 50,000 German veterans** suspected of war crimes, including members of the *Waffen-SS*, have been receiving benefits.

• **Late November 1997: Two safe-deposit boxes opened at a bank in Sao Paulo, Brazil, contain documents suggesting that assets stolen by Nazis were secretly channeled to Brazilian banks.**

• **December 1997: The Federal Reserve Bank of New York makes public secret documents showing that, early in 1952, the bank took possession of gold plates, buttons, coins, and smoking-pipe ornaments that had been stolen from victims of Nazi persecution, and later melted them into gold bars that were given to European central banks. • The U.S. State**

rendered null and void. If the Holocaust is forgotten, we will have ignored the survivors' warnings, their pleas for caring, their calls to mend the world. Then the knowledge left to us by forgetting may indeed be useless because it will leave us ignorantly indifferent to a catastrophe as real and as radically evil as it was unimaginable before it took place.

Although history never repeats itself exactly, the Holocaust shows that there is no moral or religious insurance policy, no political asset anywhere, to guarantee that

A Yiddish poster solicits funds to purchase and plant trees in the future Israel. The trees would memorialize the six million Jews who had died in the Holocaust.

"WHEN YOU STAND HERE, BE SILENT. WHEN YOU LEAVE HERE, BE NOT SILENT."

—Memorial plaque to murdered Jewish children at Bullenhuser Damm School at the former camp at Neuengamme, Germany

human destructiveness will not do its worst. But if we look, at least from time to time, into the Holocaust's pit of destruction, painful and difficult though doing so is sure to be, we will be better equipped to cope with a new century, one that has not only the potential for amazing progress and goodness but also the possibility of squandering human life in ways even more devastating than the 20th century, and the Holocaust in particular, have demonstrated. No Holocaust repercussion is more important than committing resources to education that allows the Holocaust's "useless knowledge" to drive home that life's preciousness is priceless, its beauty fragile, its justice vulnerable, its joy precarious, its future ours to determine for good or ill.

Lasting Infamy

Auschwitz survivor Elie Wiesel spoke at the White House in Washington, D.C., on April 12, 1999. Noting that "we are on the threshold of a new century, a new

millennium," he went on to ask, "What will the legacy of this vanishing century be? How will it be remembered in the new millennium?"

Even as Wiesel raised those questions, *Time* magazine was conducting a year-long Internet poll to register public opinion that will help to select the Person of the Century. Since the 1930s, *Time* has featured a person of the year, but in 1999 the stakes were higher. The Person of the Century, *Time*'s definition explained, will be the one "who, for better or worse, most influenced the course of history over the past 100 years."

At the time of this writing, the winner's identity was unknown, but *Time*'s list of leading contenders for the Person of the Century included V. I. Lenin, Winston Churchill, David Ben-Gurion, Martin Luther King, Jr., Pope John Paul II, and Adolf Hitler. *Time* provided extensive Web site information about the principal nominees. In addition to calling Hitler "the century's greatest

---

Department sets a deadline of the end of the century for completion of German reparations payments to victims of Nazi looting during the Holocaust.

● February 4, 1998: Nineteen prominent German intellectuals, historians, and authors urge German Chancellor Helmut Kohl to abandon plans for a

Holocaust memorial in Berlin. The group feels that the planned memorial is too large and artificial, and not inclusive of Gypsies, Jehovah's Witnesses, and other groups victimized by the Nazis.

● June 19, 1998: A $600 million settlement offer made by major Swiss banks to Holocaust victims whose

assets had been stolen during the war after being deposited in Swiss banks is called "humiliating" by the World Jewish Restitution Organization, and is widely derided by other Jewish groups and leaders. The three banks are Credit Suisse, Swiss Bank Corp., and Union Bank of Switzerland; *See* early August 1998.

Magda Trocmé, a French Christian who had rescued Jews, lights the eternal flame at the Yad Vashem Holocaust memorial in Jerusalem.

threat to democracy," the capsule description that headed *Time*'s entries also noted that he "redefined the meaning of evil forever."

The *Time* Web site about Hitler included the cover story from the magazine's January 2, 1939, issue. It featured Hitler as *Time*'s Man of 1938. *Time* gave Hitler credit for lifting Germany to unanticipated power in less than six years: "His was no ordinary dictatorship, but rather one of great energy and magnificent planning." But on the whole, *Time*'s story was ominous, for it stated that the most significant fact about Hitler in 1938 was that he had become "the greatest threatening force that the democ-

ratic, freedom-loving world faces today." The article contained no explicit reference to the November 1938 pogroms (*Kristallnacht*) that had savaged Jews in Germany and Austria, but it did note Hitler's racist antisemitism and called attention to the fact that Germany's Jews "have been tortured physically, robbed of homes and properties, denied a chance to earn a living, chased off the streets."

The cover of the January 2, 1939, issue of *Time* did not use a conventional photograph, but a caricature with sentiments worthy of the brave Munich journalists whom the Nazis crushed for protesting against Hitler in the late 1920s and early 1930s. The cover art, drawn by Baron Rudolph Charles von Ripper, a German Catholic who despised Nazi Germany, depicted Hitler as an organist playing a hymn of hate in a profaned cathedral while the Nazi hierarchy approvingly observes the tortured victims of the Third Reich.

The coverage of Hitler also mentioned other leaders who had acted with distinction in 1938. In the field of religion, *Time* recognized two men for their opposition to him. One was German Protestant Pastor Martin Niemöller, who was first arrested and imprisoned by the Nazis in early July 1937. He endured harsh concentration-camp conditions at Sachsenhausen and Dachau until the end of World War II. His famous personal statement remains one of the most succinct warnings from the Holocaust. "First they came for the Communists," said Niemöller, "and I did not speak up because I was not a Communist. They came for the union leaders, and I did not speak up because I was not a union leader. They came for the Jews, and I did not speak

Miep Gies helped hide Anne Frank and her family in Amsterdam. She found Anne's diary and saved the treasured book, which has touched millions of readers.

• **July 7, 1998: Volkswagen AG announces plans to establish a fund to compensate workers who were forced into slave labor at VW factories during World War II.**

• **Early August 1998: Major Swiss banks agree to pay a total of $1.25 billion to Holocaust victims whose assets had been stolen from Swiss**

bank accounts during World War II; *See* **Summer 1999.**

• **August 18, 1998: The Polish government announces a plan to terminate the lease for property near the former Auschwitz death camp held by a Christian war-victims organization. The government states that the group violated terms of the lease by erecting**

crosses on the property. The crosses have raised the ire of Jewish groups; *See* **September 20, 1998.**

• **August 19, 1998: Italy's *Assicurazioni Generali* insurance company agrees to pay $100 million to compensate Holocaust victims whose insurance policies were never honored. The settlement also requires that**

up because I was not a Jew. Then they came for me, and there was no one left to speak up for me."

The other religious leader recognized by *Time* on January 2, 1939, was 81-year-old Pope Pius XI, whose opposition to Nazism and its antisemitism proved bolder than that of Pius XII, his 1939 papal successor. *Time*'s Man of 1938 story also identified that year's "greatest single news event" as the late September conference in Munich, which turned Czechoslovakia into a German puppet state. It signaled that an extensively rearmed Germany might have its way in Europe in the near

future. "The Man of 1938," *Time* concluded, "may make 1939 a year to be remembered."

Fifty years later, Elie Wiesel, whose Holocaust experiences testify that Hitler did indeed make 1939 a year to remember, asked his questions at the White House: "What will the legacy of this vanishing century be? How will it be

Berlin's Spandau Prison remained a physical reminder of Allied justice and the Nazi criminal legacy. When its last inmate, Rudolf Hess, died in 1987, the structure was razed.

remembered in the new millennium?" Wiesel may be saddened but not surprised if *Time* names

Yom ha-Sho'ah

Yom ha-Sho'ah, or Holocaust Remembrance Day, was established by the Israeli *Knesset* (Parliament) in 1951. The date chosen for the annual commemorative event is the 27th day of the Hebrew month of Nissan, a day that falls between the

anniversary of the Warsaw Ghetto uprising (January to May 1943) and Israel's Independence Day (May 14, 1948).

In Israel, *Yom ha-Sho'ah* is marked by closing all places of entertainment and sounding a siren at 8:00 A.M. When the siren sounds, all activities throughout the country cease for a moment of silence. People stop what they are doing, even if they are driving a car, and stand in remembrance of the Jews who died during the Holocaust.

Yom ha-Sho'ah is also observed throughout the United States

(shown, 1994) and in many European locations. Commemorative ceremonies are coordinated by Jewish religious and community centers, gentile religious institutions, interfaith centers, and sectarian associations. Although there are no set rules for the observance of *Yom ha-Sho'ah*, the ceremonies typically include speakers, prayers, and candle lighting. It is common to light six candles to represent the six million Jews killed, although some ceremonies light a seventh candle to commemorate the non-Jewish victims of Nazi persecution.

Generali make public its policy records from the Nazi era.

• **August 30, 1998:** Attorneys in the United States and Germany file class-action suits against Daimler-Benz, BMW, Volkswagen, Siemens, Krupp, Audi, and six other large German and Austrian corporations that benefited during World War II from slave labor

provided by the Nazi government; *See* February 16, 1999.

• **September 20, 1998:** Ignoring pleas of Polish church and government officials, conservative Catholics erect four 13-feet-tall wooden crosses next to the former Auschwitz death camp. The act brings the number of crosses near the infamous site to about 200.

• **December 3, 1998:** A 44-nation panel meeting in Washington, D.C., agrees to U.S.-drafted principles for the return of fine art looted from Holocaust victims by the Nazis. France announces the creation of a governmental body to handle individual claims by Holocaust victims for the return of artworks.

Many Holocaust survivors have taken pains to tell their stories to the world. Here, former Resistance leader Abba Kovner gives vehement testimony at the 1961 trial of Adolf Eichmann.

Hitler its Person of the Century. Evidence for that judgment can be found at the magazine's Web site, for it is Wiesel himself who has authored the essay that accompanies the site's factual material about Hitler and the reissue of *Time*'s Man of 1938 cover story. When the 20th century is remembered, Wiesel's essay states, Hitler's will be "among the first names that will surge to mind."

Some say that Hitler's name should be blotted out forever. That sentiment is understandable, but when Wiesel decided to write about Hitler for *Time*'s Person of the Century poll, another theme came to the fore. The world can ill-afford to forget Hitler because his infamy is not just that his regime

launched, in Wiesel's words, "a war that remains the most atrocious, the most brutal and the deadliest in history." The essence of Hitler's infamy, inseparable from the war he waged, was the Holocaust.

To remember the Holocaust means not to forget Hitler. Perhaps, then, Hitler *should* be the Person of the Century. The 20th century was, after all, the bloodiest in human history. No event did more to produce that outcome than the Holocaust. No person had more to do with the Holocaust than Hitler.

Today, we remember the Holocaust not simply as part of the past, but as an event with profound implications for the present and the future. We still have much to learn, but we do know this: The Holocaust was not inevitable. It

In this scene from the 1993 film *Schindler's List,* a Nazi labor-camp commandant selects a Jewish woman prisoner to be his domestic servant. Ralph Fiennes played the commandant, who was based on sadistic Kraków camp leader Amon Goeth.

emerged from deliberate decisions made by human beings. Those decisions were neither predestined or inevitable. Whether or not Hitler is *Time* magazine's Person of the 20th Century, we must insist that no one remotely like him shall have that distinction at the end of the 21st.

The small, the helpless, the innocent: these were the victims of Adolf Hitler's Holocaust. His ardent followers exterminated millions. Those who survived, such as this Polish woman and her infant, lived with the horrors the rest of their lives.

But our insistence—and the hope and determination that must accompany it—will not lessen the horror of the Holocaust. We can, however, nurture the memories of Holocaust survivors, and dedicate ourselves to remaining sensitive and well informed; politically aware and ethically sound.

Such are the goals that *The Holocaust Chronicle* exists to serve.

• **February 16, 1999: German Chancellor Gerhard Schröder announces the $1.7 billion Remembrance, Responsibility and the Future fund. It is financed by 12 major German corporations to compensate people impressed by the Nazis into forced labor that benefited those companies during World War II. The corporations include Daimler-Benz, Volks-** wagen, BMW, Siemens, Krupp, and Audi.

• **May 26, 1999: Germany agrees that Nazi-era slave laborers from Poland should get the same compensation as those from other countries. More than 400,000 Poles are seeking a total of more than $2 billion in compensation for their slave labor.**

• **Summer 1999: Five hundred newspapers worldwide publish full-page ads with clip-out forms that will enable Holocaust survivors to apply for their share of a $1.25 billion settlement with Swiss banks. • Memoirs of high-ranking SS functionary Adolf Eichmann are opened and widely publicized.**

Appendices

TOTAL DEATHS FROM NAZI GENOCIDAL POLICIES

Group	Deaths
European Jews	5,600,000 to 6,250,000
Soviet prisoners of war	3,000,000
Polish Catholics	3,000,000
Serbians	700,000 (Croat *Ustasa* persecution)
Roma, Sinti, and Lalleri	222,000 to 250,000
Germans (political, religious, and Resistance)	80,000
Germans (handicapped)	70,000
Homosexuals	12,000
Jehovah's Witnesses	2500

DEATH CAMPS (POLAND)

Death Camps	Jewish Deaths	Commandant
Auschwitz-Birkenau	1.1 to 1.6 million	Lothar Hatjenstein, Rudolf Höss, Josef Kramer, Arthur Liebehenschel, Heinrich Schwarz
Belzec	601,500	Odilo Globocnik
Chelmno	255,000	Hans Bothmann
Majdanek	360,000	Arthur Liebehenschel
Sobibór	250,000	Franz Reichleitner, Franz Stangl, Richard Thomalla
Treblinka	750,000 to 870,000	Kurt Franz, Franz Stangl

INTERNMENT AND TRANSIT CAMPS IN WESTERN EUROPE UNDER NAZI OCCUPATION

Belgium
- Breendonck (internment): Belgian and "stateless" Jews deported to Mechelen.
- Mechelen (transit): 26,000 Jews sent to concentration camps.

France
- Beaune-la-Rolnade (internment)
- Compiègne (transit): 12,000 Jews deported to Buchenwald and Dachau.
- Drancy (transit): 74,000 indigenous and non-French Jews, and 5000 Belgian Jews, deported to Auschwitz, Majdanek, and Sobibór.
- Gurs (collection camp): 6000 non-French Jews, mostly German, deported to Drancy.
- Les Milles (transfer camp): 2000 inmates deported to Drancy and then on to Auschwitz.
- Pithiviers (internment and transit): 3700 Jewish men deported to Auschwitz.
- Rivesaltes (internment): German Jews, Roma, and Spanish Republicans deported to death camps.
- Vittel (internment): 300 Jews sent to Drancy.

Luxembourg
- Fünfbrunnen (transit): Approximately 2000 Jews from Luxembourg and Jewish refugees were deported to death and concentration camps.

Netherlands
- Vught (transit and punishment camp): 12,000 Jews deported to Westerbork.
- Westerbork (internment): 89,000 Jews and 500 Roma deported to concentration and death camps in Germany, Czechoslovakia, and Poland.

MAJOR CONCENTRATION AND LABOR CAMPS

Camp	Location	Jewish Deaths
Auschwitz I	Oswieçim, Poland	1.6 million
Bergen-Belsen	Hanover, Germany	50,000
Buchenwald	Weimar, Germany	60,000 to 65,000
Dachau	Munich, Germany	35,000
Dora-Nordhausen	Harz Mountains, Germany	8125
Mittelbau/Mittelwerk		20,000
Flossenbürg	Upper Palatine, Bavaria	27,000
Gross-Rosen	Lower Silesia, Germany	105,000
Janówska	Lvov, Ukraine	40,000
Jasenovac	Zagreb, Croatia	20,000
Kaiserwald	Riga, Latvia	10,000
Klooga	Tallinn, Estonia	2400
Mauthausen	Linz, Austria	120,000
Natzweiler-Struthof	Strasbourg, France	17,000
Neuengamme	Hamburg, Germany	55,000
Ninth Fort	Kovno, Lithuania	10,000
Pawiak Prison	Warsaw, Poland	37,000
Plaszów	Kraków, Poland	8000
Poniatowa	Lublin, Poland	15,000
Ravensbrück	Berlin, Germany	92,000
Sachsenhausen/Oranienburg	Berlin, Germany	105,000
Sajmiste/Semlin	Serbia	50,000
Sered	Slovakia	13,500 (deported to Theresienstadt)
Stutthof	Poland	65,000 to 85,000
Theresienstadt	Prague, Czechoslovakia	33,430
Trawniki	Lublin, Poland	10,000

MAJOR JEWISH GHETTOS

Ghetto	Country	Population
Amsterdam	Netherlands	100,000
Bedzin	Poland	27,000
Bialystok	Poland	35,000 to 50,000
Budapest	Hungary	70,000
Chernovtsy	Romania	50,000
Grodno	Poland	25,000
Kovno/Kaunas	Lithuania	40,000
Kraków	Poland	19,000
Lida	Belorussia	9000
Liepaja	Latvia	7400
Łódź	Poland	205,000
Lublin	Poland	34,000
Lvov	Ukraine	110,000
Minsk	Belorussia	100,000
Mir	Belorussia	2500
Novogrudok	Belorussia	6000
Radom	Poland	30,000
Riga	Latvia	43,000
Salonika	Greece	56,000
Shanghai*	China	10,000
Ternopol	Ukraine	12,500
Theresienstadt	Czechoslovakia	90,000
Vitebsk	Belorussia	16,000
Vilna	Lithuania	41,000
Warsaw	Poland	400,000 to 500,000

*The ghetto was administered by the Japanese occupational government with the assistance of the Jewish welfare organization.

Country	Jews Killed	Perc. of Country's Jews Killed
Albania	—	—[1]
Austria	50,000	36[2]
Belgium	25,000	60[3]
Belorussia	245,000	65
Bohemia/Moravia	80,000	89
Bulgaria	11,400	14[4]
Denmark	60	1.3
Estonia	1500	35
Finland	7	2.8[5]
France	90,000	26
Germany	130,000	55
Great Britain	130	[6]
Greece	65,000	80[7]
Hungary	450,000	70
Italy	7500	20[8]
Latvia	70,000	77
Lithuania	220,000	94
Luxembourg	1950	50
The Netherlands	106,000	76
Norway	870	55
Poland	2,900,000	88
Russia	107,000	11[9]
Romania	270,000	33
Slovakia	71,000	80
Spain	—	—
Sweden	—	—
Switzerland	—	—[10]
Ukraine	900,000	60
Yugoslavia	60,000	80[11]

1. Between ten to 12 Jews were deported from Albania to Bergen-Belsen.

2. When the Nazis annexed Austria in March 1938, there were 185,000 Jews living in the country. Thousands of Jews fled after the *Anschluss* and subsequent *Kristallnacht* pogrom in November 1938.

3. Only 10% of the victims were citizens of Belgium prior to the war.

4. The Jewish victims came exclusively from Thrace and Macedonia, territories awarded to Bulgaria by Hitler.

5. Out of a Jewish population approaching 2000, a small number of Jewish refugees were deported to labor camps in Estonia.

6. From 1941 to 1945, the British interned 1500 Jews destined for Palestine on Mauritius; 124 perished. In 1939, two Jews were killed by the British Navy when their ship was sunk attempting to enter Palestine. At least three Jews were deported to camps during the German occupation of Britain's Channel Islands.

7. Includes Corfu (1800), Rhodes (1540), and Salonika (42,000).

8. Jews were deported during the Nazi occupation of Italy, which began in 1943.

9. This estimate of Jewish victims is likely to increase, possibly by as much as 250,000, as scholars examine documents made available after the collapse of the former Soviet Union.

10. The Swiss policy of *refoulement*, enforced from 1938 until July 7, 1944, curtailed the flow of Jewish refugees into Switzerland. Although approximately 30,000 Jews found refuge in or passed through Switzerland, at least 10,000 Jews were turned away. Although trains destined for concentration and death camps in the East were allowed to be routed through Switzerland, its prewar Jewish population of 12,000 was not turned over to the Nazis.

11. Includes Jews from Bosnia, Croatia, Rab, and Serbia. Most Jews in the Italian Zone of Occupation were not deported or released to the Nazi or *Ustasa*.

Area of Activity	Organization	Leadership
Algeria	José Aboulker Family	José Aboulker
Auschwitz-Birkenau	Resistance, *Sonderkommando* revolt	Battle Group Auschwitz, Jewish *Sonderkommandos*
Bedzin Ghetto	underground	Jewish Youth Groups
Bialystok Ghetto	Jewish Anti-Fascist Bloc	Mordechai Tenenbaum
France	Armée Juivee	Abraham Polonski & Lucien Lublin
Germany	Baum Group	Herbert & Marianne Baum
France	Jewish Scout Movement	Robert Gamzon
Italy	Jewish Brigades	Yishuv Jews
Balkans and Austria	Jewish Parachutists	Yishuv Jews
Kovno/Kaunas Ghetto	Jewish Fighting Organization	Young Zionists and Anti-Fascist Struggle Organization
Kraków	Resistance	Zionist Youth Movements & Jewish Fighting Organization
Lida Ghetto	Bielski partisans	Bielski Brothers
Lvov Ghetto	Resistance/underground	Tadek Drotorski
Minsk Ghetto	partisan	Hersh Smolar
Minsk Ghetto	partisan	Kazinets a.k.a. "Slavek"
Mir Ghetto	underground & revolt	Shmuel Rufeisin
Novogrudok Ghetto	Bielski partisans	Bielski brothers
Riga Ghetto	underground	"Secret Cells"
Sobibór death camp	Resistance & revolt	Aleksandr Pechersky & Leon Feldhandler
Treblinka death camp	Resistance & revolt	Dr. Julian Chorazycki, Marceli Galewski, & Zelo Bloch
Vilna Ghetto	underground/United Partisan Organization	Josef Glazman & Yitzhak Wittenberg
Vilna Ghetto	partisans	Yehiel Scheinbaum
Warsaw Ghetto	Jewish Fighting Organization	Mordecai Anielewicz, Zivia Lubetkin, Yitzhak Zuckerman
Warsaw Ghetto	Jewish Military Union (Zionist Revisionists)	Pawel Frenkiel

Year	Aliya	Aliya Bet*
1933	30,327	467 (817)+
1934	42,359	NA
1935	61,854	NA
1936	29,727	NA
1937	10,536	69
1938	14,675	3041 (3079)[1]
1939	31,195	13,350 (15,217)[2]
World War II		
1939	—	2899 (4029)
1940	10,643	5806 (8306)
1941	4592	800
1942	4206	0 (889)
1943	10,063	0 (0)[3,4]
1944	15,552	3944 (4283)[5,6]
1945	15,259	—
Postwar		
1945	—	989 (989)
1946	18,760	1197 (21,673)[7]
1947	22,098	2520 (25,191)
1948	17,165	189 (21,509)

Aliya: legal immigration. *Aliya bet:* "illegal" immigration.

+The first number of the last column is the actual number of Jews who landed in Palestine. The number inside the parentheses represents the total number of Jews who attempted to enter Palestine.

1. Evian Conference held from July 6 to 15, 1938.

2. British White Paper implemented and enforced from May 17, 1939, until May 14, 1948.

3. Bermuda Conference held in April 1943.

4. Thousands of Jews were deported by the British to Athlit and Cyprus.

5. War Refugee Board established on January 22, 1944.

6. Thousands of Jews were shipped to British internment camps, and some were deported to Germany.

7. Data includes immigration up to May 14, 1948; some Jews were detained on Cyprus until that date, when the state of Israel was established.

Glossary

Abwehr (G. Self-Defense)—The German armed forces' foreign and counter-intelligence service, headed by Admiral Wilhelm Canaris. Started in 1933, it became the center of an anti-Hitler conspiracy.

Aktion (G. operation, pl. *Aktionen*)—Murderous campaigns against Jews for the purposes of deportation or execution. Most viciously employed in the Eastern Territories.

aliya (Heb. immigration)—Individuals or groups who immigrated to Palestine and, later, Israel.

aliya bet (Heb. "illegal" immigration)—Organized "illegal" immigration by clandestine Jewish organizations—for example, *Hagana* or *Irgun*—to British-controlled Palestine, 1930s to 1946.

Angriff, Der (G. *The Assault*)—Nazi newspaper founded by Joseph Goebbels in 1927. Mostly a political pamphlet, the paper served as a vehicle for his venom until 1945.

Anschluss (G. linkage)—Term used by Germans for Nazi Germany's annexation of Austria on March 13, 1938.

"Arbeit macht frei" (G. "work will set you free")—Slogan above entrance gates of a number of concentration and death camps, including Auschwitz, Dachau, and Theresienstadt. It was deceptive, since all Jews had indefinite sentences.

Arrow Cross Party (Hungarian Nyilas Party)—Pro-Nazi Fascist party that assumed power in October 1944 in Hungary. It was responsible for mass murder and deportations.

Aryan—A language grouping referring to Indo-European tongues. It was perverted by Nazis to mean a non-Jewish Nordic racial grouping.

Aryanization—The Nazi term to cover outright stealing, plundering, or takeovers of Jewish property.

Auschwitz I (Pol. Oswieçim)—Original and main Auschwitz camp in southwest Poland. Served first as Polish military barracks, then as a concentration camp largely for gentiles.

Auschwitz II (also called Birkenau, Pol. Brzezinka)—Opened in October 1941, particularly for the extermination of Jews and Roma (Gypsies). It was the site of four gas chambers.

Auschwitz III (also known as Buna-Monowitz)—Set aside as a labor camp for chemical giant I.G. Farben. It refers also to 36 subcamps.

Axis—The political, military, and ideological alliance of Nazi Germany with Italy, Japan, Finland, Hungary, Slovakia, Romania, and Bulgaria during World War II.

badge, Jewish—A six-pointed yellow Star of David, often with the word "Jude," that had to be sewn by Jews on visible garments.

Barbarossa—Hitler coined this code name (after a medieval German king) for the massive German attack on the Soviet Union, which began on June 22, 1941.

Beer Hall Putsch (G. coup)—A revolutionary attempt in Munich, Germany, on November 8, 1923, by Hitler and his followers to topple the Bavarian government. It failed and led to Hitler's arrest and brief imprisonment.

blood libel—A vicious antisemitic lie accusing Jews of killing Christian children to use their blood to make Passover matzo.

Bund (G. and Yiddish. league)—Jewish Socialist, non-Zionist organization and union founded in Vilna, Lithuania, in 1897. It prompted Jewish cultural autonomy.

death marches—With the collapse of the Eastern Front in the late fall of 1944 to 1945, the SS marched concentration-camp inmates on long, often pointless treks into the heart of Germany and Austria.

DEGESCH (acronym for German Vermin-Combating Corporation)—This subsidiary of I.G. Farben produced and distributed Zyklon B to extermination camps.

displaced persons (DPs)—Jews and others who did not wish, at war's end, to be repatriated to their former communities/countries of origin, and who were placed in DP camps.

Einsatzgruppen (G. Special Action Groups)—SS murder units that were assisted by auxiliary units from Poland, Ukraine, Lithuania, and Latvia. They were made up of 3000 troops divided into four groups.

Einsatzkommando (G. Special Squad)—Fifteen subgroups of an *Einsatzgruppe.* They organized the mass murder of Jews in the Soviet Union by shooting.

"Final Solution" *(Endlösung)*—Term used by Hermann Göring in a letter to Reinhard Heydrich that was discussed at the Wannsee Conference. It became a code term for complete murder of all Jews.

Freikorps (G. Free Corps)—A right-wing volunteer military force, comprised of former World War I veterans and unemployed youth. Started in 1919, the *Freikorps* crushed the Communist revolutionaries in Berlin and Bavaria. Later, many members joined the Nazis.

Freiwillige (G. volunteers)—Non-German collaborators who aided the SS in the mass murder of Jews.

Führer (G. leader)—Adolf Hitler was *"Der Führer,"* or dictator, of Nazi Germany. Hitler created the title after the death of President Paul von Hindenburg in August 1934.

Gau (G. district)—One of 32 regional districts, called *Gaugebiete,* set up by the Nazi Party in the Third Reich. Similar to the old *Reichstag* electoral districts.

Gauleiter (G. district leader)—Governor of a *Gau,* appointed by Hitler. Responsible for political, economic, and labor activities; civil defense; and some police duties.

Generalgouvernement—The part of eastern Poland not incorporated into Germany. It included Galicia, Radom, Warsaw, Lublin, and Kraków. Poland's 3.3 million Jews were forced into this area.

Gestapo (acronym for *Geheime Staatspolizei;* G. Secret State Police)—The political police. Had powers of incarceration without judicial review. It became the most feared entity in Nazi-controlled areas.

haavara (Heb. transfer)—An arrangement between Germany, the German Zionist Federation, and the Anglo-Palestine Bank (1932–1939) to allow the export of Jewish capital from Germany to Jewish Palestine.

Hagana (Heb. Defense Force)—An underground military group founded in 1920 by the Palestine Jewish settlement to fend off Arab attacks.

Hitlerjugend (G. Hitler Youth)—Nazi youth organization for boys 14 to 18, founded in 1922. Membership in this paramilitary indoctrination body was made compulsory in 1939.

Hlinka Guard—Militia organized by the Slovak People's Party that reigned from 1938 to 1945. It was named after Slovakian Fascist Andrej Hlinka.

Iron Guard—Romanian Fascist party. A paramilitary and political antisemitic organization, founded by Corneliu Codreanu in 1927.

Judenfrei (G. free of Jews)—Nazi euphemism for ethnic cleansing of an area by deportation or murder. An alternate term was *Judenrein.*

Judenrat (G. Jewish council, pl. *Judenräte*)—Ghetto Jewish councils set up by Nazis and under their strict control. Jewish leaders, called Elders, collaborated in Nazi plans for Jewish ghetto life.

Judenrein (G. cleansed of Jews)—*See Judenfrei.*

Jüdischer Ordnungsdienst (G. Jewish Order Service)—Jewish police in ghettos. They caused resentment among other Jews since they aided in roundups and deportations.

Kapo (It. chief or head)—An inmate in a concentration camp who assisted in the administration of the camp in return for additional rations and better living conditions.

Kriminalpolizei (Kripo; G. Criminal Police)—German police organization with duties related mainly to nonpolitical crimes, although they joined with the Gestapo and the SS against the Jews. They eventually came under the control of the SD as the *Sicherheitspolizei.*

Kristallnacht (G. Night of Broken Glass)—A violent, orchestrated pogrom against Jewish stores and synagogues on November 9–10, 1938, in Germany, Austria, and Sudetenland, Czechoslovakia.

Lebensborn (G. Fountain of Life)—SS program aimed at selective breeding to turn the German people into a "super race." There were a number of maternity centers. In 1942 *Lebensborn* was a cover for kidnapping Polish children possessed of "Aryan" traits.

Lebensraum (G. living space)—A guiding principle of German foreign policy expressed in Hitler's *Mein Kampf.* The Nazis believed they were entitled to conquer huge portions of eastern territories.

Luftwaffe (G. Air Force)—This was the title given to the German air force in World War II. Headed by Hermann Göring.

"Madagascar Plan"—A Nazi Plan, approved by Hitler in 1940, to ship four million European Jews to the French island off Africa's southeast coast. It ultimately was abandoned.

Mein Kampf (G. *My Struggle*)—Adolf Hitler's autobiography and philosophical/political creed, written in 1924 with the aid of his secretary, Rudolf Hess, in Landsberg Prison. It spelled out his plans for the Jews.

Mischlinge (G. mixed breed)—Nazi term defined in the 1935 Nuremberg Laws for those having one or two Jewish grandparents.

Muselmann (G. Muslim)—A physically and emotionally run-down concentration-camp inmate who was so weak he could not walk, work, or stand erect; he looked like a praying Muslim.

Nacht und Nebel (G. Night and Fog)—Hitler's second order, issued on December 7, 1941, which mandated the arrest and disappearance of anyone suspected of underground activities against the Reich.

Night of the Long Knives—A June 30, 1934, blood purge of top SA officers, including Ernst Röhm and Gregor Strasser, that took place due to the efforts of selected SS troops.

Nuremberg Laws—Nazi laws passed in September 1935, which took German citizenship from Jews, defined Jews racially, and prohibited Jewish-Aryan sexual relations.

Nuremberg Trial—Main trial at Nuremberg, Germany, of 22 top Nazis (November 20, 1945, to October 1, 1946) by an international tribunal of U.S., British, French, and Soviet judges.

Odessa—Secret escape organization of the SS, founded after Germany's defeat in 1945. High-level Nazis used it to escape justice.

Organization Todt—Administered by Dr. Fritz Todt, this governmental unit was set up in 1938 to construct military installations. It later employed slave labor.

Ostland (G. Eastern Territories)—These Nazi-occupied territories included Estonia, Latvia, Lithuania, and western Belorussia. They were headed by a *Reichskommissar* (German governor).

partisans—Underground resistance fighters against Nazi occupiers, particularly in rural areas.

Rassenschande (G. race defilement)—Forbidden sexual contact between German Aryans and either Jews or Slavic Eastern workers.

Rasse-und Siedlungshauptamt (G. Race and Resettlement Main Office; RuSHA)—At first, this office authenticated the Aryan ancestry of SS members. Later, it organized the settlement and welfare of the Germans' colonizing of Poland.

Reichsbahn (G. state railways)—The German state railways, which were complicit in the Holocaust by transporting Jewish victims to ghettos and concentration camps under horrendous conditions.

Reichsführer-SS (G. Reich leader of the SS)—State supreme leader of the SS. Title given to Heinrich Himmler.

Reichskommissariat (G. Reich Commissioners)—A governing division of an occupied territory of the Soviet Union headed by a Nazi official during World War II.

Reichssicherheitshauptamt (G. Reich Security Main Office)—The RSHA was set up in 1939 to combine all existing police forces: criminal police, Gestapo, SD, and SS. A sub-branch, AM VI, managed the "Final Solution."

Reichstag (G. parliament)—This central German legislative body was retained by Hitler, but it granted most of its powers in 1933 to the chancellor and became Hitler's rubber stamp.

"Righteous Among the Nations"—Gentiles who risked their lives to save Jews and who are honored at the Yad Vashem, the Holocaust museum in Jerusalem.

SA (*Sturmabteilungen;* Storm Troopers)—Led by Ernst Röhm, the "Brown Shirts" were a battling street force from 1922 to 1934. The organization faded when its leaders were executed in the Night of the Long Knives.

SD (*Sicherheitsdienst;* Security Service)—An intelligence service for the Nazi Party and SS. Headed by Reinhard Heydrich, it became a terror instrument against "enemies of the state."

Selektion (G. selection)—In ghettos, the SS selected which Jews would be deported. In camps, the SS weeded out exhausted and sick inmates for murder.

Sho'ah (Heb. mass slaughter)—This Hebrew word is preferred over "Holocaust" in Israel. It is found in Isaiah 10:3 and means destruction, complete ruination.

Sicherheitspolizei (SIPO; G. Security Police)—A police unit made up of Gestapo members and *Kriminalpolizei.*

Sonderkommando (G. Special Squads)—An *Einsatzgruppe* detachment or a Jewish forced-labor unit that cleared gas chambers or assisted in the cremation process.

SS (*Schutzstaffel*)—Started in 1925. By 1936, under Heinrich Himmler, it controlled all German police agencies. It was the major criminal organization for persecution and murder of Jews. A military arm, the *Waffen-SS,* was organized for combat duty.

Stürmer, Der (G. *The Stormer*)—A highly anti-semitic, crude, virtually pornographic paper published and edited by Julius Streicher from 1923 to 1945.

subsequent Nuremberg proceedings—Twelve trials of Nazi war criminals held from 1946 to 1949, and administered by American judges in Nuremberg, Germany. The trials focused on physicians, judges, and industrialists.

swastika—Taken by Hitler as a symbol of Aryans, this "twisted cross" became the symbol of Nazi Germany and the centerpiece of the flag of the Third Reich.

Third Reich—Term given by Hitler to his regime (1933–1945). The first Reich was the Holy Roman Empire; the second was the Kaiser Reich.

Umschlagplatz (G. transfer place)—A loading area, often a railway siding, used as an assembly staging point as Jews were placed in freight cars for deportation.

United Nations Relief and Rehabilitation Administration (UNRRA)—Refugee relief agency formed by the Allies in 1943, mainly with American funds. After World War II, under the direction of American politician Fiorello La Guardia, it aided displaced persons.

Ustasa—Croatian ultranationalist Fascist party that came to power in April 1941 with Nazi support. It was responsible for the mass murder of Serbs, Jews, and Gypsies.

Vernichtung durch Arbeit (G. destruction through work)—Concentration camps that had a deliberate policy of killing inmate laborers by starvation, brutality, and overwork.

Vichy—A spa town in central France and the site of the collaborationist French government after the defeat of Republican France in 1940.

Völkish (G. of the people)—An inherently benign term appropriated by the Nazis in the 1920s and turned into a nationalistic, antidemocratic concept with powerful antisemitic overtones. It motivated violent Nazi outbursts in the party's early years.

Volksdeutsche (G. ethnic Germans)—Germans living outside Greater Germany who were given favored treatment in Nazi-occupied areas.

Waffen-SS (G. Armed SS)—The *Waffen*, the largest branch of the SS (39 divisions), often fought at the front like regular soldiers. Many were implicated in the Holocaust.

Wannsee Conference—An 87-minute meeting held on January 20, 1942, at a villa in a Berlin suburb, attended by 15 leading Nazi bureaucrats. Reinhard Heydrich, its chairman, discussed plans to coordinate the "Final Solution."

Wehrmacht (G. defense might)—The name of Nazi Germany's army after 1935. The *Wehrmacht* assisted the SS in the "Final Solution."

Weimar Republic—The German democratic government from 1919 to 1933, located in Weimar. A severe economic depression (1929–1932) paved the way for Hitler.

Yad Vashem—The Holocaust Martyrs and Heroes Remembrance Authority. This center for Holocaust archives, museum, and memorial in Jerusalem was established in 1962 by the Israeli government.

Yellow Star—Jews were forced to wear a yellow Star of David in Nazi-controlled Europe. The patch had to be sewn on all visible clothing.

Zyklon B (hydrogen cyanide)—A poisonous gas used in the gas chambers of the Nazi extermination camps.

Further Reading

Aarons, Mark, and John Loftus. *Unholy Trinity: The Vatican, the Nazis, and the Swiss Banks.* New York: St. Martin's Griffin, 1998.

Abitbol, Michel. Catherine Zentelis, trans. *The Jews of North Africa During the Second World War.* Detroit: Wayne State University Press, 1989.

Adam, Peter. *Art of the Third Reich.* New York: Abrams, 1992.

Ainsztein, Reuben. *Jewish Resistance in Nazi-Occupied Eastern Europe, with a Historical Survey of the Jew as Fighter and Soldier in the Diaspora.* London: 1974.

Ajzensztadt, Amnon. *Endurance: Chronicles of Jewish Resistance.* Oakville, Ontario, Canada: Mosaic Press, 1987.

Allon, Yigal. *Shield of David: The Story of Israel's Armed Forces.* London: Weidenfeld and Nicolson, 1970.

Arad, Yitzhak. *Belzec, Sobibor, Treblinka: Operation Reinhard Death Camps.* Bloomington, IN: Indiana University Press, 1999.

Arendt, Hannah. *Eichmann in Jerusalem: A Report on the Banality of Evil.* New York: Viking, 1963.

_____. *The Origins of Totalitarianism.* New York: Harcourt Brace Jovanovich, 1973.

Aroneanu, Eugene, ed., trans, by Thomas Whissen. *Inside the Concentration Camps: Eyewitness Accounts of Life in Hitler's Death Camps.* Westport, CT: Praeger, 1996.

Ashman, Charles, and Robert J. Wagman. *The Nazi Hunters.* New York: Warner Books, 1990.

Bailey, George. *Germans.* New York: The Free Press, 1991.

Barnett, Victoria. *For the Soul of the People: Protestant Protest Against Hitler.* New York: Oxford University Press, 1992.

Bauer, Yehuda. *From Diplomacy to Resistance: A History of Jewish Palestine, 1939–1945.* New York: Atheneum, 1973.

_____. *A History of the Holocaust.* New York: Franklin Watts, 1982.

_____. *My Brother's Keeper: A History of the American Jewish Joint Distribution Committee, 1929–1933.* Philadelphia: Jewish Publications Society of America, 1974.

Bauminger, Aryeh. *Rising of the Krakow Ghetto.* Tel Aviv: H'menorah, 1967.

Beckman, Morris. *The Jewish Brigade: An Army with Two Masters.* Rockville Center, NY: Sarpedon, 1998.

Begin, Menachem. *The Revolt: The Story of the Irgun.* New York: Henry Schuman, 1951.

Ben-Gurion, David. *Israel: A Personal History.* New York: Funk & Wagnalls, 1971.

_____. Mordecai Nurock and Misha Louvist, trans. *The Jews in Their Land.* New York: Doubleday, 1966.

Berenbaum, Michael, ed. *Witness to the Holocaust.* New York: HarperCollins, 1997.

_____. *The World Must Know.* New York: Little, Brown & Co., 1993.

Bering, Dietz. *Stigma of Names: Anti-Semitism in German Daily Life, 1812–1933.* Ann Arbor, MI: University of Michigan Press, 1992.

Bernadac, Christian. *Camp for Women: Ravensbrück.* Geneva: Ferni Publishing House, 1978.

_____. *The 186 Steps: Mauthausen.* Geneva: Ferni Publishing House, 1978.

Bierman, John. *Righteous Gentile: The Story of Raoul Wallenberg, Missing Hero of the Holocaust.* New York: Viking, 1981.

Borchsenius, Poul. *Behind the Wall: The Story of the Ghetto.* London: Allen & Unwin, 1964.

Borkin, Joseph. *The Crime and Punishment of I.G. Farben.* New York: The Free Press, 1978.

Braham, Randolph L. *The Politics of Genocide: The Holocaust in Hungary.* New York: Columbia University Press, 1981.

Breitman, Richard. *The Architect of Genocide.* New York: Knopf, 1991.

_____. *Official Secrets.* New York: Hill and Wang, 1998.

Bresheeth, Haim, Stuart Hood, and Litza Jansz. *Introducing the Holocaust.* New York: Totem Books, 1994.

Browning, Christopher R. *Fateful Months: Essays on the Emergence of the Final Solution.* New York: Holmes & Meier, 1985.

_____. *Ordinary Men: Reserve Police Battalion 101 and the Final Solution in Poland.* New York: HarperCollins, 1992.

Bullock, Alan. *Hitler: A Study in Tyranny.* New York: Harper & Row, 1964.

Bytwerk, Randall L. *Julius Streicher.* New York: Stein & Day, 1983.

Calic, Edouard. Lowell Bair, trans. *Reinhard Heydrich.* New York: Military Heritage Press, 1982.

Caracciolo, Nicola. *Uncertain Refuge: Italy and the Jews During the Holocaust.* Champaign, IL: University of Illinois Press, 1995.

Cargas, Harry James, ed. *When God and Man Failed: Non-Jewish Views of the Holocaust.* New York: Macmillan, 1981.

Cecil, Robert. *The Myth of the Master Race: Alfred Rosenberg and Nazi Ideology.* New York: Dodd Mead, 1972.

Chary, Frederick B. *The Bulgarian Jews and the Final Solution.* Pittsburgh: University of Pittsburgh Press, 1972.

Cohen, Arthur A., ed. *Arguments and Doctrines: A Reader of Jewish Thinking in the Aftermath of the Holocaust.* New York: Harper & Row, 1970.

Cohen, Elie A. *Human Behavior in the Concentration Camp.* New York: W. W. Norton, 1953.

Cohen, Norman. *Warrant for Genocide: The Myth of the Jewish World Conspiracy and the Protocols of the Elders of Zion.* New York: Harper & Row, 1967.

Cohn-Sherbock, Dan. *The Crucified Jew: Twenty Centuries of Christian Anti-Semitism.* London: HarperCollins, 1992.

Comay, Joan. *The Diaspora Story: The Epic of the Jewish People Among the Nations.* New York: Random House, 1980.

Conference on Manifestations of Jewish Resistance. *Jewish Resistance During the Holocaust: Proceedings.* Jerusalem: Yad Vashem, 1971.

Conot, Robert E. *Justice at Nuremberg.* New York: Harper & Row, 1983.

Crankshaw, Edward. *Gestapo: Instrument of Tyranny.* New York: Putnam, 1956.

Crum, Bartley. *Behind the Silken Curtain.* Jerusalem: Milah Press, 1996.

Czech, Danuta. *Auschwitz Chronicle: 1939–1945.* New York: Henry Holt, 1990.

Dallin, Alexander. *German Rule in Russia, 1941–1945: A Study of Occupation Policies.* New York: St. Martin's, 1957.

Davies, Norman. *Europe*. New York: Oxford University Press, 1997.

Dawidowicz, Lucy S. *The Holocaust and the Historians*. Cambridge, MA: Harvard University Press, 1981.

_____. *A Holocaust Reader*. New York: Behrman House, 1976.

_____. *The War Against the Jews: 1933–1945*. New York: Holt, Rinehart and Winston, 1975.

Dear, I.C.B., ed. *The Oxford Companion to World War II*. New York: Oxford University Press, 1995.

Dekel, Efraim. *Shai: The Exploits of Hagana Intelligence*. New York: Thomas Yoseloff, 1959.

Delbo, Charlotte. *Auschwitz and After*. New Haven, CT: Yale University Press, 1995.

Dinur, Benzion, and Shaul Esh, eds. *Yad Vashem Studies on the European Jewish Catastrophe and Resistance*. 4 vols. Jerusalem: Jerusalem Post Press, 1957–1960.

Dippel, John H. *Bound Upon a Wheel of Fire: Why So Many German Jews Made the Tragic Decision to Remain in Nazi Germany*. New York: Basic Books, 1996.

Distel, Barbara, and Ruth Jakusch, eds. *Concentration Camp Dachau: 1933–1945*. Munich: Comite International de Dachau, 1978.

Dobroszycki, Lucjan, ed. *The Chronicle of the Lodz Ghetto: 1941–1944*. New Haven, CT: Yale University Press, 1984.

_____, and Barbara Kirshenblatt-Gimblett. *Image Before My Eyes: A Photographic History of Jewish Life in Poland Before the Holocaust*. New York: Schocken Books, 1977.

Domarus, Max. *Hitler: Speeches and Proclamations, 1932–1945*. Wauconda, IL: Bolchazy-Carducci, 1990.

Dorian, Emil. *The Quality of Witness: A Romanian Diary, 1937–1944*. Philadelphia: Jewish Publication Society of America, 1982.

Dundes, Alan, ed. *The Blood Libel Legend: A Casebook in Anti-Semitic Folklore*. Madison, WI: University of Wisconsin Press, 1991.

Dwork, Debórah, and Robert Jan van Pelt. *Auschwitz: 1270 to the Present*. New York: W. W. Norton, 1996.

Dworzecki, Mark. *The Jewish Camps in Estonia*. Tel Aviv: I. L. Peretz, 1970.

Edelheit, Abraham J. *The Yishuv in the Shadow of the Holocaust: Zionist Politics and Rescue Aliya, 1933–1939*. New York: Westview Press, 1996.

Edelheit, Abraham J., and Hershel Edelheit. *History of the Holocaust: A Handbook and Dictionary*. Boulder, CO: Westview Press, 1994.

Eisenbach, Artur. *Operation Reinhard: Mass Extermination of the Jewish Population in Poland*. Poznan, Poland, 1962.

Epstein, Eric Joseph, and Phil Rosen. *Dictionary of the Holocaust*. Westport, CT: Greenwood Publishing Group, 1997.

Falconi, Carlo. *The Silence of Pius XII*. London: Faber & Faber, 1970.

Feig, Konnilyn. *Hitler's Death Camps: The Sanity of Madness*. New York: Holmes & Meier, 1983.

Fenelon, Fania. *Playing for Time: An Extraordinary Personal Account of the Women's Orchestra in Auschwitz*. New York: Atheneum, 1977.

Fest, Joachim C. *The Face of the Third Reich: Portraits of the Nazi Leadership*. New York: Pantheon, 1970.

_____. *Hitler*. New York: Harcourt Brace Jovanovich, 1974.

Flood, Charles Bracelen. *Hitler: The Path to Power*. Boston: Houghton Mifflin, 1989.

Fogelman, Eva. *Conscience and Courage: Rescuers of Jews During the Holocaust*. New York: Doubleday, 1994.

Frank, Anne. Otto H. Frank and Mirjam Pressler, eds. *The Diary of a Young Girl.* New York: Doubleday, 1995.

Frazier, Nancy. *Jewish Museums of North America.* New York: John Wiley & Sons, 1992.

Freier, Recha. *Let the Children Come: The Early History of Youth Aliyah.* London: 1961.

Friedlander, Henry. *The Origins of Nazi Genocide: From Euthanasia to the Final Solution.* Chapel Hill, NC: University of North Carolina Press, 1995.

Friedländer, Saul. *Nazi Germany and the Jews, Volume 1: The Years of Persecution, 1933–1939.* New York: HarperCollins, 1997.

Gager, John G. *The Origins of Anti-Semitism: Attitudes Toward Judaism in Pagan and Christian Antiquity.* New York: Oxford University Press, 1983.

Gilbert, Martin. *Atlas of the Holocaust.* New York: Morrow, 1993.

_____. *Final Journey.* New York: Mayflower Books, 1979.

_____. *The Holocaust: A History of the Jews of Europe During the Second World War.* New York: Henry Holt, 1985.

Goebbels, Joseph. Richard Barry, trans. *Final Entries, 1945: The Diaries of Joseph Goebbels.* New York: Putnam, 1978.

_____. Fred Taylor, trans. *The Goebbels Diaries, 1939–1941.* New York: Putnam, 1983.

_____. Louis P. Lochner, trans. *The Goebbels Diaries, 1942–43.* New York: Doubleday, 1948.

Goldhagen, Daniel Jonah. *Hitler's Willing Executioners.* New York: Knopf, 1996.

Goralski, Robert. *World War II Almanac: 1931–1945.* New York: Putnam, 1981.

Gordon, Harold J., Jr. *Hitler and the Beer Hall Putsch.* Princeton, NJ: Princeton University Press, 1972.

Gribetz, Judah, Edward L. Greenstein, and Regina S. Stein. *The Timetables of Jewish History.* New York: Simon & Schuster, 1993.

Grunbaum, Irene. *Escape Through the Balkans.* Lincoln, NE: University of Nebraska Press, 1996.

Grunberger, Richard. *The 12-Year Reich.* New York: Holt, Rinehart and Winston, 1971.

Grunfeld, Frederic V. *The Hitler File.* New York: Random House, 1974.

Gutman, Israel, ed. *Encyclopedia of the Holocaust.* New York: Macmillan, 1990.

_____. *Resistance: The Warsaw Ghetto Uprising.* Boston: Houghton Mifflin, 1994.

Gutman, Israel, and Michael Berenbaum. *Anatomy of the Auschwitz Death Camp.* Bloomington: Indiana University, 1994.

Hackett, David A., ed. *The Buchenwald Report.* Boulder, CO: Westview Press, 1995.

Hamerow, Theodore S. *On the Road to the Wolf's Lair: German Resistance to Hitler.* Cambridge, MA: The Belknap Press of Harvard University Press, 1997.

Handler, Andrew, ed. and trans. *The Holocaust in Hungary: An Anthology of Jewish Response.* Tuscaloosa, AL: University of Alabama Press, 1982.

Hart-Davis, Duff. *Hitler's Games: The 1936 Olympics.* New York: Harper & Row, 1986.

Hartmann, Erich. *In the Camps.* New York: W. W. Norton, 1995.

Hatzair, Hashomer. *The Massacre of European Jewry: An Anthology.* Israel: 1963.

_____. *Youth Amidst the Ruins: A Chronicle of Jewish Youth in the War.* New York: Scopus, 1941.

Hay, Peter. *Ordinary Heroes: The Life and Death of Chana Szenes, Israel's National Heroine.* New York: Paragon House, 1989.

Hayes, Paul M. *Quisling*. Bloomington, IN: Indiana University Press, 1972.

Hecht, Ingeborg. J. Maxwell Brownjohn, trans. *Invisible Walls: A German Family Under the Nuremberg Laws*. New York: Harcourt Brace Jovanovich, 1985.

Herzberg, Abel J. Joseph Santcross, trans. *Between Two Streams: A Diary from Bergen-Belsen*. London: I. B. Tauris, 1997.

Herzstein, Robert Edwin. *The War that Hitler Won: Goebbels and the Nazi Media Campaign*. New York: Paragon House, 1987.

Hilberg, Raul. *The Destruction of the European Jews*. New York: Holmes & Meier, 1985.

_____. *Documents of Destruction: Germany and Jewry 1933–1945*. Chicago: Quadrangle Books, 1971.

_____. *Perpetrators Victims Bystanders: The Jewish Catastrophe, 1933–1945*. New York: HarperCollins, 1992.

Hillel, Marc, and Clarissa Henry. *Of Pure Blood: Hitler's Eugenics Program*. New York: McGraw-Hill, 1976.

Hillesum, Etty. Arnold J. Pomerans, trans. *An Interrupted Life: The Diaries of Etty Hillesum 1941–1943*. New York: Pantheon, 1983.

_____. Arnold J. Pomerans, trans. *Letters from Westerbork*. New York: Pantheon, 1986.

Hilsenrad, Helen. *Brown Was the Danube: A Memoir of Hitler's Vienna*. New York: Thomas Yoseloff, 1966.

Hirschmann, Ira A. *Life Line to a Promised Land*. New York: Vanguard, 1946.

Hitler, Adolf. Salvatore Attanasio, trans. *Hitler's Secret Book*. New York: Grove Press, 1961.

_____. *Hitler's Secret Conversations, 1941–1944*. New York: Farrar, Strauss and Young, 1953.

_____. *Mein Kampf*. New York: Houghton Mifflin, 1971.

Holliday, Laurel, ed. *Children in the Holocaust and World War II*. New York: Washington Square Press, 1995.

The Holocaust. Jerusalem: Yad Vashem, 1977.

Hull, David Stewart. *Film in the Third Reich*. New York: Touchstone, 1973.

Jenks, William A. *Vienna and the Young Hitler*. New York: Columbia University Press, 1960.

Justman, Stuart, and Rebecca Shope. *The Jewish Holocaust for Beginners*. New York: Writers and Reading Publishing, 1995.

Kahane, David. *Lvov Ghetto Diary*. Amherst, MA: University of Massachusetts Press, 1990.

Kamenetsky, Christa. *Children's Literature in Hitler's Germany*. Athens, OH: Ohio University Press, 1984.

Kamenetsky, Ihor. *Secret Nazi Plans for Eastern Europe: A Study of Lebensraum Policies*. New Haven, CT: Yale University Press, 1961.

Kantor, Alfred. *The Book of Alfred Kantor: An Artist's Journal of the Holocaust*. London: Piatkus, 1987.

Katz, Jacob. *From Prejudice to Destruction: Anti-Semitism, 1700–1933*. Cambridge, MA: Harvard University Press, 1980.

Katz, Robert. *Death in Rome: The Ardeatine Caves Massacre in the Eternal City of Rome*. New York: Macmillan, 1967.

Keegan, John. *The First World War*. New York: Knopf, 1999.

_____. *The Second World War*. New York: Viking, 1990.

Kenrick, Donald, ed. *In the Shadow of the Swastika: The Gypsies During the Second World War*. Hertfordshire, England: University of Hertfordshire Press, 1999.

Kershaw, Ian. *Hitler, 1889–1936: Hubris*. New York: W. W. Norton, 1998.

Klarsfeld, Beate. *Wherever They May Be!* New York: Vanguard Press, 1975.

Klee, Ernst, and Willi Dressen and Volker Riess, eds. *"The Good Old Days": The Holocaust as Seen by Its Perpetrators and Bystanders.* New York: Konecky & Konecky, 1991.

Klemperer, Victor. *I Will Bear Witness.* New York: Random House, 1998.

Koehl, Robert L. *RKFVD: German Resettlement and Population Policy 1939–1945.* Cambridge, MA: Harvard University Press, 1957.

Koehn, Ilse. *Mischling, Second Degree: My Childhood in Nazi Germany.* New York: Greenwillow Books, 1977.

Kogon, Eugen. *The Theory and Practice of Hell.* New York: Farrar, Strauss & Co., 1949.

Krakowski, Shmuel. *The War of the Doomed: Jewish Armed Resistance in Poland, 1942–1944.* New York: Holmes & Meier, 1984.

Kreis, Ernst, and Hans Speier. *German Radio Propaganda: Report on Home Broadcasts During the War.* New York: Oxford University Press, 1946.

Kuznetsov, Anatoly. *Babi Yar: A Documentary Novel.* New York: Dial Press, 1967.

Landau, Ronnie S. *The Nazi Holocaust.* Chicago: Ivan R. Dee, 1994.

Langbein, Hermann. *Against All Hope: Resistance in Concentration Camps.* New York: Paragon House, 1994.

Langer, Lawrence L. *Holocaust Testimonies: The Ruins of Memory.* New Haven, CT: Yale University Press, 1991.

Langer, Walter C. *The Mind of Adolf Hitler: The Secret Wartime Report.* New York: Basic Books, 1972.

Laqueur, Walter, and Barry Rubin, eds. *The Israel-Arab Reader.* New York: Penguin Books, 1984.

Large, David Clay. *Where Ghosts Walked: Munich's Road to the Third Reich.* New York: W. W. Norton, 1997.

Latour, Anny. Irene R. Ilton, trans. *The Jewish Resistance in France, 1940–1944.* New York: Holocaust Library, 1981.

Lazare, Lucien. *Rescue as Resistance: How Jewish Organizations Fought the Holocaust in France.* New York: Columbia University Press, 1996.

Lemmons, Russel. *Goebbels and Der Angriff.* Lexington, KY: The University Press of Kentucky, 1994.

Levi, Primo. Raymond Rosenthal, trans. *The Drowned and the Saved.* New York: Vintage Books, 1988.

_____. Ruth Feldman, trans. *Moments of Reprieve: A Memoir of Auschwitz.* New York: Summit Books, 1985.

_____. *Survival in Auschwitz.* New York: Macmillan, 1961.

Levin, Dov. Moshe Kohn and Dina Cohen, trans. *Fighting Back: Lithuanian Jewry's Armed Resistance to the Nazis, 1941–1945.* New York: Holmes & Meier, 1985.

Levine, Hillel. *Economic Origins of Anti-Semitism: Poland and Its Jews in the Early Modern Period.* New Haven, CT: Yale University Press, 1991.

_____. *In Search of Sugihara: The Elusive Japanese Diplomat Who Risked His Life to Rescue 10,000 Jews from the Holocaust.* New York: The Free Press, 1996.

Lewin, Rhoda G., ed. *Witnesses to the Holocaust: An Oral History.* Boston: Twayne, 1990.

Lewisohn, Ludwig. *Theodor Herzl: A Portrait for This Age.* Cleveland: World Publishing, 1955.

Liddell Hart, B. H. *The German Generals Talk.* New York: Morrow, 1948.

Lifton, Robert J. *Nazi Doctors: Medical Killing and the Psychology of Genocide.* New York: Basic Books, 1988.

Lipstadt, Deborah E. *Denying the Holocaust: The Growing Assault on Truth.* New York: The Free Press, 1993.

Lord Russell of Liverpool. *The Scourge of the Swastika: A Short History of Nazi War Crimes.* London: Cassell & Co., 1954.

Lukacs, John. *The Hitler of History.* New York: Knopf, 1997.

Machlin, Edda Servi. *Child of the Ghetto: Coming of Age in Fascist Italy, 1926–1946, a Memoir.* Croton-on-Hudson, NY: Giro Press, 1995.

Manchester, William. *The Arms of Krupp.* Boston: Little, Brown & Co., 1968.

Manvell, Roger, and Heinrich Fraenkel. *Himmler.* New York: Putnam, 1965.

Marrus, Michael R., and Robert O. Paxton. *Vichy France and the Jews.* New York: Basic Books, 1981.

Marszalek, J. *Majdanek: The Concentration Camp in Lublin.* Warsaw: Interpress Warsaw, 1986.

Mayer, Milton. *They Thought They Were Free.* Chicago: University of Chicago Press, 1955.

Meltzer, Milton. *Never to Forget: The Jews of the Holocaust.* New York: HarperTrophy, 1976.

Metcalfe, Philip. *1933.* New York: Perennial Library, 1988.

Meyer, Peter. *The Jews in the Soviet Satellites.* Syracuse, NY: Syracuse University Press, 1953.

Michael, Robert A. *The Holocaust: A Chronology and Documentary.* Northvale, NJ: Jason Aronson, 1998.

Michel, Henri. *The Shadow War: European Resistance 1939–1945.* New York: Harper & Row, 1972.

Millay, Edna St. Vincent. *The Murder of Lidice.* New York: Harper & Brothers, 1942.

Mitscherlich, Alexander, and Fred Mielke. *Doctors of Infamy: The Story of the Nazi Medical Crimes.* New York: Henry Holt, 1949.

Morais, Vamberto. *A Short History of Anti-Semitism.* New York: W. W. Norton, 1976.

Morse, Arthur. *While Six Million Died: A Chronicle of American Apathy.* New York: Hart Publishing, 1968.

Mosley, Leonard. *The Reich Marshal: A Biography of Hermann Goering.* New York: Doubleday, 1974.

Mosse, George, ed. *Nazi Culture.* New York: Grossett & Dunlap, 1966.

Muller, Ingo. *Hitler's Justice: The Courts of the Third Reich.* Cambridge, MA: Harvard University Press, 1991.

Müller, Melissa. Rita and Robert Kimber, trans. *Anne Frank.* New York: Metropolitan Books, 1998.

Near, Henry. *The Kibbutz Movement: A History, 1939–1977.* Ilford, Essex, England: Littman Library of Jewish Civilization, 1997.

Nicholas, Lynn H. *The Rape of Europa: The Fate of Europe's Treasures in the Third Reich and the Second World War.* New York: Knopf, 1994.

Novick, Peter. *The Holocaust in American Life.* New York: Houghton Mifflin, 1999.

O'Neill, Robert J. *The German Army and the Nazi Party, 1933–1939.* New York: Heinemann, 1966.

Outze, Borg, ed. *Denmark During the Occupation.* Copenhagen: Scandinavian Publishing, 1946.

Owings, Alison. *Frauen: German Women Recall the Third Reich.* New Brunswick, NJ: Rutgers University Press, 1993.

Padfield, Peter. *Himmler.* New York: Henry Holt, 1990.

Pauley, Bruce F. *From Prejudice to Persecution: A History of Austrian Anti-Semitism.* Chapel Hill, NC: University of North Carolina Press, 1992.

Perechodnik, Calel. Frank Fox, trans. *Am I a Murderer?* Boulder, CO: Westview Press, 1996.

Pincus, Chasya. *Come from the Four Winds: The Story of Youth Aliya.* New York: Herzl Press, 1970.

Plant, Richard. *The Pink Triangle: The Nazi War Against Homosexuals.* New York: Henry Holt, 1986.

Poliakov, Leon. *Harvest of Hate: The Nazi Program for the Destruction of the Jews of Europe.* Syracuse, NY: Syracuse University Press, 1954.

Posner, Gerald L., and John Ware. *Mengele: The Complete Story.* New York: McGraw-Hill, 1986.

Presser, Jacob. Arnold Pomerans, trans. *Ashes in the Wind: The Destruction of Dutch Jewry.* Detroit: Wayne State University Press, 1998.

Price, Morgan. *Dispatches from the Weimar Republic: Versailles and German Fascism.* London: Pluto Press, 1999.

Pulzer, Peter G. J. *The Rise of Political Anti-Semitism in Germany and Austria.* New York: John Wiley & Sons, 1964.

Quinley, Harold E., and Charles Y. Glock. *Anti-Semitism in America.* New York: The Free Press, 1979.

Rapoport, Louis. *Stalin's War Against the Jews.* New York: The Free Press, 1990.

Rashke, Richard. *Escape from Sobibor.* Boston: Houghton Mifflin, 1982.

Read, Anthony, and David Fisher. *The Fall of Berlin.* New York: W. W. Norton, 1992.

————. *Kristallnacht: The Nazi Night of Terror.* New York: Random House, 1989.

Reichmann, Eva G. *Hostages of Civilization: The Social Sources of National Socialist Anti-Semitism.* Boston: The Beacon Press, 1951.

Reinartz, Dirk, and Christian Graf von Krockow. Ishbel Flett, trans. *Deathly Still: Pictures of Concentration Camps.* New York: Distributed Art Publishers/Scalo, 1995.

Reitlinger, Gerald. *The Final Solution: The Attempt to Exterminate the Jews of Europe, 1939–1945.* New York: Beechhurst Press, 1953.

————. *The SS: Alibi of a Nation, 1922–1945.* New York: Viking, 1956.

Remak, Joachim. *The Nazi Years.* New York: Touchstone, 1969.

Rentschler, Eric. *The Ministry of Illusion: Nazi Cinema and Its Afterlife.* Cambridge, MA: Harvard University Press, 1996.

Reuth, Ralf Georg. *Goebbels.* New York: Harcourt Brace & Co., 1990

Rhodes, Anthony. *Propaganda: The Art of Persuasion, World War II.* New York: Chelsea House, 1976.

Ringelblum, Emanuel. *Notes from the Warsaw Ghetto.* New York: McGraw-Hill, 1958.

Rittner, Carol, and John Roth. *Different Voices: Women and the Holocaust.* St. Paul: Paragon House, 1993.

Robinson, Jacob, and Henry Sachs. *The Holocaust: The Nuremberg Evidence.* Jerusalem: Yad Vashem/YIVO Institute for Jewish Research, 1976.

Rogow, Arnold A. *The Jew in a Gentile World.* New York: Macmillan, 1961.

Rosenbaum, Ron. *Explaining Hitler.* New York: Random House, 1998.

Rosenberg, Alfred. *Race and Race History and Other Essays.* New York: Harper & Row, 1974.

Rossel, Seymour. *The Holocaust: The World and the Jews, 1933–1945.* West Orange, NJ: Behrman House, 1992.

Rubenstein, Richard, and John Roth. *Approaches to Auschwitz: The Holocaust and Its Legacy.* Atlanta: John Knox Press, 1987.

Rudashevski, Yitzhok. *The Diary of the Vilna Ghetto: June 1941–April 1943.* Israel: Ghetto Fighters' House, 1972.

Sanders, Ronald. *Shores of Refuge: A Hundred Years of Jewish Emigration.* New York: Henry Holt, 1988.

Sax, Benjamin, and Dieter Kuntz. *Inside Hitler's Germany: A Documentary History of Life in the Third Reich.* Lexington, MA: D. C. Heath & Co., 1992.

Schechtman, Joseph. *The Mufti and the Fuehrer: The Story of the Grand Mufti of Jerusalem and*

His Unholy Alliance with Nazi Germany. New York: Thomas Yoseloff, 1965.

Schleunes, Karl A. *The Twisted Road to Auschwitz: Nazi Policy Toward German Jews 1933–1939.* Urbana, IL: University of Illinois Press, 1970.

Scholl, Inge. Arthur R. Schultz, trans. *White Rose Munich, 1942–1943.* Middletown, CT: Wesleyan University Press, 1970.

Schur, Maxine. *Hannah Szenes, Song of Light.* Philadelphia: Jewish Publications Society, 1986.

Schwarz, Solomon M. *The Jews in the Soviet Union.* Syracuse, NY: Syracuse University Press, 1951.

Segel, Binjamin W. *A Lie and a Libel: The History of the Protocols of the Elders of Zion.* Lincoln, NE: University of Nebraska Press, 1995.

Segev, Tom. *Soldiers of Evil.* New York: McGraw Hill, 1987.

Seiden, Othniel J. *The Survivor of Babi Yar.* Boulder CO: Stonehenge, 1980.

Senesh, Hannah. *Her Life and Diary.* New York: Schocken Books, 1973.

Sereny, Gita. *Albert Speer: His Battle with Truth.* New York: Knopf, 1995.

Sevillias, Errikos. *Athens-Auschwitz.* Athens: Lycabettus Press, 1983.

Shirer, William L. *Berlin Diary.* New York: Knopf, 1941.

_____. *The Rise and Fall of the Third Reich.* New York: Simon & Schuster, 1960.

Silver, Eric. *The Book of the Just: The Unsung Heroes Who Rescued Jews from Hitler.* New York: Grove Press, 1992.

Smith, Denis Mack. *Mussolini: A Biography.* New York: Knopf, 1982.

Smolar, Hersh. Max Rosenfeld, trans. *Minsk Ghetto: Soviet-Jewish Partisans Against the Nazis.* New York: Holocaust Library, 1989.

Snyder, Louis L. *Encyclopedia of the Third Reich.* New York: Paragon House, 1989.

Stein, George H. *The Waffen-SS: Hitler's Elite Guard at War, 1939–1945.* Ithaca, NY: Cornell University Press, 1966.

Steinberg, Lucien. *Jews Against Hitler.* New York: Gordon & Cremonesi, 1978.

Steiner, Jean-François. *Treblinka: The Extraordinary Story of Jewish Resistance in the Notorious Nazi Death Camp.* New York: MJF Books, 1967.

Steinhoff, Johannes, Peter Pechel, and Dennis Showalter, eds. *Voices from the Third Reich.* Washington, DC: Regnery Gateway, 1989.

Stolzfus, Nathan. *Resistance of the Heart: Intermarriage and the Rosenstrasse Protest in Nazi Germany.* New York: W. W. Norton, 1996.

Stroop, Jürgen. *The Stroop Report.* New York: Pantheon, 1979.

Suhl, Yuri. *They Fought Back.* New York: Crown, 1967.

Sutherland, Christine. *Monica: Heroine of the Danish Resistance.* New York: Farrar, Strauss & Giroux, 1990.

Svoray, Yaron, and Nick Taylor. *In Hitler's Shadow: An Israeli's Amazing Journey Inside Germany's Neo-Nazi Movement.* New York: Doubleday, 1994.

Sweets, John F. *Choices in Vichy: The French Under Nazi Occupation.* New York: Oxford University Press, 1986.

Swiebocka, Teresa, ed. Jonathan Weber and Connie Wilsack, trans. *Auschwitz: A History in Photographs.* Bloomington, IN: Indiana University Press, 1993.

Syrkin, Marie. *Blessed Is the Match: The Story of Jewish Resistance.* Philadelphia: Jewish Publications Society, 1947.

Taylor, James, and Warren Shaw. *Dictionary of the Third Reich.* New York: Penguin, 1997.

Taylor, Telford. *Sword and Swastika: The Wehrmacht in the Third Reich.* London: Gallancz, 1953.

Tec, Nechama. *Defiance: The Bielski Partisans.* New York: Oxford University Press, 1993.

Thomas, Gordon. *Voyage of the Damned.* New York: Stein and Day, 1974.

Tokayer, Marvin, and Mary Swartz. *The Fugu Plan: The Untold Story of the Japanese and the Jews During World War II.* New York: Paddington Press, 1979.

Toland, John. *Adolf Hitler.* New York: Doubleday, 1976.

Toll, Nelly. *When Memory Speaks: The Holocaust in Art.* Westport, CT: Praeger, 1998.

Tory, Avraham, and Martin Gilbert, eds. Jerry Michalowicz, trans. *Surviving the Holocaust: The Kovno Ghetto Diary.* Cambridge, MA: Harvard University Press, 1991.

Trunk, Isaiah. *Judenrat: The Jewish Councils in Eastern Europe Under Nazi Occupation.* New York: Macmillan, 1972.

Ungerer, Tomi. *Tomi: A Childhood Under the Nazis.* Niwot, CO: TomiCo, 1998.

United States Holocaust Memorial Museum. *Historical Atlas of the Holocaust.* New York: Macmillan, 1996.

Volavkova, Hana, ed. *I Never Saw Another Butterfly: Children's Drawings and Poems from Theresienstadt Concentration Camp, 1942.* New York: McGraw-Hill, 1964.

Warmbrunn, Werner. *The Dutch Under German Occupation: 1940–1945.* Stanford, CA: Stanford University Press, 1963.

Warren, Donald. *Radio Priest Charles Coughlin: The Father of Hate Radio.* New York: The Free Press, 1996.

Wasserstein, Bernard. *Britain and the Jews of Europe, 1939–1945.* New York: Oxford University Press, 1979.

_____. *Vanishing Diaspora: The Jews in Europe Since 1945.* London: Hamish Hamilton/Penguin, 1996.

Weinberg, Jeshajahu, and Rina Elieli, in collaboration with the United States Holocaust Memorial Museum. *The Holocaust Museum in Washington.* New York: Rizzoli, 1995.

Werner, Harold. *Fighting Back: A Memoir of Jewish Resistance in World War II.* New York: Columbia University Press, 1992.

Wiesel, Elie. *The Night Trilogy.* New York: Hill and Wang, 1987.

World Jewish Congress. *The Black Book: The Nazi Crime Against the Jewish People.* New York: Duell, Sloan & Pearce, 1946.

Wyden, Peter. *Stella.* New York: Simon & Schuster, 1992.

Wyman, David S. *The Abandonment of the Jews: America and the Holocaust, 1941–1945.* New York: Pantheon, 1985.

Wyman, Mark. *DPs: Europe's Displaced Persons, 1945–1951.* Ithaca, NY: Cornell University Press, 1998.

Yahil, Leni. Ina Friedman and Haya Galai, trans. *The Holocaust: The Fate of European Jewry.* New York: Oxford University Press, 1990.

_____. *The Rescue of Danish Jewry.* Philadelphia: Jewish Publication Society of America, 1969.

Young, Peter, ed. *The World Almanac Book of World War II.* London: World Almanac Publications, 1981.

Zimmerman, Moshe. *Wilhelm Marr: The Patriarch of Anti-Semitism.* New York: Oxford University Press, 1986.

Zuckerman, Yitzhak. *A Surplus of Memory: Chronicle of the Warsaw Ghetto Uprising.* Berkeley, CA: University of California Press, 1993.

Audio Lecture Series

Childers, Thomas. *The History of Hitler's Empire.* Springfield, VA: The Teaching Co., 1994.

INDEX

Page numbers in *italic* type indicate a photograph or other visual.

724

729

733

Italy (continued)
  surrender to Allies, 477
  surrender to Germany in
    Rhodes, 478
  treaty with Japan, 203
  United States declares war
    on, 287
  Vichy occupation by, 389
Iyyar 5, 655
Izbica Lubelska (Poland)
    Ghetto, 315
Izieu (France) Children's
    Home, 520–21, 557

J

Jackson, Robert H., 580, 634,
    636, *636*, 639, 649
Jacob, Max, 514
Jacob, Simone, 522
Jacobson, Leon, 191
Jadovno (Croatia) concentration
    camp, 224
Jaffa, Palestine, *104*, 104–105
Jäger, Karl, 236, *266*, 284–85,
    671
Jaktorów (Poland) slave-labor
    camp, 469
Jamaica, *400*
Jannina, Greece, 517
Janówska (Ukraine)
    concentration/labor camp,
    308, 335, 423, 459, 466,
    467–68, 469
  killings at, 332, 456
  liquidation of corpse-burning
    squad, 492
  murders near, 456, 474
  orchestra, *391*
  sexual abuse of women by SS,
    473, 474
  Sonderkommando revolt, 499
Japan, 189, 587
  Anti-Comintern Pact, 107–8
  bombing Pearl Harbor,
    212–13, 285, *289*
  China declares war on, 287
  immigration to, 193–94
  military agreement with
    Germany, 119
  relations with Germany, 113
  Soviets declare war on, 629
  surrender of, 630
  treaty with Germany and
    Italy, 203
  visas, 201
  war declared on, 286
Jasenovac (Croatia)
    concentration camp, *232*,
    257, *356*, 414, 609
Jawiszowice (Poland) slave-
    labor camp, 343, 351
Jaworów, Poland, 360, 443

Jaworzno, Poland, 459
Jebwabne, Lithuania, 246
Jeckeln, Friedrich, 259, 643
Jedrzejów, Poland, 367
Jehovah's Witnesses, 57, 171,
    188, 409, 511, 513, 569,
    581, 685, 695
Jerusalem, 18, 20, 31, 43, 44,
    46, 115, 282, 296–97, 417,
    450–51, 619, 648, 656, 657,
    659, 684, 685, 687, 696
  anti-Jewish riots in, 39
  attacks in, 46
  capture of, 21
  District Court trial, 674
  Holocaust survivors, 679
  immigration to, 193–94
  refugees in, *195*
  West German offer of
    reparations, 667
Jesuits, 112, 138
Jesus of Nazareth, 18, 19, 20,
    43, 45, 46, 101, 117, 125,
    260, 288. *See also* Christ
Jeunesse Nationale, 42–43
Jew
  beginnings of, 18
  defined, 55, 60
  "Jew and France, The," 260,
    263, *263*
Jewelry, 558, *616*
Jewish Advertiser, The, 298
Jewish Agency Executive,
    169–170, 571
Jewish Agency for Palestine,
    154, 396, 417, 484, *631*,
    632, 666, 690
Jewish Americans, 158
Jewish Anti-Defamation
    League, 34
Jewish Antifascist Committee,
    318, 335, 389, 551, 661
Jewish athletes, 97–99
Jewish Brigade, 366, *509*, 538,
    555, 560, 566, 570, 576, *576*
Jewish Bund, 327, 328
Jewish Center, 514
Jewish Christian, 20
Jewish-Christian marriages, 594
Jewish Chronicle, 687
Jewish Combat Organization, 297
Jewish combatants, 366
Jewish Congress, 665
Jewish Councils, 149, 171, 190,
    191, 216, *221*, 237, 241,
    244, 247, 253, 262, 263,
    282, 289, 295, 297, 301,
    319, 321, 328, 339, 341,
    346, 350, 352, 385, 415,
    423, 425
Jewish Cultural Association, 172
Jewish Cultural League, 164, *164*

Jewish Distribution Committee,
    517
Jewish District of Jerusalem
    bombing, *664*
Jewish Emigration Office, 155.
    See also Emigration
Jewish Fighting Organization.
    *See Żydowska Organizacja
    Bojowa*
Jewish Historical Documentation
    Center, 673, 674
Jewish holiday removal, 77
Jewish immigration, United
    States and, 188–89
Jewish intelligentsia, 438
Jewish Joint Distribution
    Committee, 131, 132
Jewish kings, 18
Jewish Labor Committee, 71,
    89, 113
Jewish Law (France), 197
Jewish merchants, 117, *120–21*
Jewish military organization,
    529
Jewish National Council, 662
Jewish Newsletter, 124
Jewish New Year, 267
Jewish Orthodox Hospital, 585
Jewish-Palestinian paratrooper,
    565, 570, 573
"Jewish Plot, The," 388
Jewish population, postwar,
    663
Jewish professionals boycott,
    61–62
Jewish Quarter, 24, 369, 406,
    455
"Jewish question." *See* "Final
    Solution"
*Jewish Question as a Racial,
    Moral and Cultural
    Problem, The*, 29, 115
Jewish Resistance, 114, 115,
    423, 438, 447, 529, 533,
    637. *See also* Partisans;
    Resistance
Jewish Review, 85
Jewish Ritual Murder, The, 454
Jewish Scriptures, 19
Jewish Self-Help Society, 394
Jewish Social Democrat Party,
    452
Jewish State, The, 31
Jewish State Theater, Moscow,
    661
"Jewish Statute" (France), 203,
    204, 205
Jewish underground, 263, 444
    657. *See also* Jewish
    Resistance; Resistance
Jewish War Veterans of
    America, 60, 114

Jewish Winter Aid, *124*
Jewish World Pest, The, 663
Jewish World Plague, The, 152
Jewry
  citizenship stripping of, 86
  determination of, 87
  German national organization
    of, 85
"Jewry in Music," 30
Jews
  annihilation of, 304
  arresting of, 129
  civil service and, 95
  German goods, services
    boycott by American,
    60–61, 68–69, 71, *71*
  hair color and, 83
  hiding, 486
  identity cards for, 131
  Karaite, 154
  killed by Nazis, 211, 437
  killed in World War II, 581
  legal system and, 101
  Nazi propaganda about, *316*
  Olympic games and, 97–98
  police surveillance of, 105
  Polish, 100, 202
  ration cards for, 167
Jews and Their Lies, The, 42
"Jews are our misfortune, The,"
    49
Jodl, Alfred, *239*, 579, 617, *617*,
    640, 651, 652
Johanngeorgenstadt (Germany)
    camp, 608
Johst, Hanns, 57
Joint Boycott Council, 89
Joint Distribution Committee,
    400, 648. *See also*
    American Jewish Joint
    Distribution Committee
Joint Emergency Committee
    for European Jewish
    Affairs, 380, 443, 436
Joint Rescue Committee, 417
Joly, Maurice, 27
Jordan, 662, 675
Jósefváros station, *571*
Josiah Wedgewood, *646*
Journal of Historical Review,
    678
Journalists, 67, 69, 70, 80
Journal for Racial Science, 89
Joyce, William, *364*
Jozefek, Kazimierz, 511
Józefów (Poland) labor camp,
    200, 334
Jud Süss, 202, 203, 670
Judaism, 21, 43, 60, 632, 687
  badge of, 177
  communism and, 152, *153*
  exodus and, 44

Morgenthau, Henry, 426–27, 501, 502–3, *508, 518*
Morocco, 203, 380, 391
Morrison, Herbert, 369
Mościcki, Ignacy, 109
Moscow, 166, 269, 280, 328
  Declaration, 495
  saved from occupation, 302
  Soviet Union
    counteroffensive, 285
  state of siege in, 274
  ultimatum to Lithuania from, 240
Moses, 18, 44, 60
Mosley, Sir Oswald, *88*, 89
Mossad, 649, 657
Moszkowicz, Daniel, 472, 473
Moulin, Jean, 557
Mount of Olives, Palestine, *372*
Mount Scopus, *657*
Mount Sinai, 44, 60
Movement of German Christian Believers, 56, 481
Moyne, Lord Walter, 526, 529, 545, 572
Mozhaisk, Russia, 302
Mueller, Otto, *542*
Mufti, 296
Mulhouse, France, liberated by Allied troops, 573
Müller, Heinrich, 123, 155, *181*, 294, 300, 303, 395, *395*, 612
Müller, Bishop Lüdwig, 64, 288
Münchener Neueste Nachrichten, 19, 26
Mundelein, Cardinal George, 145
Muni, Paul, 115–16, 434
Munich, Germany, 23, 32, 35, 284, 430, 627, 697
  attempt on Hitler's life in, 178
  agreement, 128
  art exhibits in, 113, 117
  Beer Hall *Putsch*, 23–24, 25, *25*, 36, 41–42, 81
  Brown House, *62*
  captured by Allies, 614
  Eternal Jew exhibition, 118, *119*
  Gestapo headquarters, 181
  Himmler and, 153
  Hofbräuhaus, 38
  maternity homes, 100
  police, 395
  police president of, 105
  synagogue burning, 129
Munich Conference/Treaty, 136–37, 139, 156, 503, 697
Munich Post, 25–26, 27
Munkàcs, Hungary, 524, 527, 569
Munkaszolgàlat, 159, 324

"Murder," 567
Murrow, Edward R., *503*, 603
Muslims, 44, 227, 228, 297, 365
Mussert, Anton, 396, *396, 613*, 623, 647
Mussolini, Benito, 26, 39, 79, 81, 109, *109*, 130, 188, *243*, 312, 467, *481, 540, 607*, 613
  Berlin-Rome Axis and, 107
  execution of, 612
  Munich Conference and, 136
Mustard gas, 34, 384
My Political Awakening, 37
Myslowice labor camp, 562
My Struggle, 24, 36, 42, 44
My Testament (Hitler's), *611*
Myth of the Twentieth Century, The, 34

N

Naarden, Netherlands, 88
Nabeal, Tunisia, *391*
Nachtigall battalion, 241
Nadich, Rabbi Judah, 630
Nahariya, Palestine, 637
Nakonieczmy, Jan, 461
Naliboki Forest, 404, 492, 517
Namerring, Germany, *612*
Nancy, France, liberated by Allies, 559
Napoleon, 26
Napoleon III, 27
Napy, Ukraine, 437
Naroch Forest, 487
Narodowa Demokracja, 32
Narva (Estonia) slave-labor camp, 553
Nashashibi, Fahhri al-, 365
Nasjonal Samling, 305
Nathanya, Palestine, 658
Nationaal-Socialistische Beweging der Nederlanden, 49, 195, 396, 613
National City Bank, 666, 693
National Democratic Party, 32, 131
National Law of Citizenship, 93
National Legionary government, 201
National Liberation Movement, 547
National Military Organization, 629, 648, 649, 658
National Party, 667
National People's Rally (France), 218
National Political Educational Institutes, 63
National Radical Camp, 78, 79
National Representation of Jews in Germany, 85–87

National Self-Defense, 108
National Socialism, 19, 25, 34, 47, 49, 50, 51, 682
  abolished, 633
  ideals of, 174
  Jewish emigration and, 121–22
  mission of, 115
National Socialist Front, 689
National Socialist German Physicians' League, 46
National Socialist German Workers' Party (NSDAP), 19, 27, *28*, 36, 37, 38–39, 56, 66, 101. *See also* Nazi Party; Nazis
National Socialist League, 364
National Socialist Movement, 195, 396, 629
National Socialist Party, 75, 76, 93, 114, 627. *See also* Nazi Party; Nazis
  Masons and, 118
  paraphernalia, *67*
  rally of 1937, 114
National Socialist Physicians' League, 514
National Socialist regime, *101*
National Socialist Women's Organization, 125
National Socialist Workers Party, 35, *35*
National Socialist Youth, *62*, 83
National Socialistike Ungdom, 83
National Socialists Schoolboys League, 102
National Union for Social Justice, 44
National Unity, 305
National Worker, 57
National-Socilistische Vrouwen Organisatie, 125
Nationalists (Spanish), 35, 109
Nationalpolitische Erziehungsanstalten, 6
Nationalsozialistische Deutsche Arbeiterpartei, 38
Naturalization papers, 237
Natzweiler (Germany) concentration camp, 229, 600
  camp personnel, 647
  subcamp, 592
Natzweiler-Struthof (France) camp, 386, *458*, 461, 477, 566, *576*
Naumann, Michael, 665, *667*
Nazareth, 115
Nazi Party, 48, 71, 673
  antisemitic propaganda, 40, 202
  Austrian, 139

cadet schools, 63
Chancellery, 219, 300, 640
Congress, Nuremberg, 83
Congress of 1934, 88
Day rally, *37*
dinner party and *Kristallnacht*, 144
early opposition to, 25
Foreign Section, 100
Germany as one, 71
Globocnik joins, 467
Globke and, 277
Goebbels in, 315
infighting, 302
Kube in, 273
launch of, 43
leader, 563
made only legal German party, 67
Mengele and, 111
newspaper, 143
Nuremberg rally, 47
physicians in, 225
Protestant reformer Martin Luther and, 42
rally, 118
rally of 1935, 85
rise of, 36
RuSHA and, *155*
slogan, 18
structure, 49
Stuckart in, 92
supporters, 37
Thierack in, 390
Treaty of Versailles and, *49*
war reparations and, 20
Nazis, 36
  agent, 158
  American support for, 79
  antisemitism, 54, 113, 123, 119
  apartments occupied by Jews and, 313–14
  Argentina, 686
  attempt to seize Austria, 82, 83
  auxiliary police and, 246
  Blood Witness Day, 141
  business boycott and, 55
  communism and, 212
  concordat and, 116
  Czechoslovakia, 154
  elimination of Polish intellectuals by, 195
  emigration and, 109
  entering Czechoslovakia, 159
  euphemisms, 215
  Europe's borders under, *359*
  execution reports, 263
  expansionist policies of, 90
  extermination industry of, 508

Picture credits:
Front cover: **Archive Photos**
AKG Photo, London: 58 (bottom right), 66 (center), 71 (bottom), 164 (top & left center), 461 (right center), 544 (center); **AP/Wide World Photos:** 18, 19 (top), 24 (bottom), 61 (center), 62 (left center), 65 (left & bottom), 82 (top), 90 (bottom), 92 (bottom), 95 (bottom), 100 (top left), 105 (right center), 106 (bottom), 112, 113 (top), 117 (bottom), 128 (top & left center), 138 (left center), 143 (bottom), 152 (top), 155 (top left), 156 (bottom right), 157 (top right), 158 (top left), 159 (top), 162 (center), 175 (top left), 178 (top), 187 (bottom), 194 (top), 197 (top left), 203 (top), 213 (bottom), 217 (left center), 223 (bottom), 225 (bottom), 237 (bottom), 258 (left center), 259 (bottom), 260 (right center), 264 (top left), 268 (top right), 289 (top right), 298 (left center), 305 (right center), 354 (center), 359 (center), 365 (right center), 373 (top right), 396 (left), 398 (left center), 430 (top), 437 (center), 440 (top right), 454 (right center), 460 (top left & top right), 466 (top), 477 (top left), 478 (right center), 481 (top), 488 (top left), 519 (right), 531 (top left), 554 (bottom), 595 (top right), 596 (top), 597, 599 (right), 601 (top & bottom), 610 (right), 615 (top left), 616 (bottom), 625 (bottom right), 628 (top), 629 (top), 642 (top), 651 (bottom), 652 (top), 676 (top), 697 (top); Richard Drew: 690 (top); Jockel Finck: 677 (center); **Archive of the State Security Office, Warsaw:** 648 (top left & top right); **Archive Photos:** 16, 28 (bottom), 30 (center), 43, 44 (top), 52–53, 56 (center), 62 (right center), 70 (left center), 102 (bottom left), 125 (right center), 130 (left center), 159 (right), 193 (top right), 205 (center), 231 (top right), 252 (top right), 270 (left center), 277 (bottom), 289 (top left), 315 (right), 364 (top right), 399 (right), 535 (bottom), 555 (left), 588 (top right), 593 (left & bottom), 595 (bottom right), 598 (top left), 599 (bottom left), 600 (left), 621 (top left), 647 (top), 651 (top), 652 (center), 658 (top), 668 (bottom), 669 (top left), 673 (top); American Stock Photos: 129 (right center); Archiv Cas Oorthuys: 267 (top); Leo Baeck Institute: 113 (bottom); Deutche Presse: 482 (bottom); Express Newspapers: 88 (bottom), 443 (left); Fotos International: 698 (bottom); Bernard Gotfryd: 627 (right); G.D. Hackett: 280 (top left), 399 (top), 433 (center), 445 (center); Herbert: 114 (bottom); Imperial War Museum: 207, 499 (top left & top right), 539 (top), 540 (top left), 615 (bottom left); *The New York Times*: 99 (bottom); Popperfoto: 101 (bottom left), 107 (bottom right), 109 (center), 127 (left center), 153 (right), 159 (bottom), 254, 649 (left center); Potter Collection: 84–85, 130 (right center); Franz Stangl: 670 (top); Tallandier/Archive France: 197 (center), 204 (left), 220 (top), 263 (top right), 648 (right center); Ricardo Watson: 658 (center); Reuters: Jochen Eckel: 667 (top); Leonhard Foeger: 688 (top); Jacqueline Godany: 693 (bottom); Paul Hanna: 669 (bottom right); Jim Hollander: 669 (top right); Pawel Kopczynski: 678 (top left); Reinhard Krause: 678 (top right), 686 (bottom); Mike Segar: 690 (bottom); Mike Theiler: 694 (top); **Bildarchiv Preussischer Kulturbesitz:** 39 (bottom), 51 (bottom), 135 (left center), 285 (bottom), 286 (center), 329 (left center), 345 (left center), 403 (left center), 408 (left), 415 (right), 418 (top right), 445 (top left & top right), 446, (449 (top right), 474 (center), 501, 506, 527 (top right), 536 (bottom right), 555 (bottom right), 558 (center), 567, 589 (top left), 614 (right), 633 (bottom left), 657, 682; Imperial War Museum: 443 (top); **Bilderdienst Süddeutscher Verlag:** 19 (bottom), 26 (top), 27, 30 (left & top right), 32, 35, 37 (top), 45, 48, 49, 80 (bottom right), 81 (bottom right), 83 (bottom right), 87 (bottom), 89 (top), 92 (top right), 101 (top & bottom right), 115 (bottom), 117 (top left), 118 (top right & bottom), 119 (top), 135 (right center), 142 (top), 145 (top), 155 (bottom), 156 (left), 193 (top left), 199 (top left), 209 (center & bottom), 220 (left center), 245 (top), 248 (top right), 253 (right center), 261 (top right), 273 (left center), 275 (left center), 279 (top right), 286 (top left), 291 (top left), 294, 300, 301 (top left), 302 (center), 303 (center), 312 (top left), 313 (center), 328 (bottom), 334 (top & right center), 335 (top right), 350 (top right & right center), 366 (left), 368, 378 (center), 386 (top), 393 (center), 412, 414 (top left), 421 (top & left center), 436 (center), 443 (right center), 451 (right), 452 (top), 457 (top), 458 (right center), 462, 479 (top & right center), 490 (right center), 496 (left), 497 (top & right center), 507 (top), 510 (top right), 514 (bottom), 521 (top), 530 (top left), 531 (top right & bottom), 538 (right), 540 (right), 541 (bottom left), 542 (bottom left), 551 (top left), 554 (top), 555 (top right), 563 (right), 564 (bottom), 570 (top right), 577 (top left & top right), 589 (bottom), 590 (left), 611 (right & bottom left), 612 (bottom), 613 (right), 614 (left), 652 (bottom), 661 (top), 664 (bottom), 672 (bottom), 689, 693 (top); imo: 667 (bottom); **Bundesarchiv:** 343 (right center), 383 (top right), 503 (top left); **Center for Historical Research and Documentation on War and Contemporary Society:** 356 (left center); **Philip Drell:** 26 (bottom), 70 (top left), 153 (center), 157 (bottom), 190 (right center), 198 (top right), 348 (right center), 375 (center), 388 (top), 410 (top left), 519 (top left), 602 (bottom left), 608 (top left & right), 609 (top right & bottom), 610 (bottom left), 627 (bottom left), 660 (bottom), 679 (top); **Drew University, Center for Holocaust Study:** 604 (top left), 605 (right), 612 (top), 615 (bottom right), 622, 632 (top), 636 (bottom right); **Gideon:** 389 (center), 426, 599 (top left); **Larry Glickman:** 681 (bottom); **Gerald Gustafson Photography:** 376 (top right), 398 (right center); 416 (top left); **Kadar Gyorgy/Vanderbilt University:** 512 (bottom), 547 (left); **Beth Hatefutsoth:** 115 (top), 143 (top right), 192 (top right), 195 (top), 203 (right center), 237 (top left), 263 (top left), 309 (top right), 314, 319 (top), 321 (top left), 324 (top right & right center), 336 (top right), 357 (right center), 392 (right), 393 (top right), 401 (top left), 402 (center), 433 (top right), 466 (center & bottom right), 474 (top right), 498 (center), 516 (bottom right), 645 (top), 656 (top), 661 (bottom), 683 (top), 684 (top); Moshe Baruch, Israel: 228 (top left); Leo Forbert: 225 (top); The Furst Family, Israel: 425 (top); Zvi Kadushin: 422 (right center); The Leibowitz Family: 229 (left center); Joseph Mayerovich, Kiev: 684 (bottom); David Petel, Tel Aviv: 356 (right center); **Hulton Getty Collection:** 25 (bottom), 229 (top), 253 (top), 301 (top right), 333 (top), 523 (left), 534 (top & right), 556 (top right & bottom), 560 (top right), 588 (top left), 603 (bottom left), 616 (top left & top right), 698 (top right); **Schaffer Gyula/ Hungarian National Museum Historical Photographic Archives:** 226 (top left); **Larry Kane:** 683 (bottom); **Netherlands Photo Archives:** 511 (bottom), 512 (top right); **Państwowe Muzeum Oświecim:** 186, 215 (bottom), 408 (top), 417 (center), 467 (center); **Leni Sonnenfeld:** 638–639, 654; **Ullstein Bilderdienst:** 20, 21, 23, 24 (top), 28 (top), 31, 33, 34, 37 (bottom), 42, 44 (bottom), 47, 50, 51 (top), 71 (left center), 154 (top), 181 (top left), 233 (top), 248 (top left), 272 (left center), 275 (right center), 301 (center), 302 (top left), 306 (left), 340 (center), 344 (top left), 409 (top), 419 (center), 420 (right center), 421 (right), 424 (top left), 428 (top left), 429 (top right), 444 (top left), 447 (top), 450 (center), 467 (top left), 481 (left center & right center), 515 (top right), 553 (top right), 574, 582 (top), 583 (top), 592 (left), 611 (top left), 659 (top), 670 (right center), 685 (bottom), 686 (top); **United States Holocaust Memorial Museum Photo Archives:** 64 (top & left center), 66 (top left), 67 (top), 70 (top right & right center), 76 (top right), 77 (bottom left), 79 (top), 81 (bottom left), 83 (bottom left), 91 (top left), 94 (top), 95 (top right), 100 (bottom), 107 (top), 114 (top right), 116 (bottom), 124 (left center & right center), 132 (right center), 133 (top right & bottom), 135 (top), 138 (right center), 139 (top right), 146 (top left), 147 (top right), 154 (right center), 160 (top right), 162 (top right), 165 (top left), 178 (right center), 181 (left center), 189 (right center), 191 (top right), 192 (top left center), 204 (top), 205 (top right), 217 (top & right center), 224 (top left), 229 (right center), 243 (top right), 270 (right center), 279 (top left), 287 (left center), 318 (top right), 326 (right center), 332 (right center), 335 (center), 370 (top), 372 (right center), 380 (left center), 385 (top right), 387 (left), 397 (top), 399 (center), 403 (right), 410 (top right), 415 (top & left center), 425 (left center), 438 (right center), 447 (left center), 453 (top), 455 (center), 460 (bottom), 473 (right), 475 (top right), 479 (left center), 484 (top), 494 (top right), 495 (top), 509 (right), 511 (top right), 519 (bottom left), 534 (bottom), 546 (right), 551 (bottom right), 552 (bottom center), 556 (top left), 605 (top left), 635 (top), 672 (top), 696 (bottom), 697 (bottom); Miru Alcana: 163 (center), 518 (top right); American Jewish Archives: 358 (left), 513 (top); American Jewish Historical Society: 514 (top); American Jewish Joint Distribution Committee: 8 (bottom), 116 (top), 145 (bottom), 167 (top right), 189 (bottom center), 204 (right), 243 (bottom), 252 (left center), 400 (top), 517 (top right), 520 (top), 625 (top right), 641 (bottom), 645 (center), 646 (top), 648 (left center); AP/Wide World Photos: 122, 166 (top right), 442 (center), 502 (top right), 503 (left center), 557 (top right), 580, 591 (right), 634, 647 (right center), 653 (top), 694 (bottom); Archives of Mechanical Documentation: 104 (bottom), 222 (left center), 239 (top left), 240 (top right), 318 (bottom right); Archives Nationales de la Grand-Duche de Luxembourg: 480 (center); Archiwum Akt Nowych [Former Communist Party Archives]: 175 (center), 230 (top right), 296 (center), 321 (left center), 345 (top), 450 (top right); Arhiv Jugoslavije: 351 (top right); Frida Aronson: 413 (top); Raphael Aronson: 108 (top left), 386 (bottom); Maria Austria Institute: 548 (top right & bottom), 549 (bottom); Lisa Freund Avedon: 109 (top left); Babi Yar Society, Kiev: 271 (center), 309 (top left); Bayerische Motoren Werke: 410 (center); Bayerische Staatsbibliothek: 57; Belgium Radio and TV: 228 (top right), 355 (top); Berlin Document Center: 193 (center), 225 (left center), 266 (top right), 272 (right center), 273 (top), 374 (left), 397 (right center), 400 (right center), 520 (bottom right); Bibliothèque Historique de la Ville de Paris: 158 (top right), 161 (center & top right), 179 (top right), 195 (left center), 347 (top right), 420 (left center); Bibliothèque Nationale: 147 (top left); 261 (center); Bildarchiv Abraham Pisarek: 87 (top), 104 (top left), 105 (left center), 124 (top), 130 (top), 134 (top), 143 (top left), 172 (bottom); Bildarchiv Preussischer Kulturbesitz: 54, 59 (top), 60 (top), 61 (top right), 67 (right center), 68 (bottom), 74, 78 (top right), 117 (top right), 119 (right), 144, 146 (right), 148–149, 157 (top left), 165 (bottom left & right center), 176 (center), 180 (left center & right center), 183 (top right), 189 (top left), 190 (top right), 216 (top), 220 (right center), 221 (top left), 238 (center), 255 (top right), 258 (top), 265 (bottom), 265 (left center), 283 (top left), 284 (top right), 292–293, 323, 341 (top left), 360 (top left), 379 (top), 409 (center), 440 (top left), 449 (top left), 452 (left center), 471 (bottom); Bilderdienst Süddeutscher Verlag: 367 (right center), 395 (right), 418 (left), 617 (bottom left), 641 (top), 691 (bottom); Rachel Birenbaum: 325 (center), Gay Block and Malka Drucker: 329 (top), 491 (center); Karl Bonhoeffer-Nervenklinik: 76 (top left), 91 (bottom), 169; Bnai Brith: 307 (center); Thea Boruzk Slawner: 291 (center); Yelena Brusilovsky: 271 (top left & top right); Bundesarchiv: 25 (top), 40 (bottom), 59 (bottom), 61 (top left), 75 (top), 77, 79 (bottom right), 80 (bottom left), 82 (bottom left), 91 (top right), 103 (center), 106 (top right), 126 (right center), 128 (right center), 182 (top left), 196 (top left), 198 (center), 201 (left center), 203 (left center), 206 (center), 216 (left center), 221 (center), 242 (left center), 245 (bottom), 253 (left center), 260 (top), 261 (top left), 262 (right center), 289 (bottom), 343 (left center), 416 (top right), 434 (left center), 436 (top), 541 (top), 542 (top & right), 544 (bottom), 452 (right center), 464 (top right), 493 (top), 569 (bottom), 582 (bottom right), 587 (bottom left), 588 (bottom), 660 (top); Bundesarchiv/Allgemeiner Deutscher Nachrichtendienst Bildarchiv: 226 (center); Bundesarchiv Schweizerisches: 250 (left center); Marion I. Cassirer: 560 (left); Central State Archive of Film, Photo and Phonographic Documents: 263 (left center), 328 (top), 487 (top); Central Zionist Archives: 154 (left center), 160 (top left), 178 (left center), 208 (top), 338 (left center), 359 (left), 365 (top right), 372 (top), 375 (top left & top right), 411 (bottom), 431 (bottom), 459 (left), 475 (center), 498 (top right), 509 (top left), 570 (bottom), 576 (bottom right), 619 (left), 624 (left), 626 (top left), 631 (bottom), 662 (left center), 665 (bottom), 666, 674, 695; Centre de Documentation Juive Contemporaine: 195 (right center); Lydia Chagoll: 206 (top right), 282 (top), 319 (left & right center), 337 (left center), 361, 365 (top left), 390 (bottom right), 486 (top), 537 (top right), 624 (top right); Joseph Chwedyk: 379 (bottom); Comité International de la Croix Rouge: 402 (top), 456 (left center), 536 (top right & left); Syma Crane: 425 (right); Czechoslovak News Agency: 139 (left center), 140 (top), 179 (center), 307 (top right), 330 (right center), 331, 332 (top & left center), 333 (left), 346 (top), 508 (top left), 512 (top left), 582 (left), 624 (bottom right); Czestochowa Public Library: 369 (top left); Ada Dekhtyar: 210–211; Fred Diament: 626 (top right); District Museum of Radom: 227 (center); Documentary Film Archives: 401 (top right), 585 (bottom right); Dokumentationsarchiv des Österreichischen Widerstandes: 29, 126 (left center), 127 (top & right center), 142 (right center), 205 (top left), 246 (top left), 266 (bottom right), 276 (right center), 280 (center), 338 (right center), 357 (left), 369 (top right), 418 (bottom right), 466 (bottom left), 625 (left); Marvin Dorf: 596 (bottom right); Frania Dunska Friedman: 200 (top); ECPA Photo Cinema Video: 262 (top right), 592 (bottom); Ellen W. Echeverria: 533 (top left); Joost Elffers: 349 (top left); Erzbischofliches Ordinat Pressastelle: 274 (top); Lena Fagen: 174 (left), 518 (top left); Federation Nationale des Deportes et Internes Resistants: 230 (center), 395 (left), 453 (bottom); Peter Feigl: 510 (left); Benjamin Ferencz: 262 (left), 691 (top); Caroline Fierst: 137 (top); Fondazione Centro Di Documentatzione Ebraica Contemporranea: 628 (left); 491 (top left & top right); Spaarnestad Fotoarchief: 78 (bottom); FPG International: 146 (bottom left), 233 (bottom left), 240 (center), 382 (right center), 637 (bottom right), 640, 643 (left center); Anne Frank Stichting: 76, 335 (top left), 548 (left), 549 (top left); Richard Freimark: 8 (top), 38, 72–73, 83 (top), 109 (top right), 499 (center); Frihedsmuseet: 282 (left),

488 (top right & center), 489; Annette Fry: 388 (left center); William Gallagher: 102 (top), 139 (top left), 239 (top right), 390 (left); Gedenkstaette Bergen-Belsen: 642 (left center), 659 (bottom); Bernard Geron: 455 (top left); Jacquelyn Gervay: 522 (top left); Max-Planck Gesellschaft: 225 (right center); Ghetto Fighters' House: 209 (top), 346 (right center), 350 (top left), 363 (top right), 364 (center), 409 (left), 414 (center), 550 (top); Trudi Gidan: 455 (top right), 515 (bottom); Louis Gonda: 448 (top); Government Press Office, Lishkat Ha-Itonut: 529 (right), 662 (right center), 675, 698 (top left); Paul Grisso: 532 (top right); Dr. Charles Grosso: 177 (right); Ruth Gruber: 552 (top & bottom left), 656 (bottom); Irene Guttmann Slotkin Hizme: 467 (top right); Lutz Haase: 216 (right center); Beth Hatefutsoth: 391 (left), 530 (bottom), 566 (bottom left), 644 (right center); Hebrew Immigrant Aid Society: 662 (top); Anna and Joshua Heilman: 568 (top); Hessisches Hauptstaatsarchiv: 208 (center), 270 (top right), 272 (top), 278 (top & bottom); Norges Hjemmefrontmuseum: 385 (top left); Historical Museum of Rzeszów: 40 (top), 41, 78 (top left); Hoover Institution: 93 (bottom right), 201 (top), 509 (bottom left); Hoover Institution/American Jewish Joint Distribution Committee: 131 (center); Howard University/Art Carter Collection: 106 (top left); David S. Hull, *Film in the Third Reich: A Study of the German Cinema, 1933–1945*. University of California Press, 1969: 202 (top right); Hulton Picture Company: 58 (bottom left); Hungarian National Museum Historical Photographic Archives: 248 (center), 569 (top); Jacob Igra: 174 (top); Rafal Imbro: 297 (top & left center); Imperial War Museum: 56 (top right), 82 (bottom right), 238 (top right), 576 (left), 600 (bottom right), 606 (top), 615 (top right), 627 (top left), 632 (bottom right); International News Photo: 163 (top right); Israel Defense Forces Archives: 637 (bottom left), 646 (left center); Jewish Historical Institute: 450 (top left); Jewish Historical Museum, Yugoslavia: 226 (top right), 231 (top left), 232 (top left), 242 (right center), 283 (center), 476 (top); Jewish Museum of the Dohany Synagogue: 569 (left); Jewish State Museum, Lithuania: 257 (right center), 295 (bottom), 371 (top right); Jewish War Veterans of the United States of America, Inc.: 114 (top left), 152 (center), 153 (top), 156 (top right); Jüedisches Museum: 191 (center), 237 (center), 276 (top), 341 (top right); KZ Gedenkstatte Dachau: 513 (bottom left); KZ Gedenkstatte Neuengamme: 136 (top left), 141 (bottom), 188 (top right), 502 (right center); George Kadish: 241 (top), 273 (right center), 274 (center), 559 (right), 643 (top); Moshe Kaganovich: 404–405, 422 (left); Henny Kalkstein Reemy: 486 (left center); Jan Karski: 389 (right); Ferenc Katona: 522 (bottom); Nettie Stub Katz: 141 (top); Keren Kayemet Archives: 160 (center), 170 (top left), 619 (bottom); Aviva Kempner: 633 (right), 644 (top); Keystone: 530 (top right); Morris Kiel: 162 (left); Serge Klarsfeld: 337 (right center), 373 (top left), 394 (left), 483 (left); Julie Klein: 161 (top left); Roland Klemig: 93 (bottom left), 107 (bottom left), 315 (top left & left center), 316, 387 (right center), 390 (top right); Marion Koch: 607 (bottom); Ruth Kohn: 132 (top); Sylvia Kramarski Kolski: 471 (top); Nancy & Michael Krzyzanowski: 591 (left), 598 (bottom); Lena Kurtz Deutsch: 557 (left); Judiska Kvinnoklubben: 602 (top left); La Documentation Française: 327 (left center), 371 (top left), 398 (top); Margaret Lambert: 98; Sara Lamhaut Boucart: 508 (top right); Landesbildstelle, Berlin: 77 (top), 94 (bottom); William Landgren: 608 (bottom); Tamy Lavee: 427 (bottom); Jack Lennard Archive: 472 (top); Samson Lerner: 483 (right); Alice Lev: 581 (bottom), 630, 631 (left), 632 (bottom left), 649 (top); Jacqueline Levy: 320 (top right); Library of Congress: 39 (top), 71 (right center), 89 (bottom left & bottom right), 268 (top left); Life Picture Service: 176 (top left), 181 (top right), 219 (center); Josef Lipnicki: 642 (right center); P. Liveright: 595 (top left); Joan Liwer Wren: 202 (top left), 242 (top); Joseph Maier: 644 (left); Main Commission for the Investigation of Nazi War Crimes in Poland: 125 (top), 150, 166 (left), 170 (bottom), 171 (top), 173 (top left), 180 (top left & top right), 183 (top left & center), 184–185, 194 (right center), 222 (top), 224 (center), 230 (top right), 238 (top left), 244 (top & bottom right), 264 (bottom right), 268 (bottom), 285 (top), 287 (top), 308 (top & center), 311 (center), 325 (top left), 327 (right center), 336 (center), 339 (top left), 340 (right), 343 (top), 351 (top left), 354 (bottom), 358 (top), 360 (top right), 364 (top left), 374 (top), 376 (center), 378 (top), 381 (top & right), 382 (left center), 383 (top left), 387 (top right), 423 (top left), 434 (top), 435 (left center), 438 (top & left center), 448 (center), 451 (top & left center), 458 (left), 459 (top right), 461 (top), 464 (center), 465 (left center), 504–505, 538 (bottom left), 545 (left & bottom right), 557 (bottom right), 618 (left), 621 (bottom left); Wilfred McCarty: 623 (bottom); William O. McWorkman: 62 (top), 93 (top), 103 (top left), 288; Benjamin Meed: 297 (right center), 312 (top right & center), 423 (top right), 486 (right center); Memoire Juive de Paris: 342 (top), 507 (bottom); Flora Mendelowitz Singer: 355 (left center); Oscar Mendelsohn: 392 (left); Hanna Meyer-Moses: 484 (bottom); Ministere des Affaires Etrangeres: 619 (top right); Ministere des Anciens Combattants: 458 (top right), 510 (bottom right), 606 (bottom); Moreshet Archives: 646 (right center); Frank Morgens: 232 (top right); John W. Mosenthal: 636 (left); Al Moss: 362 (top); Sharon Muller: 283 (top right); Musee de la Resistance Nationale: 477 (top right), 573 (top left), 607 (left); Museum of the History of Photography: 459 (right center); Museum of Jewish Community of Bucharest: 233 (bottom right); Museum of Jewish Heritage/Center for Holocaust Studies: 490 (top right), 561 (top left); Museum of Modern Art, New York: 200 (left center); Museum of the Polish Army: 170 (top right); Muzej Revolucije Narodnosti Jugoslavije: 224 (top right), 232 (center), 257 (left center), 264 (top right), 267 (bottom), 311 (top), 428 (center); Muzeum Stutthof: 174 (center), 621 (top right); National Archives: 54, 55, 58 (top left), 63, 68 (top), 75 (bottom), 80 (top), 90 (top left), 94 (left), 99 (top), 102 (bottom right), 126 (top), 132 (left center), 134 (left center), 136 (top right), 151 (top), 152 (left center), 163 (top left), 167 (bottom), 171 (center), 187 (top), 198 (top left), 200 (right center), 201 (right center), 237 (top right), 247 (top & left center), 250 (right center), 286 (top right), 307 (top left), 317 (center), 341 (center), 349 (top right & center), 360 (center), 377 (left center), 380 (top), 391 (right), 406, 442 (top), 447 (right center), 449 (center), 454 (top), 477 (center), 508 (bottom), 533 (right & bottom left), 550 (left), 563 (top left), 566 (right), 573 (top right), 575 (top & bottom), 576 (top), 587 (top right), 590 (bottom right), 592 (top), 593 (top right), 595 (bottom left), 602 (right), 603 (top left), 604 (right), 610 (top left), 613 (top left), 617 (right), 618 (bottom right), 633 (top left), 635 (right & bottom left), 636 (top right), 637 (top), 650 (left), 653 (bottom), 668 (top), 692; National Archives, Kraków: 222 (right center), 327 (top); National Museum of American Jewish History: 134 (right center), 377 (right center); Nationale Mahn- und Gedenkstatte Buchenwald: 487 (bottom); New York Public Library: 123 (top); *The New York Times*: 105 (top), 136 (bottom), 166 (bottom right), 182 (right center), 217 (bottom); Novosty Press: 212, 291 (top right), 517 (top left), 629 (bottom left); Oesterreichische Gesellschaft fur Zeitgeschichte: 142 (left center); Organization of Jews in Bulgaria: 214 (top left & center), 430 (left), 435 (top), Orzagos Szechenyi Konyvtar, Budapest: 131 (top right), 478 (top); Leopold Page Photographic Collection: 465 (top), 470, 565, 679 (bottom), 685 (top); Shlomo Perel: 427 (top); Malie Perez: 432; Prof. Leopold Pfefferberg-Page: 231 (center), 303 (top right), 352 (right center); Julia Pirotte: 647 (left center); Helen Preiss: 266 (top left); Pretenkabinet-Rijksuniversiteit te Leiden: 463 (left center); Mahn und Gedenkstatte Ravensbrück: 562 (center); *The Record: News Bulletin*. United Romanian Jews of America, June 1942.: 337 (top); Rijksinstituut voor Oorlogsdocumentatie: 118 (top left), 120–121, 129 (left center), 137 (bottom), 179 (top left), 214 (top right), 218 (top left), 269, 313 (top right), 317 (top left), 325 (top right), 347 (center), 413 (bottom), 463 (top), 541 (bottom right), 561 (bottom right), 604 (bottom left), 670 (left center); Romania Library of the Academy: 243 (top left), 260 (left center); Franklin D. Roosevelt Library: 496 (right), 518 (bottom left); Morris Rosen: 123 (bottom); Albert Rosenthal: 528 (top); Janka Rosenzweig: 223 (top); Barbara Roth: 596 (left); Richard A. Ruppert: 497 (left center); Sächsische Landesbibliothek: 277 (top); Norman & Amalia Petranker Salsitz: 58 (top right), 303 (top left), 372 (left center); Susan Schaffer: 643 (right); Rafael Scharf: 234, 235, 256 (top left); Joanne Schartow: 36, 79 (bottom left); Julius Schatz: 431 (top); Lorenz Schmuhl: 110–111, 116 (bottom left), 119 (center); Victor Schnell: 511 (top left); Samuel Schryver: 257 (top), 296 (top left); Gunther Schwarberg: 573 (bottom); Schwules Museum: 66 (top right); Yoseph Schyveschuurder: 444 (top right); Arnold Shay: 202 (center), 353, 469 (top); Ruth Sherman: 218 (top right); Jack Shipper: 583 (bottom left); Sovfoto: 240 (top left), 407 (bottom), 494 (top left); Ita Spiller: 330 (top left); Stadtarchiv Bielefeld: 95 (top left); Stadtarchiv Hof: 133 (top left); Stadtarchiv Nuernberg: 92 (top left), 151 (bottom), 168 (bottom), 299 (top); Stadtarchiv Ulm: 429 (top left); State Archives of the Russian Federation: 239 (center), 251 (top & left center), 252 (right center), 320 (center), 329 (right center), 424 (top right), 437 (top right), 544 (top), 585 (top left), 621 (bottom right); State Museum of Auschwitz-Birkenau: 171 (bottom), 188 (top left), 227 (top right), 342 (center), 397 (left center), 420 (top), 422 (top), 444 (center), 500 (right), 546 (bottom), 553 (left & bottom right), 584 (bottom), 671, 680 (top); Hans Steinitz: 155 (top right); David Stoliar: 304 (top & left center); Dana Szeflan: 681 (top); Terezin Memorial Museum: 282 (right center), 376 (top left), 419 (top left & top right), 495 (bottom left), 543 (bottom), 620 (top & bottom); Jerzy Tomaszewski: 88 (top right), 168 (top left), 175 (top right), 177 (top), 218 (center), 304 (right center), 345 (right center), 382 (top), 502 (left); Avraham Tory: 241 (bottom); Harry S. Truman Library: 650 (top right); Sophie Turner-Zaretsky: 440 (center), 469 (center); Ullstein Bilderdienst: 351 (center); University of Minnesota Libraries: 430 (right center); University of New Hampshire: 383 (center); University of Southern California: 338 (top), 503 (top right); UPI/Corbis: 22; Yad Vashem Photo Archives: 9 (top), 140 (bottom), 167 (top left), 173 (bottom), 194 (left center), 196 (center), 215 (top), 219 (top left), 228 (center), 245 (center), 246 (center), 247 (right center), 276 (left center), 280 (top right), 284 (top left), 322, 326 (top), 330 (top right), 333 (right center), 334 (left center), 339 (top right & center), 346 (left center), 348 (left center), 352 (top right), 358 (right center), 362 (center), 377 (top), 388 (right), 393 (top left), 396 (right center), 407 (top), 414 (top right), 437 (top left), 472 (right center), 475 (top left), 482 (top), 485 (top left), 487 (right), 490 (left), 494 (center), 500 (left), 513 (right), 520 (left), 521 (bottom), 524 (bottom), 525, 526, 527 (top left & bottom), 528 (bottom), 546 (top left), 551 (bottom left), 568 (left & bottom right), 571 (top left), 572 (top right), 583 (right), 628 (bottom), 673 (bottom), 696 (top); Thomas Veres: 570 (left), 571 (right & bottom), 688 (bottom); Verzetsmuseum Amsterdam: 441 (top left & center), 613 (bottom left); Dr. Robert G. Waite: 581 (top); Wiener Library: 46, 86, 88 (top left), 190 (left center), 336 (top left), 538 (top), 677 (top); Wiener/Bundesarchiv/Yad Vashem Photo: 119 (left center); Archives: R. Wirth: 586, 590 (top right); Max Wischkin: 492; World Jewish Congress: 498 (top left); YIVO Institute for Jewish Research: 69 (top), 71 (top), 108 (top right), 129 (top), 168 (top right), 173 (top right), 176 (top right), 191 (top left), 196 (top right), 213 (top), 219 (top right), 246 (top right), 281, 298 (top), 299 (left center & right center), 305 (left center), 306 (right center), 313 (top left), 320 (top left), 326 (left center), 344 (top right), 348 (top), 357 (top), 363 (right center), 367 (top), 385 (center), 401 (center), 403 (top), 417 (top left), 423 (center), 424 (center), 433 (top left), 439 (top), 456 (top & right center), 461 (left center), 473 (left center), 478 (left center), 480 (left); Roger Et Viollet: 164 (right center), 284 (center); Zbiór Fotografii: 295 (top), 532 (left); Zentrale Stelle der Landesjustizverwaltungen: 256 (top right), 279 (left center); Zentrales Partei Archiv: 259 (top); Eliezer Zilberis: 503 (right center); Nachman Zonabend: 296 (top right), 363 (left); Zydowski Instytut Historyczny Instytut Naukowo-Badawczy: 408 (center); **UPI/Corbis:** 9 (bottom), 56 (top left), 59 (center), 60 (bottom), 64 (right center), 65 (top), 67 (left center), 81 (top), 90 (top right), 96–97, 100 (top right), 103 (top right), 104 (top right), 131 (top left), 138 (top), 147 (center), 158 (bottom), 172 (top), 177 (bottom), 197 (top right), 309 (center), 344 (center), 381 (left), 396 (top right), 428 (top right), 434 (right center), 515 (top left), 523 (top right), 532 (bottom), 543 (top & center), 559 (bottom left), 560 (bottom right), 561 (bottom left), 566 (top left), 572 (top left & bottom center), 577 (bottom), 584 (top), 587 (top), 594 (bottom), 600 (top right), 603 (right), 605 (bottom), 609 (top left), 618 (top right), 623 (top left), 626 (bottom), 629 (bottom right), 664 (top), 665 (top); Reuters: 676 (bottom); **U.S. Army/National Archives:** 578–579; **U.S. Army Signal Corps:** 594 (top), 598 (top right), 617 (top left); **Ed Vebell:** 650 (right center); **Yad Vashem Photo Archives:** 221 (top right), 236, 244 (bottom left), 249 (top left & top right), 251 (right center), 255 (top left, center & bottom), 256 (center), 277 (center), 287 (right center), 289 (center), 290, 302 (top right), 305 (top), 310, 317 (top right), 318 (left), 321 (top right), 340 (top), 352 (left), 354 (top), 355 (right center), 356 (top), 366 (bottom right), 367 (left center), 369 (center), 370 (center), 373 (center), 374 (center), 380 (right center), 384, 389 (top), 400 (left center), 402 (left center), 417 (top right), 435 (right), 439 (center), 441 (top right), 454 (left center), 457 (left center & right center), 463 (right), 464 (top left), 465 (right), 468, 472 (left center), 473 (top), 474 (top left), 476 (bottom), 480 (top), 485 (center & top right), 493 (bottom), 495 (right), 516 (top right & left), 524 (top left & top right), 529 (top & bottom left), 537 (left & bottom), 547 (right), 550 (bottom right), 559 (top left), 563 (bottom left), 564 (top), 585 (top right), 587 (bottom right), 601 (right), 607 (top right), 631 (top), 649 (right center), 680 (bottom); Dokumentationsarchiv Des Osterreichische: 249 (bottom); BeitLohamei Haghetast: 347 (top left), Sifriat Hapoalim: 324 (left), 366 (top right), 394 (right); Spielberg Archive: 306 (top); **André Zucca/Bibliothèque Historique de la Ville de Paris:** 411 (top), 416 (center), 517 (bottom left), 523 (bottom right).

EXPLORE THE HOLOCAUST CHRONICLE WEB SITE

For regularly updated Holocaust-related information, and for those times when you are without your copy of *The Holocaust Chronicle*, log on to *The Holocaust Chronicle* Web site at **www.holocaustchronicle.org**.

Like the book, *The Holocaust Chronicle* Web site is ideal for use by schools and universities, students, teachers, researchers, synagogues and churches, and organizations. The site will have special value to people with personal links to the Holocaust, students of Judaism and Jewish history, and anyone anxious to learn about the Holocaust, its prelude, and its aftermath.

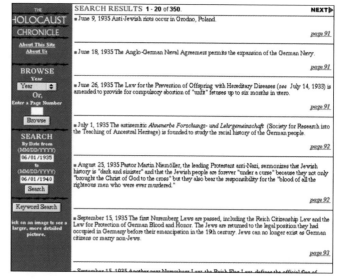

More than 100 major click-on topics—ranging from PALESTINE to POLAND, THE NAZI PARTY to JEWISH LEADERS—give the site visitor instant access to major themes. Handy pull-down menus with hundreds of subtopics key in on specific events, places, people, and issues.

Date-specific timeline events are located by typing in a span of dates; the search function will bring up all events that fall between those dates. These searches take the user to a remarkable timeline of Holocaust-related events that is unmatched in Holocaust scholarship, encompassing more than 5000 events from 1500 B.C.E. to the 21st century.

A scroll-through feature allows site visitors to read and study *The Holocaust Chronicle* page by page. The Web site contains every word of the book's text, plus a generous selection of images taken from the more than 2000 photographs and other visuals that are highlights of the book.

Because Holocaust-related developments cross international news wires almost daily, *The Holocaust Chronicle* timeline will be regularly updated. Log on often to keep track of the latest Holocaust news stories.

Whether for quick reference or deep research, **www.holocaustchronicle.org** is your window to *The Holocaust Chronicle,* and history at its most profound.